TABLE 2.2   Employment Distribution by Major Industrial Sector, 1900–1989

Year	Agriculture[a]	Goods-Producing Industries[b]	Nongovernment Services[c]	Government Services[d]
1900	38.1%	37.8%	20.0%	4.1%
1910	32.1	40.9	22.3	4.7
1920	27.6	44.8	21.6	6.0
1930	22.7	42.1	28.1	7.1
1940	18.5	41.6	31.1	8.8
1950	12.1	41.3	36.4	10.2
1960	6.6	41.4	38.8	13.2
1970	3.8	39.8	40.5	15.9
1980	3.6	32.8	46.3	17.3
1989	2.6	28.1	53.4	15.9

Note: From 1900 to 1930, "employment" refers to "gainful workers." From 1940, "employment" refers to experienced civilian labor force. Where applicable, persons not assigned to an industry were assumed to have the same employment distribution as those who were.

[a] Agriculture includes forestry and fishing.

[b] Included are manufacturing, mining, construction, transportation, communications, and public utilities.

[c] Included are trade; personal, professional, and business services; entertainment; finance; and real estate.

[d] Includes federal, state, and local government workers.

TABLE 2.4   Average Wages and Earnings of Production Workers in Manufacturing, 1914–89

Year	Weekly Earnings (current dollars)	Average Weekly Hours Paid For	Average Hourly Wage (current dollars)	Consumer Price Index (1914 = 100)[a]	Index of Real Weekly Earnings (1914 = 100)	Index of Real Hourly Wages (1914 = 100)	Annual Percentage Change in Real Hourly Wages over Previous 10 Years
1914	10.92	49.4	0.22	100	100	100	
1920	26.02	47.4	0.55	199	120	126	
1925	24.11	44.5	0.54	174	127	141	3.1[b]
1930	23.00	42.1	0.55	166	127	151	
1935	19.91	36.6	0.54	137	133	179	2.3
1940	24.96	38.1	0.66	140	163	214	
1945	44.20	43.5	1.02	179	226	259	3.7
1950	58.32	40.5	1.44	240	223	273	
1955	75.70	40.7	1.86	266	261	318	2.1
1960	89.72	39.7	2.26	295	278	348	
1965	107.53	41.2	2.61	314	314	378	1.7
1970	133.73	39.8	3.36	386	317	396	
1975	189.51	39.4	4.81	536	324	408	0.8
1980	288.62	39.7	7.27	820	322	403	
1989	429.27	41.0	10.47	1240	317	384	−0.4[c]

[a] The figures in this column should be interpreted with some caution. They are generated by pricing out a fixed "market basket" of consumer goods each year. Over time, however, new goods have become available and old ones improved in quality, so that comparability of the "baskets" used in making the index diminishes over time.

[b] Change calculated over previous 11 years.

[c] Change calculated over previous 14 years.

MODERN
LABOR
ECONOMICS

Fourth Edition

MODERN LABOR ECONOMICS
Theory and Public Policy

Ronald G. Ehrenberg
Cornell University

Robert S. Smith
Cornell University

HarperCollins*Publishers*

Sponsoring Editor: Bruce Kaplan
Project Coordination, Text and Cover Design: Carnes-Lachina Publication Services, Inc.
Cover Illustration: Susan D'Angelo
Production: Michael Weinstein
Compositor: Beacon Graphics Corporation
Printer and Binder: R.R. Donnelley & Sons Company
Cover Printer: New England Book Components

MODERN LABOR ECONOMICS, 4th Edition

Library of Congress Cataloging-in-Publication Data

Ehrenberg, Ronald G.
    Modern labor economics: theory and public policy / Ronald G.
    Ehrenberg, Robert S. Smith. -- 4th ed.
        p.   cm.
    Includes bibliographical references and index.
    ISBN 0-673-46227-7
    1. Labor economics.   I. Smith, Robert Stewart.   II. Title.
HD4901.E34   1990
331--dc20

                                    90-42613
                                         CIP

90 91 92 93 9 8 7 6 5 4 3 2 1

For Our Families, With Love

Contents

PREFACE   XV

1   INTRODUCTION   1

The Labor Market   2
Labor Economics: Some Basic Concepts   2
Plan of the Text   11

   Example 1.1   Normative Economics, Positive Economics, and the War of
      1812   9

   Appendix 1A   Statistical Testing of Labor Market Hypotheses   13

2   OVERVIEW OF THE LABOR MARKET   21

The Labor Market: Definitions, Facts, and Trends   22
How the Labor Market Works   32
Applications of the Theory   46

   Example 2.1   The Black Death and the Wages of Labor   41
   Example 2.2   A Modern Exodus from Egypt   56

3   THE DEMAND FOR LABOR   60

A Simple Model of Labor Demand   61
Modified Models of Labor Demand   75
Policy Application: Minimum Wage Legislation   82

Example 3.1   Professional Hockey: One Player's Marginal Revenue Productivity   64

Example 3.2   The Winner's Curse: Is There a Tendency to Overpay Baseball's Free Agents?   70

Example 3.3   Coal Mining   80

Example 3.4   Minimum Wages in Developing Countries   89

Example 3.5   Mandating Employee Benefits   93

Appendix 3A   Graphic Derivation of a Firm's Labor Demand Curve   97

4   LABOR DEMAND ELASTICITIES, TECHNOLOGICAL CHANGE, AND FOREIGN TRADE   106

The Own-Wage Elasticity of Demand   106
The Cross-Wage Elasticity of Demand   113
Empirical Evidence on Wage Elasticities of Demand   115
Policy Applications   121
Applying Concepts of Labor Demand Elasticity to the Issue of Technological Change   124
International Trade and the Demand for Labor: Can High-Wage Countries Compete?   126

Example 4.1   Gross Complementarity and Substitutability: The Rise and Fall of the Handloom Weavers, 1780–1850   116

Example 4.2   Are Targeted Wage Subsidies Harmful?   123

Example 4.3   Import Quotas and Employment in the Automobile Industry   132

Appendix 4A   The Elasticity of Demand for Labor and Labor Share: Understanding the Exception   137

5   QUASI-FIXED LABOR COSTS AND THEIR EFFECTS ON DEMAND   141

Nonwage Labor Costs   142
The Employment/Hours Trade-off   146
Firms' Labor Investments and the Demand for Labor   155
Training Investments   160
Hiring Investments   166
Policy Application: Why Do Employers Discriminate in Hiring?   168

Example 5.1   Recruiting and Training Longshore Crane Operators   143

Example 5.2   "Renting" Workers as a Way of Coping with Fluctuations in Product Demand   153

Example 5.3   Paying for America's Minor Leagues and Spain's "Stone Quarries"   162

Example 5.4   Paternalism in Japan — Is It Rooted in Feudalism or Economics?   169

6   SUPPLY OF LABOR TO THE ECONOMY: THE DECISION TO WORK   174

Trends in Labor Force Participation and Hours of Work   174
A Theory of the Decision to Work   179
Policy Applications   202

Example 6.1   Incentives and Absenteeism   183

Example 6.2   Primitive Cultures and Labor Supply Theory   196

Example 6.3   Disability and Economic Incentives in Three Countries   204

Appendix 6A   Child Care, Commuting, and the Fixed Costs of Working   222

7   LABOR SUPPLY: HOUSEHOLD PRODUCTION, THE FAMILY, AND THE LIFE CYCLE   227

The Theory of Household Production   227
Joint Husband–Wife Labor Supply Decisions   233
Household Production Theory and Some Social Issues   237
Life-Cycle Aspects of Labor Supply   242

Example 7.1   Household Productivity and Labor Supply in Japan   235

Example 7.2   Differences in Swiss Child-Rearing Practices Around 1800   241

Example 7.3   The Value of a Homemaker's Time   246

8   COMPENSATING WAGE DIFFERENTIALS AND LABOR MARKETS   257

A Verbal Analysis of Occupational Choice   257
A Hedonic Theory of Wages   266
Empirical Tests of the Theory of Compensating Wage Differentials   274
Policy Applications   277

Example 8.1   The Economic Implications of Flogging Workers   260

Example 8.2   Compensating Wage Differentials for the Evening and Night Shifts   266

Example 8.3   Compensating Wage Differentials in the Soviet Union   275

Example 8.4   Compensating Wage Differentials in 19th-Century Britain   282

Example 8.5   What Price Status?   285

Appendix 8A   Compensating Wage Differentials and Layoffs   294

9   INVESTMENTS IN HUMAN CAPITAL: EDUCATION AND TRAINING   299

Demand for Education by Workers   301
The Education/Wage Relationship   314
Is Education a Good Investment?   318
Applications of Human Capital Theory   330

Example 9.1   Hiroshima, Hamburg, and Human Capital   300

Example 9.2   Do Unskilled Jobs Cause Poor Mental Health?   308

Example 9.3   Valuing a Human Asset: The Case of the Divorcing Doctor   321

Example 9.4   The Socially Optimal Level of Educational Investment   327

Example 9.5   Socialists or (Human) Capitalists: Wage Differentials in the Soviet Union   331

Example 9.6   Do Families Move Up and Down the Income Distribution?   342

Appendix 9A   "Signaling" in the Labor Market   349
Appendix 9B   Measuring Inequality   355

10   WORKER MOBILITY: TURNOVER AND MIGRATION   360

The Determinants of Worker Mobility   361
Geographic Mobility   363
Voluntary Turnover   373
Policy Application: Restricting Immigration   379

Example 10.1   Job Satisfaction: An Alternative View   362

Example 10.2   "Economic" vs. "Political" Immigrants   370

Example 10.3   A Positive and Normative Theory of Quitting in 19th-Century Japan   375

Example 10.4   The Mariel Boatlift and Its Effects on Miami's Wage and Unemployment Rates   388

Example 10.5   Discouraging Immigration to Zurich in the 18th Century   390

Appendix 10A   Cohort Quality Changes, Assimilation, and the Earnings Growth of Immigrants   394

11 THE STRUCTURE OF COMPENSATION   397

The Economics of Employee Benefits   398
Implicit Contracts, Explicit Contracts, and Asymmetric Information   409
The Basis of Pay   411
Internal Labor Markets and the Level and Time Pattern of
    Compensation   420

  Example 11.1   The Wage/Benefit Trade-off in the Collective Bargaining
  Process   408

  Example 11.2   Piece Rates and Supervisory Effort in California
  Agriculture   414

  Example 11.3   Incentive Pay and Output—or "You Get What You Pay
  For"   418

  Example 11.4   The Wide Range of Possible Productivities: The Case of the
  Factory That Could Not Cut Output   421

  Example 11.5   Did Henry Ford Pay Efficiency Wages?   424

  Example 11.6   Monitoring Costs, Occupational Segregation, and Gender
  Differences in Compensation Methods in the 1890s   429

  Example 11.7   Do Professional Golf Tournaments Have Incentive
  Effects?   433

Appendix 11A   Profit Sharing and the Demand for Labor   438

12 UNIONS AND COLLECTIVE BARGAINING IN THE PRIVATE SECTOR   442

Unions and Collective Bargaining   443
How Unions Achieve Their Objectives   455
The Effects of Unions   469

  Example 12.1   Deregulation and the Airlines   453

  Example 12.2   The Rise and Fall of the Mississippi Steamboat Pilots' Union
  458

  Example 12.3   The Paradox of Large Wage Increases in Declining
  Sectors   478

  Example 12.4   Corporate Takeovers and Union Wages   485

Appendix 12A   "Monopoly Unions" or "Efficient Contracts"?   490

13 PUBLIC SECTOR LABOR MARKETS   496

A Model of a Public Sector Labor Market   501
The Growth and Effects of Public Sector Unions   504

The Effects of Arbitration Statutes on the Wages of State and Local
    Government Employees   509
Public vs. Private Pay Comparisons   511
The Effect of Expenditure- and Tax-Limitation Legislation   515
Public Sector Employment Programs   517

  Example 13.1   Final-Offer Arbitration and Police Wages in New
    Jersey   510

  Example 13.2   Are Postal Workers Overpaid?   513

Appendix 13A   Arbitration and the Incentive to Bargain   524

14   THE ECONOMICS OF DISCRIMINATION   529

What Is Discrimination?   529
Earnings Disparities by Race, Ethnicity, and Gender   531
Theories of Market Discrimination   541
State Fair Employment Practice Legislation   556
Federal Programs to End Discrimination   558

  Example 14.1   Customer Discrimination and Professional
    Basketball   546

  Example 14.2   South Africa's "Civilized Labour Policy"   555

  Example 14.3   Comparable Worth and the University   564

  Example 14.4   How Fast Can Discrimination Be Eradicated?   569

Appendix 14A   Estimating "Comparable Worth" Earnings Gaps: An
    Application of Regression Analysis   575

15   UNEMPLOYMENT   579

A Stock-Flow Model of the Labor Market   581
Types of Unemployment and Their Causes   585
The Demographic Structure of Unemployment Rates   601
Government Policy and Frictional Unemployment: The Effects of
    Unemployment Benefits on Job Search   607
Normative Issues in Unemployment   614

  Example 15.1   Advance Notice for Layoffs and Plant Shutdowns   589

  Example 15.2   International Unemployment Rate Differentials   594

  Example 15.3   Unemployment Insurance Benefits in Great Britain   611

  Example 15.4   The Unemployment Insurance Bonus Experiments   613

Appendix 15A   The Relationship Between the Unemployment Rate and Labor
    Market Flows   618

16   INFLATION AND UNEMPLOYMENT   620

Measuring Wage Inflation   620
The Inflation/Unemployment Trade-off   621
Wage Inflation, Price Inflation, Productivity, and the Long-Run
    Trade-off   638
Expected vs. Unexpected Inflation   644
Unions and Inflation   647
Structural Policies to Reduce Inflation   651

    Example 16.1   The Growth of Employment in Small Businesses: Will Wages
        Become More Downwardly Flexible?   635

    Example 16.2   The Slowdown in U.S. Productivity Growth   640

    Example 16.3   Incomes Policies During the Roman Empire   655

Appendix 16A   Does a Long-Run Trade-off Exist Between the Rate of Price
    Inflation and the Unemployment Rate?   659

ANSWERS TO ODD-NUMBERED REVIEW QUESTIONS   665

NAME INDEX   693

SUBJECT INDEX   701

Preface

OVERVIEW OF THE TEXT

Modern Labor Economics: Theory and Public Policy has grown out of our experiences over the last twenty years in teaching labor market economics and in conducting research aimed at influencing public policy. Our text develops the modern theory of labor market behavior, summarizes empirical evidence that supports or contradicts each hypothesis, and illustrates in detail the usefulness of the theory for public policy analysis. We believe that showing students the social implications of concepts enhances the motivation to learn them and that using the concepts of each chapter in an analytic setting allows students to see the concepts in action. The extensive use of detailed policy applications constitutes a major innovation in this text.

Modern Labor Economics is designed for one-semester or one-quarter courses in labor economics at the undergraduate or graduate level for students who may not have extensive backgrounds in economics. Since 1974 we have taught such courses at the School of Industrial and Labor Relations at Cornell University. The undergraduate course requires only principles of economics as a prerequisite, and the graduate course (for students in a professional program akin to an MBA program) has no prerequisites. We have found that it is not necessary to be highly technical in one's presentation in order to convey important concepts and that students with limited backgrounds in economics *can* comprehend a great deal of material in a single course. However, for students who have had intermediate microeconomics, we have included fourteen chapter appendices that discuss more advanced material or develop technical concepts in much greater detail than the text discussion permits.

Chapter 2 presents a quick overview of demand and supply in labor markets so that students will see from the outset the interrelationship of the major forces at work shaping labor market behavior. This chapter can be skipped or skimmed by students with strong backgrounds in economics or by students in one-quarter courses. Chapters 3 to 5 are concerned primarily with the demand for labor, while Chapters 6 to 10 focus on labor supply issues. Compensation, unionism, public sector labor markets, and discrimination are treated in Chapters 11–14. The final two chapters treat the issues of unemployment and inflation.

In addition to the use of public policy examples and the inclusion of technical appendices, the text has a number of important pedagogical features. First, each chapter contains one or more numbered examples that illustrate an application of that chapter's theory in a nontraditional, historical, business, or cross-cultural setting. Second, each chapter contains a number of discussion or review questions that allow students to apply what they have learned to specific policy issues. To enhance student mastery, we provide answers to the odd-numbered questions at the back of the book. Third, we identify one of six frequently misunderstood fundamentals of labor economics at the end of every chapter, and we briefly highlight and discuss a common error in perception arising from the misunderstanding. Fourth, updated lists of selected readings at the ends of chapters refer students to more advanced sources of study.

COMMENTS ON THE FOURTH EDITION

Our goal in writing *Modern Labor Economics: Theory and Public Policy* was to provide a comprehensive survey of the field of labor economics written in a style that is interesting and accessible to students of varying backgrounds. We believe this fourth edition offers improvements and innovations that should enhance its value to students and professors.

Several new applications or theoretical/empirical developments have been included in textual discussions, in a new appendix, and in 22 new numbered examples. Among the most significant additions are the following:

Chapter 1:   A statistical methods appendix.

Chapter 2:   A section defining and analyzing "economic rents."

Chapter 4:   A section on technological change and labor demand, and (moved from the appendix into the text) a section on international trade and labor demand.

Chapter 6:   A revised discussion of welfare reform.

Chapter 9:   A section on changes in the distribution of earnings (the "vanishing middle class").

Chapter 10:   New analyses of the characteristics of countries furnishing immigrants, how immigrants perform in the United States, and the effects of immigration on natives.

Chapter 12:   A section on the decline of unions.

Chapter 14:   New material on patterns and trends in race and gender wage differentials.

Chapter 15:   New analyses of wage rigidity, and a section discussing the concept of full employment.

All Chapters: At least two new review questions per chapter.

ACKNOWLEDGMENTS

Several colleagues have contributed, through their thoughtful evaluations of the third edition, to the development of the fourth. We appreciate the suggestions and criticisms of the following people:

John M. Abowd, Cornell University
Steven G. Allen, North Carolina State University
Francine D. Blau, University of Illinois at Urbana–Champaign
George Borjas, University of California, Santa Barbara
George R. Boyer, Cornell University
Charles Callahan III, SUNY, Brockport
Donald Coffin, Indiana University Northwest
Larry Davis, Northern Montana College
Gary S. Fields, Cornell University
Robert M. Hutchens, Cornell University
George H. Jakubson, Cornell University
Lawrence M. Kahn, University of Illinois at Urbana–Champaign
Mark R. Killingsworth, Rutgers University
Levis Kochin, University of Washington
Edward P. Lazear, University of Chicago
Olivia S. Mitchell, Cornell University
Donald O. Parsons, Ohio State University
Solomon W. Polachek, SUNY, Binghamton

Enormous debts are also owed to three other groups of people. First are those instrumental in teaching us the concepts and social relevance of labor economics when we were students: Frank Brechling, George Delehanty, Dale Mortensen, John Pencavel, Orme Phelps, and Mel Reder. Second are the generations of undergraduate and graduate students we have taught who have forced us to clarify our thinking and who sat through the lectures that preceded *Modern Labor Economics.* Third are the secretaries who have typed the many drafts of the manuscript: Jean Brown and Patricia Dickerson.

Ronald G. Ehrenberg
Robert S. Smith

1

Introduction

E conomic theory provides powerful, and often surprising, insights into individual and social behavior. At a purely scientific level, these insights are interesting because they help us understand important aspects of our lives. Beyond this, however, government, industry, labor, and other groups have increasingly come to understand the usefulness of the concepts and thought processes of economists in formulating social policy. This theory of behavior is simple yet compelling, and provides a systematic approach to the analysis of economic problems.

This book presents a comprehensive and understandable application of economic analysis to the behavior of, and relationship between, employers and employees. The aggregate compensation received by employees from their employers was $2,880 billion in 1989, while all *other* forms of personal income that year—from investments, self-employment, pensions, and various government welfare programs—amounted to $1,548 billion. The *employment* relationship, then, is one of the most fundamental relationships in our lives, and as such it attracts a good deal of legislative attention. A mastery of the fundamentals of labor economics is thus essential to an understanding of a huge array of social problems and programs.

As economists who have been actively involved in the analysis and evaluation of labor-related policies adopted or considered by the government, we obviously believe labor economics is useful in understanding the effects of these policies. Perhaps more important, we also believe policy analysis can be useful in teaching the fundamentals of labor economics. We have therefore incorporated such analyses into each chapter with two pedagogical purposes in mind. First, we believe that seeing the relevance and social implications of concepts studied enhances the student's motivation to learn. Second, using the concepts of each chapter in an analytical setting serves to reinforce understanding by permitting the student to see them "in action."

THE LABOR MARKET

There is a rumor that one recent Secretary of Labor attempted to abolish the term "labor market" from departmental publications. He believed it demeaned workers to regard labor as being bought and sold like so much grain, oil, or steel. True, labor is somewhat unique. Labor services can only be rented; workers themselves cannot be bought and sold. Further, because labor services cannot be separated from workers, the conditions under which such services are rented are often as important as the price. Put differently, *nonpecuniary factors*—such as work environment, risk of injury, personalities of managers, and flexibility of work hours—loom larger in employment transactions than they do in markets for commodities. Finally, a host of institutions and pieces of legislation that influence the employment relationship do not exist in other markets.

Nevertheless, the circumstances under which employers and employees rent labor services clearly constitute a market for several reasons. First, institutions have been developed to facilitate contact between buyers and sellers of labor services. This contact may come about through want ads, union hiring halls, employment agencies, placement offices, or plant personnel offices.

Second, once contact is arranged, information about price and quality is exchanged. Employment applications, interviews, and even word-of-mouth information from friends illustrate this kind of exchange in the market for labor.

Third, when agreement is reached, some kind of *contract* is executed covering compensation, conditions of work, job security, and even duration of the job. At times the contract is formal, such as with collective bargaining (union–management) agreements. At other times the agreement is unwritten and informal, with only an implied understanding between the parties based on past practices and experience. Nonetheless, it is often useful to think of the employment relationship as governed by a contract.

Labor contracts typically call for employers to compensate employees for their *time* and not for what they produce. Only 14 percent of U.S. workers receive piece-rate wages or commissions, in which compensation is computed directly on the basis of output. The vast majority are paid by the hour, week, or month. They are paid, in short, to show up for work and (within limits) to follow orders. This form of compensation requires that employers give careful attention to worker motivation and dependability in the selection and employment process.

The end result of employer–employee transactions in the labor market is, of course, the placement of people in jobs at certain rates of pay. This allocation of labor serves not only the personal needs of individuals but the needs of the larger society as well. Through the labor market, our most important national resource—labor—is allocated to firms, industries, occupations, and regions.

LABOR ECONOMICS: SOME BASIC CONCEPTS

Labor economics is the study of the workings and outcomes of the market for labor. More specifically, labor economics is primarily concerned with the behavior of employers and employees in response to the general incentives of wages, prices, profits, and nonpecuniary aspects of the employment relationship, such as working conditions. These incentives serve both to motivate and to limit individual choice. The focus in economics is on inducements for behavior that are impersonal and apply to wide groups of people.

In this book we shall examine, for example, the relationship between wages and employment opportunities, the interaction between wages, income, and the decision to work, the way general market incentives affect occupational choice, the relationship between wages and undesirable job characteristics, the incentives for and effects of educational and training investments, and the effects of unions on wages, productivity, and turnover. In the process, we shall analyze the employment and wage effects of such social policies as the minimum wage, overtime legislation, pension reform regulations, the Occupational Safety and Health Act, welfare reform, payroll taxes, unemployment insurance, immigration policies, the rise in the mandatory retirement age, and antidiscrimination laws.

Our study of labor economics will be conducted on two levels. Most of the time we shall use economic theory to analyze "what is"; that is, we shall explain people's behavior using a mode of analysis called *positive economics*. Less commonly, we shall use *normative* economic analysis to judge "what should be."

Positive Economics

Positive economics is a theory of behavior in which people are typically assumed to respond favorably to benefits and negatively to costs. In this regard, positive economics closely resembles Skinnerian psychology, which views behavior as shaped by rewards and punishments. The rewards in economic theory are pecuniary and nonpecuniary gains (benefits), while the punishments are forgone opportunities (costs). For example, a person motivated to become a surgeon because of the earnings and status surgeons command must give up the opportunity to become a lawyer and must be available for emergency work around the clock. Both the benefits and the costs must be considered in making this career choice. Likewise, a firm deciding whether to hire an additional worker must weigh the wage and salary costs against the added revenues or cost savings made possible by expanding its work force.

Scarcity. The most all-pervasive assumption underlying economic theory is that of resource *scarcity*. According to this assumption, individuals and society alike do not have the resources to meet all their wants. Hence, any resource devoted to satisfying one set of desires could have been used to satisfy another set, which means that there is a cost to any decision or action. The real cost of using labor hired by a government contractor to build a road, for example, is the production lost by not devoting this labor to the building of an airport or some other good. Thus, in popular terms, "There is no such thing as a free lunch," and we must always make choices and live with the rewards and costs these choices bring us. Moreover, we are always constrained in our choices by the resources available to us.

Rationality. The second basic assumption of positive economics is that people are *rational* in the sense that they have an objective and pursue it in a reasonably consistent fashion. When considering *persons,* economists assume that the objective being pursued is *utility maximization;* that is, people are assumed to strive toward the goal of making themselves as happy as they can (given their limited resources). Utility, of course, encompasses both pecuniary and nonpecuniary dimensions. When considering the behavior of *firms,* which are inherently nonpersonal entities, economists assume that the goal of behavior is *profit maximization.* Profit maximization is really just a special case of utility maximization in which pecuniary gain is emphasized and nonpecuniary factors are ignored.

The assumption of rationality implies a *consistency* of response to general economic incentives and an *adaptability* of behavior when those incentives change. These two characteristics of behavior underlie predictions about how workers and firms will respond to various incentives. Rationality cannot be directly proven, however, and even totally habit-bound or unthinkingly impulsive people might be forced to alter their behavior in predictable ways if the resources at their command changed.[1] Thus, while we shall maintain the assumption of rationality throughout this text, this assumption is not absolutely necessary to the derivation of at least *some* of the behavioral predictions contained herein.

The Models and Predictions of Positive Economics

Behavioral predictions in economics flow more or less directly from the two fundamental assumptions of rationality and scarcity. Workers must continually make choices, such as whether to look for other jobs, accept overtime, seek promotions, move to another area, or acquire more education. Employers must also make choices concerning, for example, the level of output and the mix of machines and labor to use in production. Economists usually assume that, when making these choices, employees and employers are guided by their desires to maximize utility or profit, respectively. However, what is more important to the economic theory of behavior is not the *particular* goal of either employees or employers; rather, it is that economic actors weigh the costs and benefits of various alternative transactions in the context of achieving *some* goal or other. For example, when analyzing race or gender discrimination (see Chapter 14), economists frequently assume that employers are maximizing *utility,* not profits. Likewise, workers' utility is normally assumed to be a function of their own consumption, but the concept of utility maximization can be expanded to include both one's own consumption and one's *ranking* relative to the consumption of others (see Chapter 8 for a discussion of status-seeking behavior in labor markets). Again, fundamental to positive economics are the assumptions that employers and employees act in purposeful and considered ways.

One may object that these assumptions are unrealistic and that people are not nearly as calculating, as well informed about alternatives, or as well endowed with choices as economists assume. Economists are likely to reply that if people are not calculating, are totally uninformed, or do not have any choices, then most predictions suggested by economic theory will not be sup-

---

1. Gary Becker, "Irrational Behavior and Economic Theory," *Journal of Political Economy* 70, no. 1 (February 1962): 1–13.

ported by real-world evidence. They thus argue that the theory underlying positive economics should be judged on the basis of its *predictions* and that there may be *enough* information, calculation, and available options to make the theory useful in explaining or predicting a wide range of behavior.

The reason we need to make assumptions and create a relatively simple theory of behavior is that the actual workings of the labor market are almost impossibly complex. Millions of workers and employers interact daily, all with their own sets of motivations, preferences, information, and perceptions of self-interest. A detailed description of the individual outcomes and the processes that determine them would clearly be of limited feasibility and usefulness. What we need to discover are general principles that provide useful insights into the labor market. These principles could not be expected to predict or explain behavior with the same accuracy as the laws of physics predict the movement of an object through space, because we are dealing with human beings capable of making choices. Nevertheless, we hope to show that a few forces are so basic to labor market behavior that they alone can predict or explain many of the outcomes and behaviors we observe in the labor market.

Any time we attempt to explain a complex set of behaviors and outcomes using a few fundamental influences, we have created a *model*. Models are not intended to capture every complexity of behavior; instead, they are created to strip away random and idiosyncratic factors so that we can focus on general principles. An analogy from the physical sciences may make the nature of models and their relationship to actual behavior more clear.

Using calculations of velocity and gravitational pull, physicists can predict where a ball will land if it is kicked with a certain force at a given angle to the ground. The actual point of landing may vary from the predicted point because of wind currents and any spin the ball might have—factors ignored in the calculations. If 100 balls are kicked, none may ever land exactly on the predicted spot, although they will tend to cluster around it. The accuracy of the model, while not perfect, may be good enough to enable a football coach to decide whether to attempt a field goal or not. The point is that we usually just need to know the *average tendencies* of outcomes for policy purposes. To estimate these tendencies we need to know the important forces at work, but we must confine ourselves to few enough influences so that calculating estimates remains feasible.

To really grasp the assumptions and predictions of economic models, it is necessary to consider a concrete example. Suppose we begin by asserting that, being subject to resource scarcity, workers will prefer high-paying jobs to low-paying ones *if* all other job characteristics are the same in each job. Thus, in pursuit of their own well-being, they will quit low-paying jobs to take better-paying ones for which they qualify if they believe sufficient improvement is likely. This principle does not imply that workers care only about wages or that all are equally likely to quit. Workers obviously care about a number of employment characteristics, and improvement in any of these characteristics makes turnover less likely. Likewise, some workers are more receptive to change than others. Nevertheless, if we hold these other factors constant and increase only wages, we should clearly observe that the probability of quitting will fall.

On the employer side of the market, we can consider a similar prediction. Firms need to make a profit to survive. If they have high turnover, their costs will be higher than otherwise because of the need to hire and train replacements. With high turnover they could not, therefore, afford to pay high wages. However, if they could reduce turnover enough by paying higher wages, it might well be worth incurring the high wage costs. Thus, both the utility-maximizing behavior of employees and the profit-maximizing behavior of firms lead us to expect low turnover to be associated with high wages and high turnover with low wages, other things equal.[2]

It is important to note several things about the above predictions:

1. The predictions emerge directly from the twin assumptions of rationality and scarcity. Employees and employers, both mindful of their scarce resources, are assumed to be on the lookout for chances to improve their well-being. The predictions are also based on the assumptions that employees are aware of, or can learn about, alternative jobs and that these alternatives are open to them. If any of these assumptions is invalid or inappropriate, the predictions would not be consistently borne out by observed behavior.

2. The prediction of a negative relationship between wages and voluntary turnover is made holding other things equal. The theory does not deny that job characteristics other than wages matter to employees or that employers can lower turnover by varying policies other than the wage rate. However, holding these other factors constant, we should observe the predicted negative relationship if the basic assumptions are valid.

3. The *assumptions* of the theory concern *individual* behavior of employers and employees, but the *predictions* are about an *aggregate* relationship between wages and turnover. The prediction is *not* that all employees will remain in their jobs if their wages are increased, but that *enough* will remain for turnover to be cut by raising wages. The test of the prediction thus lies in finding out if the predicted relationship between wages and turnover exists as one looks at aggregate data from firms or industries.

In fact, there is abundant evidence that these predictions about turnover are accurate. Two of the more convincing studies estimate that if an industry increased its wage rate by 10 percent relative to other industries, holding all other job characteristics constant, it would reduce its voluntary turnover by 3 to 20 percent.[3]

Normative Economics

Any normative statement—a statement about what *ought* to exist—is based on some underlying value. The value premise upon which normative econom-

---

2. In this example the expected relationship between wages and worker/firm behavior is clear-cut. While this is often the case, the expected relationship is not always that clear. We shall see examples of this later on—especially in Chapter 6.

3. John Pencavel, *An Analysis of the Quit Rate in Manufacturing Industry* (Princeton: Industrial Relations Section, Princeton University, 1970), and Farrell Block, "Labor Turnover in U.S. Manufacturing Industries," *Journal of Human Resources* 14, no. 2 (Spring 1979): 236–46.

ics rests is that of *mutual benefit*. A mutually beneficial transaction is one in which there are no losers and, therefore, one that everyone in society could support. A transaction can be unanimously supported when

a. All parties affected by the transaction gain;
b. Some gain and no one else loses; or
c. Some gain and some lose from the transaction, but the gainers fully compensate the losers.

When the compensation in *c* takes place, case *c* is converted to case *b*. In practice, economists often judge a transaction by whether the gains of the beneficiaries exceed the costs borne by the losers, thus making it *possible* that there would be no losers. If the losers sustain losses that the gainers could not possibly compensate, then the transaction could never be beneficial to all and the wisdom of the transaction must be questioned.

To illustrate a mutually beneficial transaction, suppose that people who formerly owned and operated small subsistence farms in West Virginia—earning the equivalent of $4,000 per year—take jobs in the growing coal-mining industry at $15,000 a year. Assuming the switch in jobs is voluntary, these workers are clearly better off. The income gain of $11,000 per year might be offset to some extent by the disagreeableness of working in a mine, but the fact that the people voluntarily choose to move into mining tells us that they believe their utility will be enhanced. Mine owners likewise enter into the transaction voluntarily, implying that they obtain at least $15,000 in output from these new workers. Such a transaction benefits the parties it affects, and as a result it benefits society as a whole. There has been an increase in social output from $4,000 to $15,000 per worker, but, more important, there has been an increase in the overall utility of workers (the miners are better off and no one else is worse off).

To illustrate a transaction that is not mutually beneficial, suppose that society sought to increase the income of these same subsistence farmers by giving them a cash allowance raised by taxing others. This program would simply transfer money from the pockets of some people to the pockets of others, with no increase in output. There would be no possibility for the gainers (farmers) to compensate the losers (those taxed), so unanimous consent about the transaction could not be secured. While economists would not say that this transaction was bad or unwarranted, it could not be justified on the grounds of mutual benefit. Some other ethical principle—not based on unanimous consent—would have to be invoked to justify it. (One such principle is that the rich should share their wealth with the poor.)

Normative economics, then, is the analysis of actual and potential transactions to see if they conform to the standard of being mutually beneficial. Transactions may fail to meet this standard—or transactions that meet the standard may not occur—for one of several reasons.

Ignorance.   First, people may be ignorant of some important facts and thus led to make decisions that are not in their self-interest. For example, a worker who smokes may take a job in an asbestos-processing plant not knowing that the combination of smoking and inhaling asbestos dust substantially increases the risk of disease. Had the worker known this, he or she would probably have stopped smoking or changed jobs, but both transactions were "blocked" by ignorance.

Transaction Barriers.   Second, there may be some barrier to the completion of a transaction that could be mutually beneficial. Often such a barrier is created by law. For example, a firm may be willing to offer overtime to production workers at rates no more than 10 percent above their normal wage. Some workers might be willing to accept overtime at the 10 percent premium. However, this transaction, which is desired by both parties, could not legally be completed in most instances because of a law (the Fair Labor Standards Act) requiring almost all production workers to be paid a 50 percent wage premium for overtime. In this case, overtime would not be worked and both parties would suffer.

Another barrier to mutually beneficial transactions may be the expense of completing the transaction. Unskilled workers facing very limited opportunities in one region might desire to move to take better jobs. Alternatively, they might want to enter job-training programs. In either case, they might lack the funds to finance the desired transaction.

Nonexistence of Market.   A third reason why transactions that are mutually beneficial may not occur is that it may be impossible or uncustomary for buyers and sellers of certain resources to transact. As an illustration, assume that a woman who does not smoke works temporarily next to a man who does. She would be willing to pay as much as 50 cents an hour to keep her working environment smoke-free, and he could be induced to give up smoking for as little as 25 cents an hour. Thus, the potential exists for her to give him 35 cents an hour and for both to benefit. However, custom or the transience of their relationship might prevent her from offering him money in this situation, in which case the transaction would not occur.

Normative Economics and Government Policy

The solution to problems that impede the completion of mutually beneficial transactions frequently involves government intervention. When law creates the barrier to a transaction, the "intervention" might be to repeal the law. Laws prohibiting women from working overtime, for example, have been repealed in recent years as their adverse effects on women have become recognized.

In other cases, however, the government might be able to undertake activities to reduce transaction barriers that the private market would not undertake. We shall cite three examples, each of which relates to a barrier discussed above.

Public Goods.   First let us take the case of the dissemination of information. Suppose that workers in noisy factories are concerned about the effects of noise on their hearing, but that ascertaining these effects would require an expensive research program. Suppose, further, that a union representing sawmill workers considers undertaking such research and financing the project by selling its findings to the many other unions or workers involved. The workers would then have the information they desire—albeit at some cost—which they could use to make more intelligent decisions concerning their jobs.

The hitch in the scheme is that the union doing the research may not have any customers *even though* others find the information it produces valuable. As soon as the union's findings are published to its own members or its first customers, the results can easily become public knowledge—and thus available *free* from newspapers or by word of mouth. Other unions may be understandably reluctant to pay for information they can get free, and the union doing the research ends up getting very little, if any, reimbursement for its expenses. Anticipating this problem, the union will probably decide not to undertake the research.

EXAMPLE 1.1
Normative Economics, Positive Economics, and the War of 1812

The advocacy of mutually beneficial transactions underlying *normative economics* has a very practical social value in the labor market: it assures a *voluntary* allocation of workers to jobs. When compulsion is necessary to fill certain jobs, society suffers the costs of recruiting and retaining unwilling workers. Sometimes these costs can be very large, as the British learned from their "impressment" of seamen in the early 1800s.

The British navy had long followed a policy of paying its ordinary seamen considerably less than they could obtain on British merchant ships. Because of the difficulties caused by these low wages in recruiting and retaining sailors, Britain's navy resorted to the often-brutal impressment of merchant seamen during times of war. Those choosing to become British merchant seamen, therefore, faced the risk of being forced to serve in the navy against their will. This risk was especially high during the war-torn years around 1800.

During this time, American merchant ships were offering seamen wages that were roughly double the wages offered on British merchant ships—and therefore much more than double the wages offered by the British navy. As one might predict from this chapter's illustrative model of *positive economics,* high wages offered by the Americans caused many British seamen to choose work on board American ships. Moreover, many opted to become naturalized U.S. citizens in the hope of avoiding impressment.

Not recognizing the rights of its subjects to change citizenship, and facing substantial shortages of naval recruits, Britain began stopping American merchant ships on the high seas and carting off seamen who were suspected of being British. This capture and impressment of sailors employed on American ships angered the United States and was one of the principal causes of the War of 1812. Truly, then, its low naval wages in fact imposed very high opportunity costs on Great Britain!

SOURCE: Michael Lewis, *A Social History of the Navy, 1793–1815* (London: George Allen and Unwin Ltd., 1960).

Information in this example is called a *public good*—a good that can be consumed by any number of people at the same time, including those who do not pay for it. Because nonpayers cannot be excluded from consuming the good, no potential customer will have an incentive to pay. The result is that the good never gets produced by a private organization. Because the government, however, can *compel* payment through its tax system, it is natural to look to the government to produce public goods. When information on occupational health hazards is to be produced on a large scale, the government is likely to have to be involved.

Capital Market Imperfections.   An example of a second type of situation in which the government might have to step in to overcome a transaction barrier involves a case in which loans are not available to finance job training or interregional moves, even though such loans might give workers facing a very poor set of choices access to better opportunities. Such loans are not typically provided by the private sector because they are not backed (secured) by anything other than the debtor's promise to pay them back. Banks cannot ordinarily afford to take the risks inherent in making such loans, particularly when the loan recipients are poor, because a number of defaults could put them out of business (or at least lower their profitability). This lack of available loans to finance worthwhile transactions represents a "capital market imperfection."

The government, however, might be willing to make loans in such situations even if it faced the same risk of default, because enabling workers to move to areas of better economic opportunity could improve social welfare and strengthen the economy. In short, because society would reap benefits from encouraging people to enter job-training programs or move to areas where their skills could be better utilized, it might be wise for the government to make the loans itself.

Establishing Market Substitutes.   A third type of situation in which government intervention might be necessary to overcome transaction barriers occurs when a market fails to exist for some reason. In the example above, a smoker and a nonsmoker were temporarily working next to each other, and their transitory relationship prevented a mutually beneficial transaction from taking place. A solution in this case might be for the government to impose the same result that a market transaction would have generated—and require the employer to designate that area a nonsmoking area.

In each case, when government does intervene, it must make sure that the transactions it undertakes or imposes on society create more gains for the beneficiaries than they impose in costs on others. Since it is costly to produce information, for example, the government should do it only if the gains are more valuable than the resources used in producing it. Likewise, the government would want to make loans for job training or interregional moves only if these activities enhanced social welfare. Finally, imposing nonsmoking areas would be socially desirable only if the gainers gained more than the losers lost. Thus, while normative economics suggests a role for government in helping to accomplish mutually beneficial transactions, the role is not an unlimited one.

PLAN OF THE TEXT

With this brief review of economics in mind, we turn now to the specific subject-matter areas of labor economics. The study of labor economics is mainly a study of the interplay between employers and employees—or between demand and supply. Chapter 2 presents a quick overview of demand and supply in the labor market, allowing students to see from the outset the interrelationship of the major forces at work shaping labor market behavior. (This chapter contains many concepts that will be familiar to students who have a background in microeconomics.) Chapters 3–5 are concerned primarily with the demand for labor, while Chapters 6–11 emphasize labor supply issues.

The special topics of unionism and discrimination are treated in Chapters 12–14. The final two chapters deal with the macroeconomic issues of unemployment and inflation.

MISCONCEPTION

"We all know that wearing gas masks is uncomfortable, but an economist would argue that, from a social perspective, mandating the use of gas masks is a cheaper way to reduce workplace health risks than is requiring that the air be purified. The reason for this is that gas masks provide equivalent protection from inhaling toxic substances and can be manufactured at considerably less total cost than ventilation systems."

Analysis

Since the goal of individuals is to maximize *utility,* the true social costs of any government program include both pecuniary and nonpecuniary costs. Gas masks may be cheaper to produce, but if they cause discomfort to workers when they are worn, that discomfort is itself part of overall social costs (like a pecuniary cost, discomfort involves a loss of utility).

Principle

The social cost of an action is the forgone utility that the action requires; the social benefit is the added utility it generates.

REVIEW QUESTIONS

1. Using the concepts of normative economics, when would the labor market be judged to be at a point of optimality? What imperfections might prevent the market from achieving this point?
2. Are the following statements "positive" or "normative"? Why?
   a. Employers should not be required to offer pensions to their employees.
   b. Employers offering pension benefits will pay lower wages than they would if they did not offer a pension program.
   c. If further immigration of unskilled foreigners is prevented, the wages of unskilled immigrants already here will rise.

d. The military draft *compels* people to engage in a transaction they would not voluntarily enter into; it should therefore be avoided as a way of recruiting military personnel.

e. If the military draft were reinstituted, military salaries would probably fall.

3. Child labor laws exist at both the federal and state levels of government in the United States. These generally prohibit children from working until age 14 and restrict younger teenagers to certain kinds of work that are not considered dangerous. Reconcile the prohibitions of child labor legislation with the principles underlying normative economic analysis.

4. What are the functions and limitations of an economic model?

5. In Chapter 1 a simple model was developed in which it was predicted that workers employed in jobs paying wages less than they could get in comparable jobs elsewhere would tend to quit and seek the higher-paying jobs. Suppose we observe a worker who, after repeated harassment or criticism from her boss, quits an $8-per-hour job to take another paying $7.50. Answer the three questions below:

a. Is this woman's behavior consistent with the economic model of job quitting outlined in the text?

b. Is there any way we can test to see whether this woman's behavior is consistent with the assumption of rationality?

c. Suppose that the boss in question had harassed other employees but that this woman was the only one who quit. Can we conclude from this that economic theory applies to the behavior of some people but not to others?

6. A few years ago it was common for the laws in many states to prohibit women from working more than 40 hours a week. Using the principles underlying normative economics, evaluate these laws.

SELECTED READINGS

Amacher, Ryan C., Tollison, Robert D., and Willet, Thomas D., eds. *The Economic Approach to Public Policy.* Ithaca, N.Y.: Cornell University Press, 1976.

Friedman, Milton. *Essays in Positive Economics.* Chicago: University of Chicago Press, 1953.

Lindbeck, Assar. *The Political Economy of the New Left: An Outsider's View.* New York: Harper & Row, 1971.

McCloskey, Donald. "The Rhetoric of Economics." *Journal of Economic Literature* 21 (June 1983): 481–517.

APPENDIX 1A

Statistical Testing of Labor Market Hypotheses

This appendix provides a brief introduction to how labor economists test hypotheses. The discussion is intentionally kept simple and presumes that the reader has no previous background in statistics. To provide a concrete example, we will discuss how one might attempt to test the hypothesis presented in Chapter 1 that, other things equal, one should expect to observe that the higher the wage a firm pays, the lower will be the voluntary labor turnover among its employees. Put another way, if we define a firm's quit rate as the proportion of its workers who voluntarily quit in a given time period (say a year), we expect to observe that the higher a firm's wages, the lower will be its quit rate, holding *other* factors affecting quit rates constant.

A UNIVARIATE TEST

In testing the above hypothesis, an obvious first step is to collect data on the quit rates experienced by a set of firms during a given year and match these data with the firms' wage rates. This type of analysis is called *univariate* because we are analyzing the effects on quit rates of just one other variable (the wage rate); the data are called *cross-sectional* because they provide observations across behavioral units at a point in time.[1] Table 1A.1 contains such information for a hypothetical set of ten firms located in a single labor market in 1990. For example, firm A is assumed to have paid an average hourly wage of $4 and to have experienced a quit rate of 40 percent in 1990.

---

1. Several other types of data are also used frequently by labor economists. One could look, for example, at how a given firm's quit rate and wage rate vary over time. Observations that provide information on a single behavioral unit over a number of time periods are called *time-series* data. Sometimes labor economists have data on the behavior of a number of observational units (e.g., employers) for a number of time periods; combinations of cross-sectional and time-series data are called *panel* data.

TABLE 1A.1   Average-Wage and Quit-Rate Data for a Set of Ten Hypothetical Firms in a Single Labor Market in 1990

Firm	Average Hourly Wage Paid	Quit Rate	Firm	Average Hourly Wage Paid	Quit Rate
A	$4	40%	F	$ 8	20%
B	4	30	G	10	25
C	6	35	H	10	15
D	6	25	I	12	20
E	8	30	J	12	10

The data on wages and quit rates are presented graphically in Figure 1A.1. Each dot in this figure represents a quit-rate/hourly-wage combination for one of the firms in Table 1A.1. Firm A, for example, is represented in the figure by point A, which shows a quit rate of 40 percent and an hourly wage of $4, while point B shows the data for firm B. From a visual inspection of all ten data points, it appears from this figure that firms paying higher wages in our hypothetical sample do indeed have lower quit rates. Although the data points in Figure 1A.1 obviously do not lie on a single straight line, their pattern suggests that, on average, there is a linear relationship between a firm's quit rate and its wage rate.

Any straight line can be represented by the general equation

$$Y = a + bX \qquad (1A.1)$$

Variable Y is the *dependent variable,* and it is generally shown on the vertical axis of the graph depicting the line. Variable X is the *independent* or *explanatory* variable, which is usually shown on the horizontal axis. The letters "a" and "b" are the *parameters* (the fixed coefficients) of the equation, with "a" representing the intercept and "b" the slope of the line. Put differently, "a" is

FIGURE 1A.1   Estimated Relationship Between Wages and Quit Rates Using Data from Table 1A.1

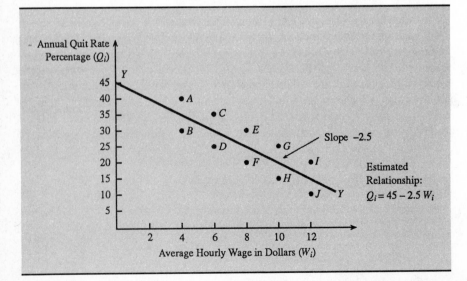

the value of Y when the line intersects the vertical axis ($X = 0$). The slope, "b," indicates the vertical distance the line travels for each one-unit increase in the horizontal distance. If "b" is a positive number the line slopes up (going from left to right); if "b" is a negative number, the line has a downward slope.

If one were to try to draw the straight line that best fits the points in Figure 1A.1, it is clear that the line would slope downward and that it would not go through all ten points. It would lie above some points and below others, and thus it would "fit" the points only with some error. We could model the relationship between the data points on the graph, then, as follows:

$$Q_i = \alpha_0 + \alpha_1 W_i + \epsilon_i \qquad (1A.2)$$

Here Q_i represents the quit rate for firm i and it is the dependent variable. The independent or explanatory variable is W_i, firm i's wage rate. α_0 and α_1 are the parameters of the line, with α_0 the intercept and α_1 the slope of the line. The term ϵ_i is a random *error term;* it is included in the model because we do not expect that the line (given by $Q_i = \alpha_0 + \alpha_1 W_i$) will connect all the data points perfectly. Behaviorally, we are assuming the presence of random factors unrelated to wage rates that also cause the quit rate to vary across firms.

We seek to estimate what the true values of α_0 and α_1 are. Each pair of values of α_0 and α_1 defines a different straight line, and an infinite number of lines can be drawn that "fit" these points. It is natural for us to ask, "Which of these straight lines fits the data the best?" Some precise criterion must be used to decide "which line fits the best," and the procedure typically used by statisticians and economists is to choose that line for which the sum (in our example, across all firms) of the squared vertical distances between the line and the individual data points is minimized. The line estimated from the data using this method, which is called *least squares regression analysis,* has a number of desirable properties.[2]

Application of this method to the data found in Table 1A.1 yields the estimated line[3]

$$Q_i = 45 - 2.5W_i \qquad (1A.3)$$
$$(5.3) \quad (.625)$$

The estimate of α_0, the intercept of the line, is 45 and the estimate of α_1, the slope of the line, is -2.5. Thus, if a firm has a wage rate of \$4/hour, we would predict that its annual quit rate would be $45 - 2.5(4)$, or 35 percent. This estimated quit/wage relationship is drawn in Figure 1A.1 as the line YY. (The numbers in parentheses will be discussed later.)

Several things should be noted about this relationship. First, taken at face value, this estimated relationship implies that firms paying their workers

---

2. These include that, on average, the correct answer for α_1 is obtained, the estimates are the most precise possible among a certain class of estimators, and the sum of the positive and negative vertical deviations of the data points from the estimated line will be zero. For a more formal treatment of the method of least squares, see any statistics or econometrics text. A good introduction for the reader with no statistical background is A. H. Studenmund and Henry Cassidy, *Using Econometrics: A Practical Guide* (Boston: Little, Brown, 1987).

3. Students with access to computer software to estimate regression models can easily verify this result.

nothing (a wage of zero) would be projected to have *only* 45 percent of their workers quit each year $(45 - 2.5(0) = 45)$, while firms paying their workers more than \$18 an hour would have negative quit rates.[4] The former result is nonsensical (why should any workers stay if they were paid nothing?) and the latter result is logically impossible (the quit rate cannot be less than zero). As these extreme examples suggest, it is dangerous to use linear models to make predictions that take one outside the range of observations used in the estimation (in the example, wages from \$4 to \$12). The relationship between wages and quit rates cannot be assumed to be linear (represented by a straight line) for very low and very high values of wages. Fortunately, the linear regression model used in the example can be easily generalized to allow for nonlinear relationships.

Second, the estimated intercept (45) and slope (-2.5) that we obtained are only estimates of the "true" relationship, and there is uncertainty associated with these estimates. The uncertainty arises partly from the fact that we are trying to infer the true values of α_0 and α_1—that is, the values that characterize the wage/quit relationship in the entire population of firms—from a sample of just ten firms. The uncertainty about each estimated coefficient is measured by its *standard error,* or the estimated standard deviation of the coefficient. These standard errors are reported in parentheses under the estimated coefficients in equation (1A.3); for example, given our data, the estimated standard error of the wage coefficient is .625 and that of the intercept term is 5.3. The larger the standard error, the greater the uncertainty about our estimated coefficient's value.

Under suitable assumptions about the distribution of ϵ, the random error term in equation (1A.2), one can use these standard errors to test hypotheses about the estimated coefficients.[5] In our example, we would like to test the hypothesis that α_1 is negative (which implies, as suggested by theory, that higher wages reduce quits) against the "null hypothesis" that α_1 is zero and there is thus no relationship between wages and quits. One common test involves computing for each coefficient a *t statistic,* which is the ratio of the coefficient to its standard error. A heuristic rule, which can be made precise, is that if the absolute value of the *t statistic* is greater than 2, the hypothesis that the true value of the coefficient equals zero can be rejected. Put another way, if the absolute value of a coefficient is at least twice the size of its standard error, one can be fairly confident that the true value of the coefficient is other than zero. In our example, the *t statistic* for the wage coefficient is $-2.5/.625$, or -4.0, which leaves us very confident that the true relationship between wage levels and quit rates is really negative.

MULTIPLE REGRESSION ANALYSIS

The discussion above has *assumed* that the only variable influencing quit rates, other than random (unexplained) factors, is a firm's wage rate. The discussion

---

4. For example, at a wage of \$20/hour the estimated quit rate would be $45 - 2.5(20)$, or -5 percent per year.
5. These assumptions are discussed in any econometrics text.

in Chapter 1 stressed, however, that the prediction of a negative relationship between wages and quit rates is made holding *all other factors constant*. As we will discuss in Chapter 10, there are many factors besides wages that systematically influence quit rates. These include characteristics both of firms (e.g., employee benefits offered, working conditions, and firm size) and of their workers (e.g., age and level of training). If any of these other variables that we have omitted from our analysis tend to vary across firms systematically with the wage rates that the firms offer, the resulting estimated relationship between wage rates and quit rates will be incorrect. In such cases, we must take these other variables into account by using a model with more than one independent variable.

To illustrate this procedure, suppose for simplicity that the only variable affecting a firm's quit rate besides its wage rate is the average age of its work force. Other things held constant, older workers are less likely to quit their jobs for a number of reasons (as workers grow older, ties to friends, neighbors, and co-workers become stronger, and the psychological costs involved in changing jobs—which often requires a geographic move—grow larger). To capture the effects of both wage rates and age, we assume that a firm's quit rate is given by

$$Q_i = \alpha'_0 + \alpha'_1 W_i + \alpha'_2 A_i + \epsilon_i \qquad (1A.4)$$

A_i is a variable representing the age of firm i's workers. Although A_i could be measured as the average age of the work force, or as the percentage of the firm's workers older than some age level, for expositional convenience we have defined it as a *dichotomous* variable. A_i is equal to 1 if the average age of firm i's work force is greater than 40, and it is equal to zero otherwise. Clearly theory suggests that α'_2 is negative, which means that whatever values of α'_1, α'_2, and W_i pertain (that is, holding all else constant), firms with work forces having an average age above 40 years should have lower quit rates than firms with work forces having an average age equal to or below age 40.

The parameters of equation (1A.4)—that is, the values of α'_0, α'_1, and α'_2—can be estimated using *multiple regression analysis*, a method that is analogous to the one described above. This method finds the values of the parameters that define the best straight-line relationship between the dependent variable and the set of independent variables. Each parameter tells us the effect on the dependent variable of a one-unit change in the corresponding independent variable, *holding the other independent variables constant*. Thus, the estimate of α'_1 tells us the estimated effect on the quit rate (Q) of a one-unit change in the wage rate (W), holding the age of a firm's work force (A) constant.

THE PROBLEM OF OMITTED VARIABLES

If we use a univariate regression model in a situation calling for a multiple regression model—that is, if we leave out an important independent variable— our results may suffer from "omitted variables bias." We illustrate this bias because it is an important pitfall in hypothesis-testing and because it illustrates the need to use economic theory to guide empirical testing.

To simplify our example, we assume that we know the true values of α'_0, α'_1, and α'_2 in equation (1A.4) and that there is no random error term in this model (each ϵ_i is zero). Specifically, we assume that

$$Q_i = 50 - 2.5W_i - 10A_i \tag{1A.5}$$

Thus, at any level of wages a firm's quit rate will be 10 percentage points lower if the average age of its work force exceeds 40 than it will be if the average age is less than or equal to 40.

Figure 1A.2 graphically illustrates this assumed relationship between quit rates, wage rates, and work force average age. For all firms that employ workers whose average age is less than 40, A_i equals zero and thus their quit rates are given by the line Z_0Z_0. For all firms that employ workers whose average age is greater than 40, A_i equals 1 and thus their quit rates are given by the line Z_1Z_1. The quit-rate schedule for the latter set of firms is everywhere 10 percentage points below the one for the former set. Both schedules indicate, however, that a \$1 increase in a firm's average hourly wage will reduce its annual quit rate by 2.5 percentage points (that is, both lines have the same slope).

Now suppose a researcher were to estimate the relationship between quit rates and wage rates but ignored the fact that the average age of a firm's workers also affects the quit rate. That is, suppose one were to omit a measure of age and estimate the following equation:

$$Q_i = a_0 + a_1W_i + \epsilon_i \tag{1A.6}$$

Of crucial importance to us is how the estimated value of a_1 will correspond to the true slope of the quit/wage schedule, which we have *assumed* to be -2.5.

FIGURE 1A.2   Relationships Between Wages and Quit Rates (Equation 1A.5)

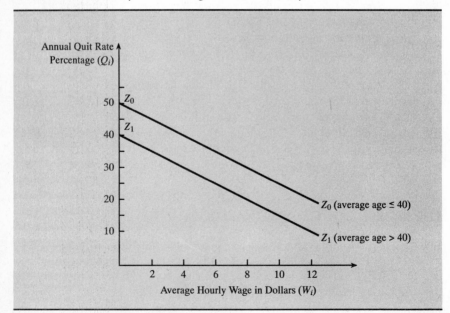

TABLE 1A.2 **Hypothetical Average-Wage and Quit-Rate Data for Three Firms That Employ Older Workers and Three That Employ Younger Workers**

| | Employ Older Workers $(A_i = 1)$ | | | Employ Younger Workers $(A_i = 0)$ | |
Firm	Average Hourly Wage	Quit Rate	Firm	Average Hourly Wage	Quit Rate
k	$ 8	20%	p	$4	40%
l	10	15	q	6	35
m	12	10	r	8	30

The answer depends heavily on how average wages and the average age of employees vary across firms. Table 1A.2 lists combinations of quit rates and wages for three hypothetical firms that employ older workers (average age greater than 40) and three hypothetical firms that employ younger workers. Given the wage each firm pays, the values of its quit rate can be derived directly from equation (1A.5).

It is a well-established fact that earnings of workers tend to increase as they age.[6] On average, then, firms employing older workers are assumed in the table to have higher wages than firms employing younger workers. The wage/quit rate combinations for these six firms are indicated by the dots on the lines $Z_0 Z_0$ and $Z_1 Z_1$ in Figure 1A.3,[7] which reproduce the lines in Figure 1A.2.

FIGURE 1A.3 Estimated Relationships Between Wages and Quit Rates from Data in Table 1A.2

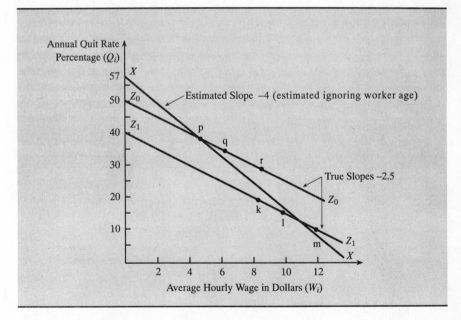

---

6. Reasons why this occurs will be discussed in Chapters 5, 9, and 11.
7. The fact that the dots fall exactly on a straight line is a graphic representation of the assumption in equation (1A.5) that there is no random error term. If random error is present, the dots would fall *around,* but not all *on,* a straight line.

When one estimates equation (1A.6) using these six data points, one obtains the following straight line:

$$Q_i = 57 - 4W_i \qquad (1A.7)$$
$$(5.1) \quad (.612)$$

This estimated relationship is denoted by the line XX in Figure 1A.3. The estimate of a_1, which equals -4, implies that every dollar increase in wages reduces the quit rate by four percentage points, yet we know (by assumption) that the actual reduction is two and a half percentage points. Our estimated response overstates the sensitivity of the quit rate to wages because the estimated equation ignored the effect that age has on quits.

Put differently, quit rates are lower in high-wage firms *both* because the wages they pay are higher, *and* because high-wage firms tend to employ older workers, who are less likely to quit. By ignoring age in the analysis, we mistakenly conclude that quit rates are more sensitive to wage changes than they actually are. Therefore, by omitting from our model an important explanatory variable (age) that both affects quit rates and is associated with wage levels, we have obtained the wrong estimate of the effect of wages on quit rates.

This discussion highlights "the other things held equal" nature of most hypotheses in labor economics. In testing hypotheses, one must control for other factors that are expected to influence the variable of interest. Typically this is done by specifying that the dependent variable is a function of a *set* of variables. This specification must be guided by economic theory, and one reason for learning economic theory is that it can guide us in testing hypotheses about human behavior. Without a firm grounding in theory, analyses of behavior can easily run afoul of omitted variables bias.

Having said this, we must point out that it is neither possible nor crucial to have data on all conceivable variables that influence (say) quit rates. As emphasized in Chapter 1, testing economic models involves looking for *average* relationships and ignoring idiosyncratic factors. Two workers with the same age and the same wage rate may exhibit different quit behaviors because, for example, one wants to leave town to avoid a dreadful father-in-law. This idiosyncratic factor is not important for the testing of an economic model of quit rates, because having a father-in-law has neither a predictable effect on quits (some fathers-in-law are desirable to be around) nor any correlation with one's wage rate. To repeat, omitted variables bias is a problem only if the omitted variable has an effect on the dependent variable (quit rate) *and* is correlated with an independent variable of interest (wages).

2

Overview of the Labor Market

E very society—regardless of its wealth, its form of government, or the organization of its economy—must make certain basic decisions. It must decide what and how much to produce, how to produce it, and how the output shall be distributed. These decisions require finding out what consumers want, what technologies for production are available, and what the skills and preferences of workers are; deciding where to produce; and coordinating all such decisions so that, for example, the millions of people in New York City and the isolated few in an Alaskan fishing village can each buy the milk, bread, meat, vanilla extract, mosquito repellent, and brown shoe polish they desire at the grocery store. The process of coordination involves creating incentives so that the right amount of labor and capital will be employed at the right place at the required time.

These decisions can, of course, be made by administrators employed by a centralized bureaucracy. The amount of information this bureaucracy must obtain and process to make the millions of needed decisions wisely and the number of incentives it must give out to ensure that these decisions are coordinated are truly mind-boggling. It boggles the mind even more to consider the major alternative to centralized decision making—the decentralized marketplace. Millions of producers striving to make a profit observe the prices millions of consumers are willing to pay for products and the wages millions of workers are willing to accept for work. Combining these pieces of information with data on various technologies, they decide where to produce, what to produce, whom to hire, and how much to produce. No one is in charge, and while imperfections impede progress toward achieving the best allocation of resources, millions of people find jobs that enable them to purchase the items they desire each year. The production, employment, and consumption decisions are all made and coordinated by price signals arising through the marketplace.

The market that allocates workers to jobs and coordinates employment decisions is *the labor market*. With over 120 million workers and about 5 million employers in the United States, thousands of decisions about career choice, hiring, quitting, compensation, and technology must be made and coordinated every day. This chapter will present an overview of what the labor market does and how it works. For those students who may already have mastered microeconomic theory, this chapter can provide a review of basic concepts.

THE LABOR MARKET: DEFINITIONS, FACTS, AND TRENDS

Every market has buyers and sellers, and the labor market is no exception: the buyers are employers and the sellers are workers. Because there are so many buyers and sellers of labor at any given time, the decisions that are made in any particular case are influenced by the behavior and decisions of others. For example, when other employers are increasing compensation, a firm may decide to do likewise to remain competitive in its ability to attract and hold workers. Likewise, a current or prospective teacher may choose to go into personnel work if he or she discovers that teachers are having a difficult time finding jobs.

The *labor market* is thus composed of all the buyers and sellers of labor. Some of these participants may not be active at any given moment in the sense of seeking new jobs or new employees, but on any given day thousands of firms and workers will be "in the market" trying to transact. If, as in the case of doctors or mechanical engineers, buyers and sellers are searching throughout the entire nation for each other, we would describe the market as a *national labor market*. If buyers and sellers only search locally, as in the case of secretaries or automobile mechanics, the labor market is a *local* one.

Some labor markets, particularly those in which the sellers of labor are represented by a union, operate under a very formal set of rules that partly govern buyer–seller transactions. In the construction and longshoring trades, for example, employers must hire at the union hiring hall from a list of eligible union members. In other unionized markets, the employer has discretion over who gets hired but is constrained by a union–management agreement in such matters as the order in which employees may be laid off, procedures regarding employee complaints, the compensation schedule, the workload or pace of work, and promotions. The markets for government jobs and jobs with large nonunion employers also tend to operate under rules that constrain the authority of management and ensure fair treatment of employees. When a formal set of rules and procedures guides and constrains the employment relationship *within* a firm, an *internal labor market* is said to exist.[1]

In many cases, of course, labor market transactions are not made within the context of written rules or procedures. Most transactions in which an employee is changing employers or newly entering the market fall in this cate-

---

1. P. Doeringer and M. Piore, *Internal Labor Markets and Manpower Analysis* (Lexington, Mass.: D. C. Heath, 1971). A more recent analysis of internal labor markets can be found in Michael L. Wachter and Randall Wright, "The Economics of Internal Labor Markets," Discussion Paper no. 70, Institute for Law and Economics, University of Pennsylvania, February 1989.

gory. Written rules or procedures generally do not govern within-firm transactions—such as promotions and layoffs—among smaller, nonunion employers. While jobs in this sector of the labor market can be stable and well-paying, many are not. Low-wage, unstable jobs are sometimes considered to be in the *secondary labor market.*[2] We will discuss the concept of secondary labor markets in greater detail in Chapters 11 and 14.

When we speak of a particular "labor market"—for taxi drivers, say—we are using the term loosely to refer to the companies trying to hire people to drive their cabs and the people seeking employment as cabdrivers. The efforts of these buyers and sellers of labor to transact and establish an employment relationship constitute the market for cabdrivers. However, neither the employers nor the drivers are confined to this market; both could simultaneously be in other markets as well. An entrepreneur with $100,000 to invest might be thinking of operating either a taxi company or a car wash, depending on the projected revenues and costs of each. A person seeking a cabdriving job might also be trying to find work as an electronics assembler. Thus, all the various labor markets that we can define on the basis of industry, occupation, geography, transaction rules, or job character are interrelated to some degree. We speak of these narrowly defined labor markets for the sake of convenience, and doing so should not suggest that people are necessarily or permanently locked in to markets that are independent of other markets.

The Labor Force and Unemployment

Figure 2.1 highlights some basic definitions concerning labor market status. The term *labor force* refers to all those over 16 years of age who are either employed, actively seeking work, or awaiting recall from a layoff. Those in the labor force who are not employed for pay are the *unemployed.*[3] People who are not employed and are neither looking for work nor waiting to be recalled from layoff by their employers are not counted as part of the labor force. The total labor force thus consists of the employed and the unemployed.

The number and identities of people in each labor market category are always changing, and as we shall see in Chapter 15, the flows of people from one category to another are sizable. As Figure 2.1 suggests, there are four major flows between labor market states:

1. Employed workers become unemployed by voluntarily *quitting* or *being laid off* (being involuntarily separated from the firm, either temporarily or permanently).
2. Unemployed workers obtain employment by *being newly hired* or *being recalled* to a job from which they were temporarily laid off.

---

2. Doeringer and Piore, *Internal Labor Markets and Manpower Analysis.*
3. The official definition of unemployment for purposes of government statistics includes those who have been laid off by their employers, those who have been fired or have quit and are looking for other work, and those who are just entering or reentering the labor force but have not found a job as yet. The extent of unemployment is estimated from a monthly survey of some 55,000 households called the Current Population Survey (CPS). Interviewers ascertain whether household members are employed, whether they meet one of the aforementioned conditions (in which case they are considered "unemployed"), or whether they are out of the labor force.

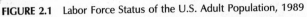

FIGURE 2.1   Labor Force Status of the U.S. Adult Population, 1989

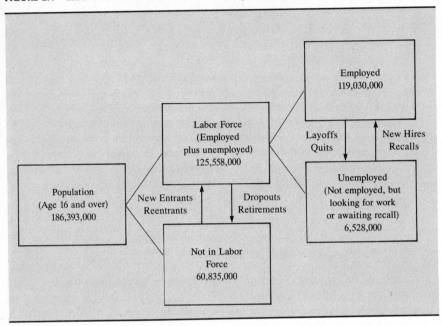

3. Those in the labor force, whether employed or unemployed, can leave the labor force by *retiring* or otherwise deciding against taking or seeking work for pay *(dropping out)*.
4. Those who have never worked or looked for a job expand the labor force by *newly entering* it, while those who have dropped out do so by *reentering* the labor force.

In 1989 there were over 125 million people in the labor force, representing 67 percent of the entire population over 16 years of age. An overall *labor force participation rate* (labor force divided by population) of nearly 67 percent is substantially higher than the rates around 60 percent that prevailed prior to the 1980s, as is shown by the data in Table 2.1. This table also indicates the most important fact about labor force trends in this century: *labor force participation rates for men are falling while those for women are increasing dramatically.* These trends and their causes will be discussed in detail in Chapters 6 and 7.

The ratio of those unemployed to those in the labor force is the *unemployment rate.* While this rate is crude and has several imperfections, it is the most widely cited measure of labor market conditions. When the unemployment rate is in the 3–4 percent range in the United States, the labor market is considered *tight*—indicating that jobs in general are plentiful and hard for employers to fill and that most of those who are unemployed will find other work quickly.[4] When the unemployment rate is higher—say, 7 percent or

---

4. Many economists now argue that labor markets are tight when unemployment is around 5 percent or even a bit more. This issue will be discussed in Chapter 15.

TABLE 2.1   Labor Force Participation Rates by Gender, 1950–1989

Year	Total	Men	Women
1950	59.9%	86.8%	33.9%
1960	60.2	84.0	37.8
1970	61.3	80.6	43.4
1980	64.2	77.9	51.6
1989	66.8	76.8	57.5

SOURCES:

1950–1980: U.S. President, *Employment and Training Report of the President* (Washington, D.C.: U.S. Government Printing Office), transmitted to the Congress 1981, Table A-1.

1989: U.S. Bureau of Labor Statistics, *Employment and Earnings* 37, no. 1 (January 1990), Tables A-1, A-2.

above—the labor market is described as *loose,* in the sense that workers are abundant and jobs are relatively easy for employers to fill. To say that the labor market as a whole is loose, however, does not imply that no shortages can be found anywhere; to say it is tight can still mean that in some occupations or places the number of those seeking work exceeds the number of jobs available at the prevailing wage.

Figure 2.2 displays the overall unemployment rate during this century (the data displayed graphically in Figure 2.2 are contained in the table inside the front cover). The data clearly show the extraordinarily loose labor market during the Great Depression of the 1930s and the exceptionally tight labor market during World War II. However, when we look at long stretches of nonwar years, excluding the years of the Great Depression, two interesting pat-

FIGURE 2.2   Unemployment Rates for the Civilian Labor Force, 1900–1989

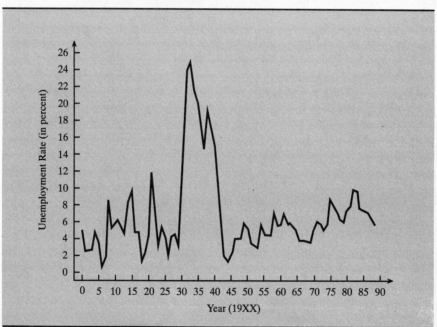

terns emerge. First, the average unemployment rate has clearly risen: it was 4.4 percent in 1900–1914, but in the most recent nonwar periods it was 5.3 percent (1954–65) and 7.0 percent (1973–89). Second, in recent years the unemployment rate has fluctuated less than it did in 1900–1914. In the years from 1900 to 1914, the average yearly change in the unemployment rate was 1.9 percentage points; in contrast, from 1954 to 1965 and from 1973 to 1989 it was 0.8 percentage points. The labor market, then, would appear to be more stable now than it was at the turn of the century, but it operates with proportionately more unemployment. Chapter 15 will present a more detailed analysis of the determinants of the unemployment rate.

Industries and Occupations: Adapting to Change

As we pointed out earlier, the labor market is the mechanism through which workers and jobs are matched. Over the years in this century, the number of some kinds of jobs has expanded and the number of others has contracted. Both workers and employers had to adapt to these changes in response to signals provided by the labor market. For example, in 1976 there were 4.3 million places of employment (establishments) in the United States. As shown in panel (a) of Figure 2.3, over the next six years alone 1.3 million (30 percent) of these were closed! Fortunately, another 1.7 million were opened. Of the 22 million manufacturing jobs in 1976, 8 million were "destroyed" over the six-year period, but 9.1 million new jobs were created (see panel b of Figure 2.3). The labor market is indeed characterized by continual churning.

FIGURE 2.3   Establishment and Job Changes, 1976–1982

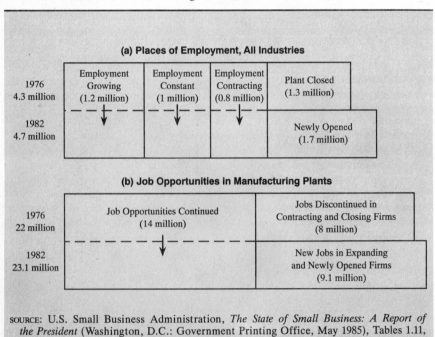

SOURCE: U.S. Small Business Administration, *The State of Small Business: A Report of the President* (Washington, D.C.: Government Printing Office, May 1985), Tables 1.11, 1.12, A1.21.

An examination of the industrial distribution of employment from 1900 to 1989 reveals the kinds of changes the labor market has had to facilitate. Table 2.2 discloses a major shift: *agricultural employment has declined drastically while employment in service industries has expanded.* Goods-producing jobs increased roughly proportionately to the increase in total employment during the first seven decades, but their share fell sharply after 1980. The largest employment increases have been in the service sector. Retail and wholesale trade, which increased from 9.2 percent of employment in 1910 to 23.2 percent in 1989, showed the largest increases in nongovernment services. However, the largest percentage increase has been in government employment, which almost quadrupled its share of total employment over the 89-year period. Some describe this shift in employment from agriculture to services as a shift from the *primary* to the *tertiary* sector (manufacturing being labeled the *secondary* sector). Others describe it as the arrival of the "post-industrial" state. In any case, the shift in employment has been accompanied by large population movements off the farms and to urban areas. These population movements have also been largely coordinated by the labor market, as Chapter 10 will show.

TABLE 2.2   Employment Distribution by Major Industrial Sector, 1900–1989

Year	Agriculture[a]	Goods-Producing Industries[b]	Nongovernment Services[c]	Government Services[d]
1900	38.1%	37.8%	20.0%	4.1%
1910	32.1	40.9	22.3	4.7
1920	27.6	44.8	21.6	6.0
1930	22.7	42.1	28.1	7.1
1940	18.5	41.6	31.1	8.8
1950	12.1	41.3	36.4	10.2
1960	6.6	41.4	38.8	13.2
1970	3.8	39.8	40.5	15.9
1980	3.6	32.8	46.3	17.3
1989	2.6	28.1	53.4	15.9

Note: From 1900 to 1930, "employment" refers to "gainful workers." From 1940, "employment" refers to experienced civilian labor force. Where applicable, persons not assigned to an industry were assumed to have the same employment distribution as those who were.

[a] Agriculture includes forestry and fishing.
[b] Included are manufacturing, mining, construction, transportation, communications, and public utilities.
[c] Included are trade; personal, professional, and business services; entertainment; finance; and real estate.
[d] Includes federal, state, and local government workers.

SOURCES:

1900–1940: U.S. Bureau of the Census, *Historical Statistics of the United States, Colonial Times to 1957,* 1960, Table D57-71.

1950: *U.S. Census of Population 1950,* Subject Reports, vol. IV, Chapter 1D, 1955, Table 15.

1960: *U.S. Census of Population 1960,* Subject Reports, PC(2)-7F, 1967, Table 1.

1970: *U.S. Census of Population 1970,* Subject Reports, PC(2)-7B, 1972, Table 1.

1980: U.S. Bureau of the Census, *Statistical Abstract of the United States,* 103d ed., 1982, Tables 624, 629.

1989: U.S. Bureau of Labor Statistics, *Employment and Earnings,* 37, no. 1 (January 1990), Tables A-25, B-1.

The combination of shifts in the industrial distribution of jobs and shifts in the production technology within each sector has also required that workers acquire new skills and work in new jobs. Table 2.3 shows that a large increase in *white-collar,* or nonmanual, jobs has taken place concurrently with a large decline in agricultural jobs. Manual workers have witnessed a small decline in their share of total employment, while personal-service workers have shown relatively modest increases since 1900. The largest single gain has come about in clerical jobs, although professional and technical jobs (teachers, engineers, lawyers, and so forth) have also increased disproportionately fast.

Labor markets must work very effectively if enormous shifts in the industrial and occupational distribution of employment are to be accomplished without long delays or undue hardship. There is disagreement over how effectively and humanely labor markets operate, but the labor market clearly plays an incredibly large and important role in society.

TABLE 2.3 Occupational Distribution of the Experienced Civilian Labor Force, 1900–1987 (in percent)

	1900	1910	1920	1930	1940	1950	1960	1970	1980	1987
White-collar workers	17.6	21.0	25.0	29.4	31.1	36.6	42.2	47.5	52.2	55.9
Professional and technical	4.3	4.6	5.4	6.8	7.5	8.6	11.3	14.6	16.1	15.8
Managers	5.9	6.5	6.6	7.4	7.3	8.7	8.5	8.1	11.2	14.6
Clerical	3.0	5.2	8.0	8.9	9.6	12.3	14.9	17.8	18.6	15.6
Sales	4.5	4.6	4.9	6.3	6.7	7.0	7.5	7.0	6.3	9.0
Manual workers	35.8	37.5	40.2	39.6	39.8	41.1	39.7	36.6	31.7	27.6
Craft workers	10.6	11.4	13.0	12.8	12.0	14.2	14.3	13.9	12.9	12.1
Operatives	12.8	14.4	15.6	15.8	18.4	20.4	19.9	17.9	14.2	11.3
Laborers (nonfarm)	12.5	11.8	11.6	11.0	9.4	6.6	5.5	4.7	4.6	4.3
Personal-service workers	9.1	9.4	7.9	9.8	11.8	10.5	11.7	12.9	13.3	13.4
Domestics	5.4	4.9	3.3	4.1	4.7	2.6	2.8	1.5	1.1	0.8
Other[a]	3.6	4.5	4.5	5.7	7.1	7.9	8.9	11.3	12.3	12.6
Farm workers	37.5	30.4	27.0	21.2	17.4	11.8	6.3	3.1	2.8	3.1
Farmers and farm managers	19.9	16.3	15.3	12.4	10.4	7.4	3.9	1.8	1.5	1.2
Farm laborers	17.7	14.2	11.7	8.8	7.0	4.4	2.4	1.3	1.3	1.9

Note: From 1900 to 1930, employment data relate to "gainful workers." From 1940 on, data relate to experienced civilian labor force. 1980s data are not strictly comparable because they relate only to the *employed* labor force aged 16 and over.

[a]Included are attendants, barbers, cooks, guards, janitors, police, practical nurses, ushers, waiters, etc.

SOURCES:
1900–1950: U.S. Bureau of the Census, *Historical Statistics of the United States, Colonial Times to 1957* (1960), Table D72-122.

1960: U.S. Bureau of the Census, *Census of Population 1960,* Subject Reports, PC(2)-7A, 1967, Table 1.

1970: U.S. Bureau of the Census, *Census of Population 1970,* Subject Reports, PC(2)-7A, 1972, Table 1.

1980: U.S. President, *Employment and Training Report of the President* (Washington, D.C.: U.S. Government Printing Office, 1981), 149.

1987: U.S. Bureau of Labor Statistics, *Employment and Earnings,* 35, no. 1 (January 1988), Table 20.

The Earnings of Labor

The actions of buyers and sellers in the labor market serve both to allocate and to set prices for various kinds of labor. From a social perspective, these prices act as signals or incentives in the allocation process, a process that relies primarily on individual and voluntary decisions. From the worker's point of view, the price of labor is important in determining income—and hence purchasing power.

Nominal and Real Wages.   The *wage rate* is the price of labor per working hour.[5] The *nominal wage* is what workers get paid per hour in current dollars; nominal wages are most useful in comparing the pay of various workers at a given time. *Real wages,* nominal wages divided by some measure of prices, suggest how much can be purchased with workers' nominal wages. For example, if a worker earns $64 a day and a pair of shoes costs $32, one could say the worker earns the equivalent of two pairs of shoes a day (real wage = $64/$32 = 2).

Calculations of real wages are especially useful in comparing the purchasing power of workers' earnings over a period of time when both nominal wages and product prices are changing. Thus, real wages are normally expressed as an *index number,* which compares the purchasing power of an hour of work to some base period (the base is set equal to 100). To understand how index numbers are constructed, refer to the next-to-last column in Table 2.4, where the index of real hourly wages in 1989 is listed as 384. This means that hourly real wages were almost exactly four times higher in 1989 than in the base year, which was chosen arbitrarily as 1914.

To arrive at an index of *real* hourly wages requires that we calculate an index of nominal wages *and* an index of prices. An index of nominal wages can be constructed for each year (with 1914 as a base) by dividing the wage in each year by $0.22—the hourly wage in 1914—and multiplying by 100. This fixes the index at 100 in 1914 and yields an index number of 4759 for 1989 [$(10.47 \div 0.22) \times 100$]. The Consumer Price Index, which is based on "pricing out" a "market basket" of goods from year to year, is 1240 for 1989 if 1914 is the base year. Dividing the price index (1240) into the index for nominal wages (4759) and multiplying by 100 gives us the figure of 384 in the table.

Wages, Earnings, Compensation, and Income.   We often apply the term *wages* to payments received by workers who are paid on a salaried basis (monthly, for example) rather than an hourly basis. The term is used this way

---

5. In this book we define the hourly wage in the way most workers would if asked to state their "straight-time" wage. It is the money a worker would lose per hour if he or she had an unauthorized absence. When wages are defined in this way, a paid holiday becomes an "employee benefit," as we note below, because leisure time is granted while pay continues. Thus, a worker paid $100 for 25 hours—20 of which are working hours and 5 of which are time off—will be said to earn a wage of $4 per hour and receive time off worth $20.

An alternative is to define the wage in terms of actual hours worked—or as $5 per hour in the above example. We prefer our definition, because if the worker seizes an opportunity to work one less hour in a particular week, his or her earnings would fall by $4, not $5 (as long as the reduction in hours does not affect the hours of paid holiday or vacation time for which the worker is eligible).

merely for convenience and is of no consequence for most purposes. It is important, however, to distinguish among wages, earnings, and income, as we do
schematically in Figure 2.4. The term *wages* refers to the payment for a *unit*
of time, while *earnings* refers to wages multiplied by the number of time units
(typically hours) worked. Thus, earnings depend on both wages and the length
of time the employee works. *Income*—the total command over resources of a
person or family during some time period (usually a year)—includes both
earnings and *unearned income,* which includes dividends or interest received
on investments and transfer payments received from the government in the
form of food stamps, welfare payments, unemployment compensation, and
the like.

Table 2.4 shows the long-run trends in earnings and wages for U.S. manufacturing production workers. While real weekly earnings were over three
times higher in 1989 than in 1914, the fall in paid weekly hours from 49 to 41
represented an additional gain in the general standard of living for workers.
Probably the best index of living standards is how much workers receive *per
hour,* and Table 2.4 shows that real hourly wages were 3.84 times higher in
1989 than in 1914, which implies that an hour of work paid for about four
times more goods and services in 1989 than in 1914. Interestingly, however,
the rate of growth of real wages has steadily dropped since 1945, and over the
1975–89 period the real wage rate actually fell for the first time this century.

The actual long-term increase in living standards attained by the ordinary worker is perhaps even greater than indicated in Table 2.4. Both wages
and earnings are normally defined and measured in terms of direct monetary
payments to employees (before taxes for which the employee is liable). *Total
compensation,* on the other hand, consists of earnings plus *employee benefits*—benefits that are either payments in kind or deferred. Examples of *pay-*

FIGURE 2.4   Relationship Between Wages, Earnings, Compensation, and Income

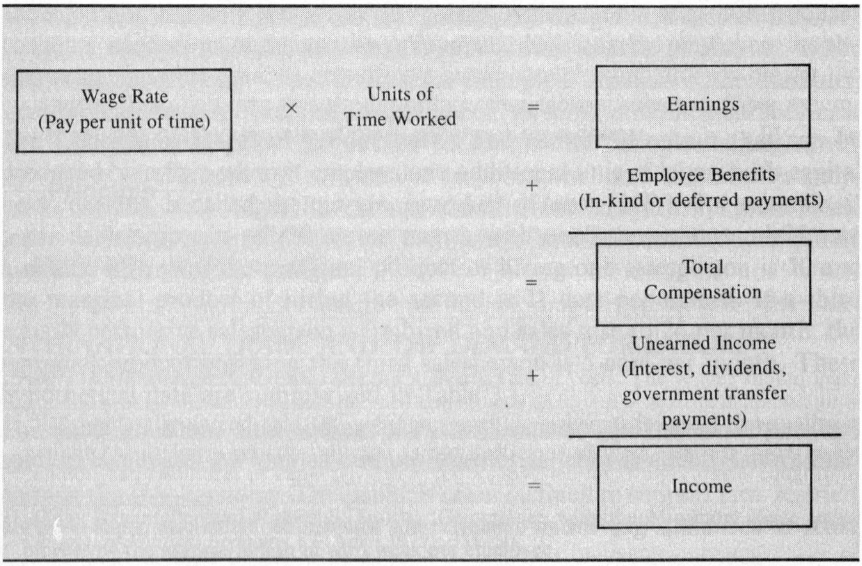

TABLE 2.4   Average Wages and Earnings of Production Workers in Manufacturing, 1914–89

Year	Weekly Earnings (current dollars)	Average Weekly Hours Paid For	Average Hourly Wage (current dollars)	Consumer Price Index (1914 = 100)[a]	Index of Real Weekly Earnings (1914 = 100)	Index of Real Hourly Wages (1914 = 100)	Annual Percentage Change in Real Hourly Wages over Previous 10 Years
1914	10.92	49.4	0.22	100	100	100	
1920	26.02	47.4	0.55	199	120	126	
1925	24.11	44.5	0.54	174	127	141	3.1[b]
1930	23.00	42.1	0.55	166	127	151	
1935	19.91	36.6	0.54	137	133	179	2.3
1940	24.96	38.1	0.66	140	163	214	
1945	44.20	43.5	1.02	179	226	259	3.7
1950	58.32	40.5	1.44	240	223	273	
1955	75.70	40.7	1.86	266	261	318	2.1
1960	89.72	39.7	2.26	295	278	348	
1965	107.53	41.2	2.61	314	314	378	1.7
1970	133.73	39.8	3.36	386	317	396	
1975	189.51	39.4	4.81	536	324	408	0.8
1980	288.62	39.7	7.27	820	322	403	
1989	429.27	41.0	10.47	1240	317	384	−0.4[c]

[a] The figures in this column should be interpreted with some caution. They are generated by pricing out a fixed "market basket" of consumer goods each year. Over time, however, new goods have become available and old ones improved in quality, so that comparability of the "baskets" used in making the index diminishes over time.

[b] Change calculated over previous 11 years.

[c] Change calculated over previous 14 years.

SOURCES: U.S. Bureau of the Census, *Historical Statistics of the United States, Colonial Times to 1970* (Washington, D.C.: U.S. Government Printing Office, 1975); U.S. Department of Labor, Bureau of Labor Statistics, *Handbook of Labor Statistics 1977,* Bulletin 1966 (Washington, D.C.: U.S. Government Printing Office, 1977); U.S. Department of Labor, Bureau of Labor Statistics, *Handbook of Labor Statistics,* Bulletin 2340 (Washington, D.C.: U.S. Government Printing Office, 1989), Tables 75, 80, 83; U.S. Department of Labor, Bureau of Labor Statistics, *Employment and Earnings,* 37, no. 1 (January 1990), Table 65.

ments in kind are employer-provided health care and health insurance, where the employee receives a service or an insurance policy rather than money. Paid vacation time is also in this category, since employees are given days off instead of cash. *Deferred* payments can take the form of employer-financed retirement benefits, including Social Security taxes, in which employers set aside money now that enables their employees to receive pensions later.

By 1988, earnings as conventionally defined constituted only 63 percent of the total compensation of manufacturing production workers. Vacations, pensions, and insurance were the largest categories of employee benefits. Because employee benefits were virtually nonexistent before 1940, we can assume that total earnings and total compensation were essentially the same in the early 1900s. If earnings in more recent years are adjusted to reflect employee benefits, we arrive at the conclusion that real compensation per hour in the late '80s was six times higher than in 1914 for the typical manufacturing worker.

The next section will shift from labor market *outcomes* over time to an analysis of how the market *operates* to generate these outcomes. This analysis of labor market functioning is the central focus of labor economics.

HOW THE LABOR MARKET WORKS

As shown diagrammatically in Figure 2.5, the labor market is one of three markets in which firms must successfully operate if they are to survive; the other two are the capital market and the product market. The labor and capital markets are the major ones in which firms' inputs are purchased, and the product market is the one in which output is sold. In reality, of course, a firm may deal in many different labor, capital, or product markets simultaneously.

The study of the labor market begins and ends with an analysis of the demand for and supply of labor. On the demand side of the labor market are employers, whose decisions about the hiring of labor are influenced by conditions in all three markets. On the supply side of the labor market are workers and potential workers, whose decisions about where (and whether) to work must take into account their other options for how to spend time.

It is useful to remember that the major labor market outcomes are related to (*a*) the *terms of employment* (wages, compensation levels, working conditions), and (*b*) *employment levels*. In analyzing both these outcomes, one must usually differentiate among the various occupational, skill, or demographic groups that make up the overall labor market. It is also important to remember that any labor market outcome is always affected, to one degree or another, by the forces of both demand and supply. To paraphrase economist Alfred Marshall, it takes both demand and supply to determine economic outcomes, just as it takes both blades of a scissors to cut cloth.

FIGURE 2.5 The Markets in Which Firms Must Operate

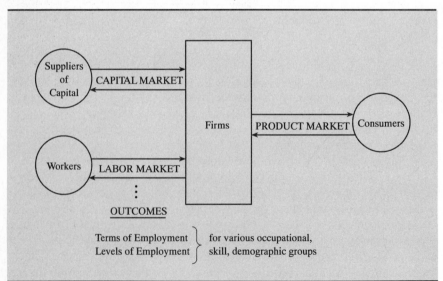

In this chapter we present the basic outlines and broadest implications of the simplest economic model of the labor market. In later chapters we shall add some complexities to this basic model and explain assumptions and implications more fully. However, the simple model of demand and supply presented here offers some insights into labor market behavior that can be very useful in the formulation of social policy. Every piece of analysis in this text is an extension or modification of the basic model presented in this chapter.

The Demand for Labor

Firms combine various factors of production—mainly capital and labor—to produce goods or services that are sold in a product market. Their total output and the way in which they combine labor and capital depend on product demand, the amount of labor and capital they can acquire at given prices, and the choice of technologies available to them. When we study the demand for labor, we are interested in finding out how the number of workers employed by a firm or set of firms is affected by changes in one or more of these three forces. To simplify the discussion, we shall study one change at a time and hold all other forces constant.

Wage Changes.   Of primary interest for most purposes is the question of how the number of employees (or total labor hours) demanded varies when wages change. Suppose, for example, that we could vary the wages facing a certain industry over a long period of time but keep the technology available, the conditions under which capital is supplied, and the relationship between product price and product demand unchanged. What would happen to the quantity of labor demanded if, say, the wage rate were *increased?*

First, higher wages imply higher costs and, usually, higher product prices. Because consumers respond to higher prices by buying less, employers would tend to reduce their level of output. Lower output levels, of course, imply lower employment levels (other things being equal). This decline in employment is called a *scale effect*—the effect on desired employment of a smaller scale of production.

Second, as wages increase (assuming the price of capital does not change, at least initially), employers have incentives to cut costs by adopting a technology that relies more on capital and less on labor. Thus, if wages were to rise, desired employment would fall because of a shift toward a more "capital-intensive" mode of production. This second effect might be termed a *substitution effect*, because as wages rise, capital is *substituted* for labor in the production process.

The effects of various wages on employment levels might be summarized in a table showing the labor demanded at each wage level. Table 2.5 illustrates such a *demand schedule*. The relationship between wages and employment tabulated in Table 2.5 could be graphed as a *demand curve*. Figure 2.6 shows the demand curve generated by the data in Table 2.5. Note that the curve has a negative slope, indicating that as wages rise, less labor is demanded.

A demand curve for labor tells us how the desired level of employment, measured in either labor hours or number of employees, varies with changes

TABLE 2.5   Labor Demand Schedule for a Hypothetical Industry

Wage Rate	Desired Employment Level
$3.00	250
4.00	190
5.00	160
6.00	130
7.00	100
8.00	70

Note: Employment levels can be measured in number of employees *or* number of labor hours demanded. We have chosen here to use number of employees.

in the price of labor when the other forces affecting demand are held constant. These other forces, to repeat, are the product demand schedule, the conditions under which capital can be obtained, and the set of technologies available. If wages change and these other factors do not, one can determine the change in labor demanded by moving up or down along the demand curve.

Changes in Other Forces Affecting Demand.   What happens when one of the other forces affecting labor demand changes?

First, suppose that *demand for the product* of a particular industry were to increase, so that at any output price, more of the goods or services in question could be sold. Suppose in this case that technology and the conditions under which capital and labor are made available to the industry do not change. Output levels would clearly rise as firms in the industry sought to maximize profits, and this *scale* (or *output*) *effect* would increase the amount of labor demanded. (As long as the relative prices of capital and labor remain unchanged, there is no *substitution effect*.)

How would this change in the demand for labor be illustrated using a demand curve? Since the technology available and the conditions under which capital and labor are supplied have remained constant, this change in product demand would increase the labor desired at any wage level that might prevail. In other words, the entire labor demand curve *shifts* to the right. This right-

FIGURE 2.6   Labor Demand Curve

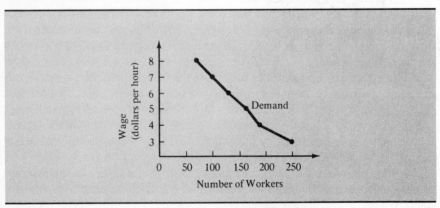

FIGURE 2.7   Shift in Demand for Labor Due to Increase in Product Demand

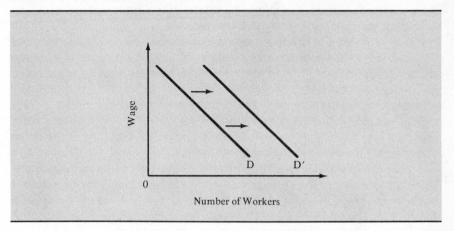

ward shift, shown as a movement from D to D' in Figure 2.7, indicates that at every possible wage rate the number of workers demanded has increased.

Second, consider what would happen if the product demand schedule, technology, and labor supply conditions were to remain unchanged, but *the supply of capital* changed so that capital prices fell to 50 percent of their prior level. How would this change affect the demand for labor?

Our method of analyzing the effects on labor demand of a change in the price of *another* productive input is familiar: we must consider the scale and substitution effects. First, when capital prices decline, the costs of producing tend to decline. Reduced costs stimulate increases in production, and these increases tend to raise the level of desired employment at any given wage. The scale effect of a fall in capital prices thus tends to increase the demand for labor at each wage level, which can be represented in Figure 2.8 by a shift to the right of the labor demand curve.

FIGURE 2.8   Shift in Demand for Labor Due to Scale Effect Resulting from Fall in Capital Prices

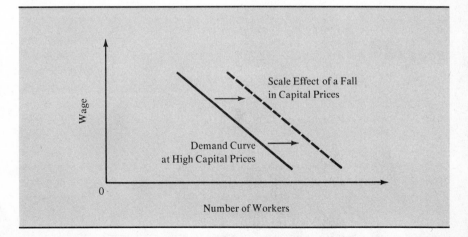

The second effect of a fall in capital prices would be a substitution effect, whereby firms adopt more-capital-intensive technologies in response to cheaper capital. Such firms would substitute capital for labor and would use less labor to produce a given amount of output than before. With less labor being desired at each wage rate, the labor demand curve tends to shift to the left, as shown in Figure 2.9. In some cases this leftward-shifting tendency of the substitution effect would be stronger than the rightward-shifting tendency of the scale effect; in other cases, the scale effect would be stronger. Thus, when the price of a substitute for labor changes, the effects on the demand for labor are not theoretically predictable (because the scale and substitution effects work in opposite directions).

The hypothesized changes in product demand and capital supply just discussed have tended to *shift* the demand curve for labor. It is important to distinguish between a *shift* in a demand curve and *movement along* a curve. A labor demand curve graphically shows the *labor desired* as a function of the *wage rate* (the wage is on one axis and the number employed is on the other). When the *wage* changes and other forces are held unchanged, one *moves along* the curve. However, when one of the *other forces* changes, the labor demand curve *shifts*. Unlike wages, these forces are not directly shown when the demand curve for labor is drawn. Thus, when they change, a different relationship between wages and employment prevails, and this shows up as a shift of the demand curve. If more labor is desired at any given wage rate, then the curve has shifted to the right. If less labor is demanded at each wage rate that might prevail, then the demand curve has shifted left.

Market, Industry, and Firm Demand.   The demand for labor can be analyzed on three levels:

1. To analyze the demand for labor *by a particular firm*, we would examine how an increase in the wage of machinists, say, would affect their employment by a particular aircraft manufacturer.

FIGURE 2.9   Shift in Demand for Labor Due to Substitution Effect Resulting from Fall in Capital Prices

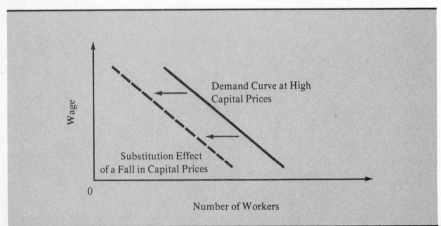

2. To analyze the effects of this wage increase on the employment of machinists *in the entire aircraft industry,* we would utilize an industry demand curve.

3. Finally, to see how the wage increase would affect the *entire labor market* for machinists, in all industries in which they are used, we would use a market demand curve.

We shall see in Chapters 3 and 4 that firm, industry, and market labor demand curves vary in *shape* to some extent because *scale* and *substitution effects* have different strengths at each level. However, it is important to remember that the scale and substitution effects of a wage change work in the same direction at each level, so that firm, industry, and market demand curves *all slope downward.*

Long Run vs. Short Run.   One can also distinguish between *long-run* and *short-run* labor demand curves. Over very short periods of time, employers find it difficult to substitute capital for labor (or vice versa), and customers may not change their product demand very much in response to a price increase. It takes *time* to fully adjust consumption and production behavior. Over longer periods of time, of course, responses to changes in wages or other forces affecting the demand for labor are larger and more complete.

In Chapters 3 and 4 we shall draw some important distinctions between short-run and long-run labor demand curves. At this point we need only point out that while these curves will differ, *they both slope downward.* Thus, an increase in the wage rate will reduce the demand for labor, although perhaps by different amounts, in both the short and the long run.

The Supply of Labor

Having looked at a simple model of behavior on the buyer (or demand) side of the labor market, we now turn to the seller (or supply) side of the market. For the purposes of this chapter, we shall assume that workers have already decided to work and that the question facing them is what occupation and what employer to choose.

Market Supply.   To first consider the supply of labor to the entire market (as opposed to the supply to a particular firm), suppose that the market we are considering is the one for secretaries. How will supply respond to changes in the wages secretaries might receive? In other words, what does the supply schedule of secretaries look like?

If the salaries and wages in *other* occupations are *held constant* and the wages of secretaries rise, we would expect to find more people wanting to become secretaries. For example, suppose that each of 100 people in a high school graduating class has the option of becoming an insurance agent or a secretary. Some of these 100 people will prefer to be insurance agents even if secretaries are better paid, because they like the challenge and sociability of selling. Some would want to be secretaries even if the pay were comparatively poor, because they hate the pressures of selling. Many, however, could see themselves doing either job; for them the compensation in each occupation would be a major factor in their decision. If secretaries were higher paid than insurance agents, more would want to become secretaries. If the pay of insurance agents were higher, the number of people choosing the insurance occupation would increase and the supply of secretaries would decrease. Of course, at some ridiculously low wage for secretaries, *no one* would want to become one.

Thus, the supply of labor to a particular market is positively related to the wage rate prevailing in that market, holding other wages constant. That is, if the wages of insurance agents are held constant and the secretary wage rises, more people will want to become secretaries because of the relative improvement in compensation (as shown graphically in Figure 2.10).

As with demand curves, each supply curve is drawn holding other prices and wages constant. If one or more of these other prices or wages were to change, it would cause the supply curve to *shift*. As the salaries of insurance agents *rise,* some people will change their minds about becoming secretaries and choose to become insurance agents. Fewer people would want to be secretaries at each level of secretarial wages as salaries of insurance agents rise. In graphic terms (see Figure 2.11), increases in the salaries of insurance agents would cause the supply curve of secretaries to shift to the left.

Supply to Firms.   Having decided to become a secretary, the individual would then have to decide which offer of employment to accept. If all employers were offering secretarial jobs that were more or less alike, the choice would be based on compensation. Any firm unwise enough to attempt paying a wage below what others were paying would find it could not attract any employees (or at least none of the caliber it wanted). Conversely, no firm would be foolish enough to pay more than the going wage, because it would be paying more than it would have to pay to attract a suitable number and quality of employees. The supply curve to a firm, then, would be horizontal, as can be seen in Figure 2.12. The horizontal supply curve to a firm indicates that at the going wage, a firm could get all the secretaries it needs. If it paid less, however, supply would shrink to zero.

The difference in slope between the market supply curve and the supply curve to a firm is directly related to the type of choice facing workers. In de-

FIGURE 2.10   Supply Curve for Secretaries

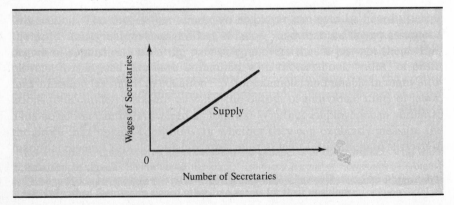

FIGURE 2.11   Shift in Labor Supply Curve for Secretaries As Salaries of Insurance Agents Rise

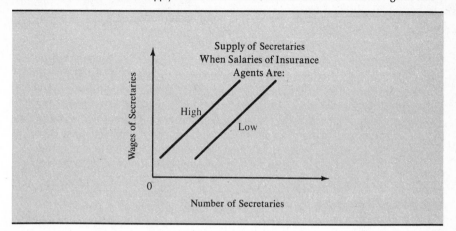

ciding whether to enter the secretarial labor market, workers must weigh both the compensation *and* the job requirements of alternative options (such as being an insurance agent). If wages of secretaries were to fall, fewer people would want to enter the secretarial market. However, not everyone would withdraw from the market, because the jobs of insurance agent and secretary are not perfect substitutes. Some people would remain secretaries after a wage decline because they dislike the job requirements of insurance agents.

Once the decision to become a secretary had been made, the choice of which employer to work for would be a choice among alternatives in which the job requirements were nearly the *same*. Thus, the choice would have to be made on the basis of compensation alone. If a firm were to lower its wage offers below those of other firms, it would lose all its applicants. The horizontal supply curve is, therefore, a reflection of supply decisions made among alternatives that are perfect substitutes for each other.

We have argued that firms wishing to hire secretaries must pay the going wage or lose all applicants. While this may seem unrealistic, it is not. If a firm

FIGURE 2.12   Supply of Secretaries to a Firm

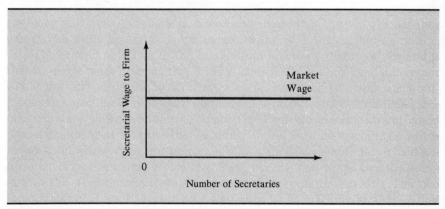

offers jobs *comparable* to those offered by other firms but at a lower level of total compensation, it might be able to attract a few applicants of the quality it desires because a few people will be unaware of compensation elsewhere. Over time, however, knowledge of the firm's poor relative pay would become more widespread, and the firm would find it had to rely solely on less qualified people to fill its jobs. It could secure quality employees at below-average pay only if it offered *noncomparable* jobs (more pleasant working conditions, longer paid vacations, and so forth). This factor in labor supply will be discussed in Chapter 8. For now, we will assume that individual firms, like individual workers, are usually *wage takers;* that is, the wages they pay to their workers must be pretty close to the going wage if they face competition in the labor market. Neither individual workers nor firms can set a wage much different from the going wage and still hope to transact. (Exceptions to this general proposition will be noted in later chapters.)

The Determination of the Wage

The wage that prevails in a particular labor market is heavily influenced by the forces of demand and supply, regardless of whether the market involves a labor union. However, because unions are labor market institutions designed to alter the market outcome, we shall first discuss wage determination in nonunionized labor markets.

The Equilibrium Wage. Recall that the market demand curve indicates how many workers employers would want at each wage rate, holding capital prices and consumer incomes constant. The market supply curve indicates how many workers would enter the market at each wage level, holding the wages in other occupations constant. These curves can be placed on the same graph to reveal some interesting information, as shown in Figure 2.13.

For example, suppose the market wage were set at W_1. At this low wage, demand is large but supply is small. More important, Figure 2.13 indicates that at W_1 demand *exceeds* supply. At this point, employers will be competing for the few workers in the market and a shortage of workers would exist. The

FIGURE 2.13 Market Demand and Supply

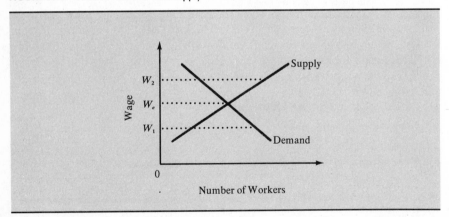

desire of firms to attract more employees would lead them to increase their wage offers, thus driving up the overall level of wage offers in the market.

As wages rose, two things would happen. First, more workers would choose to enter the market and look for jobs (a movement along the supply curve); second, increasing wages would induce employers to seek fewer workers (a movement along the demand curve). If wages were to rise to W_2, supply would exceed demand. Employers would desire fewer workers than the num-

---

EXAMPLE 2.1
The Black Death and the Wages of Labor

An example of what happens to wages when the supply of labor suddenly shifts occurred when plague—the Black Death—struck England (among other European countries) in 1348–51. Estimates vary, but it is generally agreed that plague killed between 17 and 40 percent of the English population in that short period of time. This shocking loss of life had the immediate effect of raising the wages of laborers. As the supply curve shifted to the left, a *shortage* of workers was created at the old wage levels, and competition among employers for the surviving workers drove the wage level dramatically upward.

Reliable figures are hard to come by, but many believe wages rose by 50–100 percent over the three-year period. A thresher, for example, earning two and one-half pence per day in 1348 earned four and one-half pence in 1350, while mowers receiving 5 pence per acre in 1348 were receiving 9 pence in 1350. Whether the overall rise in wages was this large or not, there was clearly a labor shortage and an unprecedented increase in wages. A royal proclamation commanding landlords to share their scarce workers with neighbors and threatening workers with imprisonment if they refused work at the pre-plague wage was issued to deal with this shortage, but it was ignored. The shortage was too severe and market forces were simply too strong for the rise in wages to be thwarted.

The discerning student might wonder at this point about the *demand* curve for labor. Did it not also shift to the left as the population—and the number of consumers—declined? The answer is that it did, but this leftward shift was not as pronounced as the leftward shift in supply. While there were fewer customers for labor's output, the customers who remained consumed greater amounts of goods and services per capita than before. The money, gold and silver, and durable goods that had existed prior to 1348 were divided among many fewer people by 1350, and this rise in per capita wealth was associated with a widespread and dramatic increase in the level of consumption, especially of luxury goods. Thus, the leftward shift in labor demand was dominated by the leftward shift in supply, and the predictable result was a large increase in wages.

SOURCES: Harry A. Miskimin, *The Economy of Early Renaissance Europe 1300–1460* (Englewood Cliffs, N.J.: Prentice-Hall, 1969); George M. Modlin and Frank T. deVyver, *Development of Economic Society* (Boston: D.C. Heath, 1946); Douglass C. North and Robert Paul Thomas, *The Rise of the Western World* (Cambridge: Cambridge University Press, 1973); Philip Ziegler, *The Black Death* (New York: Harper & Row, 1969).

ber available, and not all those desiring employment would be able to find jobs, resulting in a surplus of workers. Employers would have long lines of eager applicants for any opening. These employers would soon reason that they could fill their openings with qualified applicants even if they offered lower wages. Further, if they could pay lower wages, they would want to hire more employees. Some employees would be more than happy to accept the lower wages if they could just find a job. Others would leave the market and look for work elsewhere as wages fell. Thus, demand and supply would become more equal as wages fell from the level of W_2.

The wage rate at which demand equals supply is the *market-clearing* or *equilibrium* wage. At W_e in Figure 2.13, employers can fill the number of openings they have, and all employees who want jobs in this market can find them. At W_e there is no surplus and no shortage. All parties are satisfied, and no forces exist that would alter the wage. The market is in equilibrium in the sense that the wage will remain at W_e.

The equilibrium wage is the wage that eventually prevails in a market. Wages below W_e will not prevail, because the shortage of workers leads employers to drive up wage offers. Wages above W_e likewise cannot prevail, because the surplus leads to downward pressure on wage rates. The market-clearing wage, W_e, thus becomes the *going wage* that individual employers and employees must face. In other words, wage rates are determined by the market and "announced" to individual market participants. Figure 2.14 graphically depicts market demand and supply in panel (a), along with the demand and supply curves for a typical firm in that market in panel (b). All firms in the market pay a wage of W_e, and total employment of L equals the sum of employment in each firm.

Disturbing the Equilibrium.   What could happen to change the equilibrium (market) wage once it has been reached? Once equilibrium has been achieved,

FIGURE 2.14   Demand and Supply at the "Market" and "Firm" Level

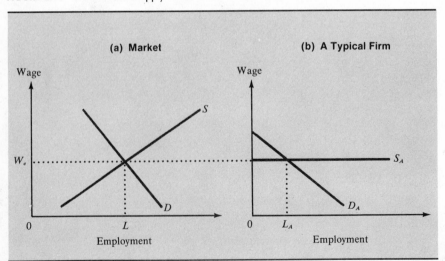

changes could arise from shifts in either the demand or the supply curve. For example, consider what might happen to the wages of secretaries (the majority of whom at present are women) if job opportunities for women in management and other prestigious fields were to improve. The greater availability and improved pay for women in these alternative careers would probably cause some women to leave the secretarial market and seek work in these other fields. Fewer women would want to become secretaries at the going wage. As Figure 2.15 shows, the market supply curve for secretaries would shift to the left.

As can be seen from Figure 2.15, after the supply curve has shifted, W_e is no longer the market-clearing wage. There is now a shortage of secretaries (because demand exceeds supply) at W_e. As employers scramble to fill secretarial jobs, the wage rate is driven up. The new equilibrium wage is W_e', which of course is higher than W_e. Better opportunities for women in management would thus lead to a smaller supply of secretaries, and to fill secretarial jobs the wage rate paid to secretaries would have to rise. The end result of the improved opportunities elsewhere would be to increase the wages of secretaries.

Shifts of the demand curve to the right would also cause wages to rise. Suppose, for example, that the increase in paperwork accompanying greater government regulation of industry causes firms to demand more secretarial help than before. Graphically, as in Figure 2.16, this greater demand would be represented as a rightward shift of the demand curve. This rightward shift would depict a situation in which, for any given wage rate, the number of secretaries desired had risen. The old equilibrium wage (W_e) would no longer equate demand and supply. If W_e were to persist, there would be a labor shortage in the secretarial market (because demand would exceed supply). This shortage would induce employers to improve their wage offers and eventually drive up the secretarial wage to W_e^*.

Both the leftward shift in supply and the rightward shift in demand initially created shortages—shortages that led to increases in the market

FIGURE 2.15   New Labor Market Equilibrium After Supply Shifts Left

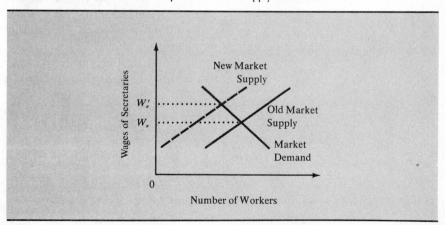

FIGURE 2.16   New Labor Market Equilibrium After Demand Shifts Right

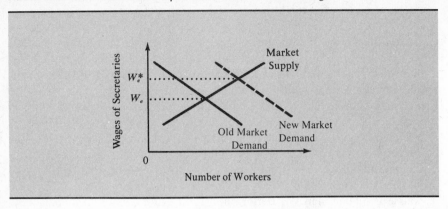

wage rate. The supply-caused shift, however, led to a fall in employment (as compared to the old equilibrium level of employment). Conversely, the demand-caused shift induced an increase in the equilibrium level of employment.

Equilibrium wages can also fall, of course. Although *money* wages are rarely cut, in a period of rising prices *real* wages can fall quite readily. Between 1976 and 1977, for example, money wages for nonagricultural production workers rose by 8 percent (from $203.70 per week to $219.91), but their real wages fell by 3 percent because prices rose by 11 percent.[6] Money wages in an occupation can also fall relative to wages in other occupations. Thus, when we speak of a declining wage rate, it can imply a decline *relative to product prices or to other wages,* as well as a fall in the money wage rate.

A fall in the equilibrium wage rate would occur if there were increased supply or reduced demand. An increase in supply would be represented by a rightward shift of the supply curve, as more people entered the market at each wage (see Figure 2.17). This rightward shift would cause a surplus to exist at the old equilibrium wage (W_e) and lead to behavior that reduced the wage to W_e'' in Figure 2.17. Note that the equilibrium employment level has increased. What could cause this rightward shift of the supply curve? For secretaries, the cause of increased supply at each wage could be a greater desire among people to become secretaries, or reductions in the wages of competing occupations (such as insurance agents in our example above).

A decrease (leftward shift) in demand would also cause a decrease in the equilibrium wage, although such a shift would be accompanied by a fall in employment, as we can see in Figure 2.18. The leftward shift of the demand curve would cause a surplus at the original equilibrium wage (W_e). When firms found the ratio of applicants to openings was greater than usual, and when workers found that jobs were harder to come by, downward pressure on the wage would exist and the market-clearing wage would fall to W_e^{**}. Money

6. U.S. President, *Economic Report of the President* (Washington, D.C.: U.S. Government Printing Office, January 1980), Tables B-36, B-49.

FIGURE 2.17 New Labor Market Equilibrium After Supply Shifts Right

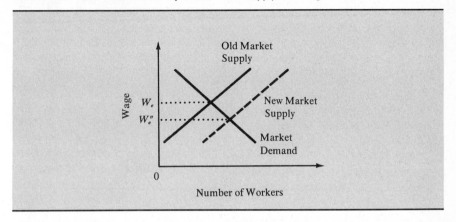

wages might go up, but any increases would be smaller than those received in other occupations. Sadly for the authors, the decline in demand for college professors brought on by a number of financial and demographic pressures in the 1970s offers an excellent example of a surplus market. The result was a 21 percent decline in real earnings for college professors over the 1971–81 period. (Starting in 1981, however, real earnings of college professors began to rise again, but the recent increases have not eradicated the large decline in real earnings since 1971.)

It is possible, of course, for equilibrium to be disturbed by shifts in both demand and supply at the same time. These simultaneous shifts might either reinforce each other or work against each other. An example of a reinforcing shift occurs when a leftward shift in demand is accompanied by a rightward shift in supply, as shown in Figure 2.19. If the demand curve alone shifted, wages would fall from W_{1-1} to W_{2-1}, but when accompanied by a rightward shift in supply, wages fall to W_{2-2}.

FIGURE 2.18 New Labor Market Equilibrium After Demand Shifts Left

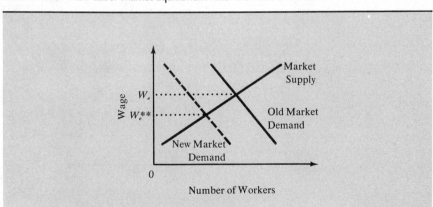

FIGURE 2.19   New Labor Market Equilibrium After Supply Shifts Right and Demand Shifts Left

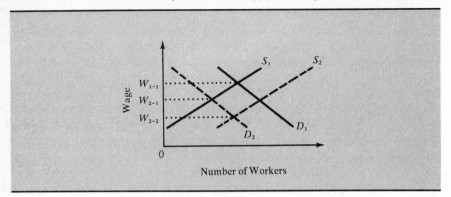

Shifts may also tend to work against each other. For example, if the invention and spread of word processors reduced the demand for people with secretarial skills at the same time that opportunities for women outside the clerical occupations were increasing, it would be difficult to predict the effects on secretaries' wages (see Figure 2.20). The leftward shift of demand would exert downward pressure on wages, while the leftward shift of supply would tend to cause wages to rise. The ultimate effect would depend on which force was greater. In panel (a) of Figure 2.20, the forces generated by the contraction of demand were dominant, and the equilibrium wage is depicted as falling from W_{1-1} to W_{2-2}. In panel (b), however, the contraction of supply was dominant, and wages are shown as rising from W_{1-1} to W_{2-2}.

APPLICATIONS OF THE THEORY

Although this simple model of how a labor market functions will be refined and elaborated upon in the following chapters, it can explain many important phenomena, including those discussed in the following sections.

FIGURE 2.20   New Labor Market Equilibria After Supply and Demand Shift Left

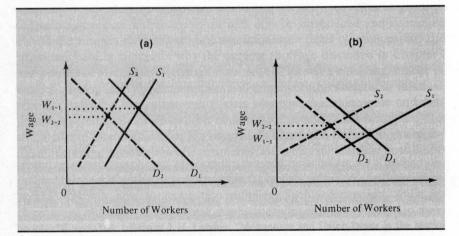

FIGURE 2.21   Labor Market Equilibrium for Teenagers After Population Increase

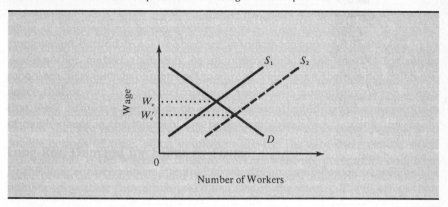

The Accommodation of "Baby Boom" Workers

During the late 1970s, the overall labor market was forced to accommodate a huge influx of new workers searching for jobs. These new entrants were born in the late 1950s, the period of the so-called baby boom. The number of 20-year-olds in the population in 1977 was 44 percent larger than the number in 1962 and as large as the numbers projected for 1992.[7] Thus, there was a bulge in the number of inexperienced workers seeking jobs. What would be the predictable effect as this bulge in supply hit the labor market?

First, new entrants are, by definition, inexperienced workers, and such workers are not very good substitutes for experienced workers. Inexperienced workers tend to be offered *entry-level jobs,* while more complicated or responsible jobs higher up the career ladder are reserved to some extent for experienced workers. Thus, the experienced and the inexperienced are, to a degree, in different labor markets.

What happens when a big bulge of population enters a labor market? The sheer increase in population shifts the supply curve to the right because more people are offering themselves for work at every wage level. Figure 2.21 illustrates this shift from S_1 to S_2. This shift in supply, if not accompanied by a correspondingly large shift in demand, will reduce wages. (Figure 2.21 shows that the equilibrium wage fell from W_e to W_e'.)

Did the baby-boom bulge in the late 1970s cause wages of inexperienced workers to fall? To answer this question we must pick a standard against which to measure the fall. Money wages rarely fall, especially when prices are rising. We could, therefore, measure whether *real wages* fell over some time period. However, real wages have tended to rise with improvements in technology—a force we would like to filter out if possible so that we can focus only on changes produced by the shift in supply.

The best way to measure the fall in the wages of inexperienced workers is to compare their wages with those of adults in their peak earnings years.

7. Data for this section were obtained from Finis Welch, "Effects of Cohort Size on Earnings: The Baby Boom Babies' Financial Bust," *Journal of Political Economy* 87, no. 5 (October 1979): S65–S98.

TABLE 2.6   Economic Position of New Entrants in Labor Force by Level of Schooling

Years of School Completed	Percent of Work Force with Less Than 5 Years of Experience in Each Schooling Category		Weekly Wages of New Entrants Relative to Peak Earners	
	1967–1969	1973–1975	1967–1969	1973–1975
8–11 years	8.9	15.4	0.53	0.46
12 years	15.0	20.8	0.63	0.55
1–3 years of college	19.0	25.2	0.59	0.52
4 or more years of college	18.7	22.9	0.63	0.54

SOURCE: From Finis Welch, "Effects of Cohort Size on Earnings: The Baby Boom Babies' Financial Bust," *Journal of Political Economy* 87, no. 5 (October 1979): S65–S98.

These adults will be the beneficiaries, along with inexperienced workers, of technological advances, but they are far enough removed from the baby boomers in experience that the bulge of new labor force entrants will not affect their wages directly. Measured against this group, earnings of new entrants fell dramatically in the 1970s.

Table 2.6 tells the story. In every educational category, the proportion of inexperienced workers in the labor force increased during the period from 1967 to 1975—a clear indication that the number of young workers was increasing faster than the number of older workers. This abnormally large rise in employment was accompanied by a 12–15 percent decline in the earnings of new workers relative to adults. Thus, as our model of labor market behavior suggests, the large increase in employment necessary to accommodate the baby-boom entrants was facilitated by a decline in their wage. The influx of inexperienced workers created a surplus at the former wage level, and as new workers competed for jobs, the wage level was driven down.

Interestingly, the decline in relative wages facing the baby boomers when they first entered the labor market has continued to plague them since. By 1984 the baby-boom workers were 25–34 years of age, and it has been estimated that from 1968 to 1984 the average household incomes of those in this age group relative to those aged 35–44 fell by 12 percent. Similar declines in relative wages for the baby-boom generation have occurred in other countries that experienced a big bulge in the postwar birthrate.[8]

Effects of Unions

Although we shall discuss the role and effects of unions on the labor market later in this text, it is important here to briefly establish that the model outlined in this chapter can also apply to unions. This analysis will look only generally at the effects of unions on wages. Later chapters will analyze

---

8. David Bloom, Richard Freeman, and Sanders Korenham, "The Labour-Market Consequences of Generational Crowding," *European Journal of Population* 3 (1987): 131–76.

union effects on wages in more detail and will also examine their effects on productivity, turnover, and wage differentials across race and gender groups.

Unions represent workers and, as such, primarily affect the *supply* curves to labor markets. They do so in two ways. First, most unions operate under labor–management agreements—called *contracts* or *collective bargaining agreements*—that permit employer discretion in the selection of workers. These contracts cover wages, other forms of compensation, working conditions, procedures for employee complaints, and rules governing promotions and layoffs. The provisions of the contracts are the result of a bargain struck between management and all workers collectively. In effect, workers band together, agree to a bargaining position, and negotiate as a group. All are bound by the final provisions of the contract, which means that all must receive the agreed-upon wage.

Many of the most prominent collective bargaining agreements, in effect, are industrywide. These agreements, which include those in the auto, steel, rubber, coal, and trucking industries, affect the supply curves in the relevant labor markets by making them horizontal. No one can get paid more or less than the wage agreed upon in the contract (see Figure 2.22).

In Figure 2.22 the supply curve without a union is S and the market-clearing wage is W_e. However, the union raises the wage above W_e to W_u, the wage specified in the contract, by preventing firms and workers from offering or accepting wages below W_u. The result is a wage above equilibrium, employment levels below those that would prevail if the wage were lower, and a "surplus" of labor (at W_u, L_s workers want work in these jobs but only L_u can find work). Because the wage cannot fall, the surplus remains and will manifest itself in long lines of workers applying for job openings with union employers.

The above analysis is based on the assumption that unions raised the wage above market-clearing levels. This is probably a useful assumption, given that unions certainly intend to do this. Not all unions have the power to affect wages much, for reasons we shall discuss in Chapter 4. If these unions agree to wages equal to W_e, the market equilibrium wage, then clearly they do not affect wage or employment outcomes in the labor market.

FIGURE 2.22   Effects on Labor Market Equilibrium of Industrywide Unions

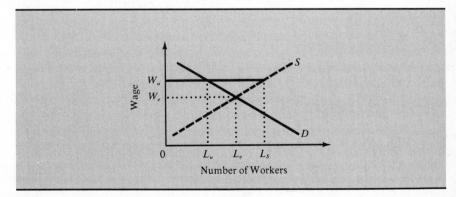

FIGURE 2.23   How Unions That Control Supply of Labor to a Market Affect Labor Market Equilibrium

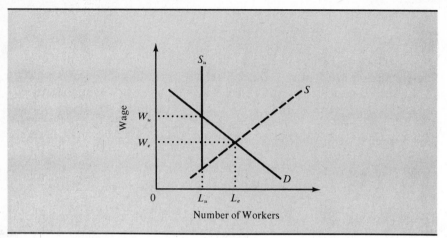

The second way in which some unions affect the supply to markets is by *directly* limiting supply. Some unions operate under agreements in which employers hire all labor from the union and in which the union controls which and how many members it lets in. The dual power of being able to restrict its membership and to require employers to hire only union members permits the union to set the level of labor supply to the market (see Figure 2.23).

In Figure 2.23, S_u represents the level of supply determined by union policy and W_u the resulting wage. S_u is drawn as a vertical line because wage increases or decreases do not affect supply. Supply is set at L_u by union policy.

The wage and employment levels under the union—W_u and L_u—can be compared to the lower wages (W_e) and higher employment levels (L_e) that would prevail in the absence of a union. The major difference between this case, in which unions control supply, and the more common situation, in which employers choose workers but make contracts with all workers collectively, is that there is no surplus of workers standing at the employer's hiring gate. The long line of disappointed people is at the union's office. Examples of labor unions that control supply are those representing skilled construction workers, longshoring workers, and theater lighting technicians.[9]

Who Is Underpaid and Who Is Overpaid?

In casual conversation one often hears a worker say that he or she is "underpaid." Just as often one hears employers claiming workers are "overpaid." Clearly, each is using a different standard for judging wages. People tend to judge the wages paid or received against some notion of what they "need," but

---

9. This is not to say that all unions that *can* control supply are equally prone to do it. Some may fear the presence of a large number of qualified workers outside the union and figure that it is better to take them in, collect their dues, and ration jobs among all members than to face stiff nonunion competition. Restricting entry into the union is *most likely* when employers *must* hire only union workers.

there is no universally accepted standard of need. A worker may "need" more income to buy a larger home or finance a recreational vehicle. An employer may "need" greater profits to pay for sending a child to college. In general, almost all of us feel we "need" more income!

Despite the difficulties of assessing needs, there are still important reasons for defining "overpaid" and "underpaid." For example, the public utilities commissions in every state must consider and approve rate increases requested by the telephone, gas, and electric companies. These companies desire increases partly to keep up with production costs, which the companies obviously want to pass on to consumers. Suppose, however, that a public utilities commission observed that the *level* of wages paid by these companies or the *increases* in such wages were "excessive." In the interests of holding down consumer prices, it might want to consider adopting a policy whereby excessive labor costs could not be passed on to consumers in the form of rate increases. Instead, it might decide that such costs should be borne by the company or its shareholders. Obviously, such a policy would require a definition of what constitutes overpayment.

We pointed out in Chapter 1 that a fundamental value of normative economics is that, as a society, we should strive to complete all those transactions that are mutually beneficial. Another way of stating this value is to say that we must strive to use our scarce resources as effectively as possible, which implies that output should be produced in the least costly manner so that the most can be obtained from such resources. This goal, combined with the labor market model outlined in this chapter, suggests a useful definition of what it means to be overpaid.

Above-Equilibrium Wages. We shall define workers as *overpaid* if their wages are higher than the market equilibrium wage for their job. Because a labor surplus exists for jobs that are overpaid, a wage above equilibrium has two implications (see Figure 2.24). First, employers are paying more than they have to in order to produce (they pay W_H instead of W_e); they could cut wages and still find enough qualified workers for their job openings. In fact, if they

FIGURE 2.24   Effects of an Above-Equilibrium Wage

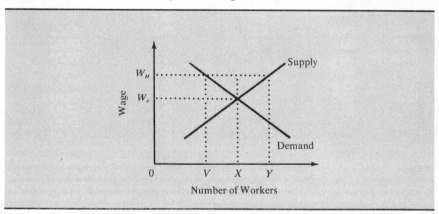

did cut wages, they could expand output and make their product cheaper and more accessible to consumers. Second, more workers want jobs than can find them (*Y* workers want jobs, and only *V* openings are available). If wages were reduced a bit, more of these disappointed workers could find work. A wage above equilibrium thus causes consumer prices to be higher and output to be smaller than is possible, and it creates a situation in which not all workers who want the jobs in question can get them.

With this definition of overpayment, the public utilities commission in question would want to look for evidence that wages were above equilibrium. The commission might be able to compare wages paid by utilities to those of comparable workers in the general labor market. Doing so would require measures of worker quality, of course—data that are hard to quantify in some cases. Alternatively, the commission could look to employee behavior for signs of above-market wages. If wages were above those for comparable jobs, current employees would be *very* reluctant to quit because they would know their chances of doing better were small. Likewise, the number of applicants would be unusually large.[10]

An interesting—although perhaps extreme—example of above-equilibrium wage rates could be seen in New York City in 1974–75. New York City sanitation workers during this period were receiving salaries of $14,770, some 60 percent higher than the $9,200 received by the area's laborers/materials handlers. Perhaps the most convincing evidence of overpayment was the waiting list of 36,849 job applicants who had passed a job-related examination—3.4 qualified applicants for each current employee! Hiring was almost nil during this period, so these numbers clearly point to a labor surplus—and thus to overpayment.[11]

To better understand the social losses attendant on overpayment, let us return to the principles of normative economics. Can it be shown that reducing overpayment will create a situation in which the gainers gain more than the losers lose? Suppose in the case of sanitation workers that *only* the wages of *newly hired* sanitation workers were lowered—to $10,000. Current workers thus would not lose, but many laborers working at $9,200 per year (the prevailing wage for them in 1974) would jump at the chance to take a $10,000-a-year job. Taxpayers, knowing that garbage-collection services could now be expanded at lower cost than before, would increase their demand for such services, thus creating jobs for these new workers.[12] Thus, some workers would gain while no one lost—and social well-being would clearly be enhanced.[13]

10. For analyses of the issue of overpayment with respect to U.S. postal workers, see Example 13.2 in Chapter 13.

11. Sharon P. Smith, *Equal Pay in the Public Sector: Fact or Fantasy,* Research Report Series no. 122 (Princeton, N.J.: Industrial Relations Section, Princeton University, 1977).

12. These new workers, of course, have wanted sanitation jobs with New York City all along, but the high wage prevented job opportunities in that field from expanding.

It should be noted that if the wages of *current* sanitation workers were lowered, city taxpayers could obtain their current level of service for less money. Their gains (in tax savings) would equal the income losses of sanitation workers, and if we were to arrange the transaction so that no one lost, the gainers would have to compensate the losers by restoring their lost income. For this reason we have assumed that salaries for current sanitation workers are not cut.

13. If the workers who switched jobs were getting paid approximately what they were worth to their former employers, these employers would lose $9,200 in output but save $9,200 in costs—and their welfare would thus not be affected. The presumption that employees are paid what they are worth to the employer is discussed at length in Chapter 3.

FIGURE 2.25   Effects of a Below-Equilibrium Wage

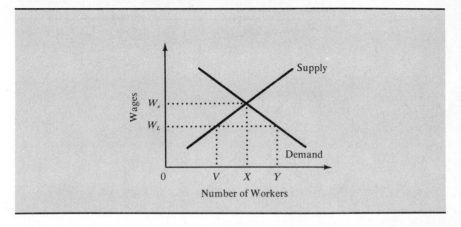

Below-Equilibrium Wages.   Employees can be defined as *underpaid* if their wage is below equilibrium. At below-equilibrium wages, employers have difficulty finding workers to meet the demands of consumers, and a labor shortage thus exists (firms want more workers than they can find at the prevailing wage). They also have trouble keeping the workers they do find. If wages were increased, output would rise and more workers would be attracted to the market. Thus, an increase would benefit the people in society in *both* their consumer and their worker roles. Figure 2.25 shows how a wage increase from W_L to W_e would increase employment from V to X (at the same time wages were rising).

Wages in the U.S. army illustrate how the market adjusts to below-equilibrium wages. Prior to 1973, when the military draft was eliminated, the government could pursue a policy of paying below-market wages to military recruits, because the resultant gap between supply and demand could be filled by conscription. This policy, which presumably was intended to keep taxpayer costs down, placed a burden—an implicit tax—on the conscripted recruits, because they were forced to turn down better options and work for an employer involuntarily. (In terms of normative economics, the government forced individuals into a transaction that was not mutually beneficial.) In 1962, for example, military cash wages to enlisted personnel came to 80 percent of the wages of comparable civilian workers, but by 1977 the requirement to compete with other employers for recruits had driven the military's wage offers up to 95 percent of civilian wages. A recent fall in the educational attainment of army recruits again has military planners considering pay increases larger than those experienced in the private sector.[14]

Economic Rents.   The concepts of underpayment and overpayment have to do with the *social* issue of producing desired goods and services in the least costly way; therefore, wages paid were compared to the *market-clearing wage*.

---

14. Richard Halloran, "Military Recruiting Hurt by Tight Labor Market," *New York Times*, August 1, 1989, A16. For analyses of the supply of military recruits, see Charles Brown, "Military Enlistments: What Can We Learn from Geographic Variation?" *American Economic Review* 75, no. 1 (March 1985): 228–34, and Charles Dale and Curtis Gilroy, "Enlistment in the All-Volunteer Force," *American Economic Review* 75, no. 3 (June 1985): 547–52.

At the level of *individuals,* however, it is often useful to compare the wage received in a job to one's *reservation wage,* the wage below which the worker would refuse (or quit) the job in question. The amount by which one's wage exceeds one's reservation wage in a particular job is the amount of his or her *economic rent.*

Rents clearly exist when wages are above the market-clearing level (we will see later in this text that above-market wages can be created by government policy, through employer design, as a result of collective bargaining agreements, or because the equilibrium wage has fallen and wages are inflexible in a downward direction). However, rents are present even when the market wage prevails. The existence of rents in this latter case is the result of differences in worker preferences, as we explain below.

Consider the labor supply curve to, say, the military. As shown in Figure 2.26, if the military is to hire L_1 people, it must pay W_1 in wages. These relatively low wages will attract to the military those who most enjoy the military culture and are least averse to the risks of combat. If the military is to be somewhat larger and to employ L_2 people, then it must pay a wage of W_2. This higher wage is required to attract those who would have found a military career unattractive at the lower wage. If W_2 turns out to be the wage that equates demand and supply, and if the military pays that wage, everyone who would have joined up for less would be receiving an economic rent!

Put differently, the supply curve to an occupation or industry is a schedule of reservation wages that indicates the labor forthcoming at each wage level. The difference between the wage actually paid and workers' reservation wages—the shaded area in Figure 2.26—is the amount of the rent. Since each worker potentially has a different reservation wage, rents may well differ for each worker in the market. In Figure 2.26, the greatest rents are received by those L_0 individuals who would have joined the military even if the wage were only W_0.

FIGURE 2.26 Labor Supply to the Military: Different Preferences Imply Different "Rents"

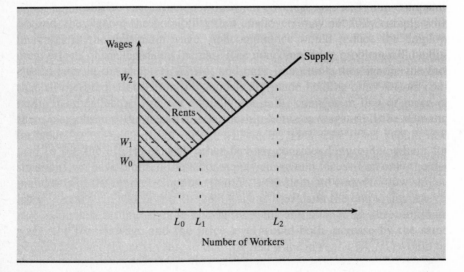

Why don't employers reduce the wage of each employee down to his or her reservation level? While capturing employee rents would seem to be lucrative, since by definition it could be done without the workers' quitting, attempting to do so would create resentment and would be extremely costly, if not impossible, to implement. Employers do not know the true reservation wages of each employee or applicant, and to find it would involve experiments in which the wage offers to each worker either started high and were cut or started low and were raised. This would be costly, and if workers realized the firm was *experimenting,* they would attempt to disguise their true reservation wages and adopt the "strategic behavior" associated with bargaining (bluffing, for example). Therefore, firms usually pay according to the job, one's level of experience or longevity with the employer, and considerations of merit—but not according to preferences. An exception to this general rule is the two-tier wage schedule that has arisen in a few cases in which the market is calling for a wage decrease and the firm does not want to cut wages for its current workers; in these cases, discussed later in Example 12.1, lower wages are paid to the firm's new entrants than were paid to its current workers when they were new. Thus, rents are extracted from new workers but no attempt is made to extract them from current employees.

Labor "Shortages": A Policy Application

The government is frequently urged to undertake programs to cope with perceived labor shortages. Underlying these proposals is usually an assumption that market forces are not working effectively to generate an adequate supply of workers to the occupations in question. For example, the fear of a "skills shortage" (a lack of well-educated, highly trained workers) that was voiced in the late 1980s grew out of an assumption that changes in the types of skills demanded would not be met by changes in skills on the supply side of the labor market unless government intervened in some way.[15] In contrast, the model of the labor market outlined in this chapter suggests that the labor market may well adjust to this need for better-educated workers without such intervention: a rightward shift in the demand for a fixed number of skilled workers would cause their wages to rise, which would both dampen demand and call forth an increased supply of such workers (once they had time to acquire the training). It is interesting to note that at the very time the fear of a skills shortage was first being voiced, the wages of more-educated workers were rising much more rapidly than average (see Chapter 9 for a more thorough discussion of how workers respond to incentives for education and training).

The calls for the government to help solve labor shortages are sometimes characterized by a tendency to define a shortage in terms that are independent of demand. According to our definition a shortage exists if, at the prevailing wage rate for a given occupation, demand exceeds supply. Frequently, however, *actual* demand is ignored and a shortage is defined with reference to what someone thinks society "needs." This latter definition of shortage ignores the economic reality, caused by resource scarcity, that our individual or

---

15. William B. Johnston and Arnold E. Packer, *Workforce 2000: Work and Workers for the 21st Century* (Indianapolis: Hudson Institute, 1987).

EXAMPLE 2.2

A Modern Exodus from Egypt

When oil prices rose dramatically in 1973 the oil-producing Arab countries greatly increased their domestic investment activities, particularly those involving construction. Because the number of construction workers demanded in these oil-producing countries far exceeded the supply available locally, construction workers from Egypt (an Arab nation, but not a major oil producer) were recruited in massive numbers. The inducement for Egyptian construction workers to emigrate, at least temporarily, was the chance to earn—tax free—wages six to ten times higher than they could earn in Egypt.

With such strong incentives to emigrate, approximately one-half (174,000) of Egypt's 354,000 construction workers left to work in other countries, representing a considerable leftward shift in the labor supply curve of the Egyptian construction industry. To this leftward shift in the labor supply curve was added a rightward shift in the labor demand curve facing the construction industry in Egypt, the result of a vigorous residential building boom in the 1970s.

The combination of a leftward-shifting supply curve and a rightward-shifting demand curve would be expected to cause construction wages to rise much faster than other wages and prices. Indeed, as the figures below indicate, the percentage increases in construction wages far outpaced wages in other sectors and consumer prices in general from 1970 to 1975:

	Increase, 1970–75
Construction wages (average)	+200%
Agricultural wages (male)	+ 90%
Manufacturing wages (private)	+ 53%
Consumer prices (urban)	+ 31%
Consumer prices (rural)	+ 42%

It is notable that, despite the emigration of 174,000 workers, the rightward shift of the labor demand curve caused construction employment in Egypt to *rise* (on net) by a total of 80,000 during this period, with many of the 254,000 new workers being recruited from the large agricultural sector. One can observe the effects of the resultant leftward shift of the labor supply curve in agriculture: wages in that sector rose almost twice as fast as wages in manufacturing employment.

SOURCE: Bent Hansen and Samir Radwan, *Employment Opportunities and Equity in Egypt* (Geneva: International Labour Office, 1982).

social needs for newer cars, cleaner air, larger houses, or more mass transit are not necessarily always translated into *demand*.

Acceptance of a need-based definition of labor shortage caused the government, in the 1960s, to initiate a $300-million program to increase the supply of professional nursing graduates by 29 percent in five years. The program was adopted after a report by the Surgeon General calculated a huge shortage of nurses based on a needs approach. The report contended that 50 percent of direct patient care should be provided by registered nurses (as opposed to nursing aides), because below this level patient satisfaction is significantly reduced. The problem with trying to increase the supply of nurses to meet this "shortage" was that, at the time, supply did not seem to be falling short of effective demand!

The hallmark of a shortage (as we have defined it) is a wage rate that rises faster than average. If demand exceeds supply at the prevailing wage, firms with unfilled vacancies attempt to attract workers by offering higher wages, and thus wages in the shortage occupation rise relative to those in occupations not experiencing a shortage. (Put differently, shortages exist because the wage rate is below market-clearing levels; the market response is for these wages to rise.) There is no evidence that, as of the mid-1960s, nursing salaries were rising faster than average.[16] The relationship of these salaries to those of all workers, all female workers, and all female professional workers remained essentially constant from 1950 to 1963, showing no tendency to rise. This fact suggests that the effective demand for nurses did not exceed supply at the prevailing wage,[17] and the essential balance between demand and supply probably explains why the supply of nurses rose by 3 percent, not 29 percent, as a result of the government program.[18] Future employment and salary prospects simply did not seem attractive enough to lure more students to the field.

What the Surgeon General and the government failed to recognize was that the problem they perceived in providing adequate patient care was one of *demand,* not supply. Nurses were in abundant enough supply to fill available jobs; it was the number of *jobs* that was the problem. Ironically, a program shifting the *demand* for nurses was initiated later in the 1960s, when Medicare and Medicaid were adopted, and the labor market responses to this program indicate a properly functioning market. Nursing salaries rose relative to those in other occupations, and the number of nurses employed rose quickly (mainly because the higher wages attracted many who were *already* trained as nurses back into the field). These responses suggest that the government's efforts to cure a "supply" problem in the nursing market using subsidies were unnecessary as well as unproductive.

Public perception that another shortage of nurses existed in the late 1980s led to the establishment of a Commission on Nursing in the Department of Health and Human Services. That Commission defined a registered nurse (RN) shortage as we have: "... a market disequilibrium between RN supply and RN demand in which the quantity of RNs demanded exceeds the supply that is forthcoming at the prevailing wage."[19] The evidence presented by the Commission overwhelmingly supported the proposition that a shortage

---

16. Donald Yett, *An Economic Analysis of the Nursing Shortage* (Lexington, Mass.: Lexington Books, 1975), 160.
17. Many economists believe the nursing labor market is dominated by just a few buyers of labor in each city, as we shall discuss in Chapter 3. While a lack of competition on the employer side of the market does have a bearing on the perception of shortages, it is nevertheless true that if hospitals were trying to hire beyond current levels, they would behave in a way that would drive nursing salaries up.
18. Yett, *An Economic Analysis of the Nursing Shortage.*
19. U.S. Department of Health and Human Services, *Secretary's Commission on Nursing, Final Report,* vol. 1 (Washington, D.C.: U.S. Government Printing Office, December 1988), 3.

was present. For example, the percentage of RN positions that hospitals (which employ more than two-thirds of all RNs) reported unfilled rose from 4.4 percent in 1983 to 11.3 percent in 1987.

This shortage in the late 1980s existed because the demand for RNs had increased at the same time that enrollments in nursing schools had declined. Among the factors responsible for reduced enrollments was the growth of employment opportunities for women in occupations that provided both higher starting salaries and greater future salary increases than nursing did. In an attempt to stem the decline in nursing school enrollments, some schools lowered their entry standards, with the result that failure rates of nursing school students on licensing exams rose to a record high of 16 percent in 1988.[20]

The Commission offered a number of recommendations to reduce the RN shortage, including the obvious one that hospitals should improve RN compensation levels. The reader may wonder why market forces did not cause this to happen independent of government intervention. One answer is that by the late 1980s payments to hospitals for Medicare and Medicaid patients, a growing share of total patients, were severely limited by federal cost containment procedures. As a result each individual hospital was reluctant to grant a larger wage increase to its RNs out of fear that the government would not fully reimburse the hospital for the cost of such an increase in the rates paid for Medicare and Medicaid patients. Not surprisingly, then, the Commission also recommended that the government reimburse hospitals at levels that would allow them to recruit and retain nurses.[21]

MISCONCEPTION

"The profits of tea plantations in Sri Lanka are very sensitive to labor costs. Therefore, that wages are relatively low on these plantations can be attributed to the fact that employers cannot afford to pay more."

Analysis

Economic theory suggests that relative wages are determined by the interaction of demand *and* supply forces. Employers are assumed to *always* want to pay workers as little as possible so that they can enhance profits by acquiring a competitive advantage in the product market. However, they can acquire a labor force only if they are offering wages high enough to attract workers from alternative employment. Wages on Sri Lankan tea plantations are low partly because, for some reason or other, the plantation workers have low alternative wage offers.

Principle

Equilibrium employment and relative wage levels are the result of both demand and supply influences.

---

20. "Upturn in Nursing School Enrollments Is First Since 1983," *Nursing World Journal* 15 (January 1989): 1.
21. *Commission on Nursing,* 27–31.

REVIEW QUESTIONS

1. The Central Intelligence Agency (CIA) finds out that compensation for coal miners in the Soviet Union is rising much faster than compensation in general in that country. It knows that the Soviet labor market is free in the sense that it relies on incentives (not compulsion) in the allocation process.

   What can the CIA infer from this sharp rise in mining wages? Can it infer that coal output is increasing? Explain your answers.

2. Analyze the impact of the following changes on wages and employment in a given occupation:
   a. A decrease in the danger of the occupation.
   b. An increase in product demand.
   c. Increased wages in alternative occupations.

3. What would happen to the wages and employment levels of engineers if government expenditures on research and development programs were to fall? Show the effect graphically.

4. Suppose a particular labor market were in equilibrium. What could happen to cause the equilibrium wage to fall? If all money wages rose each year, how would this market adjust?

5. Assume that you have been hired by a company to do a salary survey of its arc welders, who the company suspects are overpaid. Given the company's expressed desire to maximize profits, what definition of "overpaid" would you apply in this situation and how would you identify whether arc welders were, in fact, overpaid?

6. How will a fall in the civilian unemployment rate affect the supply of recruits for the volunteer army? What will be the effect on military wages?

7. Suppose a state government requires all auto mechanics in its jurisdiction to pass competency examinations before they offer their services to the public. What will this licensing requirement do to the wages and employment levels of auto mechanics in the state?

8. Suppose that the Consumer Product Safety Commission passes a regulation requiring an expensive safety device to be attached to all power lawnmowers. This device does not increase the efficiency with which the lawnmower operates. What, if anything, does this regulation do to the demand for labor of firms manufacturing power lawnmowers? Explain.

9. Suppose the Occupational Safety and Health Administration were to mandate that all punch presses be fitted with a very expensive device to prevent injuries to workers. This device does not improve the efficiency with which punch presses operate. What does this requirement do to the demand curve for labor? Explain.

10. Suppose we observe that employment levels in a certain region suddenly decline as a result of (a) a fall in the region's demand for labor, and (b) wages that are fixed in the short run. If the new demand for labor curve remains unchanged for a long period and the region's labor supply curve does not shift, is it likely that employment in the region will recover? Explain.

SELECTED READINGS

Rottenberg, Simon. "On Choice in Labor Markets." *Industrial and Labor Relations Review* 9, no. 2 (January 1956): 183–99. Lampman, Robert J. "On Choice in Labor Markets: Comment." *Industrial and Labor Relations Review* 9, no. 4 (July 1956): 636–41.

U.S. Department of Health and Human Services. *Secretary's Commission on Nursing, Final Report.* Vol. 1. Washington, D.C.: U.S. Government Printing Office, December 1988.

3

The Demand for Labor

T he demand for labor is a derived demand. In most cases, employers hire labor not for the direct satisfaction that such action brings them but rather for the contribution they believe labor can make towards producing some product for sale. Not surprisingly, then, employers' demand for labor is a function of the characteristics of demand in the product market. It is also a function of the characteristics of the production process—more specifically, the ease with which labor can be substituted for capital and other factors of production. Finally, the demand for labor is a function not only of the price of labor but also of the prices of other factors of production. This chapter and the next will illustrate how knowledge of characteristics of the demand for labor can be used in various policy applications.

For the purpose of making or evaluating social policy, the demand for labor has two important features. The first is that it can be shown theoretical-ly—and demonstrated empirically—that labor demand curves slope downward. This chapter discusses the downward-sloping nature of the demand-for-labor curve. The second is that the quantity of labor demanded has varying *degrees of responsiveness* to changes in the wage. While the quantity of labor demanded always declines as the wage increases, this decline is larger in some cases than in others. For most policy issues, the degree of responsiveness is of critical importance. Thus, Chapter 4 will discuss the forces that determine this responsiveness and suggest ways policymakers can make some guesses about the degree of responsiveness when explicit empirical estimates are not available.

When the demand for labor is analyzed, two sets of distinctions are typi-cally made. First, one must specify whether one is concentrating on demand by *firms* or on the demand curves for an entire *market*. As noted in Chapter 2, firm and market labor demand curves have different properties, although both slope downward. Second, one must specify the *time* period for which the demand curve is drawn: the short run or the long run. The *short run* is defined as a period over which a firm's capital stock is fixed; the only input that is free to be varied is labor. The *long run* is defined as a period over which a firm is free to vary all factors of production, in this case both labor and capital. This distinction between short run and long run is a conceptual one, and the two concepts do not necessarily correspond closely to any actual period of calendar time. For example, the owner of a steel mill may find that it takes several years to construct a new steel plant, in which case anything less than two years might be considered the short run. In contrast, the owner of a small firm that hires people to shovel driveways may find that he can vary his capital stock instantaneously (by buying new shovels). In this case, the firm may never face the short run; it will always be involved in making decisions about both labor and capital! However, in spite of the fact that the short run and long run do not correspond neatly to specified calendar periods of time, the distinction does allow us to be more specific about the different forces that influence the demand for labor.

A SIMPLE MODEL OF LABOR DEMAND

Our analysis of the demand for labor will begin with a simple model that yields fundamental behavioral predictions. To simplify the discussion, this model is derived using the four assumptions noted below. Later on in the chapter, two of the assumptions will be dropped to see what difference they make. A third assumption will be dropped in Chapter 5 and the fourth in Chapter 13.

The Assumptions

Our first assumption is that employers seek to maximize *profit* (the difference between the revenue they take in from the sales of their product and their costs of production). This is a standard assumption of positive economics, but it is not absolutely necessary to derive the fundamental conclusion of the chapter—namely, that the demand curve for labor is a downward-sloping function of the wage rate.[1] We shall relax this assumption in Chapter 13 when we consider the demand for labor in the public sector.

Second, we shall initially assume that firms employ two homogeneous factors of production—labor and capital—in their production of goods and services. That is, we assume that there is a two-factor *production function* that indicates how various amounts of labor (L) and capital (K) can be combined to produce output (Q):

$$Q = f(L, K) \tag{3.1}$$

In equation (3.1) f stands for "a function of" and is used to represent a *general* mathematical relationship between Q and the factors of production. The

---

1. Totally impulsive or random demand patterns are consistent with downward-sloping demand curves if people or firms have limited resources—a point made by Gary Becker in "Irrational Behavior and Economic Theory," *Journal of Political Economy* 70, no. 1 (February 1962): 1–13.

specific relationship between Q and the two factors of production depends on the technology utilized. Later in this chapter we shall relax this two-factor assumption, noting that there are many categories of labor. Firms also use other inputs besides *capital* (defined as machinery, equipment, and structures) in their production process, including materials and energy.

Third, we shall assume that the hourly wage cost is the only cost of labor. We shall initially ignore the existence of hiring and training costs, as well as those employee-benefit costs (like holiday pay, vacation pay, and sick leave as well as many forms of social insurance) that do not vary with weekly hours of work. By ignoring these costs here and assuming that the length of the work-week is fixed, we gloss over the distinction between the number of employees a firm hires and the total number of person-hours[2] of labor it employs. In Chapter 5 we shall drop our simplifying assumption and consider the question of how the firm determines its optimal workweek—as well as how hiring, training, and nonvariable employee-benefit costs affect the demand for labor.

Finally, we shall initially assume that both a firm's labor market and its product market are competitive. If the firm's labor market is competitive, we can treat the wage rate that it must pay its workers as given; if its product market is competitive, we can treat the product price it faces as given. (Both of these assumptions are relaxed later in the chapter.) The following analyses of labor demand by the firm, in both the long and the short run, are primarily verbal. The derivation of demand curves through graphic analysis is presented in the appendix to this chapter.

Short-Run Demand for Labor by Firms

In the short run, when a firm's capital stock (K) and production function are not free to vary, a firm's demand for labor (its desired level of employment) and its choice of output level are really two aspects of the same decision. That is, with capital and the production technology fixed, a decision about employment level (inputs) implies a decision about output level. Conversely, a decision about output implies a certain level of employment. This section introduces concepts needed to understand employment decisions by employers in the short run.

The Concept of Marginal Productivity.   The additional output that can be produced by a firm when it employs one additional unit of labor, with capital held constant, is called the *marginal product of labor* (MP_L). For example, if a car dealership can sell 10 cars a month with one salesperson and 21 cars a month with two, the marginal product of hiring one salesperson is 10 and the marginal product of hiring the second is 11 cars per month. If a third equally persuasive salesperson were hired and sales rose to 26 per month, the marginal product of hiring the third salesperson is 5 cars per month. These hypothetical data are summarized in Table 3.1.

Table 3.1 shows that adding an extra salesperson increased output (cars sold) in each case. As long as output *increases* as labor is added, labor's mar-

---

2. Person-hours, also called labor hours, are calculated by multiplying the number of employees by the average length of workweek per employee.

TABLE 3.1   The Marginal Product of Labor in a Hypothetical Car Dealership (capital held constant)

Number of Salespersons	Total Cars Sold	Marginal Product of Labor
0	0	
1	10	10
2	21	11
3	26	5

ginal product (the change in output brought about by adding another unit of labor) is *positive*. In our example, however, the marginal product of labor increased at first (from 10 to 11), but then fell (to 5). Why?

The initial rise in marginal product is *not* because the second salesperson is better than the first; we ruled out this possibility by our assumption (stated above) that labor is homogeneous. Rather, the rise could be the result of cooperation between the two in generating promotional ideas or helping each other out in some way. Eventually, however, as more salespeople are hired, the marginal product of labor must fall. A fixed building (remember that capital is held constant) can contain only so many customers, and thus each additional increment of labor produces progressively smaller increments of output. This law of *diminishing marginal returns* is an empirical proposition that derives from the fact that as employment expands, each additional worker has a progressively smaller share of the capital stock to work with. For expository convenience, we shall assume that the marginal product of labor is always decreasing.[3]

The Conditions for Profit Maximization.   We assume that firms seek to maximize profits. In order to accomplish this objective, a firm should employ labor up until the point that the marginal revenue (or additional revenue) it receives from hiring the last employee is just equal to its marginal (or additional) cost of employing that worker. Since a firm's profit is simply equal to revenues minus costs, *if its marginal revenue exceeds its marginal cost, overall profits can be increased by expanding employment. Analogously, if its marginal revenue is less than its marginal cost, a firm is losing money on the last unit of labor hired, and it could increase its profit by reducing employment. As a result, the only employment level that is consistent with profit maximization is that level at which the marginal revenue of hiring the last unit of labor* (MR_L) *is just equal to its marginal cost* (MC_L). These (italicized) principles can be summarized as follows:

If $MR_L > MC_L$, increase employment.   (3.2a)

If $MR_L < MC_L$, reduce employment.   (3.2b)

If $MR_L = MC_L$, do not change employment because   (3.2c)
    profits are maximized.

---

3. We lose nothing by this assumption, because we show later in this section that a firm will never be operated at a point where its marginal product of labor schedule is increasing.

EXAMPLE 3.1

Professional Hockey: One Player's Marginal Revenue Productivity

The conditions for hiring labor summarized in the text as expressions (3.2a), (3.2b), and (3.2c) presume that employers are aware of the marginal revenue product (*MRP*) of workers they hire. This awareness is most often implicit, in the sense that employers indirectly find out about the wisdom of their hiring decisions by observing profit levels. Sometimes, however, it is possible to calculate a worker's *MRP* with reasonable precision—as illustrated by a recent example from professional hockey.

In August 1988, the Los Angeles Kings of the National Hockey League purchased the contract of Wayne Gretzky, widely thought to be professional hockey's biggest star, from the Edmonton Oilers. Consistent with a point made later in this chapter about the *MRP* of baseball stars, the purchase was possible because the Kings, among hockey's worst teams at the time, anticipated that Gretzky's *MRP* would be higher with them than with the Oilers, which had been hockey's best team over the past five years.

The Kings paid the Oilers $15 million (plus first-round draft picks in 1989, 1991, and 1993) to obtain Gretzky's contract, which was renegotiated to pay him about $2 million per year for an undisclosed period of time (probably six years). After his contract expires, Gretzky can become a free agent and could be lost to the Kings.

What is the annual cost of this transaction to the Kings? Amortizing the $15 million payment over six years yields an annual cost of $2.5 million. To this must be added the interest income that could be earned on the $15 million had it not been invested in Gretzky's contract; at 10 percent, this came to $1.5 million for the first year. Adding in Gretzky's yearly pay of $2 million, it is clear that for the Kings to profit from this transaction Gretzky's yearly *MRP* with them had to exceed $6 million. Did it?

According to the Kings' owner, "We tried to do dozens of case projections before the deal happened, but it was so impossible to predict."* Given the uncertainties and the money at stake, Gretzky's first year with the Kings was a gratifying one for them. Immediately after Gretzky signed, a Los Angeles cable television company announced it would carry 60 of the Kings' 80 games instead of the 37 it had carried the season before. Into the season, the team found that home attendance and average ticket prices had increased by enough to double its "gate" revenues (which are kept entirely by the home team). In addition, advertising and merchandising income increased, with the overall result that Gretzky's financial effect on the team was estimated to be about $200,000 per game. Over the 40 home games, this effect implied that his marginal revenue productivity for the year was around $8 million!

*Larry Wigge, "Shaking Out Gretzky Deal," *The Sporting News,* February 6, 1989, 4. The information for this example was taken from this article, from one in the *New York Times* of September 2, 1988, sec. I, p. 24, and from Paul D. Staudohar, *The Sports Industry and Collective Bargaining,* 2d ed. (Ithaca, N.Y.: ILR Press, 1989), 142.

Given the assumptions that we have made, the marginal cost of a unit of labor is simply the money wage rate (W) that must be paid. The marginal revenue obtained from hiring an additional unit of labor, also called labor's *marginal revenue product* (MRP), is equal to the value of the additional output produced. MRP equals the marginal product of labor multiplied by the additional revenue that is received per unit of output (MR):

$$MR_L = MRP = (MP_L) \cdot (MR) \qquad (3.3)$$

Because we assumed that the firm sells its output in a competitive market—and hence that product price does not vary with output—the additional revenue per unit of output is simply the firm's product price (P). Thus, for firms that operate in competitive output markets, the marginal revenue product obtained from an additional unit of labor equals the product price for the firm's output multiplied by its marginal product of labor:

$$MRP = P \cdot (MP_L) \qquad (3.4)$$

The marginal revenue of labor is just equal to its marginal cost, and profits are maximized by the competitive firm, at the point at which the marginal revenue product equals the money wage:

$$P \cdot (MP_L) = W \qquad (3.5)$$

Both sides of equation (3.5)—both the marginal revenue product and the marginal cost of labor—are stated in terms of dollars. In contrast to equations (3.3) and (3.4), which are merely definitions, equation (3.5) is a behavioral condition that must be met if profits are to be maximized.

Labor Demand in Terms of Real Wages. The demand for labor can be analyzed in terms of either "real" or "money" wages. Which version of demand analysis is used is a matter of convenience only. In this and the following subsection we give examples of both.

Dividing both sides of equation (3.5) by the firm's product price yields an alternative way of stating the profit-maximizing condition, which is that labor should be hired until its marginal product equals the real wage:

$$MP_L = \frac{W}{P} \qquad (3.6)$$

The marginal product of labor is measured as units of added output per unit increase of labor. Suppose we continue to denote the money (nominal) wage rate that the firm pays per unit of labor by W and its product price per unit of output by P. These variables have dimensions of dollars per unit of labor and dollars per unit of output, respectively. Thus, the *real wage rate* that the firm pays—its money wage divided by its price level (W/P)—also has the dimension *units of output per unit of labor*. For example, if a woman is paid $10 per hour and the product she makes sells for $2, she gets paid, from the firm's point of view, five units of output per hour ($10 \div 2$). These five units represent her real wage.

Figure 3.1 shows a marginal product of labor schedule (MP_L) for a representative firm. In this figure the marginal product of labor is tabulated on the

FIGURE 3.1   Demand for Labor in the Short Run (Real Wage)

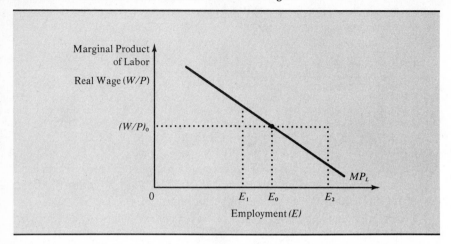

vertical axis and the number of units of labor employed on the horizontal axis. The negative slope of the schedule indicates that each additional unit of labor employed produces a progressively smaller (but still positive) increment in output. Because the real wage and the marginal product of labor are both measured in the same dimension, we can also plot the real wage on the vertical axis of Figure 3.1.[4]

Given any real wage (by the market), the firm should thus employ labor to the point at which the marginal product of labor just equals the real wage. In other words, *the firm's demand for labor in the short run is equivalent to the downward-sloping segment of its marginal product of labor schedule.*[5] To see that this is true, pick any real wage—for example, the real wage denoted by $(W/P)_0$ in Figure 3.1. We have asserted that the firm's demand for labor is equal to its marginal product of labor schedule and consequently that the firm would employ E_0 employees. Now suppose that a firm initially employed E_2 workers as indicated in Figure 3.1, where E_2 is *any* employment level greater than E_0. At the employment level E_2, the marginal product of labor is less than the real wage rate; the marginal cost of the last unit of labor hired is therefore greater than its marginal revenue product. As a result, profit could be increased by reducing the level of employment. Similarly, suppose instead that a firm initially employed E_1 employees, where E_1 is *any* employment level less than E_0. Given the specified real wage $(W/P)_0$, the marginal product of labor is greater than the real wage rate at E_1—and consequently the marginal additions to output of an extra unit of labor exceed its marginal cost. As a result, a firm could increase its profit level by expanding its level of employment.

---

4. For simplicity here we do not distinguish between the firm's product price and the overall price level. Thus, the real wage (W/P) represents here both the per-unit cost of workers (in output terms) to the firm and the purchasing power of a worker's earnings.

5. One should add here, "provided that the firm's revenue exceeds its labor costs." Above some real wage level this may fail to occur, and the firm will go out of business (employment will drop to zero).

Hence, to maximize profit, given any real wage rate, a firm should stop employing labor at the point at which any additional labor would cost more than it would produce. This profit-maximization rule implies two things. First, the firm should employ labor up to the point at which its real wage equals the marginal product of labor—but not beyond that point. Second, its profit-maximizing level of employment lies in the range where its marginal product of labor is *declining.* (If $W/P = MP_L$ but MP_L is *increasing,* then adding another unit of labor will create a situation in which marginal product *exceeds W/P.* As long as adding labor causes MP_L to exceed W/P, the profit-maximizing firm will continue to hire labor. It will stop hiring only when an extra unit of labor would reduce MP_L below W/P, which will happen only when MP_L is declining. Thus, the only employment levels that could possibly be consistent with profit maximization are those in the range where MP_L is decreasing.)

Labor Demand in Terms of Money Wages.   As shown above, one can conceptualize the demand for labor as a downward-sloping function of the real wage. In some circumstances, however, labor demand curves are more readily conceptualized as downward-sloping functions of money wages. To make the analysis as concrete as possible, we analyze the demand for department-store detectives in this subsection.

At a business conference one day, a department store executive boasted that his store had reduced theft to 1 percent of total sales. A colleague shook her head slowly and said, "I think that's too low. I figure it should be about 2 percent of sales." How can more shoplifting be better than less? The answer is based on the fact that reducing theft is costly in itself. A profit-maximizing firm will not want to take steps to reduce shoplifting if the added costs it must bear in so doing exceed the value of the savings it generates.

Table 3.2 shows a hypothetical marginal revenue product (*MRP*) schedule for department-store detectives. Hiring one detective would, in this example, save $50 worth of thefts per hour. Two detectives could save $90 worth of thefts each hour, or $40 more than hiring just one. The *MRP* of hiring a second detective is thus $40. A third detective would add $20 more to thefts prevented, and thus add $20 more to revenues.

The *MRP* does *not* decline from $40 to $20 because the added detectives are incompetent; in fact, we shall assume that all are equally alert and well

TABLE 3.2   Hypothetical Schedule of Marginal Revenue Productivity for Store Detectives

Number of Detectives on Duty During Each Hour Store Is Open	Total Value of Thefts Prevented per Hour	Marginal Value of Thefts Prevented per Hour (MRP)
0	$ 0	$—
1	50	50
2	90	40
3	110	20
4	115	5
5	117	2

trained. *MRP* declines, in part, because surveillance equipment (capital) is fixed; with each added detective, there is less equipment per person. However, the *MRP* also declines because it becomes progressively harder to generate savings. With just a few detectives, the only thieves caught will be the more obvious, less experienced shoplifters. As more detectives are hired, it becomes possible to prevent theft by the more expert shoplifters, but they are harder to detect and fewer in number. Thus, *MRP* falls because theft prevention becomes more difficult once all those who are easy to catch are apprehended.

To draw the demand curve for labor, we need to determine how many detectives the store will want to employ at a given wage. For example, at a wage of $50 per hour, how many detectives will the store want? Using the *MRP* = *W* criterion, it is easy to see that the answer is "one." At $40 per hour, the store would want to hire two, and at $20 per hour the number demanded would be three. The demand-for-labor curve that summarizes the store's profit-maximizing employment of detectives is shown in Figure 3.2.

Figure 3.2 illustrates a fundamental point: the demand-for-labor curve in the short run slopes downward because it *is* the *MRP* curve—and the *MRP* curve slopes downward because of diminishing marginal productivity. The demand curve and the *MRP* curve coincide, as demonstrated by the fact that if one were to graph the *MRP* schedule in Table 3.2, one would arrive at exactly the same curve as in our graph. When one detective is hired, *MRP* is $50; when two are hired, *MRP* is $40; and so forth. Since *MRP* always equals *W* for a profit maximizer who takes wages as given, the *MRP* and labor demand curve (expressed as a function of the money wage) must be the same.

(Another point to be made in this example is that there is some level of shoplifting that the store finds more profitable to tolerate than to eliminate. At high wages for store detectives, this level will be higher than at lower wages. To say the theft rate is too low thus implies that the marginal costs

FIGURE 3.2 The Demand for Labor in the Short Run (Nominal Wage)

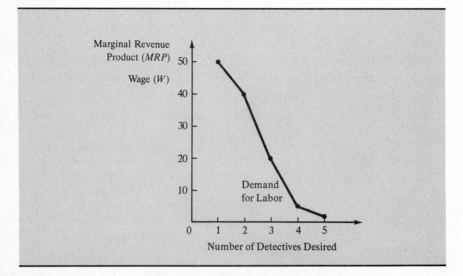

of crime reduction exceed the marginal savings generated, and the firm is therefore failing to maximize profits.)

Personal Characteristics, Marginal Productivity, and Baseball.   It is important to emphasize that the marginal product of any individual is *not* a function solely of his or her personal characteristics. As emphasized above, the marginal product of a worker depends upon the number of similar employees the firm has already hired. An individual's marginal product also depends upon the size of the firm's capital stock; increases in the firm's capital stock shift the entire marginal product of labor schedule up. It is therefore incorrect to speak of an individual's productivity as an immutable factor that is associated only with his or her characteristics, independent of the characteristics of the other inputs he or she has to work with.

The fact that one's marginal productivity is not independent of other inputs being used helps explain the allocation of certain professional baseball players across the various teams. Before 1975, professional baseball players were bound to the team for which they played. They could choose not to play baseball, of course, but they could not choose the baseball team for which they would play. Being bound to a team naturally limited their options and held down their salaries. Other teams could not bid them away from the teams to which they were bound; a player could change teams only if both owners involved agreed on the terms on which the player would be sold or traded to the new team.

In 1975 a labor relations ruling was issued (later followed by a collective bargaining agreement) that allowed certain players to become *free agents,* which meant that they could sell their services to any team. Owners initially objected to the free-agent system. One argument they advanced was that it would harm the competitive balance among the teams by enabling the best and richest teams to grab up all the star players. Our observations about marginal productivity and profit maximization can be used to evaluate and refute the owners' contention about competitive imbalance.

If team owners are profit maximizers, they will hire a star only if the extra revenue he is expected to generate is greater than his salary. That is, the star's expected *MRP* must not be lower than his wage. (That *actual MRP* may be lower than *expected MRP* is another issue, which is dealt with in Example 3.2.) If a team is *already* loaded with stars, an additional good player will not bring in very much in terms of added revenues. However, if a team has no star, or very few, the addition of the *same* good player will quite possibly generate a lot of added revenue. Thus, because the expected *MRP* of a star will probably be lower, *other things equal,* on the best teams, these teams will tend to be the least willing to put up money for the star free agents. Capital stock is one of the "other things" that must be held equal for this prediction to hold, however. For example, if team quality is held constant, a player's *MRP* will be higher on teams that have larger stadiums and larger television markets.

The above considerations suggest that the teams that will bid most aggressively for the free agents will be those that tend to have poorer records or are located in areas with large potential markets. Although there are instances to the contrary, it is interesting to note that 45 of the first 69 "star-quality" free

EXAMPLE 3.2

The Winner's Curse: Is There a Tendency to Overpay Baseball's Free Agents?

In the first nine years of baseball free agency, owners pursued free agents very aggressively. Salary levels were driven up dramatically, even for marginal players, but perhaps the most significant indicator of aggressive bidding was the use of long-term contracts. In many cases, teams saddled themselves with salary obligations to players whose careers ended before the contract period was over. For example, only two of the four free agents who signed five-year contracts in 1983 remained in the major leagues for the entire contract length, and one of those (the free agent who had signed the largest contract in 1983) played only occasionally in his fifth year and retired at year's end.

In 1985, owners apparently decided to pull back from their pursuit of free agents. None of the 62 potential free agents that year could obtain a better offer from another team, and the players charged the owners with collusion. An arbitrator eventually upheld these charges, and many of those adversely affected were enabled to become "new look" free agents in 1988 and 1989. By 1989, the free-agent market was again active, but there was a tendency to avoid the long-term contracts that had been so troublesome in earlier years.

Were the owners' mistakes prior to 1985 the result of their failure to take a businesslike approach toward running their teams? Not necessarily. They may have fallen victims to a problem often associated with auctions of all sorts: the "winner's curse."

Suppose several baseball teams are bidding for the services of a "star" player. This player's past performance is well known, but each team can only

agents (through 1990) signed with teams that had poorer records than the team they were on—and of the remaining 24, 9 signed with teams located in larger markets.[6] Thus, free agency has not had, nor could it be expected to have, harmful effects on the competitive balance of professional baseball teams.

Objections to the Marginal Productivity Theory of Demand.   Two kinds of objections are sometimes raised to the theory of labor demand introduced in this section. The first is that almost no employer can ever be heard uttering the words "marginal revenue product of labor," and that the theory assumes a degree of sophistication on the part of employers that is just not there. Employers, it is argued, are both unfamiliar with the textbook "rules" of profit maximization (as stated in equation 3.5, for example) and unable in many situations to accurately measure or value the output of individual units of labor. This objection can be answered as follows: Whether employers can verbalize the profit-maximizing conditions, or whether they can explicitly measure the marginal revenue product of labor, they must at least *intuit* them to survive in

---

6. These totals do not include two "star" free agents whose value to their teams dropped dramatically when their teams signed other free agents for their positions.

guess at his future performance (by trying to take account of such factors as age, the influence of teammates, and the effects of the ballpark in which the team plays its home games). The various teams in the bidding will probably make different estimates of future performance and translate these into team-specific estimates of marginal revenue product.

Suppose that the *average* prediction by all teams in the free-agent "auction" turns out to be *correct,* but that some teams guess low and others high. Among the teams that can most use a star player, the highest bidder will tend to be the one making the most optimistic estimate of the player's future performance. If the average estimate is correct, the winning bidder will therefore tend to be one that *overestimates* the player's future performance. No wonder that the successful bidder is frequently judged, in retrospect, to have fallen prey to the winner's curse by paying "too much"!

The "winner's curse" represents a potential, but not inevitable, danger inherent in auctions. As is seen in the baseball example, experience can provide a useful learning process, and bidders can be expected to modify their behavior to take account of this pitfall.

For a discussion of the winner's curse applied to baseball, see James Cassing and Richard W. Douglas, "Implications of the Auction Mechanism in Baseball's Free Agent Draft," *Southern Economic Journal* 47, no. 1 (July 1980): 110–21. For applications to other types of auctions, see John H. Kagel and Dan Levin, "The Winner's Curse and Public Information in Common Value Auctions," *American Economic Review* 76, no. 5 (December 1986): 894–920; Richard Thaler, "The Winner's Curse," *Journal of Economic Perspectives* 2, no. 1 (Winter 1988): 191–202; and Stuart Thiel, "Some Evidence on the Winner's Curse," *American Economic Review* 78, no. 5 (December 1988): 884–96. Thiel's article suggests the "curse" is not a significant problem in auctions for highway construction contracts.

a competitive environment. Competition will "weed out" employers who are not good at generating profits, just as competition will weed out pool players who do not understand the intricacies of how speed, angles, and spin affect the motion of bodies through space. Yet one could canvass the pool halls of America and probably not find one player who could verbalize Newton's laws of motion! The point is that employers can *know* concepts without being able to verbalize them. Those that are not good at maximizing profits will not last very long in competitive markets. Conversely, those that survive, whether they can verbalize the general concepts or not, *do* know how to maximize profits.

The second objection to the marginal productivity theory of demand is that in many cases it seems that adding labor while holding capital constant would not add to output at all. For example, one secretary and one word-processing machine can produce output, but it might seem that adding a second secretary while holding the number of word processors constant could produce nothing extra, since that secretary would have no machine on which to work. The answer to this objection is that the second secretary could address envelopes by hand—a slower process, but one that would free the secretary at the word-processing machine to type more letters per day. The two secretaries could trade off using the word-processing machine, so that neither

FIGURE 3.3 The Market Demand Curve and Effects of an Employer-Financed Payroll Tax

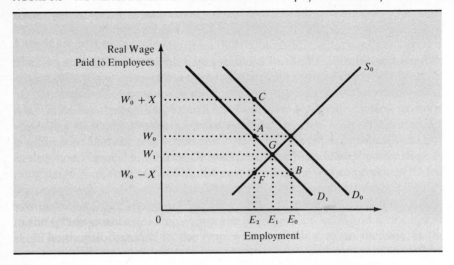

became fatigued to the extent that mistakes increased and typing speeds slowed down. The second secretary could also answer the telephone and in other ways expedite work. Thus, even with technologies that seem to require one machine per person, labor will generally have an *MRP* greater than zero if capital is held constant.

Market Demand Curves

The demand curve (or schedule) for an individual firm indicates how much labor that firm will want to employ at each real wage level. A *market demand curve* (or schedule) is just the *summation* of the labor demanded by all firms in a particular labor market at each level of the real wage.[7] If there are three firms in a certain labor market, and if at $(W/P)_0$ firm A wants 12 workers, firm B wants 6, and firm C wants 20, then the market demand at $(W/P)_0$ is 38 employees. More important, because market demand curves are so closely derived from firm demand curves, they too will *slope downward* as a function of the real wage. When the real wage falls, the number of workers that existing firms want to employ increases. In addition, the lower real wage may make it profitable for new firms to enter the market. Conversely, when the real wage increases, the number of workers that existing firms want to employ decreases, and some firms may be forced to cease operations completely.

Figure 3.3 shows a hypothetical market demand-for-labor curve (D_0) and a labor supply curve (S_0). (Disregard the curve labeled D_1 for the moment.)

---

7. If firms' demand curves are drawn as a function of the money wage, they represent (as we noted) the downward-sloping portion of the firms' marginal revenue product curves. In a competitive industry, the price of the product is "given" to the firm, and thus at the firm level the marginal revenue product of labor has imbedded in it a given product price. When aggregating labor demand to the *market* level, product price can no longer be taken as given, and the aggregation is no longer a simple summation. However, the market demand curves drawn against money wages, like those drawn as a function of real wages, slope downward—which at this point is all that is important.

The supply curve has been drawn as an upward-sloping function of the real wage, since higher real wages induce more individuals to enter this labor market. In this competitive labor market, the equilibrium real wage (W_0) and employment (E_0) levels are determined by the intersection of the labor demand and supply curves. If the real wage were lower than W_0, the number of workers that employers would want to hire would exceed the number of individuals who wanted to work. Facing unfilled positions, employers would be forced to raise their real wage offers to eliminate the job vacancies. In contrast, if the real wage were above W_0, employers would face an excess supply of applicants. The number of individuals willing to work would exceed the number of employees firms wanted to hire, and employers would eventually realize that they could reduce their real wage offers and still attract the necessary workers.[8]

Policy Application: Who Bears the Burden of the Payroll Tax?

In the United States several social insurance programs are financed by payroll taxes. Employers, and in some cases employees, make mandatory contributions of a fraction of the employees' salaries, up to a maximum level (or taxable wage base), to the social insurance trust funds. For example, the Social Security retirement, disability, and Medicare programs (OASDHI) are financed by a payroll tax paid by both employers and employees, while in most states unemployment insurance and workers' compensation insurance programs are financed solely by payroll-tax payments made by employers. It is not clear just why payroll taxes on *employers* are so heavily used in the social insurance area. There seems to be a prevailing notion that such taxes result in employers' "footing the bill" for the relevant programs, but this is not necessarily the case.

With our simple labor market model, we can show that the party making the social insurance payment is not necessarily the one that bears the burden of the tax. Suppose for expository convenience that only the employer is required to make payments and that the tax is a fixed dollar amount ($\$X$) per employee, rather than a percentage of payroll. Now consider the demand curve D_0 in Figure 3.3, which is drawn in such a way that desired employment is plotted against the real wage *employees receive*. Prior to the imposition of the tax, the wage employees receive is the same as the wage employers pay. Thus, if D_0 were the demand curve before the tax was imposed, it would have the conventional interpretation of indicating how much labor a firm would be willing to hire at any given wage. However, *after* imposition of the tax, employer wage costs would be $\$X$ above what employees received. Thus, if employees received W_0, employers would face costs of $W_0 + X$. They would no longer demand E_0 workers; rather, because their costs were $W_0 + X$, they would demand E_2 workers. Point A would become a point on a *new* demand curve, formed when demand shifted down because of the tax (remember, the wage on the vertical axis of Figure 3.3 is the wage *employees receive*, not the wage employers pay). Only if employee wages fell to $W_0 - X$ would the firm

---

8. The reduction in real wages need not occur through a reduction in money wages. Rather, all that is required during a period when prices are rising is that money wages remain constant or rise less rapidly than product prices.

want to continue hiring E_0 workers, for then *employer* costs would be the same as before the tax. Thus, point B would also be on the new, shifted demand curve. Note that, with a tax of $\$X$, the new demand curve (D_1) is parallel to the old one and the vertical distance between the two is X.

Now, the tax-related shift in the demand curve to D_1 implies that there would be an excess supply of labor at the previous equilibrium real wage of W_0. This surplus of labor would create downward pressure on the real wage, and this downward pressure would continue to be exerted until the wage fell to W_1, the point at which the quantity of labor supplied just equaled the quantity demanded. At this point, employment would also have fallen to E_1. Thus, *employees* bear part of the burden of the payroll tax in the form of *lower wage rates and lower employment levels.* The lesson is clear: The party legally liable to make the contribution (the employer) is not necessarily the one that bears the full burden of the actual cost.

Figure 3.3 does suggest, however, that employers bear at least *some* of the tax, because the wages received by employees do not fall by the full amount of the tax ($W_0 - W_1$ is smaller than X, which is the vertical distance between the two demand curves). The reason for this is that, with an upward-sloping supply curve, employees withdraw labor as their wages fall, and it becomes more difficult for firms to find workers. If wages fell to $W_0 - X$, the withdrawal of workers would create a labor shortage that would serve to drive wages to some point (W_1 in our example) between W_0 and $W_0 - X$. Only if the labor supply curve were *vertical*—meaning that lower wages have no effect on labor supply—would the *entire amount of the tax* be shifted to workers in the form of a decrease in their wages by the amount of X, as shown by supply curve S_0 in Figure 3.4.

In general, the extent to which the labor *supply* curve is sensitive to wages determines the proportion of the employer payroll tax that gets shifted to employees' wages. The less responsive labor supply is to changes in wages, the fewer the employees who withdraw from the market and the higher the proportion of the tax that gets shifted to workers in the form of a wage decrease (compare the outcomes in Figures 3.3 and 3.4). It must also be pointed out,

FIGURE 3.4 Payroll Tax Shifting with a Vertical Supply Curve

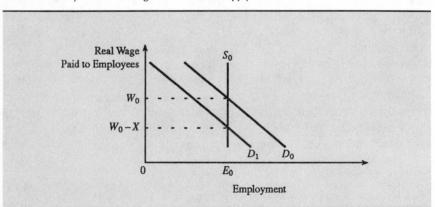

however, that to the degree employee wages do *not* fall, employment levels *will;* when employee wages do not fall much in the face of an employer payroll-tax increase, employer labor costs are increased—and this increase reduces the quantity of labor employers demand.[9]

A number of empirical studies have sought to ascertain what fraction of employers' payroll-tax costs are actually passed on to employees in the form of lower wages or lower wage increases. Although the evidence is by no means unambiguous, two studies have concluded that less than half of employers' payroll-tax contributions are actually shifted onto labor in the form of real wage decreases.[10]

MODIFIED MODELS OF LABOR DEMAND

Monopoly in the Product Market

We have assumed so far that firms take product prices as given. If a firm faced a downward-sloping demand curve for its output—so that as it expanded employment and output, its product price fell—then the marginal revenue (*MR*) it received from the last unit of output it produced would not be the product price (*P*). Rather, the marginal revenue would be less than the product price because the lower price applied to all units it sold, not just the marginal unit. As a result, equations (3.5) and (3.6) do *not* define the demand for labor in the presence of product market monopoly.

A monopoly trying to maximize profits and facing a competitive *labor* market will hire workers until its marginal revenue product (*MRP*) equals the wage rate:

$$MRP = (MR) \cdot (MP_L) = W \tag{3.7}$$

Now one can express the demand for labor in the short run in terms of the real wage by dividing equation (3.7) by the firm's product price, *P*, to obtain

$$\frac{MR}{P} \cdot MP_L = \frac{W}{P} \tag{3.8}$$

---

9. Another major influence on the extent to which payroll taxes are shifted to employees is the shape of the demand curve. If the demand curve were very sensitive to changes in labor costs, there would be relatively large employment losses and strong downward pressures on employee wages. On the other hand, if employer demand were not very responsive to labor costs, both employment losses and employee wage changes would be small.

   The analyses presented in this section so far have examined just the demand-side effects of employer payroll taxes. A complete analysis must take account of supply-curve shifts associated with benefits paid by the programs for which the taxes are collected. As we shall see in Chapters 6 and 7, the benefits made available by the Social Security, unemployment compensation, and workers' compensation systems all provide incentives for individuals to alter their labor supply behavior. To the extent that these benefits cause the labor supply curve to shift, conclusions about the wage and employment effects of programs financed by payroll taxes must be modified. For example, if the labor supply curve shifts to the right (because the benefits financed by the tax make working more attractive), wages will fall to an extent greater than that caused by shifts in the demand curve alone. However, with the larger wage decrease, the decline in employment will be moderated.

10. Ronald G. Ehrenberg, Robert Hutchens, and Robert S. Smith, *The Distribution of Unemployment Insurance Benefits and Costs,* Technical Analysis Paper no. 58, ASPER, U.S. Department of Labor, October 1978, and Daniel Hamermesh, "New Estimates of the Incidence of the Payroll Tax," *Southern Economic Journal* 45 (February 1979): 1208–19.

Since marginal revenue is always less than a monopoly's product price, the ratio (MR/P) in equation (3.8) is less than one. As such, the demand-for-labor curve for a firm that has monopoly power in the output market will lie below and to the left of the demand-for-labor curve for an *otherwise identical* firm that takes product price as given. Put another way, just as output is lower under monopoly than it is under competition, other things equal, so is the level of employment.

The *wage* rates that monopolies pay, however, are not necessarily different from competitive levels even though *employment* levels are. An employer with a product market monopoly may still be a very small part of the market for a particular kind of employee, and thus be a *price taker* in the labor market even though a *price maker* in the product market.[11] For example, a local utility company might have a product market monopoly, but it would have to compete with all other firms to hire secretaries and thus would have to pay the going wage.

There are circumstances, however, in which economists suspect that product market monopolies might pay wages that are *higher* than competitive firms would pay.[12] The monopolies that are legally permitted to exist in the United States are regulated by governmental bodies in an effort to prevent them from exploiting their favored status and earning monopoly profits. This regulation of profits, it can be argued, gives monopolies incentives to pay higher wages than they would otherwise pay for two reasons.

First, regulatory bodies allow monopolies to pass on the costs of doing business to consumers. Thus, while unable to maximize profits, the managers of a monopoly can enhance their *utility* by paying high wages and passing the costs along to consumers in the form of higher prices. The ability to pay high wages makes a manager's life more pleasant by making it possible to hire people who might be more attractive or personable or have other characteristics managers find desirable.

Second, monopolies that are as yet unregulated may not want to attract attention to themselves by earning the very high profits usually associated with monopoly. Therefore they, too, may be induced to pay high wages in a partial effort to "hide" their profits. The excess profits of monopolies, in other words, may be partly taken in the form of highly preferred workers—paid a relatively high wage rate—rather than in the usual monetary form.

The evidence on monopoly wages, however, is not very clear as yet. Some studies suggest that firms in industries with relatively few sellers *do* pay higher wages than competitive firms for workers with the same education and experience.[13] Other studies of regulated monopolies, however, have obtained mixed

---

11. A *price taker* is someone who is such a small part of a particular market that he or she cannot influence market price. Thus, to such a person, the market price is a given. A *price maker* is someone with enough monopoly power to influence prices.

12. For a full statement of this argument, see Armen Alchian and Reuben Kessel, "Competition, Monopoly, and the Pursuit of Money," in *Aspects of Labor Economics,* ed. H. G. Lewis (Princeton, N.J.: Princeton University Press, 1962).

13. James Dalton and E. J. Ford, "Concentration and Labor Earnings in Manufacturing and Utilities," *Industrial and Labor Relations Review* 30 (October 1977): 45–60; James Long and Albert Link, "The Impact of Market Structure on Wages, Fringe Benefits and Turnover," *Industrial and Labor Relations Review* 36 (January 1983): 239–50; and John S. Heywood, "Labor Quality and the Concentration-Earnings Hypothesis," *Review of Economics and Statistics* 68 (May 1986): 342–46.

results on whether wages tend to be higher for comparable workers in these industries.[14]

Monopsony in the Labor Market

When only one firm is the buyer of labor in a particular labor market, such a firm is called a *monopsonist*. Because the firm is the only demander of labor in this market, it can influence the wage rate. Rather than being a *price (wage) taker* and facing the horizontal labor supply curve that competitive firms are confronted with, monopsonists face an upward-sloping supply curve. The supply curve confronting them, in other words, is the *market* supply curve. To expand its work force, a monopsonist must increase its wage rate. (In contrast, a competitive firm can expand its work force while paying the prevailing market wage as long as that wage is not below market-clearing levels.)

The unusual aspect of a *firm's* being confronted with an upward-sloping labor supply curve is that the *marginal cost of hiring labor exceeds the wage*. If a competitive firm wants to hire 10 workers instead of 9, the hourly cost of the additional worker is equal to the wage rate. If a monopsonist hires 10 instead of 9, it must pay a higher wage to all workers *in addition to* paying the bill for the added worker. For example, suppose that a monopsonist could get 9 workers if it paid $7 per hour but that if it wished to hire 10 workers it would have to pay a wage of $7.50. The labor cost associated with 9 workers would be $63 per hour (9 times $7), but the labor cost associated with 10 workers would be $75 per hour (10 times $7.50). Hiring the additional worker would cost $12 per hour—far more than the $7.50 wage rate![15]

The fact that the marginal cost of hiring labor is above the wage rate affects the labor market behavior of monopsonists. To maximize profits, we know that any firm should hire labor until the point at which marginal revenue product equals marginal cost. Hence, the monopsonist should hire workers up to the point at which labor's marginal revenue product equals the marginal cost of hiring additional workers (MC_L),

$$MRP = MC_L \tag{3.9}$$

Since the marginal cost of hiring labor for a monopsonist is *above* the wage rate, it will stop hiring labor at some point at which marginal revenue product is above the wage rate. In terms of Figure 3.5, the monopsonist hires E_M workers because at that point marginal revenue product equals marginal labor costs (point X). However, the wage rate necessary to attract E_M workers to the firm—which can be read off the supply curve—is W_M (see point Y). Thus, wages are below marginal revenue product for a monopsonist.

If the market depicted in Figure 3.5 were competitive, each firm in the market would hire labor until marginal revenue product equaled the wage,

14. Ronald Ehrenberg, *The Regulatory Process and Labor Earnings* (New York: Academic Press, 1979); James Long and Albert Link, "The Impact of Market Structure on Wages, Fringe Benefits and Turnover," *Industrial and Labor Relations Review* 36 (January 1983): 239–50; and Michael Pergamit, "Wages in Regulated Industries," BLS Working Paper no. 152 (Washington, D.C.: June 1985).

15. We assume here that the monopsonist does not know which workers it can hire for $7.00 per hour and which workers could only be hired at $7.50. All it knows is that if it wants to hire 10 workers it must pay $7.50, while if it wants to hire 9 it can pay only $7.00. Therefore, all workers get paid the same wage.

FIGURE 3.5 The Effects of Monopsony

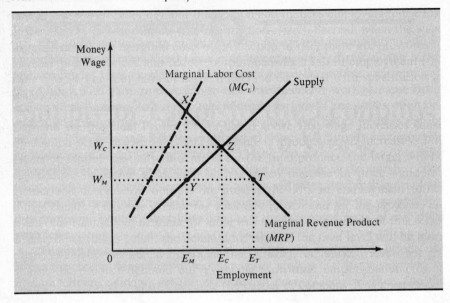

and the marginal revenue product schedule would be the demand curve for labor.[16] Thus, the wage rate would be W_C and the employment level would be E_C. Note that in a market that is monopsonized, wages and employment levels are *below* W_C and E_C.

Examples of pure monopsony in the labor market are difficult to cite: isolated coal-mining towns or sugar plantations, where the mines or sugar companies are literally the only employers, are increasingly rare. However, some employers may be large relative to the market and may, therefore, find themselves confronted with an upward-sloping supply curve.

Some economists argue that the market for registered nurses, particularly in small towns, is partially monopsonized. Hospitals employ the majority of registered nurses, and in many small towns there is only one hospital. These hospitals, it is argued, behave like monopsonists and pay lower wages than they otherwise would.[17]

If the market for registered nurses is characterized by monopsony, this situation could help explain why the nursing shortage discussed in Chapter 2 was perceived to exist even though nursing salaries were not being bid up. At wage W_M in Figure 3.5, the monopsonized employer (the hospital in this case) will hire only E_M nurses because that is where marginal revenue and marginal cost are equal. However, *if* it could do all its additional hiring at W_M, it would *like* to hire E_T. Since at W_M supply falls short of E_T, there might appear

---

16. Since a monopsonist never takes the wage rate as given, a monopsonist does not face a demand curve for labor, just as a monopolist in the product market does not face a supply curve of output.

17. Richard Hurd, "Equilibrium Vacancies in a Labor Market Dominated by Non-Profit Firms: The 'Shortage' of Nurses," *Review of Economics and Statistics* 55, no. 2 (May 1973): 234–40, and C. R. Link and J. H. Landon, "Monopsony and Union Power in the Market for Nurses," *Southern Economic Journal* 41 (April 1975): 649–59.

to be a shortage. In this case, then, hospitals find themselves in the position of wanting to hire more nurses at wage W_M—and being unable to do so—while at the same time being unwilling to raise wage offers enough to increase employment beyond E_M! The shortage is thus more apparent than real.

Another market that may be monopsonized is the market for public school teachers outside of metropolitan areas.[18] However, there is not much evidence that private firms in metropolitan areas have monopsony power. Wages that these firms pay appear to be essentially unaffected by the concentration of employment in the hands of a very few employers.[19]

Long-Run Demand for Labor by Firms

In the long run, employers are free to vary their capital stock as well as the number of workers they employ. An increase in the wage rate will affect their desired employment levels for two reasons. First, wages affect employment through a *scale* or *output effect.* A profit-maximizing firm will produce up to the point at which the marginal revenue from the last unit of output produced is just equal to its marginal cost of production. Now an increase in the wage rate tends to increase the marginal cost of production without affecting the marginal revenue. As a result, at the firm's previous equilibrium level of output, marginal cost *exceeds* marginal revenue. The firm is losing money on the last units of output that it produces, and it can increase its profits after the wage increase by cutting back on its production level. Reducing output generally will cause the firm to reduce its usage both of capital and of labor.

The second reason why an increase in the wage rate affects a firm's desired employment level in the long run is that it induces *factor substitution.* To maximize profit, a firm must minimize the cost of producing whatever level of output it produces. This cost minimization is achieved when an extra unit of output produced by adding labor (holding capital constant) costs the same as an extra unit of output produced by adding just capital. To illustrate this point, assume that a firm wants to keep its output level constant at Q but is considering changing its mix of capital and labor to see if it can reduce cost. If the marginal cost of expanding output by one unit using just labor is (say) $13 and the marginal cost using just capital is $10, then reducing the labor input and expanding capital by an appropriate amount could leave Q fixed but reduce costs by $3. That is, if the firm cut back on its use of labor by enough to reduce output by one unit, it would save $13; if it then increased capital by enough to restore this loss of output, its added costs would only be $10. The net effect would be to leave output constant but reduce costs.

The substitution of capital for labor would continue as long as the cost of adding a unit of output through employing more labor exceeds the cost of an extra unit of output produced by adding capital. Because labor would be substituted for capital (by an analogous chain of reasoning) if the cost discrepancy were reversed, it can be deduced that cost minimization is achieved only when

18. Ronald Ehrenberg and Joshua Schwarz, "Public Sector Labor Markets," in *Handbook of Labor Economics,* ed. Orley Ashenfelter and Richard Layard (Amsterdam: North-Holland, 1987), summarize the evidence on this point.
19. See Robert L. Bunting, *Employer Concentration in Local Labor Markets* (Chapel Hill: University of North Carolina Press, 1962).

EXAMPLE 3.3
Coal Mining

That wage increases have both a *scale effect* and a *factor substitution effect,* both of which tend to reduce employment, is widely known—even by many of those pushing for higher wages. John L. Lewis was president of the United Mine Workers during the 1920s, 1930s, and 1940s, when wages for miners were increased considerably with full knowledge that this would induce the substitution of capital for labor. Lewis explained:

> Primarily the United Mine Workers of America insists upon the maintenance of wage standards guaranteed by the existing contractual relations in the industry, in the interests of its own membership....But in insisting on the maintenance of an American wage standard in the coal fields the United Mine Workers is also doing its part, probably more than its part, to force a reorganization of the basic industry of the country upon scientific and efficient lines. The maintenance of these rates will accelerate the operation of natural economic laws, which will in time eliminate uneconomic mines, obsolete equipment, and incompetent management....
>
> The policy of the United Mine Workers of America will inevitably bring about the utmost employment of machinery of which coal mining is physically capable....Fair wages and American standards of living are inextricably bound up with the progressive substitution of mechanical for human power. It is no accident that fair wages and machinery will walk hand-in-hand.

SOURCE: John L. Lewis, *The Miners' Fight for American Standards* (Indianapolis: Bell Publishing Co., 1925), 40, 41, 108.

---

expanding output using labor and expanding it using capital cost just the same. In this case the firm has no incentive to change its mix of labor and capital, which is another way of saying that it is producing its output level as cheaply as it can.

To better understand factor substitution, let C represent the rental cost per period of a unit of capital equipment. Rental cost depends upon a number of things, including the purchase price of new capital equipment, the interest rate a firm must pay on borrowed funds, and various provisions that affect the income tax treatment of firms' investment expenditures (the specific formula for C need not concern us here). Now, if a firm is to minimize the cost of producing any given level of output, it must employ labor and capital up until the point that the marginal cost of producing the last unit of output is the same regardless of whether capital or labor is employed in generating that last unit. A formal way of stating this requirement is that the wage divided by the marginal product of labor (which is the cost of producing an added unit of output using just labor) must equal the cost of capital (C) divided by the marginal product of capital (MP_K):

$$(W/MP_L) = (C/MP_K) \tag{3.10}$$

We can rewrite equation (3.10) as

$$(W/C) = (MP_L/MP_K) \tag{3.11}$$

Equation (3.11) indicates that, to minimize its cost of production, a firm must employ capital and labor up until the point that their relative marginal costs are just equal to their relative marginal productivities.

Consider what happens when wages increase and capital costs do not. The increase in W/C distorts the equality in equation (3.11), and the left-hand side is now greater than the right-hand. Since the marginal cost of producing a unit of output is now greater when a firm adds new labor than when it adds new capital, the firm has an incentive to substitute capital for labor (to increase its usage of capital and decrease its usage of labor). Because the marginal productivity of a productive factor declines when its usage increases, the increased use of capital leads to a decline in the marginal product of capital, while the decreased use of labor leads to an increase in the marginal product of labor. Eventually the equality in equation (3.11) is restored, with fewer workers employed.

More Than Two Inputs

Thus far we have assumed that there are only two inputs in the production process: capital and labor. In fact, labor can be subdivided into many categories (for example, labor can be categorized by age, ethnicity, gender, race, educational level, and occupation). Other inputs that are used in the production process include materials and energy. If a firm is seeking to minimize costs, in the long run it should employ all inputs up until the point that the marginal cost of producing a unit of output is the same regardless of which input is used. This generalization of equation (3.10) leads to the somewhat obvious result that the demand for *any* category of labor will be a function not only of its own wage rate, but also of the wage rates of all other categories of labor and of the prices of capital and other inputs.

The demand curve for each category of labor will be a downward-sloping function of the wage rate paid to workers in the category, for the reasons discussed earlier. If the inputs are *substitutes in production* (that is, if the greater use of one in producing output can compensate for reduced use of the other), then increases in the prices of *other* inputs may shift the entire demand curve for a given category of labor either to the right or to the left. If an increase in the price of one input shifts the demand for *another* input to the left, as in panel (a) of Figure 3.6, the scale effect has dominated the substitution effect and the two inputs are *gross complements;* if it shifts the demand for the other input to the right, as in panel (b) of Figure 3.6, the substitution effect has dominated and the two inputs are *gross substitutes.*

If, instead, the two inputs are *complements in production,* which means that they must be used together, then reduced use of one implies reduced use of the other. In this case, there is no substitution effect, only a scale effect, and the two inputs must be gross complements.

Consider an example of a snow-removal firm in which skilled and unskilled workers are substitutes in production—snow can be removed using either unskilled workers (with shovels) or skilled workers driving snowplows. Let us focus on demand for the skilled workers. Other things equal, an increase in the wage of skilled workers would cause the firm to employ fewer of them; their demand curve would be a downward-sloping function of their

FIGURE 3.6   Effect of Increase in the Price of One Input (k) on Demand for Another Input (j), Where Inputs Are Substitutes in Production

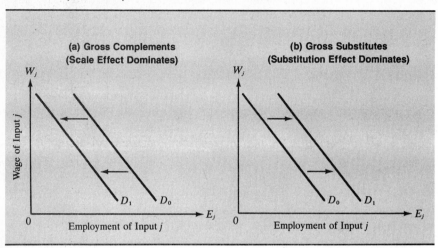

wage. If only the wage of *unskilled* workers increased, however, the employer would want fewer unskilled workers than before, and more of the now relatively cheaper skilled workers, to remove any given amount of snow. To the extent that this substitution effect dominated over the scale effect (the higher unskilled wage leads to reduced output), the demand for skilled workers would shift to the right. In this case, skilled and unskilled workers would be gross substitutes. In contrast, if the reduction in the scale of output caused employment of skilled workers to be reduced, on balance, even though skilled workers were being substituted for unskilled workers in the production process, skilled and unskilled workers would be considered gross complements.[20]

In the above firm, snowplows and skilled workers are complements in production. If the price of snowplows went up, the employer would want to cut back on their usage, which would result in a reduced demand at each wage for the skilled workers who drove the snowplows. As noted above, inputs that are complements in production are always gross complements.[21]

POLICY APPLICATION: MINIMUM WAGE LEGISLATION

History and Description

The Fair Labor Standards Act of 1938 was the first major piece of protective labor legislation adopted at the national level in the United States. Among its provisions were a minimum wage rate, or floor, below which hourly wages could not be reduced, an overtime pay premium for workers who worked long workweeks, and restrictions on the use of child labor. The minimum wage

---

20. This example highlights that *both* the production process *and* demand conditions determine whether two inputs are gross substitutes or gross complements.
21. This statement assumes that all inputs are *noninferior* inputs—i.e., that an increase in output does not reduce the usage of any input. We maintain this assumption throughout.

provisions were designed to guarantee each worker a reasonable wage for his or her work effort and thus to reduce the incidence of poverty.

When initially adopted, the minimum wage was set at $0.25 an hour and covered roughly 43 percent of all nonsupervisory wage and salary workers — primarily those employed in larger firms involved in interstate commerce (manufacturing, mining, and construction). As Table 3.3 indicates, both the basic minimum wage and coverage under the minimum wage have expanded over time. Indeed, by April of 1990, the minimum wage was set at $3.80 an hour and was scheduled to rise to $4.25 an hour in April of 1991; over 80 percent of all nonsupervisory workers were covered by its provisions.

It is important to emphasize that the minimum wage rate is currently specified in *nominal* terms and not in terms *relative* to some other wage or price index. Historically, this specification of the minimum wage has led to a pattern of changes that can be represented by Figure 3.7, where time is plotted on the horizontal axis and the value of the minimum wage relative to average hourly earnings in manufacturing is plotted on the vertical axis. Congress initially specifies the nominal level of the minimum wage (MW_0),

TABLE 3.3   Minimum Wage Legislation in the United States, 1938–91

Effective Date of Minimum Wage Change	Nominal Minimum Wage	Percent of Nonsupervisory Employees Covered[a]	Minimum Wage Relative to Average Hourly Wage in Manufacturing	
			Before	After
10/24/38	$0.25	43.4	—	0.403
10/24/39	0.30	47.1	0.398	0.478
10/24/45	0.40	55.4	0.295	0.394
1/25/50	0.75	53.4	0.278	0.521
3/1/56	1.00	53.1	0.385	0.512
9/3/61	1.15	62.1	0.431	0.495
9/3/63	1.25	62.1	0.467	0.508
9/3/64	1.25	62.6		
2/1/67	1.40	75.3	0.441	0.494
2/1/68	1.60	72.6	0.465	0.531
2/1/69	1.60	78.2		
2/1/70	1.60	78.5		
2/1/71	1.60	78.4		
5/1/74	2.00	83.7	0.363	0.454
1/1/75	2.10	83.3	0.423	0.445
1/1/76	2.30		0.410	0.449
1/1/78	2.65		0.430	0.480
1/1/79	2.90		0.402	0.440
1/1/80	3.10		0.417	0.445
1/1/81	3.35		0.403	0.435
4/1/90	3.80		0.329	0.373
4/1/91	4.25		—	—

[a]Excludes executive, administrative, and professional personnel (including teachers in elementary and secondary schools) from the base. Coverage peaked at 87.3 percent of the nonsupervisory work force in September 1977. As of 1978, however, a court decision eliminated most state and local government workers from coverage. As a result, worker coverage fell from 56,100,000 in 1976 to 51,900,000 in 1978.

FIGURE 3.7   Time Profile of the Minimum Wage Relative to Average Hourly Earnings

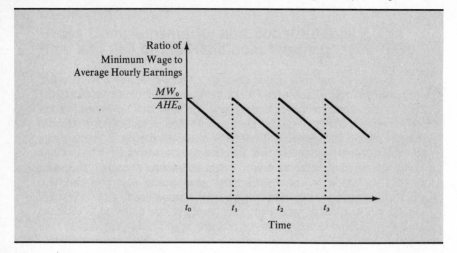

which, given the level of average hourly earnings that prevails in the economy (AHE_0), leads to an initial value of the minimum wage relative to average hourly earnings (MW_0/AHE_0). Over time this relative value declines as average hourly earnings increase as a result of inflation or productivity growth. The reduced relative value of the minimum wage creates pressure on Congress to legislate an increase in the nominal minimum wage, and after the passage of time (point t_1 in Figure 3.7) Congress returns the relative value of the minimum wage approximately to its initial level. Over time the process is repeated, and the saw-toothed time profile of relative minimum wage values portrayed in Figure 3.7 emerges. Although it varies from peak to peak, the value of the minimum wage relative to average hourly earnings in manufacturing after each legislated change was typically in the range of 0.45 to 0.50 until the 1990 change (see Table 3.3).

A Model with Uniform Coverage

Unfortunately, as with many social programs, minimum wage legislation may have unintended side effects that work against the program's goals of reducing poverty. Consider the labor market for unskilled workers and assume, initially, that all are covered by minimum wage legislation. As Table 3.3 indicates, such uniform coverage certainly would not be a reasonable assumption if we wanted to analyze minimum wage effects during the early years of the legislation. However, a model of full coverage may be more appropriate today than it once was.

Figure 3.8 represents the labor market for unskilled labor, which is in equilibrium prior to the imposition of the minimum wage with an employment level of E_0 and a *real* wage of W_0/P_0. Now suppose Congress legislates a nominal minimum wage of W_1, which is higher than W_0; this legislation will raise the real wage to W_1/P_0 and reduce to E_1 the number of employees firms

FIGURE 3.8   Minimum Wage Effects: Uniform Coverage Causes Unemployment

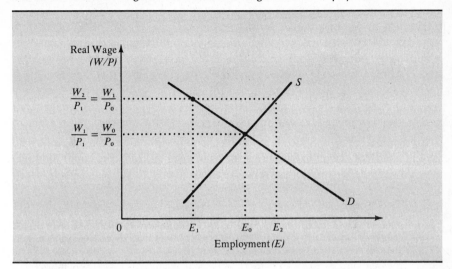

want to hire.[22] Although a larger number of workers (E_2) are willing to offer their services at that wage rate, no downward pressure is exerted on the money wage because by law the wage cannot be reduced below the nominal minimum. As a result, the immediate impact of the increase in the minimum wage is a decrease in employment and an increase in unemployment (which equals $E_2 - E_1$).[23]

Over time, the government may take actions to stimulate the economy in the hope of reducing unemployment. Such actions invariably include pursuing expansionary monetary or fiscal policies (increasing the money supply and government spending, decreasing taxes) and lead to increases in the price level. However, as the price level goes up, the real minimum wage falls, because the nominal minimum wage is being held constant. As the real wage falls, the number of workers employed increases. If Congress takes no other action but continues to pursue expansionary policies, eventually the price

22. Of course, if the legislated minimum wage were set at some level *below* W_0, it would not have any effect. For at any level of real wages below W_0/P_0 an excess demand for labor exists and employers would bid the real wage back to W_0/P_0 to fill unfilled positions.
23. The analysis here is somewhat oversimplified. The supply curve in Figure 3.8 indicates the number of workers who want to work at each real wage, under the assumption that anyone who wants to work can find employment. However, the imposition of a minimum wage that leads to a real wage (W_1/P_0) above the market-clearing level means that not all workers who want to work at that real wage can actually find employment. This reduced probability of finding employment should reduce the actual number of workers seeking employment below the level indicated by the supply curve (E_2). As a result, the actual increase in unemployment will be less than the depicted excess supply of labor $(E_2 - E_1$ in Figure 3.8). Since this complication does not fundamentally alter any of the conclusions in this chapter, we ignore it in the analysis that follows. Jacob Mincer, in "Unemployment Effects of Minimum Wage Changes," *Journal of Political Economy* 84 (August 1976): S87–S104, has presented evidence that higher minimum wage rates do lead to reduced labor force participation rates.

level will rise to P_1, where $(W_1/P_1) = (W_0/P_0)$. That is, the real value of the minimum wage will fall back to the market-clearing level, and employment will return to its initial level. While the immediate impact of the minimum wage increase was to reduce employment, over a longer period of time this employment reduction is eliminated, at the expense of a higher price level.

The story, however, does not end here. As noted above, Congress periodically increases the nominal minimum to restore its value relative to average hourly earnings. An increase, say, to W_2, where $(W_2/P_1) = (W_1/P_0)$, would again reduce employment to E_1 and create further pressure for the government to take action to reduce unemployment. What results then is a cycle of minimum wage increases inducing short-run employment losses, inflation reducing the real value of the minimum wage and restoring employment, and then an increase in the nominal minimum that starts the process all over.

Periodically proposals have been introduced into Congress to tie the minimum wage to either the consumer price level or average hourly earnings; the minimum wage would automatically increase each year to maintain a constant value relative to one of these variables. If tied to the former, the net effect of the legislation would be to fix the real wage of low-skilled labor at a level such as (W_1/P_0) in Figure 3.8. Whether such a policy is desirable for low-skilled workers as a group depends upon whether the higher real wage is sufficiently high to compensate low-skilled workers for their employment losses $(E_0 - E_1)$ and upon the income support programs, such as unemployment insurance, available to unemployed workers.

What's Wrong with the Model?

Early studies of the effects on employment of minimum wage legislation, conducted in the 1940s and 1950s, often found that employment *increased* after minimum wage increases. They concluded that there are no adverse effects of minimum wage legislation and that the model presented above is all wrong.

These studies, however, do not succeed in disproving the model for at least three reasons. First, they ignore the fact that the uniform coverage model is not applicable to the earlier period when coverage was less than complete. Second, they ignore the possibility that employers may not fully comply with increases in the minimum wage; noncompliance would reduce the employment effects of the legislated increase (the noncompliance problem will be discussed later in the chapter). Third, and most important, they ignore the fact that all the predictions from our models are made holding *other factors constant*. If other factors are not actually constant, changes in one or more of them may obscure the negative relationship between wages and the demand for labor.

To see the effects of such other factors, consider Figure 3.9, where for simplicity we have omitted the labor supply curve and focused on only the demand side of the market. Suppose that D_0 is the demand curve for low-skilled labor in year 0, in which year the real wage is W_0/P_0 and the employment level is E_0. Further assume that in the absence of any change in the minimum wage, the money wage and the price level would both increase by the same percentage over the next year, so that the real wage in year 1 (W_1/P_1) would be the same as that in year 0.

FIGURE 3.9   Minimum Wage Effects: Growing Demand Obscures Job Loss

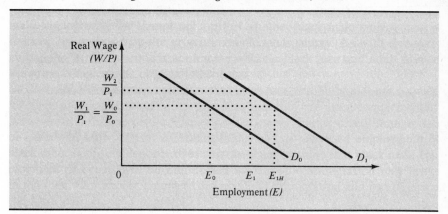

Now suppose that in year 1, two things happen. First, the minimum wage rate is raised to W_2, which is greater than W_1, so that the real wage increases to W_2/P_1. Second, because the economy is expanding, the demand for low-skilled labor shifts out to D_1. The result of these two changes is that employment increases from E_0 to E_1.

Comparisons of observed employment levels, such as E_1 and E_0 above, caused early investigators to conclude that minimum wage increases had no adverse employment effects. However, this simple before/after comparison is *not* the correct one. Rather, one should ask, "How did the actual employment level in period 1 compare to the level that *would have prevailed* in the absence of the increase in the minimum wage?" Since demand grew between the two periods, this hypothetical employment level would have been E_{1H}. E_{1H} is greater than E_1, the actual level of employment in period 1, so that $E_{1H} - E_1$ represents the loss of jobs caused by the minimum wage.

In sum, in a growing economy with complete coverage, the net effect of a one-time increase in the minimum wage is to reduce the rate of growth of employment. By focusing on only the actual employment growth, the early studies both misunderstood the implications of the model and failed to adequately estimate the adverse employment effects of the program.[24]

A Model with Incomplete Coverage

Although minimum wage coverage has grown over time, so that today about 87 percent of all nonsupervisory workers in the private sector are covered, as recently as 1965 more than one-third of private-sector workers were not covered. The major uncovered sectors then included retail trade, the service industries, and agriculture; today they include primarily employees in these

---

24. It is important to distinguish between a one-time increase in the minimum wage and recurrent increases that, because of inflation, have tended to keep the ratio of the minimum wage to the price level roughly constant after each increase in the minimum (Figure 3.7). In the case of recurrent increases, the main effect of minimum wage legislation is to decrease the average *level* of employment, rather than to decrease the average (over time) rate of growth of employment.

FIGURE 3.10 Minimum Wage Effects: Incomplete Coverage Causes Employment Shifts

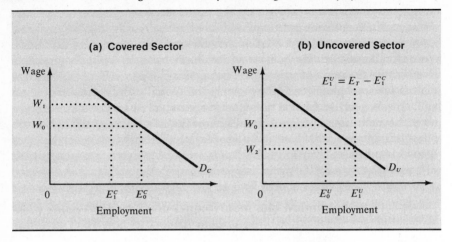

industries who work for small firms. Since coverage is less than complete, it is useful to present a model of minimum wage effects under incomplete coverage. (A similar model will appear in Chapter 12 when we discuss the effects of unions on wages.)

To simplify the discussion, we shall assume that:

a. Prices are constant (so we can talk interchangeably about real and money wages);
b. The market for unskilled labor is characterized by a vertical supply curve such that total employment of the unskilled is E_T;
c. This labor market has a covered and an uncovered sector; and
d. Unskilled workers move back and forth between sectors seeking jobs where the wages are highest.

These assumptions suggest that without a minimum wage, the wage in each sector will be the same. Referring to Figure 3.10, let us assume that this "pre-minimum" wage is W_0 and that total employment of E_T is broken down into E_0^C in the "covered" sector plus E_0^U in the other sector.

If a minimum wage of W_1 is imposed on the covered sector, all unskilled workers will prefer to work there. However, the increase in wages in that sector, from W_0 to W_1, reduces demand, and covered-sector employment will fall from E_0^C to E_1^C. Some workers who previously had, or would have found, jobs in the covered sector must now seek work in the uncovered sector. Thus, to the E_0^U workers formerly working in the uncovered sector are added $E_0^C - E_1^C$ other workers seeking jobs there. Thus, all unskilled workers in the market who are not lucky enough to find "covered jobs" at W_1 must now look for work in the uncovered sector,[25] and the (vertical) supply curve to that sector becomes

---

25. Under some circumstances it may be rational for these unemployed workers to remain unemployed for a while and to search for jobs in the covered sector. We shall discuss this possibility—which is discussed by Jacob Mincer in "Unemployment Effects of Minimum Wage Changes," *Journal of Political Economy* 84 (August 1976): S87–S104—in Chapter 12. At this point we simply note that if it occurs, unemployment will result.

EXAMPLE 3.4

Minimum Wages in Developing Countries

Does minimum wage legislation reduce employment? The answer depends at least partially on the *level* at which the minimum is set relative to prevailing wages. While in the United States the minimum has stayed at roughly 35 to 50 percent of average hourly earnings, in developing countries the minimum is sometimes set much higher. Not surprisingly, the predictions of economic theory are often borne out in situations like the one in Zimbabwe in July 1980. As the *New York Times* reported, a Zimbabwe government decision to set a minimum wage resulted in the dismissal of thousands of workers.

> SALISBURY, Zimbabwe, July 6 (Reuters)—A Government decision to set a minimum wage for workers has backfired for thousands with dismissals reported throughout the country.
>
> Officials of the ruling party of Prime Minister Robert Mugabe said today that in the Salisbury area alone more than 5,000 workers were dismissed before the minimum wage bill went into effect last Tuesday.
>
> Worst hit, according to the officials, were domestic servants and farm workers for whom the minimum had been set at $45 a month. Employees in the commercial and industrial sectors, where the minimum had been fixed at $105 a month, have also been dismissed. The officials said that every party office in the country was dealing with hundreds of workers each day complaining of unfair dismissal.

SOURCE: *New York Times*, July 7, 1980.

$E_1^U \left[= E_0^U + (E_0^C - E_1^C) = E_T - E_1^C \right]$. The increased supply of workers to that sector drives down the wage there from W_0 to W_2.

As with most laws, a partial-coverage minimum wage produces both winners and losers. The winners are those covered-sector workers who kept their jobs after the imposition of the minimum and now receive the higher minimum wage. The losers are those low-skilled workers who lost their jobs in the covered sector and now are paid lower wages in the uncovered sector. The losers also include those low-skilled workers in the uncovered sector who kept their jobs but now find their real wages depressed by the increased supply of labor to that sector. Hence, even in the context of this model, in which there are no overall employment effects, it is not obvious that the legislation is desirable on balance. The gains won by some groups must be weighed against the losses suffered by other groups before an unambiguous conclusion can be reached.

Social Losses

Besides predicting that minimum wage laws produce both gainers and losers among the poor, this chapter also predicts that such laws will create losses for society as a whole. In the case of full coverage, where government-mandated increases in the real wage create unemployment, the losses of potential output from those who are unemployed is obvious. However, there are also social losses in cases where, as in our Figure 3.10 example of partial coverage, total employment remains constant. To understand this point requires a quick review of profit-maximization principles.

A firm will hire labor until labor's marginal revenue product equals the money wage rate. In the partial-coverage example above (Figure 3.10), unskilled labor—prior to imposition of the minimum wage—would be hired in both sectors to the point at which marginal revenue product equaled W_0. Thus, if a worker were transferred from one sector to the other, the value of total output would go down by W_0 in the "sending" sector and up by W_0 in the "receiving" sector. Overall output would remain unchanged by such a transfer.

After the minimum wage is imposed on the covered sector, however, employment is reduced there until labor's marginal revenue product equals W_1. Wages in the uncovered sector, in contrast, fall to W_2; employment in that sector will thus increase until labor's marginal revenue product equals W_2. The marginal revenue product in the uncovered sector is now *below* that in the covered sector (W_2 is less than W_1), so that if a worker were transferred from the uncovered to the covered sector, output would be increased! (The value of output lost in the uncovered sector by this transfer would be W_2, while the value of output gained in the covered sector would be W_1.)

Since W_1 exceeds W_2, *the value of output* could be increased by transferring labor from the uncovered to the covered sector. This transfer would occur naturally if there were no minimum wage, because workers seeking the higher-paying jobs in the covered sector would bid down wages there and employment in that sector would expand. Transfers of labor would stop when the wages in each sector were equalized—and as we have shown above, when wages are equal in both sectors of the unskilled labor market, there are no further gains to be made by transfers of labor between the two sectors of that market.

With a minimum wage, however, labor *cannot* transfer out of the sector with the lower wage (and lower marginal revenue product) to the higher-wage sector. Wages in the latter sector cannot legally fall, and therefore employment cannot expand there. A beneficial transfer of resources is blocked, and social losses occur. Put differently, total output could be increased with no change in our total resources merely by transferring labor from one sector to another, and the effective prevention of this transfer by the minimum wage law implies social losses.

The Effects of Monopsony

This analysis of the minimum wage law has assumed that firms are sufficiently small that their hiring decisions do not affect the market wage for low-skilled workers. That is, we have assumed there is no monopsony in the market for low-skilled labor. While this assumption is probably appropriate for most employers of low-skilled labor, it is theoretically possible that monopsony exists in some communities. To understand the effects of a minimum wage on monopsonized markets, consider a "full coverage" model (with only one employer and no uncovered sector).

You will recall from our earlier discussion of the demand for labor by monopsonists that their marginal labor costs are above the wage rate. In maximizing profits, they choose an employment level (E_0 in Figure 3.11) at which marginal labor costs equal marginal revenue product (point A in Figure 3.11). The wage required to generate a labor supply of E_0 in Figure 3.11 is W_0.

Suppose now that a minimum wage of W_m is set in Figure 3.11. This minimum wage prevents the firm from paying a wage less than W_m and effectively creates a horizontal portion in the supply curve facing the firm (which is now *DACS*). The firm's marginal cost of labor curve is now *DACEM*, because up to employment level E_1 the marginal costs of labor are equal to W_m. The firm, which maximizes profits by equating marginal revenues with marginal costs (which equation remains at point A), will still hire E_0 workers, but it will pay them W_m instead of W_0. Moreover, if the minimum were set at a wage rate *between* W_0 and W_m, wages *and* employment would increase.

The apparent conclusion that a minimum wage can increase wages without reducing employment in a monopsonized market is subject to two qualifications. First, in the context of Figure 3.11, the minimum wage cannot be set above W_m if employment is to remain at least as large as E_0. Above W_m there would be employment losses. The second qualification is that the firm must remain in business in order for employment not to fall. While an employer may be the only buyer of labor in a particular market, the employing firm may also have many competitors in its product market. If its product market is competitive, its level of profits will be "normal" —which means that if profits were to fall, the firm would find it could earn more profits in another line of business. If, in our initial example (Figure 3.11), wages rose from W_0 to W_m and employment remained at E_0, the profits of the firm would clearly fall. If the fall were large enough, the firm might go out of business and all E_0 workers would lose their jobs.

FIGURE 3.11   Minimum Wage Effects Under Monopsony: Both Wages and Employment Can Increase

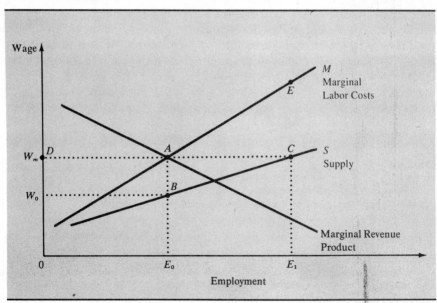

Empirical Evidence

Labor economists have devoted much effort to empirically estimating the magnitudes of the effects of minimum wage legislation on the employment levels of various age/race/gender groups.[26] Although the precise magnitudes of the relationships have yet to be pinned down, it is now widely agreed that increases in minimum wages do reduce employment opportunities, especially among teenagers. The studies use different data and often ask slightly different questions. Virtually all agree, however, that employment opportunities for teenagers have been reduced by the minimum wage, although the size of the reduction is in doubt. A careful review of the evidence concluded that a 10 percent increase in the minimum wage would reduce teenage employment by 1 to 3 percent and the employment of young adults (ages 20 to 24) by a somewhat smaller amount.[27] There is no consensus, however, on the effects of minimum wage legislation on other adults, perhaps because far fewer adults are directly affected by the minimum wage (most have wages in excess of the minimum).

Somewhat surprisingly, most research on the minimum wage has focused on its unintended adverse outcome: reductions in employment. Very little research has addressed the question of whether minimum wage legislation is achieving its intended goal of reducing the incidence of poverty. The few studies that have considered this issue have found that minimum wage legislation has only a minor effect on the distribution of income.[28] This finding is not surprising, because not all low-wage workers are members of low-income families; many low-wage workers, especially teenagers, are second earners in middle- or upper-income families. Put another way, minimum wage legislation directly affects low-wage workers, not necessarily low-income families.

The Fair Labor Standards Act has a certain political sanctity because it was the first piece of protective labor legislation adopted at the federal level; very few people would seriously argue for the repeal of the minimum wage law today. Instead, given the estimates of the adverse effects of the legislation on employment opportunities for youth, many people have recently argued that a youth subminimum (or training) wage should be instituted. Lower wages for teens, they claim, would help alleviate the teenage unemployment problem. While there appears to be empirical support for this proposition, opponents, including organized labor, point out that reducing the wages of teenagers relative to adults would encourage employers to increase their em-

---

26. For a very readable, albeit critical, nontechnical survey of economic research on the minimum wage, see Sar Levitan and Richard Belous, *More Than Subsistence: Minimum Wages for the Working Poor* (Baltimore: Johns Hopkins University Press, 1979). For a more sympathetic view, see Finis Welch, *Minimum Wages: Issues and Evidence* (Washington, D.C.: American Enterprise Institute, 1978). A more recent treatment is in Charles Brown, "Minimum Wage Laws: Are They Overrated?" *Journal of Economic Perspectives* 2, no. 3 (Summer 1988): 133–46.
27. Brown, "Minimum Wage Laws: Are They Overrated?"
28. See Richard Burkhauser and T. Aldrich Finegan, "The Minimum Wage and the Poor: The End of a Relationship," *Journal of Policy Analysis and Management* 8 (Winter 1989): 53–71. Other studies have examined the effect of minimum wages on teenagers' educational decisions, which, as we discuss in Chapter 9, have important implications for the distribution of income. See, for example, Ronald Ehrenberg and Alan Marcus, "Minimum Wages and Teenagers' Enrollment-Employment Outcomes: A Multinomial Logit Model," *Journal of Human Resources* 17 (Winter 1982): 39–58.

EXAMPLE 3.5

Mandating Employee Benefits

Recently, proposals have been put forth in the United States that, if enacted, would mandate that employers provide their employees with certain forms of nonwage employee benefits. For example, concern that many low-wage workers are not covered by health insurance has led to proposals that all employers be required to provide their employees with at least a minimal level of insurance coverage. Similarly, concern for the welfare of children has led to proposals that employers be required to provide their employees with unpaid parental leave so they can care for newborn or ill children without fear of losing their jobs.

While the benefit to employees of each proposal for mandated benefits seems clear, each also imposes a cost on employers that, unfortunately, might ultimately fall on these same employees. In the case of mandated health insurance, the cost to employers is in providing coverage for currently uncovered, primarily low-wage workers; one study suggested that a recent mandated insurance proposal would increase employers' costs for low-wage workers by 15 to 20 percent.* In the case of parental leave, employers' costs would include any loss of output suffered when workers are on leave and the costs of hiring and training temporary replacements.

As with payroll taxes, these costs on employers may be partially or fully passed on to workers in the form of lower wages. However, if they are not fully passed on (say, because minimum wage laws prevent low-wage workers' wages from being cut), inevitably employers will respond to these cost increases by cutting back employment—especially among those groups of workers (primarily low-wage) for whom the cost increases are greatest. As with proposals for minimum wage changes, then, policymakers must weigh the social benefits of proposed mandated benefits legislation against the wage and employment costs that might ultimately fall on the very group they are trying to help.

*Lawrence H. Summers, "Some Simple Economics of Mandated Benefits," *American Economic Association Papers and Proceedings* 79 (May 1989): 177–83, and Olivia S. Mitchell, "The Effects of Mandating Benefit Packages," in *Research in Labor Economics,* vol. 11, ed. Ronald Ehrenberg (Greenwich, Conn.: JAI Press, 1990).

ployment of teenagers at the expense of reduced adult employment. A youth subminimum wage was in fact instituted as part of the 1990 minimum wage change.[29] Estimates of the likely magnitude of the substitution of youths for adults will be required before intelligent policy decisions can be made with respect to future changes in this youth differential (see Chapter 4); in the language of some opponents, one should not substitute parents' unemployment for that of their children.[30]

---

29. The youth subminimum, or training, wage was set at $3.35 an hour in April of 1990 and scheduled to rise to $3.61 an hour in April of 1991. It applies to 16- to 19-year-olds only for the first six months of their first job.

30. One study that investigated this question concluded that roughly one adult job would be lost for every four teenage jobs created by a youth subminimum. See Daniel Hamermesh, "Minimum Wages and the Demand for Labor," *Economic Inquiry* 20 (July 1982): 365–80.

Two additional factors may help explain why increases in the minimum wage have not had as dramatic effects on employment or the distribution of income as one might expect. First, there is no reason to suspect that all employers comply with the legislation; only limited resources are expended on enforcement of the legislation, and the penalties for employers found to be not complying (paying covered workers less than the minimum) are quite small. Indeed, certain evidence suggests that only 50 to 70 percent of covered workers who would have earned less than the minimum in the absence of the law are actually paid the minimum. The remainder are paid a wage that is illegally low.[31]

Second, our discussion has ignored the possibility that employers may respond to increases in the minimum wage by lowering other forms of nonwage compensation that are *not* covered by the minimum wage law.[32] As Chapter 11 will discuss, nonwage forms of compensation (including holiday, vacation, and sick-leave pay, health insurance, and retirement benefits) now constitute a large, and still growing, share of total compensation. To the extent that employers can respond to increases in the minimum wage by lowering the levels (or more likely the rates of growth) of these benefits, increases in the minimum will have smaller effects on total labor costs—and hence smaller employment effects—than one might otherwise have anticipated.

MISCONCEPTION

"Each time the minimum wage has been raised total employment has continued to grow. Therefore, those who claim that the minimum wage causes job loss are simply not correct."

Analysis

Employment growth is affected by a number of factors besides the minimum wage. Many of these factors undoubtedly serve to increase employment. However, the minimum wage law could indeed cause job loss in the sense that *in its absence employment would have grown to an even greater extent!* Thus, job loss occurs if, holding other factors constant, there are fewer jobs created than there might otherwise have been.

Principle

Predictions of positive economics involve the influence of one variable on another, holding all *other* variables constant.

REVIEW QUESTIONS

1. "It is generally agreed that the volunteer army is a dismal failure—the quality of volunteers is down and the number is not sufficient to meet desired force levels.

---

31. Orley Ashenfelter and Robert S. Smith, "Compliance with the Minimum Wage Law," *Journal of Political Economy* 87 (April 1979): 335–50.
32. For a discussion of this point, see Walter J. Wessels, *Minimum Wages, Fringe Benefits, and Working Conditions* (Washington, D.C.: American Enterprise Institute, 1981).

The only alternatives are to raise the pay of volunteers or to reinstitute a draft system. Since the cost to society is clearly higher in the former than in the latter case, from an economist's perspective a draft system would be preferable." Evaluate this position.

2. Suppose the government were to subsidize the wages of all women in the population by paying their *employers* 50 cents for every hour they work. What would be the effect on the wage rate women received? What would be the effect on the net wage employers paid? (The net wage would be the wage women received less 50 cents.)

3. The Occupational Safety and Health Administration promulgates safety and health standards. These standards typically apply to machinery (capital), which is required to be equipped with guards, shields, etc. An alternative to these standards is to require the employer to furnish personal protective devices to employees (labor)—such as earplugs, hard hats, and safety shoes. *Disregarding* the issue of which alternative approach offers greater protection from injury, what aspects of each alternative must be taken into account when analyzing the possible *employment* effects of the two approaches to safety?

4. Assume that there are two grades of professional football players. There are a limited number of "stars," whom the fans most want to watch, and an unlimited number of "nonstars." There are too few stars to fully staff each team, but there are enough for a few to be on each team if an owner decided to hire them.

   a. Assume that football teams keep all the "gate" and TV revenues they generate and that players are free to choose their teams at the end of any season. Do stars earn more than nonstars? How are the wages of each group determined?

   b. Continue to assume that players are free to choose their teams, but assume now that teams agree to share *all* their gate and TV revenues equally (they put them into a "pool" and divide it equally among the team owners). What happens now to salaries of stars and nonstars?

5. Several years ago Great Britain adopted a program that placed a tax—to be collected from employers—on wages in *service* industries. Wages in manufacturing industries were not taxed. Discuss the wage and employment effects of this tax policy.

6. Suppose the government is considering imposing a payroll tax of $1 per person-hour worked to finance a massive training program for the unemployed. Will the new equilibrium wage and employment level depend upon whether it is *employers* or *employees* who are legally liable for the tax? Explain.

7. In the last decade or two the United States has been subject to huge increases in the illegal immigration of workers from Mexico, most of them unskilled, and the government has recently considered ways to reduce the flow. One policy that has been considered is to impose financial penalties on employers who are discovered to have hired illegal immigrants.

   What effect would this policy have on the employment of unskilled illegal immigrants? What effect would it have on the demand for skilled "native" labor?

8. The city of Rochester, New York, was declared a "foreign-trade zone" by the United States Department of Commerce. A foreign-trade zone is designated as "international ground," and companies in that zone are exempt from paying customs duties on component parts they import to manufacture their products. Analyze the effects of this foreign-trade-zone designation on the demand for labor in the Rochester area.

SELECTED READINGS

Ashenfelter, Orley, and Smith, Robert. "Compliance with the Minimum Wage Law." *Journal of Political Economy* 87 (April 1979).

Brown, Charles. "Minimum Wage Laws: Are They Overrated?" *Journal of Economic Perspectives* 2, no. 3 (Summer 1988).

Mincer, Jacob. "Unemployment Effects of Minimum Wage Changes." *Journal of Political Economy* 84 (August 1976).

Report of the Minimum Wage Study Commission. Washington, D.C.: U.S. Government Printing Office, 1981.

Rottenberg, Simon, ed. *The Economics of Legal Minimum Wages.* Washington, D.C.: American Enterprise Institute, 1981.

Welch, Finis. *Minimum Wages: Issues and Evidence.* Washington, D.C.: American Enterprise Institute, 1978.

APPENDIX 3A

Graphic Derivation of a Firm's Labor Demand Curve

Chapter 3 described verbally the derivation of a firm's demand-for-labor curve. This appendix will present the *same* derivation graphically. This graphic representation permits a more rigorous derivation, although our conclusion that demand curves slope downward in both the short and the long run remains unchanged.

THE PRODUCTION FUNCTION

Equation (3.1) presented the "production function" as $f(L, K)$. Figure 3A.1 illustrates this production function graphically and depicts several aspects of the production process.

Consider the convex curve labeled $Q = 100$. Along this line, every combination of labor (L) and capital (K) produces 100 units of output (Q). That is, the combination of labor and capital at point $A(L_a, K_a)$ generates the same 100 units of output as the combinations at points B and C. Because each point along the $Q = 100$ curve generates the same output, that curve is called an *isoquant* (*iso* = "equal"; *quant* = "quantity").

Two other isoquants are shown in Figure 3A.1 ($Q = 150, Q = 200$). These isoquants represent higher levels of output than the $Q = 100$ curve. The fact that these isoquants indicate higher output levels can be seen by holding labor constant at L_b (say) and then observing the different levels of capital. If L_b is combined with K_b in capital, 100 units of Q are produced. If L_b is combined with K_b', 150 units are produced (K_b' is greater than K_b). If L_b is combined with even more capital (K_b'', say), 200 units of Q could be produced.

Note that the isoquants in Figure 3A.1 have *negative* slopes, reflecting an assumption that labor and capital are substitutes. If, for example, we cut capital from K_a to K_b, we could keep output constant (at 100) by increasing labor from L_a to L_b. Labor, in other words, could be substituted for capital to maintain a given production level.

FIGURE 3A.1 A Production Function

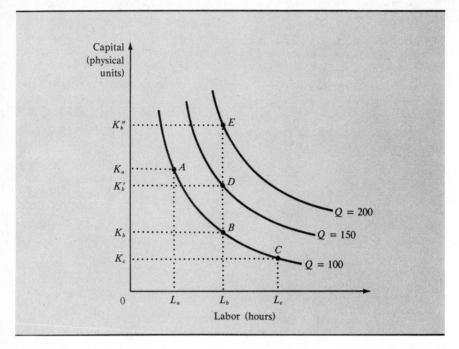

Finally, note the *convexity* of the isoquants. At point A, the $Q = 100$ iso-quant has a steep slope, suggesting that to keep Q constant at 100, a given de-crease in capital could be accompanied by a *modest* increase in labor. At point C, however, the slope of the isoquant is relatively flat. This flatter slope means that the same given decrease in capital would require a much *larger* in-crease in labor for output to be held constant. The decrease in capital permit-ted by a given increase in labor in order for output to be held constant is called the *marginal rate of technical substitution* (*MRTS*) between capital and labor. Symbolically, the *MRTS* can be written as

$$MRTS = \frac{\Delta K}{\Delta L} \,|\, \overline{Q} \tag{3A.1}$$

where Δ means "change in" and $|\overline{Q}$ means "holding output constant." The *MRTS* is *negative,* because if L is increased, K must be reduced to keep Q constant.

Why does the absolute value of the marginal rate of technical substitu-tion diminish as labor increases? When labor is highly used in the production process and capital is not very prevalent (point C in Figure 3A.1), there are many jobs that capital can do. Labor is easy to replace; if capital is increased, it will be used as a substitute for labor in parts of the production process where it will have the highest payoff. As capital becomes progressively more utilized and labor less so, the few remaining workers will be doing jobs that are hardest for a machine to do, at which point it will take a lot of capital to substitute for a worker.[1]

DEMAND FOR LABOR IN THE SHORT RUN

Chapter 3 argued that firms will maximize profits in the short run (K fixed) by hiring labor until labor's marginal product (MP_L) is equal to the real wage (W/P). The reason for this decision rule is that the real wage represents the *cost* of an added unit of labor (in terms of output), while the marginal product is the *output* added by the extra unit of labor. As long as the firm, by increasing labor (K fixed), gains more in output than it loses in costs, it will continue to hire employees. The firm will stop hiring when the marginal cost of added labor exceeds MP_L.

The requirement that $MP_L = W/P$ in order for profits to be maximized means that the firm's labor demand curve in the short run (in terms of the *real* wage) is identical to its marginal product of labor schedule (refer to Figure 3.1). Remembering that the marginal product of labor is the extra output produced by one-unit increases in the amount of labor employed, holding capital constant, consider the production function displayed in Figure 3A.2. Holding capital constant at K_a, the firm can produce 100 units of Q if it employs labor equal to L_a. If labor is increased to L'_a, the firm can produce 50 more units of Q; if labor is increased from L'_a to L''_a, the firm can produce an additional 50 units. Notice, however, that the required increase in labor to get the latter 50 units of added output, $L''_a - L'_a$, is larger than the extra labor required to produce the first 50-unit increment ($L'_a - L_a$). This difference can only mean that as labor is increased when K is held constant, each successive labor hour hired generates progressively smaller increments in output. Put differently, Figure 3A.2 graphically illustrates the diminishing marginal productivity of labor.

Why does labor's marginal productivity decline? Chapter 3 explained that labor's marginal productivity declines because, with K fixed, each added worker has less capital (per capita) with which to work. Is this explanation proven in Figure 3A.2? The answer is, regrettably, no. Figure 3A.2 is drawn *assuming* diminishing marginal productivity. Renumbering the isoquants could produce a different set of marginal productivities. (To see this, change $Q = 150$ to $Q = 200$, and change $Q = 200$ to $Q = 500$. Labor's marginal productivity would then rise.) However, the logic that labor's marginal product must eventually fall as labor is increased, holding buildings, machines, and tools constant, is very compelling. Further, as Chapter 3 pointed out, even if MP_L rises initially, the firm will stop hiring labor only in the range where MP_L is declining; as long as MP_L is above W/P and *rising*, it will pay to continue hiring.

---

1. Only a decade or two ago, most long-distance telephone calls were made through operators. Over time, operators have been increasingly replaced by a very capital-intensive direct-dialing system. Those operators who remain employed, however, perform tasks that are the most difficult for a machine to perform—handling collect calls, dispensing directory assistance, and acting as trouble-shooters when problems arise.

FIGURE 3A.2   The Declining Marginal Productivity of Labor

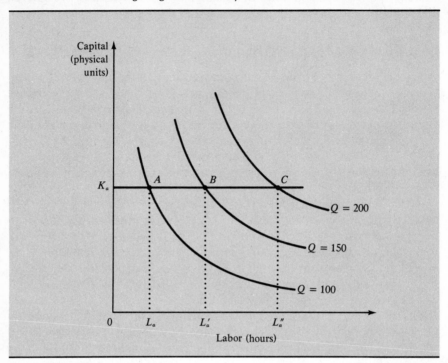

The assumptions that MP_L declines eventually and that firms hire until $MP_L = W/P$ are the bases for the assertion that a firm's short-run demand curve for labor slopes downward. The graphic, more rigorous derivation of the demand curve in this appendix confirms and supports the verbal analysis in the chapter. However, it also emphasizes more clearly than a verbal analysis can that the downward-sloping nature of the short-run labor demand curve is based on an *assumption*—however reasonable—that MP_L declines as employment is increased.

DEMAND FOR LABOR IN THE LONG RUN

Recall that a firm maximizes its profits by producing at a level of output (Q^*) where marginal cost equals marginal revenue. That is, the firm will keep increasing output until the addition to its revenues generated by an extra unit of output just equals the marginal cost of producing that extra unit of output. Because marginal revenue, which is equal to output *price* for a competitive firm, is not shown in our graph of the production function, the profit-maximizing level of output cannot be determined. However, continuing our analysis of the production function can illustrate some important aspects of the demand for labor in the long run.

Conditions for Cost Minimization

In Figure 3A.3, profit-maximizing output is assumed to be Q^*. How will the firm combine labor and capital to produce Q^*? It can maximize profits only if it produces Q^* in the least expensive way; that is, it must minimize the costs of producing Q^*. To better understand the characteristics of cost minimization, refer to the three *isoexpenditure* lines—AA', BB', DD'—in Figure 3A.3. Along any one of these lines the costs of employing labor and capital are equal.

For example, line AA' represents total costs of $1,000. Given an hourly wage (W) of $10 per hour, the firm could hire 100 hours of labor and incur total costs of $1,000 if it used no capital (point A'). In contrast, if the price of a unit of capital (C) is $20, the firm could produce at a total cost of $1,000 by using 50 units of capital and no labor (point A). All the points between A and A' represent combinations of L and K that, at $W = $10 and $C = $20, cost $1,000 as well.

The problem with the isoexpenditure line of AA' is that it does not intersect the isoquant Q^*, implying that Q^* cannot be produced for $1,000. At prices of $W = $10 and $C = $20, the firm cannot buy enough resources to produce output level Q^* and hold total costs to $1,000. The firm can, however, produce Q^* for a total cost of $2,000. Line DD', representing expenditures of $2,000, intersects the Q^* isoquant at points X and Y. The problem with these points, however, is that they are not cost-minimizing; Q^* can be produced for less than $2,000.

Since isoquant Q^* is convex, the cost-minimizing combination of L and K in producing Q^* will come at a point where an isoexpenditure line is *tangent* to the isoquant (that is, just barely touches isoquant Q^* at only one place). Point Z, where labor equals L_Z and capital equals K_Z, is where Q^* can be produced at minimal cost, *given* that $W = $10 and $C = $20. No lower isoexpenditure curve touches the isoquant, meaning that Q^* cannot be produced for less than $1,500.

FIGURE 3A.3   Cost Minimization in the Production of Q^* (Wage = $10 per Hour; Price of a Unit of Capital = $20)

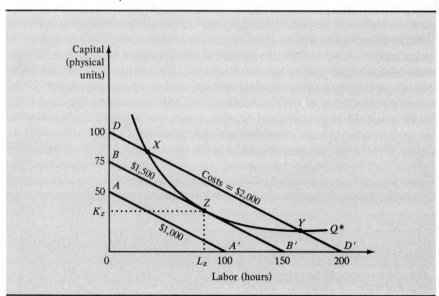

An important characteristic of point Z is that the slope of the isoquant at point Z and the slope of the isoexpenditure line are the same (the slope of a curve at a given point is the slope of a line tangent to the curve at that point). The slope of the isoquant at any given point is the *marginal rate of technical substitution* as defined in equation (3A.1). Another way of expressing equation (3A.1) is:

$$MRTS = \frac{-\Delta K/\Delta Q}{\Delta L/\Delta Q} \tag{3A.2}$$

Equation (3A.2) directly indicates that the $MRTS$ is a ratio reflecting the reduction of capital required to *decrease* output by one unit if enough extra labor is hired so that output is tending to *increase* by one unit. (The ΔQs in equation 3A.2 cancel each other and keep output constant.) Pursuing equation (3A.2) one step further, the numerator and denominator can be rearranged to obtain the following:[2]

$$MRTS = \frac{-\Delta K/\Delta Q}{\Delta L/\Delta Q} = -\frac{\Delta Q/\Delta L}{\Delta Q/\Delta K} = -\frac{MP_L}{MP_K} \tag{3A.3}$$

where MP_L and MP_K are the marginal productivities of labor and capital, respectively.

The slope of the *isoexpenditure line* is equal to the negative of the ratio W/C (in Figure 3A.3, W/C equals 10/20, or 0.5).[3] Thus, at point Z, where Q^* is produced in the minimum-cost fashion, the following equality holds:[4]

$$MRTS = -\frac{MP_L}{MP_K} = -\frac{W}{C} \tag{3A.4}$$

Equation (3A.4) is exactly the same as equation (3.11) in the text.

The economic meaning, or logic, behind the characteristics of cost minimization can most easily be seen by stating the $MRTS$ as $-\dfrac{\Delta K/\Delta Q}{\Delta L/\Delta Q}$ (see equation 3A.2) and equating this version of the $MRTS$ to $-\dfrac{W}{C}$:

$$-\frac{\Delta K/\Delta Q}{\Delta L/\Delta Q} = -\frac{W}{C} \tag{3A.5}$$

or

$$\frac{\Delta K}{\Delta Q} \cdot C = \frac{\Delta L}{\Delta Q} \cdot W \tag{3A.6}$$

Equation (3A.6) makes it very plain that to be minimizing costs, the cost of producing an extra unit of output by adding only labor must equal the cost of producing that extra unit by employing only additional capital. If these

---

2. This is done by making use of the fact that dividing one number by a second one is equivalent to *multiplying* the first by the *inverse* of the second.
3. Note that $10/20 = 75/150$, or $0B/0B'$.
4. The negative signs on each side of equation (3A.4) cancel each other and can therefore be ignored.

costs differed, the company could reduce total costs by expanding its use of the factor with which output can be increased more cheaply and cutting back on its use of the other factor. Any point where costs can still be reduced while Q is held constant is obviously not a point of cost minimization.

The Substitution Effect

If the wage rate, which was assumed to be $10 per hour in Figure 3A.3, goes up to $20 per hour (holding C constant), what will happen to the cost-minimizing way of producing output of Q^*? Figure 3A.4 illustrates the answer that common sense would suggest: total costs rise, and more capital and less labor are used to produce Q^*. At $W = $20, 150 units of labor can no longer be purchased if total costs are to be held to $1,500; in fact, if costs are to equal $1,500, only 75 units of labor can be hired. Thus, the isoexpenditure curve for $1,500 in costs shifts from BB' to BB'' and no longer is tangent to isoquant Q^*. Q^* can no longer be produced for $1,500, and the minimum-cost way of producing Q^* will rise. In Figure 3A.4 we assume that it rises to $2,250 (isoexpenditure line EE' is the one tangent to isoquant Q^*).

Moreover, the increase in the cost of labor relative to capital induces the firm to use more capital and less labor. Graphically, the old tangency point of Z is replaced by a new one (Z'), where the marginal productivity of labor is higher relative to MP_K, as equation (3A.4) explained. Point Z' is reached (from

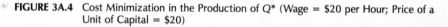

FIGURE 3A.4 Cost Minimization in the Production of Q^* (Wage = $20 per Hour; Price of a Unit of Capital = $20)

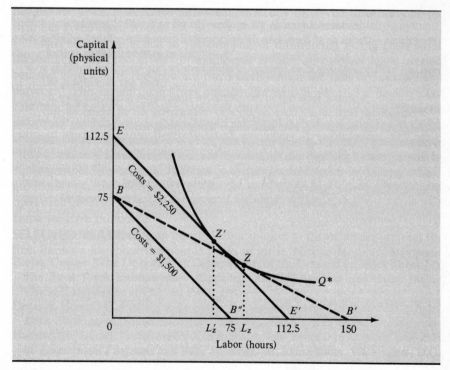

Z) by adding more capital and reducing employment of labor. The movement from L_Z to L'_Z is the *substitution effect* that is generated by the wage increase.

The Scale Effect

The fact that Q^* can no longer be produced for \$1,500, but instead involves at least \$2,250 in costs, will generally mean that it is no longer the profit-maximizing level of production. The new profit-maximizing level of production will be less than Q^* (how much less cannot be determined unless we know something about the product demand curve).

Suppose that the profit-maximizing level of output falls from Q^* to Q^{**}, as shown in Figure 3A.5. Since all isoexpenditure lines have the new slope of -1 when $W = \$20$ and $C = \$20$, the cost-minimizing way to produce Q^{**} will lie on an isoexpenditure line parallel to EE'. We find this cost-minimizing way to produce Q^{**} at point Z'', where an isoexpenditure line (FF') is tangent to the Q^{**} isoquant.

The *overall* response in the employment of labor to an increase in the wage rate has been a fall in labor usage from L_Z to L''_Z. The decline from L_Z to L'_Z is called the substitution effect, as we have noted. It results because the *proportions* of K and L used in production change when the ratio of wages to capital prices (W/C) changes. The *scale effect* can be seen as the reduction in employment from L'_Z to L''_Z wherein the usage of both K and L is cut back

FIGURE 3A.5 The Substitution and Scale Effects of a Wage Increase

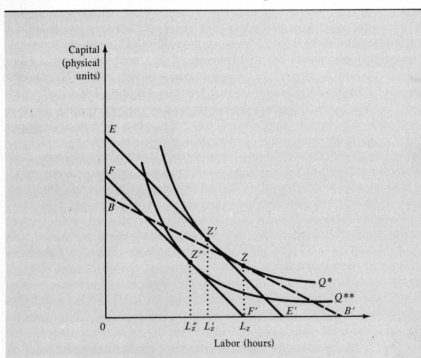

solely because of the reduced *scale* of production. Both effects are simultaneously present when wages increase and capital prices remain constant, but as Figure 3A.5 emphasizes, the effects are conceptually distinct and occur for different reasons. Together, these effects lead us to assert that the long-run demand-for-labor curve slopes downward.

4

Labor Demand Elasticities, Technological Change, and Foreign Trade

The previous chapter presented concepts fundamental to the assertion that the demand for labor is a downward-sloping function of the wage rate, in both the short run and the long run. It also addressed the issue of how changes in the prices of *other* productive factors affect the demand for labor. Put generally, Chapter 3 was concerned primarily with the *direction* of employment effects. In Chapter 4, we focus on the issue of *how responsive,* in a quantitative sense, labor demand is to changes in wages or prices of other factors of production. Clearly, knowing the *magnitude* of some policy's effects on employment is just as important as knowing the direction of those effects. It is therefore crucial to understand the factors affecting the extent to which employment responds to changes in wages or prices of other productive factors. An understanding of these concepts is also important in correctly analyzing the effects of technological change and foreign trade.

The responsiveness of labor demand to a change in wage rates is normally measured as an "elasticity," which is the percentage change in labor demand brought about by a 1 percent change in the wage rate. We define and discuss the concepts of own-wage elasticity and cross-wage elasticity below, and then move on to apply these concepts to various social issues, including the effects on employment of technological change and foreign trade.

THE OWN-WAGE ELASTICITY OF DEMAND

The *own-wage elasticity of demand* for a category of labor is defined as the percentage change in its employment (E) induced by a 1 percent increase in its wage rate (W):

$$\eta_{ii} = \frac{\%\Delta E_i}{\%\Delta W_i} \tag{4.1}$$

In equation (4.1), we have used the subscript i to denote category of labor i, η to represent elasticity, and the notation $\%\Delta$ to represent "percentage change in." Since the last chapter showed that labor demand curves slope downward, an increase in the wage rate will cause employment to decrease; the own-wage elasticity of demand is therefore a negative number. What is at issue is its magnitude. The larger its *absolute* value (its magnitude, ignoring its sign), the larger will be the percentage decline in employment associated with any given percentage increase in wages.

Labor economists often focus on whether the absolute value of the elasticity of demand for labor is greater than or less than one. If it is greater than one, a 1 percent increase in wages will lead to an employment decline of greater than 1 percent; this situation is referred to as an *elastic* demand curve. In contrast, if the absolute value is less than one, the demand curve is said to be *inelastic:* a 1 percent increase in wages will lead to a proportionately smaller decline in employment.[1] If demand is elastic, aggregate earnings (defined here as the wage rate times the employment level) of individuals in the category will decline when the wage rate increases, because employment falls at a faster rate than wages rise. Similarly, if demand is inelastic, aggregate earnings will increase when the wage rate is increased.

To see the importance of the magnitude of elasticity, let us return to our analysis of the minimum wage in a world with *complete coverage.* We saw in Chapter 3 that an increase in the minimum wage would lead to a decrease in employment, if other factors affecting employment were held constant. Does this result imply, from the perspective of low-wage workers as a group, that minimum wage increases are undesirable? The answer is ambiguous; it depends upon the extent to which the higher minimum wage for those workers who keep their jobs offsets the loss in employment that occurs. There are obvious equity issues involved here that make such comparisons difficult. However, *if* the own-wage elasticity of demand for low-skilled workers is inelastic, an increase in the minimum wage will lead to an increase in aggregate earnings for this group. This increase in aggregate earnings among the low-skilled implies that those who keep their jobs could compensate those who lose them and still be better off.[2] (The fact that *low-skilled* workers, as a *group, might* be made better off by a minimum wage law does not imply that the gains to *society* as a whole would exceed the losses. Chapter 3 addressed the issue of social losses.)

Figure 4.1 shows that the flatter of the two demand curves graphed (D_1) has greater elasticity than the steeper (D_2). Beginning with any wage (W, for example), given wage changes (to W', say) will yield greater responses in employment with demand curve D_1 than with D_2 (compare $E_1 - E_1'$ with $E_2 - E_2'$).

---

1. If the elasticity just equals -1, the demand curve is said to be *unitary elastic.*
2. Once we include transfer payments, such as unemployment insurance, in the analysis, it becomes possible for the total income of low-skilled workers (including transfer payments) to increase even if the elasticity is greater than one. See Edward Gramlich, "Impact of Minimum Wages on Other Wages, Employment, and Family Incomes," *Brookings Papers on Economic Activity,* 1976–2.

FIGURE 4.1 Relative Demand Elasticities

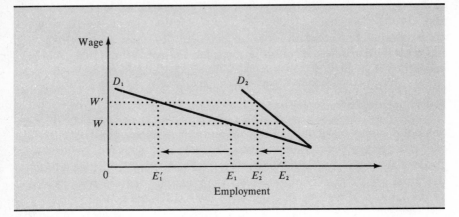

To speak of a demand curve as having "an" elasticity, however, is technically incorrect. Given demand curves will generally have elastic and inelastic ranges—and while we are usually just interested in the elasticity of demand in the range around the current wage rate in any market, one cannot fully understand elasticity without understanding that it can vary along a given demand curve.

To illustrate, suppose we examine the typical straight-line demand curve that we have used so often in Chapters 2 and 3 (see Figure 4.2). One feature of a straight-line demand curve is that, at *each* point along the curve, a unit change in wages induces the *same* response in terms of units of employment.

FIGURE 4.2 Different Elasticities Along a Demand Curve

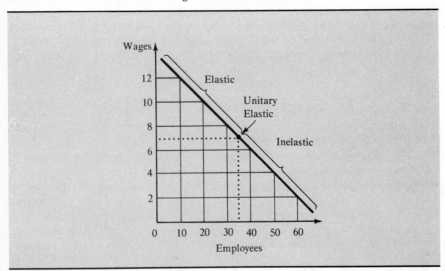

For example, at any point along the demand curve shown in Figure 4.2, a $2 decrease in wages will increase employment by 10 workers.

However, the same responses in terms of *unit* changes along the demand curve do *not* imply equal *percentage* changes. To see this point, look first at the upper end of the demand curve in Figure 4.2 (the end where wages are high and employment is low). A $2 decrease in wages when the base is $12 represents a 17 percent reduction in wages, while an addition of 10 workers when the starting point is also 10 represents a 100 percent increase in demand. Demand at this point is clearly *elastic.* However, if one looks at the same unit changes in the lower region of the demand curve (low wages, high employment), demand there is inelastic. A $2 reduction in wages from a $4 base is a 50 percent reduction, while an increase of 10 workers from a base of 50 is only a 20 percent increase. Since the percentage increase in employment is smaller than the percentage increase in wages, demand is seen to be inelastic at this end of the curve.

Thus, the upper end of a straight-line demand curve will exhibit greater elasticity than the lower end. Moreover, a straight-line demand curve will actually be elastic in some ranges and inelastic in others (as shown in Figure 4.2).

The Hicks-Marshall Laws of Derived Demand

Knowledge of own-wage elasticities of demand is very important for making policy decisions. The factors that influence own-wage elasticity can be summarized by the four "Hicks-Marshall Laws of Derived Demand"—"laws" named after the two distinguished British economists, Alfred Marshall and John Hicks, who are closely associated with their development.[3] These laws assert that, other things equal, the own-wage elasticity of demand for a category of labor is high under the following conditions:

1. When the price elasticity of demand for the product being produced is high;
2. When other factors of production can be easily substituted for the category of labor;
3. When the supply of other factors of production is highly elastic (that is, usage of other factors of production can be increased without substantially increasing their prices); and
4. When the cost of employing the category of labor is a large share of the total costs of production.

Not only are these laws generally valid as an empirical proposition, but the first three can be shown to always hold. There are conditions, however, under which the final law does not hold. (The exception to the final law is graphically derived in the appendix to this chapter.)

In seeking to explain why these laws hold, it is useful to act as if we could divide the process by which an increase in the wage rate affects the demand

---

3. John R. Hicks, *The Theory of Wages,* 2d ed. (New York: St. Martin's Press, 1966), 241–47, and Alfred Marshall, *Principles of Economics,* 8th ed. (London: Macmillan, 1923), 518–38.

for labor into two steps: First, an increase in the wage rate increases the relative cost of the category of labor in question and induces employers to use less of it and more of other inputs (the *substitution effect*). Second, when the wage increase causes the marginal costs of production to rise, there are pressures to increase product prices and reduce output, causing a fall in employment (the *scale effect*). The four laws of derived demand each deal with substitution or scale effects.

Demand for the Final Product. We noted above that wage increases cause production costs to rise and tend to result in product price increases. The greater the price elasticity of demand for the final product, the larger will be the decline in output associated with a given increase in price—and the greater the decrease in output, the greater the loss in employment (other things equal). Thus, *the greater the elasticity of demand for the product, the greater the elasticity of demand for labor will be.* One implication of this result is that, other things equal, the demand for labor at the *firm* level will be more elastic than the demand for labor at the *industry,* or market, level. For example, the product demand curves facing *individual* carpet-manufacturing companies are highly elastic because the carpet of company X is a very close substitute for the carpet of company Y. Compared to price increases at the *firm* level, however, price increases at the *industry* level will not have as large an effect on demand because the closest substitutes for carpeting are hardwood, ceramic, or some kind of vinyl floor covering—none a very close substitute for carpeting. The demand for labor is thus much more elastic for an individual carpet-manufacturing firm than for the carpet-manufacturing industry as a whole. (For the same reasons, the labor demand curve for a monopolist is less elastic than for an individual *firm* in a competitive industry. Monopolists, after all, face *market* demand curves for their product because they are the only seller in the particular market.)

Another implication of this first law is that *wage elasticities will be higher in the long run than in the short run.* The reason for this is that price elasticities of demand in product markets are higher in the long run. In the short run there may be no good substitutes for a product, or consumers may be locked into their current stock of consumer durables. However, after a period of time, new products that are substitutes may be introduced and consumers will begin to replace durables that have worn out.

Substitutability of Other Factors. As the wage rate of a category of labor increases, firms have an incentive to try to substitute other, now relatively cheaper, inputs for the category. Suppose, however, that there were no substitution possibilities; a given number of units of the type of labor *must* be used to produce one unit of output. In this case, there is no reduction in employment due to the substitution effect. In contrast, when substitution possibilities do present themselves, a reduction in employment owing to the substitution effect will accompany whatever reductions are caused by the scale effect. Hence, other things equal, *the easier it is to substitute other factors of production, the higher the wage elasticity of demand will be.*

Limitations on substitution possibilities need not be solely technical ones. For example, as we shall see in Chapter 12, unions often try to limit substitution possibilities by including specific work rules in their contracts (e.g., minimum crew size for railroad locomotives). Alternatively, the government may legislate limitations by specifying minimum employment levels for safety reasons (for example, each public swimming pool in New York State must always have a lifeguard present). Such collectively bargained or legislated restrictions make the demand for labor less elastic. Note, however, that substitution possibilities that are not feasible in the short run may well become feasible over longer periods of time, when employers are free to vary their capital stock. For example, if the wages of railroad workers went up, companies could buy more powerful locomotives and operate with larger trains and fewer locomotives. Likewise, if the wages of lifeguards rose, cities might build larger, but fewer, swimming pools. Both adjustments would occur only in the long run, which is another reason why the demand for labor is more elastic in the long run than in the short run.

The Supply of Other Factors.   Suppose that, as the wage rate increased and employers attempted to substitute other factors of production for labor, the prices of these inputs were bid up substantially. This situation might occur, for example, if one were trying to substitute capital equipment for labor. If producers of capital equipment were already operating their plants near capacity, so that taking on new orders would cause them substantial increases in costs because they would have to work their employees overtime and pay them a wage premium, they would accept new orders only if they could charge a higher price for their equipment. Such a price increase would dampen firms' "appetites" for capital and thus limit the substitution of capital for labor.

For another example, suppose an increase in the wages of unskilled workers caused employers to attempt to substitute skilled employees for unskilled employees. If there were only a fixed number of skilled workers in an area, their wages would be bid up by employers. As in the prior example, the incentive to substitute alternative factors would be reduced, and the reduction in unskilled employment due to the substitution effect would be smaller. In contrast, if the prices of other inputs did not increase when employers attempted to increase their usage, other things equal, the substitution effect—and thus the wage elasticity of demand—would be larger.

Note again that prices of other inputs are less likely to be bid up in the long run than in the short run. In the long run, existing producers of capital equipment can expand their capacity and new producers can enter the market. Similarly, in the long run more skilled workers can be trained. This observation is an additional reason why the demand for labor will be more elastic in the long run.

The Share of Labor in Total Costs.   Finally, the share of the category of labor in total costs is crucial to the size of the elasticity of demand. If the category's initial share were 20 percent, a 10 percent increase in the wage rate, other things equal, would raise total costs by 2 percent. In contrast, if its initial share were 80 percent, a 10 percent increase in the wage rate would increase total costs by 8 percent. Since employers would have to increase their product prices by more in the latter case, output, and hence employment, would fall more in that case. *Thus, the greater the category's share in total costs, the higher the wage elasticity of demand will tend to be.*[4]

Applying the Laws of Derived Demand: The Estimated Employment Effects of Black Lung Benefits

In 1969 Congress passed the Coal Mine Health and Safety Act, which, among other things, made coal miners and former coal miners with black lung disease eligible for monthly benefits. Black lung disease, which develops when lungs become clogged with coal dust, is disabling and can lead to early death. Any coal miner found eligible in the first five years of the program was to receive benefits financed by the government, but beginning in 1974 the financing of the benefits for new recipients was to fall upon the coal-mine operator for whom the recipient last worked for at least one year.

As 1974 approached, it became clear that many coal-mine operators would buy insurance against their potential liabilities and that the insurance premiums would be charged as a fraction of the operator's *payroll* costs. These premiums, which the government feared would be large, would increase the cost of hiring labor and could have very adverse effects on the employment of coal miners. How large might these effects be? Describing how one study[5] estimated these effects illustrates the practical significance of the four laws of derived demand.

The first step in estimating employment effects was to obtain an estimate of what the insurance premiums would be. The insurance industry estimated they would average about 11 percent of the payroll in underground mining and 7 percent of the payroll in strip (or surface) mining, where the problem of black lung disease is smaller.

The next step involved breaking the employment response into the *scale* and *substitution* effects. The share of labor in the total costs of underground mining was about 50 percent, so the insurance premiums in that sector would increase costs and prices by about 5.5 percent (in other words, there would be an 11 percent increase in half of the total costs). In strip mining, labor costs were only about 25 percent of total costs, so the 7 percent premium there would increase prices by only 1.7 percent. These calculations clearly made use of data on the *labor share in total cost*.

---

4. As we noted earlier, this law does not always hold. More specifically, when it is easy for employers to substitute other factors of production for the category of labor but difficult for consumers to substitute other products for the product being produced (low price elasticity of demand), this law is reversed. A graphic demonstration of this law and its exception is given in the appendix to this chapter. For a more formal treatment, see Hicks, *The Theory of Wages.*
5. From Morris Goldstein and Robert S. Smith, "The Predicted Impact of the Black Lung Benefits Program on the Coal Industry," in *Evaluating the Labor-Market Effects of Social Programs,* ed. Orley Ashenfelter and James Blum (Princeton, N.J.: Industrial Relations Section, Princeton University, 1976).

The price increases in coal that would be caused by the insurance premiums would have two effects. First, the overall price of coal would rise and cause less of it to be used. The overall elasticity of demand for coal was estimated to be −0.5 (an inelasticity caused by difficulties in substituting oil or natural gas for coal in electric power generation). Second, because underground and strip-mined coal are good substitutes for each other, the change in their *relative* prices would cause those still using coal to increase their purchases of strip-mined coal at the expense of underground coal.

The total scale effect in the *underground-coal* sector that would take place if the 11 percent and 7 percent rates were charged was an estimated 6 percent reduction in output and employment (largely because of substituting away from underground coal toward strip-mined coal). Strip mining, by virtue of the shift away from underground coal, would probably experience a 4 percent increase in employment. These calculations used estimates of the *price elasticity of demand* for both underground and strip-mined coal.

The final step in estimating the employment effects of the Black Lung Benefits Program was to estimate substitution effects. From data on the capital/labor ratios in each sector of the coal-mining industry, it appeared that a 1 percent increase in the price of labor relative to the price of capital was associated with a 1 percent increase in the capital/labor ratio used in production. (Economists define the percentage change in the ratio of factor inputs associated with a 1 percent change in the relative prices of these inputs as the "elasticity of substitution.") With this information on the *substitutability of capital and labor,* it was estimated that about 4.5 percent of employment in the underground sector would be lost to capital substitution. The corresponding losses in the strip-mining sector were estimated at 3.9 percent. (The estimate of the substitution effect was made *assuming that capital prices would remain constant.* This amounts to assuming that *the supply curve for capital* in the coal-mining industry is *horizontal.*)

The *overall* estimate of employment losses that would accompany the imposition of financial liability for black lung payments on coal operators amounted to about 8.4 percent (or almost 12,000 jobs, virtually all of which were in the underground sector). This estimate implied that even if the coal industry expanded (as it did), there would be around 12,000 fewer jobs in that industry than there would otherwise have been. While the program was never implemented in the manner assumed above, the process of making the estimates illustrates the use of the factors underlying the elasticity of labor demand curves.

THE CROSS-WAGE ELASTICITY OF DEMAND

Because firms may employ several categories of labor and capital, the demand for any one category can be affected by price changes in the others. For example, if the wages of carpenters rose, more people might build brick homes and the demand for *masons* might increase. On the other hand, an increase in carpenters' wages might decrease the overall level of home building in the economy, which would decrease the demand for *plumbers.* Finally, changes in the price of *capital* could increase or decrease the demand for workers in all three trades.

The direction and magnitude of the above effects can be summarized by examining the elasticities of demand for inputs with respect to the prices of other inputs. The *elasticity of demand for input j with respect to the price of input k* is the percentage change in the demand for input *j* induced by a 1 percent change in the price of input *k*. If the two inputs are both categories of labor, these *cross-wage elasticities of demand* are given by

$$\eta_{jk} = \frac{\%\Delta E_j}{\%\Delta W_k} \tag{4.2}$$

and

$$\eta_{kj} = \frac{\%\Delta E_k}{\%\Delta W_j}$$

If the cross-elasticities are positive (with an increase in the price of one increasing the demand for the other), the two are said to be *gross substitutes*. If these cross-elasticities are negative (and an increase in the price of one reduces the demand for the other), the two are said to be *gross complements* (refer to Figure 3.6).

It is worth restressing that whether two inputs are gross substitutes or gross complements depends on *both* the production function *and* product demand conditions. To see this, suppose we assume that adults and teenagers are substitutes in production. A decrease in the teenage wage will thus have opposite effects on adult employment. On the one hand, there is a substitution effect: for a given level of output, employers will now have an incentive to substitute teens for adults in the production process and reduce adult employment. On the other hand, there is a scale effect: a lower teenage wage provides employers with an incentive to increase employment of all inputs, including adults. The magnitude of the scale effect depends on the elasticity of product demand with respect to price; the larger this elasticity is, the larger the scale effect will be.

If the scale effect proves to be smaller than the substitution effect, adult employment will move in the same direction as teenage wages and the two groups will be gross substitutes. In contrast, if the scale effect is larger than the substitution effect, adult employment and teenage wages will move in opposite directions and the two groups will be gross complements. Knowing that two groups are substitutes in production, then, is not sufficient to tell us whether they are gross substitutes or gross complements.[6]

Both the sign and the magnitude of cross-elasticities are important for policy analysis. To return to our minimum wage example again, is the introduction of a youth subminimum, or youth differential in the minimum wage, as was done in 1990, an effective way to increase teenage employment levels? If the own-wage elasticity of demand for youth is elastic, a youth differential

---

6. As noted in Chapter 3, if two groups are complements in production, a decrease in the price of one should lead to increased employment of the other. Complements in production are always gross complements.

of 15 percent (which was roughly what was specified in the 1990 legislation) would lead to a greater than 15 percent increase in teenage employment.[7] The story does not end here, however, as one also needs to consider whether other groups would face adverse employment effects. If, for example, teens and low-skilled adult workers were gross substitutes, employment of low-skilled adults would fall if a youth differential were enacted. However, if the magnitude of the elasticity were very small, the decline in adult employment would be small and this negative side effect of the policy might not be judged serious. Estimates of the cross-wage elasticity of demand for adult labor with respect to the teenage wage are thus also required for intelligent policymaking. As discussed below, there is evidence that the own-wage elasticity of demand for teenagers is elastic; however, evidence on the size and sign of relevant adult–teenager cross-wage elasticities is generally lacking.

EMPIRICAL EVIDENCE ON WAGE ELASTICITIES OF DEMAND

Literally hundreds of studies have been published in recent years that present empirical evidence on the magnitudes of wage elasticities of demand. Some of these studies focus on the aggregate demand for labor in the economy as a whole; others focus on the demand by different industries. Some focus on the demand for different skill classes; still others focus on the demand for different age/race/gender groups. Although knowledge in a number of these areas is not very precise, it is useful to summarize what we can learn from both statistical studies and inferential analyses.

Statistical Evidence

To draw a particular demand curve with precision requires knowledge of the factors that affect derived demand: the technological possibilities given by the production function (substitutability of capital and labor, labor share in total cost), the supply curve of capital, and the elasticity of product demand. In estimating the elasticity of demand for labor, we do not want to hold these factors constant because they are all crucial in determining the *size* of the elasticity of demand. As a practical matter, however, researchers often have to estimate demand elasticities holding the *price of capital* constant.[8] This is tantamount to assuming that capital usage can be increased or decreased as wages change with no effect on the price at which capital is supplied; that is, capital supply curves are assumed to be horizontal.

Estimates of the own-wage elasticity of demand for labor, holding output constant—that is, estimates of the substitution effect—for the economy as a whole are inelastic and probably in the range of −0.15 to −0.50.[9] Moreover, at

---

7. This actually is an overestimate since it assumes all teens earn the minimum wage. In fact, many earn significantly more; their wages would not be directly affected by a youth differential. Hence, the actual reduction in the average teenage wage would be substantially less than 15 percent.

8. *Capital,* even in a given industry, encompasses so many machines, tools, supplies, and buildings that estimating a supply function is beyond the capability of the data usually available.

9. Daniel Hamermesh, "The Demand for Labor in the Long Run," in *Handbook of Labor Economics,* ed. Orley Ashenfelter and Richard Layard (Amsterdam: North-Holland, 1986).

EXAMPLE 4.1

Gross Complementarity and Substitutability: The Rise and Fall of the Handloom Weavers, 1780–1850

In the 1770s a new technique for spinning cotton yarn was developed, making it possible to produce a much stronger, higher-quality yarn than was previously available. This new spinning technology offered substantial cost reductions to producers, and the increased availability of cheaper and better yarn induced a substantial scale effect on the demand for cotton fabrics. One result of this increased demand was that the employment of handloom weavers in England's Lancashire region (where almost all of England's cotton manufacturing took place) grew from something like 40,000 in 1780 to 200,000 in 1820. These weavers, who were often women and children, worked primarily at home as self-employed subcontractors. In terms of our discussion of the cross-elasticity of demand for labor, it is clear that there was gross complementarity between handloom weaving and the new spinning technology.

By 1820, however, another technological change was taking place that would adversely affect the employment of weavers. The powerloom, which had been invented several years earlier, had been improved to the point that it began to substitute for the handloom. Powerloom weaving, which had to be done in factories, gradually replaced home-centered handloom weaving (the two were substitutes in production), and by 1851 there were only 50,000 handloom weavers left in Lancashire.

We normally think of the cross-elasticity of the demand for labor in terms of changes in the number of jobs within a particular *occupation,* and it is in this sense that handloom weaving and the powerloom were gross substitutes. However, it may also be useful to think of cross-elasticities in terms of changes in employment opportunities for workers within a particular *industry.* In this context the invention of the powerloom apparently increased the number of jobs for low-skilled workers in the cotton textile industry. The improvements in powerloom weaving had a scale effect on employment in the textile industry, and while there was a fall of 150,000 jobs in handloom weaving, the number of those employed in Lancashire's cotton mills rose from roughly 85,000 in 1820 to 275,000 in 1850. Thus, although powerloom and handloom weavers were clearly gross substitutes, the improvements in the powerloom did increase the market for cotton goods sufficiently to create other (factory) jobs in the cotton textile industry.

SOURCES: Duncan Bythell, *The Handloom Weavers* (Cambridge: Cambridge University Press, 1969); John S. Lyons, "Family Response to Economic Decline: English Cotton Handloom Weavers in Early Nineteenth-Century Lancashire," *Research in Economic History* 12 (1989): 45–91.

the level of the economy *as a whole,* scale effects are likely to be small: workers losing jobs as a result of wage increases will become self-employed in some cases; there are also often federal policies and programs designed to maintain national output and create full employment; and foreign goods and services are sometimes hard to substitute for domestic goods and services. For all

TABLE 4.1   **Representative Estimates of Long-Run Wage Elasticities of Demand, by Industry**

Industry	Long-Run Wage Elasticity
Coal mining[a]	
Underground	−0.98
Surface	−0.86
Manufacturing[b]	−0.29
Retail trade[c]	−0.34 to −1.20
State and local government[d]	
Employees in education	
sector	−1.06
Noneducation employees	−0.38

[a]Derived from estimates presented in Morris Goldstein and Robert S. Smith, "The Predicted Impact of the Black Lung Benefits Program on the Coal Industry," in *Evaluating the Labor-Market Effects of Social Programs,* ed. Orley Ashenfelter and James Blum (Princeton, N.J.: Industrial Relations Section, Princeton University, 1976).

[b]Barry Field and Charles Grebenstein, "Capital-Energy Substitution in U.S. Manufacturing," *Review of Economics and Statistics* 62 (May 1980): 207–12. This estimate is a weighted average of their individual industry estimates, using industry employment as the weights.

[c]Philip Cotterill, "The Elasticity of Demand for Low-Wage Labor," *Southern Economic Journal* 41 (January 1975): 520–25.

[d]Orley Ashenfelter and Ronald G. Ehrenberg, "The Demand for Labor in the Public Sector," in *Labor in the Public and Nonprofit Sectors,* ed. Daniel Hamermesh (Princeton, N.J.: Princeton University Press, 1975).

these reasons, the *overall* wage elasticity of demand is probably also inelastic, although it may be as large as −0.75.

The own-wage elasticities of demand at the *industry* level tend to vary widely across industries and in the main are also inelastic. Table 4.1 gives a representative set of estimates for coal mining, manufacturing, retail trade, and the state and local government sector. That the demand for employees in underground mining (located primarily in the East) is more elastic than the demand for employees in surface or strip mining (located primarily in the West) is not unexpected. Surface mining is much more capital-intensive, and labor costs are a smaller share of the total costs of production in that sector. That the estimated elasticities at the industry level tend to be in the inelastic range is also not surprising, because scale effects at that level are likely to be relatively small in many cases. The elasticity of product demand *for a firm* is very high, as mentioned earlier, but *at the industry level* it is not likely to be very large.

A third set of empirical findings suggests that the greater the level of skills embodied in a group of workers, the less elastic the own-wage elasticity of demand tends to be for the group.[10] So, for example, the own-wage elasticity of demand for highly educated workers tends to be less elastic than that for workers with less education. Similarly, the own-wage elasticity for adult males, many of whom are skilled workers, tends to be much less elastic than that for teenagers, who are primarily unskilled workers. Indeed, the available

10. See Hamermesh, "The Demand for Labor in the Long Run," for a summary of the underlying studies.

evidence suggests that the own-wage elasticity for teenagers is very elastic; it may well be in the range of -7.0 to -9.0.[11]

All of the evidence cited above has concerned *own-wage* elasticities of demand; evidence on *cross-wage* elasticities is somewhat sketchier. Research to date suggests that capital and unskilled labor are more easily substituted for each other in the production process than are capital and skilled labor; some studies suggest that capital and skilled workers are complements in production.[12] As noted above, groups that are complements in production are always gross complements (have *negative* cross-wage elasticities of demand). However, whether groups that are substitutes in production are gross substitutes (have *positive* cross-wage elasticities) depends upon the relative magnitudes of the scale and substitution effects; the substitution effect must be larger for the groups to be gross substitutes.

The evidence suggests that teenagers and adults, especially adult females, are substitutes in production.[13] Again, whether they are gross substitutes depends on the scale effect as well as on the substitution effect. In other words, we know with some certainty that if teenage wages are reduced relative to adult wages by a youth differential in the minimum wage teenagers will be substituted for adults (at least to some degree) in the production process. However, whether adult employment would go up or down depends also on the scale effect a youth subminimum would create. If scale effects are large, teenagers and adults *could* be gross complements (that is, as teenage wages fell, adult employment would rise despite the substitution against them in the production process). Unfortunately, it is not clear at this point whether teenagers and adults are gross complements or gross substitutes, although one study found that they are gross substitutes. Indeed, this study suggested that for every 100 teenagers who might be employed as a result of a youth subminimum wage, 11–33 adult workers would be displaced.[14]

Similarly, there is evidence that black men and adult women are substitutes in production.[15] Hence, if women's wages fall because of their growing relative numbers in the labor force, employers are likely to substitute women

11. Hamermesh, "The Demand for Labor in the Long Run," Table 5. As with all elasticity estimates, these estimates are for small changes in wages.

12. Ibid. Recently evidence has been offered that the degree of complementarity depends on the *age* of capital equipment. Specifically, Ann Bartel and Frank Lichtenberg, "Technology: Some Empirical Evidence," *Review of Economics and Statistics* 69 (February 1987): 1–11, present evidence that the relative demand for highly educated workers vis-à-vis less-educated workers declines as the capital stock ages. They attribute this to the comparative advantage that highly educated workers have with respect to learning and implementing new technologies; thus as the capital stock ages, the complementarity of these workers with capital declines.

13. James Grant and Daniel Hamermesh, "Labor Market Competition Among Youths, White Women and Others," *Review of Economics and Statistics* 63 (August 1981): 354–60; Mark Berger, "Changes in Labor Force Composition and Male Earnings: A Production Approach," *Journal of Human Resources* 18 (Spring 1983): 177–96; and George Borjas, "The Demographic Determinants of the Demand for Black Labor," in *The Black Youth Unemployment Crisis*, ed. Richard Freeman and Harry Holzer (Chicago: University of Chicago Press, 1986), 191–230.

14. Daniel Hamermesh, "Minimum Wages and the Demand for Labor," *Economic Inquiry* 20 (July 1982): 365–80.

15. Borjas, "The Demographic Determinants of the Demand for Black Labor."

for black men when producing any given level of output. However, since the *scale* effect of a decrease in adult women's wages will tend to *increase* black male employment, we cannot say a priori whether black male employment is reduced or increased by the growing female labor supply. As with teenagers and adults, at this point it is not known whether black men and adult women are gross complements or gross substitutes.

Finally, there is some evidence that black men and Hispanics are complements in production, which in turn implies that they are gross complements.[16] As a result, a decline in the Hispanic wage caused by increased immigration of Hispanics into the United States might lead to increased employment of black men. If this evidence proves correct, fears by some that black male employment prospects will be diminished by Hispanic immigration may prove unfounded. (For a more complete discussion of immigration and its effects on the labor market, see Chapter 10.)

Inferential Analyses

Because empirical estimates of demand elasticities that may be required for making decisions are lacking in some cases, it is sometimes necessary to try to guess what these elasticities are likely to be. In making these guesses, we can apply the laws of derived demand to predict these magnitudes for various types of labor. Consider first the demand for unionized New York City garment workers. As we shall discuss in Chapter 12, because unions are complex organizations, it is not always possible to specify what their goals are. Nevertheless, it is clear that most unions value both wage *and* employment opportunities for their members. This observation leads to the simple prediction that, other things equal, the more elastic the demand for labor, the smaller will be the wage gain that a union will succeed in winning for its members. The reason for this prediction is that the more elastic the demand curve, the greater will be the percentage employment decline associated with any given percentage increase in wages. As a result, we can expect the following:

1. Unions would win larger wage gains for their members in markets with inelastic labor demand curves;
2. Unions would strive to take actions that reduce the wage elasticity of demand for their members' services; and
3. Unions might first seek to organize workers in markets in which labor demand curves are inelastic (because the potential gains to unionization are higher in these markets).

As we shall see in Chapter 12, many of these predictions are borne out by empirical evidence.

---

16. Borjas, "The Demographic Determinants of the Demand for Black Labor," and George Borjas, "The Substitutability of Black, Hispanic, and White Labor," *Economic Inquiry* 21 (January 1983): 93–106. Further evidence that immigration in general will not harm the earnings of black males is found in George Borjas, "The Sensitivity of Labor Demand Functions to Choice of Dependent Variable," *Review of Economics and Statistics* 68 (February 1986): 58–66, and *Who Comes? American Competitiveness in the Immigration Market* (New York: Basic Books, 1989), Chapter 5.

Because of foreign competition, the price elasticity of demand for the clothing produced by New York City garment workers is extremely high. Furthermore, employers can easily find other inputs to substitute for these workers—namely, nonunion garment workers in the South (this substitution would require moving the plant to the South, a strategy that many manufacturers have followed). These facts lead one to predict that the wage elasticity of demand for New York City unionized garment workers should be very elastic, a prediction that seems to be borne out by union policies in the industry. That is, because the garment workers' union faces a highly elastic demand curve, its wage demands historically have been moderate. However, the union has also aggressively sought to reduce the elasticity of product demand by supporting policies that reduce foreign competition; in addition, it has pushed for higher federal minimum wages in order to reduce employers' incentives to move their plants to the South.

Next, consider the wage elasticity of demand for unionized airplane pilots on commercial scheduled airlines in the United States. The salaries of pilots are only a small share of the costs of operating large airplanes; they are dwarfed by the fuel and capital costs of airlines. Furthermore, substitution possibilities are limited; there is little room to substitute unskilled labor for skilled labor (although airlines can contemplate substituting capital for labor by reducing the number of flights they offer while increasing the size of airplanes). In addition, before the deregulation of the airline industry in 1978, many airlines faced no competition on many of their routes or were prohibited from reducing their prices to compete with other airlines that flew the same routes. These factors all suggest that the wage elasticity of demand for airline pilots was quite inelastic. As one might expect, pilots' wages were also quite high because their union could push for large wage increases without fear that these increases would substantially reduce pilots' employment levels. However, after airline deregulation, competition among airline carriers increased substantially, leading to a more elastic labor demand for pilots. As a result, many airlines "requested," and won, reduced wages from their pilots (see Example 12.1).

Finally, consider the wage elasticity of demand for *domestic* farm workers. This elasticity will depend heavily on the supply of immigrants, either legal or illegal, who are willing to work as farm workers at wages less than the wages paid to domestic farm workers. The successful unionization of farm workers, coupled with union or government rules that prevent illegal immigrants from accepting such employment, obviously will make the demand curve for domestic farm workers less elastic. Similarly, government regulations that either limit the quantity of foreign farm products that can be imported into the United States (quotas), place tariffs on such products, or limit foreign producers from *dumping* (selling their farm products in the United States at prices less than they charge in their own countries) will reduce the price elasticity of demand for U.S. farm products (and hence the wage elasticity of demand for domestic farm workers). This example indicates how government policies on international trade, to be more completely analyzed later in this chapter, can influence wage elasticities of demand in particular labor markets.

POLICY APPLICATIONS

Knowledge of the magnitudes and signs of wage elasticities of demand is important in many policy applications, as the discussion above and the following examples illustrate.

Investment Tax Credit to Reduce Unemployment

An *investment tax credit* allows businesses to subtract from their tax bills a certain percentage of the investments they make in new capital equipment. As such, the credit is an implicit subsidy given to employers for increasing their capital stocks. It has the effect of reducing the price of new capital equipment, which should stimulate such investments. To the extent that this increases the growth rate in the economy, such a tax credit may stimulate employment growth and reduce the unemployment rate. However, working against this scale effect is a substitution effect: the cost of capital is lower because of the tax credit, and this induces the substitution of capital for labor.

Investment tax credits were part of federal tax legislation in the early 1960s, and as late as 1986 the credit was equal to 10 percent of the purchase price for most capital investments. Tax reform legislation enacted in late 1986, however, repealed the investment tax credit. One issue of major interest is whether eliminating the investment tax credit would be expected to increase or decrease employment.

Although the overall effects of an investment tax credit on employment have not been precisely pinned down, we have a fairly good idea which groups will gain or lose most from repealing the credit. As noted above, the data seem to indicate that capital and skilled labor are less substitutable than capital and unskilled labor. Hence, as eliminating the investment tax credit increases the cost of capital, one would expect greater substitution effects, tending to increase employment levels, among the unskilled. Whether the *actual* level of employment among the unskilled will rise or not depends, as we have emphasized, on the size of the *scale* effect accompanying the increased cost of capital. However, we would expect that repealing the tax credit would cause less displacement (or more employment gains) among unskilled workers than among skilled workers.

Employment Tax Credits or Wage Subsidies

As an alternative to an investment tax credit, one might institute a system of payments to employers for increasing their employment levels. When the payment is made directly to employers (for example, when employers are rebated 50 percent of their new employees' wages), the payment is called a *wage subsidy.* If the payment is implicit, in the form of a tax credit, it is called an *employment tax credit.* The analyses, and effects, of both types of payment programs are identical, however. By reducing the price the employer pays for labor, both tend to stimulate employment.

Employment tax credits, or wage subsidy schemes, can take many forms.[17] They can apply to all new hires or only to increases in firms' employ-

---

17. See Daniel Hamermesh, "Subsidies for Jobs in the Private Sector," in *Creating Jobs: Public Employment Programs and Wage Subsidies,* ed. John Palmer (Washington, D.C.: Brookings Institution, 1978), for an extended discussion.

ment levels (in which case they are called *marginal* employment tax credits). Since firms typically hire new employees to replace employees who have quit, retired, or been involuntarily terminated, they would receive subsidies in the former case even if they maintained a constant employment level.

Employment subsidies can also be either *general* or *selective*. A general subsidy is not conditional on the characteristics of the people hired, while a selective, or *targeted*, plan makes payments conditional on hiring people from certain target groups (such as the disadvantaged). While targeted subsidies are more focused, they can have stigmatizing effects that are counterproductive (see Example 4.2).

Although European nations have had more experience with such programs than has the United States, both general and selective tax credit programs have been tried in the United States in recent years. For example, a New Jobs Tax Credit was part of the 1977 economic stimulus package passed by Congress. This general, marginal employment tax credit program was in effect only for 1977 and 1978. With limitations on the size of the credit that an employer could receive for each employee (essentially 50 percent of the worker's annual earnings up to a maximum earnings ceiling of $4,200), the plan effectively gave employers a proportionately greater subsidy for hiring unskilled and part-time labor than for hiring skilled or full-time labor.[18] Because of this, *if* the own-wage elasticities of demand are the same or larger for unskilled or part-time labor *and* if the various skill groups are gross substitutes, one would expect the employment levels of unskilled and part-time workers to be stimulated most by the program.

Early evaluations of the program indicated that it may have had some small positive effect on the overall level of employment; firms that knew of the program's existence seemed to grow more rapidly than firms that did not know.[19] However, one year into the program, less than half of all surveyed firms actually knew that the program existed, and one might conjecture that the direction of causation ran from "plans to grow rapidly" to "knowledge of the program," rather than vice versa.[20] That is, firms that were planning to expand their employment, even in the absence of the program, had an incentive to learn about the program so that they could receive the subsidy.

This example again highlights the difficulties social scientists face when they attempt to evaluate the effect of social programs. It also suggests the importance of rapidly disseminating information about the existence of programs; the passage of a law, per se, does not guarantee that employers will know about it.

---

18. For more details of the plan, see Orley Ashenfelter, "Evaluating the Effects of the Employment Tax Credit," in U.S. Department of Labor, *Conference Report on Evaluating the 1977 Economic Stimulus Package* (Washington, D.C.: U.S. Government Printing Office, 1979).

19. See Jeffrey Perloff and Michael Wachter, "The New Jobs Tax Credit—An Evaluation of the 1977-78 Wage Subsidy Program," *American Economic Review* 69 (May 1979): 173-79; John Bishop and Robert Haveman, "Selective Employment Subsidies: Can Okun's Law Be Repealed?" *American Economic Review* 69 (May 1979): 124-30; and Mark R. Killingsworth, "Substitution and Output Effects on Labor Demand: Theory and Policy Applications," *Journal of Human Resources* 20 (Winter 1985): 142-52.

20. Perloff and Wachter, "The New Jobs Tax Credit"; Bishop and Haveman, "Selective Employment Subsidies."

EXAMPLE 4.2

Are Targeted Wage Subsidies Harmful?

In 1980–81 the U.S. Department of Labor conducted an experiment in the Dayton, Ohio, area to try to estimate the effectiveness of two targeted wage subsidy plans. A number of economically disadvantaged welfare recipients, all of whom were eligible for the Targeted Jobs Tax Credit Program, were randomly assigned to three groups. The first group received vouchers that could be presented to prospective employers. These vouchers informed employers that if the disadvantaged workers were hired, the government would grant the employers tax credits equal to 50 percent of the employees' first-year salaries and 25 percent of their second-year salaries, with a maximum credit per worker of $3,000 and $1,500 per year, respectively. The second group received vouchers informing prospective employers that they would receive direct cash payments of the above amounts, rather than tax credits, for hiring workers. The third served as a control group and received no vouchers.

The experiment's purpose was to see if having disadvantaged welfare recipients inform prospective employers of their eligibility for wage subsidies would increase their labor market success; as discussed in the text, employers often failed to realize that the tax credit program existed. Moreover, since employers with zero tax liabilities (because their profits were low or they were suffering losses) would have no economic incentive to hire disadvantaged workers under a tax credit plan, it was felt that the voucher system calling for direct cash payments to employers might prove more beneficial to disadvantaged workers.

For political reasons the experiment was ended after only six months. By that time, 13.0 percent of the tax credit group and 12.7 percent of the direct cash treatment group had found employment; in this experiment direct cash payments *did not* work better than tax credits. Quite strikingly, however, 15.3 percent of the control group had found employment; this group did *better* than the two groups who advertised their eligibility for subsidies. Although the "vouchered" groups were able to offer themselves to employers at a discount, apparently employers were also made aware that they were "welfare recipients." This may have led them to conclude that people with vouchers were probably not very productive, thus reducing their willingness to hire them. That is, the voucher system may well have had a *stigmatizing* effect on members of the first two groups.

This example illustrates that the effects of targeted wage subsidy or tax credit programs will often depend upon more than the relative cost advantages they provide for the targeted groups and the underlying demand elasticities. The example also illustrates that individuals are often at least partly judged by the characteristics of the group to which they belong rather than by their own personal characteristics. (Targeted social programs should be designed in ways that minimize their stigmatizing effects. The implications of such judgments, often called *statistical discrimination,* will be more fully discussed in Chapter 14.)

SOURCE: Gary Burtless, "Are Targeted Wage Subsidies Harmful? Evidence from a Wage Voucher Experiment," *Industrial and Labor Relations Review* 39 (October 1985): 105–14.

The New Jobs Tax Credit was replaced in 1979 by a Targeted Jobs Tax Credit, a selective tax credit that subsidized the hiring of unemployed youth (ages 18–24), handicapped individuals, and welfare recipients. As with the New Jobs Tax Credit Program, many employers seemed unaware of the Targeted Jobs Tax Credit Program and did not utilize it.[21]

Evaluations of the program suggest that it probably has had a small positive effect on youth employment.[22] Little is known, however, about its impact on nontargeted groups, especially unskilled adults for whom teenagers may be quite close substitutes, and on the other targeted groups (for example, the handicapped and welfare recipients).

APPLYING CONCEPTS OF LABOR DEMAND ELASTICITY TO THE ISSUE OF TECHNOLOGICAL CHANGE

Technological change, which can encompass the introduction of new products and production techniques as well as changes in technology that serve to reduce the cost of capital (for example, increases in the speed of computers), is frequently viewed as a blessing by some and a curse by others. Those who view it positively point to the enormous gains in the standard of living made possible by new technology, while those who see technological change as a threat often stress its adverse consequences for workers. Are the concepts underlying the elasticity of demand for labor useful in making judgments about the effects of technological change?

There are two aspects of technological change that affect the demand for labor. One is product demand. *Shifts* in product demand curves will tend to shift labor demand curves in the same direction, and changes in the *elasticity* of product demand with respect to product price will tend to cause qualitatively similar changes in the own-wage elasticity of labor demand. The invention of new products (word processors, for example) that serve as substitutes for old ones (typewriters) will tend to shift the labor demand curve in the older sector to the left, causing loss of employment in that sector. If greater product substitution possibilities are also created by these new inventions, it is possible that the introduction of new products can increase the *elasticity* of product—and hence, labor—demand. Increasing the own-wage elasticity of labor demand increases the amount of job loss associated with collectively bargained wage increases, for example, and it therefore reduces the power of unions to secure large wage increases in the older sector. While benefiting people as consumers, and while providing jobs in the new sectors, the introduction of new products does necessitate some painful changes in established sectors of the economy as workers, unions, and employers must all adjust to a new environment.

---

21. See David O'Neill, "Employment Tax Credit Programs: The Effects of Socioeconomic Targeting Provisions," *Journal of Human Resources* 17 (Summer 1982): 449–59, for a discussion of the historically low utilization rates of targeted employment tax credits and other problems inherent in such programs.
22. John Bishop, *Subsidizing the Hiring and Training of the Disadvantaged* (Kalamazoo, Mich.: Upjohn Institute for Employment Research, 1989).

A second aspect of technological change is often associated with automation, or the substitution of capital for labor. For purposes of analyzing its effects on labor demand, this second aspect of technological change should be thought of as reducing the cost of capital. In some cases—the mass production of personal computers is one example—a fall in capital prices is what literally occurs. In other cases of technological change—the miniaturization of computer components, which has made possible new production techniques—an invention makes completely new technologies available. When something is unavailable, it can be thought of as having an infinite price (it is not available at any price); therefore, the availability of a new technique is equivalent to observing a decline in its price to some finite number. In either case, with a decline in its cost, capital tends to be substituted for labor in the production process.

Earlier in this chapter, we introduced the concept that the demand for a given category of labor is responsive to changes in the prices of other factors of production; in general, we refer to this responsiveness as a "cross-elasticity" (if the other factor is another category of labor, it is "cross-wage elasticity"). The *sign* of the cross-elasticity of demand for a given category of labor with respect to a fall in the price of capital depends on whether capital and the category of labor are gross substitutes or gross complements. If a particular category of labor is a substitute in production with capital, *and* if the scale effect of the reduced capital price is relatively weak, then capital and the category of labor are gross substitutes and automation reduces demand for workers in this category. For categories of labor that are not close substitutes with the new technology, however, the scale effect may dominate and the two can be gross complements. Thus, the effect of automation on the demand for *particular* categories of labor can be either positive or negative.

Under what conditions are capital and labor most likely to be gross substitutes? Our answer can be guided by the four laws of derived demand, but because these laws refer to the own-wage elasticity of demand they cannot be applied slavishly to the question of cross-elasticities.

First, the substitution effect will be stronger to the extent that *capital is a substitute for labor* in the production process and that it is relatively easy for firms to make the substitution. Moreover, if the *supply of capital is elastic,* so that the suppliers of capital do not raise their prices much in the face of increased demand, the incentives to substitute capital for labor are not diminished by rising capital costs.

Second, the scale effect will be relatively weak if there is an *inelastic product demand* and if *capital constitutes a small share of total cost* in the industry experiencing automation. The latter condition, to which an exception analogous to the one noted in footnote 4 applies, limits the extent to which the cost savings created by automation are reflected in overall reductions in the unit costs of production. The former condition limits the extent to which cost (and product price) reductions induce greater consumption of the product.

Clearly, whether capital and a given type of labor are gross substitutes depends on several factors, all of which are highly specific to particular industries and production processes. Perhaps the most that can be said generally is that, as pointed out in a prior section, unskilled labor and capital are more likely to be substitutes in production than are skilled labor and capital, which some studies have identified as complements in production. Because factors of production that are complementary must be gross complements, technological change is more likely to increase the demand for skilled than for unskilled labor.

Before concluding that technological change is a threat to the unskilled, however, three things must be kept in mind. First, even factors that are substitutes in production can be gross complements (if scale effects are large enough). Second, as illustrated in Example 4.1, substitution of capital for labor can destroy some unskilled jobs, but accompanying scale effects can create others, sometimes in the same industry.

Finally, although the fraction of all workers who are unskilled laborers has declined over the course of this century (see Table 2.3), this decline is not in itself convincing evidence of gross substitutability between capital and unskilled labor. The concepts of elasticity and cross-elasticity refer to changes in labor demand caused by changes in wages or capital prices, *holding all else constant*. That is, labor demand elasticities focus on the labor demand curve at a particular point in time. Actual employment outcomes over time are also influenced by labor *supply* behavior of workers. Thus, from simple observations of employment levels over time it is impossible to tell anything about own-wage demand elasticities or about the signs or magnitudes of cross-elasticities of labor demand.

The effects of technological change on *total* employment and on society in general are less ambiguous. Technological change permits society to achieve greater and often more varied consumption possibilities, and it leads to scale effects that both enlarge and change the mix of output. As the productive mix changes, some firms, occupations, and industries decline or are eliminated (see, for example, the data back in Table 2.2, which show declining employment shares in agriculture and goods-producing industries, where technological changes have reduced the labor required per unit of output). Other sectors of the economy—the services, for example—expand. While these dislocations can create pockets of unemployment as some workers must seek new jobs or acquire new skills, there is no evidence that technological change (over the course of this century, say) has led to permanent problems of unemployment. In fact, real wages have risen rather dramatically from their levels earlier this century (refer to Table 2.4), a rise that has been at least partly fueled by technological change.

INTERNATIONAL TRADE AND THE DEMAND FOR LABOR: CAN HIGH-WAGE COUNTRIES COMPETE?

The question of how international trade affects labor demand in the long run has been highlighted recently by the increasing importance of exports and imports in the U.S. economy. The public is often inclined to support laws restricting free trade on the grounds that lower wages and living standards in other countries inevitably cause employment losses among American workers—losses that could be mitigated only by a large decline in American living standards. This section will show that the effects of international trade on the demand for labor are analogous to the effects of technological change, that they do not depend on relative living standards, and that two countries will generally find trade mutually beneficial regardless of their respective wage rates. To keep things simple, we assume in what follows that goods and services can be traded across countries but that capital and labor are immobile (international mobility of labor is discussed in Chapter 10).

Production in the United States Without International Trade

Suppose that the available supplies of labor and capital in the United States can be combined to produce two goods, food and clothing.[23] If all inputs were devoted to food production, 200 million units of food could be produced; similarly, if all available resources were devoted to the production of clothing, 100 million units of clothing could be produced. If 15 percent (say) of the resources were devoted to food and 85 percent to clothing, 30 million units of food and 85 million units of clothing could be produced. All the possible combinations of food and clothing that could be produced in the United States are summarized graphically by line XY in Figure 4.3, which is called a "production possibilities curve."

Two things should be noted about the production possibilities curve in Figure 4.3. It is negative in slope, indicating that if more of one good is produced less of the other can be produced. It has a slope of -0.50, symbolizing the real cost of producing food: if the country chooses to produce one more unit of food, it must forgo 0.50 units of clothing. (Conversely, if it wants to produce one more unit of clothing it must give up two units of food.)[24]

The ultimate mix of food and clothing produced depends on consumer preferences. If the United States is assumed to have 100 million workers and chooses to allocate 15 percent to the production of food, incomes would average 0.30 units of food and 0.85 units of clothing per worker.

Suppose an inventor were to come along with a device that could increase the efficiency of inputs in the production of clothing, so that if all inputs were devoted to clothing 180 million units could be produced. The production possibilities curve would shift out to the dashed line (YZ) in Figure 4.3, and per capita real incomes in the United States would rise (it is possible to produce more of both food and clothing with the resources available). After this innovation, only 1.11 (200/180) units of food would have to be given up to obtain one unit of clothing.

(Note that when the real cost of clothing falls from 2 to 1.11 units of food, the *real cost* of food is *automatically* increased from 0.50 to 0.90 units

---

23. To allow a graphic presentation, the analysis will be in the context of just two goods; however, the results are applicable to more.
24. The production possibilities "curve" in Figure 4.3 is a straight line, which reflects the simplifying assumption that the ratio at which food can be "transformed" into clothing, and vice versa, never changes. This assumption is not necessary to the argument but does make it a bit easier to grasp initially.

FIGURE 4.3   Hypothetical Production Possibilities Curves, United States

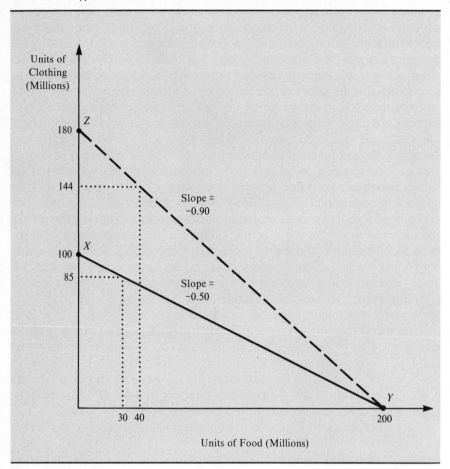

(180/200) of clothing. The reason for this food cost increase is straightforward: if a given set of inputs can now produce more clothing but the same amount of food, diverting enough from the production of clothing to produce one more unit of food will now result in a larger decline in clothing output than before. It is this decline in clothing output that is the real cost, or "opportunity cost," of producing a unit of food.)

Production in a Foreign Country Without International Trade

It would be an amazing coincidence if the rates at which food and clothing could be traded off were equal in all countries. Land quality differs, as do the quality and quantity of capital and labor. Therefore, let us assume that a country—call it China—can produce either 300 million units of food, or 500 million units of clothing, or any other combination of food and clothing along the production possibilities curve, *AB*, in Figure 4.4.

FIGURE 4.4   Hypothetical Production Possibilities Curves, China

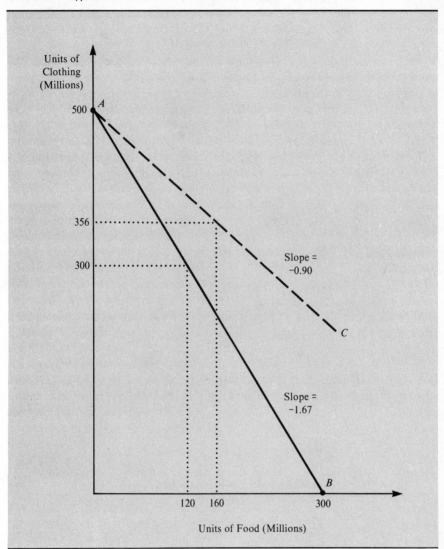

If 40 percent of its productive inputs were devoted to farming, China could produce 120 million units of food and 300 million units of clothing. With a population of, say, 500 million workers, China's average income per worker would be 0.24 units of food and 0.60 units of clothing. Clearly, then, living standards (real wage rates) are lower in China than in the United States (since the average consumption per worker of *both* food and clothing are lower in China).

After analyzing China's production possibilities curve (*AB* in Figure 4.4) it can be calculated that the real cost of a unit of food within China is 1.67 (500/300) units of clothing; to produce one more unit of food means that

1.67 fewer units of clothing can be produced. Conversely, the real price of a unit of clothing in China is 0.60 (300/500) units of food.

The Mutual Benefits of International Trade

In the absence of innovation in the clothing industry, discussed earlier, the price of food within the United States is 0.50 units of clothing and the price of clothing is 2 units of food. In contrast, the price of food in China is 1.67 units of clothing and the price of clothing is 0.60 units of food. These prices are summarized in columns (a) and (b) of Table 4.2. Because the real internal cost of food is lower in the United States than in China, while the real internal cost of clothing is higher, economists therefore say that the United States has a *comparative advantage* in producing food and that China has a *comparative advantage* in the production of clothing.

It is important to note that the real costs of each good in the two countries depend *only* on the *internal trade-offs* between food and clothing output. Despite the assumed fact, for example, that real wages in China are lower than in the United States, food is much more costly in the former country than in the latter! Further, despite the generally more productive inputs in the United States, the real cost of clothing is lower in China.

The costs listed in columns (a) and (b) of Table 4.2 make it plain that both countries could benefit from trade. China would be willing to buy food from the United States as long as it had to give up something less than 1.67 units of clothing per unit of food (its internal real cost of production). The United States would be willing to trade away food as long as it could obtain something more than 0.50 units of clothing in return (0.50 units represents what the United States can now obtain internally if it gives up one unit of food). The divergent internal values placed on food and clothing make it possible for mutually beneficial trades to take place.

TABLE 4.2   Hypothetical Costs and Quantities of Food and Clothing in the United States and China, Before and After Trade

Good	Before Trade		After Trade	
	(a) U.S.	(b) China	(c) U.S.	(d) China
Food costs	0.50 units of clothing	1.67 units of clothing	0.90 units of clothing	0.90 units of clothing
Clothing costs	2 units of food	0.60 units of food	1.11 units of food	1.11 units of food
Assumed Food consumption:				
Total	30 million	120 million	40 million	160 million
Per capita	0.30	0.24	0.40	0.32
Assumed Clothing consumption:				
Total	85 million	300 million	144 million	356 million
Per capita	0.85	0.60	1.44	0.71
World production of food	150 million		200 million	
World production of clothing	385 million		500 million	

With a lower-bound price of 0.50 units of clothing per unit of food, and an upper-bound price of 1.67, the ultimate price at which the two countries would trade is not predictable. Trade at any price in between these two bounds would benefit both countries and be preferable to each over no trade at all; however, the closer the price of food is to 0.50 units of clothing the less the United States gains and the more China benefits.

Let us assume that the bargaining strengths of the two countries are such that units of food are traded by the United States to China in return for 0.90 units of clothing. From the perspective of the United States, one unit of food can now be transformed into 0.90 units of clothing instead of just 0.50 units. In this example, trade will therefore accomplish exactly what the previously discussed technological innovation in clothing production did: it will move the production possibilities curve out and give the country a greater command over resources. In terms of Figure 4.3, trade by itself could move the production possibilities curve from XY to YZ. This outward shift allows the United States to consume more food *and* more clothing.

From the Chinese perspective, trading 0.90 units of clothing for one unit of food is equivalent to allowing the transformation of one unit of clothing into 1.11 units of food (up from 0.60 units of food). This increase represents an outward shift in the Chinese production possibilities curve (see curve AC in Figure 4.4), and the output that can be consumed by each Chinese worker clearly increases.

To obtain a sense of how trade could affect per capita consumption in our example, let us suppose that the United States specialized in food production and that China specialized in the production of clothing.[25] The United States would produce 200 million units of food, and if it consumed 40 million units the remaining 160 million units could be traded to China for 144 million units of clothing (0.9 × 160). China would produce 500 million units of clothing, exporting 144 million so that its total internal consumption of clothing would equal 356 million units. China, of course, would consume 160 million units of food under these assumptions. As can be seen from Table 4.2, where the pre- and post-trade units of production and consumption are compared, per capita real incomes rise in both countries as a result of trade. Conversely, when trade is restricted, consumers in both countries can lose (see Example 4.3).

Labor Market Implications

International trade is driven by the relative internal (real) costs of producing various goods. Conclusions from our two-good analysis of trade between the United States and China are not at all affected by the assumptions about living standards (real wages) in the two countries. If the production possibilities curves remained the same but the assumed populations of the two coun-

---

25. Complete specialization in production will occur in one or both countries if the production possibilities curves are straight lines; in these cases the internal rate of transformation between the two goods is unchanging. Specialization may not be total when the production possibilities curves are concave from below. A concave curve implies that the real costs of food production, say, rise with food output so that at some point the United States could lose its comparative advantage.

EXAMPLE 4.3

Import Quotas and Employment in the Automobile Industry

From 1970 to 1974, imported automobiles represented approximately 14 to 15 percent of all new automobiles sold in the United States. By 1981 this percentage had risen to 28 percent. This shift has been attributed to a number of factors, including a perceived decline in the relative quality of domestically produced cars and an increase in the relative price of domestic cars (due to more rapid wage growth and slower productivity growth of U.S. than of Japanese automobile workers and to exchange rate changes that reduced the prices of Japanese cars in terms of dollars). Misguided management decisions in the United States, which left Japanese producers in a better position to meet the American consumers' demand for fuel-efficient automobiles, have also been blamed.

In spite of the declining market share of domestic producers, their production and employment continued to grow throughout most of the 1970s as total automobile purchases in the United States grew. However, the recession of the late '70s hit the domestic automobile industry hard. Between 1978 and 1980 total employment in the automobile industry (including all supplier companies) fell from a little over 1 million to less than 800 thousand, a decline of over 20 percent. Profits of domestic auto producers also fell precipitously, as record losses were reported.

In the face of pressure to impose mandatory quotas on imported cars, the Reagan Administration negotiated voluntary import restraints with the Japanese government in April of 1981. An explicit purpose of these restraints was to preserve American jobs in the auto industry, since the reduced availability of Japanese cars was expected to increase the demand for U.S. automobiles and thus shift the demand for U.S. automobile workers to the right. While this in fact occurred, U.S. automobile manufacturers responded by raising their prices, using the restrictions on import competition to try to restore their profit levels. The higher domestic automobile prices reduced the number of domestic automobiles demanded; this served to partially shift the derived demand for U.S. automobile workers back to the left. In addition, U.S. automobile workers pressed for and won wage increases, which, given the position of the labor demand curve, reduced the number of automobile workers that domestic automobile producers would hire. This further reduced the employment effects of the restriction.

The net result of these actions was that the voluntary import restraints only had a small effect on domestic U.S. automobile employment. One study concluded that as of 1983 they probably had saved only about 26,000 jobs. Moreover, when one considers the higher costs consumers had to pay because the prices on both domestic and imported cars rose (the latter because Japanese producers "loaded" the cars they sent to the United States with expensive options, and consumers bid up the prices of the relatively scarce imported cars), the study added that *each* of the jobs saved probably cost American automobile purchasers about $160,000.

SOURCE: Robert Crandall, "Import Quotas and the Automobile Industry," *The Brookings Review* 2 (Summer 1984): 8–17; U.S. Department of Labor, *Employment and Earnings* (various issues).

tries had been reversed—and living standards were posited to be higher in China—trade would still have taken place and the United States would still have traded food for Chinese-made clothing.

The general conclusion one can reach from this simple model of trade is that the advent of free trade between two countries will tend to cause each to specialize in producing goods for which it has a comparative advantage and to reduce its production of goods for which its real internal costs are relatively high. Trade, just like an important technological improvement in a given industry, will tend to *shift* employment from one industry to another.[26] However, there is no reason to believe that the advent of free trade will create a permanent loss of employment in the country with higher real wages. To repeat, it is the production possibilities curves, not real-wage rates, that drive international trade.

If, within a country, individual *firms* paying very high wages are "punished" by the market and forced out of business, what prevents a high-wage *country* from being similarly punished by international trade? Put differently, if the average wages for production workers in, say, Haiti are 20 percent of the average wages in the United States, why can't Haiti undersell American producers in every product line? How can American workers hope to remain employed at high wages when faced with such low-wage competitors?

It is important to realize that Haiti has labor and capital resources that are fixed at any moment. It cannot produce *everything!* If, for example, several thousand Haitian workers are employed sewing garments for export to the United States, they are thus not available for (say) the growing and harvesting of agricultural produce. Thus, while there may be a benefit to Haiti when jobs in the garment trades open up, there is also a cost in terms of forgone output that must now be purchased from the United States (the place where dollars received from the export of clothes must ultimately be spent). Haiti will benefit from increasing the labor it devotes to garment exports *only* if it can replace its forgone production of food more cheaply.

To make the above concepts more concrete, suppose that shirts costing $10 to sew in the United States can be produced in Haiti for $2. Will American garment workers lose their jobs to foreign exports? If the food production forgone in Haiti when one additional shirt is made cannot be purchased from the United States for $2 or less, neither Haitian workers nor their country as a whole will be better off by taking the new jobs. In this case, American workers—despite their higher wages—would not lose jobs to Haitians.

If, however, the food production forgone when a shirt is produced can be purchased from the United States for $2 or less, American jobs in the garment trades will tend to be lost to Haitians. However, it is equally true that Haitian agricultural jobs are thereby lost to the much higher-paying agricultural sector in the United States!

---

26. The available evidence for unionized U.S. and Canadian manufacturing firms suggests that increased foreign competition, in the form of an increase in the share of imports in domestic markets, does lead to lower employment levels in these firms but has no major effect on the wages they pay. See, for example, John Abowd and Thomas Lemieux, "The Effects of International Trade on Collective Bargaining Outcomes: A Comparison of the United States and Canada," in *Immigration, Trade, and Labor Markets*, ed. John Abowd and Richard Freeman (Chicago: University of Chicago Press, 1990).

To repeat, international trade can cause employment to shift across industries, and these shifts may well be accompanied by unemployment if workers, employers, or market wages are slow in adapting to change. However, there is no reason to believe that the transitional unemployment associated with international trade will become permanent; trade does not condemn jobs in high-wage countries to extinction.

MISCONCEPTION

"The challenge of the 21st century will be to teach people how to use their leisure time. The availability of robots means that they will take over most routine jobs, and only a tiny fraction of the population will need to be employed. The rest will have time on their hands."

Analysis

Employers' incentives to substitute capital for labor depend on the relative prices and marginal productivities of each; the scale of output consumed depends on national wealth. Technological progress enhances national wealth (and hence consumption), but the substitution of capital for labor is not inevitable. Capital substitution drives up the marginal productivity of labor, while if there are widespread labor surpluses wages would be bid down; both factors would serve to limit the profitability of continual substitution for labor.

Principle

The choices of economic actors depend on the relative benefits and costs of the alternatives available to them.

REVIEW QUESTIONS

1. Suppose Congress had just passed a permanent tax credit applicable to the purchase of machinery. What impact would this tax reduction have on the demand for labor? Under what conditions is the demand for labor most likely to increase?
2. A national study concludes that the hourly pay received by part-time workers is always less than the hourly pay received by full-time workers in comparable jobs. It also concludes that part-time workers are disproportionately women, teenagers, the elderly, and the hard-to-employ. Thus, the study suggests that Congress pass a law compelling employers offering part-time jobs to pay the *full-time* wage rate prevailing in their area for the relevant jobs. Analyze as completely as you can the effects on both part-time and full-time workers.
3. Beginning in 1990, the federal minimum wage for 16- to 19-year-olds who are in the first six months of their first job will be lower than the minimum wage rate for other workers. Suppose, instead, that the youth differential were permanent (that is, it applied to all teenagers regardless of how long they had worked). How would a permanent youth differential affect the employment prospects of older workers who want to work part time?
4. Union A faces a demand curve in which a wage of $4 per hour leads to demand for 20,000 person-hours and a wage of $5 per hour leads to demand for 10,000 person-

hours. Union B faces a demand curve in which a wage of $6 per hour leads to demand for 30,000 person-hours, while a wage of $5 per hour leads to demand for 33,000 person-hours.

    a. Which union faces the *more* elastic demand curve?

    b. Which union will be more successful in increasing the total income (wages times person-hours) of its membership?

5. Suppose that a U.S. President is proposing to aid decaying central cities by declaring them to be "enterprise zones." The idea is for the federal government to subsidize the revenues of the eligible cities, thus allowing them to cut property taxes for businesses that subsequently open up within the zones. (Property taxes are the major source of local government revenues, and all forms of property—buildings, land, machinery—are taxed.) The aim of this program, of course, is to attract business and employment into the central city. These subsidies will not be granted to cities that are not in a state of decay. *Suburban* areas around qualified central cities would likewise be ineligible for the subsidies as long as they are not in a state of decay.

    Suppose you are an analyst concerned about the effects of this program on the employment and wage levels of low-skilled workers, both in and out of enterprise zones. What problems do you see that might keep this program from raising the employment and wages of the less-skilled? What conditions would lead to the most favorable effects (more employment, higher wages) for the less-skilled?

6. Clerical workers represent a substantial share of the U.S. work force—over 15 percent in recent years. Concern has been expressed that computerization and office automation will lead to a substantial decline in white-collar employment and increased unemployment of clerical workers. Is this concern well founded?

7. Briefly explain how the following programs would affect the elasticity of demand for labor in the steel industry:

    a. an increased tariff on steel imports;

    b. a law making it illegal to lay off workers for economic reasons;

    c. a "boom" in the machinery industry (which uses steel as an input)—causing production in that industry to rise;

    d. a decision by the owners of steel mills to operate each mill longer than has been the practice in the past;

    e. an increase in the wages paid by employers in the steel industry;

    f. the placement by the government of a tax on each ton of steel produced.

8. In 1942 the government promulgated regulations that prohibited the manufacture of many types of garments by workers who did the sewing, stitching, and knitting in their homes. If these prohibitions are repealed, so that clothing items may now be made either by workers in factories or by independent contractors doing work in their homes, what effect will repealing the prohibitions have on the labor demand curve for *factory workers* in the garment industry?

SELECTED READINGS

Borjas, George. "The Demographic Determinants of the Demand for Black Labor." In *The Black Youth Unemployment Crisis,* ed. Richard Freeman and Harry Holzer. Chicago: University of Chicago Press, 1986.

Denison, Edward F. *Accounting for Slower Economic Growth: The United States in the 1970s.* Washington, D.C.: Brookings Institution, 1979.

Hamermesh, Daniel. "Subsidies for Jobs in the Private Sector." In *Creating Jobs: Public Employment Programs and Wage Subsidies,* ed. John Palmer. Washington, D.C.: Brookings Institution, 1978.

_____. "The Demand for Labor in the Long Run." In *Handbook of Labor Economics,* ed. Orley Ashenfelter and Richard Layard. Amsterdam: North-Holland, 1986.

Perloff, Jeffrey, and Wachter, Michael. "The New Jobs Tax Credit—An Evaluation of the 1977–78 Wage Subsidy Program." *American Economic Review,* May 1979.

APPENDIX 4A

The Elasticity of Demand for Labor and Labor Share: Understanding the Exception

Footnote 4 of Chapter 4 noted that the law relating a smaller labor share with a less elastic demand curve holds only when it is easier for customers to substitute among final products than it is for employers to substitute capital for labor. While it is easy to intuitively explain why the fourth law of derived demand holds, explaining the exception to the law is somewhat more difficult. This appendix provides a graphical explanation of this exception.

It is convenient to assume the extreme case in which capital/labor substitution can occur but product substitution cannot. In this case consumers will buy the product in the same amounts, no matter what its price; hence a wage increase will lead to no scale effect. We do allow for capital/labor substitution in response to a wage change and further assume that the supply of capital curve is horizontal (perfectly elastic).

The substitutability of capital (K) and labor (L) can be measured by the *elasticity of substitution,* which is defined as the percentage change in the capital/labor ratio called forth by a 1 percent change in the ratio of wages (W) to capital costs (C):

$$\text{Elasticity of Substitution} = \frac{\%\Delta(K/L)}{\%\Delta(W/C)} \qquad (4A.1)$$

The elasticity of substitution is clearly a positive number because as W rises relative to C, capital will be substituted for labor. Expressing substitutability as an elasticity is convenient because elasticity is measured in units independent of the units in which capital and labor are measured.

Figure 4A.1 displays representative isoquants of two different (industry) production functions. *Both* these production functions have an elasticity of substitution equal to $+1$. A unitary elasticity of substitution has the property that factor shares remain constant no matter what the relative prices of capital

FIGURE 4A.1 Two Production Functions with an Elasticity of Substitution Equal to +1

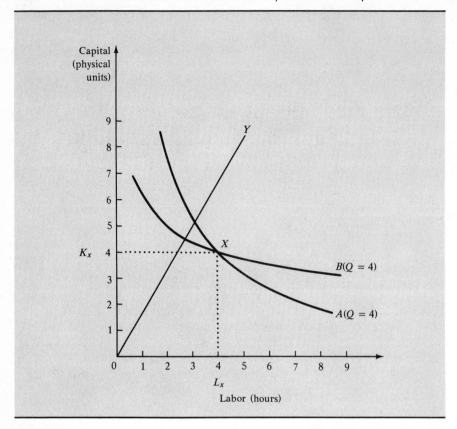

and labor are. If wages rise 10 percent relative to capital prices, the use of labor falls 10 percent relative to the use of capital, and labor's share remains constant.[1]

While isoquants A and B have different shapes, it can be understood (with some work) that their elasticities of substitution are equal. Suppose, for example, that industries A and B were both operating at point X, where the capital/labor ratio equals K_x/L_x. Industry A will be at point X if wages are relatively high compared to capital costs, while B will be there if wages are relatively low (remember from Appendix 3A that the marginal rate of technical substitution, as given by the slope of the isoquants, must equal the ratio of W to C). The equality of the elasticity of substitution for A and B means that if the factor-price ratios in each case change by the same percentage amount,

---

1. The production functions in Figure 4A.1 are both Cobb-Douglas production functions, meaning they have the form $Q = L^\alpha K^{1-\alpha}$, where α = labor's share and $1 - \alpha$ equals capital's share. All Cobb-Douglas production functions have an elasticity of substitution equal to 1. Isoquant A is the $Q = 4$ isoquant for $Q = L^{0.5}K^{0.5}$. Isoquant B is the $Q = 4$ isoquant for $Q = L^{0.25}K^{0.75}$.

their capital/labor ratios will also change by equal percentages. Since K_x/L_x held for *both* prior to the change in factor-price ratios, K/L *after* the change must also be the same. This means that K_A/L_A and K_B/L_B after adjustment must lie along the *same ray* passing through the origin of Figure 4A.1. Along a given ray (Y, for example), levels of usage of K and L vary, but the *ratio* of K to L is the same at each point. While the post-adjustment levels of capital and labor will be different in industries A and B, then, the capital/labor *ratios* will be the same if they both start at point X and experience the same *percentage changes* in W/C.

Isoquants A and B are repeated in Figure 4A.2, where it is assumed that the two industries, while having different production functions, face the *same* factor prices. Industry A responds to these factor prices by producing 4 units of output at point A', where the capital/labor ratio is K_a/L_a. Industry B responds by producing its 4 units at point B', where the capital/labor ratio is much higher (at K_b/L_b). Given that factor prices are exactly the same, the

FIGURE 4A.2 A Smaller Share of Labor in Total Costs Generates a Larger Elasticity of Demand for Labor When the Elasticity of Substitution Between Labor and Capital Exceeds the Elasticity of Product Demand

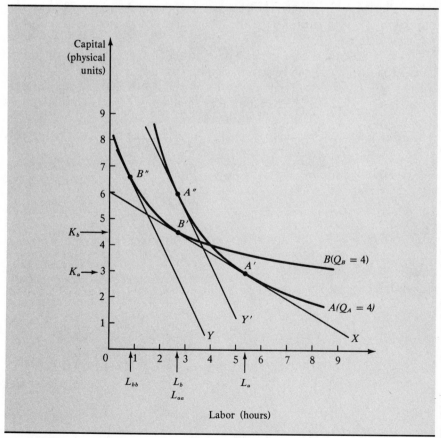

share of labor in total cost is much lower in B than A. This can easily be seen using the formula for labor share:

$$\frac{\text{Labor Share in}}{\text{Total Cost}} = \frac{WL}{WL + CK} \qquad (4A.2)$$

where W and C are the same for each industry, but K/L is much higher for industry B.

Figure 4A.2 can now be used to analyze the effects of labor share on the elasticity of demand for labor, given (a) completely inelastic product demand curves, (b) a completely elastic supply of capital, and (c) equal elasticities of substitution between K and L. Now suppose that originally W_0 and C_0 were such that isoexpenditure curve X held, but that wages increase to W_1 while C_0 remains constant. This increase in wages tilts the new isoexpenditure curves to Y and Y', both of which have the same slope of W_1/C_0. Because there is no scale effect, both industries continue producing at $Q = 4$. Industry A moves from a cost-minimizing point of A' to point A'', while B moves from B' to B''. The amount of labor used by A falls from L_a to L_{aa}—a percentage drop of roughly 50 percent, as shown in Figure 4A.2. The labor used by B drops by a smaller amount in absolute terms but by a much larger percentage owing to the smaller base; the percentage decrease in B's labor is around 70 percent in the figure. Thus B, with the smaller labor share, has a more elastic demand for labor than does A.

One senses, then, that the exception to the "labor share" law of derived demand is a result of the relatively small initial usage of labor in industries where labor share is also small (other things equal). Given equal elasticities of substitution and no scale effect (or a very small one), a change in the ratio of wages to capital prices will call forth relatively larger percentage changes in employment where labor share is smaller because of the smaller initial level of employment.

5

Quasi-Fixed Labor Costs and Their Effects on Demand

To this point in our detailed discussion of the demand for labor, we have treated all labor costs as *variable*—that is, as being strictly proportional to the length of time the employee works. Variable labor costs, such as the hourly wage rate, recur every period and, of course, can be reduced if the hours of work are reduced. Many labor costs, however, are *quasi-fixed,* in that they are not strictly proportional to hours of work. Such costs are borne by the firm on a *per-worker* basis that is largely independent of the hours each employee works. This chapter traces the effects these quasi-fixed costs have on the demand for labor.

Because quasi-fixed labor costs are generally *nonwage,* the first section discusses the nature and magnitude of nonwage labor costs. Included in our discussion are the costs to firms of hiring and training new employees, the costs of legally required social insurance programs (such as Social Security and unemployment compensation), and the costs of privately negotiated employee benefits (such as health insurance, vacation and sick-leave pay, and private pensions).

One important effect that quasi-fixed costs have on the demand for labor concerns the choice firms have between hiring more (or fewer) workers and employing those already on the payroll for longer (or shorter) hours. As discussed in the second section of this chapter, the fact that many nonwage labor costs do *not* vary at the margin with weekly hours of work explains why some employers decide to regularly work their employees overtime at legally required premium wage rates rather than increasing the level of employment—a phenomenon that has led periodically to the proposal that the legally mandated overtime premium be increased in an effort to discourage employers from authorizing overtime and to encourage them to "spread the work." The second section concludes with policy analyses of the federally mandated overtime-pay premium and of proposals to require all employers to provide their employees with health insurance.

The third section looks in detail at the nature and consequences of one important type of quasi-fixed labor cost: *investments* by firms in the hiring and training of their employees. Investments generally involve a current outlay of funds with a future payback, so that investments in workers cause firms' employment decisions to extend over multiple periods. Thus, this section discusses two critical issues: the ways current costs and future returns can be meaningfully compared, and the multiperiod criterion for profit maximization in the hiring of labor. The application of these concepts to the issue of *training* investments is made in the section that follows, in which we discuss the conditions under which these investments by a firm will meet the profit-maximizing criterion. We conclude this section with some implications for the occupational distribution of layoffs, labor hoarding, and the training effects of minimum wage laws.

Turning from training to *hiring* investments, the next section briefly discusses the choices firms face in the often costly process of selecting employees. The underlying rationale for the existence of *internal labor markets* and the use of credentials in screening employees is discussed here. Finally, we conclude with a section that analyzes some hiring practices that often appear to be discriminatory.

NONWAGE LABOR COSTS

Although simple textbook models of the labor market often refer to the hourly wage rate paid to workers as the cost of labor, substantial *nonwage* labor costs have important implications for labor market behavior. In general, they fall into two categories: hiring and training costs and employee benefits.

Hiring and Training Costs

Firms incur substantial costs in hiring and training new employees. *Hiring costs* include all costs involved in advertising positions, screening applicants to evaluate their qualifications, and processing successful applicants who have been offered jobs. One might also include the overhead costs of maintaining employees on the payroll once they have been employed in this category of costs; these costs would include record-keeping costs, the costs of computing and issuing paychecks, and the costs of providing forms to the government (such as W-2 forms to the Internal Revenue Service) giving information on employees' earnings.

New employees typically undergo formal or informal training and orientation programs. These programs may teach new skills, such as how to use a machine, that directly increase the employees' productive ability. Alternatively, orientation programs may simply provide newcomers with background information on how the firm is structured, such as who to call if a machine breaks down or how to requisition supplies. Such information, while not changing skill levels, does increase productivity by enabling workers to make more efficient use of time.

Firms incur at least three types of *training costs:*

1. The *explicit* monetary costs of employing individuals to serve as trainers and the costs of materials used up during the training process;
2. The *implicit* or opportunity costs of using capital equipment and experienced employees to do the training in less-formal training situations (for example, an experienced employee demonstrating to a new recruit how he or she does a job may work at a slower pace than normal); and
3. The *implicit* or opportunity costs of the trainee's time (individuals undergoing training are not producing as much output as they would if all of their time were devoted to production activities).

Because a large share of employers' hiring and training costs are implicit, it is rare to obtain data on the magnitude of such costs. A 1982 study of some

---

EXAMPLE 5.1
Recruiting and Training Longshore Crane Operators

The cost of recruiting and training workers means that employers must decide on an overall hiring strategy. Firms choosing a *high-wage* strategy generate many applicants for each opening and can be selective, taking only trained, experienced workers. By paying high wages they avoid the explicit and implicit costs of hiring the inexperienced. Firms choosing a *low-wage* strategy can attract only inexperienced applicants, and they must be prepared to undertake a period of training and to sustain the risks later on of losing the workers they have trained to higher-wage employers. Thus, low-wage employers save on hourly costs but must incur higher training and recruiting expenses.

In the following description of the market for shipside crane operators in California, the "house" companies (associated with a shipping line) have clearly chosen the high-wage strategy, while Marine Terminals, an independent loading company, has chosen the low-wage approach:

> Crane operating is for the most part an isolated activity, which allows individual operators to be compared. . . . A vigorous competition has resulted for the most able of these operators.
>
> To become a competent crane operator requires a combination of off-the-job training, to satisfy union seniority requirements, and on-the-job learning and experience, since the skills of crane operating are actually acquired on the job. . . . The Marine Terminals superintendent described the situation: "Marine Terminals is almost traditionally the training ground for crane operators. Marine Terminals takes people . . . who aren't skilled and trains them to drive cranes, and then some other company, once they're good, will offer them a better deal and then off they'll go." . . .
>
> In short, the house companies employ the top operators and pay them better, and the independents employ the newly qualified and incompetent operators, pay them less, and risk losing any who attain above average competence.

SOURCE: William Finlay, *Work on the Waterfront* (Philadelphia: Temple University Press, 1988), 82, 83, 84.

TABLE 5.1 Hours Devoted by Firms to Hiring and Training a New Worker During First Three Months on Job

Activity	Average Hours
Recruiting, screening, interviewing	10
Hours of formal instruction by training personnel	11
Hours spent by management in orientation, informal training, extra supervision	60
Hours spent by co-workers in informal training	27
Hours spent by new worker watching others do work	53
Total	161

SOURCES: John M. Barron, Dan A. Black, and Mark A. Lowenstein, "Job Matching and On-the-Job Training," *Journal of Labor Economics* 7, no. 1 (January 1989): 5; John Barron and John Bishop, "Extensive Search, Intensive Search and Hiring Costs: New Evidence on Employer Hiring Activity," *Economic Inquiry* 23 (July 1985): 363–82.

2,000 employers, however, collected data on the hours spent on recruiting and on both formal and informal training during a new employee's first three months on the job. The study was somewhat weighted toward establishments employing low-wage workers, and about three-quarters of the establishments surveyed employed less than 50 people. Summarized in Table 5.1, the data indicate that, on average, about 10 hours were spent per new hire on recruiting and screening activities, that 11 hours of formal training were given, that some 87 hours were devoted by supervisors and co-workers to informal training activities, and that the new employees each spent an additional 53 hours watching others perform their jobs rather than doing the work themselves. It has been estimated that the average value of time spent in hiring and training new workers during their first three months came close to 30 percent of the value that an experienced co-worker produces during that time period.[1] The study did not address training after the initial three-month period.

Employee Benefits

We have much better data, however, on the other types of *nonwage* labor costs that firms incur. *Employee benefits* include *legally required* social insurance contributions and *privately provided* benefits. Examples of legally required benefits are payroll-based payments employers must make to fund programs that compensate workers for unemployment (unemployment insurance), injury (workers' compensation), and retirement (old-age, survivors', disability, and health insurance—or "Social Security"). Examples of privately provided benefits are holiday pay, vacation and sick leave, private pensions, and private health and life insurance.

Table 5.2 gives some idea of employee benefits as a percentage of total compensation, at least among the large firms responding to a recent U.S.

---

1. John H. Bishop, "Do Employers Share the Costs and Benefits of General Training?" (Working Paper #88-08, Center for Advanced Human Resource Studies, School of Industrial and Labor Relations, Cornell University), 15.

TABLE 5.2   Employee Benefits as a Percent of Total Compensation Among Large Employers, 1986

Legally required payments		6.5
Social Security	4.4	
Workers' compensation	.8	
* Unemployment insurance	.7	
Other	.6	
Retirement		4.9
* Employer costs based on benefit formulas (defined benefit plans)	2.4	
Employer costs proportional to earnings (defined contribution plans)	1.1	
* Other (including insurance annuities and administrative costs)	1.4	
* *Insurance* (medical, life)		6.3
* *Paid rest* (coffee breaks, meal periods, set-up and wash-up time)		2.4
* *Paid vacations, holidays, sick leave*		7.3
* *Miscellaneous* (discounts on products bought, employee meals, child care)		.9
Total		28.3

* Category of costs believed by authors to be largely *quasi-fixed* (see discussion in the text).

SOURCE: U.S. Chamber of Commerce, *Employee Benefits 1986* (Washington, D.C.: U.S. Chamber of Commerce, 1987).

Chamber of Commerce survey.[2] The data indicate that nonwage benefits constitute over one-quarter of total compensation, with the largest categories being pay for time not worked (9.7%), insurance (6.3%), legally required payments (6.5%), and pensions (4.9%). These nonwage benefits have been growing over time, although in the last decade their growth has slowed. Thirty years ago, however, nonwage benefits were 19 percent of total compensation in large firms, and in the late 1940s they constituted just 13 percent of compensation.

The Quasi-Fixed Nature of Many Nonwage Costs

The distinction between wage and nonwage costs of employment is important because many nonwage costs are *costs per worker* rather than *costs per hour worked*. That is, many nonwage costs do not vary at the margin with the number of hours an employee works. Economists thus refer to them as *quasi-*

2. Benefits as a percentage of compensation varied from 25 percent for firms employing under 100 employees, to 26 percent for firms employing 100 to 5,000 employees, to 28.4 percent for those with over 5,000 workers. Because the sample average was 28.3 percent, it is reasonable to infer that most firms in the sample were in the over-5,000 category. See U.S. Chamber of Commerce, *Employee Benefits 1986* (Washington, D.C.: U.S. Chamber of Commerce, 1987).

fixed, in the sense that once an employee is hired the firm is committed to a cost that does not vary with his or her hours of work.

It should be obvious that hiring and training costs are quasi-fixed; they are associated with each new employee, not with the hours he or she works after the training period. Many benefit costs, however, are also quasi-fixed. For example, most life and medical insurance policies are paid on a per-worker basis, as is pay for time not worked (breaks, holidays, vacation, and sick leave). Some pension costs are proportional to hours worked, because some employers (those with "defined contribution" plans) agree to contribute a certain percentage of employee pay to a pension fund. However, most private sector pension plans promise benefits that are a function of years of service rather than hours of work; the costs of these "defined benefit" plans are quasi-fixed in most cases.

In the category of legally required benefits, workers' compensation costs are strictly proportional to hours worked, because they are levied as a percentage of payroll, and Social Security taxes are proportional for most employees.[3] However, the unemployment insurance payroll-tax liability is specified to be a percentage (the tax rate) of each employee's earnings up until a maximum earnings level (the taxable wage base), which in 1989 was between $7,000 and $10,000 in two-thirds of all states. Since most employees earn more than $10,000 per year, having an employee work an additional hour per week will *not* cause any increase in the employer's payroll-tax liability. Therefore, unemployment insurance costs are a quasi-fixed cost to employers.

In Table 5.2 we have indicated (by an asterisk) which nonwage costs are usually of a quasi-fixed nature. The data suggest that, at least for large employers, around 21 percent of total compensation (three-quarters of nonwage costs) are quasi-fixed. The quasi-fixed nature of many nonwage labor costs has important effects on employer hiring and overtime decisions. These effects are discussed below.

THE EMPLOYMENT/HOURS TRADE-OFF

The simple model of the demand for labor presented in the preceding chapters spoke to the quantity of labor demanded and made no distinction between the number of individuals employed by a firm and the average length of its employees' workweek. Holding all other inputs constant, however, a firm can produce a given level of output with various combinations of the number of employees hired and the number of hours worked per week. Presumably increases in the number of employees hired will allow for shorter workweeks, while longer workweeks will allow for fewer employees, other things equal.

---

3. The Social Security (OASDHI) payroll-tax liability of employers is specified as a percentage of earnings up until a maximum taxable wage base; this wage base was $51,300 in 1990. Since this level exceeds the annual earnings of most full-time employees, the employer's payroll-tax liability *is* increased when a firm employs a typical employee an additional hour per week.

In the short run, with capital and all other inputs fixed, the output (Q) a firm can produce is related to both its employment level (M) and its average workweek per employee (H) by the following production function:

$$Q = f(M, H) \tag{5.1}$$

It is reasonable to assume that both inputs in equation (5.1) have positive marginal products ($MP_M > 0$; $MP_H > 0$). That is, increasing the number of employees holding hours constant—or increasing the average workweek holding employment constant—will lead to increases in output. While remaining positive, each of these marginal products must surely decline at some point. When the number of employees is increased, this decline may be due to the reduced quantity of capital now available to each individual employee. When the hours each employee works per week are increased, the decline in marginal product may occur because after some point fatigue sets in.

Given this production function,[4] how does a firm determine its optimal employment/hours combination? Is it ever rational for a firm to work its existing employees overtime on a regularly scheduled basis, even though it must pay them a wage premium, rather than hiring additional employees?

Determining the Mix of Workers and Hours

The fact that certain labor costs are *not* hours-related and others are makes it important to examine the marginal cost an employer faces when employing an additional *worker* for whatever length workweek other employees are working (MC_M). This marginal cost will be a function of the quasi-fixed labor costs plus the weekly wage and variable (with hours) employee-benefit costs for the specified length of workweek. Similarly, it is important to examine the marginal cost a firm faces when it seeks to increase the *average workweek* of its existing work force by one hour (MC_H). This marginal cost will equal the hourly wage and variable employee-benefit costs multiplied by the number of employees in the work force. Of course, if the employer is in a situation in which an overtime premium (such as time and a half or double time) must be paid for additional hours, that higher rate is the relevant wage rate to use in the latter calculation.

Viewed in this way, a firm's decision about its optimal employment/hours combination is no different from its decision about the usage of any two factors of production, which was discussed in Chapter 3. Specifically, to minimize the cost of producing any given level of output, a firm should adjust both its employment level and its average workweek so that the costs of producing an added unit of output are equal for each:

$$\frac{MC_M}{MP_M} = \frac{MC_H}{MP_H} \tag{5.2}$$

---

4. For estimates of such a function, see Martin Feldstein, "Specifications of the Labor Input in the Aggregate Production Function," *Review of Economic Studies* 34 (October 1967): 375–86. See also Sherwin Rosen, "Short-Run Employment Variation in Class-I Railroads in the U.S., 1947–1967," *Econometrica* 36 (July–October 1968): 511–29.

Put another way, the marginal cost of hiring an additional employee (MC_M) relative to the marginal cost of working the existing work force an additional hour (MC_H) should be equal to the marginal productivity of an additional employee relative to that of extending the workweek by an hour:

$$\frac{MC_M}{MC_H} = \frac{MP_M}{MP_H} \tag{5.3}$$

The Fair Labor Standards Act (FLSA) requires that all employees covered by the legislation receive an overtime pay premium of at least 50 percent of their regular hourly wage (time and a half) for each hour per week they work in excess of 40 hours.[5] Now, while a large proportion of overtime hours are worked because of disequilibrium phenomena—rush orders, seasonal demand, mechanical failures, and absenteeism, for example—a substantial amount of overtime appears to be regularly scheduled. Equation (5.3) indicates why this scheduling of overtime may occur. Although overtime hours require premium pay, they also enable an employer to avoid the quasi-fixed employment costs associated with employing an additional worker. This point can be illustrated by considering what would happen if the overtime-pay premium were to be increased.

Policy Analysis: The Overtime-Pay Premium

Periodically proposals have been introduced in Congress to raise the overtime premium to double time.[6] The argument made to support such an increase is that even though unemployment remains a pressing national problem, the use of overtime hours has not diminished. Moreover, the argument continues, the deterrent effect of the overtime premium on the use of overtime has been weakened since the FLSA was enacted because of the growing share of hiring and training costs, employee benefits, and government-mandated insurance premiums in total compensation. As already noted, many of these costs are *quasi-fixed,* or employee-related rather than hours-related, and thus do not vary with overtime hours of work. An increase in these costs increases employers' marginal costs of hiring new employees relative to the costs of working their existing work forces overtime.

---

5. In 1978, approximately 59 percent of all workers were subject to the overtime-pay provisions of the FLSA [see U.S. Department of Labor, *Minimum Wage and Maximum Hours Standards Under the Fair Labor Standards Act* (Washington, D.C.: U.S. Government Printing Office, October 1979)]. Coverage under the law has not changed since that date. The major categories of excluded employees are executive, administrative, and professional personnel, outside salespersons, most state and local government employees, and agricultural workers.

6. For example, Congressman John Conyers of Michigan introduced HR 1784 into Congress in February 1979. To quote a supporter of the proposal, "The AFL-CIO endorses the double-time provision as a means of generating additional jobs. The evidence is persuasive that the overtime-pay requirements of the Fair Labor Standards Act have lost their effectiveness as a deterrent to regularly scheduled overtime work." (See the statement by Rudolph Oswald, Director of Research, AFL-CIO, in the minutes of the Hearings before the Subcommittee on Labor Standards on HR 1784, October 23, 1979.)

In terms of equation (5.3), the increase in quasi-fixed costs that has occurred causes an inequality between the ratio of marginal productivities and marginal costs at the old equilibrium employment/hours combination:

$$\frac{MC_M}{MC_H} > \frac{MP_M}{MP_H} \tag{5.4}$$

To restore the equality (and thus minimize costs) requires increasing the right-hand side of expression (5.4). Given our assumptions of diminishing marginal productivities, if output were to remain constant, employment would have to be reduced and hours worked per employee would have to increase. It is claimed, therefore, that the growth of these quasi-fixed costs has been at least partly responsible for increased usage of overtime hours and that an increase in the overtime premium is required to better "spread the work."[7] Such an increase, by raising the marginal cost of overtime hours relative to the marginal cost of hiring new workers, should induce employers to substitute new employees for the overtime hours employers might otherwise schedule.

Would an increase in the overtime premium prove to be an effective way of increasing employment and reducing unemployment? A number of economists have sought to answer this question. Although the overtime premium is, for the most part, legislatively fixed at a point in time, the ratio MC_M/MC_H varies across establishments because the weekly quasi-fixed costs and the straight-time wage rate vary across establishments. Economists have attempted to estimate the extent to which the usage of overtime hours varies across establishments with the ratio MC_M/MC_H, when all other factors are held constant.[8]

Once this relationship is known, it is possible to simulate the effect of an increase in the overtime premium on overtime hours per employee. For example, suppose that the statistical analyses indicated that the relationship between overtime hours and MC_M/MC_H was given by the line AB in Figure 5.1. Consider a representative firm that faced relative marginal costs of $(MC_M/MC_H)_0$ and whose employees worked an average of H_0 overtime hours per week. It is a simple matter to compute the effect on the relative marginal cost of an increase in the overtime premium to double time. If an increased premium caused a decrease to $(MC_M/MC_H)_1$, overtime hours would correspondingly fall to H_1.

Now if one *assumes* that *all* of the reduction in overtime would be converted to new full-time positions, it is possible to estimate what the effect on the employment level would be. The implied results from these studies appear in Table 5.3; these results suggest that employment increases in the range of 0.3 to 4.0 percent would result. At first glance, then, increasing the over-

---

7. For example, average weekly overtime hours of work in manufacturing averaged 2.56 hours per employee between 1956 and 1963. However, over the 1964–78 period the average rose to 3.37 hours per employee, an increase of more than 30 percent. This increase undoubtedly helped stimulate the 1979 proposal mentioned in footnote 6.
8. Since data on hiring and training costs are not widely available, these studies utilize data on the other employee benefits only.

FIGURE 5.1   Simulating the Effect of an Increase in the Overtime Premium to Double Time

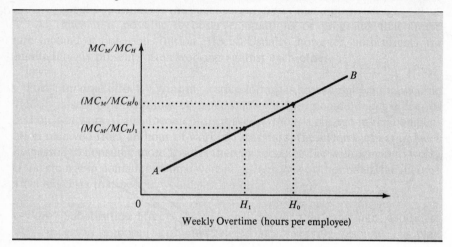

time premium to double time does seem like an effective way of increasing employment and reducing unemployment.

A complete economic analysis, however, suggests that such a conclusion would be an overly optimistic assessment of the effects of a double-time premium.[9] First, these estimates *assume* that the demand for *total* labor hours is completely inelastic with respect to its cost. That is, they ignore the fact that an increase in the overtime premium raises the average cost of labor even if all overtime is eliminated! The reason for this increase is that firms eliminating overtime and increasing employment must bear the quasi-fixed costs of employment discussed earlier. Firms using overtime *before* the imposition of the double-time premium *could* have hired more workers and reduced overtime usage earlier; the fact that they did not make this choice suggests it was a more costly one. If the double-time premium now induces this more costly choice, their labor costs will clearly rise. This increase may cause the total hours of labor hired to decrease as firms shift to more capital-intensive modes of production.

Second, even if the firms that used overtime prior to the new double-time premium shift to more capital-intensive modes of production, their unit costs of output will tend to increase (they could have chosen to substitute capital for labor *before* but decided not to—presumably because of the higher cost). If this cost increase is passed on to consumers in the form of higher prices, a reduction in the quantity of output will occur. This *scale effect* should also lead to a decline in the number of labor hours purchased by employers.

Third, these estimates ignore the responses of currently employed workers who would be simultaneously faced with an increase in the overtime premium and a reduction in their hours of work. Although we have yet to discuss the supply side of the labor market in detail, it should be obvious that one

---

9. See Ronald G. Ehrenberg and Paul L. Schumann, *Longer Hours or More Jobs? An Investigation of Amending Hours Legislation to Create Employment* (Ithaca, N.Y.: ILR Press, 1982).

TABLE 5.3   Estimated Changes in Full-Time Employment Resulting from Increasing the Overtime Premium from Time and a Half to Double Time

Study	Group	Percentage Change
Ehrenberg (1971)	1966 manufacturing production workers	+1.6
Nussbaum and Wise (1977)	1968 manufacturing production workers	+3.7
	1970 manufacturing production workers	+3.7
	1972 manufacturing production workers	+2.8
	1974 manufacturing production workers	+4.0
	1968–1974 pooled manufacturing interindustry data	+2.0
Solnick and Swimmer (1978)	1972 private nonfarm supervisory workers	+0.3 to 3.1
Ehrenberg and Schumann (1982)	1976 manufacturing production workers	0.0 to 1.5
	1976 nonmanufacturing nonsupervisory workers	1.0 to 2.3

SOURCES: Ronald G. Ehrenberg, "The Impact of the Overtime Premium on Employment and Hours in U.S. Industry," *Western Economic Journal* 19 (June 1971): 199–207; Joyce Nussbaum and Donald Wise, "The Employment Impact of the Overtime Provisions of the FLSA" (final report submitted to the U.S. Department of Labor, 1977); Loren Solnick and Gene Swimmer, "Overtime and Fringe Benefits—A Simultaneous Equations Approach" (mimeographed, 1978); Ronald G. Ehrenberg and Paul L. Schumann, *Longer Hours or More Jobs?* (Ithaca, N.Y.: ILR Press, 1982).

possible response to a reduction in overtime hours is for employed workers to *moonlight*—to seek part-time second jobs. Moonlighting would be more likely to occur if the increase in the premium resulted in a decrease in their labor earnings.[10] If increased moonlighting occurred, the creation of new jobs for the unemployed would be further reduced.

Fourth, these estimates assume either that the skill distributions of the unemployed and of those who work overtime are sufficiently similar, or that the unemployed and those working overtime are close enough substitutes in production, to permit all of the reduction in overtime to be converted into new full-time employment. However, *if* those working overtime were primarily skilled workers and the unemployed were primarily unskilled, and the substitutability of the two groups were very low, potential employment gains from raising the overtime premium might be considerably smaller than these estimates.

Finally, these estimates assume that the overtime-pay provisions of the FLSA are fully complied with and that they would continue to be fully complied with after an increase in the premium to double time. However, since an increase in the overtime premium would increase the amount employers save by *not* complying with the legislation, such an increase might well lead to a reduced compliance rate, further reducing the positive employment effects of the legislation. A number of studies indicate that noncompliance with the

---

10. Formally, this would occur if employers' demand curves for overtime hours were elastic with respect to the overtime wage.

overtime-pay provisions is currently at least in the 10 percent range.[11] That is, at least 10 percent of the individuals working overtime who are covered by the FLSA *fail* to receive a premium of at least time and a half. Hence, the possibility of increased noncompliance cannot be dismissed.

Our analysis of the wisdom of increasing the overtime premium to double time to stimulate employment growth unfortunately reminds us that policy analysis is never easy. The world is complex, and any complete analysis of a policy issue must consider a number of factors. It is in identifying what factors to consider that economic theory is so useful. Indeed, in the present case, even though the *initial* simulations suggested that a double-time premium would lead to an increase in employment, consideration of the *other* factors noted above led to a recommendation against increasing the overtime premium.[12]

Policy Analysis: Part-Time Employment and Mandated Employer Provision of Health Insurance

As discussed in Example 3.5, recently several proposals have been considered in Congress that, if enacted, would mandate that employers provide health insurance coverage for all of their employees.[13] To the extent that employers currently do not provide such coverage, adoption of this type of proposal would increase quasi-fixed employment costs and thus encourage employers to further substitute overtime hours for additional employment. Moreover, because part-time employees are less likely to be currently covered by an employer health insurance policy, adoption of this proposal would probably influence the mix of full-time and part-time employees in the economy.

Just as the usage of overtime hours has increased, part-time employment has grown as a share of total employment in most European countries and in the United States in recent years. For example, between 1955 and 1988 the percentage of employees in U.S. nonagricultural industries who were employed part time (defined as less than 35 hours per week) rose from 10.5 to 18.4.[14] Explanations for this growth have focused mainly on the supply side of the labor market and on the changing industrial composition of employment. The growing shares of married women with children in the labor force (see Chapter 6), of older workers phasing into retirement, and of students who

---

11. See Ronald G. Ehrenberg and Paul L. Schumann, "Compliance with the Overtime Pay Provisions of the Fair Labor Standards Act," *Journal of Law and Economics* 25 (April 1982): 159–81, and Brigitte Sellekaerts and Stephen Welch, "Noncompliance with the Fair Labor Standards Act: Evidence and Policy Implications," *Labor Studies Journal* 8 (Fall 1983): 124–36.

12. Ehrenberg and Schumann, *Longer Hours or More Jobs?* In Europe, much attention has been directed toward proposals to reduce the number of hours of work per week after which the overtime premium goes into effect. These proposals would increase employers' costs of working their employees relatively long hours, and the hope is that they would lead to reductions in employees' overtime hours and to more rapid employment growth. Robert Hart, *Working Time and Employment* (London: Allen and Unwin, 1986), summarizes the evidence on the wisdom of such a policy change and concludes that it is unlikely to have much effect on employment growth.

13. See Lawrence Summers, "Some Simple Economics of Mandated Benefits," *American Economic Review Papers and Proceedings* 79 (May 1989): 177–83, for a more general discussion of mandated benefits.

14. U.S. Department of Labor, *Employment and Earnings,* January 1989 and earlier issues.

EXAMPLE 5.2

"Renting" Workers as a Way of Coping with Fluctuations in Product Demand

The demand for a firm's product fluctuates from day to day, week to week, and month to month. If a firm finds it feasible to hold inventories of its finished goods, these fluctuations in demand can be absorbed by *product inventories,* thus permitting the firm to keep its employment and production levels constant during the period. That is, in periods when product demand does not absorb what is produced, the firm stores its unsold output; in periods when demand exceeds output, these stores are drawn down. Many firms, however, find that the costs of maintaining inventories are very high, and other firms produce services, which by their very nature are impossible to produce ahead of demand. How can such firms cope with fluctuating demand?

The firms might use overtime to meet fluctuations in product demand, but this option requires paying a substantial wage premium. Overtime can also lead to problems associated with fatigue, and it causes production coordination problems in some industries.

Another way to cope with fluctuating demand is to hire workers on a temporary basis when product demand is unusually high. Temporary workers can also be used to replace absent workers or those who are on vacation or on leave. As indicated in the text, however, the one-time costs of advertising an opening, screening candidates, and processing the paperwork necessary to put workers on the payroll can be quite high. If the tenure of a job is relatively short, the firm may have insufficient time to recoup these costs. In this case the firm might consider "renting" workers from a temporary-help service.

Temporary-help services specialize in screening and training workers who are then put to work in client firms that need temporary workers. The temporary-help service bills its clients, and its hourly charges are generally above the wage the client would pay if it hired workers directly—a premium the client is willing to pay because it is spared the investment costs associated with hiring. Because obtaining jobs through the temporary-help service also saves employees repeated investment costs associated with searching and applying for available temporary openings, its employees are willing to take a wage less than they otherwise would receive. The difference between what its clients are charged and what its employees are paid permits the successful temporary-help service to cover its screening and training costs. A recent survey of U.S. employers found that over three-quarters hired workers from temporary-help services in the course of a year.*

*Katharine Abraham, "Flexible Staffing Arrangements and Employers' Short-Term Adjustment Strategies," in *Employment, Unemployment, and Labor Utilization,* ed. Robert Hart (Boston: Unwin Hyman, 1988), 288–311.

need to work to finance their educations are all thought to have increased the number of workers willing to work part time. On the demand side of the market, growth in the share of service-sector employment (Table 2.3) has increased the number of jobs in which part-time workers can be easily employed.

Recently, however, attention has shifted to the role that relative costs play in the growth of part-time employment. Assuming that part-time workers and full-time workers are substitutes in production, if the hourly labor costs (wages and hours-related benefits) or the quasi-fixed costs (non–hours-related benefits and hiring/training costs) of part-time workers fall relative to those of full-time workers, part-time employment should expand relative to full-time employment. In contrast, if costs of part-time workers rise relative to those of full-time employees, part-time employment should fall relative to full-time employment.

It is well known that part-time workers' wages and benefits are often lower than those of full-time workers, and that part-time employees in some European countries are often not eligible for social insurance programs financed by payroll taxes on employers. To explain trends in the part-time share of total employment, however, it is important to analyze *changes* in the part-time/full-time hourly labor cost and quasi-fixed cost ratios. Less is known about these changes, but one study showed that employment of part-time workers in Great Britain expanded most rapidly during periods when they were covered by relatively few social insurance programs and protective regulations. Specifically, Britain's passage of the Employment Protection Act of 1975, which increased the eligibility of part-time employees for (among other things) job separation payments and maternity benefits, seemed to be associated with a slowdown in its part-time employment growth.[15] Studies that used U.S. data at a point in time have also documented that across industries in the United States, the part-time/full-time wage employment ratio *does* appear to be negatively related to the part-time/full-time wage ratio. Thus, holding other factors constant, in industries in which part-time workers' wages are lowest relative to full-time workers' wages, usage of part-time employees is highest relative to that of full-time employees.[16]

The evidence thus suggests that employers do substitute part-time for full-time employees when their relative costs change. Mandated employer-provided health insurance would be likely to increase the cost of employing part-time workers relative to that of employing full-time workers, both because the former are currently less likely to be covered by an employer-provided policy[17] and because the cost to the employer of providing a given policy would be higher for part-time employees (since the cost is spread over a smaller number of hours). As such, mandated employer-provided health insurance would probably lead employers to substitute full-time for part-time employees.

---

15. R. Disney and E. M. Szyszczak, "Protective Labor Legislation and Part-Time Employment in Great Britain," *British Journal of Industrial Relations* 22 (March 1984): 78–100.
16. Ronald G. Ehrenberg, Pamela Rosenberg, and Jeanne Li, "Part-Time Employment in the United States," in *Employment, Unemployment, and Labor Utilization,* ed. Robert A. Hart (Boston: Unwin Hyman, 1988): 256–81.
17. In one survey, employers providing medical insurance to 98 percent of full-time employees provided such insurance to just 23.6 percent of part-time workers. See U.S. Chamber of Commerce, *Employee Benefits 1986* (Washington, D.C.: U.S. Chamber of Commerce, 1987), 24.

FIRMS' LABOR INVESTMENTS AND THE DEMAND FOR LABOR

The models of the demand for labor given in Chapters 3 and 4 were static in the sense that they considered only *current* marginal productivities and *current* labor costs. If all of a firm's labor costs are variable each year, then its employment decisions each period are independent and it will employ labor *each period* to the point at which labor's marginal revenue product equals the wage. For a competitive firm, which takes product price as given, this condition reduces to employing labor each period up until the point at which labor's marginal product equals its real wage (the money wage divided by the price level). This condition is a straightforward generalization of the single-period decision rule expressed in equation (3.6) of Chapter 3.

Once we begin to consider hiring and training costs, however, the analysis changes somewhat. Hiring and training costs are usually heavily concentrated in the initial periods of employment and do not recur. Later on, however, these early investments in hiring and training raise the productivity of employees. Once the investments are made, it is cheaper for the firm to *continue* using its current workers than to hire, at the same wage rate, new ones (who would have to be trained). Likewise, with an investment required for all *new* workers, employers have to consider not only *current* marginal productivity and labor costs but also *future* marginal productivity and labor costs in deciding whether (and how many) to hire. In short, the presence of investment costs—hiring and training expenses—means that hiring decisions must take into account past, present, and future factors.

To illustrate the hiring decision in the face of labor-investment costs, let us consider a firm that is seeking to determine its employment level over a two-period horizon. To keep the discussion simple, we shall ignore employee-benefit costs and the decision about how many hours employees will work; all workers employed in a period will be assumed to work for the entire period. We shall also assume that the firm is a competitive firm that takes its product price as given. Hence, as in Chapter 3, we can express all of the firm's labor costs in real terms (money costs divided by the price level).

Now suppose the firm incurs hiring and training costs only in the initial period (period 0) and that these *direct outlays* amount to Z per worker in real terms. Suppose also that during the initial period, when workers are undergoing training, their actual marginal product schedule is lowered from MP^* to MP_0 (as shown in Figure 5.2)—in other words, $MP^* - MP_0$ represents the *implicit* costs of training in real terms. In the period subsequent to training (period 1), the marginal productivity of trained employees is higher (MP_1). Finally, suppose that the real wage a firm must pay each employee, the money wage divided by the product price, is W_0 and W_1 in periods 0 and 1, respectively; for now, we take these wages as given by the market, although we shall shortly examine how they are determined.

The Concept of Present Value

In determining its optimal employment level over the two periods, the firm clearly must consider the costs of employing workers in both periods and their

FIGURE 5.2 Multiperiod Demand for Labor

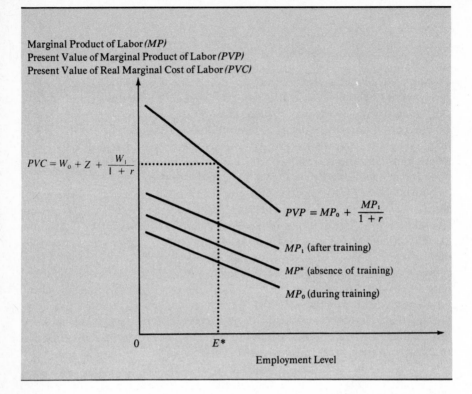

Marginal Product of Labor *(MP)*
Present Value of Marginal Product of Labor *(PVP)*
Present Value of Real Marginal Cost of Labor *(PVC)*

$$PVC = W_0 + Z + \frac{W_1}{1 + r}$$

$$PVP = MP_0 + \frac{MP_1}{1 + r}$$

MP_1 (after training)

MP^* (absence of training)

MP_0 (during training)

0 E^*

Employment Level

marginal products in both periods. A *naive* approach would be to simply add up the costs $(W_0 + W_1 + Z)$, add up the marginal products $(MP_0 + MP_1)$, and then stop hiring when the sum of the marginal products that the last worker produces over the two periods is just equal to the sum of his or her wages and hiring/training costs in real terms. This approach is naive because it ignores the fact that benefits accruing in the future are worth less to the firm than an equal level of benefits that accrue now. Similarly, costs that occur in the future are less burdensome to the firm than equal dollar costs that occur in the present.

Why should this be the case? The answer hinges on the role of interest rates. A dollar of revenue earned by a firm today can be invested at some market rate of interest so that by the second period it will be worth more than a dollar. Hence, faced with a choice of employing a worker whose marginal product is 5 in period 0 and 2 in period 1, or a worker whose marginal product is 2 in period 0 and 5 in period 1, the firm would prefer the former (if wages for the two workers were equal in each period). The sooner the product is produced and sold, the more quickly the firm can gain access to the funds, invest them, and earn interest.[18] Similarly, faced with the option of paying a $100

18. We are assuming here, of course, that the real price the firm receives for its product is constant and that the real rate of interest is positive.

wage bill today or $100 next period, the firm should prefer the second option. It could earn interest on the $100 in the first period, make the payment in the next period, and have the interest left over. If the firm had made the payment in the initial period, it could not have earned interest income.

These examples illustrate why firms prefer benefit streams in which the benefits occur as early as possible and cost streams in which the costs occur as late as possible. But how do we compare different benefit and cost streams when benefits and costs occur in more than one period? Economists rely on the concept of *present value,* which we define to be the value *now* of an entire stream of future benefits or costs.

Suppose a firm receives the sum of $$B_0$ in the current period and will receive nothing in the next period. How much money could it have in the next period if it invested $$B_0$ at a rate of interest that equals r? It would have its original sum, B_0, plus the interest it earned, rB_0:

$$B_1 = B_0 + rB_0 = B_0(1 + r) \qquad (5.5)$$

Since assets of B_1 can be automatically acquired by investing B_0 at the market rate of interest, B_0 *now and* B_1 *next period are equivalent values.* That is, a person who is offered B_0 now or B_1 in one year would regard the offers as exactly the same as long as $B_1 = B_0(1 + r)$.

Following this line of reasoning, suppose that the firm knows it will receive B_1 in the next period. What is the *current* value of that sum? Receiving B_1 in one year is equivalent to receiving a smaller amount (call it X) *now* and investing it so that it equals B_1 in a year. That is, the firm would need to have amount X now in order to invest it and wind up with principal plus interest equal to B_1 in the next period:

$$X(1 + r) = B_1 \qquad (5.6)$$

Dividing both sides by $(1 + r)$:

$$X = \frac{B_1}{1 + r} \qquad (5.7)$$

The quantity X in equation (5.7) is called the *discounted value* of B_1 earned one period in the future.

The *present value* of the firm's earnings over two periods is equal to its earnings in the initial period plus the discounted value of its earnings in the next period.[19] Returning to our two-period hiring decision example given at the start of this section, the *present value* of marginal productivity (*PVP*) can now be seen as

$$PVP = MP_0 + \frac{MP_1}{1 + r} \qquad (5.8)$$

That is, the value of a worker's marginal productivity *now* to the firm is the marginal productivity in the current period (MP_0) plus the marginal produc-

---

19. Earnings in the initial period are not discounted because they are received *now,* not in the future.

tivity in the next period *discounted* by $(1 + r)$. Likewise, the present value of the real marginal *cost* of labor (PVC) is equal to

$$PVC = W_0 + Z + \frac{W_1}{1 + r} \tag{5.9}$$

where r is the market rate of interest. W_0 and Z are not discounted because they are incurred in the current period. However, W_1 is discounted by $(1 + r)$ because it is incurred one year in the future.

The present-value calculation reduces a stream of benefits or costs to a single number that summarizes a firm's entire stream of revenues or liabilities over different time periods. For example, the PVC can be thought of as the answer to the question, "Given that a firm incurs costs per worker of $(W_0 + Z)$ this period and W_1 next period, how much does it have to set aside today to be able to cover both periods' costs?" The PVC is *less* than $W_0 + Z + W_1$ because W_1 is not owed until the latter period and any funds set aside to cover W_1 can be invested now. If the firm sets aside $W_1/(1 + r)$ to cover its labor cost in the next period and invests this amount earning a rate of return r, the interest, $r[W_1/(1 + r)]$, plus principal, $W_1/(1 + r)$, available in the next period will just equal W_1. Similarly, the PVP can be thought of as the answer to the question, "Given that a worker's marginal product will be MP_0 in this period and MP_1 next period, what is the value of that output stream to the employer today?" The PVP is less than $MP_0 + MP_1$ because if the firm were to attempt to borrow against the employee's future marginal product, it could borrow at most $MP_1/(1 + r)$ today and still afford to repay this principal plus the interest, $r[MP_1/(1 + r)]$, out of earnings in the next period.[20]

The Multiperiod Demand for Labor

The concept of present value can help clarify what determines the demand-for-labor function in our two-period model. Rather than focusing on the marginal product of labor in each period, an employee's productivity must be summarized by the *present value* of the marginal product schedule, which is drawn as the curve PVP in Figure 5.2. Similarly, rather than focusing on the hiring and training costs and the wage rates in each period separately, an employer must consider the *present value* of the marginal cost of labor (PVC). To

---

20. More generally, if the firm expects to receive benefits of $B_0, B_1, B_2, \ldots, B_n$ dollars over the current and next n periods, and if it faces the same interest rate, r, in each period, its present value of benefits (PVB) is given by

$$PVB = B_0 + \frac{B_1}{1 + r} + \frac{B_2}{(1 + r)^2} + \frac{B_3}{(1 + r)^3} + \cdots + \frac{B_n}{(1 + r)^n}$$

An analogous expression exists for the present value of costs. The reader should make sure that he or she understands why the denominator of B_2 is $(1 + r)^2$, the denominator of B_3 is $(1 + r)^3$, etc. If one thinks in terms of a series of one-period loans or investments, it should become obvious. For example, X_0 invested for one period yields $X_0(1 + r)$ at the end of the period. Let us call $X_0(1 + r) = X_1$. X_0 invested for two periods is equal to its value after one period (X_1) multiplied by $(1 + r)$—or $X_2 = X_1(1 + r)$. But $X_1 = X_0(1 + r)$, so $X_2 = X_0(1 + r)^2$. To find the present value of X_2 we divide by $(1 + r)^2$, so $X_0 = X_2/(1 + r)^2$.

maximize its present value of profits, a firm should employ labor up until the point that adding an *additional* employee yields as much as it costs (when both yields and costs are stated as present values):

$$PVP = PVC, \text{ or } MP_0 + \frac{MP_1}{1 + r} = W_0 + Z + \frac{W_1}{1 + r} \qquad (5.10)$$

Given the particular values of W_0, W_1, Z, and r that are specified in Figure 5.2, this proves to be the employment level E^*. More generally, the employer's labor demand schedule coincides with the present value of the marginal product of labor schedule.

Now, equation (5.10) merely states the familiar profit-maximizing condition, that marginal returns should equal marginal costs, in a multiperiod context. If Z were zero, for example, equation (5.10) implies that profits could be maximized when labor is hired so that $MP_0 = W_0$ and $MP_1/(1 + r) = W_1/(1 + r)$, or, since $1 + r$ is the denominator on both sides of the equation, $MP_1 = W_1$. Thus, when there are no hiring or training costs ($Z = 0$), the conditions demonstrated in Chapter 3 are sufficient to guarantee profit maximization in the multiperiod context. However, when Z is positive, which means that firms make initial investments in their workers, the conditions for maximizing profits change.

To understand the change in profit-maximizing conditions suggested by equation (5.10), suppose that in the initial period the real wage the worker receives (W_0) plus the firm's direct investment outlays (Z) exceed the extra worker's output (MP_0). We can call this difference the *net cost* to the firm of hiring an additional worker in the initial period (NC_0):

$$NC_0 = W_0 + Z - MP_0 > 0 \qquad (5.11)$$

In order for the firm to maximize the present value of its profit stream, it must thus get a net *surplus* in the subsequent period—see equation (5.10). If it does not, the firm will not have any incentive to hire the additional worker.

The discounted value of the subsequent period's surplus (G) is defined as:

$$G = \frac{MP_1}{1 + r} - \frac{W_1}{1 + r} = \frac{MP_1 - W_1}{1 + r} \qquad (5.12)$$

From equations (5.10), (5.11), and (5.12), we see that the discounted value of the subsequent-period surplus must equal the net cost (NC_0) in the initial period if the firm is to maximize profits:

$$W_0 + Z - MP_0 = \frac{MP_1 - W_1}{1 + r} \qquad (5.13)$$

A subsequent-period surplus can exist *only* if real wages in that period (W_1) lie *below* marginal product (MP_1). This surplus makes up for the fact that the employer's labor costs in the initial period ($W_0 + Z$) were above the worker's marginal product (MP_0).

To this point we have established two things. First, equation (5.10) has shown that in a multiperiod model of labor demand, the firm's demand curve is the same as the curve representing the *present value* of labor's marginal product over the periods of hire. Thus, the firm maximizes profits when the present value of its marginal labor costs equals the present value of labor's marginal product. Second, we demonstrated in equation (5.13) that maximizing profits when the firm's labor costs in the initial period exceed the worker's initial-period marginal product requires real wages in the subsequent period to be below marginal productivity in the subsequent period (so that a surplus is generated). The only times when a subsequent-period surplus is not necessary to induce the hiring of an additional employee are when investment costs (Z) are zero in the initial period or when investment costs of Z exist but the initial-period real wage is decreased to such an extent that it equals $MP_0 - Z$. In the latter case, employees pay for their own training by accepting a wage in the initial period that is decreased by the direct costs of training.

Understanding how W_0 and W_1 are determined, then, is central to the task of analyzing the demand for labor in the presence of investment costs. To fully understand the level and time profile of wages we must examine the nature of job training.

Before doing so, however, a fundamental constraint that firms face must be stressed. To obtain any workers, a firm must offer its employees a present value of earnings over their term of employment that is at least as high as can be obtained elsewhere. Letting W^* be the wage they can earn elsewhere (W^* equals their marginal productivity in the absence of training), the ability to attract workers for a two-period term requires that W_0 and W_1 satisfy the following condition:

$$W_0 + \frac{W_1}{1 + r} \geq W^* + \frac{W^*}{1 + r} \tag{5.14}$$

Note that this condition permits W_0 and W_1 to vary from the market wage (W^*) in each period, and the extent to which it varies is a matter of choice to the firm. What is not a matter of choice is the need to offer jobs for which the *present value* of pay over the two periods is equivalent to market levels. Thus, if the firm chooses to pay a very low wage rate (relative to W^*) in the initial period, it must pay a very high wage rate in the subsequent period.

TRAINING INVESTMENTS

In this section we shall consider the types of training a firm will find it profitable to undertake and trace out some important implications of training investments by firms. In the section that follows we shall analyze hiring investments.

General and Specific Training

Following Gary Becker, it is useful to conceptually distinguish between two types of training: *general training* that increases an individual's productivity *to many employers* equally, and *specific training* that increases an individual's productivity *only at the firm* in which he or she is currently employed.[21] Pure

---

21. Gary Becker, *Human Capital,* 2d ed. (New York: National Bureau of Economic Research, 1975).

general training might include teaching an applicant basic reading skills or teaching a would-be secretary how to type and use a word-processing program. Pure specific training might include teaching a worker how to use a machine that is unique to a single employer or showing him or her the organization of the production process in the plant. The distinction is primarily a conceptual one because most training contains aspects of both types; however, the distinction does yield some interesting insights.

Suppose (continuing our two-period model) that a firm offers *general* training to its employees and incurs an initial-period net cost equal to NC_0 of equation (5.11). This training increases employee marginal productivity to MP_1 in the subsequent period, and the firm scales its wages (W_1) in the subsequent period so that there is a surplus in that period whose present value (G) equals NC_0. What will happen? The trained employee is worth MP_1 to several other firms, but is getting paid less than MP_1 by the firm doing the training (so that it can obtain the required surplus). The employee can thus get *more* from some other employer, who did not incur training costs and thus will not demand a surplus, than he or she can get from the employer offering the training. This situation will induce the employee to quit after training and seek work elsewhere (for an illustration of this behavior, refer back to Example 5.1). Assuming all other conditions of employment are the same, the firm would have to pay its employees MP_1 after training to keep them from quitting.

If firms must pay a wage equal to MP_1 after training, they will not be willing to pay for general training of their employees. They either will not offer training or will force trainees to bear the full cost of their training by paying wages that are less than marginal product in the period of training by an amount equal to the direct training costs (that is, NC_0 must equal zero). Exceptions to this conclusion can be found in cases in which the employee is bound to the firm in some way or can otherwise recover its training costs (see Example 5.3). For example, the federal government requires employees it has sent to college (in Master of Business Administration programs, for example) to remain in the federal service for a specified number of years or to repay the costs of the training. Similarly, firms may offer to pay for the general training of long-term employees bound to the firm by pension rights or unique promotion opportunities (see Chapter 11 for further discussion).

In contrast, consider an individual who receives *specific training* that increases marginal productivity with the *current* employer to MP_1 in the subsequent period. Since the training is firm-specific, the trainee's marginal product in *other* firms remains at its pretraining level of MP^*; therefore, the most the employee can obtain elsewhere is W^*. The firm that trains the worker *will* have an incentive to offer (and at least partially pay for) the job training because it can pay a wage above W^* but below MP_1 in the subsequent period.

Why will it pay above W^* in the subsequent period? It will do so because if it makes an initial-period investment in the worker, it does not want the worker to quit. If it pays W^*, the worker will not have much of an incentive to stay with the firm, since he or she can get W^* elsewhere, too. The higher W_1 is compared with W^*, the less likely the worker is to quit. Why will the firm pay

EXAMPLE 5.3

Paying for America's Minor Leagues and Spain's "Stone Quarries"

The lack of employer incentives to pay for employees' general training is a problem that must be addressed by professional sports leagues. Teams often invest huge sums of money in selecting and training players, but the resulting skills can be used with *other* teams as well. If trained players can be bid away by teams with no investment costs to recoup, and if the teams making the investments are not provided with a mechanism for recovering their costs, then such training will clearly be curtailed. How can professional sports leagues be structured to provide the incentives necessary for the major league teams to scout and train players?

A major league baseball team in the United States spends about 4 million dollars each year to scout and train players, over 90 percent of whom never make it to the major leagues. Those who do typically spend four or five years in the minor leagues, with the result that the team's minor league system will "graduate" only two or three players a year to the major league club. Because the major league teams receive none of the minor league revenues, but must pay the salaries of minor league players and instructors, their yearly investment costs must be recouped by paying the few players who make it less than their marginal revenue productivity.

The recovery of scouting and training investments in baseball is facilitated by the "reserve clause," under which a player with less than six years of major league experience is not free to choose the team for which he plays. Only

less than MP_1? As noted earlier, the firm must obtain a surplus in the subsequent period to recoup its initial-period investment costs. Thus, the firm prefers a *subsequent-period* wage that is above W^* and below MP_1:

$$W^* < W_1 < MP_1 \qquad (5.15)$$

This subsequent-period wage is also preferred by employees. If, for example, they were promised a wage equal to MP_1 in the subsequent period, the lack of employer surplus would mean two things. First, employees would be required to pay the *full* cost of training in the initial period, and, second, they would live in fear of being laid off. Since their subsequent-period wage would be equal to their marginal productivity, a firm would not lose much if it laid them off—and *the workers* would lose all the investment costs incurred in the initial period. However, if the workers generated a surplus for the employer, layoff would be less likely in the post-training period.

The wage scheme in equation (5.15) thus suggests that the employer and the employee should be willing to share in the costs of specific training. If employees bear *all* the costs of training, there will be no post-training surplus to protect them from layoff. If employers bear *all* the costs, they may not be able to pay their employees enough in the subsequent period to guard against after six years can he become a "free agent" and obtain offers from other teams. Presumably, the competitive bidding process for free agents results in their salaries being roughly equal to their marginal revenue productivity. (Why?) However, since players with more than three years of major league experience are eligible for salary arbitration, and since these awards often establish pay similar to that received by free agents, players' salaries are probably close to marginal revenue productivity from their fourth year on. Thus, each team really has only three years in which it can pay its players much less than their marginal revenue productivity and thereby recover minor league costs.

In Spain, each professional soccer team also has a network of minor league teams—called its "stone quarry"—in which player development takes place. Unlike American baseball players, Spanish soccer players are free from the very start to change teams once their contracts have expired; in other words, there is no reserve clause in Spanish soccer. To preserve incentives for "major league" soccer teams to develop players, however, Spanish labor law requires that teams acquiring free agents must compensate the team from which the player came for its training and development invest-ments ("*indemnización de preparación y formación*"). This compensation is the subject of negotiation between the two teams, and if agreement cannot be reached, it is then decided by arbitration. This system clearly tries to bal-ance the rights all workers (including professional athletes) have under Spanish labor law to freely choose their employer against the need for teams to recover general training costs if the "stone quarry" system is to survive.*

*Information on the Spanish system was provided to us by a former Cornell graduate student, Miguel Rodriguez-Piñero Royo, from Madrid.

their quitting. It is in their *shared* interest to foster a long-term employment relationship, which can best be done by sharing the investment costs of the initial period.

Implications of the Theory

Layoffs. One major implication of the presence of specific training is the above-mentioned reluctance of firms to lay off workers in whom they have in-vested. We have seen that in the post-training period, wages must be less than marginal productivity if the firm is to have any incentive at all to bear some initial training costs. This gap between MP_1 and W_1 provides protection against employee layoffs, even in a recession.

Suppose a recession were to occur and cause product demand to fall. The marginal productivity associated with each employment level would fall (from MP' to MP'' in Figure 5.3). For workers whose wage was equal to marginal productivity before the recession, this fall would reduce their marginal pro-ductivity to *below* their wage—and profit-maximizing employers would reduce employment, as shown in panel (a) of Figure 5.3, in order to maximize profits under the changed market conditions. In terms of Figure 5.3(a), employment would fall from E' to E''.

For a worker whose wage was *less* than marginal productivity, owing to past specific training, the decline in marginal productivity might *still* leave such productivity *above* the wage. Firms would not be making enough surplus in the post-training period to earn back the net labor costs they incurred during the training period. However, these costs have already been spent and

FIGURE 5.3   The Effect of a Decline in Demand on Employment with General and Specific Training

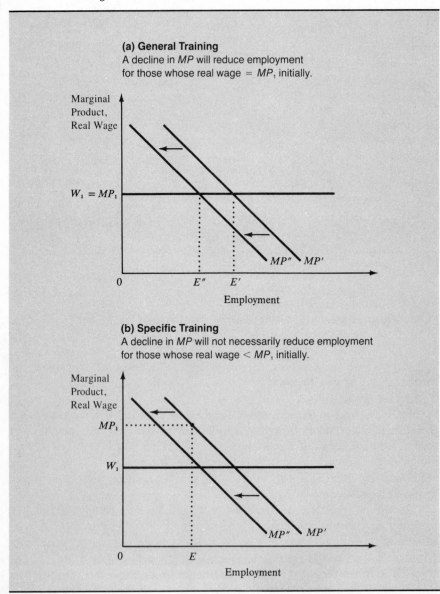

they cannot get them back. They will not hire and train *new* workers, but neither will they fire the ones they have trained. After all, these trained workers are still generating more than the company is paying them, and to lay them off would only reduce profits further. Thus, as panel (b) of Figure 5.3 shows, workers in whom their employers have invested are shielded to some extent from being laid off in business downturns. Of course, if marginal productivity fell to the point where it was below the wage, even trained workers might be laid off.[22]

Thus, this model suggests that during an economic downturn firms have an incentive to lay off workers with either no training or general training, but that it may prove profitable for firms to retain workers who have specific training. Although it is difficult to estimate the extent to which workers have specific training "imbedded" in them, there is some evidence that layoffs are lower for workers with higher skill levels, holding all other things, including their *wage rates,* constant.[23] Since the divergence between skill (productivity) and wages during the post-training period can be taken as a measure of the extent of specific training, this finding provides some support for the theory.

Labor Productivity.   A second phenomenon our revised theory of demand can help explain is the fall in average productivity—output per labor hour—that occurs in the early stages of a recession.[24] As demand and output start to fall, firms that have invested in specific training respond by maintaining their specifically trained workers on their payrolls. Such *labor hoarding* causes measured productivity to fall. Of course, the converse of this is that when demand picks up, firms can increase their output levels without proportionately increasing their employment levels because, in effect, they have maintained an *inventory* of skilled labor. Labor hoarding due to specific investments in human capital thus causes average productivity to increase in the early stages of a cyclical expansion and decrease in the early stages of a recession.

Minimum Wage Effects Again.   A third implication of our theory has to do with training effects of the minimum wage. We have seen that firms will offer *general* training only if the employees fully pay for it. For this to be the case, the employees must receive an initial-period wage that is below actual marginal productivity by an amount equal to the direct costs of training. If the minimum wage is set so that receiving such a low wage is precluded, then employers will not offer them training. They may be willing to *hire* workers, if

---

22. If the downturn is expected to be short and if marginal productivity is not too much below the wage, firms might not lay off workers and chance losing them. Why any adjustment would come in the form of layoff, rather than by temporarily reducing wages or hours of work, is discussed in Chapter 15.
23. For a summary of the evidence, see Donald O. Parsons, "Models of Labor Market Turnover: A Theoretical and Empirical Survey," in *Research in Labor Economics,* vol. 1, ed. Ronald G. Ehrenberg (Greenwich, Conn.: JAI Press, 1977). Parsons also provides evidence on the existence of a negative relationship between quit rates and specific training; as noted earlier, this is another implication of the theory.
24. See the 1977 *Employment and Training Report of the President* (Washington, D.C.: U.S. Government Printing Office, 1977), 23–25.

the minimum wage is not above their marginal productivity, but any training would have to take place off the job.

This same analysis would also hold for *specific* training. If the minimum wage prevented the training-period wage from going low enough, firms offering specific training might *not* be able to offer post-training wages that are higher than workers' alternative offers. If this is the case, trained workers will always be on the verge of quitting in the post-training period, which places the firm's initial-period investment at risk. Under these conditions, firms will have little incentive to offer specific training. Minimum wage legislation may thus reduce the number of jobs offering training options that are available to low-skilled youths and lower their rates of wage growth. In fact, there is some evidence that this has occurred.[25]

HIRING INVESTMENTS

As pointed out earlier, firms often incur significant costs in selecting employees. These costs cause them to establish institutions or behave in ways that can be explained using the concepts we have discussed. The implications of hiring costs are the subject of this section.

Credentials or Screening Devices

Since firms often bear the costs of hiring and training workers, it is in their interest to make these costs as low as possible. Other things equal, firms should prefer to obtain a work force of a given quality at the least possible cost. Similarly, they should prefer to hire workers who are fast learners because such workers could be trained at less cost. Unfortunately, it may prove expensive for firms to extensively investigate the background of every possible individual who applies for a job to ascertain his or her skill level and ability to undertake training.

One way to reduce these costs is to rely on *credentials,* or *signals,* in the hiring process, rather than intensively investigating the qualities of individual applicants.[26] For example, if *on average* college graduates are more productive than high school graduates, an employer might specify that a college degree is a requirement for the job. Rather than interviewing and testing all applicants to try to ascertain the productivity of each, the firm may simply select its new employees from the pool of applicants who meet this educational standard. Similarly, if employers believe that married men are less likely to quit their jobs than single men, or that 25-year-olds are less likely to quit than teenagers, they may want to give preferential treatment to married men and 25-year-olds over single men and teenagers in their hiring decisions.

---

25. Masanori Hashimoto, "Minimum Wage Effects and Training on the Job," *American Economic Review* 72 (December 1982): 1070–87, and Linda Leighton and Jacob Mincer, "Effects of Minimum Wages on Human Capital Formation," in *The Economics of Legal Minimum Wages,* ed. Simon Rottenberg (Washington, D.C.: American Enterprise Institute, 1981), 155–73.

26. See Michael Spence, "Job Market Signaling," *Quarterly Journal of Economics* 87 (August 1973): 355–74. See also Appendix 9A, " 'Signaling' in the Labor Market."

Such forms of *statistical discrimination,* judging individuals by *group* characteristics, have obvious costs. On the one hand, for example, some high school graduates may be fully qualified to work for a firm that insists on college graduates. Excluding them from the pool of potential applicants imposes costs on them (they do not get the job); however, it also imposes costs on the employer *if* other qualified applicants cannot be readily found. On the other hand, there may be some "lemons" among the group of college graduates, and an employer who hires them may well suffer losses while they are employed. However, if the reduction in hiring costs that arises when *signals* (such as educational credentials, marital status, or age) are used is large, it may prove profitable for an employer to use them even if an occasional lemon sneaks through. Put another way, the total costs of hiring, training, and employing workers may well be lower for some firms when hiring standards are used than when such firms rely upon more intensive investigations of applicant characteristics. (Chapter 14 will return to the issue of statistical discrimination.)

Internal Labor Markets

A major problem with the use of credentials, or screening devices, to predict which applicants will become good employees is that these credentials may only be loosely related to actual productivity on the job. Such personal attributes as dependability, motivation, honesty, and flexibility are difficult to observe using credentials, yet for many jobs such attributes may be crucial. This difficulty with screening has induced some firms to adopt a policy of hiring workers at low-level jobs, observing their behavior, and filling all upper-level jobs from within the firm—that is, filling all upper-level vacancies with people whose characteristics have been carefully observed in other jobs the firm has given them to do.

This second approach to the problem of minimizing hiring costs while maximizing the productivity of employees creates an *internal labor market,* because most jobs in the firm are filled from within the ranks of current employees.[27] The hiring done from outside the firm tends to be heavily concentrated at certain low-level "ports of entry." These jobs—such as "general laborer," "machine cleaner," and "packer" for blue-collar applicants or "management trainee" for white-collar applicants—are at sufficiently low responsibility levels that a bad employee cannot do too much damage to the firm or its equipment. However, these jobs do give the firm a chance to observe *actual* productive characteristics of the employees hired, and this information is then used to determine who stays with the firm and how fast and how high employees are promoted.

The *benefits* of using an internal labor market to fill vacancies are that the firm knows a lot about the people working for it. Hiring decisions for upper-

---

27. For a detailed discussion of internal labor markets, see Peter Doeringer and Michael Piore, *Internal Labor Markets and Manpower Analysis* (Lexington, Mass.: D. C. Heath and Co., 1971); Oliver Williamson et al., "Understanding the Employment Relation: The Analysis of Idiosyncratic Exchange," *Bell Journal of Economics* 16 (Spring 1975): 250–80; and Paul Osterman, ed., *Internal Labor Markets* (Cambridge, Mass.: MIT Press, 1984).

level jobs in either the blue-collar or the white-collar work forces will thus offer few surprises to the firm. The *costs* of using the internal labor market are associated with the restriction of competition for the upper-level jobs to those in the firm. Those in the firm may not be the best employees available, but they are the only ones the firm considers for these jobs. Firms most likely to decide that the benefits of using an internal labor market outweigh the costs are those whose upper-level workers must have a lot of firm-specific knowledge and training that can best be attained by on-the-job learning over the years. For those firms, the number of qualified *outside* applicants for upper-level jobs is relatively small. Firms in the steel, petroleum, and chemical industries tend to rely on internal labor markets to fill vacancies, while those in the garment and shoe industries do not.[28] The former group of industries has highly automated, complicated, and interdependent production technologies that can be mastered only through years on the job. The garment- and shoe-manufacturing industries employ workers who perform certain discrete crafts, skills that are not specific to one firm.

As noted earlier, firms engaged in *specific training* will want to ensure that they obtain a stable, long-term work force of employees who can learn quickly and perform well later on. For these firms, the internal labor market offers two attractions. First, it allows the firm to observe workers on the job, where it can see firsthand who learns quickly, who is easily motivated, who is dependable, and so forth, and thus make better decisions about which workers will be the recipients of later, perhaps very expensive, training. Second, the internal labor market tends to foster an attachment to the firm by its employees. They know that they have an inside track on upper-level vacancies because outsiders will not be considered. If they quit the firm, they would lose this privileged position. They are thus motivated to become long-term employees of the firm. The full implications of internal labor markets for wage policies within the firm will be discussed in the chapter on compensation (Chapter 11).

POLICY APPLICATION: WHY DO EMPLOYERS DISCRIMINATE IN HIRING?

It is commonly asserted that older workers and women are not given the same preference as *prime-age* men (men between 25 and 55) in filling many jobs, especially the better-paying ones. While this preference may be rooted in prejudice, there may also be an underlying, nondiscriminatory rationale for it. Chapter 14 will discuss discrimination, but we wish to point out here that what *appears* to be prejudice may be employer behavior designed to avoid losses on hiring and training investments.

To illustrate how the presence of hiring and training costs bears on the issue of apparent age or gender discrimination, let us assume that two people apply for a job for which the employer is intending to make an initial-period investment of Z in hiring and training costs. It is expected that one applicant

---

28. Doeringer and Piore, *Internal Labor Markets and Manpower Analysis,* 43.

EXAMPLE 5.4

Paternalism in Japan—Is It Rooted in Feudalism or Economics?

In Japan there are many large firms in which employer and employee are committed to a virtual lifetime relationship. These firms almost never lay off workers, and employees are given incentives to remain with the firm for their entire careers. Wages are more strongly linked to seniority than in the United States, pensions and paid vacations are formulated to encourage a long job tenure, and company loyalty is encouraged through the provision of "paternalistic services," such as company housing, health care, and recreational facilities.

Some view this lifelong relationship as a natural outgrowth of Japan's feudal system prior to industrial development, with its emphasis on the reciprocal loyalty of lord and vassal:

> The loyalty of the worker to the industrial organization, the paternal methods of motivating and rewarding the worker, the close involvement of the company in all manner of what seem to Western eyes to be personal and private affairs of the worker—all have parallels with Japan's preindustrial social organization.

Advocates of an alternative view of Japan's paternalism argue that the paternalistic system is based more on the need of employers to protect training investments than on feudal tradition. Those who espouse this view argue that Japan's rapid industrialization beginning around 1900 was accompanied by severe shortages of skilled factory workers. Firms competed against each other for skilled labor, and by the end of World War I this fierce competition for workers had led to annual turnover rates of 100 percent for many factories.

Faced with such a high degree of employee turnover, firms did not find it profitable to train their own workers; these workers would be gone before firms could recoup their investment costs. To reduce the need for constant recruiting, and to induce employees to have long enough job attachments to make training feasible, firms began to offer cash bonuses, company-paid pleasure trips, and shares of company profits to long-term workers. Company housing was provided, and firms took an active interest in improving the quality of worker life both on and off the job.

SOURCES: Quotation from James C. Abegglen, *The Japanese Factory: Aspects of Its Social Organization* (Glencoe, Ill.: The Free Press, 1958). The alternative view is in Koji Taira, *Economic Development and the Labor Market in Japan* (New York: Columbia University Press, 1970). Evidence that long-term employment is more prevalent in Japan than in the United States is presented in Masanori Hashimoto and John Raisian, "Employment Tenure and Earnings Profiles in Japan and the United States," *American Economic Review* 75 (September 1985): 721–36. Evidence that on-the-job training is more extensive in Japan than in the United States can be found in Jacob Mincer and Yoshio-Higuchi, "Wage Structures and Labor Turnover in the United States and Japan," *Journal of Japanese and International Economies* 2 (1988): 97–133.

will be with the firm for two periods, while the other will remain for three periods. Which will the firm prefer to hire?

If there were no cost involved in finding and training workers, firms would not care about the length of their tenure. If one worker quit, a replacement could easily be found without cost. When hiring a worker involves an initial investment by the firm, however, employers prefer to hire workers with relatively long expected tenures. The longer an employee is expected to be with the firm, the more likely it is that the firm will recoup its initial investment costs. Thus, if the two applicants in our example were alike in every respect except their expected length of tenure with the firm, the one expected to remain with the firm for three periods would be preferred.

This preference can be demonstrated by referring to equation (5.12). Equation (5.12) calculates the present value of a worker's post-training surplus (G) for a case in which he or she will be employed for just one period after training. To repeat, the present value of the surplus in cases in which there is *one* post-training period, which we shall call G_1, is calculated as:

$$G_1 = \frac{MP_1 - W_1}{1 + r} \tag{5.16}$$

If there are *two* post-training periods of employment, the present value of a firm's surplus is found by adding to G_1 the discounted value of the surplus in the second post-training period. The *undiscounted* surplus in this period is the difference between marginal productivity and wages $(MP_2 - W_2)$. However, because this surplus occurs further into the future than the first post-training period's surplus, it must be more heavily discounted when calculating present value. This is done by dividing $(MP_2 - W_2)$ by $(1 + r)^2$—the rationale for which is given in footnote 20. Thus, the present value of a surplus derived over two periods (G_2) is:

$$G_2 = \frac{MP_1 - W_1}{1 + r} + \frac{MP_2 - W_2}{(1 + r)^2} \tag{5.17}$$

It is obvious, by comparing G_2 and G_1, that the post-training surplus a firm can expect to gain from a worker increases as the expected length of the worker's tenure with the firm goes up, if other things are equal. That is, if the differences between marginal productivity and wages are the same for two workers, the one with the longer tenure will generate more post-training "surplus" for the firm.

Applicants who are very close to retirement will not be seriously considered for jobs that require large employer hiring or training investments (*unless* they accept a low post-training wage). That is, if post-training wages are equal, firms tend to prefer prime-age applicants to equally productive older ones whenever substantial employer hiring or training investments are involved, because the older applicants may retire before the firm can recoup its investment costs. Older workers could redress this imbalance in hiring preferences only by agreeing to work for a lower wage than younger applicants or by paying at least some of the hiring and training costs themselves, conditions that might raise charges of discrimination!

This same reasoning can help explain why women have not had ready access to jobs requiring sizable initial employer investments. Women—or at least *married* women—have tended to enter and leave the labor force more often than men. The result of this movement in and out of the labor force among women is that, for 1983, the average length of job tenure for males was 5.1 years, while the average woman had been on her job for 3.7 years.[29]

The shorter average job tenure among women could legitimately induce employers contemplating hiring and training investments to be wary of investing in female workers. This concern has an understandable economic rationale, but it also offers a good example of what we earlier called *statistical discrimination* (judging individuals by the characteristics of the group to which they belong). In this case, statistical discrimination could have unfortunate consequences for women who *do* plan continuous careers outside the home. For example, single (never-married) women aged 25–34 had about the same average job tenure (2.6 years) as men of that age (2.7 years) in 1978. For single women aged 35–44 the typical length of time on one's current job was 5.7 years, while for men it was only slightly higher (6.9 years). In contrast, the typical married woman worker aged 35–44 had been on her job for only 3.5 years. Thus, women who never marry are much more likely to have job tenures equivalent to those of the typical male worker, but a firm using general hiring standards (such as age and gender) might not make such distinctions.

In summary, two policy-related points can be drawn from this discussion of hiring and training investments. First, employers may have legitimate economic reasons for preferring to hire employees who are expected to have relatively long job tenures *when* there are significant employer hiring or training investments involved. Thus, it is not necessarily maliciousness or prejudice that causes older workers and women to have reduced access to jobs that typically require such investments.

The second point, however, is that individuals within groups vary, and using group averages to estimate an individual's expected tenure may do a disservice to atypical members of the group. We have seen, for example, that women who never marry have much longer job tenures than married women. Taking this fact into account when screening applicants would make hiring decisions more fair to single women, but would probably entail added costs to employers. Firms would have to collect data on their applicants to attempt accurate guesses as to which of their female applicants would remain in the labor force continuously or would never marry.

---

29. Ellen Sehgal, "Occupational Mobility and Job Tenure in 1983," *Monthly Labor Review* 107, no. 10 (October 1984): 18–23. For an earlier study, using 1978 data, see U.S. Bureau of Labor Statistics, *Job Tenure Declines As Work Force Changes,* Special Labor Force Report no. 235 (Washington, D.C.: U.S. Government Printing Office, 1979). In general, the job tenure differences between men and women have been narrowing in recent years.

MISCONCEPTION

"Reducing government subsidies for on-the-job training of ex-convicts will not hurt their employment prospects; a survey has established that the vast majority of all employers do not now hire ex-convicts at all, and most ex-convicts are either unemployed or working in unskilled jobs."

Analysis

While it may be unattractive for most businesses to hire or train most ex-convicts, this statement ignores the fact that firms differ and that some are a lot closer to hiring ex-convicts than others. Put differently, at least a few firms are "at the margin" concerning their hiring of ex-convicts, and these will be responsive to changes in government subsidies. Changes in some incentive may not affect everyone's behavior, but it is wrong to assert that *no one's* behavior will be altered when the change is implemented.

Principle

Changes in the costs and benefits of some activity will affect the behavior of those "at the margin"; they may not result in changed behavior of all actors in the market.

REVIEW QUESTIONS

1. Both low-skilled workers and high-paid college professors have high rates of voluntary quits. What do they have in common that leads to a high quit rate?
2. Wages in the U.S. Postal Service have been attacked for being higher than wages elsewhere for people of the same age and education. The Postal Service answers that it *must* pay higher wages than workers could get elsewhere in order to keep the quit rate below the quit rate in other jobs. Are there circumstances under which this argument has any merit?
3. Suppose the government wants to reduce recidivism of ex-convicts by improving their employment prospects and job stability. Suppose further that the government is considering subsidizing half of employer costs incurred in training ex-convicts for jobs. How will this subsidy affect the job prospects and stability of ex-convicts, assuming ex-convicts are the only group subsidized?
4. As noted in the text, unemployment insurance is financed through a payroll tax levied on the employer. Rather than applying to all earnings, the tax applies only to the first $7,000 to $10,000 per year an employee earns in most states. How would you expect the existence of this low taxable wage base to affect employers' relative demands for skilled and unskilled workers?
5. In presentations to the Democratic and Republican national platform committees, the AFL-CIO proposed the following changes to the Fair Labor Standards Act in 1976:
   a. Raise the federal minimum wage to $3 per hour (the minimum was then less than $3);
   b. Increase overtime pay to double the standard wage (it was then 1½ times the standard);
   c. Reduce the standard workweek to 35 hours per week.

Analyze the effects of these proposals on employment levels (number of employees) and on average weekly hours.

6. A memo from the President to her Council of Economic Advisors states, "It is one of my goals to stimulate, in any way possible, job stability. By this I mean that it seems desirable to create a situation in which workers are less likely to leave their employers, and employers are less likely to lay off workers."

   How would the President's stated goal be affected by the implementation of a policy forbidding employers from using age, race, and gender as hiring standards and instead forcing employers to use more expensive methods of determining who is most suitable for purposes of hiring and training?

7. In recent years there has been discussion of taxing employees for the nonwage benefits they receive. (At present, most benefits—medical and life insurance, for example—are not subject to the personal income tax.) If benefits such as insurance are taxed, they will become less attractive to employees, who may prefer to obtain increases in compensation in the form of wage increases rather than increases in nonwage benefits. Should this happen, what would be the likely effect on hours of work per employee per week?

8. Major league baseball teams scout and hire younger players whom they then train in the minor leagues for a period of three to five years. Very few of their trainees (perhaps 5%) actually make it to the major leagues, but if they do they are bound to the team that owns their contract for a period of six years. After six years, the player can become a "free agent" and choose any major league team on which to play. Keeping in mind that the major league teams pay the costs of, but derive no revenues from, their minor league teams, what would be the most important predictable effects of allowing players to become free agents immediately upon their entry into the major leagues?

9. The government of South Africa has attempted to attract businesses to the resettlement area of Botshabelo by offering various subsidies for firms located in that area. The most notable substantial subsidy is the government's payment of 95 percent of workers' wages up to a wage of $12 a week. Analyze the labor market implications of this wage subsidy for employment and wages, assuming that wages of full-time workers in Botshabelo average $20 per week.

SELECTED READINGS

Becker, Gary. *Human Capital*. 2d ed. New York: National Bureau of Economic Research, 1975.

Doeringer, Peter, and Piore, Michael. *Internal Labor Markets and Manpower Analysis*. Lexington, Mass.: D. C. Heath, 1971.

Ehrenberg, Ronald G., and Schumann, Paul L. *Longer Hours or More Jobs? An Investigation of Amending Hours Legislation to Create Employment*. Ithaca, N.Y.: ILR Press, 1982.

Hart, Robert. *Working Time and Employment*. London: Allen and Unwin, 1986.

Oi, Walter. "Labor as a Quasi-Fixed Factor." *Journal of Political Economy* 70 (December 1962): 538–55.

Osterman, Paul, ed. *Internal Labor Markets*. Cambridge, Mass.: MIT Press, 1984.

Spence, Michael. "Job Market Signaling." *Quarterly Journal of Economics* 87 (August 1973): 355–74.

Williamson, Oliver, et al. "Understanding the Employment Relation: The Analysis of Idiosyncratic Exchange." *Bell Journal of Economics* 16 (Spring 1975): 250–80.

6

Supply of Labor to the Economy: The Decision to Work

This and the next four chapters will focus on issues of *worker* behavior. That is, Chapters 6–10 will discuss and analyze various aspects of *labor supply* behavior. Labor supply decisions can be roughly divided into two categories. The first, which is addressed in this chapter and the next, includes decisions about whether to work at all and, if so, how long to work. Questions that must be answered include whether to participate in the labor force, whether to seek part-time or full-time work, and how long to work both at home and for pay. The second category of decisions, which is addressed in Chapters 8–10, deals with the questions that must be faced by a person who has decided to seek work for pay: the occupation or general class of occupations in which to seek offers (Chapters 8–9) and the geographical area in which offers should be sought (Chapter 10).

This chapter begins with some basic facts concerning labor force participation rates and hours of work and then moves on to analyze decisions to work for pay. This framework is useful for analyzing the structure of income maintenance programs.

TRENDS IN LABOR FORCE PARTICIPATION AND HOURS OF WORK

When a person actively seeks work, he or she is, by definition, in the *labor force*. As pointed out in Chapter 2, the *labor force participation rate* is the percentage of a given population that either has a job or is looking for one. Thus, one clear-cut statistic important in measuring people's willingness to work outside the home is the labor force participation rate.

Perhaps the most revolutionary change taking place in the labor market today is the tremendous increase in the proportion of women, particularly married women, working outside the home. Table 6.1 shows the extraordinary dimensions of this change. As recently as 1950 only 21.6 percent of married women were in the labor force. By 1960 this percentage had risen to 31.9 percent, and by 1988 it had increased to 56.7 percent—over two and a half times what it had been in 1950.

We need not dwell here on the social changes that have been associated with this increasing tendency for women to seek work outside the home. Changes in family income, child-rearing practices, and the family itself are obvious. Less obvious are the effects on the demand for education by females and on the unemployment rate, which will be discussed in Chapters 9, 15, and 16. The longer life span of females is another factor that will affect labor supply and will become an important issue, for example, in funding pension plans (see Chapter 11). Of paramount concern in this chapter are the factors that have influenced this fundamental change in the propensity of women to seek work outside the home.

A second major trend in labor force participation is the decrease in length of careers for males, as can be seen in Table 6.2. The overall labor force participation rate of men has been falling, as was noted in Chapter 2, but the really substantial decreases have been among those over 65—from 68.3 percent in 1900 down to 16.6 percent by 1989. Participation rates for men of "prime age" have declined only slightly, although among 45- to 64-year-olds there were sharp decreases in the 1930s and 1970s. Clearly, men are ending their careers earlier than they were at the beginning of this century.

Other measures reflecting the decisions people make about work are the weekly *hours* of work and the fraction of people who work *part time*—two

TABLE 6.1   Labor Force Participation Rates of Females over 16 Years of Age, by Marital Status, 1900–1988 (percent)

Year	All Females	Single	Widowed, Divorced	Married
1900	20.6	45.9	32.5	5.6
1910	25.5	54.0	34.1	10.7
1920	24.0			9.0
1930	25.3	55.2	34.4	11.7
1940	26.7	53.1	33.7	13.8
1950	29.7	53.6	35.5	21.6
1960	37.7	58.6	41.6	31.9
1970	43.3	56.8	40.3	40.5
1980	51.5	64.4	43.6	49.8
1988	56.6	67.7	46.2	56.7

SOURCES:

1900–1950: Clarence D. Long, *The Labor Force Under Changing Income and Employment* (Princeton: Princeton University Press, 1958), Table A-6.

1960–88: U.S. Department of Labor, Bureau of Labor Statistics, *Handbook of Labor Statistics*, Bulletin 2340 (Washington, D.C.: U.S. Government Printing Office, 1989), Table 6. (The data for 1960–88 are not strictly comparable to those for earlier years because they are derived from a monthly survey, not the decennial census.)

TABLE 6.2   Labor Force Participation Rates for Males, by Age, 1900–1989 (percent)

			Age Groups			
Year	14–19	16–19	20–24	25–44	45–64	Over 65
1900	61.1	—	91.7	96.3	93.3	68.3
1910	56.2	—	91.1	96.6	93.6	58.1
1920	52.6	—	90.9	97.1	93.8	60.1
1930	41.1	—	89.9	97.5	94.1	58.3
1940	34.4	—	88.0	95.0	88.7	41.5
1950	39.9	63.2	82.8	92.8	87.9	41.6
1960	38.1	56.1	86.1	95.2	89.0	30.6
1970	35.8	56.1	80.9	94.4	87.3	25.0
1980	—	60.5	85.9	95.4	82.2	19.1
1989	—	57.9	85.3	94.4	80.2	16.6

SOURCES:

1900–1950: Clarence D. Long, *The Labor Force Under Changing Income and Employment* (Princeton: Princeton University Press, 1958), Table A–2.

1960: U.S. Department of Commerce, Bureau of the Census, *Census of Population, 1960: Employment Status,* Subject Reports PC(2)–6A, Table 1.

1970: U.S. Department of Commerce, Bureau of the Census, *Census of Population, 1970: Employment Status and Work Experience,* Subject Reports PC(2)–6A, Table 1.

1980: U.S. President, *Employment and Training Report of the President, 1981* (Washington, DC: U.S. Government Printing Office, 1980), Table A2, and U.S. Bureau of Labor Statistics, *Handbook of Labor Statistics,* December 1983 (Washington, DC: U.S. Government Printing Office, 1983), Table 4 (this source was used for the rates for 16–19-year olds for 1950–80).

1989: U.S. Bureau of Labor Statistics, *Employment and Earnings* 37 (January 1990), Table 3. (The data for 1980 and 1989 are not strictly comparable to those for earlier years because they are derived from a monthly survey, not the decennial census.)

measures that also exhibit interesting patterns. It is not common for people to think of hours of work as being a *supply* variable that is subject to *employee* choice. After all, don't employers, in responding to the factors discussed in Chapter 5, establish their hours of work? They do, of course, but this does not mean that employees have no choice of, or influence on, working hours. The *weekly* hours of work offered by employers vary to some extent, so in choosing an employer a worker can also choose hours of work.[1] In 1989, 40.1 percent of nonfarm employees worked a 40-hour week, while 19.2 percent worked over 48 hours a week and 16.3 percent worked under 30 hours a week. Interestingly, diversity in the weekly work schedules among which employees can choose seems to be growing.[2] Moreover, even firms with the standard 40-hour workweek may offer different *yearly* hours of work because of different absenteeism, vacation, and holiday policies. Finally, *occupational* choice has a working-hours dimension. The weekly or yearly hours of work are different if one chooses to become a teacher rather than an accountant, a retail clerk rather than a traveling sales representative, or a Wall Street lawyer rather than a small-town lawyer.

---

1. Recent papers emphasizing the limitations on choices facing workers include William T. Dickens and Shelly Lundberg, "Hours Restrictions and Labor Supply," Working Paper no. 1638, National Bureau of Economic Research, June 1985, and Shulamit Kahn and Kevin Lang, "The Effects of Hours Constraints on Labor Supply Estimates," Working Paper no. 2647, National Bureau of Economic Research, July 1988.

2. U.S. Department of Labor, *Employment and Earnings* 37 (January 1990): 198.

Thus, by choosing their employment, workers can exercise some direct influence on their hours of work; however, most of the short-run changes in hours worked seem to emanate from the *demand* side of the market.[3] Forces on the *supply* side of the market are more prominent in explaining long-run trends in hours worked, because the birth of new firms, the introduction of new technologies and products, and the need for employers to attract new employees all ensure a more malleable, less rigid environment in the long run. If employees receiving an hourly wage of $X for 40 hours per week really wanted to work only 30 hours at $X per hour, some enterprising employer would eventually seize on their dissatisfaction and offer jobs with 30-hour weeks—ending up with a more satisfied work force in the process. Thus, the theory of labor supply is of most use in understanding long-term influences on hours worked.

Table 6.3 displays the historical change in *actual* weekly hours of work in this century after correcting for the fact that these hours tend to rise in prosperity and fall in recessions.[4] What the table shows is that weekly hours fell steadily until the 1940s, but since then have more or less stabilized. Overall, the typical manufacturing worker has 16 more hours of leisure each week than he or she had in 1901—virtually an entire waking day. Yet perhaps equally worth emphasizing is that almost all of this change came in the first 45 years of this century, much of it in the first 30 years when unions and federal legislation could not have exerted much influence. A complete explanation for this must include an analysis of factors influencing both the demand for and the supply of weekly hours per worker. The supply factors are considered in this chapter, while the demand-side influences were treated in Chapter 5.

Table 6.4 contains data on the percentage of workers who work part time voluntarily. The table clearly shows that teenagers are more likely to work part time than adults, and that among adults women choose to work part time more often than men. Trends in the propensity to choose part-time work are consistent with the labor force participation trends noted above. Specifically, as adult women increasingly work full time they are choosing to work part time less often, while teenagers (perhaps because of increased schooling) and adult men exhibit faint tendencies toward increasing part-time employment.

Because labor is the most abundant factor of production, it is fair to say that this country's well-being in the long run is heavily dependent on the willingness of its people to work. As we shall demonstrate, leisure and other ways of spending time that do not involve work for pay are also important in generating well-being; however, our economy relies heavily on goods and services

---

3. See, for example, Joseph G. Altonji and Christina H. Paxton, "Job Characteristics and Hours of Work," *Research in Labor Economics* 8 (1986); Orley Ashenfelter, "Macroeconomic Analyses and Microeconomic Analyses of Labor Supply," *Carnegie-Rochester Conference Series on Public Policy* 21 (1984): 117–56; and John C. Ham, "On the Interpretation of Unemployment in Empirical Labour Supply Analysis," in *Unemployment, Search and Labour Supply,* ed. Richard Blundell and Ian Walker (Cambridge, Eng.: Cambridge University Press, 1986), 121–42. Altonji and Paxton show, for example, that hours of work fluctuate much more over time for individuals who change employers than they do for individuals who remain with the same employer.

4. Chapter 2 noted, when defining wages and employee benefits, that hours of *actual* work and hours for which an employee is *paid* are two different things. Since World War II, *paid* hours of work have been greater than *actual* hours of work because of the growing prevalence of paid holidays and paid vacations.

TABLE 6.3   Average Weekly Hours Actually Worked by Manufacturing Production Workers During the Peak Employment Years in Each Business Cycle, 1900–1979 (excluding 1940–45)

	Average Hours Worked	Average per Decade Decline in Hours Worked
1901	54.3	
1906	55.0	
1913	50.9	
1919	46.1	2.2
1923	48.9	
1926	47.8	
1929	48.0	4.6
1948	38.8	
1953	38.6	
1956	38.2	0.4
1969	38.3	
1973	38.0	
1979	37.5	

SOURCE: The data for 1901–1956 were taken from Ethel Jones, "New Estimates of Hours of Work Per Week and Hourly Earnings, 1900–1957," *Review of Economics and Statistics* 45 (November 1963): 374–85. Data for 1969–79 were calculated from the *Annual Survey of Manufacturers,* which contains worker hours actually worked (exclusive of vacations, sick leave, and holidays). The table ends with 1979, because as of 1990 it was unclear whether another cyclical employment peak had yet been reached.

produced for market transactions. Therefore, it is important to understand the *work-incentive* effects of higher wages and incomes, different kinds of taxes, and various forms of income maintenance programs.

The question of work incentives, for example, will become critically important as our population—through longer life spans and a declining birthrate—gradually becomes older. When this happens, there will be a period when the support of a large number of retirees will rest on a relatively small number of people of working age. Their ability to assume this financial burden and still maintain current standards of living obviously depends on the age at which older people retire and the percentage of the working-age population in the labor force.

TABLE 6.4   Percentages of Nonagricultural Employee Groups in Voluntary Part-Time Status, Selected Years

	All Workers	Male Workers, Age 20+	Female Workers, Age 20+	Both Sexes, Age 16–19
1965	10.6	—	—	—
1970	13.3	4.1	20.8	47.3
1975	13.8	4.4	20.7	46.7
1980	13.9	4.7	19.7	47.6
1985	13.3	4.7	18.6	50.7
1989	13.8	5.1	18.8	54.7

Note: A part-time worker is one who works between 1 and 34 hours per week. Voluntary part-timers are those who work part time because of family or school responsibilities.
SOURCE: U.S. Department of Labor, *Employment and Earnings,* various issues.

A THEORY OF THE DECISION TO WORK

The decision to work is ultimately a decision about how to spend time. One way to use one's available time is to spend it in pleasurable leisure activities. The other major way in which people use time is to work.[5] One can work around the home, performing such *household production* as raising children, sewing, building, or even growing food. Alternatively, one can work for pay and use one's earnings to purchase food, shelter, clothing, and child care.

Because working for pay and engaging in household production are two ways of getting the same jobs done, we shall initially ignore the distinction between them and treat work activities as working for pay. We shall therefore be characterizing the decision to work as a choice between leisure and working for pay. Most of the crucial factors affecting work incentives can be understood in this context, but insight into labor supply behavior can be enriched by a consideration of household production as well; this we do in Chapter 7.

If we regard the time spent eating, sleeping, and otherwise maintaining ourselves as more or less fixed by natural laws, then the discretionary time we have (16 hours a day, say) can be allocated to either work or leisure. Since the amount of discretionary time spent on leisure is time not spent on working, and vice versa, the *demand for leisure* can be considered the reverse side of the coin labeled *supply of labor*. It is actually more convenient to analyze work incentives in the context of the demand for leisure, because one can apply the standard analysis of the demand for any good to the demand for leisure, and then simply subtract leisure hours from total discretionary hours available to obtain the *labor supply* effects.

A Verbal Analysis of the Labor/Leisure Choice

Since we have chosen to analyze work incentives in the context of the demand for leisure, it is instructive to briefly consider the factors that affect the demand for any good. Basically, the demand for a good is a function of three factors:

1. The *opportunity cost* of the good (which is often equal to *market price*),
2. One's level of *wealth*, and
3. One's set of *preferences*.

For example, consumption of heating oil will vary with the *cost* of such oil; as that cost rises, consumption tends to fall unless one of the other two factors intervenes. As *wealth* rises, people generally want larger and warmer houses that obviously require more oil to heat.[6] Even if the price of energy and the level of personal wealth were to remain constant, the demand for energy could rise if a falling birthrate and lengthened life span resulted in a higher

---

5. Another category of activity is to spend time acquiring skills or doing other things that enhance one's future earning capacity. These activities will be discussed in Chapters 9 and 10.
6. When the demand for a good rises with wealth, economists say the good is a *normal good*. If demand falls as wealth rises, the good is said to be an *inferior good* (traveling or commuting by bus is sometimes cited as an example of an inferior good).

proportion of the population being aged and therefore wanting warmer houses. This change in the composition of the population amounts to a shift in the overall *preferences* for warmer houses and thus leads to a change in the demand for heating oil.

To summarize, the demand (D) for a "normal good" (see footnote 6) can be characterized as a function of opportunity costs (C) and wealth (V):

$$D = f(\bar{C}, \overset{+}{V}) \tag{6.1}$$

where f—the particular relationship between demand and the variables C and V for an individual—depends on preferences. The notation above C and V indicates the direction in which the demand for a good is expected to go when the variable in question *increases, holding the other one constant.* The demand would move in the opposite direction if C or V were to decrease.

Note: Economists usually assume that preferences are given and are not subject to immediate change. For policy purposes, the changes in C and V, not changes in the function f, are of paramount interest to us in explaining changes in demand because C and V are more susceptible to change by government policy. For the most part, we shall assume preferences are *given* and *fixed* at any point in time.[7]

To apply this general analysis of demand to the demand for leisure, we must first ask, "What is the opportunity cost of leisure?" The cost of spending an hour watching television is basically what one could earn if one had spent that hour working. Thus, the opportunity cost of an hour of leisure is very closely related to one's *wage rate*—so closely related, in fact, that to simplify the analysis we shall say that leisure's opportunity cost *is* the wage rate.[8]

Next, we must understand and be able to measure wealth. Naturally, wealth includes a family's holdings of bank accounts, financial investments, and physical property. Workers' skills can also be considered assets, since these skills can be, in effect, rented out to employers for a price. The more one can get in wages, the larger is the value of one's human assets. Unfortunately, it is not usually possible to directly measure people's wealth. It is much easier to measure the *returns* from that wealth, because data on total *income* are readily available from government surveys. Economists thus often use total income as an indicator of total wealth, since the two are conceptually so closely related.[9]

---

7. On occasion the government attempts to influence consumption patterns of people by changing preferences rather than prices. For example, rather than raising cigarette taxes to discourage cigarette consumption, the federal government in the 1970s prohibited cigarette manufacturers from advertising on television and even sponsored radio and television campaigns against smoking. The effectiveness of these attempts to change preferences is difficult to assess.

8. This assumes that individuals can work as many hours as they want at a fixed wage rate. While this assumption may seem overly simplistic, it will not lead to wrong conclusions with respect to the issues analyzed in this chapter. More rigorously, it should be said that leisure's *marginal* opportunity cost is the *marginal* wage rate (the wage one could receive for an extra hour of work).

9. The best indicator of wealth is one's *permanent*, or long-run potential, *income.* One's current income may differ from one's permanent income for a variety of reasons (unemployment, illness, unusually large amounts of overtime work, etc.). For our purposes here, however, the distinction between current and permanent income is not too important.

If we replace the general demand function in equation (6.1) with the *demand for leisure function,* it would become equation (6.2) if leisure were a normal good:

$$D_L = f(\bar{W}, \overset{+}{Y})\tag{6.2}$$

where D_L is the demand for leisure hours, W is the wage rate, Y is total income, and f (as before) depends on preferences people have for leisure independent of W and Y. The signs over W and Y indicate what happens to the demand for leisure if the variable in question increases, holding the other variable constant.

If income increases, holding wages (and f) constant, equation (6.2) asserts that the demand for leisure goes up. Put differently, *if income increases, holding wages constant, desired hours of work will go down.* (Conversely, if income is reduced while the wage rate is held constant, desired hours of work will go up.) Economists call the response of desired hours of leisure to changes in income, with wages held constant, the *income effect.* The income effect is based on the simple notion that as incomes rise, holding leisure's opportunity cost constant, people will want to consume more leisure (which means working less).

Because we have assumed that time is spent either in leisure or in working for pay, the income effect can be expressed in terms of the *supply of working hours* as well as the demand for leisure hours. Because the ultimate focus of this chapter is labor supply, we choose to express this effect in the context of supply.

Using algebraic notation, we define the income effect as the change in hours of work (ΔH) produced by a change in income (ΔY), holding wages constant ($\overline{W}$):

$$\text{Income Effect} = \left.\frac{\Delta H}{\Delta Y}\right|_{\overline{W}} < 0\tag{6.3}$$

We say the income effect is *negative* because the *sign* of the *fraction* in equation (6.3) is *negative.* If income goes up (wages held constant), hours of work fall. If income goes down, hours of work increase. The numerator (ΔH) and denominator (ΔY) in equation (6.3) move in opposite directions, giving a negative sign to the income effect.

Equation (6.2) also suggests that *if income is held constant, an increase in the wage rate will reduce the demand for leisure, thereby increasing work incentives.* (Likewise, a decrease in the wage rate will reduce leisure's opportunity cost and the incentives to work, holding income constant.) This *substitution effect* occurs because as the cost of leisure changes, income held constant, leisure and work hours are substituted for each other.

In contrast to the income effect, the substitution effect is *positive.* Because this effect is the change in hours of work (ΔH) induced by a change in the wage (ΔW), holding income constant ($\overline{Y}$), the substitution effect can be written as:

$$\text{Substitution Effect} = \left.\frac{\Delta H}{\Delta W}\right|_{\overline{Y}} > 0\tag{6.4}$$

Because numerator (ΔH) and denominator (ΔW) always move in the same direction, at least in theory, the substitution effect has a positive sign.

At times it is possible to observe situations or programs that create pure income or pure substitution effects. Usually, however, both effects are simultaneously present, often working against each other.

A "Pure" Income Effect. Winning a state lottery is an example of the income effect by itself. The winnings enhance one's wealth (income) *independent* of the hours of work. Thus, income is increased *without* a change in the compensation received from an hour of work. In this case, the income effect induces the person to consume more leisure, thereby reducing the willingness to work. (If the change in nonlabor income were *negative,* on the other hand, the income effect suggests that people would work *more.*)

A "Pure" Substitution Effect. In the 1980 Presidential campaign, candidate John Anderson proposed a program aimed at conserving gasoline. His plan consisted of raising the gasoline tax but offsetting this increase by a reduced Social Security tax payable by individuals on their earnings. The idea was to raise the price of gasoline without reducing people's overall spendable income.

For our purposes, this plan is interesting because it creates a pure substitution effect on labor supply. Social Security revenues are collected by a tax on earnings, so reductions in the tax are, in effect, increases in the wage rate.[10] For the average person, however, the increased wealth associated with this wage increase is exactly offset by increases in the gasoline tax.[11] Hence, wages are increased while income is held more or less constant. This program would thus create a substitution effect that induces people to work more hours.

Both Effects Occur When Wages Rise. While the above examples illustrate situations in which the income or the substitution effect is present by itself, normally both effects are present, often working in opposite directions. The presence of both effects working in opposite directions creates ambiguity in predicting the overall labor supply response in many cases. Consider the case of a person who receives a wage increase.

The labor supply response to a simple wage change will involve *both* an income effect and a substitution effect. The *income effect* is the result of the worker's enhanced wealth (or potential income) after the increase. For a given level of work effort, he or she now has a greater command over resources than before (because more income is received for any given number of hours

---

10. Social Security taxes are levied on yearly earnings up to some maximum—$51,300 in 1990. Once that maximum level is reached within a year, no more Social Security taxes are paid. People whose yearly earnings exceed the base experience no change in the marginal opportunity cost of leisure because an additional hour of work per year is not subject to Social Security taxes anyway. However, the marginal opportunity cost of leisure would be increased for many, if not most, workers.

11. An increase in the price of gasoline will reduce the income people have left for expenditures on nongasoline consumption only if the demand for gasoline is inelastic. In this case, the percentage reduction in gasoline consumption is smaller than the percentage increase in price: total expenditures on gasoline would thus rise. Our analysis assumes this to be the case.

of work). The *substitution effect* results from the fact that the wage increase raises the opportunity costs of leisure. Because the actual labor supply response is the *sum* of the income and substitution effects, we cannot predict the response in advance; theory simply does not tell us which effect is stronger.

EXAMPLE 6.1
Incentives and Absenteeism

Absenteeism is a serious problem for employers because absent employees may cause disruptions in a firm's operations. Employees may be absent either because of serious illnesses or personal problems (e.g., a death in the family) that prevent them from coming to work, because of more minor illnesses or personal problems (when they have some discretion about whether to come to work), or because some days they simply feel like consuming additional leisure time. Can the economic theory of labor supply help explain the latter two types of absences and thus the patterns of absenteeism we observe in the economy?

As documented in Chapter 5, employee benefits form a large proportion of total compensation. In some cases, these benefits have included paid sick leave, which serves as an obvious inducement for a certain amount of absenteeism. Because workers can call in sick for a specified number of days per year without losing any pay, it is not surprising that studies of absenteeism among public school teachers find that it is greater in districts with more generous paid sick-leave provisions.

However, benefits frequently contain incentives for greater absenteeism independent of paid sick leave. An absence often causes a worker to lose his or her daily wage, but the value of many employee benefits, such as health insurance or holiday pay, is invariant with respect to an absence. Thus, when additional compensation is paid in the form of employee benefits rather than wages, an *income effect* on the demand for leisure is created *without a corresponding substitution effect*.

The increased use of benefits has had a possibly profound effect on the incentive to come to work on days when one is feeling slightly ill, needs a "break," or has a personal problem. The increased compensation that has accompanied economic growth tends to induce greater consumption of all normal goods, including leisure; however, to the extent that employee benefits are increased instead of wages, the price of leisure is not raised. Thus, the changing structure of compensation suggests that relatively stronger income effects, and correspondingly weaker substitution effects, on the demand for leisure have been accompanying economic growth in recent years.

Absenteeism is one way leisure is consumed. As such, it is not surprising that studies find that absenteeism appears to be higher when compensation packages are weighted toward employee benefits rather than wages.

SOURCES: Donald Winkler, "The Effects of Sick-Leave Policy on Teacher Absenteeism," *Industrial and Labor Relations Review* 33 (January 1980): 232–40; Ronald G. Ehrenberg et al., "School District Leave Policies, Teacher Absenteeism, and Student Achievement," *Journal of Human Resources* (forthcoming); Steven G. Allen, "Compensation, Safety and Absenteeism: Evidence from the Paper Industry," *Industrial and Labor Relations Review* 34 (January 1981): 207–18.

If the *income* effect is dominant, the person will respond to a wage increase by decreasing his or her labor supply. This decrease will be *smaller* than if the same change in wealth were due to an increase in *nonlabor* wealth, because the substitution effect is present and acts as a moderating influence. However, when the *income* effect dominates, the substitution effect is not large enough to prevent labor supply from *declining*. It is entirely plausible, of course, that the *substitution* effect will dominate. If so, the actual response to wage increases will be to *increase* labor supply.

Should the substitution effect dominate, the person's labor supply curve—relating, say, desired hours of work to wages—will be *positively sloped*. That is, labor supply will increase with the wage rate. If, on the other hand, the income effect dominates, the labor supply curve will be *negatively sloped*. Economic theory cannot say which effect will dominate, and in fact individual labor supply curves could be positively sloped in some ranges of the wage and negatively sloped in others. In Figure 6.1, for example, the person's desired hours of work increase (substitution effect dominates) when wages go up as long as wages are low (below W^*). However, at higher wages, further increases result in reduced hours of work (the income effect dominates); economists refer to such a curve as "backward-bending."

While economic theory is unable to predict whether the income or the substitution effect will dominate in an individual's labor supply curve, it can bring some useful insights to bear on important policy issues. The work-incentive effect of the personal income tax is an important case in point.

Tax Rate Cuts and "Supply-Side" Economics. The election of Ronald Reagan as President in 1980 brought to power an administration persuaded that high rates of inflation (that is, rising prices) and lagging labor productivity could be at least partially overcome by cutting taxes in such a way that investment and work effort would be stimulated. The use of tax rate cuts and tax-related investment incentives to drive *actual output* up to its potential has

FIGURE 6.1 An Individual Labor Supply Curve Can Bend Backwards

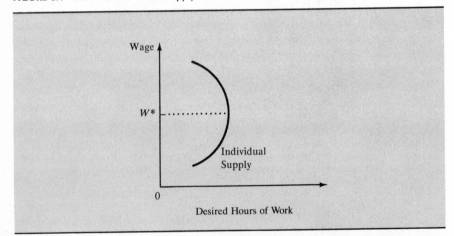

long been accepted by many economists and policymakers as a technique for overcoming recessionary forces.[12] However, the use of tax rate cuts to stimulate the growth of *potential output* is central to what has come to be called supply-side economics. An important element of the supply-side strategy proposed by President Reagan was to make large across-the-board cuts in personal income tax rates in the belief that such cuts would, among other things, increase the incentive of people to work:

> According to supply-siders, large tax rate cuts would cause an increase in investment and work effort that would reduce fundamental inflationary pressures.[13]

Is the belief of supply-siders that income tax rate cuts will increase work effort theoretically sound? Suppose, first, that Congress were to lower the income tax rates of lower-income workers but not cut the level of government services provided for this group. A decrease in their income tax rates would be equivalent to an increase in wages, because the workers would take home more income for each hour of work. This wage increase would generate an income and substitution effect, and theoretical reasoning alone cannot predict which effect will dominate. If the substitution effect dominated, labor supply would increase; if the income effect were dominant, the tax cuts would be accompanied by a *fall* in labor supply! The issue is ultimately an empirical question.[14]

The supply-siders who claim that reducing income tax rates increases work incentives have a valid point, however, when one considers *general* income tax rate reductions. Let us examine, for example, how a general 10 percent reduction in income tax rates might be handled. While a cut in tax rates would, of course, increase workers' wage rates, it would have the *initial* effect of reducing by 10 percent the revenues available to government. Unless the government were trying to combat a recession and accompanying unemployment, it might respond to reduced revenues by cutting back on various services it formerly provided: mail delivery on Saturday, educational subsidies, and road construction funds, for example. Thus, while *wages* would be increased, real income would be held more or less constant by the cut in government services. Workers would have more take-home income but fewer government-provided services.[15] There would be a substitution effect but no overall

---

12. A recession is said to occur when *actual* national output declines, thereby falling below potential output. A recession is accompanied by resource unemployment of both labor and capital. A widely (though not universally) accepted technique for ending a recession is for the government to spend more than it collects in taxes.
13. "Reagan's Top Problem: Braking Inflationary Expectations," *Business Week,* December 1, 1980, 110. In the summer of 1981 Congress voted to cut taxes 25 percent over 3 years and to adjust tax brackets for inflation thereafter. In 1986, Congress adopted several other changes in the income tax code, with a primary focus on further reducing tax rates.
14. Later this chapter will show that the income effect may dominate for men but not for married women.
15. One alternative to cutting services, at least initially, is to borrow money. However, borrowing from banks increases the money supply, and this would tend to be inflationary in the absence of resource unemployment associated with a recession. A rise in *prices* would lower the real wage and mitigate any substitution effects (if before-tax money wages remained constant).

FIGURE 6.2   The Aggregate Labor Supply Curve Is Upward-Sloping at a Point in Time

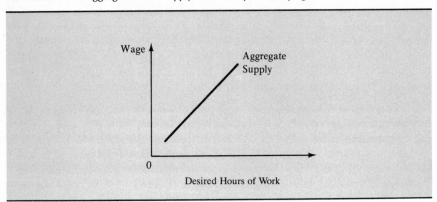

income effect, and the aggregate labor supply curve would be upward-sloping, as shown in Figure 6.2.[16]

In 1986 Congress passed further tax legislation that served to lower tax rates on individuals while eliminating certain deductions and raising corporate taxes enough to maintain the same tax revenue (hence holding workers' real incomes constant).[17] The empirical significance of any resulting substitution effects have yet to be determined, but evidence cited later in this chapter suggests such effects will probably be greater for women than men.

A Graphic Analysis of the Labor/Leisure Choice: The Fundamentals

This section introduces indifference curves and budget constraints—material that may already be familiar to students with a background in these fundamentals. Graphic analysis requires a level of rigor that is more convincing

---

16. This point is also made in James Gwartney and Richard Stroup, "Labor Supply and Tax Rates: A Correction of the Record," *American Economic Review* 73 (June 1983): 446–56. However, the fact that some groups in the population may be more affected by spending cuts than others, despite the overall constancy of real income, leads to the possibility that an overall income effect may indeed exist. See David M. Betson and David Greenberg, "Labor Supply and Tax Rates: Comment," *American Economic Review* 76 (June 1986): 551–56. However, the essential point still stands: income effects from the tax cut will tend to be offset by income effects associated with the spending cuts.

17. The increase in labor supply caused by the tax cut would serve to increase people's money incomes and reduce their consumption of leisure. Some of the increased earnings would be spent on goods or services, and some would go to the government in the form of taxes. However, whether the increased goods or services are provided privately or by the government, the happiness they generate is offset by the reduced consumption of leisure time. In the short run, then, increased goods and services are offset by reduced consumption of leisure, leaving workers' real incomes approximately constant.

  In the *long run,* however, real national wealth could be increased *if* the increase in goods and services were channeled into *investment* activities and not immediately consumed. Wage increases that accompany the growth of national wealth *do* generate income effects. However, real national welfare could be increased *only* in the long run and only if current investments were to increase.

than verbal analysis and incorporates visual aids that make the analysis easier to understand. The graphic analysis here, however, is simply a more rigorous, visible repetition of our verbal analysis; hence, none of the conclusions or definitions reached above will be changed in any way.

Preferences.   Let us assume that there are two major categories of goods that make people happy—leisure and money income (which can, of course, be used to buy other goods). Collapsing all goods into two categories allows our graphs to be drawn in two-dimensional space.

Since both leisure and money can be used to generate satisfaction (or *utility*), these two goods are to some extent substitutes for each other. If one were forced to give up some money income—by cutting back one's hours of work, for example—there would be some increase in leisure time that could be substituted for this lost income to keep the person as happy as before. A very thoughtful consumer/worker, in fact, could reveal a whole *variety* of combinations of money income and leisure hours that would yield him or her this same level of satisfaction.

To understand how preferences can be graphed, suppose a thoughtful consumer/worker were asked to decide how happy he or she would be with a daily income of $64 combined with 8 hours of leisure (point *a* in Figure 6.3). This level of happiness could be called utility level *A*. Our consumer/worker could name *other combinations* of money income and leisure hours that would *also* yield utility level *A*. Assume that our respondent named five other combinations. All six combinations of money income and leisure hours that yield utility level *A* are represented by heavy dots in Figure 6.3. The curve connecting these dots is called an *indifference curve,* a curve connecting the various combinations of money income and leisure that yield equal utility. (The term *indifference curve* is derived from the fact that, since each point on the curve yields equal utility, a person is truly indifferent about where on the curve he or she will be.)

Our worker/consumer could no doubt achieve a higher level of happiness if he or she could combine the 8 hours of leisure with an income of $100 per day, instead of just $64 a day. This higher satisfaction level could be called utility level *B*. The consumer could name other combinations of money income and leisure that would also yield *this* higher level of utility. These combinations are denoted by the *X*s in Figure 6.3 that are connected by a second indifference curve.

Indifference curves have certain specific characteristics that are reflected in the way they are drawn:

1. Utility level *B* represents more happiness than level *A*. Every level of leisure consumption is combined with a higher income on *B* than on *A*. Hence our respondent prefers all points on indifference curve *B* to any point on curve *A*. A whole *set* of indifference curves could be drawn for this one person, each representing a different utility level. Any such curve that lies to the northeast of another one is preferred to any curve to the southwest because the northeastern curve represents a higher level of utility.

FIGURE 6.3 Two Indifference Curves for the Same Person

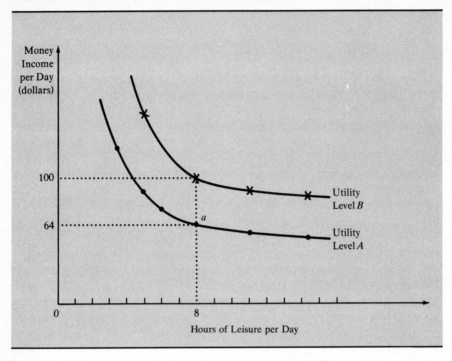

2. Indifference curves *do not intersect.* If they did, the point of intersection would represent *one* combination of money income and leisure that yielded *two* different levels of satisfaction. We assume our worker/consumer is *not* so inconsistent in stating his or her preferences that this could happen.

3. Indifference curves are *negatively sloped,* because if either income or leisure hours are increased, the other is reduced in order to preserve the same level of utility. If the slope is steep, as at segment *LK* in Figure 6.4, a given loss of income need not be accompanied by a large increase in leisure hours in order to keep utility constant.[18] When the curve is relatively flat, as at segment *MN* in Figure 6.4, a given decrease in income must be accompanied by a large increase in the consumption of leisure to hold utility constant. Thus, when indifference curves are relatively steep, people do not value money income as highly as when such curves are relatively flat; when they are flat, a loss of income can only be compensated for by a large increase in leisure if utility is to be kept constant.

4. Indifference curves are *convex*—steeper at the left than at the right. This shape reflects the assumption that when money income is rela-

---

18. Economists call the change in money income needed to hold utility constant when leisure hours are changed by one unit the *marginal rate of substitution* between leisure and money income. This marginal rate of substitution can be graphically understood as the slope of the indifference curve at any point. At point *L*, for example, the slope is relatively steep, so economists would say that the marginal rate of substitution at point *L* is relatively high.

FIGURE 6.4   An Indifference Curve

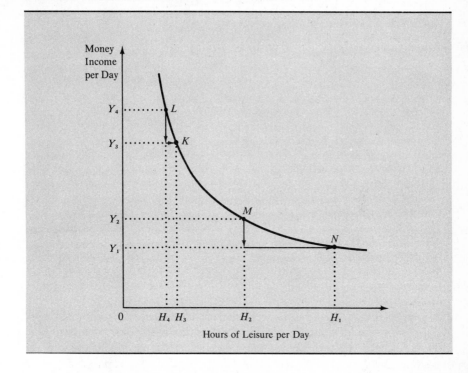

Hours of Leisure per Day

tively high and leisure hours are relatively few, leisure is more highly valued than when leisure is abundant and income relatively scarce. At segment LK in Figure 6.4, a great loss of income (from Y_4 to Y_3, for example) can be compensated for by just a little increase in leisure, whereas a little loss of leisure time (from H_3 to H_4, for example) would require a relatively large increase in income to maintain equal utility. What is relatively scarce is more highly valued.

Conversely, when income is low and leisure is abundant (segment MN in Figure 6.4), income is more highly valued. Losing income (by moving from Y_2 to Y_1, for example) requires a huge increase in leisure for utility to remain constant. To repeat, what is relatively scarce is assumed to be more highly valued.

5. Finally, different people have different sets of indifference curves. The curves drawn in Figures 6.3 and 6.4 were for *one person*. Another person would have a completely different set of curves. People who value leisure more highly, for example, would have had indifference curves that were generally steeper (see Figure 6.5a). People who do not value leisure highly would have relatively flat curves (see Figure 6.5b).[19] Thus, individual preferences can be portrayed graphically.

---

19. The two curves shown in Figure 6.5 should be compared in *slope* only. Levels of utility for two people cannot be compared, because happiness is not objectively measurable. Figure 6.5 simply shows that people with different preferences have indifference curves with different *slopes*.

FIGURE 6.5 Indifference Curves for Two Different People

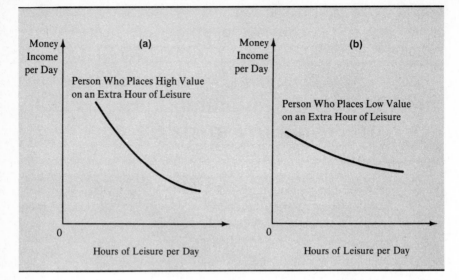

Income and Wage Constraints. Now, everyone would like to maximize his or her utility, which would be ideally done by consuming every available hour of leisure combined with the highest conceivable income. Unfortunately, the resources anyone can command are limited. Thus, all that is possible is to do the best one can, given limited resources. To see these resource limitations graphically requires superimposing constraints on one's set of indifference curves to see which combinations of income and leisure are available and which are not.

Suppose the person whose indifference curves are graphed in Figure 6.3 had no source of income other than labor earnings. Suppose, further, that he or she could earn $8 per hour. Figure 6.6 includes the two indifference curves shown in Figure 6.3 as well as a straight line (*DE*) connecting combinations of leisure and income that are possible for a person with an $8 wage and no outside income. If 16 hours per day are available for work and leisure and if this person consumes all 16 in leisure, then money income will be zero (point *D* in Figure 6.6). If 8 hours a day are devoted to work, income will be $64 per day (point *M*), and if 16 hours a day are worked, income will be $128 per day (point *E*). Other points on this line—for example, the point of 15 hours of leisure (1 hour of work) and $8 of income—are also possible. This line, which reflects the combinations of leisure and income that are possible for the individual, is called the *budget constraint.* Any combination to the right of the budget constraint is not achievable; the person's command over resources simply is not sufficient to attain these combinations of leisure and money income.

The *slope* of the budget constraint is a graphic representation of the wage rate. One's wage rate is properly defined as the increment in income (ΔY) derived from an increment in hours of work (ΔH):

$$\text{Wage Rate} = \frac{\Delta Y}{\Delta H} \qquad (6.5)$$

FIGURE 6.6 Indifference Curves and Budget Constraint

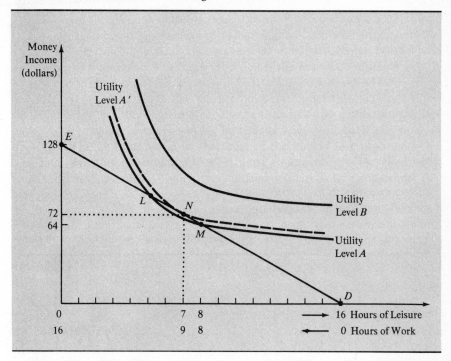

Now, $\Delta Y/\Delta H$ is exactly the slope of the budget constraint (in absolute value).[20] Figure 6.6 shows how the constraint rises $8 for every one-hour increase in work: if the person works zero hours, income per day is zero; if the person works one hour, $8 in income is possible; if he or she works 8 hours, $64 in income can be achieved. The constraint rises $8 for every unit increase in hours of work because the wage rate the person commands is $8 per hour. If the person could earn $16 per hour, the constraint would rise twice as fast and therefore be twice as steep.

It is clear from Figure 6.6 that our consumer/worker cannot achieve utility level B. He or she can achieve *some* points on the indifference curve representing utility level A—specifically, those points between L and M in Figure 6.6. However, if our consumer/worker is a utility maximizer, he or she

---

20. The vertical change for a one-unit change in horizontal distance is the definition of *slope*. *Absolute value* refers to the magnitude of the slope, disregarding whether it is positive or negative. The budget constraint drawn in Figure 6.6 is a straight line (and thus has a constant slope). Economically, a straight-line budget constraint reflects the assumption that the wage rate at which one can work is fixed, and that it does not change with the hours of work. Shelly Lundberg, "Tied Wage-Hours Offers and the Endogeneity of Wages," *Review of Economics and Statistics* 67 (August 1985): 405–10, finds evidence that jobs requiring longer hours pay higher wages, so that the actual budget constraint may be convex (with the slope rising in absolute value as more hours are worked). However, the major theoretical implications derived from using a straight-line constraint would be unchanged by employing a convex one, so we are using the fixed-wage assumption for ease of exposition. A review of the reasons for, and theoretical implications of, nonlinear budget constraints is given in John Pencavel, "Labor Supply of Men: A Survey," in *Handbook of Labor Economics,* ed. Orley Ashenfelter and Richard Layard (Amsterdam: North-Holland, 1986).

will realize that a utility level *above A* is possible. Remembering that an infinite number of indifference curves can be drawn between curves *A* and *B* in Figure 6.6, one representing each possible level of satisfaction between *A* and *B*, we can draw a curve (*A'*) that is northeast of curve *A* and just *tangent* to the budget constraint. Any movement along the budget constraint *away* from the tangency point places the person on an indifference curve lying *below A'*.

An indifference curve that is just tangent to the constraint represents the highest level of utility that the person can obtain given his or her constraint. It is the most northeast curve with an achievable point on it, and no curve superior to it can be reached. If this highest possible curve is denoted as utility level *A'* in Figure 6.6, then point *N* represents the utility-maximizing combination of leisure and income. Thus, our consumer/worker is best off, given his or her preferences and constraints, working 9 hours a day, consuming 7 hours of leisure, and having a daily income of $72. All other possible combinations, such as 8 hours of work and $64 of income, yield lower utility.

The Decision Not to Work. In the example discussed above and illustrated in Figure 6.6, a point of tangency (*N*) existed between the individual's indifference curve and the budget constraint. That point of tangency indicated the utility-maximizing labor/leisure combination. What happens if there is no point of tangency? What happens, for example, when a person's indifference curves are at every point more steeply sloped than the budget constraint (see Figure 6.7)?

If indifference curves that represent an individual's preferences are very steeply sloped, it indicates that the person places a very high value on extra hours of leisure (see Figure 6.5a). A very high hourly wage would be required

FIGURE 6.7 The Decision Not to Work Is a "Corner Solution"

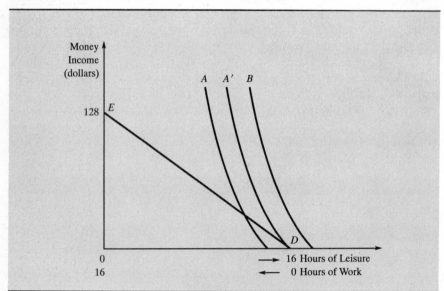

to compensate the person for an hour of *lost* leisure (that is, an hour of work). If the increase in money income required to compensate the worker for an hour of work (to keep utility constant) is greater than the wage rate at every feasible number of leisure hours, then the person will simply choose not to work. Figure 6.7 indicates that utility is maximized at point *D*, a point of zero hours of work. Point *D* is *not* a tangency point; there can be no tangency if the indifference curve has no points at which the slope equals the slope of the budget constraint. Thus, utility in Figure 6.7 is maximized at a *corner,* a point at the extreme end of the budget constraint. At this point (*D*) the person chooses not to be in the labor force.

The Income Effect.   Suppose now that the person depicted in Figure 6.6 receives a source of income independent of work. Suppose, further, that this *nonlabor* income amounts to about $36 per day. Thus, even if this person worked zero hours per day, his or her daily income would be $36. Naturally, if the person worked more than zero hours, his or her daily income would be equal to $36 plus earnings (the wage multiplied by the hours of work).

Our person's command over resources has clearly increased, as can be shown by drawing a new budget constraint to reflect the nonlabor income. As shown by the broken line in Figure 6.8, the end points of the new constraint are point *d* (zero hours of work and $36 of money income) and point *e* (16 hours of work and $164 of income—$36 in nonlabor income plus $128 in earnings).

FIGURE 6.8   Indifference Curves and Budget Constraint (with an increase in nonlabor income)

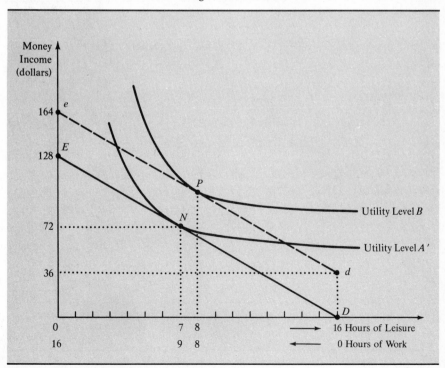

Note that the new constraint is *parallel* to the old one. Parallel lines have the same slope; since the slope of each constraint reflects the wage rate, we can infer that the increase in nonlabor income has not changed the person's wage rate.

We have just described a situation in which a pure *income effect* should be observed. Income (wealth) has been increased, but the wage rate has remained unchanged. The previous section noted that if wealth increased and the opportunity cost of leisure remained constant, the person would consume more leisure and work less. We thus concluded that the income effect was negative; as income went up (holding wages constant) hours of work went down, or as income went down (holding wages constant) hours of work went up. This negative relationship is illustrated graphically in Figure 6.8.

When the old budget constraint was in effect (solid line), the person's highest level of utility was reached at point *N*, where he or she worked 9 hours a day. With the new constraint (dashed line), the optimum hours of work are 8 per day. The new source of income, because it does not alter the wage, has caused an income effect that results in one less hour of work per day.

Income and Substitution Effects with a Wage Increase. Suppose that, instead of increasing one's command over resources by receiving a source of nonlabor income, the wage rate for another person were to be increased from

FIGURE 6.9 Wage Change with Substitution Effect Dominating

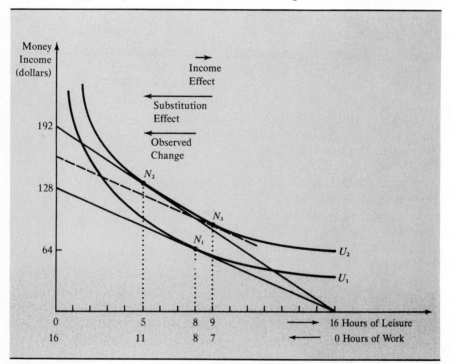

$8 to $12 per hour. This increase, as noted earlier, would cause *both* an income and a substitution effect; the person would be wealthier *and* face a higher opportunity cost of leisure. Both effects can be illustrated graphically (see Figures 6.9 and 6.10).

Figures 6.9 and 6.10 illustrate the *observed effects* of the wage change as well as the two hidden *components* of the observed change: the income and substitution effects. Figure 6.9 illustrates the case in which the observed response is to increase the hours of work; in this case the substitution effect is stronger than the income effect. Figure 6.10 illustrates the case in which the income effect is stronger and the response to a wage increase is to reduce the hours of work. Both cases are plausible. Theory tells us in what direction the income and substitution effects should go, but it does not tell us which effect will be stronger. The difference between the two cases lies *solely* in the shape of the indifference curves (preferences); the budget constraints, which reflect wealth and the wage rate, are exactly the same.

Figures 6.9 and 6.10 show a new budget constraint. We are assuming that no source of nonlabor income exists for the person depicted, so both the old and new constraints in each diagram are anchored at the same place—zero income for zero hours worked. However, the new constraint rises 50 percent faster than the old constraint, reflecting the 50 percent increase in the wage rate (from $8 to $12 per hour). The left endpoint of the new constraint is now

FIGURE 6.10   Wage Change with Income Effect Dominating

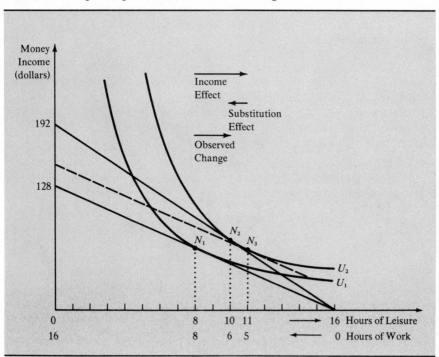

EXAMPLE 6.2
Primitive Cultures and Labor Supply Theory*

Primitive cultures, which are often thought to be so tradition-bound as to be outside the purview of economic analysis, have some characteristics in common. One is that, for the most part, their members work little more than is required for subsistence; anthropologists frequently describe labor resources in primitive cultures as "underutilized." A second is a strong tradition of gift-giving. Partly to communally share the risks of ill health or bad luck, and partly to generate social harmony in an environment in which power is decentralized and conflicts are not mediated by formalized government, these societies often develop the expectation that those with surplus goods will freely share them with others.

Are primitive peoples so tradition-bound that changes in behavior either never occur or are unexplainable by economic theory? During the period from 1933 to 1953, the steel axe replaced the stone axe among the Siane tribe of New Guinea. One of the Siane men's jobs was to clear and fence land used for cultivation, and steel axes made it possible to do this in one-third the time previously taken. This introduction of steel represented an increase in the real wages of Siane men, because consumption per hour of work rose. Thus, we have an opportunity to observe how their labor supply behavior changed when their "budget constraint" changed.

According to one study, the supply of hours to work activities dropped from 80 percent of a Siane man's day to 50 percent over the 20-year period. Not surprisingly, the declines in work hours were greatest in clearing and fencing. While there was an increase in the time devoted to home crafts, Siane men generally opted to consume more leisure in the face of the increased real wage.

If economic theory is applied to an analysis of this change, we must conclude that the income effect of the wage increase dominated the substitution effect. Interestingly, the relatively weak substitution effect may have had something to do with the tradition of gift-giving; because surplus goods were always shared, work effort beyond that required for subsistence may truly have had a net wage rate close to zero. One anthropologist, commenting on the system of gift-giving, argued as follows:

> Under this system people are less likely to want or be able to accumulate material wealth—especially money. They have little incentive to work harder or produce more than the next person if they can have a particular item simply by openly admiring it, thereby encouraging the owner to display his generosity by giving it. They are unlikely to work hard to acquire a particularly desirable item if they may eventually have to give it away.

*See Review Question 9 at end of chapter.

SOURCES: Quotation from Brian Lockwood, *Samoan Village Economy* (Melbourne: Oxford University Press, 1971), 208. Other sources include Marshall Sahlins, *Stone Age Economics* (Chicago: Aldine-Atherton, 1972), 17, 21, and R. F. Salisbury, *From Stone to Steel* (Melbourne: Melbourne University Press, 1962), 108, 146. We are grateful to Professor Davydd J. Greenwood for suggesting references to us on this topic.

at $192 (16 hours of work times $12 per hour) rather than at $128 (16 hours times $8).

In Figure 6.9, the new constraint implies that utility level U_2 is the highest that can be reached, and the tangency at point N_2 suggests that 11 hours of work per day is the optimum. When the old constraint was in effect, the utility-maximizing hours of work were 8 per day. Thus, the wage increase has caused the person's hours of work to increase by 3 per day.

This observed effect, however, masks the underlying forces at work. These underlying forces are, of course, the income and substitution effects. These forces are not directly observable, but they are there (and working against each other) nonetheless. A physical analogy can be used to explain how these forces work.

Suppose a riderless boat is set adrift in the Mississippi River on a day when the wind is blowing *across* the river. The river's current carries the boat downstream, but the crosswind also exerts a force that blows the boat east. We observe where the boat is when it passes under a certain bridge. While we can *observe* where the boat crosses under the bridge, we cannot directly see the two independent forces that together dictate where the boat ends up. There is the influence of the current and of the wind, and for some purposes it may be useful to measure these effects separately. How would we do it?

We would measure the influence of the current by asking ourselves, "Where would the boat have passed under the same bridge if there had been no wind?" This hypothetical question holds two elements constant: the wind (zero velocity) and the bridge under which the boat passes. The answer to the question is thus designed to identify the "pure" effect of the current. The influence of the wind could be measured by comparing where the boat actually crossed under the bridge with where it *would have crossed* had there been no wind.

Turning now to Figure 6.9, we shall identify the income effect (as we did the current effect) by asking, "What would have been the change in the hours worked if the person had reached indifference curve U_2 (the bridge) by a change in *nonlabor* income with *no* change in the wage rate (no wind)?"

We answer this question by moving the old constraint to the northeast while maintaining its original slope (reflecting the old wage of $8), which holds the wage constant. By definition, we must hold the wage constant when dealing with the income effect. However, moving the old constraint hypothetically allows nonlabor income to increase so that the person arrives at the new level of utility. The constraint in Figure 6.9 (dashed line) depicts this hypothetical constraint, which is tangent to indifference curve U_2 at N_3. This tangency suggests that had the person received nonlabor income, with no change in the wage, sufficient to reach the new level of utility, he or she would have *reduced* work hours from 8 (N_1), to 7 (N_3) per day. This shift is graphic proof that the income effect is negative, assuming that leisure is a normal good.

The substitution effect can be measured once the pure effect of the wage change is known. We measure the substitution effect as the difference between where the person ends up and where he or she *would* have ended up without a wage change.[21] *With* the wage change, the person represented in Figure 6.9 ended up at point N_2, working 11 hours a day. *Without* the wage change, the person would have arrived at point N_3, working 7 hours a day. The wage change by *itself* (holding utility, or real wealth, constant) caused work hours to increase by 4 per day. This increase demonstrates that the substitution effect is positive.

To summarize, the observed effect of raising wages from $8 to $12 per hour increased the hours of work in Figure 6.9 from 8 to 11 per day. This observed effect, however, is the *sum* of two component effects. The income effect, which operates because an increased wage increases one's real wealth, tended to *reduce* the hours of work from 8 to 7 per day. The substitution effect, which captures the pure effect of the change in leisure's opportunity cost, tended to push the person toward 4 more hours of work per day. The end result was an increase of 3 in the hours worked each day.

Figure 6.10 can be analyzed in the same way. Here the *observed* effect of the increased wage is a *reduction* in hours of work from 8 to 6 per day (points N_1 to N_2). This change is the result of an income effect, which by itself tended to *decrease* by 3 hours the hours of work per day, and a substitution effect, which tended to *increase* working hours by 1 per day. The net result of these forces is, of course, a reduction in hours of work by 2 per day.

The differences in the observed effects of a wage increase between Figures 6.9 and 6.10 are due to differences in the shape of the indifference curves—or, in other words, to different preferences. The substitution and income effects worked in their predicted directions in both cases, but their relative strengths are a function of preferences (which are reflected in the shape and placement of the indifference curves).

Although theory cannot predict whether the income effect or the substitution effect will dominate, the income effect of any given wage change is *larger* for individuals who are *working many hours* for pay than for those who are working few hours. Changes in income represent changes in one's command over resources, and a wage increase clearly fosters greater increases in wealth the more hours one works. (In terms of our graphic analysis, it can be seen from Figures 6.9 and 6.10 that the budget constraint representing a wage of $12 per hour lies further to the northeast of the one representing an $8 wage in its upper portion, where more hours are worked.)

---

21. The analysis here measures the income effect first and then portrays the substitution effect as the difference between the person's actual hours of work and the amount he or she would have worked with just a pure income effect. An alternative approach is to measure the substitution effect first (along the old indifference curve) and then think of the income effect as the movement (with the new wage constant) to the new indifference curve. The two alternatives are equally correct methods of graphically portraying income and substitution effects. We have chosen to show the income effect first here, because it more neatly fits our river-boat-bridge analogy. Back in Appendix 3A, however, in an analogous representation of substitution and scale effects on the demand side of the market, it was more convenient to show the substitution effect first.

Empirical Findings on the Labor/Leisure Choice

This chapter has argued, both verbally and graphically, that the income effect on labor supply is negative and that the substitution effect is positive. While these predictions are often useful for policy purposes, as we saw in the discussions of the work-incentive effect of the income tax, it is also important to know *how large* the two effects are. It is the *relative size* of each effect that determines the ultimate *observed* effect.

Evidence on the absolute and relative sizes of income and substitution effects can be obtained in two ways:

1. The *time-series study* can be used to look at *trends* in labor force participation rates and hours of work over time.
2. The *cross-sectional study* can be used to analyze the patterns of labor supply across individuals at a given point in time.

Time-Series Studies.   Chapter 2 pointed out that real hourly wages rose four-fold from 1914 to 1989. Associated with that rise was a rather sharp decline in the labor force participation rate of older men, clearly reflecting a trend toward earlier retirement. One can also observe substantial declines in hours of work. One might be tempted to conclude from these trends that the income effect dominates the substitution effect, meaning that when wages rise, the propensity to work will fall.

There are three potential objections to, or problems with, the conclusion that the income effect is larger than the substitution effect. First, the earlier retirement of men can be seen as a function of the greater availability of pensions and/or disability payments. Pensions pay older people for not working, thereby creating incentives not to work at an elderly age; disability payments go largely to older workers and represent an alternative source of income for those with health problems who choose not to work.[22]

A second disturbing fact that raises questions about the relative strength of the income and substitution effects is the much smaller decline in weekly hours of work after World War II. Has the income effect grown weaker relative to the substitution effect? Not necessarily, for at least two reasons. First, hours of work are *jointly* determined by employers and employees, and while rising real wages may be inducing employees to want to work less, a number of developments have led employers to offer incentives for workers to work longer hours (these forces were discussed in Chapter 5). It is important to remember that countervailing forces may well be coming from the *demand* side of the market in determining hours of work. Second, the increase in hours of

---

22. For a recent paper on retirement and public pensions, see Donald O. Parsons, "Male Retirement Behavior in the United States, 1930–1950" (unpublished paper, Economics Department, The Ohio State University, November 1987). On the topic of disability and labor force participation, see John Bound, "The Health and Earnings of Rejected Disability Insurance Applicants," *American Economic Review* 79, no. 3 (June 1989): 482–503.

paid work among married women can influence the working hours of their husbands independently of the male wage. We discuss this issue in Chapter 7 in the context of household production and *family* labor supply decisions.

The third problem is that, while we cannot rule out the possibility that the income effect dominates the substitution effect for males, interpreting the dramatic rise in participation rates among women becomes difficult. One possible explanation is that preferences among women changed, particularly after their heavy involvement in the labor market during World War II. For example, the stigma against working wives or mothers weakened. This change in preferences may explain some of the rising propensity of women to work, but it does not explain the *cause* of the changing preferences. Since women's attitudes may be most strongly influenced by the sheer increase in the number of working women, understanding what started the increase in the first place is fundamental.

Another explanation for the growing proportion of working women is based on the observation that women really have a tripartite choice of how to spend time: leisure, market work, and nonmarket (household) work (see Chapter 7 for further discussion of this tripartite choice). The availability of automatic washers and dryers, frost-free refrigerators, and prepared foods, to name a few labor-saving conveniences, has reduced the time required to perform household tasks. The ability to perform these tasks faster reduces the savings from staying home instead of working for pay. Thus, yet another force is at work affecting the incentives of women to work for pay.

Finally, since wives often work in the home more, and for pay less, than men and unmarried women, the income effect for them tends to be smaller and the substitution effect larger. The plausibility of a smaller income effect rests on the observation that, at any point in time, many married women are out of the labor force and many others are working less than full time. Thus, as noted before, a given wage increase will generate a smaller income effect than it would if virtually all were working for pay full time. A larger substitution effect is plausible for married women because household and market work are close substitutes, whereas market work and leisure are not, as we argue below.

Suppose that women and men have roughly the same preferences regarding leisure and work. These two ways to spend time are substitutes, but not close substitutes. Thus, a change in the opportunity cost of leisure may not elicit a large change in the supply of working hours for either sex; leisure and work are simply too different for a large responsiveness to changes in opportunity costs to be observed. However, there are two types of *work* activity, market work (for pay) and household work, and there is a high degree of substitutability between *these* alternatives. If market work is performed, household chores are hired out to specialists (baby sitters, cleaning services) or done by machines (electric dishwashers). If household work is substituted for market work, these costs of hiring out tasks are saved. Thus, doing household work oneself and hiring out these chores while working for pay represent two ways of getting the same job done. They are very close substitutes, so when the incentives to pursue one alternative change, a large response in time spent doing the other can be expected. Because married women have traditionally performed household work to a greater extent than have men and unmarried women, we would expect this second influence (the substitution between work activities) on the overall substitution effect to be more important for married women. The substitution effect observed in the above studies is thus plausibly larger for married women. (Chapter 7 will return to the issue of household and market work in more detail.)

It is easy to see that looking at *trends* in the propensity of people to work for evidence on the relative strength of income or substitution effects is not completely satisfactory. Because so many other factors that affect these propensities are involved over time, isolating income and substitution effects is impossible. Indeed, the growth of pensions, changes in employer desires concerning hours of work, time-saving household inventions, and changed attitudes toward working women all cloud our analysis of trends.

Cross-Sectional Studies.   Numerous studies of labor supply behavior have relied on cross-sectional data. These studies basically analyze labor force participation or annual hours of work as they are affected by wage rates (the slope of the budget constraint) and unearned income (how far out the constraint lies). The most reliable and informative studies are those done on large samples of men, primarily because the labor supply behavior of women is complicated by child-rearing and household work arrangements for which data are sketchy at best. The findings discussed here are of *nonexperimental studies*—studies in which variations in wages and incomes are *observed,* rather than *generated,* by the researchers. (Findings from experimental studies are summarized later in this chapter in the discussion of income maintenance programs.)

Most studies of male labor supply behavior indicate that the income effect dominates the substitution effect, and thus that men have (individual) negatively sloped supply curves. There is as yet no consensus about the exact *size* of the labor supply response, but it appears to be relatively small. One careful review study claims that, once various statistical and definitional problems are accounted for, the effect of raising a man's wage by 10 percent would be a 1–2 percent reduction in his labor supply. This observed effect is the result of something like a 2.5 percent reduction resulting from the income effect and roughly a 1 percent increase associated with the substitution effect.[23]

The estimates for women usually indicate that the *substitution* effect dominates, yielding a positively sloped labor supply curve for women. Studies comparable to those for men (noted above) have generally found similar in-

---

23. George Borjas and James Heckman, "Labor Supply Estimates for Public Policy Evaluation," *Proceedings of the Industrial Relations Research Association* (1978), 320–31. John Pencavel, "Labor Supply of Men: A Review," presents similar summary estimates but adds the observation that such estimates frequently are imprecise, are of diverse magnitude, and imply a negative substitution effect. He cautions that empirical support for the theory of labor supply is as yet rather tenuous.

come effects among women, but the substitution effects for women are much larger than those for men, the likely reasons for which were mentioned earlier.[24]

It is interesting, and somewhat heartening, that the results of nonexperimental, statistically sophisticated cross-sectional studies generally support the observations based on trends over time. Namely, the income effect appears to dominate for males and the substitution effect appears dominant for females. As noted earlier, the relatively larger substitution effect among women probably reflects the traditional household role of married women, rather than gender-related differences in work/leisure preferences.

POLICY APPLICATIONS

Virtually all government income maintenance programs—from welfare payments to unemployment compensation—have work-incentive effects, and the direction and size of these effects are often critical issues in constructing and enacting such programs. As a society, we have decided to help those among us who are economically disadvantaged for one reason or another. However, it is important to understand how income maintenance programs can affect willingness to work. This section on policy applications will discuss the labor supply implications of unemployment insurance, workers' compensation, and welfare programs and their alternatives.

Income Replacement Programs

Unemployment insurance, workers' compensation, and disability insurance might be called *income replacement programs.* Unemployment insurance benefits are paid to workers who have been laid off, permanently or temporarily, by their employers. Workers' compensation is paid to employees who have been injured on the job, while disability benefits are paid to former workers whose physical or mental disabilities are judged severe enough to prevent their holding down a job. All three programs are intended to compensate workers for earnings lost owing to their inability to work.[25]

---

24. Mark Killingsworth, *Labor Supply,* Cambridge Surveys of Economic Literature (Cambridge, England: Cambridge University Press, 1983), offers a very comprehensive review of what the author calls "first- and second-generation" estimates of income and substitution effects.

A recent study, which reviews many other studies, claims that the income and substitution effects for men and married, *working* women are more or less the same; see Thomas A. Mroz, "The Sensitivity of an Empirical Model of Married Women's Hours of Work to Economic and Statistical Assumptions," *Econometrica* 55, no. 4 (July 1987): 765–800. Articles on women's labor supply in the United States and 11 other countries appear in the *Journal of Labor Economics,* January 1985 supplement. Jacob Mincer, "Intercountry Comparisons of Labor Force Trends and of Related Developments: An Overview," *Journal of Labor Economics* 3, no. 1 (January 1985 supplement): S1–S32, summarizes these studies by noting that they predominantly find that substitution effects outweigh income effects.

25. For a complete description of these programs, see C. Arthur Williams, Jr., John G. Turnbull, and Earl F. Cheit, *Economic and Social Security: Social Insurance and Other Approaches,* 5th ed. (New York: John Wiley & Sons, 1982). We shall return to the workers' compensation and unemployment insurance programs in the chapters on compensating differentials (Chapter 8) and unemployment (Chapter 15).

Complete Replacement?   Given that the unemployment insurance, workers'
compensation, and disability insurance programs are intended to replace lost
earnings, it may seem a bit odd, if not callous, that all three programs in the
United States typically replace roughly just *half* of before-tax lost earnings.[26]
Many benefits paid out under these programs are not taxed, so the fraction of
after-tax earnings replaced is often somewhat higher than 50 percent. However, lost employee benefits are not replaced, so lost compensation is far from
completely replaced. Why?

The reason for incomplete earnings replacement has to do with work incentives. Both injured and unemployed workers have some discretion regarding how long they will remain out of work. A man with a lacerated arm might
be able to carry out his normal duties with some discomfort after a few days
of recuperation, or he might choose to wait until his wound is completely
healed before returning to work. An unemployed woman might accept the
first offer of work she obtains, or she may prefer to wait a while and see if she
can generate a better offer. In both cases the worker has the legal latitude to
decide (within some limits) when to return to work. These decisions will obviously be affected by work incentives inherent in the income replacement
programs affecting them (see Example 6.3).

Replacing *all* of lost income could result in *overcompensation* by generating a higher level of utility than before the loss of income,[27] and would motivate the recipients of benefits to remain out of work as long as possible.
Figure 6.11 shows that before employment ceased, the person earned E_0 and
had a level of utility equal to U_1. If, when employment ceases, the worker receives benefits equal to E_0, he or she will be at point T on a higher indifference curve. Before work ceased, the worker earned E_0 and had 8 hours of
leisure, whereas at T he or she has E_0 in income and 16 hours of leisure per
day. In this case, the recipient would be better off not working than working.
Thus, full earnings replacement could clearly inhibit program beneficiaries
from returning to work at the earliest possible time.

Actual Income Loss vs. "Scheduled" Benefits.   A second issue in income replacement programs is how to structure workers' compensation for permanent
disabilities. Should workers who are either totally or partially disabled receive
benefits that replace their *actual* lost earnings, or should they receive benefits
according to some impersonal schedule appropriate for people with their disability? One might initially think that replacing actual losses is more fair, but
in almost all states those with permanent disabilities are compensated without
reference to actual losses. We show below that if actual losses were to be completely compensated, such a program would create an enormous disincentive
to work.

---

26. Unemployment insurance and workers' compensation programs are run at the state level
and thus vary in their characteristics across states. Benefits in both programs are bounded
by minimums and maximums.
27. We are assuming here that the psychic costs of injury or layoff are small. It could be argued that complete income replacement is justified on the grounds that it compensates for
large psychic losses, but our analysis of work-incentive effects would be unchanged.

Example 6.3

Disability and Economic Incentives in Three Countries

Most economically advanced countries have "disability" programs to compensate workers who suffer from a condition that prevents their continuing to work. The aim of these programs is to care for those unable to work, but the determination of who is disabled is not just a medical issue. Some with a given physical or mental handicap continue to work, while others with an identical diagnosis do not; and some countries have far higher percentages of "disabled" workers than others of comparable per capita income and medical resources. Why?

The effects of physical or mental handicaps on the ability to work are at least partly a matter of incentives. Many handicapped people can learn new skills or can, though perhaps with significant inconvenience or exertion, perform well in a variety of jobs. The social policy question is thus not just one of ability to work; it is also one of how much effort or inconvenience society is willing to require of handicapped workers. Programs that pay relatively small disability benefits implicitly require more of handicapped workers than do programs that are more generous, because the former make it more attractive to work than to receive disability benefits (normally, one cannot—by law—do both).

In the United States, for example, workers who formerly earned pay equal to the national average receive about half of their former pay if they cease work and qualify for disability benefits. In Sweden and the Netherlands, workers formerly earning average pay find that disability programs replace some 70 to 90 percent of former earnings. Not surprisingly, the proportion of older people in each country receiving disability is directly related to the above replacement rates:

| | | Percent of Each Group Receiving Disability in 1980 | |
	Replacement Rates for Median Earner	Age 45–59	Age 60–64
United States	49%	8.3%	28.5%
Sweden	69–88	9.9	38.2
The Netherlands	77–80	26.5	58.5

While the work ethic, economic opportunities, and the availability of other programs clearly affect the percentages of people receiving disability across countries (Sweden, for example, is strongly committed to rehabilitation and job placement of the disabled), the fact that in the Netherlands one of every four workers aged 45–59 is considered disabled is by itself sufficient to raise questions about the effect of economic incentives on disability.

source: Richard Burkhauser, "Disability Policy in the United States, Sweden, and the Netherlands," in *Disability and the Labor Market: Economic Problems, Policies, and Programs* (Ithaca, N.Y.: ILR Press, 1986).

FIGURE 6.11   Full-Earnings Replacement Overcompensates Workers

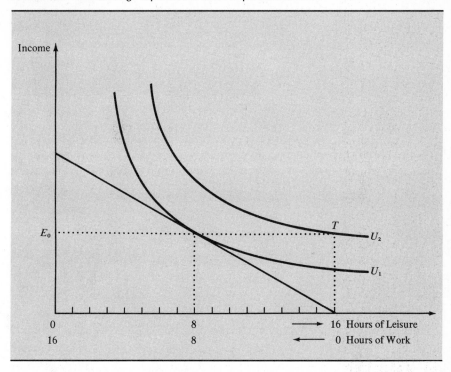

Suppose a manual worker became partially disabled by an injury on the job. Suppose this worker lost three fingers on one hand and must now seek work in jobs that pay less than he earned before. Generally speaking, an injury of this magnitude may well cause changes in both a worker's indifference curves and the "market" budget constraint facing the worker. Assume the new preferences and budget constraint are shown in Figure 6.12. If our injured worker earned E_0 before injury and workers' compensation replaced all earnings loss up to E_0, the workers' compensation budget constraint facing this worker would be like the solid-line constraint ($ABCD$) drawn in Figure 6.12. This income replacement constraint has a vertical segment (AB), which indicates that if the person does not work at all, he receives a benefit equal to E_0. If he does earn money by taking a job, the difference between E_0 and his actual earnings becomes his disability benefit. Thus, as long as his actual earnings are below E_0, his benefit is such that his total income remains at E_0, which is why the segment BC is horizontal at E_0. The segment CD corresponds to his "market" (unsubsidized) constraint when earnings are above E_0.

The interesting thing about Figure 6.12 is that, for many people, B—a point of no work at all—is the point of maximum utility. Throughout the horizontal segment, BC, the individual's effective wage is zero (as reflected by BC's zero slope). If our worker were to earn an extra \$10, the government

FIGURE 6.12   Budget Constraint with Actual Income Replacement

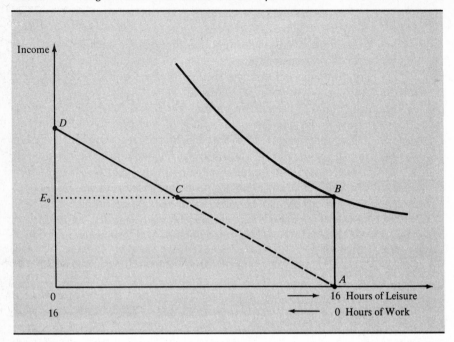

would reduce his benefits by \$10. In a very real sense, any earnings would be "taxed" away completely in the form of a dollar-for-dollar reduction in benefits. When people cannot increase their income by working, there is usually no incentive to work.

One way to avoid the disincentives inherent in replacing *actual* lost earnings for disabled workers is to grant benefits according to some schedule drawn up with reference to the disability but without regard to the individual's actual earnings loss. For example, in New York State, a worker losing the first three fingers of one hand receives two-thirds of his or her before-injury weekly wage for a period of 101 weeks, irrespective of his or her actual earnings during or after this 101-week period.[28] Other states compensate permanent, partial disabilities in a similar manner.

Using an impersonal schedule of disability benefits preserves at least some incentive to work because benefits are not reduced if earnings increase. The benefits received become a grant of nonwage income, and they do not alter the recipient's effective wage rate (price of leisure).

Figure 6.13 includes the "market" constraint (AD) and the "actual earnings loss" constraint ($ABCD$) previously depicted in Figure 6.12. Now assume that, instead of actual earnings loss, disability benefits for our disabled worker equal E_0 no matter how much or how little he earns after the injury. His new constraint is thus ABJ. This new constraint is parallel to AD, his "market"

---

28. New York State, *Workmen's Compensation Law* (Hempstead, N.Y.: Workmen's Compensation Board, 1970), 65.

FIGURE 6.13   Comparing Budget Constraints of Two Disability Programs

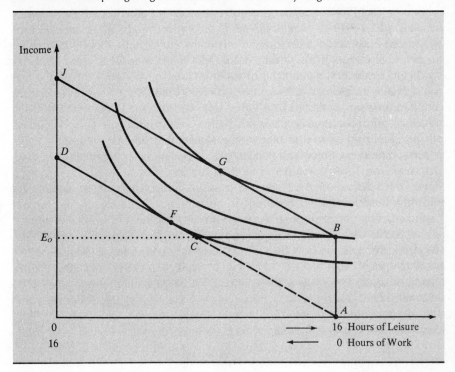

constraint (*ABJ* is everywhere E_0 higher than constraint *AD*), reflecting the fact that this form of compensation for injury does not alter his effective wage rate.

Figure 6.13 provides a graphic demonstration that there are greater incentives to work if benefits are "scheduled" than if benefits are calculated to completely replace earnings losses. Our injured worker maximizes utility at point *G* rather than at point *B*, even though both disability benefit programs depicted pay equal benefits for those who cannot or do not choose to work.

The conclusion that scheduled payments offer stronger work incentives than benefits based on actual losses becomes even stronger if the scheduled benefits are reduced below E_0. As benefits are reduced, the constraint *ABJ* moves closer to *AD*, and the point of utility maximization moves farther from *G* and closer to *F* (the utility-maximizing point in a world without disability benefits). Maximum work incentives are retained when there is no income transfer program, a situation in obvious conflict with the overall *goal* of helping workers who find themselves economically disadvantaged.[29]

While the basic aim of such programs is to restore income to disadvantaged workers, it is important to preserve work incentives as much as possible.

---

29. Chapter 8 will show that workers who are injured may have been compensated *in advance* of injury by having higher wages (due to the risk inherent in their job) than they would otherwise have had. These *compensating wage differentials* must also be taken into account when establishing programs for post-injury compensation.

If we take AD as the budget constraint when no benefit program exists and point F as the corresponding optimum work effort, it is easy to see from Figure 6.13 that "scheduled" benefits cause only an income effect. The constraint moves out to ABJ, but it does not change slope. Work effort declines, since point G is to the right of point F, but it does not cease.[30]

On the contrary, if actual earnings loss were to become the benefit, there would be an income effect *and* a substitution effect, and *both* would work in the *same* direction. The benefits would simultaneously increase income while *reducing* the effective wage rate to zero (in the segment BC of constraint $ABCD$). The presence of a zero wage rate would reduce the price of leisure to zero and be a powerful disincentive to work. It is not surprising that payments for partial disabilities are generally "scheduled."

Income Maintenance Programs

Income maintenance programs, more popularly known as "welfare" or "relief" programs, have the goal of *raising* the income of the poor to some minimum acceptable level. They thus differ from income replacement programs, which are aimed at *restoring* lost income. Because poverty is generally an income-related concept, the benefits paid out under income maintenance programs generally are affected by the level of the beneficiary's actual income. As we shall see, income-conditioned benefits inevitably reduce work incentives below what such incentives would be with no income support system for the poor. They simultaneously increase income while reducing the price of leisure (the effective wage rate), both of which should cause the demand for leisure to increase and the supply of labor to fall. This fact is the root of much of the controversy welfare programs have generated over the years. Welfare payments have taken two forms in this country, as described below.

The Basic Welfare System.   In recent years welfare has taken the form of a guaranteed annual income. A welfare worker determines the "needed" income of the eligible person or family, based on family size, area living costs, and local welfare regulations. Actual earnings are generally subtracted from this needed level, and a check is received each month for the difference. If earnings go up, welfare benefits go down, dollar for dollar.[31] This creates a budget constraint like $ABCD$ in Figure 6.14, where total income is Y_n (the "needed" income) as long as the person is subsidized. People on welfare have no incentive to work, because there is a zero wage (segment BC) over most normal hours of work, and they end up at point B.

Thus, the basic welfare system serves to increase the income of the poor by moving the budget constraint out from AC to ABC; this shift creates an *income effect* tending to reduce labor supply from points E to F in Figure 6.14.

---

30. An exception to this statement would be a situation in which a person's indifference curves were such that a "corner solution," as in Figure 6.7, was obtained.
31. This statement is true after the first 4 months of work. During the first 4 months, the welfare recipient is allowed to "keep" the first $30 earned each month plus one-third of earnings above that (that is, above $30, welfare payments are reduced by 67 cents for each dollar earned). While this aspect could be incorporated into our analysis, we ignore it for sake of brevity; however, see Review Question 3 at the end of the chapter.

FIGURE 6.14   Income and Substitution Effects for the Basic Welfare System

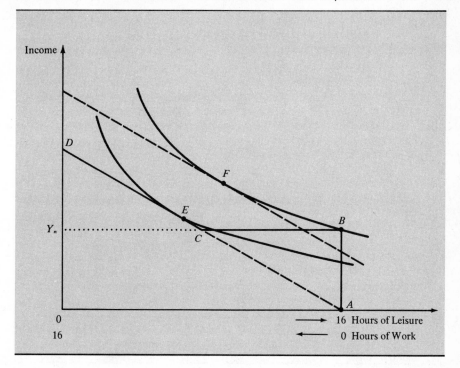

However, it *also* causes the wage to effectively drop to zero: every dollar earned is matched by a dollar reduction in welfare benefits. This dollar-for-dollar reduction in benefits induces a huge *substitution effect,* causing those accepting welfare to reduce their hours of work to zero (point *B*). Of course, if a person's indifference curves were sufficiently flat so that the curve tangent to segment *CD* passed *above* point *B* (see Figure 6.15), then that person's utility would be maximized by choosing work instead of welfare.

The Revised Welfare System.   Beginning in late 1990, the welfare system described above was modified to include a work requirement of 16 hours a week (for at least 6 months a year) for welfare recipients whose children are more than three years old. It is unclear just how many welfare recipients actually will be required to work, for two reasons. One is that there is a rather lengthy "phase-in" period for the work requirement during most of the 1990s.[32] The other is that persons who cannot find work can satisfy the requirement by attending a job-training program. Despite the slow pace at which this requirement is likely to be implemented, it is nevertheless interesting to consider the work-incentive effects of this kind of reform.

---

32. One estimate is that even by 1997, persons in only 6 percent of welfare families will be required to work. See Mickey Kaus, "Is It Hype or True Reform?" *Newsweek,* October 10, 1988, 45.

FIGURE 6.15 The Basic Welfare System: A Person Not Choosing Welfare

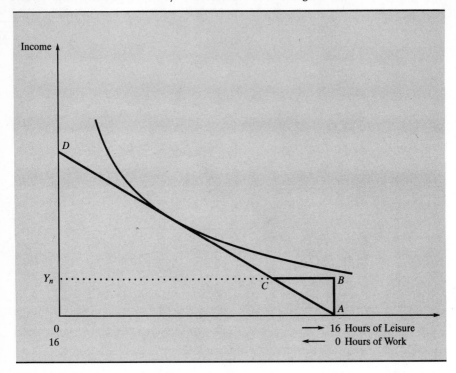

Suppose the government were to require people to work 3 hours a day to qualify for welfare. This requirement is equivalent to saying that if they work less than that they face their "market" constraint. That is, at less than 3 hours of work per day they are not eligible for welfare and must rely solely on labor market earnings for their income. In terms of Figure 6.16, they face segment *AB* in the region in which hours of work total less than 3.

At the point at which they work 3 hours per day, they become eligible for welfare if they are poor enough to otherwise qualify. Thus, after 3 hours of work they qualify for welfare payments that bring their total income up to Y_n; however, if they work more than 3 hours a day their welfare check is reduced one dollar for each dollar of earnings. These facts are reflected in segment *CD* of the constraint in Figure 6.16. Of course, if their earnings rise above Y_n they no longer qualify for welfare and are on segment *DE* of their "market" constraint.

The work-incentive effects of the "work requirement" modification just described can be inferred from studying Figure 6.16. If indifference curves are steep enough so that utility is maximized at point *C*, those on welfare will desire to work 3 hours a day, but no more than that. If indifference curves are flat enough so that the curve tangent to segment *DE* passes *above* point *C*, then, analogous to the result in Figure 6.15 for the old welfare system, the

FIGURE 6.16   The Welfare System with a Work Requirement

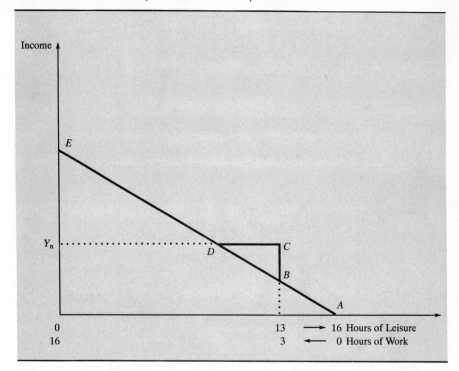

person would choose not to receive welfare. Thus, the effect of the work requirement will be to induce welfare recipients to work, but as long as they are
on welfare they will want to work only the minimum hours needed to qualify.

With respect to the above conclusion, two points need to be made. First,
working the minimum number of hours needed to qualify does not imply that
welfare recipients are "lazy"; they are *induced* to choose that level of work by
the budget constraint implicit in the program. Second, we must stress that *actual* hours of work might differ from *desired* hours if there are limitations that
employers place on the hours of jobs for which they hire. The final section of
this chapter, however, presents evidence that workers with incentives to work
part time are remarkably able to find jobs that bring them close to their
desired hours.

Welfare Dilemmas.   Lest the student believe there is an obviously better solution to the problem of work incentives for those on welfare, let us consider
a widely debated one: the "negative income tax." Noting the disincentive effects of the zero effective wage rate for those receiving welfare under the current system, proponents of the negative income tax approach to welfare
reform advocate a much smaller reduction in welfare payments for each dollar
of earnings. In fact, they advocate reduction rates that are close to the tax

FIGURE 6.17   Budget Constraint with a "Negative Income Tax"

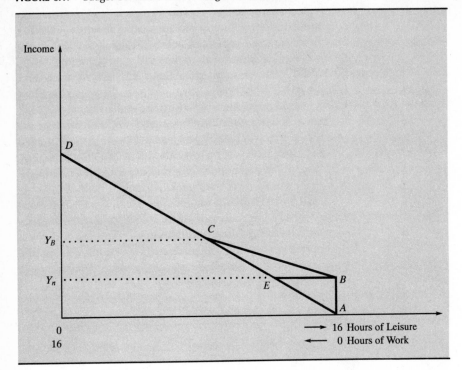

rates of regular taxpayers (hence, the term "negative income tax").[33] For example, in the Presidential election of 1972, candidate George McGovern proposed a plan that would have reduced welfare payments by only 25 cents for each dollar earned.

A lower rate by which welfare benefits are reduced when earnings are increased does strengthen the work incentives of those already on welfare. It raises their effective wage rate above zero so that, to take the McGovern proposal as an example, they would get to keep 75 percent of what they earn. (Because only 25 percent of earnings would be "taxed" away in the form of welfare-benefit reductions, it can be said that the McGovern proposal had an "implicit tax rate" of 25 percent.)

The increase in the effective wage rate of welfare recipients under a negative income tax type of welfare program can be seen in Figure 6.17, in which the constraint under the basic welfare system is shown as *ABED*. If the bene-

---

33. The proposal's name was coined by Milton Friedman, *Capitalism and Freedom* (Chicago: University of Chicago Press, 1962). Friedman proposed to integrate welfare into the income tax system, with those earning over a certain level of income paying positive taxes and those earning below that level paying negative taxes (that is, receiving money from the government).

fit for a family with no earnings were unchanged (that is, if it were kept at level AB, which equals the "needed" income of Y_n), the constraint under a negative income tax type of reform would be $ABCD$. The student will note that the slope of segment BC is nonzero, signifying a nonzero effective wage rate for those on welfare.

The increased effective wage clearly would entice many welfare recipients away from the "corner solution" of no work (point B) that exists under the basic welfare system. Many would maximize utility along segment BC and would work, at least part time. Further, unlike the revised system of required work hours, the negative income tax approach would provide a *continuum* of work incentives; recipients would not all have incentives to stop work when some minimum work requirement was fulfilled.

The negative income tax approach, however, illustrates two dilemmas of welfare reform. First, it allows families with incomes well above the poverty level (Y_n) to receive benefits. As can be seen in Figure 6.17, families with incomes as high as Y_B can receive benefits.[34] Income level Y_B is called the "break-even" level of income, because above it no welfare subsidies can be obtained (the person is on segment CD of the constraint in Figure 6.17). Below Y_B the family will be eligible for subsidies, and utility will be maximized along segment BC. Holding the zero-earnings level of benefits (segment AB) constant, a lower implicit tax rate means a higher break-even level of income.

Another dilemma is that, because any welfare subsidy is conditioned on income, and because income is to some extent under the control of an individual, some people previously above the break-even level of income might reduce their labor supply (and income) enough to qualify for a given subsidy. This possibility is illustrated in Figure 6.18. Prior to the subsidy, the person depicted maximized utility at point L, working 9 hours per day. After the subsidy is instituted and the constraint moves to $ABCD$, this person finds that utility is maximized at point M, where hours of work are many fewer. Point M is a point of lower money income than point L, but the increased leisure time more than makes up for the lost income. To generalize, in instituting reforms designed to increase the work incentives of those now on welfare, the government cannot ignore the effects of reforms on the work incentives of those *not* now on welfare!

Empirical Studies of Welfare and Work Incentives. The student will recall that when workers become newly eligible for an income maintenance subsidy, they face a dual incentive to reduce their hours of work. They receive added income, which produces an income effect that serves to reduce labor supply. Obviously, the more generous the level of benefits, the larger this income effect will be. They also receive a reduction in their effective wage rate; in the current program their effective wage is reduced to zero, but even in negative income tax schemes their effective wage while on welfare lies below their

---

34. In the McGovern proposal, families with incomes up to the nationwide median were eligible for government subsidies!

FIGURE 6.18   Some May Reduce Hours of Work and Money Income Under a
Negative Income Tax Program

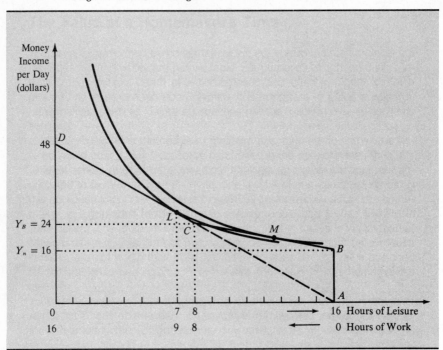

market wage (note that the slope of *BC* in Figure 6.17 is flatter than the slope
of *AD*). This reduction in the effective wage rate creates a substitution effect
that also serves to reduce labor supply.[35]

Although making welfare benefits available to people who were not previously eligible for them will clearly decrease their work incentives, the relevant policy question is: By how much will their work incentives be decreased?
Some studies used estimates of income and substitution effects obtained from
nonexperimental data in the late 1960s to answer this question. These studies
imply that, for males, a guaranteed (zero earnings) benefit of about 75 percent
of the poverty level (which was $3,300 per year in 1967) and a 50 percent
implicit tax rate would cause male labor supply to decrease by 8–15 percent.[36]

---

35. Like any wage reduction, the welfare-induced reduction in the effective wage, *taken by itself*, will tend to reduce income. This tendency, however, is swamped by the effects of the
newly available welfare subsidy—as can be easily seen in Figure 6.17 by the fact that the
new constraint for low-income people (*ABC*) lies to the northeast of the old (*AC*). When a
constraint shifts to the northeast in our diagrams, it signifies that the person has a greater
command over resources, which is the very essence of increased income.
36. Borjas and Heckman, "Labor Supply Estimates for Public Policy Evaluation," 331.

Experimental data, however, can also be used to estimate the size of income and substitution effects. Four large social experiments were conducted in New Jersey, Seattle-Denver, Gary (Indiana), and rural North Carolina in the late 1960s and early 1970s for the purpose of measuring labor supply responses to various income maintenance policies. They were conceived and funded because researchers and policymakers did not want to rely solely on estimates derived from the nonexperimental studies cited above.

While the details in each experiment varied, the negative income tax programs offered to the people in the experiments had benefit guarantee levels (benefits with zero earnings) ranging from 50 to 125 percent of the poverty level.[37] The implicit tax rates on earnings in each experiment ranged from 30 to 80 percent. The typical response for males in these experiments was to reduce labor supply by 3–5 percent. The somewhat smaller response than the cross-sectional prediction above is perhaps due to the known and limited duration of each experiment (responses might have been larger if recipients knew the program would be available to them indefinitely) and to the fact that some participants were unaware of the implicit tax rates they faced.

In examining the labor supply response of females in these experiments, it is useful to recall two facts from the nonexperimental studies. First, the estimates of income and substitution effects for women are much less precise than for men; second, the substitution effect for market work appears to be larger. Since the substitution effect of income maintenance programs induces a withdrawal of labor supply, it is not surprising that the labor supply responses of women in the experiments tended to be larger than for men. For wives, the typical response was for labor supply to decline by a bit over 20 percent, while for single women who headed households the labor supply reduction was typically in the 13–16 percent range. The responses of youth were similar to those of married women.[38]

---

37. Poverty-level incomes are those below which the federal government considers a family to be living in poverty. These income thresholds are defined for farm and nonfarm families separately and are also calculated by family size and the age/gender of the household head. The threshold in each case is based on the 1963 cost of an inexpensive, but nutritionally sound, food plan designed by the Department of Agriculture. This cost was multiplied by 3, reflecting an assumption that families of three or more persons spend one-third of their income on food, and has been adjusted upward each year since 1963 by changes in the Consumer Price Index. For a nonfarm family of four, the 1976 poverty threshold was $5,815, up from $3,128 in 1963; by 1989 changes in the Consumer Price Index implied a poverty level of around $12,675 per year. (See U.S. Bureau of the Census, Current Population Reports, *Consumer Income,* Series P-60, no. 115, issued July 1978, for a more detailed explanation of poverty thresholds.)

38. Philip K. Robins, "A Comparison of the Labor Supply Findings from the Four Negative Income Tax Experiments," *Journal of Human Resources* 20, no. 4 (Fall 1985): 567–82. For other reviews of these experimental findings, see Pencavel, "Labor Supply of Men: A Review"; Michael C. Keeley, *Labor Supply and Public Policy: A Critical Review* (New York: Academic Press, 1981); Killingsworth, *Labor Supply;* and Robert Moffitt and Kenneth Kehrer, "The Effect of Tax and Transfer Programs on Labor Supply: The Evidence from the Income-Maintenance Experiments," in *Research in Labor Economics,* ed. R. Ehrenberg (Greenwich, Conn.: JAI Press, 1981).

Thus, the labor supply effects of expanded welfare coverage are not likely to be innocuous. At some point, society will have to decide whether the improvements in social equity that result from more generous welfare programs are counterbalanced by the social losses attendant on reduced labor supply.[39] In making this decision, of course, society may feel quite differently about reductions in market work by some groups (say, mothers of small children) than about labor supply reductions of other groups.

Worker Adjustment to Incentives

The discussion of work incentives inherent in income replacement and income maintenance programs assumed that workers are well informed about program characteristics—that is, that they have some intuitive understanding of the budget constraint facing them. It also assumed that workers face a sufficiently large array of choices that they can find a set of working hours close to their utility-maximizing set. Students often have a healthy skepticism about the degree to which these assumptions approximate reality. The following example suggests that workers *do* have sufficient knowledge and choice to accommodate their behavior to a given set of work incentives.[40]

Wisconsin, like other states, has an unemployment compensation program that pays unemployed workers a weekly benefit. These benefits are different for different recipients, depending primarily on their pre-unemployment earnings. There is a minimum and a maximum weekly benefit, but for most workers the unemployment benefit is about one-half of prior earnings. Also like most other states, Wisconsin has a method of allowing for partial benefits to be paid to unemployed workers who obtain part-time or low-wage work during their period of eligibility for unemployment benefits. Unlike most other states, however, Wisconsin's partial benefit scheme is such that recipients can only receive one of three unemployment benefits: their full weekly benefit, a benefit equal to half their full weekly benefit, or zero. This partial benefit program contains some interesting work incentives.

The typical recipient of unemployment compensation in Wisconsin can earn up to one-fourth of his or her pre-unemployment earnings with *no loss of benefits.* Since recipients can, in effect, keep all their earnings up to that point (see point X in Figure 6.19), their effective wage rate equals their market wage. This element of the program is graphed in Figure 6.19 as segment CD, which is parallel to the market constraint (AB).

However, once current earnings rise above the critical level of one-fourth of prior earnings, benefits are reduced to one-half the weekly benefit. This abrupt drop in benefits causes an equally abrupt drop in total income. Since

39. The general issue of equity vs. output considerations is treated in a readable manner by Arthur Okun, *Equality and Efficiency: The Big Trade-Off* (Washington, D.C.: The Brookings Institution, 1975).
40. This example is taken from Raymond Munts, "Partial Benefit Schedules in Unemployment Insurance: Their Effect on Work Incentive," *Journal of Human Resources* 5 (Spring 1970): 160–76.

FIGURE 6.19   Partial Unemployment Benefits in Wisconsin

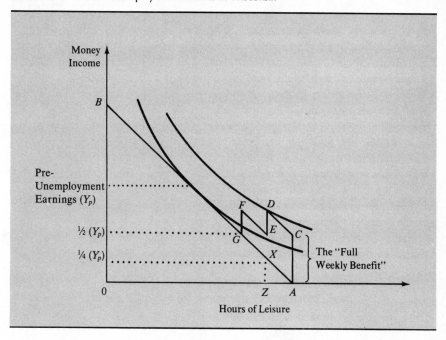

working an extra hour past point Z causes income to drop, the wage, in effect, becomes *negative*, as segment DE in the figure illustrates.

Benefits equaling one-half the full entitlement are paid, then, to recipients who earn between one-fourth and one-half of their prior earnings. When earnings rise just beyond the one-half point (see G), all unemployment benefits cease and the constraint becomes the "market constraint," as segments EF, FG, and GB illustrate. Figure 6.19 shows a saw-toothed constraint in which the market wage alternates with extremely negative wage rates.

A quick look at Figure 6.19 indicates that, for many people, point D is the utility-maximizing combination of leisure hours and income. People who are not fortunate enough to obtain a job where they can earn exactly one-fourth of their prior earnings will try to choose the next best position, which is likely to be at points along the upper portions of CD or near point F. Points along most of EF and the lower portions of CD are clearly inferior, in terms of utility, to other points along the constraint running from C to G.

While it is true that most of those receiving unemployment benefits are completely unemployed, it is interesting to observe whether those who *are* able to find part-time work adjust their behavior as indicated above. In other words, *do* people tend to cluster most at point D, where earnings are just equal to one-fourth of their prior wages? Are there more people at point F and the upper portions of CD than along the rest of the constraint running from C to G?

The answer to both these questions—at least for 1967, when a study of the questions was undertaken—is yes. In Figure 6.20, segment *CDEFG* of Figure 6.19's budget constraint is superimposed on the distribution of those actually receiving partial unemployment benefits, demonstrating that by far the biggest cluster of people is at point *D*, earning 20–25 percent of their prior earnings. Further, the concentrations of people increase as one moves to the upper ends of each segment (*CD* and *EF*), with two-thirds of all partial-benefits recipients at either *F* or the upper half of *CD*. Thus, it appears that workers who do find partial employment while receiving unemployment benefits have the knowledge and inclination to adjust their behavior to the constraints (and the related incentives) facing them.

FIGURE 6.20 Distribution of Partial Benefits in Wisconsin (1967), by Earnings Level

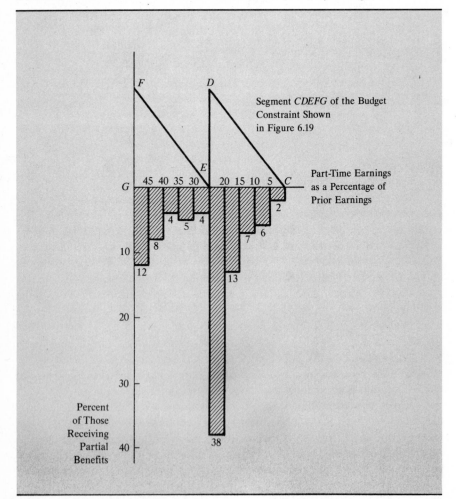

MISCONCEPTION

"When one looks at rising absenteeism and the downward trend in the labor force participation of males, one must conclude that the 'work ethic'— especially among men—in this country is dying. People just aren't the same any more."

Analysis

People's decisions about work effort, like their decisions about other economic transactions, depend on their wealth and the prices (incentives) they face, not just on their basic preferences. The declining labor supply of males may well be a function of their growing wealth (an outward movement of their budget constraint), not a change in their basic preferences (as reflected in their indifference curves).

Principle

People with a stable set of preferences can be induced to change their behavior if their command over resources and/or the prices they face change.

REVIEW QUESTIONS

1. Is the following statement true, false, or uncertain: "Leisure must be an inferior good for an individual's labor supply curve to be backward-bending." Explain your answer.

2. The way the workers' compensation system works now, employees permanently injured on the job receive a payment of X each year whether they work or not. Suppose the government were to implement a new program in which those who did not work at all got $0.5X$ but those who did work got $0.5X$ plus workers' compensation of 50 cents *for every hour worked* (of course, this subsidy would be in addition to the wages paid by their employers). What would be the change in work incentives associated with this change in the way workers' compensation payments were calculated?

3. In footnote 31 it was noted that during the first 4 months of work, a welfare recipient is allowed to "keep" the first $30 earned plus one-third of earnings above $30. Put differently, during the first 4 months of work, the government makes no reduction in welfare benefits for the first $30 of earnings each month; however, welfare benefits are reduced by 67 cents for each dollar earned in excess of $30. See if you can draw the *monthly* budget constraint for a woman who can make $6 per hour, has 300 hours per month to allocate between labor and leisure, and can receive welfare benefits of $600 per month if she does not work at all.

4. Suppose the Social Security disability insurance (DI) program was structured so that otherwise eligible recipients lost their *entire* disability benefit if they had any labor market earnings at all. Suppose, too, that Congress was concerned about the *work disincentives* inherent in this program, and that the relevant committee was

studying two alternatives for increasing work incentives among those disabled enough to qualify for it. One alternative was to *reduce* the benefits paid to all DI recipients but make no other changes in the program. The other was to maintain the old benefit levels (for those who received them) but allow workers to earn $300 per month and still keep their benefits; those who earned over $300 per month would lose all DI benefits.

Analyze the work-incentive effects of both alternatives. (The use of graphic analyses will be of great help to you.)

5. The Secretary of Labor received the following memo from a member of the President's staff:

"The growth of interest in worker-owned enterprises raises some important questions relating to profit sharing. If workers with no previous investment income begin to receive a portion of profits, the effects on labor supply could be large. Would you please have your staff prepare an analysis of the labor supply implications of widespread worker participation in profits? The paper should cover the direction of the labor supply effects as indicated by theory and the likely ways in which these labor supply effects could be manifested. In particular, however, I am interested in a comparison of the labor supply effects of alternative bases upon which profits can be shared among workers. Which basis or bases have the smallest labor supply effects?"

Write the analysis avoiding the use of undefined jargon words. In other words, explain the concepts and hypotheses fully.

6. François Mitterrand, the president of France, instituted a number of programs designed to appeal to his "blue-collar" constituency. He raised the income tax rate applicable to the rich and expanded the free, government-provided social service programs to all (medical services and education being prominent among these). Analyze the work-incentive effects of Mitterrand's programs.

7. Suppose there is a proposal to provide poor people with housing subsidies that are tied to their income levels. These subsidies will be in the form of vouchers the poor can turn over to their landlords in full or partial payment of their housing expenses. The yearly subsidy will equal $2,400 as long as earnings do not exceed $8,000 per year. The subsidy is to be reduced 60 cents for every dollar earned in excess of $8,000; that is, when earnings reach $12,000, the person is no longer eligible for rent subsidies.

Draw an arbitrary budget constraint for a person assuming that he or she receives no government subsidies. Then draw in the budget constraint that arises from the above housing subsidy proposal. After drawing in the budget constraint associated with the proposal, analyze the effects of this proposed housing subsidy program on the labor supply behavior of various groups in the population.

8. The Tax Reform Act of 1986 was designed to reduce the marginal tax rate (the tax rate on the last dollars earned) while eliminating enough deductions and loopholes so that total revenues collected by the government could remain constant. Analyze the work-incentive effects of tax reforms that lower marginal tax rates while keeping total tax revenues constant.

9. Example 6.2 described some general characteristics of primitive cultures and the effect of an increase in real wages on the labor/leisure choices in one such society (the Siane of New Guinea). Draw a budget constraint relevant to the labor/leisure choices of Siane men before the introduction of the steel axe; this constraint should reflect the tradition of gift-giving described in Example 6.2. Next, draw the constraint that can be inferred from the labor/leisure choices of Siane men after the introduction of the steel axe.

SELECTED READINGS

Cain, Glen G., and Watts, Harold W., eds. *Income Maintenance and Labor Supply.* Chicago: Markham, 1973.

Ellwood, David T. *Poor Support: Poverty in the American Family.* New York: Basic Books, 1988.

Keeley, Michael C. *Labor Supply and Public Policy: A Critical Review.* New York: Academic Press, 1981.

Killingsworth, Mark R. *Labor Supply.* Cambridge, Eng.: Cambridge University Press, 1983.

Moffitt, Robert, and Kehrer, Ken. "The Effect of Tax and Transfer Programs on Labor Supply: The Evidence from the Income Maintenance Experiments." In *Research in Labor Economics,* vol. 4, ed. Ronald G. Ehrenberg. Greenwich, Conn.: JAI Press, 1981. Pp. 103–50.

Pechman, J. A., and Timpane, P. M., eds. *Work Incentives and Income Guarantees: The New Jersey Income Tax Experiment.* Washington, D.C.: The Brookings Institution, 1975.

Pencavel, John. "Labor Supply of Men: A Review." In *Handbook of Labor Economics,* ed. Orley Ashenfelter and Richard Layard. Amsterdam: North-Holland, 1986.

APPENDIX 6A

Child Care, Commuting, and the Fixed Costs of Working

This appendix generalizes the static model of labor supply discussed in Chapter 6 to include *costs of working*.[1] These costs typically include both monetary *and* time components. For example, the commute to work involves both time and such monetary outlays as fares on public transportation or the costs of operating an automobile. Similarly, in addition to paying for child care, a working parent often must spend time transporting a child back and forth to the place where the care is provided.

For expository convenience, we will analyze the effects of monetary and time costs of work separately. We will also treat these costs as being fixed, in the sense that they will be assumed not to vary with the number of hours an individual actually works. At first glance this latter assumption may seem overly restrictive, as child-care costs often do depend on the number of hours that care is given. However, the astute student will realize that introducing hours-related costs of work is analytically equivalent to reducing the wage rate. Since we have already stressed how wage changes affect hours of work in the text, we lose little by focusing on the fixed costs of work here.[2]

---

1. Our discussion draws heavily on Mark Killingsworth, *Labor Supply* (Cambridge: Cambridge University Press, 1983), 23–27.
2. It is of course straightforward to introduce into the model money costs of work that vary directly with hours worked. So, for example, a decrease in hourly child-care costs would be equivalent to an increase in the hourly wage, and it would have both income and substitution effects. Based upon existing estimates of labor supply functions one can then simulate directly what the effects of subsidies for child care costs (such as the tax credits for child-care expenses) would be on the labor supply of married women with children. One sophisticated study that does this is James Heckman, "Effect of Child Care Programs on Women's Work Effort," in *Economics of the Family: Marriage, Children, and Human Capital,* ed. Theodore W. Schultz (Chicago: University of Chicago Press, 1974), 491–518. Another study, Siv Gustafsson and Frank Stafford, "Daycare Subsidies and Labor Supply in Sweden," Center for Economic Policy Research, Discussion Paper no. 279 (London, October 1988), found that provision of high-quality public day care in Sweden encourages female labor force participation, as does a lower price for child care.

FIXED MONETARY COSTS OF WORKING

Consider first the case of fixed *monetary* costs of work. Figure 6A.1 shows several indifference curves for an individual who has nonlabor income in the amount aT. If this individual chooses not to work at all, he or she will locate at point a and have a utility level of U_1. If the individual does choose to work, we assume that a fixed per-period cost of ab is incurred. Hence, if the individual works, the budget line starts from point b, not from a.

How large does the wage rate need to be to induce the person depicted in Figure 6A.1 to work for pay—and for how many hours will he or she work at this wage? The absolute value of the slope of the budget line represents the wage rate. Rotating hypothetical budget lines around point b, we eventually reach tangency (at point C) with the indifference curve that represents the

FIGURE 6A.1 Work/Leisure Choice with Fixed Money Costs of Working

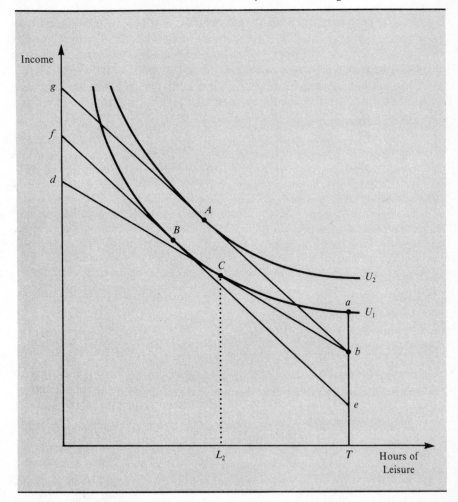

individual's utility level, U_1, if he or she doesn't work at all. At point C the individual is receiving a wage equal to the absolute value of the slope of budget line bd, is working $T - L_2$ hours, and is just indifferent to not working. Any decrease in this wage will cause the individual to drop out of the labor force, because utility level U_1 will no longer be attainable if he or she works any hours. Thus, the wage represented by the slope of bd is the person's *reservation wage*—the lowest wage for which he or she will work.

This fixed-cost model thus provides an explanation for why we tend to observe that even part-time workers do not work a very small number of hours a week.[3] Given the fixed costs of work, individuals receiving a wage close to the minimum they require and who work only a small number of hours would not do as well in terms of utility as they would if they didn't work at all.

What would happen to the minimum hours of work and to reservation wages if the fixed costs were to increase to, say, ae in Figure 6A.1? As is graphically illustrated by the fact that the budget line starting at point e and tangent to U_1—line ef—has a steeper slope than does bd, an increase in the fixed costs of work will tend to raise the reservation wage of potential workers. It can also be noted that the tangency point of budget line ef with indifference curve U_1 is at point B, which because it lies to the left of point C implies that those who work will work longer and consume fewer leisure hours than was the case with fixed costs of ab.

How will an increase in these fixed costs of working affect workers who, when fixed costs were ab, could earn enough by working that they were not close to choosing the option of dropping out of the labor force? Suppose, for example, workers facing fixed working costs of ab could earn the wage implied by budget line bg in Figure 6A.1. These workers would locate at point A and could thereby achieve utility level U_2. Since points on curve U_2 are superior to points on curve U_1, they clearly prefer working to being out of the labor force.

However, if the fixed costs of work were to increase from ab to ae, and wages were to remain constant, the relevant budget line for these workers becomes ef. Now they can achieve only utility level U_1, the same utility they can get by not working. If they continue to work they will desire to work more hours (the increase in fixed cost causes an income effect in this case). These workers, however, may decide *not* to work and to drop out of the labor force, because the rise in the fixed monetary costs of work has increased their reservation wage to the point at which it equals their actual wage.

Increasing fixed costs of work, then, will tend to increase the hours of work for some workers but cause others to drop out of the labor force. Conversely, decreasing fixed costs (for example, by subsidizing commuting or child-care costs) would decrease hours of work for some workers but induce others to enter the labor force. On balance, the net effect on labor supply of such policy changes is ambiguous a priori; empirical estimates are required to pin down the direction of the net effect.

---

3. Average weekly hours of part-time employees in nonagricultural establishments in the United States were about 20 in the early 1980s.

FIXED TIME COSTS OF WORKING

Consider next the case of a fixed *time* cost of working, associated perhaps with commuting or transporting children to day care. In Figure 6A.2 an individual again has nonlabor income in the amount aT and, if this individual does not work at all, will have a utility level of U_1. Now suppose that if the individual does work, he or she incurs fixed time costs in the amount ab. In this case, the maximum number of hours a day available for work or leisure is no longer T but rather T_1. The individual's budget line thus starts at point b if he or she works, and its slope is minus the wage rate. If this budget line is bc the individual will locate at point A and work $T_1 - L_1$ hours.

If the individual's wage rate were lower, the budget line would rotate around point b and become flatter than the slope of bc. If the budget line were bh, the individual *could* maximize utility by locating at point D and by working $T_1 - L_2$ hours. At this point, however, the individual's utility is equal to U_1, the utility level he or she would attain from *not* working, so he or

FIGURE 6A.2 Work/Leisure Choice with Time Costs of Working

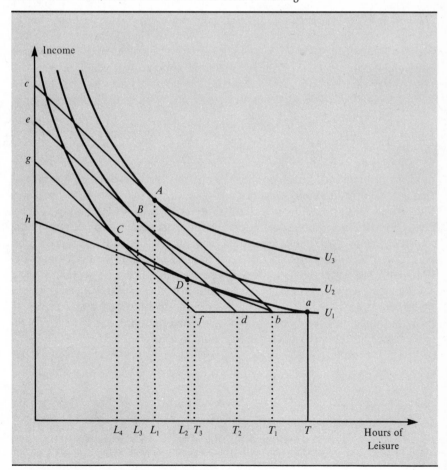

she would be indifferent between working and not working. Any lower wage would clearly induce the individual to drop out of the labor force, as utility level U_1 could no longer be attained by working. Thus, this individual will never work less than $T_1 - L_2$ hours, and it can be seen that fixed *time* costs of work also help explain why we rarely observe individuals working only small numbers of hours per week.

Suppose now that the fixed time costs of work increase from ab to ad, perhaps because of increased traffic congestion faced by commuters. A worker originally facing budget line bc now faces budget line de, will locate at point B, and will work $T_2 - L_3$ hours while consuming L_3 hours of leisure. As long as leisure and income are both assumed to be normal goods, hours of *both* work and leisure time will be reduced by the increase in time costs of work.[4] Further increases in the time cost of work will lead to further reduction in hours of work. Indeed, as drawn in Figure 6A.2, if the time costs reached af, the individual would locate at point C, work $T_3 - L_4$ hours, and have a utility level of U_1. Since this is just equal to the level of utility at point a, any further increase in the fixed time costs of work would cause the individual to drop out of the labor force.

Conversely, this model suggests that anything that decreases the time costs of work will lead to increases in hours of work, *ceteris paribus.* So, for example, if a firm agreed to provide day care of equivalent quality to that which its employees' children were receiving elsewhere, and to charge an equivalent price, it would reduce employees' time cost of work (getting children to day care is now easier) and would increase the hours its employees are willing to work at the wages they are paid.

POLICIES AFFECTING BOTH MONETARY AND TIME COSTS

Combining the insights we have obtained from the fixed *money* and *time* cost models outlined above, it is possible to analyze the effects of policy changes that affect both simultaneously. For example, the introduction of a costly new high-speed mass transit system that is financed by high fares may simultaneously reduce the time costs and increase the monetary costs of commuting to work. The former change should increase the desired hours of work for existing labor force participants and tend to increase the labor force participation rate. The latter change should also increase hours of work for those workers who remain in the labor force, but it would tend to reduce the labor force participation rate. Thus, while average hours of work for workers previously in the labor force would tend to rise, the effect of these changes on the labor force participation rate is indeterminate a priori.

---

4. Note that leisure falls from L_1 to L_3 while hours of work fall from $T_1 - L_1$ to $T_2 - L_3$ or by $(T_1 - T_2) - (L_1 - L_3)$ hours. The increase in fixed time costs of work has an income effect that reduces the worker's demand for both leisure and the goods income will buy (if leisure and these goods are normal goods). Given a constant wage rate, a fall in income implies that hours of work have been reduced.

7

Labor Supply: Household Production, the Family, and the Life Cycle

I n Chapter 6 the theory of labor supply focused on *individuals* who were choosing between *labor* and *leisure*. This chapter will recast labor supply theory to take into account the interdependency of family members' decisions and the fact that much of the time spent at home is on *production*, not consumption, activities. It will also stress the interdependency of individuals' labor supply decisions across different stages of their lives. This theory of labor supply in the context of "household production" and life-cycle decisions can yield many useful insights into labor supply behavior and related policy issues.[1]

THE THEORY OF HOUSEHOLD PRODUCTION

Although many adults are unmarried at some points in their lives, most do marry and form family units. The family thus becomes a very basic decision-making entity in society, and many important decisions concerning both consumption patterns and labor supply are made in a *family* context. Our task in this chapter is to find out in what ways the implications of the individual

---

1. Models of household production are based on the pioneering work of Gary Becker, "A Theory of the Allocation of Time," *Economic Journal* 75 (September 1965): 493–517. Another early study in this area is by Reuben Gronau, "The Measurement of Output of the Nonmarket Sector: The Evaluation of Housewives' Time," in *The Measurement of Economic and Social Performance,* ed. Milton Moss (New York: National Bureau of Economic Research, 1973), 163–89.

labor supply theory in Chapter 6 are modified or expanded by consideration of the *family.*

We shall assume that many commodities the family consumes are produced, or can be produced, at home. Food and energy are combined with preparation time to produce the meals from which family enjoyment is derived. A vacuum cleaner and time are combined to contribute to an orderly home. Food, clothing, and supervision time all contribute to the growth of children, whom the parents hope to enjoy. Thus, a marriage partner who stays at home may be engaged more in the production of commodities from which the family derives utility than in the direct consumption of leisure.

A Model of Household Production

Household production models explicitly recognize that both consumption and production take place in the home. The family unit, then, must make two kinds of decisions: *what* to consume and *how to produce* what it consumes. Consider the second decision first by analyzing a family that does not have to worry about what to consume because it consumes only one commodity: meals. This family derives its utility only from the quantity and quality of food it eats. We shall drop the assumption about consuming just one commodity later, but the assumption permits us to make several basic points in an easily understood fashion.

Meals that yield equal utility can be produced in several ways. A family can buy prepared foods and simply warm them at home, in which case minimum time is spent in preparation and a maximum of market goods are consumed. The meal could be prepared at home with food bought from a market, or it could be prepared at home with food grown or made at home, which obviously represents a lot of preparation time. Since any combination of goods and household time can produce meals that are equally valuable (in terms of producing utility) to the family, we can draw a curve that represents all the time/goods combinations that can produce meals of equal utility. Such a curve can be called a utility *isoquant,* where *iso* means "equal" and *quant* means "quantity" (of utility). Two isoquants are depicted in Figure 7.1 as M_0 and M_1.

Several things should be noted about the isoquants in Figure 7.1. First, along M_0 the utility provided by family meals is constant. The utility produced by the time/goods combinations along M_1 is also constant, but it is greater than the utility represented by M_0 because meals produced by such combinations are of higher quality (involving more inputs of goods and time).

Second, the isoquants M_0 and M_1 are both *negative* in slope and *convex* (as viewed from below) in shape. The *negative* slope reflects an assumption that time and goods are substitutes in the production of meals. If household time is reduced, meal production can be held constant by increasing the purchase of goods. Thus, if a family decides not to grow its own food, it can buy food instead—or if it decides to spend less time cooking food, it could still maintain the same utility from meals by using a microwave oven to heat prepared foods.

The *convexity* of the isoquants reflects an assumption that as household meal-preparation time continues to fall, it becomes more difficult to make up for it with goods. If the family spends a lot of time in meal preparation, it

FIGURE 7.1   The Production of Family Meals

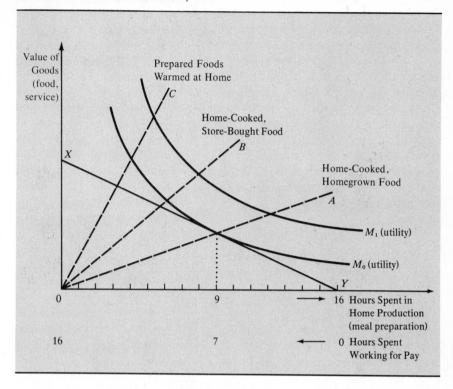

will be easy to replace some of that time with just a few goods (store-bought food easily replaces homegrown food, for example). However, when preparation time is very short to begin with, a further cut in such time may be very difficult to absorb and still keep utility constant. Thus, it will take many goods—a large increase in food quality, for example—to substitute for reduced cooking time.

Finally, along any one ray (A, B, or C) emanating from the origin of Figure 7.1, the ratio of goods to household preparation time in the production of meals is constant. When time and goods are combined in the ratio along ray A, time-intensive meals are produced using homegrown food. Meals produced with the time/goods ratio along B are home-cooked, using store-bought food, and the time/goods ratio along ray C represents the use of prepared foods.

The utility-maximizing mode of producing meals depends on the wage rate, nonwage income, and family preferences. In Figure 7.1 the budget constraint of a woman whose husband is disabled and cannot work, who has no nonwage income, and who has a relatively low wage is depicted by XY. The figure suggests that the utility-maximizing mode of meal preparation is to use homegrown food, for the simple reason that when one has a low wage, time-intensive activities are relatively inexpensive. Time spent weeding, tilling, canning, and freezing does not cost a lot, in terms of forgone earnings (goods), in this case. Thus, in the example shown, 9 hours a day would be spent at home, 7 hours performing work for pay, and meal production on isoquant M_0 represents the highest level of utility that can be attained.

Figure 7.2 shows what will happen if the budget constraint in Figure 7.1 shifts because of an increase in *nonwage* income. What happens to the wife's propensity to work outside the home if the family begins to receive governmental payments for the husband's disability? This income grant does not change the wife's wage rate, so the new budget constraint facing the family has the same slope as constraint XY in Figure 7.1. However, the new constraint ($X'Y'$ in Figure 7.2) lies above the old one and reflects a pure *income effect*. Because it is wealthier, the family will want to enjoy higher-quality meals. It will have more money with which to buy goods, but it will also decide to have the wife spend more time at home to prepare the meals (remember, both goods and time are valuable in producing meals). She may change

FIGURE 7.2   Production of Family Meals: The Income Effect

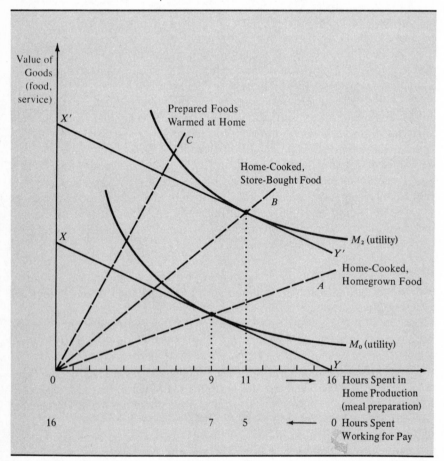

the time/goods ratio, as shown in Figure 7.2, by a movement from ray *A* to ray *B*, depending on the shape of the isoquants.

Before discussing the changes that result from a change in the wife's wage, let us pause to make two points. First, the income effect in this household production model has exactly the same sign as the effect in the labor/leisure model discussed in Chapter 6. Second, the amount of work for pay and the mode of household production are jointly determined; that is, they are affected by the same constraint and are made as part of the same decision. Emphasizing household production rather than leisure, therefore, does not change our conclusion about the effects of income on labor supply in this case. Emphasizing production rather than leisure, however, does highlight the interrelated nature of decisions concerning family "household production" and decisions about labor supply.

Let us continue for a moment with our example in Figure 7.2 of a wife whose husband is disabled and unemployed. If he remains disabled but she obtains a wage increase, what will happen to her labor supply? Quite simply, there will be two opposing effects (as we found in the "leisure" model previously). The *income effect,* as above, will tend to drive her away from market work and toward more time at home, where she can spend more time in activities (meal preparation) that enhance family utility. However, the *substitution effect* will tend to push her out of the home and toward more work for pay. When her wages are increased, time spent at home preparing meals becomes more expensive than it was before. Thus, she will tend to move away from time-intensive modes of production to modes that rely more on goods, thus freeing her for more "market" work. The overall observed effect of her wage increase on her labor supply cannot be predicted based on theory alone.

Household Production and Consumption

We have just seen that when a family member is engaged in household production, an increase in the wage rate will have two effects. There will be an income effect that induces the family to consume more household "output" and tends to push the household producer out of market work and into the home. However, there is also a substitution effect that induces the family to produce its household output in a less time-intensive fashion, which tends to drive the household producer into working more for pay outside the home. Thus, *substitution in the (household) production process* occurs. How large is this substitution effect?

Recall from Chapter 6 that the substitution effect is graphically depicted by changing the slope of the budget constraint, keeping it tangent to a given indifference curve. If the relevant indifference curve (isoquant) is gently curved, as in panel (a) of Figure 7.3, the substitution effect will be larger than when the indifference curve is abruptly bent, as in panel (b). What will cause it to bend suddenly? In terms of our model, the curve will exhibit a rapid change in slope when it becomes *difficult to substitute goods for time* without loss of utility. (To prove this to yourself, ask, "If an hour of time at home is given up, what amount of goods will have to be added to keep utility con-

FIGURE 7.3   Large vs. Small Substitution Effects

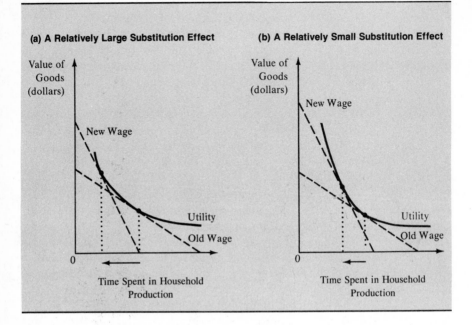

(a) A Relatively Large Substitution Effect   **(b) A Relatively Small Substitution Effect**

stant?" When it is difficult to substitute goods for time, it will take many added goods to keep utility constant.)[2]

Married women have traditionally been engaged in household production as well as household consumption. Married men have tended to be less involved in household production, and a higher proportion of their time at home has been spent in consumption, or leisure, activities. As men's wages rise, they experience a substitution effect in *consumption* that tends to push them away from time-intensive forms of consumption and towards more goods-intensive consumption. When women's wages rise, however, there are substitution effects in both *production* and *consumption*. Women will tend to consume less time-intensive commodities, but as household producers they *also* adopt less time-intensive modes of production. They substitute day care, frozen foods, and microwave ovens for household production time; this substitution effect in production is more or less added to the one in consumption to yield a stronger overall substitution effect than is observed for men.

---

2. Students should be able to convince themselves that the limiting case in which no substitution is possible involves an isoquant that is L-shaped; in this case no change in the wage rate will change the optimum mix of inputs. The limiting case of *perfect* substitution involves an isoquant that is a negatively sloped straight line; in this case a change in the wage rate could cause the family to flip-flop from the use of only one input to using only the other.

JOINT HUSBAND–WIFE LABOR SUPPLY DECISIONS

We have just seen that analyzing the labor supply of *individuals*—in this case a wife whose husband is unable to work either inside or outside the home—when the choice is between market and household work yields the same implications as when the choice involves leisure (as in Chapter 6). However, introducing the household as the primary locus of consumption raises the issue of *family* decision making. More specifically, if husband and wife can both work either inside or outside the home, their labor supply decisions are interdependent to some extent.

The proper way to model family decision making is not entirely clear, unfortunately, and economists have adopted various approaches.[3] The most common approach up to now assumes that the marriage partners have a collective set of preferences and thus behave as a single unit. The other major approach assumes that each partner has a separate set of preferences, and that each seeks to maximize his or her own individual utility subject to a family budget constraint. This approach often includes the assumption that the marriage partners bargain with each other in the decision-making process, and that one may have more power than the other over the ultimate outcomes.[4]

While these decision-making models have somewhat different implications (see footnote 8 later in this chapter), they all acknowledge that family labor supply decisions are jointly made. This being the case, there are a number of considerations that must be taken into account by the spouses, whatever their decision-making style. In the subsections that follow we discuss some of these factors.

Who Stays at Home?

Consider a family trying to decide which spouse will stay home and engage in "household production" full time. This family needs to answer two questions: Who is relatively more productive at home? Who is relatively more productive in market work? The answer to the first question depends upon who can produce more commodities (more utility) for a given amount of goods and home production time. The answer to the second question depends upon who can generate the greater command over goods by working for pay. Simply put, if a

---

3. These approaches are usefully summarized in Mark R. Killingsworth, *Labor Supply* (Cambridge, Eng.: Cambridge University Press, 1983), 29–38.
4. See Marilyn Manser and Murray Brown, "Marriage and Household Decision-Making: A Bargaining Analysis," *International Economic Review* 21, no. 1 (February 1980): 31–44, and Marjorie McElroy and Mary Jean Horney, "Nash-Bargained Household Decisions: Toward a Generalization of the Theory of Demand," *International Economic Review* 22, no. 2 (June 1981): 333–49. The international trade model presented in Chapter 4 can also be usefully applied, by analogy, to the family. Each partner can be viewed as having a comparative advantage in producing one or more commodities from which the family derives utility; if so, the family can enhance its command over commodities by deciding to have each partner specialize in his or her area of comparative advantage.

family decides it must have one spouse at home, it will find that its total resources are maximized if the primary household producer is the spouse who is relatively more productive there than in the marketplace.

For example, a family deciding who should stay home and perform most of the child rearing would want to consider the gains and losses attendant on either the husband or wife performing this task. The losses from staying home are related to the market wage of each, while the gains depend on their enjoyment of, and skill at, child rearing. (Since enjoyment of the parenting process increases utility, we can designate both higher levels of enjoyment *and* higher levels of skill as indicative of greater "productivity" in child rearing.) The wage rate for women, perhaps because of discrimination, is usually below that for men. (Discrimination will be treated in Chapter 14; other reasons for male/female wage differences are dealt with in Chapters 8 and 9.) It is also likely that, because of socialization, wives are usually more productive than husbands in child rearing. If a given woman's wage rate is lower than her husband's and the woman is more productive in child rearing, it is clearly better for the woman to raise the children. The family gives up less in market goods and gains more in child rearing.

Modeling the choice of who stays home to raise children as influenced by relative productivities is not meant to imply that customs are not important in shaping preferences or in limiting choices concerning household production; clearly they are.[5] What the theory of household production emphasizes is that child-rearing arrangements will probably change as wages and home productivities change. If discrimination against women is eliminated or if gender roles in childhood become less distinct for boys and girls, we could well observe more men rearing children in the future.

Do Both Spouses Work for Pay?

It is clearly not necessary, of course, that either husband or wife stay at home full time. Many household chores, from cooking and cleaning to child care, can be hired out or otherwise performed in a goods-intensive manner. The considerations underlying the decision about whether both should work can be best understood by looking at Figure 7.4. The utility isoquants there (U_1 and U_2) represent the various combinations of household time and goods that can be used to generate family (or individual) utility of two levels (level 1 and level 2).

As long as an extra hour of market work by both husband and wife creates the ability to buy more goods than are required to make up for the hour of lost home production time, both spouses can enhance family resources if they work for pay that extra hour. In terms of Figure 7.4, if a person spending H_0 hours at home decides to work an extra hour for pay, so that H_1 hours are now spent at home, he or she will gain BD in goods.[6] Since an increase of only

---

5. For a discussion of this issue, see Claire Brown, "An Institutional Model of Wives' Work Decisions," *Industrial Relations* 24, no. 2 (Spring 1985): 182–204.
6. We are talking here of *after*-tax spending power. The value of what one produces at home is not taxed, but earnings in the marketplace are—a difference that forces us to focus here on wages and earnings *net* of taxes.

EXAMPLE 7.1
Household Productivity and Labor Supply in Japan

One of the fundamental insights of household production theory is that one's labor supply behavior is, in part, a function of productivity at home relative to that in the marketplace (as reflected in one's wage rate). While formal exposition of the theory is a recent development in economics, the behavior it seeks to explain is not. Many developing countries employ people in their industrial cities who have recently migrated from family farms and whose labor is valuable there at harvest time. In terms of household production theory, the harvest-related increase in their productivity back on the farm temporarily reduces the relative advantage of market (paid) work; the result is they quit or absent themselves from their factory jobs at this time of year and go back home to help out.

An example of the above behavior can be found in Japan early in this century. Many cotton-spinning mills lost 30 percent of their work force in August, stimulating factory owners to adopt countermeasures. Koji Taira describes the situation as follows:

It was widely recognized that the seasonal fluctuations were closely related to labor requirements on farms, since the factory operatives were predominantly from farm households. From the point of view of the farm households, the value of work on the farm during busy periods was much higher than the regular wages at the factory. The essence of countermeasures on the part of the factory, therefore, was to offer such inducements as might make staying on the job more attractive than returning to the farm during such periods. A variety of inducements developed that were based on this premise. One was to grant bonuses to those who stayed on their jobs during the months of peak activity on the farm. Another was a profit-sharing plan of one kind or another that was related to length of period of consecutive work. The third was a variety of devices such as company-paid pleasure trips, participation in company-sponsored lotteries, and recreational opportunities granted only to workers remaining on the job during busy seasons on the farm.

SOURCE: Koji Taira, *Economic Development and the Labor Market in Japan* (New York: Columbia University Press, 1970), 122.

BC in goods is required to compensate for the lost hour of home production to keep utility constant, family resources are clearly increased if the person works for pay. In other words, at point *A* the person is relatively more productive in the marketplace than at home. Thus, decisions about family labor supply must be made in full consideration of the market and household productivities of both marriage partners.

As we saw earlier in this chapter, the level of household income can also be expected to affect the labor supply of each partner (with lower income levels inducing more market work, other things equal). This income effect apparently plays a prominent role in affecting the labor supply of married women who face relatively high probabilities of marital dissolution. Namely, the *prospect* of reduced income associated with separation and divorce induces

FIGURE 7.4   Home vs. Market Productivities

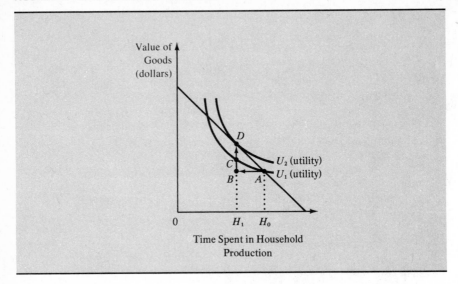

them to gradually increase their hours of work and labor force participation rates *prior to* separation, and the separation itself is associated with a relatively large jump in hours worked and participation rates.[7]

The Joint Decision and Cross-Effects

We have seen that family labor supply decisions are the outcomes of a process that jointly considers the household and market productivities of each spouse. However, one spouse's productivity in both production and consumption at home is affected by the *other* spouse's labor supply to the market, so that modeling the joint decision is quite complex. For example, if a married woman decides to increase her hours worked outside the home, her husband's marginal productivity for a given number of hours at home may rise as he takes over chores she once performed. Thus, if both wife and husband are *substitutes* in the household *production* of commodities, one's increased labor supply may tend to decrease the labor supply of the other.

7. William R. Johnson and Jonathan Skinner, "Labor Supply and Marital Separation," *American Economic Review* 76, no. 3 (June 1986): 455–69.

The more general issue of the forces that influence marital dissolution rates has been a subject of some interest to economists; a pioneering theoretical and empirical study that uses a generalization of the framework developed in this chapter is Gary S. Becker, Elisabeth M. Landes, and Robert T. Michael, "An Economic Analysis of Marital Instability," *Journal of Political Economy* 85, no. 6 (December 1977): 1141–88. One implication of this approach is that higher incomes available to women will create an "independence effect" and increase their divorce probabilities (allowing them to substitute their own resources for their husbands' time and income in the production of desired consumption goods). In fact, studies of the negative income tax experiments discussed in Chapter 6 show that these income transfer programs did lead to an increase in female participants' probabilities of divorce. See, for example, Lyle P. Groeneveld, Nancy Brandon Tuma, and Michael T. Hannan, "The Effects of Negative Income Tax Programs on Marital Dissolution," *Journal of Human Resources* 15, no. 4 (Fall 1980): 654–74.

On the other hand, both spouses may be *complementary* in the *consumption* of commodities. That is, if the woman above takes a job that involves working until 8:00 P.M. each night, her husband may decide that dinners at 6:00 P.M. have less utility than before, and as a result, he might decide that the benefits of working later outweigh the utility lost by so doing. In this case, one spouse's decision to increase hours worked for pay may induce the other spouse to likewise increase labor supply.

Theory cannot predict whether the spouses are substitutes or complements in household production and consumption; similarly, it is impossible to say which cross-effect will dominate if their signs conflict. Thus, the question of how one spouse's labor supply will respond to changes in the labor supply of the other is essentially an empirical one, and there is as yet no real consensus about the sizes and signs of these cross-effects for husbands and wives.[8] However, as will be seen in the next section, the dominant cross-effect may well vary with family circumstances.

HOUSEHOLD PRODUCTION THEORY AND SOME SOCIAL ISSUES

The theory presented thus far in this chapter can be used to analyze some important social and policy issues. In this section we shall look at the effects on family labor supply of health problems, recessions, and income maintenance programs. Note that in each case, questions of the cross-effects discussed in the preceding section are critical.

Health and Labor Supply

An analysis of the market and household productivities of a husband and wife must consider the effects of *health* on labor supply. While a man who tires quickly because of a respiratory problem may be capable of performing market work at reduced hours or wages, his affliction renders his *market* time less productive than that of a healthy person. However, his marginal contribution to production at home, where resting in between tasks is possible, may not be affected much at all. If he and his wife are substitutes in household production, his changed relative productivity between home and the marketplace may induce him to become the principal household producer and her to become the primary wage earner. Indeed, there is some evidence that slightly

---

8. For reviews of these issues, see Killingsworth, *Labor Supply;* Marjorie B. McElroy, "Appendix: Empirical Results from Estimates of Joint Labor Supply Functions of Husbands and Wives," in *Research in Labor Economics,* vol. 4, ed. Ronald G. Ehrenberg (Greenwich, Conn.: JAI Press, 1981), 53–64; and Shelly Lundberg, "Labor Supply of Husbands and Wives: A Simultaneous Equations Approach," *Review of Economics and Statistics* 70 (May 1988): 224–34.

We mentioned earlier that the two basic approaches economists have taken to modeling the family's decision-making process have somewhat different implications. One implication of the model that assumes the spouses have a collective set of preferences is that the effect of increases in the wife's wage (income held constant) on the husband's labor supply would be the same as the effects on the wife's labor supply of increases in the husband's wage. The empirical studies cited above tend to reject this built-in assumption about the symmetry of the two cross-effects, thus casting doubt on the relevance of this model of family decision making.

disabled workers do tend to replace their spouses as primary household producers.[9] One cannot theoretically predict with any certainty that this change in roles will occur, however, for at least two reasons. First, his becoming disabled may *increase* his wife's marginal productivity at home if he needs extra care. Second, if the time of each is *complementary in consumption,* his increased time at home would tend to increase her time at home.

Here again, labor supply decisions are viewed by a utility-maximizing family as matters of choice, not custom or necessity. While custom or necessity is obviously important in some cases, viewing labor supply decisions as matters of choice provides insight into how government policies or general economic trends can change such decisions. For example, if there is discrimination against women and if this discrimination decreases so that their market wages improve relative to those for men, the labor supply withdrawal of unhealthy men might become more pronounced, for the reasons noted above. For the same reasons, it could become more common for women to be the primary breadwinners in two-adult families.

The "Discouraged" vs. the "Additional" Worker

Changes in one spouse's productivity, either at home or in market work, can alter the family's basic labor supply decision. Consider, for example, a family in which market work is performed by the husband and in which the wife is employed full time in the home. What will happen if a recession causes the husband to become unemployed?

The husband's market productivity declines, at least temporarily. He may be a highly specialized worker and unable to find similar work at the moment. The drop in his market productivity relative to his household productivity (which is unaffected by the recession) makes it more likely that the family will find it beneficial for him to engage in household production. If the wage his wife can earn in paid work is not affected, the family *may* decide that, to try to maintain the family's prior level of utility (which might be affected by both consumption and *savings* levels), *she* should seek market work and *he* should substitute for her in home production for as long as the recession lasts. He may remain a member of the labor force as an unemployed worker awaiting recall, and as she begins to look for work, she becomes an "added" member of the labor force. Thus, in the face of falling family income, the number of family members seeking market work may increase. This potential response is akin to the income effect in that, as family income falls, fewer commodities are consumed—and less time spent in consumption tends to be matched by more desired hours of work for pay.

At the same time, however, we must look at the *wage rate* someone without a job can *expect* to receive if he or she looks for work. This expected wage, denoted by $E(W)$, can actually be written as a precise statistical concept:

$$E(W) = \pi W \tag{7.1}$$

9. Richard Conley, *The Economics of Vocational Rehabilitation* (Baltimore: Johns Hopkins University Press, 1965), 70.

where W is the wage rate of people who have the job and π is the probability of obtaining the job if out of work. For someone without a job, the price of an hour at home—the opportunity cost of staying home—is $E(W)$. The reduced availability of jobs that occurs when the unemployment rate rises causes the expected wage of those without jobs to fall sharply for two reasons. First, an excess of labor supply over demand tends to push down real wages (for those with jobs) during recessionary periods. Second, the chances of getting a job fall in a recession. Thus, both W and π fall in a recession, causing $E(W)$ to decline. Noting the *substitution effect* that accompanies a falling expected wage, some have argued that people who would otherwise have entered the labor force become "discouraged" in a recession and tend to remain out of the labor market. Looking for work has such a low expected payoff for them that such people decide that spending time at home is more productive than spending time in job search. The reduction of the labor force associated with discouraged workers in a recession is a force working against the "added-worker" effect—just as the substitution effect works against the income effect.

It is possible, of course, for both the "added-worker" and "discouraged-worker" effects to coexist, because "added" and "discouraged" workers will be different groups of people. Which group predominates, however, is the important question. If the labor force is swollen by "added workers" during a recession, the published unemployment rate will likewise become swollen (the added workers will increase the number of people looking for work). If workers become "discouraged" and drop out of the labor market after having been unemployed, the decline in people seeking jobs will depress the unemployment rate. Knowledge of which effect predominates is needed in order to make accurate inferences about the actual state of the labor market from the published unemployment rate.

We know that the added-worker effect does exist, although a recent study finds it to be rather small.[10] The added-worker effect is confined, however, to the relatively few families whose normal breadwinner loses a job (the overall unemployment rate rarely goes above 10 percent), and as more and more women become regularly employed for pay, the added-worker effect will tend to both decline and become increasingly confined to teenagers. In contrast, the fall in expected real wages occurs in nearly *every* household, and since the substitution effect is strong for married women, it is not surprising that studies have consistently found the discouraged-worker effect to be large and dominant.[11] Other things equal, *the labor force tends to shrink during recessions and grow during periods of economic recovery.*

The dominance of the discouraged-worker effect creates what some call the "hidden" unemployed—people who would like to work but who believe that jobs are so scarce that looking for work is of no use. Because they are not

---

10. Shelly Lundberg, "The Added Worker Effect," *Journal of Labor Economics* 3, no. 1 (January 1985): 11–37.
11. The landmark study on this topic is Jacob Mincer, "Labor Force Participation and Unemployment: A Review of Recent Evidence," in *Prosperity and Unemployment*, ed. R. A. Gordon and M. S. Gordon (New York: John Wiley & Sons, 1966).

looking for work, they are not counted as unemployed in government statistics. Focusing on the period 1979–81, when the overall official unemployment rate went from 5.8 percent to 7.6 percent, can give some indication of the size of hidden unemployment.

In 1979 an average of 6.1 million people were counted as unemployed at any given time, representing 5.8 percent of the labor force. In addition, 772,000 people indicated that they wanted work but were not seeking it because they felt jobs were unavailable to them. This group constituted 1.2 percent of those adults not in the labor force. In 1981 the number of people officially counted as unemployed was 8.3 million (7.6 percent of the labor force), but there were 1.1 million others among the "hidden" unemployed. These people represented 1.7 percent of those adults not in the labor force. The rise in the percentage of those out of the labor market for job-related reasons is evidence of the discouraged-worker effect. Incidentally, if "discouraged workers" were counted as unemployed members of the labor force, the unemployment rate would have been 6.5 percent in 1979 and 8.5 percent in 1981.[12] To count these workers, however, would overlook the possibility (raised later in this chapter) that some of them desire only an intermittent labor force attachment and time their periods out of the labor force to coincide with periods when expected wages are low.[13]

How Will an Income Maintenance Program Affect Work Incentives?

Family labor supply models can also be applied to the analysis of the effects of income maintenance programs. Our model in Chapter 6 implied that income maintenance programs clearly reduce work incentives because they simultaneously increase income and reduce the effective wage rate. While this effect may be true for the family unit as a whole, it does *not* follow that *both* husband and wife will supply fewer hours to the labor market, primarily because of the possibility that the spouses are substitutes in household production.[14]

Consider the *wife's* response to a family income maintenance subsidy and assume she is initially the primary "household producer." The *increase* in family *income* will encourage the family to consume more of all normal goods, including both "pure" leisure and other household-produced commodities. These manifestations of the income effect suggest that total family hours at home will tend to rise. The *decline* in her effective *wage rate* induces the family to adopt more time-intensive modes of household production, indica-

---

12. To say that including "discouraged workers" in unemployment statistics would change the published unemployment rate does not imply that it *should* be done. For a summary of the arguments for and against counting discouraged workers as unemployed, see the final report of the National Commission on Employment and Unemployment Statistics, *Counting the Labor Force* (Washington, D.C., 1979), 44–49.

13. Most "discouraged workers" seldom test the market. A 1984 study found that only 44 percent had looked for work in the past year, and one-third had not worked in the past five years (many, however, were youths). See Paul Flaim, "Discouraged Workers: How Strong Are Their Links to the Job Market?" *Monthly Labor Review* 107, no. 8 (August 1984): 8–11.

14. For a more rigorous and complete analysis of this issue, see Mark R. Killingsworth, "Must a Negative Income Tax Reduce Labor Supply? A Study of the Family's Allocation of Time," *Journal of Human Resources* 11 (Summer 1976): 354–65.

EXAMPLE 7.2

Differences in Swiss Child-Rearing Practices Around 1800

Household production theory emphasizes the interrelated nature of household production and labor market activity. It views choices concerning both household and labor market activities as functions of family preferences, wage rates, and wealth (or its derivative, income). One important household activity is the rearing of children, and we show below how differences in labor market opportunities and wealth in Switzerland around 1800 caused differences in child-rearing practices.

In the late 18th and early 19th centuries, a lucrative and vigorous "cottage industry" developed in the rural highlands near Zurich, with households in this industry performing spinning and weaving operations at home. In the households that owned their own land and had relatively spacious accommodations, equipment was brought into the home and the spinning and weaving activities provided a remunerative activity for all household members, including children. In these households it became common for parents to set a quota for spinning or weaving that was required before children were free to play; the quota that had to be met before leisure was possible became known as the *Rast* (rest).

Among the poorer, landless families, this system of *Rast* became very different. Because of rapid population growth and prohibitions against increasing the housing supply, these families could not secure accommodations large enough to house spinning and weaving equipment for the entire family. In these households children were a "burden" in two senses. They were a net drain on family wealth, and the time required for their upbringing became more and more costly as the parents' earning power increased. As a result of their low level of wealth, their growing cost of child rearing, and their children's low productivity at home, these families tended to board their children in the homes of wealthier families. In effect, these children were placed in "market" instead of household work, and they were expected to pay (by spinning and weaving) for their own upkeep. The money required by the boarding family to maintain the child was called the *Rast*.

In short, child-rearing practices—and the meaning of *Rast*—varied with differences in wealth (especially in the form of housing) and household productivity. Consistent with the theory of household production, labor market and household decisions were interrelated and affected by both wealth and the opportunity cost of time.

SOURCE: Rudolf Braun, "Early Industrialization and Demographic Change in the Canton of Zurich," in *Historical Studies of Changing Fertility,* ed. Charles Tilly (Princeton: Princeton University Press, 1978), 289–334.

tive of a substitution effect that also works in the direction of reduced family labor supply. Both effects depend, of course, on her *remaining* the primary household producer.

The income maintenance program, however, also reduces the take-home wage of her *husband,* and this change could result in the family's deciding that the husband should become the primary household producer. Suppose, for example, that both husband and wife have the same market wage but the wife is relatively more productive at home when just a few total hours of family time are spent there. Initially, then, the family decides that *she* should do the household production. Suppose, however, that the husband has household skills, such as carpentry and plumbing skills, that can be put to best use when time at home is substantial. When the family decides to allocate more total hours of family time to household production, his household skills become relatively more valuable, and the family may decide *he* should become the primary household producer. (The likelihood of this decision is increased if the family, for example, is renovating a very old house.) He might thus reduce his market labor supply, but she might increase hers.

Thus, it is theoretically possible that the availability of an income maintenance program could cause *overall* family labor supply to fall while at the same time inducing one family member to *increase* his or her labor supply. To say that it is a *possibility* should not imply, of course, that it is a theoretical prediction or that it actually occurs. The empirical results on this issue are still inconclusive.[15]

LIFE-CYCLE ASPECTS OF LABOR SUPPLY

Because market productivity (wages) and household productivity vary over the life cycle, people vary the hours they supply to the labor market over their lives. In the early adult years relatively fewer hours are devoted to work than in later years, and more time is devoted to schooling. In the very late years people fully or partially retire, though at varying ages. In the middle years most males are working full time, but many women have careers that are interrupted by years at home raising small children. While the issue of schooling is dealt with in Chapter 9, the model of household production discussed in this chapter can help us understand both the labor force behavior of married women and decisions about retirement.

The Interrupted Careers of Married Women

The basic premise of the household production model is that people are productive in two places: in the home and in a "market" job. Their decisions about whether to seek market work and for how many hours are a function of their *relative* productivities in both places. As long as an extra hour of market work allows the person to buy more goods than are required to make up for the hour of lost production time at home, the person will work for pay that extra hour.

The marginal home productivity of parents greatly increases when young children are present. The increase in household productivity can be represented graphically by a steeper tilt to one's utility isoquants. In Figure 7.5, the married woman depicted has utility isoquants like U when without children,

---

15. See Chapter 6 for citations of numerous labor supply studies based on income maintenance experiments, and footnote 8 in this chapter for reviews of empirical studies on cross-effects.

FIGURE 7.5   Household Productivity Can Change over the Life Cycle

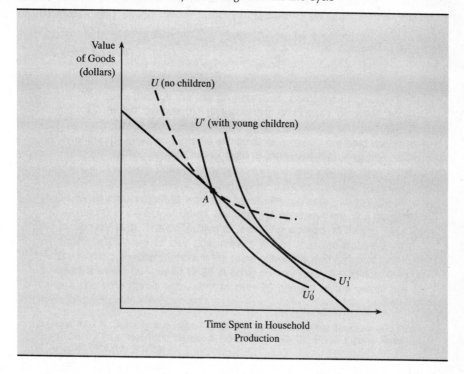

but with young children at home her isoquants take on a steeper slope (compare the slopes of U and U_0' at point A). The steeper slope of the U' "family" of isoquants results in a tangency point to the right of point A; thus, her hours devoted to household production tend to increase and those devoted to market work tend to decrease. As the children grow older, her isoquants tilt back toward U, and she begins to seek more work for pay.

The Substitution Effect and When to Work over a Lifetime

Just as deciding *who* will work at home at various stages in a family's life involves comparing market and home productivities of husband and wife, deciding *when* to work over the course of one's life involves comparing market and home productivities *over time*. The basic idea here is that a person will tend to perform the most market work when his or her earning capacity is high relative to home productivity. Conversely, people will engage in household production when their earning capacity is relatively low.

Suppose a sales representative working on a commission basis knows that his potential income is around $30,000 in a certain year, but that July's income potential will be twice that of November's. Would it be rational for him to schedule his vacation (a time-intensive activity) in November? The answer depends on his market productivity relative to his "household productivity" for the two months. Obviously his market productivity, his wage rate, is higher in July than November, which means that the opportunity costs of a vacation are greater in July. However, if he has children who are free to vacation only in July, he may decide that his household productivity (in terms of utility) is so much greater in July than November that the benefits of vacationing in July outweigh the costs. If he does not have children of school age, the utility generated by a November vacation may be sufficiently close to that of a July vacation that the smaller opportunity costs make a November vacation preferable.

Similar decisions are probably made over longer periods of time, perhaps one's entire life. As Chapter 9 will show, market productivity (which is reflected in one's wage) starts low in the young adult years, rises rapidly with age, then tails off and even falls in the later years, as shown in panel (a) of Figure 7.6. *If* home productivity is more or less constant over the years, then we should find people working (for pay) hardest in their middle years and least in the early and late years, as illustrated in panel (b) of Figure 7.6. Likewise, the consumption of very time-intensive commodities will occur in one's early and late years, a prediction more or less confirmed when one observes the ages of Americans traveling in Europe. That such travelers are primarily young adults and the elderly is clearly related to the fact that, for these

FIGURE 7.6   Life-Cycle Allocation of Time

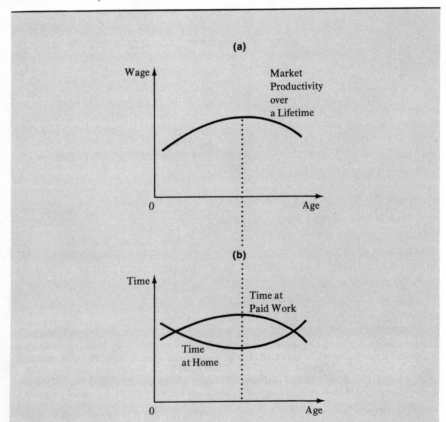

groups, opportunity costs are lower. They make the time to go because, at these stages in their lives, time is relatively inexpensive.

The decision about *when* to do one's work for pay over the life cycle focuses on the productivity and cost of time—in other words, the *substitution effect*. Without explicitly saying so, we have been looking in this subsection at persons or families of given wealth and analyzing how they arrange market and household production over their lives in response to changing productivities in each place. In this context, the income effect is of little relevance.

For example, once one's educational level, general occupation, and probable inherited wealth are known, one's overall lifetime wealth can be foretold with reasonable accuracy. If a woman of wealth level X knows she wants to take a trip to Kenya at least once in her life, the question is not *whether* to take it, but *when*. The "when" partly depends on the factors discussed above, which emphasize substitution effects.[16] Empirical research on intertemporal substitution effects has only recently begun, but to date the estimated effects, while generally supportive of the theory, appear to be small.[17]

The Choice of Retirement Age

As suggested above, some labor supply decisions are more concerned with *when* to work for pay than with *how much* work to do over a lifetime. Decisions about *when* to work largely turn on the substitution effect. Retirement decisions, however, concern the *quantity* of paid hours of work performed in a lifetime, and are clearly affected by both income and substitution effects.

A *life-cycle* perspective is necessary to correctly analyze retirement decisions, in large part because *yearly retirement benefits, lifetime* earnings, and *lifetime* expected pension benefits are all influenced by the age of retirement.[18] Thus, if one thinks of household productivity as a partial function of pension benefits (which are what one can "earn" by refraining from market work), the commodities that can be produced at the margin by staying home (retiring) vary with one's retirement age. Also, because one's market wage tends to change each year, both market *and* household productivity vary with the age of retirement, and as we argued earlier, it is because of these yearly variations that we must adopt a life-cycle perspective.

To simplify the analysis, we initially assume that retirement is associated with the total cessation of market work. We can then model workers' choices about retirement age as a function of their (discounted) expected *lifetime nonwork income* as of the earliest year in which they can retire and the *gain* in (discounted) lifetime total (work plus nonwork) income that could be obtained by working longer and postponing retirement. The first factor affects the height of segment AB in Figure 7.7, where age 62 is assumed (for illustrative

---

16. Another factor, of course, is the extent to which the trip will permanently increase her utility (through pleasant memories, for example).

17. See Pencavel, "Male Labor Supply: A Review," and Joseph Altonji, "Intertemporal Substitution in Labor Supply: Evidence from Micro Data," *Journal of Political Economy* 94 (June 1986): S176–S215.

18. The analysis in this section borrows heavily from Olivia S. Mitchell and Gary S. Fields, "The Effects of Pensions and Earnings on Retirement: A Review Essay," *Research in Labor Economics,* ed. R. Ehrenberg (Greenwich, Conn.: JAI Press, 1982), 115–55.

EXAMPLE 7.3

The Value of a Homemaker's Time

The services performed by homemakers are not sold in the marketplace, but this does not imply they are not valuable. For purposes of settling claims involving the wrongful death of a homemaker, and often in cases in which property must be divided upon divorce, it is important to place a value on homemakers' services. Three approaches can be taken in evaluating these services.

Market Prices. One method is to measure how much a homemaker's services would cost if they were to be purchased in the marketplace. Thus, the "market" costs of child care, cleaning, cooking, and other services are aggregated to form an overall estimate. The results of one careful study using this approach imply that the value of services performed by a full-time homemaker, in a two-adult family with two children under age 6, was $16,770 in 1989 dollars. The problem with this method is that in cases in which market services are available but not purchased, the household must believe such services are not worth their cost; for these households, the value assigned by the market-prices approach overstates the value of the homemaker's services.

Opportunity Costs. A second method is to estimate what the homemaker would have been able to earn if she (or he) had worked for pay. Of course, many married women do not work for pay at all, which implies they value the services they provide at home at *more* than their potential market earnings. Using the forgone wage to estimate the value of their services thus results in an underestimate. An estimate of the value of a typical homemaker's services using this approach comes to about $9,490 per year in 1989 (after taxes and work-related expenses).

Self-Employment Approach. A third method is to treat homemakers as self-employed individuals who can either increase hours at home if their marginal household productivity (*MHP*) exceeds their market wage (*W*) or reduce hours at home if *W* exceeds *MHP*. If *MHP* exceeds *W* even when hours of work for pay are zero, the homemaker works full time at home; if *W* exceeds *MHP* even when working full time for pay, the person works full time outside the home. If a person is at home part of the time and also works part time for pay, theory suggests that *MHP* and *W* must be equal.

Thus, for those homemakers who work for pay part time, we can infer that the value of their *marginal* productivity at home is equal to their net market wage. Using this wage as an estimate of their marginal household productivity, it is possible to estimate a production function for the value of household services. Applying this production function to full-time homemakers, it has been estimated that the typical homemaker working exclusively in the home produces services worth (in 1989 terms) $21,900 to the family. Full-time married homemakers *with children under age 6* were estimated to produce services worth $29,130 in 1989.

SOURCE: William H. Gauger and Kathryn E. Walker, "The Dollar Value of Household Work," Information Bulletin 60, New York State College of Human Ecology, Cornell University, 1979; Reuben Gronau, "Home Production—A Forgotten Industry," *Review of Economics and Statistics* 62 (August 1980): 408–15; Carmel Ullman Chiswick, "The Value of a Housewife's Time," *Journal of Human Resources* 16 (Summer 1982): 413–25.

FIGURE 7.7   Choice of Optimum Retirement Age

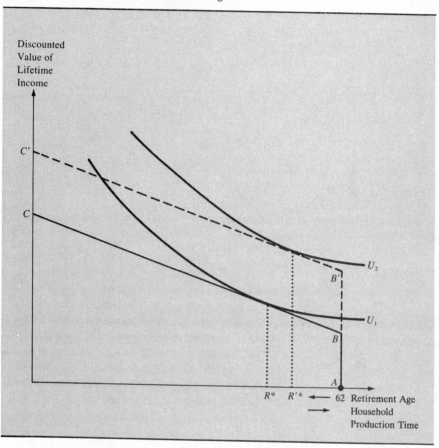

purposes only) to be the earliest possible retirement age. The second factor affects the *slope* of BC in Figure 7.7; for convenience, we assume the gain from working an added year to be constant and thus represent it with a straight line (we discuss this assumption below). The optimum retirement age, R^*, is clearly affected by the shape of the constraint ABC *and* the person's preferences (represented by curves U_1 and U_2) regarding income (goods) and years of retirement (household time).

When nonwork income (which includes pension benefits) at age 62 is larger, holding constant the gain in income beyond age 62, the vertical portion of the constraint is lengthened and the constraint shifts *up* to $AB'C'$. Because segment $B'C'$ is parallel to segment BC (by the assumption that the gain in income beyond age 62 remains constant), there is a pure income effect that induces the person to retire earlier. When AB' is one's expected lifetime income if age 62 is the retirement age, R'^* becomes the optimum age of retirement. Thus, we should expect wealthier people or people with more generous pension benefits as of age 62 to retire earlier, other things equal.

The gains in lifetime income from delaying retirement are represented by the slope of segment BC, as noted earlier. These gains are complex to calculate because they are the sum of added *working* income plus changes in ex-

TABLE 7.1 **Social Security Payments When Retirement Is Postponed past Age 62, Males* (1989 dollars)**

	Retirement Age						
	62	63	64	65	66	67	68
Yearly Social Security Benefit	$7,344	$8,076	$8,688	$9,312	$9,684	$10,056	$10,428
Present Value at Age 62 of Expected Lifetime Benefits	$102,888	$105,228	$104,844	$103,584	$98,760	$93,444	$87,648

*Yearly benefits are for males born in 1927 whose yearly earnings in 1989 dollars were $24,000 throughout their careers; see Hay/Huggins Company, *1989 Social Security Summary* (Philadelphia: Hay/Huggins Company, Inc., 1989), Table XVII. Present values (using a discount rate of 2 percent) and life expectancies are calculated as of age 62.

pected lifetime pension benefits. Generally, the later one retires, the higher will be one's *yearly* pension benefit[19] but the fewer years one will collect that benefit. Table 7.1 shows the yearly and discounted lifetime Social Security benefits a typical male worker would anticipate at alternative retirement ages, assuming that he ceased all market work upon retirement (the case of Social Security recipients who work after officially retiring will be discussed in the next subsection) and that the real rate of interest is 2 percent. While yearly benefits rise with retirement age, expected total (discounted) lifetime benefits peak at age 63.[20] While this typical worker may add more to discounted lifetime income by working than any drop in discounted lifetime pension benefits takes away, thus guaranteeing a negative slope to segment *BC* in Figure 7.7, the slope of this segment need not be a constant as we have drawn it (that is, *BC* need not be a straight line). Our graphic simplification notwithstanding, it is still interesting to see how retirement age is affected by changes in the lifetime income gains from delaying retirement.

If the above gains were to grow as a result of changes in the structures of pension plans, so that the expected present value of pensions grew with retirement age and segment *BC* took on a steeper slope, would people retire later? Theory cannot tell us, because the steeper slope to *BC* creates income and substitution effects that work in opposite directions. A greater income gain from continuing to work makes household time more expensive, and by itself this leads to a substitution effect that pushes in the direction of later retirement. On the other hand, greater lifetime income creates an income effect tending to encourage greater consumption of commodities and thus more time spent at home (earlier retirement).

19. This is not always the case, as we shall discuss in Chapter 11. Some firms pressure employees to retire early by cutting yearly pension benefits for those who do not.
20. Because the Social Security adjustments for retirement before age 65 are the same for men and women, despite differences in life expectancies, the analogous present value of benefits for women is maximized at age 65 (using a 2 percent discount rate).

Empirical estimates of responses in the age of retirement to changes in both nonwork income at the earliest retirement age and the net gains from postponing retirement are not abundant. One careful study, however, found that (as expected) increased lifetime nonwork income *by itself* reduces the retirement age. This same study found that increased gains from postponing retirement cause retirement age to *increase,* thus suggesting the dominance of the substitution effect. The degree of responsiveness is rather small, however, so large changes in the structure of pension plans would probably have to be made to elicit much of a change in retirement age.[21]

An interesting development related to private pensions typically received by manual workers is that between 1975 and 1980 the present value of pension benefits associated with early retirement was increased more generously than the present value of benefits at normal retirement age.[22] In terms of Figure 7.7, segment *AB* of the original budget constraint was lengthened while the slope of segment *BC* was flattened. The combination of these effects can be confidently predicted to lower the age of retirement; indeed, one can only surmise that companies were trying to induce their older manual workers to retire earlier![23]

Policy Application: The Social Security Retirement Test

The preceding subsection dealt with the choice of a utility-maximizing retirement age and assumed that retirement was associated with the cessation of all market work activities. This subsection deals with another decision retirees must make: whether to work after declaring retirement and qualifying for Social Security. Thus, we change our focus from one in which retirement age is an issue and it is assumed that people do not work after retirement, to one in which we assume people have already declared their retirement and filed for Social Security and then must decide whether to work for pay full time, part time, or not at all.[24]

---

21. Olivia S. Mitchell and Gary S. Fields, "The Economics of Retirement Behavior," *Journal of Labor Economics* 2 (January 1984): 84–105, and Gary S. Fields and Olivia S. Mitchell, "The Effects of Social Security Reforms on Retirement Ages and Retirement Incomes," *Journal of Public Economics* 25 (1984): 143–59. These calculations assume a real discount rate of 2 percent. A review of theoretical and empirical studies of retirement behavior can be found in Edward P. Lazear, "Retirement from the Labor Force," in *Handbook of Labor Economics,* ed. Orley Ashenfelter and Richard Layard (Amsterdam: North-Holland, 1986).
22. Edward P. Lazear, "Pensions as Severance Pay," in *Financial Aspects of the United States Pension System,* ed. Zvi Bodie and John B. Shoven, A National Bureau of Economic Research Project Report (Chicago: University of Chicago Press, 1983), 57–90.
23. See Lazear, "Pensions as Severance Pay," 83, and Laurence J. Kotlikoff and David A. Wise, "The Incentive Effects of Private Pensions," in *Issues in Pension Economics,* ed. Zvi Bodie, John Shoven, and David Wise (Chicago: University of Chicago Press, 1987), 283–336.
24. A complete analysis of retirement behavior would model the retirement-age and work-after-retirement decisions *jointly,* instead of separately as we do. This task is beyond the scope of this text because estimates of lifetime income changes must account for the effects of the "retirement test" (discussed in this subsection) on Social Security benefits. A graphic analysis thus becomes very difficult. The interested student might begin an investigation into this joint decision by reading Lawrence H. Thompson, "The Social Security Reform Debate," *Journal of Economic Literature* 21 (December 1983): 1425–67; Gary Burtless and Robert Moffitt, "The Joint Choice of Retirement Age and Postretirement Hours of Work," *Journal of Labor Economics* 3, no. 2 (April 1985): 209–36; and Alan Gustman and Thomas Steinmeier, "Partial Retirement and the Analysis of Retirement Behavior," *Industrial and Labor Relations Review* 37, no. 3 (April 1984): 403–15.

Nearly everyone who has worked for 10 years and has reached 62 years of age qualifies for a Social Security pension. The size of the pension depends, within upper and lower limits, on the person's average monthly earnings while working and on the age of retirement, with those retiring at age 62, for example, receiving less per month than those retiring at 65 (as we saw in Table 7.1).

One interesting feature of the Social Security system in the United States is that there is a "retirement test" that determines the benefits one can receive. To receive full benefits, one must qualify as being "retired," which in 1990 meant earning less than $9,360 per year for those 65 or older. (This limit is increased slightly each year, is lower for people under 65, and does not apply to those over age 70.) For those earning more than $9,360 per year in 1990, Social Security retirement benefits were reduced by 33 cents for every dollar earned *above* $9,360. Thus, if a person's "full" Social Security benefit was $7,000 and he or she earned $9,600 per year at age 65, the Social Security benefit received would have been reduced by $80 (0.33 × 240) to $6,920.

The existence of the retirement test has long been a subject of controversy. Supporters of the retirement test maintain that Social Security is a program to help older people without jobs meet their financial needs and that the costs of giving benefits to those older people who have a decent labor income would be burdensome to those of working age who finance the program through a payroll tax. Opponents argue that retirees have earned their benefits through years of paying a payroll tax and that they are entitled to them in old age, regardless of their circumstances. Opponents further assert that *removing* the retirement test would *increase* work incentives among the elderly.[25] Indeed, these opponents were successful in changing, effective in 1990, the reduction of benefits for those earning over the allowable limit from 50 cents per "excess" dollar to 33 cents.

As illustrated in Figure 7.8, the retirement test in 1990 separated the budget constraint facing Social Security recipients aged 65 and over into three segments. Along segment *CD* a recipient kept his or her market earnings (which can be read off line *AB*) and the full Social Security benefit (*AC*). Once earnings reached $9,360 in 1990, Social Security benefits were cut 33 cents for every additional dollar of earnings—reflected in the flatter segment *DE* (which has a slope two-thirds that of *AB*). At some point (*E* in Figure 7.8) earnings are so high that Social Security benefits were reduced to zero; at that point people were on the market constraint (segment *EB*), and although they had successfully applied for Social Security, their benefit was zero. Depending on one's preferences, the optimum hours of paid work put in by a Social Security recipient would be located along segment *CD* (person *X* in panel a), segment *DE* (person *Y* in panel b), or segment *EB* (person *Z* in panel c).

Would *eliminating* the retirement test increase work incentives? We analyze this question by first looking at the immediate effects of the elimination on people who have qualified for Social Security. We then return to a life-

---

25. See, for example, Marshall R. Colberg, *The Social Security Retirement Test: Right or Wrong?* (Washington, D.C.: The American Enterprise Institute for Public Policy Research, 1978), for a review of this and other arguments concerning the retirement test.

FIGURE 7.8   Budget Constraint Relevant to Social Security Retirement Test in 1990

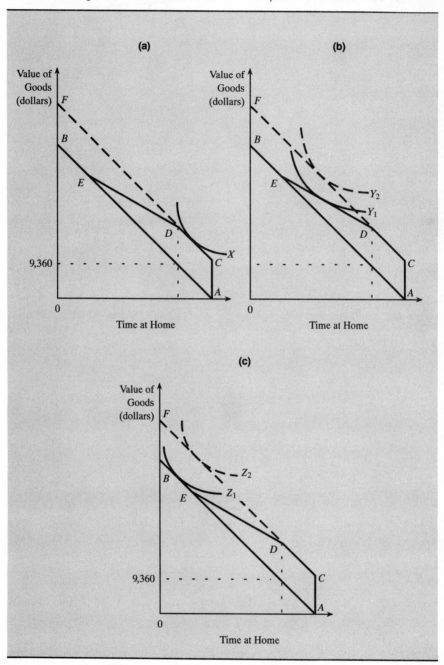

cycle perspective and analyze the effects on younger workers who are now only *future* Social Security recipients.

Immediate Effects on Social Security Recipients.   For those who qualify for Social Security benefits at or near the time when the retirement test is eliminated, any increase in benefits resulting from the change would increase wealth. These people receive added benefits but do not have to face years of increased payroll taxes to finance them (their future working years are limited).

Figure 7.8 shows that removing the retirement test would change the budget constraint facing these older people from *ACDEB* to *ACF*. This change preserves the market wage rate, essentially granting elderly people an income supplement independent of their work effort. People with preferences like *X* in panel (a)—people who earned less than $9,360 before the retirement test was removed—would be unaffected. Their work incentives would be the same as before the change. People with preferences like *Z* in panel (c) would have *reduced* work incentives. They would face a pure income effect (their wage rate would not change), which would induce them to work less. However, for people affected by the portion of the old constraint labeled *DE* in panel (b), constraint *ACF* represents a wage increase, and there would be *both* an income and a substitution effect. Which effect dominates cannot be foretold by theory. If the income effect dominated, people with preferences like *Y* would have *reduced* work incentives, and the *overall* effect of eliminating the retirement test would be to reduce hours of work by the elderly. If the substitution effect dominated, labor supply by people like *Y* would increase, and the overall effect would be unknown in advance.

Life-Cycle Effects.   The life-cycle effects of removing the retirement test are more complicated, but still relatively straightforward, if we confine our analysis to the question of yearly hours of work before and after successfully applying for Social Security benefits. Eliminating the retirement test would clearly increase the total benefits paid out to Social Security recipients, but the increased benefits younger workers could expect to receive in old age would be paid for by higher current payroll taxes. The life-cycle effect on workers of paying this higher payroll tax would depend on which segment of constraint *ACDEB* would have been relevant after age 65 had the retirement test not been removed.

Consider workers of average earning power.[26] For workers constrained by segment *CD* in their old age, neither benefits nor wages while on Social Secu-

---

26. For workers with average wage rates, Social Security benefits are roughly equivalent to Social Security payroll taxes. Low-wage workers obtain proportionately higher benefits, and high-wage workers proportionately lower benefits, relative to their taxes paid out. Focusing the analysis on the average wage earner is sufficient for our purpose, which is to illustrate the usefulness of the theory in policy analysis.

rity change. However, the added payroll tax they must pay in their younger years reduces their wage rate, causing income and substitution effects. Depending on which effect is dominant, labor supply in one's younger years may be increased or decreased, while in the years on Social Security labor supply is unchanged.

Older workers who are affected by segment *DE* of the Social Security constraint will receive increased benefits in old age, but these benefits will tend to be offset by larger taxes in their younger years. Their *lifetime wealth* may thus be largely unaffected by this change — or, to put it differently, removing the retirement test will tend to have essentially *no income effect* on the labor supply of these workers *over their lifetime*. Where these workers will be affected is in their allocations of labor supply over their lifetimes.

The increased payroll taxes for those on segment *DE* lower their wages during their prime years while increasing their wages in old age. This change in relative wages, *in the presence of constant wealth,* would tend to cause a reallocation of household (time-intensive) activities from old age to prime age. Thus, instead of waiting until old age to take one's European tour, some people may seize on the reduced disparity between wage rates in prime age and old age as sufficient reason to take this tour earlier in life. For the people affected by *DE*, then, labor supply will tend to decrease in one's prime years and increase in one's years on Social Security.

Finally, for those affected by segment *EB* — people who apply for Social Security and then work so much they do not receive any benefits — wages decrease (because of the increased payroll tax) but lifetime wealth tends to increase. The reason for this increase is simple. Before the retirement test was eliminated, they paid Social Security taxes but received no benefits; in effect, then, their taxes paid for the benefits to others. After the retirement test was eliminated, their subsidy to others ended — so that despite their reduced wages, lifetime wealth increased (as they got some of their taxes back in benefits). The reduced wages and increased lifetime wealth would drive these people toward less work at all stages in their lives.

The overall labor supply effects of removing the retirement test from the Social Security program cannot be predicted from theory. For some workers (such as *X*) the effects in *old age* are nil, but removing the test would create income and substitution effects in their prime years that have opposite tendencies on labor supply. For other workers, there may be some reallocation of labor from one's prime years to one's older years, but theory cannot tell us whether this shift will be one for one. For still others, lifetime labor supply may fall. What we *can* say is that people who argue that removing the retirement test will increase labor supply are being simplistic — unless, of course, they have some empirical evidence that resolves the theoretical ambiguities.[27]

---

27. Burtless and Moffitt's careful empirical analyses suggest that the earnings test has had only modest effects on the age of retirement, but a large effect on post-retirement hours of work.

MISCONCEPTION

"The growth of married women's participation in the labor force has converted a previously untapped resource into a powerful engine for economic betterment."

Analysis

The fact that married women are working more hours for pay than they previously did implies that they are either engaging less in household production or consuming less leisure. Neither of these alternative uses of time is unproductive in the important sense of generating utility. Therefore, while the fact they have voluntarily chosen to work for pay suggests they believe such a choice yields more utility than alternative allocations of time, it cannot be said that those engaged in these alternatives are an untapped resource.

Principle

The social cost of an action is the forgone utility that the action requires; the social benefit is the added utility it generates.

REVIEW QUESTIONS

1. Suppose that 5 percent unemployment is defined as "full employment" and currently unemployment is 7 percent. Suppose further that we have the following information:

Unemployment Rate	Labor Force	Unemployment	Employment
5 percent	6,000	300	5,700
7 percent	5,600	392	5,208

   a. What is the amount of "hidden" unemployment when the unemployment rate is 7 percent?
   b. If the population is 10,000, what change occurs in the participation rate as a result of the marginal change in the unemployment rate?
   c. What is the economic significance of hidden unemployment? Should measured and hidden unemployment be added to obtain a "total unemployment" figure?
2. Several studies have indicated that for prime-age males, the income effect of a wage increase tends to dominate the substitution effect. Other recent studies point out that hourly wages tend to rise over the early stages of the life cycle (the young receive lower wages than the middle-aged) *and* that young males tend to work fewer hours than middle-aged males, *ceteris paribus.* Employing a theory of life-cycle allocation of time, explain the apparent discrepancy.
3. In the first debate of the 1976 Presidential campaign, candidate Jimmy Carter argued, "While it is true that much of the recent rise in employment is due to the entrance of married women and teenagers into the labor force, this influx of people into the labor force is itself a sign of economic decay. The reason these people are now seeking work is because the primary breadwinner in the family is out of work and extra workers are needed to maintain the family income." Comment.

4. Some American observers have worried about a supposed decline in the "work ethic" among U.S. workers. The thesis (as yet unproven) of these observers is that U.S. workers are less interested in working than they used to be and that in the long run our national output per capita might fail to grow if gains in productivity are offset by reductions in working hours or labor force participation rates. These observers conclude: "A constant per capita output of goods and services is a sure sign of economic decay. It implies that economic progress is halted—that improvements in human welfare stop. It is unthinkable that our society would tolerate such stagnation in human progress."

Suppose the *factual* premise of these observers is true. That is, suppose improvements in the marginal productivity of workers over time are offset by declining work hours and participation rates so that gross national product per capita remains constant. Use economic theory to evaluate the *conclusion* drawn by these observers that this represents a stoppage of improvements in human welfare.

5. Suppose day-care centers charge working parents for each hour their children spend at the centers. Suppose, too, that the federal government passes legislation that subsidizes half of the hourly cost per child (so that the hourly cost per child now borne by the parents is cut in half). Would this policy cause an increase in the labor supply of parents with small children? Would it induce an overall increase in labor supply?

6. Is the following statement true, false, or uncertain? Why? "If a married woman's husband gets a raise, she tends to work less, but if *she* gets a raise, she tends to work more."

7. Suppose that, as the ratio of the working population to the retired population continues to fall, the voters approve a change in the way Social Security benefits are calculated—a way that effectively reduces every retired person's benefits by half. This change affects everyone in the population, no matter what their age or current retirement status, and it is accompanied by a 50 percent reduction in payroll taxes. What would be the labor supply effects on those workers who are very close to the typical age of retirement (62 to 65)? What would be the labor supply effects on those workers just beginning their careers (workers in their twenties, for example)?

8. Suppose that, under state law, the financial settlement in a divorce case that does not involve dependent children depends upon the economic contribution each marriage partner made up to the date of divorce. Thus, if the wife contributed half of the couple's initial assets and earned an income equal to her husband's throughout the years, she would be determined to qualify for half of the assets at the date of divorce. Based on what you have learned in Chapter 7, how could an equitable settlement be determined in the case of a woman who stayed home, raised the family's children, and never worked for pay?

SELECTED READINGS

Becker, Gary. "A Theory of the Allocation of Time." *Economic Journal* 75 (September 1965): 493–517.

Fields, Gary S., and Mitchell, Olivia S. *Retirement, Pensions and Social Security.* Cambridge, Mass.: MIT Press, 1984.

Ghez, G. R., and Becker, G. S. *The Allocation of Time and Goods over the Life Cycle.* New York: Columbia University Press, 1975. Chapter 3.

Gronau, Reuben. "The Measurement of Output of the Nonmarket Sector: The Evaluation of Housewives' Time." In *The Measurement of Economic and Social Performance,* ed. Milton Moss. New York: National Bureau of Economic Research, 1973, Pp. 163–89.

Layard, Richard, and Mincer, Jacob, eds. *Journal of Labor Economics* 3 (January 1985, pt. 2).

Lazear, Edward P. "Retirement from the Labor Force." In *Handbook of Labor Economics,* ed. Orley Ashenfelter and Richard Layard. Amsterdam: North-Holland, 1986.

Mincer, Jacob. "Labor Force Participation and Unemployment: A Review of Recent Evidence." In *Prosperity and Unemployment,* ed. Robert A. Gordon and Margaret S. Gordon. New York: John Wiley & Sons, 1966.

Thompson, Lawrence. "The Social Security Reform Debate." *Journal of Economic Literature* 21 (December 1983): 1425–67.

8

Compensating Wage Differentials and Labor Markets

C hapters 6 and 7 analyzed workers' decisions about *whether to seek employment* and *how long to work*. Chapters 8 and 9 will analyze workers' decisions about the industry, occupation, or firm in which they will work. This chapter will emphasize the influence on job choice of such daily, *recurring* job characteristics as working environment, length of commute from home to work, and risk of injury. The following chapter will analyze the effects of required educational *investments* on occupational choice.

This chapter will present a verbal as well as a graphic analysis of occupational choice that emphasizes the importance of both wages and nonpecuniary job characteristics in the allocation of labor to meet social needs. The empirical research on wage patterns will also be examined to see if job choices and the allocation of labor really are made along the lines suggested by these analyses. The final section applies the concepts of this chapter to two very important and controversial government programs: occupational safety and health regulation and affirmative action plans for women and minorities. An appendix considers the relationship between wages and layoffs.

A VERBAL ANALYSIS OF OCCUPATIONAL CHOICE

One of the major functions of the labor market is to provide the signals and the mechanisms by which workers seeking to maximize their utility can be matched to employers trying to maximize profits. Matching is a formidable task, because workers have varying skills and preferences and because employers offer jobs that differ in skill content and working environment. The process of finding the worker–employer pairings that are best for each is truly one of trial and error, and whether the process is woefully deficient or reasonably satisfactory is a question implicitly underlying this and the succeeding three chapters.

The assumption that workers are attempting to maximize utility implies that they are interested in both the pecuniary and the nonpecuniary aspects of their jobs. On the one hand, we expect that higher compensation levels in an occupation (holding job tasks constant) would attract more workers to that occupation.[1] The reason for this was discussed in Chapter 2. Different occupations have different tasks, and workers have different preferences concerning these duties. At a given level of pay only certain numbers of workers will be interested in a particular occupation, but if the level of pay were to rise, others would become attracted to it. On the other hand, it is clear from the factors just discussed that pay is not all that matters; occupational tasks and how workers' preferences mesh with those tasks are critical elements in the matching process.[2] The focus of this chapter is on how the labor market accommodates worker preferences.

If all jobs were *exactly alike* and located in the *same place,* an individual's decision about where to seek work would be relatively simple. He or she would attempt to obtain a job where the expected compensation was highest. Any differences in compensation would cause workers to seek work with the highest-paying employers and avoid applying for work with the low-paying ones. The high-paying employers, having an abundance of applicants, might decide they were paying more than they had to in order to staff their vacancies. The low-paying employers would have to raise wage offers in order to compete for workers. Ultimately, if the market works without hindrance, wages of all employers would equalize.

All jobs are not the same, however. Some jobs require much more education or training than others. Some jobs are in clean, modern offices, and others are in noisy, dusty, or dangerous factories. Some permit the employee some discretion over the pace of work at various points throughout the day, while others involve highly rigid assembly-line work. Some are challenging and call for decision making by the employee; others are monotonous. The influence of educational and training requirements will be discussed at length in the next chapter; we will discuss here the ways variations in job characteristics influence individual choice and the observable market outcomes of that choice.

---

1. See, for example, recent studies of physicians' choices of specialty: Jeremiah E. Hurley, "Physicians' Choices of Specialty, Location, and Mode: A Reexamination Within an Interdependent Decision Framework," unpublished Ph.D. diss., University of Wisconsin–Madison, 1987, and Gloria J. Bazzoli, "Specialty Choices of Female Physicians: Response to Intrinsic Job Characteristics or to Economic Advantages?" (unpublished paper, Peat Marwick Main & Co., 1987). Evidence that workers weigh likely *future* occupational demand conditions can be found in a study of the choice to become a teacher; see Gary A. Zarkin, "Occupational Choice: An Application to the Market for Public School Teachers," *Quarterly Journal of Economics* 100, no. 2 (May 1985): 409–46.

2. These factors have an interesting application to the choice of criminal activity. Whether one views such choices in a consumption context or as a matter of occupational choice, it is clear that preferences, the rewards of alternative activities, and expected benefits (net of expected punishments) are crucial to the model. For a comprehensive review of economists' work in this area, see Helen Tauchen, Ann Dryden Witte, and Harriet Griesinger, "Deterrence, Work, and Crime: Revisiting the Issues with Birth Cohort Data," Working Paper no. 2508, National Bureau of Economic Research, Cambridge, Mass., February 1988.

Individual Choice and Its Outcomes

Suppose several unskilled workers have received offers from two employers. Employer X pays $5 per hour and offers clean, safe working conditions. Employer Y also pays $5 per hour, but offers employment in a dirty, noisy factory. Which employer would the workers choose? Most would undoubtedly choose employer X, because the pay is the same while the job is performed under less disagreeable conditions.

Clearly, however, $5 is not an equilibrium wage in both firms.[3] Because firm X finds it very easy to attract applicants at $5, it will "hold the line" on any future wage increases. Firm Y, however, must either clean up the plant, pay higher wages, or do both if it wants to fill its vacancies. Assuming it decides not to alter working conditions, it must clearly pay a wage *above* $5 to be competitive in the labor market. The *extra* wage it must pay to attract workers is called a *compensating wage differential* because the higher wage is paid to compensate workers for the undesirable working conditions. If such a differential did not exist, firm Y could not attract the unskilled workers that firm X can obtain.

Suppose that firm Y raises its wage offer to $5.50 while the offer from X remains at $5.00. Will this 50-cent-per-hour differential—an extra $1,000 per year—attract *all* the workers in our group to firm Y? If it did attract them all, firm X would have an incentive to raise its wages and firm Y might want to lower its offers a bit; the 50-cent differential in this case would *not* be an equilibrium differential.

More than likely, however, the 10 percent higher wage in firm Y would attract only *some* of the group to firm Y. Some people are not bothered by dirt and noise as much as others are, and these people may decide to take the extra pay and put up with the poorer working conditions.[4] Others, however, are very sensitive to noise or allergic to dust, and they may decide that they would rather get paid less than expose themselves to such working conditions. If both firms could obtain the quantity and quality of workers they wanted, the 50-cent differential *would* be an equilibrium differential, in the sense that there would be no forces causing the differential to change.

The desire of workers to avoid unpleasantness or risk, then, should force employers offering unpleasant or risky jobs to pay higher wages than they would otherwise have to pay. Put another way, in order to attract a work force, these employers will have to pay higher wages to their workers than firms that offer pleasant, safe jobs to comparable workers. This wage differential serves two related, socially desirable ends. First, it serves a *social* need by giving people an incentive to voluntarily do dirty, dangerous, or unpleasant work. Likewise, the existence of a compensating wage differential imposes a

---

3. There may be a few people who really are indifferent to noise and dirt in the workplace. We assume here that these people are so rare, or firm Y's demand for workers is so large, that Y cannot fill all its vacancies with just those who are totally insensitive to dirt and noise.

4. The assertion that people are affected differently by noise is documented in *Community Reaction to Airport Noise,* vol. 1 (report to the National Aeronautics and Space Administration prepared by Tracor, Inc., of Austin, Texas), July 1971. This study showed, for example, that around 10 percent of people are "highly susceptible" to noise annoyance, while around half are "highly adaptable" to airport noises.

financial penalty on employers who have unfavorable working conditions. Second, at an *individual* level, it serves as a reward to workers who accept unpleasant jobs by paying them more than comparable workers in more pleasant jobs.

The Allocation of Labor.   Society has a number of jobs that are unavoidably nasty or would be very costly to make safe and pleasant (coal mining, deep-sea diving, and coke-oven cleaning are examples). There are essentially two ways to recruit the necessary labor for such jobs. One is to compel people to do these jobs (the military draft is the most obvious American example of forced labor). The second way is to induce people to do the jobs voluntarily.

Most modern societies rely mainly on incentives, compensating wage differentials, to recruit labor to unpleasant jobs voluntarily. Workers will mine coal, collect garbage, and bolt steel beams together 50 stories off the ground because, compared to alternative jobs for which they could qualify, these jobs pay well. The 1,500 commercial deep-sea divers in the United States, for example, who are exposed to the dangers of drowning, the rigors of construction

---

EXAMPLE 8.1
The Economic Implications of Flogging Workers

In Korea during the 16th and 17th centuries a new printing technology was developed. This new technology involved the use of movable type, which allowed for more flexibility in the printing of documents than did carving each page in wood blocks. The problem with movable type, however, was that the Korean language required thousands of different characters, and storing the characters and "composing" them into pages was a staggering task.

Korean printers during this era were illiterate, and the Korean government was so concerned about the accuracy and appearance of documents printed using the new technology that it promulgated the following regulations:

> The supervisor and compositor shall be flogged thirty times for an error per chapter; the printer shall be flogged thirty times for bad impression, either too dark or too light, of one character per chapter.

It is said that Korean documents had a reputation for quality, but that the Koreans found it very difficult to recruit compositors and printers!

We do not know how Korean print shops solved their recruiting problem, but the harsh discipline inflicted on workers would have forced one of three alternatives upon them. One strategy could have been to *compel* people to work as compositors or printers; this method of recruitment would have required the use of government power and/or the use of force (see Example 1.1). The second alternative could have been to raise the wages of printers and compositors by enough to attract volunteers to those occupations (see Example 8.4). Third, employers could have removed or altered the harsh conditions that served as an impediment to recruitment.

SOURCE: Daniel J. Boorstin, *The Discoverers* (New York: Random House, 1983), 505–8.

work with cumbersome gear, a lonely and hostile work environment, and several physiological disorders as a result of compression and decompression, made $20,000 to $45,000 per year in the mid-1970s, or about 20 to 170 percent more than the average high school graduate.

As another example, the *failure* to pay sufficiently high wages to U.S. military personnel has created occasional difficulties in recruiting and retaining such people. While the pay for military recruits with less than two years of service was 14 percent above the pay for civilian youth right after the draft was eliminated in 1973, the relative pay advantage had fallen to 2 percent by 1979. This fall in relative pay for recruits was accompanied by a severe decline in the quantity and quality of enlistees, despite the decline in civilian job opportunities that accompanied a large rise in the unemployment rate over that six-year period. By 1982 both the quality and the quantity of enlistees had improved, owing partly to a very high civilian unemployment rate, but probably mostly to pay raises that increased the pay for recruits to 18 percent above that for civilian youths. If the government wants to maintain armed services without resorting to the draft, it is clear that military pay must remain at a level sufficient to compensate for the hazards and inconveniences of military life.[5]

Compensation for Workers.   Compensating wage differentials also serve as *individual* rewards by paying those who accept bad or arduous working conditions more than they would otherwise receive. In a parallel fashion, those who opt for more pleasant conditions have to "buy" them by accepting lower pay. For example, if a person takes the $5.00-per-hour job with firm X, he or she is giving up the $5.50-per-hour job with less pleasant conditions in firm Y. The better conditions are being bought, in a very real sense, for 50 cents per hour.

Thus, compensating wage differentials become the prices at which good working conditions can be purchased by, or bad ones sold to, workers. Contrary to what is commonly asserted, a monetary value *can* often be attached to events or conditions whose effects are primarily psychological in nature. Compensating wage differentials provide the key to the valuation of these nonpecuniary aspects of employment.

In the area of occupational health and safety policy, there is continuous debate about whether to make machines safer or protect the worker from machine hazards with personal protective devices.[6] For example, high noise levels can eventually damage the hearing of workers. The Department of Labor has favored reducing noise levels through engineering changes, such as putting mufflers on or baffles around noisy machines. Employer representatives have consistently claimed that such engineering changes are inordinately expensive and that compelling workers to wear earplugs would preserve workers' hear-

---

5. "The Retention Problem," *Wall Street Journal,* March 19, 1980, 24, and an unpublished table provided to us by Robert Lockman, Center for Naval Analyses. What is pleasant or unpleasant is determined in the market at the *margin.* For example, even if most people dislike outdoor work, there might be enough who do not mind it to fill outdoor jobs without a compensating wage differential.

6. The debate about whether or not the government should be involved at all in occupational safety and health is discussed later in this chapter.

ing at much less cost. Because resources are scarce, our society would like to achieve hearing protection at minimum cost, but we must be sure to count *all* the costs. One cost of wearing earplugs is *psychic:* most people find them very uncomfortable to wear. The cost of this discomfort *must* be counted along with the purchase price of earplugs in arriving at the total cost of wearing earplugs.

How could we put a dollar value on earplug discomfort? A straightforward way to determine this would be to find a set of employers who *require* the use of earplugs as a condition of employment and to compare the wages they pay to those of *comparable* firms that *do not require* the wearing of earplugs. If workers find earplugs more uncomfortable than the noise, wages in the firms that require their use should be higher, and this wage differential is an estimate of the value workers place on this discomfort.

Suppose, for example, that the research showed that companies requiring earplugs pay 10 cents an hour, or $200 per year, more than *otherwise similar* firms pay for *comparable* labor.[7] Workers accepting work with such companies are indicating by their behavior that they are willing to take $200 per year as compensation for the discomfort they must bear; that is, the cost of the discomfort to them is equal to, or less than, $200 per year. Those refusing to work at the plant place a value higher than that on their discomfort costs, because $200 is insufficient to compensate them. Thus, the cost of discomfort at the margin is $200 per year (to induce one more worker to wear earplugs would require added compensation of about $200 per year).

Before concluding that the psychic costs of wearing earplugs are $200 per year, we must remember that our hypothetical findings are for the marginal worker. People differ in the amount of discomfort they feel and in the value they place on what they feel. Those most likely to take the extra pay in return for having to wear earplugs are those who are least sensitive to discomfort or most willing to trade discomfort for money. If we were to compel *all* workers in noisy factories to wear earplugs, we would be forcing earplugs on some for whom the costs of discomfort exceeded $200.

As this example illustrates, compensating wage differentials are the price at which various *qualitative* job characteristics are bought and sold. As such, they offer a way of placing a value on things most people think of as "noneconomic." This illustration, of course, does not prove that compensating wage differentials exist or that they are equilibrium prices; these issues will be discussed later in the chapter.

Assumptions and Predictions

We have seen how a simple theory of job choice by individuals leads to the *prediction* that compensating wage differentials will be associated with various job characteristics. Positive differentials (higher wages) will accompany "bad" characteristics, while negative differentials (lower wages) will be associated with "good" ones. However, it is very important to understand that this prediction can *only* be made *holding other things equal.*

---

7. Firms may be willing to do this if they believe requiring the use of earplugs will reduce workers' compensation claims for hearing loss in the future.

Our prediction about the existence of compensating wage differentials grows out of the reasonable assumption that if a worker has a choice between a job with "good" working conditions and a job of equal pay with "bad" working conditions, he or she will choose the "good" job. If the employee is an unskilled laborer, he or she may be choosing between an unpleasant job spreading hot asphalt or a more comfortable job in an air-conditioned warehouse. In either case, he or she is going to receive something close to the wage rate unskilled workers typically receive. However, our theory would predict that this worker would receive *more* from the asphalt-spreading job than from the warehouse job.

Thus, the predicted outcome of our theory of job choice is *not* that employees working under "bad" conditions receive more than those working under "good" conditions. The prediction is that, *holding worker characteristics constant,* employees in bad jobs receive higher wages than those working under more pleasant conditions. The characteristics that must be held constant include all the other things that influence wages: skill level, age, race, gender, union status, region of the country, and so forth. Because there are many influences on wages *other* than working conditions, our theory leads us to expect employers offering "bad" jobs to pay higher wages than employers offering "good" jobs to *comparable* workers. This theory is based on three assumptions.

Assumption 1: Utility Maximization.   Our first assumption is that workers seek to maximize their *utility,* not their income. If workers sought to maximize income, they would always choose the highest-paying job available to them. This behavior would eventually cause wages to be equalized across the jobs open to any set of workers, as stated earlier.

In contrast, compensating wage differentials will only arise if some people do *not* choose the highest-paying job offered, preferring instead a lower-paying but more pleasant job. This behavior allows the employers offering the lower-paying, pleasant jobs to be competitive. Wages do not equalize in this case. Rather, the *net advantages*—the overall utility from the pay and the psychic aspects of the job—tend to equalize for the marginal worker.

Assumption 2: Worker Information.   The second assumption implicit in our analysis is that workers are aware of the job characteristics of potential importance to them. Whether they know about them before they take the job or find out soon after taking it is not too important. In either case, a company offering a "bad" job with no compensating wage differential would have trouble recruiting or retaining workers, trouble that would eventually force it to raise its wage.

It is quite likely, of course, that workers would quickly learn of dust, dirt, noise, rigid work discipline, and other obvious bad working conditions. It is equally likely that they would *not* know the *precise* probability of being laid off, say, or of being injured on the job. However, even with respect to these probabilities, their own direct observations or word-of-mouth reports from other employees could give them enough information to evaluate the situation with some accuracy. For example, the proportions of employees considering their work dangerous have been shown to be closely related to the actual injury rates published by the government for the industries in which they work.[8] This finding illustrates that, while workers probably cannot state the precise probability of being injured, they do form accurate judgments about the relative risks of several jobs.

Where predictions may disappoint us, however, is with respect to *very* obscure characteristics. For example, while we now know that asbestos dust is highly damaging to worker health, this fact was not widely known 40 years ago. One reason information on asbestos dangers in plants was so long in being generated is that it takes more than 20 years for asbestos-related disease to develop. Cause and effect were thus obscured from workers and researchers alike, creating a situation in which job choices were made in ignorance of this risk. Compensating wage differentials for this danger thus could not possibly have arisen at that time. Our predictions about compensating wage differentials, then, hold only for job characteristics that workers know about.

Assumption 3: Worker Mobility. The final assumption implicit in our theory is that workers have a range of job offers from which to choose. Without a range of offers, workers would not be able to select the combination of job characteristics they desired or avoid the ones to which they did not wish exposure. A compensating wage differential for risk of injury, for example, simply could not arise if workers were able to obtain only dangerous jobs. It is the act of choosing safe jobs over dangerous ones that forces employers offering dangerous work to raise wages.

One manner in which this choice can occur is for each job applicant to receive several job offers from which to choose. However, another way in which choice could be exercised is for workers to be (at least potentially) highly mobile. In other words, workers with few concurrent offers could take jobs and continue their search for work if they thought an improvement could be made. Thus, even with few offers at any *one* time, workers could conceivably have relatively wide choice over a *period* of time, which would eventually allow them to select jobs that maximized their utility.

While there are no general data on the number of concurrent offers a typical job applicant receives, job mobility among American workers is relatively high. The reported quit rate in manufacturing is normally 1–2 percent per month, or about 12–24 percent per year. With job openings from quits and from general business expansion, manufacturing businesses newly hire 3 percent of their employees each month. Turnover is so great, in fact, that the median length of job tenure is 3.2 years, meaning that half of all workers have been with their current employer less than three and a half years.[9]

---

8. W. Kip Viscusi, "Labor Market Valuations of Life and Limb: Empirical Evidence and Policy Implications," *Public Policy* 26 (Summer 1978): 359–86. An interesting study of how workers' perceptions of risk are changed by new information is found in W. Kip Viscusi and Charles J. O'Connor, "Adaptive Responses to Chemical Labeling: Are Workers Bayesian Decision Makers?" *American Economic Review* 74, no. 5 (December 1984): 942–56.

9. Max L. Carey, "Occupational Tenure in 1987: Many Workers Have Remained in Their Fields," *Monthly Labor Review* 111, no. 10 (October 1988): 3–12, Table 5.

TABLE 8.1   Annual Occupational Change Rates for Those Employed in 1982 and 1983

	Percentage of Those Employed in 1982 Who Were Working in a Different Occupation[a] in 1983	
	Men	Women
All Ages	9.3	10.1
Age: 18–19	29.0	26.0
20–24	21.3	20.1
25–34	11.5	11.9
35–44	6.7	7.8
45–54	4.8	4.9
55–64	3.1	3.8

[a]Occupations were defined narrowly as "accountant," "attorney," "day-care attendant," "huckster-peddler," and so forth.

SOURCE: Ellen Sehgal, "Occupational Mobility and Job Tenure in 1983," *Monthly Labor Review* 107, no. 10 (October 1984): 18–23.

Another way to understand the amount of choice workers have in the job market is to look at occupational mobility over time. Consider Table 8.1, which displays yearly rates of occupational change for men and women employed in both 1982 and 1983. The data indicate that for men and women as a whole, and for those aged 25–34, the proportions working in a different occupation when surveyed in 1982 and again in 1983 lay in the range of 9–12 percent. For those over age 35 the percentages changing occupations were lower, and for those below age 24 the percentages were much higher. Some of this occupational mobility was voluntary and some was initiated by employers, but what is of significance for assessing the extent of mobility is that the typical worker employed in 1982 had over a 9 percent chance of being employed in a different occupation just a year later.[10]

The next section will present a graphic exposition of the theory of compensating wage differentials that has just been described verbally. This graphic analysis incorporates employer behavior, which has not yet been explicitly considered, and visually illustrates some important conclusions. Economists have labeled the following analysis a *hedonic theory of wages*— that is, a wage theory based on the assumption of *philosophical hedonism* that workers strive to maximize utility (happiness).[11]

---

10. The data in Table 8.1 do not necessarily reflect changes of employer, because they include those who changed occupations while remaining with the same employer, and they exclude those who changed employers but remained in the same occupation.
11. The philosophy of hedonism is usually associated with Jeremy Bentham, a philosopher of the late-18th century who believed people always behaved in ways that they thought would maximize their happiness. The analysis that follows is adapted primarily from Sherwin Rosen, "Hedonic Prices and Implicit Markets," *Journal of Political Economy* 82 (January/February 1974): 34–55.

EXAMPLE 8.2

Compensating Wage Differentials for the Evening and Night Shifts

Roughly 25 percent of production workers living in metropolitan areas work on the evening or night shifts. This percentage has been stable for two decades, but it varies by industry. Over 50 percent of the workers in the cotton and synthetic textiles, cigarette, and glass container industries work in the evening or at night. Because evening and night work requires sleeping and leisure patterns that differ from the norm, one might expect that firms scheduling such work would have to pay a wage premium to attract workers. Indeed, a 1984 study found that 90 percent of evening and night workers received higher pay than their daytime co-workers; evening workers earned 23 cents per hour more and night workers 30 cents per hour more in manufacturing industries. Given an average manufacturing wage of $9.18 in 1984, shift workers received wages that were about 3 percent higher than they would have received if they had worked during the day.

SOURCE: Sandra L. King and Harry B. Williams, "Shift Work Pay Differentials and Practices in Manufacturing," *Monthly Labor Review* 108, no. 12 (December 1985): 26–33.

A HEDONIC THEORY OF WAGES

Business firms offer, and employees accept, jobs that may differ greatly in their level of responsibility, pace of work, security from layoff, work environment, and so forth. Job characteristics that workers consider undesirable should have a positive compensating wage differential associated with them, while those that are desired should be purchased by employees in the form of lower wages. To simplify our discussion, we shall analyze just one dimension— risk of injury on the job—and *assume* that the compensating wage differentials for every *other* dimension have already been established. This assumption allows us to clearly see the outcomes of the job selection process with respect to *one* undesirable dimension (injury risk); since the same analysis could be repeated for every other dimension, our conclusions are not obscured by it. To obtain a complete understanding of the job selection process and the outcomes of that process, it is necessary, as always, to consider both the employer and employee sides of the market.

Employee Considerations

Employees, it may safely be assumed, dislike the risk of being injured on the job. A worker who is offered a job for $8 per hour in a firm in which 3 percent of the work force is injured each year would achieve a certain level of utility from that job. If the risk of injury were increased to 4 percent, holding other job characteristics constant, the job would have to pay a higher wage to produce the same level of utility (except in the unlikely event that the costs of

FIGURE 8.1   A Family of Indifference Curves Between Wages and Risk of Injury

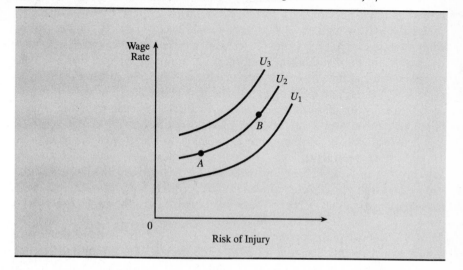

wage loss, medical treatment, and suffering caused by the added injuries were completely covered by the firm or its insurance company after the fact).[12]

Other combinations of wage rates and risk levels could be devised that would yield the same utility as the $8/hour–3 percent risk offer. These combinations can be connected on a graph to form an indifference curve (for example, the curve U_2 in Figure 8.1). Unlike the indifference curves drawn in Chapters 6 and 7, those in Figure 8.1 slope upward because risk of injury is a "bad" job characteristic, not a "good" (such as leisure, for example). In other words, if risk increases, wages must rise if utility is to be held constant.

As in the previous chapters, there is one indifference curve for each possible level of utility. Because a higher wage at a given risk level will generate more utility, indifference curves lying to the northwest represent higher utility.[13] Thus, all points on curve U_3 in Figure 8.1 are preferred to those on U_2, and those on U_2 are preferred to U_1. The fact that each indifference curve is

12. Compensating wage differentials provide for *ex ante*—"before the fact"—compensation related to injury risk. Workers can also be compensated (to keep utility constant) by *ex post*—or after-injury—payments for damages. Workers' compensation insurance provides for *ex post* payments, but these payments are typically incomplete. There is no way to compensate a worker for his or her own death, and workers' compensation does not cover the psychic costs of disfigurement due to permanent impairment. Moreover, the lost income associated with temporary impairments is not *completely* replaced by workers' compensation. Because not all injury-related losses are completely compensated *ex post,* compensating wage differentials must exist *ex ante* for worker utility to be held constant in the face of increased risk.

13. When two "goods" were on the axes of our graphs, as in Chapters 6 and 7, indifference curves lying to the northeast represented higher levels of utility (people wanted more of each). When a "bad" is on the horizontal axis (as in Figure 8.1) and a "good" on the vertical axis, people with more of the "good" and less of the "bad" are unambiguously better off, and this combination is achieved by moving in a northwest direction on the graph.

convex (when viewed from below) reflects the normal assumption of diminishing marginal rates of substitution. At point B of curve U_2, the person receives a relatively high wage and faces a high level of risk. He or she will be willing to give up a lot in wages to achieve a given reduction in risk because risk levels are high enough to place one in imminent danger, and the consumption level of the goods that are bought with wages is already high. However, as risk levels and wage rates fall, the person becomes less willing to give up wages in return for the given reduction in risk; the danger is no longer imminent, and consumption of other goods is not as high.

People differ, of course, in their aversion to the risk of being injured. Those who are very sensitive to this risk will require large wage increases for any increase in risk, while those who are less sensitive will require smaller wage increases to hold utility constant. The sensitive workers will have indifference curves that are steeper at any level of risk than those of workers who are less sensitive, as illustrated in Figure 8.2. At risk level R_1, the slope at point C is steeper than at point D. Point C lies on the indifference curve of a worker who is highly sensitive to risk, while point D lies on an indifference curve of one who is less sensitive. Of course, each person has a whole family of indifference curves that are not shown in Figure 8.2, and each will attempt to achieve the highest level of utility possible.

Employer Considerations

Employers are faced with a wage/risk trade-off of their own that derives from three assumptions. First, it is presumably costly to reduce the risk of injury facing employees. Safety equipment must be placed on machines, production time must be sacrificed for safety training sessions, protective clothing must be furnished to workers, and so forth. Second, competitive pressures will pre-

FIGURE 8.2   Representative Indifference Curves for Two Workers Who Differ in Their Aversion to Risk of Injury

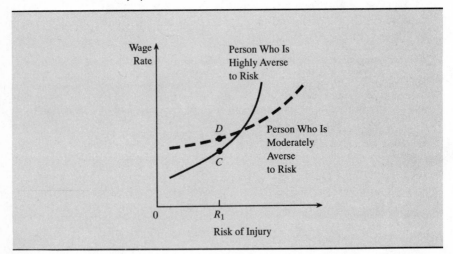

sumably force many firms to operate at *zero profits* (that is, at a point at which all costs are covered and the rate of return on capital is about what it is for similar investments).[14] Third, all *other* job characteristics are presumably given or already determined. The consequence of these three assumptions is that, if a firm undertakes a program to reduce the risk of injury, it must reduce wages to remain competitive.

Thus, forces on the employer side of the market tend to cause low risk to be associated with low wages and high risk to be associated with high wages, *holding other things constant.* These "other things" may be employee benefits or other job characteristics; assuming they are given will not affect the validity of our analysis (even though it may seem at first unrealistic). The major point is that if a firm spends *more on safety,* it must spend *less on other things* if it is to remain competitive.[15] The term *wages* can thus be thought of as shorthand for "terms of employment" in our theoretical analyses.

The employer trade-offs between wages and levels of injury risk can be graphed through the use of *isoprofit curves,* which show the various combinations of risk and wage levels that yield a given level of profits (*iso* means "equal"). Thus, all the points along a given curve, such as those depicted in Figure 8.3, are wage/risk combinations that yield the *same* level of profits. Curves to the southeast represent higher profit levels because with all other items in the employment contract given, each risk level is associated with a *lower* wage level. Curves to the northwest represent, conversely, lower profit levels.

Note that the isoprofit curves in Figure 8.3 are concave (from below). This concavity is a graphic representation of our assumption that there are diminishing marginal returns to safety expenditures. Suppose, for example, that the firm is operating at point *M* in Figure 8.3, a point where the risk of injury is high. The first expenditures by the firm to reduce risk will have a relatively high return, because the firm will clearly choose to attack the safety problem by eliminating the most obvious and cheaply eliminated hazards. Because the risk (and accompanying cost) reductions are relatively large, the firm need not reduce wages by very much to keep profits constant. Thus, the isoprofit curve at point *M* is relatively flat. At point *N*, however, the curve is steeply sloped, indicating that wages will have to be reduced by quite a bit if the firm is to maintain its profits in the presence of a program to reduce risk. This large wage reduction is required because, at this point, further increases in safety are very costly; all the easy-to-solve safety problems have been dealt with.

We also assume that employers differ in the ease (cost) with which they can eliminate hazards. We have just indicated that the cost of reducing risk levels is reflected in the *slope* of the isoprofit curve. In firms where injuries

---

14. If returns are permanently below normal, it would benefit the owners to close down the plant and invest their funds elsewhere. If returns are above normal, investors will be attracted to the industry and profits will eventually be driven down by increased competition.

15. We *could* focus on the trade-off between safety and employee benefits or safety and other working conditions, because certainly our theory would predict that such trade-offs exist. However, we choose to focus on the *wage* trade-off because wages are easy to measure and form the largest component of compensation.

FIGURE 8.3   A Family of Isoprofit Curves for an Employer

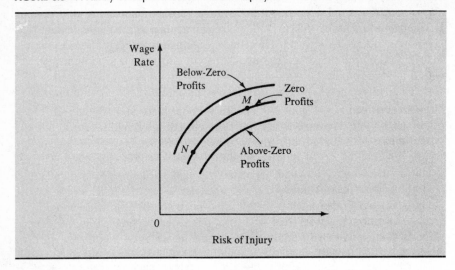

are costly to reduce, large wage reductions will be required to keep profits constant in the face of a safety program; the isoprofit curve in this case will be steeply sloped. The isoprofit curve of one such firm is shown as YY' in Figure 8.4. The isoprofit curves of firms where injuries are easier to eliminate are flatter. Note that curve XX' in Figure 8.4 is flatter at each level of risk than YY'; this indicates that firm X can reduce risk more cheaply than firm Y.

The Matching of Employers and Employees
The aim of employees is to achieve the highest possible utility from their choice of a job. If they receive two offers at the same wage rate, they will choose the lower-risk job. If they receive two offers in which the risk levels are equal, they will accept the offer with the higher wage rate. More generally, they will choose the offer that falls on the highest, or most northwest, indifference curve.

In obtaining jobs, employees are constrained by the offers they receive from employers. Employers, for their part, are constrained by two forces. On the one hand, they cannot make outrageously lucrative offers because they will be driven out of business by firms whose costs are lower. On the other hand, if their offered terms of employment are very low, they will be unable to attract employees (who will choose to work for other firms). These two forces compel firms in competitive markets to operate on their zero-profit isoprofit curves.

To better understand the offers firms make, refer to Figure 8.4, where two different firms are depicted. Firm X, the firm that can cheaply reduce injuries, can make higher wage offers at low levels of risk (left of point R) than can firm Y. Because it can produce safety (reduce risk) more cheaply, it can pay higher wages at low levels of risk and still remain competitive. Any point

FIGURE 8.4   The Zero-Profit Curves of Two Firms

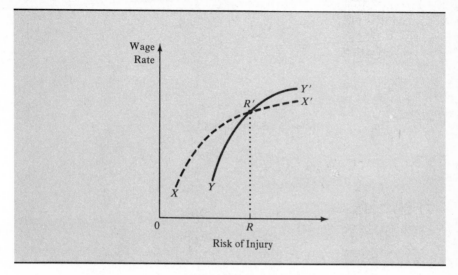

along segment *XR'* will be preferred by employees to any point along *YR'* because, for given levels of risk, higher wages are paid.

At higher levels of risk, however, firm Y can outbid firm X for employees. Firm X does not save much money if it permits the risk level to rise above *R*, because risk reduction is so cheap. Because firm Y *does* save itself a lot by operating at levels of risk beyond *R* (it may be a sawmill where risk reduction is prohibitively costly), it is willing to pay relatively high wages at high risk levels. Since offers along *R'Y'* will be preferable to those along *R'X'*—again, because higher wages at any level of risk are paid by firm Y—employees working at high-risk jobs will work for Y.

Graphing worker indifference curves and employer isoprofit curves together can show which workers choose which offers. Figure 8.5 contains the zero-profit curves of two employers (X and Y) and the indifference curves of two employees (A and B). Employee A maximizes utility (along A_2) by working for employer X at wage W_{AX} and risk level R_{AX}, while person B maximizes utility by working for employer Y at wage W_{BY} and risk level R_{BY}.

Looking at A's choice more closely, we see that if he or she took the offer B accepted—W_{BY} and R_{BY}—the level of utility achieved would be A_1, which is less than A_2. Person A values safety very highly, and wage W_{BY} is just not high enough to compensate for the high level of risk. Person B, whose indifference curves are flatter (signifying he or she is less averse to risk), finds the offer of W_{BY} and R_{BY} on curve B_2 superior to the offer A accepts. Person B is simply not willing to take a cut in pay to W_{AX} in order to reduce risk from R_{BY} to R_{AX}, because that would place B on curve B_1.

The matching of A with firm X and B with firm Y is thus not accidental or random. Firm X can generate safety relatively cheaply and does not reduce cost much by operating at high risk levels. Since X can "produce" safety more

FIGURE 8.5 Matching Employers and Employees

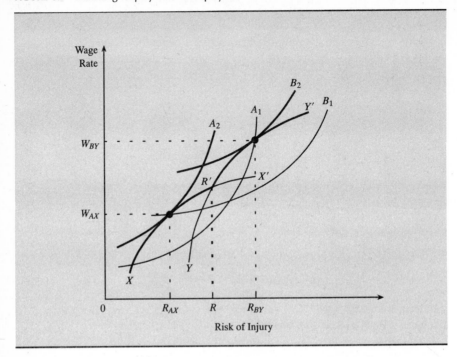

cheaply than Y, it is logical that X will be a low-risk producer who attracts employees, like A, who value safety highly. Likewise, employer Y generates a lot of cost savings by operating at high risk levels and can thus afford to pay high wages and still be competitive. Y attracts people like B, who have a relatively strong preference for money wages and a relatively weak preference for safety. Firm Y, then, has a comparative advantage (over X) in offering high-risk, high-paying jobs.[16]

The Offer Curve. The above job-matching process, of course, can be generalized beyond the case of two employees and two employers. To do this it is helpful to note that in Figures 8.4 and 8.5, the only offers of jobs to workers with a chance of being accepted lie along $XR'Y'$. The curve $XR'Y'$ can be called an "offer curve," because only along $XR'Y'$ will offers employers can afford to make be potentially acceptable to employees. The concept of an offer curve is useful in generalizing our discussion beyond two firms, because a single offer curve can summarize the potentially acceptable offers any number of firms in a particular labor market can make.

Consider, for example, Figure 8.6, which contains the zero-profit isoprofit curves of firms L through Q. We know from our discussions of Figures 8.4 and 8.5 that employees will accept offers along only the most northwest seg-

---

16. The issue of whether society should allow firm Y to operate at high-risk levels is examined later in this chapter.

ments of this set of curves; to do otherwise would be to accept a lower wage at each level of risk. Thus, the potentially acceptable offers will be found along the thickened curve of Figure 8.6, which we shall call the offer curve. The more types of firms there are in a market, the smoother this offer curve will be; however, it will always slope upward because of our twin assumptions that risk is costly to reduce and that employees must be paid higher wages to keep their utility constant if risk is increased. In some of the examples that follow, the offer curve is used to summarize the feasible, potentially acceptable offers employers are making in a labor market, because using an offer curve saves our diagrams from becoming cluttered with the isoprofit curves of many employers.

Major Insights.   Our hedonic model generates two major insights. The first is that wages rise with risk, other things equal. According to this prediction, there will be compensating wage differentials for job characteristics that are viewed as undesirable by workers whom employers must attract. Second, workers with strong preferences for safety will tend to take jobs in firms where safety can be generated most cheaply. They thus tend to seek out and accept safer, lower-paying jobs. Workers who are not as averse to accepting risk will seek out and accept the higher-paying, higher-risk jobs offered by firms that find safety costly to "produce." The second insight, then, is that the job-matching process—if it takes place under the conditions of knowledge and choice—is one in which firms and workers offer and accept jobs in a fashion that makes the most of their strengths and preferences.

FIGURE 8.6   An Offer Curve

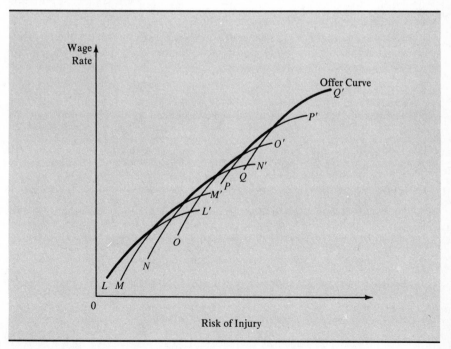

Before employing the above hedonic model to analyze labor market problems, it is useful to establish the empirical credibility of the theory of compensating differentials. The major empirically testable prediction of this theory is that, other things being equal, wages are higher in jobs with disagreeable characteristics.

EMPIRICAL TESTS OF THE THEORY OF COMPENSATING WAGE DIFFERENTIALS

The prediction that there are compensating wage differentials for undesirable job characteristics is over 200 years old. Adam Smith, in his *Wealth of Nations,* published in 1776, proposed five "principal circumstances which . . . make up for a small pecuniary gain in some employments, and counterbalance a great one in others." One of these, the constancy of employment, is discussed in the appendix to this chapter. Another two will be discussed in other chapters: the difficulty of learning the job (Chapter 9) and the probability of success (Chapter 11). Our discussion in this chapter, while it could draw upon any of Smith's "principal circumstances" to illustrate the concept of compensating wage differentials, will focus on his assertion that "the wages of labour vary with the ease or hardship, the cleanliness or dirtiness, the honourableness or dishonourableness of the employment."[17]

One would think that 200 years is a sufficient period of time over which to have accumulated substantial evidence concerning an important prediction. Unfortunately, the prediction has been seriously tested only in the last fifteen years, and only in a limited way. The reasons for this lack of evidence are twofold. First, the prediction is that, *other things equal,* wages will be higher in unpleasant or dangerous jobs. The prediction can be tested validly only if the researcher is able to control for the effects of age, education, gender, region, race, union status, and all the other factors that typically influence wages. Only when the effects of these factors on wages are known can the researcher filter out the *separate* influence on wages of (say) injury risk.[18]

---

17. See Adam Smith, *Wealth of Nations* (New York: Modern Library, 1937), Book I, Chapter 10. The fifth "principal circumstance" is "the small or great trust which be reposed in the workmen." This job characteristic has not been widely studied in the context of compensating wage differentials, but positive compensating wage differentials have been found for supervisory jobs. See, for example, Martha S. Hill, "Authority—A Job Quality with Greater Benefits for Men than Women," Working Paper Series, Survey Research Center, University of Michigan, 1983.

18. It is especially important to control for these other influences because safety is probably a normal good (meaning that higher-income workers desire more of it). A *simple* correlation of risk levels and earnings is thus negative—not positive as predicted by theory. However, the simple correlation fails to account for all the *other* factors that influence earnings. Only if the influence of these factors can be accounted for would we expect to obtain the predicted positive relationship between earnings and risk.

The adequacy of studies in which the wage/risk relationship is inferred from a cross section of workers has been challenged by several authors on the grounds that there are many unmeasured characteristics whose omission from the data set could bias the results. These authors propose the use of longitudinal data in which two or more observations on each worker are recorded, permitting unmeasured, person-specific characteristics to be controlled for. See, for example, Charles Brown, "Equalizing Differences in the Labor Market," *Quarterly Journal of Economics* 94 (February 1980): 113–34, and Greg Duncan and Bertil Holmlund, "Was Adam Smith Right After All? Another Test of the Theory of Compensating Wage Differentials," *Journal of Labor Economics* 1 (October 1983): 366–79.

EXAMPLE 8.3

Compensating Wage Differentials in the Soviet Union

In the Soviet Union, where production is centrally planned but labor is recruited voluntarily through the use of incentives, compensating wage differentials have arisen despite the philosophical emphases on wage equality and the altruistic dedication of individuals to the state. Workers in the Far North, where the Siberian winter is extraordinarily harsh, are paid wages and supplements 60–180 percent higher than in the populated areas of central, southern, and western Russia. Only part of this differential is to compensate workers for the higher costs of living in northern Siberia; the higher real wage serves as an inducement to work in a harsh environment.

Coal mining in the Soviet Union, like coal mining elsewhere, is a dangerous but necessary task. The difficulties of recruiting workers to mining have led the Soviet authorities to pay coal miners wages that are *double* those of factory workers. Further, miners in the most unhealthy and arduous jobs work 30 hours a week, compared to 36 in other mining jobs; in addition, they receive a one-time bonus equivalent to over 25 percent of the yearly pay for manufacturing workers.

SOURCES: Paul R. Gregory and Robert C. Stuart, *Soviet Economic Structure and Performance*, 2d ed. (New York: Harper & Row, 1981), 190–92; Radio Liberty Research, June 11, 1979 (RL 179/79).

Statistical procedures can control for these other factors, but these procedures require large data samples and the use of computers, and only in the last fifteen years or so have the necessary data and computers been widely available to researchers.

The second problem that has hindered the empirical testing for compensating wage differentials is the problem of specifying, in advance of these tests, job characteristics that are generally regarded as disagreeable. For example, while some people dislike outdoor work and would have to be paid a premium in order to accept it, others prefer such work and dislike desk jobs. Similar observations can be made about such job characteristics as repetitiveness, chances to make decisions, and amount of physical exertion. Tests of the theory require selecting job characteristics on which there is widespread agreement about what is "good" or "bad" at the margin. For this reason, many of the most credible and convincing tests of the theory have dealt with the level of *danger* on the job. While people may respond with different intensities to danger, it is difficult to believe that anyone prefers injury to safety; danger is an unambiguous "bad." The risk of injury is also objectively measured from injury rates published by occupation or, more commonly, by industry.

The strongest evidence of compensating wage differentials for on-the-job danger relates to the risk of *fatal* injury. Several studies using different sets of data from the United States, Great Britain, Sweden, and Korea have found that wages are positively associated with the risk of being killed on the job, other things equal. The results vary in magnitude and are rather sensitive to changes in the sample of workers used for estimation; however, for the most part they suggest that workers receive between $35 and $500 more per year for every one-in-ten-thousand increase in the risk of being killed on the job.[19] (One death for every 10,000 workers is roughly the yearly average for steel mills, while a rate of 10 deaths per 10,000 workers is the average for logging camps.) While these estimates seem small, they do imply that a plant with 1,000 employees could save between $35,000 and $500,000 in wage costs *per year* if it undertook a safety program that would save one life every ten years.

When testing for compensating differentials associated with *nonfatal* injuries, one must take into account that injured workers are at least partially compensated through the workers' compensation system.[20] Holding the generosity of workers' compensation benefits constant, increases in risk of nonfatal injury should be associated with increased wages; however, holding risk constant, increasing the generosity of such insurance payments should serve to reduce wages because injury-related losses are now smaller. Thus, tests of the theory in the context of nonfatal injuries must include data on both risk and workers' compensation. Such tests have generally offered some support for the theory, but the results are not consistently strong.[21] It may be that the

---

19. Eight studies are reviewed in Robert S. Smith, "Compensating Wage Differentials and Public Policy: A Review," *Industrial and Labor Relations Review* 32 (April 1979): 339–52. See also Alan Marin and George Psacharopoulos, "The Reward for Risk in the Labor Market: Evidence from the U.K. and a Reconciliation with Other Studies," *Journal of Political Economy* 90 (August 1982): 827–53; Stuart Dorsey, "Employment Hazards and Fringe Benefits: Further Tests for Compensating Differentials," in *Safety and the Work Force,* ed. John D. Worrall (Ithaca, N.Y.: ILR Press, 1983); Duncan and Holmlund, "Was Adam Smith Right After All?"; Sung-Joong Kim, "Compensating Wage Differentials for Job Hazards in Korea," unpublished master's thesis, New York State School of Industrial and Labor Relations, Cornell University, 1985; and Michael J. Moore and W. Kip Viscusi, "Doubling the Estimated Value of Life: Results Using New Occupational Fatality Data," *Journal of Policy Analysis and Management* 7, no. 3 (Spring 1988): 476–90. The range of estimates cited in the text is expressed in 1988 dollars.

   For an example of the sensitivity of the estimates to the sample employed, compare William Dickens, "Differences Between Risk Premiums in Union and Nonunion Wages and the Case for Occupational Safety Regulations," *Papers and Proceedings: American Economic Review* 74, no. 2 (May 1984): 320–23, and Alan Dillingham and Robert Smith, "Union Effects on the Valuation of Fatal Risk," *Proceedings of the Industrial Relations Research Association, Thirty-Sixth Annual Meeting* (1984): 270–77. See also Alan Dillingham, "The Influence of Risk Variable Definition on Value-of-Life Estimates," *Economic Inquiry* 23, no. 2 (April 1985): 277–94, and J. Paul Leigh, "Data on Occupational Fatalities Fail to Provide Evidence for Compensating Wages," unpublished paper, Department of Economics, San Jose State University, 1989.
20. Workers' compensation payments are also made in cases involving death, but obviously they cannot compensate the victims themselves.
21. On this subject see Stuart Dorsey and Norman Walzer, "Workers' Compensation, Job Hazards, and Wages," *Industrial and Labor Relations Review* 36, no. 4 (July 1983): 642–54; Richard J. Arnould and Len M. Nichols, "Wage-Risk Premiums and Workers' Compensation: A Refinement of Estimates of Compensating Wage Differentials," *Journal of Political Economy* 91, no. 2 (1983): 332–40; W. Kip Viscusi and Michael Moore, "Workers' Compensation: Wage Effects, Benefit Inadequacies, and the Value of Health Losses," *Review of Economics and Statistics* 69, no. 2 (May 1987): 249–61; and John Ruser, "Workers' Compensation Benefits and Compensating Wage Differentials," U.S. Bureau of Labor Statistics Working Paper no. 153, 1985. For a paper that also distinguishes between the *probability* of injury and the *duration* of the recovery period see Daniel S. Hamermesh and John R. Wolfe, "Compensating Wage Differentials and the Duration of Wage Loss," *Journal of Labor Economics* 8, no. 1 (pt. 2, January 1990): S175–S197.

losses that can be expected each year by the typical worker are too small to statistically distinguish their effects from those of the other forces that influence wages.[22]

POLICY APPLICATIONS

The insights of hedonic wage theory can be applied to some very critical social issues: the federal occupational safety and health program and affirmative action plans for hiring minorities.

Occupational Safety and Health

Are Workers Benefited by the Reduction in Risk?   In 1970 Congress passed the Occupational Safety and Health Act, which directed the U.S. Department of Labor to issue and enforce safety and health standards for all private employers. The stated goal of the act was to ensure the "highest degree of health and safety protection for the employee."[23]

Despite the *ideal* that employees should face the minimum possible risk in the workplace, implementing this ideal as social *policy* is not necessarily in the best interests of workers. Our hedonic model can show that reducing risk in some circumstances will lower the workers' utility levels. Consider Figure 8.7.

Suppose a labor market is functioning about like our textbook models, in that workers are well informed about dangers inherent in any job and are mobile enough to avoid risks they do not wish to take. In these circumstances, wages will be positively related to risk (other things equal), and workers will sort themselves into jobs according to their preferences. This market can be modeled graphically in Figure 8.7, where, for simplicity's sake, we have assumed there are two kinds of workers and two kinds of firms. Person A, who is very averse to the risk of injury, works at wage W_{AX} and risk R_{AX} for employer X. Person B works for employer Y at wage W_{BY} and risk R_{BY}.

Now suppose the Occupational Safety and Health Administration (OSHA), the Department of Labor agency responsible for implementing the federal safety and health program, promulgates a standard that, in effect, says that risk levels above R_{AX} are illegal. The effects, although unintended and perhaps not immediately obvious, would be detrimental to employees like B. Reducing risk is costly, and the best wage offer a worker can obtain at risk R_{AX} is W_{AX}. For B, however, wage W_{AX} and risk R_{AX} generate *less utility* than did Y's offer of W_{BY} and R_{BY}. Figure 8.7 shows that X's offer of W_{AX} and R_{AX} lies on indifference curve B_1, whereas Y's old (now illegal) offer was on the higher curve B_2.

---

22. The statistical problem is one of distinguishing the influence of injuries from all the other influences, including random ones, on wages. It is a little bit like trying to locate the position of Pluto in the sky from one's backyard. When Pluto is close to the earth, the moon is merely a crescent, there is no haze, and the city is dark, it can be done. If the moon is full, Pluto is far from the earth, and ground light and haze are present, Pluto's weak light signal cannot be seen or "filtered" out from that of all the other stars or planets.
23. Section 6(b)(5) of the Occupational Safety and Health Act.

FIGURE 8.7   The Effects of Government Regulation on a Perfectly Functioning Labor Market

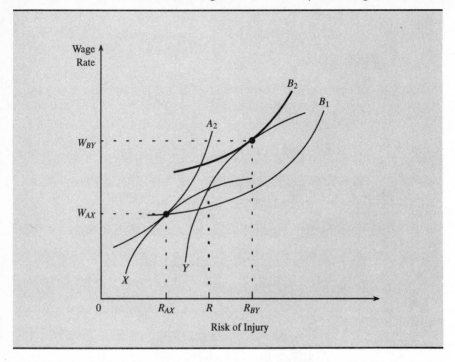

When the government mandates the reduction of risk in a market where workers are compensated for the risks they take, it penalizes workers like B, who are not terribly sensitive to risk and appreciate the higher wages associated with higher risk. The critical issue, of course, is whether workers have the knowledge and choice necessary to generate compensating wage differentials. Many people believe that workers are uninformed, unable to comprehend different risk levels, or immobile, and thus that most do not choose risky jobs voluntarily. If this belief were true, government regulation *could* make workers better off. Indeed, while the evidence of a positive relationship between wages and risk of death should challenge the notion that information and mobility are *generally* insufficient to create compensating differentials, there are specific areas in which problems obviously exist. For example, the introduction each year of new workplace chemicals whose effects on humans may be unknown for two or more decades (owing to the long gestation periods for most cancers and lung diseases) clearly presents substantial informational problems to affected labor market participants.

To say that worker utility *can* be reduced by such programs does not, of course, imply that it *will* be reduced. The outcome depends on how well the unregulated market functions and how careful the government is in setting its standards for risk reduction. The following section will analyze a government program implemented in a market that has *not* generated enough information about risk for employees to make informed job choices.

How Strict Should OSHA Standards Be?   Consider a labor market, like that mentioned previously for asbestos workers, in which ignorance or worker immobility hinders labor market operation. Let us suppose also that the government becomes aware of the health hazard involved and wishes to set a standard regulating worker exposure to this hazard. How stringent should this standard be?

The crux of the problem in standard setting is that reducing hazards is costly; the greater the reduction, the more it costs. While businesses bear these costs initially, they ultimately respond to them by cutting costs elsewhere and raising prices (to the extent that cutting costs is not possible). Since labor costs constitute the largest cost category for most businesses, it is natural for firms facing large government-mandated hazard-reduction costs to hold the line on wage increases or to adopt policies that are the equivalent of reducing wages: speeding up production, being less lenient with absenteeism, reducing employee benefits, and so forth. It is also likely, particularly in view of any price increases (which, of course, tend to reduce product demand), that employment will be cut back. Some of the job loss will be in the form of permanent layoffs that force workers to find other jobs—jobs they presumably could have had before the layoff but chose not to accept. Some of the loss will be in the form of cutting down on hiring new employees who would have regarded the jobs as their best employment option.

Thus, whether in the form of smaller wage increases, more difficult working conditions, or inability to obtain or retain one's first choice in a job, the costs of compliance with health standards will fall on employees. Employees will bear these costs in ways that reduce their earnings below what they *would have been in the absence of OSHA.* These losses may not be immediate or very obvious, since it is hard to know what wages would have been without the OSHA standard. However, the obscurity of this outcome of government regulation does not justify ignoring it. A graphic example can be used to make an educated guess about whether worker utility will be enhanced or not as a result of the increased protection from risk mandated by an OSHA health standard.

Figure 8.8 depicts a worker who believes she has taken a low-risk job, when in fact she is exposing herself to a hazard that has a relatively high probability of damaging her health in 20 years. She receives a wage of W_1 and *believes* she is at point A, where the risk level is R_1 and the utility level is U_1. Instead, she is in fact at point B, receiving W_1 for accepting (unknowingly) risk level R_2; she would thus experience lower utility (indifference curve U_0) if she knew the extent of the risk she was taking.

Suppose now that the government discovers that her job is highly hazardous. The government could simply inform the affected workers and let them move to other work. However, if it has little confidence in the ability of workers to understand the information or to find other work, the government could pass a standard that limits employee exposure to this hazard. But what level of protection should this standard offer?

If the government forces the risk level down to R', the best wage offer the woman in our example could obtain is W' (at point D on the offer curve). Given the market, no employer would or could pay her more at risk level R',

FIGURE 8.8   A Worker Accepting Unknown Risk

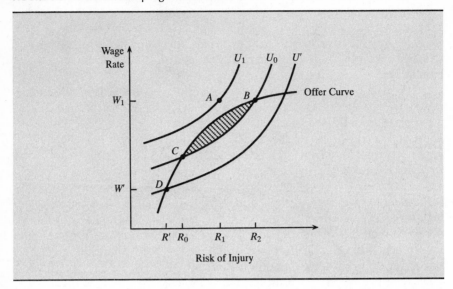

other things equal. Point D, however, lies on indifference curve U', which represents a lower level of utility than she is in fact getting now (U_0). She would be worse off under the government-imposed standard. On the other hand, if the government forced risk levels down to a level between R_0 and R_2, she would be better off because she would be able to reach an indifference curve above U_0 (see shaded area of Figure 8.8).

How can one estimate, in a practical way, how much wage loss workers would be willing to bear in exchange for a reduction in risk and still feel at least as well off as they are currently? The answer lies in estimating compensating wage differentials in markets that appear to work. Suppose, in a properly functioning market, that workers facing risk level R_1—the one our hypothetical worker *thought* she was facing in Figure 8.8—accept wage cuts of $500 per year for reductions in the yearly death rate of 1 in 10,000 (this represents the upper estimates reported on page 276). These workers appear to feel that, other things equal, $500 is a price they are willing to pay for this reduction in risk. Thus, as noted earlier in the case of earplug use, compensating wage differentials can be used to estimate the value workers place on seemingly intangible aspects of their jobs. The use of such differentials should not be oversold, because the difficulties of establishing which markets are properly functioning are considerable. However, estimating compensating wage differentials is probably the best way of finding out what value workers attach to various job characteristics.[24]

Since one cannot rule out the possibility—indeed, the likelihood—that one way or another workers will ultimately pay for the costs of their reduced workplace risks, economists argue strongly that the government should con-

24. See E. J. Mishan, "Evaluation of Life and Limb: A Theoretical Approach," *Journal of Political Economy* 79, no. 4 (July/August 1971): 687–705.

duct studies to estimate whether the value workers place on risk reduction is commensurate with the costs of the program. These studies are called *benefit/cost* studies, and they weigh the costs of a program against the value workers (or other beneficiaries) attach to the benefits of reduced risk. Estimates of compensating wage differentials can be very useful in estimating these benefits.

Consider the OSHA standard that reduced the exposure of 90,000 asbestos workers to two fibers of asbestos per cubic centimeter of air. Inhaling airborne asbestos fibers is strongly and persuasively associated with several types of cancer; it is expected that the two-fiber standard will reduce yearly asbestos-related deaths by 4 per 1,000 workers. The *lower* estimates of compensating differentials associated with the risk of death (mentioned on page 276) suggest that asbestos workers would probably be willing to pay *at least* $1,400 per year for this four-in-one-thousand reduction in risk.[25] Because the estimated yearly costs of complying with the asbestos standard were roughly comparable to this conservative estimate of benefits, it seems reasonably certain that the workers benefited by the standard would be willing to bear any of the program's costs that are shifted to them.[26] Thus, the asbestos standard almost certainly improves the welfare (utility) of asbestos workers.

As another example of benefit/cost analysis, consider two alternative standards limiting the exposure of chemical workers to *acrylonitrile,* a substance used in making acrylic fibers and a certain type of resin. Exposure to acrylonitrile is believed to increase one's chances of contracting cancer; reducing worker exposure from 20 parts per million (ppm) of air to 2 ppm would reduce the yearly risk of cancer-related deaths by 8.4 per 10,000 exposed workers. We know from our estimates of compensating differentials that the *most* we can assume workers would be willing to give up to obtain this reduction in risk is about $4,200 per year.[27] Since obtaining this new level of risk would cost $5,400 per worker (per year), it is conceivable that the standard would improve worker utility if workers bore the costs, but the costs would probably outweigh the benefits.

On the other hand, reducing acrylonitrile exposure to 1 ppm would reduce the death rate by 9 per 10,000 exposed workers at a yearly cost of $48,000 per worker. Given that the most workers seem willing to pay for a 9-in-10,000 reduction in risk is $4,500 per year, there is no chance that a 1-ppm standard could improve their utility if they bore the costs. Thus, while a 2-ppm standard may be worth promulgating, a 1-ppm standard would not be.[28]

---

25. The figure of $1,400 arises from multiplying the lower estimate of $35 for a one-in-ten-thousand reduction in death risk by a factor of 40 (to bring it up to a four-in-one-thousand reduction).
26. Russell Settle, "Benefits and Costs of the Federal Asbestos Standard," Paper delivered at a Department of Labor Conference on Evaluating the Effects of the Occupational Safety and Health Program, March 18–19, 1975. Cost estimates from this paper were converted to current dollars using the Consumer Price Index.
27. This figure is obtained by multiplying the upper estimate of $500 for a one-in-ten-thousand reduction by 8.4.
28. This analysis is based on data reported in James Miller, "Occupational Exposure to Acrylonitrile," statement before the Occupational Safety and Health Administration on behalf of Vistron Corporation, Washington, D.C., 1978. Cost estimates were converted to current dollars using the Consumer Price Index.

Perhaps because of the high costs and small benefits, OSHA chose to set the acrylonitrile standard at 2 ppm.

Judging OSHA Under Alternative Norms.   In our analysis of OSHA above, we argued that a safety or health standard is socially desirable only if the value workers place on risk reduction is commensurate with the costs of com-

EXAMPLE 8.4

Compensating Wage Differentials in 19th-Century Britain

English mill towns in the mid-1800s were often beset by violence and unhealthy living conditions. Infant deaths, a common indicator of health conditions, averaged over 200 per 1,000 live births in English towns, a rate well above those that typically prevail today in the poorest countries. Violence was also a common part of life, and corporal punishment was often used by factory supervisors against child laborers.

It is interesting, however, that the conditions varied from town to town and factory to factory. Infant mortality rates ranged from 110 to 344 in English towns in 1834, and not all factories used corporal punishment as a means of industrial discipline. These differences in conditions have led economic historians to wonder whether workers' *information* and *choices* back then were sufficient to generate compensating wage differentials for the more unpleasant or unhealthy sectors of employment.

More specifically, workers were leaving rural areas to work in towns during this era, and the towns and factories in which conditions were unhealthy would be less attractive to potential migrants. If workers had reasonably good information on health conditions and could obtain work in several places, they would tend to gravitate toward the more pleasant places. Factories in the more squalid towns, and those that used corporal punishment, would have had to offer higher wages to compete for migrants.

While data from the 1800s are such that research results are probably only suggestive, two intriguing findings have emerged. First, it appears that once the cost of living and regional wage differences are accounted for, in areas where infant mortality rates were 10 percent greater than average, the unskilled wage was 2–3 percent higher than average. It also appears that boys who worked in factories where corporal punishment was used received wages some 16–18 percent higher than boys of the same age, experience, and literacy who worked in plants where violence was not used. (Because workers receive compensating wage differentials only if employers are willing to pay them, one must entertain the notion that the threat, and use, of corporal punishment raised productivity by 16–18 percent.)

SOURCES: Jeffrey G. Williamson, "Was the Industrial Revolution Worth It? Disamenities and Death in 19th-Century British Towns," *Explorations in Economic History* 19 (1982): 221–45; Clark Nardinelli, "Corporal Punishment and Children's Wages in Nineteenth Century Britain," *Explorations in Economic History* 19 (1982): 283–95. We are indebted to Professor Ronald Warren, University of Virginia, for suggesting this general topic as an example.

plying with the standard. As was shown above, the value workers place on risk reduction can be estimated, in theory at least, from knowledge of compensating wage differentials. However, even if compensating wage differentials were accurately calculated from observations in a market characterized by both widespread information and choice, there are still objections to their use in assessing the benefits of OSHA standards. These objections will be discussed in this and the following subsection.

First, compensating wage differentials reflect the preferences of only those directly involved in the employer–employee contract. It is frequently argued that members of society who are not directly affected by the risk-reduction program might be willing to pay *something* for the benefits that accrue to those who *are* directly affected. Presumably, this "willingness to pay" is strongest for family members, relatives, and close friends and weakest for strangers. However, even strangers would have some interest in reducing injury and disease if they were taxed to subsidize the medical treatment of those who are injured or become ill. Thus, it is argued, the benefits of OSHA standards extend beyond the direct beneficiaries to other external parties whose willingness to pay should also be counted.

The major issue for policymaking is not whether these external benefits exist, but how large they are and whether they are already included in the willingness to pay of those directly benefited by an OSHA standard. For example, one could plausibly argue that a worker's *family* might be heavily involved in his or her choice of jobs so that compensating wage differentials *already* reflect family preferences. Put differently, the opinions and preferences of family members and close relatives *could* affect the indifference curves of the workers directly at risk and thus play a role in determining what jobs such workers choose at what wages. To date, no research has addressed this issue.

Also unclear at present is the degree to which medical care for job-related injuries and illnesses is subsidized by parties who are not direct beneficiaries of an OSHA standard. Workers' compensation insurance premiums, for example, are established at the *industry* level and are subject to some modification based on the experience of the individual firm in that industry; it seems unlikely that one industry's workers subsidize the medical treatment of injured workers in other industries. Since OSHA standards apply to *entire industries,* it does not appear probable that subsidies by external parties through workers' compensation are very large. However, because most occupational *illnesses* are not effectively covered by workers' compensation, treatment of those who contract a disease from their work is paid for by them, their insurance, or public subsidies (Medicare and Medicaid).[29] The likelihood that external parties subsidize the treatment of those directly at risk of occupa-

---

29. When a worker contracts lung cancer, it is usually very difficult to tell whether the cause was job related, due to personal habits, related to residential location, or a combination of all three. Because it cannot usually be proven to be job related, workers' compensation does not apply.

tional disease is thus very high; what is unknown at present is the magnitude of the subsidy.[30]

A second argument against using only the apparent willingness of workers to pay for risk reduction as a measure of its benefit is that workers really may not know what is best for themselves in the long run. Society frequently prohibits (or at least tries to prohibit) people from indulging in activities that are dangerous to their welfare; laws against the use of narcotics and gambling are two examples. Some argue that OSHA standards limiting exposure to dangerous substances or situations fall into the category of preventing workers from doing harm to themselves by being lured into dangerous work; therefore, it is argued that to ask how much they value risk reduction is irrelevant. The conflict between those who claim that workers know what is best for themselves and those who claim they do not can only be resolved on philosophical grounds.

However, one offshoot of the argument that workers do not know what is best for themselves deserves special mention. Some argue that worker preferences are molded by the environment in which they were raised and that there is no reason to take that environment as "given" or unchangeable. Once all workers at risk are required to wear protective clothing and equipment, and once they are prevented from taking certain risks on the job (in return for higher pay, perhaps), their attitudes and preferences will change. A few years ago, for example, wearing hard hats was considered "sissified," but today it is not. Thus, OSHA standards are regarded as an engine for changing worker, as well as employer, attitudes and behavior.

How far one wants to go in imposing present costs on workers to induce a change of attitude is a philosophical issue. We should add, however, that the value judgment underlying normative economics—that of mutual benefit, or making some better off and no one else worse off—is usually interpreted as applying to *current* (observed) preferences. Thus, the policy analyses of this text, by taking indifference curves and the current set of prices (compensating wage differentials, for example) as given, have implicitly assumed that workers know what is best for themselves.

The Implications of Status-Seeking.[31]   A third argument against relying on compensating wage differentials as a measure of willingness to pay for risk reduction is grounded in the interesting notion that, in choosing occupations and employers, workers are concerned about their *relative status* in addition to earnings and their "consumption" of safety. Our hedonic model assumed that workers derive utility from the consumption of both safety and the goods their earnings can buy, but it is possible that they also derive satisfaction from

---

30. This ignorance need not prevent us from making benefit estimates, however. We could, for example, calculate benefits in two ways: We could first assume no subsidy and use compensating wage differentials as discussed in the text. Alternatively, we could assume a 100 percent subsidy of medical costs and add to the willingness to pay implied by the compensating differentials the medical cost savings associated with the OSHA standard. These calculations would at least indicate the range into which benefits are likely to fall.
31. The considerations in the rest of this subsection originate in Robert H. Frank, *Choosing the Right Pond: Human Behavior and the Quest for Status* (New York: Oxford University Press, 1985), 136–42.

EXAMPLE 8.5

What Price Status?

The quest for status in one's job, like the consumption of other amenities, conceivably can lead to the creation of compensating wage differentials. The status being sought may be "global"—that is, indicative of one's relative standing in society—or it may be a "local" concern related to one's standing in a narrowly defined group with which one has almost daily contact.

To the extent that workers are concerned about global status, firms that are prestigious should find it easier to attract workers than their less prestigious counterparts. The ease with which internationally acclaimed universities, for example, can attract and retain professors suggests that they can recruit them at lower wages than their less prestigious counterparts would have to pay. The status conferred by these famous universities becomes part of one's compensation package; when status is lacking, a higher wage must be paid to compensate for its absence.

Local status, however, may also be a factor in the job selection process. Suppose, for example, that workers derive utility from being ranked highly among their day-to-day associates: they enjoy the deference shown by their colleagues and the roles they are asked to play as team leaders or problem solvers. If such local status is a concern, workers of a given quality will prefer employment in a firm hiring less able colleagues to a job in which their co-workers have greater ability. Thus, to induce a person concerned with local status to work with more able co-workers requires a higher wage than it would take to induce the same person to work with a less able group. Those who choose to work with people who have less ability end up paying for their high local status by accepting a lower wage.

Does the labor market show evidence of status-related wage differences? We do not know, frankly, but theory raises the intriguing possibility that status-seekers pay a price for their place in the employment hierarchy. Further, if the higher-ranking people in a firm receive a lower wage—and the lower-ranked workers a higher wage—than each would otherwise receive, theory also suggests that status-seeking narrows the wage differentials that might otherwise exist between the best and worst workers in a group.

SOURCE: Robert H. Frank, *Choosing the Right Pond: Human Behavior and the Quest for Status* (New York: Oxford University Press, 1985).

achieving a certain status *relative* to their peers. They may want their children to go to colleges that are at least as good as the ones attended by others in their reference group, or they may want a house that is as large or as nicely appointed as those of their friends or acquaintances. The key characteristic of a concern about relative standing is that the consumption of *others,* not just one's *own* consumption levels, affects utility.

The importance of concerns about status to the measurement of willingness to pay for additional safety is that these concerns may lead workers to place an emphasis on consuming "conspicuous" goods that others can observe. Thus, money income and the goods it will buy (cars, housing, the proper schools for children) tend to be emphasized more than goods—such as safety in the workplace—that are hard to observe and are thus more or less irrelevant to the determination of one's ranking in a group. The illustration developed below demonstrates how a concern for the conspicuous can lead workers to behave in a way that systematically *understates* their *true* willingness to pay for risk reduction.

Let us assume that persons A and B comprise a reference group for each other, and that each must choose between a high-wage, low-safety (HW-LS) job and one offering low wages and high safety (LW-HS). In the payoff matrix shown in Figure 8.9, it can be seen that each receives 12 units of happiness if they both choose LW-HS, and 9 units if they both choose HW-LS. In both cases, they have equal status, because their consumption levels are equal; as long as their status is equal each prefers (by assumption) the low-wage, high-safety job. If they could both coordinate their behavior and agree to choose LW-HS, their total utility would be maximized.

The problem is that each worker suspects that if he or she chooses LW-HS, the other will choose the high-wage job and secure the added status associated with higher earnings. Let us look more closely at the payoff matrix in Figure 8.9. Since A cannot be sure what B will do, she will want to consider all options. If B were to choose LW-HS, A would find it better to choose HW-LS; choosing LW-HS would yield her 12 units of happiness, but choosing HW-LS—by increasing the conspicuous part of her consumption package (her money wage)—would yield her 14 units of happiness. Similarly, if B were to choose HW-LS, A would find it advantageous to choose HW-LS, thereby securing 9 units of happiness rather than the 7 units associated with LW-HS. Thus, no matter what choice B makes, once he has committed himself A can make herself better off by choosing HW-LS.

The individual incentives to choose HW-LS also exist for person B, as one can see by analyzing what his best options are *given* A's choices (the payoff matrix is symmetric). Thus, *without coordinating their behavior,* both A and B (because of their concerns for conspicuous goods) would be induced to choose high-wage, low-safety jobs. These choices are not socially optimal, because when both choose HW-LS their total utility is *lower* than when each chooses the low-wage, high-safety job![32]

Here, then, is the essence of the third argument for not relying on the "willingness to pay" estimates implied by compensating wage differentials. An uncoordinated market may fail to accomplish all mutually beneficial transactions when relative status is a factor motivating worker behavior, because it *can* lead to more emphasis on conspicuous goods than workers really want. Thus, in effect, workers may find it in their interests to *collectively* agree, through safety legislation, to consume more safety at lower wages than an unfettered free market would provide. The rationale is that by constraining everyone to choose LW-HS, no one is permitted to reap the individual benefits of choosing HW-LS, and it prevents a status-seeking game that ultimately has no winners.

---

32. The payoff matrix in Figure 8.9 is known as the "Prisoner's Dilemma." This name derives from the situation in which two conspirators in a crime are captured and interrogated separately. If neither talks, both will be freed and each will get one-half of the loot; however, if one implicates the other he is freed, the other is jailed, and the freed suspect collects all the loot. If they cannot communicate, both will confess and both will be jailed.

FIGURE 8.9 Payoff Matrix: Two-Person Game with Suboptimal Market Outcome

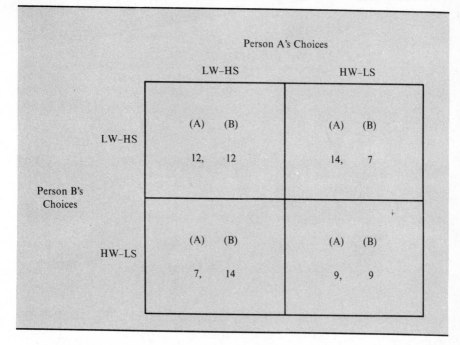

When evaluating this rationale for not relying completely on compensating wage differentials as indicators of willingness to pay for safety, it must be noted that the example above is a *possibility,* not an inevitability, when status-seeking is present. More specifically, status-seeking will lead to the "wrong" social outcome (HW–LS) only when preferences for status are strong relative to preferences for safety. If the desire for safety had been stronger and the payoff matrix in Figure 8.10 had held instead of the one in Figure 8.9, both workers would choose the low-wage, high-safety job despite their concerns for status.[33] Thus, status-seeking behavior will not *always* cause workers to overemphasize conspicuous goods.

Affirmative Action Planning

In an effort to end discriminatory hiring practices, all large firms doing business with the federal government are required to prepare *affirmative action plans* listing their goals for the hiring of women and minorities for the coming years. If these goals are set too low or if approved goals are not met, the firm could conceivably lose its government contracts. Thus, setting realistic goals is important.

In order to construct and evaluate a realistic affirmative action plan for hiring employees, firms must know the *availability* of women and minorities. The concept of availability used by the government has been interpreted in

---

33. That safety is more important than status in Figure 8.10 can be seen by looking at the pay-offs to A. If B chooses LW–HS, A receives 12 units of happiness if she chooses LW–HS, but only 11 if she chooses HW–LS. The combination of less safety but more status *reduces* her happiness. In Figure 8.9, that same combination was assumed to *increase* her utility.

FIGURE 8.10   Payoff Matrix: Two-Person Game with Optimal Market Outcome

		Person A's Choices	
		LW–HS	HW–LS
Person B's Choices	LW–HS	(A) (B) 12, 12	(A) (B) 11, 9
	HW–LS	(A) (B) 9, 11	(A) (B) 8, 8

basically two ways:

1. The percentage of minorities or women among those who have the skills required by a specific job group or who are capable of acquiring them;
2. The percentage of minorities or women who can be expected to become available during the period in which the ultimate goal is to be achieved.[34]

A construction contractor seeking to hire 20 carpenters for a big job may be required to establish a goal of having 6 blacks among them if 30 percent of *all* carpenters in the city are black. Alternatively, an automobile manufacturer that will be hiring 20 beginning mechanical engineers may be required to set a goal of having 5 women among them if 25 percent of *new graduates* in mechanical engineering are female. The definition of availability to be used is the one that makes more sense in the situation.

While this flexibility in defining availability undoubtedly helps achieve the goal of setting realistic targets for firms, the government has usually ignored another aspect of availability: the *interest of workers* in a particular employer. In the case of locally recruited minority workers, for example, the government has typically used the percentage of qualified minorities in the entire city or metropolitan area as the measure of availability, regardless of

---

34. U.S. Department of Labor, Office of Federal Contract Compliance Programs, *Compliance Manual* (October 18, 1978).

how far away they may live from the place of employment. This measure of availability disregards the fact that people prefer to work near home, other things equal, and that their interest in applying for jobs diminishes as the commuting distance rises. Commuting costs, in terms of both time and money, are seen by workers as negative aspects of employment — aspects to be avoided unless adequate compensation for them is received. Failure to take them into account when trying to measure availability works against the intention of setting realistic hiring goals.

The Timken Company.   An illustration of the severity of the commuting issue arose in 1976, when the government declared the Timken Company ineligible to receive government contracts.[35] The reason for debarment was that Timken's plant in Bucyrus, Ohio, set its minority hiring goals based on a 16-mile recruiting radius, an area with a 0.6 percent minority population, and refused to include the town of Mansfield, which was 25 miles from its plant and contained 15 percent minorities. The government concluded that 25 miles — 35 to 45 minutes by car — was a reasonable commuting distance and that Mansfield should thus be included for goal-setting purposes. Characteristically, the government's hiring goal for Timken assumed that workers in Mansfield were as interested in a job at Timken as workers in Bucyrus. The government thus calculated its measure of availability by drawing a 25-mile radius around the plant and calculating the percentage (3.5 percent) of minorities living in that entire area.

Timken took the case to court and won a reversal. The court, looking at the jobs available in Mansfield and the commuting pattern of its residents, decided that workers living in Mansfield were unlikely to want to commute to Bucyrus. In this decision, the court relied on a survey of 12 major employers in Bucyrus, none of whom restricted the geographic range of their hiring, which showed that only four Mansfield residents out of 2,300 workers were working in the Bucyrus firms.

While it is clear that the government was wrong in weighting Mansfield and Bucyrus residents equally in computing Timken's availability, it is not clear that the court was correct in rejecting Mansfield as part of Timken's natural recruiting area.

A Hedonic Model of Commuting.   We asserted earlier that the cost of commuting to work is viewed by workers as a disadvantage; the higher the cost is, the greater are the disadvantages of the job. In this respect, commuting costs are like the risk of injury, to be avoided unless compensation is received. Thus, we would expect that workers, in order to keep their utility constant, would require higher wages to commute longer distances to otherwise identical jobs.

Figure 8.11 shows worker commuting preferences graphically by drawing indifference curves that are upward-sloping and convex (similar to indifference curves in the analysis of risk of injury). Workers with the greatest aversion to commuting (like employee A) have the steepest curves because they

---

35. *Timken Company* v. *Vaughn* 413 F. Supp. 1183 (N.D., Ohio 1976).

require the greatest wage increases to commute longer distances. Workers with the weakest aversion to commuting (like employee B) have the flattest indifference curves.

On the employer side of the market, there is also a positive relationship between wages and the commuting distances of their workers. Consider a firm that is dissatisfied with its pool of job applicants and wants to enlarge this pool so it can be more selective in hiring. One solution is to raise its wage offers in order to attract more applicants. This higher wage offer will, among other things, attract applicants who live farther from the plant. The higher wage offer serves to overcome the commuting costs for these workers.

How high the firm is willing to raise its wage offer depends on how much more productive its work force will be. A large, sophisticated assembly-line plant may be willing to raise its wages a lot to increase the size of its labor market, because it can select the most skilled *and* the most dependable workers. Unsteady workers, or those prone to absenteeism, can impose high costs on an assembly-line producer. These large, sophisticated firms (like Z in Figure 8.11) have the steepest isoprofit curves. A smaller firm looking for workers of the same general skill, but lacking a highly interdependent production process, may not obtain a very big increase in productivity if it hires only the most dependable workers. Thus, it may not find that increasing the size of its labor market is as beneficial; this type of small firm (like Y) has a flatter isoprofit curve.

FIGURE 8.11   A Hedonic Model of Commuting

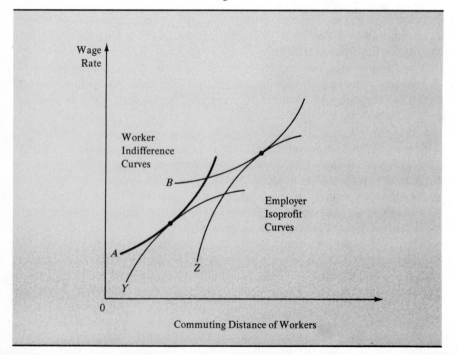

Figure 8.11 suggests two conclusions of interest in the context of antidiscrimination programs. First, there is a *positive* relationship between wages and commuting distances, other things equal. High-wage firms will have geographically larger recruiting areas than low-wage employers.[36] What this means for affirmative action planning is that the firm's wage policy—whether its pay rate is high, average, or low for the skills it hires—should play a role in determining the size of its labor market and the availability of minorities or women.

In the Timken case, for example, Mansfield may well have been in Timken's legitimate recruiting area (even if it was not for the other 12 employers) *if* Timken's wage rates were higher than average for the jobs involved. Mansfield workers would not, under any circumstances, be considered as available as Bucyrus workers, but an important consideration—the wage rate—was ignored by the court in defining the availability of minorities to Timken. This consideration, however, was taken into account in a 1979 court decision, wherein it was held that residents of the District of Columbia were not effectively in the labor pool of a suburban employer because, in part, the employer's wages were lower than those paid in the district.[37]

The second major conclusion suggested by Figure 8.11 is that workers facing a given set of choices will select wage offers and commuting distances based on their preferences. People who place a high value on working close to home will accept lower wage offers. These lower offers serve as a compensating wage differential for the desirable characteristic of being able to commute to work quickly and cheaply.

This second conclusion is significant for antidiscrimination policy because women typically work closer to home than men. It can be argued that women, because they usually have primary family responsibility for meal preparation and child rearing, apparently place a premium on being able to work close to home. Under this line of argument, it is preferences that induce women to work closer to home. It can also be argued, however, that because of discrimination, women are confined to jobs in which gains to an employer from a larger applicant pool are not commensurate with the costs of increased wages. If so, the dispersion of wages in a given labor market may be smaller for women than for men, and women's incentives to seek offers farther from home are thus relatively low. This argument suggests that discrimination may cause the wage/distance "offer curve" facing women to be flatter than the corresponding one for men, which (for a given set of preferences) would cause women to choose job offers closer to home.[38] Whether driven by preferences

36. For studies on this topic, see Philip S. Borba, "Factors That Influence the Home-to-Work Dispersion of Workers in a Local Labor Market, with an Application to the External Labor Market Availability of Protected Class Workers," Ph.D. diss., Cornell University, 1982; Janice F. Madden, "Urban Wage Gradients: Empirical Evidence," *Journal of Urban Economics* 18 (November 1985): 291–301; and Eric A. Hanushek, "Do Wages Vary in Cities? An Empirical Study of Urban Labor Markets," Working Paper no. 91, Department of Economics, University of Rochester, June 1987.

37. *U.S.* v. *County of Fairfax* 19 FEP Cases 753 (E.O., Va. 1979).

38. Borba, "Factors That Influence the Home-to-Work Dispersion of Workers in a Local Labor Market," p. 148, finds that the wage/distance offer curve is steeper for white males than for all workers combined, but his study did not analyze men and women separately.

(related to household productivity) or a flatter offer curve, shorter commutes for women imply that at least some of the lower earnings they experience relative to men compensates for their shorter average commutes. Therefore, a complete measure of wage discrimination (see Chapter 14) must take some account of differential commuting distances.

MISCONCEPTION

"Economists know the price of everything and the value of nothing. Life is full of intangibles, like safety and health, that are too precious to value in terms of dollars."

Analysis

Certain minimum levels of such goods as food and safety are essential to the preservation of the species. Beyond these levels, however, society must decide how much of each to produce. The problem is that resources used to produce more of each can also be used to produce *other* goods that enhance the quality of life. The costs of producing an additional unit of any item reflect what producers must pay to bid the needed resources away from their alternative uses; therefore, prices *do* reflect people's willingness to pay for small changes in the allocation of resources among alternative uses. Put differently, comparing prices (including compensating wage differentials) will reveal the relative values people place on marginal changes in the allocation of resources.

Principle

The social cost of an action is the forgone utility that the action requires; the social benefit is the added utility it generates.

REVIEW QUESTIONS

1. Is the following true, false, or uncertain: "Certain occupations, such as coal mining, are inherently dangerous to workers' health and safety. Therefore, unambiguously, the most appropriate government policy is the establishment and enforcement of rigid safety and health standards." Explain your answer.
2. Statement 1: "Business executives are greedy profit maximizers, caring only for themselves." Statement 2: "It has been established that workers doing filthy, dangerous work receive higher wages, other things equal." Can both of these statements be generally true? Why?
3. It has often been claimed that an all-volunteer army would be entirely made up of soldiers from minority groups or disadvantaged backgrounds. Using what you have learned in this chapter, analyze the reasoning and assumptions underlying this claim.
4. "The concept of compensating wage premiums for dangerous work does not apply to industries like the coal industry, where the union has forced all wages and other compensation items to be the same. Since all mines must pay the same wage, owners of dangerous mines will have to pay the same wage as owners of safe mines. Therefore, compensating differentials cannot exist." Is this statement correct? (As-

sume wages and other forms of pay must be equal for dangerous and nondangerous work and consider the implications for individual labor supply behavior.)

5. "There are three methods of allocating labor across a spectrum of jobs that may differ substantially in working conditions. One is the use of force, one is the use of trickery, and one is the use of compensating wage differentials." Comment.

6. Some employers offer jobs for which overtime is mandatory. Others offer jobs for which overtime hours are usually available to workers if they wish to work them, and still others offer jobs for which overtime hours are not commonly worked. Suppose a careful study of wages found that jobs for which overtime hours are commonly available pay lower wages than jobs for which overtime is not usually worked (after controlling for all other factors affecting the wage rate). Moreover, jobs for which overtime is required are found to pay wages comparable to those found in jobs for which overtime is unusual, again controlling for all other factors affecting wages. What would the results of these studies tell us about worker attitudes regarding overtime? Why?

7. In 1986 the federal government was considering the removal of prohibitions on the production of various garments and apparel items by independent contractors working out of their homes. These prohibitions had been in effect since 1942, at which time the government decided that many homeworkers were being exploited by garment manufacturers who paid them extremely low wages. Those who, in 1986, favored retaining the prohibitions argued that homeworkers (primarily women) would end up getting considerably less than factory workers. These supporters of the 1942 prohibitions asserted that the earnings differential between factory and homeworkers is a measure of the degree to which the latter are exploited. Evaluate this assertion.

8. Suppose we observe a city in which highway workers are required to give the Supervisor of Highways an under-the-table payment of X dollars per year. Suppose we were to compare the wages paid by this city with the market-clearing wage paid to comparable workers in the area. Would we expect wages paid to highway workers by this city to be higher or lower than the market wage? Would we expect the salary paid by the city to its Supervisor of Highways to be above or below market? Explain.

SELECTED READINGS

Brown, Charles. "Equalizing Differences in the Labor Market." *Quarterly Journal of Economics* 94 (February 1980): 113–34.

Duncan, Greg, and Holmlund, Bertil. "Was Adam Smith Right After All? Another Test of the Theory of Compensating Wage Differentials." *Journal of Labor Economics* 1 (October 1983): 366–79.

Frank, Robert. *Choosing the Right Pond: Human Behavior and the Quest for Status.* New York: Oxford University Press, 1985.

Rosen, Sherwin. "Hedonic Prices and Implicit Markets." *Journal of Political Economy* 82 (January–February 1974): 34–55.

Smith, Adam. *Wealth of Nations.* New York: Modern Library, 1937. Book I, Chapter 10.

Smith, Robert S. "Compensating Wage Differentials and Public Policy: A Review." *Industrial and Labor Relations Review* 32 (April 1979): 339–52.

———. *The Occupational Safety and Health Act: Its Goals and Its Achievements.* Washington, D.C.: The American Enterprise Institute for Public Policy Research, 1976.

Viscusi, W. Kip. *Risk by Choice.* Cambridge, Mass.: Harvard University Press, 1983.

APPENDIX 8A

Compensating Wage Differentials and Layoffs

As mentioned in the chapter text, one of the circumstances identified by Adam Smith under which compensating wage differentials would arise relates to the "constancy or inconstancy of employment." While there is evidence, as we shall see, to support this prediction, the relationship of wages to layoff probabilities is by no means as simple as Smith thought. In particular, there are three issues relevant to the analysis, all of which we shall discuss briefly.[1]

UNCONSTRAINED CHOICE OF WORK HOURS

Suppose that, in the spirit of Chapters 6 and 7, employees are free to choose their hours of work in a labor market that offers an infinite choice of work hours. Given the wage a particular worker can command and his or her non-wage income, the utility-maximizing choice of working hours would be selected. For the person depicted in Figure 8A.1, the utility-maximizing choice of work hours is H^*, given his or her offered wage rate (W^*) and level of nonwage income (assumed here to be zero).

If H^* is thought of in terms of yearly work hours, it is easy to understand that a worker may *prefer* a job involving layoff! Suppose H^* is 1,500 hours per year, or essentially three-quarters of the typical "full-time" job of 2,000 hours. One could work 6 hours a day, 5 days a week, for 50 weeks a year, or one could work 8 hours a day, 5 days a week, for 9 months and agree to be laid off for 3 months. Which alternative holds more appeal to any given individual depends on his or her preferences with respect to large blocks of leisure or household time, but it is clear that many people value such large blocks. Teachers, for example, typically work full time during a 9-month school year,

---

1. The analysis in this appendix draws heavily upon John M. Abowd and Orley Ashenfelter, "Anticipated Unemployment, Temporary Layoffs, and Compensating Wage Differentials," in *Studies in Labor Markets,* ed. Sherwin Rosen (Chicago: University of Chicago Press, 1981), 141–70.

FIGURE 8A.1   Choice of Hours of Work

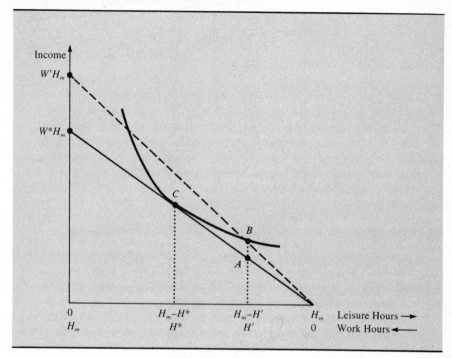

and then some of them vacation during the summer. Many other jobs, from construction trades to work in canning factories, involve predictable seasonal layoffs, and workers in these jobs may have chosen them because they value the leisure or household production time accompanying the layoffs.

Putting the point differently, the theory of compensating wage differentials suggests they will be positive only when a job characteristic is regarded as bad by the marginal worker. Predictable blocks of leisure or household time accompanying seasonal layoffs may not be regarded as bad by the marginal worker. In fact, workers in some markets may see layoffs as a mechanism through which they can best achieve their desired yearly hours of work.

CONSTRAINED HOURS OF WORK

Suppose that the worker depicted in Figure 8A.1 is offered a choice between a job offering wage W^* and hours H^*, and one offering fewer hours than desired because of a predictable layoff each year that reduces hours of work to H'. Clearly, if the wage for the latter job remains at W^*, the worker's utility will be reduced by taking the job offering H' hours because he or she will be on an indifference curve passing through point A. The job offering W^* and H^* is thus clearly preferred at W^*.

However, suppose that H' is offered at a wage of W', where W' exceeds W^* by enough so that point B can be reached. Point B, where the wage is W' and hours of work are H', is on the *same* indifference curve as point C (the utility-maximizing point when W^* is the offered wage). Point B is not a point of utility maximization at a wage offer of W',[2] but if the worker is offered an unconstrained choice of hours at wage rate W^*, or a wage of W' where working hours are *constrained* to equal H', he or she would be indifferent between the two job offers.

In the above example, $(W' - W^*)$ is the compensating wage differential that would have to arise for the worker to consider a job where hours of work were constrained to lie below those otherwise desired. Many people view layoffs as an event that prevents workers from working the number of hours they would otherwise desire to work. If this is the case, and if these layoffs are predictable and known with certainty, such as layoffs accompanying model changeovers in the auto industry, then compensating wage differentials associated with the predictable, certain layoff rate would arise in a well-functioning labor market (that is, one where workers are informed and mobile).[3]

The Effects of Uncertain Layoffs

In the above section, we assumed that layoffs were predictable and known with certainty. In most cases, however, they are not. While one might expect layoff rates to be higher in some industries than in others, they are in fact often subject to considerable random fluctuation *within* industries over the years. This *uncertainty* of layoffs is itself another aspect of affected jobs that is usually thought to be a negative feature and for which a compensating wage differential might arise.

Suppose that utility is measurable and is a function only of income, so that it can be graphed against income (Y), as in Figure 8A.2.[4] Suppose also that the person depicted is offered a job for which a wage of W' and yearly hours of H' are known *with certainty*. The utility associated with these H' hours is a function of his or her income at H' hours of work: $W'H'$ (again assuming no nonwage income).

Now suppose there is another job paying W' in which the *average* hours of work per year are H' but half the time H_h is worked and half the time H_ℓ is worked. Although we have assumed that $0.5\,H_h + 0.5\,H_\ell = H'$, so that over the years the person averages H' hours of work, it turns out that with the con-

---

2. It is not a point of tangency; that is, at a wage of W' the worker depicted in Figure 8A.1 would prefer to work more than H' hours if he or she were free to choose work hours. We have assumed in the discussion that the choice is *constrained* so that hours cannot exceed H'.

3. A similar argument can be used to predict that workers will receive compensating wage differentials if they are forced to work longer hours than they would otherwise prefer. For the argument and evidence in support of it, see Ronald G. Ehrenberg and Paul L. Schumann, "Compensating Wage Differentials for Mandatory Overtime," *Economic Inquiry* 22 (December 1984).

4. Although economists typically work with *ordinal* utility functions, which specify the relative ranking of alternatives without assigning each alternative a numerical value of utility, the analysis of choice under uncertainty requires the use of *cardinal* utility functions (ones in which each alternative is assigned a specific numerical value of utility). It is far beyond the scope of this text to fully discuss the properties of such functions; the interested reader is referred to other sources such as R. Duncan Luce and Howard Raiffa, *Games and Decisions* (New York: John Wiley & Sons, 1957). A similar analysis of another topic can be found in the appendix to Chapter 13.

FIGURE 8A.2   The Choice Between H' Hours with Certainty and H' Hours on Average

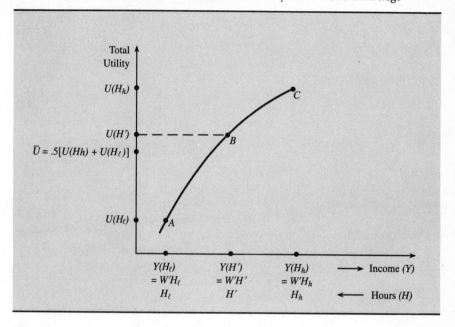

vex utility function we have drawn, the person's average utility is *below* $U(H')$. To understand this we must look closely at Figure 8A.2.

When the person's working hours are H_h, which is half the time, he or she earns $W'H_h$, and this income yields a utility of $U(H_h)$. Thus, half the time the worker will be at point C enjoying utility level $U(H_h)$. The other half of the time, however, the person will be working H_ℓ hours, earning $W'H_\ell$ in income, and be at point A enjoying utility of $U(H_\ell)$. His or her average utility is thus $\overline{U}$, which is $\overline{U} = 0.5\,U(H_h) + 0.5\,U(H_\ell)$. Note that $\overline{U}$, which is midway between $U(H_h)$ and $U(H_\ell)$ in our example, lies *below* $U(H')$—the utility derived from a job paying W' and employing the person for H' *with certainty* every year.

Why is $\overline{U} < U(H')$ even though H' hours are worked on *average* in both cases? The answer lies in the convexity of the utility function, which economists define as exhibiting *risk aversion*. Moving from H' to H_h covers the same absolute distance as moving from H' to H_ℓ, but the changes in utility are not the same in *magnitude*. In particular, moving from H' to H_h (points B to C) in the good years adds *less* to utility than moving from H' to H_ℓ (points B to A) in the bad years takes away. Put differently, the convexity of the total utility curve in Figure 8A.2 implies diminishing marginal utility of income. Thus, in the unlucky years, when hours are below H', there is a relatively big drop in utility (as compared to the utility associated with H' hours), while in the lucky years the added income increases utility by a relatively small amount.

The upshot of this discussion is that when workers are averse to risk— that is, when their utility functions are convex so that they in essence place a larger value on negative changes from a given level of income than they do on positive changes of equal dollar magnitude—they would prefer a job paying

W' and offering H' hours with certainty to one paying W' and offering only H' hours on average. Thus, to compensate them for the loss in utility associated with *risk aversion,* they would require a wage above W' for the job offering H' hours only on average.

THE OBSERVED WAGE/LAYOFF RELATIONSHIP

The discussion above centered on worker preferences regarding layoffs. For compensating wage differentials to arise, of course, employers must be willing to pay them. That is, employers must profit from being able to lay off workers, and if we are to observe firms pursuing a high-wage/high-layoff strategy, their gains from layoff must exceed their costs of higher wages.

The discussion above also neglected unemployment insurance (UI) payments to laid-off workers. This topic is discussed in some detail in Chapter 16. Here we need note only that if UI payments fully compensate laid-off workers for their lost utility, compensating wage differentials will not arise. Compensating wage differentials will arise only if UI payments do not fully compensate laid-off workers.

One study that looked very carefully at the relationship between wages and layoffs suggests that the compensating wage differential for an average probability of layoff is around 4 percent of wages, with over 80 percent of this differential related to the aversion to risk associated with the variability (uncertainty) in layoff rates facing workers over time. Workers in the high-layoff industries of automobile manufacturing and construction received estimated compensating wage differentials ranging over the early 1970s from 6 to 14 percent and 6 to 11 percent, respectively.[5]

---

5. These estimates are from the Abowd and Ashenfelter article in footnote 1 of this appendix. Similar evidence for the late 1970s can be found in Robert H. Topel, "Equilibrium Earnings, Turnover, and Unemployment: New Evidence," *Journal of Labor Economics* 2, no. 4 (October 1984): 500–522. For those interested in how the presence of compensating wage differentials and UI benefits affects workers' choices of jobs when layoff probabilities differ across jobs, see Robert M. Hutchens, "Layoffs and Labor Supply," *International Economic Review* 24 (February 1983): 37–55.

9

Investments in Human Capital: Education and Training

Chapters 6, 7, and 8—on the decision to work and job choice—emphasized the effects of *current* wages and psychic income on worker decisions. Many labor supply choices, however, require a substantial initial *investment* on the part of the worker. Recall that investments, by definition, entail an initial cost that one hopes to recoup over some period of time. Thus, for many labor supply decisions, *current* wages and working conditions are not the only deciding factors. Modeling these decisions requires developing a framework that incorporates investment behavior.

Workers undertake three major kinds of investments: education and training, migration, and search for new jobs. All three investments involve an initial cost, and all three are made in the hope and expectation that the investment will pay off well into the future. To emphasize the essential similarity of these investments to other kinds of investments, economists refer to them as investments in *human capital,* a term that conceptualizes workers as embodying a set of skills that can be "rented out" to employers. The knowledge and skills a worker has—which come from education and training, including the training that experience yields—generate a certain *stock* of productive capital. However, the *value* of this amount of productive capital is derived from how much these skills can earn in the labor market. Job search and migration are activities that increase the value of one's human capital by increasing the price (wage) received for a given stock of skills.

Society's total wealth should therefore be thought of as a combination of both human and nonhuman capital. Human capital includes accumulated investments in such activities as education, job training, and migration, whereas nonhuman wealth includes society's stock of land, buildings, and machinery. Total wealth in the United States was estimated at $15.6 trillion in 1973, or

EXAMPLE 9.1

Hiroshima, Hamburg, and Human Capital

An insight into the relative magnitudes and importance of physical and human capital is obtained by noting some interesting facts concerning severely war-damaged cities. The atomic attack on Hiroshima destroyed 70 percent of its buildings and killed about 30 percent of the population. Survivors fled the city in the aftermath of the bombing, but people began returning within 24 hours; within three months two-thirds of the city's surviving population had returned. Because the air-burst bomb left the city's underground utility networks intact, power was restored to surviving areas one day after the bombing. Through railway service began again in two days, and telephone service was restarted in a week. The U.S. Strategic Bombing Survey estimated that plants responsible for three-quarters of the city's industrial production (many of these were located on the outskirts of the city and were undamaged) could have begun normal operations within thirty days.

In Hamburg, Germany, a city of around 1.5 million in the summer of 1943, Allied bombing raids over a ten-day period in July and August destroyed about half of the buildings in the city and killed about 3 percent of the city's population. Although there was considerable damage to the water supply system, electricity and gas service were adequate within a few days after the last attack, and within four days the telegraph system was again operating. The central bank was reopened and business had begun to function normally after one week, and postal service was resumed within twelve days of the attack. The Strategic Bombing Survey reported that within five months Hamburg had recovered up to 80 percent of its former productivity.

The speed and success of recovery from these disasters has prompted one economist to offer the following two observations:

> (1) the fraction of the community's real wealth represented by visible material capital is small relative to the fraction represented by the accumulated knowledge and talents of the population, and (2) there are enormous reserves of energy and effort in the population not drawn upon in ordinary times but which can be utilized under special circumstances such as those prevailing in the aftermath of disaster.

SOURCE: Jack Hirshleifer, *Economic Behavior in Adversity* (Chicago: University of Chicago Press, 1987), 12–14, 78–79.

about $75,000 for every man, woman, and child. Of this, 52 percent, or $39,000 per capita, took the form of *human* wealth.[1] Thus, investments in human capital are enormously important in our society (see Example 9.1 for a further indication of the relative importance of human capital).

The expected *returns* on human capital investments are, as noted, a higher level of earnings, greater job satisfaction over one's lifetime, and a greater

1. U.S. Congress, Joint Economic Committee, *Economic Growth and Total Capital Formation* (Washington, D.C.: U.S. Government Printing Office, February 18, 1976).

appreciation of nonmarket activities and interests. Generally speaking, the investment *expenditures* can be divided into three categories:

1. *Out-of-pocket* or *direct* expenses include tuition and books (education), moving expenses (migration), and gasoline (job search).
2. *Forgone earnings* are another source of cost because during the investment period it is usually impossible to work, at least not full time.
3. *Psychic losses* are a third kind of cost incurred because education is difficult and often boring, because job search is tedious and nerve-wracking, and because migration means saying goodbye to old friends.

This chapter will analyze educational investments and their labor market implications. Because most such investments are closely related to the supply of labor to a particular occupation or set of occupations, this aspect of human capital theory adds more depth to the analysis of occupational choice begun in the last chapter. Chapter 10 deals with turnover and migration; other aspects of job search are treated in Chapter 15.

DEMAND FOR EDUCATION BY WORKERS

There are many ways in which workers, or potential workers, can enhance their earning capacity through education. They can attend high school, junior college, or college. They can go to a trade school or technical institute. They can enter an apprenticeship program or acquire skills on the job. Since the analysis of the demand for any of these types of education or training is essentially the same, this section will analyze the demand for a college education as an illustration and application of human capital theory.

People want to attend college when they believe they will be better off by so doing. For some, the benefits may be short-term: they like the courses or the life-style of a student. Students attending for these reasons regard college as a *consumption good*—that is, they are going to college primarily for the satisfaction it provides during the period of attendance. Others, however, attend college because of the *long-term* benefits it provides. These benefits are partly in the form of higher earnings, partly in the form of gaining access to more interesting, challenging, or pleasant jobs, and partly in the form of prestige or enhanced enjoyment of nonmarket activities. Attendance for the long-term benefits, or *investment behavior,* is the behavior this chapter seeks to analyze.

An Overview of the Benefits and Costs of an Educational Investment

Calculating the benefits of an investment over time requires the progressive discounting of benefits lying further into the future (see Chapter 5). Benefits that are received in the future are worth less to us now than an equal amount of benefits received today for two reasons. First, if people plan to consume their benefits, they prefer to consume earlier. (One is relatively sure of being able to enjoy such consumption now, but the uncertainties of life make future enjoyment problematic.) Second, if people plan to invest the monetary benefits rather than use them for consumption, they can earn interest on the investment and enlarge their funds in the future. Thus, no matter how people intend to use their benefits, they will discount future receipts to some extent.

As Chapter 5 explained, the present value of a stream of yearly benefits (B) over time (T) can be calculated as follows:

$$\text{Present Value} = \frac{B_1}{1 + r} + \frac{B_2}{(1 + r)^2} + \frac{B_3}{(1 + r)^3} + \cdots + \frac{B_T}{(1 + r)^T} \quad (9.1)$$

where the interest rate (or discount rate) is r. As long as r is positive, benefits into the future will be progressively discounted. For example, if $r = 0.06$, benefits payable in 30 years would receive a weight that is only 17 percent of the weight placed on benefits payable immediately ($1.06^{30} = 5.74$; $1/5.74 = 0.17$).

The costs of going to college are normally incurred over a relatively short period of time. These costs include the direct costs of tuition, fees, and books, the forgone earnings attendant on being a full-time student, and the psychic costs of studying and being examined. The total costs of going to college are thus very high, with the monetary costs alone (direct costs plus forgone earnings) in the range of $12,000–$25,000 per year in 1990.

A person considering college has, in some broad sense, a choice between two streams of income over his or her lifetime. Stream A begins immediately but does not rise very high; it is the earnings stream of a high school graduate. Stream B (the college graduate) has a negative income for the first four years (owing to college tuition costs), followed by a period when the salary is less than what the high school graduate makes, but then it takes off and rises above stream A. Both streams are illustrated in Figure 9.1. (Why these streams are *curved* will be discussed later in this chapter.) The streams shown in the figure are stylized so that we can emphasize some basic points. Actual earnings streams will be shown in Figures 9.11 and 9.13.

Obviously, the earnings of the college graduate would have to rise above those of the high school graduate to induce someone to invest in a college education (unless, of course, the psychic or consumption-related returns were large). The gross benefits, the difference in earnings between the two streams, must total much more than the costs because such returns are in the future and are therefore discounted. For example, suppose it costs $20,000 per year to obtain a four-year college education and the real interest rate (the nominal rate less the rate of inflation) is 2 percent. The after-tax returns—if they were the same each year—must be $2,920 in constant-dollar terms (that is, after taking away the effects of inflation) each year for 40 years in order to justify the investment on purely monetary grounds. These returns must be $2,920 because $80,000 invested at a 2 percent interest rate can provide a payment (of interest and principal) totaling $2,920 a year for 40 years.[2]

---

2. This calculation is made using the *annuity formula*:

$$Y = X \frac{1 - [1/(1 + r)^n]}{r}$$

where Y equals the total investment ($80,000 in our example), $X =$ the yearly payment ($2,920), $r =$ the rate of interest (0.02), and $n =$ the number of years (40). In this example, we treat the costs of a college education as being incurred all in one year rather than being spread out over four—a simplification that does not alter the magnitude of required returns much at all.

FIGURE 9.1   Alternative Income Streams

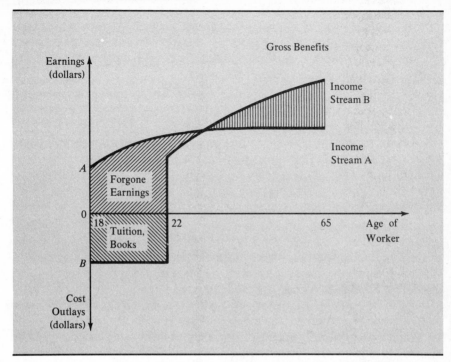

A Formal Model of Choice and Its Implications

The preceding discussion emphasized that investing in a college education is worthwhile if the present value of the benefits (monetary and psychic) is at least as large as the costs. In mathematical terms this criterion can be expressed as

$$\frac{B_1}{1 + r} + \frac{B_2}{(1 + r)^2} + \cdots + \frac{B_T}{(1 + r)^T} \geq C \qquad (9.2)$$

where C equals the total costs of a college education and B equals the yearly differences in earnings between college and high school graduates.

There are two ways one can measure whether the criterion in equation (9.2) is met. Using the *present-value method*, one can specify a value for the discount rate, r, and determine if the present value of benefits is greater than or equal to costs. Alternatively, one can adopt the *internal-rate-of-return method*, which asks, "How large could the discount rate be and still render college profitable?" Clearly, if the benefits are so large that even a very high discount rate would render college profitable, then the project is worthwhile. In practice, one calculates this internal rate of return by setting the present value of benefits equal to costs and solving for r. The internal rate of return is then compared to the rate of return on other investments. If the internal rate of return exceeds the alternative rates of return, the investment project is considered profitable.[3]

In deciding whether to attend college, no doubt few students make the very precise calculations suggested in equation (9.2). Nevertheless, if they make less formal estimates that take into account the same factors, four predictions concerning the demand for college education can be made:

1. Present-oriented people are less likely to go to college than forward-looking people (other things equal).
2. Most college students will be young.
3. College attendance will increase if the costs of college fall (other things equal).
4. College attendance will increase if the gap between the earnings of college graduates and high school graduates widens (again, other things equal).

Present-Orientedness. Psychologists use the term *present-oriented* to describe people who do not weight future events or outcomes very heavily. While all people discount the future with respect to the present, those who discount it more than average—or, at the extreme, ignore the future altogether—could be considered present-oriented. In terms of equations (9.1) and (9.2), a present-oriented person is one with a very high discount rate (r).

Suppose one were to calculate investment returns using the *present-value method*. If r is large, the present value of benefits associated with college will be lower than if the discount rate being used is smaller. Thus, a present-oriented person would impute smaller benefits to college attendance than one who is less present-oriented, and those who are present-oriented would be less likely to attend college. Using the *internal-rate-of-return method* for evaluating the soundness of a college education, one would arrive at the same result. If a college education earns an 8 percent rate of return but the individuals in question are so present-oriented that they would insist on a 25 percent rate of return before investing, they would likewise decide not to attend.

The prediction that present-oriented people are less likely to attend college than forward-looking ones is difficult either to substantiate or to disprove. The rates of discount that people use in making investment decisions are rarely available, because such decisions are not made as formally as equation (9.2) implies. However, the model does suggest that people who have a high propensity to invest in education will also engage in other forward-looking behavior. Certain medical statistics tend to support this prediction.

In the United States there is a strong statistical correlation between education and health status.[4] People with more years of schooling have lower

---

3. For our purposes here, the present-value and internal-rate-of-return methods may be considered interchangeable in evaluating investment alternatives. In *some* circumstances, however, the two methods would not provide identical rankings of investment opportunities. See J. Hirshleifer, "On the Theory of Optimal Investment Decision," *Journal of Political Economy* 66 (August 1958): 329–52.
4. The analysis of the correlation between education and health status is taken from Victor Fuchs, "The Economics of Health in a Post-Industrial Society," *The Public Interest* (Summer 1979): 3–20.

mortality rates, fewer symptoms of disease (such as high blood pressure, high cholesterol levels, abnormal X-rays), and a greater tendency to report themselves to be in good health. This effect of education on health is independent of income, which appears to have no effect of its own on health status except at the lowest poverty levels. Is this correlation between education and health a result of better use of medical resources by the well-educated? It appears not. Better-educated people undergoing surgery choose the same doctors, enter the hospital at the same stage of disease, and have the same length of stay as less-educated people of equal income.

What *may* cause this correlation is a more forward-looking attitude among those who have obtained more education. People with lower discount rates will be more likely to attend college, and they will *also* be more likely to adopt forward-looking habits of health. They may choose healthier diets, be more aware of health risks, and make more use of preventive medicine. This explanation for the correlation between education and health is not the only plausible one, but it receives some direct support from British data on cigarette smoking.[5] From 1958 to 1975, the proportion of men in the most highly educated groups who smoked fell by 50 percent. During the same time period, the proportion of smokers in the more poorly educated class remained unchanged. It is unlikely that the less-educated group was uninformed of the smoking dangers revealed during that period. It is more likely that they were less willing to give up a present source of pleasure for a distant benefit. Thus, we have at least some evidence that people who invest in education also engage in *other* forward-looking behavior.

Age.   Given similar *yearly* benefits of going to college, young people have a larger present value of *total* benefits than older workers simply because they have a longer remaining work life ahead of them. In terms of equation (9.2), T for younger people is greater than for older ones. We would therefore expect younger people to have a greater propensity than older people to obtain a college education or engage in other forms of training activity. This prediction is parallel to the predictions in Chapter 5 about which workers employers will decide to invest in when they make decisions about hiring or specific training.

Costs.   A third prediction of our model is that human capital investments are more likely when costs are lower. The major monetary costs of college attendance are forgone earnings and the direct costs of tuition, books, and fees. (Food and lodging are not always opportunity costs of going to college because a large portion of these costs would have to be incurred in any event.) Thus, if forgone earnings or tuition costs fall, other things equal, we would expect an increase in college enrollments. Similarly, if offers of financial aid

---

5. It could be, for example, that healthy people, with longer life spans, are more likely to invest in human capital because they expect to experience a longer payback period. Alternatively, one could argue that the higher incomes of college graduates later in life mean they have more to lose from illness than do non–college graduates.

to college applicants rise, other things equal, we would expect more accepted applicants to enroll in college.[6]

The costs of college attendance offer an additional reason why we observe older people attending less often than younger people. As workers age, they acquire levels of experience and maturity that employers are willing to reward with higher wages. Because older workers thus command higher wages (on average), their opportunity costs of college attendance are higher than those for younger students.[7] Older people are thus doubly discouraged from attending college: their forgone earnings are relatively high and the period over which they can capture benefits is comparatively short.

The psychic costs of going to college cannot be ignored. While these costs cannot be easily observed, they are likely to be related to ability. People who learn easily and who do well in school have an easier and more pleasant time in college than people who do not.

In any set of market transactions, some people are *at the margin,* which means that they are close to the point of not transacting. For example, consider a downward-sloping demand curve for education, where the number of people attending college is drawn as a function of its money costs (see Figure 9.2). If the money costs were X_0, we would observe that N_0 people would go to college. If the costs were raised to X_1, only N_1 would decide to attend. The people deciding to drop out when costs rise to X_1 are those who were closest to not going when costs were X_0. They are the ones who had the hardest time making up their minds at X_0—in other words, those who came closest to deciding not to go when costs were X_0.

Who are the people closest to the margin regarding the decision to go to college? In part, they are people for whom the psychic costs of studying and being examined are relatively high, people who do not especially like school. This group—who, we have argued, might consist to a large extent of less able students—is thus likely to be the most responsive to changes in the money costs of education. (See Appendix 9A for a more complete discussion of this issue.) Indeed, studies that have analyzed the effects of college location on college attendance show that males of moderate ability are much more responsive to college location than those of high ability. That is, whether a college is available in one's hometown seems to matter a lot more to moderate-ability students than it does to high-ability students.[8]

6. For evidence that these relationships exist, see Charles F. Manski and David Wise, *College Choice in America* (Cambridge, Mass.: Harvard University Press, 1983), and Ronald G. Ehrenberg and Daniel Sherman, "Optimal Financial Aid Policies for a Selective University," *Journal of Human Resources* 19 (Spring 1984): 202–30.
7. This discussion is related to our discussion of the life-cycle supply of labor in Chapter 7. When wages are low, people engage in time-intensive activities.
8. C. A. Anderson, M. J. Bowman, V. Tinto, *Where Colleges Are and Who Attends* (New York: McGraw-Hill, 1972). Given that loans to attend college are not always available, the *financial resources* of the investor are also an important factor in the decision to invest. Thus, people in families with modest wealth are closer to the margin regarding the educational decision, other things equal, than those with more wealth. For a recent article on the issue of financial access to colleges, see Jere R. Behrman, Robert A. Pollak, and Paul Taubman, "Family Resources, Family Size, and Access to Financing for College Education," *Journal of Political Economy* 97 (April 1989): 398–419.

FIGURE 9.2   The Demand for a College Education

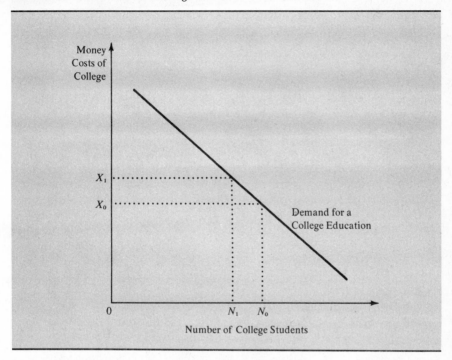

Earnings Differentials.   The fourth prediction of human capital theory is that the demand for education is positively related to the *returns*—that is, to the increases in lifetime earnings or psychic benefits that a college education allows. In practice, this prediction can be tested only with reference to money returns, since psychic returns are unobservable.[9]

As can be seen in Table 9.1, the income differentials enjoyed by recent college graduates over high school graduates of the same age (25–34) fell by some 14 percent from the late 1960s to the late 1970s. This fall reflected a relative surplus of college graduates during the 1970s. Since then, however, the earnings of recent college graduates have grown much faster than those of high school graduates in the same age group, and by 1985 the income ratios were as high as or higher than they had been in the late 1960s. Have these changes in relative earnings been accompanied by changes in college enrollments? As the student might expect by now, answering this question is a bit complex.

For men, the fall and later rise in the college/high school income ratio is reflected directly in their college enrollment rates. However, the enrollment rate in 1985 did not begin to approach 1968's rate despite a larger earnings dif-

---

9. There is evidence, although it is somewhat weak, that better-educated workers are more likely to describe themselves as satisfied with their jobs. See Daniel Hamermesh, "Economic Aspects of Job Satisfaction," in *Essays in Labor Market Analysis,* ed. Orley Ashenfelter and Wallace Oates (New York: John Wiley & Sons, 1977), 53–72. *Quantifying* job or nonjob psychic benefits, however, is still not possible.

EXAMPLE 9.2

Do Unskilled Jobs Cause Poor Mental Health?

It is frequently asserted that the mental health of low-skilled workers is poorer than it is for higher-skilled workers of the same age. For example, a study of factory workers in the automobile industry found that 56 percent of middle-aged *skilled* workers had good mental health, while only 26 percent of middle-aged workers in repetitive, semiskilled jobs exhibited good mental health. The figures were 58 percent and 10 percent, respectively, for younger workers, and for both age groups there was a steady downward fall in the percentages of those with good mental health as one moved down the skill ladder between skilled and repetitive semiskilled jobs.* The conclusion generally drawn from such findings is that the boring, uncreative nature of jobs requiring little skill causes workers to lose self-esteem and to adopt negative attitudes toward life.[†]

It is entirely possible, however, that the causal connection between skill level and mental health is the reverse. For example, in the above-mentioned study of automobile workers, the following characteristics were included (with others) as indicative of poor mental health: a "live for today" attitude, a belief that success is due to luck and pull, a belief that one can't do much to shape one's future, and a lack of optimism. People with these characteristics are probably much less likely to undertake costly human capital investments with distant payoffs. Lack of self-esteem raises the perceived costs of education or training, while a lack of optimism or a present orientation limits the expected benefits. Thus, workers with these characteristics are much less likely to undertake human capital investments and become skilled. While human capital theory cannot be used to prove the causation runs from poor mental health (as defined by the researchers) to lower skill levels, it *can* be used to raise questions about the standard interpretation of the observed association between skill level and measures of mental health.

*Arthur Kornhauser, *Mental Health of the Industrial Worker* (New York: John Wiley & Sons, 1965), 57.

[†]Kornhauser, p. 76, and George Strauss and Leonard R. Sayles, *Personnel: The Human Problems of Management* (Englewood Cliffs, N.J.: Prentice-Hall, 1972), 21.

ferential. A major reason for higher enrollment rates in 1968 probably lies in the military draft exemption given to college students at that time. When draft laws were altered in the early 1970s, the draft-related incentives to remain in college were eliminated. Thus, part of the large decline in male enrollment rates from 1968 to 1978 was draft-related, but a careful study of college enrollments during that period concluded that much of the decline for males was also caused by changes in earnings patterns.[10]

10. Richard Freeman, "Overinvestment in College Training?" *Journal of Human Resources* 10, no. 3 (Summer 1975): 287–311. In measuring the benefits of a college education (see equation 9.1), the earnings of high school graduates are *subtracted* from those of college graduates, yielding a difference that must be adjusted for inflation if the benefits of schooling are to be compared over time. The ratios used in Table 9.1 need not be adjusted, and they are presented for ease of comparison across years; however, it is possible for differences (and hence the incentives to attend college) to grow even when the ratios fall! Over the period we analyze (1968 to 1978), both the ratios and the real differences fell.

TABLE 9.1 Changes in College Enrollments and the College/High School Income Differential, by Gender

	Ratio of Median Incomes of College Graduates to High School Graduates, Ages 25–34[a]		Percentage of 20- to 21-Year-Olds Enrolled in College	
	Male	Female	Male	Female
1968	1.31	1.41	45.0%	21.5%
1978	1.11	1.22	31.7	27.5
1985	1.36	1.40	36.5	34.1

[a]For year-round, full-time workers. Data on *earnings* would have been preferable to use, but these were unavailable for 1968; however, the earnings ratios for the latter two years are close to the corresponding income ratios and move in the same direction over time.

SOURCES: U.S. Bureau of the Census, *Money Income of Families and Persons in the United States,* Current Population Reports P-60, no. 66 (Table 41), no. 123 (Table 50), no. 156 (Table 35); U.S. Department of Education, Center for Education Statistics, *Digest of Education Statistics,* relevant years, Tables 4, 6.

Among women, college enrollment rates rose from 1968 to 1978 despite the falling college/high school income ratio. This increase continued a long-standing tendency for female college enrollment rates to rise, a rise that can itself be understood by use of human capital theory. Because women's labor force participation rates and hours worked outside the home have increased over time, the period over which their human capital investment returns can be received has lengthened, and such investments have become more attractive. Interestingly, however, during the 1968–78 period, when the earnings advantage of college graduates was falling, female college enrollment rates were growing 0.6 percentage points per year, while such rates grew at over 0.9 percentage points per year during the period (1978–85) when the earnings advantage was growing. Thus, for women as well as men, college enrollments do seem responsive to the college/high school earnings differential.

Earnings Differences and the Demand for Education

As we have just seen, the demand for education is influenced by the differences in earnings made possible by an educational investment. However, the returns to education are themselves affected by the number of people who attend school. To obtain an overall picture of how enrollments and returns are interrelated, it is necessary to return briefly to our simple model of the labor market.

Figure 9.3 shows the labor market demand for, and supply of, college graduates. We know why the demand curve for labor slopes downward, but why does the supply curve for college graduates in Figure 9.3 slope upward? The reason, discussed earlier in this chapter, is that college is costly. If college graduates typically earned relatively low wages, few people would want to attend college. If the earnings of college graduates were to rise, more would want to attend college. If they were to rise still more, even greater numbers would enroll.

What would happen if the demand for college graduates were to shift outward, so that more such graduates were demanded at any given wage? Fig-

FIGURE 9.3   The Market for College Graduates with a Shift in Demand

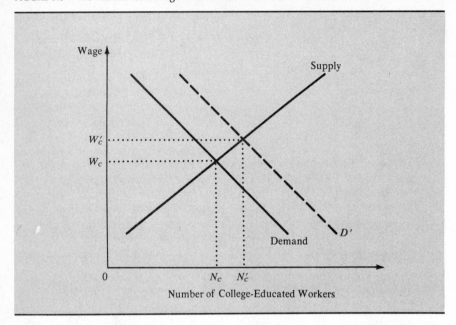

ure 9.3 illustrates that if the demand curve shifted to D', the wages of college graduates would rise from W_C to W_C'. This increase in the wages of college graduates would serve as an incentive for more people to attend college, and the number of college graduates would rise.

What would happen if, on the other hand, the supply of college graduates were to shift to the right, indicating that more people wanted to attend college for any given wage level that could be attained by graduates? Such a shift might occur, for example, if the government were to subsidize students in college or to exempt students from the military draft. Figure 9.4 shows that the outward shift in the supply of college graduates drives wages down to W_C'', a reduction that serves to moderate the increase in enrollments (as W_C falls to W_C'', the movement along S' suggests that fewer people decide to attend).

Unfortunately, the adjustment of college enrollments to changes in the returns to education is not always smooth or rapid, particularly in special fields, like engineering and law, that are highly technical. The problem is that if engineering wages (say) were to go up suddenly in 1993, the supply of graduate engineers would not be affected for three or four years (owing to the time it takes to learn the field). Likewise, if engineering wages were to fall, those students enrolled in an engineering curriculum would understandably be reluctant to immediately leave the field. They have already invested a lot of time and effort and may prefer to take their chances in engineering rather than devote more time and money to learning a new field.

The inability to respond immediately to changed market conditions can cause *boom-and-bust cycles* in the market for highly technical workers. If educational planners in government or the private sector are unaware of these cy-

FIGURE 9.4   The Market for College Graduates with a Shift in Supply

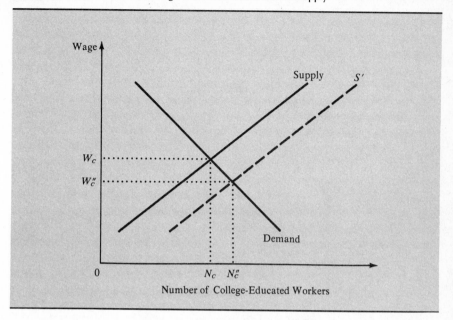

cles, they may seek to stimulate or reduce enrollments at times when they should be doing exactly the opposite, as illustrated below.

Suppose the market for engineers is in equilibrium, where the wage is W_0 and the number of engineers is N_0 (see Figure 9.5). Let us now assume that the demand curve for engineers shifts from D_0 to D_1. Initially, this increase in the demand for engineers does *not* induce the supply of engineers to increase beyond N_0, because it takes a long time to become an engineer once one has decided to do so. Thus, while the increased demand for engineers causes more people to decide to enter the field, the number available for employment *at the moment* is N_0. These N_0 engineers, therefore, can *currently* obtain a wage of W_1 (in effect, there is a vertical supply curve, at N_0, for a few years until the supply of engineering graduates is increased).

Now W_1, the *current* engineering wage, is above W_e, the new *long-run* equilibrium wage caused by the intersection of D_1 and S. The market, however, is unaware of W_e, observing only W_1. If people are myopic and assume W_1 is the new equilibrium wage, N_1 people will enter the engineering field (see Figure 9.6). When these N_1 all graduate, there will be a *surplus* of engineers (remember that W_1 is *above* long-run equilibrium).

With the supply of engineers now temporarily fixed at N_1, the wage will fall to W_2. This fall will cause students and workers to shift *out* of engineering, but that effect will not be fully felt for a few years. In the meantime, note that W_2 is below long-run equilibrium (still at W_e). Thus, when supply *does* adjust, it will adjust too much—all the way to N_2. Now there will be another shortage of engineers, because after supply adjusts to N_2, demand exceeds supply at a wage rate of W_2. This causes wages to rise to W_3, and the cycle repeats itself.

FIGURE 9.5 The Labor Market for Engineers

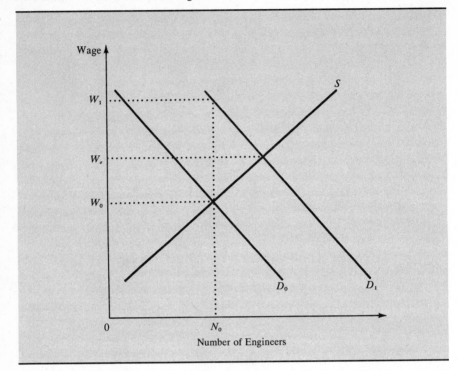

Over time, the swings become smaller, and eventually equilibrium is reached. Because the adjustment path in Figure 9.6 looks somewhat like a cobweb, the adjustment process described above is sometimes called a *cobweb model.*

Critical to cobweb models is the assumption that workers form myopic expectations about the future behavior of wages.[11] In our example, they first assume that W_1 will prevail in the future and ignore the possibility that the occupational choice decisions of others will, in four years, drive the wage below W_1. Just how workers (and other economic actors, such as investors and taxpayers) form expectations about future wage (price) levels is very important to the understanding of many key issues affecting the labor market. While we discuss some of these issues in Chapter 16, and hence will return to the topic of expectations at that point, it is useful to introduce some basic concepts here.

---

11. Also critical to cobweb models is that the demand curve be flatter than the supply curve; if it is not, the cobweb "explodes" when demand shifts and an equilibrium wage is never reached. An exploding cobweb model is an example from economics of the phenomenon of "chaos," which has attracted much scientific attention recently. For a general introduction to this fascinating topic, see James Gleick, *Chaos* (New York: Penguin Books, 1987). For an article on chaos in the economic literature, see William J. Baumol and Jess Benhabib, "Chaos: Significance, Mechanism, and Economic Applications," *Journal of Economic Perspectives* 3, no. 1 (Winter 1989): 77–106.

FIGURE 9.6   The Labor Market for Engineers: A Cobweb Model

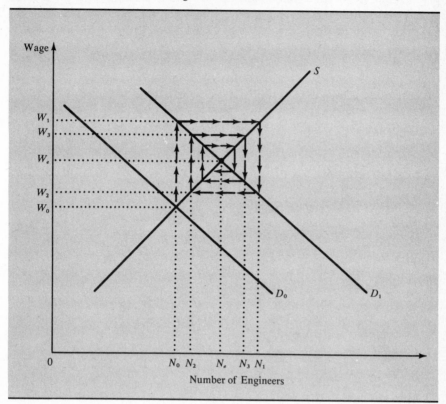

The simplest and most naive way to predict future wage levels is to assume that what is observed today is what will be observed in the future; this naive assumption, as noted above, underlies the cobweb model. A more sophisticated way to form predictions about the future is with an *adaptive expectations* approach. Adaptive expectations are formed by setting future expected wages equal to a weighted average of current and past wages. While more weight may be given to current than past wages in forecasting future wage levels, changes in those levels prior to the current period are not ignored; thus, it is likely that wage expectations formed adaptively do not alternatively "overshoot" and "undershoot" the equilibrium wage as much as those formed using the naive approach. If adaptive expectations, however, also lead workers to first overpredict and then underpredict the equilibrium wage, cobweb-like behavior of wages and labor supply will still be observed (although the fluctuations will be of a smaller magnitude if the predictions are closer to the mark than those made naively).

The most sophisticated way to predict future market outcomes is to use a full-blown model of the labor market. Those who believe in the *rational expectations* method of forming predictions about future wages assume that workers do have such a model in their heads, at least implicitly. Thus, they will realize that a marked increase in the earnings of engineers (say) is likely to be temporary, because supply will expand and eventually bring the returns to an investment in engineering skills in line with those for other occupations. Put differently, the rational expectations model assumes workers behave as if they have taken (and mastered!) a good course in labor economics and that they will not be fooled into over- or underpredicting future wage levels.

Clearly, how people form expectations is an important empirical issue. In the case of engineers and lawyers, periodic fluctuations in supply that characterize the cobweb model have been found.[12] Whether these fluctuations are the result of naive expectations or not, the lesson to be learned from cobweb models should not be lost on government policymakers. If the government chooses to take an active role in dealing with labor shortages and surpluses, it must be aware that, because supply adjustments are slow in highly technical markets, wages in those markets tend to *over*adjust. In other words, to the extent possible, governmental predictions and market interventions should be based on rational expectations. For example, at the initial stages of a shortage, when wages are rising toward W_1 (in our example), the government should be pointing out that W_1 is likely to be *above* the long-run equilibrium. If instead it attempts to meet the current shortage by *subsidizing* study in that field, it will be encouraging an even greater *surplus* later on. The moral of the story is that a complete knowledge of how markets adjust to changes in demand or supply is necessary before one can be sure that government intervention will do more good than harm.

THE EDUCATION/WAGE RELATIONSHIP

The preceding section used human capital theory to explore the demand for education, particularly college education. This section will investigate in more detail the effects of education on earnings and will explore several policy issues to which human capital theory can be applied.

A Hedonic Model of Education and Wages

The preceding section argued that the prospect of improved lifetime earnings served as a major inducement for people to invest in an education or training program. Indeed, unless education is acquired purely for purposes of consumption, people will not undertake an investment in education or training without the expectation that, by so doing, they can improve their stream of lifetime earnings or psychic rewards. However, in order to obtain these higher benefits, *employers* must be willing to pay for them. Therefore, it is necessary to examine both sides of the market to fully understand the prediction made

---

12. Richard B. Freeman, "A Cobweb Model of the Supply and Starting Salary of New Engineers," *Industrial and Labor Relations Review* 29 (January 1976): 236–46, and "Legal Cobwebs: A Recursive Model of the Market for New Lawyers," *Review of Economics and Statistics* 57 (May 1975): 171–79. Gary Zarkin, "Occupational Choice: An Application to the Market for Public School Teachers," *Quarterly Journal of Economics* 100 (May 1985): 409–46, and Aloysius Siow, "Occupational Choice Under Uncertainty," *Econometrica* 52, no. 3 (May 1984): 631–45, use rational expectations models of occupational choice.

FIGURE 9.7   Indifference Curves for Two Different Workers

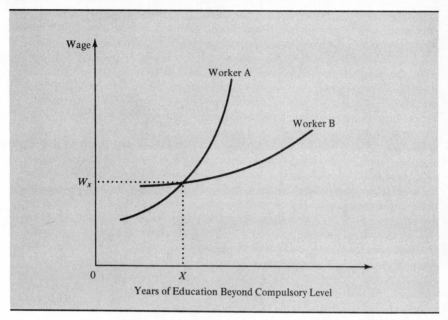

over 200 years ago by Adam Smith that wages rise with the "difficulty and expense" of learning the job.[13]

Supply (Worker) Side.   Consider a group of people who have chosen selling as a desired career. These salespersons-to-be have a choice of how much education or training to invest in, given their career objectives. In making this choice they will have to weigh the returns against the costs, as pointed out in the previous section. Crucial to this decision is how the *actual* returns compare with the returns each would *require* in order to invest.

Figure 9.7 shows the indifference curves between yearly earnings and education for two workers, A and B. To induce A or B to acquire X years of education would require the assurance of earning W_x after beginning work. However, to induce A to increase his or her education beyond X years (holding utility constant) would require a larger salary increase than B would require. A's greater aversion to making educational investments could be explained in several ways. Person A could be older than B, thus having higher forgone earnings and fewer years over which to recoup investment costs. Person A could be more present-oriented and thus more inclined to discount future benefits heavily, or could have less ability in classroom learning or a greater dislike of schooling. Finally, A may find it more difficult to finance additional schooling. Whatever the reason, this analysis points up the important fact that people differ in their propensity to invest in schooling.

13. See Adam Smith, *Wealth of Nations,* Book I, Chapter 10. The five "principal circumstances" listed by Smith as affecting wages were first discussed in Chapter 8.

FIGURE 9.8 Isoprofit Curves for Two Different Firms

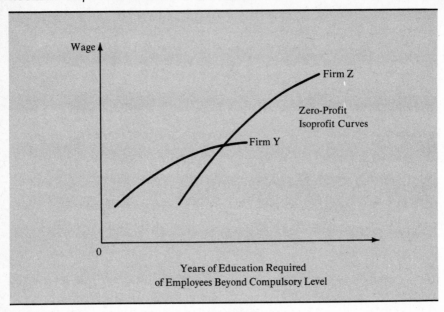

Demand (Employer) Side. On the demand side of the market, employers must consider whether they are willing to pay higher wages for better-educated workers. If they are, they must also decide how much to pay for each additional year. Figure 9.8 illustrates employers' choices about the wage/education relationship. Employers Y and Z are *both* willing to pay more for better-educated sales personnel (to continue our example) because they have found that better-educated workers are more productive.[14] Thus, they can achieve the same profit level by paying either lower wages for less-educated workers or higher wages for more-educated workers. Their isoprofit curves are thus upward-sloping (see Chapter 8 for a description of isoprofit curves).

The isoprofit curves in Figure 9.8 have three important characteristics:

1. For each firm the curves are concave; that is, they get flatter as education increases. This concavity results from the assumption that, at some point, the added benefits to the employer of an additional year of employee schooling begin to decline. In other words, we assume that schooling is subject to diminishing marginal productivity.

2. The isoprofit curves are the *zero-profit curves*. Neither firm can pay higher wages for each level of education than those indicated on the curves; if they did so, their profits would be negative and they would cease operations.

3. The added benefits from an extra year of schooling are smaller in firm Y than in firm Z, causing Y to have a flatter isoprofit curve. Firm Y,

---

14. Whether schooling causes workers to be more productive or simply reflects—or "signals"— higher productivity is not important at this point, but we do address this issue later on.

for example, may be a discount department store in which "selling" is largely a matter of working a cash register. While better-educated people may be more productive, they are not *too* much more valuable than less-educated people; hence, firm Y is not willing to pay them much more. Firm Z, on the other hand, may sell technical instruments for which a knowledge of physics and customer engineering problems is needed. In firm Z, additional education adds a relatively large increment to worker productivity.

Market Determination of the Education/Wage Relationship

Putting both sides of the market for educated workers together, it is clear that the education/wage relationship will be positive, as indicated in Figure 9.9. Worker A will work for Y, receiving a wage equal to W_{AY} and obtaining X_1 years of education. The reason for this matching is simple. Firm Z cannot pay higher wages (for each level of education) than those shown on the isoprofit curve in Figure 9.9, for the reasons noted above. Clearly, then, worker A could never derive as much utility from Z as he or she could from Y; working for firm Z would involve a loss of utility to worker A. For similar reasons, worker B will accept work with firm Z, obtain X_2 years of schooling, and receive higher pay (W_{BZ}).

When examined from an overall social perspective, the positive wage/education relationship is the result of a very sensible sorting of workers and employers performed by the labor market. Workers with the greatest aversion to investing in education (A) will work for firms where education adds least to employee productivity (Y). People with the least aversion to educational investment (B) are hired by those firms most willing to pay for an educated work force (Z).

FIGURE 9.9 The Education/Wage Relationship

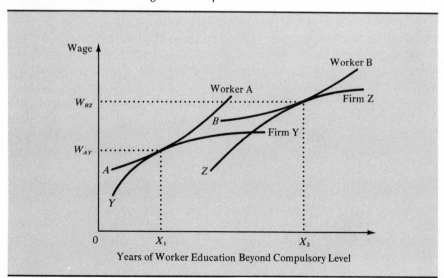

Note: If employers were unwilling to pay higher wages for more-educated workers, no education-related differentials would exist and employer isoprofit curves would be horizontal. Without a positive education/wage relationship, employees would have no incentive to invest in an education (see Figure 9.10).

The relationship between education and earnings is well documented and can be observed graphically in Figure 9.11. This figure presents *age/earnings profiles*—or lifetime earnings patterns—for males at five levels of schooling. Two conclusions are immediately obvious:

1. Better-educated males earn more than less-educated males at each post-schooling age level, as predicted by our theory.
2. The age/earnings profiles for workers with more education are steeper than the profiles of workers with less education. That is, the differences in earnings associated with education tend to widen as workers grow older. In the early years the earnings gap is small. Workers who have gone to college have not had a chance to acquire the work experience of those who have been working rather than attending college. Later, after they have had a chance to gain experience, their earnings rise much more sharply. (A more detailed discussion of *why* age/earnings profiles are steeper for more-educated workers will be presented later in this chapter.)

IS EDUCATION A GOOD INVESTMENT?

It is well established that workers with more education tend to earn higher wages. However, an individual deciding whether to go to college would naturally ask, "Will I increase my monetary and psychic income enough to justify the costs of going to college?" Further, government policymakers trying to

FIGURE 9.10   Unwillingness of Firm to Pay for More Education of Employees

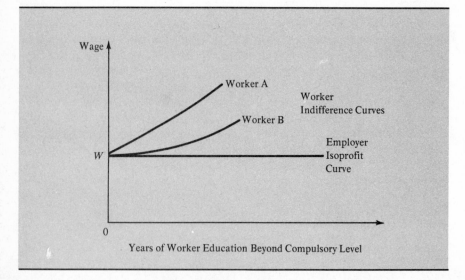

FIGURE 9.11   Total Money Earnings (Mean), for Full-Time, Year-Round Male Workers, 1987

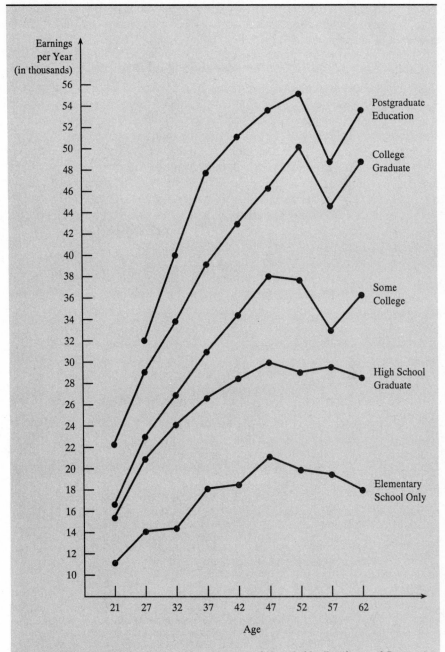

SOURCE: U.S. Bureau of the Census, *Money Income of Households, Families, and Persons in the United States: 1987,* Current Population Reports, Series P-60, no. 162, Table 36.

decide whether to expand educational facilities or subsidize increased enrollments must ask, "Will the benefits of improved productivity outweigh the
costs?" The next two subsections deal with *individual* and *social* returns from
educational investments.

Is Education a Good Investment for Individuals?

Individuals about to make an investment in a college education are typically
committing themselves to costs of at least $12,000 per year. Is there evidence
that this investment pays off for the typical student? Several studies have
tried to answer this question by calculating the internal rates of return to educational investments. While the methods and data used vary, these studies
normally estimate benefits by calculating earnings differentials at each age
from age/earnings profiles such as those in Figure 9.11. (*Earnings* are usually
used to measure benefits because higher wages and more-stable jobs are both
payoffs to more education.) The *rate of return* is that discount rate that equates
the present value of benefits to the cost of acquiring the level of education in
question. It should be stressed that all such studies have analyzed only the
monetary, not the psychic, costs of and returns on educational investments.

The rates of return typically estimated for the United States generally fall
in the range of 5–15 percent (after adjusting for inflation).[15] These findings
are interesting because most other investments generate returns in the same
range. Thus, it appears, at least at first glance, that an investment in education
is about as good as an investment in stocks, bonds, or real estate. This conclusion must be qualified, however, by recognizing that there are systematic biases in the estimated rates of return to education. These biases, which are of
unknown size, work in opposite directions.

The Upward Bias. The typical estimates of the rate of return on further
schooling overstate the gain an individual student could obtain by investing in
education because they are unable to separate the contribution that *ability*
makes to higher earnings from the contribution made by *schooling*.[16] The
problem is that (*a*) people who are smarter, harder-working, and more dynamic

15. For a review of rate-of-return studies, see George Psacharopoulos, "Returns to Education:
A Further International Update and Implications," *Journal of Human Resources* 20, no. 4
(Fall 1985): 583–604. For a study that analyzes the recent rise (reflected in Table 9.1) in
the returns to educational investments, see John Bound and George Johnson, "Changes in
the Structure of Wages During the 1980s: An Evaluation of Alternative Explanations,"
Working Paper no. 2983, National Bureau of Economic Research, May 1989.

16. Another source of upward bias has been pointed out by C. M. Lindsay, "Measuring Human Capital Returns," *Journal of Political Economy* 79 (November/December 1971): 1195–
1215. Lindsay reasons that if human capital investments earn a normal rate of return, they
do not change the wealth of those who invest; post-investment returns, in other words, just
make up for the costs of investment. Human capital investments, however, do raise wages,
and hence the price of leisure. As the principles of labor supply in Chapters 6 and 7 suggested, an increased wage with unchanged wealth would cause hours of leisure consumed
to fall. Thus, human capital investments cause an increased price, and reduced consumption, of the important consumer good we call "leisure." Some of the differential in earnings we observe between those with more human capital and those with less is offset by
utility lost by the former group when leisure is reduced. To count the entire earnings differential as a return on the investment without correcting for lost leisure overstates the
real gains (that is, those expressed in terms of *utility*) to human capital investments.

EXAMPLE 9.3

Valuing a Human Asset: The Case of the Divorcing Doctor

State divorce laws typically provide for the assets acquired during marriage to be divided in some equitable fashion. Such laws in the State of New York recognize, among the assets to be divided, the asset value of human capital investments made by either spouse during the period of marriage. How these acquired human capital values are estimated can be illustrated by the following example.

Dr. Doe married his wife right after he had acquired a license to practice medicine as a general practitioner. Instead of opening a general (family) practice, however, Dr. Doe undertook specialized training to become a surgeon. During his training (residency) period, the income of Dr. Doe and his wife was much lower than it would have been had he been working as a general practitioner (thus both spouses were investing, albeit to different degrees, in Dr. Doe's human capital). Shortly after his residency was completed and he had acquired board certification as a general surgeon, Dr. Doe and his wife decided to divorce. She sued him for an equitable division of the asset value of his certification as a general surgeon. How can this asset value be estimated?

The asset value of Dr. Doe's certificate as a general surgeon is the present value of his estimated *increase in lifetime earnings* made possible by the investment undertaken during marriage. In the absence of a specific work history as a surgeon, the most reasonable estimate of his increase in yearly earnings is calculated by subtracting from what the typical general surgeon earns in a year the average earnings of general practitioners (which is an estimate of what Dr. Doe could have earned in the absence of his training as a surgeon). In 1988, the earnings median of general surgeons was $135,000, while the earnings median of general practitioners was $91,000, implying a yearly earnings differential of $44,000.* Assuming a remaining worklife of 25 years and a real interest rate (which takes account of what inflation will do to the earnings differential) of 2 percent, the present value of the asset Dr. Doe "acquired" as the result of his surgical training comes to $858,440. (It would then be up to the court to divide this asset equitably between the two divorcing spouses.)

*The earnings data used are national medians for doctors with office practices in 1988. They were obtained with permission of the Medical Economics Company from "Why Some Colleagues' Fees Are Sky High" by Arthur Owens, *Medical Economics* (February 19, 1990): 200–205. The formula used to calculate present value is the one given in footnote 2 of this chapter, where $X = \$44,000$, $r = 0.02$, and $n = 25$.

are more likely to obtain more schooling, and (*b*) such people might be more productive, and hence earn higher-than-average wages, even if they did not complete more years of schooling than others. When measures of ability are not observed or accounted for, the studies attribute *all* the earnings differentials associated with college to college itself and none to ability, even though *some* of the added earnings college graduates typically receive would probably be received by an equally able high school graduate who did not attend college.

Most studies attempting to identify the separate effects of ability and schooling have concluded that the effects of ability are relatively small—accounting for, at most, one-fifth of observed earnings differentials.[17] However, these studies have used aptitude-test scores, such as IQ or mathematical reasoning, as measures of ability, and these measures are primarily designed to predict success in school, not in the workplace. Success in the world of work is also affected by interpersonal skills, work habits, motivation, and resourcefulness—attributes that are not easily measured by a test.

One interesting attempt to control for all the unmeasured aspects of ability used data on twins.[18] When the researcher first calculated rates of return on an added year of education ignoring any controls for ability, the estimated return was 8 percent. When he looked only at earnings differences between identical twins—people with a common *genetic and environmental* background—with different levels of schooling, he found that the rate of return on schooling dropped to 3 percent. While no one study is conclusive, the results do suggest that part of the earnings differentials associated with higher levels of schooling arise because inherently abler persons tend to obtain more schooling.[19]

The Downward Bias.   By focusing only on the earnings differentials associated with an educational investment, the studies of returns to educational investments ignore other aspects of the returns on schooling. First, some benefits of college attendance are not necessarily reflected in higher productivity, but rather in an increased ability to understand and appreciate the behavioral, historical, and philosophical foundations of human existence. While these benefits may be difficult to measure, they exist nonetheless.

Second, most rate-of-return studies fail to include employee benefits; they measure money earnings, not total compensation. Because employee benefits as a percentage of total compensation tend to rise as money earnings rise, ignoring benefits tends to create a downward bias in the estimation of rates of return to education. The size of this bias is largely unknown at present.[20]

Third, some of the job-related rewards of college are captured in the form of psychic or nonmonetary benefits. Jobs in executive or professional occupations are probably more interesting and pleasant than the more routine jobs typically available to people with less education. While executive and

17. See, for example, Gary Becker, *Human Capital* (New York: National Bureau of Economic Research, 1975); Zvi Griliches and William M. Mason, "Education, Income, and Ability," and John C. Hause, "Earnings Profile: Ability and Schooling," both in *Journal of Political Economy* 80, no. 3 (May/June 1972).
18. Paul Taubman, "Earnings, Education, Genetics, and Environment," *Journal of Human Resources* 11, no. 4 (Fall 1976): 447–61.
19. Zvi Griliches, "Sibling Models and Data in Economics: Beginnings of a Survey," *Journal of Political Economy* 87 (October 1979): S37–S64, reviews several studies attempting to estimate rates of return on schooling from data on siblings. This article suggests that much of the drop from an estimated 8 percent rate of return to an estimated 3 percent rate is a statistical artifact rather than the result of controlling for heredity and environment.
20. Greg J. Duncan, "Earnings Functions and Nonpecuniary Benefits," *Journal of Human Resources* 11, no. 4 (Fall 1976 ˈ52–83.

professional jobs do pay more than others, the total benefits of these jobs are probably understated when only earnings differences are analyzed.

An interesting example of the role nonmonetary costs and benefits play in schooling decisions can be seen in the fact that there is near-universal agreement that conventionally calculated rates of return fall as educational level rises. That is, the rate of return on a high school education is higher than for a college education, and higher yet than the average returns from going to graduate school. This fact can be understood when psychic benefits and costs are accounted for. Referring back to Figure 9.9, one is reminded that students who acquire the most education are, on average, the ones who dislike school the least. They may also be the ones who, because of their higher learning abilities, derive the most psychic benefits from college. They thus require a smaller monetary incentive to attend college than do their less able colleagues.[21]

Selection Bias. A third source of bias in the standard estimates of rates of return on education arises from what has become known in recent years as the *selectivity* problem.[22] Briefly put, one who decides to go to college and become a manager, rather than terminate schooling with high school and become a mechanic, may do so in part because he or she has very little mechanical aptitude; thus, becoming a mechanic might yield this person *less* income than would be earned by others who chose to become mechanics rather than go to college. Likewise, those who go to college may have aptitudes that generate more income in managerial jobs than could have been earned in those jobs by terminal high school graduates if they had acquired the college education needed to qualify for the managerial jobs.

The significance of these considerations is that the measured rate of return on a college education may *understate* the actual return for those who choose to attend college. Likewise, the measured rate of return may *overstate* the return that would have been received by those terminating schooling with high school had they instead chosen to attend college. To understand these points, return to equation (9.2), where the benefits of a college education in year t were given as B_t. The term B_t is conventionally measured as follows:

$$B_t = E_{C,t}^C - E_{H,t}^H \qquad (9.3)$$

where E_C^C represents the earnings in a college-level job of those who choose to go to college, and E_H^H represents the earnings in a high-school-level job of those who choose not to go to college.

Now, had the person who chose to attend college instead terminated schooling at high school, he or she would have earned E_H^C (where E_H^C is perhaps *less* than E_H^H). Thus, the benefits in year t to those who chose college (B_t^C) are

$$B_t^C = E_{C,t}^C - E_{H,t}^C \qquad (9.4)$$

21. It may also be true that students from poor families, who lack the financial resources to obtain much education, require a higher rate of return on their educational investments than do students from families in which wealth is more abundant.
22. The discussion in this subsection is based on Robert J. Willis and Sherwin Rosen, "Education and Self-Selection," *Journal of Political Economy* 87 (October 1979): S7–S36.

—a sum *greater* than the measured benefit in equation (9.3). Thus, the benefits of going to college to those who choose to go may be greater than is indicated by the measured rate of return.

Similarly, if those who chose not to attend college were to alter their decisions, the earnings they could expect in year t would be $E_{C,t}^{H}$. The considerations in this subsection suggest that *their* post-college earnings ($E_{C,t}^{H}$) might be *less* than the earnings of those who did decide to attend college ($E_{C,t}^{C}$). Since the benefits of a college education to those who decided not to attend (B_{t}^{H}) are

$$B_{t}^{H} = E_{C,t}^{H} - E_{H,t}^{H} \qquad (9.5)$$

it is apparent by comparing equations (9.3) and (9.5) that B_{t}^{H} is less than B_{t}. Thus, the potential rate of return to those who decided not to go to college may well be less than the measured rate of return.

The Willis-Rosen study mentioned in footnote 22 calculated estimates of the rate of return to schooling beyond high school for those who did not go beyond high school and those who did. Taking into account both measured differences in ability and the selectivity bias discussed in this section, they estimated a rate of return of 9.9 percent for those attending college. For those who did not go beyond high school, the rate of return they could have obtained from going to college was estimated to be 9.3 percent. While this is not a large difference, it is a reminder that when abilities are diverse, the principle of comparative advantage is an important factor in making choices about schooling and occupations.

It is difficult to summarize the findings on the question of whether education is a sensible investment for an individual. Considering only monetary costs and benefits, rates of return on educational investments are modest (once ability is accounted for), but not out of line with the "real" returns on many other types of investments. Moreover, if benefits other than money earnings were measured, the estimated returns on education would probably be higher.

Is Education a Good Social Investment?

The United States spends roughly 7 percent of its gross national product on formal education (primary, secondary, and college). If forgone earnings of high school and college students were included, this figure would rise to 10 percent.[23] In part these expenditures are justified by our need for a literate citizenry, speaking a common language and sharing a common culture. In part, however, education, especially at the secondary and college levels, is justified on the grounds that it enhances worker productivity. Interestingly, an early Soviet economist, S. G. Strumilin, wrote in 1929:

> A long time ago we had already arrived at the conclusion, that the expenditure of the state budget to raise the cultural level of the country ought to be considered along with the expenditures on technical reconstruction of pro-

---

23. The forgone earnings of high school and college students have been estimated to equal 60 percent of the *direct* cost outlays at those schooling levels. See Theodore Schultz, *The Economic Value of Education* (New York: Columbia University Press, 1963).

duction as capital expenditures and as equal in terms of their importance to our economy.[24]

There are some fields, such as mechanics and engineering, in which education clearly has a social payoff in the form of increased productivity. Recently, however, some critics have suggested that, to a large degree, education acts merely as a "sorting device." They argue that rather than making workers more productive, the educational process is merely a screening device that reveals to employers the productive characteristics *already inherent* in prospective workers (we touched on this issue earlier in the discussion of the relationship between education and ability).

Employers, as noted in Chapter 5, are faced with the problem of ascertaining the quality of their job applicants. If they hire people for a trial period to see how they work out, they may face the costs of terminating low-quality employees and recouping the losses associated with their mistakes. An alternative procedure is to screen applicants through interviews, evaluations from previous employers, or work-related tests. These procedures themselves are costly, of course. They take time and money, and may still give imprecise readings of applicant quality.

Employers may also use data on applicant education as a screening tool. To do well in school requires both a capacity to learn and a willingness to work. The intellectual abilities required to succeed in school are obviously more closely correlated with the requirements for success in some jobs than in others; however, workers who are better able to learn in school are probably easier to train and more flexible in the workplace than others. The discipline required in school—promptness, willingness to follow directions, adherence to deadlines—is very similar to the discipline required to perform well in most jobs. In a real sense, schooling is the "work" of youth and may well be a good test of ability to succeed later on.

The argument of those who regard education *only* as a sorting device goes beyond the argument that employers use educational attainment to screen applicants. Such critics of education assert that schooling does *nothing* to alter productive characteristics, that it does not increase knowledge of the kind useful to employees, and that it does not impart useful attitudes or work habits. In short, they say, nothing happens to students while in school that affects productivity later on. The educational system is seen as simply a filter that has the effect of *signaling* which people are likely to be most productive.[25] (For a discussion of signaling, see Appendix 9A.)

It should be recognized that even if schooling were only a screening device, it could have social, as well as private, value. Employers need a reliable method by which to select employees. Obviously, sorting millions of

---

24. Arcadius Kahan, "Russian Scholars and Statesmen on Education as an Investment," in *Educational and Economic Development,* ed. C. A. Anderson and M. J. Bowman (Chicago: Aldine Publishing Co., 1965), 10.
25. If this were all that schools did, they would not do much to alter the influences of family background and thus would not be terribly useful in breaking down existing class distinctions or providing a vehicle for social mobility. For an elaboration of this point, see Samuel Bowles and Herbert Gintis, *Schooling in Capitalist America: Educational Reform and the Contradictions of Economic Life* (New York: Basic Books, 1976).

workers into various categories of ability is an enormous job for any society, and sorting on the basis of schooling may be a very efficient means of doing this. The people most likely to acquire more schooling are the ones for whom schooling entails the least psychic cost, and as we have argued, this group will tend to be heavily populated by the ablest people. Investment in schooling, then, sends a *signal* to the labor market that one has a certain level of ability. The costs of investing in schooling purely for its signaling value generate net *private* benefits if the increased wage a graduate can obtain outweighs the costs. Schools in this case would have net *social* value if the decision to attend and the success one attained in school sent accurate signals about productive characteristics to employers in the least costly way.

Whether schooling is purely a sorting device or adds to productivity is not a particularly important question for individuals. Whatever role schools play, additional schooling does enhance one's lifetime income. Where the issue of screening is important is at the social level. If the only purpose of schools is to screen, why encourage the expansion of schooling? If 40 years ago being a high school graduate signaled above-average intelligence and work discipline, why incur the enormous costs of expanding college attendance only to find out that now these qualities are signaled by having a bachelor's degree? The issue is of even more importance in less developed countries, where mistakes in allocating extremely scarce capital resources could be disastrous (see Example 9.4).

Unfortunately, direct evidence on the role schooling plays in society is almost impossible to obtain.[26] Advocates of the screening viewpoint, for example, assert that the fact that rates of return for college *graduates* are higher than for college *dropouts* is evidence that schooling is a screening device.[27] They argue that what is learned in school is proportional to the time spent there and that an added bonus (rate of return) just for a diploma is proof of the screening hypothesis. Advocates of the view that schooling enhances human capital counter that one who graduates after four years probably has learned more than four times what the freshman dropout has learned. They argue that dropouts are more likely to be poorer students—the ones who overestimated their returns on schooling and quit when they discovered their mistake. Thus, their relatively low rate of return is associated not with their dropping out but with their *reason* for dropping out.[28]

---

26. Recent papers on this topic highlight the difficulties and come to varying conclusions. Kevin Lang and David Kropp, "Human Capital Versus Sorting: The Effects of Compulsory Attendance Laws," *Quarterly Journal of Economics* 101, no. 3 (August 1986): 609–24, and Andrew Weiss, "High School Graduation, Performance, and Wages," *Journal of Political Economy* 96, no. 4 (August 1988): 785–820, argue that their evidence supports the screening hypothesis; M. Boissiere, J. Knight, and R. Sabot, "Earnings, Schooling, Ability, and Cognitive Skills," *American Economic Review* 75, no. 5 (December 1985): 1016–31, find support for the human capital hypothesis.

27. Dropouts naturally have lower incomes than graduates, but because they have also invested less, it is not clear that their *rates of return* should be lower.

28. See Barry Chiswick, "Schooling, Screening, and Income," in *Does College Matter?* ed. Lewis Solomon and Paul Taubman (New York: Academic Press, 1973), and Charles F. Manski and David Wise, *College Choice in America*, Chapter 8.

EXAMPLE 9.4

The Socially Optimal Level of Educational Investment

In addition to asking whether schooling is a good social investment, we could also ask, What is the socially optimal *level* of schooling? The general principle guiding our answer to this question is that society should increase or reduce its educational investments until the marginal rate of return (to society) equals the marginal rate of return on other forms of capital investment (investment in physical capital, for example).

The rationale for the above principle is that if society has some funds it wants to invest, it will desire to invest them in projects yielding the highest rates of return. If an investment in physical capital yields a 20 percent rate of return and the same funds invested in schooling yield (all things considered) only a 10 percent return, society will clearly prefer to invest in physical capital. As long as the two rates of return differ, society could be made better off by reducing its investments in low-yield projects and increasing them in those with higher rates of return.

The text has discussed many of the difficulties and biases inherent in esti-mating rates of return to schooling. However, the general principle of equat-ing the rates of social return on all forms of investments is still a useful one to consider. It suggests, for example, that capital-poor countries should invest in additional schooling only if the returns are very high—higher, in all proba-bility, than the rates of return required for optimality in more-capital-rich countries. Indeed, the rates of return to both secondary schooling and higher education appear to be generally higher in less-developed countries than in developed countries. One review estimated that the rate of return on sec-ondary schooling investments was 11 percent for a developed country (on average), while for a less-developed country it was 15 to 18 percent. Compa-rable rates of return on investments in higher education were 9 percent and 13 to 16 percent, respectively.

SOURCE: George Psacharopoulos, "Returns to Education: A Further International Update and Implications," *Journal of Human Resources* 20, no. 4 (Fall 1985): 583–604.

To take another example, proponents of the human capital view of edu-cation sometimes argue that the fact that earnings differentials between col-lege and high school graduates continue to grow supports their view. They argue that if schooling were just a screening device, employers would rely on it *initially*, but as they accumulated direct information from experience with their employees schooling would play a smaller role in determining earnings. Screening advocates could counter that continued growth in earnings differ-entials and the continued association of schooling and earnings only illustrate that educational levels are a *successful* sorting device; in other words, that workers with higher levels of attainment in school do make more productive workers.

Finally, it has been argued that the 1940–65 change in skill requirements for a large number of jobs was very small, yet the educational requirements for obtaining those jobs rose dramatically.[29] Thus, while shoe salespeople in 1965 performed the same job as in 1940, they were required to have more education because of the general inflation in levels of educational attainment. While this seems like persuasive evidence in favor of the screening hypothesis, it ignores the fact that the real earnings of sales personnel rose. While the job requirements were the same—fitting and selling shoes—the salesperson of the 1960s had a higher real marginal product than his or her counterpart of the 1940s. This higher marginal productivity could have been achieved by harder work and improved store layout or it could have been the result of more knowledgeable sales personnel. Exactly how the increase was obtained is unknown, but one cannot rule out improvements in human capital as a partial cause.

Thus, just about any evidence offered to support one side of the argument can be accommodated by the other side. Perhaps the best resolution of this issue relies on economic reasoning. We know, for example, that college is very expensive and that to induce students to attend requires a reasonable return on their investment. Thus, to obtain college graduates, employers must pay them wages high enough to compensate them for their investment. If their investment costs are $80,000, employers must pay them wages whose lifetime present value is at least $80,000 higher than they would be paid if they had not attended.[30] In short, hiring a college graduate costs an employer at least $80,000 more in the long run than hiring a high school graduate (in present-value terms).

Now, the college graduate may in fact be worth $80,000 more because of his or her productive characteristics. However, if these characteristics existed prior to college and were unaffected by college, it would pay the firm to find its *own* method of sorting high school graduates in order to find the best potential workers. As long as the methods it used were as reliable and cost less than a college education ($80,000 per worker), it would be profitable to adopt them. The firm could pay lower wages to its workers because these workers would be spared the expense of college.

The fact that firms have not generally substituted their own screening devices for the educational requirements widely used suggests one of two things. Either education *does* enhance worker productivity or it is a *cheaper* screening tool than any other that firms could use. In either case, the fact that employers are willing to pay a high price for an educated work force *seems* to suggest that education produces social benefits.

Government Training Programs

Questions about the social benefits and costs of educational investments can be extended from general schooling to *particular* job training programs. Beginning in the early 1960s, the federal government became heavily involved in programs to increase worker skills. In 1978, for example, 856,000 workers were enrolled in federally funded classroom or on-the-job training programs, at a cost of close to $2,000 per trainee on the average. One need not be a hard-

29. See Ivar Berg, *Education and Jobs: The Great Training Robbery* (New York: Praeger Publishers, 1970).

30. If some of the benefits of college attendance are *consumption* goods, the investment costs that employees must recoup are, of course, less than $80,000.

bitten cynic to ask, "Are these programs worth their cost?" At times the answer seems to be a clear-cut no.

During the 1960s, one government training program was aimed primarily at blacks in the poverty-stricken Mississippi-delta area. When delta training programs were geared to produce more than 8,000 trainees a year, available jobs for trainees were opening up at a rate of 3,000 per year.[31] Given this lack of job openings, the programs became, in effect, welfare programs, valued for the stipend they paid trainees rather than their future benefits. Trainees had no incentive to graduate and tried to stay in the program as long as possible.

While it can be argued that enhancing the incomes of poor delta blacks is itself a worthy enterprise, training programs may not be efficient means of doing this. They require society to pay the salaries of instructors (who are not poor) and to purchase capital equipment, funds that might better be used if they were given directly to the poor.

The intent of a properly conceived job skills training program is to enhance private and social productivity by training workers to do jobs that are in demand. Some policymakers have followed a *personnel planning* approach in deciding how many workers, in what fields, to train. This personnel planning approach asks employers how many persons with certain kinds of qualifications they will need, projects the numbers likely to be supplied by other sources, and recommends filling the gap with government training programs. While this method, if successfully used, should avoid the problems mentioned in the case of the delta trainees, it does suffer the fatal flaw of ignoring *costs:*

> The manpower planner who plans supply to match demand asks the *wrong* questions. He asks, "What is the absorptive capacity of the economy for persons with different skills and educational attainments?" and does not consider the costs of schooling at all. If employers say (or his calculations lead him to believe) that an extra graduate would be hired, the manpower planner directs the education system to produce an extra graduate. He does not ask, "What is the nature of the work the graduate will perform and what benefits will he confer on society?" Nor does he ask, "How much will it cost society to educate another graduate? Do the benefits justify the costs?"[32]

The only way one can be sure that investments in training programs are socially productive is to weigh their costs against the increases in productivity they permit. Since theory implies that marginal productivity and wages are roughly equal, one can look at the wage increases of trainees to obtain an approximation of productivity increases. For example, if a worker would have earned $8,000 per year had she not had training and earns $8,600 a year after training, the program has pretty clearly increased her productivity by $600 per year. This yearly benefit to her (and society) must then be weighed against the cost of training in order to see if the rate of return is as large as it would be if the funds had been invested elsewhere.

---

31. Michael J. Piore, "Negro Workers in the Mississippi Delta: Problems of Displacement and Adjustment," in *Perspectives on Poverty and Income Distribution,* ed. James G. Scoville (Lexington, Mass.: D. C. Heath, 1971), 151–57.
32. Gary S. Fields, "Private and Social Returns to Education in Labour Surplus Economies," *Eastern Africa Economic Review* 4, no. 1 (June 1972): 43.

Weighing costs against returns is not an easy job, primarily because one must find some way of estimating what trainees would have earned in the absence of the program. One way to make such an estimate is to project the earnings based on past earnings trends, taking note of earnings trends among comparable workers who did not enter the training program. A comprehensive study of 13,000 people who received training in 1964 under the federal Manpower Development and Training Act (MDTA) found that, for males, yearly increases in earnings were in the $150–$500 range, with the effects declining by half over a five-year post-training period. For females the gains were in the $300–$600 range, with no decline over time.[33]

Do these returns justify the costs? The costs per student in this program were $1,800. If a 10 percent rate of return on this investment were to be earned indefinitely, the gains would have to amount to $180 a year. The results for men roughly meet this standard, while those for women clearly exceed it. Thus, the MDTA program appears to have been a good investment in 1964, although the results indicate that training for females was a better investment and should, therefore, have been expanded.

Unfortunately, later classes of trainees did not experience as high rates of return as the 1964 class.[34] Whether and what types of government-sponsored training programs represent good social investments are questions that do not have conclusive answers at the moment, mainly because making estimates of what recipients would have earned in the absence of the programs is so open to different approaches. However, there is general agreement that the gains from such training are largest for women and the economically disadvantaged.[35]

APPLICATIONS OF HUMAN CAPITAL THEORY

The theory of human capital can be used to explain several interesting phenomena in the labor market. This section will apply the theory to post-schooling investments in training, the labor force behavior of women, and the distribution of earnings.

Post-Schooling Investments and Age/Earnings Profiles

Schooling is largely a full-time, formally organized activity. However, there are less formal kinds of human capital investments that are more difficult to observe. These investments take the form of training that normally occurs in

---

33. Orley Ashenfelter, "Estimating the Effect of Training Programs on Earnings," *Review of Economics and Statistics* 60, no. 1 (February 1978): 47–57.

34. For a review of studies evaluating government training and employment programs, see Lauri J. Bassi and Orley Ashenfelter, "The Effect of Direct Job Creation and Training Programs on Low-Skilled Workers," in *Fighting Poverty: What Works and What Does Not,* ed. Sheldon H. Danziger and Daniel H. Weinberg (Cambridge, Mass.: Harvard University Press, 1986), and Burt S. Barnow, "The Impact of CETA Programs on Earnings," *Journal of Human Resources* 22, no. 2 (Spring 1987): 157–93. See also Robert LaLonde, "Evaluating the Econometric Evaluations of Training Programs with Experimental Data," *American Economic Review* 76, no. 4 (September 1986): 604–20.

35. For a study on how training affects employment probabilities, see David Card and Daniel Sullivan, "Measuring the Effect of Subsidized Training Programs on Movements In and Out of Employment," *Econometrica* 56, no. 3 (May 1988): 497–530. A side effect of training is the displacement of other workers; for an analysis of whether this is a social cost, see Robert Smith, "The Economics of Job Displacement," in *Disability and the Labor Market,* ed. Monroe Berkowitz and M. Anne Hill (Ithaca, N.Y.: ILR Press, 1986).

EXAMPLE 9.5

Socialists or (Human) Capitalists: Wage Differentials in the Soviet Union

The principles of human capital theory are neither unknown nor ignored in the Soviet Union. To increase the incentives of its workers to obtain more training and improve their skills, the government announced in early 1987 that it was going to revise its schedule of wages to create a wider gap between skilled and unskilled workers. The previous wage schedule, adopted in the early 1970s, had reduced the average salary differential between engineers, for example, and factory workers to 10 percent—down from the 46 percent differential that had existed in the 1960s. In commenting on the salary compression built into the schedule adopted in the 1970s, Leonid Kostin, First Deputy Chairman of the State Committee for Labor and Social Issues, said:

> Obviously, this does nothing to stimulate the professional improvement of workers even though the nature of production and the requirements of scientific and technical progress call for people with the highest qualifications.

In terms of human capital theory, Mr. Kostin's reasoning is that for workers to undertake human capital investments, the benefits of improved wages must be large enough to offset the costs of training.

SOURCE: Theodore Shabad, "Soviet Moves to Pay More to Better Workers," *New York Times,* March 8, 1987, 8.

the workplace. Some of this "training" is *learning by doing* (as one hammers nails month after month, one's skills naturally improve), but much of it takes place on the job, under close supervision, or consists of a formal program in the workplace. All forms of training are costly in the sense that the productivity of learners is low, and all represent a conscious *choice* on the part of the employer to accept lower current productivity in exchange for higher output later. It has been estimated that the average worker acquires the equivalent of at least two years of college in on-the-job training and that the annual cost of such training amounts to 3 percent of gross national product![36]

Who bears the cost of on-the-job training? You will recall that Chapter 5 argued that the cost of *specific training,* training of use *only* to one's employer, is shared by the worker and the firm. The employee might be paid a wage greater than marginal product (*MP*) during the training period, but after training the employee's wage is below *MP* (but above what the employee could get elsewhere). In the case of general training, in which employees acquire skills usable elsewhere, they alone pay the training costs.

How do employees pay the costs of general training provided by their employer? They work for a wage lower than they would get if they were not receiving training. Their wage is equal to their *MP,* which is, of course, decreased during the training period when trainees require close supervision or time off

---

36. Jacob Mincer, "On-the-Job Training: Costs, Returns, and Some Implications," *Journal of Political Economy* (Supplement 1962): 50–79.

the job to engage in classroom learning. Why do employees accept this lower wage? They accept it for the same reason that some decide to obtain schooling: in the expectation of improving the present value of their lifetime earnings. In other words, employees incur current investment costs (lower wages) to obtain increased earnings later.

The Timing of Post-Schooling Investments. This chapter has demonstrated that if people are going to invest in themselves, they will tend to undertake most of the investments at younger ages for two reasons:

1. Investments made at younger ages have a longer period over which to capture returns and thus tend to have higher total benefits.
2. One big cost of investing in education and training is forgone earnings, and this cost rises as one gets older and earnings become higher (if for no other reason, because of learning by doing).

Consequently, putting off human capital investments lowers the returns on such investments.

It is not surprising to find, then, that schooling, largely a full-time activity, is followed by on-the-job training, normally a part-time activity. Further, we also find that job training declines with age, being most heavily concentrated in one's early years on the job when opportunity costs are lower. However, in the case of job training, where scholarships and loans are not available and where the training is part-time, investment will not take place all at once. Too much current consumption would have to be forgone by the ordinary worker if one's entire lifetime amount of job training were acquired completely in the first two years of one's career. Thus, employees tend to parcel out their job training over a number of years but gradually reduce such training as time goes by.

Timing of Investment and Age/Earnings Profiles. The above theory of post-schooling investments helps explain why age/earnings profiles are concave: rising more rapidly at first, then flattening out, and ultimately falling (see Figure 9.12). Earnings, low at first because of training investments, rise quickly as new skills are acquired. However, as workers grow older, the pace of training investment slows and so does the rate at which productivity increases. At the end of one's working life, skills may have depreciated, as a result of lack of continued investment and the aging process, to the extent that retirement, semi-retirement, or a change in jobs is necessary for many workers. This depreciation contributes to the downturn in *average* earnings near retirement age.

The Fanning Out of Age/Earnings Profiles by Education. As noted earlier in this chapter, the differences in average earnings between people of the same age but different educational levels increase over time (see Figure 9.11). This phenomenon is also consistent with what human capital theory would predict.

The answer to the question, "Who will invest most in post-school training?" should be familiar by now. Those who expect the highest benefits and learn most quickly will do the most investing in job training. The fact that

FIGURE 9.12   Age/Earnings Profile

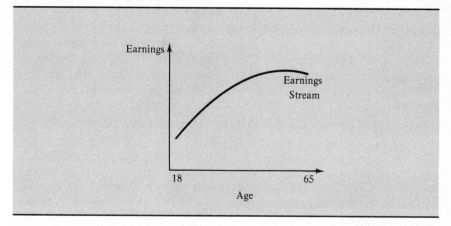

they learn rapidly shortens the training period, which both reduces investment costs and increases the duration of benefits. But who are these fast learners? They are most likely the people who, because of their abilities, were best able to reap benefits from formal schooling! Thus, human capital theory leads us to expect workers who invested more in schooling to also invest more in post-schooling job training.

The tendency of the better-educated workers to invest more in job training explains why their age/earnings profiles start low, rise quickly, and keep rising after the profiles of their less-educated counterparts have leveled off. Their earnings rise more quickly because they are investing more heavily in job training, and they rise for a longer time for the same reason. In other words, people with the ability to learn quickly select the ultimately high-paying jobs where much learning is required and thus put their abilities to greatest advantage.[37]

Women and the Acquisition of Human Capital

As implied in Chapters 6 and 7, the career pattern of many married women has tended to consist of distinct stages. First there is a period of employment preceding childbirth. Following the birth of the first child is a period of non-participation in the labor force, followed by a return to labor market participation, often on a part-time or temporary basis. A study conducted on data collected in the 1960s found that the first stage of participation usually lasted 3 or 4 years and that the second stage of nonparticipation usually lasted 7 years, although it is likely that the former period has lengthened and the latter shortened. Overall, the expected worklife of women at age 20 was 27.2 years

---

37. A recent paper that analyzes, in a more sophisticated way, the propositions about job training and earnings presented in this section is Jacob Mincer, "Job Training, Wage Growth, and Labor Turnover," Working Paper no. 2690, National Bureau of Economic Research, August 1988.

in 1980, up from 21.3 years in 1970; in contrast, the average man at age 20 could be expected to work for 36.8 years in 1980 (down from 37.3 in 1970).[38]

The interrupted nature of many women's careers has had profound implications for their acquisition of education and training. First, because women's careers are usually shorter than men's, they have less time to reap the rewards of investments in human capital. This lowers the benefits of investments in schooling and training, rendering women less likely than men to make such investments.

Second, the interruptions add further incentives to avoid certain kinds of investments. During the period of nonparticipation in the labor market, skills depreciate and the continuity of experience is broken. Previous investments in human capital may become almost useless, especially in highly technical, ever-changing fields such as law, medicine, engineering, and research. Thus, many women in the prematernal years might be expected to avoid investments that will lose their value during the years of child rearing.

Human capital theory therefore predicts that women will acquire less schooling and less training than men. The evidence is generally consistent with these predictions, but rapid changes have been occurring. The above predictions of human capital theory, it must be remembered, are for "traditional" women—those who have, or expect to have, interrupted labor market careers. To the extent that women's expectations concerning their jobs are changing, these predictions will be less and less supported by the data.

Women and Schooling.   When one considers the reduced benefits traditional women receive from a human capital investment relative to those for men, it is not surprising that, historically, relatively fewer of them attended college. Table 9.2 demonstrates that as late as 1971, women—who made up 50–51 percent of high school graduates—made up only about 42 percent of college students. Slightly fewer women went on to obtain master's degrees, and far fewer women obtained professional and doctoral degrees. By 1985, however, women and men were almost equally represented among high school, college, and master's graduates. Only at the professional and doctoral level were women underrepresented in 1985, and even there the proportion of women had increased markedly in 14 years.

The data in Table 9.2 thus suggest a marked change in the relative benefits and costs of investments in higher education among younger women. Gender differences in major fields of study persist, though, suggesting that young women are still more likely than men to choose occupations in which interrupted careers are less damaging. For example, Table 9.3 reveals that in 1983 women were much more likely than men to major in education and much less likely to major in business or engineering. However, shifts away from tradition can be seen even here, with a big rise in female business majors from 1969 to 1983.

---

38. These data are taken from Jacob Mincer and Solomon Polachek, "Family Investments in Human Capital: Earnings of Women," *Journal of Political Economy* 82, no. 2 (March/April 1974): S76–S108, and Shirley Smith, "Revised Worklife Tables Reflect 1979–80 Experience," *Monthly Labor Review* 108, no. 8 (August 1985): 23–30.

TABLE 9.2   Percentages of Women in Selected Educational Categories, 1971 and 1985

Category	1971	1985
Graduating seniors, high school	50.5	50.2
College students	41.8	52.5
Graduating seniors, bachelor's degree	43.4	50.7
Graduating with master's degree	40.1	49.9
Graduating with professional degree (medicine, law)	6.3	32.8
Graduating with doctoral degree	14.3	34.1

SOURCES: U.S. National Center for Education Statistics, *Digest of Education Statistics 1987,* Tables 69, 101, 150.

Women and Job Training. Besides reduced incentives to invest in certain types of schooling, women have had fewer incentives than men to invest in job training. As a result, women have not typically found themselves in jobs with steep age/earnings profiles. While we lack the data necessary to track the earnings of individual women through time, we can plot (as we did for men) average earnings of each age group. As Figure 9.13 shows, the age/earnings profiles for women are relatively flat: older women do not appear to earn much more than younger women. We can conclude from this that experience-related increases in productivity have not had a big influence on women's wages, which implies that the acquisition of job training has not been very widespread among women.

One reason for the lack of job training among traditional women may be their shorter and more interrupted careers, which reduces both their incentives and the incentives of their employers to engage in such training. Another reason, however, may be various forms of discrimination (see Chapter 14, "The Economics of Discrimination," for further discussion of women's earnings). Nevertheless, at least some of the differences between the earnings of men and women are due to differences in the acquisition of human capital. The magnitude of these differences will be addressed in Chapter 14.

TABLE 9.3   Percentages of Bachelor's and Master's Degrees Conferred, by Selected Major Field of Study and Gender, 1969 and 1983

	1969				1983			
	Bachelor's		Master's		Bachelor's		Master's	
	Men	Women	Men	Women	Men	Women	Men	Women
Business	21	3	16	1	27	19	32	13
Engineering	10	a	12	a	16	2	12	1
Education	9	36	27	53	5	15	16	42
Health professions	1	5	2	3	2	11	3	9
All majors	100	100	100	100	100	100	100	100

[a]Negligible.

SOURCES: U.S. National Center for Education Statistics, *Digest of Education Statistics 1970* (1970), Table 117; *Digest of Education Statistics 1987,* Table 153.

FIGURE 9.13 Total Money Earnings (Mean), Full-Time Female Workers, 1987

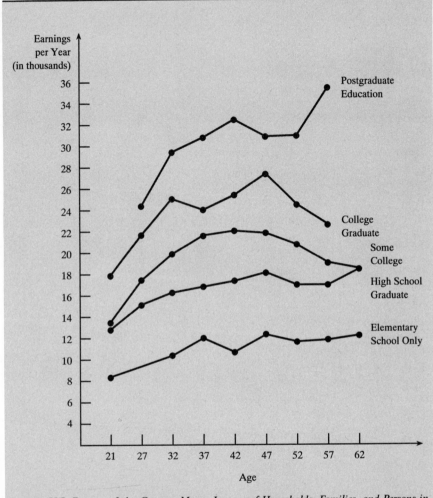

SOURCE: U.S. Bureau of the Census, *Money Income of Households, Families, and Persons in the United States: 1987,* Current Population Reports, Series P-60, no. 162, Table 36.

Human Capital and the Distribution of Earnings

Society is often as interested in the *distribution* of income as it is in the average *level* of income. For example, it is frequently asserted that the United States is a rich country, but one in which advantaged workers are rewarded handsomely while those less fortunate receive a very small portion of the national wealth. To evaluate this assertion that the outcome of our market system is unfair requires data on the *distribution* of income. Such distribution data are needed to answer questions like, "How much more does the top 10 percent of the population make than the bottom 10 percent?"

FIGURE 9.14   Income Distribution with Perfect Income Equality

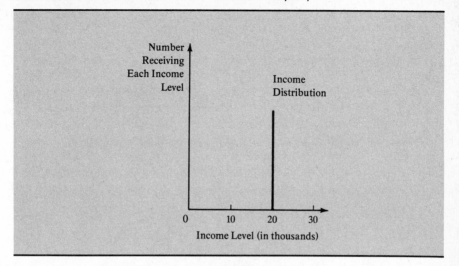

This section presents a few basic facts about the distribution of both family *income* and individual *earnings* in the United States and uses human capital theory to explain certain characteristics of the distribution of *earnings*. Earnings are considered separately from income because income can include rents, dividends, interest, and income maintenance payments that are not the result of labor market transactions and are therefore not the subject of human capital theory.[39]

Statistical Concepts.   To understand certain basic concepts related to the distribution of income (or the distribution of earnings) it is helpful to think in graphic terms. Consider a simple plotting of the number of people receiving each given level of income. If everyone made the same income—say $20,000 per year—there would be no dispersion or disparities in income. The graph of the income distribution would look like Figure 9.14.

If there *were* disparities in the income people received, these disparities could be relatively large or relatively small. If the average level of income received was $20,000 and virtually all people received incomes very close to the average, the *dispersion* of incomes would be small. If the average was $20,000 but some made much more and some much less, the dispersion of incomes would be large. In Figure 9.15 two hypothetical income distributions are illustrated. While both distributions are centered on the same average level of income ($20,000), distribution A exhibits smaller dispersion than distribution B. Incomes in B are more widely dispersed and thus exhibit a *greater degree of*

---

39. Because the availability of loans for human capital investments is imperfect, students from wealthy families face fewer constraints in making such investments than do others. Thus, financial and human wealth are interconnected to some extent.

inequality. Appendix 9B discusses alternative approaches to the measurement of income inequality.

While for most purposes the degree of income dispersion is of most importance in judging equality, it is also interesting to inquire whether the distribution of incomes (or earnings) is *symmetric* or not. If the distributions are symmetric, as in Figure 9.15, then as many people earn $X less than average as earn $X more than average. Put differently, the dispersion of incomes for the poorest half of society mirrors the dispersion for the richest half if the distribution is symmetric. If the distribution is not symmetric, we say it is *skewed,* meaning that one part of the distribution is bunched together and the other part is relatively dispersed (see Figure 9.16). In fact, the actual distributions of income and earnings in the United States are skewed to the right, as is the distribution depicted in Figure 9.16, meaning that they are bunched at the left (at the lower levels of income) and widely dispersed at the higher income levels.

Skewness is an important characteristic of the distribution of income or earnings, because the concept suggests another dimension of fairness. For example, many less developed countries do not have a sizable middle class. Such countries have a huge number of very poor families and a tiny minority of very wealthy families. Thus, the distribution of income in these countries, normally considered unfair, is highly skewed to the right.

The Distribution of Income.   Family incomes in the United States are disparate, and there has been a trend toward greater inequality since the mid-1960s. Note from Table 9.4 that the 20 percent of families with the lowest incomes obtained less than 5 percent of the total income received in 1987, while the top 20 percent obtained more than 40 percent of the total income in that year. These disparities in incomes are not unlike those in other countries

FIGURE 9.15   Symmetric Distributions of Income with Different Degrees of Dispersion

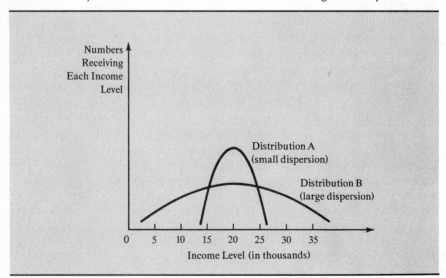

FIGURE 9.16   Distribution of Income That Is Skewed to the Right

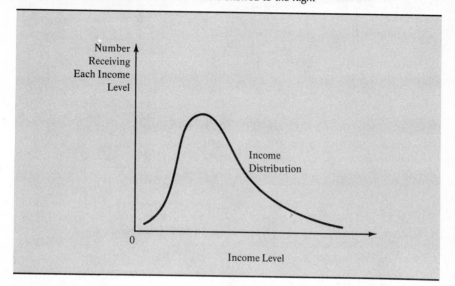

(see Table 9.5). Further, if the data are adjusted for taxes paid and noncash benefits received from government transfer programs, the percentage of total income received by the bottom group of families is increased by over 2 percentage points and the percentage received by the upper group is reduced by some 4 percentage points.[40] Nevertheless, the unmistakable growth in the disparity of family incomes in the recent decade or so has raised the concern that the United States is losing its middle class and becoming polarized into two groups: the well-to-do, holding down professional or executive jobs, and less-educated workers, who have been displaced from manufacturing jobs and relegated to low-paying jobs in the service sector.[41]

In evaluating assertions about the "vanishing middle class," it must be noted that a major part of the growing inequality in family incomes is explained not by jobs but by changes in families themselves (namely, the growth of single-parent households).[42] When assessing claims about the distribution of jobs or wages, we must therefore turn our attention away from family incomes and toward an analysis of individual *earnings*.

The Dispersion of Earnings.   The 1987 distribution of wage and salary earnings for men aged 25–64 is graphed in Figure 9.17. (The distribution of earnings for men of this age group is less affected by variations in hours of work,

40. Frank Levy, *Dollars and Dreams* (New York: Norton, 1988), 195–96.
41. Barry Bluestone and Bennett Harrison, *The Deindustrialization of America* (New York: Basic Books, 1982), and Bennett Harrison, Charles Tilly, and Barry Bluestone, "Wage Inequality Takes a Great U-Turn," *Challenge* (March/April 1986): 26–32.
42. Charles M. Beach, "The 'Vanishing' Middle Class? Evidence and Explanations," Industrial Relations Centre, Queen's University, Kingston, Ontario, 1988. When a family is split into two households by divorce or separation, its income is split and the number of lower-income households tends to proliferate.

TABLE 9.4   Distribution of Pre-Tax, Money Incomes Among Families, 1947–1987

Income Level	Percent of Aggregate Income Received				
	1947	1957	1967	1977	1987
Total families	100.0	100.0	100.0	100.0	100.0
Lowest fifth	5.0	5.1	5.5	5.2	4.6
Second fifth	11.9	12.7	12.4	11.6	10.8
Third fifth	17.0	18.1	17.9	17.5	16.9
Fourth fifth	23.1	23.8	23.9	24.2	24.1
Highest fifth	43.0	40.4	40.4	41.5	43.7
Top 5 percent	17.5	15.6	15.2	15.7	16.9
Median family income (in 1987 dollars)	15,422	20,053	27,004	30,025	30,853

Note: The income (before taxes) boundaries of each fifth of families, arranged by income in 1987, were: lowest fifth, under $14,450; second fifth, $14,450 to $25,100; third fifth, $25,101 to $36,600; fourth fifth, $36,601 to $52,910; highest fifth, over $52,910; top 5 percent, over $86,300.

SOURCE: U.S. Bureau of the Census, *Money Income of Households, Families, and Persons in the United States: 1987*, Current Population Reports, Series P-60, no. 162, Tables 11, 12.

and thus more reflective of variations in wage rates, than the earnings of any other group.) It is obvious from Figure 9.17 that there is considerable dispersion (as well as skewness) in the earnings of this group.

It is not surprising, of course, that earnings vary. This chapter has shown, for example, that much of the higher earnings received by the well-educated and highly trained is a return on their investments in human capital. In fact, in any society in which people can make themselves more productive only through a costly investment of time and money, we would expect to observe earnings differentials. Not *all* the observed dispersion in earnings is related to the normal returns on human capital investments, but *some* dispersion is to be expected when these investments are being made by some people and not by others.

TABLE 9.5   Percentage of National Income Received by the Lowest- and Highest-Income Households in Ten Countries

Country (Year)	Percentage of National Income Received by	
	Lowest 20 Percent	Highest 20 Percent
Germany (1978)	7.9	39.5
Hong Kong (1980)	5.4	47.0
Hungary (1982)	6.9	35.8
Israel (1979)	6.0	39.9
Japan (1979)	8.7	37.5
Mexico (1977)	2.9	57.7
Sweden (1981)	7.4	41.7
Switzerland (1978)	6.6	38.0
United Kingdom (1979)	7.0	39.7
United States (1980)	5.3	39.9

SOURCE: The World Bank, *World Development Report 1986* (New York: Oxford University Press, 1986), Table 24.

FIGURE 9.17   Distribution of Wages and Salaries, Men Aged 25–64, 1987

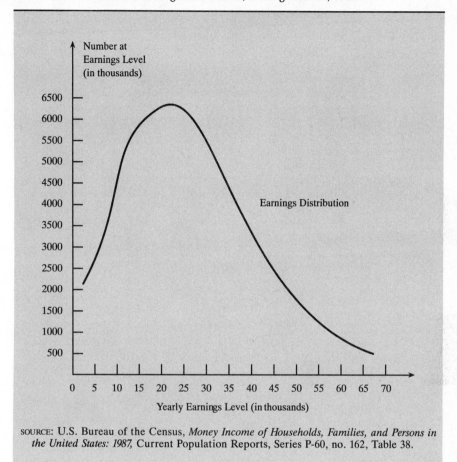

SOURCE: U.S. Bureau of the Census, *Money Income of Households, Families, and Persons in the United States: 1987,* Current Population Reports, Series P-60, no. 162, Table 38.

Another portion of the overall dispersion in earnings among men aged 25–64 is the result of combining men of different ages in the same distribution. We know that productivity increases over time, so older men typically earn more than younger men. This source of dispersion is probably not of much concern to society, because everyone's income follows the pattern of being relatively low in the younger years.

What may be of more concern is the dispersion of earnings *within* age groups. Here human capital theory offers a clear-cut prediction. When people are young, the job training in which some are investing keeps their earnings close to (or below) what those who are not investing receive. As time passes, however, the earnings of those who have invested are raised considerably above the earnings of those who have not. We noted this phenomenon when we examined age/earnings profiles: earnings "fan out" with age. Hence, because of the acquisition of more human capital by some than by others, the dispersion of earnings among older workers is expected to be greater than among younger workers.

EXAMPLE 9.6

Do Families Move Up and Down the Income Distribution?

As indicated in Tables 9.4 and 9.5, the distributions of family income in the United States and other countries are characterized by a good deal of inequality in any given year. These distributions are constructed, of course, by measuring the incomes of a cross section of families at a single point in time.

It is equally interesting, however, to follow specific families through time to see if they stay in the *same place* in the income distribution. If there is considerable movement up and down the income distribution by these families over the years, then the inequality observed at any point in time is tempered by the fact that, for many, their status is temporary. A longitudinal study of particular American families, involving comparisons of their place in the 1971 income distribution with their place in the 1978 income distribution, found considerable movement, as indicated below:

Of Those Families in the 1971 Income Quintiles Below:	The Below Percentages Were in the Indicated Income Quintiles in 1978:					
	Highest	Second	Third	Fourth	Lowest	Total
Highest	48.5	29.5	14.0	4.5	3.5	100%
Second	22.0	31.5	25.5	15.0	6.0	100%
Third	14.0	18.5	30.5	23.5	13.5	100%
Fourth	9.0	13.5	21.5	34.5	21.5	100%
Lowest	6.0	7.0	9.5	22.0	55.5	100%

The numbers above show that, of those in the lowest fifth of the income distribution in 1971, 55 percent were still in the lowest fifth in 1978; 22 percent had moved up one quintile, while 13 percent had made it to the upper two quintiles. Likewise, less than half of those in the upper fifth in 1971 were still there in 1978; most of the rest had moved down one quintile, but 8 percent had fallen to the bottom two quintiles. As can be seen from the underlined figures, which represent those families that were in the same quintile in both years, the income-distribution ranking occupied by specific families is generally more likely to change over time than it is to stay the same.

Why is there so much movement up and down the income distribution in such a short period of time (7 years)? Because it is family income that was measured, changes in family composition owing to marriage, divorce, or adult children leaving or re-entering the home can produce substantial changes in incomes. Further, entry and exit from the labor force associated with household production decisions, life-cycle changes, or disability and retirement can significantly affect family incomes, as can involuntary changes in employment status associated with unemployment. However, some of the changes are undoubtedly due to human capital factors mentioned or discussed in this chapter: earnings changes associated with acquiring or reaping the benefits of training or educational investments, relative changes in given occupational or regional wage rates, and the change in occupational choices made by individual workers.

SOURCE: Mark Lilla, "Why the 'Income Distribution' Is So Misleading," *Public Interest* 77 (Fall 1984): 62–76.

Put differently, the overall disparity in earnings is a combination of differences in average earnings across educational/demographic groups and differences in earnings among those *within* each of these groups. Human capital theory is central to an understanding of wage differences across educational groups, and it helps to explain at least some of the differences across age/gender groups. To fully explain earnings dispersion, however, one must also take into account discrimination, economic "rents" to individuals in groups to which entry is limited (unions, age cohorts, those with unique abilities), differences in hours worked, regional differences in wages and living costs, compensating wage differentials, and disequilibrium phenomena associated with recession, structural change, or random events.

Most of the above factors have been analyzed in attempts to understand changes in the earnings distribution in recent years. It is fair to say that no consensus has been reached regarding the magnitude of increased earnings inequality or its cause. The results of various analyses are highly dependent on the measure of earnings used; on whether groups are disaggregated by gender, age, or employment status; on the period of analysis; on the measure of inequality used (for some understanding of this issue, see Appendix 9B); and on how one handles such statistical issues as the treatment of missing sample observations.[43] Nevertheless, most observers would seem to agree on the following two points.[44]

First, there has been at least *some* growth in the disparity of earnings among men (although not necessarily women). A crude way to observe this growth in inequality is to calculate the ratio of wage and salary earnings of men at the boundary of the top 20 percent of the distribution to those at the boundary of the bottom 20 percent. In 1987, this ratio was 3.0 ($41,300/$13,588) for men aged 25–64, whereas a decade earlier it had been 2.5 ($22,119/$8,730). Note that the gap between these two points in the wage and salary distribution widened both proportionately and absolutely.

Second, the increased disparity has probably been caused more by changes *within* industries than by shifts in jobs from manufacturing to the service sector. To some extent these within-sector changes are due to the increased incidence of part-time and part-year work schedules associated with the deep recession of the early 1980s and the structural changes (for example, the decline of unions) brought about by increased world competition. There are also strong indications that the earnings of more highly educated workers have risen relative to those with less education.[45] Table 9.1 documented this rise

43. McKinley L. Blackburn and David E. Bloom, "Earnings and Income Inequality in the United States," *Population and Development Review* 13, no. 4 (December 1987): 575–609.
44. See Blackburn and Bloom, "Earnings and Income Inequality"; John Bound and George Johnson, "Changes in the Structure of Wages During the 1980s: An Evaluation of Alternative Explanations"; W. Norton Grubb and Robert H. Wilson, "Sources of Increasing Inequality in Wages and Salaries, 1960–80," *Monthly Labor Review* (April 1989): 3–13; Levy, *Dollars and Dreams,* 95–97; and Beach, "The 'Vanishing' Middle Class?"
45. Kevin M. Murphy and Finis Welch, "The Structure of Wages" (Los Angeles: Unicon Research Corporation, 1987); Chinhui Juhn, Kevin Murphy, and Brooks Pierce, "Wage Inequality and the Rise in Returns to Skill," Paper presented at the NBER Universities Research Conference, December 8–9, 1989, Cambridge, Mass.

from 1978 to 1985 for both men and women, and the returns to education continued their sharp growth into the late 1980s. By 1987, the income ratio of male college graduates, aged 25–34, to high school graduates of the same age reached 1.40 (compared to 1.11 in 1978); for women, the comparable ratio was 1.46 (up from 1.22 in 1978).

The rising relative pay of better-educated workers is consistent with the "vanishing middle class" hypothesis, which sees our economy as moving toward a polarized wage structure (good, "high-tech" jobs and low-paying service jobs). Human capital theory, however, suggests that a less pessimistic view may be warranted. As we have seen, the earnings advantage enjoyed by more-educated workers rises and falls, mostly because changes in this earnings differential call forth changes in post–high school enrollments. Because a larger supply of more highly educated workers eventually competes away any abnormally high returns to an educational investment, we can expect the disparity of earnings across educational levels to narrow again in the future.

Skewness of Earnings.   It has been a puzzle to people why the distribution of earnings is skewed. *If* ability is distributed symmetrically and is reflected in productivity, it would seem that earnings should be symmetrically distributed. Human capital theory suggests at least two reasons why, even if there *were* a symmetric distribution of ability, one would expect to find earnings skewed to the right.

First, it is true that *if* ability were symmetrically distributed and no one invested in education or training in order to enhance his or her productivity, the earnings distribution would be symmetric. However, the people who make investments that increase their earnings later in life tend to be high-ability people. Thus, while low-ability people tend to go through their careers with their productivity relatively unchanged by investment, high-ability people augment their productivity by investments. The more ability they have, the more they tend to invest. Thus, education and training tend to increase the earnings of workers in some rough proportion to their abilities, which extends—or *skews*—the distribution at the upper earnings levels.

Second, the discounting process aids the above forces in skewing the distribution of earnings. A person attending graduate school for one year after graduating from college incurs a greater cost and has a shorter time over which to obtain benefits than an undergraduate who decides to continue work toward a bachelor's degree for one more year. The graduate student has higher opportunity costs and is also older and just that much closer to retirement. Therefore, those considering ever-larger investments in schooling will require ever-larger payoffs per year (in the form of earnings increments). This need for ever-larger payoffs in order to encourage greater investments in human capital tends to skew the distribution of earnings. In effect, the larger costs and smaller remaining career life discourage most people from continuing to invest, which serves to more handsomely reward those who do undertake the investment (since they are "scarce"). Since these latter people tend to be those of highest ability (they are the ones who can learn with the most ease), the "rich get richer" and the distribution becomes skewed.

While one may be tempted to conclude from this analysis that human capital investments make the distribution of earnings more unequal than it would otherwise be, one must first consider two mitigating factors. First, human capital theory suggests that some of the inequality observed in earnings is a normal return on a prior investment; that is, it is compensation for an earlier period in one's life when earnings were low because time was being spent in the acquisition of human capital. Second, if access to colleges were severely limited, the lucky few able to advance themselves would reap very large rewards. This limitation on opportunities would impart an extreme skewness to the earnings distribution (a very few would get a lot, and most would earn very little). Thus, although human capital acquisition will impart a rightward skew, widespread availability of educational and training opportunities serves to reduce the skewness relative to what it would be with only limited access to these opportunities.

Policy Application: Human Capital and Earnings in Regulated Industries

Human capital theory can be useful in analyzing policy issues related to employee earnings. One such issue arises in the state regulation of monopolies. State commissions that regulate public utilities (such as telephone, electric, and gas companies) must decide whether all the costs that the utilities incur should be legitimately charged to consumers. It would be obvious to the commission that some costs should not be charged to consumers. For example, if an executive of a company had chartered a plane to take his family on a winter vacation to the Bahamas, surely that cost would be disallowed. Or if a construction contract were awarded to the friend of the president of a local utility without being submitted to competitive bidding, a commission might want to examine that contract closely to make sure the price charged was comparable to what other contractors in the area would have charged.

Deciding whether or not labor costs should be charged to consumers is more difficult. On the one hand, it is often conjectured that employers in regulated industries have less incentive to "bargain tough" with the unions that may represent their employees than do employers in nonregulated industries because, historically, regulatory commissions have allowed utilities to pass all labor cost increases on to consumers (in the form of higher utility prices). If such an argument is valid, it would indicate the need for commissions to carefully scrutinize utilities' wage settlements. On the other hand, it is difficult to decide what wage rates a commission should consider "just and reasonable." A utility's work force includes a number of different skill categories, as does the work force of other employers in an area, and making simple comparisons using raw wage-rate data would fail to take into account qualitative differences between work forces.

The human capital framework suggests a more appropriate comparison. According to this framework, better-educated workers receive higher wages than less-educated workers, and more-experienced workers get paid more than less-experienced workers. By statistically controlling for such worker characteristics as education and experience, it should be easier to see if employees in a regulated industry are paid more than employees in other firms. When such a comparison was made for telephone workers in New York State, it was found that the utility's employees were paid approximately 9–12 percent more than were other employees with comparable education and experience levels in the state in 1970.[46]

Such evidence in itself does not imply that a public commission should prevent a utility from passing all its labor cost increases on to consumers in the form of higher prices. For example, the wage premium might in some cases be seen as a compensating differential paid to the utility's employees for more difficult jobs or less favorable working conditions, as discussed in Chapter 8. Nevertheless, the human capital framework does provide a useful starting point for public utility commissions seeking to address the labor cost issue. In the case mentioned above, the commission decided not to limit the permissible wage increase but did reserve the right to limit future wage "pass-throughs" if similar comparative studies illustrated the need for such limits.

MISCONCEPTION

"Human capital theory says that highly educated people should earn more than those with less human capital, yet many workers with only high school educations earn more than those in the religious ministry with advanced degrees. The human capital theory of wage determination must be wrong."

Analysis

Human capital theory does *not* say that those with higher levels of educational achievement have a *moral* right to earn more. The theory *does* suggest that if education is not regarded as pure consumption, then to induce workers to obtain additional education they will have to obtain future benefits of great enough magnitude to outweigh the initial investment costs; these benefits, however, need not be solely pecuniary. In short, human capital theory is a theory of investment, not of wage determination. The theory does not claim to explain all sources of wage differentials, nor does it deny the importance of nonpecuniary factors in occupational choice. Those choosing to become religious workers may have such strong preferences for what they regard as meaningful work that they are willing to take a lower wage to do that kind of work.

Principle

Predictions of positive economics involve the influence of one variable on another, holding all *other* variables constant.

---

46. Ronald G. Ehrenberg, *The Regulatory Process and Labor Earnings* (New York: Academic Press, 1979).

REVIEW QUESTIONS

1. Women receive lower wages, on average, than men of equal age. What concepts of human capital help to explain this phenomenon? Explain. Why does the discrepancy between earnings for men and women grow with age?

2. Suppose financial aid to college students were financed by income taxes on the general population and the President cut this aid significantly (correspondingly cutting taxes). Analyzing the likely *labor market* effects of these cuts, identify the various groups that would *gain* and *lose* from these cuts over their lifetimes. Discuss your reasoning concerning each in turn. Then analyze the likely effects on the retirement ages of these groups.

3. Many crimes against property (burglary, for example) can be thought of as acts that have immediate gains but entail long-run costs (sooner or later the criminal may be caught and imprisoned). If imprisoned, the criminal loses income from both criminal and noncriminal activities. Using the framework for occupational choice in the long run, analyze what kinds of people are most likely to engage in criminal activities. What can society do to reduce crime?

4. Suppose education provided no *social* benefits of any kind; that is, it did not enhance worker productivity and did not accurately "signal" who was already more productive. What conditions would have to hold to create a positive *individual* return to education in this circumstance?

5. Why do those who argue that more education "signals" greater ability believe that the most able people will obtain the most education?

6. Most societies are concerned about the distribution of economic resources across their populations, and the focus is often on the distribution of earnings. Using human capital theory, evaluate the use of statistics on the distribution of *earnings* as a means of gauging the distribution of *wealth* in a society.

7. In many countries higher education is heavily subsidized by the government (that is, university students do not bear the full cost of their college education). While there may be good reasons for heavily subsidizing university education, there are also some dangers in it. Using human capital theory, explain what these dangers are.

8. "The vigorous pursuit by a society of tax policies that tend to equalize wages across skill groups will frustrate the goal of optimum resource allocation." Comment.

9. Suppose that you are in charge of evaluating a vocational rehabilitation program. The program has a goal of increasing the earnings capabilities of those who have become disabled, and your job is to assess whether, from a social perspective, the program is improving social welfare. What types of information would you need to make a judgment about the vocational rehabilitation program you are asked to study? How would you go about using the information you receive?

SELECTED READINGS

Becker, Gary. *Human Capital*. New York: National Bureau of Economic Research, 1975.

Bluestone, Barry, and Harrison, Bennett. *The Great U-Turn: Corporate Restructuring and the Polarization of America*. New York: Basic Books, 1988.

Borjas, George J. "Earnings Determination: A Survey of the Neoclassical Approach." In *Three Worlds of Labor Economics,* ed. Garth Mangum and Peter Philips. Armonk, N.Y.: M. E. Sharpe, 1988.

Freeman, Richard B. *The Overeducated American*. New York: Academic Press, 1976.

Levy, Frank. *Dollars and Dreams*. New York: Norton, 1988.

Manski, Charles F., and Wise, David A. *College Choice in America.* Cambridge, Mass.: Harvard University Press, 1983.

Mincer, Jacob. *Schooling, Experience and Earnings.* New York: National Bureau of Economic Research, 1974.

Mincer, Jacob, and Polachek, Solomon. "Family Investments in Human Capital: Earnings of Women." *Journal of Political Economy* 82 (March/April 1974): S76–S108.

Schultz, Theodore. *The Economic Value of Education.* New York: Columbia University Press, 1963.

Spence, Michael. "Job Market Signaling." *Quarterly Journal of Economics* 87 (August 1973): 355–74.

APPENDIX 9A

"Signaling" in the Labor Market

Chapter 9 discussed both the private and the social benefits of education and stressed that individuals will undertake an educational investment if the long-run gains to them outweigh the monetary and psychic costs. *Societal* decisions to invest in education should likewise be made only if the social gains outweigh the social losses; however, Chapter 9 noted that there is a rather lively debate about the nature and extent of the social benefits of formal education. Some believe that education *enhances* worker productivity, while others believe that, at best, education simply *reveals*—or "signals"—the inherent productivity of workers.

This appendix will delve into the signaling aspect of formal education in greater depth.[1] It will analyze the benefits and costs of educational signaling to workers and firms in an example in which it is assumed that education does *not* enhance productivity. Initially, however, it is important to understand just what signaling is and why it exists.

An employer seeking to hire workers is never completely sure of the actual productivity of any applicant, and in many cases the employer may remain unsure long after an employee is hired. What an employer *can* observe are certain *indicators* that firms have found (or otherwise believe) to be correlated with productivity: age, race, gender, experience, education, and other personal characteristics. Some of these indicators—such as race and gender—are immutable. Others, like formal schooling, can be *acquired* by workers. Indicators that can be acquired by individuals can be called *signals;* our analysis will focus on the signaling aspect of formal education.

THE FIRM'S DESIRE FOR SIGNALS

Let us suppose that firms trying to hire new employees in a particular labor market know there are two groups of applicants that exist in roughly equal proportions. One group has a productivity of 2, let us say, and the other group

---

1. This appendix is based on Michael Spence, "Job Market Signaling," *Quarterly Journal of Economics* 87 (August 1973): 355–74.

has a productivity of 1. In the absence of screening or applicant signaling, firms would be forced to assume that workers in this market had average productivities of 1.5 and would offer wages up to 1.5.

While workers in this simple example would be receiving what they were worth on *average,* any one firm could increase its profits if it were possible (at no cost) to distinguish between the two groups of applicants. When wages equal 1.5, workers with productivities equal to 1 are receiving more than they are worth. If these applicants could be identified, a firm could increase profits by rejecting their applications and hiring only those with a productivity of 2. These gains might be short-lived if other firms did the same and drove the wage for the more productive workers up to 2. However, the individual firms in a competitive market cannot control or affect the behavior of competitors, and screening would occur as each sought to obtain maximum profit.[2]

WORKER SUPPLY OF SIGNALS

To continue with our example, suppose that firms believe that an applicant who has acquired e^* or more years of schooling has a productivity of 2. An applicant with less than e^* years of formal education is believed to have a productivity of 1. Let us also assume that education does *not* enhance productivity. In what situations, if any, could this use of schooling as a screening device be productive? The answer is that educational signaling can be useful only if the costs to the worker of acquiring the signal are negatively related to productivity.

If firms use e^* as a hiring standard, applicants with schooling of e^* or greater will be preferred if wages for all workers are equal; their wages will eventually be driven up to 2, while those with less than e^* will obtain wages of 1 (see Figure 9A.1). If all applicants could acquire e^* at no cost, they would obviously do so and this screening device would fail; workers of both productivity levels would have at least e^* years of schooling. As we argued in Chapter 9, however, formal schooling is not costless. Furthermore, we also argued that the *psychic* costs of education are probably inversely related to one's ability: those who learn easily can acquire the educational signal (of e^* in this case) more cheaply than others. If—and this is crucial—those who have *lower* costs of acquiring education are *also* more productive on the job, then educational signaling can be useful.

To understand the role of costs in signaling, refer to Figure 9A.2, in which the reward structure from Figure 9A.1 is reproduced. If we assume that each year of education costs those with less productivity C and those with greater productivity $C/2$, the fundamental influences on worker choices concerning education are easily seen. Workers will want to choose a level of education at which the difference between benefits (wages) and educational costs

---

2. The phenomenon here is very similar to the entry of firms into markets with excess profits. The gains from entry are short-lived because the entry of others will drive profits down to the normal level. Individual firms, however, react to the presence of excess profits nevertheless, expecting to catch "a piece of the action" and hoping no one else will be quite as smart as they are!

FIGURE 9A.1   The Benefits to Workers of Educational Signaling

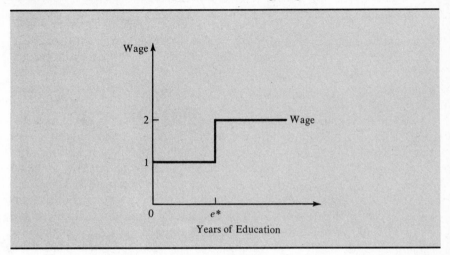

is maximized. For those with a productivity of 1 and marginal educational costs of C, the difference between wages and costs is greatest when years of schooling equal zero (distance $A0$). For those whose marginal educational costs are $C/2$, this difference is maximized at e^* (where it equals BD, which is greater than $A0$). Thus, only those with costs of $C/2$—the workers with productivities of 2—acquire e^* years of school.

FIGURE 9A.2   The Benefits and Costs to Workers of Educational Signaling

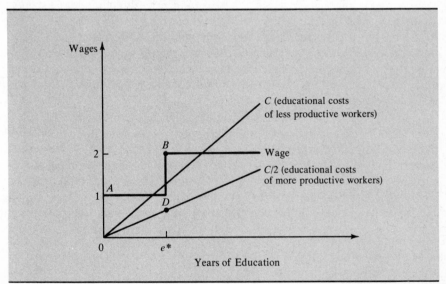

THE USEFULNESS OF EDUCATIONAL SIGNALING

Several points should be made about our simple example of signaling above. First, workers may not think of themselves as acquiring a signal if they attend school, even though in our example they are. All most workers will know is that by obtaining more education they can increase their wages, and their decision about how much education to acquire depends on the costs and returns to them.

Second, our simple example demonstrated how education could have signaling value even if it did not directly enhance worker productivity. It is necessary to stress, though, that for education to have signaling value in this case, on-the-job productivity and the costs of education must be *negatively* related. This negative relationship is by no means universally accepted, and there are even those who assert that better-educated workers are actually *less* productive.[3] However, if education is *not* a good signal for productivity, firms should eventually find this out and stop using formal schooling as a screening device! (The argument that education will survive as a signal for productivity only if it is an accurate indicator does not suggest, of course, that firms will learn about signaling errors immediately.)

Third, if the signal required by firms were reduced from e^* to e' (in Figure 9A.3), the signaling value of education would be lost. Workers of both productivity levels would find it beneficial to acquire the signal of e' because the distance $A0$ is exceeded by DG for the less productive and by DB for the more productive. Education would cease to be a good screening device for employers to use. A signal of e' could not be an equilibrium signal in the long run, because employers would eventually learn that not all workers with e' years of education have a productivity of 2. They would either have to give up on screening and pay a wage of 1.5 or increase hiring standards.

Fourth, increases in the educational signal beyond e^* in our example are not productive. A look back at Figure 9A.2 indicates that individual workers with yearly educational costs of $C/2$ have no incentives to obtain more schooling than e^*, because such schooling is costly but results in no higher wage offer. Moreover, if firms increased their minimum hiring standard from e^* to e'' (Figure 9A.3), the signaling value of education would again be lost. Even the more productive workers would not have incentives to acquire an education (because $A0$ exceeds EF), and firms could not distinguish between the two kinds of workers.

Finally, there *is* an optimum educational signal in our example: the minimum schooling level that successfully distinguishes between the two types of workers. Optimality is reached *just to the right of* e^{**} in Figure 9A.4. A required signal of just beyond e^{**} is one that will be acquired by workers of productivity 2, but it will not be acquired by those with productivity 1. If the required signal were reduced below e^{**}, both kinds of workers would acquire it and signaling value would be lost. If the required signal were increased much beyond e^{**}—to e^*, say—the signal would still be accurate but would cost more

---

3. See Ivar Berg, *Education and Jobs: The Great Training Robbery* (New York: Praeger Publishers, 1970), 85–104, which questions the social value of educational investments.

FIGURE 9A.3   Signaling Failures

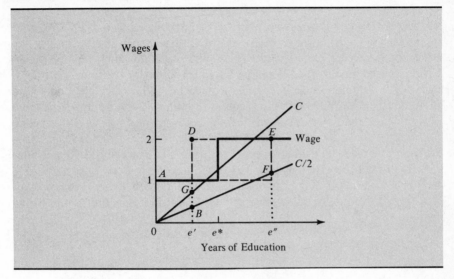

than necessary. Put differently, if e^* were required, the more productive workers would acquire it and the less productive ones would not. However, the extra $e^* - e^{**}$ years in school would entail social costs for which there were no benefits because e^{**} distinguishes between the two types of workers just as well as e^*. The critics of education mentioned in Chapter 9 argue that the escalation of educational standards has occurred for jobs in which work requirements are largely unchanged. These critics can be understood as saying that

FIGURE 9A.4   The Optimum Educational Signal

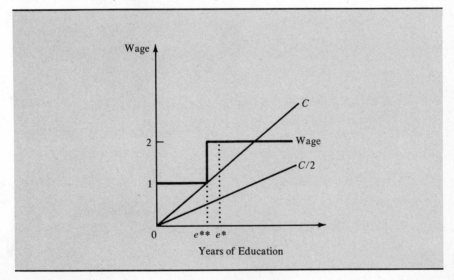

firms require e^* when e^{**} would distinguish between workers just as well and be much less costly.[4]

Are there market forces pushing the required signal toward e^{**}? We have argued that a required signal below e^{**} would be unable to discriminate between applicants and would eventually be abandoned by employers. However, if the required signal were initially e^*, there would *also* be forces pushing it back to e^{**}, although these influences take us beyond our simple model with its fixed wages. Workers who have acquired e^* years of education will be more costly to hire than workers acquiring e^{**} because they will want to recoup their educational costs. Noting their higher asking wage, some firms may experiment and hire applicants with only e^{**} years of schooling. If these latter workers proved to be just as productive as those with e^* years of schooling, the firms that experimented would be rewarded with extra profits. Other firms would eventually follow, and e^{**} would become the equilibrium hiring standard.

---

4. See Berg, *Education and Jobs,* 38–60.

APPENDIX 9B

Measuring Inequality

As indicated near the end of Chapter 9, the *distribution* of earnings or incomes attracts considerable attention. Often, economists are interested in assessing whether earnings or incomes are becoming more or less equally distributed, or in how equal they are in one country compared with another. This appendix offers a brief introduction to some of the alternative measures of distributional inequality that have been employed, and it briefly discusses their strengths and weaknesses. For expositional simplicity, we focus our discussion on inequality in *incomes;* however, the concepts discussed could also be applied to analyses of *earnings* distributions.

The most obvious measure of inequality, suggested by Figure 9.15, is the *variance* of the distribution. Variance is a common measure of dispersion, and it is calculated as follows:

$$\text{Variance} = \frac{\sum_i (E_i - \overline{E})^2}{n} \tag{9B.1}$$

where E_i represents the income of person i in the population, n represents the number of people in the population, $\overline{E}$ is the mean level of income in the population, and the symbol Σ indicates that we are summing over all persons in the population. One problem with using the variance, however, is that it tends to rise as incomes grow larger. For example, if all incomes in the population were to double, so that the ratio of each person's income to the mean (or to the income of anyone else, for that matter) remained constant, the variance would still quadruple. Clearly, variance is a better measure of the absolute than of the relative dispersion of incomes.

An alternative to the variance is the *coefficient of variation:* the square root of the variance (called the "standard deviation") divided by the mean. If all earnings were to double, the coefficient of variation, unlike the variance, would remain unchanged. The problem with this measure is that the variance (and therefore the coefficient of variation) will fall just as much if the richest person gives a dollar to the next richest one as it will if the dollar is given to the poorest person. For example, suppose there are five people in a population, with incomes of 2, 4, 6, 8, and 10 dollars, respectively. If a dollar is taken from the richest person and given to someone else, the coefficient of variation is the same whether the resultant distribution is 3, 4, 6, 8, 9 or 2, 4, 6, 9, 9. Since the most commonsense notion of equality suggests that the former distribution is more equal than the latter, because the ends of the distribution are closer together, the coefficient of variation is not widely used to measure inequality.

The most commonly used measures of distributional inequality involve dividing the distribution into quintiles.[1] As we did in Chapter 9 when attempting to assess whether it is earnings or incomes that are more equally distributed, one can simply measure the absolute or relative differences between the income level at the 20th percentile and the level at the 80th percentile. A richer and more fully descriptive measure, however, would employ data on the *share of total income* received by those *in each quintile*. Data such as these were presented earlier in Table 9.4, but a visual aid is frequently used to summarize and compare distributions. We discuss this visual aid below.

Suppose that each person in the population has the same income. In this case of perfect equality, each fifth of the population has a fifth of the total income. In graphic terms, this equality can be shown by the straight line *AB* in Figure 9B.1, which plots the cumulative share of income (vertical axis) received by each quintile and the ones below it (horizontal axis). Thus, the first quintile (with a 0.2 share, or 20 percent of all workers) would receive a 0.2 share (20 percent) of total income, the first and second quintiles (four-tenths of the population) would receive four-tenths of total income, and so forth.

If the distribution of income is not perfectly equal, then the curve connecting the cumulative percentages of income received by the cumulated quintiles—the *Lorenz curve*—is convex and lies below the line of perfect equality. For example, if the 1987 income data for the United States (in Table 9.4) are plotted in Figure 9B.1, the curve *ACDEFB* emerges. This curve displays the convexity one would expect from the clearly unequal income distribution that exists in the United States.

Comparing the equality of two different income distributions results in unambiguous conclusions if one Lorenz curve lies completely inside the other (closer to the line of perfect equality). If, for example, we were interested in comparing the American income distributions of 1967 and 1987, we could observe that plotting the 1967 data results in a Lorenz curve, *AcdefB* in Figure 9B.1, that lies everywhere closer to the line of perfect equality than the one for 1987.

If two Lorenz curves cross, however, conclusions about which one represents greater equality are not possible. Comparing curves *A* and *B* in Figure 9B.2, for example, one can see that the distribution represented by *A*

---

1. This involves ranking incomes (or earnings) in a population from lowest to highest, and then dividing them into five equal-size groups. The use of quintiles, while common, is arbitrary. One could just as easily divide the population into ten equal-size groups and base the analyses on the incomes or earnings in each *decile*.

FIGURE 9B.1   Lorenz Curves for 1967 and 1987 Distributions of Income in United States

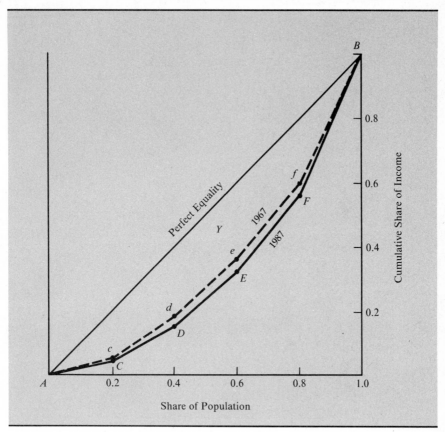

has a lower proportion of total income received by the poorest quintile than does the distribution represented by curve *B*; however, the cumulative share of income received by the lowest two quintiles (taken together) is equal for *A* and *B*, and the cumulative proportions received by the bottom three and bottom four quintiles are higher for *A* than for *B*.

Another measure of inequality, which seems at first glance to yield unambiguous answers when various distributions are compared, is the *Gini coefficient:* the ratio of the area between the Lorenz curve and the line of perfect equality (the area labeled *Y* in Figure 9B.1) to the total area under the line of perfect equality. Obviously, with perfect equality the Gini coefficient would equal zero.

One way to calculate the Gini coefficient is to split the area under the Lorenz curve into a series of triangles and rectangles, as shown in Figure 9B.3 (which repeats the Lorenz curve for 1987 shown in Figure 9B.1). Each triangle has a base equal to 0.2—the horizontal distance for each of the five quintiles—and a height equal to the percentage of income received by that quintile (the cumulative percentage less the percentages received by lower quintiles). Because the base of each triangle is the same and their heights sum to unity,

FIGURE 9B.2 Lorenz Curves That Cross

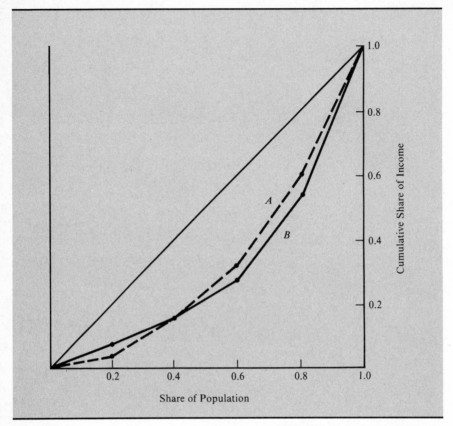

the *sum* of the areas of each triangle is always equal to $0.5 \times 0.2 \times 1.0 = 0.1$ (one-half base times height).

The rectangles in Figure 9B.3 all have one side equal to 0.2 and another equal to the cumulated percentages of total income received by the previous quintiles. Rectangle $Q_1CC'Q_2$, for example, has an area of $0.2 \times 0.046 = 0.0092$, while $Q_2DD'Q_3$ has an area of $0.2 \times 0.154 = 0.0308$. Analogously, $Q_3EE'Q_4$ has an area of 0.0646 and $Q_4FF'Q_5$ an area of 0.1128; together, all four rectangles in Figure 9B.3 have an area that sums to 0.2174.

The area under the Lorenz curve in Figure 9B.3 is thus $0.2174 + 0.1 = 0.3174$. Given that the total area under the line of perfect equality is $0.5 \times 1 \times 1 = 0.5$, the Gini coefficient for 1987 is calculated as follows:

$$\text{Gini coefficient (1987)} = \frac{0.5 - 0.3174}{0.5} = 0.3652 \qquad (9B.2)$$

For comparison purposes, the Gini coefficient for the income distribution in 1967 can be calculated as 0.3578—which, because it lies closer to zero than the Gini coefficient for 1987, is evidence of greater equality in 1967.

FIGURE 9B.3   Calculating the Gini Coefficient for 1987

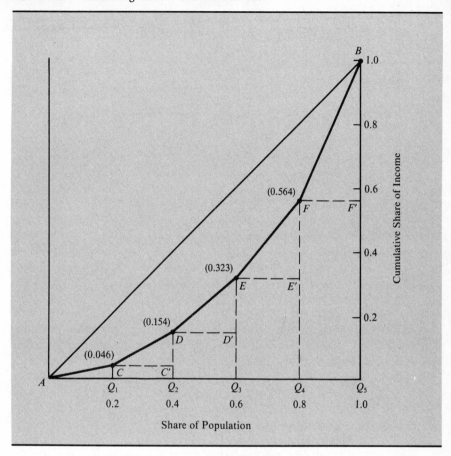

Unfortunately, the Gini coefficient will become smaller when the rich give up some of their income to the middle class as well as when they give up income in favor of the poor. That is, the Gini coefficient has some of the same drawbacks as the coefficient of variation, and it may yield a "definitive" answer about comparative equality when none is warranted. As we saw in the case of Figure 9B.2, in which the Lorenz curves being compared cross, judging the relative equality of two distributions is not always susceptible of an unambiguous answer.

10

Worker Mobility: Turnover and Migration

A salient fact about the U.S. economy is the high degree of mobility among its workers. The monthly quit rate in manufacturing industries is 1–3 percent per month, which implies a yearly turnover rate of 12–36 percent. Chapter 8 noted that at least 9 percent of workers in 1982 were employed in *different occupations* by 1983. Roughly 25 percent of all workers change the industry in which they work over a three-year period.[1] Moreover, in many cases job mobility is accompanied by geographic mobility. In a recent one-year period (1986–87), for example, almost 3 percent of employed individuals moved between states; for those in their twenties the figure was 5 percent.[2] Finally, the United States admits over 600,000 legal immigrants each year, and the discrepancy between the numbers who want to come and the numbers permitted by law is so great that hundreds of thousands more enter illegally. As of 1985, the U.S. Bureau of the Census estimated that there were between 3 and 5 million illegal immigrants who had settled in the United States.[3]

This mobility is not without its costs. Sometimes a temporary loss of income occurs between the time one job is given up and a new one, perhaps in a new place, is obtained. There are direct moving costs when migration occurs. Psychic costs are associated with leaving a familiar job or place and having to become acquainted with a new environment. There can be no doubt, then, that large monetary and psychic costs are borne each year by large num-

---

1. Lowell E. Gallaway, *Interindustry Labor Mobility in the United States, 1957 to 1960,* Social Security Administration Research Report no. 18 (Washington, D.C.: U.S. Government Printing Office, 1967), 29.
2. U.S. Bureau of the Census, *Geographical Mobility: March 1986 to March 1987,* Current Population Reports, Series P-20, no. 430 (April 1989), Table B.
3. U.S. President, *Economic Report of the President, 1986* (Washington, D.C.: U.S. Government Printing Office, 1986), 219.

bers of people wanting to improve their lot in life. In this sense mobility represents a significant investment in human capital. Costs are borne in the short run so that benefits will be possible in the long run. The human capital model of mobility described in this chapter offers some clear-cut implications about who invests in mobility and where they go.

The basic human capital model of mobility is a model of "voluntary" mobility undertaken by workers who perceive mobility to be in their self-interest. The factors influencing employer-initiated mobility—layoffs, for example— are quite different, as discussed in Chapter 5.[4] The determinants of voluntary mobility are discussed first, and later in the chapter the testable implications of human capital theory for both migration and job-quitting behavior are analyzed. The chapter will conclude with an economic analysis of immigration and its implications for national policy.

THE DETERMINANTS OF WORKER MOBILITY

The human capital model presented in Chapter 9 can be used to understand and predict worker-initiated mobility. This model views voluntary mobility as an investment in which costs are borne in some early period in order to obtain returns over a longer period of time. If the present value of the benefits associated with mobility exceeds the costs, both monetary and psychic, we assume that people will decide to change jobs or move, or both. If the discounted stream of benefits is not as large as the costs, then people will decide against such a change.

What determines the present value of the net benefits of mobility—that is, the benefits minus the costs—determines the mobility decision. These factors can be better identified by writing out the formula one would use if one were to precisely calculate these net benefits:

$$\text{Present Value of Net Benefits} = \sum_{t=1}^{T} \frac{B_{jt} - B_{ot}}{(1 + r)^t} - C \qquad (10.1)$$

where:

B_{jt} = the utility derived from the new job (j) in the year t;
B_{ot} = the utility derived from the old job (o) in the year t;
T = the length of time (in years) one expects to work at job j;
r = the rate of discount;
C = the utility lost in the move itself (direct and psychic costs); and
Σ = a summation—in this case the summation of the yearly discounted net benefits over a period running from year 1 to year T.

Clearly, the present value of the net benefits of mobility will be larger the greater is the utility derived from the new job, the less happy one is in the job of origin, the smaller are the immediate costs associated with the change, and

---

4. The distinction between "employee-initiated" and "employer-initiated" mobility is more apparent than real, as we point out later in this chapter.

EXAMPLE 10.1

Job Satisfaction: An Alternative View

In the past decade or so, managers and researchers have expressed much interest in job satisfaction, and most are inclined to view dissatisfaction as a result of employer policies concerning job tasks, working conditions, or compensation. Economists, however, view the phenomenon of job satisfaction somewhat differently. Workers are viewed as making choices of jobs and employers from among competing alternatives; if they are unhappy in a particular occupation or with a particular employer, they will be motivated to seek other employment. Moreover, as noted in Chapter 8, pecuniary and nonpecuniary aspects of jobs are viewed as substitutes for each other; higher wages, for example, might compensate for poor working conditions and lead to overall satisfaction with one's job. Thus, economists tend to view job satisfaction as an outcome of the employer/worker *matching* process and not solely as the result of employer policies. If the matching process is impeded by factors inhibiting mobility, workers may be "stuck" in jobs they dislike. If workers are aware of alternatives and are able to leave jobs that are unsatisfactory for them, they should eventually find something close to their best option.

A survey of job satisfaction around 1970 found that 47 percent of all workers were "very satisfied" with their jobs and 38 percent were "somewhat satisfied," while only 15 percent were either "not too satisfied" or "not at all satisfied." A more sophisticated statistical analysis of job satisfaction responses in this survey found that workers were more likely to indicate feelings of satisfaction as they became older and as their *actual* earnings exceeded an estimate of their *alternative* earnings.

Taken together, the above results offer some support for economists' views. The small number of people who report themselves even mildly dissatisfied, coupled with the finding that dissatisfaction falls with age, suggests that job mobility may be an antidote for dissatisfaction. It appears that employees "try out" occupations and employers and leave situations they dislike. If they realize that the job they have is on the whole better-paying than their alternatives, they express greater satisfaction and are presumably less likely to leave it. Thus, a trial-and-error process, fueled by information about one's alternatives, may well be at work producing generally satisfactory matches between workers and jobs in the long run.

SOURCE: Daniel S. Hamermesh, "The Economics of Job Satisfaction," Technical Analysis Paper no. 22, Office of the Assistant Secretary for Policy, Evaluation, and Research, U.S. Department of Labor, May 1974, Appendix. A revised version of this paper, without the appendix, was published with the same title in *Essays in Labor Market Analysis*, ed. Orley Ashenfelter and Wallace Oates (New York: John Wiley & Sons, 1978).

the longer one expects to be in the new job or live in the new area (that is, the greater is T). These observations lead to some clear-cut predictions about which groups in society will be most mobile and about the *patterns* of mobility one would expect to observe. These predictions are analyzed in the following sections on migration and quit behavior.

GEOGRAPHIC MOBILITY

When people are asked about their reasons for moving, 70–85 percent of them cite economic reasons. While about one-third of those who moved to a different area in the late 1960s or early 1970s stayed with their current employers, in about two-thirds of the cases a change in employer took place. Taking into account those who say their moves were motivated by economic factors and who also changed jobs, it appears that roughly one-half of all moves are caused by the decision to change jobs.[5] This emphasis on job change suggests that the implications of human capital theory for migration can be tested in the labor market.

Comparing Wages and Employment Opportunities

If job changes are the dominant factor motivating mobility, then we should observe people migrating from areas where wages and employment opportunities are relatively poor to areas where they are relatively good. Three interrelated patterns of internal migration can be observed in the United States over recent decades: rural-to-urban shifts, the movement of blacks, and the interregional flows of people.

Rural-to-Urban Movements.   Huge movements of people from rural to urban areas have occurred in this century as farming jobs have diminished in number. In 1910, 54 percent of the U.S. population lived in rural areas—that is, areas with fewer than 2,500 inhabitants. By 1980 this percentage had stabilized at 26 percent. In the 1960s alone, farming employment fell by 40 percent, and the rural areas of California, the Dakotas, Nebraska, and Kansas experienced population losses of 10–16 percent. Interestingly enough, the *overall* rural population fell by only 0.9 percent during the 1960s, while it rose by the same percentage (11 percent) as the urban population in the 1970s. This recent change reflects, to a large degree, the extension of suburban areas into neighboring rural counties and thus does not contradict our observation that people move to where the jobs are.

Migration of Blacks.   A dramatic characteristic of rural–urban migration in this century has been the massive movement of blacks out of the rural South to urban areas in the non-South. This movement began during World War I, when wartime production created jobs in the urbanized, industrial states in the North. In the 1920s this migration continued as 800,000 blacks left the South, headed primarily for big cities in the North. This flow was cut in half during the 1930s, when the Great Depression diminished job opportunities in the industrial sector, but rose to 1.6 million during the war-dominated 1940s. In the essentially prosperous decades of the 1950s and 1960s, 2.9 million more blacks left the South.

---

5. Ann P. Bartel, "The Migration Decision: What Role Does Job-Mobility Play?" *American Economic Review* 69 (December 1979): 775–86. See also Larry Schroeder, "Interrelatedness of Occupational and Geographical Labor Mobility," *Industrial and Labor Relations Review* 29 (April 1976): 405–11.

Undoubtedly part of the migration of blacks reflected the decline in farming employment. Many southern states had also experienced outflows of whites. More whites left the states of Alabama, Kentucky, Oklahoma, and West Virginia during the 1950s and 1960s than entered them, while Arkansas, the Carolinas, Georgia, Mississippi, and Tennessee experienced outmigration of whites in the 1950s but net in-migration of whites during the 1960s.

That the migration of blacks out of the South was not completely due to the decline in agricultural jobs is clearly indicated by the fact that while blacks were *leaving* the South during the 1960s, whites were, on balance, *flowing into* the South as jobs there expanded. Because basic federal civil rights laws concerning segregation and voting were not passed until the mid-'60s and programs aimed at eliminating job discrimination were not implemented until the late '60s, it is not far-fetched to speculate that much of the black migration out of the South was induced by perceptions of greater freedom and opportunities elsewhere. As discrimination lessened in the 1970s, however, and blacks began to share in the general economic expansion under way in the South, there was, on balance, a movement of blacks *into* the South. Between 1970 and 1980 there was a net influx of 209,000 blacks into the South—the first time this had occurred in the 20th century. This movement of blacks to the South continued in the 1980s; the net inflow in 1987, for example, was 148,000. Interestingly, migration of blacks to the South is now far greater than to any other region.[6]

Regional Migration.   Further evidence to support the view that people move from regions where opportunities are poor to regions where they are better can be found by examining regional migration. The older, slow-growing industrial states of New York, Pennsylvania, Ohio, Illinois, and Michigan are experiencing outmigration, while the faster-growing states in the South and West are the recipients of an influx of migrants. During 1986–87, for example, the Northeast and Midwest regions of the United States had a net outflow of 445,000 people, while the South and West had net inflows of 279,000 and 166,000, respectively. The net inflow to the South is a complete turnaround from the 1950s, when the region was largely rural and offered relatively few job opportunities. As the South has industrialized, *real* wages there have risen, so that by the late 1970s the real wages received by urban workers in the South exceeded those typically received by urban workers of comparable skill in each of the other regions.[7] Not surprisingly, then, the South has become the region with the highest net flows of in-migrants.

Human capital theory predicts that people will move from areas of relatively poor earnings possibilities to places where opportunities are better. While the general regional flows of people support this prediction, the predic-

---

6. U.S. Bureau of the Census, *Statistical Abstract of the United States: 1982–83* (December 1982), Table 13. Other data in this section were obtained from the *Manpower Report of the President,* 1974, 90–97; U.S. Bureau of the Census, *Statistical Abstract of the U.S.,* 99th ed. (Washington, D.C.: U.S. Government Printing Office, 1978), Table 26; and U.S. Bureau of the Census, *Geographical Mobility: March 1986 to March 1987,* Current Population Reports, Series P-20, no. 430 (April 1989), Table G.

7. Leonard G. Sahling and Sharon P. Smith, "Regional Wage Differentials: Has the South Risen Again?" *Review of Economics and Statistics* 65, no. 1 (February 1983): 131–35.

tion can also be tested by looking at the characteristics of more specific areas from which and to which people move. In general, the results of such studies suggest that the "pull" of good opportunities in the areas of destination are stronger than the "push" of poor opportunities in the areas of origin. In other words, while people are more attracted to places where earnings are expected to be better, they do not necessarily come from areas where opportunities are poorest.

The most consistent finding in these detailed studies is that people are attracted to areas where the real earnings of full-time workers are highest. One might also expect that the chances for obtaining work in a new area would also affect that area's attractiveness. One way to measure job availability in an area is to use the unemployment rate, but the studies find no consistent relationship between unemployment and in-migration, perhaps because the number of people moving with a job already in hand is three times as large as the number moving *to look* for work.[8] If one already has a job in a particular field, the area's unemployment rate is irrelevant.

Most studies have found that, contrary to what one might expect, the characteristics of the place of origin do not appear to have much net influence on migration. One reason for this finding is that while those in the poorest places have the greatest *incentives* to move, the very poorest areas also tend to have people with lower levels of wealth, education, and skills—the very people who seem least *willing* (or able) to move. To understand this phenomenon, we must turn from the issue of *where* people go to a discussion of *who* is most likely to move.

Personal Characteristics of Movers

Migration is highly selective in the sense that it is not an activity in which all people are equally likely to be engaged. To be specific, mobility is much higher among the young and the better-educated, as human capital theory would suggest.

Age.   Age is the single most important factor in determining who migrates. The peak years for mobility are the ages 20–24; 13 percent of this age group migrates across county or state lines each year. By age 35 the rate of migration is half what it was for those in their early twenties, and by age 45 it is only one-third as high.

There are two explanations for the fact that migration is an activity primarily for the young. First, the younger one is, the greater the potential returns from any human capital investment. As noted earlier, the longer the

8. John B. Lansing and Eva Mueller, *The Geographic Mobility of Labor* (Ann Arbor: Survey Research Center, University of Michigan, 1967), 37. In fact, the level of *new hires* in an area appears to explain migration flows much better than the unemployment rate; see, for example, Gary Fields, "Place to Place Migration: Some New Evidence," *Review of Economics and Statistics* 61, no. 1 (February 1979): 21–32. For a more general review of empirical findings on migration, see Michael Greenwood, "Research on Internal Migration in the United States: A Survey," *Journal of Economic Literature* 13 (June 1975): 397–433. Further, Robert H. Topel, "Local Labor Markets," *Journal of Political Economy* 94, no. 3, pt. 2 (June 1986): S111–S143, contains an analysis of how permanent and transitory shifts in an area's demand affect migration and wages.

TABLE 10.1   **Migration Rates for Men and Women 30–34, by Educational Level, 1986–87 (in percentages)**

Educational Level (in Years)	Moving Between Counties Within States		Moving Between States	
	Men	Women	Men	Women
9–11	5.8	5.7	2.8	1.8
12	4.8	3.1	2.6	2.2
13–15	4.8	4.8	3.7	3.6
16	5.1	4.5	5.2	4.8
17 or more	5.1	6.7	6.4	4.8

SOURCE: U.S. Bureau of the Census, *Geographical Mobility: March 1986 to March 1987,* Population Characteristics, Series P-20, no. 430, Table 24.

period over which benefits from an investment can be obtained, the larger the present value of these benefits.

Second, a large part of the costs of migration are psychic—the losses associated with giving up friends, community ties, and the benefits of knowing one's way around. When one is starting out as an adult, these losses are comparatively small because one is not well established in the adult world. However, as one grows older, community ties become stronger and the losses associated with leaving loom larger, thus inhibiting mobility. This line of reasoning is underscored by the fact that, within age groups, unmarried people are more likely to migrate than married ones, and married people without children are more mobile than those with children.[9]

Education.   While age is probably the best predictor of who will move, education is the single best indicator of who will move *within* an age group. As can be seen from Table 10.1, more education does make one more likely to move; however, it is a *college* education that raises the probability of migrating the most. The labor markets for college-educated workers are more likely to be regional or national than are the labor markets for those with less education.

One cost of migration is that of ascertaining *where* opportunities are and *how good* they are likely to be. If one's occupation has a national labor market, for example, it is relatively easy to find out about opportunities in distant places. Jobs are advertised in national newspapers. Recruiters from all over visit college campuses. Employment agencies make nationwide searches. In cases such as these, people usually move with a job already in hand.

However, if the relevant labor market for one's job is localized, it is difficult to find out where opportunities might be better. For a janitor in Beaumont, Texas, to find out about employment opportunities in the north-central region is like looking for the proverbial needle in a haystack. That such moves occur at all, let alone in reasonably large numbers, is testimony to the fact that people are able to acquire information despite the obstacles.

---

9. See Jacob Mincer, "Family Migration Decisions," *Journal of Political Economy* 86, no. 5 (October 1978): 749–73.

The Role of Distance

Human capital theory clearly predicts that as migration costs rise, the flow of migrants will fall. The costs of moving increase with distance for two reasons. First, as noted above, for people in local labor markets, acquiring *information* on opportunities elsewhere can be very difficult (costly). Surely it is easier to find out about employment prospects closer to home than farther away; newspapers are easier to obtain, phone calls are cheaper, friends and relatives are more useful contacts, and knowledge of employers is greater. Second, the *money costs* of transportation for the move and for trips back to see friends and relatives, and hence the *psychic costs* of the move, obviously rise with distance. Thus, one would clearly expect to find that people are more likely to move short distances than long distances.

In general, people *are* more likely to move shorter than longer distances. One study published in the late 1960s found that 34 percent of all moves were of less than 100 miles and 51 percent were of less than 200 miles. In contrast, only 17 percent were of distances between 200 and 400 miles and only 10 percent were between 400 and 600 miles in length.[10] Thus, moves over 600 miles accounted for only 22 percent of all moves. Clearly, the propensity to move far away is smaller than the propensity to stay close to home.

Related to the desire to minimize psychic and informational costs is the fact that people tend to migrate to areas where friends or relatives have previously migrated. This *chain migration* is especially evident in the stream of migration from Puerto Rico to the mainland: most Puerto Ricans go to Chicago and to the tri-state area of New York–New Jersey–Connecticut.

Interestingly, lack of education appears to be a bigger deterrent to long-distance migration than does age (other influences held constant), a fact that can shed some light on whether it is information costs or psychic costs that are the primary deterrent. As suggested by our arguments in the previous subsection, the age deterrent is closely related to psychic costs, while educational level and ease of access to information are closely linked. The apparently larger deterrent of educational level suggests that information costs have more influence on the relationship between migration and distance.[11]

Skills, the Earnings Distribution, and International Migration

To this point, our examples of factors that influence geographic mobility have related to domestic migration—movements within the United States. The influences of age, access to information, the potential gains in earnings, and distance are all relevant to international migration as well, although the international migration actually observed is often so highly regulated that not all people who want to change their country of residence can do so. One aspect of the potential gains from migration that is especially important when analyzing international flows of labor is the distribution of earnings in the sending

---

10. Lansing and Mueller, *The Geographic Mobility of Labor,* 28. Some of the moves of less than 100 miles may not have been accompanied by a job change; the explanation for these moves lies outside the realm of human capital theory.
11. Aba Schwartz, "Interpreting the Effect of Distance on Migration," *Journal of Political Economy* 81 (September/October 1973): 1153–67.

as compared with the receiving country. The relative distribution of earnings can help us predict which skill groups within a sending country are most likely to emigrate.

Some countries have a more compressed (equal) earnings distribution than is found in the United States. In these countries, the average earnings differential between skilled and unskilled workers is smaller, implying that the returns to human capital investments are lower than in the United States. Skilled and professional workers from these countries (northern European countries are most notable in this regard) have the most to gain from emigration to the United States. Unskilled workers in countries with more equality of earnings are well paid compared to unskilled workers here and thus have less incentive to move, so immigrants to the United States from these countries are *positively selected* with respect to skills (that is, they are more skilled than the average worker who remains in the country of origin).

In countries with less equal distributions of earnings than are found in the United States, skilled workers do relatively well, but there are large potential gains to the unskilled from emigrating to the United States. These unskilled workers may be blocked from making human capital investments within their own countries (and thus from taking advantage of the high returns to such investments that are implied by the large earnings differentials). Instead, their human capital investment may take the form of emigrating and seeking work in the United States. Less-developed countries tend to have relatively unequal earnings distributions, so it is to be expected that immigrants from these countries (and especially Mexico, which is closest) will be *negatively selected* with regard to skills. That is, immigrants to the United States from countries with less equal earnings distributions will be disproportionately unskilled.[12]

The Individual Returns to International and Domestic Migration

The previous sections discussed the fact that the people most likely to move are the ones with the most to gain and the least to lose by migration, and that they move to areas where their net gains are likely to be largest. Another way to test our human capital theory of migration is to see if the earnings of individual immigrants are higher than they would have been without migration. One way to proceed with calculations of these "returns" to migration is to calculate the differences in earnings received by migrants and the earnings received by workers of comparable age and education in the areas from which the migrants came. This procedure generally cannot be contemplated for international migrants owing to the lack of data,[13] so the focus of research on

12. For a more thorough discussion of this issue, see George J. Borjas, *Friends or Strangers* (New York: Basic Books, 1990), especially Chapters 1 and 7.

13. Barry R. Chiswick, *Illegal Aliens: Their Employment and Employers* (Kalamazoo, Mich.: W. E. Upjohn Institute for Employment Research, 1988), mentions two studies that compared the earnings or living standards of Mexican immigrants with the conditions under which they lived before they left. In one study it was found that living conditions, as indexed by the availability of running water and electricity, rose substantially. The other study reported that the earnings of Mexican apple harvesters in Oregon, even after deducting the costs of migration, were triple what they would have been in Mexico.

them has centered on comparisons of the earnings streams of immigrants and native-born workers; given the poverty of the countries from which less-skilled immigrants generally come, if they eventually do as well as comparable native workers here then positive returns from immigration can be inferred.

The post-immigration earnings patterns of foreign-born workers have been of interest to economists in recent years, and studies of these patterns are interesting in what they reveal and in the difficulties of interpretation they present. In general, the wages of immigrants are initially low relative to those received by native-born Americans of the same age and level of education; for example, new immigrants from Asia and Europe earned about 25 percent less than their American counterparts in 1981, and recent Latin American immigrants earned about 35 percent less. However, those from all three of these continents who had immigrated in the early 1960s, and thus had been in the United States about 20 years, earned about 8–10 percent more than comparable native-born workers in 1980.[14] Taken together, these earnings ratios seem to suggest that immigrants' earnings may grow more rapidly than those of native-born Americans with similar levels of education and experience.

The above earnings pattern invites two comments. First, the relatively low initial earnings positions of new immigrants may occur because employers regard hiring them as risky; there are difficulties in trying to evaluate their backgrounds, and language or cultural problems may reduce their productivity. After immigration, the foreign-born invest in themselves by acquiring experience in the culture and with English, and these investments appear to raise the wages they can command. (See Example 10.2.) For example, one study found that for an immigrant who does not speak English well, attaining full fluency is worth almost $2,000 per year. Over a career spanning 27 years, this investment in English proficiency would have a payoff whose present value is $36,000.[15]

Second, there is some uncertainty about whether the above patterns, observed in a cross section of men of *various ages* at a point in time, represent the pattern an *individual* immigrant can expect over his lifetime. The crux of the question is this: Do the current relative earnings of immigrants who have been here for (say) 20 years represent the relative earnings that can be expected by a group of newly arrived immigrants with similar educational backgrounds 20 years from now?[16]

For concreteness, let us focus on immigrants with 12 years of schooling. If each successive group of newcomers has about the same acquired skills, work habits, and capacity to learn, then the earnings experience of those who have gone before is a good predictor of what new arrivals can expect. If, however, the quality of each successive immigrant group (with 12 years of education) is

---

14. George J. Borjas, *International Differences in the Labor Market Performance of Immigrants* (Kalamazoo, Mich.: W. E. Upjohn Institute for Employment Research, 1988), 51.

15. Walter McManus, "Labor Market Costs of Language Disparity: An Interpretation of Hispanic Earnings Differences," *American Economic Review* 75, no. 4 (September 1985): 818–27.

16. Inflation is not an issue here, because our interest is in the earnings of immigrants *relative* to those of nonimmigrants. General inflation of wages would increase the nominal earnings of both groups.

EXAMPLE 10.2

"Economic" vs. "Political" Immigrants

Individuals who emigrate to a country like the United States presumably do so because they believe they will be improving their well-being. For some the decision is motivated primarily by economic considerations, and the timing of the move is both voluntary and planned. These individuals may be referred to as "economic" migrants. Others, however, may be forced to flee their countries because of *political* upheavals, and for these individuals the decision is likely to be less motivated by economic factors, not planned far in advance, and somewhat less voluntary (given the life-threatening prospects they may face). The latter may be referred to as "political" migrants.

What differences might we expect in the economic success of the two groups when they arrive in the United States? On the one hand, since the economic migrants' decisions were motivated by expectations of improved economic welfare, one might expect that they would initially earn more than the political migrants, who were less prepared for the move. On the other hand, members of the latter group do not have the option of ultimately returning to their homelands as the economic migrants do. Because return migration is precluded for political migrants, they have stronger incentives than economic migrants to make human capital investments that have payoffs only in the United States (economic migrants may want to preserve skills that will be useful to them if they return to their homelands). In addition, political migrants often leave all their physical or financial assets behind when they flee their homelands; as a result, they may prefer to concentrate a greater share of their subsequent investments in human (rather than physical) capital. For both reasons, one might expect political migrants to have steeper earnings profiles—more rapid earnings growth with years in the United States—than economic migrants.

In a carefully conducted study, George Borjas found substantial evidence to support these expectations. Other factors (such as age and education) held constant, Cuban male immigrants to the United States, many of whom fled their homeland after Fidel Castro came to power, appear to have lower earnings than other Hispanic male immigrants (primarily Mexicans and Puerto Ricans) in the early years after both groups arrive in the United States; however, in subsequent years they exhibit more rapid rates of earnings growth.

SOURCE: George Borjas, "The Economic Status of Male Hispanic Migrants and Natives in the U.S.," in *Research in Labor Economics,* vol. 6, ed. Ronald Ehrenberg (Greenwich, Conn.: JAI Press, 1984), 65–122.

changing, then the patterns observed in a cross section of various immigrant cohorts will misrepresent what a newly arrived group can expect.[17]

If the cross-sectional patterns of relative earnings *can* be used to represent what each new wave of immigrants can expect, then the observed patterns noted above suggest that the typical immigrant has a stronger work

---

17. We elaborate more fully on this possibility in the appendix to this chapter.

orientation or greater propensity to improve skills than his or her native-born counterparts. Given the difficulties facing immigrants, it would not be surprising if they were indeed better-than-average workers; after all, they are people with enough drive to "get ahead" that they are willing to bear these substantial psychic and monetary costs.[18]

It is a possibility, however, that the relative earnings pattern observed in a cross section of immigrants is created by a fall in the quality of immigrants over time. That is, the immigrants of 20 years ago may be of relatively higher quality than more recent cohorts of immigrants, thus accounting for the higher-than-average relative earnings of older cohorts and the lower-than-average relative earnings of more recent cohorts. One study showed that while schooling levels of immigrants have remained roughly constant during the post–World War II period, relatively more immigrants are now coming from countries whose nationals earn less in the United States; in that sense new immigrants are less productive than older, comparably educated cohorts.[19] Another comprehensive study estimated that the quality of recent immigrants to the United States, whatever their continent of origin, is lower than it was in the 1960s.[20] Thus, it may be unlikely that recent immigrants can expect to attain the relative earnings advantages in 20 years that are enjoyed today by immigrants of 20 years ago.

Still, there seems to be indisputable evidence that the earnings of immigrants grow faster over time than do the earnings of native-born workers. Given that the initial earnings of immigrants are relatively so low, however, this faster growth rate rarely permits the discounted present value of *lifetime* immigrant earnings to exceed that of comparable natives. European immigrants prior to 1975 could expect to equal or exceed the lifetime earnings of American-born workers, but Latin American immigrants prior to 1975 had expected lifetime earnings that were about 12 percent lower, and recent immigrants from Latin America can probably expect lifetime earnings that are 27 percent lower.[21]

To reiterate a point made at the beginning of this section, whether migration is a good investment depends on the earnings immigrants can attain here relative to their country of origin. Thus, despite the expectation of recent Mexican immigrants that their lifetime earnings will only total 73 percent of those earned by comparable U.S. natives, the fact that the typical resident of Mexico is able to consume only 25 percent as much as the typical resident

18. This interpretation receives support from the observation that the *children* of immigrants—people raised by parents with a presumably strong work orientation—earn 5 percent more than children of native-born parents. See Barry Chiswick, "Immigrants and Immigration Policy," in *Contemporary Economic Problems,* ed. William Fellner (Washington, D.C.: American Enterprise Institute, 1978), and Geoffrey Carliner, "Wages, Earnings and Hours of First, Second, and Third Generation American Males," *Economic Inquiry* 18 (January 1980): 87–102.
19. Barry Chiswick, "Is the New Immigration Less Skilled Than the Old?" *Journal of Economic Literature* 4 (April 1986): 168–92.
20. Borjas, *Friends or Strangers,* 108, calls the decline in immigrant productivity over the past two or three decades "the most important single feature of postwar immigration to the United States."
21. Borjas, *International Differences in the Labor Market Performance of Immigrants,* 62, 67.

of the United States implies that the migration investment still has a large monetary payoff.

Can the above conclusion be reached concerning migrants *within* the United States? Studies have found that, as a general rule, migrants do earn more than they would have earned if they had not moved. The exact size of the typical earnings differential is unclear, but earnings increases in the 10–20 percent range have been found for blacks moving out of the South.[22] There may be no *immediate* increases in income for migrants within the United States, but increases after five years are found and turn out to be large—a finding more or less consistent with the finding for foreign-born migrants. Thus, the studies of returns accruing to *individual* moves confirm the findings of research on the relationship between area-wide incentives and the *general flow* of migrants.

One other finding regarding the individual returns on migration is that the gains to *wives* from migration are much lower than the gains to husbands. For example, one study of husband–wife families who moved across state lines in 1971–72 found that the changes in present value of earnings over the next four years were $4,254 for husbands and −$1,716 for wives. (These figures compare to increases of $1,648 and $160, respectively, for nonmovers.)[23] The reason for this disparity is found in the way that family migration decisions have traditionally been made. The husband's earnings opportunities have probably been given primary weight in the decision about whether (and where) to move. The husband is thus free to move where his earnings potential is best, and it would only be by coincidence that this same place would be optimal for his wife (in terms of earnings). Thus, while *family* income seems to rise after a move, it is the husband's income that increases the most. The wife's earnings, as shown by this one study, may actually decline when migration takes place.

Return Migration

Migration, whether it is internal or international, is frequently accompanied by subsequent permanent returns to the area of origin.[24] Twenty percent of all moves are to an area in which the person had *previously* lived, and about half of these are back to one's birthplace. Thus, *return migration*—migrating back to a place from which one originated in some sense—is an important phenomenon of geographic mobility.

There are two major reasons for return migration. First, much of the migration across international borders may well be by people who intend to stay in the foreign country for only a limited period of time. These people live fru-

22. Michael J. Greenwood, "Research on Internal Migration in the United States: A Survey."
23. Solomon W. Polachek and Francis W. Horvath, "A Life-Cycle Approach to Migration: Analysis of the Perspicacious Peregrinator," in *Research in Labor Economics,* ed. Ronald Ehrenberg (Greenwich, Conn.: JAI Press, 1977), 128–29. For a study with similar findings, see Steven Sandell, "Women and the Economics of Family Migration," *Review of Economics and Statistics* 59 (November 1977): 406–14.
24. The discussion in this section is influenced by Lansing and Mueller, *The Geographic Mobility of Labor,* 34; John Vanderkamp, "Migration Flows, Their Determinants and the Effects of Return Migration," *Journal of Political Economy* 79 (September/October 1971): 1012–31; and Michael J. Piore, *Birds of Passage* (New York: Cambridge University Press, 1980).

gally, send much of their earnings back to their homeland, and return when their objectives are met. (Sometimes known as "target workers," because they often have a certain financial goal in mind and intend to return to their homeland when that goal is met, these migrants may become unexpectedly rooted in their new culture and decide to stay.)

Second, return migration may be a response by those who find either that job opportunities were not what they had expected or that the psychic costs of living without the social or economic "safety net" of friends and family were higher than they had anticipated. To say that, on average, migration is a good investment for those who decide to undertake it does not imply that it is a good investment for all. Clearly, most people *do not* migrate in any given year, presumably because they believe that, for them, it would not be a good investment. It is equally clear, however, that some migrants find out they have made a mistake. What they thought would be a good investment may turn out not to be. In these cases people will seek to leave where they are and move elsewhere, and it is understandable that they might seek to minimize costs by moving back to an area with which they are familiar.

VOLUNTARY TURNOVER

While most workers who experience geographic mobility also change jobs (although perhaps not employers), these migrants are but one part of a wider group of workers who change jobs each year with or without a change of residence. Among American male workers in the 1976–81 period, for example, 14 percent separated from their employers each year.[25] Some of these separations were voluntary in the sense that they were initiated by the employee, and some were involuntary (employer-initiated). Voluntary separations are termed *quits* and involuntary separations are *layoffs*. Layoffs can be temporary separations for economic reasons or permanent discharges, whether for cause (firing) or for economic reasons.

The human capital model outlined in this chapter focuses on *worker-initiated* mobility and yields the same types of implications for this wide class of voluntary job mobility that it did for geographic mobility. This section will focus on *voluntary* turnover—deciding whether or not to quit; some major determinants of employer-initiated turnover were discussed in Chapter 5. The related decision of *how long to search* for a new job once one has quit his or her former job is discussed in Chapter 15.

Wage Effects.   Human capital theory predicts that, *other things equal,* a given worker will have a greater probability of quitting a low-wage job than a higher-paying one. That is, workers employed at lower wages than they could obtain elsewhere are most prone to quitting. Indeed, a very strong and consistent finding in virtually all studies of worker quit behavior is that, holding worker characteristics constant, employees in industries with lower wages

25. Jacob Mincer and Yoshio Higuchi, "Wage Structures and Labor Turnover in the U.S. and Japan," *Journal of the Japanese and International Economies* 2 (1988): 97–133.

TABLE 10.2   Monthly Quit Rates (per 100 Workers) by Firm Size, Selected Industries, 1977–81 Averages

Industry	Number of Employees			
	<250 Employees	250–499	500–999	1000 and Over
All manufacturing	3.28	3.12	2.40	1.50
Food and kindred products	3.46	4.11	3.95	2.28
Fabricated metal products	3.33	2.64	2.12	1.20
Electrical machinery	3.81	3.12	2.47	1.60
Transportation equipment	3.90	2.78	2.21	1.41

SOURCE: Walter Oi, "The Durability of Worker-Firm Attachments," Report to the U.S. Department of Labor, Office of the Assistant Secretary for Policy, Evaluation, and Research, March 25, 1983, Table 1.

have higher quit rates.[26] In fact, the relationship between wages and quit rates is so strong that we argued in Chapter 2, and shall argue again in Chapter 13, that an unusually low quit rate is often a reliable signal of an above-equilibrium wage rate. (See Example 10.3 for some normative implications of quit behavior.)

In thinking about the relationship between quit rates and wages, it is useful to bear in mind a constant theme throughout this text: that market outcomes are the result of both worker *and* employer behavior. While workers may decide to quit if their wages fall below what they could get elsewhere, *employers* often have incentives to reduce quits by raising wages. While we may talk of a quit as "worker-initiated," the fact that an employer did not choose to take steps to retain potential quitters would seem to imply that the employer believed keeping them was not worth the cost. For example, Japanese firms offer more firm-specific training than U.S. firms and offer their workers much larger wage increases as employee tenure with the firm increases; the result is an average yearly separation rate that is one-fourth the U.S. average.[27] Thus, the distinction between "worker-initiated" and "employer-induced" quits is quite ambiguous. To expand on this point, we shall briefly discuss the relationship between quit rates and firm-specific human capital investments in the context of both *firm-size* and *gender* differences in quit rates.

From Table 10.2, it can be seen that *quit rates tend to decline as firm size increases.* One explanation offered for this phenomenon is that large firms offer more possibilities for transfers and promotions.[28] Another, however, builds

---

26. Donald O. Parsons, "Models of Labor Market Turnover: A Theoretical and Empirical Survey," in *Research in Labor Economics,* ed. Ronald Ehrenberg (Greenwich, Conn.: JAI Press, 1977), 185–223. George Borjas and Sherwin Rosen, "Income Prospects and Job Mobility of Younger Men," also in *Research in Labor Economics* (1980), ed. Ronald Ehrenberg, 159–81, found that the gains to job-changers were larger than the gains that *would* have been received by those who did *not* change jobs *if* they had decided instead to quit and take other jobs. This finding is similar to that cited in footnote 22 of Chapter 9 relating to "selection bias" in returns on education. See Christopher J. Flinn, "Wages and Job Mobility of Young Workers," *Journal of Political Economy* 94, no. 3, pt. 2 (June 1986): S88–S110, for an analysis of longitudinal data on quit behavior and wages.

27. Mincer and Higuchi, "Wage Structures and Labor Turnover in the U.S. and Japan."

28. Arthur M. Ross, "Do We Have a New Industrial Feudalism?" *American Economic Review* 48 (1958): 903–20.

EXAMPLE 10.3
A Positive and Normative Theory of Quitting in 19th-Century Japan

Is modern labor economics, in both its positive and its normative modes, culture bound? Does the theory presented in this book pertain only to circumstances as they are now in the United States? Despite our emphasis on the analysis of current American policy issues, economic behavior is so general, and the need for markets so pervasive, that the theory presented here as *modern labor economics* is neither American nor necessarily modern.

For example, in the years just before 1900 when Japan was just beginning to industrialize, labor turnover rates (as noted in Example 5.4) were very high owing to persistent labor shortages. In 1898 a conference of business and government leaders was held to discuss the problems underlying this high turnover and the need for legislation concerning it. In the course of these discussions, Shoda Heigoro, a Mitsubishi executive, articulated the "modern" theory of job-quitting behavior—in both its positive *and* its normative aspects:

> Since it is the nature of man to be tempted by better opportunities, it is impossible to keep workers without adequate provisions. That is, if a worker desires to go to another factory because of better pay there, his present employer should allow him to go. If the employer wanted to keep the worker, he should raise wages so that the worker would see no reason to move. Were I censured for this statement on the ground that the competitive spiraling of wages would damage the profits of factory owners and retard industrial progress, I would rebut by calling attention to the simple logic of demand and supply in the market. Factory operatives, engineers, machinists, and other workers in modern industries are scarce in Japan today, because these occupations unlike the traditional crafts emerged only recently. It is true that their relative scarcity enables them to command relatively higher wages than other types of labor. But this very fact of high wages also induces more workers to flow into these occupations....
>
> Therefore, if the forces of demand and supply worked normally, the increase in their number would in time reduce their wages. But this subsequent decrease in their wages would spell no hardship for them, because workers would move into these occupations only insofar as the advantages there were sufficient to make them willing to move.... Thus, in my opinion, it is highly necessary that factory owners should acquiesce in the economic motives of workers in seeking high wages and better occupations....

SOURCE: Koji Taira, *Economic Development and the Labor Market in Japan* (New York: Columbia University Press, 1970), 118.

on the fact that large firms generally pay higher wages.[29] This explanation asserts that large firms tend to have highly mechanized production processes, where the output of one work team is highly dependent on that of production groups preceding it in the production "chain." Larger firms, it is argued, have greater needs for dependable and steady workers because employees who shirk

29. Walter Oi, "The Fixed Employment Costs of Specialized Labor," in *The Measurement of Labor Cost,* ed. Jack E. Triplett (Chicago: University of Chicago Press, 1983).

TABLE 10.3   Job Tenure by Age and Gender, 1983

Age	Percent with Less Than 1 Year with Employer		Percent with More Than 10 Years with Employer		Median Job Tenure (years)	
	Men	Women	Men	Women	Men	Women
16–24	56.1	56.7	—	—	1.5	1.5
25–34	27.6	33.1	11.5	8.3	3.8	3.2
35–44	16.8	24.3	42.3	22.5	7.7	4.6
45–54	11.1	15.5	60.6	38.2	13.2	6.9
55–64	8.9	10.8	68.2	52.1	16.9	10.3

SOURCE: Ellen Sehgal, "Occupational Mobility and Job Tenure in 1983," *Monthly Labor Review* 107, no. 10 (October 1984): 18–23.

their duties can impose great costs on a highly interdependent production process. Large firms, then, establish "internal labor markets" for the reasons suggested in Chapter 5; that is, they hire workers at entry-level jobs and carefully observe such hard-to-screen attributes as reliability, motivation, and attention to detail. Once having invested time and effort in selecting the best workers for its operation, a large firm finds it costly for such workers to quit. Thus, large firms pay high wages to reduce the probability of quitting because they have substantial firm-specific screening investments in their workers.[30]

It is well established that *female workers have higher propensities toward quitting* than male workers, a fact at least partially revealed by the data in Table 10.3. In large part, this differential propensity probably reflects lower levels of firm-specific human capital investments. We argued in Chapter 9 that the interrupted careers of "traditional" women workers rendered many forms of human capital investment less beneficial than would otherwise be the case, and reduced levels of firm-specific training could account for lower wages, lower job tenures, and higher quit rates.[31] In fact, once the lower wages and shorter careers of women are controlled for, there appears to be no difference between the sexes in the propensity to quit a job.[32] Indeed, one study of employee behavior at a single firm found that females were *less* likely to quit than otherwise identical, equally paid males employed in the same jobs.[33]

Cyclical Effects.   Another implication of the theory is that workers will have a higher probability of quitting when it is relatively easy for them to obtain a better job quickly. Thus, when labor markets are *tight* (jobs are more plentiful

---

30. This argument is developed more fully and elegantly in Walter Oi, "The Durability of Worker-Firm Attachments," Report prepared for the U.S. Department of Labor, Office of the Assistant Secretary for Policy, Evaluation, and Research, March 25, 1983.

31. Jacob Mincer and Boyan Jovanovic, "Labor Mobility and Wages," in *Studies in Labor Markets*, ed. Sherwin Rosen (Chicago: University of Chicago Press, 1981).

32. Francine Blau and Lawrence Kahn, "Race and Sex Differences in Quits by Younger Workers," *Industrial and Labor Relations Review* 34 (July 1981): 563–77, and W. Kip Viscusi, "Sex Differences in Worker Quitting," *Review of Economics and Statistics* 62 (August 1980): 388–98.

33. Andrew Weiss, "Determinants of Quit Behavior," *Journal of Labor Economics* 2 (July 1984): 371–87. Weiss argues that to the extent that (a) males and females were treated equally in the firm, and (b) males faced better job alternatives outside the firm than did females (see Chapter 14 for evidence on sex discrimination), then (c) males at the firm should be expected to have higher quit rates than otherwise identical females in the firm.

FIGURE 10.1   The Quit Rate and Labor Market "Tightness"

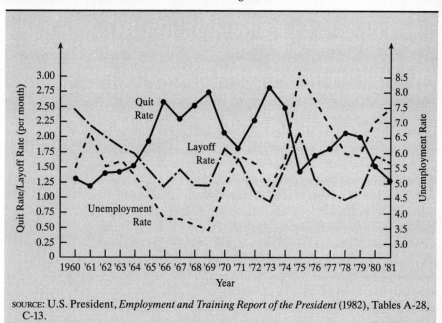

SOURCE: U.S. President, *Employment and Training Report of the President* (1982), Tables A-28, C-13.

relative to job-seekers), one would expect the quit rate to be higher than when labor markets are *loose* (few jobs are available and many workers are being laid off). This prediction is confirmed in studies of time-series data.[34] Quit rates tend to rise when the labor market is tight and fall when it is loose. One measure of tightness is the unemployment rate; the negative relationship between the quit rate and unemployment can be readily seen in Figure 10.1. Another measure of labor market conditions is the layoff rate, which tends to rise in recessions and fall when firms are expanding production. It, too, is inversely correlated with the quit rate (see Figure 10.1).

Unexpected Outcomes.   While human capital theory predicts that, on average, workers will flow from jobs with lower wages to those with higher wages (other things equal), it does not imply that mistakes are never made. Like other investments, human capital investments involve a substantial element of risk. A person might quit a job thinking better opportunities are abundant only to find that he or she was misinformed. The risk of turnover, however, can be decreased if a worker who intends to quit lines up another job first. One study of "quitters" in 1966–67 found that those who quit only after another job had been obtained—about 50–60 percent of all quitters—increased their wages by 10.7 percent on average.[35] This same study found that for those

34. Parsons, "Models of Labor Market Turnover," 185–223.
35. J. Peter Mattila, "Job Quitting and Frictional Unemployment," *American Economic Review* 64 (March 1974): 235–39.

who quit one job and were unemployed for a while, the average wage increase was almost nil. While the utility of the latter group of quitters could still have been increased by *nonwage* factors, it does seem likely that at least some of this group received returns below what they expected.

Age and Job Tenure. Earlier this chapter argued that people tend to invest more heavily in human capital early in their careers. In many cases younger people have lower opportunity costs and a longer period over which to recoup such costs. The data on *all* forms of job mobility clearly indicate that turnover falls as age rises, but is this true for *voluntary* mobility? The answer appears to be yes. Studies that have investigated differences in quit rates among various industries have generally found that, other things (wages, for example) equal, quit rates are higher when the proportion of younger workers is greater.[36]

The relationship between age and worker mobility can also be inferred from data on job tenure (the length of time an employee has been with an employer). As can be seen from Table 10.3, the percentage of male workers who have been with their employers for less than one year falls with age, while the median number of years with one's current employer rises with age. By retirement age, roughly two-thirds of all male workers have been with their employers for ten years or more. While the data for female workers show much lower job tenure, a similar relationship between mobility and age can be seen.

What appears to prevail, then, is a pattern suggested in Example 10.1. Namely, there is very high mobility when workers are young, as mutually satisfactory worker/firm attachments are being sought; however, once these attachments are found, mobility decreases markedly. One study, for example, found that most employees work for about ten employers in the course of their careers, with eight of these jobs being held before the age of 40.[37] Other studies that use data on individual workers find that the probability that a worker will quit tends to decline with job tenure.[38]

Presumably, the decline of quits with tenure reflects a job-matching process in which workers do not always have good information about all of the characteristics of jobs that they are offered. Only after accepting a job and starting work does a worker begin to accumulate better information. Workers who realize, after the fact, that they have not made a "good match" will quit their jobs and seek employment elsewhere. Workers with long tenure will disproportionately be those who believe they have made "good matches" and

36. Parsons, "Models of Labor Market Turnover," 209, and Farrell E. Block, "Labor Turnover in U.S. Manufacturing Industries," *Journal of Human Resources* 14 (Spring 1979): 236–46.

37. Robert Hall, "The Importance of Lifetime Jobs in the U.S. Economy," *American Economic Review* 72 (September 1982): 716–24.

38. Jacob Mincer and Boyan Jovanovic, "Labor Mobility and Wages," in *Studies in Labor Markets,* ed. Sherwin Rosen (Chicago: University of Chicago Press, 1981), and Robert Topel and Michael Ward, "Job Mobility and the Careers of Young Men," *Quarterly Journal of Economics,* forthcoming. Mark Meitzen, "Differences in Male and Female Job-Quitting Behavior," *Journal of Labor Economics* 4 (April 1986): 151–67, finds that for a sample of youths in the early stages of their careers, this result holds for males but not for females. He conjectures that the latter may occur because it takes women time to learn whether they will be discriminated against (see Chapter 14).

thus will have low quit rates. Hence, quit rates will decline with job tenure as a result of the job-matching process.[39]

Costs of Quitting.   Another prediction of human capital theory is that quit rates will be higher when the costs of quitting are lower. For example, workers in rural areas who change employers may well have to move their residences if they want to find a job in the same industry or occupation. Job-changers who live in large cities have a much wider choice of jobs in their fields and have a much lower probability of having to move. Because job changing is thus less costly for residents of large cities, one would expect turnover to be higher in these larger cities. Indeed, we do find that industries in which employment is more concentrated in larger cities have higher quit rates, other things (wages and ages of workers, for example) equal.[40]

POLICY APPLICATION: RESTRICTING IMMIGRATION

Nowhere are the analytical tools of the economist more important than in the area of immigration policy; the lives affected by immigration policy number in the millions each year. After a brief outline of the history of U.S. immigration policy, this section will analyze in detail the consequences of illegal immigration, a problem currently attracting widespread attention.

U.S. Immigration History

The United States is a rich country, a country whose wealth and high standard of living make it an attractive place for immigrants from nearly all parts of the world. For the first 140 years of our history as an independent country, the United States followed a policy of essentially unrestricted immigration (the only major immigration restrictions were placed on Asians and on convicts). The flow of immigrants was especially large after 1840, when industrialization here and political and economic upheavals in Europe made immigration an attractive investment for millions. As one can see from Table 10.4, officially recorded immigration peaked in the first decade of the 20th century, when the *yearly* flow of immigrants was more than 1 percent of the population.

In 1921, however, Congress adopted the Quota Law, which set annual quotas on immigration on the basis of nationality. These quotas had the effect of reducing immigration from eastern and southern Europe. This act was followed by other laws in 1924 and 1929 that further restricted immigration from southeastern Europe. These various revisions in immigration policy were motivated, in part, by widespread concern over the alleged adverse impact on

---

39. A formal model of turnover and the job-matching process is presented in Boyan Jovanovic, "Job Matching and the Theory of Turnover," *Journal of Political Economy* 87 (October 1979): 972–90. Jacob Mincer, "Job Training, Wage Growth, and Labor Turnover," Working Paper no. 2690, National Bureau of Economic Research, August 1988, argues that the decline in quit rates with job tenure reflects mainly an accumulation of firm-specific training.

40. Parsons, "Models of Labor Market Turnover," and Bloch, "Labor Turnover in U.S. Manufacturing."

TABLE 10.4   Officially Recorded Immigration: 1820 to 1988

Period	Number (in thousands)	Annual Rate (per thousand of U.S. population)	Year	Number (in thousands)	Annual Rate (per thousand of U.S. population)
1820–1830	152	1.2	1981	597	2.6
1831–1840	599	3.9	1982	594	2.6
1841–1850	1,713	8.4	1983	560	2.4
1851–1860	2,598	9.3	1984	544	2.3
1861–1870	2,315	6.4	1985	570	2.4
1871–1880	2,812	6.2	1986	602	2.5
1881–1890	5,247	9.2	1987	602	2.5
1891–1900	3,688	5.3	1988	643	2.6
1901–1910	8,795	10.4			
1911–1920	5,736	5.7			
1921–1930	4,107	3.5			
1931–1940	528	0.4			
1941–1950	1,035	0.7			
1951–1960	2,515	1.5			
1961–1970	3,322	1.7			
1971–1980	4,389	2.0			

SOURCE: U.S. Immigration and Naturalization Service, *Annual Report;* U.S. Bureau of the Census, *1989 Statistical Abstract of the United States,* Table 6; and John W. Wright, ed., *The Universal Almanac 1990* (New York: Andrews and McMeel), 247.

native employment of the arrival of unskilled immigrants from eastern and southern Europe.

In 1965 the passage of the Immigration and Nationality Act abolished the quota system based on national origin that so heavily favored northern and western Europeans. Under this law there is no restriction on the immigration of those who are spouses, children, or parents of adult citizens. In addition, there are a restricted number of immigrants who can settle here for other reasons; family reunification reasons are given first preference (about 80 percent of restricted immigration is for this reason), and the filling of labor scarcities accounts for most of the rest.[41] An immigrant in the latter category must obtain a labor certificate approved by the U.S. Department of Labor after an investigation to verify that the applicant is qualified for the job, that there is a shortage of workers for that job in the area, and that the terms of employment are average or better.

While the 1965 change in immigration policy did achieve its goal of making immigration less overtly discriminatory, the policy still imposes a ceiling on immigrants that is far below the numbers who wish to come. The fact that immigration to the United States is viewed as a very worthwhile investment for many more people than are allowed to take advantage of it has created incentives for people to live in the country illegally.

---

41. U.S. President, *Economic Report of the President, 1986* (February 1986), 217–19. Under the Refugee Act of 1980 the President, in consultation with Congress, annually determines the number and regional allocation of *refugees* (another immigrant category).

Illegal immigration can be divided into two categories of roughly equal size: immigrants who enter legally but overstay or violate the provisions of their visas, and those who enter the country illegally. About 9 million people enter the United States each year, as students or visitors usually, under non-immigrant visas.[42] Once here, the foreigner can look for work, although it is illegal to work at a job under a student's or visitor's visa. If the "student" or "visitor" is offered a job, he or she can apply for an "adjustment of status" to become a permanent resident (based on the existence of a labor certificate). Immigrants from the Eastern Hemisphere are allowed to remain in the United States while their adjustment-of-status applications are being evaluated.

Immigrants from the Western Hemisphere are required to return home while their adjustment-of-status applications are being processed. The backlog of people awaiting entry is such that, in recent years, the delay in re-entering the United States as a legal permanent resident is longer than most job offers will wait. Thus, the affected immigrants have incentives to take the jobs and work here illegally while awaiting approval of their status change.

Moreover, there are other ways of illegally immigrating to the United States. Immigrants from the Caribbean often enter through Puerto Rico, whose residents are U.S. citizens and thus allowed free entry to the mainland. Others walk across the Mexican border. Still others are smuggled into the United States or use false documents to get through entry stations. For obvious reasons, it is difficult to establish the number of illegal immigrants who have come to the United States; however, the report of the Select Commission on Immigration and Refugee Policy, submitted in 1981, placed the total number of illegal residents at below 6 million, possibly in the range of 3.5–5 million (a range consistent with the Bureau of the Census estimate reported earlier).[43]

Despite the lack of precise knowledge about the dimensions of illegal immigration, the fact remains that by the 1980s it had become a very prominent policy issue. The Secretary of Labor estimated in late 1979 that if only *half* of the jobs held by illegal aliens were given to U.S. citizens, the unemployment rate would drop from 6 percent to 3.7 percent. Similar beliefs led Congress in 1986 to pass an act substantially reforming immigration policy. The act, for the first time, imposed penalties on *employers* who knowingly hire illegal aliens; previously, the penalties for illegal employment (deportation) fell only on the illegally employed workers. The newly imposed sanctions against employers included fines that can range from $250 to $10,000 per illegal worker, with penalties escalating throughout that range for repeated offenses. Jail terms are prescribed for "pattern and practice" offenders. The reform act also granted amnesty (and legal immigrant status) to all those who had been in the United States illegally since the end of 1981, and illegal aliens who had worked in agriculture for over 90 days per year were granted the right to apply for immigrant status even if they came after 1981. All told, some 2.7 million people applied for amnesty under the provisions of the act.

---

42. U.S. President, *Economic Report of the President, 1986* (February 1986), 217–19.
43. Select Commission on Immigration and Refugee Policy, *U.S. Immigration Policy and the National Interest* (Washington, D.C.: U.S. Government Printing Office, 1981), 36.

The dual policies of employer sanctions and amnesty for long-term illegal aliens are controversial, because they entail consequences for employers, consumers, taxpayers, and workers of varying skill levels and ethnicities. The policies people advocate are based on their beliefs about the consequences of immigration. Nearly everyone with an opinion on this subject has an economic model implicitly or explicitly in mind when addressing these consequences; the purpose of the remainder of this chapter is to make these economic models explicit and to evaluate them.

Naive Views of Immigration

There are two opposing views of illegal immigration that can be considered naive. One view, which is widely held in the government, is that every illegal immigrant deprives a citizen or legal alien of a job. For example, a Department of Labor official told a House committee studying immigration, "I think it is logical to conclude that if they are actually employed, they are taking a job away from one of our American citizens."[44] According to this view, if x illegal aliens are deported and others kept out, the number of unemployed Americans would decline by x.

At the opposite end of the policy spectrum is the equally naive argument that the illegals perform jobs no American citizen would do:

> You couldn't conduct a hotel in New York, you couldn't conduct a restaurant in New York ... if you didn't have rough laborers. We haven't got the rough laborers anymore....Where are we going to get the people to do that rough work?[45]

Both arguments are simplistic because they ignore the slopes of the demand and supply curves. Consider, for example, the labor market for the job of "rough laborer"—any job most American citizens find distasteful. Without illegal immigrants, the restricted supply of Americans to this market would imply a relatively high wage (W_1 in Figure 10.2). N_1 citizens would be employed. If illegal aliens entered the market, the supply curve would shift outward and perhaps flatten (implying that immigrants were more responsive to wage increases for rough laborers than citizens were). The influx of illegals would drive the wage down to W_2, but employment would increase to N_2.

Are Americans unwilling to do the work of rough laborers? Clearly, at the market wage of W_2, many more aliens are willing to work at the job than U.S. citizens. Only N_3 citizens would want these jobs at this wage, while the remaining supply ($N_2 - N_3$) is made up entirely of aliens. If there were no immigrants, however, N_1 Americans would be employed at wage W_1 as rough laborers. Wages would be higher, as would the prices of the goods or services produced with this labor, but the job would get done. The only "shortage" of American citizens is at the low wage of W_2; at W_1 there is no shortage (see Chapter 2 for further discussion of labor shortages).

---

44. Elliott Abrams and Franklin S. Abrams, "Immigration Policy—Who Gets In and Why?" *Public Interest* 38 (Winter 1975): 25.
45. Abrams and Abrams, "Immigration Policy—Who Gets In and Why?" 26.

FIGURE 10.2   Demand and Supply of Rough Laborers

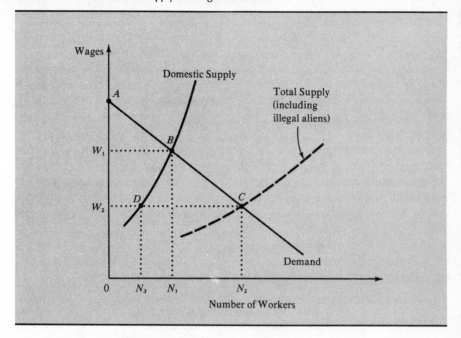

Would deporting those illegal aliens working as rough laborers create the same number of jobs for U.S. citizens? The answer is clearly no. If the $N_2 - N_3$ aliens working as laborers were deported and all other illegal aliens were kept from the market, the number of Americans employed as laborers would rise from N_3 to N_1 and their wages would rise from W_2 to W_1 (Figure 10.2). $N_2 - N_1$ jobs would be destroyed by the rising wage rate associated with deportation. Thus, while deportation would increase the employment and wage levels of Americans in the laborer market, it would certainly not increase employment on a one-for-one basis.

There is, however, one condition in which deportation *would* create jobs for American citizens on a one-for-one basis: when the federal minimum wage law creates a surplus of labor. Suppose, for example, that the supply of American laborers is represented by ABS_1 in Figure 10.3 and the total supply is represented by ACS_2. Because an artificially high wage has created a surplus, only N of the N' workers willing to work at the minimum wage can actually find employment. If some of them are illegal aliens, sending them back—coupled with successful efforts to deny other aliens access to these jobs—would create jobs for a comparable number of Americans. However, the demand curve would have to intersect the domestic supply curve (ABS_1) at or to the left of point B to prevent the wage level from rising (and thus destroying jobs) after deportation. In addition, all laborers would have to be paid the minimum wage, an unlikely eventuality given the lack of compliance noted in Chapter 3.

The analyses above ignore the possibility that if low-wage immigrant labor is prevented from coming to the jobs, employers may transfer the jobs to countries with abundant supplies of low-wage labor. If this were to occur, un-

FIGURE 10.3 Demand and Supply of Rough Laborers with a Minimum Wage

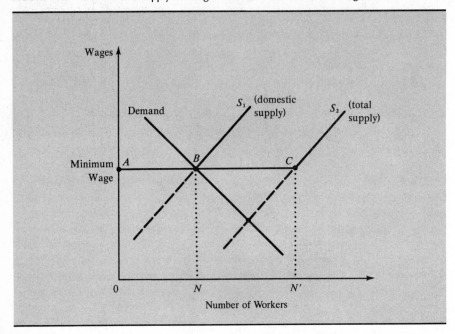

skilled workers in this country would continue to feel downward pressure on their wages and employment opportunities even if illegal immigration were to cease. Thus, it may well be the case that unskilled American workers are in competition with foreign unskilled workers anyway, whether those workers are employed in the United States or elsewhere. However, not all unskilled jobs can be moved abroad, because not all outputs can be imported (most unskilled services, for example, must be performed at the place of consumption); therefore, the analyses that follow will continue to focus on situations in which the "export" of unskilled jobs is infeasible or very costly.

An Analysis of the Gainers and Losers

Some claim that, while perhaps not reducing citizen-held jobs one-for-one, large immigrant flows are indeed harmful to American workers. This view is probably the dominant force behind our restrictive immigration policy and the consequent concern about illegal immigration.

The argument is based primarily on a single-market analysis like that contained in Figure 10.2, where only the effects on the market for rough labor are examined. As far as it goes, the argument is plausible. When immigration increases the supply of rough laborers, both the wages and the employment levels of American citizens working as laborers are reduced. The total wage bill paid to American laborers falls from $W_1 0 N_1 B$ in Figure 10.2 to $W_2 0 N_3 D$. Thus, some American workers leave the market in response to the reduced wage, and those who stay earn less. If the Americans employed as laborers are the target of antipoverty efforts, the influx of immigrants could frustrate such efforts by reducing their wages, employment levels, or working hours.

Even if unskilled immigration were to adversely affect domestic laborers, however, it would be a mistake to conclude that it is necessarily harmful to Americans as a *whole*. First, immigration of "cheap labor" clearly benefits consumers using the output of this labor. As wages are reduced and employment increases, the goods and services produced by this labor are increased in quantity and reduced in price.

Second, employers of rough labor (to continue our example) are obviously benefited, at least in the short run. In Figure 10.2, profits are increased from W_1AB to W_2AC. This rise in profitability will have two major effects. By raising the returns to capital, it will serve as a signal for investors to increase investments in plant and equipment (the investment funds could be attracted from overseas as well as from domestic sources). Increased profits will also induce more people to become employers. The increases in capital and the number of employers will eventually drive profits down to their normal level, but in the end the country's stock of capital is increased and opportunities are created for some workers to become owners.

Third, our analysis of the market for laborers assumed that the influx of immigrants had no effect on the demand curve (which was held fixed in Figure 10.2). This is probably not a bad assumption when looking at just one market, because the fraction of earnings immigrant laborers spend on the goods and services produced by rough labor may be small. However, immigrants do spend money in the United States, and this added demand creates job opportunities for others (see Figure 10.4). Thus, workers who are not close substi-

FIGURE 10.4 Market for All Labor Except Unskilled

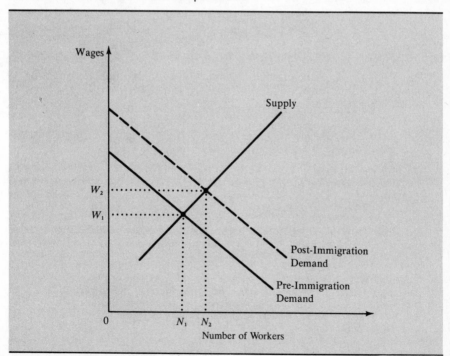

tutes for unskilled immigrant labor may benefit from immigration because of the increase in consumer demand attendant on this addition to our working population.

(Note: Recall from Chapter 3 that if the demand for skilled workers increases when the wage of unskilled labor falls, the two grades of labor would be *gross complements*. Assuming skilled and unskilled labor are substitutes in the production process, the only way they could be gross complements is if the *scale effect* of a decline in the unskilled wage dominated the substitution effect. In the case of immigration one may suppose the scale effect to be very large, because as the working population rises, aggregate demand is increased. While theoretical analysis cannot *prove* that the demand for skilled workers is increased by unskilled immigration if the two grades of labor are substitutes in the production process, it can offer the above observation that an increase in demand for skilled workers remains a distinct possibility. Of course, for any type of labor that is *complementary* with unskilled labor in the production process—supervisory workers, for example—immigration does represent a clear-cut gain.)[46]

It has been estimated that immigration between 1975 and 1985 increased the supply of workers with less than 12 years of schooling by 17 percent for men and 21 percent for women; there were no such increases from immigration in other educational groups.[47] This large overall increase in unskilled labor supply was heavily concentrated in particular "host" cities and areas, so its wage and employment effects on natives should be observable by comparing labor market outcomes in these host areas with those elsewhere. Such studies generally indicate that immigration's effects on native wages in the host cities are very small, even among groups with a high proportion of unskilled workers. A *doubling* of immigrants in a local labor market, for example, is likely to depress the wages of natives, including young blacks, by 2 percent, at most. Estimates are that the wages of women would *increase* by a comparable amount! The group of workers most affected by an increase in an area's immigrant population are other immigrants; a doubling of immigration would probably reduce their wages by about 20 percent.[48]

The estimated effects of increased immigration on the levels of employment and unemployment among natives in the host city are similarly small. However, these findings for host areas may mask pressures on wages and em-

46. For an interesting empirical investigation of the substitutability between immigrants and nonimmigrant labor, see Jean B. Grossman, "The Substitutability of Natives and Immigrants in Production," *Review of Economics and Statistics* 64 (November 1982): 596–603. A detailed analysis of the economic effects of immigration can be found in the *Economic Report of the President, 1986,* Chapter 7. For a theoretical analysis of the likely effects of various policies to restrict illegal immigration of unskilled labor, see Wilfred J. Ethier, "Illegal Immigration: The Host-Country Problem," *American Economic Review* 76 (March 1986): 56–71. A review of theoretical and empirical issues raised by immigration can be found in Michael J. Greenwood and John M. McDowell, "The Factor Market Consequences of U.S. Immigration," *Journal of Economic Literature* 24, no. 4 (December 1986): 1738–72.

47. Lawrence F. Katz, George J. Borjas, and Richard B. Freeman, "On the Labor Market Effects of Immigration and Trade," Paper presented at the National Bureau of Economic Research Conference on the Determinants and Effects of Immigration on the U.S. and Source Economies, January 15–16, 1990.

48. See Borjas, *Friends or Strangers,* Chapter 5, for references to, and a summary of, these studies.

ployment elsewhere. There is a strong possibility that natives may leave (or, if considering migration, avoid) the areas experiencing an influx of immigrants;[49] if this happens, the effects of immigration on the employment and wages of natives will spread beyond the host areas. (See Example 10.4 for a corroborating "case study" of the Mariel boatlift's effects on Miami in the early 1980s.)

Do the Overall Gains from Immigration Exceed the Losses?

Theory suggests that immigration may lower the earnings of resident groups with whom the immigrants are most substitutable, but that the real incomes of other resident groups could be increased. Is it possible to assess whether, among natives, the gainers gain more than the losers lose? Put differently, can economic theory guide our thinking about the effects of immigration on the *aggregate* income of natives in the receiving country?

If immigrants are paid a wage equal to the value of their marginal product (*MP*) and are not subsidized by native taxpayers, then the aggregate income of U.S. citizens *will* increase as a result of immigration. Recall that total product—the area under the marginal product curve—is greater than wages paid. Only for the last unit of labor employed, where MP = Wage, is there no surplus or profit generated. Thus, as long as immigrants get paid a wage equal only to their *MP*, the aggregate income of citizens cannot be reduced.

One way in which the native-born population, taken as a whole, *can* lose from immigration is if the immigrants obtain government services or payments in excess of the payroll, income, sales, and property taxes they pay. Because many government programs are essentially aids to the poor—public health, welfare, and unemployment insurance, to name just three—there is a distinct possibility that immigrants, especially the unskilled and those with less favorable labor market outcomes, will receive public subsidies. However, the presence of illegal aliens among the less-skilled group of immigrants probably serves to limit their public subsidization, because illegals are generally ineligible for many public welfare programs. Moreover, the taxes immigrants pay, directly or indirectly, also serve to reduce the burden of certain "overhead" expenses to U.S. citizens—expenses, like those for national defense and road construction, that the presence of immigrants does not increase.

Overall, do immigrants pay at least as much in taxes as they receive in public services and income subsidies? The evidence to date is sketchy, but it suggests that, generally speaking, immigrants have "paid for themselves" when it comes to public taxation and expenditures.[50] The lack of net subsi-

49. Randall K. Filer, "The Impact of Immigrant Arrivals on Migratory Patterns of Native Workers," and Stephen G. Bronars, "Immigration, Internal Migration, and Economic Growth, 1940–1980," Papers presented at the National Bureau of Economic Research Conference on the Determinants and Effects of Immigration on the U.S. and Source Economies, January 15–16, 1990.

50. Borjas, *Friends or Strangers,* Chapter 9. A study in Texas found that illegal residents made very little use of social and welfare services, with the exception of health services; however, they appeared to pay for these latter services (see *Economic Report of the President, 1986,* 232). See also Kevin F. McCarthy and R. Burciaga Valdez, *Current and Future Effects of Mexican Immigration in California* (Santa Monica, Calif.: Rand Corporation, 1986).

EXAMPLE 10.4

The Mariel Boatlift and Its Effects on Miami's Wage and Unemployment Rates

Between May and September of 1980, some 125,000 Cubans were allowed to emigrate to Miami from the port of Mariel in Cuba. Leaving in flotillas of privately chartered boats, these immigrants—half of whom permanently settled in Miami—increased Miami's overall labor force by 7 percent in under half a year. Because two-thirds of "the Mariels" had not completed high school, and because unskilled workers made up about 30 percent of Miami's work force, it is likely that the number of *unskilled* workers in Miami increased by 16 percent or more during this short period! Such a marked and rapid increase in labor market size is highly unusual, but it provides an interesting "natural experiment" on the consequences of immigration for a "host" area.

As discussed in the text, the effects of immigration on host areas are more complex than those associated with a simple shift in supply. The demand for labor itself shifts as a result of an influx of consumer/workers, and there also may be adjustments in locational decisions by present or potential residents of an area. In the case of the Mariel boatlift, the effects on the wages and unemployment rates of unskilled workers in Miami were surprisingly small.

If immigration has negative effects on wages in the receiving areas, we would expect to observe that the wages of Miami's unskilled workers fell relative to the wages of its skilled workers and relative to the wages of unskilled workers in otherwise comparable cities. Neither relative decline occurred; in fact, the wages of unskilled black workers in Miami actually rose relative to wages of unskilled blacks in four comparison cities (Atlanta, Los Angeles, Houston, and Tampa). Similarly, the unemployment rate among low-skilled blacks in Miami improved, on average, relative to that in other cities during the five years following the boatlift. Among Hispanic workers, there was a predictable increase in Miami's unemployment rate relative to that in the other cities in 1981, but from 1982 to 1985 the Hispanic unemployment rate in Miami fell faster than in the comparison cities.

What accounts for the absence of adverse pressures on the wages and unemployment rates of unskilled workers? Concurrent rightward shifts in the demand curve for labor probably tended to offset the rightward shifts in labor supply curves. However, it also appears that some residents may have left Miami in response to the influx of immigrants and that other potential migrants went elsewhere; the rate of Miami's population growth after 1980 slowed considerably relative to that of the rest of Florida, so that by 1986 its population was roughly equal to what it was projected to be by 1986 *before* the boatlift. For locational adjustments of residents and potential in-migrants to underlie the lack of wage and unemployment effects, these adjustments would have to have been very rapid. Their presence reinforces the theoretical prediction, made earlier in this chapter, that migration flows are sensitive to economic conditions in both sending and receiving areas.

SOURCE: David Card, "The Impact of the Mariel Boatlift on the Miami Labor Market," *Industrial and Labor Relations Review* 43, no. 2 (January 1990): 245–57.

dization implies that immigration may well have *increased* the aggregate income of the native populace, but whether it will continue to do so is a legitimate question. As mentioned earlier, immigrants in recent years have been less skilled and less successful in the labor market relative to their native counterparts. It also seems to be the case that the probability of an immigrant's being on welfare, given his or her economic circumstances, grows with the time spent in the United States (apparently, "learning one's way around" also includes learning how one qualifies for public programs).[51] Thus, there is no guarantee that any past benefits immigrants may have conferred on the native populace will continue.

If the aggregate income of the resident population is increased by immigration, then the gainers gain more than the losers lose. You will recall from Chapter 1 that when the gains are larger than the losses, a mutually beneficial transaction is possible. The immigrants gain from their move to this country and, on balance, the resident population gains. In fact, the gains are large enough that the beneficiaries could compensate those who lose from immigration and *still* be better off.

Whether a policy of unrestricted immigration would be advisable probably depends on three factors:

1. The possibility that those hurt by it could actually receive compensation;
2. The probability that immigrants would remain unsubsidized; and
3. The desirability of programs designed to reduce or deny subsidies to immigrants.

Since many social programs are aimed at the poor, compensation to unskilled workers for their losses associated with immigration of the unskilled may be fairly automatic, coming in the form of unemployment compensation, public housing, food stamps, job retraining, and welfare payments. Compensation to skilled workers (if the immigrants are predominantly skilled) would be less automatic and might have to take the form of a special program.[52]

The reservations many have about unrestricted immigration center on points 2 and 3, especially as they relate to immigration of those most likely to receive public subsidies (see Example 10.5). Illegal immigrants *are* denied access to certain public welfare programs because of their undocumented status, but they also represent what some view as an "underclass" who cannot vote and who do not have full citizenship rights. An alternative used in Europe— "guest worker" programs—also denies permanent residence and citizenship rights to immigrants; in addition, these workers can be required to leave the

---

51. See Borjas, *Friends or Strangers,* 141.
52. Such a program already exists for those hurt by foreign imports. The Trade Adjustment Assistance Program identifies those hurt and compensates them through job retraining, subsidies to move to other areas, and special unemployment insurance payments. While this program has been criticized as generally unsuccessful in several respects, it does serve as an example of a program specifically designed to compensate those who lose as a consequence of a public policy.

EXAMPLE 10.5

Discouraging Immigration to Zurich in the 18th Century

Agricultural towns in Switzerland during the 18th century typically had common areas used for grazing, the collection of firewood, and other purposes. Realizing that the free access to common property by newcomers to the community would amount to a subsidy that could make natives worse off, the Swiss in the canton of Zurich imposed a settlement fee (an *Einzugsgeld*) on immigrants. Designed to discourage immigration and compensate natives for any losses, the *Einzugsgeld* was higher in towns with larger amounts of common property.

Towns in the canton also vested a limited number of houses (not families) with the rights to use common property. The restricted number of rights made it doubly difficult for immigrants, who had to pay the settlement fee *and* find living quarters that allowed them the right to use the town's common property. Clearly, farmers in the canton believed that free access to common property by immigrants represented a subsidy to newcomers that should be avoided.

SOURCE: Rudolf Braun, "Early Industrialization and Demographic Change in the Canton of Zurich," in *Historical Studies of Changing Fertility*, ed. Charles Tilly (Princeton: Princeton University Press, 1978), 289–334.

country at the government's will. Thus, ensuring that poor, unskilled immigrants remain unsubsidized means denying them the rights of other citizens and legal aliens. While the immigrants themselves are obviously willing to pay the price when they immigrate, some worry that they or their foreign-born children may not be willing to pay this price indefinitely.

The Consequences of Emigration

The consequences of emigration are generally the reverse of those for immigration. The country loses a productive resource, and those remaining are deprived of the surplus (total product less wages) produced by the emigrants. The groups most competitive with the emigrants are helped by their departure, but the aggregate income of the residents who remain will be smaller. Emigration may also involve a loss of capital by the country of origin, especially the loss of human capital. It is frequently asserted that less-developed countries face a "brain drain"—a loss of highly trained doctors, scientists, artists, and so forth. Not only does the country of origin lose the services of talented people, but it must also invest resources in the training and education of their replacements.[53]

---

53. For comprehensive analyses of the brain drain, see Herbert G. Grubel and Anthony Scott, *The Brain Drain* (Waterloo, Ont.: Wilfrid Laurier University Press, 1977), and J. N. Bhagwati and M. Partington, eds., *Taxing the Brain Drain* (Amsterdam: North-Holland, 1976).

There are two important exceptions to the above tendency for the countries of origin to lose. First, if the emigrants are owners of capital and are forced by the government to leave this capital behind, the remaining population could benefit (in much the same way the Black Death benefited the survivors, as pointed out in Chapter 2). Some governments, most notably Cuba's, have permitted middle-class workers to leave under these conditions.

The second exception applies to economies in which there is a permanent labor surplus. Many believe that in very poor countries the supply of labor is so large relative to demand that the equilibrium wage is below a socially acceptable minimum (perhaps the subsistence level). If the minimum must be paid, a labor surplus is created (see Figure 10.5). If surplus workers leave, the country obviously gains. These workers were not producing anything, but they had to be kept alive by transfer payments from others. Emigration is a clear-cut help to those who remain.

Labor surpluses in less-developed countries can also be created by the high wages paid in the industrial, urban sector. These wages are set high to attract foreign labor with the requisite skills and must by law be paid to native workers also. Hoping to be lucky enough to obtain these jobs, migrants flock to the cities, where they form sizable groups of unemployed, surplus workers. If a country were not willing to let the industrial wage for native workers fall to the point of market equilibrium, emigration would be an attractive solution to the resulting problem of a labor surplus.

FIGURE 10.5 A "Labor-Surplus" Market

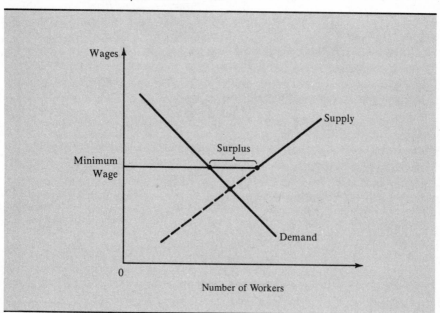

MISCONCEPTION

"Americans won't do stoop labor."

Analysis

Americans may not supply their services to jobs requiring stoop labor at current wage rates, but there is *some* (higher) wage rate at which at least some supply would be forthcoming!

Principle

People with a stable set of preferences can be induced to change their behavior if their command over resources and/or the prices they face change.

REVIEW QUESTIONS

1. The following four paragraphs were taken from an Associated Press story on December 8, 1979:

   WASHINGTON (AP)—Treasury Secretary G. William Miller said Friday that the Senate Banking Committee version of the Chrysler aid bill is "unworkable," in part because the automaker might lose many of its best workers.

   Miller said the most objectionable feature of the committee bill is a requirement that Chrysler workers accept a three-year wage freeze in exchange for $1.25 billion in federal loan guarantees for Chrysler.

   "Under the proposed bill, efforts to aid Chrysler would fail, because conditions of the bill simply could not be met," he said, adding that the wage freeze would impose "a disproportionate financing burden on the workers of the company."

   "The terms of the bill would substantially impair the operations of the Chrysler Corporation, risk loss to the company of many of its most able employees, and seriously damage the morale and productivity of the workers essential to the company's future success," he said.

   Suppose you are a staff worker for an important senator trying to evaluate Secretary Miller's contention that a wage freeze would cause Chrysler to lose its best employees. Write an essay evaluating Miller's contention. Start with a coherent statement of the theory relevant to Miller's assertion and then analyze all the conditions necessary for Miller's assertion to be true.

2. As you know, thousands of illegal immigrants are working in the United States. Suppose the United States increases the penalties for illegal immigration to include long jail sentences for illegal *workers*. Analyze the effects of this increased penalty on the wages and employment levels of *all* affected groups of workers.

3. Suppose a Presidential commission on immigration policy had made the following report:

   "As a compromise between those on our commission who wish to make it illegal for an employer to hire 'undocumented' (that is, illegal) aliens and those who wish to continue the current practice (where it is not illegal), we propose that

a. a tax be placed on any employer who hires an undocumented alien in the amount of $1 for every hour that alien is employed, and

b. the revenues be used to finance job-training programs for American citizens who have low skill levels."

Assume that the program above could be carried out feasibly. Analyze the effects the program would have on employment and earnings of both illegal aliens and American citizens. (In writing your answer, assume that it is not currently illegal to hire undocumented workers and that only limited job training is available.) Would this proposal tend to reduce the influx of illegal immigrants? Why?

4. One way for the government to facilitate economic growth is for it to pay workers in depressed areas to move to regions where jobs are more plentiful. What would be the labor market effects of such a policy?

5. Other things equal, firms usually prefer their workers to have low quit rates. However, from a social perspective, quit rates can be too low. Why do businesses prefer low quit rates, and what are the social disadvantages of having such rates "too low"?

6. For the last 100 years coal-mine operators in South Africa have recruited migrant workers from other African countries to work in their mines for a specified period (for example, three years). These miners have been housed in male-only dormitories and have not been permitted to live with their families. Recently, the migrant workers and their unions have resisted this policy of separating workers from their families, and in a few instances workers have defied company policy and moved their wives and children into their rooms. If the migrant workers are successful in their efforts to live with their families, what are the likely labor market consequences?

7. "Wage differentials across states in labor markets that are national in scope will be smaller than wage differentials across states in labor markets that are local in nature." Comment.

SELECTED READINGS

Borjas, George. *Friends or Strangers.* New York: Basic Books, 1990.

———. *International Differences in the Labor Market Performance of Immigrants.* Kalamazoo, Mich.: W. E. Upjohn Institute for Employment Research, 1988.

Chiswick, Barry. *Illegal Aliens: Their Employment and Employers.* Kalamazoo, Mich.: W. E. Upjohn Institute for Employment Research, 1988.

———. "Illegal Immigration and Immigration Control." *Journal of Economic Perspectives* 2, no. 3 (Summer 1988): 101–15.

Greenwood, Michael J. "Research on Internal Migration in the United States: A Survey." *Journal of Economic Literature* 13, no. 2 (June 1975): 397–433.

Greenwood, Michael J., and McDowell, John M. "The Factor Market Consequences of U.S. Immigration." *Journal of Economic Literature* 24, no. 4 (December 1986): 1738–72.

Parsons, Donald O. "Models of Labor Market Turnover: A Theoretical and Empirical Survey." In *Research in Labor Economics,* ed. Ronald Ehrenberg. Greenwich, Conn.: JAI Press, 1977. Pp. 185–223.

Pencavel, John. *An Analysis of the Quit Rate in Manufacturing Industry.* Princeton, N.J.: Industrial Relations Section, Princeton University, 1970.

Piore, Michael J. "The 'New Immigration' and the Presumptions of Social Policy." *Proceedings of the Industrial Relations Research Association.* Madison, Wis.: Industrial Relations Research Association, 1974. Pp. 350–58.

APPENDIX 10A

Cohort Quality Changes, Assimilation, and the Earnings Growth of Immigrants

As noted in the text, comparisons at a point in time of the earnings of relatively new immigrants to the United States and the earnings of older immigrants who have been here for a while suggest that the earnings of immigrants grow quite rapidly as they accumulate labor market experience in the United States. Indeed, these comparisons suggest that the assimilation of immigrants is so rapid that within a relatively short period of time their earnings exceed those of native-born Americans with comparable measured characteristics (e.g., education and labor market experience). That immigrants eventually earn more, on average, than otherwise comparable native-born Americans has been hypothesized to be caused by their being a select, highly motivated group.[1]

Recently, however, some researchers have challenged the view that individual immigrants' earnings grow more rapidly than those of native-born Americans, arguing that it is incorrect to draw conclusions about earnings growth rates from earnings data on a cross section of individuals of different ages at a point in time. The use of such cross-sectional data will overstate the earnings growth rates of individual immigrants *if* the quality, or productivity, of recent immigrant cohorts is systematically lower than that of cohorts who have been in the United States for a while.[2] (This change in cohort quality might occur, for example, if the least successful immigrants return to their country of origin after some period of time.)

1. Barry Chiswick, "The Effect of Americanization on the Earnings of Foreign-Born Men," *Journal of Political Economy* 86 (October 1978): 897–921.
2. George Borjas, "Assimilation, Changes in Cohort Quality, and the Earnings of Immigrants," *Journal of Labor Economics* 3 (October 1985): 463–89; George Borjas, *International Differences in the Labor Market Performance of Immigrants* (Kalamazoo, Mich.: W. E. Upjohn Institute for Employment Research, 1988).

To see why this is true, refer to Figure 10A.1, in which we have drawn hypothetical age/earnings profiles for three groups: immigrants who turned age 25 in 1970, immigrants who turned 25 in 1980, and native-born Americans. To keep things simple, we ignore increases in earnings due to inflation or economy-wide productivity growth over time and assume that earnings grow at a constant rate over an individual's lifetime (from Chapter 9, we know that earnings growth rates actually decline as individuals age). We have placed the logarithm of earnings on the vertical axis because when earnings are expressed in logarithmic terms, a straight line in the figure represents a constant rate of growth of earnings.

Line *aa'* is the assumed age/earnings profile for immigrant males who were age 25 in 1980. It shows (the logarithm of) the level of earnings that they will earn at each age during their work lives. Line *cc'* is the assumed profile for immigrant males who turned age 25 in 1970. The earnings of these immigrants are assumed to grow over their lifetimes at the same rate as those of the more recently arrived immigrants; hence, the slopes of *aa'* and *cc'* are equal. Line *cc'* lies above *aa'* because of the assumption that more recently arrived immigrants (those who turned 25 in 1980) are of lower quality or productivity than immigrants who arrived earlier (those who turned 25 in 1970).

Suppose that the quality of native-born males does not change over time, that their earnings actually grow *at the same rate* as those of immigrants, and that native-born workers earn more than immigrants at age 25. Given the other assumptions we have made (e.g., no inflation or economy-wide productivity growth), the age/earnings profile for native-born males *regardless of the*

FIGURE 10A.1   Hypothetical Age/Earnings Profiles for Native-Born Americans and for Immigrants Who Turned 25 in Either 1970 or 1980

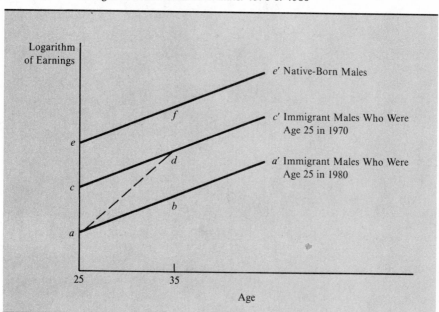

year they turn age 25 can be drawn as ee'. That is, ee' shows (the logarithm of) the earnings a native-born male will receive each year during his lifetime.

Now suppose that rather than having access to data on individuals' earnings over their lifetimes, a researcher has access only to information on the 1980 earnings of individuals who are ages 25 and 35 in that year. Can we infer from these cross-sectional data the earnings path for individual immigrants and native-born workers? The 25-year-old native-born male in 1980 will be at point e, and his 35-year-old native-born counterpart will be at point f in Figure 10A.1. The estimated earnings growth rate for individual native-born males that one would obtain from these data is the slope of ef—which in fact is the actual growth rate. Given the assumptions we have made, the earnings growth rate for individual native-born males *can* be inferred from these *cross-sectional* data.

Unfortunately, the same cannot be said for immigrant males. The immigrant male who is 25 in 1980 would be at point a. However, the immigrant male who is 35 in 1980—and hence was 25 in 1970—would be at point d. The slope of the line, ad, joining these points is greater than the true growth rate of individual immigrant earnings. This overestimate occurs because the immigrant who is 35 in 1980 has both ten years more experience than the immigrant who is 25 in 1980 *and* is of higher quality. Hence, because (by assumption) the quality of recent immigrant cohorts is lower than that of older cohorts, comparisons of earnings of immigrants of different ages in a single year's cross section will *overstate* the true rate of earnings growth that can be expected by any individual immigrant.

=11=

The Structure of Compensation

Chapters 6 and 7 examined factors influencing the decision to work for pay and the desired hours of work. Chapters 8 and 9 analyzed the day-to-day and human capital aspects, respectively, of occupational choice. Chapter 10 discussed human capital aspects of voluntary job and geographic mobility. We now turn to a discussion of yet another set of factors influencing job choice and work effort decisions: employer compensation policies both at one point in time and over several periods of time.

What ultimately matters to workers in making labor supply decisions is the total compensation they receive per unit of time worked. This total compensation paid to employees consists of far more than hourly, weekly, or monthly pay for time worked. There are numerous *employee benefits,* offered in varying combinations by employers, that have value to employees but are not paid to them in the form of currently spendable cash. Employers can also offer, explicitly or implicitly, different bases for computing or timing pay over one's career. These various forms of compensation affect employee behavior and labor market outcomes in interesting ways.

This chapter begins by describing and analyzing the consequences of employee benefits. One particular policy application is then discussed in some detail: namely, the issue of pension fund regulation by the federal government. The chapter also discusses various methods of compensation that provide strong incentives for employees to maximize their productivity and remain attached to a firm for long periods of time. These methods include paying above market-clearing compensation levels (or what have become known as "efficiency wages"), offering compensation profiles that increase with experience more rapidly than does workers' productivity, and relating compensation directly to some measure of individual or group output rather than solely to time worked. As we shall see, several of these methods may arise as a natural consequence of internal labor markets. Moreover, one of these methods used to stimulate worker productivity—profit or revenue

TABLE 11.1 **Employer Costs for Employee Benefits as a Share of Total Compensation in Private Industry in 1988**

Category	Percentage Share of Employee Compensation	
Paid Leave		7.0
Vacation Pay	3.5	
Holiday Pay	2.4	
Sick Leave	0.9	
Other Leave with Pay (includes maternity)	0.3	
Insurance (health, life, sickness, accident)		5.6
Retirement and Savings		3.3
Pensions	2.8	
Savings and Thrift Plans	0.5	
Legally Required		8.8
Social Security	5.9	
Federal Unemployment Insurance	0.2	
State Unemployment Insurance	0.8	
Workers' Compensation	1.7	
Other Legally Required	0.2	
Other Benefits (including severance pay, supplemental unemployment benefits, merchandise discounts in department stores, and bonuses)		1.0
Total Benefits		25.7

SOURCE: U.S. Bureau of Labor Statistics, *Employment Cost Indexes and Levels, 1975–88*, Bulletin 2319 (Washington D.C.: December 1988), Table 10.

sharing—has some fascinating and potentially important implications for stabilizing the demand for labor over a business cycle; these implications are analyzed in the appendix to this chapter.

THE ECONOMICS OF EMPLOYEE BENEFITS

As noted in Chapter 5, the proportion of total compensation coming in the form of cash payments to workers has fallen over time as the use of employee benefits has risen. Data on employee benefits obtained from a representative sample of private firms in 1988 are presented in Table 11.1, and they suggest that among the most expensive, in terms of their costs to employers, are paid vacations and holidays, health and life insurance, pension contributions, and sick leave. In addition to these privately provided benefits, publicly mandated benefits that employers must at least partially fund, including Social Security, unemployment compensation, and workers' compensation, represented 8.8 percent of total compensation costs in 1988. Employer costs for maternity or parental leave currently represent substantially less than 1 percent of total compensation costs, as do employer costs for subsidizing employee child care (a newly emerging benefit not included in the data in Table 11.1).[1]

---

1. See Janet Norwood, "Measuring the Cost and Incidence of Employee Benefits," *Monthly Labor Review* (August 1988): 3–8.

Table 11.2 presents similar data on employee benefits as a share of total compensation over a number of years for a sample of primarily large firms that respond to periodic U.S. Chamber of Commerce surveys (some of these data have previously appeared in Table 5.2). This table provides a number of insights. First, the proportion of total compensation devoted to employee benefits is considerably higher now than in the 1940s or 1950s. Second, the most rapidly growing employee benefits are private pensions and insurance. Third, employee benefits represent a slightly higher proportion of total compensation in manufacturing than in all industries generally (manufacturing workers tend to work in larger, better-paying, and more-unionized firms).

What accounts for the growth and size of employee benefits? What are the consequences of this growth and size? To answer these questions, we must examine both the employee and employer sides of the market.

Employee Preferences

The distinguishing feature of most employee benefits is that they compensate workers in a form *other* than currently spendable cash. In general, there are two broad categories of such benefits. First and largest are *payments in kind*— that is, compensation in the form of some commodity. As we have seen, it is very common for employers to partly or completely pay for insurance policies of one kind or another on behalf of their employees. Slightly less obvious as payments in kind are paid vacations and holidays. A woman earning $15,000 per year for 2,000 hours of work can have her hourly wage increased from $7.50 to $8.00 by either a straightforward increase in current money payments or a reduction in her working hours to 1,875 with no reduction in yearly earnings. If her raise comes in the form of an increase in money payments, she will receive $1,000 (before taxes) more in yearly income that she can use to buy a variety of things (she could even buy time off by giving money back to her employer in exchange for days off). However, if she receives her raise in the form

TABLE 11.2   Employee Benefits as a Percentage of Total Compensation (for firms in U.S. Chamber of Commerce survey), 1948–86

Categories of Compensation	All Industries				Manufacturing		
	1948	*1959*	*1977*	*1986*	*1959*	*1977*	*1986*
Pay for leave time (vacations, holidays, sick leave, personal days)	5.7	7.8	9.7	9.7	7.7	9.1	9.5
Pensions and insurance	3.7	5.9	9.3	11.2	5.1	9.4	12.6
Legally required contributions to Social Security, workers' compensation, and unemployment insurance	2.8	3.4	6.2	6.5	3.7	7.2	6.1
Other (including bonuses and profit sharing)	1.1	1.5	1.6	0.9	1.3	1.1	1.3
Total employee benefits	13.3	18.6	26.8	28.3	17.8	26.8	29.5

SOURCE: U.S. Chamber of Commerce, *Employee Benefits* (Washington, D.C.: Economic Policy Division, U.S. Chamber of Commerce), 1948, 1959, 1977, 1986.

of paid vacation time, she is in fact being paid in the form of a commodity: leisure time.

The second general type of employee benefit is *deferred compensation,* compensation that is earned now but will be paid in the form of money later on. Employer contributions to employee pension plans make up the largest proportion of these benefits.

Payments in Kind.   It is a well-established tenet of economic theory that, *other things equal,* people would rather receive $X in cash than a commodity that costs $X. The reason is simple. With $X in cash the person can choose to buy the particular commodity or choose instead to buy a variety of other things. Cash is thus the form of payment that gives the recipient the most discretion and the most options in maximizing utility. In-kind payments are inherently more restrictive, and while they generate utility, they do not ordinarily generate as much as cash payments of equal monetary value.

As might be suspected, however, "other things" are not equal. Specifically, in-kind payments offer employees a sizable tax advantage because, for the most part, they are not taxable under current income tax regulations. The failure to tax important in-kind payments is a factor that tends to offset their restrictive nature in affecting employee demands for in-kind payments. A worker may prefer $1,000 in cash to $1,000 in some in-kind payment, but if his or her income- and payroll-tax rates total 25 percent, the comparison is really between $750 in cash and $1,000 in the in-kind benefit.

Deferred Compensation.   Like payments in kind, deferred-compensation schemes enjoy a tax advantage over current cash payments. With deferred payments the tax advantage is that the compensation is not taxed until it is received by the worker. In the case of pensions, for example, employers contribute currently to a pension fund, but employees do not obtain access to this fund until they retire. Neither the pension fund *contributions* made on behalf of employees by employers nor the *interest* that compounds when these funds are invested is subject to the personal income tax. Only when the retirement benefits are received does the ex-worker pay taxes, but because of lower income and special tax advantages given the elderly, the tax rates actually paid are often relatively low.

Because of the above-noted tax advantages accorded to pension fund contributions, employees wishing to save for old age have incentives to do so through a pension fund, rather than receiving cash payments and saving from that (although workers whose employers do not offer a pension plan can obtain the same tax advantages by establishing their own Individual Retirement Accounts). Saving through a pension fund defers the taxation of part of one's compensation (the pension fund contributions) until old age and permits funds for retirement to accumulate on a tax-free basis. What one *loses* with saving through a pension fund is the ability to currently control one's assets: by putting money into a pension fund, one is forgoing the ability to use that money now for routine or emergency needs.

Again, then, two opposing forces are at work on the demand for employee benefits by employees. With both kinds of benefits there is a loss of discretion in spending one's total compensation, which tends to render such benefits inferior to cash payments in generating utility. On the other hand, the special tax advantages accorded to both kinds of benefits as compared with cash payments tend to increase the demand for them.[2]

Before turning to a discussion of employer preferences regarding benefits, it is interesting to note that the presence of labor unions appears to increase the share of total compensation devoted to employee benefits.[3] As we mention when discussing this issue in Chapter 12, one possible reason for this effect is that unions may be more effective than employers at identifying the desire for a given employee benefit among workers. It may also be that by raising wages, unions place their members in higher tax brackets and make it more likely that they will become permanently attached to the firm; both of these factors should increase the desirability of employee benefits. Moreover, if union leaders are politically more responsive to the preferences of older, longer-term members than to those of younger, more mobile workers, the preferences of the former group will tend to dominate in the negotiating process.[4] Thus, while tax advantages may be the driving force behind the relatively recent growth of employee benefits, unions appear to facilitate this growth.

Employer Preferences

Suppose employers are totally indifferent about whether to spend $X on wages or $X on benefits. Both expenditures are of equal sums of money and are equally deductible as a business expense. If so, the composition of total compensation is a matter of indifference to them; only the level of compensation is of concern.

The easiest way to depict the willingness of a firm to offer employee benefits is through the use of isoprofit curves (introduced in Chapter 8). Suppose a firm offers a certain type of job for which it must pay at least $X in total compensation to attract workers. Suppose also that if it paid more than $X, its profits would fall below zero. Thus, it must compensate its workers $X per year to remain competitive in both the labor and the product markets. However, if the *composition* of total compensation is a matter of indifference to

2. Stephen Woodbury, "Substitution Between Wage and Nonwage Benefits," *American Economic Review* 73 (March 1983): 166–82, shows that wages and benefits (especially pensions) are viewed by workers as very good substitutes, and that tax rate increases play a large role in explaining the growth of benefits. A smaller role is found, however, by Robert Turner, "Are Taxes Responsible for the Growth in Fringe Benefits?" *National Tax Journal* 40 (June 1987): 205–20.
3. Richard B. Freeman, "The Effect of Unionism on Fringe Benefits," *Industrial and Labor Relations Review* 34 (July 1981): 489–509.
4. For evidence on this issue, see Stanley M. Nealey, "Pay and Benefit Preference," *Industrial Relations* 3 (October 1963): 17–28. Other evidence that the preferences of younger and older workers diverge can be found in Jonathan Eaton and Harvey Rosen, "Agency, Delayed Compensation and the Structure of Executive Remuneration," *Journal of Finance* 38 (December 1983): 1489–1505.

the firm, it will be willing to offer any combination of wages and benefits that totals $X in value. The various compensation packages a firm is willing to offer fall along the zero-profit isoprofit curve drawn between wages and benefits (see Figure 11.1).

Any combination of wages and benefits along the isoprofit curve shown in Figure 11.1 would yield the firm equal profits (assuming it could recruit workers). Thus, it is willing to offer $X in wages and no employee benefits, benefits that cost (say) $300 and wages that equal $(X − 300), or any other combination totaling $X in cost. The slope of the isoprofit curve is *negative,* reflecting the fact that the firm can increase benefits only if it reduces wages (again, because of competitive pressures). Further, in this case the isoprofit curve has a slope of −1, which reflects employer indifference about the composition of compensation. If employees want a health insurance policy costing $300, it will cost them $300 in wages.

There are some reasons to expect that firms might offer benefits to their employees on something other than the dollar-for-dollar basis assumed above. For one, by increasing compensation in the form of benefits rather than wages, employers can often avoid taxes and required insurance payments that are levied as a fraction of payroll. Social Security taxes and workers' compensation premiums are examples of costs that generally increase with salaries and wages but not with employee benefits, thus making it more costly for an employer to increase compensation by increasing salaries than by increasing

FIGURE 11.1   An Isoprofit Curve Showing the Wage/Benefit Offers a Firm Might Be Willing to Make to Its Employees: A Unitary Trade-off

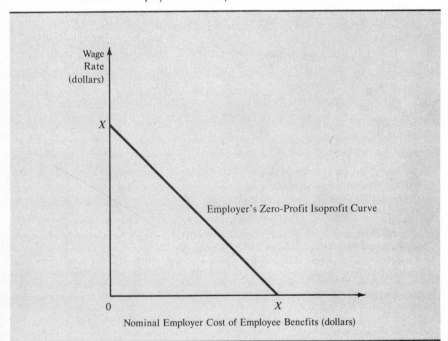

benefits.[5] Payroll taxes thus tend to flatten the isoprofit curve shown in Figure 11.1 (a $300 increase in benefits could be accompanied by a reduction in wages of only $280, and the firm would be equally profitable).

There are also more subtle factors that might cause firms to offer benefits to their employees on something other than the dollar-for-dollar basis in Figure 11.1. Some benefits allow firms to attract a certain kind of worker in situations in which the use of wage rates would be of questionable legal validity. For example, suppose a firm prefers to hire mature adults, preferably those with children, in the hopes of acquiring a stable, dependable work force. Attempting to attract these people by offering them higher wages than it offers to single, younger, or much older adults would risk charges of discrimination. Instead, the firm can accomplish the same effect by offering its employees benefits that are of much more value to the group it is trying to attract than to others. For example, offering *family* coverage under a health insurance plan has the effect of compensating those with families more than others because single or childless people cannot really take advantage of the full benefit. Offering dental insurance covering orthodontia or tuition assistance for children who attend college accomplishes similar purposes. Thus, at times employee benefits allow the firm to give preferential treatment to a group it wants to attract without running afoul of discrimination laws.

The preferential treatment given to some groups of workers, however, has become of increasing concern to employees as benefits have grown in importance. Many families, for example, have dual earners and have no need for two family medical insurance policies. To take into account the biases in many employee benefit plans, some 22 percent of the nation's largest employers have adopted *cafeteria plans,* which allow workers to choose among two or more benefits up to some dollar limit; as of 1986, however, less than 2 percent of all private sector employees were covered by cafeteria plans.[6] One firm implementing such a plan found that only 10 percent of its employees elected to receive the same benefits offered by its old program.[7]

Another subtle reason why a firm may prefer to put an extra dollar of compensation into benefits rather than wages (and have a flatter isoprofit curve than is shown in Figure 11.1) is found whenever the government regulates profits or controls wages. Regulated monopolies or governmental bodies, for example, fearing that the granting of large wage increases would call forth an investigation or outrage public opinion, could hide an increase in compensation by granting increases in benefits that are difficult to cost out: a nicer work environment, shortened days in the summer, time off for religious observances, top-quality food in the company cafeteria for bargain prices, low-cost

---

5. The argument that the presence of Social Security taxes levied on the employer increases the costs of granting salary increases holds only for workers who earn less than the maximum taxable earnings base, which in 1990 was $51,300. Earnings beyond $51,300 in 1990 were not subject to the Social Security tax.

6. William C. Banks, "The Way We'll Work: Shorter Hours, Bigger Bonuses," *Money* 14, no. 11 (November 1985): 158, and Employee Benefit Research Institute, *Fundamentals of Employee Benefit Programs,* 3d ed. (Washington, D.C.: Employee Benefit Research Institute, 1987), 274.

7. "Making Job Benefits Flexible," *New York Times,* March 13, 1981, D1, D3, and Hay/Huggins *Bulletin* (June 1984).

loans to employees for buying a home, and so forth.[8] Similar behavior will occur among firms that are having trouble recruiting employees during a period when the government is attempting to control wages to fight inflation. Wages are easy to observe and measure, but many benefits are very difficult to observe and quantify and can thus be used to increase compensation without violating wage controls.[9] Examples of benefits that are difficult for wage control boards to monitor are increased rest times on the job, rules increasing crew sizes in dangerous activities, and better recreational facilities for employees.

On the other hand, as noted earlier in Example 6.1, some employee benefits could conceivably increase absenteeism, thus reducing the firm's profitability. Life insurance, health insurance, and pensions, for example, are all awarded to current employees regardless of their actual hours of work during the year (assuming they work enough to keep their jobs). If an increase in compensation comes in the form of increasing one of these benefits, workers' *incomes* are increased in the sense that they need to save less for "rainy days" and are thus freer to spend their cash income. However, this enhancement of income is accomplished without an increase in the price of leisure because the hourly wage has not risen. Recall from Chapter 6 that increased income with no change in the price of leisure causes people to want to work less. In this case workers will not quit their jobs, but they may be absent from work more often. The connection between absenteeism and an employee benefit is even more obvious in the case of paid sick leave.[10]

Apart from the possibility of contributing to absenteeism, some benefits compress the differentials in compensation between skilled and unskilled workers, thereby reducing the incentives of employees to obtain training for skilled positions.[11] Benefits such as medical insurance and free or discounted merchandise are of equal value to people of similar-size families, no matter how much they earn. Because their value thus represents a larger percentage of a low-wage worker's compensation, such benefits tend to compress earnings differentials between skilled and unskilled workers.

---

8. For further arguments along this line, see Armen Alchian and Reuben Kessel, "Competition, Monopoly, and the Pursuit of Money," in *Aspects of Labor Economics,* ed. H. G. Lewis (Princeton, N.J.: Princeton University Press, 1962). See also our discussion in Chapter 13 of employee benefits in the public sector.

9. For a brief discussion of the difficulties inherent in controlling employee benefits, see John Dunlop, "Wage and Price Controls As Seen by a Controller," *Proceedings of the Industrial Relations Research Association* (Madison, Wis.: Industrial Relations Research Association, 1975), 457–63.

10. See Steven G. Allen, "Compensation, Safety, and Absenteeism: Evidence from the Paper Industry," *Industrial and Labor Relations Review* 34 (January 1981): 207–18, and also his "An Empirical Model of Work Attendance," *Review of Economics and Statistics* 63 (February 1981): 77–87. For evidence on teacher absenteeism, see Donald R. Winkler, "The Effects of Sick-Leave Policy on Teacher Absenteeism," *Industrial and Labor Relations Review,* 33, no. 2 (January 1980): 232–40, and Ronald G. Ehrenberg, et al., "School District Leave Policies, Teacher Absenteeism, and Student Achievement," *Journal of Human Resources,* forthcoming.

11. See Chapter 9 for the complete argument on how wage differentials affect the incentives of workers to acquire human capital.

FIGURE 11.2   Alternative Isoprofit Curves Showing the Wage/Benefit Offers a Firm Might Be Willing to Make to Its Employees: Nonunitary Trade-offs

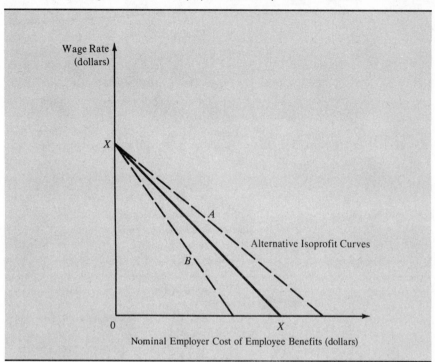

The major point of our analysis of benefits from the employer's perspective is that a dollar spent on benefits could cost employers more or less than a dollar nominally spent on wages or salaries.[12] When benefits enhance productivity more than a similar expenditure on wages would, the isoprofit curve in Figure 11.1 will flatten. Figure 11.2 shows this as isoprofit curve *A*. When benefits increase other costs or reduce productivity, the isoprofit curve will steepen. In this case (curve *B* in Figure 11.2) a $300 benefit would have to be accompanied by a $320 fall in wages, say, to keep profits constant.

The Joint Determination of Wages and Benefits

The offer curve in a particular labor market can be obtained by connecting the relevant portions of each firm's zero-profit isoprofit curve, as done in Chapter 8 (see Figure 8.6). When all firms have isoprofit curves with a slope of −1, the offer curve is a straight line with a negative and unitary slope. One

---

12. Many benefits, like pensions and paid vacations, become more generous as the worker's tenure with the firm increases. In fact, in most firms, workers are not even eligible to receive retirement benefits unless they have worked at least 5 years for the firm. These policies are clearly designed to reduce costly turnover, but they are more a matter of the *timing* of compensation than anything else. We shall discuss issues regarding the timing of compensation later in this chapter.

FIGURE 11.3   Market Determination of the Mix of Wages and Benefits

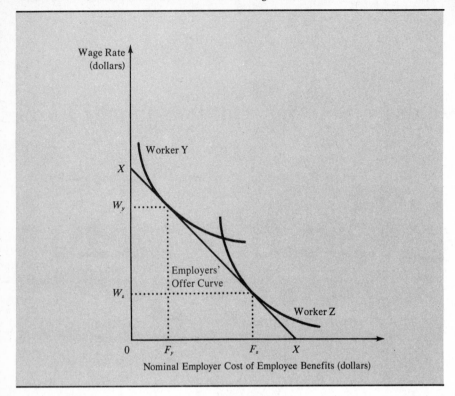

such offer curve is illustrated in Figure 11.3, and the only difference between this curve and the zero-profit isoprofit curve in Figure 11.1 is that the latter traced out *hypothetical* offers *one* firm could make, while this one traces out the *actual* offers made by *all* firms in this labor market. Of course, if firms have isoprofit curves whose slopes are different from −1, the offer curve will not look like that depicted in Figure 11.3. However, whatever its shape or the absolute value of its slope at any point, it will slope downward.

Employees, then, face a set of wage/benefit offers that imply the necessity for making trade-offs. Those employees (like worker Y in Figure 11.3) who attach relatively great importance to the availability of currently spendable cash will choose to accept offers in which total compensation is largely in the form of wages. Employees who may be less worried about current cash income but more interested in the tax advantages of benefits will accept offers in which employee benefits form a higher proportion of total compensation (see the curve for worker Z in Figure 11.3).[13] Thus, employers will tailor their com-

---

13. The indifference curves in Figure 11.3 are drawn with the typical convexity. One assumption underlying this convexity is that as *benefits* increase, the decrease in currently spendable cash that one is willing to bear declines, owing to the loss of discretionary control in spending one's income. The other assumption is that as *current wages* increase and workers advance into higher income tax brackets, the tax advantages offered by benefits become ever more attractive (which causes the indifference curves to steepen).

pensation packages to suit the preferences of the workers they are trying to attract. If their employees tend to be young, poor, or present-oriented, for example, their compensation packages may be heavily weighted toward wages and include relatively little in the way of pensions and insurance. Alternatively, if they are trying to attract people in an area where family incomes are high and hence employee benefits offer relatively large tax savings, firms may offer packages in which benefits constitute a large proportion of the total.

Figure 11.3 shows that workers receiving more generous benefits pay for them by receiving lower wages, other things being equal. Further, if employer isoprofit curves have a unitary slope, a benefit that costs the employer $1 to provide will cost workers $1 in wages. In other words, economic theory suggests that workers pay for their own benefits.

Actually observing the trade-off between wages and employee benefits is not easy. Because firms that pay high wages usually also offer very good benefits packages, it often appears to the casual observer that wages and employee benefits are *positively* related. Casual observation in this case is misleading, however, because it does not allow for the influences of *other factors,* such as the demands of the job and the quality of workers involved, that influence total compensation. The other factors are most conveniently controlled for statistically, and the few statistical studies on this subject tend to support the prediction of a negative relationship between wages and benefits.[14]

The policy consequences of a negative wage/benefits trade-off are enormously important, because government legislation designed to improve employee benefits might well be paid for by workers in the form of lower future wage increases.

Policy Application: Pension Reform Legislation

Pension plans provided by employers are of two general types: *defined contribution* plans and *defined benefit* plans. The less common are *defined contribution* plans, in which the employer merely promises to contribute a certain amount each year to a fund to which the employee has access upon retirement. The fund is increased each year by employer, and perhaps also employee, contributions and by returns from investments made by the fund's managers. One's retirement benefits depend solely on the size of the fund at the age of retirement.

More common are *defined benefit* pension plans, in which the employer promises employees a certain benefit upon retirement. This benefit may be a

---

14. Empirical studies of the trade-offs between wages and pensions are few in number. Many of the studies that do exist indicate workers pay, perhaps dollar for dollar, for their pensions in the form of lower wages. For a review of these studies, see Ronald Ehrenberg and Robert Smith, "A Framework for Evaluating State and Local Government Pension Reform," in *Public Sector Labor Markets,* ed. Peter Mieszkowski and George E. Peterson (Washington, D.C.: The Urban Institute, 1981). However, not all studies done in this area have found the predicted trade-offs, perhaps because of data problems. For a discussion of data requirements for estimating these trade-offs, see Robert Smith and Ronald Ehrenberg, "Estimating Wage-Fringe Trade-offs: Some Data Problems," in *The Measurement of Labor Cost,* ed. Jack E. Triplett, National Bureau of Economic Research, Conference on Research in Income and Wealth, Studies in Income and Wealth, vol. 48 (Chicago: University of Chicago Press, 1983).

EXAMPLE 11.1
The Wage/Benefit Trade-off in the Collective Bargaining Process

At times, the wage/benefit trade-off can be directly observed in the collective bargaining process, although management and unions are usually reluctant to explicitly acknowledge that workers might be paying for their own employee benefits. In 1950, however, the United Automobile Workers (the UAW) called a strike against Chrysler over the issue of pensions. Chrysler had promised a pension benefit to its workers for the first time, but it had not promised to put aside current funds to guarantee retirees that they would obtain benefits in the future. Fearing that Chrysler could become bankrupt in the future, the UAW wanted this pension promise to be backed up with current funding, and it called a strike. (In the early 1980s Chrysler did teeter on the edge of bankruptcy, although by 1983 the company was again solvent.) The union's last offer to Chrysler before the strike is an excellent illustration of a wage/benefit trade-off: it asked Chrysler either to pay 6 cents per hour (per worker) to a pension fund and 4 cents to buy medical insurance or to give workers a 10-cents-per-hour raise in wages.

SOURCE: *The Daily Labor Report,* January 17, 1950, A-17.

---

fixed sum per month or a fixed fraction of one's earnings prior to retirement. In either case employers guarantee the size of the pension benefit, and it is up to them to make sure that the funds are there when the promised benefits need to be paid.

The *vesting* provisions of any pension plan are the rules about who becomes eligible to receive a pension. If a plan is unvested, any worker who quits the company before retirement age loses all rights to a pension benefit. Once workers are vested, they can receive a pension from company X even if they quit X before retirement age and work elsewhere. How much they receive from X at retirement, of course, depends on their length of service with X and their preretirement earnings; however, the point is that they receive *something* from X upon retirement if they are vested.

In 1974 Congress passed the Employee Retirement Income Security Act (ERISA), which, among other things, required private sector employers to adopt liberalized vesting rules. The Tax Reform Act of 1986 required even more liberalized (earlier) vesting beginning in 1989. The intent of these mandated changes was to help employees by making it more likely that they would receive pensions in their old age. However, as we have seen with other programs designed to help workers, good intentions can sometimes be undone by unintended side effects. What are the side effects of liberalized vesting provisions?

From the employees' perspective, rules that entitle them to become vested, or vested sooner, enhance their welfare if nothing else in the compensation package is changed. They are not penalized as much for voluntarily leaving an employer, nor are they as economically vulnerable to being fired. However, the value different workers attach to liberalized vesting may vary widely. The Tax Reform Act of 1986, for example, requires full vesting after 5 years of service, as compared to the 10-year vesting required under ERISA.[15] Employees who plan on working for a given employer less than 5 years do not benefit at all from the liberalized vesting; neither do workers who have more than 10 years of service with the company. However, workers who might want to change employers after 5 to 10 years of service, or who might be fired during that period, stand to gain from liberalized vesting.

From the employers' perspective, the new vesting rules impose costs because they make it possible for more workers to qualify for pensions. Will firms simply absorb these costs, or will they force workers to pay for their more liberal pension benefits in the form of lower wages? Our theory suggests that employers probably will not—and in a competitive market cannot—absorb the added pension costs. Those firms for which pension costs are increased will have to hold the line on future wage increases to remain competitive in the product market, and over time the wages they pay will fall below the level that would have held had it not been for the pension reform legislation.[16] Alternatively, firms whose expected pension costs rise because of vesting may choose to offset this rise with a reduction in promised pension benefits. In either case, theory suggests that it is the workers who bear the cost of the mandated change in vesting.

IMPLICIT CONTRACTS, EXPLICIT CONTRACTS, AND ASYMMETRIC INFORMATION

Agreements between employers and employees concerning job duties and compensation can be considered contracts, whether or not they are formally written. An *explicit contract,* such as a formal written agreement between a union and a firm, specifies what transactions or events will occur when some contingency arises. Thus, such contracts may spell out how the firm is to respond if layoffs are necessary or what is to be done when a job vacancy occurs.

Nonunion employees, however, typically do not work under explicit contracts. These employees, who constitute a majority of American workers, have relationships with their employers that are governed by *implicit contracts.* An implicit contract is a set of shared, informal understandings about how firms and workers will respond to contingencies.[17]

---

15. The vesting referred to here is known as "cliff vesting," in which a worker suddenly goes from being unvested to being fully vested. Both ERISA and the Tax Reform Act allowed for *partial* vesting plans, under which a fractional right to a pension upon retirement is granted earlier than 10 or 5 years, respectively, but full vesting occurs somewhat later.

16. The two studies that have looked at the effects of vesting on wages have both found that nonvesting (public) employers pay higher wages, other things equal, than ones who vest. See Ehrenberg and Smith, "A Framework for Evaluating State and Local Government Pension Reform," for more details.

17. For a more detailed analysis of implicit contracts, see Robert Flanagan, "Implicit Contracts, Explicit Contracts and Wages," *American Economic Review Papers and Proceedings* 74 (May 1984): 345–49, or Sherwin Rosen, "Implicit Contracts," *Journal of Economic Literature* 23 (September 1985): 1144–75.

The major difference between explicit and implicit contracts is that provisions of the former are legally enforceable, whereas those of the latter may or may not be. This distinction, however, may not be quite as significant as it first appears, because the *market* could provide a means for enforcing implicit contracts. More specifically, if either employer or employee acquires a reputation for breaking the promises inherent in implicit agreements, others will be less willing to transact with them in the future. Thus, differences between the two contracts in enforceability are mostly a matter of degree.[18] Moreover, since drawing up a list of all foreseeable contingencies and specifying rules for responding to them would be very costly to both parties, even employment relationships governed largely by explicit contracts remain implicit to some extent.

Over the years, but especially lately, labor economists have been interested in the forces that shape some fundamental characteristics common to explicit and implicit contracts in the labor market. For example, economic theory has been used to explain the following compensation phenomena:

1. Wages are typically tied to hours of work, rather than to units of output produced;
2. Nominal wages are rarely reduced, even in the nonunion sector, so when the demand-for-labor curve shifts left during a recession, the labor market typically adjusts through layoffs;
3. Workers typically receive higher wages as they become older, but are then required—or offered a large "bribe" (a pension)—to fully retire from their companies at a specified age; and
4. Firms—especially large ones—frequently offer compensation packages that appear to have a value above market-clearing levels.

Analyses of these phenomena tend to stress three themes: (*a*) there are costs associated with agreeing upon or adjusting contract provisions; (*b*) the two parties may have different attitudes toward fluctuations in income; and (*c*) there are costs associated with enforcing contractual promises. The impli-

---

18. See H. Lorne Carmichael, "Reputation in the Labor Market," *American Economic Review* 74 (September 1984): 713–25, for an interesting analysis of the role reputation plays.

In most European nations workers have some protection against "unjust dismissals." In contrast, the doctrine of *employment-at-will,* under which employers (and employees) have the right to terminate an employment relationship at any time, has historically prevailed in the United States. Those not subject to this doctrine in the United States have included unionized workers with contract provisions governing discharges, tenured teachers, and workers under some civil service systems.

Recently, however, a number of state courts have adopted public policy and/or implicit contract exceptions to the doctrine. The former prevent an employee from being discharged for an action that is consistent with public policy (e.g., reporting the violation of an OSHA standard), while the latter prevent discharges "without cause" if actions taken by an employer (e.g., oral statements, established past practices, or statements in a personnel manual) implicitly promise such protection. The adoption by the courts of implicit contract exceptions to the employment-at-will doctrine seems to make it less likely that employers will unilaterally break promises. However, since these exceptions increase employers' costs of discharging workers, they obviously will alter employers' behavior in a number of ways (e.g., hiring standards, employment levels). For a full discussion of these issues, see Ronald Ehrenberg, "Workers' Rights: Rethinking Protective Labor Legislation," in *Rethinking Employment Policy,* ed. Lee Bawden and Felicity Skidmore (Washington, D.C.: Urban Institute Press, 1989).

cations of enforcement costs have received much attention in recent years, and we shall briefly outline this theme here before moving on to analyses of the above phenomena.

Each party to a contract is interested in holding the other to its promises; thus, it is very important to know when a contingency covered by the contract has really occurred. A contract may specify, for example, that employees who steal company property or shirk their duties can be fired, but a given firm might find it very difficult to prove who has violated rules on stealing or shirking, or to what extent. Likewise, a contract may permit the wage rate to be reduced during times of economic distress, but workers, lacking access to the company's records, may find it difficult to ascertain just how much distress their employer is facing.

Put differently, one of the problems facing each party in enforcing a contract is that the other party may have greater information about a particular contingency. In this respect, access to information is *asymmetric.* Moreover, the party with the greater information may have incentives to mislead the other: a firm that is actually prospering during a recession may claim it is being hurt so that it can reduce wages, just as a shirking worker will attempt concealment. Because this asymmetry of information makes cheating possible, and because monitoring by the other party is often very costly, ways must be found to make contracts *self-enforcing.* That is, incentives must be built in to labor contracts that induce both parties to refrain from cheating the other when each has the opportunity to do so.

In the remainder of this chapter we shall examine economic analyses of phenomena 1, 3, and 4 above. That is, we shall consider why labor contracts typically pay workers for their time instead of their output; why workers who appeared at age 64 to be highly paid, highly valued members of a production team were often required to retire at age 65 (prior to passage of federal legislation in 1978 that prohibited such requirements); and why workers often appear to be paid above market-clearing wage levels. We shall defer our consideration of phenomenon 2—nominal wage inflexibility over a business cycle—until Chapter 15. In analyzing each of these compensation phenomena, we shall bring to bear one or more of the three analytical themes mentioned above.

THE BASIS OF PAY

The agreements between employers and employees concerning job duties and compensation can be considered *contracts,* whether or not they are formally written. As mentioned briefly in Chapter 1, there are two basic types of pay provisions in labor contracts. One rewards employees for the *time* they work, and the other rewards them for some *result* of their work.[19] Some contracts, however, contain a hybrid system of rewards.

---

19. This distinction concerning labor contracts is analyzed in Herbert A. Simon, "A Formal Theory of the Employment Relationship," *Econometrica* 19, no. 3 (July 1951): 293–305, and more recently in Joseph E. Stiglitz, "Incentives, Risk, and Information: Notes Toward a Theory of Hierarchy," *Bell Journal of Economics* 6 (Autumn 1975): 552–79.

The most common reward structure is payment for time worked, with about 86 percent of U.S. employees paid either by the hour or by the month. When employees are paid for time at work, it becomes management's challenge to motivate them not to shirk during that time. An alternative that would appear to alleviate the problem of shirking is payment by results, or incentive pay.

Piece-rate pay, under which workers earn a certain amount for each item produced, is the most common form of individually based incentive pay for production workers.[20] Another system linking earnings to individuals' output is payment by *commission,* under which workers (usually salespeople) receive a fraction of the value of the items they sell. *Gainsharing* plans, which have grown in popularity recently, are *group*-incentive plans that at least partially tie earnings to gains in group productivity, reductions in cost, increases in product quality, or other measures of group success. *Profit-sharing* and *bonus* plans attempt to relate workers' pay to the profits of their firm or subdivision; this form of pay also rewards work *groups* rather than individuals. Under all these systems, workers are paid at least somewhat proportionately to their output or to the degree their employer prospers. Because such payment schemes would appear to serve as such an obvious incentive to work industriously, one is led to wonder why time-based pay systems are so dominant.[21] Selecting the basis for pay, however, is ultimately a matter of satisfying the interests of both employer and employee, and we turn now to an analysis of some factors affecting the choice of a pay system.

Employee Preferences

If employees were told that their average earnings over the years under a time-payment system would be equal to their earnings under an individual incentive-pay scheme, they would probably choose to be paid on a *time* basis. Why? Earnings under a piece-rate or commission system depend on the thought and energy one is able to bring to the job. There are days and even weeks in any person's life when he or she is depressed, preoccupied, tired, or otherwise distracted from maximum work effort. There are other periods when one is exceptionally productive. If employees are paid on a piece-rate basis, their earnings could be highly *variable* over time because of the somewhat uncontrollable swings in productivity. The variability in income could cause anxiety owing to the possibility that several low-productivity months

---

20. A variant of piece-rate pay is the allowance of a *standard time* to complete a given task. A worker who finishes the task more *quickly* is paid for the full standard time regardless of how little time was actually spent; if the worker takes *longer* to complete the task, pay reverts to an *hourly* basis.

21. While the focus here is on the work-*incentive* aspects of various pay schemes, another important subject of analysis is how they affect the demand for labor. This topic is introduced in the appendix to this chapter. A theoretical analysis of the choice between piece rates and time-based pay can be found in Edward P. Lazear, "Salaries and Piece Rates," *Journal of Business* 59, no. 3 (July 1986): 405–31, and a theoretical and empirical analysis can be found in Charles Brown, "Firms' Choices of Method of Pay," in *Do Compensation Policies Matter?* ed. Ronald Ehrenberg (Ithaca, N.Y.: ILR Press, 1990).

could be strung together, making it difficult to meet mortgage payments and other obligations.

Because of this anxiety about less productive periods of time, employees might prefer the certainty of time-based pay to the uncertainty of piece-rate pay if both schemes paid the same average wage over time. In order to induce employees to accept piece-rate pay, employers would have to pay higher average wages over time; that is, a compensating differential would have to exist to compensate workers for the anxiety associated with variations in their earnings. Conversely, to obtain more certainty in their stream of earnings, employees would probably be willing to accept a somewhat lower average wage.

Employer Considerations

The willingness of employers to pay a premium in order to induce employees to accept piece rates depends on the costs and benefits to employers of incentive-pay schemes. If workers are paid with piece rates or commissions they bear the consequences of low productivity, as noted above; thus, employers can afford to spend less time screening and supervising workers (see Example 11.2). If workers are paid on a *time* basis, the *employer* accepts the risk of variations in their productivity. When they are exceptionally productive, profits increase; when they are less productive, profits decline. Employers, however, may be less anxious about these *variations* than employees are. They typically have more assets and can thus weather the lean periods more comfortably than can individual workers. More important, perhaps, employers usually have several employees, and the chances are that not all will suffer the same swings in productivity at the same time (unless there is a morale problem in the firm). Thus, employers may not be as willing to pay for income certainty as are workers.

Employers must also consider, however, that incentive-pay schemes are likely to increase worker productivity in two ways. First, because workers bear (or share) the risk of low productivity, incentive-pay schemes are likely to attract the most productive workers within each occupation. Put differently, schemes that reward high productivity implicitly punish low productivity; thus, firms offering such pay schemes will tend to attract those who anticipate the highest rewards. Second, because workers (whatever their quality) directly benefit from their own diligence under incentive-pay schemes, they have incentives to work harder than if paid only for their time. A full analysis, however, of these productivity-related incentives and the costs of implementing them must take into account differences between *individual* and *group* incentive-pay plans.

Individual Rewards: Piece Rates and Commissions

The use of piece rates varies considerably by industry. Data on their usage are difficult to obtain, but as Table 11.3 indicates for the 1970s, they seem most prevalent in clothing manufacturing. Other data from the 1970s found that nearly half of the production workers in U.S. auto-repair shops were paid incentive rates: roughly one-quarter received some fraction of the labor costs charged to the customer (they were paid by *commission,* in essence), and

EXAMPLE 11.2

Piece Rates and Supervisory Effort in California Agriculture

We have emphasized that piece-rate pay schemes allow employers to operate with relatively little supervisory effort. In some cases workers paid under pure piece rates work, essentially as subcontractors, out of their homes; these workers are not directly supervised at all. Others paid pure piece rates work in factories, but supervision may be relatively loose. For example, a contemporary account of work in a California cannery in the 1920s described worker behavior that, on the one hand, seems like a major absence of industrial discipline, but on the other can be looked upon as an early example of *flexible time* (in which firms allow workers, within limits, to set their own work schedules):

> One cannery checker...complained that the piece-rate system instilled a sense that each woman was "in business for herself," and, as a consequence, piece workers often came late and left the cannery early. Preparation workers were likely to leave if incoming produce slacked off or was of less workable quality.

Pure piece-rate pay schemes at times also allow firms to hire workers whose capabilities or work habits render their productivity so low or so variable that they would not ordinarily be hired by a firm paying time-based wages. Consider this description of "hiring standards" in California's harvest labor market around 1950:

> Differences in skill, age, and sex become matters of relative indifference, provided only that the elementary distinction between a ripe grape or a ripe peach and a green one can be communicated. Thus California agriculture is able to provide productive employment for men, women, and children, for the experienced and inexperienced, for alcoholic derelicts from the "slave" markets, and for the skilled Filipino, at a labor cost per unit of output which does not vary widely.

SOURCES: Martin Brown and Peter Philips, "The Decline of Piece Rates in California Canneries: 1890–1960," *Industrial Relations* 25, no. 1 (Winter 1986): 81–91; Lloyd H. Fisher, *The Harvest Labor Market in California* (Cambridge, Mass.: Harvard University Press, 1953), 8–11.

the other quarter were paid a flat rate *(piece rate)* for each kind of repair performed.[22]

The big advantage of these compensation schemes from the employer's perspective is that they induce employees to adopt a set of work goals that are consistent with those of their employer. Employees paid a piece rate are motivated to work quickly, while those paid by commission are induced to very thoroughly evaluate the servicing needs of the firm's customers. Moreover, these inducements exist without the need for, and expense of, close monitoring by the firm's supervisors. Auto-repair shops, however, provide a specific example of several general disadvantages to individually based incentive-pay

---

22. Sandra King, "Incentive and Time Pay in Auto Dealer Repair Shops," *Monthly Labor Review* 98, no. 9 (September 1975): 45–48.

TABLE 11.3   The Percentage of Production Workers Paid at Least Partially Under Piece-Rate Schemes, Selected Manufacturing Industries, 1972–76

Industry	Percentage of Workers
Highest	
Work clothing	80 %
Footwear	73
Men's and boys' shirts	72
Men's and boys' suits and coats	71
Children's hosiery	65
Women's hosiery	62
Men's hosiery	57
Cigars	45
Lowest	
Paints	0
Synthetic fibers	1
Glass containers	1
Fabricated structural steel	3
Prepared meat	3
Misc. plastic	3
Paperboard containers	3.5
Meat packing	4

SOURCE: Eric Seiler, "Piece Rate vs. Time Rate: The Effect of Incentives on Earnings," *Review of Economics and Statistics* 66, no. 3 (August 1984), Table 1.

schemes. These general problems include maintaining quality standards, misusing equipment, setting the rate, and measuring output.

Maintaining Quality Standards. Workers paid by the job are motivated to work quickly, but they are also motivated to have minimal regard for quality. Workers paid by commission are motivated to be so thorough in ferreting out servicing needs that they may fix things that are not broken. Both bases for compensation thus create a need for close supervisory attention to the quality of work performed, a need and an expense that in many cases will offset other supervisory savings associated with incentive pay.[23]

Equipment Misuse. Allied to the problem of work quality is the problem of equipment misuse. Workers receiving incentive pay are motivated to work so quickly that machines or tools are often damaged or otherwise misused. It is often asserted, for example, that piece-rate workers disengage safety devices on machinery in their desire to maximize output. This problem is mitigated to the extent that equipment damage causes *downtime* that results in lost employee earnings. Many firms using piece rates require workers to provide their *own* machines or tools.

23. The piece rate's inducement to emphasize quantity over quality is antithetical to a "quality revolution," associated with W. E. Deming, that has attracted growing interest recently. For a summary of the managerial philosophy that emphasizes quality, including the use of statistical process control techniques, see Alan Hodgson, "Deming's Never-Ending Road to Quality," *Personnel Management* (July 1987): 40–44.

Setting the Rate. A third problem, probably more often associated with piece rates than with commissions, is setting the rate. For example, it may be standard practice in the auto-repair industry to assume that an engine tune-up will require two hours of work and to translate this time requirement into a "per job" piece rate. Suppose, however, that some new tool or electronic device is adopted that reduces the time required for a tune-up. A new piece rate will have to be adopted, but how do the shop's owners determine the standard time requirement for tune-ups now? The best way may be to observe mechanics using the new devices, but if these workers know they are being observed for purposes of setting a new rate, they will probably deliberately work slowly so that the time requirement is overestimated. The problem is compounded in industries facing frequent changes in products or technology. In the women's apparel industry around the turn of the century, for example, it was common to have seasonal strikes over piece rates coinciding with seasonal changes in fashions.[24]

Measuring Output. A fourth reason why individual incentive-pay schemes are not more widely used is the problem of measuring and motivating individual *output*. The output of an auto mechanic, a salesperson, or a dressmaker is relatively easy to measure in terms of quantity, but what about that of an office manager or an auto assembly-line worker? The manager has a number of duties and deals with a multitude of problems; combining them into a single index of output would be next to impossible. Assembly-line workers, on the other hand, may have an easily counted output, but it is not individually controlled. In both cases, *individual* incentive pay would be arbitrary or useless; however, *group* incentives might be attractive in these situations.

Group Incentive Pay

When individual output is hard to monitor or control, or when individual incentive plans are detrimental to output quality, firms sometimes adopt group incentive-pay schemes to more closely align the interests of employer and employee. These plans may tie at least a portion of pay to some component of profits (group productivity, product quality, cost reductions) or they may directly link pay with the firm's overall profit level.[25] In still other cases workers might *own* the firm and split the profits among themselves, or more commonly, be partially compensated in shares of company stock.[26]

---

24. Louis Levine, *The Women's Garment Workers* (New York: B.W. Huebsch, 1924), 42. The observation that a stable technology is important for the success of an incentive-pay system is also made by Sumner H. Slichter, James J. Healy, and E. Robert Livernash, *The Impact of Collective Bargaining on Management* (Washington, D.C.: The Brookings Institution, 1960), 519.

25. Pay based on company profits also represents a way firms have of controlling their real wage costs. When the product price of a given firm goes up with prices in general, firms may seek to adopt a policy of tying their wage increases to some aggregate measure of prices (such as the Consumer Price Index). However, when an industry's product prices are declining relative to prices in the aggregate, firms in the industry may find profit-sharing plans advantageous. Under these plans the compensation of their workers is closely tied to the firm's profitability, and increases are granted only if the firm is profitable.

26. For a detailed treatment of worker-owned enterprise, the most widespread example of which is in Yugoslavia, see Jaroslav Vanek, *The General Theory of Labor-Managed Market Economies* (Ithaca, N.Y.: Cornell University Press, 1970).

One drawback to group incentives is that groups are composed of individuals, and it is at the individual level that decisions about shirking are ultimately made. A person who works very hard to increase group output or the firm's profits winds up splitting the fruits of his or her labor with all the others, who may not have put out extra effort. Group incentives, then, are sometimes no incentive at all. People come to realize that they can reap the rewards of someone else's hard work without doing any extra work of their own, and that if they do put out extra work, the rewards mainly go to others. Such schemes thus give workers incentives to cheat on their fellow employees by shirking.

In very small groups, however, cheating may be easy to detect, and group punishments, such as ostracism, can be effectively used to eliminate it. In these cases, group incentive-pay systems can accomplish their aims. However, if the group of workers receiving incentive pay is large, cheating (shirking) probably cannot be effectively handled. Group incentive-pay schemes thus become less effective as group size increases.[27]

As suggested by Example 11.3, the *basis* upon which incentive payments are made is very important in determining the overall profitability of the firm. For example, consider a firm wishing to maximize profits over the *long run* and trying to decide how to compensate its executives in such a way that this long-term goal will be achieved. If it adopts a yearly profit-sharing plan in which a fraction of year-end profits is given to each executive, its executives may be induced to pursue strategies designed to maximize profits in the current period. These short-run strategies may not be consistent with long-run profit maximization, but the executives involved may use their short-run performances to obtain positions with other firms before the long-run consequences of their strategies are fully observed.

Perhaps for these reasons, 40 percent of the 200 largest industrial companies in the United States give their executives rights to future payments that are directly tied to company performance over a *multiyear* period.[28] Ninety-five percent of all these long-term "performance attainment" plans base their awards on some measure of company prosperity over a period of 3–5 years, apparently in the belief that a period of less than 3 years is too short to measure long-term performance, while more than 5 years would represent so long a delay in receiving rewards that their motivational effects would be weakened.

A number of recent studies have gone beyond the formal pay practices for executives in the largest corporations to look at executive pay generally. In particular, these studies are concerned with whether executive earnings are tied, implicitly or explicitly, to the economic performance of firms.[29] Some studies define performance in terms of accounting measures of profits, while

27. Evidence on the productivity effects of profit sharing is reviewed in Martin Weitzman and Douglas Kruse, "Profit Sharing and Productivity," in *Paying for Productivity,* ed. Alan S. Blinder (Washington, D.C.: Brookings Institution, 1990).
28. Lawrence C. Bickford, "Long-Term Incentives for Management; Part 6: Performance Attainment Plans," *Compensation Review* (Third Quarter, 1981): 14–29.
29. See, for example, Jonathan Leonard, "Executive Pay and Corporate Performance," Kevin Murphy, "Relative Performance Evaluation for Chief Executive Officers," and John Abowd, "Does Performance-based Compensation Affect Subsequent Corporate Performance?" in *Do Compensation Policies Matter?* ed. Ronald Ehrenberg.

EXAMPLE 11.3

Incentive Pay and Output—or "You Get What You Pay For"

The effects of incentive-pay schemes depend on just what "output" is being paid for. There is a (probably apocryphal) story that when Soviet farm labor was compensated according to the number of acres planted, plowing was done too hastily and seeds were sown too far apart for high productivity. In an effort to improve output, the Soviet Union began to compensate farm workers on the basis of yield per acre. This caused farmers to invest too many resources (time, fertilizer) per acre and not plant extensively enough, and costs rose. Only when they seized upon the idea of paying farmers on the basis of the difference between the value of output and the costs of production (that is, *profit*) did farmers have the incentive to take into account output *and* costs.

Another example comes from Great Britain. Instead of paying dentists on the basis of "contact hours" with patients, the British National Health Service decided (for a while) to compensate them on the basis of cavities filled. The result was that the incidence of tooth decay identified by dentists increased substantially and the time it took to fill cavities dropped from 18 to 6 minutes per filling. It is obvious that this new basis for payment was of questionable benefit to patients.

Finally, a study of lawyers was made to see how the time they spent on civil cases was affected by the basis upon which their fee was calculated. The study compared the behavior of lawyers who charge an hourly fee with that of lawyers who charge on a contingency basis (that is, charge the client a percentage of the damages they are able to win from the party they are suing). In cases involving modest sums of money ($10,000 or less), lawyers paid an hourly fee tended to put in more preparation time than did contingent-fee lawyers; the reverse was true in cases in which the sums involved were greater. This pattern of effort is to be expected: the payment to lawyers charging hourly fees is independent of outcome, whereas the payoffs to contingent-fees lawyers—and hence their efforts—rise with the stakes involved.

SOURCES: Assar Lindbeck, *The Political Economy of the New Left* (New York: Harper & Row, 1971), 71; John Pencavel, "Piecework and On-the-Job Screening" (Department of Economics, Stanford University, June 1975), 4; Herbert M. Kritzer, William L. F. Felstiner, Austin Sarat, and David M. Trubek, "The Impact of Fee Arrangement on Lawyer Effort," *The Law and Society Review* 19, no. 2 (1985): 251–78.

others use the *total return* (dividends plus capital gains) on the firms' stocks. Virtually all studies find a strong positive correlation between compensation changes and firm performance. Moreover, there is some evidence that the way executive compensation is structured affects firm performance. Two studies showed that firms whose executives' compensation was at least implicitly tied to firm performance subsequently outperformed other firms.[30] Other

---

30. Leonard, "Executive Pay and Corporate Performance," and Abowd, "Does Performance-based Compensation Affect Subsequent Corporate Performance?"

studies show that the adoption of executive performance attainment plans leads to improved short-run stock market performance of these firms. Apparently the stock market believes that performance attainment plans will increase profits.[31]

Earnings Under Piece and Time Rates

Two observations lead to the prediction that workers on incentive pay earn more per hour than comparable workers paid on a time basis. First, if workers have a preference for being paid on a time basis, employers will have to pay a premium, a compensating wage differential, to induce them to accept an incentive-pay scheme. This earnings differential would compensate workers for accepting the risks associated with incentive pay. Second, the workers most likely to accept a job with incentive pay are those most likely to be successful at it: the fastest, most intense workers within each occupational group.

Although there are few studies of this issue, the prediction that incentive-pay workers earn more appears to hold up. A 1960s study of punch-press operators in Chicago found that piece-rate workers earned about 9 percent more per hour of work than did those paid an hourly wage. Research by the Bureau of Labor Statistics found that auto-repair workers paid on an incentive basis earned 20–50 percent more per hour than those paid on a time basis. Finally, another study estimated that piece-rate workers in the footwear and men's and boys' suit and coat industries earned 14–16 percent more than comparable workers receiving time-based pay. Only a small part of this latter differential could be attributed to a compensating wage differential; most of the differential was associated with greater productivity.[32]

Other Kinds of Incentive Pay

Although used relatively infrequently, incentive-pay schemes other than piece rates, commissions, gainsharing, and profit sharing have also been devised to solve particular production problems. For example, a firm attempting to induce employees to avoid injuries on the job might give a quarterly bonus to any worker who remained uninjured during that quarter.

Some of the most imaginative incentive-pay systems have been directed at the problem of absenteeism. Two in particular have achieved notice in the oral tradition of labor economics. A manufacturing plant during the 1940s coped with absenteeism by holding a daily raffle. The prizes were various consumable and durable items of special value to householders during those

---

31. See, for example, J. Brickley, S. Bhagat, and R. Lease, "The Impact of Long-Run Managerial Compensation Plans on Shareholder Wealth," *Journal of Accounting and Economics* 7 (April 1985): 115–29. An alternative explanation for these findings, however, is that executives may push for the adoption of these plans only when they believe the performance of the firm is likely to be good. If this occurs, adoption may *signal* to the stock market that the firm expects "good times" ahead. The resulting observed improvement in stock market performance may reflect only this signal, not any anticipated incentive effects.

32. John Pencavel, "Work Effort, On-the-Job Screening, and Alternative Methods of Remuneration," in *Research in Labor Economics,* vol. 1, ed. Ronald Ehrenberg (Greenwich, Conn.: JAI Press, 1977), 225–58; King, "Incentive and Time Pay in Auto Dealer Repair Shops," 46; and Eric Seiler, "Piece Rate vs. Time Rate: The Effect of Incentives on Earnings," *Review of Economics and Statistics* 66, no. 3 (August 1984): 363–76.

shortage-prone years. However, to have a chance to win, a worker had to be present. Absenteeism apparently fell dramatically.

Another scheme was adopted by an automobile manufacturer. This involved awarding daily points to each employee who was present for work—points that could be accumulated and redeemed for prizes, such as tickets to popular vacation attractions. The wrinkle in this plan was that the points were given not to the worker, but to the worker's spouse. With the spouse helping to monitor worker attendance, it is said that absenteeism problems were greatly reduced.

INTERNAL LABOR MARKETS AND THE LEVEL AND TIME PATTERN OF COMPENSATION

Given the difficulties and disadvantages of implementing the common forms of individual or group incentive pay, firms might consider methods of motivating workers using a time-based pay system. One approach to motivating workers within the context of time-based pay involves close supervision. If close supervision is impossible or very costly, two other approaches might be considered. Workers can be paid above what they could get elsewhere, thereby creating an incentive for them to work hard enough to maintain their jobs and continue to qualify for the above-market wage. Alternatively, workers can be offered delayed rewards—promotions, large pay increases, or generous pensions—only *after* years of diligent effort. Approaches that combine time-based wages and relatively low supervisory efforts suggest the existence of a *long-term relationship* between employer and employee.

That many workers, after a period of "job shopping," establish a long-term relationship with an employer was suggested in Chapter 10. It has been estimated, for example, that over half of all men and one-fourth of all women find employers for whom they will work at least 20 years. Moreover, 8 percent of men in the 45-to-59-year-old age group have worked for only one employer over their entire work history.[33] Most of the long-term employment that characterizes much of the American labor market is found in large firms with *internal labor markets,* wherein higher-level jobs are exclusively or primarily filled from within the organization.

Internal Labor Markets and Employee Pay

Recall from Chapter 5 that firms sometimes create an *internal labor market,* wherein hiring is done only at certain *entry-level jobs,* and all other jobs are filled from within the firm. This hiring and promotion system serves in part as a substitute for the difficult task of screening job applicants with respect to crucial personal characteristics. Workers are hired at low levels of responsibil-

---

33. Robert E. Hall, "The Importance of Lifetime Jobs in the U.S. Economy," *American Economic Review* 72 (September 1982): 716–24. See also George Akerlof and B. G. M. Main, "An Experience-Weighted Measure of Employment and Unemployment Durations," *American Economic Review* 71 (December 1981): 1003–11, and Walter Oi, "The Durability of Worker-Firm Attachments," Report prepared for the U.S. Department of Labor, Office of the Assistant Secretary for Policy, Evaluation, and Research, March 25, 1983, 16.

EXAMPLE 11.4

The Wide Range of Possible Productivities: The Case of the Factory That Could Not Cut Output

The effects of incentive pay on productivity depend in part on the degree to which greater efforts by workers can potentially result in increased output. There may be some operations in which employee output is not very elastic with respect to effort, but as illustrated by this example, there are other environments in which the range of potential worker productivities is surprisingly wide.

In 1987, a manufacturer of airguns ("BB guns") in New York State found that its sales were lagging behind production. Wanting to cut production by about 20 percent without engaging in widespread layoffs, the company decided to temporarily cut back from a five-day work schedule to a four-day workweek. To its amazement, the company found that, despite this 20 percent reduction in working hours, production levels were not reduced. That is, its workers produced as many airguns in four days as they had during the five-day workweek!

Central to the problem of achieving its desired output reduction was that the company paid its workers on a piece-rate basis. Faced with the prospect of a temporary cut in their earnings, its workers reduced time on "breaks" and increased their pace of work sufficiently to maintain their previous levels of output (and earnings). The company was therefore forced to institute artificial caps on employee production; when these individual output quotas had been met, the worker was not allowed to produce more.

The inability to cut output, despite cutting back on hours of work, suggests how wide the range of possible worker productivity can be in some operations. Clearly, then, careful attention by management to the motivation and morale of employees can have important consequences, both privately and socially!

ity and then observed over time to determine their actual productive characteristics. As we argued in Chapter 10, once the firm has discovered who the productive, dependable workers are, it wants to retain them. Internal labor markets can be useful in constructing compensation systems designed to motivate workers when close daily supervision is costly. These systems require worker efforts to be monitored over long periods of time, so that even if shirking in any one period is not likely to be detected, it will be observed eventually if it exists.

If employees are hired with the expectation that they will spend an entire career with a firm—an expectation that is certainly encouraged by a policy of promoting only from within—then the critical element in their choice of an employer is the *present value of their career earnings.* That is, they will be concerned about their likely earnings over their entire *career,* not just the pay on the job for which they are initially hired. A firm with an internal labor market must therefore offer a *stream* of earnings over time whose overall present value is at least equivalent to that offered by other firms competing in the same labor market.

To say that the present value of an earnings stream must be at least equivalent to that paid elsewhere does *not* imply that the wages offered for each job or at each stage in one's career must be at least equal to those paid by other firms. Firms that pay low wages initially but offer high earnings later on may be very competitive with firms offering initially higher wages but not raising them much over time. For example, suppose a firm offered a ten-year job sequence where the workers were paid $15,000 in each of the first five years and $18,000 for the next five years. Using a discount rate of 2 percent, an income stream with the same present value could be achieved by a labor market competitor who offered $10,000 for each of the first five years and paid $23,500 per year for the last five!

Besides having to offer workers a stream of earnings that is sufficient to attract their services, the firm with an internal labor market must also keep its pay within a zone that allows it to compete successfully with its product market competitors. It can pay higher than market wages and compete in the product market only if its workers are more productive, less likely to quit, or cheaper to supervise.

Thus, it should be clear that firms offering workers *careers,* and not just jobs, have some latitude in setting the level and sequencing of compensation within the general context of having to remain competitive in both labor and product markets. We now turn to more detailed analyses of the major compensation-based approaches to worker motivation when time wages are paid.

Efficiency Wages

In situations where the potential for long-term attachment between workers and firms exists, it may prove profitable for employers to pay workers *above* what the workers can earn elsewhere. One rationale for this was discussed in Chapter 5 when hiring and training investments were analyzed: there, the payment of higher wages was seen to be profitable for employers if it led to reduced turnover and consequent greater savings in hiring and training costs. It has also been emphasized in various chapters that high compensation levels allow a firm to assemble a quality work force; high pay generates so many applicants that hiring only the best is a feasible strategy.

Still another rationale relates to the difficulties employers face in monitoring employee work effort under time-based compensation arrangements. As discussed above, employees working under a time-based compensation scheme do not face the same direct incentives to work hard as do employees under a piece-rate or incentive system. In some situations, it may prove very costly for employers to supervise and monitor the effort levels of workers receiving time-based pay. Moreover, if the employer is paying hourly wages equal to what employees could earn elsewhere, they face no particularly strong incentive not to shirk. If at great cost the employer succeeded in repeatedly observing shirking and discharged the offending workers, the workers could obtain comparable employment elsewhere. Put another way, the cost to workers of shirking is relatively low when they are paid only what they could earn elsewhere.

Suppose instead that the firm were to pay its workers above what they could earn elsewhere. This obviously would increase the firm's labor costs, but such a scheme offers the firm at least two types of benefits. First, workers now would face an incentive not to shirk, for if they were caught and discharged they would lose (in present-value terms) the difference between the higher earnings at the firm and their potential earnings elsewhere, over the entire period they had expected to remain with the firm. To the extent that the employees responded by working harder, the firm's revenues would increase. Second, since the firm would now know that its workers would be shirking less, it could save money by devoting fewer resources to supervising and monitoring their behavior.[34]

Raising compensation above the level that workers can earn elsewhere obviously has both benefits and costs to the employer. While initial increases in pay may well serve to increase the profits of the firm, after a point the costs to the employer of further increases may well exceed the benefits. The pay level at which the marginal benefits to the employer of a further increase just equal the marginal costs is the level that will maximize profits. This has become known recently as the *efficiency wage*.[35]

Note that the payment of wages above what workers could earn elsewhere makes sense here only because workers expect to have long-term employment relationships with firms. If workers switched jobs every period they would face no incentive to reduce shirking when a firm paid above-market wages, because firing someone who is going to quit anyway is not an effective penalty; as a result firms would have no incentive to pursue an efficiency-wage policy. Thus, high-wage policies of the type described here are likely to arise only in situations where structured internal labor markets exist. Moreover, other things equal, the longer workers' expected tenure with the firm, the greater is the financial loss if a shirking worker is fired and hence the more likely it is that such schemes will have their intended effects.[36]

---

34. The argument actually is a bit more complicated, since the willingness of workers to shirk depends not only on the "penalty" (loss of high wages) they will face if caught but also on the probability they will get caught. Reduced employer monitoring presumably will reduce this probability. For simplicity, we ignore this complication in the text; introducing it into more formal models does not change any of the conclusions that follow.

35. It should be clear that the efficiency "wage" refers to all forms of compensation, not just cash wages. Besides inducing lower turnover, the acquisition and retention of higher-quality employees, and more employee effort with less supervisory input, it has also been argued that the "gift" of high wages by an employer encourages a reciprocal "gift" of high effort by employees. For further discussions of efficiency wages, see George A. Akerlof, "Gift Exchange and Efficiency Wages: Four Views," *American Economic Review* 74 (May 1984): 78–83; Lawrence Katz, "Efficiency Wage Theories: A Partial Evaluation," in *NBER Macroeconomics Annual, 1986,* ed. Stanley Fischer (Cambridge, Mass.: MIT Press, 1986); and Joseph E. Stiglitz, "The Causes and Consequences of the Dependence of Quality on Price," *Journal of Economic Literature* 25, no. 1 (March 1987): 1–48. A critical evaluation of the theory and evidence on efficiency wages is found in Kevin M. Murphy and Robert H. Topel, "Efficiency Wages Reconsidered: Theory and Evidence," in *Advances in the Theory and Measurement of Unemployment,* ed. Yoram Weiss and Gideon Fishelson (London: Macmillan, 1990).

36. The payment of above market-clearing, efficiency wages by some firms can also be shown to lead to unemployment in the economy; this point will be elaborated upon in Chapter 16. See Janet Yellen, "Efficiency Wage Models of Unemployment," *American Economic Review* 74 (May 1984): 200–208.

EXAMPLE 11.5

Did Henry Ford Pay Efficiency Wages?

The 1908–14 period saw the introduction of "scientific management" and assembly-line production processes at the Ford Motor Company. The change in production methods led to a change in the occupational composition of Ford's work force, and by 1914 most of its workers were relatively unskilled and foreign-born. Although these changes proved extremely profitable, worker dissatisfaction was high. In 1913 turnover rates reached 370 percent (370 workers had to be hired each year to keep every 100 positions filled), which was high even by the standards of the Detroit automobile industry at the time. Similarly, absenteeism typically averaged 10 percent a day. However, while Henry Ford was obviously having difficulty retaining and eliciting effort from workers, he had little difficulty finding replacements: there were always long lines of applicants at the factory gates. Hence, Ford's daily wage in 1913 of about $2.50 was at least at the competitive level.

In January of 1914, Ford instituted a $5.00-a-day wage; this doubling of pay was granted only to workers who had been employed at the company for at least six months. At roughly the same time, residency in the Detroit area for at least six months was made a hiring standard for new job applicants. Since the company was limiting the potential applicant flow and was apparently not screening job applicants any more carefully after the pay increase, it appears the motivation for this extraordinary increase in wages was not to increase the quality of new hires.

It is clear, however, that the increase *did* affect the behavior of existing employees. Between March of 1913 and March of 1914, the quit rate of Ford employees fell by 87 percent and their discharges by 90 percent. Similarly, the absentee rate fell by a factor of 75 percent during the October 1913 to October 1914 period. Morale and productivity increased and the company continued to be profitable.

There is some evidence that at least initially, however, Ford's productivity gains were less than the wage increase. Historians have pointed to the non-economic factors that influenced Ford's decision, including his paternalistic desire to teach his workers good living habits. (For workers to receive these increases, investigators from Ford first had to certify that they did not pursue life-styles that included behavior like excessive gambling or drinking.) While the wage increase thus probably did not lead to a wage level that maximized the company's profits (a smaller increase probably would have done that), the policy did have a substantial positive effect on worker turnover, effort, morale, and productivity.

SOURCE: Daniel Raff and Lawrence Summers, "Did Henry Ford Pay Efficiency Wages?" *Journal of Labor Economics* 5 (October 1987): S57–S86.

Pay in Large Firms

The theoretical association between internal labor markets and efficiency wages may help to explain the very strong empirical relationship between wage levels and firm size. It appears, for example, that workers in manufacturing firms with 100–500 workers receive wages that are 6 percent higher than those of workers in smaller firms who have the same measurable human capital characteristics; workers in firms of over 500 workers earn about 12 percent more.[37]

A variety of hypotheses have been advanced to explain this positive relationship between wage levels and employer size, but at the moment none seems entirely satisfactory.[38] It has been argued that large firms have more rigid, impersonal work environments, and that they must therefore pay a compensating wage differential to their workers; however, a significant size-related differential persists even when measurable working conditions have been held constant. It has been argued that large firms need workers who have intrinsic qualities that are hard to measure (motivation and dependability, for example), but a significant size-related wage differential also survives after controlling for these unmeasurables.[39] Likewise, the arguments that large firms "hide" monopoly profits by paying above-market wages (refer to Chapter 3) and that they pay high wages just to keep out labor unions seem unable to completely explain the differential. Thus, while our understanding of the wage differences associated with employer size is incomplete, the greater possibilities for the existence of efficiency wages among larger firms may have something to do with it.[40]

Employment Contracts and the Sequencing of Pay

Employers with internal labor markets also have options for *sequencing* workers' pay while still offering jobs with at least the same *present value* of career compensation as paid by the market generally.[41] It may be beneficial to both employer and employee to arrange workers' pay over time so that employees are "underpaid" early in their careers and "overpaid" later on. This sequencing of pay will increase worker productivity and enable firms to pay *higher* present

---

37. Wesley Mellow, "Employer Size and Wages," *Review of Economics and Statistics* 64, no. 3 (August 1982): 495–501.
38. The discussion in this paragraph is based on Charles Brown and James Medoff, "The Employer Size–Wage Effect," *Journal of Political Economy* 97 (October 1989): 1027–59.
39. Controlling for worker characteristics that are impossible to measure is done by tracking the wage *changes* of workers who have moved between small and large firms. Clearly, workers' intrinsic qualities do not change over short periods of time, so that the observed wage changes cannot be attributable to these qualities; rather, it is reasonable to infer that they are associated with changes in the size of one's employer. As longitudinal data—data on the same workers in different years—have become available, analyses of person-specific wage changes over time have been used to control for worker characteristics that affect productivity but are unobservable to the researcher.
40. Another empirical regularity for which our understanding is incomplete concerns wage differences *across industries*. As with the size-related patterns, the differences in wages across industries persist even after controlling for measurable and unmeasurable employee characteristics, working conditions, and unionization. Moreover, industry-related differentials appear to be fairly consistent over time and across countries. Theories of efficiency wages are again being challenged to explain these facts. For a review of the issues, see Richard Thaler, "Anomalies: Interindustry Wage Differentials," *Journal of Economic Perspectives* 3 (Spring 1989): 181–93.
41. Our discussion here draws on Edward Lazear, "Why is There Mandatory Retirement?" *Journal of Political Economy* 87, no. 6 (December 1979): 1261–84. For a review of issues raised in this and succeeding sections, see H. Lorne Carmichael, "Self-Enforcing Contracts, Shirking, and Life Cycle Incentives," *Journal of Economic Perspectives* 3, no. 4 (Fall 1989): 65–83.

values of compensation than otherwise, for two reasons. An understanding of these reasons takes us back to the problem of creating self-enforcing contracts in the presence of asymmetric information.

First, employment contracts that underpay workers in the early years of their careers and overpay them later on will appeal most to workers who intend to establish long-term relationships with their employers and work diligently enough to avoid being fired before their deferred rewards can be collected. Thus, in the absence of knowledge by employers of which applicants are diligent and not likely to quit, a pay scheme featuring deferred compensation appears to be a clever mechanism to force employees to reveal information about themselves that employers otherwise could not obtain.[42]

Second, a company that pays poorly to begin with but well later on increases the incentives of its employees to work industriously. Once in the job, an employee has incentives to work diligently in order to qualify for the later overpayment. The employer need not devote as many resources to supervision each year as would otherwise be the case, because the firm has several years in which to identify shirkers and withhold from them the reward. Workers are less likely to take chances and shirk their responsibilities, because the penalties for being caught and fired are forfeiture of a large reward. Because all employees work harder than they otherwise would, their total compensation tends to be higher also.

One feasible compensation-sequencing scheme would pay workers *less* than their marginal product early in their careers and *more* than their marginal product later on. This scheme, however, must satisfy two conditions. First, the present value of the earnings streams offered to employees must be at least equal to alternative streams offered to workers in the labor market; if not, the firm cannot attract the workers it wants. Since pay that is deferred into the future is discounted, deferred sums must be larger the higher is the discount rate, or *present-orientedness,* of workers (see Chapter 9). Second, the scheme must also satisfy the equilibrium conditions that firms maximize profits and do not earn supernormal profits. If profits are not maximized, the firm's existence is threatened; if firms make supernormal profits, new firms will be induced to enter the market. Thus, in neither case would equilibrium exist.

These two conditions will be met if hiring is done until the present value of one's career-long marginal product equals the present value of one's career earnings stream. (This career-long condition is the multiyear analogue of the single-year profit conditions discussed in Chapter 3 and the two-year profit-maximization criteria discussed in Chapter 5.) Thus, for firms choosing the "underpayment now, overpayment later" compensation scheme to be competitive in both the labor and the product markets, the present value of the yearly amounts by which marginal product (*MP*) *exceeds* compensation early on must equal the present value of the later amounts by which *MP falls short* of pay.

The above compensation plan is diagrammed in Figure 11.4. We assume that *MP* rises slightly over one's career, but that in the first t^* years of employment compensation remains below *MP*. At some point in one's career with the

---

42. Walter Oi, "The Durability of Worker-Firm Attachments," 41–45.

firm—year t^* in the diagram—compensation begins to exceed *MP*. From t^* until retirement in year r is the period during which diligent employees are rewarded by receiving compensation in excess of what they could receive elsewhere (namely, their *MP*). For the firm to be competitive in both the labor and the product markets, the *present value* of area A in the diagram must equal the *present value* of area B. (Area B is larger than area A in Figure 11.4 because sums received further in the future are subjected to heavier discounting when present values are calculated.)

To be sure, there are risks to both parties in making this kind of agreement. Employees agreeing to this compensation scheme take a chance that they may be fired without cause or that their employer may go bankrupt before they have collected their reward in the years beyond t^*. It is easy to see that employers will have some incentives to renege, since older workers are being paid a wage that exceeds their immediate value (at the margin) to the firm.

On the other hand, employers who do not wish to fire people face the risk that older, "overpaid" employees will stay on the job longer than is necessary to collect their reward—that is, stay on longer than time r in Figure 11.4. Knowing that their current wage is greater than the wage they can get elsewhere, since it reflects payment for more than current output, older employees will have incentives to keep working longer than is profitable for the firm.

A partial solution to these problems of risk is to agree on a formal employment contract that has two elements. One element protects older employees from arbitrary discharge by stipulating the grounds under which employees can be discharged and guaranteeing "seniority rights" for older

FIGURE 11.4 A Compensation Scheme Designed to Increase Worker Motivation

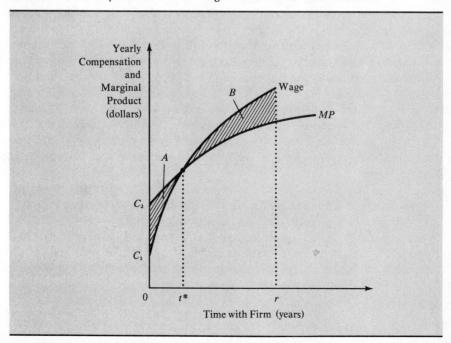

workers. According to these seniority provisions, workers with the shortest durations of employment with the firm are usually laid off first when the firm cuts back its work force. Without these seniority rights, firms might be tempted to lay off older workers, whose wages are greater than *MP*, and keep the younger ones, who are paid less than *MP* at this point in their careers.

The second element of a formal employment contract designed to reduce the risk inherent in this compensation plan is some form of retirement clause. Unless firms can induce workers to retire before the present value of area *B* in Figure 11.4 exceeds that of *A*, or unless they can force older employees to accept wage cuts so that after year *r* their wages equal *MP*, employers will not agree to the compensation-sequencing plan under discussion.

In some instances, formal employment contracts have included a mandatory retirement age, which prior to 1978 was normally set at age 65. Under these agreements employees had to retire at age 65 whether they wanted to or not. In other cases there may be inducements offered for voluntary early retirement. A study of pension plans in 190 of the *largest* companies in the United States (employing about one-quarter of all workers) found that it is common for the present value of pension benefits, summed over the expected lifetime of the retirees, to decline as retirement is postponed. For example, for workers with defined benefit plans in 1980 who retired after 20 years of service with yearly earnings of $25,000, the present value of retirement benefits at normal retirement age was $43,244. However, if retirement had occurred 5 years before normal retirement age, the present value of pension benefits would have been $55,604, and if retirement had been taken 8 years early, the present value of benefits would have totaled $57,200.[43]

In making an early-retirement decision, one must compare the utility generated by one's income and leisure streams if retirement occurs at 65 (say) with that generated by early retirement and its associated streams of leisure and pension income. When the stream of pension income associated with early retirement is increased in some way, the utility associated with early retirement is enhanced. Inducing early retirement by essentially bribing people to retire makes economic sense when older employees are paid more than they are currently worth.

Formal, explicit agreements cannot remove risks altogether, however. There is, on the employee side, no assurance that the firm will be in business during the employee's older years. Even large, once-profitable firms go bankrupt, close down plants, or are bought out by other firms—all of which can have the effect of reducing jobs or wage opportunities for older workers in the firm. While most *pension* promises are backed up by a separate fund that remains even if the employer goes bankrupt, there is really nothing to back up a promise of future pay increases. On the employer side, mandatory retirement agreements can be, and have been, voided by federal legislation. Amendments made to the Age Discrimination in Employment Act in 1978 and 1986, for example, have now effectively precluded mandatory retirement for most workers.

---

43. Edward Lazear, "Pensions as Severance Pay," in *Financial Aspects of the United States Pension System,* ed. Zvi Bodie and John Shoven (Chicago: University of Chicago Press, 1983). Since benefits are fixed nominally, Lazear uses a discount rate of 10 percent.

Thus, *explicit* contracts safeguarding the deferral of earnings to late in one's career are not riskless. Even more risky are *implicit contracts,* which are understood to exist but which have not been formally written and signed by both parties. In these contracts the employee is protected from arbitrary dismissal mainly by the employer's need to recruit *other* workers. If a certain em-

---

EXAMPLE 11.6

Monitoring Costs, Occupational Segregation, and Gender Differences in Compensation Methods in the 1890s

Female manufacturing workers at the turn of the century were far more likely to be paid by piece rates than were male manufacturing workers. For example, approximately 47 percent of all female operatives in manufacturing were paid by piece rates or some other variant of incentive pay in 1890, while only 13 percent of males were so paid. What caused these differences?

One possibility is that these differences arose because firms were trying to minimize the costs of monitoring and supervising workers. In situations in which it is difficult to supervise workers, firms can pursue several alternatives. On the one hand, employers can offer either above-market wage levels (efficiency wages) or deferred-compensation schemes (including wage profiles that increase with job tenure). Both of these strategies provide workers with incentives to work hard and not to shirk, for if they are caught shirking they stand to lose a job whose pay exceeds what they could earn elsewhere. On the other hand, if an individual's output is easy to measure, employers can pay workers by piece rates (or some other variant of incentive pay) rather than paying them for the time they are at work.

Given the frequent difficulty of measuring an individual worker's output, efficiency wages or deferred-compensation schemes often will be the preferred alternative for firms to use. In order for such schemes to have the desired incentive effects, however, employees must have strong labor force attachment and relatively long expected tenure with a firm. The shorter an employee's expected tenure with a firm, the smaller is the discounted present value of wage losses suffered if he or she is caught shirking.

At the turn of the century, the typical female labor force participant had a very short expected job tenure and labor force attachment. Women tended to enter the labor force (if at all) prior to marriage and then to leave it permanently shortly thereafter. Indeed, as noted in Table 6.1, the labor force participation rate of married women in 1900 was only 5.6 percent. Not surprisingly, then, employers may have been reluctant to employ women in occupations in which monitoring costs were high and an individual's output was difficult to measure. As a result, women in the labor force at the beginning of the 20th century often found themselves in occupations in which either monitoring costs were low or output could be so readily measured that piece-rate compensation schemes could be implemented.

SOURCE: Claudia Goldin, "Monitoring Costs and Occupational Segregation by Sex: A Historical Analysis," *Journal of Labor Economics* 4 (January 1986): 1–27.

ployer gains a reputation for firing older workers despite an implicit agreement not to do so, that employer will have trouble recruiting new employees (as noted earlier), which is some incentive to adhere to the implicit contract. However, if the company is in permanent decline, if it faces an unusually adverse market, or if information on its employment policies is not easily available, incentives to renege on implicit contracts are probably very strong.

Pensions as Deferred Payments

One way to ensure that employees receive their delayed reward is to provide pensions. According to statistics published by the Bureau of Labor Statistics, those retiring at age 65 in 1984, after 20 years of service with their employer and with yearly earnings of $25,000, received an average yearly benefit of $4,608. While this sum is not overwhelmingly large, a yearly payment of this size beginning at age 65 and lasting 15 years (the average life expectancy of a 65-year-old) requires a fund of $35,056 to finance it at a 10 percent rate of interest. Thus, giving pensioners $4,608 per year from age 65 until death is equivalent to giving the average retiree a lump-sum payment of $35,056. If the pension benefits were more generous, the lump-sum equivalent would increase proportionately. For example, the typical worker earning $25,000 per year and retiring in 1984 with 30 years of service received $6,660 per year in retirement benefits, with a lump-sum equivalent of $50,616.[44]

It is obvious, then, that pensions represent the equivalent of a deferred payment to workers at the end of their careers. Under ERISA, the money to finance this payment must be set aside each year by the employer in a separate fund so that employees have some assurance of receiving their reward even if the firm goes bankrupt. As discussed in this chapter, firms offering their employees pensions must pay lower wages, other things equal, to remain competitive. Thus, pensions offer a mechanism whereby spendable pay is low during one's working years but a reward is received later on.

The strongest incentives for diligence under a pension scheme would exist if the pension were not vested. Nonvested employees can be threatened with loss of a pension up to the day before retirement. Vesting, however, modifies the incentive effects of this compensation scheme somewhat. After 1989, most private sector employees with pensions must be vested after five years, so that the threat of losing all rights to their pension is, strictly speaking, only there for the first five years. This in itself may be a long enough time to motivate and observe reliable work habits, but even being fired after becoming vested entails loss. A vested worker fired by firm X may be able to obtain a pension from X at retirement, but this pension will be smaller to the extent that one's tenure with X is shorter. To receive a *full* pension benefit would require the worker to qualify for a pension with *another* firm—a process that will normally take five more years. Thus, while vesting softens the threat of

---

44. Donald G. Schmitt, "Today's Pension Plans: How Much Do They Pay?" *Monthly Labor Review* 108, no. 12 (December 1985): 19–25. The 10 percent discount rate was chosen for reasons cited in footnote 43. The study cited in footnote 43 was of very large firms; the one cited here presents national averages.

being fired for cause after five years, it does not remove all the incentive to work honestly and diligently throughout one's career.

Promotion Tournaments

Another form of worker motivation within the context of internal labor markets might best be called a *promotion tournament*. Suppose a group of entering management trainees were hired with the expectation that *one* of them would become a high-ranking corporate officer and make an extraordinary sum of money each year. The employees who did not make it to the top would be guaranteed a spot in the firm somewhere, but they would not achieve such high earnings.

Now, if everyone knew in advance who would be promoted, this scheme would not be incentive-producing nor would it have aspects of a tournament. However, if no one knew in advance who would "win" but all were told that winning the top job depended on hard work, all would be attracted by the large salary (or prestige) and work hard to get it. Here, as in the previous schemes, the prospect of obtaining large sums toward the end of one's career offers incentives for diligent work throughout earlier years.

In this scheme, however, not all diligent workers get the prize at career's end; only the winner does. Further, once the prize has been awarded and the losers are known, they no longer have the same strong incentives to work hard. Moreover, the employer, knowing the losers have reduced incentives, has every reason to want to get rid of them. Dangling a lucrative job in front of everyone increases the incentives of all, even the eventual losers, to work hard; once the prize has been awarded, the losers are of substantially less value to the firm.

The problem for the employer is that employees may not be willing to enter this tournament unless even the losers are treated relatively well. A firm known for firing older mid-level managers may not be able to attract a large enough group of young management trainees from which to produce an excellent corporate officer in the future. For this reason, a firm may be tempted to agree to essentially guarantee the losers desirable jobs somewhere in the organization.

Since workers whose wages are less than or equal to their marginal product do not need any guarantee of job security, it is most likely true that the losers of promotion tournaments have wages or salaries that *exceed* marginal product. If this is the case, the employer will obviously want to offer strong incentives for these employees to retire at a certain point. Again, then, a mandatory retirement clause or inducements to retire voluntarily may be an essential ingredient in the running of a promotion tournament.

Hypothesizing that promotion tournaments exist helps explain three phenomena that are widely observed in the labor market. First, it helps explain why, after a number of candidates are carefully considered for a top executive job, one is selected and paid perhaps three times what the others receive. Is it because he or she is three times as productive as the others? If so, the others would not have been serious contenders for the job. The huge pay differential most likely exists to serve as an incentive for younger employees to work hard so they can win the next tournament.[45] Second, the existence of tournaments helps explain why corporations sometimes tolerate *deadwood,* older employees who obviously are not going to be promoted and who clearly are not as productive as they used to be. Such deadwood is the unfortunate cost to the firm of running a successful tournament. Third, because deadwood can be tolerated for a while but not indefinitely, there have arisen mandatory retirement rules or other inducements for employees to retire before they might otherwise decide to do so.

Promotion tournaments are situations in which an individual's compensation depends only on his or her output *relative* to that of other competitors. In addition to the situation of corporate executives discussed above, such compensation structures appear to exist for young college professors who may be thought of as competing with colleagues for tenure, to salespeople whose bonuses often depend upon their performance relative to that of their co-workers, and to competitors in a professional sports tournament (such as golf; see Example 11.7) whose prize money depends on their rank relative to their competitors', not on their absolute scores.

When it is difficult to monitor worker effort and there are random shocks that influence the *absolute* level of output of all competitors (e.g., bad weather faced by golf players, or a heat wave that increases the sales of all air-conditioner salespeople), tournaments are thought to be a desirable way of compensating people because of the incentives they provide for participants to expend effort.[46] Of course, the benefits firms obtain from using tournament-type compensation schemes decline when participants can enhance their positions by sabotaging others. Thus, if it is possible for a participant to reduce another's output, we should not expect to observe payment according to relative performance.[47]

Federal Policy on Mandatory Retirement Reconsidered

This chapter has argued that "underpaying" employees in the early stages of their careers and "overpaying" them later serves as an incentive for employees to work industriously. Because workers are more productive, employers can offer them an income stream whose percent value is increased over what it would otherwise be. While employees can command more compensation because they, as individuals, work harder, they benefit *additionally* by a system that causes *other* employees to also work more diligently.

As we have pointed out, however, overpaying workers is something a firm cannot tolerate indefinitely. Thus, for this payment scheme to work—and it must work for both parties in order for each to have incentives to agree

45. This argument is advanced by Edward Lazear and Sherwin Rosen, "Rank-Order Tournaments as Optimum Labor Contracts," *Journal of Political Economy* 89 (October 1981): 841–64, and Sherwin Rosen, "Prizes and Incentives in Elimination Tournaments," *American Economic Review* 76 (September 1986): 701–15.

46. Lazear and Rosen, "Rank-Order Tournaments as Optimum Labor Contracts," and Rosen, "Prizes and Incentives in Elimination Tournaments."

47. Edward Lazear, "Pay Equality and Industrial Politics," *Journal of Political Economy* 97 (June 1989): 561–81.

EXAMPLE 11.7

Do Professional Golf Tournaments Have Incentive Effects?

One way to test whether tournament-type reward structures have desired incentive effects is to focus on professional golf tournaments, because information on the incentive structure players face (the prize distribution) and their output (the players' scores) are both available. In particular, most tournaments on the men's Professional Golfers' Association Tour have the same structure of prize money by rank, although the level of total prize money varies across tournaments. The figure below summarizes the structure. A key element in it is that the marginal return from improving one's performance by one rank is much higher for people who are close to the leaders after three rounds than it is for people who are far from the leaders. Furthermore, since the structure of prizes is constant across tournaments, the larger the level of the total prize money, the greater the incentive all players have to "play hard."

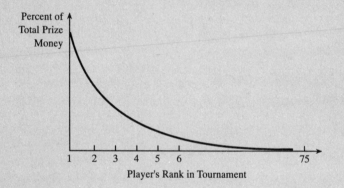

Player's Rank in Tournament

These facts suggest two ways to test whether tournaments have incentive effects. First, one can focus on men's tournaments as a whole and ask if, other things held constant (e.g., the weather, the course difficulty, the quality of the player and his opponents), higher total prize money in a tournament leads to lower player scores (remembering low scores mean better performance in golf). Second, one can focus on the last round of tournaments and ask if, other things equal (including how well the player has performed on earlier rounds), a player's performance on the last (fourth) round in a tournament is better when he is closer to the leader after the third round.

In fact, analyses of data from both the 1984 Professional Golfers' Association Tour and the 1987 European Professional Golfers' Association Tour provide positive answers to both questions. The level and structure of prize money in professional golf tournaments do influence player performance.

SOURCE: Ronald G. Ehrenberg and Michael L. Bognanno, "Do Tournaments Have Incentive Effects?" *Journal of Political Economy*, forthcoming, and Ehrenberg and Bognanno, "The Incentive Effects of Tournaments Revisited: Evidence from the European PGA Tour," *Industrial and Labor Relations Review* 43, no. 3 (February 1990): 74-S–88-S.

to it—firms must be able to terminate the overpayment at the point where it is no longer profitable in the long run.

One way to end the overpayment is to reduce the wage rate of older workers after a certain age to a wage that more closely corresponds to their marginal product. Reducing the wage rate in this way would almost surely raise charges of age discrimination, reflecting a prevailing social value that workers' nominal wages should not be reduced under any but the most extraordinary circumstances. Why society has adopted this particular value is an interesting—and open—question.[48]

A social "rule" against wage cutting suggests that the "underpay now, overpay later" scheme will be adopted only if older workers can be subjected to mandatory retirement (or otherwise induced to retire) by their employers. In most cases such retirement will mean no work at all; in other cases the employees might be able to find work at a lower wage rate with some other employers. In either case the affected employees have absorbed wage cuts, and because these cuts—when seen from the workers' perspective in old age— have been forced on them, they are likely to feel worse off. They may even support legislation to outlaw mandatory retirement, which is exactly what happened with the 1978 and 1986 amendments to the Age Discrimination in Employment Act, which eliminated mandatory retirement for most workers.

Who gains and who loses from this abolishment of mandatory retirement? It is clear that employers lose, but is it equally clear that employees gain? Surely people who are currently near retirement gain. However, their gain lies in the fact that governmental authority has been used to break a key element of a contract from which they benefited in the past. The fact that firms can no longer enforce a critical element of their old contracts removes from them the incentive to agree to future contracts of the same type. Thus, younger employees may be harmed by the forced elimination of mandatory retirement. In fact, the gains to older employees occur only *once*—to the group that is allowed to break its contract. Future generations of older workers do not gain, since their employment contracts and compensation schemes will be made under the new rules of the game.[49]

Why Do Earnings Increase with Experience?

Several explanations for the tendency of earnings to increase with a worker's tenure with a firm have been offered in Chapter 5 and this chapter. The first explanation is that increased earnings are a reward for workers' investment in implicit and explicit training during the early years of their career. The second is that the use of earnings profiles that increase with experience serves to motivate workers and reduce shirking. To these a third can be offered, namely that workers with long job tenures tend to be workers who have made good "job matches" and thus are more productive, on average, than otherwise

---

48. Chapter 15 discusses the related question of why employers react to decreases in demand by laying off workers rather than cutting their wages.
49. For further analysis of the winners and the losers, see Ronald G. Ehrenberg, "Retirement Policy, Employment, and Unemployment," *American Economic Review* 69, no. 2 (May 1979): 131–36.

identical workers with shorter job tenures.[50] Is it possible to ascertain which of these three explanations is correct?

In fact, a number of recent econometric studies provide support for *each* of these explanations. One study found that earnings increase most rapidly with seniority for workers during the stages of their careers in which they are undergoing formal or informal training.[51] Two other studies found that a large share of the apparent return to experience comes about because the more experienced workers have made better job matches, although a fourth study disputes this finding.[52] Finally, a fifth study has provided evidence in favor of the incentive compensation argument.[53]

These findings illustrate that the various theories of the relationship between earnings and experience are not mutually exclusive. To say that one explanation appears to have support does *not* imply that the others are unimportant. Rather, it appears that *each* of the theories provides a partial explanation for the increase of earnings with job tenure.[54]

MISCONCEPTION

"The way to get power over workers is to underpay them."

Analysis

If management *already* has power over workers because workers' ability to go to other jobs is severely limited by unemployment or monopsony, then low wages may result. However, paying low wages is definitely not the way to *acquire* power if management currently lacks it. Underpaid workers have no incentives to tolerate demanding requirements from management, because their current job is not better (and may be worse) than one they could find elsewhere. However, if workers are paid *more* by one firm than they could get elsewhere, they *will* tolerate heavy demands from their supervisors before deciding to quit. One way to *acquire* power over workers, therefore, is to overpay, not underpay, them.

Principle

The choices of economic actors depend on the relative benefits and costs of the alternatives available to them.

---

50. Boyan Jovanovic, "Job Matching and the Theory of Turnover," *Journal of Political Economy* 87 (October 1979): 972–90.
51. James N. Brown, "Why Do Wages Increase with Tenure?" *American Economic Review* 79, no. 5 (December 1989): 971–91.
52. Joseph Altonji and Robert Shakotko, "Do Wages Rise with Job Seniority?" *Review of Economic Studies* 54 (November 1987): 437–59; Katharine Abraham and Henry Farber, "Job Duration, Seniority and Earnings," *American Economic Review* 77 (June 1987): 278–97; and Robert Topel, "Wages Rise with Job Seniority," *Journal of Political Economy*, forthcoming.
53. Robert Hutchens, "A Test of Lazear's Theory of Delayed Payment Contracts," *Journal of Labor Economics* 5 (October 1987, pt. 2): S153–S170.
54. See Robert Hutchens, "Seniority, Wages, and Productivity: A Turbulent Decade," *Journal of Economic Perspectives* 3, no. 4 (Fall 1989): 49–64.

REVIEW QUESTIONS

1. There is a law that compensation of federal government employees must be comparable to that of private sector employees of similar skills who perform similar duties. Suppose that pay in the two sectors were compared by measuring salaries or wages of a "typical" worker in each sector (one, say, with 10 years of experience). In what respects would this approach be deficient?

2. In 1981 the President's Commission on Pension Policy proposed that every employee in the country be covered by a Minimum Universal Pension (MUP). This pension would vest immediately and would be fully *portable*. (That is, all workers would qualify for a pension no matter how many employers they worked for in their lifetime or how long they worked for each. Currently, employees are not eligible to receive any private pension benefits at age 65 unless they have worked for an employer 5 years.) What impact would a MUP have on labor costs and productivity?

3. Suppose mandatory retirement laws were abolished and firms undertook various strategies to induce *voluntary* retirements at age 65. Some of these possible strategies are listed below. The firm's objectives are to unambiguously increase the incentives for people over 65 to retire, but to do so in a way that offers the strongest incentives to the *least productive* of the older workers to retire. (For our purposes, the least productive will be defined as the workers no other firm would want at anything close to their current wage. Productive workers, even though elderly, could get jobs elsewhere at close to their current wage.) Evaluate each of the following strategies to determine whether it will accomplish the firm's objectives:
   a. Cut the wages of all workers after the age of 65.
   b. Provide a large lump-sum payment to anyone who quits his or her employment *at the firm* at age 65.
   c. Increase the monthly pension benefit of anyone who *retires* (and does not work elsewhere) at age 65.

4. In 1982 the State of New York paid its employees for only 50 of the 52 weeks they worked. This 4 percent pay cut was accomplished by increasing pay periods from 14 to 15 days apart for 14 pay periods (the other 11 pay periods were the normal 14 days). The two weeks of pay not given to employees was placed in a fund to be paid (with interest) when employees quit or retired.

   While the purpose of this scheme may have been to "force" employees to lend money to their state employer, the *effects* of schemes like this on quits and retirements may not be neutral. Explain.

5. Many states, particularly in the Snowbelt, have experienced the problem of "runaway" firms (firms that close down operations within their borders and move to another state, usually in the Sunbelt). Some states have adopted policies to discourage firms from closing operations and leaving the state. One such policy is to require firms closing down to pay *severance pay* to their workers. That is, if a firm permanently closes down operations within the state's borders, it is required to pay a lump-sum payment to its former employees. What are the labor market effects of requiring firms in this situation to give severance pay to employees?

6. The "employment-at-will" doctrine is one that allows employers to discharge workers for any reason whatsoever. This doctrine has generally prevailed in the United States except where modified by union agreements or by laws preventing age, race, or gender discrimination. Recently, however, the courts and lawmaking bodies have begun to erode the employment-at-will doctrine by moving closer to the notion that one's job becomes a property right that the worker cannot be deprived of unless there is a compelling reason. If employers lose the right to discharge workers without good cause, what effects will this have on the labor market?

7. Company X announces a plan to test all employees for drugs on a periodic basis. If employees whose tests are positive are found, upon further investigation, to be drug users, they will be fired. Analyze the likely effects of this policy on company X's hiring, supervisory, and wage costs.

SELECTED READINGS

Akerlof, George A., and Yellen, Janet L., eds. *Efficiency Wage Models of the Labor Market.* New York: Cambridge University Press, 1986.

Allen, Steven G. "Compensation, Safety and Absenteeism." *Industrial and Labor Relations Review* 34 (January 1981): 207–18.

Blinder, Alan, ed. *Paying for Productivity: A Look at the Evidence.* Washington, D.C.: Brookings Institution, 1990.

Ehrenberg, Ronald, ed. *Do Compensation Policies Matter?* Ithaca, N.Y.: ILR Press, 1990.

Ehrenberg, Ronald, and Smith, Robert. "A Framework for Evaluating State and Local Government Pension Reform." In *Public Sector Labor Markets,* ed. Peter Mieszkowski and George E. Peterson. Washington, D.C.: The Urban Institute, 1981.

Flanagan, Robert. "Implicit Contracts, Explicit Contracts and Wages." *American Economic Review Papers and Proceedings* 74 (May 1984): 345–49.

Lazear, Edward. "Why Is There Mandatory Retirement?" *Journal of Political Economy* 87 (December 1979): 1261–84.

Pencavel, John. "Work Effort, On-the-Job Screening, and Alternative Methods of Remuneration." In *Research in Labor Economics,* vol. 1, ed. Ronald Ehrenberg. Greenwich, Conn.: JAI Press, 1977. Pp. 225–58.

Rosen, Sherwin. "Implicit Contracts." *Journal of Economic Literature* 23 (September 1985): 1144–75.

APPENDIX 11A

Profit Sharing and the Demand for Labor

Chapters 3–5 of this text analyzed the demand for labor assuming that workers were paid time-based wages (that is, paid by the hour, week, month, or year). In Chapter 11, various forms of incentive-pay systems were discussed, but their implications for labor demand were not analyzed. Because linking pay to results may become more widespread as our economy adjusts to a changing global economic environment, it is important to understand the effects of incentive pay on the demand for labor. In this appendix, we analyze the effects of profit sharing, the most widespread of these "contingent compensation" schemes, on the demand for labor. In particular, we focus on the assertion that profit sharing helps avert unemployment in business downturns.[1]

Roughly 25 percent of American workers have at least part of their compensation tied to the profitability of their employers. For these workers, profit-sharing distributions by their employers amount to between 5 and 10 percent of earnings. Most profit sharing is in conjunction with time-based wages or salaries, and most profit-sharing distributions are made to employee deferred accounts (which are the equivalent of individual retirement funds, to which workers have limited current access). In analyzing the effects of profit sharing on the demand for labor, we will assume that employers use predetermined formulas to calculate their distributions each year;[2] the critical element of these formulas is the "share parameter," the fraction of profits that employers set aside for distribution to workers.

---

1. This assertion was made in a widely acclaimed book by Martin Weitzman, *The Share Economy* (Cambridge, Mass.: Harvard University Press, 1984).
2. In actual practice, predetermined formulas are rarely used, especially in small businesses. Most profit sharers do make distributions proportional to profits, however, so the assumption of a fixed-share parameter does not violate reality in any important way. See James Chelius and Robert Smith, "Profit Sharing and Employment Stability," in *Do Compensation Policies Matter?* ed. Ronald Ehrenberg (Ithaca, N.Y.: ILR Press, 1990).

PROFIT SHARING WITH A WAGE GUARANTEE: THE LONG RUN

It is crucial to understand that, no matter what "mix" of guaranteed wages and profit sharing a firm offers its workers, workers' expected total compensation with an employer must be sufficient to attract (and keep) workers away from alternative places of employment. It is true that if employees prefer time-based wages to a system that generates some variability in earnings, use of the latter system would have to be accompanied by a compensating wage differential to offset its perceived disadvantages to workers.[3] The central point, however, is that the total compensation a profit-sharing firm must pay its workers is ultimately market-determined. In what follows, this market-clearing level of compensation will be denoted by W^*.

If a profit-sharing firm wants to offer W_g as a guaranteed time-based wage, it must select its profit-sharing parameter (s', say) so that when the share component is added to W_g the sum brings workers' expected pay up to W^*. In the simple case in which the profit-sharing pool is split equally among workers, the total payments to each worker must satisfy the following condition:

$$W_g + \frac{s'(PQ^* - W_g L^* - CK^*)}{L^*} = W^* \qquad (11A.1)$$

where P is the price at which output can be sold and Q^*, L^*, and K^* are, respectively, the profit-maximizing levels of output, labor, and capital. The expression in parentheses in equation (11A.1), of course, is expected profits as calculated before share payments are made to workers; when multiplied by s' and divided by L^*, the per-worker bonus is indicated.

Thus, in deciding its optimum scale of output and optimum levels and mix of capital and labor, a profit-sharing firm, like others, will regard the market wage rate (W^*) as its long-run cost of obtaining labor. Once its optimum output and levels of inputs are determined, it can set its guaranteed wage and profit-sharing parameter to ensure that its workers' earnings are equivalent to this market-determined level of compensation.

It is also important to remember that, at the firm's profit-maximizing level of employment, the marginal revenue product of labor (product price, P, times labor's marginal physical product, MP_L)[4] must equal the market wage. If the marginal revenue product of labor exceeds the market wage for labor (W^*), the firm will want to expand its operations, hire more labor, and produce more output in the long run. Similarly, if the firm's marginal revenue product of labor is less than the going wage, it could improve its long-run profits by planning to reduce employment and its scale of output. Thus, the only

---

3. Firms might choose to offer profit sharing and pay a compensating differential if they believe that such a pay system will increase productivity or reduce turnover.
4. For expositional convenience, the profit-maximizing conditions are discussed in the context of a competitive firm.

time the firm is satisfied with its long-run levels of output and employment is when the marginal revenue product of labor is equal to the market wage:

$$P \cdot MP_L = W^* \tag{11A.2}$$

PROFIT-SHARING WITH A WAGE GUARANTEE: THE SHORT RUN

In the short run (when W^*, W_g, and s' are all fixed), a firm combining profit sharing with a guaranteed wage will find that, abstracting from hiring costs, if it adds an extra worker to its work force it bears the cost of the guaranteed wage, W_g, plus a fraction (s') of the resulting addition to profit. Thus, its marginal cost of labor (MC_L) is as follows:

$$MC_L = W_g + s'(P \cdot MP_L - W_g) \tag{11A.3}$$

In equation (11A.3), the expression $P \cdot MP_L - W_g$ represents the *addition* to the firm's profits (before sharing) caused by hiring one more worker. Because the marginal revenue product of labor is equal to the market wage for a profit-maximizing firm, and because the guaranteed wage must lie below the market wage, the term $P \cdot MP_L - W_g$ must clearly be greater than zero when the firm is producing its long-run, profit-maximizing level of output.

The firm will want to hire an additional worker in the short run if the marginal revenue product of labor exceeds the marginal cost. That is, the firm will want to continue hiring as long as the following condition is met:

$$P \cdot MP_L > W_g + s'(P \cdot MP_L - W_g) \tag{11A.4}$$

Rearranging expression (11A.4), it can be shown that a profit-sharing firm will find it can enhance profits by hiring an additional worker as long as labor's marginal revenue product exceeds the guaranteed wage:

$$P \cdot MP_L(1 - s') > W_g(1 - s') \tag{11A.5}$$

or

$$P \cdot MP_L > W_g$$

Intuitively, as long as $P \cdot MP_L > W_g$, the firm finds hiring another worker is profitable because it is able to keep a fraction $(1 - s')$ of any additional net revenues generated by the new employee.

IMPLICATIONS FOR EMPLOYMENT

At first blush, it is tempting to conclude that a profit-sharing firm will be "labor-hungry," always on the lookout for workers to add to its payrolls. Theory, however, does not support the implication that profit-sharing firms will behave differently from those paying time-based wages in the *long run*. Both types of firms must have roughly equal compensation levels in the long run, and facing the same long-run prices for capital and labor will cause them to choose the same K^* and L^*. In the *short run*, a profit-sharing firm in a market with full employment faces two problems in expanding beyond L^*: attracting new workers and keeping the ones it has. Both problems are created by the fact that, with MP_L falling and s' fixed, hiring beyond L^* reduces total compensation per worker *below W**.[5]

The really important implication to come out of our analysis of the profit-sharing firm concerns how it will behave in a business downturn. Suppose we assume that a firm operating at its long-run profit-maximizing scale of output is faced with a decline in product demand. If it paid its workers entirely with guaranteed (fixed) wages equal to the market wage (W^*), its original marginal revenue product of labor would equal W^*; thus, when the fall in product-market demand reduced labor's marginal revenue product, the latter would fall below W^* and the firm would lay off workers.

The firm paying under a profit-sharing system would not be as quick to reduce employment. If the profit-sharing firm started from a position in which labor's marginal revenue product equaled W^*, its guaranteed wage would lie below the original marginal revenue product of labor:

$$P \cdot MP_L > W_g \tag{11A.6}$$

The business downturn facing the firm would cause a fall in labor's marginal revenue product (the left-hand side of expression 11A.6), but the firm would not have incentives to reduce its employment level unless the *new* marginal revenue product fell below W_g. Theory thus predicts that workers in some profit-sharing firms—those in which marginal revenue productivity does not fall below W_g—are "cushioned" against being let go when the firm faces adversity.

Are the above theoretical predictions of greater employment stability during business downturns actually observed when profit-sharing firms are compared to others? On the whole, it does appear that profit-sharing firms are less likely to lay off workers when product demand falls. Although the evidence to date is not conclusive, two studies using data on U.S. firms have found evidence consistent with the theory.[6] Among nonsupervisory workers in 1977, for example, layoff rates were 4 percent among employees with profit sharing and 7 percent for comparable workers in non-sharing firms. Moreover, in the small-business sector, profit-sharing firms facing product demand declines in 1987 did not cut employment as much as did comparable non-sharing employers.

---

5. Because MP_L falls as more workers are hired, additions to the pool of profits set aside for profit sharing are smaller than the average bonus paid out—which serves to decrease the amounts paid per worker.

6. See James Chelius and Robert Smith, "Profit Sharing and Employment Stability," and Douglas Kruse, "Profit Sharing and Economic Variability: Microeconomic Evidence" (Department of Economics, Harvard University, 1987).

12

Unions and Collective Bargaining in the Private Sector

O ur analysis of the workings of labor markets has, for the most part, omitted any mention of the role of labor unions and collective bargaining. Because many people have strong and conflicting opinions about the role of unions in our society, it is often difficult to remain objective when discussing them. Some individuals view labor unions as forms of monopolies that, while benefiting their own members, impose substantial costs on other members of society. In contrast, other individuals view unions as *the* major means by which working persons have improved their economic status and as important forces behind much social legislation.

In recent years less than 15 percent of all individuals in the labor force and 20 percent of all employees on nonagricultural payrolls have been union members. These percentages are considerably lower than those found in most other Western countries. In addition, the United States is one of the few Western countries in which labor unions are not intimately and uniformly associated with one political party (such as the Labour Party in England, which is dominated by trade unionists). While unions play an important role in our society, their influence is probably not as pervasive as either their supporters or their opponents would have us believe.

This chapter initially presents a brief discussion of the nature of unions and the collective bargaining process and the major pieces of labor legislation that have shaped collective bargaining in the private sector in the United States. (Public sector labor markets and collective bargaining will be discussed in Chapter 13.) The chapter then presents a simple conceptual model of the forces that influence the level of unionization and shows how this model can be used to explain the historical pattern of union membership in the United States.

The chapter will then discuss how unions seek to achieve their bargaining goals. After reviewing the Hicks-Marshall laws of derived demand, initially discussed in Chapter 4, to analyze the factors that limit a union's ability to improve the economic well-being of its members without causing a substantial fraction of them to lose their jobs, the chapter will turn to a discussion of how, given such constraints, unions can translate their bargaining goals into actual outcomes. (An appendix to the chapter addresses the issue of whether the wage/employment combinations that result under collective bargaining tend to lie on, or off, employers' demand-for-labor curves.)

The chapter also examines the effects unions have had on wage *and* non-wage outcomes. Neoclassical economists have traditionally focused on estimating the amount by which unions have increased the wages of their members *relative* to the wages of comparable nonunion workers, and they have argued that such wage differentials lead to inefficiencies that have a negative effect on society. Recently, however, analytical labor economists have begun to rediscover the variety of roles that unions play and have concluded that unions may play many positive roles that leave society as a whole better off.[1] This chapter contrasts the evidence that supports both views of unions' effects.

UNIONS AND COLLECTIVE BARGAINING

Labor unions are collective organizations whose primary objectives are to improve the pecuniary and nonpecuniary conditions of employment of their members. Unions can be classified into two types: an *industrial* union represents most or all of the workers in an industry or firm regardless of their occupations, and a *craft* union represents workers in a single occupational group. Examples of industrial unions are the unions representing automobile workers, steel workers, bituminous coal miners, and rubber workers; craft unions include those representing the various building trades, printers, and dockworkers.

Although most unions are members of the American Federation of Labor–Congress of Industrial Organizations (AFL-CIO), this federation of unions is not involved in the collective bargaining process per se. In some industries—for example, automobile and steel—bargaining is done primarily at the *national* level. In others, such as construction, bargaining is done at the *local* level. In either case, bargaining can be *multiemployer,* in which case an agreement is reached simultaneously with a number of employers, or bargaining can take place separately with individual employers. The structure of bargaining in our economy influences both the ability of unions to accomplish their objectives and the inflationary process (as discussed in Chapter 16).

Collective bargaining typically covers a much wider range of issues than simply the issue of wage rates. Among the issues usually included are other pecuniary conditions of employment (such as vacation pay, health insurance,

---

1. This "new" view of unions is summarized by two of its exponents in a nontechnical fashion in Richard B. Freeman and James L. Medoff, "The Two Faces of Unionism," *Public Interest* 57 (Fall 1979): 69–93.

pensions, and the like), as well as nonpecuniary conditions of employment, including job security provisions (such as seniority rules or rules governing layoffs) and working conditions (such as workplace safety, rights to refuse overtime, and methods of production). Unions also help employers administer the provisions of union contracts while collective bargaining agreements are in effect and provide individual employees with a means of communicating their concerns to management. The tendency of some observers to focus on the pecuniary aspects of collective bargaining agreements to the neglect of the nonpecuniary aspects and the roles unions play while a contract is in effect can lead to an incomplete analysis of the effects of unions.

Modern Labor Legislation in the United States

Public attitudes and federal legislation have not always been favorably disposed toward labor unions and the collective bargaining process. For example, during the early part of the 20th century, employers were often able to claim that unions acted like monopolies in the labor market and hence were illegal under existing antitrust laws. Such employers were often able to get court orders or injunctions that prohibited union activity and aided them in stopping union organization drives. In addition, employers were often able to require potential employees to sign *yellow dog contracts,* contracts in which employees agreed not to join a union as a condition of accepting employment. Given this environment, it is not surprising that the fraction of the labor force who were union members stood at less than 7 percent in 1930.

Since that date, four major pieces of federal labor legislation have shaped the collective bargaining process in the private sector, the ability of unions to increase their membership, and the way unions operate. These laws and some of their salient provisions are listed in Table 12.1.

Two laws were products of the Depression. The Norris-LaGuardia Act, enacted in 1932, for all practical purposes outlawed the antiunion practices of employers discussed above. The National Labor Relations Act (NLRA), or Wagner Act, of 1935 went far beyond the earlier act by requiring employers to bargain with unions that represented the majority of their employees and by asserting that it was illegal for employers to interfere with their employees' right to organize collectively. The National Labor Relations Board (NLRB) was established by the NLRA and given power both to conduct elections to see which union, if any, employees wanted to represent them and to investigate claims that employers were either violating election rules or refusing to bargain with elected unions.[2] In the event violations were found, the NLRB was given further power to order violators to "cease and desist"; these orders were to be enforced by the courts.

After World War II the pendulum shifted decidedly in an antiunion direction. The Taft-Hartley Act of 1947 restricted some aspects of union activity. Perhaps its most famous provision is Section 14B, which permits individual states to pass *right-to-work laws.* These laws prohibit the require-

---

2. Actually, the NLRA was much less prolabor than our brief discussion indicates; the NLRA also gave the NLRB power to investigate employers' claims that their employees, or unions, were violating provisions of the act.

TABLE 12.1   Major Pieces of Federal Labor Legislation Governing Collective Bargaining in the Private Sector

Date	Law	Some Salient Provisions
1932	Norris-LaGuardia Act	1. Restricted employers' uses of court orders and injunctions as weapons to combat union organizing drives. 2. Prohibited "yellow dog" contracts, contracts in which potential employees had to agree *not* to join a union as a condition of employment.
1935	National Labor Relations (Wagner) Act	1. Defined unfair labor practices for both employers and employees. In particular, employers are required to bargain with unions representing the majority of their employees, and may not interfere with employees' rights to organize. 2. The National Labor Relations Board (NLRB) was established to settle many labor/management disputes. The NLRB was given power to investigate alleged unfair labor practices, to order violators to cease and desist, and to have its orders enforced by the courts. The NLRB was also given the right to conduct elections to see which unions, if any, employees wanted.
1947	Labor-Management Relations (Taft-Hartley) Act	1. Restricted some aspects of union activity. Section 14B permits states to pass right-to-work laws; these prohibit the requirement that persons become (or refrain from becoming) union members as a condition of employment.
1959	Labor-Management Reporting and Disclosure (Landrum-Griffin) Act	1. Designed to protect the rights of union members, it increases union democracy. It includes provisions for periodic reporting of union finances and provisions that regulate union elections.

ment that a person become, or promise to become, a union member as a condition of employment. By 1982 some 19 states, located primarily in the South, Southwest, and Plains areas, had passed such laws.

Finally, in 1959 Congress passed the Landrum-Griffin Act. This law, which was designed to protect the rights of union members in relation to their leaders, contained provisions that increased union democracy. As argued below, such provisions may well have had the side effect of increasing the level of strike activity in the economy.

A Model of the Level of Unionization

Table 12.2 presents data on union membership from 1930 through 1988. For the years since 1968 the table also includes data on membership in employee associations, such as the National Education Association (NEA). The primary purposes of employee associations historically have not related to collective bargaining; for example, the NEA has long been primarily concerned with professional standards and improving the quality of education students re-

TABLE 12.2   Union and Association Membership in the United States, 1930–88

	Union Membership Only			Union and Association Membership		
Year	Total (in thousands)	Percentage of Labor Force	Percentage of Nonagricultural Employment	Total (in thousands)	Percentage of Labor Force	Percentage of Nonagricultural Employment
1930	3,401	6.8	11.6			
1932	3,050	6.0	12.9			
1934	3,088	5.9	11.9			
1936	3,989	7.4	13.7			
1938	8,034	14.6	27.5			
1940	8,717	15.5	26.9			
1942	10,380	17.2	25.9			
1944	14,146	21.4	33.8			
1946	14,395	23.6	34.5			
1948	14,300	23.1	31.9			
1950	14,300	22.3	31.5			
1952	15,900	24.2	33.3			
1954	17,022	25.4	33.7			
1956	17,490	25.2	33.2			
1958	17,029	24.2	33.2			
1960	17,049	23.6	31.5			
1962	16,586	22.6	29.9			
1964	16,841	22.2	28.9			
1966	17,940	22.7	28.1			
1968	18,916	23.0	27.9	20,721	25.2	30.5
1970	19,381	22.6	27.3	21,248	24.7	30.0
1972	19,435	21.8	26.4	21,657	24.3	29.4
1974	20,119	21.7	25.8	22,809	24.5	29.1
1976	19,634	20.3	24.5	22,662	23.4	28.3
1978	20,246	19.7	24.0	22,880	22.3	27.1
1980				22,366	20.9	24.7
1982				19,763	17.9	22.1
1984				17,340	15.3	18.8
1986				16,975	14.4	17.5
1988				17,002	14.0	16.8

SOURCE: U.S. Bureau of Labor Statistics, *Directory of National Unions and Employee Associations, 1979,* Bulletin 2079 (Washington, D.C.: U.S. Government Printing Office, 1980); U.S. Bureau of the Census, *Historical Statistics of the United States: Colonial Times to 1970* (Washington, D.C.: U.S. Government Printing Office, 1975); Bureau of National Affairs, *Directory of U.S. Labor Organizations,* 1984–85 ed. (Washington, D.C.: BNA Books, 1984); U.S. Department of Labor, *Employment and Earnings* (January 1985, 1987, 1989).

ceive. However, these associations have become increasingly involved in the collective bargaining process.

Data on union membership are notoriously poor; nevertheless, Table 12.2 yields some striking patterns. First, union membership, both in absolute terms and as a percentage of the labor force (and of nonagricultural employment), grew steadily during both the 1930s and World War II. The former result was somewhat surprising to analysts, since prior to the 1930s periods of high unemployment were typically associated with declining union strength.[3] After a

---

3. For evidence and a discussion of the pre-1930s view, see John R. Commons, *The History of Labor in the United States,* vol. 3 (New York: Macmillan, 1918).

TABLE 12.3   Results of Representation Elections and Decertification Polls Supervised by the National Labor Relations Board

Fiscal Year	Union Elections	Percent Won by Union	Decertification Votes	Percent Lost by Union
1971	8,362	53.2	401	69.6
1973	9,369	51.1	453	69.5
1975	8,577	48.2	516	73.4
1977	9,484	46.0	849	76.0
1979	8,043	45.0	777	75.0
1981	7,512	43.1	856	74.9
1983	4,405	43.0	922	74.8
1985	4,614	42.4	865	75.6
1987	4,069	43.9	755	76.2

SOURCE: *Annual Report of the National Labor Relations Board,* Appendix Table 13 (various years).

slight dip in the immediate postwar period, union strength reached a peak of 25 percent of the labor force in the mid-1950s. However, since that time the share of union members in both total nonagricultural employment and the labor force has declined steadily. By 1978 union membership stood at about 20 percent of the labor force—a 30-year low. While inclusion of employee association members in Table 12.2 raises this estimate somewhat, it does not alter the underlying trend, which has continued since. Indeed, by 1988 less than 15 percent of the labor force were union or employee association members.

Further evidence of this trend can be found in the National Labor Relations Board certification and decertification vote data for 1971–87 found in Table 12.3. These data indicate that the number of elections in which unions have sought the right to represent unorganized workers, which fluctuated between 8,000 and 9,500 a year during the 1970s, declined in the 1980s. The *share* of the elections that unions actually won has fallen steadily during the period, from over 50 to under 45 percent. Furthermore, the annual number of *decertification votes*—votes in which union claims to represent a majority of workers in a firm were challenged—has roughly doubled, with the share of these votes lost by unions increasing slightly to more than 75 percent during this period.

A simple model of the demand for and supply of union activity can be used to explain the forces that influence union strength.[4] On the demand side, employees' demand to be union members will be a function of the "price" of union membership; this price includes initiation fees, monthly dues, the value of the time an individual is expected to spend on union activities, etc. Other things equal, the higher the price, the lower the fraction of employees that will want to be union members, as represented by the demand curve D_0 in Figure 12.1.

---

4. This model is based upon the approach found in Orley Ashenfelter and John Pencavel, "American Trade Union Growth, 1900–1960," *Quarterly Journal of Economics* 83 (August 1969): 434–48, and John Pencavel, "The Demand for Union Services: An Exercise," *Industrial and Labor Relations Review* 24 (January 1971): 180–91.

FIGURE 12.1   The Demand for and Supply of Unionization

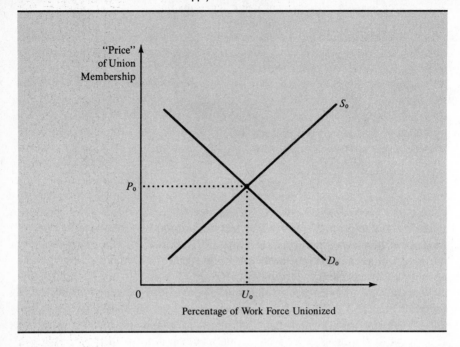

It is costly to represent workers in collective bargaining negotiations and to supervise the administration of union contracts. Moreover, union organizing campaigns require resources, and as unions move from organizing workers who are the most favorably inclined towards unions to those who are the least favorably inclined, the cost of making a sufficiently strong case to win a union representation election increases. Therefore, it is reasonable to conclude that, other things equal, on the supply side of the market the willingness of unions to provide union services is an upward-sloping function of the price of union membership, as represented by the supply curve S_0 in Figure 12.1. The intersection of these demand and supply curves yields an equilibrium percentage of the work force that is unionized (U_0) and an equilibrium price of union services (P_0).

What are the forces that determine the *positions* of the demand and supply curves? Anything that causes either the demand curve *or* the supply curve to shift to the right will increase the level of unionization in the economy, other things equal. Conversely, if either of these curves shifts to the left, other things equal, the level of unionization will fall. Identifying the factors that shift these curves enables one to explain *changes* in the level of unionization in the economy over time.

On the demand side, it is likely that individuals' demand for union membership is positively related to their perceptions of the *net benefits* from being union members. For example, the larger the wage gain they think unions will win for them, the further to the right the demand curve will be and the higher the level of unionization. Another factor is *tastes;* if individuals' tastes for union membership increase, perhaps because of changes in social attitudes or the introduction of labor legislation that protects the rights of workers to join unions, the demand curve will also shift to the right.

On the supply side, anything that changes the *costs* of union organizing activities will affect the supply curve. Introduction of labor legislation that makes it easier (harder) for unions to win representation elections will shift the supply curve to the right (left). Changes in the industrial structure that make it more difficult to organize the work force will also shift the curve to the left and reduce the level of unionization.

The rapid growth in unionization that took place during the 1930s was a product of both the changing legal environment (the Norris-LaGuardia and Wagner Acts) and changing social attitudes towards unions induced by the Great Depression—changes that shifted both the demand and the supply curves to the right.[5] The growth continued during the World War II years as low unemployment rates reduced workers' fears of losing their jobs if they indicated prounion sentiments (shifting the demand curve to the right). Unemployment increased after the end of World War II, shifting the demand curve back to the left, while the passage of the Taft-Hartley Act made it more difficult for unions to increase membership in right-to-work states and shifted the supply curve further to the left. Both shifts served to decrease the percentage unionized.

Explaining the Decline in Union Membership

The decline in unionization rates that has taken place in the United States since the mid-1950s, and the recent acceleration in that decline, can be at least partially explained by five factors related to the demand for, or supply of, union services: demographic changes in the labor force, a shifting industrial mix, a heavier mix of employment in states in which the environment is not particularly favorable for unions, increased competitive pressures, and increased employer resistance to union organizing efforts.[6]

Demographic Changes. The fraction of the labor force that is female has increased substantially (see Chapter 6), and women historically have tended not to join unions. The benefits from union membership are a function of in-

---

5. It is difficult to identify the effect of the laws per se, as they were determined by societal attitudes themselves. However, as noted both above and below, prior to and after the Depression, periods of high unemployment have been associated with weakening union membership, which leads one to suspect that the changing legal environment induced by the Depression, which reduced employees' fears of being fired for union activities, did have a substantial effect on union growth during the 1930s.

6. For a recent discussion of the factors underlying the rise and fall of unionization rates in the United States, see the essays by Edward P. Lazear, Richard B. Freeman, and Melvin W. Reder in *The Journal of Economic Perspectives* 2, no. 2 (Spring 1988): 59–110. Social legislation may also reduce unionization if it leads to the government's providing workers with benefits that previously were provided only through collective bargaining. See George Neumann and Ellen Rissman, "Where Have All the Union Members Gone?" *Journal of Labor Economics* 2 (April 1984): 175–92, for evidence that this may be occurring in the United States. For quantitative estimates of the extent to which the factors discussed in this section are responsible for the decline in unionization see Henry Farber, "The Recent Decline of Unionization in the United States," *Science* 238 (November 1987): 915–20.

TABLE 12.4 Union and Association Membership by Industry in 1988

Industry	Number of Union Members (in thousands)	Number of Employees on Payrolls (in thousands)	Percentage of Employees That Are Union Members
Manufacturing	4,516	20,430	22.1
Mining	133	711	18.7
Construction	1,096	5,193	21.1
Transportation and public utilities	2,001	6,053	33.1
Wholesale and retail trade	1,386	20,597	6.7
Finance, insurance, and real estate	178	6,812	3.5
Service	1,365	22,944	5.9
Government	6,298	17,175	36.7

SOURCE: U.S. Bureau of Labor Statistics, *Employment and Earnings* (January 1989), 226.

dividuals' expected tenure with firms; seniority provisions, job security provisions, and retirement benefits are not worth much to individuals who expect to be employed at a firm for only a short while. *In the past,* women tended to have shorter expected job tenure than men and to have more intermittent labor force participation. As a result, their expected benefits from joining unions were lower; an increase in their share in the labor force would shift the aggregate demand curve for union membership to the left.[7]

Changing Industrial Mix. A second factor in the decline of union membership is the shift in the industrial composition of employment, discussed in Chapter 2. A substantial decline in the relative employment shares of manufacturing, mining, construction, transportation, and public utilities and, conversely, a substantial increase in the share of employment in wholesale and retail trade, finance, insurance, real estate, and the service industries, has occurred since the mid-1950s. Indeed, the former group fell from 48.9 percent of nonagricultural payroll employment in 1955 to 29.4 percent by 1988. During the same period the latter group rose from 37.8 percent to 54.2 percent. As Table 12.4 indicates, the industries in the former group are the most heavily unionized in the private sector, while the industries in the latter group are the least unionized. The shifting industrial composition of employment has led to a distribution that is weighted more heavily towards industries that are not heavily unionized.

Why does the latter set of industries tend not to be unionized? These industries tend to be highly competitive ones, with high price elasticities of demand. As discussed in Chapter 3, other things equal, industries with high price elasticities of demand also have high wage elasticities of demand. High wage elasticities limit unions' abilities to increase their members' wages with-

---

7. We emphasize "in the past" here. Changing labor force patterns, with a greater share of women now having permanent attachment to the labor force, will likely increase their propensity to become union members.

out substantial employment declines also occurring. As such, the net benefits individuals perceive from union membership may be lower in these industries, and an increase in their importance in the economy would shift the demand for union services to the left in Figure 12.1, thereby reducing the percentage of the work force that is unionized.[8]

Regional Shifts in Employment.   A third factor that may have contributed to the decline in union strength is the movement in population and employment that has occurred since 1955 from the industrial Northeast and Midwest—the Snowbelt—to the Sunbelt of the South. As noted earlier, the Taft-Hartley Act permitted states to pass right-to-work laws. Such laws raise the costs of increasing union membership, since individuals who accept employment with a firm cannot be compelled to become union members as a condition of employment. In terms of Figure 12.1, these laws shift the supply curve of union services to the left, thereby reducing the level of unionization. Most Sunbelt states have right-to-work laws.

Table 12.5 presents data on the extent of unionization that existed in 1982 in right-to-work and other states. The data indicate quite clearly that right-to-work states are the ones in which union strength is the lowest. In 11 of the 19 right-to-work states, the proportion of nonagricultural employees who were union members was less than 15 percent. In contrast, in 26 of the other 31 states, the proportion exceeded 15 percent. While right-to-work states are not uniformly identical to those in the Sunbelt, there is considerable overlap. As a result, between 1955 and 1982 the proportion of employees working in right-to-work states increased from 24.1 to 31.8 percent. This shifting geographic distribution of the work force, coupled with the existence of these laws, undoubtedly had the effect of depressing union membership.

It is not at all obvious, however, that the decline in unionization occasioned by the move to the Sunbelt can be attributed to right-to-work laws per se. The extent of unionization in right-to-work states tended to be lower than that in other states even before the passage of the laws. These laws may only reflect attitudes towards unions that already exist in these communities.[9] The

---

8. These industries also tend to be populated by small establishments. The demand for unionization is thought to be lower for employees who work in small firms, since they often feel less alienated from their supervisors. Similarly, since it is more costly to try to organize 1,000 workers spread over 100 firms than it is to organize 1,000 workers at one plant, it is often thought that the supply of union services would shift down as the share of employment going to small firms increases. Both of these factors tend to suggest (in terms of Figure 12.1) that unionization will decline as the share of employment occurring in small establishments increases, providing another reason why the shift in industrial distribution of employment has affected the extent of unionization.

9. Numerous econometric studies have sought to estimate the effect of right-to-work laws on union strength, wages, and industrial conflict. A good survey of these studies is William Moore and Robert Newman, "The Effect of Right-to-Work Laws: A Review of the Literature," *Industrial and Labor Relations Review* 38 (July 1985): 571–86. While most, including Henry Farber, in "Right-to-Work Laws and the Extent of Unionization," *Journal of Labor Economics* 2 (July 1984): 319–52, conclude that these laws have little or no effect, some, such as David Ellwood and Glenn Fine, in "The Impact of Right-to-Work Laws on Union Organizing," *Journal of Political Economy* 95 (April 1987): 250–73, find a substantial effect from the laws.

TABLE 12.5   Percent of Nonagricultural Employees That Are Union Members, 1982

Right-to-Work States	Union Members (percent)	Other States	Union Members (percent)
Alabama	18.2	Alaska	30.4
Arizona	12.8	California	25.4
Arkansas	13.2	Colorado	18.0
Florida	9.6	Connecticut	18.9
Georgia	12.7	Delaware	20.3
Iowa	20.4	Hawaii	31.4
Louisiana	13.8	Idaho	16.1
Mississippi	19.3	Illinois	27.5
Nebraska	16.3	Indiana	25.1
Nevada	22.1	Kansas	12.0
North Carolina	8.9	Kentucky	20.4
North Dakota	14.2	Maine	18.5
South Carolina	5.8	Maryland-D.C.	18.6
South Dakota	10.3	Massachusetts	19.7
Tennessee	17.3	Michigan	33.7
Texas	12.5	Minnesota	24.5
Utah	16.8	Missouri	26.6
Virginia	10.9	Montana	21.7
Wyoming	15.9	New Hampshire	12.3
		New Jersey	19.9
		New Mexico	12.8
		New York	35.8
		Ohio	27.4
		Oklahoma	12.9
		Oregon	27.5
		Pennsylvania	27.0
		Rhode Island	19.4
		Vermont	11.9
		Washington	32.9
		West Virginia	28.9
		Wisconsin	24.5

SOURCE: From *Union Sourcebook: Membership, Structure, Finance, Directory,* First Edition 1985 by Leo Troy and Neil Sheflin. Copyright © 1985 by Leo Troy and Neil Sheflin. Reprinted by permission.

increasing influx of Snowbelters into the Sunbelt may eventually lead to a change in public attitudes *and* the repeal of some of these laws.

Competitive Pressures.   A fourth factor is increased foreign competition in manufacturing and the deregulation of the airline, trucking, and telephone industries (see Example 12.1). In these industries, which tended to be highly unionized, increased product market competition has served to increase the price elasticities of product demand, and hence the wage elasticities of labor demand. To the extent that union members' wages did not fall substantially in the face of increased product market competition, unionized employment within these industries could have been expected to fall. Indeed, the share of unionized employment in these previously heavily unionized industries has fallen substantially in the last decade as competition from both for-

EXAMPLE 12.1

Deregulation and the Airlines

Prior to 1978, regulation of the airline industry prohibited price competition between airlines that flew the same route, and it granted airlines that had no competitors on a route a form of monopoly power by limiting the entry of new carriers. Such regulation tended to reduce the price elasticity of demand for each airline's flights, which in turn strengthened unions in the industry by reducing the wage elasticity of demand for airline employees. Under the Airline Deregulation Act of 1978, however, price competition was permitted on routes with more than one carrier, and new airlines, which were often nonunion and had lower labor costs, began to compete with the existing carriers. As a result, revenue and employment fell substantially for the established, unionized carriers; one study suggests that their employment of mechanics had fallen by 15 to 20 percent as of 1983 because of deregulation.

These forces led the established airlines to "request" that their unions make *concessions,* in the form of reduced compensation and longer workweeks, in exchange for at least implicit promises that employment levels would be maintained. In some cases concessions were made voluntarily by the unions, in the sense that new contracts were written that agreed to temporary or permanent concessions. In at least one case, however, an airline (Continental) filed for bankruptcy and unilaterally reduced its employees' wages by almost 50 percent in an attempt to compel the unions to negotiate new contracts.

Concessions often took the form of *two-tier wage structures,* in which newly hired employees were temporarily or permanently paid according to a lower wage scale than previously hired employees. Over 60 percent of the settlements negotiated in 1985 by the established airline carriers contained such provisions. These provisions had the effect, of course, of reducing the costs of newly hired employees relative to more senior employees.

By 1987, the real earnings of pilots had fallen 17 percent below their levels in 1978, while the real earnings of airline mechanics had fallen by about 13 percent. Because the decline in real earnings among U.S. full-time male workers in this period was 4 percent, and the decline among all nonsupervisory workers was 10 percent, one can conclude that, as expected, increased product market competition in the airline industry reduced the relative wages of pilots and mechanics. (The real earnings of flight attendants fell only by 5 percent, perhaps because of increased opportunities in other occupations for the women who typically had been recruited for these jobs.)

SOURCES: "Airlines in Turmoil," *Business Week,* October 10, 1983, 98–102; David Card, "The Impact of Deregulation on the Employment and Wages of Airline Mechanics," *Industrial and Labor Relations Review* 39 (July 1986): 527–38; Sanford Jacoby and Daniel Mitchell, "Management Attitudes Toward Two-Tier Pay Plans," *Journal of Labor Research* 7 (Summer 1986): 221–37; Bureau of National Affairs, "Facts for Bargaining," no. 1062, February 13, 1986; David Card, "Deregulation and Labor Earnings in the Airline Industry," Working Paper no. 247, Industrial Relations Section, Princeton University, January 1989.

eign firms and new, nonunion employers in the deregulated industries has increased.[10]

By making labor demand curves more elastic, increased competitive pressures reduce the benefits to workers of collective action, hence shifting the demand curve for union membership to the left. Moreover, increased product market competition may well call forth *employer* responses that affect workers' demand for unions. For example, if firms find that foreign competition has intensified, they may seek to relocate in areas where workers are less likely to unionize; similarly, they may seek to employ workers in demographic groups whose demands for union membership are relatively low. Both of these employer responses may at least partially underlie factors discussed above. Moreover, increased competition may cause employers to resist union organizing efforts more vigorously, which could well increase the costs of such efforts and shift the supply curve of union services to the left.

Employer Resistance. Employers can, and often do, play an active role in opposing union organizing campaigns, using both legal and illegal means. For example, under the National Labor Relations Act it is legal for employers to present arguments to employees detailing why they think it is in the workers' best interests to vote against a union and for employers to hire consultants to advise them how to best conduct a campaign to prevent a union from winning an election. On the other hand, it is illegal for an employer to threaten to withhold planned wage increases if the union wins the election or for a firm to discriminate against employees involved in the organizing effort. If a union believes an employer is involved in illegal activities during a campaign, it can file an unfair labor practices charge with the National Labor Relations Board which, if sustained, can lead the NLRB to issue a "cease and desist" order. Although the evidence is somewhat ambiguous, it appears that both legal and illegal employer resistance to union organizing efforts reduces the chance that such efforts will succeed.

Since the early 1970s employer resistance to union organizing campaigns has increased. As noted in Table 12.3, the share of elections won by unions has decreased. In addition, the volume of unfair labor practice charges filed by unions with the NLRB has soared dramatically. Some people attribute these trends to a changing attitude of employers toward unions; they argue that employers are now more disposed, on purely ideological grounds, to maintain "union-free" workplaces.

Others suggest, however, that the change in employer behavior is not due to a changing ideology per se but rather to an increase in the expected costs that employers perceive they will face if unions win elections. During the 1970s and early 1980s wages of unionized workers grew more rapidly than the

---

10. For example, unionized employees were approximately 40 percent of manufacturing employment a decade ago, whereas in 1988 they constituted only 22 percent. Evidence that the effects of foreign competition are felt primarily in union members' employment levels, not in their wages, is found in John Abowd and Thomas Lemieux, "The Effects of International Trade on Union Wages and Employment: Evidence from the U.S. and Canada," in *Immigration, Trade, and Labor Markets,* ed. John Abowd and Richard Freeman (Chicago: University of Chicago Press, 1990).

wages of nonunion workers just as competition from foreign producers increased sharply. Thus, the perceived economic benefits to nonunion employers of keeping their workplaces nonunion increased. This factor, it is argued, has encouraged them to increasingly and aggressively combat union election campaigns, through both legal and illegal means (the "penalty" for committing an unfair labor practice is virtually nonexistent for first offenders).[11]

HOW UNIONS ACHIEVE THEIR OBJECTIVES

Union Policies to Ease Market Constraints

Many theories of union behavior attempt to formalize the view that unions are organizations that seek to maximize some well-defined objective function.[12] Indeed, several studies have even attempted to econometrically estimate the parameters of such an objective function.[13] As noted above, unions play many roles in addition to negotiating wage rates for their members; hence, it is not surprising that there is no widespread agreement on what specifically is a union's objective function. Nevertheless, it is generally agreed that in most cases unions value not only the wage and employee benefits and working conditions they can achieve for their members but also their members' employment levels. As a result, the position and wage elasticity of the labor demand curve are fundamental *market constraints* that limit the ability of unions to accomplish their objectives.

To see this, ignore employee benefits and working conditions for the moment and consider Figure 12.2, which shows two demand curves, D_e^0 and D_i^0, that intersect at an initial wage W_0 and employment level E_0. Suppose a union seeks to raise the wage rate of its members to W_1. To do so would require employment to fall to E_e^1 if the union faced the relatively elastic demand curve D_e^0, or to E_i^1 if it faced the relatively inelastic demand curve D_i^0. Other things equal, the more elastic the demand curve for labor is, the greater will be the reduction in employment associated with any given increase in wages.

11. William T. Dickens, "The Effect of Company Campaigns on Certification Elections: Law and Reality Once Again," *Industrial and Labor Relations Review* 36 (July 1983): 560–75; Robert Flanagan, *Labor Relations and the Litigation Explosion* (Washington, D.C.: Brookings Institution, 1987); and Henry Farber, "The Decline in Unionization in the United States: What Can Be Learned from Recent Experience," *Journal of Labor Economics* 8, no. 1, pt. 2 (January 1990): S75–S105.

12. See Wallace Atherton, *Theory of Union Bargaining Goals* (Princeton, N.J.: Princeton University Press, 1973), for an extensive discussion of the various theories. A classic debate took place more than 40 years ago between John Dunlop, *Wage Determination Under Trade Unions* (New York: Macmillan, 1944), and Arthur Ross, *Trade Union Wage Policy* (Berkeley: University of California Press, 1948), on whether it was meaningful to analyze unions in terms of how they maximize well-defined objective functions. Dunlop argued yes and Ross no, the latter articulating an alternative political model of union behavior. Here we shall follow in Dunlop's footsteps, although we shall return to the Ross view below.

13. See Henry Farber, "Individual Preferences and Union Wage Determination: The Case of the United Mine Workers," *Journal of Political Economy* 86 (October 1978): 923–42; J. N. Dertouzos and J. H. Pencavel, "Wage and Employment Determination Under Trade Unionism: The International Typographical Union," *Journal of Political Economy* 89 (December 1981): 1162–81; and John Pencavel, "The Trade-off Between Wages and Employment in Trade Union Objectives," *Quarterly Journal of Economics* 99 (May 1984): 215–31.

FIGURE 12.2 Effects of Demand Growth and Wage Elasticity of Demand on the Market Constraints Faced by Unions

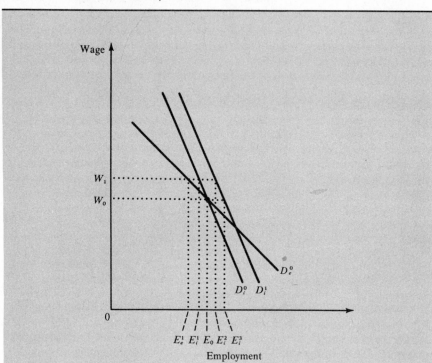

Suppose now that the demand curve D_i^0 shifts out to D_i^1 while the negotiations are under way, owing perhaps to growing demand for the final product. If the union succeeds in raising its members' wage to W_1, there will be no absolute decrease in employment in this case. Rather, the union will have only slowed the rate of growth of employment to E_i^2 instead of E_i^3. More generally, other things equal, the more rapidly the labor demand curve is shifting out (in), the smaller (larger) will be the reduction *in employment* or the reduction *in the rate of growth of employment* associated with any given increase in wages. Hence, unions' ability to raise their members' wages will be strongest in rapidly growing industries with inelastic labor demand curves. Conversely, unions will be weakest in industries in which the wage elasticity of demand is highly elastic and in which the demand curve for labor is shifting in.

Many actions that unions take are direct attempts to relax the market constraints they face: either to increase the demand for union labor or to reduce the wage elasticity of demand for their members' services. The laws of derived demand discussed in Chapter 4 implied that three important determinants of the wage elasticities of demand were the price elasticity of demand for the final product, the ease of substituting other inputs for union members in the production process, and the responsiveness of the supply of other inputs to their prices. Other things equal, if price elasticities of demand for the final product are less elastic, if it is difficult to substitute other inputs for union labor, and if the supplies of other inputs are relatively unresponsive to their prices, a more inelastic demand for union labor will result.

As noted in Chapter 4, the wage elasticity of demand for labor is more elastic in the long run. In the short run there may be only limited foreign competition in the output market while, as American automobile manufacturers realized in the late 1970s and the 1980s, in the long run foreign competition may increase, increasing the price elasticity of demand for output. In the short run production technologies may be fixed; in the long run labor-saving technologies may be introduced. Finally, in the short run the supplies of alternative inputs may be fixed, while in the long run—because of immigration, the training of other nonunion workers, or the production of new capital equipment—they may be more responsive to price. As a result, the market constraints unions face are more severe in the long run than in the short run; as illustrated in Example 12.2, large wage gains won today may lead to substantial employment losses in the future. Such constraints are the primary reason why the economic gains that unions have won for their members are, in fact, relatively modest. (This discussion has assumed that unions and employers will always agree to wage/employment combinations that lie on the demand-for-labor curve. The appendix to this chapter discusses why this might not occur.)

Altering the Demand for Union Labor

Attempts by unions to shift the demand curve for union labor to the right and to reduce the wage elasticity of demand have taken many forms. Many of these attempts have *not* occurred through the collective bargaining process per se. Rather, they have occurred through union support of legislation that at least indirectly achieved union goals and through direct public relations campaigns to increase the demand for products produced by union members.

Turning first to policies to shift the demand for the final product, at times unions have lobbied for quotas or tariffs on foreign-produced goods that would limit the amount of these goods sold in the United States. Both the steelworkers and the automobile workers sought such forms of protection during the late 1970s and the 1980s. The automobile workers also supported *domestic content* legislation proposals in the 1980s; these proposals would require that imported automobiles contain certain minimum percentages of American-made components. Other unions have sought to directly influence people's tastes for the products they produce. The International Ladies Garment Workers' Union (ILGWU) sought, for many years, to encourage people to "Buy American," featuring the song "Look for the Union Label" in some of its television ads.

Unions have also sought, by means of legislation, to pursue strategies that increase the costs of other inputs that are potential substitutes for union members. For example, as noted in Chapter 3, labor unions have been among the

EXAMPLE 12.2

The Rise and Fall of the Mississippi Steamboat Pilots' Union

Unions can enhance their power, at least in the short run, by engaging in activities that reduce the substitutability of nonmembers for union workers. In the long run, however, these efforts are often futile because new technologies and products can effectively displace union workers. These observations are illustrated by Mark Twain's description of the Mississippi steamboat pilots' union in the 1800s.

As described by Mark Twain in *Life on the Mississippi,* a primary tactic used by the Pilots' Benevolent Association was to share information on the shifting shoals and currents of the river *only* with other unionized pilots:

> It was a rigid rule of the association that its members should never, under any circumstances whatever, give information about the channel to any "outsider." By this time about half the boats had none but association pilots, and the other half had none but outsiders. At the first glance one would suppose that when it came to forbidding information about the river these two parties could play equally at that game; but this was not so. . . . [T]he outsiders had a hard time of it. . . . [They had] no particular place to meet and exchange information, no wharf-boat reports, none but chance and unsatisfactory ways of getting news.

The superiority of the information possessed by union members eventually led underwriters to insist, as a condition of their insuring the cargo, that only union pilots be used. The result was a very powerful union—until high wages and technological innovation led to the substitution of capital for labor:

> The organization seemed indestructible. It was the tightest monopoly in the world. By the United States law, no man could become a pilot unless two duly licensed pilots signed his application; and now there was nobody outside of the association competent to sign. Consequently the making of pilots was at an end. Every year some would die and others become incapacitated by age and infirmity; there would be no new ones to take their places. In time, the association could put wages up to any figure it chose. . . .
>
> [T]he pilots' association was now the compactest monopoly in the world, perhaps, and seemed simply indestructible. And yet the days of its glory were numbered. First, the new railroad stretching up through Mississippi, Tennessee, and Kentucky, to Northern railway centres, began to divert the passenger travel from the steamers. . . . [T]he railroads intruding everywhere, there was little for steamers to do . . . but carry freights; so straightway some genius from the Atlantic coast introduced the plan of towing a dozen steamer cargoes down to New Orleans at the tail of a vulgar little tug-boat; and behold, in the twinkling of an eye, as it were, the association and the noble science of piloting were things of the dead and pathetic past!

SOURCE: Mark Twain, *Life on the Mississippi* (first published, 1883), Chapter XV. We thank Professor Levis Kochin, University of Washington, for suggesting Twain's chapter to us.

primary supporters of higher minimum wages.[14] While such support may be motivated by a concern for the welfare of low-wage workers, increases in the minimum wage also raise the relative costs to employers of less-skilled non-union workers, thereby both increasing the costs of the products they produce and reducing employers' incentives to substitute nonunion workers for more-skilled union workers.

An example of such a strategy is union support for the Davis-Bacon Act and other forms of prevailing-wage legislation. These require that wages paid to construction workers on projects that are federally financed or federally assisted through loans, or whose financing is insured by the federal government, be set at least equal to the prevailing wage in the area as determined by the Secretary of Labor. Since typically the prevailing wage has been set equal to the union wage scale, the net effect is to eliminate any cost advantage the nonunion construction workers may have, thereby increasing the demand for union labor.[15]

Another example of how unions can influence the demand for union labor is the union position on immigration policy. The AFL-CIO has been quite explicit, both historically and in recent years, about its concern that immigrants depress wages and provide competition for unionized American workers. Indeed, with respect to the problem of illegal immigration in the early 1980s, the AFL-CIO asserted that

> while the nation should continue its compassionate and humane immigration policy, it is apparent that large numbers of illegal immigrants are being exploited by employers, thus threatening hard-won wages and working conditions. U.S. immigration policy should foster re-unification of families and provide haven for refugees from persecution, while taking a realistic view of the job opportunities and the needs of U.S. workers.[16]

It is not surprising, then, that unions have historically supported legislation restricting immigration, especially during recessionary periods.[17]

Union attempts to restrict the substitution of other inputs for union labor typically occur by means of the collective bargaining process. Some unions, notably those in the airline, railroad, and printing industries, have sought and

---

14. For evidence that union support for minimum wage legislation is often transformed into pro–minimum wage votes by members of Congress, see James Kau and Paul Rubin, "Voting on Minimum Wages: A Time-Series Analysis," *Journal of Political Economy* 86 (April 1978): 337–42; Jonathan Silberman and Garey Durden, "Determining Legislative Preferences on the Minimum Wage," *Journal of Political Economy* 84 (April 1976): 317–30; and James Cox and Ronald Oaxaca, "The Determinants of Minimum Wage Levels and Coverage in State Minimum Wage Laws," in *The Economics of Legal Minimum Wages,* ed. Simon Rottenberg (Washington, D.C.: American Enterprise Institute for Public Policy Research, 1981).
15. See Robert Goldfarb and John Morrall III, "The Davis-Bacon Act: An Appraisal of Recent Studies," *Industrial and Labor Relations Review* 34 (January 1981): 191–207, and Steven Allen, "Much Ado About Davis-Bacon: A Critical Review and New Evidence," *Journal of Law and Economics* 26 (October 1983): 707–36, for a more complete discussion of the act and analysis of its effects.
16. *The AFL-CIO Platform Proposals: Presented to the Democratic and Republican National Conventions 1980* (Washington, D.C.: AFL-CIO, 1980), 14.
17. F. Ray Marshall, Allan King, and Vernon Briggs, *Labor Economics: Wages, Employment, and Trade Unionism,* 4th ed. (Homewood, Ill.: Richard D. Irwin, 1980), 196.

won guarantees of minimum crew sizes (for example, at least three pilots are required to fly certain jet aircrafts). Such *staffing requirements* prevent employers from substituting capital for labor.[18] Other unions have won contract provisions that prohibit employers from *subcontracting* for some or all of the services they provide. For example, a union representing a company's janitorial employees may win a contract provision preventing the firm from hiring external firms to provide it with janitorial services. Such provisions may limit the substitution of nonunion for union workers. Craft unions, especially those in the building and printing trades, often negotiate specific contract provisions that restrict the functions that members of each individual craft can perform, thereby limiting the substitution of one type of union labor for another. Finally, craft unions also limit the substitution of unskilled union labor for skilled union labor by establishing rules about the maximum number of *apprentice* workers—workers who are learning the skilled trades—that can be employed relative to the experienced *journeymen* workers.

Apprenticeship rules also limit the supply of skilled workers to a craft. Indeed, they represent only one of several ways in which unions or employee associations may restrict entry into an occupation. Another way is to control the accreditation of outside institutions that provide training; the American Medical Association's accreditation of medical schools is an example. A third way of restricting entry into an occupation is to lobby for state occupational licensing laws.[19]

From Market Constraints to Bargaining Power

How do unions persuade employers to agree to changes that reduce the wage elasticity of demand or shift the demand curve for union labor to the right? Given the elasticity and position of demand curves, how are unions able to bargain for, and win, real wage increases when in most cases an increase in the price of an input reduces a firm's profits?[20]

In some cases a union and an employer may agree to a settlement in which real wages are increased in return for the union's agreeing to certain work rule changes that will result in increased productivity. If such an agreement is explicit and tied to the resulting change in productivity, the process is often referred to as *productivity bargaining*.[21] More typically, however, unions are able to win management concessions at the bargaining table because of the unions' ability to impose costs on management. These costs typically take the form of work slowdowns and strikes. A *strike* is an attempt to deny the

---

18. In cases in which these requirements call for the employment of employees whose functions are redundant—for example, fire stokers in diesel-operated railroad engines—*featherbedding* is said to take place. For an economic analysis of this phenomenon, see Paul Weinstein, "The Featherbedding Problem," *American Economic Review* 54 (May 1964): 145–52.

19. See, for example, Alex Maurizi, "Occupational Licensing and the Public Interest," *Journal of Political Economy* 82 (March/April 1974): 399–413.

20. It is easy to show, in the context of a simple textbook model of the behavior of firms, that an increase in the price of labor will reduce a firm's profits. However, this conclusion takes the firm's production function as given and does not consider other ways in which unions may increase productivity.

21. See Allan Flanders, ed., *Collective Bargaining* (Baltimore, Md.: Penguin Books, 1969), 317–68, for a description of productivity bargaining.

firm the labor services of all union members. Craft unions often have the added weapon of explicitly controlling the labor supply curve that firms face by means of previously negotiated or legislated entry restrictions described above.

Whether a strike, or a threat of a strike, will enable a union to win a concession from management depends upon the following factors:

1. The profitability of the firm and its ability to raise prices without losing its market (clearly unions in concentrated industries will be better off than those in competitive industries on this score);
2. The ability of the union to impose costs on the firm, which depends on whether the firm can stockpile its product in anticipion of a strike (thus avoiding the loss of customers during a strike), and whether nonunion supervisory employees can operate a plant during a strike;
3. Whether the firm has the financial resources to withstand the losses it would incur during a strike; and
4. Whether the union members have the financial resources to withstand their loss of income during a strike.[22]

If strikes involve costs to both union members and employers, why do they ever occur? It would seem that if both parties were aware of these costs, they would have an incentive to reach a settlement before a strike results. In fact, most models of the collective bargaining process focus on the likely division of the spoils between management and employees and ignore the determinants of strike activity.

The first, and also simplest, model of the bargaining process was developed by Sir John Hicks.[23] Suppose that management and labor are bargaining over only one issue—the size of the wage increase to be granted. How would the percentage increase that the union demands and the increase that the employer is willing to grant vary with the expected duration of a strike?

On the employer side of the market, the longer a strike lasts, the more costly it becomes in terms of lost customers. This increasing cost suggests that, as a strike progresses, an employer should be willing to increase the wage offer; this willingness is denoted by the upward-sloping *employer concession schedule, EC,* in Figure 12.3.

On the employee side, the attitudes of union members may harden, and they may actually increase their wage demands during the early part of a strike. However, after some point the loss in income they are suffering begins to color their attitudes, and they should begin to reduce their wage demands. This reduction is indicated by the *union resistance curve, UR,* in Figure 12.3, which eventually becomes downward-sloping.

---

22. Two states, New York and Rhode Island, allow all workers on strike to collect unemployment benefits (after a waiting period), while other states allow strikers to receive benefits if certain conditions prevail. For evidence that such benefits may affect strike activity, see John Kennan, "The Effect of Unemployment Insurance Payments on Strike Duration," in National Commission on Unemployment Compensation, *Unemployment Compensation: Studies and Research* (Washington, D.C.: U.S. Government Printing Office, 1981), and Robert Hutchens, David Lipsky, and Robert Stern, *Strikers and Subsidies: The Influence of Government Transfer Programs on Strike Activity* (Kalamazoo, Mich.: W. E. Upjohn Institute for Employment Research, 1989).
23. John R. Hicks, *The Theory of Wages,* 2d ed. (New York: St. Martin's Press, 1966), 136–57.

FIGURE 12.3   Hicks' Bargaining Model and Expected Strike Length

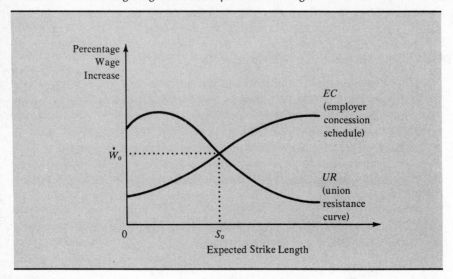

As the strike proceeds, the union's demands decrease and the employer's offer increases until at strike duration S_0 the two coincide. At this point a settlement can be reached, the parties may agree upon a wage increase of $\dot{W}_0$, and the strike may be terminated. Of course, *if* each party were aware of the position and shape of the other party's curve, each would know in advance of the strike what the size of the ultimate settlement would be. In this case, it would make sense to agree to a settlement of $\dot{W}_0$ *prior* to the strike so that *both* parties could avoid incurring the costs associated with the strike.

If such a settlement could be made in advance, why would strikes ever occur? One reason is that information is actually imperfect; one or both sides in the negotiation often fail to convey the true shape and position of their schedule to the other party.[24] A second reason is that, to enhance their bargaining positions and retain the credibility of the threat of a strike, unions may have to periodically use the weapon; a strike may be designed to influence *future* negotiations.[25] Finally, strikes may be useful devices by which the internal solidarity of a union can be enhanced against a common enemy—the employer.[26]

---

24. In the words of Hicks, "The majority of strikes are doubtless the results of faulty negotiations" (Hicks, *The Theory of Wages,* 146). Martin Mauro, "Strikes as a Result of Imperfect Information," *Industrial and Labor Relations Review* 35 (July 1982): 522–38, attempts to test the imperfect information explanation, and Edward Montgomery and Mary Ellen Benedict, "The Impact of Bargainer Experience on Teacher Strikes," *Industrial and Labor Relations Review* 42, no. 3 (April 1989): 380–92, find that strikes are shorter and less likely in situations in which the chief bargainers are more experienced.
25. Lest one carry this "rusty weapon" argument too far, the reader should consider its implication for the use of nuclear weapons.
26. Richard Walton and Robert McKersie, *A Behavioral Theory of Labor Negotiations* (New York: McGraw-Hill, 1965), 32.

TABLE 12.6   Work Stoppages in the United States, 1953–87

Year	Unemployment Rate	Number of Strikes		Estimated Percentage of Working Time Lost	
		All	Involving More Than 1000 Workers	All	Strikes Involving More Than 1000 Workers
1953	2.9	5091		0.22%	
1955	4.4	4320		0.22	
1957	4.3	3673		0.12	
1959	5.5	3708		0.50	
1961	6.7	3367		0.11	
1963	5.7	3362		0.11	
1965	4.5	3963		0.15	
1967	3.8	4595		0.25	
1969	3.5	5700		0.24	
1971	5.9	5138		0.26	
1973	4.9	5353		0.14	
1975	8.5	5031		0.16	
1977	7.0	5600		0.17	
1979	5.8	4800	235	0.15	0.09%
1981	7.6		145		0.07
1983	9.6		81		0.08
1985	7.2		54		0.03
1987	6.2		46		0.02

SOURCE: U.S. Bureau of Labor Statistics, *Handbook of Labor Statistics 1980,* Bulletin 2070 (Washington, D.C.: U.S. Government Printing Office, 1980), Table 167, and *Handbook of Labor Statistics 1985,* Bulletin 2217 (Washington, D.C.: U.S. Government Printing Office, 1985), Table 123; U.S. Bureau of Labor Statistics, *Current Wage Developments* (March 1988), 36.

The major problem with these explanations of when strikes occur is that, in the main, they do not enable one to predict whether a strike will occur in a particular contract negotiation and, more important, they offer only limited insights into why the aggregate level of strike activity should vary over time. Table 12.6 presents data on work stoppages in the United States during a recent 35-year period. These data suggest that strike activity, as measured by the number of strikes or the percentage of estimated working time lost, is cyclical, increasing when unemployment rates are low and decreasing when unemployment rates are high. A model of strike activity that can explain this observed pattern of behavior is needed.

A Political Model of Strike Activity

Although there is no universally accepted model of strike activity, Orley Ashenfelter and George Johnson have built upon Arthur Ross's earlier work and developed what is essentially a political model of strike activity.[27] Their approach illustrates how the maximization models of economists can be gen-

27. Arthur Ross, *Trade Union Wage Policy* (Berkeley: University of California Press, 1948), and Orley Ashenfelter and George Johnson, "Bargaining Theory, Trade Unions, and Industrial Strike Activity," *American Economic Review* 59 (March 1969): 35–49. A more recent test of the model is found in Henry Farber, "Bargaining Theory, Wage Outcomes, and the Occurrence of Strikes," *American Economic Review* 68 (June 1978): 262–71.

eralized to incorporate noneconomic variables and allows us to analyze the effects of the Landrum-Griffin Act on the level of strike activity.

The Ashenfelter-Johnson model is based upon the premise that it is inappropriate to view the collective bargaining process as involving only two parties, an employer and a union. Rather, they acknowledge that different members of the union will have different, and sometimes conflicting, objectives. Their focus is on the divergence in objectives between union members and union leaders. While union members are concerned primarily with their pecuniary and nonpecuniary conditions of employment, union leaders are also concerned about the survival and growth of the union *and* their own personal political survival.

Union leaders, who have been actively involved with management in the bargaining process, have much better information than rank-and-file union members about the employer's true financial position and the maximum wage settlement the union will be able to extract. If this settlement is smaller than the settlement the membership wants, the union leaders face two options.

On the one hand, union leaders can return to their members, try to convince them of the employer's true financial picture, and recommend that management's last offer (the maximum that they know they can achieve) be accepted. The danger they face with this option is that the members may vote down the recommendation, accuse the leaders of selling out to management, and ultimately vote them out of office.

On the other hand, union leaders can return to their members and recommend that the members go out on strike. This recommendation will allow them to appear to be strong, militant leaders, even though the leaders themselves know that the strike will not lead to a larger settlement. After a strike of some duration, however, in accordance with the notion of the union resistance curve in Figure 12.3, union members will begin to moderate their wage demands, and ultimately a settlement for which the union leader will receive credit will be reached. Since the latter strategy is the one that is more likely to maintain the union's strength *and* keep the leaders in office, it is the strategy leaders may opt for even though it is clearly not in their members' best interests in the short run (the members have to bear the costs of the strike).

This model can provide insights into the forces that affect the frequency and duration of strike activity. In panel (a) of Figure 12.4, curve UR represents union members' minimum acceptable percentage wage increase ($\dot{W}$) as a function of the length of a strike; this curve is nothing more than the Hicks union resistance curve. To simplify the discussion, we have assumed that curve UR always declines with strike length. In this diagram $\dot{W}_i$ is the union members' initial wage demand (the amount they would settle for without a strike) and $\dot{W}_m$ is the minimum amount they would ever settle for. Depending upon economic conditions and the members' hostility to management, $\dot{W}_m$ may be positive, zero, or even negative; the last possibility would occur if union members felt they had to take a pay cut to preserve their jobs.

Panel (b) of Figure 12.4 plots the employer's present value of profits (PVP) as a function of the length of a strike. An increase in strike duration has two offsetting effects. In the immediate period, the employer loses profits because the firm loses some sales. However, in the future the firm's profits

FIGURE 12.4 Graphic Representation of the Ashenfelter-Johnson Model of Strike Activity

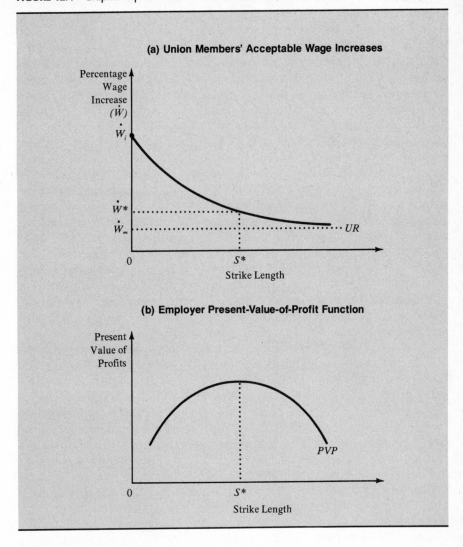

(a) Union Members' Acceptable Wage Increases

Percentage
Wage
Increase
$(\dot{W})$

$\dot{W}_i$

$\dot{W}^*$

$\dot{W}_m$ .... UR

0   S^*

Strike Length

(b) Employer Present-Value-of-Profit Function

Present
Value of
Profits

PVP

0   S^*

Strike Length

may be higher because the longer strike means that the employees will be willing to settle for smaller wage increases (from panel a of Figure 12.4). In panel (b), initially the second effect dominates, but ultimately—since the union wage demands fall less rapidly (in absolute terms) and lost sales begin to mount up—the former effect dominates. That is, the employer's present value of profits first increases and then decreases with strike duration.

Suppose the employer's goal is to maximize the firm's present value of profits, and suppose the employer knows the position and shape of the curves in Figure 12.4. The employer can maximize the firm's present value of profits by offering the union a wage increase of $\dot{W}^*$ after a strike of length S^*. At that point the union members will accept the offer and the strike will end. If the *PVP* curve in Figure 12.4 were always negatively sloped, the employer would either settle prior to a strike or go out of business if paying $\dot{W}_i$ would cause the firm to suffer losses.

Changing the model's parameters influences the probability of occurrence and the expected duration of a strike. For example, if the union's initial wage demand $(\dot{W}_i)$ increases, other things equal, a strike will have a greater payoff to the employer and the expected duration will increase. Similarly, an increase in the rate at which the union's wage demands decline over time, other things equal, will increase the employer's payoff from prolonging the strike. In contrast, an increase in the union members' minimum acceptable wage demand $\dot{W}_m$ (sometimes called the union's *resistance point*) will reduce the employer's gain from incurring a strike, other things equal, and will reduce the probability that a strike will occur.

The Ashenfelter and Johnson model—which assumed that the above parameters are influenced by the unemployment rate in the economy, by past changes in wage rates and prices, and by the profit rates of corporations—is able to explain why increases in the unemployment rate lead to reduced strike activity.[28] In the context of their model, an increase in the unemployment rate is assumed to reduce the initial wage demands of unions, $\dot{W}_i$, because it reduces the probability that workers can find temporary part-time jobs while on strike.

Ashenfelter and Johnson also found that, after statistically controlling for the unemployment rate, profits, and past wage and price changes, the level of strike activity (as measured by the number of strikes per year) tended to decline during 1952–67. However, the decline took a particular form: while the pattern was downward from 1952 to 1959, the number jumped up in 1959 before resuming its downward trend (see Figure 12.5).[29]

The general decline in strike activity in the U.S. economy has been attributed by many observers to the maturation of industrial relations in the United States; fewer strikes are now caused by the parties' misunderstanding each other's intentions or by the need to use a strike today to enhance bargaining power tomorrow.[30] The increase in 1959 coincided with the passage of the Landrum-Griffin Act. By increasing union democracy, this act increased the chances that union leaders would be voted out of office if they failed to satisfy union members' expectations at contract negotiation time. In the context of the model presented here, making union leaders more accountable to membership would increase the probability that leaders would recommend going on strike to their members, rather than trying to sell the rank and file on an unacceptable contract. To return to a previous theme, social programs and legislation often have unintended side effects; the Landrum-Griffin Act may well have unintentionally led to an increase in the level of strike activity in the economy.

---

28. Ashenfelter and Johnson, "Bargaining Theory," 42–46. A more recent empirical investigation of strike activity, using a similar model, can be found in Susan B. Vroman, "A Longitudinal Analysis of Strike Activity in U.S. Manufacturing: 1957–1984," *American Economic Review* 79 (September 1989): 816–26.

29. Ashenfelter and Johnson, "Bargaining Theory," 47.

30. Except in recent years, it is difficult to observe a steady trend in the measures of strike activity for 1953–87 presented in Table 12.6. One must remember, however, that all the other variables (unemployment, wage and price changes, profits) were changing during this period. The trends Ashenfelter and Johnson observe are found after one statistically controls for these other factors.

FIGURE 12.5   Ashenfelter and Johnson's Estimated Time Trend in Strike Activity

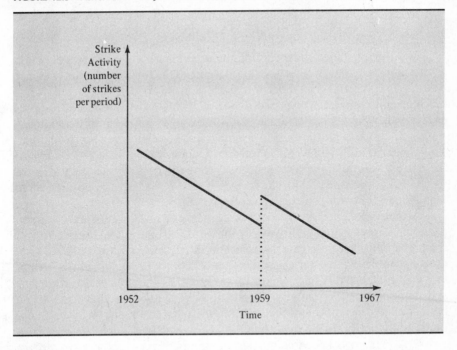

The model presented in this section does not pretend to be the ultimate model of strike activity. It focuses only on strikes that result from disagreements over economic issues, ignoring strikes that may result from conflict over recognition procedures, grievance procedures, unsafe working conditions, and the like. It also makes certain assumptions that, while sometimes plausible, are unlikely to always be true. For example, in essence this model suggests that union leaders and management implicitly collude to the detriment of union members. Union leaders are assumed to be willing to recommend a strike that will impose costs (in the form of lost income) on members, even though they know that the strike will not increase management's ultimate wage offer. Management is assumed to fully know union members' resistance curve. Finally, union members are assumed to be ignorant, in the sense that they never learn how the bargaining process is actually working. Nonetheless, the model provides useful insights into the bargaining process and an explanation of why the Landrum-Griffin Act and the unemployment rate should be expected to influence the level of strike activity.

Alternative Models of Strike Activity

Recently, several alternative models of strike activity have been developed that help to explain variations in patterns of strike activity across individual firms and industries.[31] These models abstract from the union leader/union

---

31. See John Kennan, "Strikes and Bargaining," in *Handbook of Labor Economics,* ed. Orley Ashenfelter and Richard Layard (Amsterdam: North-Holland, 1986), for a survey of models of strike activity.

member dichotomy that the political model of the last section made. They also reject that model's assumption that union members are passive participants in the strike-determination process; rather, they assume that unions are trying to maximize some well-defined objective function.

The first of these models, called the *asymmetric information* model, explicitly assumes that at least one of the parties in the negotiation does not have perfect information about the shape and position of the other's resistance or concession schedule (see Figure 12.3).[32] In such situations, the process of bargaining per se may increase the accuracy of the information each party has about the other party's schedule and ultimately lead to a solution. The greater the initial level of uncertainty, however, the longer the bargaining process will take. By raising the costs to the parties of extending bargaining, a strike increases the incentive each has to reveal its true position more rapidly, and leads to a quicker solution.

An implication of this model is that increased uncertainty about an employer's willingness and ability to pay for wage increases should increase both the probability that a strike will occur and the duration of the strike.[33] Other things equal, the more variable a firm's profitability is over time, the greater one might expect this uncertainty to be, and thus the greater the incidence and duration of strike activity. Empirical evidence does in fact suggest that both the incidence and duration of strike activity are higher in firms whose profitability varies widely over time.[34]

A second model focuses on the *total costs* of a potential strike to the parties.[35] Other things equal, the more costly a strike is, the smaller is the "size of the pie" that will be left to be distributed between the employer and the union in any settlement. In situations where costs of strikes are high, this model predicts that the parties will strive to establish *bargaining protocols* that will help to avert future strikes;[36] that is, they will seek to structure the bargaining process in ways that reduce the chances that future strikes will occur. For example, the parties might agree to start bargaining well in advance of a contract expiration, to limit the number of contract items they will discuss, or to submit the dispute to binding arbitration if they fail to reach agreement on their own.

What determines how costly a strike will be to the parties? In part, it depends upon whether inventories of the product can be built up prior to the strike to substitute for lost output during the strike: strikes will be particularly costly to producers of perishable products, for whom such substitution is impossible. In part, it also depends on the willingness of consumers to postpone

---

32. See, for example, Beth Hayes, "Unions and Strikes with Asymmetric Information," *Journal of Labor Economics* 2 (January 1984): 57–83.
33. Joseph Tracy, "An Empirical Test of an Asymmetric Information Model of Strikes," *Journal of Labor Economics* 5 (April 1987): 149–73.
34. Joseph Tracy, "An Empirical Test . . . ," and Tracy, "An Investigation into the Determinants of U.S. Strike Activity," *American Economic Review* 76 (June 1986): 423–36.
35. See Kennan, "Strikes and Bargaining," and Melvin Reder and George Neumann, "Conflict and Contract: The Case of Strikes," *Journal of Political Economy* 88 (October 1980): 867–86.
36. Reder and Neumann, "Conflict and Contract: The Case of Strikes."

their purchases of the product from a firm that is on strike: strikes will be particularly costly if there are domestic or foreign competitors who produce the same, or easily substitutable, products or if consumers cannot delay their purchases of the product. In part, finally, it depends upon subsidies that the firm or the union might receive from third-party sources during a strike: strikes will be less costly if such subsidies are present.[37]

Empirical evidence also provides support for this "total cost" model. One study showed that in situations in which it was easy to vary inventory levels over time, strikes were more likely to occur.[38] A second study focused on strikes of schoolteachers in Pennsylvania, where such strikes are legal. Teachers lose pay for each day they are on strike in Pennsylvania *unless* the school district reschedules the lost school days; in the latter case the cost of the strike to the workers involved is minimal. Not surprisingly, the study showed that the more likely a district was to reschedule lost school days if a strike occurred, the more likely it was that a strike would be observed.[39] Finally, within the heavily unionized manufacturing sector, the incidence of strike activity is much higher in durable manufacturing (e.g., automobiles), where the postponement of consumer purchases of goods is often easily possible, than it is in nondurable manufacturing (e.g., food), for which postponement of purchases is much less feasible.[40]

THE EFFECTS OF UNIONS

The Theory of Union Wage Effects

Suppose one had data on the wage rates paid to two groups of workers who were identical in every respect except for the fact that one group was unionized and the other was not. Let W_u denote the wage paid to union members and W_n the wage paid to nonunion workers. If the difference between the two could be attributed solely to the presence of unions, then the *relative wage advantage* (R) that unions would have achieved for their members would be given, in percentage terms, by

$$R = (W_u - W_n)/W_n \tag{12.1}$$

37. As an example, between 1958 and 1978 the airline industry had a "Mutual Aid Agreement." If one airline was struck, the pact called for other airlines to make payments to help defray its lost revenue. As the generosity of the plan increased over time, and hence the costs of a strike to any given airline declined, not surprisingly the frequency and duration of strikes in the industry increased. For a discussion of this pact, including why it ultimately broke down, see S. Herbert Unterberger and Edward C. Koziara, "The Demise of Airline Strike Insurance," *Industrial and Labor Relations Review* 34 (October 1980): 82–89.

38. Reder and Neumann, "Conflict and Contract: The Case of Strikes."

39. See Craig Olson, "The Role of Rescheduled School Days in Teacher Strikes," *Industrial and Labor Relations Review* 37 (July 1984): 515–28. We discuss dispute resolution in the public sector in Chapter 13, for Pennsylvania is an exception: in most states public sector strikes are illegal.

40. See, for example, U.S. Bureau of Labor Statistics, *Handbook of Labor Statistics 1973*, Bulletin 1790 (Washington, D.C.: U.S. Government Printing Office, 1973), Table 158, for industry strike-frequency data between 1956 and 1971.

FIGURE 12.6   Spillover Effects of Unions on Wages and Employment

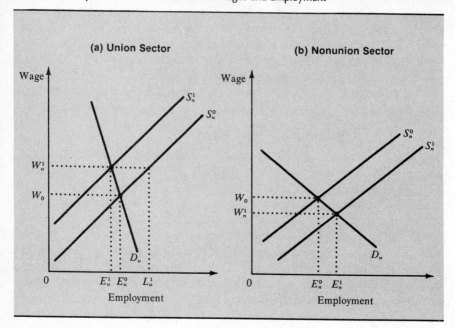

Contrary to what one might expect, this relative wage advantage does *not* represent the absolute amount, in percentage terms, by which unions would have increased the wages of their members, because unions both directly and indirectly affect *nonunion* wage rates also. Moreover, one cannot a priori state whether estimates of R will overstate or understate the absolute effect of unions on their members' real wage levels. (This section focuses on the union effects on wage *levels;* Chapter 16 will discuss union effects on the *rate of wage change.*) Figure 12.6 presents a simple two-sector model of the labor market. Except for the fact that the labor supply curves are upward-sloping in both sectors, this model is identical to the one used in Chapter 3 to analyze the effects of the minimum wage in the presence of incomplete coverage; the analyses here will proceed along similar lines.[41]

Panel (a) is the union sector and panel (b) is the nonunion sector. Suppose initially, however, that both sectors are unorganized. If mobility is relatively costless, workers will move between the two sectors until wages are equalized between them. With demand curves D_u and D_n, workers will move between sectors until the supply curves are S_u^0 and S_n^0, respectively. The

---

41. Much of the discussion in this section is based upon the pioneering work of H. G. Lewis, *Unionism and Relative Wages in the United States* (Chicago: University of Chicago Press, 1963). In Figure 12.6 and those that follow, our analysis employs a two-sector model with labor supply curves to each sector. Remember that a labor supply curve to one sector is drawn holding the wages in other sectors (the "alternative wages") constant; whenever the wage in one sector changes, the labor supply curve to the other sector may shift. We *sometimes* ignore this complexity below to keep our exposition as simple as possible and to highlight the various behaviors that might occur in either sector in response to unionization.

common equilibrium wage will be W_0, and employment will be E_u^0 and E_n^0, respectively, in the two sectors.

Now suppose a union succeeds in organizing workers in the first sector and also succeeds in raising their wage to W_u^1. This increased wage will cause employment to decline to E_u^1 workers in the union sector, resulting in $L_u^1 - E_u^1$ unemployed workers in that sector. These workers have several options; one is to seek employment in the nonunion sector. If all the unemployed workers *spill over* into the nonunion sector, the supply curves in the two sectors will shift to S_u^1 and S_n^1, respectively. Unemployment will be eliminated in the union sector; in the nonunion sector, however, an excess supply of labor will exist at the old market-clearing wage, W_0. As a result, downward pressure will be exerted on the wage rate in the nonunion sector until the labor market in that sector clears at a *lower* wage, W_n^1, and a higher employment level, E_n^1.

In the context of this model, the union has succeeded in raising the wages of its members who kept their jobs. However, it has done so by shifting some of its members to lower-wage jobs in the nonunion sector and, because of this spillover effect, by actually lowering the wage rate paid to individuals initially employed in the nonunion sector. As a result, the observed union *relative wage* advantage (R_1), computed as

$$R_1 = (W_u^1 - W_n^1)/W_n^1 \qquad (12.2)$$

will tend to be greater than the true *absolute* effect of the union on its members' real wage. This true absolute effect (A), stated in percentage terms, is defined as

$$A = (W_u^1 - W_0)/W_0 \qquad (12.3)$$

The relative effect will not necessarily be larger than the absolute effect, however, because there are several other responses that employees or employers can make. Employers in the nonunion sector may be concerned that unions will subsequently try to organize their employees, and may view a union as undesirable if unionization both increases their wage costs and limits their managerial flexibility. As such, they may try to "buy off" their employees by offering them wage increases to reduce the probability that the employees will vote for a union.[42] Because of the costs associated with union membership, noted earlier, some wage less than W_u^1 but higher than W_0 would presumably be sufficient to assure employers that the majority of their employees would not vote for a union (assuming that the employees are happy with their nonwage conditions of employment).

The implications of such *threat effects*—nonunion wage increases resulting from the threat of union entry—are traced in Figure 12.7. The increase in wage in the union sector, and resulting decline in employment there, is again assumed to cause the supply of workers to the nonunion sector to shift to S_n^1. However, in response to the threat of union entry, nonunion employers are assumed to *increase* their employees' wages to W_n^*, which lies between W_0 and

---

42. For a more formal discussion of this possibility, see Sherwin Rosen, "Trade Union Power, Threat Effects, and the Extent of Organization," *Review of Economic Studies* 36 (April 1969): 185–96.

FIGURE 12.7   Threat Effects of Unions on Wages and Employment

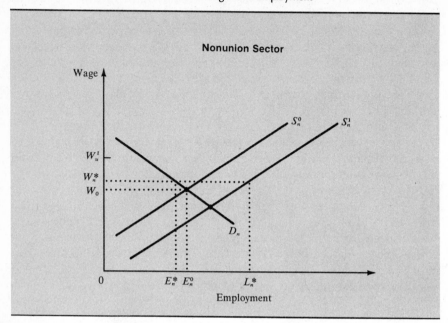

W_u^1. This wage increase causes employment to decline to E_n^*; at the higher wage nonunion employers demand fewer workers. Moreover, since the nonunion wage is now not free to be bid down, an excess supply of labor, $L_n^* - E_n^*$, exists, resulting in unemployment. Finally, because the nonunion wage is now higher than the original wage, the observed union relative wage advantage:

$$R_2 = (W_u^1 - W_n^*)/W_n^* \qquad (12.4)$$

is smaller than the absolute effect of unions on their members' real wages.

One might question whether workers who lose their jobs in the union sector as a result of the union's increasing the wage rate will necessarily seek jobs in the nonunion sector. Even with a fixed employment level in the union sector, job vacancies occur as a result of retirements, deaths, and voluntary turnover (including quits to take other jobs in the same area, geographic migration, and temporary departures from the labor force). It may pay union members to remain attached to the union sector *and* temporarily unemployed if they will ultimately obtain a job in the union sector. Indeed, it may actually pay some employed nonunion workers to quit their jobs and move to the union sector if they might obtain a relatively higher-paying union job in the future. Such decisions lead to *wait unemployment:* workers rejecting lower-paying nonunion jobs and waiting for higher-paying union jobs to open up.[43]

---

43. See Jacob Mincer, "Unemployment Effects of Minimum Wages," *Journal of Political Economy* 84 (July/August 1976, pt. 2): S87–S104. Although Mincer discusses minimum wage effects, union-imposed "minimum wages" can be analyzed analogously.

Workers will move between the union and nonunion sectors until their *expected earnings* in each are equal. If one ignores complications such as the costs of union membership, the presence of unemployment insurance benefits for some unemployed workers, employee benefits, and the like, expected earnings will be equal when the wage rate paid in each sector multiplied by the fraction of each period (F) that individuals in the sector expect to be employed are equal, or when

$$W_u F_u = W_n F_n \tag{12.5}$$

Figure 12.8 illustrates the process. If threat effects are ignored, the consequences of an increase in the union wage to W_u^1 would be a decline in employment in the union sector to E_u^1, a shift in the supply curves to S_u^1 and S_n^1, a resulting decrease in nonunion wages to W_n^1, and an increase in nonunion employment to E_n^1. Since there is no unemployment in this situation, F_u and F_n are both equal to unity. Hence, labor market equilibrium, as indicated in equation (12.5), would require that wages be equal in the two sectors. But they are *not;* W_u^1 is greater than W_n^1. Hence, individuals' expected earnings are higher in the union sector.

The above difference in expected earnings would induce some individuals to move from the nonunion sector to wait for jobs in the union sector. This movement leads to an increase in expected earnings in the nonunion sector (as supply decreases there, wages are bid up) and a decrease in expected earnings in the union sector (as supply increases there, the probability of obtaining

FIGURE 12.8   Wait Unemployment (nonunion wage falls)

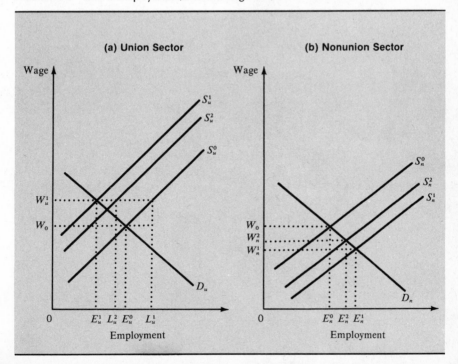

a job in that sector decreases). Eventually expected earnings are equalized between the two sectors by this process.

We have *assumed* that expected earnings are equalized in Figure 12.8 at the points at which the supply curves in the two sectors are S_u^2 and S_n^2. The resulting wage in the nonunion sector is W_n^2, and the resulting employment level is E_n^2. *Wait unemployment* now exists in the union sector; its level is given by $L_u^2 - E_u^1$. Finally, although W_n^2 is greater than W_n^1, W_n^2 is less than W_0. Thus, if the union relative wage advantage is measured as

$$R_3 = (W_u^1 - W_n^2)/W_n^2 \tag{12.6}$$

it will again be larger than the true absolute effect of the union on its members' real wage levels.

Of course, we have assumed that the expected earnings would be equalized as indicated in Figure 12.8. Under certain assumptions, the equalization may not occur until after the supply of labor to the union sector has shifted to the *right* of its initial position and after the supply of labor in the nonunion sector has shifted to the *left* of its initial position. This situation is more likely to occur if the labor demand curve in the union sector is inelastic. An inelastic demand curve would cause *expected earnings* $(W_u^1 F_u)$ in the union sector to increase immediately after the increase in the union *wage* because employment losses are so small. This immediate rise in expected earnings induces

FIGURE 12.9 Wait Unemployment (nonunion wage increases)

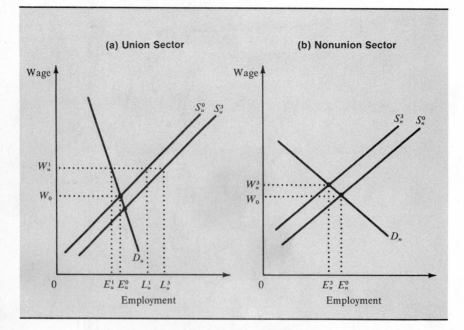

FIGURE 12.10   Union "Shifts" the Demand Curve

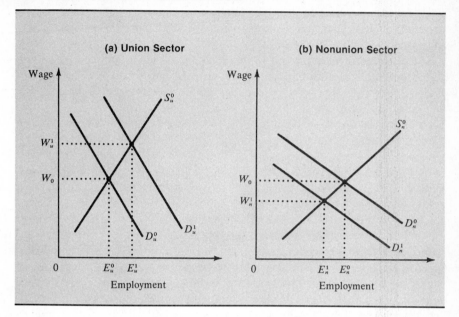

employees to migrate from the nonunion to the union sector.[44] As Figure 12.9 indicates, supply in the union sector shifts right (to S_u^3) and supply in the nonunion sector shifts left (to S_n^3). In this situation, wait unemployment would increase to $L_u^3 - E_u^1$, and the nonunion wage would increase to W_n^3, which is greater than W_0. The union relative wage advantage in this case, which is computed as

$$R_4 = (W_u^1 - W_n^3)/W_n^3 \qquad (12.7)$$

would be less than the absolute effect of unions on their members' real wages.

One final case will complete our discussion. Suppose the union increases its members' wages by increasing the demand for union labor, using any of the methods discussed in the previous section. Figure 12.10 illustrates an increase in the demand for labor in the union sector to D_u^1. If this increase comes at the expense of the demand for labor in the nonunion sector, the latter curve will fall, say to D_n^1. Initially the effect is to increase both wages (W_u^1) and employment (E_u^1) in the union sector and decrease wages (W_n^1) and employment (E_n^1) in the nonunion sector. The ultimate change in the nonunion wage,

---

44. See Mincer, "Unemployment Effects of Minimum Wages," and Edward Gramlich, "The Impact of Minimum Wages on Other Wages, Employment, and Family Incomes," *Brookings Papers on Economic Activity,* 1976–2, 409–51, for a more complete discussion of when this is likely to occur.

however, will depend upon the extent to which threat effects or wait unemployment is important. So again, estimates of the union *relative* wage effects alone tell us little about the *absolute* effects of unions on their members' real wage levels.

Because unions *are* present in the economy, at any point in time all one can observe are the union and nonunion wage rates (W_u and W_n). One can*not* observe the wage that would have existed in the absence of unions, W_0. Hence, direct estimates of a union's effects on the absolute level (A) of its members' real wages—see equation (12.3)—cannot be obtained. Care must be taken not to mistake relative wage effects for absolute wage effects.[45]

Evidence of Union Wage Effects

Economists have expended considerable effort to estimate the extent to which unions have raised the wages of their members relative to the wages of comparable nonunion workers in the private sector. These studies have tended to use data on large samples of individuals and have attempted to separate wage differentials caused by unionization from wage differentials caused by differences in personal characteristics and differences in industry and occupation of employment. That is, these economists have sought to ascertain how much more union members get paid than nonunion workers, after controlling for any differences between the two groups in other factors that might be expected to influence wages.

The various studies use several data bases that span various years, and they often employ different statistical methodologies.[46] As such, they do not yield a single unambiguous estimate of the extent to which union members' wages exceed the wages of comparable nonunion workers in the private sector. Perhaps the best estimate is that the union relative wage advantage, on average, lies in the range of 10 to 20 percent. These union wage effects, however, are neither constant over time nor constant across groups.[47]

For example, a study by Orley Ashenfelter, summarized in Table 12.7, suggests that the estimated union relative wage advantage in the private sector rose substantially between 1967 and 1975, from 11.6 to 16.8 percent. The year 1967 was one of low unemployment; the year 1975 was one of high unem-

45. This discussion has assumed a partial equilibrium model. Once one considers a general equilibrium framework and allows capital to move between sectors, even more possibilities may exist. On this point, see Harry Johnson and Peter Mieszkowski, "The Effects of Unionization on the Distribution of Income: A General Equilibrium Approach," *Quarterly Journal of Economics* 84 (November 1969): 539–61.

46. For surveys of these estimates, see Richard Freeman and James Medoff, *What Do Unions Do?* (New York: Basic Books, 1984); H. Gregg Lewis, *Union Relative Wage Effects: A Survey* (Chicago: University of Chicago Press, 1986); and Barry T. Hirsch and John T. Addison, *The Economic Analysis of Unions: New Approaches and Evidence* (Boston: Allen and Unwin, 1986). Some of the more ambitious studies also attempt to control for the fact that unionization and wages may be simultaneously determined; as noted earlier, workers' decisions to join a union are partially based on the expected gains from union membership. See, for example, Lung-Fei Lee, "Unionism and Wage Rates: A Simultaneous-Equations Model with Qualitative and Limited Dependent Variables," *International Economic Review* 19 (June 1978): 415–33.

47. Lewis, *Union Relative Wage Effects,* Chapter 9. As the evidence cited in Table 12.7 suggests, this study concludes that the union relative wage effect probably increased between 1967 and 1978.

TABLE 12.7   Estimated Union/Nonunion Relative Wage Effects, 1967, 1973, and 1975

	Percentage Union Wage Effect			Percentage Unionized		
	1967	1973	1975	1967	1973	1975
All workers	11.6	14.8	16.8	23	26	25
White men	9.6	15.5	16.3	31	33	31
Black men	21.5	22.5	22.5	32	37	37
White women	14.4	12.7	16.6	12	14	14
Black women	5.6	13.2	17.1	13	22	22

SOURCE: From *Econometric Contributions to Public Policy,* edited by Richard Stone and William Peterson. © International Economic Association 1978 and reprinted by permission of St. Martin's Press Inc. and Macmillan, London and Basingstoke.

ployment. Since unionized workers' wages tend to be less responsive to labor market conditions than nonunion workers' wages (see Chapter 16), this result is not surprising; the union relative wage advantage tends to be larger during recessionary periods.[48] More recent studies suggest that the union relative wage advantage increased significantly during the early and mid-'80s, a period of sharply elevated unemployment, especially among unionized workers.[49] Agreeing to these increases may be seen as an instance of management failure. However, large increases in union wages at this time may also reflect, as hypothesized in Example 12.3, the increase in union power that exists at least in the early stages of economic contraction.

The estimates in Table 12.7 also suggest that unions have helped to improve the relative economic positions of black males. On the one hand, the estimated relative wage effects are larger for black men than for white men; being a union member enhances black men's earnings by more than it does white men's. On the other hand, the percentage of black men who are union members also appears to be slightly larger than the comparable percentage for white men.[50] On balance, then, in spite of well-publicized conflicts between some unions and civil rights organizations over union seniority rules and the use of racial quotas, unions appear to have improved the economic well-being of black men relative to that of white men.

48. Lewis, *Unionism and Relative Wages,* provides evidence that this relationship appeared to hold during the 1930–60 period as well.
49. See Peter Linneman and Michael Wachter, "Rising Union Premiums and Declining Boundaries Among Noncompeting Groups," *American Economic Association Papers and Proceedings* 76 (May 1986): 103–8; and William Moore and John Raisian, "Union–Nonunion Wage Differentials in the Public Administration, Educational and Private Sectors," *Review of Economics and Statistics* 69 (November 1987): 608–15. In the late 1980s unions were more likely to agree to wage concessions than in the early 1980s. For example, from 1980 to 1984, 17 percent of union workers covered by newly bargained agreements took nominal wage cuts, while from 1985 to 1988 those taking such cuts rose to 28 percent. See Linda A. Bell, "Union Concessions in the 1980s," *Federal Reserve Bank of New York Quarterly Review* (Summer 1989): 44–58.
50. Indeed, although the percentage of employed white males who were union members had fallen to 19.9 percent in 1988, the comparable percentage for black males remained over 6 percentage points higher at 26.1 percent. See U.S. Department of Labor, *Employment and Earnings* (January 1989), Table 59.

EXAMPLE 12.3

The Paradox of Large Wage Increases in Declining Sectors

The fact that union members' wages grew more rapidly in the 1970s and early 1980s appears paradoxical against the backdrop of a declining union employment share and the increased resistance to unions among nonunion employers. The ten manufacturing industries with the highest growth in wages between 1970 and 1980 had higher rates of union membership and lower output growth rates than the manufacturing sector as a whole. Indeed, the increase in the pay of steelworkers was the highest of all, rising during the '70s just as the steel industry was experiencing a wrenching decline in output of 16 percent! What explains the ability of unions to negotiate large wage increases from industries that are in relative, if not absolute, decline?

One possibility is that when industries that are capital-intensive experience declining demand for output (or at least not a growing one), their ability to substitute capital for labor in response to wage increases is diminished. Capital can be most easily substituted for labor when output is expanding and new capital is being purchased; once machinery and production processes are "in place," however, the substitution possibilities are substantially diminished. It is true that even with constant production levels substitution could occur when capital needed to be replaced, but much of the capital in manufacturing is long-lived and highly industry-specific (so that selling it "used" is not attractive). The result is that the demand for labor may be less elastic in contracting industries than in growing ones!

Rapidly rising wages exacerbate the contraction of output, however, and it is clear that when firms cannot cover their variable costs plant closings become imminent. At this point (or when a majority of union members face the threat of permanent layoff) unions have incentives to engage in an "end-game" strategy and to agree to wage concessions in an effort to preserve the firms for which their members work. For example, following their extraordinary wage gains in the 1970s, unionized steelworkers since 1982 have traded away wage gains for increased job security.

SOURCE: Colin Lawrence and Robert Z. Lawrence, "Manufacturing Wage Dispersion: An End Game Interpretation," *Brookings Papers on Economic Activity,* 1985–1, 47–106.

In contrast, Table 12.7 emphasizes that female workers are considerably less likely to be union members than are males. Although in some years women who are union members appear to have gained as much as *white* men who are union members compared to their nonunion counterparts, on balance the *overall* effect of unions is to reduce women's wages relative to men's, perhaps by as much as 2.9 percent in 1975.[51]

51. Ashenfelter, "Union Relative Wage Effects." The relative wage effect for women is caused by the average union/nonunion wage differential among women and their below-average rates of unionization. By 1988, the percentage of employed black females who were union members was roughly comparable to the white male percentage, but the white female percentage was only 11.5 percent. See U.S. Department of Labor, *Employment and Earnings* (January 1989), Table 59.

The estimates cited above are of the relative wage advantage (R) that unions have achieved for their members in comparison to nonunion workers. These estimates do not indicate what effects unions have had on the absolute real wage levels of their members. In other words, the estimates do not reveal how unions have influenced *nonunion* workers' wages. The limited evidence on this point, although ambiguous, suggests that unions may well depress the wages of nonunion workers; the *spillover effect* modeled in Figure 12.6 appears to dominate over the *threat* and *wait-unemployment effects* modeled in Figures 12.7 and 12.9.[52] That is, other things equal, the wages of nonunion workers are lower in cities in which the percentage of workers who are union members is high. Thus, estimates of the relative wage effects of unions may well be greater than their effects on the absolute level of their members' real wages.

One might think that the above evidence suggests that unions increase the dispersion of labor earnings, increasing the wages of high-paid union members and decreasing the wages of lower-paid nonunion workers. In fact, however, several studies indicate that unions actually tend on balance to *decrease* the dispersion of labor earnings. For example, it is now well known that rates of return to education and job training are lower in the union than in the nonunion sector; these lower payoffs in the union sector cause the earnings there to be more equal among workers with different human capital investments than would otherwise be the case.[53] Other studies find that union wage policies designed to standardize wage rates within and across establishments significantly reduce the extent of wage dispersion among workers covered by union contracts,[54] and that unions also reduce the relative wage advantage of white-collar workers over blue-collar workers. Indeed, one study suggests that these equalizing effects dominate over the more widely known effects on union/nonunion worker wage differentials, and it concludes that, on balance, unions appear to reduce wage dispersion in the United States.[55] Finally, another study suggests that, other things equal, inequality of earnings within metropolitan areas tends to be less widespread in areas in which the extent of unionization is high.[56]

Evidence of Union Total Compensation Effects

Estimates of the extent to which the wages of union workers exceed the wages of otherwise comparable nonunion workers may prove misleading for two rea-

---

52. Lawrence Kahn, "The Effect of Unions on the Earnings of Nonunion Workers," *Industrial and Labor Relations Review* 31 (January 1978): 205–16.

53. Farrell Bloch and Mark Kuskin, "Wage Determination in the Union and Nonunion Sectors," *Industrial and Labor Relations Review* 31 (January 1978): 183–92, and Greg M. Duncan and Duane E. Leigh, "Wage Determination in the Union and Nonunion Sectors: A Sample Selectivity Approach," *Industrial and Labor Relations Review* 34 (October 1980): 24–35. The view that the returns to seniority are lower in the union sector is challenged in Katharine Abraham and Henry Farber, "Returns to Seniority in Union and Nonunion Jobs: A New Look at the Evidence," *Industrial and Labor Relations Review* 42 (October 1988): 3–19.

54. Richard Freeman, "Union Wage Practices and Wage Dispersion Within Establishments," *Industrial and Labor Relations Review* 36 (October 1982): 3–21.

55. Richard Freeman, "Unionism and the Dispersion of Wages," *Industrial and Labor Relations Review* 34 (October 1980): 3–23.

56. Thomas Hyclak, "The Effects of Unions on Earnings Inequality in Local Labor Markets," *Industrial and Labor Relations Review* 33 (October 1979): 77–84.

sons. First, such estimates ignore the fact that wages are only part of the compensation package. It has often been argued that employee benefits, such as paid holidays, vacation pay, sick leave, and retirement benefits, will be higher in firms that are unionized than in nonunion firms. The argument states that, because tastes for the various benefits differ across individuals and because there is no easy way to communicate the preferences of the average employee to the employer in a nonunion firm, nonunion firms tend to pay a higher fraction of total compensation in the form of money wages. Recent empirical evidence tends to support this contention; employee benefits and the share of compensation that goes to benefits do appear to be higher in union than in nonunion firms.[57] Ignoring benefits may therefore understate the true union/nonunion total compensation differential.

In contrast, ignoring *nonpecuniary* conditions of employment may cause one to overstate the effect of unions on their members' overall welfare levels compared to those of nonunion workers. For example, studies have shown that for blue-collar workers, unionized firms tend to have more-structured work settings, more-hazardous jobs, less-flexible hours of work, faster work paces, and less employee control over the assignment of overtime hours than do nonunion firms.[58] This situation may arise because production settings that give rise to interdependence among workers and the demand for specific work requirements by employers also give rise to unions. That is, the decision to vote for unions may be heavily influenced by these nonpecuniary conditions of employment. While unions often strive to affect these working conditions, they do not always succeed. Part of the estimated union/nonunion earnings differential may be a premium paid to union workers to compensate them for these unfavorable working conditions. Indeed, one study estimates that two-fifths of the estimated union/nonunion earnings differential reflects such compensation, suggesting that the observed union/nonunion earnings differential may overstate the true union/nonunion differential in overall levels of welfare.[59]

The true union/nonunion total compensation differential may also be overstated when comparisons are made between unionized and nonunion employees *at a point in time* if unobserved (to the researcher) differences in ability systematically exist between the two groups. That is, if unionized workers tend to be more able, but this fact cannot be controlled for in the statistical analyses, part of the measured compensation differential will reflect the greater ability of union workers, rather than union power. Attempts to handle this problem have included using *longitudinal data* — data on individuals for a number of periods—and observing how compensation changes with changes

57. Richard Freeman, "The Effect of Trade Unions on Fringe Benefits," *Industrial and Labor Relations Review* 34 (July 1981): 489–509, and William Alpert, "Unions and Private Wage Supplements," *Journal of Labor Research* 3 (Spring 1982): 179–90.
58. Greg Duncan and Frank Stafford, "Do Union Members Receive Compensating Wage Differentials?" *American Economic Review* 70 (June 1980): 355–71, and J. Paul Leigh, "Are Unionized Blue-Collar Jobs More Hazardous Than Nonunionized Blue-Collar Jobs?" *Journal of Labor Research* 3 (Summer 1982): 349–57.
59. Duncan and Stafford, "Do Union Members Receive Compensating Wage Differentials?"

in union status. Such studies tend to find smaller but still positive union/nonunion total compensation differentials.[60]

The Traditional View of Union Effects on Productivity and Output

According to the traditional neoclassical view, although unions may improve the welfare of their members by improving their pecuniary and nonpecuniary conditions of employment, their overall effects on the economy at large are negative. Three reasons are given to support this view.

First, to the extent that unions succeed in driving a wedge between the wage rates of comparable-quality workers who are employed in the union and nonunion sectors, there is a loss of output. Recall from Chapter 3 that the demand curves for labor reflect the marginal product of labor. If the "spillover" model in Figure 12.6 holds, the union wage, W_u, exceeds the nonunion wage, W_n, and the marginal product of labor is higher in the union sector than in the nonunion sector. Consequently, output could be increased if labor were reallocated from the nonunion sector to the union sector, where its marginal product is higher. Just as with the minimum wage (see Chapter 3), then, unions cause a misallocation of workers: too many workers are employed in the nonunion sector and too few in the union sector. Of course, if the union wage gain also induces some unemployment (see Figures 12.7, 12.8, and 12.9), the loss of output due to these idled resources must also be considered.

Second, union-negotiated contract provisions that establish staffing requirements or other restrictive work practices limit firms from employing capital and labor in the most efficient ways and may cause output losses. Several examples of such provisions include minimum crew sizes on jet aircrafts, maximum apprentice/journeymen ratios in construction, provisions limiting subcontracting or mandatory assignment of overtime, and requirements that redundant employees be employed (fire stokers in diesel-operated railroad engines, typesetters in printing plants where type is set by computer). By limiting substitution possibilities or forcing firms to use redundant inputs, unions reduce output below its maximum achievable level.

Third, unions are thought to reduce output because strikes called either at the time that collective bargaining is occurring (to influence the settlement) or during the term of a contract (to protest the way the contract is being administered) result in lost workdays. In this view, if strikes were eliminated, output would increase.

Actual empirical estimates of the magnitudes of these alleged losses are few and far between. In an often-cited study, Albert Rees estimated that society lost no more than 0.3 percent of gross national product because of the creation of wage differentials between comparable-quality union and nonunion

60. Richard Freeman, "Longitudinal Analyses of the Effects of Trade Unions," *Journal of Labor Economics* 2 (January 1984): 1–26; and Solomon Polachek, Phanindra Wunnava, and Michael Hutchins, "Union Effects on Wages and Wage Growth," *Economic Letters* 21 (1986): 279–303.

workers.[61] Rees also estimated that the loss of output due to restrictive work practices was possibly as large. Finally, Table 12.6 indicated that the estimated percentage of working time lost due to strikes over the 27-year period from 1953 to 1979 averaged 0.2 percent. Summing these three figures yields a ballpark estimate of a loss in output of less than 0.8 percent due to these three factors. Of course, whether one considers this an acceptable or unacceptable cost depends upon the benefits that one believes society as a whole receives from unionization.

An Alternative View of Union Effects on Productivity and Profits

Recently labor economists have begun to rediscover the possibility that unions may also have positive influences on productivity.[62] The analyses of Richard Freeman and James Medoff and their associates are based heavily on the assumption that unions function as institutions of *collective voice* operating within structured internal labor markets.[63] That is, because unions can communicate the preferences of workers on various issues directly to management and can help establish work rules and seniority provisions in the context of structured internal labor markets, they can contribute to increases in productivity in a number of ways.

First, by providing workers with a direct means to voice their discontent to management and by establishing job rights based upon seniority, unions may reduce worker discontent, thus reducing voluntary turnover (quit rates). As discussed in Chapter 5, reductions in job turnover increase employers' incentives to provide their employees with *firm-specific training*, which will lead to increased productivity. Considerable evidence suggests that unions do in fact reduce quit rates.[64] Moreover, seniority systems weaken the rivalry be-

61. Albert Rees, "The Effects of Unions on Resource Allocation," *Journal of Law and Economics* 6 (October 1963): 69–78. Rees's estimate also included consideration of output losses due to union effects on intra-industry wage differentials—for example, requiring all unionized firms in an industry to pay the same wage. A more recent study on the output losses associated with union wage effects finds them to be about half the size of the Rees estimates. See Robert H. DeFina, "Unions, Relative Wages, and Economic Efficiency," *Journal of Labor Economics* 1 (October 1983): 408–29.

62. For a discussion of the evidence supporting this view, see Richard B. Freeman and James L. Medoff, "The Two Faces of Unionism," *Public Interest* 57 (Fall 1979): 69–93. A more detailed discussion is found in their *What Do Unions Do?* (New York: Basic Books, 1984). Note that, to the extent that employers react to union wage gains by restricting employment and substituting capital for labor, labor's marginal product will rise (although total production costs will also rise). The discussion below considers whether there are additional union-induced effects on labor's marginal productivity.

63. Albert Hirschman, *Exit, Voice and Loyalty* (Cambridge: Harvard University Press, 1973), and Richard Freeman, "Individual Mobility and Union Voice in the Labor Market," *American Economic Review* 66 (May 1976): 361–68, provide discussions of unions' role as institutions of collective voice. Oliver Williamson, Michael Wachter, and Jeffrey Harris, in "Understanding the Employment Relation: Analysis of Idiosyncratic Exchange," *Bell Journal of Economics* 6 (Spring 1975): 250–80, emphasize the interrelationship between unions and internal labor markets.

64. See Richard B. Freeman, "The Exit-Voice Trade-off in the Labor Market: Unionism, Job Tenure, Quits, and Separations," *Quarterly Journal of Economics* 94 (June 1980): 643–73, and James Medoff, "Layoffs and Alternatives Under Trade Unions in United States Manufacturing," *American Economic Review* 69 (June 1979): 380–95.

TABLE 12.8   Estimates of the Impact of Unionism on Productivity in
U.S. Industries

Industry/Year of Data	Estimated Impact of Unions on Productivity (percent)
(a) All U.S. manufacturing, 1972	20 to 25
(b) Wooden household furniture, 1972	15
(c) Cement, 1953–76	6 to 8
(d) Underground bituminous coal, 1965	25 to 30
(e) Underground bituminous coal, 1975	−20 to −25
(f) Construction, 1972	17 to 22
(g) Construction, office buildings, 1973–74	30
(h) Construction, retail stores and shopping centers, 1976–78	51

SOURCES OF ESTIMATES: (a) Charles Brown and James Medoff, "Trade Unions in the Production Process," *Journal of Political Economy* 86 (June 1978): 355–78. (b) John Frantz, "The Impact of Trade Unions on Productivity in the Wood Household Furniture Industry" (Honors Thesis, Harvard University, 1976). (c) Kim Clark, "The Impact of Unionization on Productivity: A Case Study," *Industrial and Labor Relations Review* 33 (July 1980): 451–69. (d)–(e) Richard Freeman, James Medoff, and Marie Connerton, "Industrial Relations and Productivity: A Case Study of the U.S. Bituminous Coal Industry" (mimeographed, Harvard University, 1979). (f) Steven Allen, "Unionized Construction Workers Are More Productive," *Quarterly Journal of Economics* 99 (May 1984): 251–74. (g) Steven Allen, "Unionization and Productivity in Office Building and School Construction," *Industrial and Labor Relations Review* 39 (January 1986): 187–201. (h) Steven Allen, "Unions and Efficiency in Private Sector Construction: Further Evidence," *Industrial Relations* 27 (Spring 1988): 232–40.

tween inexperienced and experienced employees and consequently increase the amount of informal on-the-job training that the latter are willing to give to the former.[65]

Second, by increasing the economic rewards of employment and providing grievance mechanisms, unions may directly enhance productivity by increasing worker morale, motivation, and effort. Third, unions provide an explicit mechanism by which labor can point out possible changes in work rules or production techniques that will benefit both labor and management.

Numerous studies have been undertaken in recent years that attempt to estimate the net effect of unions on productivity. Some of these studies are summarized in Table 12.8. The methodological approach used in all but the Clark (c) and the later Allen (g, h) studies is to estimate the extent to which value of output per worker *(value added)* is associated with the level of unionization in an industry or establishment at a point in time, after controlling for other factors expected to influence productivity.[66] (The Clark and later Allen studies use data on the physical volume of output, and Clark also looks at how productivity changes after a plant becomes unionized.)

These studies suggest that union workers are more productive than nonunion workers in manufacturing. Indeed, the size of the productivity differential appears to be large enough to offset the estimated union/nonunion

---

65. See Peter Doeringer and Michael Piore, *Internal Labor Markets and Manpower Analysis* (Lexington, Mass.: D. C. Heath, 1971).

66. Value added is the difference in dollar terms between the sales price of a product and the value of the materials that went into making it.

wage differential; that is, the unit labor cost of unionized manufacturing workers does not appear to exceed the unit labor cost of nonunion workers. This result provides an explanation of how high-wage union firms and lower-wage nonunion firms can coexist in a competitive industry.

In the bituminous coal industry, positive union productivity differentials were found in 1965, but substantial negative ones appeared in 1975. Indeed, in 1975 unionized workers were estimated to be 20 to 25 percent *less* productive than nonunion workers in the industry. This decline in relative productivity has been attributed to the well-known breakdown of the United Mine Workers' (UMW) national leadership that occurred in the late 1960s and early 1970s, which resulted in deteriorating industrial relations practices, including increased occurrence of *wildcat* (unauthorized) strikes over local issues.[67] These results emphasize that the effects of unions on productivity are neither constant nor always positive; they vary across industries and time periods as industrial relations practices vary.

The Allen studies cited in Table 12.8 find surprisingly large union productivity differentials in construction—surprising because in the construction industry unions were widely thought to have adverse effects on productivity owing to their restrictive work rules (limits on apprentice/journeymen ratios, limits on the jobs members of each craft can do, etc.). He attributes the differential, however, to better training in union apprenticeship programs, changes in the occupational mix induced by unions (e.g., fewer supervisors), reduced screening and recruitment costs for contractors, and greater use of technologies and materials that economize on labor usage.

On balance, then, the studies summarized in Table 12.8 suggest that unions have *increased* productivity in certain industries, although this judgment is by no means unanimous.[68] There is also no consensus on whether these increases more than offset the loss of gross national product caused by union effects on wage structures and union strike activity. These studies suggest, however, that like most questions in economics, whether unions have had a net positive or negative effect on output is an empirical question. The answer is not as obvious as either the supporters or opponents of unions would have one believe.

---

67. Richard Freeman, James Medoff, and Marie Connerton, "Industrial Relations and Productivity: A Case Study of the U.S. Bituminous Coal Industry" (mimeographed, Harvard University, 1979).
68. Some economists question the findings of these studies. See Barry T. Hirsch and John T. Addison, *The Economic Analysis of Unions,* 192–208, for criticism of these findings and citations to other studies that fail to find positive effects. Moreover, even if unions increase productivity at a point in time, they may slow down the rate of productivity growth if their unwillingness to accept new production techniques leads them to discourage employers from investing in research and development. Evidence that unionization is often associated with slower rates of productivity growth is surveyed in Hirsch and Addison, and evidence that unions reduce innovative activity is found in Barry T. Hirsch and Albert N. Link, "Labor Union Effects on Innovative Activity," *Journal of Labor Economics* 4 (Fall 1987): 323–32. Moreover, Steven Allen, "Declining Unionization in Construction: The Facts and the Reasons," *Industrial and Labor Relations Review* 41, no. 3 (April 1988): 343–59, finds that even in construction, unionization appeared to be negatively related with productivity growth during the 1972–82 period.

EXAMPLE 12.4

Corporate Takeovers and Union Wages

During the 1980s, corporate takeover activity in the form of mergers, acquisitions, and leveraged buyouts increased to a level that was perhaps the highest experienced in the United States in the last fifty years. Corporate "raiders" and other proponents of the activity argued that takeovers (or at least the threat of them) were necessary to stimulate improved management performance. Opponents worried that takeovers would actually lead to decreased corporate efficiency and that high debt burdens assumed in leveraged buyouts would force corporations to be preoccupied with generating revenue to cover short-run debt payments rather than focusing on longer-run objectives.

Both organized labor and the general public have expressed concern that acquisitions are bad for workers. In part, this perception comes from experience with a small number of well-publicized and hostile takeovers in the airline industry. However, these experiences may be atypical of the broader set of corporate takeovers and, if an acquisition leads to improved corporate performance, workers as a group may benefit.

A number of recent studies have addressed the question of whether workers gain or lose from corporate takeovers. One study of takeovers of Michigan firms during the 1978–84 period found relatively small effects, with wage and employment levels tending to move in opposite directions and tending to offset each other. A second study, which used establishment-level census data for manufacturing plants in 1977 and 1982, found that takeovers resulted in the decline of employment and earnings among central office administrative workers. Neither of these studies, however, distinguished between unionized and nonunionized environments.

A third study used data from 1976 through 1987 on major collective bargaining agreements, and it estimated the effects of takeovers on union wage scales. This study found that after a takeover, yearly union wage increases were one percentage point lower than one would otherwise have predicted. While this finding suggests that union wages are reduced, on average, by takeovers, the estimated effect is rather modest and may simply reflect the dissipation of economic rents (see Chapter 2) that previously accrued to unionized workers. The author of this study attributed the reduction in wage gains after takeover to better negotiating skills among the new managers.

SOURCES: Charles Brown and James Medoff, "The Impact of Firm Acquisitions on Labor," in *Corporate Takeovers: Causes and Consequences,* ed. Alan Auerbach (Chicago: University of Chicago Press, 1988); Frank Lichtenberg and Donald Siegel, "The Effect of Take-Overs on the Employment and Wages of Central-Office and Other Personnel," National Bureau of Economic Research Working Paper no. 2895 (Cambridge, Mass., March 1989); Joshua Rosett, "An Empirical Investigation of Corporate Takeovers, Management Changes, Union Wages, and Employee and Target Firm Shareholder Wealth" (Ph.D. diss., Princeton University, June 1989). Rosett's data do not permit him to examine employment effects.

It is interesting to note that some of these studies suggest that unions increase productivity more than they increase wages, which leads to the possibility that profitability is greater in firms that are organized by unions. This intriguing possibility does not accord well with the substantial efforts of most firms to oppose demands for recognition by unions and of employer organizations to oppose proposed labor law reforms that might facilitate the process of union organization. If unions improve the competitive position of firms, why are they not welcomed by managers?

One hypothesis is related to the fact that unions place substantial constraints on the prerogatives and discretion that managers value. Managers may therefore oppose unionization, despite its potentially beneficial productivity effects, to protect their power and discretion. Since it is difficult for shareholders to monitor managerial performance, it may be possible for managers to take actions (such as resisting unions and their beneficial effects) that may be in their best interests but not in the interests of the shareholders.

Two ways to resolve this issue are to examine the evidence on both the effects shareholders expect unions to have on the performance of a firm and the actual effects of unions on profitability. With respect to shareholder behavior, there is considerable evidence that new publicly available information on factors influencing the profitability of a corporation is quickly reflected in stock prices. Therefore, announcements of union organizing drives and victories in representation elections should increase the equity value of the firm (if the effect on profitability is believed to be positive) or decrease the stock price (if the effect is believed to be negative). One study of 253 NLRB representation elections between 1962 and 1980 found that stock prices fell in response to both the announcement that a petition for election had been filed with the NLRB and the certification of a union as bargaining agent.[69] Similarly, announcements of a union wage settlement that is larger than anticipated should decrease the stock market value of the corporation. One recent study found that a negative relationship does exist and is essentially dollar-for-dollar.[70]

With respect to the profitability of union and nonunion firms, it is important to distinguish between different product market structures. If the effect of unions is to reduce the profitability of firms in a competitive industry, those firms will earn less than normal profits and an exodus of firms from the industry will continue until the product price increases sufficiently to restore a normal rate of return. In equilibrium, therefore, the profitability of the surviving unionized and nonunionized firms should be the same. In concentrated industries, however, firms may earn excess profits in equilibrium and a union may be able to capture some of these profits. Several recent studies indicate that unions in fact do reduce profits (consistent with the shareholder expecta-

69. Interestingly, the fall in the stock price when a petition was filed (before the campaign and election) was larger in cases in which the union ultimately won the election than in cases in which the union lost, a result that the authors interpret as indicating that the market is able to anticipate the outcome of the election. See Richard S. Ruback and Martin B. Zimmerman, "Unionization and Profitability: Evidence from the Capital Market," *Journal of Political Economy* 92 (December 1984): 1134–57.
70. John Abowd, "The Effect of Wage Bargains on the Stock Market Value of the Firm," *American Economic Review* 79 (September 1989): 774–800.

tions discussed above), but in equilibrium the reduction of profits is observed only in concentrated industries.[71] While some of the evidence is still preliminary, it appears that the general impact of unions *is* to reduce profits and that stockholders are aware of this impact.

MISCONCEPTION

"No one can doubt the obvious: unions raise wages!"

Analysis

Unions may raise wages of their members relative to those in the nonunion sector, but the higher wages will be associated with reduced employment unless other services rendered by unions offset this rise in labor's cost. Reduced employment for labor in the union sector may actually *reduce* the expected earnings of other workers, however, by increasing the supply of workers seeking jobs in the nonunion sector.

Principle

Equilibrium employment and relative wage levels are the result of both demand and supply influences.

REVIEW QUESTIONS

1. Suppose that a proposal for tax reductions associated with the purchase of capital equipment is up for debate. Suppose, too, that union leaders are called upon to comment on the proposal from the perspective of how it will affect the welfare of their members as workers (not consumers). Will they all agree on the effects of the proposal? Explain your answer.
2. The head of a large national union is trying to decide where he should concentrate his efforts at organizing a union. He perceives three options: firm A, firm B, or firm C. The three firms are identical except that:
   a. Firm A faces a perfectly elastic (horizontal) supply curve of labor and a rather inelastic demand curve for its output.
   b. Firm B behaves as a monopsonist (faces an upward-sloping supply curve of labor) and faces a perfectly elastic (horizontal) demand curve for its output.
   c. Firm C faces a perfectly elastic supply curve of labor and a perfectly elastic demand curve for its output.
   This union head would like to know where a new union will pay off most in terms of large wage gains with only small reductions in the numbers of workers. Rank the three options from best to worst, giving reasons for your ranking.
3. Is the following statement true, false, or uncertain? "The host of empirical studies that indicate that unions raise the wages of their members by 10 to 20 percent relative to the wages of comparable nonunion workers imply that unions have a negative effect on national output." Explain your answer.

---

71. See John T. Addison and Barry T. Hirsch, "Union Effects on Productivity, Profits, and Growth: Has the Long Run Arrived?" *Journal of Labor Economics* 7 (January 1989): 72–106, for a review of these studies.

4. Unionized plumbers are in unions that control the size of their membership. Wages are kept high by keeping membership highly qualified and therefore small. Employers needing or wanting to employ union labor must hire from the ranks of union membership. Suppose there is a plumbers' union in each of two cities. City A has an ordinance that states that all plumbing installations and repairs must be performed by union members. City B has no such ordinance. Analyze as completely as you can the effects of city A's ordinance on workers, consumers, and the general well-being of society. (*Hint:* You can gain insight into this question by comparing cities A and B.)

5. The Jones Act mandates that at least 50 percent of all U.S. government-financed cargo must be transported in U.S.-owned ships and that any U.S. ship leaving a U.S. port must have at least 90 percent of its crew composed of U.S. citizens. What would you expect the impact of this act to be on the demand for labor in the shipping industry and the ability of seamen's unions to push up the wages of their members?

6. Some collective bargaining agreements contain "union standards" clauses that prohibit the employer from subcontracting with firms that pay wages below those specified in the agreement. That is, the employer is prohibited from "farming out" work normally done in the plant to other firms (the subcontractors) if the subcontractors pay less than the union wage.

   a. What is the union's rationale for seeking a union standards clause?

   b. Under what conditions will a union standards clause most likely be sought by a labor union?

7. A recent publication of the AFL-CIO stated, "There is accumulating evidence that unionized workers are more productive than nonunion workers and that unionization raises productivity in an establishment. This suggests that employers and American society generally should take a much more positive approach to unionism and collective bargaining." Comment on this quotation.

8. In the mid-1970s the teachers' union of a large American city was told that the city's financial difficulties made it necessary to cut payroll costs for teachers by 10 percent. The city gave the teachers' union a choice: it could accept a 10 percent cut in the salaries paid to teachers and suffer no employment losses, or it could keep salaries constant and accept a 10 percent cut in employment levels (and a corresponding 10 percent increase in class sizes). Generalizing from the political model of strike activity given in Chapter 12, in which the major actors are employers, workers, and union leaders (elected by majority rule), please perform the following tasks:

   a. Predict and explain the union's decision, assuming that its collective bargaining agreement with the city specifies that any layoffs will occur among those teachers most recently hired.

   b. Explain whether the decision in (a) would have been different if the collective bargaining agreement had specified that all layoffs would occur on a random basis, independent of seniority, teaching field, or any other teacher characteristics.

9. In Germany temporary layoffs and dismissals on short notice are often illegal. A dismissal is illegal if it is "socially unjustified," and it is considered "socially unjustified" if the worker could be employed in a different position or establishment of the firm even if retraining is required. Workers illegally dismissed may sue their employers. What are the likely consequences of this German law for the ability of German unions to raise wages?

SELECTED READINGS

Ashenfelter, Orley, and Johnson, George. "Bargaining Theory, Trade Unions, and Industrial Strike Activity." *American Economic Review* 59 (March 1969): 35–49.

Ashenfelter, Orley, and Pencavel, John. "American Trade Union Growth, 1900–1960." *Quarterly Journal of Economics* 83 (August 1969): 434–48.

Atherton, Wallace. *Theory of Union Bargaining Goals.* Princeton, N.J.: Princeton University Press, 1973.

Freeman, Richard B., and Medoff, James L. *What Do Unions Do?* New York: Basic Books, 1984.

Hirsch, Barry T., and Addison, John T. *The Economic Analysis of Unions: New Approaches and Evidence.* Boston: Allen and Unwin, 1986.

Lewis, H. G. *Union Relative Wage Effects: A Survey.* Chicago: University of Chicago Press, 1986.

APPENDIX 12A

"Monopoly Unions" or "Efficient Contracts"?

In our discussion of how unions achieve their objectives, we assumed that unions value their members' compensation and employment levels and that their ability to achieve their objectives is constrained by the labor demand curve. It is straightforward to formalize the notion of a union's maximizing a utility function subject to the constraint of a labor demand curve, just as one can formalize the idea of a consumer's maximizing a utility function subject to a budget constraint. However, as we shall see, the solution to such a maximization process is not an *efficient contract* in that it is not *pareto optimal*. That is, there are alternative wage/employment combinations that will leave *both* the employer and the union better off.[1]

Figure 12A.1 shows the demand curve D for union members as a function of their wage; for simplicity we ignore all other pecuniary (employee benefits) and nonpecuniary (working conditions) characteristics of employment. We assume that the union values both the wages and the employment of its members and that it can aggregate its members' preferences so we can meaningfully speak of a union utility function that depends on these two variables. This utility function is summarized in Figure 12A.1 by the family of indifference curves U_0, U_1, U_2, U_3. Each curve represents a locus of employment/wage combinations about which the union is indifferent. The indifference curves are negatively sloped, because to maintain a given utility level the union must be compensated for a decline in one variable (employment or wages) by an increase in the other. They exhibit the property of diminishing marginal rates of substitution (they are convex to the origin) because it is assumed that the rate at which the union is willing to trade off wages for employment along an

---

1. This point was noted many years ago by Wassily Leontief, "The Pure Theory of the Guaranteed Annual Wage Contract," *Journal of Political Economy* 54 (February 1946): 76–79, and stressed recently by Ian McDonald and Robert Solow, "Wage Bargaining and Employment," *American Economic Review* 71 (December 1981): 896–908.

indifference curve declines as employment of its members increases. Finally, higher indifference curves represent higher levels of union utility.

Suppose that, in the absence of a union, market forces would cause the wage to be W_0 and employment to be E_0 (point a in Figure 12A.1). How does collective bargaining affect this solution? One possibility is that the union and employer will agree on a higher wage rate and then, given the wage rate, the employer will determine the number of union members to employ. Given a bargained wage rate, the employer will maximize profits and determine employment from the demand curve. Since the union presumably knows this, its goal is to maximize its utility function subject to the constraint that its wage/employment combination will lie on the demand curve.

In terms of Figure 12A.1, the union will seek to move to point b, where indifference curve U_2 is just tangent to the labor demand curve. At this point wages would be W_U and employment E_U. Given the constraint of the labor demand curve, point b represents the highest level of utility the union can attain.

This model, in which the union sets the wage subject to the knowledge that the employer will then determine employment from the demand curve, is often referred to as the *monopoly union* model. Since unions negotiate over wages in many collective bargaining negotiations, but not explicitly over employment levels, some economists feel it may be a useful analytic tool. What bothers other economists, however, is that point b is *not* an *efficient contract* in that it is not *pareto optimal*. That is, there is a whole set of wage/employment combinations that at least one of the two parties to the contract would prefer and that also leave neither party worse off than it is at point b.

FIGURE 12A.1 Union Maximizes Utility Subject to the Constraint of the Demand for Labor Curve

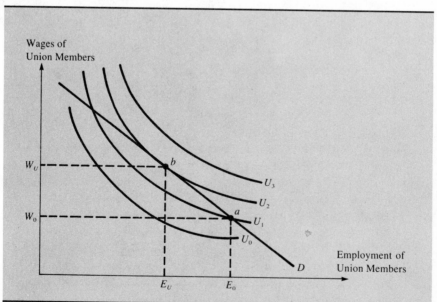

To see this, we must recall from Chapter 3 that the labor demand curve is defined by the employer's choosing the employment level to maximize profits at each wage rate. Now, starting at a point like point a on the demand curve with the wage set at W_0, if the employer were to expand or contract employment, profits would fall. To keep profits from falling would require a lower wage rate. Expanding or contracting employment further would require a still lower wage rate to keep profits at the same level.

One can formalize this by reintroducing the concept of *isoprofit curves*, first discussed in Chapter 8. Here an isoprofit curve is a locus of wage/employment combinations along which an employer's profits are unchanged. Figure 12A.2 shows three isoprofit curves for the employer whose labor demand curve is D. As discussed above, each curve reaches a maximum at its intersection with the demand curve; as we move along a given isoprofit curve in either direction away from the demand curve, wages must fall to keep profits constant. A higher isoprofit curve represents a lower level of employer profits because the wage associated with each level of employment is greater along the higher curve. So, for example, the employer would prefer any point on I_0, which includes the original wage/employment combination (point a), to any point on I_2, which includes the monopoly union wage/employment solution (point b).

Figure 12A.3 superimposes the family of employer isoprofit curves from Figure 12A.2 onto the family of union indifference curves from Figure 12A.1 and illustrates why the monopoly union solution, point b, is not an *efficient*

FIGURE 12A.2 Employer Isoprofit Curves

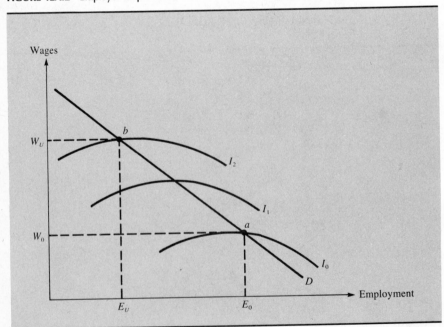

contract. Suppose, rather than locating at point b, the parties negotiated a contract that called for them to locate at point d, where the wage rate (W_d) would be lower but employment of union members (E_d) higher. At point d the union would be better off since it would now be on a higher indifference curve, U_3, while the firm would be no worse off, since it still would be on isoprofit curve I_2.

Similarly, suppose that rather than negotiating a contract to wind up at b, the parties agreed to a contract that called for them to locate at point e, with a wage rate of W_e and an employment level of E_e. Compared to the monopoly union solution (point b) the union is equally well off, since it remains on indifference curve U_2, but now the firm is better off because it has been able to reach isoprofit curve I_1. Because I_1 lies below I_2, it represents a higher level of profits.

In fact, there is a whole set of contracts that both parties will find at least as good as point b; these are represented by the shaded area in Figure 12A.3. Among this set, the ones that are *pareto optimal* (or efficient contracts)—contracts in which no party can be made better off without hurting the other— are the ones in which employer isoprofit curves are just tangent to union indifference curves, such as points d and e. Indeed, there is a whole locus of such points, and they are represented in the figure by the positively sloped curve ed. Each point on this curve represents a tangency of a union indifference curve and an employer isoprofit curve; these are points at which the em-

FIGURE 12A.3   The Contract Curve—The Locus of "Efficient Contracts"

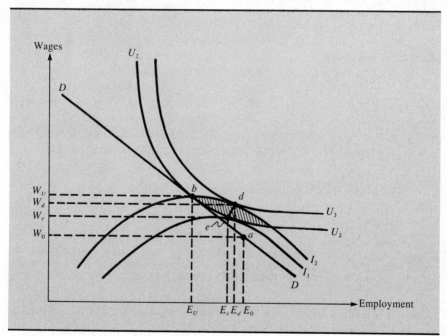

ployer and the union are equally willing to substitute wages for employment at the margin (so that no more mutually beneficial trades are possible).

All of the points on *ed*, which is often called the *contract curve* (or locus of efficient contracts), will leave both parties at least as well off as at point *b*, and at least one party better off. However, the parties are not indifferent to where along *ed* the settlement is reached. As one moves from point *e* to point *d*, wages and employment both rise, increasing union members' utility but decreasing the employer's profits. Obviously the union would prefer to be close to *d* and the employer close to *e*. Where on the contract curve a settlement actually occurs in this model depends upon the bargaining power of the parties.[2]

How realistic is the *efficient-contract* model as a description of the wage-determination process in unionized workplaces in the United States? The efficient-contract model requires that unions bargain over *both* wages and employment levels. Now, some labor contracts in the United States do explicitly cover employment levels as well as wages. For example, many contracts that cover public school teachers specify maximum class size or minimum teacher/student ratios. However, the vast majority of union contracts in the private sector contain no explicit provisions guaranteeing employment levels.[3]

To say that few *explicit* employment level guarantees exist is not to say, however, that *implicit* agreements are not present. In a world of uncertain future labor demand, it may be very difficult to specify in a written contract exactly how employment will be contingent on future labor demand during the contract period.[4] Instead, it is likely that the negotiations over wages will contain some implicit understandings between the employer and the union about how both parties expect employment to be influenced by the wage settlement. Hence, even in the absence of explicit contract guarantees with respect to employment, it is conceivable that the process of collective bargaining does lead to efficient contracts.

If one cannot use data on the existence of explicit employment guarantees in labor contracts to evaluate whether the efficient-contract model is correct, how can one decide whether the efficient-contract or monopoly union model is a better representation of the unionized wage-determination process? The answer is that the two models sometimes yield different implications about how the equilibrium wage will vary in response to changes in variables that affect

2. For an attempt to model how bargaining power affects the nature of contract settlements, see Jan Svejnar, "Bargaining Power, Fear of Disagreements, and Wage Settlements: Theory and Empirical Evidence from U.S. Industry," *Econometrica* 54 (September 1986): 1055–78.

3. In 1980, only 11 percent of major private sector collective bargaining agreements had such guarantees. See U.S. Bureau of Labor Statistics, *Characteristics of Major Collective Bargaining Agreements, January 1, 1980,* Bulletin 2095 (Washington, D.C.: U.S. Government Printing Office, May 1981).

4. The demand for teachers throughout any one school year is quite predictable once fall enrollment figures are known, which may explain the frequency of employment guarantees (in the form of class size provisions) in teachers' contracts.

either the demand curve for labor or union preferences. A number of recent studies that analyze wage outcomes for union workers in several industries provide some evidence in support of the efficient-contract model.[5]

5. Orley Ashenfelter and James Brown, "Testing the Efficiency of Employment Contracts," *Journal of Political Economy* 94, no. 3, pt. 2 (June 1986): S40–S87; Thomas MaCurdy and John Pencavel, "Testing Between Competing Models of Wage and Employment Determination in Unionized Markets," *Journal of Political Economy* 94, no. 3, pt. 2 (June 1986): S3–S39; Randall Eberts and Joe Stone, "On the Contract Curve: A Test of Alternative Models of Collective Bargaining," *Journal of Labor Economics* 4 (January 1986): 66–81; David Card, "Efficient Contracts with Costly Adjustment: Short-Run Employment Determination for Airline Mechanics," *American Economic Review* 76 (December 1986): 1045–71; Jan Svejnar, "Bargaining Power . . . "; and John Abowd, "The Effect of Wage Bargains on the Stock Market Value of the Firm," *American Economic Review* 79 (September 1989): 774–800.

13

Public Sector Labor Markets

W hy does the study of public sector labor markets in the United States warrant a separate chapter in this text? One reason is that federal, state, and local governments differ from most private sector employers in that profit maximization is unlikely to be an objective of governmental units.[1] Therefore, labor market models based upon the assumption of profit maximization are clearly inappropriate for the government sector; alternative models must be developed. As this chapter will show, it is *not* necessary to assume profit maximization in order to deduce that the demand for public employees is a downward-sloping function of their wage rate.

A second reason is that employment expanded more rapidly between 1951 and 1975 in the state and local government (SLG) sector than in any other sector of the economy. While civilian employment by the federal government (when expressed as a percentage of total nonagricultural employment) actually declined slightly during the period, SLG employment rose from 8.5 percent in 1951 to 15.5 percent in 1975 of total nonagricultural payroll employment (see Table 13.1). Indeed, the absolute number of state and local government employees almost tripled during this period, rising from 4.1 to 11.9 million. Although the share of SLG employment in total employment has declined slightly since 1975, the absolute number rose to over 14.7 million in 1989. The importance of the sector suggests that attention should be directed to analyses of it.

A third reason is that the pattern of unionization and the laws governing collective bargaining, dispute resolution, and wage determination differ between the public and private sectors. In contrast to the decline in the fraction of private sector workers who are union members, which was discussed in

---

1. For an interesting analysis of the private nonprofit sector, see Burton Weisbrod, *The Non-profit Economy* (Cambridge, Mass.: Harvard University Press, 1988).

TABLE 13.1   Government Employment in the United States: 1951–89

Year	Total Nonagricultural Payroll Employment (in thousands)	Federal Civilian Employment (in thousands)	State and Local Government (SLG) Employment (in thousands)	Federal Government as Percentage of Total	SLG as Percentage of Total
1951	47,819	2,302	4,087	4.8	8.5
1953	50,202	2,305	4,340	4.6	8.6
1955	50,641	2,187	4,727	4.3	9.3
1957	52,853	2,217	5,399	4.2	10.2
1959	53,268	2,233	5,850	4.2	11.0
1961	53,999	2,279	6,315	4.2	11.7
1963	56,653	2,358	6,868	4.2	12.1
1965	60,765	2,378	7,696	3.9	12.7
1967	65,803	2,719	8,672	4.1	13.2
1969	70,384	2,758	9,437	3.9	13.4
1971	71,214	2,696	10,185	3.8	14.3
1973	76,790	2,663	11,068	3.5	14.4
1975	76,945	2,748	11,937	3.6	15.5
1977	82,471	2,721	12,399	3.3	15.0
1979	89,823	2,773	13,174	3.1	14.7
1981	91,156	2,772	13,259	3.0	14.5
1983	90,200	2,774	13,096	3.1	14.5
1985	97,519	2,875	13,519	2.9	13.9
1987	102,200	2,943	14,067	2.9	13.8
1989	108,573	2,988	14,739	2.8	13.6

SOURCE: *1982 Employment and Training Report of the President* (Washington, D.C.: U.S. Government Printing Office, 1982), Table C-1, and *1990 Economic Report of the President* (Washington, D.C.: U.S. Government Printing Office, 1990), Table C-43.

Chapter 12, public sector union membership grew rapidly through the mid-1970s and, after experiencing a slight decline in the late 1970s, has remained fairly stable since then. For example, between 1958 and 1976 the proportion of federal employees belonging to unions increased from 23.2 to 41.5 percent, before falling back to 36.8 percent in 1983.[2] Similarly, as can be seen from column (a) of Table 13.2, the proportion of SLG employees belonging to unions or other bargaining organizations (such as the National Education Association, which over time has increasingly behaved like a union) rose from 24.3 percent in 1962 to 39.9 percent in 1976, before declining to 32.5 percent in 1983. More recent data from other sources, which are not strictly comparable (columns b and c of Table 13.2), suggest that since 1984 the percentage of SLG employees belonging to bargaining organizations or covered by contracts has remained roughly constant.

One factor that affected the growth in public sector unionization was a change in public attitudes and legislation governing bargaining in the public

---

2. John F. Burton, Jr., and Terry Thomason, "The Extent of Collective Bargaining in the Public Sector," in *Public Sector Bargaining*, 2d ed., ed. Benjamin Aaron et al. (Washington, D.C.: Bureau of National Affairs, 1989), Table 1. Because changes in the way the data were reported after 1983 made data for later years noncomparable, we have ceased our comparisons as of that date.

TABLE 13.2   State and Local Government Employees Belonging to Bargaining Organizations or Covered by Contracts

Year	Percentage Belonging to Bargaining Organizations		Percentage Covered by a Contract
	(a)	(b)	(c)
1962	24.3		
1964	25.0		
1966	24.8		
1968	24.9		
1970	30.1		
1972	33.7		
1974	37.1		
1976	39.9		
1978	35.7		
1980	34.1		
1982	33.5		
1983	32.5	36.7	45.5
1984		35.8	43.9
1986		36.0	43.2
1988		36.7	43.6

SOURCES: John F. Burton, Jr., and Terry Thomason, "The Extent of Collective Bargaining in the Public Sector," in *Public Sector Bargaining,* 2d ed., ed. Benjamin Aaron et al. (Washington, D.C.: Bureau of National Affairs, 1988), Table 2 (col. a); U.S. Bureau of Labor Statistics, *Employment and Earnings,* January 1985, Table 53; January 1987, Table 60; and January 1989, Table 60 (cols. b and c). The percentages in column (a) are based on membership data reported by bargaining organizations, while those in columns (b) and (c) are based on responses of individuals to Current Population Survey questions.

sector. In the private sector the rights of workers to organize and bargain collectively have been guaranteed since the National Labor Relations Act, but laws governing bargaining in the public sector are of much more recent vintage. Executive Order 10988 issued by President John F. Kennedy in 1962 legitimized collective bargaining in the federal sector for the first time, providing federal workers with the rights to join unions and bargain over working conditions, but not wages. While this executive order has been modified several times, most federal employees' wages are still not determined by the collective bargaining process.[3] Instead, they are determined through comparability legislation, first passed in 1962, which ties the wages of most federal civilian workers to the results of government surveys of wages of "comparable" private workers, subject to possible Presidential or congressional modification.[4] The influence of federal unions on wages operates, then, primarily

3. There were some major exceptions—namely, postal workers and employees of federal government authorities, such as the Tennessee Valley Authority (TVA). In each of these cases the prices of the products or services produced (mail delivery, hydroelectric power) can be raised to cover the cost of the contract settlement. In other federal agencies, salaries are paid out of general revenues.

4. See Sharon Smith, *Equal Pay in the Public Sector: Fact or Fantasy* (Princeton, N.J.: Industrial Relations Section, Princeton University, 1977), for a more complete description of the comparability process in the federal sector. Federal blue-collar workers' wages are also determined, in the main, by the comparability process, with comparisons in this case being made at the local labor market level.

through the political pressure they can exert on the President and Congress to approve wage increases that the surveys suggest are warranted.

Favorable state legislation for SLG employee collective bargaining began with a 1959 law in Wisconsin; prior to that date collective bargaining was effectively prohibited in the state and local sector. By 1986 most industrial states had adopted statutes that permitted SLG employees to participate in determining their wages and conditions of employment, although not all employees in each state were covered by the laws.[5] While these statutes were being adopted, and at the same time that employment and unionization were growing in the SLG sector, SLG employees' earnings also started to rise relative to the earnings of private sector employees (see Table 13.3). From the mid-1950s to 1970, SLG employees' average earnings improved relative to those of private employees by 16–20 percent.[6] During the 1970s earnings of SLG workers tended to fall relative to those of their private sector counterparts, but as of 1988 SLG employees' relative earnings stood at all-time highs.[7]

The growth in the relative earnings position of SLG employees during the 1960s, coupled with the growing strength of public employee unions, their increased militancy, and the trend towards allowing SLG employees to bargain over wage issues, led to fears that inflationary wage settlements would continue in the sector and aggravate the financial problems faced by state and local governments. These fears were explicitly based upon the belief that many public services are essential, and that this implied that the wage elasticity of demand for public employees was very inelastic. To many, the logical conclusion was that, in the absence of market constraints that would limit the wage demands of public employees, limitations should be placed on their collective bargaining rights.[8]

Although by 1981 nine states did grant the right to strike in one form or another to selected public employee groups, most continued historic prohibitions against strikes. The states that prohibited strikes, however, often provided assistance to local governments and unions in settling contract disputes, with a number of states adopting forms of binding arbitration as the terminal

---

5. See Richard B. Freeman, "Unionism Comes to the Public Sector," *Journal of Economic Literature* 24 (March 1986): 41–86, for a more complete discussion of the evolution of legislation governing bargaining in the public sector.
6. Note that 1.29 divided by 1.11 equals 1.16, and 1.24 divided by 1.03 equals 1.20, which imply 16 percent and 20 percent increases, respectively.
7. The comparisons in Table 13.3 are subject to a number of qualifications. They focus only on wages, ignoring employee benefits and differences in working conditions. Furthermore, they do not control for differences in skill level or occupational mixes between the public and private sectors. When the average earnings of workers in the two sectors are compared, we find that in 1988 the average annual earnings of SLG employees exceeded those of manufacturing production workers by 29 percent (column 2). This percentage tells us nothing about how the earnings of a worker with a given skill level would compare in the two sectors. Average earnings in the SLG sector might exceed those in the private sector, even if the wage rate paid in each occupation were the same in both sectors, simply because the public sector tends to employ relatively more high-skilled workers. Similarly, when one observes changes in the ratios in columns 1 and 2, one should be aware that they may reflect changes in the relative occupational mixes across the two sectors, as well as changes in the relative compensation levels.
8. See, for example, H. Wellington and R. Winter, "The Limits of Collective Bargaining in Public Employment," *Yale Law Journal* 69 (June 1969): 1107–27.

TABLE 13.3 Earnings Ratios, SLG Employees to Private Sector Employees, 1956–88

| | Private Sector Comparison Group | |
| | Nonagricultural Nonsupervisory Workers[a] | Manufacturing Production Workers[b] |
Year	(1)	(2)
1956	1.11	1.03
1958	1.12	1.04
1960	1.14	1.06
1962	1.19	1.10
1964	1.19	1.11
1966	1.21	1.14
1968	1.27	1.20
1970	1.29	1.24
1972	1.24	1.20
1974	1.27	1.21
1976	1.25	1.17
1978	1.19	1.10
1980	1.21	1.10
1982	1.24	1.12
1984	1.29	1.17
1986	1.38	1.24
1988	1.41	1.29

[a]Average annual earnings of SLG workers divided by average annual earnings of private nonagricultural, nonsupervisory workers.

[b]Average annual earnings of SLG workers divided by average annual earnings of manufacturing workers.

sources: Based on U.S. Department of Labor, *Employment and Earnings* (various issues), and U.S. Bureau of Census, *Public Employment in (Year)* (various issues). Average annual earnings of private sector workers are estimated as 2,000 times their average hourly earnings during the year. Average annual earnings for SLG employees are computed as 12 times the average monthly earnings of full-time SLG employees in October of the year.

stage in their impasse procedures.[9] How these alternative institutional arrangements operate and affect economic outcomes is, of course, worthy of discussion.[10]

A final reason why public sector labor markets warrant separate treatment is that they represent an area toward which much of our public policy has recently been directed. To take one example, during the 1970s and early

---

9. For more details on state laws governing dispute resolution in the state and local sectors, see Richard Freeman, "Unionism Comes to the Public Sector," Tables 13 and 15.

10. Some definition of terminology may be useful. An *impasse* is a situation in which the parties cannot agree on the terms of a collective bargaining agreement. State public employment relations agencies provide three types of assistance to the parties. *Mediators* are individuals who attempt to assist the parties to negotiate with each other by serving as intermediaries when personal conflicts prevent negotiations from occurring or by making suggestions that both parties may find acceptable. *Factfinders*, after hearing both parties' positions, issue oral or written statements to the parties about the types of settlements they believe are justified by the evidence (facts). Such positions taken by impartial third parties often influence the positions taken by the parties in the negotiations. Finally, *arbitrators* issue formal rulings about what they believe the settlement should be; in many cases state law or prior agreement by the parties dictates that if the negotiations go to arbitration, the arbitrator's decision will be binding.

1980s attempts were made to reduce unemployment by means of public service employment (PSE) programs. Starting with the Emergency Employment Act of 1971 and continuing under the Comprehensive Employment and Training Act (CETA), the federal government provided funds to state and local governments to increase their employment levels, in the hope that the availability of extra public sector jobs would provide job opportunities for the unemployed. By 1978, 569,000 individuals were reported employed on PSE program funds; these employees constituted some 3.3 percent of total SLG employment. While this program was terminated by the Reagan Administration in 1982, it is important to know what its effects were.

To take another example, growing concern over the fiscal condition of state and local governments and the increased state and local tax burden borne by taxpayers led to the passage of expenditure- and tax-limitation legislation in a number of states in the late 1970s. The most notable was Proposition 13 in California, which drastically reduced local property taxes and limited the ability of all governmental units in the state to increase their revenues.

For all these reasons, the objective of this chapter is to present a simple analytical framework that can be used to discuss public sector labor markets and then use the framework to analyze the following:

1. Why SLG employment grew so rapidly between 1950 and 1975, but has fallen in relative terms since then.
2. Why the relative earnings of SLG employees similarly rose between 1950 and the early 1970s and fell for a while thereafter.
3. Why unionization in the public sector grew so rapidly through 1975 and remained roughly constant in the 1980s.
4. What the effects of unions have been on wage and nonwage outcomes in the SLG sector.
5. What the effects of comparability legislation have been on federal employees' wages.
6. Whether the form of impasse procedure used affects the size of wage settlements in the SLG sector and what determines whether the procedure is used by the parties.
7. What the likely effects of expenditure- and tax-limitation legislation on public sector labor markets are.
8. What the net job creation effects of public employment programs were.

A MODEL OF A PUBLIC SECTOR LABOR MARKET

What are the forces that affect the level of employment and wages in a given governmental unit? Turning first to the demand side of the market, we have already indicated that profit maximization is an untenable assumption to make when analyzing the public sector. Suppose instead that there is a single decision maker (or group of decision makers) who makes decisions on the level and cost of governmental services in accordance with the wishes of voters who elect him or her to office.[11] Presumably voters are concerned with both the level of public services they receive and the resources left to them, after paying for these services through taxes or user charges, that can be used to consume private goods and services. Assume also, for simplicity, that the level of public services is proportional to the number of public employees who are hired.[12]

Decisions made by the representative public decision maker in an effort to maximize a utility function form the basis for the demand for public employees. The decision maker weighs the level of public services provided against the burden financing this level places on taxpayers, subject to a budget constraint that takes into account the prices of both public and private goods and services and the total resources available to the community. Without going through the details of such a maximization problem, it should be obvious that an increase in the cost of public services should reduce the quantity of services demanded (other things equal), just as an increase in the price of a consumer good leads a consumer to reduce his or her purchases of that good. Hence, an increase in the wage rate of public employees should lead governmental employers to demand fewer of them. Put another way, other things equal, the demand for public employees *is* a downward-sloping function of their wage rate despite the departure from an assumption of profit maximization.

Figure 13.1 shows a representative public sector labor demand curve (D_0). This curve has been drawn in *per capita* terms (public employees as a percentage of the population) in recognition of the fact that the flow of public services that an individual citizen receives from a given number of public employees depends upon the number of other individuals in the community that he or she has to "share" these public services with.[13] The position of the demand curve depends on a number of factors. Increases in the total resources available in the community, as measured perhaps by per capita family income or per capita grants from higher levels of government, will shift the demand for public employees to the right. Similarly, factors that increase the community's tastes for public services, such as a rise in the school-age population, will also shift the demand curve to the right.

Turning to the supply side, one can treat the supply of individuals to public sector jobs in the same framework used in Chapters 2 and 8 to analyze

---

11. There is extensive literature in economics on how decisions are made in the public sector. Under certain conditions in an open democratic political system, the preferences of the median voter on an issue will become the preferences of the decision makers. See Anthony Downs, *An Economic Theory of Democracy* (New York: Harper & Row, 1957), and Gordon Tullock, *Towards a Mathematics of Politics* (Ann Arbor: University of Michigan Press, 1967). However, not all economists believe that public sector decision making can be modeled in such a way. See, for example, Melvin Reder, "The Theory of Employment and Wages in the Public Sector," in *Labor in the Public and Private Nonprofit Sectors,* ed. Daniel Hamermesh (Princeton, N.J.: Princeton University Press, 1975), 1–48.

12. Such an assumption, which ignores the possibility of substituting capital for labor in producing public services, is made only for expository purposes and does not affect our final conclusion.

13. In the case of some government goods or services, however, one citizen's consumption does not reduce the amount available to others. National defense is an example of such a *pure public good* (refer to Chapter 1 for a definition of "public goods").

FIGURE 13.1   The Public Sector Labor Market and the Growth of Public Employment

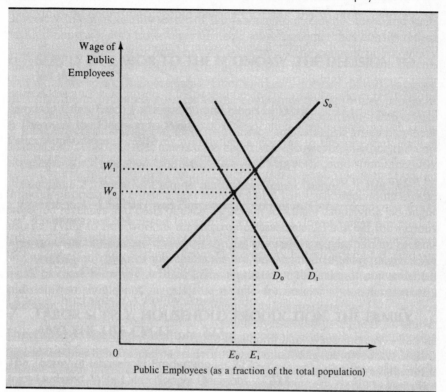

Public Employees (as a fraction of the total population)

labor supply to other occupations or industries. Other things equal, the higher the wage paid to public employees, the greater the fraction of the population that would be willing to work for the local government, as indicated by the upward-sloping labor supply curve (S_0) in Figure 13.1. The position of this curve is presumably determined by individuals' tastes for jobs in the public sector, by the wages and nonwage conditions of employment that are offered by other governmental and private employers, and by the nonwage conditions of employment offered by the particular governmental units. One important condition of employment, to which we shall return later, is job security. If the probability of being laid off in the future were to increase, for example, one would expect fewer people to be willing to work for the governmental employer, in which case the labor supply curve would shift to the left.[14]

Given the demand curve, D_0, and the supply curve, S_0, E_0 public employees per capita are hired and are paid a wage of W_0. At any wage less than W_0, the demand for public employees would exceed the supply, governmental units would have unfilled positions (job vacancies), and pressure would be exerted to raise the wage to attract more applicants. At any level of wages above

14. See Orley Ashenfelter, "Demand and Supply Functions for State and Local Government Employment," in *Essays in Labor Market Analysis,* ed. Orley Ashenfelter and Wallace Oates (New York: Halstead Press, 1979), 1–16.

W_0, there would be an excess supply of applicants, and astute public employers would realize that they could attract the desired work force at a lower real wage. Since funds used to hire public employees have alternative uses in the public and private sectors, this excess supply would create downward pressure on the real wage. Hence, the wage/employment combination (W_0, E_0) would be an equilibrium one.[15]

Suppose the demand curve for public employees were to shift out to D_1 in Figure 13.1. As indicated there, *both* public employees' wages and their per capita employment levels would increase. Between 1950 and 1970 median family income, measured in 1974 dollars, increased substantially in real terms from $6,800 to $12,531, as did per capita federal grants to state and local governments (from $33 to $137). Both of these factors should have increased the demand for SLG employees. Similarly, the proportion of the population that was of elementary-school age through college age (5 through 21) increased from 26.1 to 32.9 percent during the period, which should have increased the demand for SLG educational employees. Together, these three forces were undoubtedly largely responsible for most of the growth in employment and relative wages of SLG employees that occurred during the period (see Tables 13.1 and 13.3). However, between the mid-1970s and the mid-1980s the school-age population declined as a proportion of the population and real family incomes did not increase substantially. In retrospect, then, it is not surprising that the relative employment level and wages of SLG employees either declined or remained roughly constant during the latter period.

THE GROWTH AND EFFECTS OF PUBLIC SECTOR UNIONS

The simple demand-and-supply model of union membership presented in Chapter 12 (see Figure 12.1) can be used retrospectively to provide some insight into why unionization in the public sector grew so rapidly between 1960 and the mid-1970s and why, after a slight decline, it has remained roughly constant since then. During the 1960 to mid-1970s period, changing public attitudes and the evolution of labor legislation relating to collective bargaining in the public sector, described earlier in the chapter, reduced the costs of organizing public employees (shifting the supply of union services to the right) and probably increased the benefits public employees perceived from union membership (shifting the demand for union membership to the right). Both forces would lead to an increase in union strength. Similarly, the decline in the relative earnings position of SLG employees that occurred in the mid-1970s, along with the slowdown in the rate of growth of employment, may have strengthened the desires of public employees to turn to unions in hopes of re-

---

15. As noted in Chapter 3, there is some evidence that, *outside* of metropolitan areas, a monopsony model of public sector labor markets may be the relevant one to use. In general, however, the simple demand-and-supply model presented in the text is sufficient for our purposes. In major metropolitan areas in which scores of different local governments may employ workers in the same occupation (such as teachers), it is clear that the monopsony model is not relevant. Later in the chapter we consider the possibility that the existence of excess supplies of applicants will not put downward pressures on public sector wages.

gaining their former relative earnings positions and winning job security clauses in their contracts. Because these forces all increased the net benefits public employees perceived from union membership, they tended to shift the demand for unions further to the right. In contrast, since the mid-1970s there have been far fewer changes in state laws relating to public sector collective bargaining, and the imposition of tax and expenditure limitations in several states could have tended to reduce employees' perceptions of the benefits from joining a union (pushing the demand for union membership back to the left).[16]

This analysis naturally leads one to wonder what the effects of unions have been on wages and nonwage contract outcomes in the SLG sector. As in the private sector, a key determinant of the ability of public sector unions to raise their members' wages is the wage elasticity of demand for SLG employees. If a public sector union succeeds in raising wages above the market-clearing level (W_0) to W_u in Figure 13.2, the result will be the loss of jobs $E_0 - E_u$; the magnitude of this loss will depend upon the wage elasticity of demand. The larger this loss, the less likely it is that those unions that value both the wage and the employment levels of their members will push for large wage gains. Of course, if the demand for labor were shifting out rapidly in the SLG sector, as it was through the mid-1970s, fear of job loss would be less likely to constrain the wage demands of SLG employees' unions.

Wage Elasticity of Demand

As noted earlier, the conventional wisdom has been that, because many forms of public services are both essential and monopolized, the demand for public employees is wage inelastic. This supposed wage inelasticity of demand implies that market forces would not constrain public employees' wage demands. However, one can easily think of possibilities for substituting capital for labor in the provision of public services (for example, police patrol cars could be substituted for officers on the beat, or snowblowers could be substituted for snow-removal workers with shovels). Further, private firms can provide the same services as are now provided publicly (for example, garbage pickup could be subcontracted to private employers, or private companies could be hired to handle janitorial services in public buildings). Moreover, given the limited resources that state and local governments can command, an increase in the relative price of one service should lead a government to substitute other services that would become relatively cheaper (for example, minimally supervised playground programs could be substituted for summertime instructional programs in sports or crafts). In other words, while a local government does not have the option of moving its plant to a nonunion area (that is, fleeing to the Sunbelt), it can substitute capital for labor, change its services, or subcontract with private firms if it feels its labor costs are too high. Hence, it

---

16. See Ronald Ehrenberg and Joshua Schwarz, "Public Sector Labor Markets," in *Handbook of Labor Economics,* ed. Orley Ashenfelter and Richard Layard (Amsterdam: North-Holland, 1986); Freeman, "Unionism Comes to the Public Sector"; and Linda Edwards, "The Future of Public Sector Unions: Stagnation or Growth?" *American Economic Association Papers and Proceedings* 79 (May 1989): 161–65, for surveys of the empirical literature on union growth in the public sector.

FIGURE 13.2   The Effects of Unions in the Public Sector: Excess Applicants

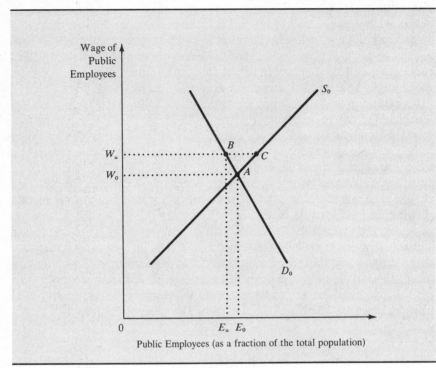

Public Employees (as a fraction of the total population)

is *not* obvious a priori that the wage elasticities of demand for all categories of state and local government employees are inelastic.

Five studies have presented estimates of the wage elasticities of demand for 11 functional categories of state and local government employees, and these studies are summarized in Table 13.4. In the main, these estimates suggest that demand curves for labor in the SLG sector *are* inelastic. However, the estimated elasticities do not appear substantially lower in absolute value than the private sector wage elasticities of demand that were summarized in Table 4.1. Regardless of these estimates, one should remember that public employees are also voters and, through the political process, seek to increase (shift) the demand for their own services.[17] To the extent that they are successful, the employment loss that would be associated with any wage increase would be smaller than if the demand curve had not been shifted out.[18]

Union Wage Effects

Numerous studies have attempted to estimate what the effect of SLG employee unions has been on their members' wages relative to the wages of

17. See Paul Courant, Edward Gramlich, and Daniel Rubinfeld, "Public Employee Market Power and the Level of Government Spending," *American Economic Review* 69 (December 1979): 806–17, for a treatment of this point.

18. See Jeffrey Zax and Casey Ichniowski, "The Effect of Public Sector Unionism on Pay, Employment, Department Budgets and Municipal Expenditures," in *When Public Sector Workers Unionize*, ed. Richard Freeman and Casey Ichniowski (Chicago: University of Chicago Press, 1988).

TABLE 13.4   Estimates of Wage Elasticities of Demand for Labor in the State and Local Sector

Category	(1)	(2)	(3)	(4)	(5)
Education	−1.06	−0.08 to −0.57	−0.57 to −0.82	−.89	
Noneducation	−0.38				
Streets and highways	−0.09	−0.44 to −0.64			
Public welfare	−0.32	−0.33 to −1.13			
Hospitals	−0.30	−0.30 to −0.51			
Public health	−0.12	−0.26 to −0.32			
Police	−0.29	−0.01 to −0.35			
Fire	−0.53	−0.23 to −0.31			
Sanitation and sewage	−0.23	−0.40 to −0.56			
Natural resources	−0.39	−0.39 to −0.60			
General control and financial administration	−0.28	−0.09 to −0.34			
All categories					−.53

SOURCES: (1) Orley Ashenfelter and Ronald Ehrenberg, "The Demand for Labor in the Public Sector," in *Labor in the Public and Nonprofit Sectors,* ed. Daniel Hamermesh (Princeton, N.J.: Princeton University Press, 1975), Table 6. (2) Ronald G. Ehrenberg, "The Demand for State and Local Government Employees," *American Economic Review* 63 (June 1973): 366–79. (3) Robert J. Thornton, "The Elasticity of Demand for Public School Teachers," *Industrial Relations* 18 (Winter 1979): 86–91. (4) Hui S. Chang and Yu Hsing, "A Note on the Demand for Faculty in Public Higher Education," *Industrial Relations* 21 (Spring 1982): 256–60. (5) Orley Ashenfelter, "Demand and Supply Functions for State and Local Government Employment," in *Essays in Labor Market Analysis,* ed. Orley Ashenfelter and Wallace Oates (New York: Halstead Press, 1979).

otherwise comparable nonunion public employees. One detailed study of noneducational municipal employees suggested that average monthly earnings of municipal employees represented by unions or employee associations exceeded those of otherwise comparable nonorganized employees by 2–16 percent in 1967.[19] These estimates are no higher, and are perhaps even lower, than the union relative wage effects observed in the private sector. Numerous studies, which use data from later periods and include analyses of educational employees' earnings, confirm this result. That is, unions in the SLG sector appear to have had more moderate effects on the relative wages of their members than unions in the private sector.[20]

As emphasized, however, wages are not identical to total compensation. In addition to those reasons presented in the previous chapter, there are other

---

19. Ronald G. Ehrenberg and Gerald S. Goldstein, "A Model of Public Sector Wage Determination," *Journal of Urban Economics* 2 (April 1975): 223–45. This study also showed that the magnitude of the union relative wage effect for a given category of municipal employees (such as police) depended upon the extent of unionization of other categories of municipal employees (such as firefighters) in the city *and* the extent of organization of municipal employees in neighboring cities. That is, both occupational and geographic wage comparisons appear to be made when public sector unions set their wage demands. In the context of our public sector labor market model, one can explain these results by noting that the supply curve of, say, police to city A will shift to the left as the wages of police in a neighboring city, or the wages of other categories of municipal employees in city A, increase. This shift would, other things equal, increase the wages of police in city A.
20. For surveys of recent studies, see Ronald G. Ehrenberg and Joshua L. Schwarz, "Public Sector Labor Markets," and H. G. Lewis, "Union/Nonunion Wage Gaps in the Public Sector," in *When Public Sector Workers Unionize.*

reasons to believe that the effects of public sector unions on nonwage benefits may well exceed their effects on wages. On the one hand, public employees' wages are much more visible to the public than are their benefits. The public may be more aware of the cost of a $500 increase in annual starting salaries, which is well publicized, than they are of an increase in health insurance costs (due to an increase in premiums or improved coverage) that will also cost $500 per employee. For this reason, it may be politically easier for governmental negotiators to make concessions on employee-benefit items than on wages.

Moreover, while the costs of increased wages must be borne in the present, the costs of improved employee benefits are often either unknown at the time of settlement or are borne only in the future. For example, the true cost of agreeing to pay 100 percent of employees' health insurance expenses depends upon future increases in health insurance rates. To take another example, if public employee pension plans are not fully funded, the costs of agreeing to more generous retirement provisions today will become evident only in the future, when employees begin to take advantage of these provisions.[21] Since government officials' tenures in office are often short, and since they typically depart from office well before the true costs of such employee benefits become known, it is in their *short-run* political interests to win favor with public employee unions by agreeing to increased benefits, since the short-run costs of such agreements to taxpayers may well be small.[22]

For both of these reasons, then, one might expect that the effects of public sector unions on employee benefits would be larger than their effects on wages. Although the limited empirical evidence on this point is not clear-cut, it does suggest that this has occurred.[23]

Union Effects on Productivity

Although it is often difficult to measure productivity in the public sector, a number of recent studies have sought to estimate what the effects of public sector collective bargaining have been on productivity. One study that focused on municipal public libraries found no union/nonunion productivity differentials for a variety of measures of library output.[24] Another study found that teachers' unions appeared to be associated with higher test scores for average students but lower test scores for below- and above-average students.[25]

---

21. A survey by the National Association of State Retirement Administrators, *Survey of Systems 1989* (Salt Lake City, 1989), found that state and local pension fund assets were about 87 percent of accrued liabilities in 1989.

22. We say short run because in the long run facts become known. The best example of this occurred in New York City, where Mayor Lindsay agreed to generous benefit packages for New York City employees during the late 1960s and early 1970s. Many people subsequently blamed him for all the financial problems the city experienced in the mid-1970s, and when he ran for U.S. Senator in the Democratic primary in 1980, he finished well behind the winner.

23. See Ronald Ehrenberg and Joshua Schwarz, "Public Sector Labor Markets," and Richard Freeman, "Unionism Comes to the Public Sector," for surveys of the relevant literature.

24. Ronald G. Ehrenberg, Daniel R. Sherman, and Joshua L. Schwarz, "Unions and Productivity in the Public Sector: A Study of Municipal Libraries," *Industrial and Labor Relations Review* 36 (January 1983): 199–213.

25. Randall Eberts and Joe Stone, *Unions and Public Schools: The Nonwage Effect of Collective Bargaining in American Education* (Lexington, Mass.: D. C. Heath, 1984).

Finally, two studies adopted a more indirect approach and found that teacher absenteeism tended to be higher in school districts where union contracts called for a generous sick-leave policy.[26] Clearly, as with the private sector studies discussed in Chapter 12, there is no consensus about how public sector unions affect productivity.

THE EFFECTS OF ARBITRATION STATUTES ON THE WAGES OF STATE AND LOCAL GOVERNMENT EMPLOYEES

One reason why the effect of SLG employee unions on their members' wages is not substantially larger may be that SLG employees' rights to strike are seriously limited. Many states explicitly prohibit strikes by SLG employees, substituting alternative forms of impasse resolution instead. Some states have adopted *binding arbitration* as the final stage of their impasse procedure for some categories of public employees, most notably those in the essential police and firefighter areas.[27]

Such binding arbitration legislation is typically opposed by municipal government officials, who argue that arbitration takes the final decision over public employees' wages out of the hands of elected officials and leads to inflated wage settlements. Several studies have analyzed the consequences of arbitration statutes and concluded that the use of arbitration may compress differentials across cities (since arbitrators tend to award larger increases in cities in which public employees are paid relatively low wages than they do in cities in which public employees' wages are relatively high), but that, on average, the wage settlements that go to the arbitration stage are no higher than the wage settlements in otherwise comparable cities that do not go to arbitration (see Example 13.1).[28] That is, if the average percentage wage settlement in cities that went to arbitration, $\dot{W}_A$, in a particular bargaining round is compared to the average percentage wage settlement in otherwise comparable cities that did not go to arbitration, $\dot{W}_N$, the difference (D) is roughly zero:

$$D = \dot{W}_A - \dot{W}_N = 0 \tag{13.1}$$

One might be tempted to conclude that the arbitration process per se has had no effect on the size of the average wage settlement in the public sector. However, this conclusion assumes that the rates of wage increase in cities in which negotiations did not go to arbitration ($\dot{W}_N$) are the same as they would have been in the absence of the arbitration statute, which is not necessarily correct. The existence of the arbitration statute per se may well alter the size of wage settlements even in cities in which the parties do not go to arbitration.

26. Donald Winkler, "The Effect of Sick Leave Policy on Teacher Absenteeism," *Industrial and Labor Relations Review* 33 (January 1980): 232–40, and Ronald G. Ehrenberg et al., "School District Leave Policies, Teacher Absenteeism, and Student Achievement," *Journal of Human Resources,* forthcoming.

27. By 1984 at least 20 states had adopted some form of binding arbitration for police and firefighter contract-dispute resolution. See Richard Freeman, "Unionism Comes to the Public Sector," Table 15.

28. See Ronald Ehrenberg and Joshua Schwarz, "Public Sector Labor Markets," for a review of these studies.

EXAMPLE 13.1

Final-Offer Arbitration and Police Wages in New Jersey

Arbitration in public sector wage disputes generally takes two forms. Some states use *conventional arbitration,* in which the arbitrator (or arbitration panel) may choose either the union's wage demand, the government's wage offer, or a compromise between the two. Because arbitrators may compromise by "splitting the difference" when settling on a pay scale, it is hypothesized that the possibility of going to conventional arbitration drives both parties to submit divergent offers. The more disparate the offers, the lower the chances that a settlement will be reached before going to arbitration.

To reduce the tendency of both sides to "ask for the moon" prior to arbitration, some jurisdictions have instituted *final-offer arbitration,* under which the arbitrator (or arbitration panel) must choose either the union's or the government's offer; no compromise is allowed. The theory underlying final-offer arbitration is it will induce both parties to moderate their offers, for it is the "more reasonable" offer that is likely to be chosen by the arbitrator.

In New Jersey, the parties to a public sector collective bargaining dispute may choose either conventional or final-offer arbitration. A study of the salary determination of municipal police officers in New Jersey revealed that employer proposals were chosen by the arbitrator only a third of the time; however, the wage increases provided for in these proposals were significantly *lower* than the average wage increases received by police officers in disputes that did *not* go to arbitration. Union proposals were selected by the arbitrator in two-thirds of the disputes that went to final-offer arbitration, but the wage increases provided by these proposals were no larger than the increases received by similarly situated police officers elsewhere in the state. Unions won more arbitrations because, on average, they submitted relatively conservative final offers, while employers were winning less frequently but gaining more from the arbitrations in which they did win. Judged by this evidence, the police unions in New Jersey were taking fewer chances than public sector employers.

SOURCE: Orley Ashenfelter and David Bloom, "Models of Arbitrator Behavior: Theory and Evidence," *American Economic Review* 74 (March 1984): 111–24. Evidence presented in Orley Ashenfelter, "Arbitrator Behavior," *American Economic Review Papers and Proceedings* 77 (May 1987): 342–46, suggests that in other states (e.g., Iowa) unions did not always win more than half of final-offer arbitrations.

For example, if municipal government labor negotiators fear there is some chance that arbitrators will award settlements that are substantially more generous than would otherwise occur, they may try to induce a settlement prior to the arbitration stage by offering their employees a wage package in excess of what they would have offered in the absence of the statute.[29] Such

---

29. Even if it expected that, on average, an arbitrated settlement would be higher, the union might agree to such a settlement because of its uncertainty about how the arbitrator would rule (that is, there is some chance that his or her settlement would be lower). Put another way, "A bird in the hand may well be worth two in the bush." This phenomenon is discussed in more detail in the appendix to this chapter.

an action would cause the estimated differential D to *understate* the effect of the arbitration statute on wages. Conversely, if public employers believed, and public employee unions concurred, that arbitrators were likely to award low settlements, management might offer—and unions might accept—an offer lower than management would have offered in the absence of the statute. While one cannot ascertain a priori whether the existence of the arbitration statute per se increases or decreases the size of wage settlements in cities that do not go to arbitration, it is very likely that the presence of an arbitration statute *does* affect the negotiations when settlement is made prior to arbitration.[30] Empirical studies do in fact suggest that the availability of an arbitration statute in a state leads public employees' wages to be higher, on average, than they otherwise would be.[31]

Of course the question of why contract negotiations are ever resolved prior to arbitration remains. In bargaining situations in which strikes are permitted, it is the costs a strike will impose on both parties that give them an incentive to agree on a contract prior to a strike. What types of costs do the parties avoid by settling prior to arbitration when a strike is not permitted? The answer appears to be that uncertainty about the decision an arbitrator will make provides the parties with an incentive to settle on their own. That is, both parties may prefer to achieve a certain outcome on their own, rather than bear the costs associated with not knowing with certainty the decision an arbitrator will make. This point is developed much more completely in the appendix to this chapter.

PUBLIC VS. PRIVATE PAY COMPARISONS

As noted early in the chapter, the pay of most federal government white-collar workers is determined through a comparability process that ties their wages to the results of a government survey of wages of "comparable private workers," subject to possible Presidential and congressional modification. As a result of this process, however, do comparably qualified workers performing comparable work in the public and private sectors receive equal total compensation?[32] This question is difficult to answer, because the comparability survey currently focuses on wages and gives only limited attention to both nonwage benefits and nonpecuniary forms of compensation. Moreover, the jobs performed in the public and private sectors are not always directly comparable, and subjective decisions must often be made on how a job should be classified.

Instead of focusing on the earnings of workers with comparable *job characteristics,* which (as noted above) is often impossible to do, one could focus on the earnings paid to workers who have comparable *measured personal characteristics,* such as education and experience, in the public and private

---

30. For a more complete discussion of this point in the context of a simple bargaining model, see Henry S. Farber and Harry C. Katz, "Interest Arbitration, Outcomes, and the Incentive to Bargain," *Industrial and Labor Relations Review* 33 (October 1979): 55–63.

31. See, for example, Peter Feuille and John Delaney, "Collective Bargaining, Interest Arbitration and Police Salaries," *Industrial and Labor Relations Review* 39 (January 1986): 228–40.

32. This discussion draws heavily on Sharon P. Smith, *Equal Pay in the Public Sector: Fact or Fantasy* (Princeton, N.J.: Industrial Relations Section, Princeton University, 1977).

sectors. In one of the earliest and most detailed empirical studies on the subject, Sharon Smith compared the earnings of government workers with those of comparable employees in the private sector.[33] Smith's comparisons, which pertained to state and local government employees as well as federal employees, are summarized in Table 13.5. As of 1975, individuals who worked for the federal government appeared to receive wages that were 13–20 percent higher than the wages received by private sector workers with comparable personal characteristics. The differentials for state and local government employees in relation to private sector employees were much more modest, and, in the case of white males, the differentials were actually negative. That is, white males employed in the state and local sector appeared to receive lower wages than workers with comparable measured personal characteristics in the private sector.

Studies that make federal/private earnings comparisons using data from the late 1970s and early 1980s tend to find similar patterns of results. Whether the focus was on all federal workers or on Postal Service workers in particular (see Example 13.2), women in the federal sector appeared to receive earnings that were roughly 20 percent higher than the earnings of females with comparable measured characteristics in the private sector, while the analogous earnings differentials for males was in the range of 0 to 12 percent.[34] Attempts to control for unmeasured differences in productivity between workers in the two sectors invariably have led to smaller estimates of the federal/private sector differentials.[35]

Earnings comparisons like those in Table 13.5 may not accurately reflect total compensation comparisons, because they ignore employee benefits and other nonpecuniary conditions of employment. For example, they do not take into account the possibility that public employees may have more (or less) difficult jobs, better (or worse) employee benefits, and higher (or lower) job stability than their private sector counterparts.[36] Furthermore, they do not take

33. Smith, *Equal Pay in the Public Sector*. More recent results are reported in Sharon Smith, "Are State and Local Government Workers Overpaid?" in *The Economics of Municipal Labor Markets*, ed. Werner Hirsch and Anthony Rufolo (Los Angeles: UCLA Press, 1983), 59–89; Steven F. Venti, "Wages in the Federal and Private Sectors," in *Public Sector Compensation*, ed. David Wise (Chicago: University of Chicago Press, 1987); Martin Asher and Joel Popkin, "The Effect of Gender and Race Differentials in Public–Private Wage Comparisons: A Study of Postal Workers," *Industrial and Labor Relations Review* 38 (October 1984): 16–25; Jeffrey Perloff and Michael Wachter, "Wage Comparability in the U.S. Postal Service," *Industrial and Labor Relations Review* 38 (October 1984): 26–35; and Alan Krueger, "Are Public Sector Workers Paid More Than Their Alternative Wage? Evidence from Longitudinal Data and Job Queries," in *When Public Sector Workers Unionize*.

34. Steven Venti, "Wages in the Federal and Private Sectors"; Martin Asher and Joel Popkin, "The Effect of Gender and Race Differentials..."; and Jeffrey Perloff and Michael Wachter, "Wage Comparability in the U.S. Postal Service."

35. Steven Venti, "Wages in the Federal and Private Sectors," and Alan Krueger, "Are Public Workers Paid More Than Their Alternative Wage?"

36. The limited evidence available suggests that, other things equal, both employee benefits and job stability are higher in the government than in the private sectors. See, for example, Smith, *Equal Pay in the Public Sector;* Farrell Bloch and Sharon Smith, "Human Capital and Labor Market Employment," *Journal of Human Resources* 12 (Fall 1977): 550–60; Joseph F. Quinn, "Pension Wealth of Government and Private Sector Workers," *American Economic Review* 72 (May 1982): 283–87; and Steven Allen, "Unions and Job Security in the Public Sector," in *When Public Sector Workers Unionize*. Thus, the comparisons in Table 13.5 may *understate* public sector compensation relative to that in the private sector.

EXAMPLE 13.2
Are Postal Workers Overpaid?

Earnings comparison studies of the type described in this section are not done solely as academic exercises; they have begun to find their way into public sector collective bargaining negotiations. During the 1981 national negotiations between the U.S. Postal Service and the unions representing its employees, and also during the subsequent arbitration of the dispute (the parties were required to go to binding arbitration if they could not reach a settlement on their own), each side presented an analysis of how the wages of postal workers compared to those of "otherwise comparable workers" in the private sector. Given the adversarial nature of such proceedings, it is not surprising that the two analyses reached different conclusions, even though they used the same underlying data. The reason for this is that they each defined "otherwise comparable workers" differently.

Analysts hired by the unions argued that average wages were higher in the Postal Service than in many private sector industries because the Postal Service pays nonwhites and women wages similar to those it pays comparable white men, while race and gender differentials often occur in the private sector (see Chapter 14 for evidence on this). Also, they asserted that the postal wage for white males was about the same as the average wage paid to comparable white males employed in the private sector. They argued that the latter comparison is the relevant one to use during wage negotiations to assess pay "comparability" in any public agency that follows a nondiscriminatory wage policy and, as a result, concluded that at the start of the negotiations postal workers' earnings were about the same as those of "comparable" private sector workers.

In contrast, analysts hired by the U.S. Postal Service argued that the Postal Reorganization Act requires that the Postal Service pay wages comparable to those paid in the private sector and that nothing in the law suggests that pay comparisons be restricted to white males. When they included all race/gender groups in the analyses and contrasted Postal Service workers' earnings with the earnings of all employees in the private sector, they concluded that, on average, postal workers enjoyed roughly a 21 percent wage advantage over comparable private sector workers.

Whether either of these studies actually influenced the Postal Service negotiations or the subsequent arbitration decision is difficult to judge. They do illustrate quite well, however, some of the difficulties involved in making judgments about comparability.

SOURCES: Martin Asher and Joel Popkin, "The Effect of Gender and Race Differentials on Public–Private Wage Comparisons: A Study of Postal Workers," *Industrial and Labor Relations Review* 38 (October 1984): 16–25; Jeffrey Perloff and Michael Wachter, "Wage Comparability in the U.S. Postal Service," *Industrial and Labor Relations Review* 38 (October 1984): 26–35; J. Joseph Loewenberg, "The 1984 Postal Arbitration: Issues Surrounding the Award," *Monthly Labor Review* (June 1986): 31–32.

into account the possibility that public employers may deliberately pursue a high-wage policy to reduce turnover and increase productivity.

Nevertheless, it is interesting to ask why the wage premium paid to public employees in relation to private employees appears to be larger in the federal

TABLE 13.5   Implied Estimated Percentage Differences Between the Wages of Government and Private Sector Employees in 1975

	Percentage by Which Government Wages Exceed Private Sector Wages for Comparable Workers		
Category	Federal Employees	State Employees	Local Government Employees
By gender			
Male	13 to 15	−3 to −11	−4 to −9
Female	18 to 20	6 to 7	1 to 2
By race and gender			
White male	16	−4	−7
Nonwhite male	17	12	3
White female	25	7	1
Nonwhite female	21	9	4

SOURCE: Based on Sharon P. Smith, *Equal Pay in the Public Sector: Fact or Fantasy* (Princeton, N.J.: Industrial Relations Section, Princeton University, 1977), Tables 3.7 and 6.4.

than in the state and local sectors. One possible explanation is that taxpayer information about the effect on tax rates of a wage increase for public employees is much more easily obtained and understood at the state and local level than at the federal level. It may also be easier to hold local politicians accountable for such financial decisions; each federal legislator is just one out of hundreds of representatives who vote on scores of issues besides federal pay legislation. Pressure to hold down public employee wage scales may thus be greater at the state and local level than it is at the federal level.

One may also ask whether equal pay for equal work in the public and private sectors is a reasonable criterion upon which to base federal employee compensation. If one defines *pay* to include all current and expected future wage and nonwage benefits and all conditions of employment, it is likely that, with free mobility of labor, workers will allocate themselves across sectors until pay is equalized. However, it does not follow that *current wage rates* should thus be equalized. Indeed, if public employees received wages equal to or higher than those of private employees and had more desirable nonwage benefits and conditions of employment, one should expect to see long queues of applicants for public sector jobs and very low quit rates for existing public employees. Although occasionally there are reports of job vacancies in the public sector, in the main one's impression is that there are fairly long lists of applicants for most public sector jobs.[37] Furthermore, there is some evidence that quit rates in the public sector are lower than quit rates in the private sector, even after one adjusts for differences in the characteristics of individuals em-

---

37. For example, Sharon Smith, in *Equal Pay in the Public Sector,* reports that in September 1974 over 42,000 individuals had passed tests to become police officers in New York City and were awaiting assignment (p. 20). To take another example, the *Wall Street Journal* reported on March 24, 1981, that the New York City Postmaster had received 225,000 applications for 2,500 jobs. Alan Krueger, "The Determinants of Queues for Federal Jobs," *Industrial and Labor Relations Review* 41 (July 1988): 567–81, finds evidence that the queue for federal jobs lengthens as wages in the federal sector rise relative to wages in the private sector.

ployed in the two sectors.[38] Long queues of applicants and very low quit rates are both consistent with the notion that government workers receive higher pay than comparable private sector workers.

THE EFFECT OF EXPENDITURE- AND TAX-LIMITATION LEGISLATION

In June 1978 California voters overwhelmingly adopted Proposition 13, a state constitutional amendment that rolled back property taxes and drastically limited the ability of all levels of government in the state to increase their tax revenues in the future. Since that date, attempts to limit state and local government spending or taxing have proliferated, and in a number of cases these attempts have been successful.[39]

The simple demand-and-supply model developed in this chapter can help illustrate the likely effects of such legislation on public sector labor markets.[40] Suppose that initially the demand and supply of public employees were D_0 and S_0, respectively, in Figure 13.3. In this case, ignoring for the moment the effect of union-won increases in wages (and queues for public jobs), equilibrium would be at point A, with the wage/employment combination (W_0, E_0).

The first-round effect of expenditure- or tax-limitation legislation is no different from the effect of any other decline in a community's ability, or willingness, to pay for public employees. The demand for public employees will decline to, say, D_2; if nothing else occurs, equilibrium will be reached at point B with the lower wage and employment combination (W_2, E_2).

This is not the end of the story, however. Expenditure- and tax-limitation legislation undoubtedly reduces public employees' expectations about the level of their *future* wages and also increases the probability that they will be laid off for financial reasons in the future. These changes reduce the desirability of being a state or local government employee. As a result, the supply curve shifts to S_2; equilibrium now occurs at point D, with the wage/employment combination (W_3, E_3). Although employment has *fallen* still further, public employees' wages have now *risen* above W_2.

Whether the final wage, W_3, is greater or less than the initial wage, W_0, is an open question and depends upon whether the shift in supply dominates the shift in demand. If the supply shift does dominate, as in Figure 13.3, public employees' wages will actually rise above their initial level; their employment, however, will fall by more than the shift in the demand curve (point D lies to the left of point C). Although the legislation *may* serve to reduce public em-

38. James E. Long, "Are Government Workers Overpaid? Alternative Evidence," *Journal of Human Resources* 17 (Winter 1982): 123–31. See, however, Richard A. Ippolito, "Why Federal Workers Don't Quit," *Journal of Human Resources* 22 (Spring 1987): 281–99, for a dissenting view that emphasizes the difference between the federal and private sectors in the timing of compensation over employees' work lives.

39. For a discussion of the causes and effects of such legislation, see "Proceedings of a Conference on Tax and Expenditure Limitations," *National Tax Journal* 32 (June 1979).

40. See Ronald G. Ehrenberg, "The Effect of Tax Limitation Legislation on Public Sector Labor Markets," *National Tax Journal* 32 (June 1979): 261–66, for a more complete discussion.

FIGURE 13.3   The Effect of Expenditure- or Tax-Limitation Legislation on Employment and Wages in the Public Sector

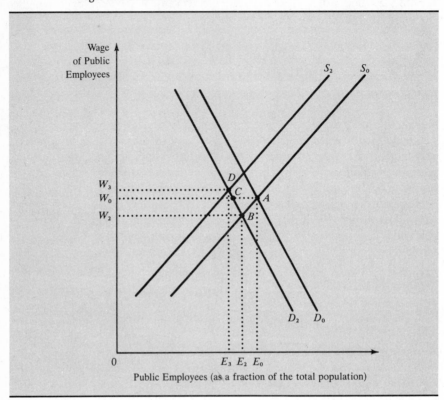

ployees' wages, it unambiguously reduces their employment levels and the flow of public services.[41]

Figure 13.4 introduces public employee unions into the analysis. Suppose at the outset that a public employee union had succeeded in keeping the wage rate at W_u, which lies above the equilibrium level. In this case employment would initially be E_u^0. The fall in demand to D_2 caused by the expenditure- or tax-limitation legislation would cause public employment to fall to E_u^1, but unless the union agreed to a reduced wage scale, wages would remain at W_u. As drawn, the reduction in labor supply to S_2 would have *no* effect on wages or employment; it would serve only to reduce the excess supply of labor. Of course, if the leftward shift in supply were large enough, employment would fall still further and wages would rise above the level set by the union.

While public employee unions could still push for higher wages at the expense of lower employment levels, the expenditure- or tax-limitation legisla-

---

41. This last statement ignores the possibility that public employee productivity might increase in response to the legislation. See Ehrenberg, "The Effect of Tax Limitation Legislation," for a discussion of why this might occur. Evidence that state tax-limitation legislation has led to lower wages is found in Joseph Gyourko and Joseph Tracy, "Public Sector Bargaining and the Local Budgetary Process," National Bureau of Economic Research Working Paper no. 2915 (1989).

FIGURE 13.4   The Effect of Expenditure- or Tax-Limitation Legislation with Unions in the Analysis

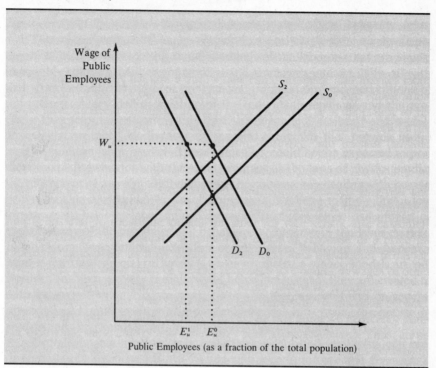

Public Employees (as a fraction of the total population)

tion would reduce their ability to use the political process to shift out the demand for public employees.[42] One could reasonably project, then, that an additional effect of such legislation may be to reduce the size of the union wage effects observed in the state and local sector.

PUBLIC SECTOR EMPLOYMENT PROGRAMS

The final focus of this chapter is on the *net job creation effects* of public employment programs, or the extent to which funds provided to state and local governments by the federal government to increase their employment levels actually serve to expand employment. As noted earlier, these funds were provided during the decade of the 1970s, first under the Emergency Employment Act of 1971 and then under the Comprehensive Employment and Training Act (CETA).

Ignoring for a moment private sector labor markets, suppose that all the unemployed workers in the economy have attached themselves to the public sector labor market and that the wage in that market is rigid downward in the *short run*. Figure 13.5 shows that, at the prevailing SLG employee wage (W_0),

---

42. Not surprisingly, public employees are overwhelmingly against expenditure- and tax-limitation legislation. See Paul Courant et al., "Why Voters Support Tax Limitation Amendments: The Michigan Case," *National Tax Journal* 33 (March 1980): 1–20.

FIGURE 13.5   A Public Sector Employment Program

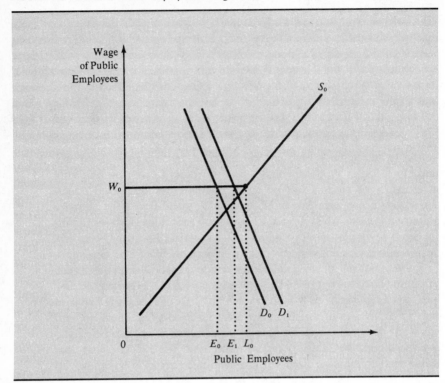

the supply of workers to the SLG sector exceeds the demand for SLG employees; employment is E_0, and $L_0 - E_0$ individuals who want work cannot find it. If, through a public employment program, such as that administered under CETA, the federal government provides funds to SLGs to expand their employment, the demand for labor will shift to the right (to, say, D_1). SLG employment will expand to E_1, and unemployment will be reduced.[43]

The key issue in evaluating such a program is the extent to which the demand curve actually shifts to the right in response to the program. If, given the prevailing public sector wage, W_0, funds are provided to create 100 new SLG positions, will the demand curve actually shift to the right by 100 positions? The answer in general is no. Since SLG decision makers have other goals in addition to increasing public employment expenditures—goals such as increasing other government expenditures, reducing local taxes, and reducing local debt—it is logical to hypothesize that they will use at least a portion of the public employment program funds to hire people they would have hired even in the absence of the program (thus freeing up their own resources for the above-mentioned alternative uses). Put another way, the public employ-

---

43. If the demand curve should shift horizontally by more than $L_0 - E_0$, or if the initial SLG employee wage were a market-clearing one, the reader should be able to show that the SLG employee wage would also increase. Surprisingly, only one study has attempted to analyze the effect of these programs on public sector wage levels, and that study proved inconclusive. See Lauri Bassi, "Estimating the Impact of Job Creation Programs on Public Sector Wages" (Working Paper, Princeton University, 1979).

ment program funds might at least partially *displace* regular SLG expenditures on public employees, thereby reducing the net job creation effect of the program.[44]

One may wonder how such a *displacement effect* (or *fiscal substitution*) could occur if by law the public employment program funds can be used only to expand SLG employment levels. The answer is that as long as SLG officials would have planned to expand their employment even in the absence of the program, program monitors have no direct way of ascertaining whether the jobs created by the program would have been created in its absence.[45] Since the annual growth of SLG employment exceeded the increase in the number of public employment program positions in every year covered by Table 13.1, it is possible that such displacement or fiscal substitution occurred.

Numerous attempts have been made to estimate the displacement effects of public employment programs. A number of empirical studies have used either aggregate time-series data or cross-sectional data on local government employment to estimate the effects of various factors on the demand for SLG employees, including such factors as public employee wage rates, community income levels, *and* the number of public employment positions funded. Although the estimated effects of the program vary widely with the models and data used in these studies, a reasonable consensus would be that at least 30 to 50 percent of program funds ultimately displace local government funds.[46] That is, no more than 50 to 70 percent of these funds actually go towards increasing SLG employment.[47]

---

44. Even if such displacement is complete, program funds will still have a stimulative impact, even if they are implicitly spent on nonlabor items, used to retire a local debt, or used to reduce local taxes. If the funds have this stimulative impact, the effects of the program will be similar to those of any other general increase in government spending or decrease in taxes. However, they will not necessarily benefit the unemployed workers at whom such programs are targeted.
45. There are literally thousands of state and local governments in the United States, and it would be nearly impossible to obtain direct information on their planned employment levels in the absence of the public employment programs. Clearly, local officials have no incentive to report that they planned to expand employment; such an action would limit their ability to implicitly shift public employment funds to other uses.
46. See, for example, George Johnson and James Tomola, "The Fiscal Substitution Effects of Alternative Approaches to Public Service Employment," *Journal of Human Resources* 12 (Winter 1977): 3–26; Michael Borus and Daniel Hamermesh, "Estimating Fiscal Substitution by Public Service Employment Programs," *Journal of Human Resources* 13 (Fall 1978): 561–65; and Charles Adams et al., "A Pooled Time-Series Analysis of the Job Creation Impact of Public Service Employment Grants to Large Cities," *Journal of Human Resources* 18 (Spring 1983): 283–94. The Johnson-Tomola paper provides an interesting case study of how research affects public policy. Later studies (such as Borus and Hamermesh) showed its precise estimates of displacement to be incorrect. However, the study was well publicized in Washington, and the mere fact that Johnson and Tomola raised the displacement issue stimulated Congress to redesign the CETA program in an effort to minimize displacement (essentially by limiting individuals' participation in part of the public employment program to a fixed term). Later studies, such as Adams et al., found that the redesign did tend to reduce displacement. As this example demonstrates, the publicity a study gets is often as important as its scientific substance.
47. Researchers using alternative methodologies have concluded that the net job creation effects may be larger. See, for example, Richard Nathan et al., *Public Service Employment* (Washington, D.C.: Brookings Institution, 1981). These estimates are based on subjective perceptions of trained field observers of what local government employment would have been in the absence of the program.

So far, however, our analysis of the net employment creation effects of a public employment program has ignored the private sector. After considering the interaction between public and private labor markets, one can see that the net job creation effects may be even less than the 50 to 70 percent figure cited above. Our analysis of this issue assumes the existence of an above-equilibrium, downward-rigid wage in the public sector and the accompanying presence of "wait unemployment" there.

In Figure 13.6, simple demand and supply models have been drawn for private and public sector labor markets. Suppose that the demand and supply curves in the private sector are initially given by D_{PR}^0 and S_{PR}^0, respectively, and that equilibrium occurs at the market-clearing wage/employment combination (W_{PR}^0, E_{PR}^0). Suppose also that the public sector demand and supply curves are given by D_{PB}^0 and S_{PB}^0, respectively. The public sector wage rate, however, is again assumed to be fixed in the short run at the level W_{PB}^0. As a result, employment will initially be E_{PB}^0 in the public sector, and the excess supply of labor to the public sector is given by $L_{PB}^0 - E_{PB}^0$.

In order to have an equilibrium situation, in the sense that unemployed workers in the public sector have no incentive to search for jobs in the private sector, the expected level of earnings (we ignore all nonwage forms of compensation) must be the same in both sectors. Therefore, the wages in each sector,

FIGURE 13.6   An Analysis of the Effects of a Public Employment Program: Responsive Supply in the Private Sector

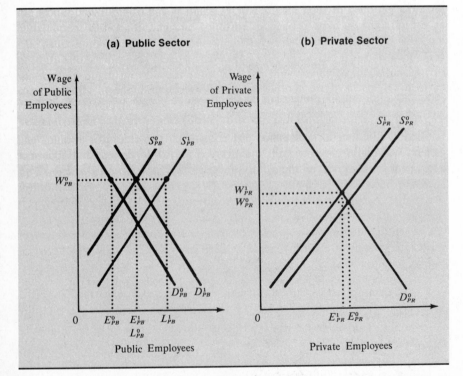

multiplied by the fraction of time (F) that individuals attached to each sector expect to be employed, must be equal:

$$W^0_{PB} F^0_{PB} = W^0_{PR} F^0_{PR} \tag{13.2}$$

Since there is an excess supply of labor in the public sector, F^0_{PB} is less than one, while the market-clearing assumption in the private sector guarantees (in this framework) that F^0_{PR} is equal to one. As a result, it must be initially true that the public sector wage exceeds the private sector wage:

$$W^0_{PB} > W^0_{PR} \tag{13.3}$$

Suppose that the federal government now provides funds to SLGs to expand their employment levels and that the result of this public employment program is to shift the demand curve in the public sector to D^1_{PB}. The first-round effect of the program is to increase SLG employment to E^1_{PB}, eliminating the excess supply of labor. This shift, however, also eliminates the equality in equation (13.2). Since the elimination of the excess supply of labor in the public sector increases the fraction of time that workers attached to that sector expect to be employed, it must now be true that

$$W^0_{PB} F^1_{PB} > W^0_{PR} F^0_{PR} \tag{13.4}$$

where F^1_{PB} is the fraction of time employees attached to the SLG sector now expect to be employed. (In our simple model where there is no unemployment when demand equals supply, F^1_{PB} would equal one.)

The situation depicted in expression (13.4) is not an equilibrium; the expected earnings level is now higher in the public than in the private sector. Therefore, some *employed* private sector workers have an incentive to quit their jobs to search for the now relatively more attractive public sector jobs. This quitting behavior is reflected by a leftward shift in the supply curve of labor to the private sector and a rightward shift in the supply curve to the public sector. As a result, an excess demand for labor in the private sector now exists at W^0_{PR}, and employers there are forced to bid up wages and to reduce employment levels. This shift out in the labor supply curve to the public sector creates an excess supply of labor there, reducing the expected fraction of the period that workers attached to the public sector will find employment. These shifts continue until equilibrium is restored and expected earnings are again equal in the two sectors:

$$W^0_{PB} F^2_{PB} = W^1_{PR} F^0_{PR} \tag{13.5}$$

This equilibrium is shown in Figure 13.6 as occurring when the supply curves are S^1_{PB} and S^1_{PR} in the two sectors ($F^0_{PR} = 1$, $F^2_{PB} < 1$, and $W^0_{PB} > W^1_{PR}$).

Note that the increase in *total* (public plus private) employment that results is less than the increase in SLG employment because some private sector employees have quit their jobs to search (or wait) for jobs in the SLG sector. The net employment effects of the program are overestimated, then, if one focuses only on what happens to SLG employment and fails to measure employment changes in the private sector that are induced by the program. Note also that the market reactions to the program have induced higher private sector wages. Is it at all surprising, then, that business organizations, especially those that represent employers whose work forces might find public employment program positions desirable, are vocal opponents of such legislation? Such programs are simply not in these employers' self-interest.

MISCONCEPTION

"Jobs are what make our economy grow, and the government has a responsibility to encourage growth by providing jobs."

Analysis

Because the ultimate end of economic activity is to enhance people's utility, growth occurs when *useful* goods and services are produced. Jobs can be provided by having some workers dig holes and others fill them up again, but this would not create economic growth. Thus, discussion of growth must center on what is produced and not on jobs per se.

Principle

The social cost of an action is the forgone utility that the action requires; the social benefit is the added utility it generates.

REVIEW QUESTIONS

1. Explain why the demand curve for public sector employees slopes downward. Do your explanations hold for both the long run and the short run?
2. You have been asked to oversee a study of the comparability of federal government and private sector employee compensation. List and explain the factors this study should take into account.
3. Referring to the four factors influencing the elasticity of demand for labor, spell out why the labor demand curve in the public sector is likely to be more or less elastic than demand curves in the private sector.
4. Congresswoman X states, "I support the granting of federal funds to our cities for the purpose of hiring additional city workers. Last year the federal government authorized payments to support 200 additional police officers in city Y, bringing its total force to 2,200. This can only mean that city Y's residents were being given 10 percent more protection than they would otherwise have received, and that 200 more people were employed in city Y than would otherwise have been employed." Analyze Congresswoman X's conclusions about the effects of federal grants.
5. In a school board election in Anytown, USA, the union representing the city teachers organized a drive to elect two write-in candidates. Taking advantage of a projected low turnout, the union selected these candidates the night before the election and passed word to its members to write in their names on election day. Both candidates were elected.

   What unique characteristic of public sector unionization does this behavior illustrate? What problems are posed by this characteristic?
6. Many municipalities in the United States have residency requirements (laws that require municipal employees to reside in the municipality in which they are employed). The goals of these laws are to provide jobs for municipal residents and to

assure the ready availability of municipal employees for work in emergencies (e.g., to have off-duty firefighters nearby in case of a major fire). What is the likely impact of such laws on municipal government employment and wage levels, in both the absence and the presence of public employee unions?

7. In the middle of 1984 the U.S. Postal Service, a governmental corporation, was engaged in negotiations with unions representing its 600,000 employees. The unions were demanding a 55 percent increase in compensation over a three-year period, and they argued that workers were entitled to a portion of the $2 billion in surpluses the Postal Service had earned since 1982. At the time the negotiations were going on, several private companies were planning to offer telecommunications services that would send coast-to-coast messages electronically. Thus, there appeared to be a very real possibility that in coming years many letters, bills, and payments would be transmitted almost instantaneously using computers, word processors, or electronic typewriters.

    What effects would this new telecommunications technology be expected to have on the outcome of the negotiations between the Postal Service and its workers?

8. It is often asserted that governmental officials should be paid high salaries so that they will be less inclined to become involved in corrupt activities (taking bribes, for example). Evaluate this argument in terms of the concepts learned in this course.

9. Suppose that a city government has long *required* its employees to live within the city limits. Would the knowledge of this requirement be useful in evaluating whether the city's wage rates are above the market wage in that area? Explain.

SELECTED READINGS

Ehrenberg, Ronald G., and Schwarz, Joshua L. "Public Sector Labor Markets." In *Handbook of Labor Economics,* ed. Orley Ashenfelter and Richard Layard. Amsterdam: North-Holland, 1986.

Freeman, Richard B. "Unionism Comes to the Public Sector." *Journal of Economic Literature* 24 (March 1986): 41–86.

Freeman, Richard B., and Ichniowski, Casey, eds. *When Public Sector Workers Unionize.* Chicago: University of Chicago Press, 1988.

Smith, Sharon. *Equal Pay in the Public Sector: Fact or Fantasy.* Princeton, N.J.: Industrial Relations Section, Princeton University, 1977.

Wise, David, ed. *Public Sector Payrolls.* Chicago: University of Chicago Press, 1987.

APPENDIX 13A

Arbitration and the Incentive to Bargain

What incentive do the parties to collective bargaining negotiations have to settle their negotiations on their own rather than go to arbitration and have an outside party impose a settlement? The answer may well be that the uncertainty about an arbitrator's likely decision imposes costs on both parties and that these costs provide them with an incentive to come to an agreement on their own. This appendix provides a simple model that illustrates this proposition; it highlights the roles of both *uncertainty* about an arbitrator's likely decision and the parties' *attitudes towards risk* in determining whether a negotiation will wind up in arbitration.[1]

Consider a simple two-party bargaining problem in which the parties, A and B, are negotiating over how to split a "pie" of fixed size. Each party's utility function depends only on the share of the pie that it receives. Figure 13A.1 plots the utility function for party A. When A's share of the pie is zero, A's utility (U_A) is assumed to be zero, and as A's share (S_A) increases, A's utility increases. Crucially, this utility function is also assumed to exhibit the property of *diminishing marginal utility;* equal increments in S_A lead to progressively smaller increments in U_A.[2] As we shall show below, this is equivalent to assuming that the party is *risk averse,* which means that the party would prefer the certainty of having a given share of the pie to an uncertain outcome that, on average, would yield the same share.

Now suppose party A believes that, on average, the arbitrator would award it one-half of the pie if the negotiations went to arbitration. If it knew with certainty that the arbitrator would do this, party A's utility from going to arbitration would be $U_A(\frac{1}{2})$—or point a in Figure 13A.1. Suppose, however, that party A is uncertain about the arbitrator's decision and instead believes the arbitrator will assign it one-quarter of the pie with probability one-half, or

---

1. The discussion here is a simplified version of some of the material found in Henry S. Farber and Harry C. Katz, "Interest Arbitration, Outcomes, and the Incentive to Bargain," *Industrial and Labor Relations Review* 33 (October 1979): 55–63.
2. Refer to Appendix 8A, especially note 4, for an introduction to this use of cardinal utility functions.

FIGURE 13A.1   Utility Function for a Risk-Averse Party: Uncertainty About Arbitrator's
Decision Leads to a Contract Zone

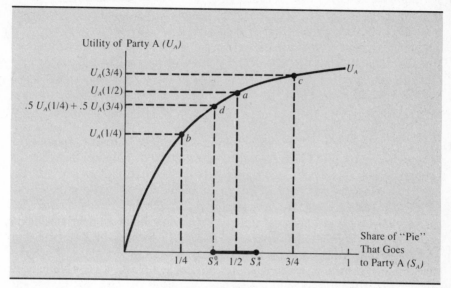

three-quarters of the pie also with probability one-half. Utility in these two
states is given by $U_A(\frac{1}{4})$, point b, and $U_A(\frac{3}{4})$, point c, respectively. Although,
on average, party A expects to be awarded one-half of the pie, its average or
expected utility in this case is $.5U_A(\frac{1}{4}) + .5U_A(\frac{3}{4})$—which, as Figure 13A.1 indicates, is *less* than $U_A(\frac{1}{2})$. This reflects the fact that party A is risk averse,
and prefers a certain outcome to an uncertain outcome that yields the same
expected share.

Note that if party A were awarded the share S_A^0 with certainty, it would
receive the same utility level it receives under the uncertain situation, where
it expects, with equal probability, the arbitrator to award it either one-quarter
or three-quarters of the pie. Indeed, it would prefer any certain share above
S_A^0 to bearing the cost of the uncertainty associated with having to face the
arbitrator's decision. The set of contracts it would potentially voluntarily agree
to, then, is the set S_A such that

$$S_A^0 \le S_A \le 1 \qquad S_A^0 < \frac{1}{2} \qquad (13A.1)$$

Suppose party B is similarly risk averse and has identical expectations
about what the arbitrator's decision will look like. It should be obvious, using
the same logic as above, that the set of contracts, S_B, that party B would
potentially voluntarily agree to is given by a similar expression:

$$S_B^0 \le S_B \le 1 \qquad S_B^0 < \frac{1}{2} \qquad (13A.2)$$

Now, any share that party B voluntarily agrees to receive implies that B is
willing to give party A one minus that share. Since the minimum share B
would agree to receive, S_B^0, is less than one-half, it follows that the maximum
share B would voluntarily agree to give A in negotiations, S_A^* (which equals

$1 - S_B^0$), is greater than one-half. Party B potentially would be willing to voluntarily agree to any settlement that gives party A a share of less than S_A^*.

Referring to Figure 13A.1, observe that party A would be willing to voluntarily agree to contracts that offer it at least S_A^0, while party B would be willing to agree to contracts that give party A S_A^* or less. Hence, the set of contracts that *both* parties would find preferable to going to arbitration (and thus *potentially* would voluntarily agree to) is given by all the shares for A (S_A) that lie between these two extremes:

$$S_A^0 \le S_A \le S_A^* \tag{13A.3}$$

This set of potential voluntary solutions to the bargaining problem is indicated by the bold line segment on the horizontal axis of Figure 13A.1 and is called the *contract zone*. As long as both parties are risk averse and are uncertain what the arbitrator will do, a contract zone will exist.

The extent of the parties' *uncertainty* about the arbitrator's decision and the extent of their *risk aversion* are important determinants of the size of the contract zone. To see this, first suppose that party A continues to expect that, on average, the arbitrator will assign it one-half of the pie, but now believes that this will occur by receiving shares of one-eighth and seven-eighths with equal probability. Figure 13A.2 indicates its utility in each of these states (points e and f) and shows that, while its expected share is still one-half, the greater uncertainty (or "spread" of possible outcomes) has led to a reduction in its expected utility. Indeed, now party A would be as happy to receive the share S_A^1 with certainty as it would to face the risks associated with going to arbitration. Since S_A^1 is less than S_A^0, the size of the contract zone has increased. Hence, increased uncertainty about the arbitrator's decision leads to a larger contract zone.

Next consider Figure 13A.3, where we have drawn a utility function for a *risk-neutral* party. A risk-neutral party has a linear utility function because its utility depends only on its expected share, not the uncertainty associated with the outcome. So, for example, in Figure 13A.3 party A gets the same utility from having a share of one-half with certainty as it does from facing an arbitrated outcome in which there is equal probability that the arbitrator will award it either a share of one-quarter or a share of three-quarters. As a result, faced with the possibility of going to arbitration, there is no share less than one-half that party A would voluntarily agree to settle for prior to arbitration. If party B had similar expectations about the arbitrator's behavior and was similarly risk neutral, it also would refuse to settle for any share of less than one-half, which on average is what it expects to win from the arbitrator. Hence, the contract zone would reduce to one point, the point where both parties receive a share of one-half. The only voluntary agreement the parties will reach is what they expect to receive on average if they go to arbitration. (This illustrates how the arbitration process per se may influence the nature of negotiated settlements.)

More generally, one can show that as a party's risk aversion increases (the utility function becomes "more curved"), the size of the contract zone will increase. Hence, increases in either the parties' risk aversion or their

FIGURE 13A.2   Increased Uncertainty About Arbitrator's Decision Increases Size of Contract Zone

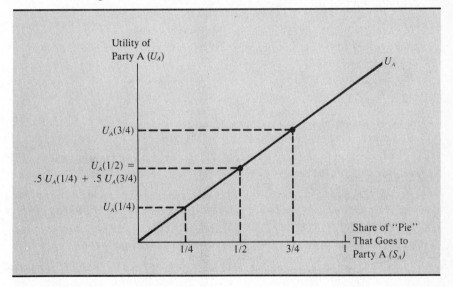

FIGURE 13A.3   Utility Function for a Risk-Neutral Party: Contract Zone Is Reduced to a Single Point

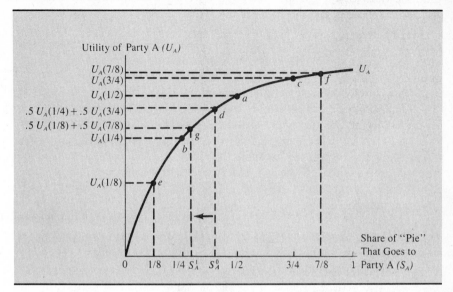

uncertainty about the arbitrator's decision will increase the size of the contract zone.

Larger contract curves mean that there are more potential settlements that *both* parties would prefer to an arbitrated settlement, and some people have argued that this increased "menu" of choices increases the probability that the parties would settle on their own prior to going to arbitration.[3] An immediate implication of this result is that, if one believes it is preferable for the parties to settle on their own, the arbitration system should be structured so that the arbitrator's behavior does *not* become completely predictable. That is, the parties must face some uncertainty about the arbitrator's potential decisions.

Remember, however, that the implications of the model are derived from the assumption that the probability of reaching a negotiated settlement is positively related to the size of the contract zone. Not all economists agree with this view.[4] To see why, suppose that there is only one point in the contract zone—only one bargaining outcome that both parties consider preferable to an arbitrated solution. Some argue that it should be easier for the parties to agree on that point than it would be for them to agree on one point out of 500 in a contract zone, all of which differed in their distribution of the pie between the parties. Without the assumption of the positive correlation between the size of the contract zone and the probability of reaching a negotiated settlement, many of the model's results concerning when negotiations are likely to go to arbitration vanish.[5]

---

3. Farber and Katz, "Interest Arbitration, Outcomes, and the Incentive to Bargain."
4. Vincent Crawford, "Arbitration and Conflict Resolution in Labor-Management Bargaining," *American Economic Review* 71 (May 1981): 205–10.
5. Models of the type described above can be generalized to address a variety of additional issues. These include how arbitrators' notions of intrinsic fairness influence the offers the parties are willing to make in bargaining, whether *conventional* arbitration or *final-offer* arbitration (where the arbitrator must choose one of the party's offers as his decision) provides greater incentives for the parties to bargain, and how differences in the degree of risk aversion between the two parties will influence the fraction of the arbitrated awards each party wins and the size of the arbitrated awards. For these models, the interested reader is referred to Henry Farber, "An Analysis of Final-Offer Arbitration," *Journal of Conflict Resolution* 24 (December 1980): 683–705, and Farber, "Splitting the Difference in Interest Arbitration," *Industrial and Labor Relations Review* 35 (October 1981): 70–77. Empirical papers based on these frameworks include Orley Ashenfelter and David Bloom, "Models of Arbitrator Behavior: Theory and Evidence," *American Economic Review* 74 (March 1984): 111–24; Max Bazerman and Henry Farber, "Arbitrator Decision Making: When Are Final Offers Important?" *Industrial and Labor Relations Review* 39 (October 1985): 76–89; Henry Farber and Max Bazerman, "The General Basis of Arbitrator Behavior: An Empirical Analysis of Conventional and Final-Offer Arbitration," *Econometrica* 54 (July 1986): 819–44; and David Bloom, "Empirical Models of Arbitrator Behavior Under Conventional Arbitration," *Review of Economics and Statistics* 68 (November 1986): 578–85. The May 1987 issue of the *American Economic Association Papers and Proceedings* also contains a set of papers dealing with arbitrator behavior.

14

The Economics of Discrimination

W e have learned that wages differ across individuals or jobs for numerous reasons. They vary with the amount of general or specific training, with job and locational characteristics, and with age. They also vary with employee benefits and compensation schemes, and, of course, they vary with the extent of unionism. Many of these sources of wage differentials may be regarded either as necessary in the allocation of labor or as socially legitimate on other grounds. There are, however, sizable wage differentials that appear to be associated solely with race and gender, and these differentials are often thought to be synonymous with widespread discrimination against minorities—especially blacks and Hispanics—and against women. This chapter discusses the evidence and theories of discrimination and concludes with an analysis of government policy in this area.

WHAT IS DISCRIMINATION?

The term *discrimination* is often used imprecisely because the relationship between *prejudice* and discrimination often is unclear. One might assert, for example, that a firm with two racially segregated branch offices is discriminating by failing to integrate both offices, even if workers in both branches are paid the same wages and have the same opportunities for advancement. This assertion raises the question of whether discrimination is always present when there is prejudice or just when some harm comes from this prejudice. Conversely, some people allege that discrimination exists in cases in which prejudice may not. For example, a firm offering specific training may prefer to hire younger workers who will stay with the firm long enough for it to recoup training costs. Is this age discrimination or good business?

Another confusing issue is whether discrimination can be identified by inequality of *achievement* or inequality of *opportunity.* Is an accounting firm located in a small, mostly white town guilty of discrimination if it has no black auditors on its staff? Would the answer change if the firm could show it had advertised job openings widely and had made the same offers to blacks as to whites, but that the offers to blacks had been rejected?

Finally, just what standards are to be used to judge equality? Consider the 1972–73 data on college teachers in the humanities contained in Table 14.1. The overall average salary paid to black professors was slightly below the salaries paid to whites for at least two reasons. First, a lower proportion of blacks had received doctorates, and, of those who had, fewer had obtained them at distinguished universities. The relatively lower levels of educational attainment among blacks thus held down their average salary. Second, among those teachers without doctorates, blacks received lower salaries than whites. However, if one looks at salaries among professors with doctorates in the humanities from distinguished universities, we see that blacks earned *more* than whites. The same was true among those with doctorates from less distinguished universities.

Do the data in Table 14.1 suggest that blacks in academia were discriminated against? One could answer yes, either because they earned less overall, or because they had lower levels of preparation for their jobs, or because there were so few blacks in college teaching (2.5 percent of college professors were black, whereas blacks constituted about 8 percent of the overall employed population at large). Others might argue that there was no evidence of discrimination against blacks with doctorates after controlling for quality of preparation.

It is obvious from the questions raised by Table 14.1 that discrimination can occur in many forms and places. If it occurs in the labor market, workers with equal preparation and productivity receive different wages. If it occurs among educational institutions, students of equal ability are treated differently and emerge from formal schooling with unequal educations. If it occurs in childhood, young children with equal potential are raised with quite different aspirations and attitudes. Discrimination can also occur in a variety of other settings: the housing market, various product markets, and treatment under the law.

The kind of discrimination this chapter will analyze in most depth is discrimination in the labor market. This emphasis should not imply that other forms of discrimination are unimportant or unrelated to labor market discrimination. Indeed, *past* labor market discrimination may have been instrumental in causing the poverty or attitudes that are *now* manifest in child-rearing

TABLE 14.1   Mean Annual Salaries of Full-Time College Faculty in the Humanities, 1972 and 1973

	Black		White	
	Number	*Salary*	*Number*	*Salary*
All full-time faculty	2,177	$15,034	85,904	$15,572
Doctorate from distinguished university	89	20,259	9,765	16,832
Doctorate from other university	173	17,262	17,894	15,790
No doctorate	1,915	14,590	58,245	15,293

SOURCE: American Council on Education.

practices, school achievement levels, and career or gender role aspirations. However, since the focus of our analysis is on *current labor market discrimination,* we shall lump all *other* forms of discrimination into a more general category we shall call *premarket differences.*

An operational definition of *current labor market discrimination* is "the valuation in the labor market of personal characteristics of the worker that are unrelated to productivity."[1] This definition recognizes that one's value in the labor market depends on all the demand *and* supply factors affecting marginal productivity. However, when factors that are *unrelated* to productivity acquire a positive or negative value in the labor market, discrimination can be said to occur. Race and gender are currently the most prominent of these factors alleged to be unrelated to productivity, but physical handicaps, religion, sexual preferences, and ethnic heritage are also on the list.

Three points should be noted about the above definition. First, the emphasis in identifying discrimination is on measurable market outcomes, such as earnings, wages, occupational attainment, or employment levels. While prejudicial attitudes may be felt by members of one group toward those of another, these feelings must be accompanied by some *action* that results in a different market outcome for us to assert that discrimination is present.

Second, we are not concerned with the routine random differences in outcomes that are matters of luck. Rather, the concept of discrimination encompasses only those differences that are so systematic that they do not cancel each other out within large groups.

Finally, our definition of labor market discrimination suggests an operational way to distinguish between *labor market* and *premarket* factors that cause earnings differentials. Differentials that derive from differences in average *productivity* levels across demographic groups, for example, can be categorized as *premarket* in nature. Differentials that are attributed to race or gender, *holding productivity constant,* can be said to be evidence of labor market discrimination.

It is very important for policy purposes to measure the relative size of labor market and premarket factors that lead to systematic earnings differences among various population groups. Any attempts to combat discrimination must be grounded in accurate information concerning the *source* of that discrimination; otherwise, effective antidiscrimination programs cannot be formulated. If the evidence points to a significant amount of labor market discrimination, programs aimed at employers and the hiring/promotion process may be effective. If, however, most of any systematic earnings differences related to race or gender appear to be rooted in premarket factors, then programs aimed at education, training, and the process of socializing children will be required.

EARNINGS DISPARITIES BY RACE, ETHNICITY, AND GENDER

There have been, and continue to be, strikingly large income disparities between most minorities and whites and between men and women. These differ-

---

1. Kenneth J. Arrow, "The Theory of Discrimination," *Discrimination in Labor Markets,* ed. Orley Ashenfelter and Albert Rees (Princeton, N.J.: Princeton University Press, 1973), 3.

TABLE 14.2 Black/White Ratio of Median Income for Full-Time, Year-Round Workers, 1955–87

Year	Black/White Income Ratio	
	Males	Females
1955	0.61	0.51
1960	0.66	0.68
1965	0.63	0.68
1970	0.70	0.84
1975	0.77	0.98
1980	0.70	0.93
1987	0.71	0.91

SOURCE: U.S. Bureau of the Census, *Money Income of Households, Families, and Persons in the United States,* Consumer Income Series P-60 (1984, no. 151, Table 28; 1987, no. 162, Table 27). Data before 1987 refer to persons aged 14 or older; data for 1987 refer to persons aged 15 or older.

ences are a cause of widespread social concern about discrimination, its sources, and possible remedies. This chapter will analyze various theories and their consequences for antidiscrimination policies after first describing the race and gender differences in earnings that actually exist. (We focus below on *earnings* differences for the practical reason that data on *total compensation,* which would be preferable because of the inclusion of employee benefits, are not generally available by race and gender.)

Racial and Ethnic Differences

Blacks. In 1987 the earnings of the typical male, year-round black worker were 71 percent of his white counterpart's. As indicated by Table 14.2, this disparity in incomes is smaller than that observed in the 1950s and 1960s, but it is larger than the differential in 1975. Table 14.2 suggests that considerably more earnings equality has been achieved among women since the 1950s and 1960s, although recent disparities have also been larger than those in 1975.

While these ratios and their trends are very interesting and important, they do not help us identify the immediate *source* of the disparities. Are the differences primarily due to *current labor market discrimination,* or are they the result of *premarket factors?* Blacks in the labor market have tended to be less educated, on average, than whites, and changes in this *premarket* factor alone could cause the ratios in Table 14.2 to vary over time.[2] For example, declines in schooling differentials between blacks and whites account for much of the relative wage growth of black males over the last few decades.[3] Moreover, variations in the rates of return to schooling can help explain why the overall black/white earnings ratio is lower now than in 1975: the falling rate of return to schooling in the 1970s (see Chapter 9) helped equalize the earnings of the less educated and the more educated, while the rising rates of return to

---

2. As noted in Chapter 9, one's choice of education is influenced by expected labor market earnings over the life cycle. Hence, ensuring that market discrimination against blacks is reduced or eliminated should serve as an incentive for blacks to stay in school longer.

3. James P. Smith and Finis R. Welch, "Black Economic Progress After Myrdal," *Journal of Economic Literature* 27 (June 1989): 519–64.

TABLE 14.3   Black/White Weekly Wage Ratios For Males, by Education and Experience, 1980

Years of Education	Years of Experience			
	5	15	25	35
8–11	0.87	0.78	0.77	0.79
12	0.83	0.80	0.78	0.78
13–15	0.89	0.81	0.75	0.74
16+	0.88	0.81	0.71	0.65

SOURCE: Adapted from "Black Economic Progress After Myrdal" by James P. Smith and Finis R. Welch, *Journal of Economic Literature,* June 1989. Copyright © 1989 by the American Economic Association. Reprinted by permission.

schooling in recent years have had the opposite effect. Can we tell how much of the overall differential in average earnings is due to differences in the characteristics that affect productivity and how much is due to labor market discrimination?

To measure the extent of market discrimination, one must answer the following question: "What would be the black/white earnings ratio if blacks and whites had the same productive characteristics?" In other words, if blacks (on average) had the same education, training, experience, turnover rate, health and marital status, and region of residence as whites, what would be the ratio of their earnings to those of whites? The answers to this question vary with the data sample and methodology employed, but they do establish a range within which the true ratio probably lies.

From Table 14.3 one can obtain at least a sense of what earnings differentials are like after controlling for two major premarket factors: education and experience. Two patterns stand out in this table. First, black/white earnings differences among males of comparable education and experience are smaller than the overall ratio (in Table 14.2) in all but one case, a phenomenon suggesting that premarket differences are important in explaining the overall differential. For example, among workers with 15 years of experience, the black/white earnings ratio for all educational groups is around 0.80. If this age group is representative, then the two measurable human capital factors of schooling and experience alone would have accounted for 10 of the 30-percentage-point difference between black and white male earnings noted in Table 14.2 (for 1980).

The second notable pattern in Table 14.3 is that earnings disparities are much smaller for new labor market entrants than for the more experienced, a factor that could have at least three explanations. If black men obtain less on-the-job training than white men, their earnings would be closer to those of whites earlier in their careers than later (see the discussion at the end of Chapter 9).[4] Alternatively, the quality of the schooling received by blacks could have improved in the 1970s, yielding the increased earnings ratios for

---

4. One way to assess this explanation is to see if the black/white earnings ratios for *given age cohorts* always fall as the cohorts age. Smith and Welch, "Black Economic Progress After Myrdal," present such ratios in their Table 11. For the cohort beginning work in 1955, there was an *increase* in the black/white earnings ratio as they aged, but for the cohort starting work in 1965, the earnings ratio tended to be lower 10 years later. Only in the latter case are the ratios consistent with the on-the-job training explanation.

younger cohorts of black men. Finally, in addition to the above "premarket" explanations, current labor market discrimination could have been reduced sufficiently over time that younger blacks now have opportunities unavailable to earlier generations.

In short, the data in Table 14.3 indicate that premarket differences account for at least one-third of the observed 30-percentage-point earnings gap between black and white men, but they also suggest that other premarket factors could be involved. Several studies have attempted to more carefully control for the age/earnings profiles implied by on-the-job training, as well as for such other factors as region of residence, union status, and a host of other factors thought to affect wage rates. Two studies using data from the late 1960s estimated that, in the absence of measurable differences in productive characteristics, black males would have earned between 85 and 90 percent of what white males earned.[5] A study using data from the mid-1970s implied that, in the absence of premarket differences, black males would have earned wages that were 88 percent of those earned by white males.[6] Finally, studies using data from 1979–80 have suggested that once premarket factors have been accounted for, black males earn between 83 and 94 percent as much as white males.[7]

If the wages of black men are 85 to 90 percent of the wages of white men, once productive characteristics are controlled for, then over half of the 30-percentage-point overall differential in earnings can be attributed to premarket factors. The remaining differential, however, may be a biased estimate of the extent of current labor market discrimination because researchers simply do not have complete data on the productive characteristics of individuals or groups. Researchers can measure age, education, and, in many cases, experience, but they rarely have data on school quality, work habits, aspirations, degree of alienation, and other intangibles that clearly affect one's productivity. These intangibles, moreover, *may* vary across race (or gender) owing to such premarket factors as social treatment, socioeconomic status of one's parents, and cultural background. If the unmeasured characteristics tend to depress the productivity of minorities or women relative to that of white males, attributing all of the unexplained difference in average earnings to current labor market discrimination will clearly overstate the extent of that discrimination. *Some* of the unexplained differential may be the result of unmeasured productive characteristics and thus may be more appropriately labeled *premarket* in nature. Of course, if the unmeasured characteristics tend to raise the productivity of minorities or women relative to that of white men, attributing all the unexplained differences in earnings to current labor market discrimination will understate the extent of that discrimination.

5. Robert J. Flanagan, "Labor Force Experience, Job Turnover, and Racial Wage Differentials," *Review of Economics and Statistics* 56 (November 1974): 521–29, and A. S. Blinder, "Wage Discrimination—Reduced Form and Structural Estimates," *Journal of Human Resources* 8 (Fall 1973): 436–55.
6. Mary Corcoran and Greg Duncan, "Work History, Labor Force Attachment, and Earnings Differences Between the Races and Sexes," *Journal of Human Resources* 14, no. 1 (Winter 1979): 3–20.
7. Saul Hoffman and Charles Link, "Selectivity Bias in Male Wage Equations: Black and White Comparisons," *Review of Economics and Statistics* 66 (May 1984): 320–24, and Leonard A. Carlson and Caroline Swartz, "The Earnings of Women and Ethnic Minorities, 1959–79," *Industrial and Labor Relations Review* 41 (July 1988): 530–46.

After estimating the portion of the *average* race/gender earnings differential that is explained by differences in average productive characteristics, one is left with a residual, or unexplained, portion. One part of the residual may be the result of current labor market discrimination, but the effects of any unmeasurable (or at least unmeasured) differences in average productive characteristics show up in the residual also. Because of this methodological defect, which is mainly the result of the difficulties of measuring all characteristics that affect productivity, accurate measures of the extent of labor market discrimination do not exist. Assuming that *all* the unexplained residual is due to discrimination, we can estimate the effects discrimination *might* have; however, we are unable to say if actual labor market discrimination is below or above these estimates.

Hispanics. In 1987, male Hispanics who worked full time, year-round had incomes averaging only 65 percent those of white, non-Hispanic males. Moreover, this percentage appears to be dropping: it was 74 in 1976, 71 in 1980, and 69 in 1984.[8] However, as suggested by our discussion of immigrants in Chapter 10, to estimate what fractions of these wage differences are due to differences in productive characteristics we need to control for proficiency in English, time in the United States, or both. Studies controlling for these factors, in addition to other human capital characteristics, suggest that language proficiency may be the biggest influence on Hispanic/non-Hispanic wage differentials;[9] one study, indeed, found that language proficiency explained virtually all the Hispanic/non-Hispanic wage differences.[10]

Asians. The issue of discrimination against Asians in the United States has not attracted much attention, probably because of their relatively high incomes. For example, the earnings among males of Asian ancestry were equal,

---

8. U.S. Bureau of the Census, *Money Income in 1976 of Families and Persons in the United States,* Consumer Income Series P-60, no. 114 (July 1978), Table 55; *Money Income of Families and Persons in the United States: 1978,* Series P-60, no. 123 (June 1980), Table 62; *Money Income of Households, Families, and Persons in the United States,* Series P-60 (1980, no. 132, Table 58; 1984, no. 151, Table 26; 1987, no. 162, Table 27).

9. Cordelia W. Reimers, "Labor Market Discrimination Against Hispanic and Black Men," *Review of Economics and Statistics* 65 (November 1983): 570–79. The findings are generally corroborated by an earlier study by James D. Gwartney and James E. Long, "The Relative Earnings of Blacks and Other Minorities," *Industrial and Labor Relations Review* 31 (April 1978): 336–46. See also Geoffrey Carliner, "Returns to Education for Blacks, Anglos, and Five Spanish Groups," *Journal of Human Resources* 11 (Spring 1976): 172–84; George Borjas, "The Earnings of Male Hispanic Immigrants in the United States," *Industrial and Labor Relations Review* 35 (April 1982): 343–53; Gilles Grenier, "The Effects of Language Characteristics on the Wages of Hispanic-American Males," *Journal of Human Resources* 19 (Winter 1984): 35–52; and Carlson and Swartz, "The Earnings of Women and Ethnic Minorities."

10. Walter McManus, William Gould, and Finis Welch, "Earnings of Hispanic Men: The Role of English Language Proficiency," *Journal of Labor Economics* 1 (April 1983): 101–30. Indeed, in a later article, McManus estimated that the present value of the loss to Hispanic men from not being fluent in English ranged from $19,000 to $36,000 per man. The failure of these workers to make the investments in language necessary to reap the benefits of fluency McManus attributes to limited horizons (for older immigrants), borrowing constraints, or very high discount rates (for illegal immigrants—who also may have relatively short time horizons). See Walter McManus, "Labor Market Costs of Language Disparity: An Interpretation of Hispanic Earnings Differences," *American Economic Review* 75 (September 1985): 818–27.

TABLE 14.4   Ratio of Female/Male Wage and Salary Income for Year-Round, Full-Time White Workers

Year	Ratio of Female/Male Income
1955	0.65
1964	0.59
1967	0.58
1970	0.59
1973	0.56
1977	0.58
1980	0.59
1983	0.64
1987	0.65

SOURCE: U.S. Bureau of the Census, *Money Income of Households, Families, and Persons in the United States,* Consumer Income Series P-60 (1984, no. 151, Table 38; 1987, no. 162, Table 27).

on average, to those of white males in 1980 (Asian women made 13 percent more than white women). These data do not rule out current labor market discrimination against males of Asian ancestry because they do not control for productive characteristics. Once differences in premarket factors have been accounted for, it seems clear that men of Japanese ancestry have earnings comparable to those of white men, while men of Filipino ancestry have earnings 10–15 percent lower. Estimates of earnings for men of Chinese descent vary between 90 and 100 percent of those for comparable white males, and the earnings of Asian Indians and Vietnamese men are within 2 percent of the earnings of comparable whites.[11]

Gender Differences

Differences in earnings between female and male workers are large. The average white, female, full-time worker earns just 65 percent of what her male counterpart earns. As one can see from Table 14.4, this ratio has followed a U-shaped pattern since the mid-1950s, remaining below 0.6 throughout the 1960s and 1970s and only recently approaching its pre-1960 level. However, movements in the ratio have been relatively small, and explaining the sizable disparity that remains between the average earnings of men and women is of considerable interest.[12]

There are several factors other than labor market discrimination that could cause this large disparity. First, because the market-work life of a woman historically has been shorter than that of a man, women have had fewer incentives to invest in schooling and post-schooling training that is

11. Barry Chiswick, "An Analysis of the Earnings and Employment of Asian-American Men," *Journal of Labor Economics* 1 (April 1983): 197–214, and Carlson and Swartz, "The Earnings of Women and Ethnic Minorities."

12. Recent articles analyzing the trend in female/male earnings are June O'Neill, "The Trend in the Male–Female Wage Gap in the United States," *Journal of Labor Economics* 3, no. 1, pt. 2 (January 1985): S91–S116; Victor R. Fuchs, "Women's Quest for Economic Equality," *Journal of Economic Perspectives* 3 (Winter 1989): 25–41; James P. Smith and Michael Ward, "Women in the Labor Market and in the Family," *Journal of Economic Perspectives* 3 (Winter 1989): 9–23; Francine D. Blau and Andrea H. Beller, "Trends in Earnings Differentials by Gender, 1971–81," *Industrial and Labor Relations Review* 41 (July 1988): 513–29; and Carlson and Swartz, "The Earnings of Women and Ethnic Minorities."

TABLE 14.5   Female/Male Median Earnings Ratios, by Age, for Full-Time, Year-Round Workers

	Age Group				
Year	20–24	25–34	35–44	45–54	55–64
1967	0.75	0.62	0.54	0.57	0.61
1977	0.77	0.68	0.55	0.54	0.56
1987	0.88	0.74	0.65	0.58	0.58

SOURCE: U.S. Bureau of the Census, *Current Population Reports,* Consumer Income Series P-60 (1967, no. 64, Table 19; 1977, no. 118, Table 46; 1987, no. 162, Table 34).

specifically oriented to the labor market.[13] (They, in essence, prepare for two careers—one at home and one in the labor market—and are thus typically less specialized than men.) The lack of on-the-job training, as noted in Chapter 9, is one reason why the age/earnings profiles for women are so flat, creating a greater disparity between the earnings of women and men as they grow older. The effects of flatter age/earnings profiles among women can be seen in Table 14.5, which shows the clear tendency for female/male earnings ratios to decline with age.

Second, because of traditional home responsibilities, women are less likely than men to work overtime or to choose occupations that offer jobs with high pay but long hours. For example, among married white women professionals (18 or more years of schooling) with at least one child under 12 at home, only 10 percent work more than 2,250 hours per year; in contrast, 50 percent of their husbands do. Overall, it has been estimated that the weekly hours worked by women who work full time throughout the year are 8–10 percent lower than those worked by comparable men. Home responsibilities also mean that women usually work closer to home than do men, a fact (as argued in Chapter 8) that implies lower wages.[14]

Finally, historically wives have tended to "follow" husbands when the husbands decided on the geographic location of their jobs (a fact noted in Chapter 10). Husbands, in effect, have been relatively free to choose their best offer, while wives have usually done the best they could *given* their geographical location. This sort of family decision-making behavior has also tended to reduce women's earnings.[15]

---

13. As noted in Chapter 9 (footnote 38), the expected work life of a woman at age 20 was 27.2 years in 1980, whereas for men it was 36.8. Solomon Polachek, "Occupational Segregation and the Gender Wage Gap," *Population Research and Policy Review* 6 (1987): 47–67, argues that expected labor market intermittency has caused women (at least in the past) to select occupations in which the penalties for intermittency are lowest; these, he argues, are the occupations with the flattest age/earnings profiles.

14. June O'Neill, "The Trend in the Male–Female Wage Gap in the United States"; Victor Fuchs, "Women's Quest for Economic Equality"; and Michelle White, "Sex Differences in Urban Commuting Patterns," *American Economic Review Papers and Proceedings* 76 (May 1986): 368–72.

15. Evidence that geographic migration usually causes husbands' earnings to rise but wives' earnings to fall was cited earlier (Chapter 10) based on Polachek and Horvath, "A Life Cycle Approach to Migration," in *Research in Labor Economics,* vol. 1, ed. Ronald Ehrenberg (Greenwich, Conn.: JAI Press, 1977). Other articles on the same topic are Robert H. Frank, "Why Women Earn Less: The Theory and Estimation of Differential Overqualification," *American Economic Review* 68 (June 1978): 360–73, and Mincer and Polachek, "Family Investments in Human Capital." Of course, increased female labor market attachment suggests that such patterns will not necessarily persist in the future.

While the above *premarket* differences are not immediately generated by *labor market* discrimination, they will be *affected* by the presence of such discrimination. If current market discrimination exists, the resulting lower wage for women strengthens incentives for them to be the ones who engage in *household production*. The expectation that women will be the ones to stay home with children, for example, is probably the major reason behind each of the three premarket forces above. Anything that reduces the disproportionate share of women in household production will tend to increase their incentives to acquire human capital, work longer hours for pay, and select their jobs from a wider area. Thus, even though premarket differences are clearly important and are deeply rooted in factors other than current labor market discrimination, measuring the extent of labor market discrimination and taking steps to end it are of obvious importance.

One way to obtain a sense of the extent of market discrimination is to look at the relative earnings of women who have never married. These women are not engaged in raising children and, unless involved in caring for a parent or sibling, do not have the household duties that usually befall married women. They tend to work almost as many hours per year as the average man, and they also exhibit concave age/earnings profiles.[16] Despite these closer similarities to men, however, the average income of never-married white women aged 25–64 is just 70 percent of that earned by the average man in that age group (as compared to 62 percent for married women).[17]

Before concluding that market discrimination is immediately responsible for most of the earnings gap between men and women, however, it is important to remember that within the age group 25–64 the typical never-married person is probably younger and has had less labor market experience than the typical married person. It is also important to realize that human capital decisions are based on *expected* career life, and many never-married women may have expected to become married when basic schooling or occupational decisions were made. In short, previously prevailing social expectations about women's role in household production may also have influenced the human capital decisions of women who ultimately decided not to marry, causing their earnings to be lower than otherwise. Finally, the group of never-married adults is likely to contain a higher proportion of disabled persons than is found in the married group. Thus, while *some* of the 30 percent earnings differential for never-married women may be due to current labor market discrimination, it is unlikely that *all* of the difference can be so attributed.

The best way to estimate the effects of market discrimination on the basis of gender is to perform the same kind of analysis reported earlier for black and white males. Thus we must ask, "What would the female/male earnings ratio be, on average, if women had the same education, training, experience, hours of work, commuting distance, turnover rate, and other productive char-

---

16. Victor Fuchs, "Differences in Hourly Earnings Between Men and Women," *Monthly Labor Review* 94, no. 5 (May 1971): 9–15.
17. These ratios are for full-time, year-round white workers aged 25–64 in 1984. See U.S. Bureau of the Census, *Money Income of Households, Families, and Persons in the United States: 1987,* Consumer Income Series P-60, no. 162, Table 33.

TABLE 14.6   Representation of Women in Ten High-Paying and Ten Low-Paying Occupations, 1970 and 1982

	Percent Female	
Occupation	*1970*	*1982*
High-paying		
Stock and bond sales agents	8.6	22.7
Managers and administrators, n.e.c.[a]	11.6	19.5
Bank officials and financial managers	17.4	37.2
Sales representatives, manufacturing	8.5	17.5
Designers	23.5	25.9
Personnel and labor relations workers	31.2	49.7
Sales representatives, wholesale	6.4	13.1
Computer programmers	22.7	31.9
Low-paying		
Practical nurses	96.3	95.1
Hairdressers and cosmetologists	90.4	87.0
Cooks, except private household	62.8	46.7
Health aides, except nursing	83.9	86.7
Nurses' aides	84.6	85.7
Sewers and stitchers	93.8	95.0
Farm laborers	13.2	10.6
Child-care workers, except private household	93.2	89.1
All occupations	37.7	40.0

[a]The initials n.e.c. mean "not elsewhere classified."

SOURCES: Sharon Smith, "Men's Jobs, Women's Jobs and Differential Wage Treatment," *Job Evaluation and EEO: The Emerging Issues,* Papers presented at the Industrial Relations Counselors Colloquium, September 14–15, 1978, Atlanta, Georgia (New York: Industrial Relations Counselors 1979), 67–84; Earl F. Mellor, "Investigating Differences in Weekly Earnings of Women and Men," *Monthly Labor Review* 107 (June 1984): 17–28.

acteristics as their male counterparts?" Studies that have attempted to answer this question have generally concluded that differences in education, experience, union status, and other personal and job attributes account for one-third to two-thirds of the earnings differences between men and women.[18] Thus, it appears that current *labor market* discrimination can account for no more than two-thirds of the earnings gap between men and women.

One aspect of alleged current labor market discrimination against women is *occupational segregation*—the reservation of some jobs for men and others (mostly lower-paying ones) for women. Some dimensions of this segregation and its effects can be seen in Table 14.6, which presents for 1970 and 1982 the share of women in a variety of high-paying and low-paying occupations. Two things are especially notable in the table. First, very few of the high-paying

---

18. Corcoran and Duncan, "Work History, Labor Force Attachment, and Earnings Differences Between the Races and Sexes"; Mincer and Polachek, "Family Investments in Human Capital: Earnings of Women"; Sharon P. Smith, *Equal Pay in the Public Sector: Fact or Fantasy* (Princeton, N.J.: Industrial Relations Section, Princeton University, 1977); and Elaine Sorenson, "The Wage Effects of Occupational Sex Composition: A Review and New Findings," in *Comparable Worth: Analysis and Evidence,* ed. M. Anne Hill and Mark R. Killingsworth (Ithaca, N.Y.: ILR Press, 1989), 57–79.

occupations employed women to an extent even close to their overall proportion among all employed workers (40 percent in 1982). On the other hand, women were heavily *over*represented in the low-paying occupations. Second, in the twelve years from 1970 to 1982, the proportion of women in most of the high-paying jobs rose much faster than their overall proportion among the employed, while their proportions in the lower-paying generally fell.

How much of the current market discrimination against women takes the form of occupational segregation and how much takes the form of different wages *within* given occupations? A crude answer to this question can be obtained by estimating the wage women would make if they had productive characteristics similar to those of the average male. Comparing this estimated wage to the average male wage will yield an estimate of overall market discrimination. If we then estimate the wage women would receive if they had the same productive characteristics *and* the same *occupational* distribution as men, we can calculate the wage disparities caused solely by occupational differences. The most recent studies, based on data from the late 1970s and mid-1980s, suggest that equalizing the occupational distribution of men and women with the same human capital characteristics would reduce the earnings gap by 6 to 8 percentage points.[19]

It would appear, then, that perhaps half of the overall 35 percent differential between the earnings of men and women is due to premarket factors. Of the remaining 18 percent, which could be due to current market discrimination, roughly 7 percentage points appears to be the consequence of occupational segregation. Thus, once occupational and human capital factors are accounted for, an "unexplained" differential of something like 10 percentage points remains, suggesting that within the same occupation, women receive only 90 percent of the wage received by comparable men.

Interestingly, an "unexplained" residual gap of about 10 percentage points between otherwise identical men and women is consistent with findings from a different kind of study done for 1981. This study used data from firms of 100 or more employees, and it found that within narrowly defined occupational grades the ratio of female to male earnings tended to range from 0.84 to 1.03 (see Table 14.7). The higher ratios were found among the highly skilled professions of accountant and attorney; for the occupation of accounting clerk, which more closely approximates a job that is typical in its duties and level of pay, the ratios within grade level averaged 0.89.

Besides indicating the pay discrepancies that generally exist even within grades in the same occupation, the data in Table 14.7 suggest again the impor-

19. Sorenson, "The Wage Effects of Occupational Sex Composition: A Review and New Findings." Morley Gunderson, "Male–Female Wage Differentials and Policy Responses," *Journal of Economic Literature* 27 (March 1989): 46–72, reviews several conclusions about gender-related wage differentials that are warranted from prior studies, including that the occupational distribution accounts for much more of the gender wage gap than do pay differences within the same jobs in the same establishments. For earlier works on the topic of occupational segregation, see Ronald Oaxaca, "Male–Female Wage Differentials in Urban Labor Markets," *International Economic Review* 14, no. 3 (October 1973): 693–709; Julianne M. Malveaux, "Moving Forward, Standing Still: Women in White-Collar Jobs," in *Women in the Workplace,* ed. Phyllis A. Wallace (Boston: Auburn House, 1982), 101–34; and Andrea H. Beller, "Occupational Segregation by Sex: Determinants and Changes," *Journal of Human Resources* 17 (Summer 1982): 371–92.

TABLE 14.7   Female/Male Earnings Ratios in Medium-Sized and Large Firms,[a] Selected Occupations, 1981

Occupation	Earnings Ratio	Average Monthly Earnings	% Female in Occupation
Accountant I	.99	$1,377	46
II	.98	1,679	34
III	.96	1,962	19
IV	.95	2,402	11
V	.90	2,928	5
All accountants	.83	[b]	23
Attorney I	1.03	1,873	28
II	.97	2,338	24
III	.95	3,031	13
IV	.94	3,738	9
All attorneys	.78	[b]	15
Accounting clerk I	.94	798	95
II	.89	953	94
III	.89	1,121	91
IV	.84	1,407	82
All accounting clerks	.82	[b]	92

[a]For most industries, firms had to have at least 100 employees to be included in the sample.
[b]Not reported.
SOURCE: Mark Sieling, "Staffing Patterns Prominent in Female–Male Earnings Gap," *Monthly Labor Review* 107, no. 6 (June 1984): 29–33.

tant role of occupational distribution in understanding the gender gap in pay: women were less represented in the higher-paying grades in each of the three occupations shown. This underrepresentation in the higher grades of an occupation could plausibly result from a variety of factors discussed above: labor force intermittency (lower levels of job tenure among women), employer bias against women in the promotion process, or the only recent entry of women into previously male-dominated occupations.

THEORIES OF MARKET DISCRIMINATION

As argued in the previous section, one cannot rule out the presence of substantial discrimination against women and minorities in the labor market. Before one can design policies to end discrimination, one must understand the *sources* and *mechanisms* causing it. The goal of this section is to lay out and evaluate the different theories of discrimination proposed by economists.

Three general sources of labor market discrimination have been hypothesized, and each source suggests an associated model of how discrimination is implemented and what its consequences are.[20] The first source of discrimina-

---

20. Two of the three general models were labeled by Kenneth Boulding, "Toward a Theory of Discrimination," in *Equal Opportunity and the AT&T Case,* ed. Phyllis Wallace (Cambridge, Mass.: MIT Press, 1976).

tion is *personal prejudice,* wherein employers, fellow employees, or customers dislike associating with workers of a given race or sex.[21] The second general source is *statistical prejudgment,* whereby employers project onto *individuals* certain perceived *group* characteristics. Finally, there are models according to which the desire for, and use of, *monopoly power* is the source of discrimination. While all the models generate useful, suggestive insights, none has been convincingly established as superior.

Personal Prejudice

Employer Discrimination.   Suppose that white male *employers* are prejudiced against women and minorities but that (for simplicity's sake) customers and fellow employees are not prejudiced. This prejudice may take the form of aversion to associating with women and minorities, it may be manifested as a desire to help fellow white males whenever possible, or it may be motivated by status considerations and take the form of occupational segregation. In whatever form, this prejudice is assumed to result in the discriminatory treatment of women and minorities. Further, we assume for the purposes of this model that the women and minorities in question have the same productive characteristics as white males. (This assumption directs our focus to market discrimination by putting aside premarket factors.)

If employers have a decided preference for hiring white males in high-paying jobs despite the availability of equally qualified women and minorities, they will act *as if* the latter were less productive than the former. By virtue of our assumption that the women and minorities involved are equally productive in every way, the devaluing of their productivity by employers is purely subjective and is a manifestation of personal prejudice. The more prejudiced an employer is, the more actual productivity will be discounted.

Suppose that MP stands for the actual marginal productivity of all workers in a particular labor market and d represents the extent to which this productivity is subjectively devalued for minorities and women. In this case, market equilibrium for white males is reached when their wage (W_M) equals MP:

$$MP = W_M \tag{14.1}$$

For the women and minorities, however, equilibrium is achieved only when their wage (W_F) equals their *subjective* value to firms:

$$MP - d = W_F, \text{ or} \tag{14.2}$$

$$MP = W_F + d \tag{14.2a}$$

Since the actual marginal productivities are equal by assumption, equations (14.1) and (14.2a) are equal to each other, and one can easily see that W_F must be less than W_M:

$$W_M = W_F + d, \text{ or} \tag{14.3}$$

---

21. The models of personal prejudice are based on Gary S. Becker, *The Economics of Discrimination,* 2d ed. (Chicago: University of Chicago Press, 1971).

$$W_F = W_M - d \qquad (14.3a)$$

What this says algebraically has a very simple economic logic: if the actual productivity of women and minorities is devalued by employers, workers in these groups must offer their services at lower wages than white males to compete for jobs.

This model of employer discrimination has two major implications, as illustrated by Figure 14.1, which is a graphic representation of equation (14.2a). Figure 14.1 shows that a discriminatory employer faced with a wage rate of W_F for women and minorities will hire N_0, for at that point $MP = W_F + d$. *Profit-maximizing* employers, however, will hire N_1; that is, they will hire until $MP = W_F$. The effects on profits can be readily seen in Figure 14.1 if one remembers that the area under the MP curve represents total product (or total revenues) of the firm, with capital held constant. Subtracting the area representing the wage bill of the discriminatory employer ($0EFN_0$) yields profits for these employers equal to the area $AEFB$. Profits for a nondiscriminatory employer, however, are AEG. These latter employers hire women and minorities to the point where their marginal product equals their wage, while the discriminators end their hiring short of that point. Discriminators thus give up profits in order to indulge their prejudices.

The second implication of our employer discrimination model concerns the size of the gap between W_M and W_F. The determinants of this gap can best be understood using a graph of the supply of jobs to women or minorities (see Figure 14.2). In a labor market in which workers of equal productivity are seeking jobs, the supply of job opportunities for women and minorities will be

FIGURE 14.1   Equilibrium Employment of Women and Minorities in Firms That Discriminate

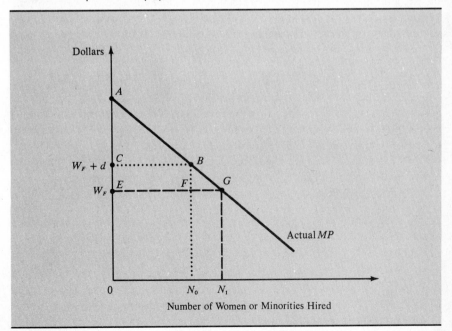

FIGURE 14.2 The Supply of Jobs to Women and Minorities

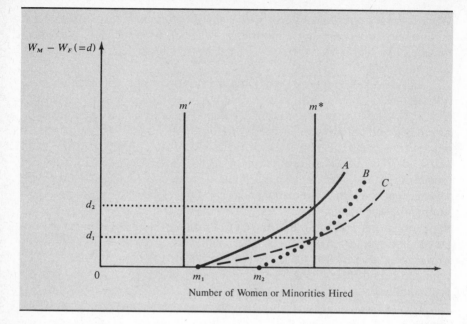

Number of Women or Minorities Hired

a function of the gap ($W_M - W_F = d$) between their wages and those of white males. As shown in Figure 14.2, some employers will hire women and minorities even if their wages equal $W_M(d = 0)$. These are the nondiscriminatory (profit-maximizing) employers, and supply curve $0m_1A$ assumes they account for m_1 jobs in the market. If there are fewer than m_1 minorities or women seeking employment in that labor market (m', say), they would all be hired by the nondiscriminators and no discrimination would be evident. W_F would equal W_M, and women and minorities would not have to deal with those who devalued their services.

If the supply of women and minorities were greater than the number that could be absorbed by the nondiscriminatory employers (m^*, say), then a wage gap would have to arise for all of them to become employed. Curve $0m_1A$ shows that if the number of women and minorities seeking jobs were to increase from m' to m^*, the required gap would rise from zero to d_2. Thus, the gap depends in part on the sheer size of the groups against whom there is personal prejudice. If the number of women or minorities seeking jobs were to rise beyond m^*, the difference between W_M and W_F would become greater than d_2.

The equilibrium gap between W_M and W_F, however, also depends on the distribution and extent of employer prejudice against women or minorities. If the number of nondiscriminatory employers grew (or if the number of jobs offered by such employers grew), the supply-of-jobs curve in Figure 14.2 would shift to the right from $0m_1A$ to $0m_2B$. This shift would reduce the observed wage disparity at m^* from d_2 to d_1. The same reduction in market discrimination could also occur if the number of nondiscriminators stayed constant but the *discriminatory preferences* of the others were *reduced*. If this were to happen, discriminatory employers would require less of a wage disparity to hire a given level of women or minorities, and the supply-of-jobs curve would shift to something like $0m_1C$ in Figure 14.2.

The most disturbing implication of the employer discrimination model is that discriminators seem to be maximizing *utility* (satisfying their prejudices) instead of *profits*. This practice should immediately raise the question of how they survive. Firms in competitive product markets *must* maximize profits just to make a normal rate of return on invested capital. Those who do not make this return will find they can earn a better return by investing some other way—a way, perhaps, that does not involve hiring workers. Conversely, since profit-maximizing (nondiscriminatory) firms would normally make more money from a given set of assets than would discriminators, we should observe nondiscriminatory firms buying out others and gradually taking over the market. In short, if competitive forces were at work in the product market, firms that discriminate would be punished and discrimination could not persist unless their owners were willing to accept below-market rates of return.

Because a firm that discriminates will have higher costs than one that doesn't, employer discrimination is most likely to persist, therefore, when owners or managers have the ability and the incentive to pursue a goal other than profit maximization. In Chapter 3 (p. 75) and again in Chapter 9 (p. 345), for example, we argued that firms subject to government regulation of prices or profits may find it attractive to hide excess profits from the public by engaging in costly practices that enhance the utility of their owners or managers. The extra costs of utility-maximizing (as opposed to profit-maximizing) practices are hidden from regulators and can be passed along to consumers if the product market is sufficiently monopolized; were these practices abandoned, profits would rise and government regulators might insist on product-price decreases.[22] It is perhaps no coincidence that the most compelling study of the relationship between product market competition and discrimination was in the regulated industry of banking; this study found that the fewer the number of banks competing in a geographical area, the smaller was the share of female employment.[23]

Customer Discrimination. A second personal prejudice model stresses *customer* prejudice as a source of discrimination. Customers may prefer to be served by white males in some situations and by minorities or women in others. If their preferences for white males extend to jobs requiring major responsibility—such as physician, stockbroker, or airline pilot—and their

22. We are indebted to Professor Levis Kochin for emphasizing this point to us. For early writings on this subject, see Becker, *The Economics of Discrimination,* 48; Ray Marshall, "The Economics of Racial Discrimination: A Survey," *Journal of Economic Literature* 12 (September 1974): 864; and David P. Taylor, "Discrimination and Occupational Wage Differences in the Market for Unskilled Labor," *Industrial and Labor Relations Review* 21 (April 1968): 375–90.
23. Orley Ashenfelter and Timothy Hannan, "Sex Discrimination and Product Market Competition: The Case of the Banking Industry," *Quarterly Journal of Economics* 101 (February 1986): 149–73.

EXAMPLE 14.1

Customer Discrimination and Professional Basketball

Customer (fan) discrimination appears to affect salaries in the National Basketball Association. While 72 percent of NBA players are black, and while overall average salaries are equal for blacks and whites, there is evidence from two studies that if black and white players were equally skilled, the white players would earn from 16 to 23 percent more. That is, if white and black players are matched, so that they have the same offensive and defensive statistics and the same experience, white players average from one-sixth to one-fourth more in salary. Why?

Discrimination among basketball fans may be at least part of the answer. These same studies found that replacing a black player with a white one of equal skill raised attendance and revenues by amounts roughly comparable to the 16–23 percent premium paid to whites! Moreover, teams appeared to respond to fan prejudice in another way: in the three NBA cities with the largest proportion of white residents, 39 percent of the players were white; in the three NBA cities with the lowest proportion of white residents, only 18 percent of the players were white.

SOURCES: Lawrence Kahn and Peter Sherer, "Racial Differences in Professional Basketball Players' Compensation," *Journal of Labor Economics* 6 (January 1988): 40–61; Timothy Tregarthen, "Racism in the NBA: The Premium for White Players," *The Margin* 4 (March/April 1989): 4–6.

preferences for women and minorities are confined to less responsible jobs—receptionist or flight attendant, say—then occupational segregation that works to the disadvantage of women and minorities will occur. Further, if women or minorities are to find employment in the jobs for which customers prefer white males, they must either accept *lower wages* or be *more qualified* than the average white male. The reason for this is that their value to the firm is lower than that of *equally qualified* white males because of customers' preferences for white males.

In testing for the presence of customer discrimination, an obvious group to analyze is the self-employed, a group whose incomes are both directly dependent on the behavior of customers and clearly unaffected by employer prejudices. A careful analysis of 1980 census data estimated that if self-employed black men had had the same characteristics as self-employed white men in 1980, they would have earned about 19 percent less.[24] Customer dis-

---

24. George Borjas, "Consumer Discrimination and Self-Employment," *Journal of Political Economy* 97 (June 1989): 581–605. In a previous study, Borjas found that federal agencies serving heavily minority-oriented constituencies hired greater fractions of minorities than agencies whose constituents are mainly white: employment with the Department of Housing and Urban Development was 27 percent minority, while that with the Department of Agriculture was 10 percent minority. See George J. Borjas, "The Politics of Racial Discrimination in the Federal Government," *Journal of Law and Economics* 25 (October 1982): 271–99.

crimination thus cannot be ruled out. Moreover, it is notable that this 19 percent "residual" gap among the self-employed was greater than the 11 percent gap the same study estimated for otherwise comparable black and white salaried employees!

Employee Discrimination.   A third source of discrimination based on personal prejudice might be found on the supply side of the market, where white male workers may avoid situations in which they will have to interact with minorities or women in ways they consider inappropriate. For example, they may resist taking orders from a woman, sharing responsibility with a minority member, or working where women or minorities are not confined to low-status jobs.

If white male workers have these discriminatory preferences, they will tend to quit (or avoid) employers who employ women or minorities on a nondiscriminatory basis. Employers, if they wish to hire or retain white males, will have to pay them more than they would if they confined women and minorities to their "traditional," lower-status jobs. In some cases employers may be able to avoid the higher costs of employing white males by running plants segregated by race or gender. Segregated plants, however, are not always legally or economically feasible. Thus, the costs to employers of hiring women or minorities in certain jobs may be elevated by employee discrimination, serving to reduce demand and lower wages for women and minorities in those jobs.

It is interesting to note that this model of employee discrimination predicts that white males working in integrated environments will receive higher wages than those with exactly the same productive characteristics who work in segregated environments. If we could observe locales in which there were no minority workers, say, we would expect that differences in pay among white men of comparable education and experience would be small. However, in areas where blacks are found in sufficient numbers that many whites must work in integrated plants, we should observe that the wages received by white males of equal human capital will *vary* according to whether they work in segregated or integrated firms. Thus, the theory suggests that the wages received by white males within any given human capital category will show *greater similarity* when integrated work forces are rare than when some whites work in integrated environments and some do not. When one looks at U.S. data, one does in fact find that, other things equal, white men's wages are more similar in states where the minority population is small—and where, presumably, few whites work in integrated plants—than they are where the minority population is large. Moreover, this finding seems to be true of both Northern and Southern states when they are considered separately.[25]

The interesting thing about the above finding is that neither the employer nor the customer model of discrimination predicts that *white* men's

---

25. Barry R. Chiswick, "Racial Discrimination in the Labor Market: A Test of Alternative Hypotheses," *Journal of Political Economy* 81, no. 6 (November 1973): 1330–52. It should be noted that the inequality of *minority* earnings does not vary according to their proportion in the population, a finding that seems to rule out the existence of some other, unmeasured force causing greater inequality in high-minority states.

wages will become *more varied* if discrimination exists. If white males are preferred for particular higher-paying jobs, their wages will be higher than if discrimination were nonexistent. However, the fact that their wages are *higher* does not imply they are more *dissimilar*. White males who, in the absence of discrimination, would have wages clustering around some lower level instead have wages clustering around some higher level. The point is that their wages continue to cluster. Nevertheless, the above finding offers only indirect support for the employee discrimination model, and it is also consistent with predictions of the "monopoly power" model outlined below. Hence, convincing evidence for the existence of employee discrimination cannot be claimed.

Statistical Discrimination

Another source of discrimination might be the kind and quality of information used in making hiring decisions.[26] Employers must try to *guess* the potential productivity of applicants, but rarely will they know what actual productivity will be. The only information available to them at the time of hire is information that is thought to be *correlated* with productivity: education, experience, age, test scores, and so forth. These correlates are imperfect predictors of actual productivity, however, and employers realize this. To some extent, then, they supplement information on these correlates with a subjective element in making hiring decisions, and this subjective element could *look* like discrimination even though it might not be rooted in personal prejudice.

Statistical discrimination can be viewed as a part of the *screening problem,* which arises when observable personal characteristics that are correlated with productivity are not perfect predictors. By way of example, suppose two types of workers apply for a secretarial job: those who can type 70 words per minute (wpm) over the long haul and those who can type 40 wpm. These actual productivities are unknown to the employer, however. All the employer observes are the results of a 5-minute typing test administered to all applicants. What are the problems created by the use of this test as a screening device?

The problems relate to the fact that some typists who can really type only 40 wpm on the job will be lucky and score higher than 40 on the test. Others who can really type 70 wpm on the job will be unlucky and score less than 70 on the test. The imperfection of the test as a predictor will cause two kinds of errors in hiring decisions: some "good" applicants will be rejected, and some "bad" workers will be hired.

Figure 14.3 shows the test-score distributions for both groups of workers. Those who can actually type 70 wpm score 70 on average, but half score less.

26. The considerations developed in this section are more formally and completely treated in Dennis J. Aigner and Glen G. Cain, "Statistical Theories of Discrimination in Labor Markets," *Industrial and Labor Relations Review* 30, no. 2 (January 1977): 175–87. A similar theory is developed in M. A. Spence, "Job Market Signaling," *Quarterly Journal of Economics* 87, no. 3 (August 1973): 355–74. Shelly J. Lundberg and Richard Startz, "Private Discrimination and Social Intervention in Competitive Labor Markets," *American Economic Review* 73, no. 3 (June 1983): 340–47, consider the social gains that can be theoretically obtained from regulating a labor market characterized by statistical discrimination.

FIGURE 14.3   The Screening Problem

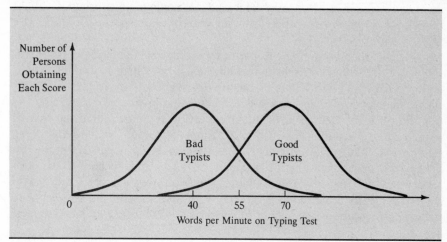

Likewise, half of the other group score better than 40 on the test. If an applicant scores 55, say, the employer does not know if the applicant is a good (70 wpm) or bad (40 wpm) typist. If those scoring 55 are automatically rejected, the firm will be rejecting some good workers, and if it needs workers badly, this policy will entail costs. Likewise, if it accepts those scoring 55, some bad workers will be hired.

In an effort to avoid the above dilemma, suppose the employer does some research and finds out that applicants from a particular business school are specifically coached to perform well on 5-minute typing tests. Thus, applicants who can actually type X words per minute over a normal day will tend to score *higher* than X wpm on a 5-minute test as a result of the special coaching (that is, they will appear better than they really are). Recognizing that students from this school are likely to have test scores above their long-run productivity, the firm might decide to reject all applicants from this school who score 55 or below (on the grounds that, for most, the test score overestimates their ability), even though some who score less than 55 really can do better.

The general lesson of this example is that, in effect, firms will use both *individual* data (test scores, educational attainment, experience) and *group* data in making hiring decisions when the former are not perfect predictors of productivity. However, this use of group data can give rise to market discrimination because people with the same *measured productive characteristics* (test scores, education, etc.) will be treated differently on a systematic basis depending on *group* affiliation.

The relevance of the above discussion to the problem of discrimination against minorities and women is that race and gender may well be the group information used to supplement individual data in making hiring decisions. If the group data bear no relationship to actual productivity, or if the screening devices used are known to be less predictive for some groups than others, then we really have a case of discrimination rooted in personal prejudice or monopoly power. However, we have shown that the use of group data to modify individual information may be based on nonmalicious grounds. Might these grounds legitimately apply from an employer's perspective to minorities and women?

Suppose that, *on average,* minorities with high school educations are discovered to be less productive than white males with high school educations owing to differences in schooling quality. Or suppose that, because of shortened career lives, women with a given education level are, *on average,* less valuable to firms than men of equal education (refer to our discussion of women and job training in Chapter 5). Employers might employ this group information to modify individual data when making hiring decisions, just as they did in our hypothetical example of the business school above. The result would be that white males with given measured characteristics would be systematically preferred over women or minorities with the same characteristics, a condition that would be empirically identified as labor market discrimination.

One unfortunate side effect of using group data to supplement individual data is that, while it could lead employers to the correct hiring decisions on average, it assigns a group characteristic to people who may not be typical of the group. There are women who will have long, uninterrupted careers, just as there undoubtedly would be graduates of the business school mentioned above who do not test well and thus perform more poorly on tests than they could do on the job. There will also be minority high school graduates of substantial ability who would have gone to college had not family poverty intervened. These atypical group members are stigmatized by the use of group data. They may have actual productivity equal to that of those who are hired, but because of the group association they do not get the job.[27]

Thus, *statistical discrimination* could lead to a systematic preference for white males over others with the same *measured* characteristics, and it could also create a situation in which minorities or women who are the equals of white males in *actual* productivity are paid less because of the above-mentioned group stigma. Both problems are caused by the use of group data in making hiring decisions, but this use need not be motivated by prejudice. The results, however, have the same appearance and effects as if prejudice were present.

An important implication of this model of statistical discrimination is that the use of group data will become a more costly screening device as members of each group become more dissimilar. For example, as greater proportions of women desire to work in full-time, year-round careers and do not intend to drop out of the labor force to raise children, employers using gender as a handy index of labor force attachment will find themselves making costly mistakes. They will reject many female applicants who have a permanent labor force attachment (in whom an investment in specific training would be very worthwhile), and they may accept male applicants who are less productive. In either case, firms using incorrect screening devices will have lower profits

---

27. The discussion here has obvious relevance to the "signaling" issue discussed in Chapter 9. Minorities, for example, may be *too poor* to acquire the necessary "signal" in many cases where their ability would indicate they should.

than those that adopt appropriate screens. Thus, as *premarket* differences between the races or sexes narrow, the use of race or sex *group* data should lessen and statistical discrimination should gradually disappear.

Monopoly Power Models

The persistence of large race/gender earnings disparities has led some labor economists to wonder whether the above models are really appropriate. These economists are dissenters from the orthodox view that labor markets are essentially competitive; instead, they advance *monopoly power theories* of discrimination. Inherent in these more radical views of the labor market is the assertion that discrimination exists and persists because it is *profitable* for the discriminators.

While monopoly power theories of discrimination vary from each other in emphasis, they tend to share the feature that race or gender is collectively used to divide the labor force into *noncompeting* groups, creating or perpetuating a kind of worker caste system. These theories clearly suggest that competitive forces fail to operate in the labor market.[28] Three versions of these models are outlined below.

Crowding.   Occupational segregation, especially by gender, is pervasive. One study of 373 establishments, done within the last decade, found that in 60 percent of these places there was not a single job category in which both men and women were employed. Substantial segregation was found at most of the remaining 40 percent.[29] Similarly, a study of job segregation for 1974 found that men were significantly overrepresented in 163 of 267 major occupations (61 percent) and women in 85 (or 32 percent). In only 19 occupations (7 percent) were men and women represented in proportions close to their proportions in the work force.[30] Moreover, over 40 percent of all women employed in 1980 were found in just 7 occupations (secretarial, retail sales, food preparation and service, teaching, health and personal services, bookkeeping, and professional nursing). These facts have caused some to argue that, because the occupations available to women are relatively limited, those who want to work for pay are in *crowded* labor markets and as a result face lower wages.

Graphically, the "crowding hypothesis" is very simple and can be easily seen in Figure 14.4. Panel (a) illustrates a market in which supply is small relative to demand and the wage (W_H) is thus relatively high. Panel (b) depicts a market in which crowding causes supply to be large relative to demand, resulting in a wage (W_L) that is comparatively low.

While the effects of crowding are easily seen, the phenomenon of crowding itself is less easily explained. If men and women were equally productive in a given job or set of jobs, for example, one would think that the lower wage

---

28. For a summary of these views, see Glen G. Cain, "The Challenge of Segmented Labor Market Theories to Orthodox Theory: A Survey," *Journal of Economic Literature* 14 (December 1976): 1215–57.

29. Barbara R. Bergmann, "Does the Market for Women's Labor Need Fixing?" *Journal of Economic Perspectives* 3 (Winter 1989): 43–60.

30. Andrea Beller, "Occupational Segregation by Sex: Determinants and Changes," *Journal of Human Resources* 17 (Summer 1982): 371–92. A sex is considered overrepresented if its share in the occupation is 5 percentage points above its share in the employed labor force.

FIGURE 14.4   Labor Market "Crowding"

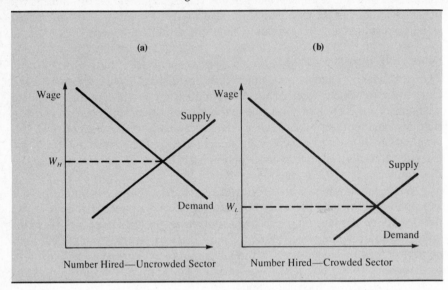

(a)

(b)

Number Hired—Uncrowded Sector   Number Hired—Crowded Sector

of women would make it attractive for firms now employing men to seek out female workers instead, and this profit-maximizing behavior would eventually eliminate any wage differential. The failure of crowding, or occupational segregation, to disappear suggests the presence of noncompeting groups, as we noted above, but we are still left with trying to explain why such groups exist. Over the past 70 years various possible explanations have been put forth: the establishment of some jobs as "male" and others as "female" through social custom,[31] differences in aptitude that are either innate or acquired,[32] and different supply curves of men and women to noncompeting (monopsonistic) employers.[33] None of these explanations is complete in the sense of getting at the ultimate source of discrimination.[34]

Dual Labor Markets.   A variant of the crowding hypothesis with more recent origins is the view, held by some economists, that there is a *dual labor market.* Dualists see the overall labor market as divided into two noncompeting sectors: a *primary* and a *secondary* sector.[35] Jobs in the primary sector offer relatively high wages, stable employment, good working conditions, and opportunities for advancement. Secondary sector jobs, however, tend to be

31. Millicent Fawcett, "Equal Pay for Equal Work," *Economic Journal* 28 (March 1918): 1–6.
32. F. Y. Edgeworth, "Equal Pay to Men and Women for Equal Work," *Economic Journal* 32 (December 1922): 431–57.
33. Joan Robinson, *The Economics of Imperfect Competition* (London: Macmillan and Co., 1934), 301–4.
34. An excellent history of crowding theories is provided in Janice F. Madden, *The Economics of Sex Discrimination* (Lexington, Mass.: Lexington Books, 1973), 30–36. The crowding hypothesis is nicely advanced also in Barbara Bergmann, "The Effect on White Incomes of Discrimination in Employment," *Journal of Political Economy* 79 (March–April 1971): 294–313.
35. Michael J. Piore, "Jobs and Training: Manpower Policy," in *The State and the Poor,* ed. S. Beer and R. Barringer (Cambridge, Mass.: Winthrop Press, 1970).

low-wage, unstable, dead-end jobs with poor working conditions, and the returns to education and experience are thought to be close to zero in this sector. Of key importance to the dualists' approach is that mobility between sectors is thought to be limited. Workers relegated to the secondary sector are tagged as unstable, undesirable workers and are thought to have little hope of acquiring primary sector jobs.

Historically, dualists continue, a large proportion of minorities and women have been employed in the secondary sector, and this leads to perpetuation of discrimination against them. Minorities and women, it is argued, are discriminated against because they tend (as a group) to have unstable work histories, but these histories are themselves a result of being unable to break into the primary labor market.

The dual labor market description of discrimination does not really explain what initially caused women and minorities to be confined to secondary jobs. Some Marxist economists view the existence of noncompeting sectors as at least partially due to attempts by capitalists to divide labor and thus to discourage organized opposition to the capitalist system;[36] this theory of discrimination is discussed later in the section on collusive action. Some economists operating within more neoclassical frameworks view the existence of two sectors, and the assignment of workers to the two sectors, as arising because of differences in monitoring costs between categories of workers.[37] As discussed in Chapter 11, firms may use "efficiency wages" or steeply sloped age/earnings profiles (characteristics of the primary sector) as compensation strategies to motivate workers and discourage shirking. These strategies deliberately encourage—and are predicated upon—a long-term relationship between workers and the firm. For workers with relatively short expected tenure, direct monitoring of work effort is required; there are no incentives for firms to adopt high-wage or delayed-compensation strategies.

To the extent that females have historically entered and left the labor force frequently (because of marriage and/or childbearing), an explanation of why they might initially have been assigned to the secondary sector is self-evident.[38] Why minorities were initially confined to the secondary sector is less obvious in the neoclassical framework. Recent empirical evidence does suggest, however, that there are two distinct sectors of the labor market—one in which education and experience are associated with higher wages and one in which they are not—and that nonwhites are more likely to be in the latter sector.[39]

---

36. See, for example, David Gordon, Richard Edwards, and Michael Reich, *Segmented Work, Divided Workers* (Cambridge, Eng.: Cambridge University Press, 1982), who assert, "The segmentation of labor forged and reproduced materially based division among U.S. workers that inhibited the growth of a unified working class movement" (p. 3).
37. See, for example, Jeremy Bulow and Lawrence Summers, "A Theory of Dual Labor Markets with Application to Industrial Policy, Discrimination and Keynesian Unemployment," *Journal of Labor Economics* 4 (July 1986): 376–414.
38. See Example 11.6 and Claudia Goldin, "Monitoring Costs and Occupational Segregation by Sex: A Historical Analysis," *Journal of Labor Economics* 4 (January 1986): 1–27.
39. William Dickens and Kevin Lang, "A Test of Dual Labor Market Theory," *American Economic Review* 75 (September 1985): 792–805, and William Dickens and Kevin Lang, "Testing Dual Labor Market Theory: A Reconsideration of the Evidence," National Bureau of Economic Research, Working Paper no. 1670, July 1985.

Such evidence in favor of the dual labor market hypothesis offers an explanation of why discrimination persists. It calls into question the levels of competition and mobility that exist and suggests that the initial existence of noncompeting race/sex groups will be self-perpetuating.[40] In short, the dual labor market hypothesis is consistent with any of the models of discrimination analyzed above; what it does suggest is that if any of these theories *are* applicable, we cannot count on natural market forces to eliminate the discrimination that results.

Collusive Action. Other nonorthodox theories claim that white employers collude and become monopsonists with respect to the hiring of minority labor. Minorities are subjugated and held immobile while monopsonistic wages are forced on them.[41] One of the more cogent and complete *power theories* of discrimination argues that prejudice and the conflicts it creates are inherent in a capitalist society because they serve the interests of owners.[42] Even if the owners of capital did not conspire to *create* prejudice, they nevertheless find that if it continues they can enhance their profits. Workers divided by race or gender are harder to organize and, if they *are* unionized, are less cohesive in their demands. Further, antagonisms on the shop floor deflect attention from grievances related to working conditions. Hence, it is argued that owners of capital gain, while *all* workers—but particularly minorities and women—lose from discrimination.

Two pieces of evidence are cited to support this theory. First, in areas in which black/white earnings differentials are largest, the income inequality among *whites* is also greatest, other things equal (the greater inequality of white income is attributed to *owner/worker* income disparities). This kind of finding was mentioned above when we discussed employee discrimination, and there the greater inequality among whites was attributed to wage differences among white *workers*. Thus, this first piece of evidence seems more or less consistent with a theory of employee discrimination, as well as with the power model.[43]

The second piece of evidence cited to support this power theory is that where black/white earnings differences are greatest, the percentage of the labor force that is unionized tends to be smallest. The strength of this argu-

---

40. That the forces of competition should at least gradually end arbitrary wage differentials is a consistent theme in economic analysis. However, the persistence of wage differentials across industries, even when all other measurable factors affecting wages are accounted for, represents another area in which some have argued that labor market outcomes are inconsistent with economic theory. See footnote 40 in Chapter 11 and William T. Dickens and Kevin Lang, "The Reemergence of Segmented Labor Market Theory," *Papers and Proceedings of the American Economic Association* 78 (May 1988): 129–34.
41. Lester Thurow, *The Economics of Poverty and Discrimination* (Washington, D.C.: The Brookings Institution, 1969).
42. Michael Reich, "The Economics of Racism," in *Problems in Political Economy: An Urban Perspective,* ed. David M. Gordon (Lexington, Mass.: D.C. Heath, 1971), 107–13.
43. A major difference between the Chiswick study of employee discrimination and Reich's test of the power model is that the former related white income inequality to the percentage of nonwhites in the population, while the latter related it to the ratio of nonwhite to white earnings. Which is the more appropriate test is a matter beyond the scope of this text; however, we should note that observed earnings ratios can reflect human capital differences as well as current discrimination. This issue illustrates the importance of *theoretical* analysis in both the execution and the interpretation of empirical studies.

EXAMPLE 14.2
South Africa's "Civilized Labour Policy"

Discrimination is ultimately the consequence of barriers to job opportunities. One technique for establishing barriers is to use government power in serving the interests of special groups at the expense of others. Sometimes the use of governmental authority is blatantly discriminatory—witness South Africa's "Colour Bar Act" of 1911 authorizing the establishment of a maximum ratio of African to white employees in that country's mines. In other cases, governments can achieve special privileges for favored groups through subtler means; an example of these means can be seen in South Africa's "civilized labour policy" of the early 1920s.

During World War I nonwhites in South Africa, despite overt discrimination in the labor market, were able to make inroads into jobs previously held by whites. In 1922, a bitter strike by white miners arose over their desire to return to prewar hiring patterns, and in 1924 a coalition government came into power with a mandate to protect "civilized" (or "European") standards from being eroded by competition from Africans and other nonwhites with low standards of living. The cornerstone of this policy was the Wage Act of 1925. Passed in the name of preventing "sweat shops" and encouraging industrial efficiency, the Act set up a Wage Board that was empowered to establish wages in various nonunion jobs (unionized wages were already set at the national level). The wages the board concentrated upon were for those jobs in which whites faced competition from nonwhites (although the Act was amended in 1937 to cover jobs in which "Coloured" and "Asiatic" workers were facing competition from Africans).

By setting relatively high wages for the skilled trades in which whites were employed, incumbent white artisans were able to keep nonwhites out of these jobs while appearing to adhere to high-sounding principles and not obtrusively invoking the issue of color. One critic of South Africa's racial policies has argued that the "civilized labour policy" was built upon the economic reality that social background and inferior educational facilities, along with discrimination in apprenticeship programs, prevented nonwhites—Africans in particular—from attaining the skill levels of whites. Thus, the only hope nonwhites had of securing jobs held by whites was to offer their services in these occupations at lower wages. The "civilized labour policy" prevented this, thereby creating a barrier to the advancement of nonwhites and effectively lowering their wages by "crowding" them in noncovered jobs:

> When the standard wage-rate is forced above the free market level (whether through legal enactment or the strike threat), thereby reducing the output which can be produced profitably, it must have the effect of preventing the entry of subordinate races or classes into the protected field or of actually excluding them from it. This has been by far the most effective method of preserving white privileges, largely because it can be represented as nondiscriminatory.

SOURCE: W. H. Hutt, *The Economics of the Colour Bar* (London: Andre Deutsch Limited, 1964).

ment decreases, however, when one realizes that the *causation* might be *reversed*. Rather than more racism causing less unionization, it could be that more unionization causes race discrimination to diminish. Evidence on this point was mentioned in Chapter 12.

Like the orthodox theories of discrimination, then, the monopoly power theories can muster only weak empirical support. They also share with the orthodox theories problems of logical consistency or completeness. If discrimination is created or at least perpetuated by capitalists, how does one account for its existence in precapitalist or socialist societies? It may be true that if all white employers conspire to keep women and minorities in low-wage, low-status jobs, they can all reap monopoly profits. However, if employers A through Y adhere to the agreement, employer Z will always have incentives to *break* the agreement! Z can hire women or minorities cheaply because of the agreement among *other* employers not to hire them, and Z can enhance profits by hiring these otherwise equally productive workers to fill jobs that A through Y are staffing with high-priced white males. Since every other employer has the same incentives as Z, the conspiracy will tend to break down unless cheaters can be disciplined in some way. The dual labor market and power theorists do not tell us how the conspiracy is maintained and coordinated among the millions of U.S. employers. Thus their theories, like the orthodox ones, are less than completely satisfactory.

Evaluation of Discrimination Theories

Our analysis of the different theories of discrimination suggests that current labor market discrimination is the result of forces that hinder *competition* or labor market *adjustments* to competitive forces. Some theories—the "power" models—postulate the existence of noncompetitive or monopoly elements at the outset. The "orthodox" theories do not, but they have trouble explaining how current labor market discrimination can persist. The market should punish employers who discriminate or who fail to change their screening methods as the average characteristics of minorities or women change. A competitive market should drive employers to adopt *segregated* workplaces if employee discrimination exists; if customer discrimination exists, customers who discriminate will be punished by having to pay the higher prices associated with being served only by white males.

It would thus appear that all models of discrimination agree on one thing: any persistence of labor market discrimination is the result of forces or motivations that are blatantly noncompetitive or very slow to adjust to competitive forces. While no one model can be demonstrated to be superior to the others in explaining the facts, the various theories and the facts they seek to explain suggest that government intervention could be useful in eliminating the noncompetitive (or sluggish) influences.

STATE FAIR EMPLOYMENT PRACTICE LEGISLATION

Since the 1930s, about 30 states have enacted *fair employment practice laws* prohibiting discrimination in employment on the basis of race, creed, color, or national origin. (Unlike the federal legislation discussed below, the state laws did not address employment discrimination by gender.) These state laws normally established enforcement commissions and provided for fines and/or imprisonment for violators of the law.

Under state fair employment practice legislation, it is normally illegal for an organization to do at least one of the following: refuse employment or discharge employees because of race, or discriminate in compensation or other terms of employment by race. Our discussion of theories of market discrimination earlier in the chapter suggests that if a law contains only one of these provisions, it is likely to be ineffective in reducing labor market discrimination. That analysis predicted that even prejudiced employers would hire minority workers if they could be "compensated" by paying minorities less than their marginal product. Therefore, a state law that does not address discrimination in compensation permits prejudiced employers to comply with the law by hiring minorities but paying them less than other workers of comparable quality. On the other hand, an equal-pay-for-equal-work law that only forbids wage discrimination is likely to reduce the relative employment of minorities (and either increase their relative unemployment or reduce their rate of labor force participation) unless it is accompanied by a requirement forbidding employment discrimination, since prejudiced employers will be less willing to hire minorities if they are unable to practice wage discrimination. With sufficient enforcement, laws that forbid both employment and wage discrimination may reduce discrimination in the labor market by raising the cost of such actions to violators.

How effective have state fair employment practice laws been in reducing discrimination? Some studies have found that, after accounting for differences in human capital between whites and nonwhites, the relative wages and occupational positions of nonwhites are higher in states with fair employment practice laws than in states that have not passed such laws. However, such findings raise a basic question of causality when they do not consider the way legislation is established. Fair employment practice laws are passed by the vote of legislators, who must represent the preferences of their constituencies to remain in office. When we find that the relative earnings of minorities are higher in states with fair employment practice laws, does that represent the impact of the law or a tendency of such laws to be passed in states where prejudice is relatively low (reflected in part by the higher relative wages received by minorities)? There is some evidence that it represents the latter. Indeed, the existence of state fair employment practice legislation appears to have little or no effect on racial earnings differentials, once independent measures of prejudice and the extent of unionization in a state are controlled for. (A measure of prejudice independent of earnings differentials is clearly needed to sort out the issue of causation; one measure used is electoral support for political candidates who are known to oppose civil rights or equal opportunity legislation. Unions have been shown to increase the relative earnings of minorities, and because fair employment laws tend to be found in states with above-average levels of unionization, studies attempting to find the separate effects of fair employment practice laws must filter out the effects of unions on earnings differentials.)[44]

FEDERAL PROGRAMS TO END DISCRIMINATION

The federal government has enforced two sets of rules in an attempt to eliminate market discrimination. One is a *nondiscrimination* requirement imposed on almost all employers. The other is a requirement that federal contractors engage in *affirmative action* — that is, actively seek out minorities and women to staff their vacancies.

Equal Pay Act of 1963

Over the years prior to the 1960s, sex discrimination was officially sanctioned by so-called *protective labor laws,* which limited women's total hours of work and prohibited them from working at night, lifting heavy objects, and working during pregnancy. Not all states placed all these restrictions on women, but the effect of these laws was to limit the access of women to many jobs. These laws were overturned by the Equal Pay Act of 1963, which also outlawed separate pay scales for men and women using similar skills and performing work under the same conditions.

The act was seriously deficient as an antidiscrimination tool, however, because it said nothing about equal opportunity in hiring and promotions. This flaw can be easily understood by a quick review of our theories of discrimination. If there is prejudice against women from whatever source, employers will treat female employees as if they were less productive or more costly to hire than equally productive males. The market response is for female wages to fall below male wages, because otherwise women cannot hope to be able to successfully compete with men in obtaining jobs. The Equal Pay Act took a step toward the elimination of wage differentials, but by so doing it tended to suppress a market mechanism that helped women obtain greater access to jobs.[45] The act failed to acknowledge that if labor market discrimination is to be eliminated, legislation must require *both* equal pay *and* equal opportunities in hiring and promotions for people of comparable productivity.

Title VII of the Civil Rights Act

Some defects in the Equal Pay Act of 1963 were corrected the next year. Title VII of the Civil Rights Act of 1964 made it unlawful for any employer "to refuse to hire or to discharge any individual, or otherwise to discriminate against any individual with respect to his compensation, terms, condition, or privileges of employment, because of such individual's race, color, religion, sex or national origin." Union practices were also addressed by the new legislation. Historically, it had been very difficult for racial minorities to obtain

---

44. See William M. Landes, "The Economics of Fair Employment Laws," *Journal of Political Economy* 76 (August 1968): 507–52.
45. Some critics of the Equal Pay Act of 1963 argued that its motivation was to help men compete with lower-paid women. See Nancy Barrett, "Women in the Job Market: Occupations, Earnings, and Career Opportunities," in *The Subtle Revolution,* ed. Ralph E. Smith (Washington, D.C.: The Urban Institute, 1979), 55.

admission into certain craft unions representing workers in the skilled trades—an exclusion that denied minorities access to both the skills training provided through union apprenticeship programs and the employment opportunities dispensed through union hiring halls. Unions representing workers in large industries were generally more integrated, although in a few unions the quality of representation in collective bargaining and in the administration of the labor agreement varied by race. Title VII made it unlawful for any labor organization to exclude individuals from membership, to segregate membership, to refuse to refer for employment, or to discriminate in admission to apprenticeship programs on the basis of race, color, religion, sex, or national origin.

This broad statement of a national policy favoring nondiscriminatory employment practices was qualified in certain respects, however. First, Title VII was not retroactive; it was written to apply to acts of discrimination occurring after its effective date of July 1, 1965. Second, the law permits exceptions to its general requirement of nondiscrimination "where religion, sex, or national origin is a bona fide occupational qualification reasonably necessary to the normal operation of a business." In practice this applies to a limited number of situations (for example, certain jobs in religious organizations, nursing homes in which the patients are of predominantly one sex, etc.). Third, Title VII permits an employer to differentiate wages and other employment conditions "pursuant to a bona fide seniority system...provided that such differences are not the result of an intention to discriminate." Finally, no party subject to the statute is required to grant preferential treatment to any group because of existing imbalances in the work force. As will become clear below, the last two qualifications have raised difficult issues for the application of the law.

Title VII applies to all employers in interstate commerce with at least 25 employees and is enforced by the Equal Employment Opportunity Commission (EEOC), which has the authority to mediate complaints, encourage lawsuits by private parties or the U.S. Attorney General, or (since 1972) bring suits itself against employers that have violated the law. In order to expand the impact of the law, the courts permitted individual plaintiffs to expand their suits into "class actions" in which the potential discriminatory impact of an organization's employment practices on an entire group of workers is assessed by the courts.

Over the years, the federal courts have fashioned two standards of discrimination that may be applied when discriminatory employment practices are alleged—*disparate treatment* and *disparate impact.* Disparate treatment occurs under Title VII if individuals are treated differently (for example, paid different wages or benefits) because of their race, sex, color, religion, or national origin, and if it can be shown that there was an intent to discriminate. While this is probably the more obvious approach to defining discrimination, it is not the definition that the courts have relied on most frequently. The difficulty raised by this standard is that personnel policies that appear to be neutral in the sense that they ignore race, gender, etc., may nevertheless perpetuate the effects of past discrimination. For example, word-of-mouth recruiting (a seemingly neutral policy) in a plant with a largely white work force would be suspect under Title VII even if the selection of new employees from among the applicants was done on a nondiscriminatory basis, since the racial composition of the applicants is likely to be influenced by the recruiting method.

The concern with addressing the present effects of past discrimination led to the "disparate impact" standard. Under this approach it is the result, not the motivation, that matters. Personnel policies that appear to be neutral but lead to different impacts by race, gender, etc., are prohibited under Title VII unless they can be related to job performance.[46] For example, employers may use tests and educational standards to screen applicants, but these tests must be validated against job performance. In the words of the Supreme Court, "Tests must measure the person for the job; not the person in the abstract." Job application forms may ask about *convictions* but not *arrests* (arrest rates among minorities tend to be higher, but the courts reason that it is conviction that is important to the employer). Marital status cannot be used as a screening device unless it is applied uniformly to both sexes and is clearly a job-related requirement. In interpreting Title VII, the federal courts have generally taken the position that neutral (for example, colorblind or sexblind) personnel practices that carry forward the effects of past discrimination constitute present discrimination. As a result, plaintiffs, employers, and the courts have become interested in how closely the race or gender composition of groups selected for employment, promotion, training, or termination accords with the race or gender composition of the pool of workers available for selection.

The adoption of the disparate impact standard by the courts as a standard of discrimination has mounted a significant challenge to employer personnel screening devices. As noted in Chapter 5, when it is extremely costly to ascertain the qualifications of individual applicants, employers have an incentive to rely on screening devices that sort job applicants on the basis of the "average" characteristics of a group, rather than according to individual merit. While the use of screening devices often results in lower costs of personnel administration, it also gives rise to the statistical discrimination discussed earlier in this chapter. In taking the position that workers must be judged on the basis of their individual abilities, rather than average group characteristics, the courts have launched a strong assault against mechanisms of statistical discrimination, and one consequence of this assault has been higher private costs of human resource management.[47]

---

46. *Willie S. Griggs* v. *Duke Power Company* 401 U.S. 424 (1971). In *Wards Cove* v. *Atonio* 109 S.Ct. 2115 (1989), the Court held that an employer using recruiting, selection, or promotion procedures that generate disparate impact must provide a plausible explanation of how they relate to job performance. However, if there is a question whether the procedures serve "legitimate employment goals," the burden is now on the *plaintiff* (the employee) to persuade the judge that the goals are *not* legitimate. (The Civil Rights Act of 1990, if enacted as originally proposed, would shift the burden of proof back to the employer.)

47. One must be careful to distinguish here between the costs to employers (*private* costs) and the costs to society (*social* costs) of statistical discrimination. Although employers' private costs for human resource management may be low because of statistical discrimination, the costs to society may be high if qualified applicants are rejected simply because of the group they are members of. While prohibiting statistical discrimination may increase the private costs of human resource management, it may decrease the social costs.

In certain instances, the application of the disparate impact standard and other efforts to combat labor market discrimination have been limited by some of the express qualifications written into Title VII. In recent years two particularly difficult issues have arisen in the application of the law: the treatment of seniority arrangements perpetuating the effects of past discrimination and the adoption of a "comparable worth" standard by which to judge pay equality when occupations are segregated.

Seniority.   Most unionized firms and many nonunion firms use seniority as a consideration in allocating promotion opportunities. Moreover, employees are frequently laid off in order of reverse seniority, the least senior first, in a recession. It was partially in recognition of the historically important role of seniority in American personnel arrangements that Congress appeared to exempt seniority systems from challenge under Title VII. Yet seniority systems have the strong potential for perpetuating the effects of past discrimination. We have seen how occupational segregation—the tendency of women or minorities to be restricted to relatively low-wage jobs despite qualifications for higher positions—has been one historical mechanism of discrimination in the labor market.

In many instances, particularly in the South, job segregation was accompanied by departmental seniority arrangements. That is, seniority was computed as time employed in a department, not as time employed in the plant or company. When companies sought to break down historical patterns of job segregation to comply with Title VII, two types of adjustment occurred: women and minorities were moved within a company from low-wage jobs to higher-wage jobs in other departments, and women and minorities were hired by companies into some jobs for the first time. Under either mechanism, women and minorities ended up with relatively low seniority under departmental seniority systems.

Many of these adjustments occurred during the late 1960s, when the general demand for labor was high. With the less favorable economic circumstances of the 1970s, however, firms began to lay off workers, and under departmental seniority arrangements a disproportionate number of those laid off were minorities and women. In many of these cases, individuals with very little departmental seniority had more *plant* seniority than workers who retained their jobs in the high-wage departments, and they might have been able to retain their jobs if they had the seniority that they had accrued in their former departments. Departmental seniority arrangements resulted in a disparate impact on women and minorities and perpetuated the effects of past discrimination. The resulting Title VII litigation presented the courts with a quandary. Under the disparate impact standard, the seniority systems were discriminatory, but the language of Title VII explicitly permitted "bona fide seniority systems." The lower courts tended to resolve the quandary by taking the position that a seniority system was not "bona fide" if it discriminated, and that under the prevailing definition of discrimination, only plant-wide seniority systems were "bona fide." When the Supreme Court considered the issue, however, it reversed the appellate courts and held that the language in

Title VII permitted even departmental seniority systems that perpetuated the effects of discrimination.[48]

Minorities and women who were hired for the first time following passage of Title VII were susceptible to layoff under either plant or departmental seniority. Some were individuals who had been victims of hiring discrimination prior to the passage of the law or who did not apply for employment because the company had a reputation for discriminating. In litigation arising out of these cases, plaintiffs often argued that the appropriate remedy was an award of seniority retroactive to the date when the individual would have been hired if the company had not practiced discrimination. (This is sometimes referred to as "fictional seniority.") On this issue the Supreme Court has ruled that fictional seniority is an appropriate remedy for individuals who can demonstrate that they were victims of unlawful discrimination. However, the Supreme Court has argued that it is not appropriate to dismiss current employees as part of the remedy for past discrimination.[49] It has also ruled that laying off more senior white employees instead of more recently hired minorities in order to preserve racial balance is unconstitutional.[50]

Comparable Worth. We noted earlier in this chapter that women are disproportionately employed in certain jobs and occupations in which wages are relatively low. Some have argued that the wages in these jobs are low because they are filled to a large extent by women, who are the victims of market discrimination. To the extent that the labor market is biased against women, it is argued further that discrimination is perpetuated by using the market as a basis for paying, say, clerical workers (a job historically filled largely by women) less than, say, maintenance workers (a job historically filled largely by men). The remedy proposed is to pay women or minorities their "comparable worth"—that is, the intrinsic value of their jobs. However, the intrinsic value of a job would be established by comparison of its importance to some other (presumably more highly paid) job predominantly held by males, rather than by reference to market wages. (See the appendix to this chapter for more details on procedures for making these comparisons.)

How much of the wage difference between two jobs can be attributed to the fact that one is largely staffed by women and the other by men? The evidence reviewed earlier in this chapter indicates that a significant portion of the wage difference between men and women reflects differences in human capital investments and other qualifications. The amount of the difference that might be attributed to discrimination is likely to vary from job comparison to job comparison. Another important influence on wage differences between jobs was discussed in Chapter 8—nonpecuniary conditions of work. To the extent that working conditions vary substantially between jobs held predominantly by men and those held predominantly by women, one would ex-

---

48. *International Brotherhood of Teamsters* v. *United States* 431 U.S. 324, 14 FEP 1514 (1977).
49. *Franks* v. *Bowman Transportation* 424 U.S. 747, 12 FEP Cases 549 (1976), and *Fire Fighters Local 1784* v. *Stotts*, U.S. S.Ct, no. 82–206, June 12, 1984.
50. *Wygant* v. *Jackson Board of Education*, U.S. S.Ct, no. 84–1340, May 19, 1986.

pect the wages to vary as well. All these factors must be considered in estimating how much of the wage differential between "male" jobs and "female" jobs is the result of market discrimination. A further difficulty in trying to construct an operational approach to the proposed comparable worth remedy is evaluating the intrinsic worth of different job requirements or characteristics. Existing job evaluation procedures may not be free of bias in the weights they assign to these characteristics.[51]

In addition to the operational difficulties with the comparable worth concept, the concept raises several fundamental policy questions. For example, is it likely to be more effective to use the law to break down occupational barriers caused by discriminatory job segregation or to develop a compensation scheme (via comparable worth) that may leave job segregation unchanged? Will raising the wage rates of traditional "female" occupations reduce women's incentives to seek occupational advancement? Will raising women's wages have an adverse effect on female employment levels?[52] Answers to these questions will be important components of any complete evaluation of comparable worth.

As yet, the major push for comparable worth has come not in the private sector, but rather in state and local government. A number of state and local governments have conducted, or are in the process of conducting, formal job evaluation surveys to see if "female" occupations are "underpaid"; the appendix to this chapter illustrates in a simplified fashion how this is done. Other state or local governments have begun to implement comparable worth salary adjustments through the collective bargaining process.[53]

---

51. See Donald J. Treiman and Heidi L. Hartmann, eds., *Women, Work and Wages: Equal Pay for Jobs of Equal Value* (Washington, D.C.: National Academy Press, 1981). For a more recent discussion of comparable worth that spans a variety of disciplines, and both proponents and opponents, see M. Anne Hill and Mark R. Killingsworth, eds., *Comparable Worth: Analyses and Evidence* (Ithaca, N.Y.: ILR Press, 1989); Robert T. Michael, Heidi L. Hartmann, and Brigid O'Farrell, eds., *Pay Equity: Empirical Inquiries* (Washington, D.C.: National Academy Press, 1989); and Mark R. Killingsworth, *The Economics of Comparable Worth* (Kalamazoo, Mich.: W. E. Upjohn Institute for Employment Research, 1990).

52. In general, increasing the wage rate for a group should lead to a decline in the group's employment. The one exception to this rule is if employers behave as monopsonists; we showed in the context of our discussion of the minimum wage (Chapter 3) that in this situation one could set a minimum wage above the current wage (within a certain range) without suffering any employment losses. A number of studies cited in Chapter 3 also suggest that registered nurses and public school teachers, both traditionally female occupations, have their wages depressed because their employers have some monopsony power. For these groups, at least, comparable worth wage adjustments might not lead to employment losses. Empirical evidence that the effects on female employment of comparable worth wage adjustments in the state and local government sector are likely to be small are presented in Ronald G. Ehrenberg and Robert S. Smith, "Comparable Worth Wage Adjustments and Female Employment in the State and Local Sector," *Journal of Labor Economics* 5 (January 1987): 43–62.

53. See Ronald G. Ehrenberg and Robert S. Smith, "Comparable Worth in the Public Sector," in *Public Compensation,* ed. David Wise (Chicago: University of Chicago Press, 1987). Ronald G. Ehrenberg, "Empirical Consequences of Comparable Worth," in *Comparable Worth: Analyses and Evidence,* ed. Hill and Killingsworth, and Mark R. Killingsworth, *The Economics of Comparable Worth,* summarize what empirical studies have found these adjustment effects on women's wages and employment levels to be.

EXAMPLE 14.3

Comparable Worth and the University

Some of the difficulties involved with the concept of *comparable worth* can be illustrated by an example in which gender does not even enter. Consider the labor market for university professors in the fields of computer science and English, and suppose that initially the demand and supply curves for both are given by D_{0C} and S_{0C}, and D_{0E} and S_{0E}, respectively. As the figure indicates, in this circumstance the same wage (W_0) will prevail in both markets, and N_{0C} computer science professors and N_{0E} English professors will be hired. Suppose also that in some objective sense the quality of the two groups of professors is equal.

Presumably this is a situation that advocates of comparable worth would applaud. Both types of professors require the same amount of training, represented by a Ph.D., and both are required to engage in the same activities, teaching and research. Unless one is willing to assign different values to the teaching and research produced in different academic fields, one must conclude that the jobs are truly comparable. Hence, if the two groups are equal in quality, equal wages would be justified according to the concept of comparable worth.

Suppose now, however, that the demand for computer science professors rises to D_{1C} as a result of the increasing numbers of students who want to take computer science courses. Suppose at the same time the demand for English professors falls to D_{1E} because fewer students want to take elective courses in English. At the old equilibrium wage rate there is now an excess demand for computer science professors of $N_{1C} - N_{0C}$ and an excess supply of English professors of $N_{0E} - N_{1E}$.

How can universities respond? One possibility is to let the market work; the wage of computer science professors will rise to W_{1C} and that of English professors will fall to W_{1E}. Employment of the former will rise to N_{2C} while employment of the latter will become N_{2E}.

Another possibility is to keep the wages of the two groups of professors equal at the old wage rate of W_0. Universities could respond to the excess demand for computer scientists and the excess supply of English professors by lowering hiring standards for the former and raising them for the latter. Since the average quality of English professors would then exceed the average quality of computer scientists, the wage paid per "quality-unit" would now be higher for the computer scientists. Hence, true comparable worth—equal pay for *equal-quality* workers performing comparable jobs—would not be achieved. Moreover, employment and course offerings in this situation would not change to meet changing student demands.

Alternatively, some advocates of comparable worth might argue that universities should respond by raising the wages of *all* professors to W_{1C}. While this would eliminate the shortage of computer science professors, it would exacerbate the excess supply of English professors, raising it to $N_{4E} - N_{3E}$. Universities would respond by drastically reducing the employment of English professors even further to N_{3E} (and reducing course offerings). Moreover, the excess supply again would permit universities to raise hiring

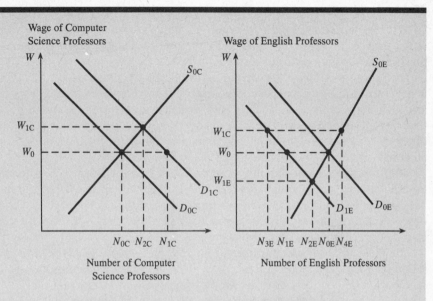

The Market for Computer Science and English Professors

standards for English professors, so again average quality would rise. As a result, once more the wage per quality-unit of English professors would be less than that of computer science professors, and again true comparable worth would not be achieved.

The message one takes away from this example is that it is difficult to "trick the market." In the face of changing relative demand conditions, either wage differentials for the two types of professors must be allowed to arise or quality differentials will arise. In neither case, however, can comparable worth be achieved. Put another way, the value of a job cannot be determined independently of market conditions.

How have universities actually responded to the changing relative demand conditions for faculty in the fields portrayed in this example? Some evidence can be found from data on faculty salaries, by academic field, obtained each year from a survey of public universities and colleges conducted by Oklahoma State University. In the academic year 1976–77 respondents reported average salaries for new assistant professors of $15,526 in computer science and $13,321 in English and literature. By 1988–89, average starting salaries of the former had risen by 156 percent to $39,746, while those for the latter had risen only 93 percent to $25,773. As a result, while the typical new assistant professor in English and literature earned 85.8 percent of what the average new assistant professor in computer science earned in 1976–77, he or she earned only 64.8 percent by 1988–89. Relative starting salaries of assistant professors in academia did adjust quite rapidly, then, to changing relative demand conditions.

SOURCE: Data are from W. Lee Hansen, "Changing Faculty Salaries," in *American Professors*, ed. H. Bowen and J. Schuster (New York: Oxford University Press, 1986), Table 6.10, and Hirschel Kasper, "High Education Goals: Low Salary Increases," *Academe* 75 (March–April 1989), Table III.

The Federal Contract Compliance Program

In 1965 the Office of Federal Contract Compliance Programs (OFCCP) was established to monitor the hiring and promotion practices of federal contractors (firms supplying goods or services to the federal government). OFCCP requires contractors above a certain size to analyze the extent of their underutilization of women and minorities and to propose a plan to remedy any such underutilization. Such a plan is called an *affirmative action plan*. Contractors submitting unacceptable plans or failing to meet their goals are threatened with cancellation of their contracts and their eligibility for future contracts, although these drastic steps are rarely taken.

Affirmative action planning is intended to commit firms to a schedule for rapidly overcoming unequal career opportunities afforded women and minorities. Such planning affects both *hiring* and *promotion* practices, but it also raises numerous philosophical and practical questions that tend to make the planning process highly controversial.

Suppose an insurance company is attempting to construct an affirmative action plan with regard to secretaries. Its first step in setting hiring goals is to decide what number of minorities are "available" and what fraction they constitute of all available workers. If blacks, say, constitute 9 percent of the labor supply available to the firm, then it might seem to be a simple matter of setting a goal of 9 percent. However, the planner must resolve some serious questions.

First, should the pool of black secretaries be estimated based on the firm's *actual applicant* pool? The answer is probably no, since any discriminatory practices in the past will discourage black applicants currently. Further, affirmative action planning is intended to force companies to *change* their hiring practices. On the other hand, as was pointed out in Chapter 8, a firm's location within a city can attract more or fewer black applicants, depending on how far from the firm blacks live and the level of compensation offered. Moreover, as we saw in Chapter 11, the mix of employee benefits in the total compensation package can alter the attractiveness of an employer to women, the young, and the poor.[54] Thus, to some extent the *potential* pool of *interested* applicants is a legitimate consideration.

Should the potential pool be estimated from the fraction of all *trained secretaries* in the area who are black? If we are interested in eradicating *market* discrimination, this may be the logical measure, since it would force firms to hire black secretaries in the same proportion as they are found in the labor market. However, years of discrimination may have induced blacks to avoid training for this occupation, with the result that blacks may be substantially underrepresented in the secretarial labor market.

Should firms then be compelled to hire black secretaries in proportion to their numbers in the adult *population* of the city at large? This goal implicitly sets out to eliminate all discrimination, both market and premarket, but if blacks are underrepresented in the occupation, the attainment of this goal is impractical in the short run. Firms attempting to hire more black secretaries

54. For a review of the economic factors affecting "availability," see Ronald Ehrenberg and Robert Smith, "Economic and Statistical Analysis of Discrimination in Hiring," *Proceedings of the Thirty-Sixth Annual Meeting of the Industrial Relations Research Association* (Madison, Wis.: Industrial Relations Research Association, 1984).

than are available would have two choices. They could hire black high school graduates and train them in secretarial skills. Remember, however, that such training is *general* in nature, so the firms would not offer it unless the workers involved paid for it in some way. Without training as an option, firms would simply try to bid against each other for the services of existing black secretaries, which would drive up their wages. The higher wage rates would induce more blacks to seek secretarial training, and their underrepresentation in the occupation would disappear in the long run.

While population-based goals would appear to fight both kinds of discrimination, they might in fact fight neither. It stands to reason that if hiring goals are set beyond the immediate reach of firms, each will individually fail to meet them. Can the government reasonably punish firms for failing to hire beyond the numbers currently available? If it cannot, then failure to meet goals will not result in punishment, which seems to remove the incentive for firms to take energetic steps to integrate their work forces.

A final issue in hiring has to do with how the goals are applied. If black secretaries, to continue our example, are 9 percent of the available pool, does that mean that 9 percent of all *newly hired* secretaries should be black? This goal might seem reasonable from a firm's point of view, but if labor turnover is low it would take a very long time for the 9 percent of *new hires* to accumulate to the point where blacks were 9 percent of the firm's total secretarial work force. Since the Civil Rights Act of 1964 prohibits workers of one race from being fired to make room for those of another, getting rid of employment imbalances must occur through new hiring. However, only if aggrieved groups are *favored* in hiring can the effects of past discrimination be eradicated quickly.

Favoritism in hiring not only raises the issue of *reverse discrimination,* wherein whites or males can assert they are being discriminated against because of race or sex, but also raises the issue of how firms, as a whole, can hire women or blacks in proportions greater than their current availability. The courts have yet to resolve the considerable tension between Title VII's standard of nondiscrimination, which protects all groups from disparate treatment, and the OFCCP's standard of affirmative action.

It is testimony to the difficulty of these questions about affirmative action planning that the government's requirements for calculating "availability" are rather vague. The OFCCP has proposed that, for purposes of affirmative action planning, federal contractors compute availability of minorities and women using either of two methods: the "civilian labor force" method or the "four-factor" method.[55] Under the former alternative, availability is estimated from the percentages of women and minorities in the *metropolitan area*'s civilian labor force. The "four-factor" alternative would require the contractor to devise estimates by taking into account the following considerations:

1. The percentage of minorities and women in the civilian labor force in the *immediate labor area* (defined as the geographic area

55. Bureau of National Affairs, Labor Relations Reporter, *Fair Employment Practices Manual* 401:5005. OFCCP's proposal is a revision of its 1974 guidelines for federal contractors, under which eight factors were considered. As of this writing the revised guidelines have not yet been implemented.

> from which employees and applicants may reasonably commute to the establishment);
> 2. The percentage of minorities and women with requisite skills in the *immediate labor area;*
> 3. The percentage of minorities and women with requisite skills in the *relevant recruitment area* (defined as the geographic area from which the contractor may reasonably recruit its employees, including areas not contiguous to the immediate labor area); and
> 4. The percentage of minorities and women among those promotable or transferable within the contractor's organization.

Contractors can assign weights of their own choosing (including weights of zero) to each of the four factors, as long as the weights are justified in writing and sum to 100 percent.

A brief analysis of the above requirements will show that they raise several questions. First, the civilian labor force method differs from factor 1 of the "four-factor" method in the definition of geographic area over which to calculate populations. Which is the less arbitrary definition for availability purposes: the metropolitan area or the "immediate labor area" (which may be larger or smaller than the metropolitan area)? Also, given the various costs of commuting discussed at the end of Chapter 8, should everyone in the defined area be assumed equally "available" for work at a given plant?

Second, factors 1 and 2 under the "four-factor" alternative differ in the attention given to *existing* skills, raising the issue discussed above concerning the goals of the contract compliance program. Is the aim of the program to eliminate only current *market* discrimination against those already in a given skill group, or should it directly address the issue of *premarket* differences in skill acquisition among race or sex groups?

Third, factor 3 is intended to apply to firms hiring in occupations that have regional or national labor markets. However, if contractors are required, as a matter of course, to adopt nontraditional hiring practices that are likely to yield more female or minority applicants, is it unreasonable to expect them to recruit regionally or even nationally for workers they normally recruit locally?

Finally, several questions can be raised about factor 4. If few minorities or women are at the office-manager rank in an organization, is the firm obliged to offer special managerial training courses for them? Should such training be equally available to interested white males? What if the interest in managerial positions varies by race or sex? Are companies supposed to promote on a nondiscriminatory basis, with the result that imbalances in its *higher*-level jobs will remain for years into the future? Instead, must employers hurry women and blacks along the promotional ladder faster than normal so that these higher-level imbalances will go away more quickly? These are the dilemmas inherent in the government's contract compliance program.

Effectiveness of Federal Antidiscrimination Programs

A question of obvious interest is just how effective the two federal antidiscrimination programs have been in increasing the relative earnings of minorities and women. The question is not easy to answer, however, because we

EXAMPLE 14.4

How Fast Can Discrimination Be Eradicated?

To illustrate the possible rate of progress in minority employment within a firm, let us take a numerical example. Suppose there is a job group that contains 1,600 employees, 100 (6.25 percent) of whom are black. Suppose, further, that this is an entry-level job group (so that all replacements come from new hires) and that the yearly turnover rate is 20 percent. Finally, assume that blacks represent 12 percent of the firm's available labor pool for this job.

The firm in question must hire 320 new workers for this job group each year. If 12 percent (about 38) of those hired each year are black, how long will it take before 12 percent (192) of the 1,600-person work group is black? Another, perhaps more significant, question is: How fast will the racial composition of the work group change? These questions have no obvious answers, because if blacks and whites have the same turnover rate (of 20 percent), the organization is both losing and hiring blacks each year.

One way to answer the above questions is to simulate employee turnover each year. The accompanying table shows that in the first year 20 blacks quit and 38 (12 percent of the 320 new hires) are hired. The net gain in blacks raises their level of employment in the group to 118 and their percentage of employment to 7.37 (from 6.25). In year 2, 38 blacks are again hired and about 24 quit, representing a net gain of 14, and by the end of the year the work group is 8.25 percent black. As this process continues, there are net additions to the black component of the work force each year, but these additions get smaller and smaller.

Of special interest in this example is the fact that it takes about 10 years of *nondiscriminatory hiring* for the percentage of blacks in the work group to get close to the goal of 12 percent. (The rate of progress would be approximately cut in half if the turnover rate were 10 percent instead of 20 percent.) Thus, if the proportion of blacks among new hires is equal to their proportion in the available labor pool and if their turnover rates are no lower than those of whites, the long-run goal of employment equality will take many years to achieve once nondiscriminatory hiring is begun. This mathematical fact illustrates why those charged with administering antidiscrimination programs are simultaneously besieged by shouts of frustration and calls for patience.

Change in the Racial Composition of a 1,600-Person Job Group (20% Yearly Turnover Rate)

		Year					
	0	1	2	3	4	5	10
Number of blacks							
Loss		20	24	26	29	31	36
New hires		38	38	38	38	38	38
Net gain		18	14	12	11	7	2
Cumulative level	100	118	132	144	155	162	181
Percent black	6.25	7.37	8.25	9.00	9.69	10.12	11.31

must make some guesses as to what earnings differentials *would have been* in the absence of these programs.

As we have seen, the ratio of black to white incomes has risen since 1960 (see Table 14.2), especially in the mid-1970s. Has this rise in the ratio been a result of government efforts, or have other forces been working to accomplish this result? Three other forces are commonly cited. First, an improvement in the *educational attainment* of black workers relative to that of whites during this period is thought to have played an important role in raising the ratio of black to white income. Second, the evidence that the *quality* of schooling received by blacks improved from 1960 to 1970 more than it did for whites lends further impetus to the increase in relative earnings.[56] Finally, blacks have historically experienced relative gains in periods of low unemployment and suffered disproportionately in periods of economic distress. The late 1960s were a period of very full employment, which could have helped increase the black/white earnings ratio from 1960 to 1970. However, general business conditions in the 1970s and 1980s were not as good as in the late 1960s, so improvements then are unlikely to have been solely the result of overall business conditions.

Two types of studies have attempted to distinguish the effects of the government programs from the other factors that affect relative earnings: time-series studies and analyses of federal contractors.

Time-Series Studies. There seems to have been a significant upturn in the black/white earnings ratio after the EEOC was created in 1964—an upturn that was independent of both the effects of *educational* gains by blacks and changes in the *unemployment rate*.[57] However, it also appears that the labor force participation rate of blacks fell relative to that of whites after 1964, a year in which many income maintenance programs began to become more generous.[58] If, as seems likely, the blacks with the lowest wages were the ones who left the labor market, their exit would increase the average wage paid to blacks and give the *appearance* of improvement. Some—probably less than half—of the post-1964 improvement is due to this latter factor.[59] Thus, there seems to be at least *some* evidence that post-1964 government efforts to lessen discrimination helped blacks.

Analysis of Federal Contractors. If the contract compliance program administered by OFCCP is effective, we should observe that the economic status of

---

56. Smith and Welch, "Black Economic Progress After Myrdal."
57. See Richard Freeman, "Changes in the Labor Market for Black Americans," *Brookings Papers* (1973): 67–120, and Richard Butler and James Heckman, "The Government's Impact on the Labor Market Status of Black Americans: A Critical Review," *Equal Rights and Industrial Relations* (Madison, Wis.: Industrial Relations Research Association, 1977), 235–80.
58. Butler and Heckman, "The Government's Impact on the Labor Market Status of Black Americans."
59. Charles Brown, "The Federal Attack on Labor Market Discrimination: The Mouse That Roared?" in *Research in Labor Economics,* vol. 5 (1982), ed. Ronald Ehrenberg, 32–68. Evidence that Title VII lawsuits have played a significant role in increasing black employment is found in Jonathan S. Leonard, "Antidiscrimination or Reverse Discrimination: The Impact of Changing Demographics, Title VII, and Affirmative Action on Productivity," *Journal of Human Resources* 19 (Spring 1984): 145–74.

blacks improves faster among federal contractors than noncontractors. Several studies have tested this hypothesis, and some have even distinguished whether or not the contractors involved had been subjected to a compliance review by the government (the government does not have the resources to inspect the affirmative action plans of *all* its contractors). The results suggest that blacks and other minorities have made faster gains in contractor firms.[60]

One problem in assessing the *overall* effects of OFCCP, however, is that because the contract compliance program relates only to *some* employers (contractors), the gains in (say) black employment among these firms may come at the expense of losses among noncontractors. Eligible blacks may just be bid away from noncontractors, although it should be pointed out that anyone successfully bid away from a former employer must have experienced an expected gain in utility. Perhaps more serious is the problem that becoming or remaining a federal contractor is a voluntary decision. Firms that perceive the costs of affirmative action to be high may simply choose not to be contractors. The contract compliance program may end up concentrating its efforts on the firms within which discrimination is a relatively small problem.

A final reason to temper optimism about the government's efforts to end discrimination is that it appears that the gains of white women have not matched those of blacks among contractors.[61] The growth of white female employment relative to total employment was slower among federal contractors than among noncontractors in the early 1970s, before women were a focus of the contract compliance program; but between 1974 and 1980 the growth of white female employment among contractors was significantly greater (although smaller than the gains for blacks). Why the gains among white women are smaller has not yet been convincingly explained; however, there is other evidence that women have been helped by the contract compliance program. One study, for example, looked at *quit rates,* rather than wages or employment ratios, as an index of perceived well-being. What it found (for 1978–79) was that, in industries in which federal contracts comprised a larger fraction of total sales and the OFCCP had initiated more compliance reviews, women had lower quit rates than would be expected, given their wages and other factors affecting quits.[62] The inference is that women in these industries perceived themselves to be better off than women elsewhere.

In summary, it appears that some of the gains registered by blacks since 1964 may be due to efforts by the EEOC and OFCCP, but the effects of these programs on women appear mixed. Effects on other minorities have not been extensively studied.

---

60. For a comprehensive review of these studies, see Jonathan Leonard, "The Effectiveness of Equal Employment Law and Affirmative Action Regulation," in *Research in Labor Economics,* vol. 8, pt. B (1986), ed. Ronald Ehrenberg.

61. Jonathan S. Leonard, "Women and Affirmative Action," *Journal of Economic Perspectives* 3 (Winter 1989): 61–75, and Gunderson, "Male–Female Wage Differentials and Policy Responses."

62. Paul Osterman, "Affirmative Action and Opportunity: A Study of Female Quit Rates," *Review of Economics and Statistics* 64 (November 1982): 604–12. Corroborating evidence is found in Andrea Beller, "The Impact of Equal Opportunity Policy on Sex Differentials in Earnings and Occupations," *American Economic Review Papers and Proceedings* 72 (May 1982): 171–75.

MISCONCEPTION

"A subsidy to firms that hire disadvantaged minorities will be less effective in promoting minority employment if employers are prejudiced."

Analysis

An increase in minority employment is stimulated by employer subsidies if more are hired than *otherwise* would have been hired in the subsidy's absence. The intent of a new subsidy would be to induce *changes,* whatever the levels from which one starts. The presence of discrimination will affect the *level* of pre-subsidy employment, but it does not follow that prejudiced employers' *changes* in hiring would be any less responsive to a subsidy than would be their induced changes in the absence of discrimination.

Principle

People with a stable set of preferences can be induced to change their behavior if their command over resources and/or the prices they face change.

REVIEW QUESTIONS

1. Assume that women live longer than men, on the average. Suppose an employer hires men and women, pays them the same wage for the same job, and contributes an equal amount per person toward a pension. However, the promised monthly pension after retirement is smaller for women than for men because the pension funds for them have to last longer. According to the *Manhart* decision by the Supreme Court, the above employer would be guilty of discrimination because of the unequal monthly pension benefits after retirement.
   a. Comment on the Court's implicit definition of discrimination. Is it consistent with the definition normally used by economists? Why or why not?
   b. Analyze the economic effects of this decision on men and women.
2. Assume there is a central city school district in which the student population is predominantly black. Surrounding the central city are predominantly white suburban school districts. Together, the central city and suburban school districts can be thought of as a local labor market for teachers. Other things being equal, black teachers in this labor market are equally willing to work in central city and suburban schools, but white teachers prefer suburban schools and are reluctant to accept jobs in the central city. There are too few black teachers to completely staff central city schools, and teachers generally have choices in the jobs they can accept.
   If federal law requires equal salaries for teachers of all races *within* a given school district but allows salaries to vary across school districts, will black teachers earn more, less, or the same salary as they would if white teachers were not prejudiced against black students? (Note: The prejudice of white teachers extends only to students, not to black teachers as co-workers. Note also: The chain of reasoning required in this answer should be made explicit in your answer.)
3. Suppose government antidiscrimination laws require employers to disregard marital status and gender in screening and hiring workers.
   a. Disregarding the employers who are engaged in discrimination, which employers will be most affected by this ruling?

    b. What alternatives do these employers have in coping with the problems created by this decision?

    c. What are the likely consequences of each alternative on employment levels and job stability among these employers?

4. Suppose the government has two methods of awarding contracts to firms. One is competitive, with the award going to the lowest bidder (who cannot then charge more than his or her bid). The other is noncompetitive, with the award going to a selected contractor who is reimbursed for actual costs incurred plus a certain percentage for profits. Suppose, too, that government contractors must hire a certain quota of minorities, many of whom require general training to be fully productive. Suppose also that federal legislation prevents the employer from shifting the costs of this general training to the minority employees. If you were an already-trained minority worker, which method of contract award would you prefer? Why?

5. The Defense Department is expanding its purchases of equipment from the private sector, and of course the firms with which it contracts must adhere to a policy of affirmative action (the hiring of minorities and women in increased proportions in the better jobs, and equal pay for equal work). The current administration is convinced that minorities and women in the firms with which the Defense Department (DOD) will now contract are subject to discrimination, but it is not sure whether the *source* of the discrimination is fellow *employees* or *customers*. It is interested in knowing how the enforcement of affirmative action regulations will affect the *unit labor costs* (the labor costs per unit of output) of the firms with which it deals. Will the *source* of discrimination make a difference to the administration's estimates of what happens to costs?

    (Answer this question assuming the only possible sources of discrimination are *employees* or *customers*. Also assume in answering the question that white males earn more than others of comparable quality, that discrimination may take place by confining women and minorities to low-wage jobs, and that prior efforts to eradicate discrimination in the industries with which DOD is dealing were entirely unsuccessful. Finally, assume that DOD will become the sole customer of the firms with which it contracts. Analyze the effects and consequences of the two types of discrimination, and then analyze what will happen to unit labor costs when DOD steps into the picture.)

6. You are involved in an investigation of charges that a large university in a small town is discriminating against female employees. You find that the salaries for professors in the nearly all-female School of Social Work are 20 percent below average salaries paid to those of comparable rank elsewhere in the university. Is this university exhibiting behavior associated with *employer* discrimination?

7. Suppose a city pays its building inspectors $12 an hour and its public health nurses $8 an hour. Assume that building inspectors are all male, that the nurses are all female, and that the wages paid to each occupation reflect the forces of supply and demand (which themselves may reflect discrimination in the labor market at large). Suppose that the city council passes a comparable worth law that in effect requires the wages of public health nurses to be equal to the wages of building inspectors. Evaluate the assertion that this comparable worth policy would primarily benefit high-quality nurses and low-quality building inspectors.

8. In the 1920s South Africa passed laws that effectively prohibited black Africans from working in jobs that required high degrees of skill; skilled jobs were reserved for whites. Analyze the consequences of this law for black and white South African workers.

9. Suppose that the United States were to adopt, on a permanent basis, a wage subsidy to be paid to employers who hire black, disadvantaged workers (those with rela-

tively little education and few marketable skills). Analyze the potential effectiveness of this subsidy in overcoming (*a*) current labor market discrimination against blacks, and (*b*) premarket differences between blacks and whites in the long run.

SELECTED READINGS

Aigner, Dennis J., and Cain, Glen G. "Statistical Theories of Discrimination in Labor Markets." *Industrial and Labor Relations Review* 30 (January 1977): 175–87.

Becker, Gary. *The Economics of Discrimination.* 2d ed. Chicago: University of Chicago Press, 1971.

Borjas, George, and Tienda, Mary, eds. *Hispanics in the U.S. Economy.* New York: Academic Press, 1985.

Cain, Glen G. "The Challenge of Segmented Labor Market Theories to Orthodox Theory: A Survey." *Journal of Economic Literature* 14 (December 1976): 1215–57.

Carlson, Leonard A., and Swartz, Caroline. "The Earnings of Women and Ethnic Minorities, 1959–79." *Industrial and Labor Relations Review* 41 (July 1988): 530–46.

Ehrenberg, Ronald, and Smith, Robert. "Economic and Statistical Analysis of Discrimination in Hiring." *Proceedings of the Thirty-Sixth Annual Meeting of the Industrial Relations Research Association.* Madison, Wis.: Industrial Relations Research Association, 1984.

Freeman, Richard. "Black Economic Progress After 1964: Who Has Gained and Why?" In *Studies in Labor Markets,* ed. Sherwin Rosen. Chicago: University of Chicago Press, 1981. Pp. 247–94.

Fuchs, Victor R. "Women's Quest for Economic Equality." *Journal of Economic Perspectives* 3 (Winter 1989): 25–41.

Gunderson, Morley. "Male–Female Wage Differentials and Policy Responses." *Journal of Economic Literature* 27 (March 1989): 46–72.

Hill, M. Anne, and Killingsworth, Mark R., eds. *Comparable Worth: Analysis and Evidence.* Ithaca, N.Y.: ILR Press, 1989.

Killingsworth, Mark R. *The Economics of Comparable Worth.* Kalamazoo, Mich.: W. E. Upjohn Institute for Employment Research, 1990.

Leonard, Jonathan. "The Effectiveness of Equal Employment Law and Affirmative Action Regulation." In *Research in Labor Economics,* vol. 8, pt. B, ed. Ronald Ehrenberg. Greenwich, Conn.: JAI Press, 1986.

Reich, Michael. "The Economics of Racism." In *Problems in Political Economy: An Urban Perspective,* ed. David M. Gordon. Lexington, Mass.: D. C. Heath, 1971. Pp. 107–13.

Smith, James P., and Welch, Finis R. "Black Economic Progress After Myrdal." *Journal of Economic Literature* 27 (June 1989): 519–64.

APPENDIX 14A

Estimating "Comparable Worth" Earnings Gaps: An Application of Regression Analysis

Although many economists have difficulty with the notion that the "worth" of a job can be established independently of market factors, formal job evaluation methods have existed for a long time. The state of Minnesota is one of the few states that have actually begun to implement "comparable worth" pay adjustments for their employees based on such an evaluation method. The purpose of this appendix is to give the reader an intuitive feel for how one might use data from job evaluations to estimate whether discriminatory wage differentials exist.[1]

Minnesota, in conjunction with Hay Associates, a prominent national compensation consulting company, began an evaluation of state government jobs in 1979. Initially evaluated were 188 positions in which at least 10 workers were employed and which could be classified as either *male* (at least 70 percent male incumbents) or *female* (at least 70 percent female incumbents) positions. Each position was evaluated by trained job evaluators and awarded a specified number of *Hay Points* for each of four job characteristics or factors: required know-how, problem solving, accountability, and working conditions. The scores for each factor were then added to obtain a total Hay Point, or job evaluation, score for each job. These scores varied across the 188 job titles from below 100 to over 800 points.

Given these objective job evaluation scores, the next step is to ask what the relationship is between the salary (S_i) each male job pays and its total Hay Point (HP_i) score. Each dot in Figure 14A.1 represents a male job, and this figure plots the monthly salary for each job against its total Hay Point score. On average, it is clear that jobs with higher scores receive higher pay.

---

1. For a more complete discussion of the Minnesota job evaluation and comparable worth study, see *Pay Equity and Public Employment* (St. Paul, Minn.: Council on the Economic Status of Women, March 1982).

FIGURE 14A.1   Estimated Male "Comparable Worth" Salary Equation

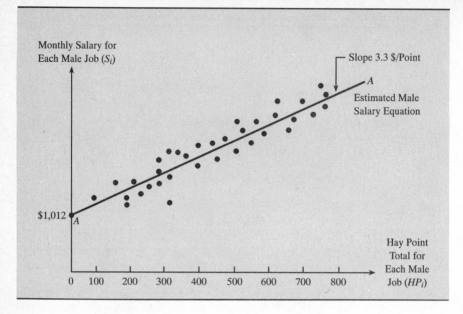

Although these points obviously do not all lie on a single straight line, it is natural to ask what straight line fits the data best. An infinite number of lines can be drawn through these points, and some precise criterion must be used to decide which line fits best. As discussed in Appendix 1A, the procedure typically used by statisticians and economists is to choose that line for which the sum (across data points) of the squared vertical distances between the line and the individual data points is minimized. The line estimated from the data using this method—the *method of least squares*—has a number of desirable statistical properties.[2]

Application of this method to data for the *male* occupations contained in the Minnesota data yielded the estimated line[3]

$$S_i = 1012 + 3.3\ HP_i \tag{14A.1}$$

So, for example, if male job i were rated at 200 Hay Points, we would predict that the monthly salary associated with job i would be $1,012 + (3.3)(200)$, or $1,672. This estimated male salary equation is drawn in Figure 14A.1 as line AA.

Now, if the value of a job could be determined solely by reference to its job evaluation score, one would expect that, in the absence of wage discrimination against women, male and female jobs rated equal in terms of total Hay Point scores would pay equal salaries (at least on average). Put another way,

---

2. See Appendix 1A.

3. These estimates are obtained in Ronald Ehrenberg and Robert Smith, "Comparable Worth in the Public Sector," in *Public Compensation,* ed. David Wise (Chicago: University of Chicago Press, 1987).

FIGURE 14A.2   Using the Estimated Male "Comparable Worth" Salary Equations to Estimate the Extent of Underpayment of Female Jobs

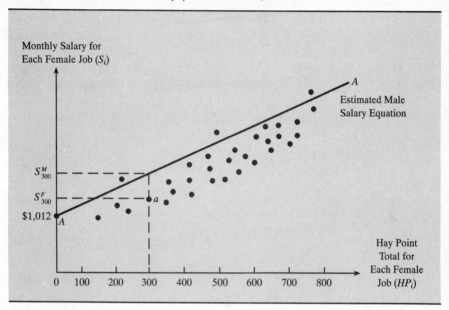

the same salary equation used to predict salaries of male jobs could be used to provide predictions of salaries for female jobs, and any inaccuracies in the prediction would be completely random. Hence, a test of whether female jobs are discriminated against is to see if the salaries they pay are systematically less than the salaries one would predict they would pay, given their Hay Point scores and the salary equation for male jobs.

Figure 14A.2 illustrates how this is done. Here each dot represents a salary/Hay Point combination for a female job. Superimposed on this scatter of points is the estimated male job salary equation, AA, from Figure 14A.1. The fact that the vast majority of the data points in Figure 14A.2 lie below the male salary line suggests that female jobs tend to be underpaid relative to male jobs with the same number of Hay Points. For example, the female job that is rated at 300 Hay Points (point a) is paid a salary of S_{300}^F. However, according to the estimated male salary line, if that job were a male job it would be paid S_{300}^M. The difference in percentage terms between S_{300}^M and S_{300}^F is an estimate of the "comparable worth" earnings gap—the extent of under-payment—for the female job. Indeed, calculations suggest that the average (across all the female occupations) "comparable worth" earnings gap in the Minnesota data was over 16 percent.[4]

This brief presentation has glossed over a number of complications that must be addressed before such estimates can be considered estimates of wage

4. See Ehrenberg and Smith, "Comparable Worth in the Public Sector." Analogous estimates for four other states are presented there and in Elaine Sorensen, "Implementing Compar-able Worth: A Survey of Recent Job Evaluation Studies," *American Economic Review Papers and Proceedings* 76 (May 1986): 364–67.

discrimination against female jobs.[5] These include issues relating to the reliability and/or potential sex bias in the evaluation methods, whether salaries and Hay Point scores may be related in a nonlinear fashion, whether the *composition* of any given total Hay Point score (across the four sets of job characteristics) affects salaries, and whether variables other than the job evaluation scores can legitimately affect salaries. Nonetheless, it should give the reader a sense of how "comparable worth wage gap" estimates are computed.

5. For a more complete discussion of these issues and recent empirical studies relating to comparable worth, see Ehrenberg and Smith, "Comparable Worth in the Public Sector"; Hill and Killingsworth, eds., *Comparable Worth: Analyses and Evidence;* Michael, Hartmann, and O'Farrell, eds., *Pay Equity: Empirical Inquiries;* and Killingsworth, *The Economics of Comparable Worth.*

15

Unemployment

As noted in Chapter 2, the population can be divided into those people in the labor force (L) and those not in the labor force (N). The labor force consists of those people who are employed (E) and those who are unemployed but would like to be employed (U). The concept of unemployment is somewhat ambiguous, since in theory virtually anyone would be willing to be employed in return for a generous enough compensation package. Economists tend to resolve this dilemma by defining unemployment in terms of an individual's willingness to be employed at some prevailing market wage. Government statistics take a more pragmatic approach, defining the unemployed as those who are on temporary layoff waiting to be recalled by their previous employers or those without a job who have actively searched for work in the previous month (of course, "actively" is not precisely defined).

Given these definitions, the unemployment rate (**u**) is measured as the ratio of the number of the unemployed to the number in the labor force:

$$\mathbf{u} = \frac{U}{L} \tag{15.1}$$

Much attention is focused on how the national unemployment rate varies over time and how unemployment rates vary across geographic areas and age/race/gender/ethnic groups.

It is important, however, to understand the limitations of unemployment rate data. They *do* reflect the proportion of a group that, at a point in time, actively wants to work but is not employed. For a number of reasons, however, they *do not* necessarily provide an accurate reflection of the economic hardship that members of a group are suffering.[1] First, individuals who are not ac-

---

1. This discussion draws heavily on the final report of the National Commission on Employment and Unemployment Statistics, *Counting the Labor Force* (Washington, D.C.: U.S. Government Printing Office, 1979), and Glen G. Cain, "Labor-Force Concepts and Definitions in View of Their Purposes," in *Concepts and Data Needs* (Appendix Volume I to the Commission's final report).

tively searching for work, including those who searched unsuccessfully and then gave up, are not counted among the unemployed (see Chapter 7). Second, unemployment statistics tell us nothing about the earnings levels of those who are employed, including whether these exceed the poverty level. Third, a substantial fraction of the unemployed come from families in which other earners are present—for example, many unemployed are teenagers—and the unemployed often are not the primary source of their family's support. Fourth, a substantial fraction of the unemployed receive some income support while they are unemployed, either in the form of government unemployment compensation payments or private supplementary unemployment benefits. Finally, unemployment rate data give us information on the fraction of the labor force that is not working but tell us little about the fraction of the population that is employed.

To emphasize the last point, Table 15.1 contains data on the aggregate unemployment rate, the labor force participation rate, and the *employment rate*—the last being defined as employment divided by *population*—for 1948, 1958, 1968, 1978, and 1988. The unemployment rate rose from 3.8 percent in 1948 to 6.6 percent in 1958, but because the aggregate labor force participation rate rose by 0.7 percentage points during the period, the employment rate (the fraction of the population that is employed) fell by only 1.2 percentage points. In contrast, while between 1968 and 1978 the unemployment rate once again rose (this time from 3.6 to 6.1 percent), the employment rate actually *rose* during the decade because of the relatively large increase in the labor force participation rate (over 3 percentage points) that occurred during 1968–78. Between 1978 and 1988, both the labor force participation rate and the employment/population ratio increased once again, while the unemployment rate fell. Clearly, the fraction of the labor force unemployed and the fraction of the population employed can move independently of each other!

Nonetheless, the unemployment rate remains a useful indicator of labor market conditions. This chapter will be concerned with the causes of unemployment; with why the unemployment rate varies over time, regions, or age/

TABLE 15.1   Civilian Labor Force Participation, Employment, and Unemployment Rates

Year	Unemployment Rate (U/L)	Labor Force Participation Rate (L/POP)	Employment Rate (E/POP)
1948	3.8	58.8	56.6
1958	6.6	59.5	55.4
1968	3.6	59.6	57.5
1978	6.1	63.2	59.3
1988	5.5	65.9	62.3

U = number of people unemployed.
L = number of people in the labor force.
E = number of people employed.
POP = total population.
SOURCE: U.S. Department of Labor, *Employment and Earnings,* January 1989, 160.

race/gender/ethnic groups; and with how various government policies affect, in an either intended or unintended manner, the level of unemployment.

The next section begins with a simple conceptual model of a labor market that emphasizes the importance of considering the *flows* between labor market states (for example, the *movement* of people from employed to unemployed status) as well as the *number* of people in each labor market state (for example, the *number* of the unemployed). Knowledge of the determinants of these flows is crucial to any understanding of the causes of unemployment.

The chapter will then move on to discuss how unemployment arises. Economists conceptually categorize unemployment as being *frictional, structural, demand-deficient* (cyclical), or *seasonal* in nature. After defining each type of unemployment and discussing its causes, we shall focus on policy issues that are raised by the discussion. Among the issues that will be considered are how the unemployment insurance system and unemployment are interrelated, why unemployment rates vary across age/race/gender/ethnic groups, why the "full employment" unemployment rate has risen since 1960, and why firms lay off workers rather than reducing their wages in a recession. The chapter will conclude by discussing some normative issues relating to unemployment, including whether teenagers who were unemployed suffer long-run losses from such experiences.

A STOCK-FLOW MODEL OF THE LABOR MARKET

Data on the number of people who are employed, unemployed, and not in the labor force are provided each month from the national Current Population Survey (CPS).[2] As Figure 15.1 indicates, in 1988 (when the overall unemployment rate averaged 5.5 percent) there were 114.9 million employed, 6.4 million unemployed, and 63.3 million adults aged 16 and over not in the labor force during a typical month. The impression one gets when one traces these data over short periods of time is that of relative stability; for example, it is highly unusual for the unemployment rate to change by more than a few tenths of a percentage point from one month to the next.

Focusing only on these *labor market stocks* and their net month-to-month changes, however, masks the highly dynamic nature of labor markets. Each month a substantial fraction of the unemployed leave unemployment status, either finding a job or dropping out of the labor force. For example, in each month of 1988 approximately 1.8 million unemployed individuals found employment (the flow denoted by *UE* in Figure 15.1), and 1.4 million of the unemployed dropped out of the labor force (the flow denoted by *UN*). These numbers represent the proportions 0.287 (P_{ue}) and 0.214 (P_{un}) of the stock of the unemployed, respectively; thus, one can conclude that approximately 50 percent of the individuals who were unemployed in a given month in 1988 left unemployment by the next month. These individuals were replaced in

2. The next two paragraphs draw heavily on Ralph E. Smith, "A Simulation Model of the Demographic Composition of Employment, Unemployment, and Labor Force Participation," in *Research in Labor Economics,* vol. 1, ed. Ronald Ehrenberg (Greenwich, Conn.: JAI Press, 1977).

FIGURE 15.1 Labor Market Stocks and Flows: 1988 Monthly Averages

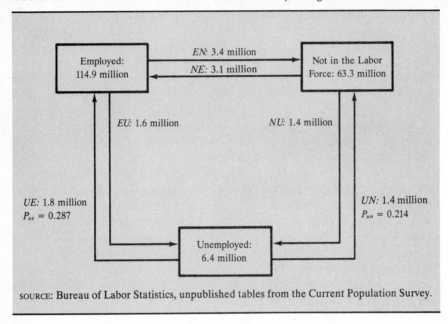

SOURCE: Bureau of Labor Statistics, unpublished tables from the Current Population Survey.

the pool of unemployed by roughly equivalent flows of individuals into unemployment from the stocks of employed individuals (the flow *EU*) and those not in the labor force (the flow *NU*).[3] The flow *EU* consists of individuals who voluntarily left or involuntarily lost their last job, while the flow *NU* consists of people entering the labor force. Finally, Figure 15.1 also indicates that each month there is considerable direct movement between employment and out-of-labor-force status.

When one thinks of the unemployed, the image of an individual laid off from his or her previous job often springs to mind. However, the view that such individuals constitute all, or even most, of the unemployed is incorrect. Table 15.2 provides some data that bear on this point for a period during the 1970s and 1980s in which the unemployment rate varied between 4.9 and 9.7 percent. Only in the high unemployment years of 1980, 1982, and 1984 were more than half of the unemployed job-losers. In each year, more than one-third of the unemployed came from out-of-labor-force status—that is, they were individuals who were either entering the labor force for the first time (*new entrants*) or individuals who had some previous employment expe-

---

3. Actually, in 1988 the flow of people from employment into unemployment was less than the flow out of unemployment into employment. As might be expected, then, the unemployment rate was declining during most of the year.

   We should note that these gross-change numbers are believed to suffer from serious measurement error problems that lead to overestimates of the extent of movement between unemployment and out-of-labor-force status. See Paul Flaim and Carma Hogue, "Measuring Labor Force Flows: A Special Conference Examines the Problems," *Monthly Labor Review* (July 1985): 7–15, for a discussion of these problems. While the reader should keep this in mind, these problems do not affect any of the conclusions we reach in this chapter.

TABLE 15.2   Categories of Unemployment

		Percent of Unemployed Who Were:			
Year	Unemployment Rate	Job-Losers	Job-Leavers	Reentrants	New Entrants
1970	4.9	44.3	13.4	30.0	12.3
1972	5.6	43.1	13.1	29.8	13.9
1974	5.6	43.5	14.9	28.4	13.2
1976	7.7	49.8	12.2	26.0	12.1
1978	6.1	41.6	14.1	30.0	14.3
1980	7.1	51.9	11.6	25.2	11.4
1982	9.7	58.7	7.9	22.3	11.1
1984	7.5	51.8	9.6	25.6	13.0
1986	6.9	48.9	12.3	26.2	12.5
1988	5.5	46.1	14.7	27.0	12.2

SOURCE: U.S. Department of Labor, *1982 Employment and Training Report of the President* (Washington, D.C.: U.S. Government Printing Office, 1982), Table A-36; U.S. Department of Labor, *Monthly Labor Review,* various issues.

rience and were reentering the labor force after a period of time out of the labor force (*reentrants*). Recent evidence suggests, though, that many reentrants are actually job-losers who dropped out of the labor force for a short time. Finally, although the vast majority of individuals who quit their jobs obtain new jobs prior to quitting and never pass through unemployment status, in each year (save for 1982 and 1984) at least 10 percent of the unemployed were voluntary job-leavers.[4]

Similarly, when one thinks of an individual on layoff, one may envision an individual who has permanently lost his or her job and who finds employment with a new employer only after an exhaustive job search and a long period of unemployment. However, the evidence suggests that a substantial fraction (approximately 70 percent) of those individuals who *lost* their last job are on *temporary layoff* and ultimately return to their previous employer, many after only a relatively short spell of unemployment.[5] Why some individuals "cycle" between employed and unemployed status, maintaining attachment to a single employer, will be discussed below.

Although ultimately public concern focuses on the level of unemployment, to understand the determinants of this level one must analyze the flows of individuals between the various labor market states. A group's unemploy-

4. For evidence that most quits do not involve a spell of unemployment, see J. Peter Mattila, "Job Quitting and Frictional Unemployment," *American Economic Review* 64 (March 1974): 235–39. Evidence that many reentrants were job-losers is found in Kim Clark and Lawrence Summers, "Labor Market Dynamics and Unemployment: A Reconsideration," *Brookings Papers on Economic Activity,* 1979–1, 13–60.

5. For evidence on the magnitude of temporary layoffs, see Martin Feldstein, "The Importance of Temporary Layoffs: An Empirical Analysis," *Brookings Papers on Economic Activity,* 1975–3, and Robert Topel, "Inventories, Layoffs and the Short-Run Demand for Labor," *American Economic Review* 72 (September 1982): 769–88. Since many of those who are temporarily laid off are rehired rather quickly, at any point in time most layoff unemployment is actually made up of individuals who will not be recalled. On this, see Lawrence Katz and Bruce Meyer, "Unemployment Insurance, Recall Expectations and Unemployment Outcomes," National Bureau of Economic Research Working Paper no. 2594 (May 1988).

ment rate might be high because its members have difficulty finding jobs once unemployed, because they have difficulty (for voluntary or involuntary reasons) remaining employed once a job is found, or because they frequently enter and leave the labor force. The appropriate policy prescription to reduce the unemployment rate will depend upon which one of these labor market flows is responsible for the high rate.

Somewhat more formally, one can show that if labor markets are roughly in balance, with the flows into and out of unemployment equal, the unemployment rate (**u**) for a group depends upon the various labor market flows in the following manner:

$$\mathbf{u} = F(\overset{+}{P}_{en}, \bar{P}_{ne}, \bar{P}_{un}, \overset{+}{P}_{nu}, \overset{+}{P}_{eu}, \bar{P}_{ue}) \tag{15.2}$$

Here F means "a function of," P_{en} = fraction of employed who leave the labor force, P_{ne} = fraction of those not in the labor force who enter the labor force and find employment, P_{un} = fraction of unemployed who leave the labor force, P_{nu} = fraction of those not in the labor force who enter the labor force and become unemployed, P_{eu} = fraction of employed who become unemployed, and P_{ue} = fraction of unemployed who become employed. So, for example, if there were initially 100 employed individuals in a group and 15 of them became unemployed during a period, P_{eu} would equal 0.15. (The exact formula for equation 15.2 and its derivation are found in the appendix to this chapter.)

A plus sign over a variable in equation (15.2) means that an increase in that variable will increase the unemployment rate, while a minus sign means that an increase in the variable will decrease the unemployment rate. The equation thus asserts that, other things equal, increases in the proportions of individuals who voluntarily or involuntarily leave their jobs and become unemployed (P_{eu}) or leave the labor force (P_{en}) will increase a group's unemployment rate, as will an increase in the proportion of the group that enters the labor force without first having a job lined up (P_{nu}). Similarly, the greater the proportion of individuals who leave unemployment status, either to become employed (P_{ue}) or to leave the labor force (P_{un}), the lower a group's unemployment rate will be. Finally, the greater the proportion of individuals who enter the labor force and immediately find jobs (P_{ne}), the lower a group's unemployment rate will be.[6]

The various theories of unemployment discussed in subsequent sections all essentially relate to the determination of one or more of the flows represented in equation (15.2). That is, they provide explanations of why the proportions of individuals who move between the various labor market states vary over time, across geographic areas, or across age/race/gender/ethnic groups. Equation (15.2) can help explain why unemployment rates rise in recessions, how and why unemployment rates are influenced by the unem-

---

6. For an intuitive understanding of why each of these results holds, recall the definition of the unemployment rate in equation (15.1). A movement from one labor market state to another may affect the numerator or the denominator, or both, and hence the unemployment rate. For example, an increase in P_{en} does not affect the number of unemployed individuals directly, but it does reduce the size of the labor force. According to equation (15.1), this reduction leads to an increase in the unemployment rate.

FIGURE 15.2   The Full-Employment Rate of Unemployment

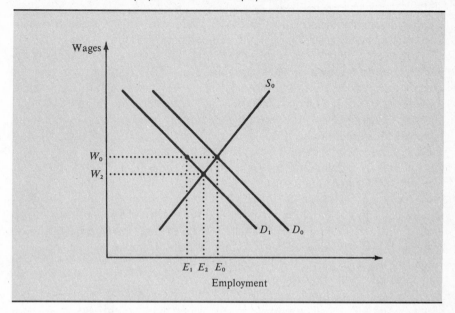

ployment insurance system, and how other government policies are likely to affect the unemployment rate.

Equation (15.2) and Figure 15.1 also make clear that social concern over any given level of unemployment should focus on both the incidence of unemployment (on the fraction of people in a group who become unemployed) and the duration of spells of unemployment. Society is probably more concerned if small groups of individuals are unemployed for long periods of time than if many individuals rapidly pass through unemployment status. Until recently, it was widely believed that the bulk of measured unemployment could be attributed to the fact that many people were experiencing short spells of unemployment. However, recent evidence suggests that, while many people do pass quickly through the unemployed state, most unemployment is due to prolonged spells of unemployment for a relatively small number of individuals.[7]

TYPES OF UNEMPLOYMENT AND THEIR CAUSES

Frictional Unemployment

Suppose a competitive labor market is in equilibrium in the sense that, at the prevailing market wage, the quantity of labor demanded just equals the quantity of labor supplied. Figure 15.2 shows such a labor market, in which the demand curve is D_0, the supply curve is S_0, employment is E_0, and the wage rate is W_0. Thus far the text has treated this equilibrium situation as one of

---

7. Kim B. Clark and Lawrence H. Summers, "Labor-Market Dynamics and Unemployment: A Reconsideration," *Brookings Papers on Economic Activity,* 1979–1, 13–60.

full employment and has implied that there is no unemployment associated with it. However, this implication is not completely correct. Even in a market-equilibrium or full-employment situation there will still be some *frictional unemployment,* because some people will be "between jobs."

Frictional unemployment arises because labor markets are inherently dynamic, because information flows are imperfect, and because it takes time for unemployed workers and employers with job vacancies to find each other. Even if the size of the labor force is constant, in each period there will be new entrants to the labor market searching for employment while other employed or unemployed individuals are leaving the labor force. Some people will quit their jobs to search for other employment (see Chapter 10). Moreover, random fluctuations in demand across firms will cause some firms to close or lay off workers at the same time that other firms are opening or expanding employment (see Figure 2.3 back in Chapter 2). Because information about the characteristics of those searching for work and the nature of the jobs opening up cannot instantly be known or evaluated, it takes time for job matches to be made between unemployed workers and potential employers. Hence, even when, in the aggregate, the demand for labor equals the supply, frictional unemployment will still exist.

The level of frictional unemployment in an economy is determined by the flows of individuals into and out of the labor market and the speed with which unemployed individuals find jobs. This speed is determined by the prevailing economic institutions, and institutional changes can influence the level of frictional unemployment. For example, as we shall show later in this chapter, a rise in the level of unemployment insurance benefits will tend to lengthen the duration of time it takes unemployed workers to find work. Or, to take another example, instituting a computerized job-bank system in which job applicants at the U.S. Employment Service are immediately informed of all listed jobs for which they are qualified might reduce the time it takes them to find jobs. This system would increase the probability that an unemployed worker would become employed in any period (increase P_{ue}) and hence, as indicated by equation (15.2), would *decrease* the unemployment rate. On the other hand, one should be aware that if the time it takes unemployed workers to find jobs decreases, more employed workers may consider quitting their jobs to search for better-paying employment; this response would increase P_{eu} and tend to *increase* the unemployment rate. (This latter example should remind us again that well-intentioned social programs often have unintended adverse side effects.)

Structural Unemployment

Structural unemployment arises when changes in the pattern of labor demand cause a mismatch between the skills demanded and supplied in a given area or cause an imbalance between the supplies of and demands for workers across areas. *If* wages were completely flexible *and* if costs of occupational or geographic mobility were low, market adjustments would quickly eliminate this type of unemployment. However, in practice these conditions may fail to hold, and structural unemployment may result.

Our by now familiar two-sector labor market model, represented by Figure 15.3, can be used to illustrate this point. For the moment we shall assume the sectors refer to markets for occupational classes of workers; later we shall assume that they are two geographically separate labor markets. Suppose that market A is the market for production workers in the automobile industry and market B is the market for skilled computer specialists, and suppose that initially both markets are in equilibrium. Given the demand and supply curves in both markets, (D_{0A}, S_{0A}) and (D_{0B}, S_{0B}), the equilibrium wage/employment combinations in the two sectors will be (W_{0A}, E_{0A}) and (W_{0B}, E_{0B}), respectively. Because of differences in training costs and nonpecuniary conditions of employment, the wages need not be equal in the two sectors.

Now suppose that the demand for automobile workers falls to D_{1A} as a result of foreign import competition, while the demand for computer specialists rises to D_{1B} as a result of the increased use of computers. If real wages are inflexible downward in market A because of union contract provisions, social norms, or government legislation, employment of automobile employees will fall to E_{1A}. Employment and wages of computer specialists will rise to E_{1B} and W_{1B}, respectively. Unemployment of $E_{0A} - E_{1A}$ workers would be created in the short run.

If automobile employees could costlessly become computer specialists, these unemployed workers would quickly "move" to market B, where we assume wages are flexible, and eventually all the unemployment would be elim-

FIGURE 15.3   Structural Unemployment Due to Inflexible Wages and Costs of Adjustment

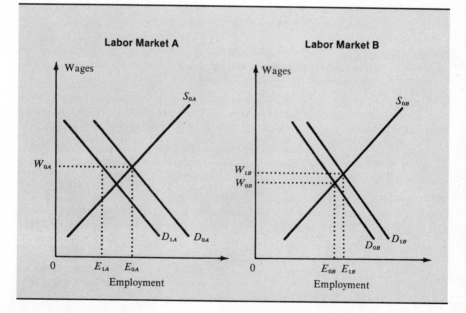

inated.[8] Structural unemployment arises, however, when costs of adjustment are sufficiently high to retard or even prevent such movements. The cost to displaced individuals—many in their fifties and sixties—may prove to be prohibitively expensive, given the limited time horizons they face. Moreover, it may be difficult for them to borrow funds to finance the necessary job training.

Geographic imbalances can be analyzed in the same framework. Suppose we now assume that market A refers to a Snowbelt city and market B to a Sunbelt city, both employing the same type of labor. When demand falls in the Snowbelt and unemployment increases because wages are not completely flexible, these unemployed workers may continue to wait for jobs in their city for at least three reasons. First, information flows are imperfect, so workers may be unaware of the availability of jobs hundreds of miles away. Second, the direct money costs of such a move, including moving costs and the transaction costs involved in buying and selling a home, are high. Third, the psychological costs of moving long distances are substantial because friends and neighbors and community support systems must be given up. As noted in Chapter 10, such factors inhibit geographic migration, and migration tends to decline with age. These costs are sufficiently high that many workers who become unemployed as a result of plant shutdowns or permanent layoffs express no interest in searching for jobs outside their immediate geographic area.[9]

Structural unemployment arises, then, because of changing patterns of labor demand that occur in the face of both rigid wages and high costs of occupational or geographic mobility.[10] In terms of Figure 15.1, structurally unemployed workers have a low probability of moving from unemployed to employed status (low P_{ue}), and any social policies that increase this probability should reduce the level of structural unemployment (other things equal). Examples of such policies include the provision of subsidized training, the provision of information about job market conditions in other areas, and the provision of relocation allowances to help defray the costs of migration.

---

8. Actually, this statement is not quite correct. As noted in Chapter 12 when analyzing the effects of unions using a similar model, *wait unemployment* may arise. That is, as long as the wage rate in market A exceeds the wage rate in market B and unemployed workers in market A expect that normal job turnover will eventually create job vacancies in A, it may be profitable for them to remain attached to market A and wait for a job in that sector. See footnote 15 below for a more complete discussion of wait employment.

9. See, for example, Robert Aronson and Robert McKersie, *Economic Consequences of Plant Shutdowns in New York State* (Ithaca, N.Y.: New York State School of Industrial and Labor Relations, 1980). A summary of the evidence on the losses workers suffer from plant shutdowns or permanent layoffs is found in Daniel Hamermesh, "What Do We Know About Worker Displacement in the U.S.?" *Industrial Relations* 28 (Winter 1989): 51–60.

10. For recent evidence on the magnitude of structural unemployment in the U.S. economy, see Katharine Abraham, "Structural/Frictional vs. Deficient Demand Unemployment," *American Economic Review* 73 (September 1983): 708–24; David Lilien, "Sectoral Shifts and Cyclical Unemployment," *Journal of Political Economy* 90 (August 1982): 777–93; and Katharine Abraham and Lawrence Katz, "Cyclical Unemployment: Sectoral Shifts or Aggregate Disturbances," *Journal of Political Economy* 94 (June 1986): 507–22. Lilien argues that shifts in employment growth rates across industrial sectors in the United States are responsible for a form of short-run structural unemployment and much of the apparent cyclical variation in unemployment rates. Abraham and Katz challenge this interpretation.

EXAMPLE 15.1

Advance Notice for Layoffs and Plant Shutdowns

In July of 1988, the *Worker Adjustment and Retraining Notification Act (WARN)* was enacted. *WARN* required employers of 100 or more workers to provide employees and local government officials with 60 days' advance notice before they shut down or make large-scale layoffs. Most European nations and Canadian provinces enacted legislation relating to plant shutdowns and large-scale layoffs much earlier, and their legislation typically is more "protective" of workers (requiring in some cases that displaced workers also be given severance pay). Prior to the passage of *WARN,* surveys suggested that very few workers in the United States actually received meaningful advance notice of impending displacement.

One way to interpret advance-notice legislation is as an attempt to reduce both frictional and structural unemployment. On the one hand, advance notice provides workers with opportunities to search for new jobs prior to their displacement; this should facilitate their job search process and thus reduce frictional unemployment. On the other hand, it provides workers with time to try to prevent their displacement (by offering wage concessions, for example) and to consider the acquisition of new job skills prior to displacement, which should serve to reduce structural unemployment.

One study, prior to *WARN,* of the effects of plant closings in Maine on local area unemployment rates found that when an employer voluntarily provided advance notice, the closing's effects on the local area's unemployment rate were smaller. A second study, which focused on individual workers displaced prior to the passage of *WARN,* found that advance notice increased the chances that these workers found new employment without suffering any spell of unemployment.

Opponents of advance-notice legislation have argued that it increases the likelihood that troubled plants will have to close. If closing is a strong possibility, but not yet a certainty, such plants may still be required to give notice. Giving notice could encourage their best (most mobile) workers to quit, reduce morale, and lower the chances that buyers will place new orders, that banks will supply new credit, and that suppliers will continue to provide services. The legislation thus makes it more difficult for distressed firms to solve their problems or to sell their plants to potential buyers. Further, opponents argue that by effectively increasing the costs of closing, the legislation discourages new plants from opening and old ones from expanding, thereby inadvertently retarding employment growth. To date, however, there is very little empirical evidence to support these claims (however, see Example 15.2 for claims concerning European unemployment).

SOURCES: Nancy Folbre, Julia Leighton, and Melissa Roderick, "Plant Closings and Their Regulation in Maine, 1971–1982," *Industrial and Labor Relations Review* 37 (January 1984): 185–97; Ronald Ehrenberg and George Jakubson, *Advance Notice Provisions in Plant Closing Legislation* (Kalamazoo, Mich.: W. E. Upjohn Institute for Employment Research, 1988). The latter source also summarizes in detail the prior empirical literature on advance notice.

Each of these policies is part of the Trade Adjustment Assistance Program, which was initiated under the Trade Expansion Act of 1962 and modified under the Trade Act of 1974. This program was designed to aid individuals who became unemployed because of changes in product demand brought about by foreign competition, and it also provided for an expanded form of unemployment compensation benefits (the effects of unemployment compensation on unemployment will be discussed later in the chapter). The available evidence indicates, however, that, perhaps because of restrictive eligibility rules, this program has had little effect on increasing the probability that these structurally unemployed workers will find employment.[11]

On a more general level, since the early 1960s the federal government has been heavily involved in policies to reduce structural unemployment. These policies include the provision of relocation allowances to unemployed workers residing in depressed areas (under the Area Redevelopment Act of 1959), the provision of classroom and on-the-job training to both disadvantaged and unemployed workers (under the Manpower Development and Training Act of 1962), the provision of both training and public sector employment opportunities (under the Comprehensive Employment and Training Act of 1973), and, most recently, an emphasis on public/private cooperation in the provision of training (under the Job Training Partnership Act of 1982, or JPTA). During the late 1980s approximately one million people a year received training under the JPTA.[12] Although evidence on the effectiveness of these programs is mixed, several studies suggest that some have succeeded in increasing the earnings or employment probabilities of those individuals who were enrolled in the programs.[13]

To this point in our analysis of the structural causes of unemployment, we have implicitly attributed mismatched labor demands and supplies to the high costs of adjustments on the *supply* side of the labor market. However, it has recently been postulated that at least some unemployment may be attributed to profit-maximizing behavior of *employers*. Specifically, it has been argued that structural unemployment may also arise if some employers are paying above market-clearing (or *efficiency*) wages to reduce employee turnover and/or shirking and to increase productivity.[14] Workers employed at other lower-paying firms could not obtain employment at a high-wage firm by

11. See, for example, George R. Neumann, "The Labor Market Adjustment of Trade-Displaced Workers: The Evidence from the Trade Adjustment Assistance Program," in *Research in Labor Economics,* vol. 2 (1978), ed. Ronald Ehrenberg, and Walter Corson and Walter Nicholson, "Trade Adjustment Assistance for Workers: Results of a Survey of Recipients Under the Trade Act of 1974," in *Research in Labor Economics,* vol. 4 (1981), ed. Ronald Ehrenberg.

12. U.S. General Accounting Office, *Job Training Partnership Act: Services and Outcomes for Participants with Different Needs* (Washington, D.C.: U.S. General Accounting Office, June 1989), 13.

13. See, for example, Burt S. Barnow, "The Impact of CETA Programs on Earnings: A Review of the Literature," *Journal of Human Resources* 22 (Spring 1987): 157–93.

14. The concept of efficiency wages was discussed in Chapter 11. Our argument here draws on, and abstracts from, many of the complications discussed in the articles in George Akerlof and Janet Yellen, eds., *Efficiency Wage Models of the Labor Market* (Cambridge, Eng.: Cambridge University Press, 1986), and Andrew Weiss, "Efficiency Wage Models of Unemployment" (mimeographed, Department of Economics, Boston University, September 1988).

offering to work at some wage between the low (market-clearing) and the high (efficiency) wage level, because the high-wage employers would want to maintain their wage advantage to discourage turnover and shirking. Voluntary decisions by these employers, then, would prevent their wage rates from falling.

Employees in the low-wage firms would still prefer to work at a high-wage firm and, as long as there is some normal turnover at the latter (which implies that future job vacancies will exist), some employees from low-wage firms may quit their jobs, "attach" themselves to the high-wage sector, and "wait" for job vacancies to occur. That is, using reasoning similar to that used in Chapter 12 in the discussion of the effects of union-imposed above-market wages, one can show that if some firms pursue an efficiency wage policy, a form of *wait unemployment* will arise.[15]

Demand-Deficient (Cyclical) Unemployment

Frictional and structural unemployment can arise even when, in the aggregate, the overall demand for labor equals the supply. Frictional unemployment arises because labor markets are dynamic and information flows are imperfect; structural unemployment arises because of geographic or occupational imbalances in demand and supply. *Demand-deficient unemployment* is associated with fluctuations in business activity (the "business cycle"), and it occurs when a decline in aggregate demand in the output market causes the *aggregate* demand for labor to decline in the face of downward inflexibility in real wages.

Returning to our simple demand and supply model of Figure 15.2, suppose that a temporary decline in aggregate demand leads to a shift in the labor demand curve to D_1. If real wages are inflexible downward, employment will fall to E_1, and $E_0 - E_1$ additional workers will become unemployed. This employment decline occurs when firms temporarily lay off workers (increasing P_{eu}) and reduce the rate at which they replace those who quit or retire (decreasing P_{ne} and P_{ue}). That is, flows into unemployment increase while flows into employment decline.

---

15. Suppose that employees are *risk neutral* (that is, they do not lose utility if their earnings *fluctuate* over time around some mean value). In equilibrium, they would move from the low-wage to the high-wage sector and remain as unemployed job-seekers as long as the expected wage from choosing to "wait" exceeds the expected wage of searching for work while employed in the low-wage sector. Put algebraically, a worker who is unemployed will "wait" for a high-wage job if

$$P_e W_e > P_0 W_e + (1 - P_0) W_0$$

where W_e and W_0 are the wages in the high- and low-wage sectors (respectively), P_e is the probability of finding a job paying W_e if one is unemployed, and P_0 is the probability of finding a high-wage job if employed in the low-wage sector. Presumably P_e is greater than P_0 because individuals can search for work more intensively if they are not employed.

The above inequality can be rewritten as

$$(P_e - P_0) W_e > W_0 (1 - P_0)$$

and, as one can see from this latter expression, whether one chooses wait unemployment depends on the increased probability of finding a high-wage job if unemployed ($P_e - P_0$) as well as on the difference between W_e and W_0.

One appropriate government response to demand-deficient unemployment is to pursue macroeconomic policies to increase aggregate demand; these policies include increasing the level of government spending, reducing taxes, and increasing the rate of growth of the money supply. Another policy is to use labor market programs that focus more directly on the unemployed. Examples here include temporary employment tax credits for firms and public sector employment programs, which were discussed in Chapters 4 and 13, respectively. A third policy recently advocated involves the "vaccination" of the economy against demand-deficient unemployment through increasing the profit-sharing component of total compensation and moving away from such heavy reliance on time-based wage payments.[16] The effects of profit sharing on employment stability in business downturns was presented in the appendix to Chapter 11; for the remainder of this chapter we will continue to assume the dominance of the time-based wages that tend to be downwardly inflexible.

Of course, it still remains for us to explain *why* employers respond to a cyclical decline in demand by temporarily laying off some of their work force rather than reducing their employees' real wages. If the latter occurred, employment would move to E_2 and real wages to W_2 in Figure 15.2. Although employment would be lower than its initial level, E_0, there would be no measured demand-deficient unemployment, because $E_0 - E_2$ workers would have dropped out of the labor force in response to this lower wage. Explanations for why employers are more likely to lay off workers than to reduce wages fall into two categories: those that focus on why cutting wage rates may be costly and those that explore reasons why layoffs are relatively inexpensive. We address each explanation below.

The Rigidity of Wages. The absence of widespread reductions in money wage rates during periods of declining aggregate demand has long been a puzzle to economists. The puzzle has two parts: why firms find it more profitable to reduce employment rather than wages, and why workers facing unemployment are apparently unwilling to take wage cuts to save their jobs. The hypotheses concerning wage rigidity that have come to the forefront recently address both aspects of the puzzle.

According to one explanation for rigid money wages, employers are not free to unilaterally cut nominal wages because of the presence of unions. This cannot be a complete explanation, however, because less than one-fifth of American workers are represented by unions (see Chapter 12), and unions could, in any case, agree to temporary wage cuts to save jobs instead of subjecting their members to layoffs. Why they fail to make such arrangements is instructive. A temporary wage reduction would reduce the earnings of all workers, while layoffs would affect, in most cases, only those workers most recently hired. Because these workers represent a minority of the union's membership in most instances, because union leaders are elected by majority rule, and because these leaders are most likely drawn from the ranks of the more

---

16. Martin Weitzman, *The Share Economy* (Cambridge, Mass.: Harvard University Press, 1984).

experienced workers (who are often immune from layoff), unions tend to favor a policy of layoffs rather than one that reduces wages for all members.[17] A variant of this explanation is the "insider-outsider" hypothesis, which sees union members as "insiders" who have little or no concern for nonmembers or former members now on layoff ("outsiders"); these insiders gain from keeping their numbers small and may choose to negotiate wages that effectively prevent the recall or employment of outsiders (see Example 15.2).[18]

Layoffs do occur in nonunion firms, although perhaps less frequently than in unionized ones.[19] There are several reasons why even nonunion employers may well prefer layoffs to wage reductions when demand falls. First, in the presence of firm-specific human capital investments, which often lead to structured internal labor markets (see Chapter 5), employers have incentives both to minimize voluntary turnover and to maximize their employees' work effort and productivity. Across-the-board temporary wage reductions would increase all employees' propensities to quit and could lead to reduced work effort on their part. In contrast, layoffs affect only the least experienced workers, the workers in whom the firm has invested the smallest amount of resources. It is likely, then, that the firm will find choosing the layoff strategy a more profitable alternative.[20]

Second, employers with internal labor markets frequently promise, at least implicitly, a certain path of earnings to employees over their careers. As we saw in Chapter 11, firms may pay relatively low salaries to new employees with the "promise" (expectation) that if they work diligently these employees will be paid relatively high wages toward the end of their careers. The firm's promises are, of necessity, conditional on how well it is performing, but the firm has more accurate information on the true state of its demand than do its workers. If a firm asks its employees to take a wage cut in periods of low demand, the employees may believe that the employer is falsely stating that demand is low and, noting that the employer loses nothing by the wage cut, resist the request. If, instead, a firm temporarily lays off some of its workers, it loses the output these workers would have produced, and workers may therefore accept such an action more readily. Put another way, the *asymmetry*

---

17. See James Medoff, "Layoffs and Alternatives Under Trade Unions in United States Manufacturing," *American Economic Review* 69 (June 1979): 380–95, for evidence. This hypothesis suggests that unions are much more likely to bargain for wage reductions when projected layoffs exceed 50 percent of the union's membership. For evidence that this occurred in the early 1980s, see Robert J. Flanagan, "Wage Concessions and Long-Term Union Flexibility," *Brookings Papers on Economic Activity,* 1984–1, 183–216.

18. Robert M. Solow, "Insiders and Outsiders in Wage Determination," *Scandinavian Journal of Economics* 87 (1985): 411–28.

19. See Medoff, "Layoffs and Alternatives Under Trade Unions," for evidence that layoff rates are higher in union than nonunion firms, other things equal.

20. See, for example, Janet Yellen, "Efficiency Wage Models of Unemployment," *American Economic Review Papers and Proceedings* 74 (May 1984): 200–205, and H. Lorne Carmichael, "Efficiency Wage Models of Unemployment: A Review," *Economic Inquiry* (forthcoming, 1990). An alternative explanation for the presence of temporary layoffs in employment situations that involve specific human capital, which stresses the inability to specify contracts that are fully contingent on all states of the world, is found in Robert Hall and Edward Lazear, "The Excess Sensitivity of Layoffs and Quits to Demand," *Journal of Labor Economics* 2 (April 1984): 233–59.

EXAMPLE 15.2

International Unemployment Rate Differentials

Comparisons of unemployment rates across nations are difficult because the exact definition of unemployment differs across nations. It is possible, however, to adjust the unemployment data reported by various industrial countries so that the data correspond approximately to the U.S. definition, and adjusted unemployment rates are reported in the table below.

Nation	1975	1978	1981	1986
United States	8.5	6.1	7.6	7.0
Canada	6.9	8.3	7.5	9.6
Australia	4.9	6.3	5.8	8.1
Japan	1.9	2.3	2.2	2.8
France	4.2	5.3	7.5	10.7
Germany	3.4	3.4	4.1	9.0
Great Britain	4.5	6.2	10.4	11.9
Italy	3.0	3.7	4.3	11.1
Sweden	1.6	2.2	2.5	2.7
Netherlands	5.2	5.2	9.3	14.6

Note: The definitions of unemployment have been adjusted to approximate the U.S. concept of unemployment.

SOURCE: Joyanna Moy, "Recent Trends in Unemployment and the Labor Force: 10 Countries," *Monthly Labor Review* 108 (August 1985): 9–22, Table 2; Joyanna Moy, "An Analysis of Unemployment and Other Labor Market Indicators in 10 Countries," *Monthly Labor Review* 111 (April 1988): 39–50.

of information between employers and employees makes layoffs the preferred policy.[21]

Third, firms with internal labor markets, and therefore long employer–employee job attachments, may be encouraged by the risk aversion of older employees to engage in seniority-based layoffs (last hired, first laid off) rather than wage cuts for all its workers. That is, the desire to have a constant income stream, rather than a fluctuating one with the same average value over time, is something for which older, more experienced workers may be willing to pay.[22] Thus, if the risks of income fluctuation are confined to one's initial years of employment, the firm may be able to pay its experienced workers

21. See, for example, Sanford Grossman, Oliver Hart, and Eric Maskin, "Unemployment with Observable Aggregate Shocks," *Journal of Political Economy* 91 (December 1983): 907–28; Sanford Grossman and Oliver Hart, "Implicit Contracts, Moral Hazard and Unemployment," *American Economic Review Papers and Proceedings* 71 (May 1981): 301–7; and Costas Azariadis, "Employment with Asymmetric Information," *Quarterly Journal of Economics* 98 (Supplement, 1983): 157–72.
22. This line of reasoning follows that in Costas Azariadis, "Implicit Contracts and Underemployment Equilibria," *Journal of Political Economy* 83 (December 1975): 1183–1202, and Martin Baily, "Wages and Employment Under Uncertain Demand," *Review of Economic Studies* 41 (January 1974): 37–50.

While country-specific institutions may largely account for the consistently low rates of unemployment in Sweden and Japan, the pattern within this table that has received the most attention recently is the dramatic increase in unemployment from 1975 to 1986 outside the United States. The reasons for this increase that have received the most widespread support are the more restrictive aggregate-demand policies outside the United States (reflecting greater concerns about inflation), and the greater tendencies in other industrialized countries for unemployment increases to persist. This latter phenomenon, called "hysteresis," deserves at least a brief explanation.*

Other industrialized countries are much more heavily unionized and have more costly restrictions regarding the laying off or firing of employees than does the United States. When unemployment rises (because of an oil crisis, perhaps), two chain reactions may occur. First, exploiting the reduced substitutability of capital for labor (see Example 12.3), unionized "insiders" may ignore the interests of unemployed "outsiders," unless bargaining is highly centralized, and demand wage increases sufficiently high that new hiring becomes impossible. Second, the high, government-imposed costs of closing plants or laying off workers, coupled with lower voluntary turnover induced by higher unemployment, may make it more risky for new firms (which often fail) to open and hire unemployed workers. Thus, the longer high unemployment lasts, the more difficult it becomes for employment to grow unless either market forces are allowed to work or labor unions, as they have done in some of the countries with highly centralized wage bargaining, also speak for the unemployed "outsiders."

*A brief summary of the hysteresis argument, with references to earlier papers, can be found in Olivier J. Blanchard and Lawrence H. Summers, "Beyond the Natural Rate Hypothesis," *American Economic Review* 78 (May 1988): 182–87.

wages lower than otherwise would be required. Of course, during the initial period, workers will be subject to potential earnings variability and may demand higher wages then to compensate them for these risks. However, if the fraction of the work force subject to layoffs is small, on average employers' costs could be reduced by seniority-based layoffs.

Fourth, it will be noted that all three of the above "explanations" are centered on firms with internal labor markets, which may be roughly thought of as large employers. One is then tempted to ask why those laid off from large firms do not seek work in small firms. These firms pay lower wages and have few of the reasons cited above to avoid reducing them further when aggregate demand falls; hence, increased employment in these jobs would lower the average nominal wage paid in the economy and help reduce unemployment. Some theorists believe that the failure of unemployed workers to flock to low-wage jobs derives from their sense of status (their relative standing in society). These economists postulate that individuals may prefer unemployment in a "good" job to employment in an inferior one, at least for a period longer than the typical recession.[23] It is this sense of status that prevents the

23. See Alan S. Blinder, "The Challenge of High Unemployment," *American Economic Review Papers and Proceedings* 78 (May 1988): 1–15.

expansion of jobs and the further reduction of wages in the low-wage sectors during recessionary periods.

Unemployment Compensation. The incentives for both employers and employees to prefer temporary layoffs to fluctuations in real wages are affected by two characteristics of the unemployment insurance (UI) system: the *tax treatment of UI benefits* and the system's *method of financing benefits.*[24] The unemployment insurance system is actually a system of individual state systems and, although the details of the individual systems differ, one can easily sketch the broad outlines of how they operate.

Today virtually all private sector employees are covered by a state UI system. When such workers become unemployed, their eligibility for unemployment insurance benefits is based upon their previous labor market experience and reason for unemployment. With respect to their experience, each state requires unemployed individuals to demonstrate "permanent" attachment to the labor force, by meeting minimum earnings or weeks-worked tests during some base period, before they can be eligible for UI benefits. In all states, covered workers who are laid off *and* meet these labor market experience tests are eligible for UI benefits. In some states workers who voluntarily quit their jobs are eligible for benefits, while in only two states (New York and Rhode Island) are strikers eligible for benefits. Finally, new entrants or reentrants to the labor force and workers fired for cause are, in general, ineligible for benefits.

After a waiting period, which is one or two weeks in most states, an eligible worker can begin to collect UI benefits. The structure of benefits is illustrated in Figure 15.4, where it can be seen that benefits are related to an individual's previous earnings level.[25] As shown in panel (a), all eligible unemployed workers are entitled to at least a minimum benefit level, B_{min}. After previous earnings rise above a critical level, W_{min}, benefits increase proportionately with earnings up to a maximum earnings level W_{max}, past which benefits remain constant at B_{max}. Thirteen states also have dependents' allowances for unemployed workers, although in some of these states the dependents' allowance cannot increase an individual's weekly UI benefits above B_{max}.

---

24. A more complete description of the characteristics of the UI system is found in National Foundation for Unemployment Compensation and Workers' Compensation, *Highlights of State Unemployment Compensation Laws, January 1989* (Washington, D.C.: National Foundation for Unemployment Compensation and Workers' Compensation, 1989). The connection between temporary layoffs and these characteristics of the UI system was pointed out in Martin Feldstein, "Temporary Layoffs in the Theory of Unemployment," *Journal of Political Economy* 84 (October 1976): 937–58; empirical evidence on the relationship was provided in Robert Topel, "On Layoffs and Unemployment Insurance," *American Economic Review* 73 (September 1983): 541–59. In most states employees working reduced hours are not eligible for UI benefits; this explains why layoffs rather than hours reductions are typically used to adjust employment to cyclical-demand changes. See Randall Wright and Julie Hotchkiss, "A General Model of Unemployment Insurance With and Without Short-Time Compensation," in *Research in Labor Economics,* vol. 9 (1988), ed. Ronald Ehrenberg, 91–131.

25. Benefits are calculated across states in at least three ways: as a percentage of annual earnings, as a percentage of previous weekly earnings, and as a percentage of an individual's earnings during his or her "high" earnings quarter during the past year. For our purposes, such distinctions are unimportant.

FIGURE 15.4   Weekly Unemployment Insurance Benefits as a Function of Previous Earnings

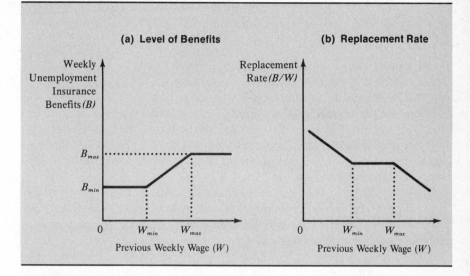

An implication of such a benefit structure is that the ratio of an individual's UI benefits to previous earnings varies according to his or her past earnings—see panel (b). This ratio is often called the *replacement rate,* the fraction of previous earnings that the UI benefits replace. Over the range between W_{min} and W_{max}, where the replacement rate is constant, most states aim to replace around 50 percent of an unemployed worker's previous earnings. It is important to stress that up until 1978 *UI benefits were not subject to the federal income tax;* since then, however, UI benefits have been increasingly subject to taxation, and federal tax reform legislation passed in 1986 made all UI benefits taxable starting in 1987.

Once UI benefits begin, an unemployed individual's eligibility for continued benefits depends upon his or her making continual "suitable efforts" to find employment; the definition of suitable efforts varies widely across states. In addition, there is a maximum duration of receipt of benefits that is of fixed length in some states and varies in other states with a worker's prior labor market experience (workers with "more permanent attachment" being eligible for more weeks of benefits). Periodically Congress also passes temporary legislation that extends the length of time unemployed workers can receive benefits in states in which the unemployment rate is high, but the maximum total duration of eligibility for benefits did not exceed 65 weeks during the 1970s and 1980s.

The benefits paid out by the UI system are financed by a payroll tax. Unlike the Social Security payroll tax, in all but four states the UI tax is paid solely by employers.[26] The UI tax payment (T) that an employer must make

---

26. Recall from our discussion in Chapter 3 that this fact tells us nothing about who really bears the burden of the tax.

for each employee is given by

$$T = tW \quad \text{if } W \leq W_B \tag{15.3a}$$

and

$$T = tW_B \quad \text{if } W > W_B \tag{15.3b}$$

where t is the employer's UI tax rate, W is an employee's earnings during the calendar year, and W_B is the *taxable wage base,* the level of earnings after which no UI tax payments are required. In 1989 the taxable wage base ranged from \$7,000 to \$10,000 in about two-thirds of the states; thus, depending upon the state, employers had to pay UI taxes on the first \$7,000 to \$10,000 of each employee's earnings. The other one-third of the states had taxable wage bases that were somewhat higher.

The employer's UI tax rate is determined by general economic conditions in the state, the industry the employer is operating in, and the employer's *lay-off experience.* The last term is defined differently in different states; the underlying notion is that since the UI system is an insurance system, employers who lay off workers frequently and make heavy demands on the system's resources should be assigned a higher UI tax rate. This practice is referred to as *experience rating.*

Experience rating is typically *imperfect* in the sense that the marginal cost to an employer of laying off an additional worker (in terms of a higher UI tax rate) is often less than the added UI benefits the system must pay out to that worker. Imperfect experience rating is illustrated in Figure 15.5, which plots the relationship between an employer's UI tax rate and that firm's layoff experience. (We shall interpret *layoff experience* to mean the probability that employees in the firm will be on layoff. Clearly, this probability depends both on the frequency with which the firm lays off workers and the average duration of time until they are recalled to their positions.)

Each state has a minimum UI tax rate, and below this rate—t_{min} in Figure 15.5—the firm's UI tax rate cannot fall. After a firm's layoff experience reaches some critical value ℓ_{min}, the firm's UI tax rate rises with increased layoff experience over some range. In each state there is also a ceiling on the UI tax rate, t_{max}, and after this tax rate is reached additional layoffs will not alter the firm's tax rate.[27] The system is *imperfectly* experience-rated because for firms below ℓ_{min} or above ℓ_{max}, variations in their layoff rate have no effect on their UI tax rate.[28] Further, over the range in which the tax rate is increasing with layoff experience, the increase is not large enough in most states to make the employer's marginal cost of a layoff (in terms of the increased UI taxes the firm must pay) equal to the marginal UI benefits the laid-off employees receive.

---

27. In actuality the UI tax rate changes discretely (as a step function) over the range ℓ_{min} to ℓ_{max}, not continuously as drawn in Figure 15.5. For expository convenience, we ignore this complication.
28. Such a system of UI financing leads to interindustry subsidies, in which industries (such as banking) with virtually no layoffs still must pay the minimum tax, and these industries subsidize those industries (such as construction) that have very high layoffs but pay only the maximum rate.

FIGURE 15.5   Imperfectly Experience-Rated Unemployment Insurance Tax Rate

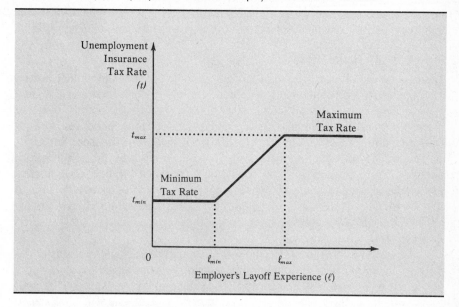

The key characteristics of the UI system that influence the desirability of temporary layoffs are the *imperfect experience rating* of the UI payroll tax and the *federal tax treatment* of UI benefits that workers receive. To understand the influence of these characteristics, suppose first that the UI system were constructed in such a way that its tax rates were perfectly experience-rated and the benefits it paid out (for example, half of previous earnings) were completely taxable. A firm laying off a worker would have to pay added UI taxes equal to the full UI benefit received by the worker, so it saves just half of the worker's wages by the layoff; the *worker's* spendable income would be cut in half if he or she were laid off.

Now suppose instead that the UI tax rate employers must pay is totally independent of their layoff experience (no experience rating) and that UI benefits are not subject to any personal income taxes. A *firm* saves a laid-off worker's *entire* wages because its UI taxes do not rise as a result of the layoff. The worker still gets a benefit equal to half of prior earnings, but since these benefits are not taxable, his or her spendable income drops by *less* than half. Thus, compared to a UI system with perfect experience rating and completely taxable benefits, it is easy to see that a system with incomplete experience rating and no taxation of benefits will tend to enhance the attractiveness of layoffs to both employer and employee.[29] While the taxation of all UI benefits

29. This statement is not always true, since the unemployed workers often lose employee benefits and the ability to take advantage of on-the-job training options. Research by Robert H. Topel, "Equilibrium Earnings, Turnover and Unemployment: New Evidence," *Journal of Labor Economics* 2, no. 4 (October 1984): 500–522, indicates that unemployment insurance increases the probability of layoff and reduces the probability of leaving unemployment—with the former effect being the stronger. He also finds both effects are stronger for temporary than for permanent layoffs.

beginning in 1987 increased the costs to workers of layoffs, the persistence of imperfect experience rating continues to increase the level of demand-deficient unemployment over what it would be with perfect experience rating.

Seasonal Unemployment

Seasonal unemployment is similar to demand-deficient unemployment in that it is induced by fluctuations in the demand for labor. Here, however, the fluctuations can be regularly anticipated and follow a systematic pattern over the course of a year. For example, the demand for agricultural employees declines after the planting season and remains low until the harvest season. Similarly, the demand for construction workers in Snowbelt states falls during the winter months. Finally, the demand for production workers falls in certain industries during the season of the year when plants are retooling to handle annual model changes; examples here include both the Detroit automotive industry (new car models) and the New York City apparel industry (new fashion designs).

The issue remains, why do employers respond to seasonal patterns of demand by laying off workers rather than reducing wage rates or hours of work? All the reasons cited for the existence of cyclical unemployment and temporary layoffs for cyclical reasons also pertain here. Indeed, one study has shown that the expansion (in the early 1970s) of the unemployment insurance system that led to the coverage of most agricultural employees was associated with a substantial increase in seasonal unemployment in agriculture.[30]

One may question, however, why workers would accept jobs in industries in which they knew in advance they would be unemployed for a portion of the year. For some workers, the existence of UI benefits along with the knowledge that they will be rehired as a matter of course at the end of the slack demand season may allow them to treat such periods as paid vacations. However, since UI benefits typically replace less than half of an unemployed worker's previous gross earnings and even smaller fractions for high-wage workers (see Figure 15.4), most workers will not find such a situation desirable. To attract workers to such seasonal industries, firms will have to pay workers higher wages to compensate them for being periodically unemployed. In fact, casual observation suggests that the hourly wages of construction workers are substantially higher than the hourly wages of comparably skilled manufacturing workers who work more hours each year. More formally, recent econometric studies confirm that, other things held constant (including workers' skill levels), wages are higher in industries in which workers' expected annual durations of unemployment are longer.[31] (For a more complete analysis of this issue, see Appendix 8A.)

---

30. Barry Chiswick, "The Effect of Unemployment Compensation on a Seasonal Industry: Agriculture," *Journal of Political Economy* 84 (June 1976): 591–602.

31. John Abowd and Orley Ashenfelter, "Anticipated Unemployment, Temporary Layoffs, and Compensating Wage Differentials," in *Studies in Labor Markets,* ed. Sherwin Rosen (Chicago: University of Chicago Press, 1981), 141–70, and Robert H. Topel, "Equilibrium Earnings, Turnover, and Unemployment: New Evidence," *Journal of Labor Economics* 2 (October 1984): 500–522. Topel also shows that, other things equal, high UI benefits *reduce* the compensating wage differential paid for the risk of unemployment.

The existence of wage differentials that compensate workers in high-unemployment industries for the risk of unemployment makes it difficult to evaluate whether this type of unemployment is voluntary or involuntary in nature. On the one hand, in an *ex ante* ("before the fact") sense, workers have voluntarily agreed to be employed in industries that offer higher wages *and* higher probabilities of unemployment than offered elsewhere. On the other hand, once on the job (*ex post,* or "after the fact") employees prefer to remain employed rather than becoming unemployed. Such unemployment may be considered either voluntary or involuntary, then, depending upon the perspective one is taking.

THE DEMOGRAPHIC STRUCTURE OF UNEMPLOYMENT RATES

The Full-Employment Unemployment Rate

The *full-employment* (or *natural*) rate of unemployment is difficult to define precisely, and there are several alternative concepts from which to choose. Some define the natural rate of unemployment as that rate at which wage and price inflation are either stable or at acceptable levels. Another defines full employment as the rate of unemployment at which job vacancies equal the number of unemployed workers, and yet another defines it as the level of unemployment at which any increases in aggregate demand will result in no further reductions in unemployment. A variant of the latter defines the natural rate as the unemployment rate at which all unemployment is voluntary (frictional and perhaps seasonal). Finally, a recent definition of the natural rate is that rate at which the level of unemployment is unchanging and both the flows into unemployment and the duration of unemployment are normal.[32]

All the various definitions above try to define in a specific way a more general concept of full employment as the rate that prevails in "normal" times. If we assume that frictional and seasonal unemployment exist even in labor markets characterized by equilibrium (i.e., markets having neither excess demand nor excess supply), it is clear that the natural rate of unemployment is affected by such factors as voluntary turnover rates among employed workers, movements in and out of the labor force, and how long it takes for the unemployed to find acceptable jobs. These latter factors vary widely across demographic groups, so the natural rate during any period is strongly influenced by the demographic composition of the labor force.

Table 15.3 presents data on unemployment rates for various age/race/gender/ethnic groups in 1988. The patterns indicated in Table 15.3 for 1988 are similar to the patterns for other years: high unemployment rates for teens and young adults of each race/gender group relative to older adults in these groups; black unemployment rates roughly double white unemployment rates for most age/gender groups, with Hispanic-American unemployment rates

---

32. James Tobin, "Inflation and Unemployment," *American Economic Review* 62 (March 1972): 1–18, and John Haltiwanger, "The Natural Rate of Unemployment," in *The New Palgrave,* ed. J. Eatwell, M. Milgate, and P. Newman (New York: Stockton Press, 1987), 610–12.

TABLE 15.3   Unemployment Rates in 1988 by Demographic Groups

Age	White Male	White Female	Black Male	Black Female	Hispanic Male	Hispanic Female	All
16–17	16.1	14.4	34.4	35.9	29.5	24.5	
18–19	12.4	10.8	31.7	29.6	19.5	18.9	
20–24	7.4	6.7	19.4	19.8	9.2	10.7	
25–54	3.8	3.9	8.9	9.4	6.5	6.6	
55+	3.0	2.5	5.4	4.5	6.8	4.3	
Total	4.7	4.7	11.7	11.7	8.1	8.3	5.5

SOURCE: U.S. Department of Labor, *Employment and Earnings* 36 (January 1989), Table 44. "Hispanic" refers to individuals of Hispanic origin; depending upon their races these individuals are included in both the white and black population group totals.

falling between the white and black rates; and female unemployment rates slightly higher than male rates for adults aged 25 to 54 but often lower for the other groups. The high unemployment rates of black teenagers, which ranged between 29.6 and 35.9 percent in 1988, have been of particular concern to policymakers and have led to numerous programs during the late 1970s and 1980s to reduce nonwhite teenage unemployment.

Over recent decades, the age/race/gender/ethnic composition of the labor force has changed dramatically with the growth in labor force participation rates of females and substantial changes in the relative size of the teenage, black, and Hispanic populations. Between 1960 and 1988 the proportion of the labor force that was female grew from 33.4 to 45.0 percent. Similarly, between 1973 (when statistics were first collected) and 1988, the Hispanic-American labor force more than doubled in size (three times the national average rate of growth) to over 7.3 percent of the total labor force. In contrast, while between 1960 and 1978 the proportion of the labor force that was black grew from 11.1 to 12.0 percent and the proportion that was teenage grew from 7.0 to 9.5 percent, by 1988 the black proportion had fallen back to 10.9 percent and the teenage proportion had fallen back to 6.6 percent.[33]

Until quite recently, women tended to have higher unemployment rates than men.[34] As a result, the increases in the relative labor force shares of women, blacks, Hispanics, and teenagers through 1978 were increases in the shares of groups that had relatively high unemployment rates; this led to an increase in the overall unemployment rate associated with any given level of labor market tightness. Indeed, one investigator concluded that demographic shifts in the composition of the labor force from the 1960s to the late 1970s probably raised the overall unemployment rate at least 1 percentage point for

---

33. See U.S. Department of Labor, *Employment and Earnings* 36 (January 1989), Tables 1–3, 39, and earlier years' issues.

34. The fact that female unemployment rates now tend to be less than or equal to male rates is at least partially due to the growth of employment over the last decade in sectors such as services that employ proportionately many females, and to the "collapse" over the last decade of manufacturing, in which proportionately more males have been historically employed. See Barry Bluestone and Bennett Harrison, *The Great U-Turn: Corporate Restructuring, Laissez-Faire and the Threat to America's High Wage Society* (New York: Basic Books, 1988), for an extensive discussion of employment shifts in the U.S. economy.

any given level of overall labor market tightness.[35] These demographic changes also led to an increase in the *full employment* (or *natural*) rate of unemployment—defined here as the unemployment rate that is consistent with a zero excess demand for labor. While an aggregate unemployment rate of 4 percent was considered a reasonable goal for policymakers in the 1960s, by the late 1970s policymakers and academic economists rarely referred to targets below 5.5 to 6.0 percent.

Over the last decade, however, a number of demographic forces have probably worked to reduce both the unemployment rate associated with any level of overall labor market tightness and the full-employment unemployment rate.[36] The shares of both teenagers and blacks in the labor force have declined. In addition, while the share of women in the labor force has continued to expand, female unemployment rates have fallen relative to male rates because much of U.S. employment growth has occurred in sectors, such as the service sector, that employ proportionately more females.

Why Do Unemployment Rates Vary Across Groups?

Calculations such as those just referred to take the age/race/gender/ethnic structure of unemployment rates as fixed, and hence it is natural to ask why this structure exists.[37] As equation (15.2) and equation (15A.7) in the appendix indicate, a group's unemployment rate might be high because its members have difficulty finding jobs once unemployed, because they have difficulty (for voluntary or involuntary reasons) remaining employed once a job is found, or because they frequently enter and leave the labor force. The appropriate policy prescriptions will depend on the relative size of these monthly flows from one labor market state to another and on which of the flows is most responsible for the high rate.

One data source that is helpful in making such a determination is the monthly Current Population Survey (CPS). Since three-quarters of the individuals in the CPS sample one month are also included in the sample the next month, it is possible to compute the number of individuals in a particular age/race/gender group who move between various labor market states in a month. Since 1967, when definitional changes in the CPS occurred, these monthly *gross-flow data* have been tabulated by the Bureau of Labor Statistics (BLS), although they have not been published. Dividing these gross flows by the size of the appropriate group in the previous month yields estimates of the probability that an individual of a given age, race, and gender will go from

35. James Tobin, "Stabilization Policy Ten Years After," *Brookings Papers on Economic Activity,* 1980–1, 19–72. Other researchers have argued that increased generosity of social insurance programs, such as unemployment insurance, welfare benefits, and food stamps, which are received only if the individual is unemployed or family income is below certain levels, have contributed to higher unemployment rates. That is, unemployed workers may now have smaller incentives to find employment quickly.
36. Richard Krashevski, "What Is So Natural About High Unemployment?" *American Economic Association Papers and Proceedings* 78 (May 1988): 289–93.
37. This section draws heavily on Ronald G. Ehrenberg, "The Demographic Structure of Unemployment Rates and Labor Market Transition Probabilities," in *Research in Labor Economics,* vol. 3 (1980), ed. Ronald Ehrenberg, 241–93.

one labor market state to another; these probabilities are called *transition probabilities.*

Table 15.4 presents estimates of the *average monthly transition probabilities* (the proportion of individuals in each labor market state who leave that state for each other state by the next month) for 20 age/gender and race/gender cohorts from January 1987 to December 1988.[38] Thus, if interested in estimating the probability that a 16- to 19-year-old male would move from employment to unemployment in one month, one would find from the table that P_{eu} is 0.045. Put differently, 4.5 percent of male teenagers who are employed in one month will be unemployed the next. Likewise, one can learn from the table that 10.5 percent of male teenagers employed in one month will be out of the labor force the next (the value of P_{en} for that demographic group is 0.105).

The data in Table 15.4, combined with the use of equation (15A.7) in the appendix, allow us to estimate the extent to which a relatively high unemployment rate for a group is caused by the values of each of its transition probabilities. Put another way, this information can be used to determine by how much a group's relative unemployment rate would change if we replaced any one of its transition probabilities with the comparable probability for a reference group (such as white adult males) that has a relatively low unemployment rate. Since different governmental policies are likely to affect different transition probabilities, this determination may suggest the types of policies to stress when seeking to alter the demographic structure of unemployment rates.

High teenage unemployment rates (relative to adult male unemployment rates) stem primarily from the high probability that teenagers will leave employment to move out of the labor force (P_{en}) and that teenagers will move into unemployment from either employment (P_{eu}) or out-of-labor-force (P_{nu}) status.[39] Teens, then, move into and out of the labor force frequently and often lose or voluntarily leave their jobs. Involuntary job loss occurs more frequently for teenagers than for adults, both because teenagers typically have low seniority and are vulnerable to layoffs and because they are much more likely to be discharged for cause, as they often have not yet learned the limits of acceptable behavior on the job.[40] Higher voluntary job-leaving of teens reflects the low quality of jobs many teens have, the normal job-matching pro-

---

38. We are grateful to Francis Horvath of the U.S. Bureau of Labor Statistics for providing these data to us. Similar data for all the age/gender/race groups found in Table 15.3 unfortunately were not available to us owing to small sample sizes. Also unavailable were data on the transition probabilities of Hispanic-Americans. However, data similar to those in Table 15.2 suggest that a greater share of the Hispanic unemployed are laid off or discharged than is true for the white unemployed. See Gregory DeFreitas, "A Time-Series Analysis of Hispanic Unemployment," *Journal of Human Resources* 21 (Winter 1986): 24–43, Table 5. A higher probability of job loss for Hispanics than for whites would partially explain the former's higher unemployment rates.

39. For a discussion of how government policies in another country (Sweden) affected these parameters, and hence the teenage/adult unemployment ratio, see Linda Leighton and Siv Gustafsson, "Differential Patterns of Unemployment in Sweden," in *Research in Labor Economics,* vol. 6 (1984), ed. Ronald Ehrenberg.

40. For example, Peter Jackson and Edward Montgomery, "Layoffs, Discharges and Youth Unemployment," in *The Black Youth Unemployment Crisis,* ed. Richard Freeman and Harry Holzer (Chicago: University of Chicago Press, 1986), offer evidence that frequent absenteeism was often the reason that black teens in Boston gave for their being discharged.

TABLE 15.4   Average Monthly Transition Probabilities (January 1987–December 1988)

	P_{eu}	P_{en}	P_{ue}	P_{un}	P_{ne}	P_{nu}
All Males						
16–19	0.045	0.105	0.289	0.304	0.126	0.075
20–24	0.031	0.032	0.343	0.144	0.157	0.080
25–34	0.018	0.009	0.317	0.108	0.134	0.103
35–44	0.012	0.006	0.301	0.097	0.094	0.075
45–54	0.010	0.008	0.265	0.114	0.071	0.042
55–59	0.009	0.015	0.218	0.153	0.047	0.020
60–64	0.007	0.036	0.189	0.266	0.029	0.010
65+	0.004	0.103	0.194	0.399	0.016	0.002
All Females						
16–19	0.033	0.120	0.284	0.339	0.112	0.068
20–24	0.020	0.045	0.278	0.267	0.101	0.067
25–34	0.012	0.030	0.240	0.257	0.067	0.039
35–44	0.009	0.026	0.247	0.249	0.073	0.032
45–54	0.008	0.027	0.255	0.249	0.054	0.019
55–59	0.006	0.035	0.232	0.262	0.035	0.009
60–64	0.006	0.058	0.232	0.317	0.023	0.005
65+	0.005	0.108	0.143	0.443	0.008	0.001
Males						
White	0.015	0.020	0.321	0.145	0.056	0.026
Nonwhite	0.027	0.030	0.230	0.201	0.060	0.054
Females						
White	0.012	0.039	0.295	0.258	0.043	0.017
Nonwhite	0.019	0.041	0.164	0.316	0.045	0.042

P_{eu} = fraction of employed who become unemployed.
P_{en} = fraction of employed who leave the labor force.
P_{ue} = fraction of unemployed who become employed.
P_{un} = fraction of unemployed who leave the labor force.
P_{ne} = fraction of those not in the labor force who enter the labor force and find employment.
P_{nu} = fraction of those not in the labor force who enter the labor force and become unemployed.
SOURCE: Bureau of Labor Statistics, unpublished tables from the Current Population Survey.

cess (see Chapter 10), and the fact that some teens quit their jobs as soon as they have earned enough to buy a specific item they were working for (e.g., a stereo).[41]

The major causes of high nonwhite male unemployment (relative to white male unemployment) are the group's high probabilities of voluntarily or involuntarily leaving employment and either becoming unemployed (P_{eu}) or leaving the labor force (P_{en}). Nonwhite males also have relatively low probabilities of finding a job once unemployed (P_{ue}). The high nonwhite female unemployment rate (relative to the white female unemployment rate) is due primarily to the group's relatively high probability of leaving employment and becoming unemployed (P_{eu}) and a relatively low probability of finding a job once unemployed (P_{ue}).

---

41. Paul Osterman, *Getting Started: The Youth Labor Market* (Cambridge, Mass.: MIT Press, 1980), presents evidence on the first jobs held for a sample of Boston youth. Very few required any skills or offered any opportunities to learn on the job.

A number of potential explanations have been offered for why nonwhites, especially nonwhite teenagers, have greater difficulty finding employment than whites. Some revolve around the methods of job search used. For example, it has been argued that nonwhites rely on institutions such as the U.S. Employment Service to find jobs, while whites tend to find jobs through friends and neighbors.[42] Others focus on the growing concentration of nonwhite youths in the central cities, while employment opportunities have been moving to the suburbs and nonmetropolitan areas. However, the data indicate that nonwhite teenage unemployment rates are higher than white teenage unemployment rates in all types of geographic areas (central city, suburban, and nonmetropolitan).[43] Moreover, even if nonwhite youths were reallocated across areas so that, in each, their proportionate representation relative to that of white youths was the same, the data suggest that the overall black/white teenage unemployment rate differential would fall by less than a tenth.

Other explanations revolve around more traditional supply and demand factors, including the relative growth in the nonwhite teenage population coupled with increases in the minimum wage, the growth of the adult female labor supply (see Chapter 4 for evidence on the substitutability of adult females and black teenagers), the possibly reduced willingness of nonwhite teens to accept low-wage jobs, the reduction in the size of the armed forces, employer prejudice against nonwhite teens, and the possibly lower-quality education that nonwhite teens receive, especially in inner-city areas, that may reduce their perceived attractiveness to employers.[44] It is clear, however, that no single explanation is sufficient to account for the much higher rates of nonwhite teenage unemployment.

Furthermore, focusing on the relative unemployment rates of black teenagers does not fully capture the magnitude of their *nonemployment* problem. For example, while the employment/population ratio for 18- and 19-year-old white males remained roughly constant during the 1955–84 period at about 0.60, the comparable ratio for minority 18- and 19-year-old males fell from 0.66 to only 0.33.[45] The reasons for this decline, unfortunately, are not well understood.

---

42. Paul Osterman, "Racial Differentials in Male Youth Unemployment," in U.S. Department of Labor, *Conference Report on Youth Unemployment: Its Measurement and Meaning* (Washington, D.C.: U.S. Government Printing Office, 1978), and Harry J. Holzer, "Search Method Used by Unemployed Youth," National Bureau of Economic Research Working Paper no. 1859, March 1986.

43. U.S. Department of Labor, *1978 Employment and Training Report of the President* (Washington, D.C.: U.S. Government Printing Office, 1978), 73, and David Ellwood, "The Spatial Mismatch Hypothesis: Are There Teenage Jobs Missing in the Ghetto?" in *The Black Youth Unemployment Crisis,* ed. Richard Freeman and Harry Holzer.

44. Evidence on minimum wage effects was discussed in Chapter 3. For evidence that black teens may have higher wage aspirations relative to their market opportunities than white teens of comparable characteristics, see Harry Holzer, "Reservation Wages and Their Labor Market Effects for Black and White Male Youths," *Journal of Human Resources* 21 (Spring 1986): 157–77.

45. Albert Rees, "An Essay on Youth Joblessness," *Journal of Economic Literature* 25 (June 1986): 613–28, Table 2.

Cyclical Variations in Unemployment Rates Across Groups and the Persistence of Unemployment

Not only do unemployment rates vary across groups at a point in time, but the relationship between the unemployment rates of different groups varies over the business cycle. Specifically, the unemployment rates of teenagers, females, nonwhite males, and Hispanics are much more sensitive to fluctuations in aggregate demand than are the unemployment rates of adult white males.[46] In part this reflects that those hired last have less seniority and thus are the first to be laid off in a downswing. In part also, it reflects the increased difficulty that members of these groups face finding employment in a downswing.

A temporary shock to the economy that lasts only one period will in fact cause unemployment to rise above its full-employment level for a number of periods.[47] The reason for this is that in a recession the unemployment pool is disproportionately made up of individuals who have a low probability of finding employment (low P_{ue}), such as teenagers and nonwhite males. Moreover, as an expansion begins, these people's share in the stock of unemployment goes up, both because adult white males (with high P_{ue}) are the first to find employment and because the expansion induces more teenagers to join the labor force.[48] Given the relatively low probabilities that these people have of finding a job, the aggregate unemployment rate declines only gradually, and above-"normal" unemployment will persist for a while even after the shock is over.

GOVERNMENT POLICY AND FRICTIONAL UNEMPLOYMENT: THE EFFECTS OF UNEMPLOYMENT BENEFITS ON JOB SEARCH

As noted earlier in the chapter, because information about job opportunities and workers' characteristics is imperfect, it will take time for job matches to be made between unemployed workers and potential employers. Other things equal, the lower the probability that unemployed workers will become employed in a period (the lower P_{ue} is), the higher will be their expected duration of unemployment and the higher will be the unemployment rate.

Critics of the unemployment insurance system often point out that the existence of UI benefits reduces the costs of being unemployed and may prolong the time that unemployed workers spend searching for jobs.[49] Supporters of the UI system respond that an explicit purpose of the UI system when it was founded in the late 1930s was to provide unemployed workers with

---

46. See Kim Clark and Lawrence Summers, "Demographic Differences in Cyclical Employment Variation," *Journal of Human Resources* 16 (Winter 1981): 61–79, and Gregory DeFreitas, "A Time-Series Analysis of Hispanic Unemployment," *Journal of Human Resources* 21 (Winter 1986): 24–43.

47. See Michael Darby, John Haltiwanger, and Mark Plant, "Unemployment Rate Dynamics and Persistent Unemployment Under Rational Expectations," *American Economic Review* 75 (September 1985): 614–37.

48. Kim Clark and Lawrence Summers, "Demographic Differences . . ."

49. Martin Feldstein, "The Economics of the New Unemployment," *Public Interest* 33 (Fall 1973): 3–42.

temporary resources to enable them to turn down low-wage jobs that were not commensurate with their skill levels and to keep searching for better jobs.[50] That is, many believe that while the existence of UI benefits might prolong spells of unemployment, such benefits also might lead to higher post-unemployment wages and better job matches, and better job matches might reduce subsequent job turnover, thus providing a further benefit to society.

Before we turn to the empirical evidence on these points, analyzing a formal model of job search will yield implications about a variety of labor market phenomena in addition to the role of UI benefits in job search.[51] This model will make the key assumption that wages are associated with the characteristics of jobs, not with the characteristics of the specific individuals who fill them.[52]

Suppose that employers differ in the set of minimum hiring standards they use. Hiring standards may include educational requirements, job training, work experience, performance on hiring tests, etc. For expositional convenience, suppose this set of attributes can be summarized in a single variable, K, which will denote the minimum skill level a job requires. Associated with each job is a wage, $W(K)$—a wage that is a function of the required skill level and not of the particular characteristics of the people hired. We assume that the wage rate is an increasing function of the minimum required skill level and that two employers using the same hiring standard will offer the same wage.

Because different employers have different hiring standards, there will be a distribution of wage offers associated with job vacancies in the labor market. This distribution of wage offers is denoted by $f(W)$ in Figure 15.6. As one moves to the right in the figure, the minimum required skill level and offered wage on a job increase. Since $f(W)$ represents a *probability distribution* of wage offers, the area under the curve sums to one (that is, the distribution contains 100 percent of all wage offers in the market). Each wage offer (on the horizontal axis) is shown in relation to that offer's share in the distribution (on the vertical axis).

Now suppose a given unemployed individual has skill level K^*. Since no firm will hire a worker who does not meet its hiring standards, the maximum wage that this individual could hope to receive is $W^*(K^*)$. An individual who knew which firms had a hiring standard of K^* would apply to them and, since the individual meets their hiring standards, would be hired at a wage of W^*, assuming a vacancy existed.

50. William Haber and Merrill Murray, *Unemployment Insurance in the American Economy* (Homewood, Ill.: Irwin, 1966), 26–35.

51. Our discussion here draws heavily on Dale T. Mortensen, "Job Search, the Duration of Unemployment, and the Phillips Curve," *American Economic Review* 60 (December 1970): 846–62. Dale T. Mortensen, "Models of Search in the Labor Market," in *Handbook of Labor Economics*, ed. Orley Ashenfelter and Richard Layard (Amsterdam: North-Holland, 1986), and Theresa Devine and Nicholas Kiefer, *Empirical Labor Economics: The Search Approach* (New York: Oxford University Press, 1990), provide surveys of the theoretical and empirical literature on job search models.

52. Such an assumption has been made in another context by Lester Thurow, *Generating Inequality* (New York: Basic Books, 1975).

FIGURE 15.6   Choice of Reservation Wage in a Model of Job Search

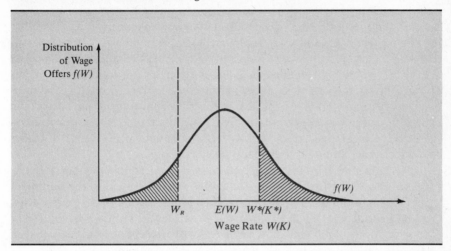

Suppose, instead, that job market information is imperfect in the sense that, while the individual knows the shape of the distribution of wage offers, $f(W)$, he or she does *not* know what each individual firm's wage offer or hiring standard will be. One can conceptualize job search as a process in which the person randomly knocks on the doors of personnel departments of firms. If the firm's hiring standard exceeds K^*, the person is rejected for the job. However, if the hiring standard is K^* or less, the person is offered the job. While the individual might find it advantageous to accumulate a number of job offers and then accept the best, job-seekers—especially those at the lower end of the skill ladder—are not always allowed such a luxury. Rather, they must instantly decide whether or not to accept a job offer, because otherwise the offer will be extended to a different applicant.

How does an unemployed worker know whether to accept a particular job offer? One strategy is to decide on a *minimum acceptance* (or *reservation*) *wage* and then to accept only those offers above this level. The critical question then is, "How is this reservation wage determined?"

To answer this question, suppose W_R is the reservation wage that is chosen (in Figure 15.6) by a person who has skill level K^*. Now observe that this individual's job application will be rejected by any firm that offers a wage higher than $W^*(K^*)$; the person will not meet its minimum hiring standards. Similarly, the person will reject any job offers that call for a wage less than W_R. Hence, the probability that he or she will find an acceptable job in any period is simply the unshaded area under the curve between W_R and W^*. The higher this probability, the lower the expected duration of unemployment. Given that the person finds a job, his or her expected wage is simply the weighted average of the job offers in the W_R to W^* range. This average (or expected) wage is denoted by $E(W)$ in Figure 15.6.

If the individual were to choose a slightly higher reservation wage, his or her choice would have two effects. On the one hand, since the person would now reject more low-wage jobs, his or her expected wage (once employed) would increase. On the other hand, rejecting more job offers also decreases the probability of finding an acceptable job in any given period, thus increasing the expected duration of unemployment. Put another way, higher reservation wages lead to the costs of longer expected spells of unemployment, but also to the benefits of higher expected wages once a job is found. Each unemployed individual will choose his or her reservation wage so that, at the margin, the expected costs of longer spells of unemployment just equal the expected benefits of higher post-unemployment wages. That is, the reservation wage should be chosen so that the marginal benefit from a higher reservation wage just equals its marginal cost.

This simple model and associated decision rule lead to a number of implications. First, as long as the reservation wage is not set equal to the minimum wage offered in the market, the probability of finding a job will be less than one and hence some *search unemployment* will result. *Search unemployment* occurs when an individual does not necessarily accept the first job that is offered—a rational strategy in a world of imperfect information.[53]

Second, since the reservation wage will always be chosen to be less than the wage commensurate with the individual's skill level, $W^*(K^*)$, virtually all individuals will be *underemployed* once they find a job (in the sense that their expected earnings will be less than W^*). This underemployment is a cost of imperfect information; better labor market information would improve the job-matching process.

Third, otherwise identical individuals will wind up receiving different wages. Two individuals with the same skill level should choose the same reservation wage and should have the same *expected* post-unemployment wage. However, the wages they actually wind up with will depend upon pure luck—the wage offer between W_R and W^* they happen to find. In a world of imperfect information, then, no economic model can explain all the variation in wages across individuals.

Fourth, anything that reduces the cost of an individual's being unemployed should lead the person to increase his or her reservation wage, and should thus lead to longer durations of unemployment and higher expected post-unemployment wages. Since higher UI benefits reduce individuals' costs of unemployment, increasing such benefits should be associated with longer spells of unemployment (see Example 15.3) and higher post-unemployment wages. Higher UI benefits should also increase the probability that temporarily laid-off workers await recall rather than accepting other lower-paying jobs.[54]

---

53. Voluntary search unemployment is but one form of frictional unemployment, and frictional unemployment is but one form of overall unemployment; thus, only a portion of unemployment is of the voluntary search nature. Indeed, the data suggest that many unemployed workers never reject any job offer; see, for example, U.S. Bureau of Labor Statistics, Bulletin 1886, *Job Seeking Methods Used by American Workers* (Washington, D.C.: U.S. Government Printing Office, 1975).
54. Lawrence Katz and Bruce Meyer, "Unemployment Insurance, Recall Expectations, and Unemployment Outcomes."

EXAMPLE 15.3

Unemployment Insurance Benefits in Great Britain

Evidence that more generous unemployment insurance (UI) benefits lead to higher levels of unemployment is not confined to the United States. For example, Daniel Benjamin and Levis Kochin have found three pieces of information that seem to confirm the relationship for Great Britain during the period between World Wars I and II:

1. Increases in the aggregate British unemployment rate, even after controlling for the level of aggregate demand, were associated with increases in the British UI replacement rate over the 1920–38 period.
2. Teenagers, many of whom were either not eligible for UI benefits during this period or received very low benefits relative to their wages, had unemployment rates that were only a fraction of the adult unemployment rate. Further, the unemployment rate jumped markedly at ages 18 and 21, when UI benefits increased.
3. In 1932, the year a change in the British UI regulations reduced the possibility that unemployed married women could receive UI benefits, the unemployment rate for married women dropped sharply relative to the rate for males.

SOURCE: See Daniel Benjamin and Levis Kochin, "Searching for an Explanation of Unemployment in Interwar Britain," *Journal of Political Economy* 87 (June 1979): 441–78. Several comments, which challenge some of their findings, appear in the April 1982 issue of the journal.

Numerous studies have sought to estimate the effects of UI benefits on durations of unemployment and post-unemployment wages.[55] In the main, these studies use data on individuals and exploit the fact that replacement rates (the fraction of previous earnings that UI benefits replace) vary both *within* states, with individuals' previous earnings levels (see Figure 15.4), and *across* states. Evidence from these studies suggests quite strongly that higher UI replacement rates are associated with longer durations of unemployment; raising the replacement rate from 0.4 to 0.5 of previous weekly earnings may increase the average spell of unemployment by a half-week to one week. In

---

55. See, for example, Ronald G. Ehrenberg and Ronald L. Oaxaca, "Unemployment Insurance, Duration of Unemployment and Subsequent Wage Gain," *American Economic Review* 66 (December 1976): 754–66; Nicholas Kiefer and George Neumann, "An Empirical Job Search Model with a Test of the Constant Reservation Wage Hypothesis," *Journal of Political Economy* 87 (February 1979): 89–107; and John Ham and Samuel Rea, Jr., "Unemployment Insurance and Male Unemployment Duration in Canada," *Journal of Labor Economics* 5 (July 1987): 325–53. Gary Solon, "Work Incentive Effects of Taxing Unemployment Benefits," *Econometrica* 53 (March 1985): 295–306, shows that the change in federal income tax law that made some UI benefits count in taxable income resulted in shorter durations of unemployment. Since taxation of benefits is equivalent to a reduction in the benefit level, this result was expected.

contrast, the evidence on the effects of post-unemployment wages is much more mixed. For example, one study found that higher replacement rates were associated with higher post-unemployment wage rates for adults but not for teenagers.[56]

Fifth, anything that increases individuals' discount rates, or their need for current income relative to future income, should lead to lower reservation wages and hence to shorter expected durations of unemployment and lower post-unemployment wages. Thus, unemployed individuals from poor families may be more likely to settle for lower-paying jobs than will equally skilled unemployed individuals from higher-income families.

Sixth, the shorter the length of time that an individual expects to be employed, the smaller will be the payoff to job search activities and hence the lower will be the reservation wage. This lower reservation wage will lead to shorter durations of unemployment and lower post-unemployment wages for individuals with short expected job tenure.

Seventh, anything that causes unemployed workers to intensify their job search (to knock on more doors per day) will reduce the duration of unemployment, other things equal. More efficient collection/dissemination of information on both jobs and applicants can increase the speed of the search process for all parties in the market; enhanced computerization among employment agencies is one example of an innovation that could reduce unemployment. However, recognizing (from Chapters 6 and 7) that even unemployed workers have alternative uses for their time, another way to induce more search intensity is to directly reward those who spend more time productively searching for employment. For example, in an attempt to increase time allocated to search activities, some states have experimented with providing bonuses, through their unemployment insurance systems, to those who found jobs "quickly" (see Example 15.4).

Finally, increases in skill level—say, by means of participation in a government job-training program— will have two effects on unemployed workers. On the one hand, their W^* will increase, which, other things equal, will increase the proportion of jobs they are qualified for, decrease their expected duration of unemployment, and increase their expected post-unemployment wage. On the other hand, an increase in skill level will induce them to raise their reservation wage, which will increase the proportion of low-wage job offers they turn down and tend to increase both their expected duration of unemployment and their expected post-unemployment wage. Thus, while unambiguously increasing expected post-unemployment wages, an increase in skill levels has an ambiguous effect on the duration of unemployment. This final implication has direct bearing on how one should evaluate the effective-

---

56. Ehrenberg and Oaxaca, "Unemployment Insurance." The results for teens may imply that (a) unemployed teens do not search actively for work, (b) unemployed teens' job search is not productive, perhaps because of the narrow range of job opportunities they face, or (c) unemployed teens may search for jobs that offer greater training options and possible higher future wages, although not higher current wages. The available data do not permit one to determine which of these alternatives is correct.

EXAMPLE 15.4

The Unemployment Insurance Bonus Experiments

Between mid-1984 and mid-1985 the State of Illinois conducted a *claimant bonus* experiment to test whether providing cash bonuses to unemployment insurance (UI) recipients who found a new job "quickly" would be an effective way of reducing their durations of unemployment without adversely affecting their post-unemployment wages. The idea was that the promise of a cash bonus for rapid reemployment would cause UI recipients to increase the fraction of time they spent searching for new employment and that they would thus find acceptable jobs more quickly.

UI recipients in the experiment were randomly assigned to two groups. The first served as a control group and received regular UI benefits. Members of the second group were promised an additional cash bonus of $500 if they found a full-time job within eleven weeks and held that job for at least four months. Given that individuals were randomly assigned to the two groups, one would expect the two groups to exhibit, on average, roughly equivalent durations of unemployment and post-unemployment wages in the absence of any "bonus effect."

It turned out that people eligible for the bonus experienced one less week of unemployment, on average, than did members of the control group. Further, their post-unemployment wages were about the same as those among the control group. Thus, it appeared that offering the cash bonus to UI recipients achieved its goal. Policymakers were sufficiently interested in considering the possibility of reforming the UI system to include bonuses for rapid reemployment that further experiments involving the concept were conducted in the states of New Jersey, Pennsylvania, and Washington.

At the same time the claimant bonus experiment was undertaken, Illinois also undertook an *employer bonus experiment.* In this experiment, the UI recipients were again randomly assigned to two groups, and one group was told that if they found full-time employment within eleven weeks and held that job for at least four months, their *employers* would receive a $500 cash bonus. The intent here was to provide a subsidy to employers (see Chapter 4) in the hope that this would stimulate faster reemployment for unemployed workers. The results of this experiment suggested that the promise of an employer bonus did *not* significantly reduce the average duration of unemployment. Whether eligible recipients had difficulty explaining the potential subsidy to employers or whether their eligibility somehow made employers think they were less productive (see Example 4.2) is unclear.

SOURCES: Stephen Woodbury and Robert Spiegelman, "Bonuses to Workers and Employers to Reduce Unemployment: Randomized Trials in Illinois," *American Economic Review* 77 (September 1987): 513–30; Bruce Meyer, "Implications of the Illinois Reemployment Bonus Experiments for Theories of Unemployment and Policy Design," National Bureau of Economic Research Working Paper no. 2783 (Cambridge, Mass., December 1988). For a summary of a similar experiment in New Jersey, see Walter Corson, Paul Decker, Shari Miller Dunston, and Anne Gordon, "The New Jersey Unemployment Insurance Reemployment Demonstration Project: Final Evaluation Report" (U.S. Department of Labor, Employment Training Administration, 1989).

ness of government-sponsored training programs. One should *not* evaluate them on the basis of the initial post-program employment experience of program graduates; these individuals may rationally remain unemployed for a while, searching for jobs commensurate with their new skill levels. Rather, evaluations should be based on the longer-run experiences of program graduates.[57]

NORMATIVE ISSUES IN UNEMPLOYMENT

Is unemployment a serious problem? Certainly some level of frictional unemployment is unavoidable in a dynamic world fraught with imperfect information. Moreover, as we have seen, the parameters of the UI system encourage both additional search unemployment and temporary layoff (cyclical and seasonal) unemployment. Nonetheless, when unemployment rises above its full-employment or natural level, resources are being wasted. Some 30 years ago Arthur Okun pointed out that every 1-percentage-point decline in the aggregate unemployment rate was associated with a 3-percentage-point increase in the output our society produces. That relationship appears to have held up through 1975, although since 1975 it is more in the range of a 2-percentage-point increase in output. Even this last number, however, suggests the great costs our society pays for excessively high rates of unemployment.[58] Thus, while it is unlikely that zero unemployment would be an optimal rate, policies to reduce cyclical unemployment (in a noninflationary manner) are clearly desirable. Improving the functioning of labor markets would also reduce frictional and structural unemployment; however, the benefits of reduced unemployment must be weighed against the costs generated by the policies designed to accomplish this objective in each case.[59]

In addition to concern over the cost of unemployment, society should also be concerned about the distribution of unemployment across age/race/gender/ethnic groups. As Table 15.3 indicated, the incidence of unemployment is higher among nonwhites and Hispanics than whites, and among teens than nonteens. We have traced the labor market flows that are associated

---

57. An additional reason for doing this is that program effects may depreciate over time. For example, after completion of a training program, unemployed workers may be able to find a job. However, if they lose that job, the program may have no further positive effect on them. In this case, the short-run effects of a program might exceed its long-run effects. Knowledge of how long program effects last is clearly important.

58. Arthur Okun, "Potential GNP: Its Measurement and Significance," reprinted in *The Political Economy of Prosperity,* ed. Arthur Okun (Washington, D.C.: Brookings Institution, 1970). Recent evidence suggests that the relationship is more in the range of 2.2 to 1. See Robert J. Gordon and Robert E. Hall, "Arthur M. Okun 1928–1980," *Brookings Papers on Economic Activity,* 1980–1, 1–5. It is important to stress that the effects of a decrease in unemployment on output will depend upon whether the decrease in unemployment is due to an increase in employment (given the labor force) or a decrease in the labor force (given employment).

59. An additional cost of unemployment is that it is often associated with increased incidence of physical and mental ailments. For a summary of some of the evidence on this point, see Frank Tippit, "The Anguish of the Jobless," *Time,* January 18, 1982, 90. For a more careful study whose results lead one to question the effects of unemployment on mental health, see Anders Bjorklund, "Unemployment and Mental Health: Some Evidence from Panel Data," *Journal of Human Resources* 20 (Fall 1985): 469–83.

with some of these differentials. The major cause of high nonwhite adult male unemployment rates is the high probability that members of that group will leave or lose their jobs to become unemployed, and the fact that they remain attached to the labor force suggests that their unemployment problem is serious and that the case for government intervention is strong.

What about the high teenage unemployment rates, especially those of nonwhite teens? Is the high unemployment rate for teens a serious problem that policymakers should address? Some doubt the seriousness of the problem, pointing out that unemployment rates decline rapidly as youths reach their early twenties (see Table 15.3). To these doubters, high teenage unemployment rates are symptomatic of the process of job turnover and search that occurs when new entrants to the labor force seek to acquire information about labor markets and their own productive ability. Moreover, proponents of this view could note that approximately 50 percent of unemployed 16- to 19-year-olds and 90 percent of unemployed 16- to 17-year-olds are enrolled in school. Of in-school unemployed youths, 50 percent were searching only for temporary jobs in 1976 and only 10 percent had become unemployed by losing their previous job.[60] Finally, they could cite evidence that teenage unemployment is not always associated with low family incomes. For example, data from the *1976 Survey of Income and Education,* a large national survey conducted by the Census Bureau, indicate that less than 26 percent of unemployed youths aged 16 to 24 came from families whose family income fell below the poverty line.[61]

Of course, these arguments neglect a number of important points. First, a substantial body of evidence indicates that youth unemployment is highly correlated with youth criminal activity; thus, there are costs to society, as well as to the youths, of youth unemployment. Second, much youth unemployment is concentrated among nonwhite youths, and the distributional implications of this fact may be unacceptable to society, especially given the higher correlation between youth unemployment and poverty that exists for nonwhites. Finally, the effects of youth unemployment may be long-lasting, and unemployed teenagers may face reduced long-run earnings and employment prospects compared to teenagers who do not suffer unemployment. Although unemployment rates decline rapidly with age for younger adults, individuals who suffered unemployment as teenagers might be "scarred" in the sense of having relatively higher probabilities of adult unemployment or commanding relatively lower adult wage rates.

Somewhat surprisingly, until recently there was no evidence on the long-run effects of teenage unemployment. Those studies that have attempted to identify whether the experience of unemployment per se matters in the long

---

60. See Arvil Adams and Garth Mangum, *The Lingering Crisis of Youth Unemployment* (Kalamazoo, Mich.: W. E. Upjohn Institute, 1978), Chapter 3.

61. U.S. Congressional Budget Office, *Youth Unemployment: The Outlook and Some Policy Strategies* (Washington, D.C.: U.S. Government Printing Office, April 1978), Appendix Table A-5. It is worth noting, however, that this table also indicates that youth unemployment rates decline with family income and that more than 45 percent of unemployed *nonwhite* youths come from families with family incomes below the poverty line. Put another way, youth unemployment is much more highly correlated with poverty for nonwhites than it is for whites.

run have yielded ambiguous results, some finding that an early employment experience has a positive effect on later employment for teens but others finding very little effect.[62] Thus, our knowledge of whether teenage unemployment has long-run scarring effects is still quite imprecise.

MISCONCEPTION

"We should attack the problem of unemployment by compelling workers to retire at age 55; this would open up jobs for younger workers who now have trouble finding them."

Analysis

Unemployment levels higher than some "natural" level are socially costly because productive resources are underutilized. However, to legislatively *compel* productive workers to quit working is *equally* costly even if each older worker's departure were to ultimately create an opening for an unemployed younger worker. A policy that achieves *increased* utilization of idle resources, not merely a *redistribution* of idleness, would be far more beneficial to society.

Principle

The social cost of an action is the forgone utility that the action requires; the social benefit is the added utility it generates.

REVIEW QUESTIONS

1. A presidential hopeful is campaigning to raise unemployment compensation benefits and lower the full-employment target from a 6 percent to a 5.5 percent unemployment rate. Comment on the compatibility of these goals.
2. Government officials find it useful to measure the nation's "economic health." The unemployment rate is currently used as a major indicator of the relative strength of labor supply and demand. Do you think the unemployment rate is becoming more or less useful as an indicator of labor market tightness? What other measures might serve this purpose better?
3. The unemployment rate is a stock concept (something like the amount of water in a lake at a given time). The level of unemployment goes up or down as the *flows* into unemployment exceed or are slower than the flows out of unemployment. Is it important for policy purposes to accurately measure the *flows* into and out of unemployment, or is knowing the *level* of unemployment enough for most purposes? Justify your answer.
4. Is the following assertion true, false, or uncertain? "Increasing the level of unemployment insurance benefits will prolong the average length of spells of unemploy-

---

62. David Ellwood, "Teenage Unemployment: Permanent Scars or Temporary Blemishes"; Mary Corcoran, "The Employment, Wage, and Fertility Consequences of Teenage Women's Nonemployment"; and Robert Meyer and David Wise, "High School Preparation and Early Labor Force Experience"; all in *The Youth Labor Market Problem: Its Nature, Causes, and Consequences,* ed. Richard B. Freeman and David A. Wise (Chicago: University of Chicago Press, 1982), 349–85, 391–423, and 277–344.

ment. Hence, a policy of raising UI benefit levels is not socially desirable." Explain your answer.

5. Recent empirical evidence suggests that unemployed workers' reservation wages decline as their spells of unemployment lengthen. That is, the longer they have been unemployed, the lower are their reservation wages. Explain why this might be true.

6. In the 1970s Sweden adopted several new labor market policies affecting layoffs. Three were notable: (1) Plants that provided in-plant training instead of laying off workers in a recession received government subsidies; (2) All workers had to be given at least one month's notice before being laid off, and the required time in the average plant was two to three months; (3) Laid-off workers had to be given first option on new jobs with the former employer. What probable effects would these policies, taken as a whole, have on wages, employment, and unemployment in the long run?

7. In recent years the federal government has introduced and then expanded a requirement that unemployment insurance beneficiaries pay income tax on their unemployment benefits. Explain what effect you would expect this taxation of UI benefits to have on the unemployment rate.

8. It was pointed out in Chapter 11 that the present value of benefits in many pension plans is greater if a person retires before the normal retirement age. In short, there is a large inducement for many private sector workers to retire early. What effect will increasing the inducements to retire early have on the unemployment rate of older men? Fully explain your answer, making use of the assumption that retired workers withdraw from the labor force and do not seek or obtain other jobs.

SELECTED READINGS

Clark, Kim B., and Summers, Lawrence. "Labor Market Dynamics and Unemployment: A Reconsideration." *Brookings Papers on Economic Activity,* 1979–1, 13–60.

Freeman, Richard, and Holzer, Harry, eds. *The Black Youth Unemployment Crisis.* Chicago: University of Chicago Press, 1986.

Freeman, Richard, and Wise, David. *The Youth Labor Market Problem: Its Nature, Causes, and Consequences.* Chicago: University of Chicago Press, 1982.

Lang, Kevin, and Leonard, Jonathan, eds. *Unemployment and the Structure of Labor Markets.* New York: Basil Blackwell, 1987.

National Commission on Employment and Unemployment Statistics. *Counting the Labor Force.* Washington, D.C.: U.S. Government Printing Office, 1979.

Rees, Albert. "An Essay on Youth Joblessness." *Journal of Economic Literature* 24 (June 1986): 613–28.

The Relationship Between the Unemployment Rate and Labor Market Flows

The objective of this appendix is to formally derive the exact equation whose implications are summarized in text equation (15.2). This equation relates a group's unemployment rate (**u**) to the proportions of its members that move between employment, unemployment, and not-in-the-labor-force status each month. As in equation (15.2), let P_{ij} denote the proportion of individuals in a group in labor market state i that move to labor market state j during the period, where the different states are employed (e), unemployed (u), and not in the labor force (n). The numbers of people in each of these states at the start of a period are denoted by E, U, and N, respectively.

Labor market equilibrium is defined as a situation in which the number of employed individuals and the number of unemployed individuals both remain constant over time. In this case, the number of unemployed people at the start of a period who obtain jobs plus the number of people out of the labor force at the start of a period who obtain jobs are just equal to the number of people employed at the start of the period who become unemployed or drop out of the labor force during the period. That is,

$$P_{ue}U + P_{ne}N = (P_{eu} + P_{en})E \qquad (15A.1)$$

$$\underset{\text{the number}}{\underbrace{\text{who become employed}}} = \underset{\text{the number}}{\underbrace{\text{who leave employment}}}$$

Similarly, in equilibrium the number of people who become unemployed during the period (because of losing or leaving their previous jobs or unsuccessfully entering the labor force) just equals the number who leave unemployment (either because they found a job or because they left the labor force):

$$P_{eu}E + P_{nu}N = (P_{ue} + P_{un})U \qquad (15A.2)$$

$$\underset{\text{the number}}{\underbrace{\text{who become unemployed}}} = \underset{\text{the number}}{\underbrace{\text{who leave unemployment}}}$$

This appendix is based on Stephen T. Marston, "Employment Instability and High Unemployment Rates," *Brookings Papers on Economic Activity,* 1976–1, 169–203.

Multiplying (15A.1) by P_{nu} and (15A.2) by P_{ne} and then subtracting (15A.2) from (15A.1), one obtains:

$$P_{ue}P_{nu}U - P_{eu}P_{ne}E = (P_{eu} + P_{en})P_{nu}E - (P_{ue} + P_{un})P_{ne}U \qquad (15A.3)$$

or

$$[P_{ue}P_{nu} + P_{ne}(P_{ue} + P_{un})]U = [P_{eu}P_{ne} + P_{nu}(P_{eu} + P_{en})]E \qquad (15A.4)$$

Hence, in equilibrium the numbers of unemployed and employed individuals, solving from equation (15A.4), are related by

$$
\begin{aligned}
E &= U \frac{[P_{ue}P_{nu} + P_{ne}(P_{ue} + P_{un})]}{[P_{eu}P_{ne} + P_{nu}(P_{eu} + P_{en})]} \\
&= U \frac{[(P_{ne} + P_{nu})P_{ue} + P_{ne}P_{un}]}{[(P_{ne} + P_{nu})P_{eu} + P_{nu}P_{en}]}
\end{aligned}
\qquad (15A.5)
$$

The unemployment rate is now defined as the number of unemployed individuals divided by the sum of the unemployed and the employed:

$$\mathbf{u} = \frac{U}{(U + E)} \qquad (15A.6)$$

Substituting (15A.5) into (15A.6) and simplifying yields:

$$\mathbf{u} = \frac{1}{1 + \left[\dfrac{(P_{ne} + P_{nu})P_{ue} + (P_{ne})(P_{un})}{(P_{ne} + P_{nu})P_{eu} + (P_{nu})(P_{en})}\right]} \qquad (15A.7)$$

Thus, a group's unemployment rate depends upon the flow of its members between all three labor market states. Moreover, one can show that this equation implies that increases in P_{eu}, P_{en}, and P_{nu} all lead to increases in the unemployment rate, while increases in P_{ue}, P_{un}, and P_{ne} all lead to decreases in the unemployment rate.

16

Inflation and Unemployment

Throughout most of the 1970s and early 1980s the United States was faced with relatively high rates of wage and price *inflation* (that is, with relatively rapid and generally pervasive increases in wages and prices). Further, these increases were taking place in the context of high unemployment rates, so the country seemed to suffer the consequences of both inflation *and* unemployment at the same time. Simultaneously high rates of inflation and unemployment challenged the long-held belief that inflation would diminish if unemployment rose—a belief that seemed to have held out hope that government fiscal or monetary policies could be skillfully used to maneuver the economy to tolerable levels of both inflation and unemployment. Fortunately, by 1989 both inflation and unemployment had returned to more modest levels.

The causes and consequences of inflation, and the fiscal and monetary policies to remedy it, are beyond the scope of labor economics. Our intent in this chapter is to analyze the relationship between inflation and unemployment so that the connections between what happens in the labor market and what happens to prices in general are more clearly understood. Moreover, because our focus is on the labor market, we shall emphasize the price of labor—the wage rate—when discussing the issue of inflation.

MEASURING WAGE INFLATION

The overall rate of *wage inflation* in the economy is the annual percentage rate of increase in some composite measure of hourly earnings in the economy. The construction of such an index is a considerable task because *average* hourly earnings can change, even if the wage scales for every individual *job* remain constant. For example, if there is a shift in the distribution of employment towards high-wage industries (such as construction) and away from low-wage industries (such as retail trade), average hourly earnings will increase. Similarly, if there is a shift towards increased usage of highly paid skilled workers and away from lower-paid unskilled workers, average hourly earnings will increase. To take another example, if the age distribution of the work force shifts towards relatively fewer lower-paid new entrants, average hourly earnings will increase. Finally, if more overtime hours for which premium pay is received are worked relative to straight-time hours, average hourly earnings will again increase, other things equal.

The problem involved in all these examples is that average hourly earnings in the economy ($\overline{W}$) are a weighted average of the earnings of individuals in each industry/occupation/experience group (W_i). The weight assigned to each group's earnings (β_i) depends upon the fraction of all hours worked in the economy by individuals in the group and the fraction of hours worked by that group for which overtime pay is received. Changes in average hourly earnings may therefore reflect changes in the weights as well as changes in the wage scales of each group. Focusing simply on the growth of average hourly earnings, then, may give one a misleading impression of what is happening to wage scales for particular jobs.[1]

To partially take the above problem into account, government statisticians have constructed an index of adjusted average hourly earnings for nonsupervisory workers in the private nonagricultural sector. This index, which controls for changes in the industrial composition of employment and changes in overtime hours in manufacturing, is one of the most comprehensive measures of wage changes available.[2] As Table 16.1 indicates, between 1963 and 1989 this index increased at annual percentage rates of roughly 3 to 9 percent.

THE INFLATION/UNEMPLOYMENT TRADE-OFF

For many years economists believed that stable negative relationships, or *trade-off curves,* existed between the rates of wage (and price) inflation, on the one hand, and the overall unemployment rate in the economy, on the other. That is, higher levels of unemployment were thought to be associated with lower rates of wage and price inflation, and vice versa. The relationship

---

1. To see this point more clearly, suppose that there are n different industry/occupation/experience groups in the economy. Then average hourly earnings of all workers are given by

$$\overline{W} = \sum_{i=1}^{n} W_i \beta_i$$

and the percentage change in average hourly earnings is *approximately* equal to

$$\dot{\overline{W}} \approx \sum_{i=1}^{n} \dot{W}_i \beta_i + \sum_{i=1}^{n} W_i \dot{\beta}_i + \sum_{i=1}^{n} \dot{W}_i \dot{\beta}_i$$

where percentage change is indicated by a dot over a variable. Even if all wage rates were constant ($\dot{W}_i$ equal to zero for all i), average hourly earnings could still change if the weights changed, for in this case

$$\dot{\overline{W}} = \sum_{i=1}^{n} W_i \dot{\beta}_i$$

2. The index only partially controls for the problem of distinguishing between changes in wage scales and changes in the composition of employment because it makes no adjustment for changes in the *occupational* or *age* distributions of the work force.

TABLE 16.1   Unemployment Rate and Percentage Change in Earnings and Prices in the United States

Year	Percent Change in Adjusted Hourly Earnings of Nonsupervisory Workers in the Private Nonagricultural Sector	Unemployment Rate	Percent Change in the GNP Deflator
1963	2.8	5.5	1.6
1964	2.8	5.0	1.5
1965	3.6	4.4	2.7
1966	4.3	3.7	3.6
1967	5.0	3.7	2.6
1968	6.1	3.5	5.0
1969	6.7	3.4	5.6
1970	6.6	4.8	5.5
1971	7.2	5.8	5.7
1972	6.2	5.5	4.7
1973	6.2	4.8	6.5
1974	8.0	5.5	9.1
1975	8.4	8.3	9.8
1976	7.2	7.6	6.4
1977	7.6	6.9	6.7
1978	8.1	6.0	7.3
1979	8.0	5.8	8.9
1980	9.0	7.0	9.0
1981	9.1	7.5	9.7
1982	6.8	9.5	6.4
1983	4.6	9.5	3.9
1984	3.4	7.4	3.7
1985	3.0	7.1	3.0
1986	2.2	6.9	2.6
1987	2.5	6.1	3.2
1988	3.5	5.4	3.3
1989	4.0	5.2	4.1

SOURCE: *1990 Economic Report of the President* (Washington, D.C.: U.S. Government Printing Office, 1990), Tables C3, C39, and C44. The unemployment rate differs from that in Figure 2.2 because the labor force includes the resident armed forces.

between unemployment and wage inflation was dubbed the *Phillips curve,* after the noted economist who was an early observer of its existence.[3] The Phillips curve was thought to provide a range of feasible options for policymakers; through the appropriate use of monetary or fiscal policy, they could choose any unemployment/inflation combination along the curve. For example, a paper in 1959 by two well-known economists claimed that in 1960 the country could choose among the following alternatives (illustrated in Figure 16.1): 8 percent unemployment and zero wage inflation, 5–6 percent unemployment and 2–3 percent wage inflation, and 3 percent unemployment and 7 percent wage inflation.[4]

3. See A.W. Phillips, "The Relation Between Unemployment and the Rates of Change of Money Wage Rates in the United Kingdom, 1862–1957," *Economica* 25 (November 1958): 283–99.
4. Paul A. Samuelson and Robert M. Solow, "Our Menu of Policy Choices," in *The Battle Against Unemployment,* ed. Arthur M. Okun (New York: W. W. Norton, 1965), 71–76.

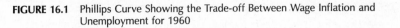

FIGURE 16.1   Phillips Curve Showing the Trade-off Between Wage Inflation and Unemployment for 1960

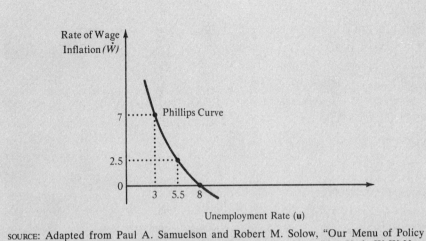

SOURCE: Adapted from Paul A. Samuelson and Robert M. Solow, "Our Menu of Policy Choices," *The Battle Against Unemployment,* ed. Arthur M. Okun (New York: W. W. Norton, 1965), 74. Used by permission of the publisher.

Unfortunately, the well-defined, stable set of choices once thought to exist appears to have vanished. Table 16.1 contains data on both the unemployment rate and wage inflation from 1963 to 1989. These data indicate that during the 1960s a negative association did appear to exist between the unemployment rate and the rate of wage inflation. Indeed, the steady tightening of labor markets and decreasing unemployment rates of the late 1960s were associated with increasing rates of wage inflation. However, during the 1970s the relationship appears, at first glance, to have broken down; one often observes simultaneous increases in the rate of unemployment and the rate of wage inflation during that decade. The result is that, while an unemployment rate of 5.5 percent was associated with a wage inflation rate of 2.8 percent in 1963, the same unemployment rate was associated with wage inflation rates of 6.2 to 8.0 percent during the 1970s. In contrast, during the late 1980s one often observed simultaneous decreases in the rates of unemployment and wage inflation, and in 1988 unemployment of nearly 5.5 percent was associated with wage inflation of 3.5 percent! These relationships suggest that the belief in a stable negative trade-off between inflation and unemployment is unwarranted.

An alternative interpretation of these data, however, is that, while a trade-off between the rates of inflation and unemployment exists at a *point in time,* the *position* of the trade-off curve is determined by a number of other factors that can change over time. The net effect of these other factors was to shift the trade-off curve shown in Figure 16.1 *upward and to the right* between 1960 and the early 1980s. Thus, the trade-off society faced in the early 1980s lay everywhere above the one that prevailed during the 1970s, which in turn was itself higher than the curve that prevailed during the 1960s (see Figure 16.2). Put another way, the argument underlying Figure 16.2 is that

FIGURE 16.2 The Changing Trade-off Between the Rate of Wage Inflation and the Level of the Unemployment Rate

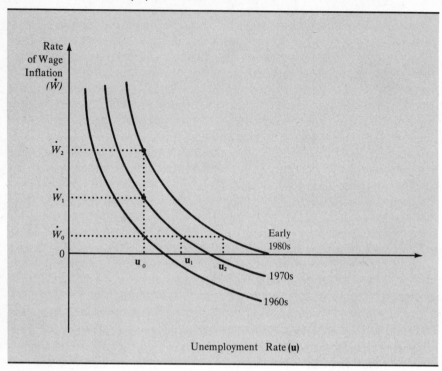

progressively higher rates of wage inflation ($\dot{W}_0$, $\dot{W}_1$, and $\dot{W}_2$) became associated over time with any given level of unemployment (u_0 in Figure 16.2). Conversely, progressively higher unemployment rates (u_0, u_1, u_2) became associated with any given level of wage inflation ($\dot{W}_0$). Indeed, some economists suggest that between 1960 and 1980, the trade-off may have shifted to the right by as much as 3 percentage points.[5] In recent years, however, the trade-off curve appears to have shifted back to the left.

It is also possible that the Phillips curve has become flatter over the years, so that the decrease in wage inflation accompanying a 1-percentage-point increase in the unemployment rate is now smaller than it once was. Any growth in the downward rigidity of wages would cause a reduction in the effectiveness of traditional macroeconomic policies to combat inflation, and would increase the importance of alternative labor market policies.

Our discussions in this chapter center on the issue of trade-offs between inflation and unemployment. In the remainder of this section we present a simple conceptual model that examines why the trade-off between wage inflation and unemployment may exist and identifies the forces that may have caused the trade-off to shift over time. This model provides a framework that is then used to discuss the various labor market policies that might enable policymakers to shift the trade-off curve in a more favorable direction.

This chapter will also discuss the relationship between wage and price behavior and consider the conditions under which a stable, long-run trade-off between *price* inflation and unemployment will occur. Although *at a point in time* a trade-off may exist between the rate of *wage* inflation and the unemployment rate, it does not necessarily follow that *in the long run* a stable trade-off exists between the rate of *price* inflation and the unemployment rate. Indeed, many macroeconomists argue that this long-run trade-off curve is vertical and that attempts to keep the unemployment rate artificially low will lead to ever-accelerating rates of inflation.[6]

This chapter then considers the role of unions and the collective bargaining process. It explores why changing institutional arrangements, in particular the spread of *multiyear agreements* with *cost-of-living escalator clauses,* may have been partially responsible for the growing insensitivity of inflation to the unemployment rate.

The final section of the chapter returns to the central issue of how government policies might reduce the rate of inflation associated with any given level of unemployment. This section focuses on the various *incomes policies* that have been pursued in the United States since 1960—policies in which the government has tried directly to influence wages and prices by specifying "desired wage and price behavior," sometimes with enforcement mechanisms tied to the program. After discussing the available evidence on the effectiveness of these programs, we conclude with a discussion of whether an expansion of profit sharing as a basis for pay might reduce the rates of wage and price inflation in the economy.[7]

The Basic Model

Figure 16.3 represents wage determination in a competitive labor market.[8] For simplicity we shall *initially* take product prices as fixed so that the demand and supply curves can be drawn in terms of the money wage (W) rather than the real wage. In this labor market, the equilibrium wage is W_0 and the equilibrium employment level is E_0. We know from earlier chapters that whenever the wage is above W_0 it will fall, and that whenever it is below W_0 it will rise, to restore equilibrium.

How rapidly will the wage rate change when it is away from its equilibrium value? It seems reasonable to assume that the speed at which the wage rate changes is related to the extent to which the labor market is in disequilibrium, as measured by the excess demand for labor. Thus, although the wage rate will be increasing whenever it is below W_0 and a positive excess demand

---

6. See, for example, Milton Friedman, "The Role of Monetary Policy," *American Economic Review* 58 (March 1968): 1–17, and *Rational Expectations — Fresh Ideas That Challenge Some Established Views of Policy Making* (Minneapolis, Minn.: Federal Reserve Bank of Minneapolis, 1977). The appendix to this chapter details these arguments.

7. See, for example, Martin Weitzman, *The Share Economy* (Cambridge, Mass.: Harvard University Press, 1983).

8. This section initially draws heavily on Richard Lipsey, "The Relation Between Unemployment and the Rate of Change in Money Wage Rates in the United Kingdom, 1862–1957: A Further Analysis," *Economica* 27 (February 1960): 1–31.

FIGURE 16.3 The Relationship Between Wage Changes and the Excess Demand for Labor: Prices Held Constant

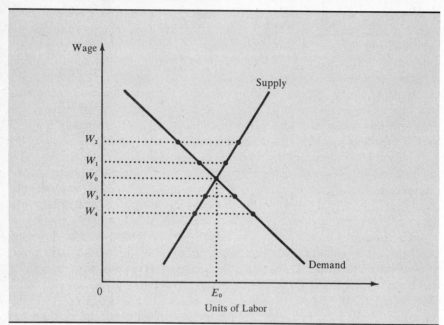

for labor exists, it is likely to be increasing more rapidly when it is at W_4 in Figure 16.3 than when it is at W_3. Similarly, while the wage rate will be falling whenever it is above W_0 and an excess supply (or negative excess demand) for labor exists, it is likely to be falling more rapidly when it is at W_2 than when it is at W_1.

The simplest possible way to formalize this idea is to assume that the percentage rate of change of wages ($\dot{W}$) is proportional to the excess demand for labor (X). Because a given *absolute* difference between quantity demanded and quantity supplied of labor ($D - S = 1,000$, say) would indicate a greater degree of disequilibrium if 10,000 people were seeking work than if 100,000 were in the market, we will measure excess demand as $(D - S)/S$, so that

$$\dot{W} = \alpha X = \alpha[(D - S)/S] \qquad (16.1)$$

This relationship is depicted in panel (a) of Figure 16.4; the larger α is, the faster wages adjust to disequilibrium. Note that when supply exceeds demand, X—and hence $\dot{W}$—will be negative. (One could, of course, allow the responses to be nonsymmetric to excess demands and excess supplies. For example, if wages are *sticky* in a downward direction, α would be smaller and the curve flatter in the region of excess supply that lies to the left of the vertical axis. However, for expository convenience we shall ignore this complication here.)

Unfortunately, because the excess demand for labor is usually not observable, it is necessary to replace it with an observable variable, such as the un-

FIGURE 16.4   Derivation of the Trade-off Between the Rate of Wage Inflation and the Unemployment Rate

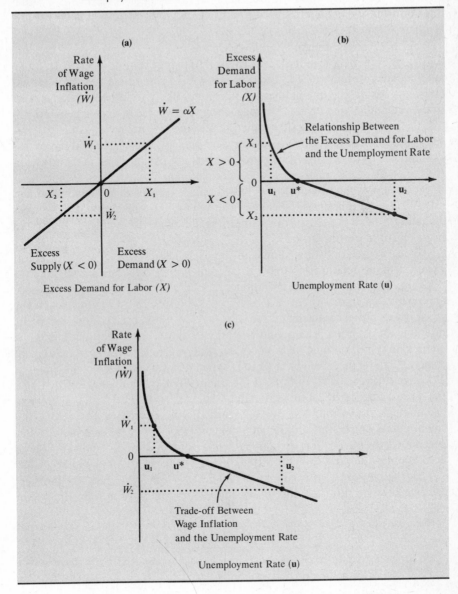

employment rate, when empirically analyzing wage changes. What is the relationship between the excess demand for labor and the unemployment rate (**u**)? We know from Chapter 15 that some unemployment exists even when labor markets are in balance, with the overall quantity of labor demanded just equal to the overall quantity supplied ($X = 0$). This frictional unemployment occurs because normal job turnover and movements of people into and out of the labor market take place in circumstances where information is imperfect and job matching takes time. In panel (b) of Figure 16.4, u^* is the unemployment rate that exists when the excess demand for labor is zero; this is often referred to in the economics literature as the *natural* or *full-employment rate of unemployment* (see Chapter 15).[9]

As the excess demand for labor increases and labor markets become tighter, the unemployment rate will fall. Although the time it takes to make job matches can be reduced, it will probably take some time to fill job vacancies. As a result, the unemployment rate is not likely to fall below some positive level, and as that level is approached, any increases in excess demand will call forth progressively smaller reductions in the unemployment rate. The result is a nonlinear relationship between the unemployment rate and the excess demand for labor, as drawn in the $X > 0$ region of panel (b). In contrast, in the region of excess supply (below the horizontal axis, where $X < 0$), increases in excess supply may well lead to proportional increases in the unemployment rate. Thus, the relationship between the unemployment rate and the excess demand for labor is perhaps linear in the region of excess supply, as illustrated in panel (b) of Figure 16.4.

The two relationships shown in panels (a) and (b), the wage inflation/excess demand relationship and the unemployment rate/excess demand relationship, contain all the information required to derive the wage inflation/unemployment trade-off curve shown in panel (c). Refer in Figure 16.4 to the point where the excess demand for labor is zero. From panel (a) we know the rate of wage inflation is zero, and from panel (b) we know that the unemployment rate is u^*. Thus, one point on our wage inflation/unemployment trade-off curve in panel (c) is $(0, u^*)$. When the excess demand for labor is X_1, wage inflation is $\dot{W}_1$ in (a) and the unemployment rate is u_1 in (b). When the excess supply of labor is X_2, the wage inflation rate is $\dot{W}_2$ in (a) and the unemployment rate is u_2 in (b). Thus, $(\dot{W}_1, u_1)$ and $(\dot{W}_2, u_2)$ are two additional points on the inflation/unemployment trade-off curve in panel (c). Repeating the argument for all possible values of the excess demand for labor leads one to trace out the entire trade-off curve in panel (c) of Figure 16.4.

In the context of this simple labor market model, the trade-off between the rate of wage inflation and the unemployment rate arises from the postu-

---

9. *Insider-outsider* models, discussed briefly in Chapter 15, challenge the notion that there is a unique natural rate of unemployment. If it is costly for firms to replace their incumbent workers (the insiders) with unemployed outsiders owing, for example, to the presence of specific training, then unionized insiders may be able to raise their wages above market-clearing levels and ignore the presence of unemployed outsiders. In such models, unemployment may persist for long periods of time, and the equilibrium unemployment rate will tend to rise as unemployment persists (a phenomenon known as "hysteresis"). Some people have used this type of model to try to explain the persistence of high unemployment rates in Europe (see Example 15.2).

    Extensive discussion of such models is beyond the scope of this text. For discussions, the interested reader can consult Lawrence F. Katz, "Some Recent Developments in Labor Economics and Their Implications for Macroeconomics," *Journal of Money, Credit and Banking* 20 (August 1988, pt. 2): 507–22; Robert J. Gordon, "Hysteresis in History: Was There Ever a Phillips Curve?" *American Economic Association Papers and Proceedings* 79 (May 1989): 220–25; and Olivier J. Blanchard and Lawrence H. Summers, "Hysteresis and the European Unemployment Problem," in *NBER Macroeconomics Annual, 1986*, ed. Stanley Fisher (Cambridge, Mass.: MIT Press, 1986): 15–77.

lated responsiveness of wages to the excess demand for labor. However, there are numerous forces affecting the *position* of the curve that traces out the aggregate relationship between the unemployment rate and the rate of wage inflation. Four of these forces are the current and expected rates of price inflation, the age/gender distribution of the labor force, the growth rates of employment and the labor force, and the dispersion of unemployment rates across markets.

Forces Affecting the Wage Inflation/ Unemployment Trade-off

Price Inflation.   So far we have assumed the price level to be fixed. However, current and expected future rates of price inflation clearly influence the rate of *money*-wage inflation associated with any given level of excess demand for labor. Since both the demand and the supply curves of labor are functions of the *real*-wage rate, an increase in the *price* level requires a proportional increase in the *money-wage* rate simply to keep the real wage and the excess demand for labor constant. The relationship between wage changes and the excess demand for labor described in Figures 16.3 and 16.4 actually refers to changes in the real wage (prices were assumed fixed while wages changed). Hence, the effect of price inflation is to *increase* the rate of money-wage inflation associated with any given level of the excess demand for labor.

Our discussion so far has assumed that labor markets are competitive and that all real wages are renegotiated continually as labor market conditions change. Later in the chapter we shall introduce several institutional features of the collective bargaining process in the United States into our discussion. Here we shall consider how the introduction of one such feature, contracts that are negotiated only periodically, affects the analysis. From employees' perspectives, past price changes may influence wage demands during contract negotiations because they signify that real wages are below the level employees expected *if* such price changes were not fully anticipated at the time of the previous contract negotiations. Expected future price changes may also matter because they translate money-wage changes into expected real-wage changes. Similarly, from employers' perspectives, past and expected future price changes may affect their willingness to increase wages, as increases in output prices, *ceteris paribus,* reduce real wages and hence employers' costs of doing business.

Unambiguously, then, higher *expected* price changes should lead to higher wage changes in a world where wages are adjusted only periodically. It is unclear, however, whether an extra 1 percent increase in expected price inflation will automatically lead to an extra 1 percent increase in money wages; this depends, among other things, on the relative bargaining power of employees and employers and the institutional process by which wages are set. For now, let us assume that a 1 percent increase in the expected rate of price inflation ($\dot{P}^e$) shifts the rate of money-wage inflation associated with a given excess demand for labor up by γ percent, where γ may be less than or equal to one.[10] That is,

$$\dot{W} = \alpha X + \gamma \dot{P}^e \qquad 0 \leq \gamma \leq 1 \tag{16.2}$$

Equation (16.2) is illustrated by Figure 16.5. If the upward shift in the relationship between $\dot{W}$ and X in Figure 16.5 is translated back to panel (a) of Figure 16.4 and its implications for panel (c) are traced through panel (b), it should become clear that increases in the expected rate of price inflation cause the whole wage inflation/unemployment trade-off curve in panel (c) to shift up.[11]

Age/Gender Composition of the Labor Force. Chapter 15 noted that teenagers tend to have higher unemployment rates than adults, that nonwhites tend to have higher unemployment rates than whites, and that women aged 25–54, who a decade ago had higher unemployment rates than men of comparable age, recently have had roughly equivalent rates of unemployment. The aggregate unemployment rate associated with any given degree of labor market *tightness,* or excess demand for labor, is simply the weighted average of the unemployment rates for the various age/gender groups, with the weights being the share of the group in the overall labor force. During the 1960s and 1970s the shares of teenagers and women in the labor force increased because of the growing share of teenagers in the population and increasing female labor force participation rate. Since these groups had higher than average unemployment rates, the overall unemployment rate associated with any level of the excess demand for labor also increased, as illustrated in Figure 16.6, in the 1970s.[12]

---

10. For simplicity, we have focused here only on expected price inflation and ignored past price inflation per se. We also have restricted γ to be no greater than one; this need not always be the case. Many leading modern macroeconomists, in particular those working in what is sometimes called the *new classical macroeconomics* tradition, assert almost as a matter of first principles that γ must equal unity. That is, they argue that if labor markets are competitive and real wages adjust to clear labor markets, then changes in the expected inflation rate must lead to equal percentage changes in money-wage rates to keep real wages at their market-clearing levels. We discuss some of their views and attempts to obtain evidence on the actual magnitude of γ later in the chapter. Here we simply note that the simple labor market model sketched above abstracts from a host of institutional features found in labor markets in which contracts are negotiated only periodically between unions and employers and in which employers may pay above market-clearing wages (see Chapters 11 and 12). While we obviously would not go as far as one labor economist (now a university president), who, in dismissing the relevance of competitive labor market models, is widely reputed to have said, "The invisible hand is all thumbs in the labor market," we see no reason to maintain here that γ must be unity. As will become clear later, its magnitude is of fundamental importance in determining whether there is a trade-off between inflation and unemployment in the long run.

11. Of course, since wages are a substantial fraction of production costs, increases in the rate of wage inflation should lead, other things equal, to increases in the rate of price inflation. This interdependency will be discussed later in the chapter.

12. An early exposition of the importance of this factor is found in George Perry, "Changing Labor Markets and Inflation," *Brookings Papers on Economic Activity,* 1970–3, 411–41. Since 1980 the share of females and nonwhites in the labor force has continued to increase, but the share of teenagers has declined (see Table 16.2).

FIGURE 16.5   Price Inflation Shifts Up the Wage-Inflation/Excess-Demand-for-Labor Relationship

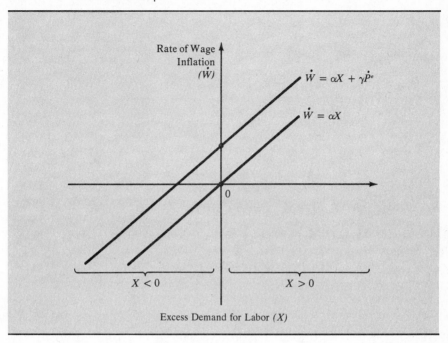

An increase in the level of unemployment associated with each level of the excess demand for labor implies, other things equal, that a higher unemployment rate will be associated with each rate of wage inflation. Put another way, the changing age/gender composition of the labor force caused the wage inflation/unemployment trade-off curve to shift up. At any level of the aggregate unemployment rate, the rate of wage inflation was higher than before. Furthermore, as indicated in Figure 16.6 (and in Chapter 15), the full-employment unemployment rate also has increased (from **u*** to **u**** in Figure 16.6).

In recent years, as the unemployment rates of women have approached those of men and as the share of teenagers in the labor force has fallen, the overall unemployment rate associated with any level of excess demand for labor has probably declined. This decline will tend to reduce the rate of wage inflation associated with each rate of unemployment.

The Growth of Employment and the Labor Force.   Another factor that might cause the excess-demand-for-labor/unemployment-rate relationship to shift up is the growth rate of employment and the labor force. Other things equal, the more rapidly aggregate employment is growing, the greater the number of job vacancies employers will have to fill. Even if the labor force is growing to keep pace with employment opportunities, rapid expansion may make it more difficult to match workers and jobs and, since voluntary and involuntary job turnover is highest among new employees, rapid expansion also

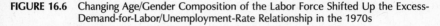

FIGURE 16.6   Changing Age/Gender Composition of the Labor Force Shifted Up the Excess-Demand-for-Labor/Unemployment-Rate Relationship in the 1970s

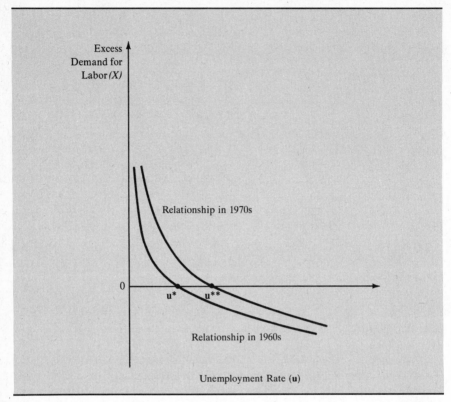

increases the need to hire replacements, compounding employers' problems. Because of this, one might expect to observe a larger excess demand for labor associated with any given unemployment rate when employment is growing rapidly than when it is growing slowly.

In fact, both the civilian labor force and employment grew considerably faster during the 1970s than during the 1960s. There is evidence that the job vacancy rates (measured often by indices of help-wanted advertisements) associated with any given unemployment rate were also higher in the 1970s.[13] Between 1980 and 1989, however, the growth rates of the labor force and employment fell back to roughly their levels during the 1960s.

The Dispersion of Unemployment Rates.   The model of the wage inflation/unemployment trade-off that we have presented applies to a *single* labor market. To obtain the wage inflation/unemployment trade-off for the *economy,* one must aggregate all the individual labor market relationships. If the unem-

---

13. James L. Medoff, "U.S. Labor Markets: Imbalance, Wage Growth, and Productivity in the 1970's," *Brookings Papers on Economic Activity,* 1983–1, 87–120, and Katharine Abraham, "Structural/Frictional vs. Demand Deficient Unemployment," *American Economic Review* 73 (September 1983): 708–24.

ployment rate differs across labor markets, the aggregate rate of wage inflation associated with any given level of aggregate unemployment may be higher than it would be if the unemployment rate were the same in all markets.

To see why this is true, suppose there were only two labor markets in the whole economy, that they were identical in size, and that the same wage inflation/unemployment trade-off curve (represented by T_0 in Figure 16.7) existed in both. Given any overall level of unemployment, the aggregate rate of wage inflation is approximately equal to the average of the rates of wage inflation in the two markets.[14] If initially the unemployment rate were **u*** in *each* market, the rate of wage inflation in each would be zero, as would the overall rate of wage inflation.

Suppose now that the unemployment rate increases to **u*** + ε in the first market and falls to **u*** − ε in the second market, where ε is any positive number. Since the two markets are equal in size, the overall unemployment rate will remain at **u***. However, wages will fall at the rate of $\dot{W}_H$ in the high-unemployment market and rise at the rate of $\dot{W}_L$ in the low-unemployment market. As Figure 16.7 indicates, $\dot{W}_L$ is larger than $\dot{W}_H$ in absolute value; hence, the average rate of wage inflation in the economy, $(\dot{W}_H + \dot{W}_L)/2$, is positive. The dispersion in unemployment rates has led to a higher overall rate of wage inflation. Indeed, increasing the dispersion in the unemployment rates (increasing ε) would lead to an even higher overall rate of wage inflation.[15]

Why does this result occur? In our simple example it occurs because the relationship between the excess demand for labor and the unemployment rate is steeper to the left of the full-employment unemployment rate than to the right (as explained earlier in relation to Figure 16.4).[16] As a result, there is more upward pressure put on wages in the tight labor market by an ε-percentage-point *decline* in unemployment than there is downward pressure put on wages in the loose labor market by an ε-percentage-point *rise*. Thus, growth in the dispersion of unemployment between the two sectors causes the average rate of wage inflation to increase. Because it is the differential rates of wage change in the expanding and declining sectors that underlie this source of wage inflation, anything that reduces upward wage pressures in the expanding sectors, or enhances downward wage pressures in the declining sectors, will serve to reduce the overall rate of wage inflation (see Example 16.1).

Figure 16.7 shows that an increase in the dispersion of unemployment rates will increase the aggregate rate of wage inflation (in this model) for any aggregate unemployment rate less than the full-employment rate (**u*** in Fig-

---

14. We say "approximately" because once the unemployment rate differs between the two markets, a slightly higher weight should be assigned to the low-unemployment market, which will have relatively more *employed* workers.

15. The role of geographic dispersion in unemployment rates was emphasized early by Lipsey and by G.C. Archibald, "The Phillips Curve and the Distribution of Unemployment," *American Economic Review* 59 (May 1969): 124–34. The importance of dispersion of unemployment across age/gender groups was emphasized in George Perry, "Changing Labor Markets and Inflation."

16. It is not necessary to have identical wage inflation/unemployment trade-off curves in the two markets. (On this see Archibald, "The Phillips Curve and the Distribution of Unemployment.") For example, if both curves are linear, as long as the wage-inflation/excess-demand-for-labor relationship is flatter in the market that has the higher unemployment rate, the same result will occur.

FIGURE 16.7 A Wider Dispersion of Unemployment Rates Increases the Wage Inflation Associated with a Given Aggregate Unemployment Rate

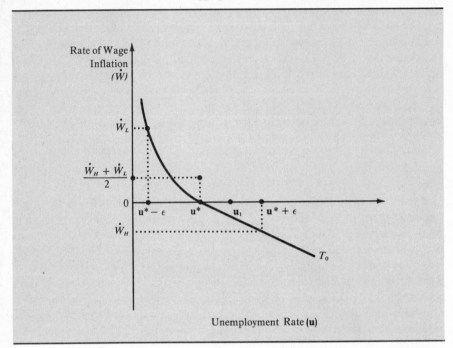

ure 16.7). Since the unemployment-rate/excess-demand-for-labor relationship was assumed to be linear to the right of $\mathbf{u}^*$, small increases in the dispersion of unemployment rates around an aggregate unemployment rate like $\mathbf{u}_1$ in Figure 16.7 will not necessarily lead to increases in the aggregate rate of wage inflation. However, if the dispersion is large enough that the nonlinear segment of T_0 is reached by the lower-unemployment market, then the aggregate rate of wage inflation will increase.

In sum, over a wide range of values of the unemployment rate, increases in the dispersion of unemployment rates across labor markets will increase the aggregate rate of wage inflation associated with the aggregate unemployment rate. Put another way, increases in the dispersion of unemployment rates can cause the aggregate wage inflation/unemployment trade-off curve to shift up. (While we have not defined precisely a *labor market* here, it is natural to think in terms of geographic markets. However, one could similarly analyze labor markets segmented by skill, age, gender, race, or industry.)

Reasons for Shifts in the Trade-off Curve over Time

Were the four major factors discussed above responsible for the upward shift of the short-run wage inflation/unemployment trade-off throughout the 1960s, 1970s, and early 1980s? Have they influenced the apparent downward shift in recent years? First, as Table 16.1 indicated, the percentage rate of change in the gross national product (GNP) *implicit price deflator,* a broad

EXAMPLE 16.1

The Growth of Employment in Small Businesses: Will Wages Become More Downwardly Flexible?

Large employers are increasingly subcontracting with smaller firms for services formerly performed by their own employees, and they are hiring more temporary or part-time workers (as indicated in Chapter 5). From 1980 to 1988 the number of workers employed in business service firms or employed less than full time grew much faster than employment generally. Consistent with this trend has been a rising fraction of workers in very small places of employment and a sharp reduction in the proportion of workers in places employing 500 or more employees. In 1973, 24.1 percent of civilian employment was in firms with fewer than 20 employees, while in 1986 the percentage had risen to 26.9 percent. In contrast, 25.4 percent of workers in 1973 were employed in firms with more than 500 employees, but by 1986 that share had dropped to 19.8 percent.

Although research is lacking on this issue, there are good reasons to hypothesize that the growing proportion of workers in small firms, coupled with the reduced proportion of workers in very large ones, might serve in two ways to generate more downward flexibility in wages during periods of business slowdown. First, as we discussed in Chapter 15, there are several reasons why large firms find that reducing wages in business downturns is less attractive than reducing employment; however, it was argued that these reasons are much less compelling for small businesses.

Second, the small-business sector is characterized by much more entry and exit of firms than is the large-business sector. For example, over the entire 1976–82 period the rates of entry and exit among single-plant firms with 500 or more employees were around 6 percent, while the rates among single-plant firms with fewer than 20 employees were three times higher; for establishments in multiplant firms the rates for the smaller group were 1.5 times higher than for the over-500 category. Thus, a higher proportion of job losses in the small-business sector are permanent layoffs, and a higher proportion of employment gains in a recovery period are in jobs with newly opening firms. These new employers are unconstrained by previous wage policies, and if the market-clearing wage has indeed fallen, they are freer than continuing employers to offer the lower wage to the workers they hire.

If workers are increasingly employed by sectors in which wages are downward-flexible, then the slope of the Phillips curve (at least that portion to the right of the natural rate of unemployment) will steepen. This could mean reductions in the extent to which the inter-sectoral dispersion of unemployment contributes to wage inflation, and over a business cycle it could lead to a lower average rate of wage inflation.

SOURCES: Richard Belous, "How Human Resource Systems Adjust to the Shift Toward Contingent Workers," *Monthly Labor Review* 112 (March 1989): 7–12; U.S. President, *The State of Small Business* (Washington, D.C.: U.S. Government Printing Office, 1987; U.S. Bureau of the Census, *County Business Patterns,* 1973 and 1986.

TABLE 16.2   White Female, Teenage, and Nonwhite Shares of the Labor Force

Year	White Female Share	Teenage Share	Nonwhite Share
1960	.290	.070	.111
1965	.305	.079	.112
1970	.332	.087	.111
1975	.346	.095	.116
1980	.365	.088	.125
1985	.376	.068	.135
1989	.382	.064	.141

SOURCES: U.S. Department of Labor, *1982 Employment and Training Report of the President* (Washington, D.C.: U.S. Government Printing Office, 1982), Table A4; U.S. Bureau of Labor Statistics, *Employment and Earnings* 37 (January 1990), Tables 3 and 4.

measure of the prices of all goods produced in the economy, trended upward through 1981 and then declined to a lower rate during the late 1980s.[17] To the extent that past price changes affect expectations of *future* price changes, this should have first shifted the trade-off curve out (as employees incorporated the expected price increases into their wage demands through the early 1980s) and then back in (as expected price inflation fell, in the late 1980s).

Second, as noted earlier in this chapter and in Chapter 15, during the 1960s and 1970s there was an increase in the fraction of the labor force subject to higher-than-average unemployment rates. As Table 16.2 indicates, between 1960 and 1980 the share of teens in the labor force rose from 7.0 to 8.8 percent and the share of white women from 29.0 to 36.5 percent, while the nonwhite share increased only slightly. Such demographic shifts alone probably increased the overall rate of unemployment associated with any given level of wage inflation, perhaps by as much as 1 percentage point during the 1965–80 period.[18]

In contrast, between 1980 and 1989, the share of teenagers in the labor force fell to 6.4 percent. While the share of females and nonwhites in the labor force increased slightly during this period, female unemployment rates have fallen relative to male unemployment rates, as much of U.S. employment growth during the period has occurred in sectors, such as the service sector, that employ proportionately more women. On balance, these changes probably reduced the fraction of the labor force subject to higher-than-average unemployment rates, which contributed to shifting the trade-off curve back to the left.

Third, as noted above, there is evidence that the rapid growth of employment and the labor force during the 1970s caused the job vacancy rate associ-

---

17. Another widely publicized price index is the Consumer Price Index (CPI), a measure of the cost of living for urban households published monthly by the Bureau of Labor Statistics. This index is the one that is typically used to calculate cost-of-living increases due under union contracts with cost-of-living escalator clauses. Because the GNP deflator and the CPI measure different things, year-to-year percentage changes in the two indices often differ. However, over longer periods of time they yield roughly the same picture about the upward trend in the inflation rate.

18. James Tobin, "Stabilization Policy Ten Years After," *Brookings Papers on Economic Activity,* 1980–1, 19–72.

ated with any given rate of unemployment to increase. One study suggested that these changes may have caused the wage inflation/unemployment trade-off to shift up by as much as one-half to one percentage point during the 1960–80 period.[19]

Finally, there is substantial evidence that the dispersion in the demographic distribution of unemployment rates rose during the 1960–80 period. In particular, the unemployment rates of teenagers rose relative to those of adult white males, and those of nonwhite teenagers rose relative to those of white teenagers. On the one hand, this increase in demographic dispersion apparently did not have a substantial impact on the aggregate wage inflation/unemployment trade-off curve.[20] On the other hand, during the 1970s there was an increase in the dispersion of employment growth rates across *industrial* sectors that is thought to have contributed to the increase in the full-employment unemployment rate during that period.[21]

Improving the Trade-off: What Can We Do?

The analyses above suggest ways government policies can reduce the rate of wage inflation associated with any given unemployment rate:

1. They can attempt to reduce the rate of wage inflation associated with any level of excess demand for labor, or shift the curve in panel (a) of Figure 16.4 or in Figure 16.5 down.
2. They can attempt to reduce the unemployment rate associated with any given level of the excess demand for labor, or shift the curve in panel (b) of Figure 16.4 down.
3. Finally, they can attempt to reduce the geographic or demographic dispersion of unemployment rates.

A number of policy tools are potentially available to achieve each goal.

Turning to the wage-inflation/excess-demand-for-labor relationship first, one obvious objective here is to reduce the expected rate of growth of prices. Over long periods of time this goal is accomplished primarily by restrictive monetary or fiscal policy. In the short run, *incomes policies*—policies by which the government tries directly to control or influence wage and price levels by the specification of standards governing when prices or wages can be changed—may also have an effect. Examples here include wage/price guidelines and temporary wage/price freezes. (A later section of this chapter will discuss incomes policies in some detail.)

The wage-inflation/excess-demand-for-labor relationship may also be, and has been, shifted down through government policies that increase the competitiveness of labor markets and remove institutional barriers that reduce the downward flexibility of wages. Examples of such policies include eliminating or relaxing the Davis-Bacon Act (discussed in Chapter 12) and deregulating certain industries, such as airlines, telephone, and trucking, that historically

---

19. Medoff, "U.S. Labor Markets," 110–11.
20. For econometric evidence on this point, see Robert J. Gordon, "Can the Inflation of the 1970s Be Explained?" *Brookings Papers on Economic Activity,* 1977–1, 353–74.
21. See David Lilien, "Sectoral Shifts and Cyclical Unemployment," *Journal of Political Economy* 90 (August 1982): 777–93.

had been regulated in ways that tended to reduce competition (see Chapter 12 for a discussion of the airline experience).

With respect to reducing the rate of unemployment associated with any given level of excess demand for labor, the goal here would be to improve the efficiency of labor markets.[22] Many policies related to this goal were discussed in Chapter 15; they include improving job market information, improving the "job-matching services" offered by the U.S. Employment Service and private employment agencies, and increasing government-sponsored training programs to help reduce skill bottlenecks. One caution here, however, is that policies designed to reduce the unemployment rate may actually serve to increase it. For example, if potential job-leavers—workers who feel some dissatisfaction with their jobs—knew that the government was actively pursuing a policy to reduce the length of time unemployed workers spent out of work, this knowledge might increase the probability that these workers would quit their jobs. One would have to balance the benefits obtained from shorter durations of unemployment against the costs of a higher incidence of unemployment before deciding if such policies were worthwhile to implement.

The government can seek to reduce the geographic dispersion of unemployment rates by providing information about jobs in other areas to unemployed workers, by providing relocation allowances and subsidies for job search in different areas, and by administering public employment and training-program budgets in a way that increases allocations to areas with above-average unemployment rates.[23] The government can also seek to reduce the dispersion of unemployment rates across occupational, industrial, or demographic groups by targeting employment and training programs, wage subsidies, tax credits, and relocation allowances on the groups with high unemployment rates.

WAGE INFLATION, PRICE INFLATION, PRODUCTIVITY, AND THE LONG-RUN TRADE-OFF

To move from the relationship between *wage* inflation and unemployment to an understanding of the relationship between *price* inflation and unemployment requires a model of how producers determine their product prices. The simple model presented here highlights the role of labor productivity growth in the inflationary process and shows how increases in the growth of labor productivity can help reduce price inflation.

Suppose producers determine their product prices by using a *constant percentage markup* over unit labor cost rule. That is,

$$P = k \cdot ULC \tag{16.3}$$

---

22. A long-time advocate of such policies is Charles Holt. See, for example, Charles Holt et al., "Manpower Proposals for Phase III," *Brookings Papers on Economic Activity,* 1971–3, 703–22. For a more critical evaluation of these policies, see Robert Hall, "Prospects for Shifting the Phillips Curve Through Manpower Policy," *Brookings Papers on Economic Activity,* 1971–3, 659–701.

23. Employment and training program funds are often administered in this way.

where P represents product price, ULC represents unit labor cost—the labor cost of producing one unit of output—and k, which is a constant that is greater than one, represents the markup. Presumably k varies across firms as the share of labor cost in total costs of production varies (with smaller labor cost shares leading to larger values of k). It is also likely that k varies with the price elasticity of demand for the firms' products.[24] Although typically the size of markups does vary over the course of a business cycle, for expositional convenience we shall ignore this fact here.[25]

Unit labor costs are equal to the costs per labor hour divided by output per labor hour (q), or labor productivity. Suppose, for simplicity, that we ignore all labor costs other than straight-time wages. Then labor costs per labor hour are equal to the wage rate (W) and

$$ULC = W/q \tag{16.4}$$

Substituting equation (16.4) into equation (16.3) and making use of the facts that (a) the percentage change in the *product* of two variables equals the *sum* of the percentage changes of the two variables, and (b) the percentage change in the *ratio* of two variables equals the percentage change in the numerator *minus* the percentage change in the denominator, one obtains

$$\dot{P} = \dot{k} + \dot{W} - \dot{q} \tag{16.5}$$

Here a dot over a variable represents a percentage change, and thus $\dot{q}$ is the rate of growth of output per labor hour (or the rate of labor productivity growth).

Over time, the size of markups may change; for example, the drastic increase in the relative prices of energy since 1973 surely has led to increases in k. However, since this is a text in labor economics, not macroeconomics, we shall ignore this complication and assume that k remains constant (the constancy of k implies that labor's share of output also remains constant). Under this assumption,

$$\dot{P} = \dot{W} - \dot{q} \tag{16.6}$$

Equation (16.6) asserts that the rate of price inflation equals the rate of wage inflation minus the rate of labor productivity growth. Thus, if wages increase at the rate of productivity growth *and* if markups do not change, prices will remain constant. Put another way, given any rate of wage inflation, an increase in the rate of growth of productivity will lead to a reduction in the rate of growth of prices if markups are constant.

Moreover, if one characterizes the trade-off between wage inflation and unemployment as $\dot{W} = f(\mathbf{u}) + \gamma \dot{P}^e$, where f means "a function of," then one can substitute $f(\mathbf{u}) + \gamma \dot{P}^e$ for $\dot{W}$ in equation (16.6) to obtain

$$\dot{P} = f(\mathbf{u}) + \gamma \dot{P}^e - \dot{q} \tag{16.7}$$

---

24. Although we do not do so here, one can formally show that these statements are true for a profit-maximizing monopolist who faces a constant average-cost curve. In this case, the less elastic the price elasticity of demand for output, the greater k will be.

25. For evidence on the cyclical variability of markups, see Robert J. Gordon, "The Impact of Aggregate Demand on Prices," *Brookings Papers on Economic Activity,* 1975–3, 613–63.

That is, as Figure 16.8 indicates, as long as productivity growth is positive, the price inflation/unemployment trade-off that exists at any time lies everywhere below the wage inflation/unemployment trade-off, with the vertical difference between the two curves being equal to the rate of labor productivity growth.

The Slowdown in Productivity Growth and Stagflation

During the late 1970s and 1980s, one often read in the popular press that the slowdown in the rate of growth of labor productivity in the United States was at least partially responsible for high rates of price inflation that were associated with high rates of unemployment—a phenomenon commonly referred to as *stagflation*. While Example 16.2 addresses the *causes* of this slowdown in

---

EXAMPLE 16.2
The Slowdown in U.S. Productivity Growth

One measure of productivity that is customarily used is *labor productivity*, or output per hour of labor employed. As suggested in Table 16.3, between 1948 and 1974 labor productivity grew at a rate averaging over 2.3 percent per year in the nonfarm business sector. Between 1975 and 1988, however, it grew at a rate of about 1.2 percent per year. This slowdown in the rate of growth of productivity is disturbing because the rate of growth of labor productivity is directly related to both the rate of growth of real wages and the rate of price inflation in the economy.

Economists have expended considerable effort to try to understand the causes of the slowdown in productivity growth. Although it is not fully understood, a number of factors have been postulated to contribute to it. While there are no universally agreed-upon reasons for the slowdown, the following factors have been analyzed: changes in the age/gender composition of the labor force, which affects how much experience the average worker has; changes in the quality of the labor input (the quality and quantity of human capital); changes in the industrial composition of employment away from sectors, like manufacturing, in which capital is easily substituted for labor; government-mandated investments in environmental protection and occupational safety and health, which do not lead to increases in measured output of goods and services; a decline in research and development expenditures; and measurement problems.

SOURCES: J. R. Norsworthy, Michael Harper, and Kent Kunze, "The Slowdown in Productivity Growth: Analysis of Some Contributing Factors," *Brookings Papers on Economic Activity,* 1979–2, 387–423; Thomas Weisskopf, Samuel Bowles, and David M. Gordon, "Hearts and Minds: A Social Model of U.S. Productivity Growth," *Brookings Papers on Economic Activity,* 1983–2, 381–441; Martin N. Baily and Robert J. Gordon, "The Productivity Slowdown, Measurement Issues, and the Explosion of Computer Power," *Brookings Papers on Economic Activity,* 1988–2, 347–420; Wayne Gray, "The Cost of Regulation: OSHA, EPA, and the Productivity Slowdown," *American Economic Review* 77 (December 1987): 998–1006; William Gullickson and Michael J. Harper, "Multifactor Productivity in U.S. Manufacturing, 1949–83," *Monthly Labor Review* 110 (October 1987): 18–28; John Bishop, "Is the Test Score Decline Responsible for the Productivity Growth Decline?" *American Economic Review* 79 (March 1989): 178–97.

FIGURE 16.8   The Relationships Between the Rates of Wage and Price Inflation, Unemployment, and (1) the Expected Rate of Price Inflation ($\dot{P}^e$) and (2) the Rate of Productivity Growth ($\dot{q}$)

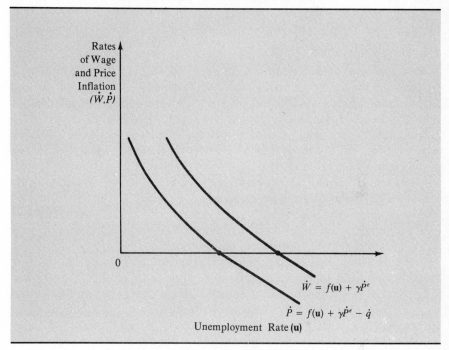

the growth of labor productivity, Table 16.3 presents data on its *magnitude* and *pattern*. For the private nonfarm business sector, productivity grew at about 2.7 percent per year over the 1948–64 period. However, from 1965 to 1974 productivity growth fell to 1.8 percent a year, and during 1975–82 it fell further to 0.7 percent a year. These shifts alone would cause the short-run aggregate price inflation/unemployment trade-off curve to be about 2 percentage points higher during the late 1970s and early 1980s than it was during the 1950s and early 1960s (see equation 16.7). This figure should, however, be contrasted with the 5 to 10 percent annual rates of increase in the GNP deflator that occurred during the late 1970s and early 1980s. Thus, while the slowdown in productivity growth contributed to the worsening inflation/ unemployment trade-off between 1960 and 1980, it was not the entire cause; the other factors we have mentioned clearly were important. During the 1983–88 period, productivity growth rose to 1.9 percent a year. As noted in

TABLE 16.3   Average Annual Rate of Labor Productivity Growth in the U.S. Private Nonfarm Business Sector (Percent Change Per Year)

1948–54	1955–64	1965–74	1975–82	1983–88
2.8	2.6	1.8	0.7	1.9

SOURCE: *1990 Economic Report of the President* (Washington, D.C.: U.S. Government Printing Office, 1990), Table C47.

Chapter 5, productivity growth tends to increase as unemployment declines, so it is difficult to ascertain whether the recent upturn in productivity growth represents only a cyclical improvement or also a reversal of the downward trend. To the extent that the latter has occurred, this will contribute to an improved inflation/unemployment trade-off.

The Long-Run Trade-off

Although *at a point in time* a trade-off exists between the rate of price inflation and the unemployment rate, it does not necessarily follow that *in the long run* a stable trade-off exists. Indeed, one school of thought argues that attempts to keep the unemployment rate artificially low—below the rate that is consistent with zero price inflation (when the expected rate of price inflation is zero)—will lead to ever-accelerating rates of inflation.[26] The reason for this acceleration is that attempts to reduce the unemployment rate through monetary or fiscal policy will lead to higher rates of wage and price inflation in the short run (see panel c of Figure 16.4 and Figure 16.8). To the extent that *expectations* of inflation are conditioned by *actual* rates of inflation, such policies will increase the expected rate of price inflation, and the rates of wage and price inflation will continue to spiral upwards.

Whether this process will lead to ever-accelerating rates of wage and price inflation or ultimately to constant rates of wage and price inflation depends crucially on the responsiveness of money-wage increases to the expected rate of price inflation. In terms of our model, if all expected price increases are fully reflected in higher wages ($\gamma = 1$ in equation 16.2), no long-run trade-off exists; attempts to force unemployment below its natural rate will cause ever-accelerating rates of inflation. To *stabilize* the inflation rate would require returning the unemployment rate to its natural rate. Hence, in this case, society can temporarily reduce the unemployment rate only at the cost of permanently higher rates of price inflation. To bring these higher rates of inflation *down* requires a further temporary increase in the unemployment rate.

In contrast, if expected price increases are *not* fully reflected in higher wage increases ($\gamma < 1$), a stable long-run trade-off between price inflation and unemployment will exist. That is, a constant rate of inflation will eventually become associated with any level of unemployment. (These propositions are formally derived in the appendix to this chapter.)

A key question for policymakers, then, is the extent to which expected increases in prices do lead to increases in wages. Empirical evidence on this question is ambiguous, and some economists assert that it is nearly impossible to answer the question from statistical estimates of γ in equations such as (16.7).[27] While some macroeconomists strongly assert that γ is equal to one, others assert that γ is less than one and that a stable long-run trade-off does exist. Moreover, these latter economists assert that between 1960 and 1980 γ appeared to grow in size, leading to a less favorable short-run trade-off (in the

---

26. See Friedman, "The Role of Monetary Policy," and Edmund Phelps, "Phillips Curves, Expectations of Inflation, and Optimal Unemployment Over Time," *Economica* 34 (August 1967): 254–81, for early expositions of this view.

27. See, for example, Robert Lucas, "Econometric Testing of the Natural Rate Hypothesis," in *The Econometrics of Price Determination,* ed. Otto Eckstein (Washington, D.C.: Board of Governors of the Federal Reserve System, 1972), 5–15.

sense that, given any level of expected price inflation, the short-run trade-off curve was higher in the early 1980s than it was in the 1960s). Their evidence also appears to indicate that the short-run curve was flatter; thus, the marginal effect of a change in the unemployment rate on inflation appeared to be smaller than it once was.[28]

One must caution, however, that these latter economists' conclusions are drawn from empirical studies in which the expected rate of price inflation is assumed to adapt with a lag to past rates of price inflation; *adaptive expectations* of inflation are formed by "looking backwards," using only information on the past. In these studies, the expected rate of price inflation, which appears in equations such as (16.2) and (16.7), is replaced by a vector of past inflation rates; tests of whether γ is less than one are based upon whether the coefficients on the past price-inflation variables sum to less than one.[29]

Critics of this approach, who include many leading macroeconomists, argue that this is not an adequate test of whether a long-run trade-off curve exists. As described in more detail in the appendix to this chapter, they argue that inflationary expectations are not formed solely with reference to past inflation rates (adaptive expectations); rather, they reason that individuals use information on other variables that they can currently observe (e.g., the size of the government budget deficit), as well as their own views about what future government policies will be, to determine their expectations of inflation. If such an expectation scheme, often called *rational expectations,* is appropriate (in the sense that expectations of inflation are formed on the basis of all available information that it is profitable for individuals to consider), the use of prior inflation rates in equations such as (16.2) or (16.7) conveys no information about whether a stable, negatively sloped, long-run trade-off curve between price inflation and unemployment exists.[30]

---

28. See, for example, George Perry, "Inflation in Theory and Practice," *Brookings Papers on Economic Activity,* 1980–1, 207–42.

29. Phillip Cagan, "The Monetary Dynamics of Hyperinflation," in *Studies in the Quantity Theory of Money,* ed. Milton Friedman (Chicago: University of Chicago Press, 1956), was an early expositor of the adaptive expectations framework. In its simplest form, the expected inflation rate is assumed to be equal to the expected inflation rate in the previous period plus a multiple (m, between 0 and 1) times the gap between the actual and expected inflation rates in the previous period:

$$\dot{P}^e = \dot{P}^e_{-1} + (1 - m)(\dot{P}_{-1} - \dot{P}^e_{-1}) \text{ or}$$

$$\dot{P}^e = m\dot{P}^e_{-1} + (1 - m)\dot{P}_{-1}$$

That is, the expected inflation rate is assumed to be a weighted average of the previous period's expected and actual inflation rates. The larger m is, the less weight is given to the previous period's actual inflation rate in forming the current period's expected rate. By algebraic manipulation, one can also show that this is equivalent to assuming that the current expected inflation rate is a weighted average of all prior periods' inflation rates, with the weights declining geometrically towards zero.

30. The term "rational expectations" was introduced by John Muth, "Rational Expectations and the Theory of Price Movements," *Econometrica* 29 (July 1961): 315–35. A good set of papers that discuss its relevance for the unemployment/inflation trade-off issue is Robert Lucas and Thomas Sargent, eds., *Rational Expectations and Econometric Practice* (Minneapolis: University of Minnesota Press, 1981). More elementary discussions are presented in many modern intermediate-level macroeconomics texts. See, for example, Michael Darby and Michael Melvin, *Intermediate Macroeconomics* (Glenview, Ill.: Scott, Foresman, 1986), or Robert Hall and John Taylor, *Macroeconomics: Theory, Performance and Policy* (New York: W. W. Norton, 1986).

TABLE 16.4 Average Annual Rate of Increase and Variance in the Rate of Increase of the GNP Price Deflator over Successive Five-Year Periods

Period	Average Annual Increase	Variance in the Annual Increase[a]
1960–64	1.5	0.181
1965–69	3.9	1.831
1970–74	6.3	2.859
1975–79	7.9	2.158
1980–84	6.6	6.571
1985–89	3.2	0.533

[a]The variance is calculated by (1) computing the average (mean) annual increase for the five-year period, (2) calculating the difference between the increase for each year and the above average, (3) squaring the differences in step 2 and summing them over five years, and (4) dividing the sum in step 3 by 5. If yearly price increases start to vary much from each other, the calculated variance will rise.

SOURCE: *1990 Economic Report of the President* (Washington, D.C.: U.S. Government Printing Office, 1990), Table C3.

EXPECTED VS. UNEXPECTED INFLATION

Our discussion of the inflation/unemployment trade-off has so far assumed that labor market tightness and unemployment determine the rate of inflation, not vice versa. We also stressed the role of *expected* (or *anticipated*) inflation rates and ignored the role of *unexpected* (or *unanticipated*) inflation rates. This section will return to the simple model of job search presented in the preceding chapter to show how unexpected rates of wage and price inflation can cause a temporary decline in the unemployment rate, but that fully expected inflation will have no causal effect on unemployment. Thus, when considering the inflation/unemployment trade-off, the direction of causation may run from *unanticipated* inflation to the unemployment rate.[31]

As the actual rate of price inflation trended upward during the 1960s, 1970s, and early 1980s (see Table 16.1), inflation also became much more variable. Table 16.4 presents data on the variance of the inflation rate over successive five-year periods, and the variance clearly increased from the early 1960s to the mid-1980s. Therefore, individuals' ability to predict the actual inflation rate may well have declined, leading to an increased likelihood that *actual* wage- or price-level changes would differ from *expected* ones. As we will show, such a discrepancy tends to flatten the short-run inflation/unemployment trade-off curves.

Suppose that the initial distribution of money-wage offers facing a representative individual is given in panel (a) of Figure 16.9. Let the maximum wage commensurate with the individual's skill level be W^*, and suppose that the individual rationally chooses W_R^0 as his or her minimal *acceptance* (or *reservation*) *wage*. As noted in Chapter 15 (Figure 15.6), the area to the right of W^* under the wage distribution represents the proportion of jobs he or she

---

31. Variants of the search-theoretic model of the inflation/unemployment trade-off presented here were first presented in several papers in *Microeconomic Foundations of Employment and Inflation,* ed. Edmund Phelps (New York: W. W. Norton, 1970).

FIGURE 16.9   Effect of Anticipated and Unanticipated Wage Inflation on Reservation Wages and Unemployment

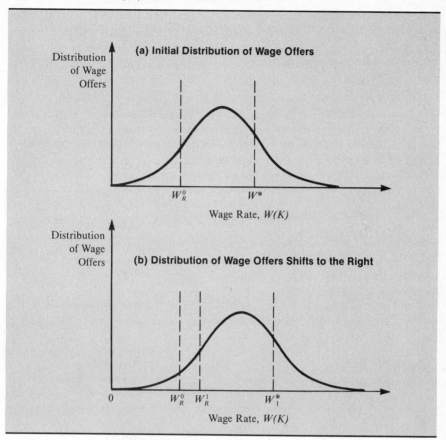

is not qualified for and the area to the left of W_R^0 represents the proportion of jobs he or she will not accept. Together, then, the two areas tell us the probability that this representative individual will not find employment in any period and, thus, what the expected unemployment rate will be.

Suppose that there is a general increase in wages and prices that shifts the whole distribution of wage offers to the right but that the workers are initially *unaware* that this shift has occurred. If this inflation was truly unanticipated there would be no reason for workers to increase their acceptance wage. If they keep their acceptance wage at W_R^0, the probability that they will reject a job offer is reduced (the area to the left of W_R^0 after the shift in the distribution is reduced, as can be seen in panel b). Because the proportion of jobs for which these individuals are qualified remains constant, W^* shifts up by the same proportion as the rest of the wage distribution (to W_1^* in panel b). Thus, the probability of finding a job will increase and the unemployment rate will fall—and the greater the unexpected shift in the wage distribution the greater will be the fall in the unemployment rate. A short-run trade-off exists between unanticipated inflation and unemployment, with the direction of causation running from the former to the latter in this model.

Once the individual becomes aware of the overall wage inflation that has occurred, however, the trade-off ceases to exist. Individuals will revise their acceptance wage upward to W_R^1 in an effort to maintain their wage relative to others' and to obtain the benefits of the general increase in wage offers. As the reservation wage increases from W_R^0 to W_R^1, the area to the left of W_R^1 in panel (b) will be identical to the area to the left of W_R^0 in panel (a), and the unemployment rate will return to its full-employment level, u^*. Since unemployed individuals alter their acceptance-wage decisions in response to expected inflation, changes in the anticipated rate of inflation will not lead to permanent changes in the unemployment rate.

The trade-offs that are implied by this model are plotted in Figure 16.10. When inflation is unanticipated by job-searchers, there is a negative trade-off, T^u, with the direction of causation running from the rate of unanticipated inflation to the unemployment rate. When inflation is fully anticipated, no trade-off exists and the level of anticipated inflation has no causal effect on the unemployment rate (as indicated by the curve T^e). To the extent that inflation is fully anticipated in the long run, no long-run trade-off will exist between inflation and unemployment.

In summary, as the rate of price inflation trended upward during the 1960s, 1970s, and early 1980s, it also became somewhat more variable; thus it

FIGURE 16.10 Trade-off Between Inflation and Unemployment: Expected vs. Unexpected Wage Inflation

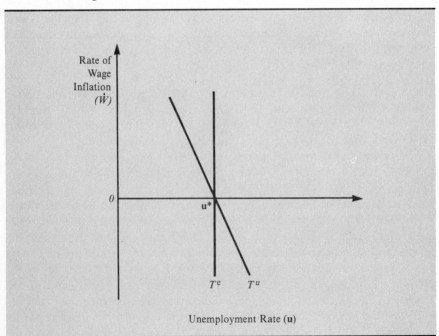

became more difficult to anticipate the actual inflation rate. The model presented in this section would suggest, then, that over this period the curve showing the change in unemployment caused by wage inflation would begin to look more like T^u than T^e. Put another way, the fact that individuals became less able to fully anticipate the actual inflation rate may have contributed to the flattening of the trade-off curves between wage or price inflation and the unemployment rate that occurred between 1960 and 1980.[32]

During the late 1980s, as the rate of price inflation fell, the variability of inflation also declined substantially. As Table 16.4 indicates, during the 1985–89 period the variance in the annual inflation rate fell to 0.533, which was lower than the variances experienced in the four immediately preceding periods. This suggests that it became easier for people to anticipate the actual inflation rate and thus that the trade-off curves between wage or price inflation and unemployment probably became steeper in the late 1980s.

UNIONS AND INFLATION

Less than 20 percent of employed workers are union members (see Chapter 12). In spite of this fact, unions and the collective bargaining process in the United States are thought to exert a considerable influence on the position and shape of the wage inflation/unemployment trade-off curve for a number of reasons.

Wage Patterns and Norms

First, in several industries—such as steel, automobile, mining, trucking, and telephone—collective bargaining negotiations are conducted at the national level and are well publicized in the media. The resulting settlements are often thought to set a pattern for wage settlements in less heavily unionized indus-

---

32. An alternative model that yields similar short-run and long-run trade-off curves is the *intertemporal substitution* model of labor supply discussed in Chapter 7. Recall that in this framework workers allocate their labor supply across periods to maximize an intertemporal utility function and, other things equal, will increase their labor supply in periods when real wages are temporarily high. Now, in the context of this model, unexpected price inflation leads to higher nominal wages, which workers may incorrectly perceive as being equivalent to higher real wages. To the extent they believe these real-wage increases will not persist for many periods, it makes sense for them to temporarily increase their labor supply "to take advantage" of the perceived higher real wages. In the short run, then, labor supply will increase; if these additional workers find employment, unemployment will drop. In the long run, however, as workers fully anticipate inflation, they realize that the increased nominal wages do not reflect increased real wages. As a result labor supply will decrease and unemployment will return to its original level.

The intertemporal labor supply approach to the inflation/unemployment trade-off curve was first introduced by Robert Lucas and Leonard Rapping, "Real Wages, Employment, and Inflation," *Journal of Political Economy* 77 (September/October 1969): 721–54. To be valid as an explanation for a negatively sloped, short-run trade-off curve, workers' labor supply must be quite responsive to short-run fluctuations in perceived real wages. However, as noted in Chapter 7, the available evidence from both micro and macro data suggests that intertemporal labor supply responses to short-run changes in perceived real wages are actually very small. [A good summary of the evidence is found in Orley Ashenfelter, "Macroeconomic Analyses and Microeconomic Analyses of Labor Supply," *Carnegie-Rochester Conference Series on Public Policy* 21 (1984): 117–56.]

tries and in the nonunion sector because of either imitative behavior in the former or attempts to compete for labor and keep unions out in the latter.[33] Our model suggests that if the economic conditions facing firms and unions in only a few key industries heavily influence the rate of wage inflation in other sectors, the effect of the *aggregate* unemployment rate on inflation will be reduced.

Evidence to support this view is mixed, however. On the one hand, during the 1970s wages in the above-mentioned highly unionized industries grew substantially relative to wages in the rest of the economy, suggesting that the settlements reached in these industries do not automatically spill over to other industries.[34] Wage patterns did appear to exist among firms *within* certain industries, such as automobiles, during much of the postwar period, but even these patterns broke down in the concession bargaining of the early 1980s, when firms in these industries faced different economic circumstances. For example, the United Automobile Workers granted larger concessions to the Chrysler Corporation, which was on the verge of bankruptcy, than to the General Motors Corporation and the Ford Motor Company, which were not. (When Chrysler turned a profit in 1983 and began to pay off loans ahead of schedule, however, workers at Chrysler were able to win back some of their earlier concessions.) More generally, formal tests of whether key wage bargains, or union wage gains in general, set a pattern for the rest of the economy have not reached definitive conclusions.[35]

On the other hand, some economists have recently argued that the position of the wage inflation/unemployment trade-off curve is determined not by expectations of price inflation (which may change continuously as economic conditions change) per se, but rather by a *wage norm,* or a generally accepted standard for rates of wage increases.[36] Such a norm is thought to be affected little by short-run cyclical conditions, such as small variations in actual inflation rates; rather, it is thought to be shifted only by extreme economic developments such as major recessions or prolonged expansions. In part, the norm may reflect the behavior of large unionized *and* nonunionized firms seeking to maintain their relative wage positions. Empirical evidence suggests that models using proxies for wage norms predict recent inflationary behavior better than models using past rates of price inflation as proxies for the expected

33. For an early exposition of this view, see Otto Eckstein and Thomas Wilson, "The Determination of Money Wages in American Industry," *Quarterly Journal of Economics* 76 (August 1962): 379–414.

34. See Daniel Mitchell, *Unions, Wages, and Inflation* (Washington, D.C.: Brookings Institution, 1980), and Marvin Kosters, "Wage and Price Behavior: Prospects and Policies," in *Contemporary Economic Problems, 1977,* ed. William Fellner (Washington, D.C.: American Enterprise Institute for Public Policy Research, 1977), 159–203.

35. See Daniel Mitchell, "Union Wage Determination: Policy Implications and Outlook," *Brookings Papers on Economic Activity,* 1978–3, 537–82; Robert Flanagan, "Wage Interdependence in Unionized Labor Markets," *Brookings Papers on Economic Activity,* 1976–3, 635–73; and Susan Vroman, "Direction of Wage Spillovers in Manufacturing," *Industrial and Labor Relations Review* 36 (October 1982): 102–12.

36. See George Perry, "Shifting Wage Norms and Their Implications," *American Economic Review Papers and Proceedings* 76 (May 1986): 245–48, and George Perry, "Inflation in Theory and Practice," *Brookings Papers on Economic Activity,* 1980–1, 207–42.

rate of price inflation; however, the wage-norm relationship seems to hold primarily in the union sector.[37]

The existence of a *wage norm* that is relatively insensitive to small variations in economic conditions has important implications.[38] It suggests that fiscal and/or monetary policy can be used to stimulate the economy over some range without fear that it will lead the short-run trade-off curve to shift up rapidly and further exacerbate any inflation that exists. However, in extreme times (deep recessions or prolonged booms) that lead to changes in wage norms, the short-run trade-off curve may shift up or down quite rapidly. This notion of wage norms also suggests that the causes of price-level increases may affect how wages respond to price inflation. For example, price increases that accompany a prolonged boom are more likely to increase wage norms than are price increases caused by exogenous shocks, such as the oil-price shocks of the '70s.

Multiyear Contracts

Second, union contracts have increasingly become multiyear in nature, calling for wage increases not only at the time the contract is signed but also in subsequent years. While these increases may well be sensitive to the unemployment rate at the time the contract is signed—or, more precisely, to unions' and employers' *expectations* of the unemployment rate over the term of the contract—the contractual increases are not directly affected by the *actual* unemployment rate during the duration of the contract. Furthermore, these contracts tend to be staggered; only a fraction are negotiated each period.[39]

Formal econometric analyses indicate that wage increases specified in the *first* year of multiyear union contracts appear to be about as sensitive to the unemployment rate as wage increases in the nonunion sector. However, *deferred* wage increases specified in union contracts—those that occur in the second or third year of multiyear contracts—do not appear to be related to the actual unemployment rates during those years.[40] Hence, the increasing frequency of long-term union contracts in the economy *does* reduce the sensitivity of the overall rates of wage and price inflation to the unemployment rate, making the trade-off curves flatter.

Cost-of-Living Adjustments

Third, accompanying the growth of multiyear contracts has been the growth of *cost-of-living adjustment (COLA) clauses* in union contracts—clauses that call for wages to be automatically adjusted periodically as the price level changes. Approximately 20 percent of workers covered by major collective

---

37. See George Perry, "What Have We Learned About Disinflation?" *Brookings Papers on Economic Activity,* 1983–2, 587–602; Daniel Mitchell, "Union vs. Nonunion Wage Norm Shifts," *American Economic Review Papers and Proceedings* 76 (May 1986): 249–52; and Daniel Mitchell, "Shifting Wage Norms in Wage Determination," *Brookings Papers on Economic Activity,* 1985–2, 575–99.

38. George Perry, "Shifting Wage Norms and Their Implications."

39. For a formal analysis of how *staggered contracts* affect the inflationary process, see John Taylor, "Staggered Wage Setting in a Macro Model," *American Economic Review Papers and Proceedings* 69 (May 1979): 108–13.

40. Mitchell, "Union Wage Determination."

bargaining agreements (those that cover 1,000 or more workers) had such provisions in their contracts in 1966. By the early 1980s this proportion had grown to over 60 percent, although it declined to under 50 percent in the late 1980s as inflationary pressures eased.[41]

Escalator clauses typically give workers less than 100 percent protection against price inflation. Such contracts usually call for wages to increase by less than 1 percent for each 1 percent increase in prices, and sometimes *caps*—or maximum allowable cost-of-living increases—are also specified. Nevertheless, their existence should increase the sensitivity of wage inflation to price inflation, and the evidence bears this out; union wage changes, especially those in contracts that call for cost-of-living escalators, appear to be more sensitive to price changes than do nonunion wage changes.[42] As noted earlier, larger values of γ in equation (16.2) lead to a higher short-run price inflation/unemployment trade-off curve. Hence, the growth in prevalence of cost-of-living escalator clauses in union contracts may well have contributed to the upward shift in the short-run trade-off curves that took place between 1960 and 1980.

Wage Imitation

A final reason why unions are thought to influence the position and shape of the trade-off curve is that union members are clearly concerned about maintaining their wage position relative to what they perceive are the wages of their *peer groups*. At the national level, for example, automobile workers look at the wage gains won in the steel industry, and vice versa. Whichever union settles first may set a pattern for the other union to follow in its negotiations, regardless of economic conditions in the latter industry. If this occurs, the responsiveness of wage and price inflation to unemployment would again be reduced.

Wage gains in several large national industries, such as automobile, steel, and rubber, clearly are highly correlated. However, it is difficult to disentangle the above *wage imitation* hypothesis from the hypothesis that wages in these industries are affected by a common set of variables. After all, steel is a major component of automobiles, as is rubber for the tires. It would, therefore, not be surprising to find that wage changes for workers in the three industries are highly correlated. Attempts to formally test whether wage imitation occurs among unions in these and other industries have not met with success.[43]

41. See Ronald G. Ehrenberg, Leif Danziger, and Gee San, "Cost of Living Adjustment Clauses in Union Contracts: A Summary of Results," *Journal of Labor Economics* 1 (July 1983): 215–45; Wallace Hendricks and Lawrence Kahn, "Cost-of-Living Clauses in Union Contracts: Determinants and Effects," *Industrial and Labor Relations Review* 36 (April 1983): 447–60; and David Card, "An Empirical Model of Wage Indexation Provisions," *Journal of Political Economy* 94 (June 1986, pt. 2): S144–S175, for discussions of the forces that caused this growth over time. As part of the concession bargaining that took place during the mid-1980s many contracts (such as those in telecommunications) began to eliminate COLA provisions.

42. Mitchell, "Union Wage Determination," and Hendricks and Kahn, "Cost-of-Living Clauses in Union Contracts."

43. See, for example, Robert Flanagan, "Wage Interdependencies in Unionized Labor Markets," *Brookings Papers on Economic Activity,* 1976–3, and Y. P. Mehra, "Spillovers in Wage Determination in U.S. Manufacturing Industries," *Review of Economics and Statistics* 58 (August 1976): 300–312.

Our discussion suggests, then, that the collective bargaining process per se may well have contributed to the flattening and shifting up of the short-run inflation/unemployment trade-off curves that occurred between 1960 and 1980. The increased prevalence of multiyear contracts was partially responsible for the flattening, and the increased use of cost-of-living escalator clauses was implicated in the upward shift. The effects of key settlements or other imitative behavior are uncertain, although there is some evidence that, in the aggregate, *wage norms* that change rather infrequently—not expectations of price inflation per se—may affect the wage inflation rate.

STRUCTURAL POLICIES TO REDUCE INFLATION

Earlier in the chapter we discussed briefly the types of policies that government could undertake to reduce the unemployment/inflation trade-off. These included policies to make labor markets more competitive by reducing barriers to the downward flexibility of wages, improving information flows to available workers, enlarging job-training programs, and subsidizing the relocation or employment of the structurally unemployed. In this section we consider in detail two structural policies whose implications take us back to fundamental theoretical principles: *incomes policies* and the use of *share wages*. Incomes policies are policies in which the government tries to directly influence wage and price behavior by specifying *desired behavior*. Sometimes the policies are completely voluntary, and sometimes enforcement mechanisms are built in to increase or guarantee compliance. Share wages are systems of compensation that involve a significant use of revenue or profit sharing among owners and workers.

Incomes Policies in the United States

During the 1960–80 period, a period over which the inflation/unemployment trade-off curve steadily shifted out, the United States tried several different types of incomes policies. In the early Kennedy-Johnson years (1962–66), the Council of Economic Advisors tried to educate the public on the relationship between the rate of wage inflation, the rate of price inflation, and the rate of productivity growth—see equation (16.6). The council observed that if money-wage growth were held on average to the rate of labor productivity growth in the economy and if markups did not change, then prices would remain stable. The council suggested in 1964 that the trend rate of growth of productivity was roughly 3.2 percent per year (but compare this with the estimates in Table 16.3) and urged that employers and unions voluntarily limit their wage settlements to this level. This limitation would cause unit labor costs to rise in firms in which productivity growth was below average, leading to increases in prices there. However, unit labor costs would fall in firms with above-average rates of productivity growth, leading to price declines there (if profit margins remained constant). On average, then, prices would remain stable, and both nominal and real wages would increase 3.2 percent per year.

The guideposts worked reasonably well from 1962 to 1965 in the sense that the average rate of increase in wages was in fact below 3.2 percent during the period.[44] However, as labor markets tightened in the mid-1960s and the price inflation rate rose above 2 percent, the guideposts broke down and in 1967 the program was abandoned.

The next experience with incomes policies occurred during the Nixon administration in August 1971. In response to increasing rates of price inflation (which averaged all of 5.3 percent in 1970), increasing unemployment, and a deteriorating trade balance, a comprehensive economic policy was announced. "Phase I," which lasted 90 days, called for a freeze—i.e., a zero rate of increase—on virtually all wages and prices. Phase I was followed in November 1971 by Phase II, which set standards for wage increases of 5.5 percent a year. If productivity grew at 3 to 3.5 percent a year and if profit margins were maintained, prices would then grow at 2 to 2.5 percent a year—see equation (16.6). Compliance was required by law under the program. However, a sufficient number of exemptions were granted that average hourly earnings growth was well above 5.5 percent a year (see Table 16.1). The program was terminated in January 1973 and replaced by a voluntary program of controls with no enforcement mechanism.

Finally, in October 1978 the Carter administration announced a voluntary system of wage standards to help reduce inflation. Average hourly earnings and employee benefits per company were to increase at a rate of no more than 7 percent a year; for contracts with cost-of-living escalator clauses, compliance was evaluated at an assumed 6 percent price inflation rate over the life of the contract.[45] Several groups of workers were exempted from having to satisfy the standards, including low-wage workers.

Contract settlements under the Carter program were monitored by the Council on Wage and Price Stability. However, its enforcement power was limited to calling violations of the voluntary standards to public attention. Other arms of government—Congress and the President—contributed to enforcement of the standards, however, through implicit or explicit threats that firms violating the standards would lose government contracts. Threats of other government action were made to particular industries; these included relaxation of import quotas (steel), deregulation (trucking), and sale of government stockpiles (copper) if wage settlements in these industries were not in compliance. As inflation continued to accelerate in 1979, the levels of permissible wage increases were raised for 1980. After the defeat of President Carter in the 1980 election, the program was terminated.

Did U.S. Incomes Policies Work?

Numerous attempts have been made to determine whether the Kennedy-Johnson wage/price guideposts and the Nixon Phase II economic program actually did hold the rates of wage and price inflation below the levels that

---

44. This does not imply that the guideposts *caused* wage increases to average less than 3.2 percent. Evidence on their effect on the wage-inflation rate will be discussed below.

45. The Carter policy did *not* apply on a *company* basis but on an *employee-group* basis within each company. The three types of employee groups considered were supervisors, nonunion–nonsupervisory employees, and workers covered by each collective bargaining agreement.

would have existed in the *absence* of the programs. It is worth emphasizing that these studies do *not* compare actual levels of wage and price inflation during the periods that the incomes policies were in effect with levels of inflation during the *previous* periods. Since the forces that affect inflation, such as unemployment rates and expected rates of inflation, change over time, such comparisons would be meaningless. Put another way, such comparisons could not disentangle the change in inflation rates caused by the incomes policies from the change in inflation rates caused by changes in other variables.

Rather, the methodology used in these studies is to use historical data to estimate generalizations of the inflation/unemployment trade-off curves specified earlier in this chapter and then to ask if these estimated relationships systematically changed during the periods that the incomes policies were in effect. That is, the researchers tried to determine whether the rates of inflation that were *predicted* using the historical relationship between unemployment and inflation (after controlling for the age/gender distribution of the labor force, the dispersion of unemployment rates, and expected inflation rates) really did exceed the *actual* inflation rates that occurred. If *predicted* rates of inflation exceeded *actual* rates, one could argue that the incomes policies were effective in bringing down inflation.

The answers these studies yielded are somewhat ambiguous. For example, George Perry found that the rate of wage inflation was some 0.6 to 1.2 points lower during the Kennedy-Johnson guidepost period than his model would otherwise have predicted, but Robert J. Gordon found that the guideposts had no effect on the rate of wage inflation.[46] In contrast, Gordon found that the rate of wage inflation was held down during the Nixon Phase II incomes policy period—a result other researchers have also found.[47]

In evaluating these studies, however, one must remember that the fact that the rate of wage inflation appeared to be lower than a model predicted during the period the policy was in effect does not imply that the policy *caused* the reduction in the rate of inflation. Factors not included in the model that reduce the rate of wage inflation might have occurred at the same time. For example, the period during which the Kennedy-Johnson wage/price guideposts were in effect (1962–66) was one of increased import competition for American steel manufacturers and one of rapid expansion of government-sponsored employee-training programs to remove skill bottlenecks. Both these forces should have reduced the rate of wage inflation, the former by in-

46. Perry's initial study was George Perry, "Wages and the Guideposts," *American Economic Review* 57 (September 1967): 897–904. Additional results are found in George Perry, "Inflation in Theory and Practice," *Brookings Papers on Economic Activity,* 1980–1, 207–42. Gordon's results are in his "Comment," *Brookings Papers on Economic Activity,* 1980–1, 249–57.
47. See Robert Gordon, "Wage Price Controls and the Shifting Phillips Curve," *Brookings Papers on Economic Activity,* 1972–2, 385–421, and his "Comment." See also Bradley Askin and John Kraft, *Econometric Wage and Price Models: Assessing the Impact of the Economic Stabilization Program* (Lexington, Mass.: D. C. Heath, 1974). More recently, John Hagens and R. Robert Russell, "Testing for the Effectiveness of Wage Price Controls: An Application to the Carter Program," *American Economic Review* 75 (March 1985): 191–207, found smaller effects than Perry during the Kennedy-Johnson guidepost period and that a "catch-up" occurred *after* the Nixon incomes policy. They could not, however, identify the effects of the Carter incomes policy.

creasing the resistance of U.S. steel manufacturers to union wage demands and the latter by reducing the excess demand for labor. It is thus not an easy task to ascertain what the effects of incomes policies really are.

Why Are Incomes Policies Unpopular Among Economists?

Independent of the evidence on the effectiveness of incomes policies in moderating the rates of wage and price inflation, many economists are opposed to their use because the policies create inequities and social losses in the economy.[48] The scope of this text does not permit our cataloguing the case against incomes policies, but a few arguments can be mentioned.

First, rigid guidelines or standards implicitly freeze the distribution of income and create inequities. For example, individuals who have recently received large increases gain relative to those whose increases will be constrained by the policies. Unless most individuals are happy with their relative income positions at the time the policy is imposed and there is a social consensus on the need for the policy, the policy will invariably break down.

Second, such policies may create social losses, because rapidly expanding sectors of the economy that face personnel shortages are prevented from bidding up wages to attract labor (in terms of the normative principles articulated in Chapter 1, controls on prices and wages serve to prevent some mutually beneficial transactions from taking place). Once exceptions to these controlled levels of prices and wages are systematically granted for the above reason, as was done in Phase II of the Nixon economic policy, the process of controlling wage increases becomes highly politicized, and the exceptions may be used to justify wage increases that exceed the standard in cases when waiving the standard is not justified by economic conditions. More generally, incomes policies tend to be unevenly applied to different groups; those with political power gain relative to those without it.

Finally, the administrative costs of incomes policies that contain enforcement procedures may be enormous. Simply costing out tens of thousands of labor contracts to ascertain compliance is no trivial task, especially when numerous employee benefits are involved—many of those costs can only be actuarially estimated or guessed at, as is true with pensions. The resources devoted both by government agencies to monitor the programs and by private employers to assure that they are in compliance may represent a substantial cost to society.

Share Wages

Instead of paying workers conventional, time-based wages, it has recently been proposed that employers pay workers *share wages*—that is, wages based upon revenue or profit sharing. It can be argued that share wages alter the demand for labor so as to make employment more stable in business downturns; this issue was analyzed in detail earlier (Appendix 11A). Besides reducing un-

---

48. A now classic article that presents the case against incomes policies more completely is Milton Friedman, "What Price Guideposts?" in *Guidelines, Informal Controls, and the Market Place,* ed. George Shultz and Robert Alibers (Chicago: University of Chicago Press, 1966), 17–40.

EXAMPLE 16.3
Incomes Policies During the Roman Empire

The use of incomes policies to combat inflation is not a recent innovation — and neither is the inflexibility in resource allocation caused by policies that fix prices. In the year A.D. 301, after years of severe inflation, the Emperor Diocletian issued an edict fixing maximum prices and wages for the whole Roman Empire. Maximum wages were specified for more than 130 different categories of labor, and severe punishment was threatened to anyone who violated the standards.

One would expect that the establishment of a rigid occupational wage structure with a maximum wage specified for each occupation would have had two effects. First, workers would have sought to leave occupations where compensation levels were fixed at relatively low levels (considering the work involved) and would have sought employment where wages happened to be fixed at relatively higher levels. These occupational flows could not be accompanied by wage changes (because wages were fixed), so one would expect that permanent surpluses and shortages would have developed. Second, some workers might have decided that the prevailing maximum wage scales did not offer sufficiently high rewards for their labor force participation and would have chosen not to participate. Either effect would have led to a reduction in the overall level of output.

Diocletian was apparently well aware of these potential difficulties and tried to head them off by restricting both occupational mobility and labor force participation decisions. Each worker was effectively tied to his job, and it was required that his children be brought up to succeed him. Not surprisingly, however, the removal of individuals' freedom of choice coupled with the wage ceilings effectively killed any incentives workers had to work hard or exhibit initiative. According to R.H. Barrow, "Production fell, and with it the standard of living; the rigid uniformity of a lifeless and static mediocrity prevailed."

SOURCES: H. Mitchell, "The Edict of Diocletian: A Study of Price Fixing in the Roman Empire," *Canadian Journal of Economics and Political Science* 13 (February 1947): 1–12; R.H. Barrow, *The Romans* (Baltimore: Penguin Books, 1949), 177.

employment, share wages also have the potential to reduce the rates of wage and price inflation in the economy.

The critical characteristic of a share basis for paying workers is that a firm's labor costs become, at least in part, a function of its performance. Under such schemes, the firm agrees to set aside a certain fraction of its profits (or revenues) in a fund that will then be split among its employees. If its product demand falls, either from a general recession or from a permanent shift away from its products, the firm's labor costs fall without its having to lay off workers. If its profits rise when demand is strong—because it can raise product prices—its workers receive an automatic wage increase. It is the sharing, among firms and workers alike, of profit reductions in the bad times and profit increases in the periods of "boom" that has the potential to bring down wage and price inflation.

Conventional economic theory predicts that when product demand falls, the prices of affected goods and services should fall; falling product prices and reduced output levels should also cause wages to be adjusted downward. Thus, wage and price levels ought to be falling in periods of recession. Two problems in achieving the conventionally predicted adjustments are that many firms use markup pricing and that nominal wage rates are not customarily reduced when business is slack. Because labor costs are an important component of total cost, the absence of wage reductions when business is slack implies that prices will not be reduced either.[49]

If share wages constitute a substantial portion of employee compensation, the wages paid to each worker will fall automatically when product demand slackens and firms' revenues are decreased.[50] This fall in the unit cost of labor will permit (encourage) firms using markup pricing to reduce product prices in periods or sectors characterized by slack demand.

How will product price increases of share firms compare with those of conventional firms when business is brisk? Suppose that a conventional firm selling items of equipment for $100 apiece realizes that it can now get $110 for them. If it altered its traditional markup and charged $110, its profits would rise by $10 per item; a firm contemplating such an increase would have to balance this $10 rise in profits per unit of output against the *costs* of the price increase (reprinting price lists and possible loss of customer "goodwill" when the traditional markup is raised). The share firm, however, must—by the very nature of its pay scheme—share the $10 rise in profits with its workers. If, for example, the share firm had agreed to put 40 percent of its profits into the compensation pool, then it could keep only $6 of the added $10 in revenues per unit of output. If there are costs to raising prices, the share firm is more likely than the conventional firm to find that these costs outweigh the benefits.[51]

By making it more likely that firms would reduce prices in periods of slack demand and less likely that firms would raise them in periods of strong

---

49. For a simple economic model of price and wage "stickiness" in the downward direction, see Arthur Okun, *Prices and Quantities* (Washington, D.C.: Brookings Institution, 1981).

50. It was argued in Appendix 11A that share firms faced with a downward shift in product demand are a lot less likely to lay off workers than are firms that pay conventional wages. With falling revenues and a generally constant number of employees, it is clear that the unit cost of labor falls.

51. Price inflation can also result from upward "pushes" from the cost side even when demand pressures are not particularly strong. If conventional wages, for example, are raised above market-clearing levels, firms paying these wages will usually mark up product prices and cut output. A share firm, however, is "labor-hungry" at its long-run profit-maximizing level of output (for a detailed discussion, see Appendix 11A). Its problem is that, in equilibrium, it cannot obtain the additional workers it wants, because to expand employment beyond its long-run optimum would drive wages down below market-clearing levels. However, if its wages were to rise above equilibrium (due to a negotiated settlement, say), then its search for additional workers *would* bear fruit. As these additional workers are added to the firm's work force, output grows and the average wage received by employees falls—reducing pressures to raise product prices. Thus, even in periods of "cost-push" inflation (stagflation), share systems appear to offer the prospect of reducing the rates of price increases below those found when conventional wages are paid.

demand, share systems have been suggested by some economists as a structural change in the economy worth contemplating. The suggestion that the economy could be "vaccinated" against stagflation by the widespread adoption of share systems has started a lively debate in recent years. Critics range from those who question the feasibility of implementing share systems to those who argue that the claims of share wage supporters have been overstated. Advocates encouraging (usually through tax incentives) the widespread adoption of share wages contend that, at the very least, share systems would not make stagflation worse and would stand a good chance of improving the economy's performance vis-à-vis unemployment and inflation.[52]

MISCONCEPTION

"All price increases are inflationary and are therefore to be discouraged."

Analysis

Inflation is defined as a rise in the *general* level of prices; it is equivalent to a fall in the value of money. Changes in *relative* prices, however, are what guide the allocation of resources in a market system—reflecting, as they do, the forces of supply and demand. Thus, not all price increases are inflationary or are to be discouraged.

Principle

Equilibrium employment and relative wage levels are the result of both demand and supply influences.

REVIEW QUESTIONS

1. Why are the size of wage increases and the unemployment rate thought to be negatively related? How (and why) is this negative relationship affected by price inflation and the rising labor force participation of women? What can the government do to reduce the wage inflation associated with any level of unemployment?

2. Some years ago Great Britain instituted three related policies. First, it increased unemployment compensation benefits. Second, the government agreed to pay lump-sum benefits owed to anyone permanently fired by his or her employer. (Assume that previously the *employers* paid these benefits.) Third, the government placed a tax, to be paid by employers, on wages in *service* industries (wages in manufacturing were not taxed).

   a. Analyze the effects of these three policies on the labor market.

   b. Judging from the effects of these programs, what is (are) the *goal(s)* implicit in these policies?

---

52. For a flavor of the discussion, see Martin L. Weitzman, *The Share Economy* (Cambridge, Mass.: Harvard University Press, 1983); a set of articles reviewing the Weitzman book appearing in *Industrial and Labor Relations Review* 39, no. 2 (January 1986): 285–90; and William Nordhaus, "Can The Share Economy Conquer Inflation?" *Quarterly Journal of Economics* 103 (February 1988): 201–17.

3. Suppose the government were to adopt an incomes policy that allows workers to receive wage increases each January equal to the increase in the cost of living during the previous 12 months but *no* other increases. Would such a scheme help reduce the rate of inflation?

4. Some members of Congress have supported legislation requiring the federal government to undertake massive employment programs as long as the overall unemployment rate is above 4 percent. Evaluate such a program with respect to its effects on inflation.

5. "Incomes policies that specify that workers should receive percentage wage increases equal to their rate of productivity growth are doomed to failure because they will cause management's share of output to continually fall." Is this statement true, false, or uncertain? Explain your answer.

6. Evaluate the statement, "The slowdown in the rate of productivity growth in the United States is the primary factor responsible for simultaneous high rates of unemployment and inflation."

7. In an effort to reduce foreign competition, many labor leaders and others have proposed "domestic content" legislation. Such laws would require that certain products sold in the United States (automobiles, for example) be made mainly with American-made parts and American labor. The laws would provide that no more than X percent of the value of the final product could be produced by foreigners.

   What would be the effects of such laws on inflation in the short run (one year, say)? In the long run?

8. "Government regulation of safety and health, as well as its policies to raise wages of women and minorities, have driven up employer costs and therefore should be opposed as inflationary." Comment.

9. It has been argued that the widespread adoption of compensation systems that would tie workers' pay more closely to the profits of their employers would help cure high rates of inflation. Explain how profit sharing could reduce the overall rate of price inflation in the U.S. economy.

SELECTED READINGS

Flanagan, Robert. "Wage Interdependencies in Unionized Labor Markets." *Brookings Papers on Economic Activity,* 1976–3, 635–73.

Friedman, Milton. "The Role of Monetary Policy." *American Economic Review* 58 (March 1968): 1–17.

Katz, Lawrence. "Some Recent Developments in Labor Economics and Their Implications for Macroeconomics." *Journal of Money, Credit and Banking* 20 (August 1988, pt. 2): 507–22.

Medoff, James. "U.S. Labor Markets: Imbalance, Wage Growth, and Productivity in the 1970s." *Brookings Papers on Economic Activity,* 1983–1, 87–120.

Mitchell, Daniel. *Unions, Wages, and Inflation.* Washington, D.C.: Brookings Institution, 1980.

Okun, Arthur, and Perry, George, eds. "Innovative Policies to Slow Inflation." *Brookings Papers on Economic Activity,* 1978–2.

Perry, George. "Shifting Wage Norms and Their Implications." *American Economic Review Papers and Proceedings* 76 (May 1986): 245–48.

APPENDIX 16A

Does a Long-Run Trade-off Exist Between the Rate of Price Inflation and the Unemployment Rate?

We have assumed that the short-run trade-off curve is given by

$$\dot{P} = f(\mathbf{u}) - \dot{q} + \gamma \dot{P}^e \qquad \gamma \leq 1 \tag{16A.1}$$

Whether a long-run trade-off exists between the rate of price inflation and the unemployment rate depends crucially on how responsive money-wage changes are to expectations of price inflation (which is captured by the parameter γ in our model) and on how expectations of price inflation are formed. To see the importance of the role of the responsiveness of wage changes to inflationary expectations, suppose for simplicity that the expected rate of price inflation in a period is determined by a very simple form of *adaptive expectations;* namely, assume that it is equal to the actual rate of price inflation that occurred in the previous period:

$$\dot{P}^e = \dot{P}_{-1} \tag{16A.2}$$

Consider first the case when expected price increases are *not* fully reflected in wage increases, and to take a specific example, suppose that γ is equal to ½. In this case, the short-run price inflation/unemployment trade-off is given by

$$\dot{P} = f(\mathbf{u}) - \dot{q} + \tfrac{1}{2}\dot{P}_{-1} \tag{16A.3}$$

If initially there were no price inflation in the economy, the trade-off curve would then be

$$\dot{P} = f(\mathbf{u}) - \dot{q} \tag{16A.4}$$

Figure 16A.1 provides a graphic representation of equation (16A.4), where T_0 is drawn as a straight line for expositional convenience. Note that if the unemployment rate were kept at $\mathbf{u}_0$, there would be no price inflation in the

FIGURE 16A.1   A Stable Long-Run Trade-off Between Price Inflation and the Unemployment Rate: $\dot{P} = f(\mathbf{u}) - \dot{q} + \frac{1}{2}\dot{P}_{-1}$

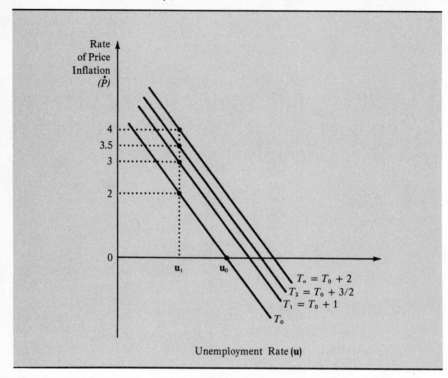

economy. (Note also that if labor productivity growth is positive, the price inflation/unemployment trade-off will lie below the wage inflation/unemployment trade-off, and hence $\mathbf{u}_0$ will typically be *less than* the full-employment unemployment rate, $\mathbf{u}^*$. This statement ignores complications caused by the dispersion in unemployment rates.)

Now suppose that the government pursues a stimulative aggregate demand policy and reduces the unemployment rate to $\mathbf{u}_1$. As drawn in Figure 16A.1, this policy would yield a 2 percent rate of price inflation—which, from equation (16A.3), would shift the short-run trade-off in the next period up by 1 percentage point ($2 \times \frac{1}{2}$). This new curve is represented by T_1 in Figure 16A.1, and if the government sought to keep the unemployment rate at $\mathbf{u}_1$, the inflation rate would rise to 3 percent. However, this inflation rate would shift the trade-off in the next period up to T_2, which is $\frac{3}{2}$ (that is, $3 \times \frac{1}{2}$) of a percentage point above the original trade-off, T_0. If government again tried to keep the unemployment rate at $\mathbf{u}_1$, the rate of price inflation in the following period would rise to 3.5 percent.

This process of upward-shifting short-run trade-off curves would continue as long as the unemployment rate was kept at $\mathbf{u}_1$. Note, however, that because less than the expected price inflation rate is passed on in the form of higher wages ($\gamma < 1$), the magnitude of the shift becomes progressively smaller. Indeed, the inflation rate will eventually reach 4 percent, at which point the trade-off curve will have shifted to T_n, which is 2 percentage points above T_0. If the government then kept unemployment at u_1, inflation in the next period would again be 4 percent and the upward spiral would stop. Hence, the inflation/unemployment combination $(4, u_1)$ is a point on the long-run trade-off curve. One could repeat this line of reasoning for other unemployment rates and trace out the entire long-run trade-off curve.

More succinctly, the long-run trade-off will be the locus of inflation/unemployment combinations for which the *actual* rate of price inflation $(\dot{P})$ equals the *expected* rate of inflation $(\dot{P}^e)$. In terms of equation (16.7) in the text, one can replace the expected inflation rate by the actual rate to obtain

$$\dot{P} = f(\mathbf{u}) + \gamma\dot{P} - \dot{q} \qquad (16A.5)$$

Solving for the actual rate of inflation, one obtains:

$$\dot{P} = \frac{f(\mathbf{u})}{1 - \gamma} - \frac{\dot{q}}{1 - \gamma} \qquad (16A.6)$$

Equation (16A.6) is the long-run price inflation/unemployment trade-off curve in our model. If wages respond at all to expected rates of price inflation (that is, if $\gamma > 0$), the long-run trade-off curve (T_L) will be steeper than the short-run trade-off curves, as indicated in Figure 16A.2. Note in Figure 16A.2

FIGURE 16A.2 The Relationship of the Short-Run and Long-Run Trade-off Curves ($\gamma = \frac{1}{2}$)

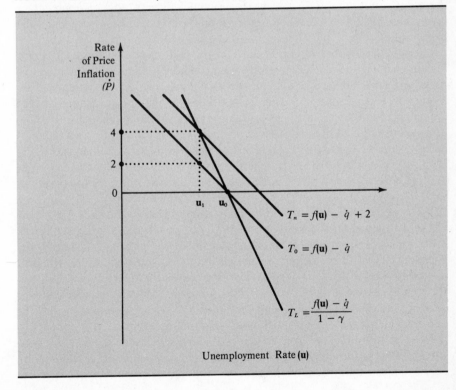

that the inflation/unemployment combinations of $(4, \mathbf{u}_1)$ and $(0, \mathbf{u}_0)$—each representing points where $\dot{P} = \dot{P}_e$—are both on T_L.

Put another way, increasing the unemployment rate by 1 percentage point will "buy" a larger reduction in inflation in the long run than it will in the short run if $\gamma > 0$. This difference in slope between the long-run and short-run trade-offs increases as γ becomes larger. Furthermore, the larger γ is, the greater will be the effect of a change in the rate of productivity growth on the long-run inflation rate, with decreases in productivity growth causing the long-run trade-off curve to shift up by more than would be the case if γ were smaller. Moreover, if $\gamma < 1$, a stable long-run relationship between $\dot{P}$ and $\mathbf{u}$ would exist.

If γ equals one, however, there is no stable long-run trade-off between the rate of price inflation and the rate of unemployment. Attempts to reduce the unemployment rate below $\mathbf{u}_0$ will lead to ever-accelerating rates of price inflation. To see this, we shall now assume that all the expected increase in prices is transmitted into higher wages ($\gamma = 1$). As a result, the short-run trade-off curve is given by

$$\dot{P} = f(\mathbf{u}) - \dot{q} + \dot{P}_{-1} \tag{16A.7}$$

The curve T_0 in Figure 16A.3 represents the relationship in equation (16A.7) when the economy is originally at $\mathbf{u}_0$ and the past inflation rate is zero. Suppose now that aggregate demand policy is pursued to reduce the unemployment rate to $\mathbf{u}_1$, and an inflation rate of 2 percent initially results. In this case, the short-run trade-off in the next period (T_1) shifts up by 2 percentage points, and if $\mathbf{u}_1$ is maintained, the inflation rate would be 4 percent in the next period.

It should be obvious that, because of the one-for-one feedback from current price inflation to next period's wage inflation, the short-run trade-off curve will shift up vertically—*and* the actual rate of price inflation will *increase*—by 2 percentage points *every* period as long as the government keeps the unemployment rate at $\mathbf{u}_1$. The attempt to keep the unemployment rate below $\mathbf{u}_0$ thus leads to ever-increasing rates of price inflation; no stable rate of inflation can be maintained. (In terms of equation 16A.6, the long-run trade-off is infinite when $\gamma = 1$ because the denominator is zero.) For this reason $\mathbf{u}_0$ is often referred to in such models as the *nonaccelerating inflation rate of unemployment,* or the *NAIRU*.

To get the process of accelerating inflation to stop in this model, the government must return the unemployment rate to the NAIRU. In Figure 16A.3, if the unemployment rate is maintained at $\mathbf{u}_1$ for periods 0, 1, 2, and 3, the inflation rate will be 8 percent in period 3 and the trade-off curve will shift up to T_4 in period 4. *If* the government then allows the unemployment rate to rise to $\mathbf{u}_0$ in period 4, the inflation rate will remain at 8 percent. The trade-off curve in period 5 will be the same as the one in period 4, and as long as the unemployment rate stays at $\mathbf{u}_0$, the inflation rate will remain at 8 percent. To reduce the inflation rate back to zero, the government could tolerate a massive increase in the unemployment rate (to $\mathbf{u}_2$) for one period, at which point $\dot{P} = 0$ and unemployment could be returned to $\mathbf{u}_0$. Alternatively, the govern-

FIGURE 16A.3   No Stable Long-Run Trade-off Between Price Inflation and the Unemployment Rate: $\dot{P} = f(u) - \dot{q} + \dot{P}_{-1}$

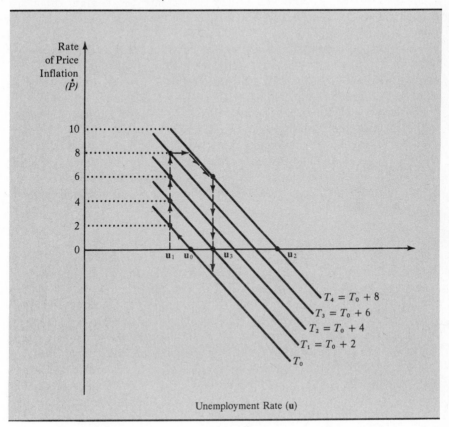

ment could let unemployment increase to u_3 for 4 periods, after which the economy would be back on T_0 and unemployment could be returned to u_0 (note the downward arrows in Figure 16A.3).

If this model is correct, a short-run trade-off exists between the rate of price inflation and the level of the unemployment rate, but no such trade-off exists in the long run. Society can *temporarily* reduce the unemployment rate at the cost of *permanently* higher rates of price inflation. To bring these higher rates of inflation down requires a temporary increase in the unemployment rate.

Of course, both these models assume that individuals *naively* base their expectations of inflation only on the actual rate of inflation that occurred in the previous period. Another school of thought argues that individuals' expectations are formed *rationally* in the sense that they take account of all available information that is relevant, *including* the direction in which government policy is moving. Such *rational expectations* theorists argue that, when formed rationally, people's expectations may frustrate the attempt by government to use aggregate-demand policies.[1] While a complete discussion of the rational expectations view would take us far into the domain of macroeconomics, we can illustrate its implications for the existence of the long-run trade-off curve quite simply.

Suppose initially that expectations of inflation are zero and the government takes action to stimulate the economy with the goal of reducing the unemployment rate. If individuals are aware of this action and the nature of the short-run trade-off (equation 16A.1), they will see that lower unemployment would imply a higher inflation rate. Hence, their expectations of inflation would increase and the short-run trade-off curve would shift up, possibly even before any effect on unemployment was felt. But with a higher short-run trade-off curve, individuals would realize that achieving the desired reduction in unemployment that the government is aiming for would require a still higher inflation rate. As a result, expectations of inflation would again increase, the short-run trade-off curve would again shift up, and the process would repeat itself.

Obviously γ remains a key parameter in the model. If γ is less than one, a stable long-run trade-off remains, although it should be clear that the stable higher inflation rate associated with a lower unemployment rate may be reached much more quickly in a world of rational expectations than it would if the short-run trade-off curve did not shift up until *after* the government succeeded in reducing unemployment. If γ equals one, once again no stable long-run trade-off exists. It should be stressed that the rational expectations viewpoint does *not* necessarily imply that γ equals one. It is conceivable that, in a world in which collective bargaining takes place and contracts are negotiated periodically, workers may have rational expectations about inflation but do not have the bargaining power to win contracts that fully compensate them for anticipated inflation. As noted in the text, however, many macroeconomists accept almost as a matter of first principles that γ does equal one and that no stable long-run trade-off exists.

---

1. For a clear exposition of the rational expectations approach, see *Rational Expectations — Fresh Ideas That Challenge Some Established Views of Policy Making* (Minneapolis, Minn.: Federal Reserve Bank of Minneapolis, 1977), and Robert Lucas and Thomas Sargent, eds., *Rational Expectations and Econometric Practice* (Minneapolis, Minn.: University of Minnesota Press, 1981).

Answers to Odd-Numbered
Review Questions

CHAPTER 1

1. The basic value premise underlying normative analysis is that if a given transaction is beneficial to the parties agreeing to it and hurts no one else, then accomplishing that transaction is said to be "good." This criterion implies, of course, that anyone harmed by a transaction must be compensated for that harm (a condition tantamount to saying that all parties to a transaction must voluntarily agree to it). The labor market will reach a point of optimality when all mutually beneficial transactions have been accomplished. If there are mutually beneficial transactions remaining unconsummated, the labor market will not be at a point of optimality.

   One condition preventing the accomplishment of a mutually beneficial transaction would be *ignorance*. A party to a transaction may voluntarily agree to it because he or she is uninformed about some adverse effect of that transaction. Likewise, a party to a potential transaction may fail to enter into the transaction because he or she is uninformed about a benefit of the transaction. Informed individuals may fail to consummate a transaction, however, because of underlying *transaction barriers*. These may arise because of government prohibitions against certain kinds of transactions, imperfections in the market's ability to bring buyers and sellers together, or the nonexistence of a market where one could potentially exist.

3. The prohibitions of child labor laws would seem to violate the principle of mutual benefit by outlawing certain transactions that might be voluntarily entered into. However, there are at least two conditions under which such prohibitions would be consistent with the principles of normative economics. First, the children entering into an employment transaction may be uninformed of the dangers or the consequences of their decision to work in a particular environment. By their very nature children are inexperienced, and society frequently adopts legislation to protect them from their own ignorance.

   Second, society may adopt child labor legislation to protect children from their parents. A child forced by a parent to work in a dangerous or unhealthy environment has not voluntarily agreed to the employment transaction. Thus, a law prohibiting such a child from engaging in certain employment would not be violating the principle of mutual benefit when parental compulsion was present.

5. a. This behavior is entirely consistent with the model of job quitting described in the text. Workers are assumed by economic theory to be attempting to maximize

utility (happiness). If all other aspects of two jobs are *similar,* this theory predicts that workers will prefer a higher-paying to a lower-paying job. However, two jobs frequently differ in many important respects, including the work environment, personalities of managers, and the stresses placed on employees. Thus, one way to interpret this woman's behavior is that she was willing to give up 50 cents an hour to be able to work in an environment freer of stress.

b. There is no way to prove that her behavior was grounded in "rationality." Economists define rationality as the ability to make considered decisions that are expected (at the time the decision is made) to advance one's self-interest. We cannot tell from any one individual act whether the person involved is being rational or not. Certainly, as described above, this woman's decision to quit could be interpreted as a move calculated to increase her utility (or level of happiness). However, it could also be that she became uncontrollably angry and made her decision without any thought of the consequences.

c. Economic theory does not predict that everyone will act alike. Since economic agents are assumed to maximize utility, and since each person can be assumed to have a unique set of preferences, it is entirely consistent with economic theory that some workers would respond to a given set of incentives and that others would not. Thus, it could not be correctly concluded from the situation described that economic theory applied to one group of workers but not to another. It might well be that the other workers were less bothered by stress and that they were not willing to give up 50 cents an hour to avoid this stress.

CHAPTER 2

1. Unless coal-mining wages in the Soviet Union are being set administratively, without reference to market forces (a possibility ruled out by assumption in this question), the rise in coal-mining wages could be caused by either (or both) of two factors: a rightward shift in the demand curve for coal miners or a leftward shift in the supply curve of coal miners. If the demand for coal miners had shifted to the right, then coal-mining employment would rise—and with it coal-mine output. However, if the increased wage has been caused by a leftward shift in supply, then there would be reduced employment associated with the rising wage, and presumably reduced output. Thus, the CIA cannot infer from the fact that coal-mining wages have increased that coal-mining output has also increased.

3. Many engineers are employed in research and development tasks. Therefore, if a major demander of research and development were to reduce its demand, the demand curve for engineers would shift left, causing wages and employment of engineers to fall.

5. If the wages for arc welders are above the equilibrium wage, the company is paying more for its arc welders than it needs to and as a result is hiring fewer than it could. Thus, the definition of overpayment that makes most sense in this case is one in which the wage rate is above the equilibrium wage.

   A ready indicator of an above-equilibrium wage rate is a long queue of applicants whenever a position in a company becomes available. Another indicator is an abnormally low quit rate as workers (in this case arc welders) who are lucky enough to obtain the above-equilibrium wage cling tenaciously to their jobs.

7. The licensing requirement will increase the difficulty of becoming a mechanic and therefore shift the supply curve of mechanics to the left. This shift will tend to in-

crease the wages of mechanics and reduce their employment (as the least-qualified mechanics are forced to drop out of the market).

9. This regulation essentially increases the cost of capital, and as such it will have an ambiguous effect on the demand curve for labor. On the one hand, the increased cost of capital will increase the cost of production and cause a scale effect that will tend to depress employment. On the other hand, this regulation will increase the cost of capital relative to labor and could stimulate the substitution of labor for capital. Thus, the substitution effect will work to increase employment while the scale effect will work to decrease it. Which effect is stronger cannot be known a priori.

CHAPTER 3

1. This line of reasoning confuses the budgetary cost of achieving any desired force level with the social costs—the costs borne by society. Consider the figure below, where we have arbitrarily drawn a vertical demand curve to reflect the assumption that the military always wants E_1 soldiers regardless of the cost. The supply curve is drawn as an upward-sloping function of the military wage; this assumes that preferences for military service vary across the population and that as the military wage increases, more and more people find military service an attractive career alternative.

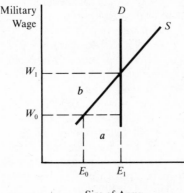

Size of Army

Suppose initially that the military wage is set at W_0, that only E_0 people volunteer, that the total military wage bill is $W_0 E_0$, and that there is a perceived "shortage" of $E_1 - E_0$. If a draft system were instituted and $E_1 - E_0$ individuals were compelled to join the army, the *additional* budgetary cost (ignoring the cost of running the draft system) would be $W_0(E_1 - E_0)$, or rectangle a in the figure. If instead the military wage rate were allowed to rise to induce people to join voluntarily, it would have to rise to W_1 to eliminate the "shortage"—and the additional budgetary cost would be $W_1 E_1 - W_0 E_0$ (this is the sum of rectangles a and b in the figure).

Obviously the budgetary cost is higher in the second case, but the true costs to society need not be. This is because, by forcing the $E_1 - E_0$ workers to join the armed forces in the draft-system case, but paying them less than they would require to voluntarily join, we are implicitly levying a tax on them. We are also levying an implicit tax on the E_0 workers, who would have been paid the wage of W_1 if the volunteer army were in effect but instead only receive W_0. The sum of these implicit taxes just equals rectangle b.

3. The potential employment effects of OSHA standards differ with the type of approach taken. If the standards apply to capital (machinery), they will increase the cost of capital equipment. This increase in cost has a scale effect, which will reduce the quantity demanded of all inputs (including labor). On the other hand, it also provides employers with an incentive to substitute labor (which is now relatively cheaper) for capital in producing any given desired level of output. This substitution will moderate the decline in employment.

In contrast, requiring employers to furnish personal protective devices to employees increases the cost of labor. In this case, employers have an incentive to substitute now relatively cheaper capital for labor when producing any given level of output (as above, the increased cost of production causes a scale effect that also tends to reduce employment).

Other things equal, then, the employment reduction induced by safety standards will be greater if the personal protective device method is used. However, to fully answer the question requires information on the costs of meeting the standards using the two methods. For example, if the "capital" approach increases capital costs by 50 percent while the "personal protective" approach increases labor costs by only 1 percent, the scale effect in the first method will probably be large enough that the greater employment loss will be associated with the first method.

5. The wage and employment effects in both service industries and manufacturing industries must be considered. In the service sector the wage tax on employers can be analyzed in much the same way as payroll taxes are analyzed in the text. That is, a tax on wages, collected from the employer, will cause the demand curve to shift leftward *if* the curve is drawn with respect to the wage employees take home. At any given hourly wage that employees take home, the cost to the employer has risen by the amount of the tax. An increase in cost associated with any employee wage dampens the employer's appetite for labor and causes the demand curve to shift down and to the left.

The effects on employment and wages depend upon the shape of the labor supply curve. If the labor supply curve is upward-sloping, both employment and the wage employees take home will fall. If the supply curve is vertical, employment will not fall but wages will fall by the full amount of the tax. If the supply curve is horizontal, the wage rate will not fall but employment will.

The reduced employment and/or wages in the service sector should cause the supply of labor to the manufacturing sector to shift to the right (as people formerly employed in the service sector seek employment elsewhere). This shift in the supply curve should cause employment in manufacturing to increase even if the demand curve there remains stationary. If the demand curve does remain stationary, the employment increase would be accompanied by a decrease in manufacturing wages. However, the demand for labor in manufacturing may also shift to the right as consumers substitute away from the now more expensive services and buy the now relatively cheaper manufactured goods. If this demand shift occurs, the increase in employment would be accompanied by either a wage increase or a smaller wage reduction than would occur if the demand curve for labor in manufacturing were to remain stationary.

7. The imposition of financial penalties on employers who are discovered to have hired illegal immigrants essentially raises the cost of hiring them. The employers now must pay whatever the prevailing wage of the immigrants is, and they also face the possibility of a fine if they are discovered to have illegally employed workers. This penalty can be viewed as increasing the cost of hiring illegal workers so that

this cost exceeds the wage. This effect can be seen as a leftward shift of the demand curve for illegal immigrants, thus reducing their employment and wages.

The effects on the demand for skilled "natives" depend on whether skilled and unskilled labor are gross substitutes or gross complements. Raising the cost of unskilled labor produces a scale effect that tends to increase the cost of production and reduce skilled employment. If skilled and unskilled labor are *complements in production,* the demand for skilled labor will clearly shift to the left as a result of the government's policy. However, if they are *substitutes* in production, the increased costs of unskilled labor would stimulate the substitution of skilled for unskilled labor. In this case, the demand for skilled labor could shift either right (if the substitution effect dominated the scale effect) or left (if the scale effect dominated).

CHAPTER 4

1. A permanent tax credit applicable to the purchase of machinery would increase the demand for capital. Its effect on the demand for labor would depend upon both scale and substitution effects. On the one hand, the lower price of capital will induce firms to increase output; this scale effect will lead to an increase in the demand for labor. On the other hand, the lower price of capital will also lead to substitution effects. Categories of labor that are substitutes for capital in production *could* see their demand decreased *if* the substitution effect dominates; if the scale effect dominates, their demand would rise. For categories that are complementary with capital in production there is no substitution effect, so their demand clearly will rise.

   The empirical evidence cited in the text suggests that skilled labor and capital are complements in production, while unskilled labor and capital are substitutes in production. Hence, skilled labor would probably gain more than unskilled labor from a tax credit applicable to the purchase of machinery.

   The conditions under which any substitution effects *against* labor would be small relative to the scale effect are as follows: a small degree of technical substitutability between capital and labor, an inelastic supply of capital, a large share of capital in total costs, and an elastic product demand curve. The conditions under which scale effects would be small relative to substitution effects against labor would be exactly the reverse of those above.

3. A youth differential in the minimum wage has both scale and substitution effects. A reduction in the wage paid to teenagers encourages employers to expand output and hence the usage of all other inputs. If teenagers and adults are complements in production, the demand for older workers will clearly rise. In contrast, if teenagers and older adults compete for the same jobs (that is, if they are substitutes in production), the youth differential encourages employers to substitute teenagers for older workers and could cause the demand for older workers to fall. Without information about the relative magnitudes of the scale and substitution effects, the net effect on older workers' employment is ambiguous.

5. Subsidizing the revenues of eligible cities will allow these cities to cut property taxes and therefore lower the cost of capital to new businesses. This policy, then, is tantamount to a subsidy of capital, and it should induce new businesses—especially capital-intensive ones—to locate in the city. This subsidy will therefore shift the demand for unskilled labor to the right *if* unskilled labor is used in the production process. However, to the extent that the new businesses would have located in the

city *anyway,* the capital subsidy may either increase or decrease the demand for labor that would have otherwise obtained. The reason for this arises from the fact that, if capital and unskilled labor are *substitutes in production,* they may be either gross complements or gross substitutes. If the former, the capital subsidy will cause the employers who had planned to open businesses in the city to demand *more* unskilled labor than they had originally planned on (the scale effect dominates); if the latter, they would use less unskilled labor.

One problem caused by the enterprise zone policy is that it provides capital subsidies for some parts of metropolitan areas and not others. Therefore, some of the increased economic activity that might take place with an enterprise zone policy will be activity that formerly was being conducted in non-decaying areas. Thus, even if employment were to rise in the decaying areas by *X,* employment in the metropolitan area or in society itself is not necessarily rising by *X;* some of the increased employment in the decaying areas might well be provided by jobs that were formerly—or would otherwise have been—in suburban or non-decaying areas.

The elasticity of supply of unskilled labor to the enterprise zone areas is also a factor affecting employment and wages there. If the supply-of-labor curve is relatively horizontal and there is increased demand for unskilled workers in the enterprise zone areas, that increase in demand will call forth very little in the way of a wage increase, but it will stimulate a relatively large increase in employment. If, on the other hand, the supply-of-labor curve to the enterprise zone areas is steeply pitched, wages would be driven up by a shift to the right in the demand curve for labor in that area but employment would not increase very much.

7. a. An increased tariff on steel imports will tend to make domestic *product* demand, and therefore the demand for domestic labor, more inelastic.
    b. A law forbidding workers from being laid off for economic reasons will discourage the substitution of capital for labor and therefore tend to make the own-wage elasticity of demand for labor more inelastic.
    c. A "boom" in the machinery industry will *shift* the product demand curve in the steel industry to the right, thereby shifting the labor demand curve to the right. The effects of this shift on the own-wage elasticity of demand for labor cannot be predicted (except that a parallel shift to the right of a straight-line demand curve will *reduce* the elasticity at each wage rate).
    d. Because capital and labor are most substitutable in the long run, when new production processes can be installed, a decision to delay the adoption of new technologies reduces the substitutability of capital for labor and makes the labor demand curve more inelastic.
    e. An increase in wages will move the firm *along* its demand-for-labor curve and does not change the shape of that curve. However, if the demand curve happens to be a straight line, movement up and to the left along the demand curve will tend to increase elasticity in the range in which firms are operating.
    f. A tax placed on each ton of steel output will tend to shift the demand-for-labor curve to the left, but will not necessarily change its elasticity. Again, however, if the demand curve happened to be a straight line this leftward shift would tend to increase the elasticity of demand for labor at each wage rate.

CHAPTER 5

1. What low-skilled workers and high-paid college professors have in common is that neither group receives much firm-specific training. The former group can be thought of as having received no training and the latter group as having received highly

general training. In either case, we know that the workers' marginal productivity in their current firm is the same as their marginal productivity with other firms. In competitive labor markets, the latter will represent the wage other firms will be willing to pay them. As a result, if the wage at their current firm falls below their marginal productivity, both types of workers have an incentive to quit their jobs.

One might contrast the behavior of these groups with the behavior of individuals who have received a good deal of firm-specific training. We know from the text that (a) by the definition of specific training, the marginal productivity of these individuals at their current firm exceeds their marginal productivity elsewhere, and (b) their wage at the current firm is less than their marginal productivity there. As long as this wage is greater than their potential marginal productivity elsewhere, these workers have reduced incentives to quit their jobs.

3. The government subsidy reduces the costs of specific training borne by the employer, thus encouraging those offering specific training to ex-convicts to hire more such workers. The surplus between marginal product and real wage in the post-training period need not be as large now, so that for specifically trained ex-convicts, labor's new marginal productivity can be closer to wages.

Thus, it is clear that the subsidy enhances the *employment* of ex-convicts. What it does to job *stability* depends on which group of ex-convicts one is considering. For ex-convicts who previously received (or would have received) unsubsidized specific training, stability is reduced. Their marginal productivity is now closer to their real wage than it was (or would have been), so any recessionary declines in labor demand are now more likely to drive their marginal productivity *below* their wage. They are thus more likely to be laid off now than they were before (if a recession occurs).

However, for ex-convicts who would not have been trained by their employers before and now receive training (as a result of the expansion of training owing to the subsidy), job stability is enhanced. They now receive specific training not received before, so they are now in a post-training situation in which marginal productivity *exceeds* the wage. This "buffer" improves their job stability, since labor demand could fall to some extent without driving marginal productivity below wages.

5. a. As detailed in Chapter 3, an increase in the federal minimum wage should have an adverse effect on employment. This effect would be largest for low-skilled groups. Groups that are gross substitutes in employment with low-skilled workers would see their employment levels increase.
   b. As detailed in Chapter 5, an increase in the overtime premium would increase the cost of overtime hours relative to additional employment and thus encourage the substitution of additional employment for overtime hours. Before one concludes that employment will increase, however, one must remember all the qualifications of the chapter. These include the facts that an increase in the overtime premium increases the cost of labor, which should lead to a *substitution* of capital for labor and a reduced usage of labor (due to the *scale* effect of lower output); that skill bottlenecks may arise; that noncompliance may occur; and that increased moonlighting by existing employees may prevent any additional employment of initially nonemployed individuals.
   c. Reducing the standard workweek from 40 to 35 hours would have both substitution and scale effects. On the one hand, by requiring the overtime premium to go into effect after 35 hours, the change increases the marginal cost of long workweeks relative to additional employment and encourages the substitution of

additional employment for overtime hours. On the other hand, by increasing the cost of labor, the change encourages a substitution of capital for labor and causes output and hence employment to fall. Thus, the net effect of the proposed policy change on employment is ambiguous. Sharing the work this way does not necessarily increase employment.

7. Employee benefits such as insurance impose *per-worker* costs on the employer, while wages impose *hourly* costs. If hourly costs of labor rise and per-worker costs remain the same or fall, employers will tend to substitute added workers for added hours per worker if they must increase labor input.

9. The effect of the wage subsidy will clearly be to increase the demand for labor, and depending on the shape of the supply curve this wage subsidy will increase employee wages or employment levels (or both) above what they would have been in the absence of such a subsidy. Another interesting aspect of the wage subsidy, however, is that only the first $12 a week of workers' wages are subsidized. If normal weekly earnings of full-time workers are $20 a week, then the $12 limit will tend to induce firms to expand labor-hours by hiring part-time workers rather than working the ones they have for longer hours. Thus, this subsidy will tend to increase employment and reduce the average hours worked by employees. It subsidizes the marginal cost of hiring *workers* rather than the marginal cost of expanding *hours* per full-time worker.

CHAPTER 6

1. False. An inferior good is defined as one that people consume less of as their incomes rise (if the price of the good remains constant). A labor supply curve is drawn with respect to a person's wage rate. Thus, for a labor supply curve to be backward-bending, the supply curve must be positively sloped in some range and then become negatively sloped in another. A typical way of illustrating a backward-bending supply curve is as follows:

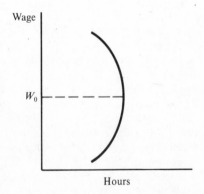

Along the positively sloped section of this backward-bending supply curve, the substitution effect of a wage increase dominates the income effect, and as wages rise the person increases his or her labor supply. However, after the wage reaches W_0 in the above figure, further increases in the wage are accompanied by a reduction in labor supply. In this negatively sloped portion of the supply curve, the income effect dominates the substitution effect.

In this answer we have assumed that the income effect is negative and that, therefore, leisure is a normal good. Had we assumed leisure to be an inferior good, as asserted in this statement, the increases in wealth brought about by increased wages would have worked *with* the underlying substitution effect and caused the labor supply curve to be unambiguously positively sloped.

3. The constraint for the program described is *ABCDE* in the figure below. At 300 hours of leisure (zero hours of work), monthly income is $600, which is represented by segment *AB*. Earnings up to $30 (5 hours of work) do not reduce the welfare subsidy; therefore, the effective wage equals the market wage, and segment *BC* is parallel to the "market" constraint of *AE*.

After 5 hours of work, additional earnings are "taxed away," in the form of benefit reductions, at the rate of 67 cents per dollar of earnings. Hence, segment *CD* has a slope that is 1/3 the slope of segment *AE*. Above an income of $930, the person is no longer eligible for benefits and the market constraint (*DE*) is relevant.

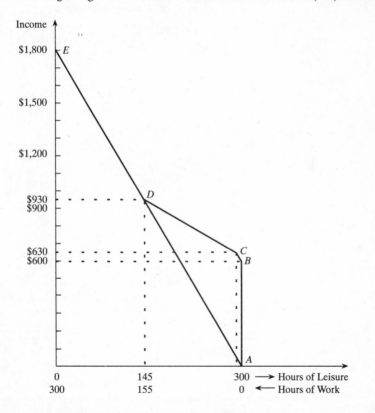

5. A major distinction between bases for distributing profits is whether hours of work are included. If profits are distributed on the basis of hours worked per year, then profit sharing is tantamount to an increase in the wage rate. An increase in the wage rate would cause an income effect tending toward reduced work incentives and a substitution effect tending to increase them. Although the net outcome is not predictable, both forces would be at work.

On the other hand, if hours of work do not form the basis for profit sharing, then with daily wages held constant, profit sharing would cause a pure income effect clearly tending to reduce work incentives. If profits are distributed on a per-worker basis or in some proportion to one's hourly wage rate, they do not effectively increase the price of leisure (because they are not based on hours of work). If either of these bases were employed, there would be solely an income effect, tending to reduce work incentives.

Of course, work incentives would not ordinarily be reduced by profit sharing to the point where the worker quit, because then the worker would no longer have access to the profits being distributed. However, one feasible way for workers to reduce their supply of effort under a profit-sharing plan would be through absenteeism.

7. In the figure below, the straight line *AB* represents the person's market constraint (that is, the constraint in a world with no subsidies). *ACDEB* is the constraint that would apply if the housing subsidy proposal became effective.

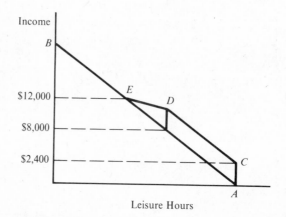

The effects on labor supply depend upon which segment of *ACDEB* the person finds relevant. There are four possible cases. First, if the indifference curves are very steeply pitched (reflecting a strong desire to consume leisure), the housing subsidy proposal will not affect work incentives. The person strongly desiring leisure would continue to not work (would be at point *C*), but would receive the housing subsidy of $2,400. The second case occurs when the person has a tangency along segment *CD*. Along this segment the person's effective wage rate is the same as the market wage, so there is a pure income effect tending to reduce work incentives.

If the person has a tangency point along segment *DE*, there are likewise reduced incentives to work because the income effect caused by the northeast shifting out of the budget constraint is accompanied by a *reduction* in the effective wage rate. Finally, those with tangency points along *EB* will not qualify for the housing subsidy program and therefore will not alter their labor supply behavior. (An exception to this case occurs when a person with a tangency point *near* point *E* before the initiation of the housing subsidy program now has a tangency point along segment *DE* and, of course, works less than before.)

9. From Example 6.2 we know that Siane men (1) work little more than is required for a subsistence level of income; (2) have an effective wage rate of close to zero for

work effort that takes them above the subsistence level of income (due to gift-giving customs); (3) substantially reduced their work effort in the face of real wage increases; but (4) did increase time spent on craft production after steel axes were introduced. Points (1) and (2) suggest a budget constraint with a sharp flattening (a "kink") at around the subsistence level of income. Point (4) implies that the slope of the budget constraint for income levels above subsistence, while it may be relatively flat, is not zero; if gift-giving generated an effective wage of zero above subsistence levels of income, Siane men would *only* engage in subsistence work. In the diagram below, ABC represents the old budget constraint; note its much flatter slope at income levels above the subsistence level (Y_s). The real wage increase associated with steel axes is reflected in segment AB' of the new budget constraint, which is shown as $AB'C'$. The new budget constraint also has a "kink" at Y_s and is relatively flat in the range of $B'C'$.

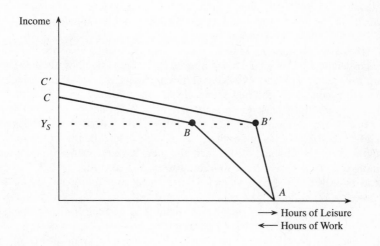

CHAPTER 7

1. a. 400 (6,000–5,600).
   b. The labor force participation rate drops from 60 percent to 56 percent—a reduction of 4 percentage points.
   c. One implication of hidden unemployment is that the unemployment rate may not fully reflect the degree of joblessness. That is, some people who want to work but do not have work are not counted as unemployed because they place such a low probability on obtaining employment that they stop looking for work. While this observation may suggest that hidden unemployment should be included in the published unemployment figures, to do so would imperil the objectivity of the unemployment rate and call into question the theoretical underpinnings of our measure of unemployment. Economic theory suggests that unemployment exists if there are more people willing to work at the going wage than there are people employed at that wage. If economic conditions are such that at the going wage one decides time is better spent in household production, say, than in seeking market work, it can be argued that the person in question has in fact dropped out of the labor force.

3. Jimmy Carter's statement reflects the "additional-worker hypothesis." Stated briefly, this hypothesis suggests that, as the economy moves into a recession and

some members of the labor force are thrown out of work, other family members currently engaged in household production or leisure will enter the labor force to try to maintain family income. While Carter's statement of the additional-worker hypothesis is an apt description of that hypothesis, his statement fails to reflect the fact that studies show the "discouraged-worker" effect dominates the added-worker effect (that is, as the economy moves into a recession and workers are laid off, the labor force shrinks, on balance).

5. To parents who already have small children, this subsidy of day care is tantamount to an increase in the wage rate. That is, each hour of work brings in more take-home earnings now than it did before. This increase in the take-home wage rate will cause both an income and a substitution effect, the net result of which is not theoretically predictable. If the substitution effect is dominant, then the change in policy would increase the labor supply (there is some evidence that the substitution effect is dominant for married women). If the income effect is dominant, then this increase in the take-home wage rate might cause a reduction in labor supply among parents with small children.

   However, the above changes in household *production* may also be accompanied by changes in household *consumption*. For younger families, the subsidy of day care may reduce the cost of having children enough that some may decide to increase the number of children they want to raise. Because the presence of small children tends to increase the productivity of at least one spouse in the home, an increase in the number of children per family could reduce the labor supply of at least one spouse over his or her life cycle. For example, a family with a six-year-old child may, in the absence of this federal policy, have planned on the mother's rejoining the labor force after a six-year absence and returning to full-time employment. However, if the new policy is implemented, this family may decide to have another child and have the mother work part time.

   While the effects on parents with small children hinge on the dominance of the substitution or the income effect, the effects of this policy on other members of the population are a bit more complicated. For those past childbearing age or those who do not plan more children, this policy change would cause an increase in their taxes. (Some segment of society must pay for this program.) Assuming the taxes that pay for this program are raised primarily through the individual income tax, this program would result in a decrease in take-home wages for those segments of the population who must bear the cost of the program without obtaining corresponding benefits. Thus, this segment experiences a net decrease in wage rates, and in mirror image of the above analysis, the effects on their labor supply depend on the dominance of the income or substitution effect.

7. For workers close to retirement age this change in government policy creates a significant decrease in post-retirement income. The basic post-retirement pension has been cut in half, so these workers experience a substantial income effect that would drive them in the direction of more work (delayed retirement).

   For very young workers, the reduction in pension benefits facing them in their retirement years is offset by a reduction in payroll taxes (which, of course, acts as an increase in their take-home wage rate). Thus, if one assumes that these workers will pay for their retirement benefits through the payroll taxes they pay over their careers, this change in Social Security will leave their lifetime wealth unaffected. What it will do, however, is increase their wages during their working years, causing a pure substitution effect and an increase in labor supply. This increase in wages without any corresponding increase or change in lifetime wealth may well cause these people to delay retirement as they near the traditional retirement age.

CHAPTER 8

1. False. Whether government policy is required in a particular labor market depends on how well that market is functioning. If the outcomes of the market take into account worker preferences (with full information and choice) and the preferences of other parties affected by coal-mine safety, then the labor market decisions will lead to utility maximization among workers. In this case, efforts by government to impose a level of safety greater than the market outcome could lead to a reduction in worker welfare. The reason for this, simply put, is that it is costly for employers to reduce injuries in environments that are "inherently dangerous." If a firm is to reduce injuries, it must invest resources toward that end, and it can remain competitive with other industries or firms only if it can sell its products at a price (which must at least cover costs) no higher than its competitors'. The increase in cost associated with increased safety must be offset either by cuts elsewhere (including cuts in labor costs) or by increases in product prices. In the latter case, of course, the downward-sloping nature of product demand curves suggests a reduction in employment. Thus, there is a good chance that workers will feel the effects of the increased investment in safety on their wages and/or employment levels. Whether these costs imposed on workers are outweighed by the benefits of greater safety is, of course, the central social question.

   If the market is functioning perfectly, then the costs and benefits of greater safety will have been weighed appropriately by private decision makers. If, however, the private decision makers do not weigh all the costs and benefits of greater safety, there is a very good chance that the market outcome will not be socially optimal. In this case, an appropriate setting of governmental standards could improve the utility of workers.

   Of course, if society does not trust workers' preferences or seeks to change those preferences, it would not want to rely on the market even if it were functioning perfectly, because the market would reflect worker preferences.

3. The supply curve to the military is often characterized as, or assumed to be, upward-sloping. At low wages the military can attract those who either have poor alternative offers of employment or genuinely prefer military life. To attract others, the military must offer higher wages—that is, offer wages that sufficiently compensate workers for turning down other job offers or for accepting the adverse conditions of military life. This higher wage is, in fact, a compensating differential that would be required to overcome many people's aversion to military life. In short, if the military wants to attract an all-volunteer army made up of people from the so-called advantaged sectors of the population, it must pay higher wages. The background of applicants depends very much on the wages or salaries the military is offering.

5. A society unwilling to use force or trickery to fill jobs that are dangerous or otherwise have adverse working conditions must essentially "bribe" workers into these jobs. That is, workers must voluntarily choose these jobs over other alternatives they have. To induce workers to choose a dangerous or dirty job over a safer, cleaner one requires that the former be made more attractive than the latter in other dimensions—and one way is to have elevated compensation levels. These increased levels of compensation are what in this chapter we have called compensating wage differentials.

   These compensating wage differentials will arise when job conditions differ *if* workers are well informed and can select from an adequate number of job choices. If workers are without *choice,* then society is using force. Workers are forced to take what is offered through the threat of being jailed or of not being able to obtain a means of livelihood. Thus, if choice is absent or severely restricted, society is in effect using force to allocate labor. (There is undoubtedly a fine line between being forced into something and voluntarily choosing an option, and the student is not here required to make this distinction.)

If, instead of lacking choice, workers lack *information* about working conditions in the jobs from which they have to choose, then society is in effect using trickery to allocate labor. That is, if workers are ignorant of true working conditions and remain ignorant of these conditions for a long period after they have taken a job, they have not made their choices with full information. They have been "tricked" into making the choices they have made.

7. Men and women who work in their homes do not have to bear the expenses of commuting and child care that factory workers do. Moreover, many prefer the flexibility of working at home to the regimen of a factory, because they can perform farming chores or do other household tasks that would be impossible to do during their shift at the factory. These intrinsically desirable or cost-saving aspects of home work suggest that the same level of utility could be reached by home workers at a lower wage rate than received by factory workers. Thus, at least *part* of the higher wage paid to factory workers is a compensating wage differential for the cost and inconvenience of factory employment.

CHAPTER 9

1. Understanding why women receive lower wages than men of comparable age requires an analysis of many possible causes, including discrimination. This answer will explore the insights provided by human capital theory.

   Women have traditionally exhibited interrupted labor market careers, thus shortening the period of time over which educational and training investments can be recouped. The shorter market-work lives of women have until recently been a factor causing women to acquire less formal education, on average, than men. Even recently, when educational attainment levels between men and women have equalized, women graduates are still bunched in occupations for which an interrupted working life is least damaging. Lower educational levels and "occupational bunching" are undoubtedly associated with lower wages.

   The fact that female age/earnings profiles are essentially flat, while men have age/earnings profiles that are upward-sloping and concave, can also be explained by human capital analysis. If men acquire more education or on-the-job training in their early years than do women, their wages will be relatively depressed by these investments (this will cause wages of men and women at younger ages to be more equal than they would otherwise be). In their later years, those who have made human capital investments will be recouping them, and this will cause the wages of men and women to become less equal.

   Thus, while human capital theory may not be the only explanation for the facts noted in this question, it can shed some light on them.

3. The commission of a crime like burglary is essentially the mirror image of human capital investment. With an investment, costs are incurred in the short run so that benefits may be obtained in the long run. With a crime like burglary, the benefits are obtained in the short run and costs may be borne in the long run. A person choosing criminal activity may well be one who is very present-oriented—that is, one who has a high discount rate and thus places a heavy discount on future costs and benefits. Thus, one's discount rate is probably a factor in decisions about crime.

It is also likely that those who choose criminal activities are the least productive in noncriminal jobs. These people have the least to lose by being imprisoned and the most to gain by trying their hand at some criminal act.

Society might consider three general types of programs to reduce crime. One is to increase the earnings opportunities for less advantaged citizens. Another is to undertake programs that would reduce the probability of a crime's being successful (programs to install burglar alarms, neighborhood watch groups, etc.). Finally, society might consider increasing the costs of crime to apprehended criminals. The theory in this chapter suggests that there are several ways the costs might be increased: increasing the *severity* of punishment, increasing the *likelihood* of apprehension and punishment, and *speeding up* the punishment by reducing the time between apprehension and punishment (this last will increase the expected present value of a crime's cost).

5. One cost of educational investment is related to the time students need to devote to studying in order to ensure success. People who can learn quickly are going to have lower costs of obtaining an education. If one assumes that learning ability and ability in general (including productive capacity in a job) are correlated, then the implication of human capital theory is that the most able people, other things being equal, will obtain the most education.

7. Government subsidies will, of course, lower the costs to individuals of obtaining an education (of making a human capital investment). Reduced university costs will, from an individual perspective, raise the individual rate of return to making an investment in education. This will induce more people to attend college than would have attended otherwise. Students who would, in the absence of a college subsidy, have required a post-college earnings differential (as compared to that of a high school graduate) of $2,000 per year may now be induced to attend college if the earnings differential is only $1,000 per year. From a social perspective, however, the increase in productivity of $1,000 per year may be insufficient to pay back society for its investments in college students.

Put differently, the subsidy may induce more investment in university education than is socially warranted (that is, the social rate of return on the human capital investment may be below the rate of return on nonhuman capital investments). Society, of course, could guard against this tendency toward overinvestment by restricting access to university positions and rationing the positions available so that they go to the abler students (those who would obtain the greatest net increase in productivity from a given human capital investment).

9. From a social perspective, judging the vocational rehabilitation program amounts to evaluating whether the benefits of the program are greater than the costs. Since the intent of the program is to increase the earnings capacity of disabled workers, the benefits are best measured as the *increases* in earnings achieved by students going through the program. Thus, the information required for evaluation involves (a) information on costs of the training program (most of which are borne in the short run), (b) the earnings after graduating from the program (these earnings will often continue for several periods so that estimates of long-run post-training earnings are required), and (c) estimates of what the program's enrollees would have earned in the absence of the program.

With the above information in hand the evaluator would calculate the present value of the cost of the program and compare that to the present value of the program's benefits. The benefits are measured each year as the difference in earnings after training and the estimated earnings in the absence of training. Since the present value of benefits will be sensitive to the discount rate chosen, a fourth critical element in the evaluation would be the selection of an appropriate rate of discount. In cases in which all the costs of training are borne in the first year, the evaluation would take the following form:

$$V = \sum_t \frac{(B_{at} - B_{bt})}{(1 + r)^t} - C$$

where C = the cost of the vocational rehabilitation program, B_{at} represents the earnings after training in the year t, B_{bt} represents the estimated earnings in the absence of training, r represents the rate of discount, and Σ is the summation operator. If $V > 0$, the program contributes to social welfare because the present value of benefits exceeds the cost. If $V < 0$, the costs of the program exceed the benefits and the program reduces social welfare.

CHAPTER 10

1. Secretary Miller is implicitly using a human capital model of worker mobility. He is arguing that if Chrysler wages are frozen at a time when other wages are rising, the workers at Chrysler will become increasingly dissatisfied and more likely to quit. Those workers likely to receive better wage offers elsewhere are probably going to be Chrysler's better workers, so that a wage freeze imposed on all Chrysler workers could, indeed, increase the likelihood that the best employees will quit.

Miller's theory, however, may be overly simplistic. What is important to workers trying to decide whether to quit is the expected wage elsewhere—that is, the wage they could receive multiplied by the probability they could obtain an offer at that wage. Moreover, Miller is forgetting that wages in the auto industry are much higher than wages in most other industries, so that even with the three-year freeze, Chrysler workers may still be receiving higher wages than they could expect to receive in industries other than the automobile industry. If the other auto companies are not hiring workers, even the best Chrysler workers may not be able to find a better job elsewhere.

For Miller's predictions to be correct, Chrysler would have to be paying a wage somewhat close to the market wage (so that the freeze would clearly drag Chrysler wages below wages elsewhere), and other job offers must be abundant enough that those who quit have relatively good expectations of receiving other offers.

3. A payroll tax levied on employers for every illegal alien hired would shift their demand curves to the left (see Chapter 3), which would tend to reduce their employment levels and also reduce the wages that an employer is willing to pay them. If the supply curve were vertical, the wages of illegal aliens would fall by $1 per hour and neither their employment nor the demand for unskilled natives (who we assume to be their closest substitutes) would change. If, however, the supply curve of aliens were upward-sloping and illegal aliens and natives were otherwise *perfect* substitutes, illegal aliens could remain employed only if the demand for unskilled natives shifted to the right enough to increase the "native" wage. In short, if the supply curve of illegal aliens were upward-sloping, this tax should increase the wages of native unskilled workers (as aliens drop out of the market) and reduce the wages of illegal immigrants. Because of the lower wage for illegal aliens, this proposed tax should result in a reduced flow of "illegals"; the returns to their migration investments would have fallen. Likewise, the higher wages for native unskilled workers would induce more natives to become (or remain) unskilled workers.

The above tendency for employment among "native" unskilled workers to increase is mitigated by the policy of subsidizing job training for the less skilled. This subsidy reduces the cost of job training for them and raises its net returns, thus tending to increase the flow of unskilled workers to jobs requiring more skill. This can be graphically depicted by a leftward shift in the supply curve of native workers to the unskilled market and a rightward shift of the supply curve to the skilled market. By themselves, these shifts will increase the unskilled wage, reduce unskilled employment, and reduce the skilled wage (while increasing skilled employment).

5. One factor inducing quit rates to be low is that the cost of job changing may be high (pension losses, seniority losses, and difficulties finding information about other jobs are examples of factors that can increase the cost of quitting). If there are cost barriers to mobility, then employees are more likely to tolerate adverse conditions within the firm without resorting to leaving.

Firms also are more likely to provide their employees with firm-specific training if quit rates are low. Thus, if firms need to train their employees in firm-specific skills, they clearly prefer a low quit rate.

Finally, firms prefer low quit rates because hiring costs are kept to a minimum. Every time a worker quits, a replacement must be hired, and to the extent that finding and hiring a replacement is costly, firms want to avoid incurring these costs.

From a social perspective, the disadvantage of having a low quit rate is related to the failure of the market to adjust quickly to shortages and surpluses. Changing relative demands for labor require constant flux in the employment distribution, and factors that inhibit change will also inhibit adaptation to new conditions.

Further, high costs of quitting will be associated not only with lower quit rates but also with larger wage differentials across firms or regions for the same grade of labor. Since firms hire labor until marginal productivity equals the wage they must pay, these large wage differentials will also be accompanied by large differentials in marginal productivities within the same skill group. As discussed first in Chapter 3, if marginal productivities differ widely, the national output could be increased by reallocating labor so that marginal productivities are equalized.

7. Wage differentials across states and regions are essentially signals for migration to take place, and migratory movements should tend to eliminate these differentials. The fact that migration requires the expenditure of resources to acquire information on wage offers in various regions means that these wage differentials will not be eliminated instantaneously. In national labor markets, new entrants into the labor market can more easily obtain information about offers in several regions, and therefore migration across regions is relatively responsive to existing wage differentials. In local labor markets, which are not set up for interregional recruitment, migration across regions will be more sluggish because the costs of acquiring information across regions are higher. Therefore, it would not be surprising if jobs in local labor markets exhibited higher interregional wage variation than jobs in national labor markets.

CHAPTER 11

1. This approach to measuring comparability is deficient in at least three ways. First, by comparing only salaries and wages, it ignores employee benefits, which form a substantial part of the total compensation package. If generous federal government employee benefits were accompanied by a somewhat lower wage rate because of

the negative trade-off suggested by economic theory, comparing salaries and wages would give the erroneous impression that federal government workers were undercompensated relative to private sector workers.

Second, by comparing pay and job categories at a certain point in one's career (let's say 10 years of experience), we ignore the time sequencing of pay. What is of utmost importance in comparing compensation is compensation over one's entire career. If the rapidity of promotion differs in the two sectors, or if use of some kind of pay-sequencing scheme differs, the compensation at 10 years of experience may look quite different, even when career-long compensation is similar.

Third, differences in working conditions may lead one sector or the other to have compensating wage differentials.

3. a. Cutting the wages of all workers after the age of 65 reduces wages for both the productive and the nonproductive. The nonproductive workers probably could not receive better offers elsewhere, but the productive ones might. Thus, cutting wages of all workers would induce the most-productive to quit.

   b. Providing a lump-sum payment to anyone who quits employment at the firm would again induce the most productive workers to quit (since they could take the lump sum provided by the firm and perhaps get a high-paying job at some other firm). The least productive workers could not obtain a high-paying job elsewhere, so quitting employment at the firm would be less desirable for them than for productive workers.

   c. Increasing the monthly benefit of anyone who retired and did not work elsewhere would be at least neutral between productive and nonproductive workers. Both would receive the same post-retirement (at the firm) benefit, so incentives to quit employment at the firm would be the same for both sets of workers.

5. Severance pay clearly increases the costs of the firms' closing down, and should therefore inhibit closings in the short run. However, because all firms have some probability of failing, the requirement that severance pay be given to employees if they do fail will increase their expected labor compensation costs. Put differently, the requirement that a firm pay this particular form of benefit to its employees will raise the cost of employing labor, other things equal, especially in firms that face a high risk of failure.

   One effect of a severance pay requirement is to put downward pressure on wage rates (as firms in industries with high business failure rates strive to remain competitive in the product market with firms in states that do not have this requirement). This change in the compensation mix away from current pay and toward deferred pay *may* make jobs in industries with high business failure rates less attractive to those workers who were formerly most attracted to these industries. (Firms in these industries could have offered this mix before and chose not to.) Unless the compensation mix now attracts a (different) group of equally productive employees, firms in industries with high business failure rates will face higher unit costs of production and tend to avoid setting up new operations in states where severance pay is required.

   It should be pointed out that if employees in industries with high business failure rates are deceived about (or ignorant of) the riskiness of their jobs, their utility may be enhanced by the change in compensation or the enforced selection of other jobs. The analysis here is similar to that in the text relating to pension reform.

7. While the costs of testing employees and firing drug users would tend to increase a firm's labor costs, the new policy would make the firm attractive only to drug-free

workers. In the face of this policy, any applicants to the firm would "signal" their nonuse of drugs, and the firm may find that applicants are easier (less costly) to evaluate and that a drug-free work force is less expensive to supervise. Thus, the effects on hiring and supervisory costs are ambiguous, with the cost-increasing tendencies stronger in the short run than in the long run.

The effects on wages are also uncertain. On the one hand, if drug use is prevalent among the firm's potential workers, drug testing may restrict the firm's flow of applicants and reduce its current work force to such an extent that it would have to raise wages to recruit the desired number of workers. Moreover, the testing procedure itself may be unpleasant or obnoxious to workers who do not use drugs, and these workers may have to receive a compensating wage differential in order for them to find work with company X as appealing as it was before. On the other hand, it is also possible that the greater homogeneity of the company's work force will enable those workers who remain to achieve higher levels of utility from the work environment, thereby putting downward pressure on wages (that is, drug-free workers may be willing to pay for the knowledge that their coworkers are also drug-free).

CHAPTER 12

1. This question is similar to question 1 in Chapter 4. Since a reduction in the price of capital equipment will stimulate the purchase of capital equipment, a union should be concerned whether its members are gross complements or gross substitutes with capital. In the former case, the proposed policy (reducing the price of capital) would cause the demand for union members to rise, while in the latter their demand would fall. Other things equal, the more rapidly the demand for labor is shifting out, the smaller will be the reduction in employment associated with any union-induced wage gain (assuming the collective bargaining agreement lies on the labor demand curve). Hence, unions representing groups that are gross complements (substitutes) with capital would benefit (lose) from the policy change. (See Appendix 12A for a discussion of cases in which the agreement does not lie on the firm's labor demand curve.)

Evidence cited in the text suggests that capital and skilled labor may be gross complements, but capital and unskilled labor are gross substitutes. This suggests that union leaders representing the latter type of workers will be opposed to the legislation, while union leaders representing the former may favor it.

3. The traditional neoclassical view is that union/nonunion wage differentials reflect marginal productivity differentials among similar workers, and thus their existence represents a misallocation of resources. To estimates of this output loss are typically added losses due to restrictive work practices and strike activity.

The alternative neoinstitutionalist viewpoint, associated most closely with Richard Freeman and James Medoff, stresses the productivity-enhancing effects of unions. These include reduced turnover, increased training, and increased morale. The net effect of unions on output depends on an empirical measurement of all these forces. Some evidence is presented in the chapter.

Advanced students might also challenge the econometric evidence that produces union/nonunion wage differentials in the range of 10 to 20 percent. As noted in the text, such estimates do not always fully control for unobserved differences in "ability" between union and nonunion workers, and part of the observed wage differential may merely compensate unionized workers for their relatively unfavorable working conditions. To the extent that true union/nonunion wage differentials are smaller, the negative allocative effects of unions will be smaller.

5. The provisions of the Jones Act affect the demand for labor in the U.S. shipping industry in at least two ways. First, the provision that 50 percent of all U.S. government cargo must be transported in U.S.-owned ships makes the price elasticity of demand for U.S. shipping in the output market less elastic. Second, the restriction that at least 90 percent of the crews of U.S. ships must be U.S. citizens reduces the ability of ship owners to substitute foreign seamen for U.S. citizens. Both changes cause the wage elasticity of demand for U.S. seamen to be less elastic than it would otherwise be.

To the extent that the U.S. shipping industry is heavily unionized and there is little competition between union seamen and nonunion seamen (a reasonable assumption), the wage elasticity of demand for union seamen would be less elastic under the Jones Act. As is stressed in the text, inelastic labor demand curves permit unions to push for increases in their members' wages without fear of large employment losses, at least in the short run.

7. There are several reasons why unions may raise worker productivity. One of the more obvious is that, as wages are increased, firms cut back employment and substitute capital for labor. Both actions tend to raise the marginal productivity of labor. To survive in a competitive market, profit-maximizing firms must raise the marginal productivity of labor whenever wages increase.

Another reason unions raise productivity is that the high wages unionized employers offer attract a large pool of applicants, and employers are able to "cream" the best applicants. Moreover, the reduction in turnover that we observe in unionized plants increases firms' incentives to provide specific training to their workers, and the seniority system that unions typically implement encourages older workers to show younger workers the "ropes" (they can do so without fear that the younger workers will compete for their jobs when fully trained).

Because many of these sources of increased productivity are responses by firms to higher wages, they tend to mitigate the effects of unionization on costs. Some nonunion firms deliberately pay high wages to attract and retain able employees, and they often pursue this strategy even without the implicit threat of becoming unionized. However, the fact that firms generally pay the union wage only after their employees become organized suggests that they believe unions raise labor costs to a greater extent than they raise worker productivity.

What the quotation in question 7 overlooks is that increases in productivity must be measured against increases in costs. If unions enhance productivity to a greater extent than they increase costs of production, then clearly employers should take a much less antagonistic approach to unions. If, however, enhancements in labor productivity are smaller than increases in labor costs, employer profitability will decline under unionization.

9. This law makes it more difficult and more costly to substitute capital for labor. Any worker replaced by capital (or another substitute factor of production) must be retrained and employed elsewhere in the firm, which clearly raises the cost of this substitution. Thus, this law tends to reduce the elasticity of demand for union labor, and it increases the ability of unions to raise wages without reducing their members' employment very much.

CHAPTER 13

1. The key point here is that a profit maximization assumption is not required to derive downward-sloping demand-for-labor curves in the public sector. The text discusses how the assumption that governmental units act as if they are maximizing utility (which is a function of both privately and publicly produced goods and services), subject to a resource constraint, will lead to downward-sloping labor demand curves.

   Just as in the private sector, one might reasonably expect wage elasticities of demand to be larger in the long run than in the short run. In the long run, one can more easily substitute privately produced goods and services for public ones (e.g., subcontract for garbage pickup), and can more easily substitute capital without bidding up its price (e.g., buying a lot of computers). So although the demand curve for labor in the public sector will slope downward in both the short and long run, it will be more elastic in the latter case.

3. The empirical estimates of wage elasticities of demand in the public sector summarized in this chapter are, on average, very similar in magnitude to the private sector elasticities summarized in Chapter 4. Hence, there is no single right answer to this question; rather, the student can pick out a particular public employee group and apply the four Hicks-Marshall laws of derived demand to it. As an example, consider the following arguments for professors at public universities.

   First, although obtaining a college degree is becoming more common, empirical evidence suggests that the enrollment decisions of many students are sensitive to the prices they must pay to attend college. To the extent that the demand for public higher education is more elastic, the wage elasticity of demand for professors at public universities will be greater.

   Second, it is possible to substitute graduate assistants for professors and to increase student/faculty ratios by allowing class size to increase. The more easily other inputs can be substituted for professors, the greater will be the wage elasticity of demand for professors.

   Third, the supply of these other inputs (e.g., graduate assistants) appears to be very elastic; many universities could expand their usage substantially without increasing the price they would have to pay assistants. This, too, should make the wage elasticity of demand for professors greater.

   Finally, college professors represent a considerable share of the university budget. Because they are an important share of the cost, this factor also will tend to increase their wage elasticity.

   On balance, then, all four factors suggest that the wage elasticity of demand for college professors may be great.

5. Public sector unions are uniquely able to affect product demand and/or factor substitution possibilities (e.g., class size limits). Public sector employment is relatively large, and unions often form a cohesive lobbying group. Thus, union behavior can frequently affect the outcomes of elections and/or legislation within the governmental jurisdiction. While any union can engage in lobbying and/or political action, public sector unions are probably even more potent because their wages and employment levels are directly set by governmental policy. Thus, they can more directly shift to the right the demand curve for their services than can unions in the private sector.

A problem that this school board election raises in the collective bargaining context is whether there are, in fact, two independent parties bargaining with each other. If the labor unions can "stack" the boards or councils that decide on matters of compensation, then one must question whether labor is bargaining with management or with itself. However, the short-run gain that may be obtained through an overt use of political action may be offset by voter backlash in the long run, and it is therefore not clear that public sector unions will be tempted to use these tactics generally. They may have to adopt strategies that are more similar to those followed by private sector unions (that is, the use of public persuasion).

7. The new technology offers a substitute for the services provided by the U.S. Postal Service. Thus, the availability of the technology tends to increase the elasticity of the product demand curve facing the Postal Service, and thus the elasticity of demand for Postal Service workers.

   More specifically, the increase in the elasticity of the product demand curve comes about because of the availability of substitute services. Consumers may become more responsive to the price of mail service (in the sense that, if the price of first-class mail rises noticeably, they may instead transmit messages or bills electronically). Increased elasticity of demand for mail service increases the elasticity of demand for labor (postal workers) and will reduce the power of unions to raise wages. The reduction in union power should result in wage settlements that are below what otherwise would have prevailed (had the electronic telecommunications alternatives been absent).

9. If this residency requirement is binding and city workers are forced to live in housing they would otherwise have rejected, or if potential workers are reluctant to apply for city jobs because of this requirement, the city will be forced to pay a compensating wage differential. This analysis suggests that the residency requirement causes an increase in the cost of labor to the city—a cost that is unnecessary unless the residency requirement enhances worker productivity. Of course, it also may be that the city's wages historically have been so far above the market that city jobs remained attractive despite the residency requirement. In this case the residency requirement could be used to ration job applicants. In either case, then, the residency requirement suggests an above-average wage rate.

CHAPTER 14

1. a. Current labor market discrimination typically is said to exist when compensation levels paid to one demographic group are lower than those paid to another demographic group that is exactly comparable in terms of productive characteristics. Using this definition in the context of this question, there would be no discrimination because both men and women would receive equal yearly compensation while working. This equal yearly compensation would, in fact, result in a pension fund for each man and woman that would have exactly the same present value at retirement age. However, because women live longer than men on average, this retirement fund would be paid out over a longer period of time and thus would be paid out to retired women in smaller yearly amounts. The Supreme Court definition of discrimination would seem to stress the receipt of unequal yearly incomes by retirees who were comparable in productive characteristics but not comparable in terms of expected life spans. The Supreme Court decision would require employers to put aside more pension funds for women

because of the requirement that women must receive equal yearly pension benefits over their longer life spans. Thus, the Supreme Court requires that working
women have greater yearly compensation (while working) than comparable men.

b. The *Manhart* decision essentially mandates greater labor costs for women than
for men of comparable productive characteristics, and by raising the firm's
costs of hiring women, it could give firms incentives to substitute male for
female workers (or capital for female workers). This would tend to reduce the
employment of women.

3. a. Firms frequently use marital status and gender to estimate how long a job applicant might be expected to remain with them. Those that offer specific training
or find that hiring new employees requires substantial investments are especially
sensitive to the expected tenure of workers in their firms. Thus, they are among
the firms most affected by this ruling.

b. These firms have two general options open to them in adjusting to the antidiscrimination law. One is to undertake the implementation of alternative screening devices designed to estimate the expected length of employee tenure. The
other is to essentially drop efforts to estimate expected employee tenure and adjust their behavior to the fact that those employees hired may now have shorter
expected tenures.

c. If a firm undertakes to use alternative screening devices, it may find that its
costs of hiring have been increased. These alternatives presumably existed before and were rejected as more costly than the use of marital status and gender
as indicators of expected tenure. If so, then the hiring investment in each worker
must necessarily increase and, unless offset by a reduced wage rate, will cause
quasi-fixed labor costs of the firm to rise. If labor costs do rise, then there will
be scale and substitution effects working in the direction of a smaller work force
within the firm. Because it is the quasi-fixed labor costs that rise, firms will tend
to increase hours per worker and reduce the number of workers.

If a firm decides to adjust its behavior to reflect the fact that new workers
may have shorter expected tenures, then again it may keep training investments
the same but lower the post-training wage (to recoup its training costs more
quickly). However, it may also decide that training is not as profitable as it once
was and reduce training provided to new employees. If this option is followed,
there will be a smaller gap between marginal productivity and the wage rate,
which could reduce job stability over the business cycle. Finally, if neither wages
nor training investments can be feasibly reduced, the firm will again face higher
labor costs and would have to respond by reducing its work force.

In general, if hiring investments are increased (first option), if employment
is reduced, or if wages are reduced, the gap between marginal productivity and
wages will tend to rise—reflecting the more costly investments in workers—and
job stability should be enhanced. If, however, as noted above, the firm decides
to reduce investments in employees, then job stability will be reduced.

5. With *customer* discrimination, the productivity of women and minorities was artificially reduced by customer prejudice (which may have dictated they be employed in
menial jobs below their true potential). If the government becomes the sole customer and insists that women and minorities be employed in greater numbers in
higher-paying jobs, their wages will rise but so will their output. The source of discrimination is removed, and unit labor costs do not rise.

With *employee* discrimination, white male workers (who we assume for the
purposes of this question are prejudiced) must be paid a compensating wage differ-

ential to work in integrated plants. If employers are forced to increase their level of integration in the nonmenial jobs, white males will have to be paid a larger compensating differential to keep them with the firm. Since the "equal pay" requirement exists, *all* workers would have to receive the higher wage paid to white males and unit labor costs would rise.

7. When nursing wages are raised above market-clearing levels a surplus of nursing applicants will arise. Because the supply of nurses at above-market wages is greater than the demand, the city will be facing a long queue of applicants each time it has a nursing vacancy. The high wages, of course, will attract not only a large *number* of applicants but also a large number of very *high-quality* applicants; the fact that applicants are so plentiful allows the city to select only the best. Therefore, comparable worth may reduce the number of nursing jobs available, but it will also tend to raise the demand for high-quality nurses.

   Since the wages of nurses are tied to those of building inspectors, the city will be very reluctant to raise the wages of building inspectors even if there are shortages. Rather than raising wages as a recruiting device for building inspectors, the city may be tempted to lower its hiring standards and to employ building inspectors it would previously have rejected. Thus, employment opportunities for low-quality building inspectors may be enhanced by the comparable worth law.

9. a. A wage subsidy paid to employers who hire disadvantaged black workers will shift the demand curve for such workers (stated in terms of the employee wage) to the right. This shift can cause employment to increase, the wage rate paid to black disadvantaged workers to increase, or both. The mix of wage and employment changes will depend on the shape of the supply curve of these workers. The changes in wages and employment induced by the subsidy will tend to overcome the adverse effect on unskilled blacks of *current* labor market discrimination.
   b. Increasing the wages and employment opportunities of unskilled black workers will reduce incentives of these workers to invest in the training required to become skilled. Thus, one consequence of a wage subsidy just for *unskilled* black workers is that the subsidy may induce more blacks to remain unskilled than would otherwise have been the case. Thus, while helping to overcome *current* labor market discrimination, the subsidy may increase premarket disparities between whites and blacks by reducing the incentives of blacks to acquire training for the skilled trades.

CHAPTER 15

1. The two policy goals are not compatible in the short run. An increase in unemployment compensation benefits reduces the costs to unemployed workers of additional job search; this will lead them to extend their duration of unemployment and search for better-paying jobs. In the short run, increasing unemployment compensation benefits will increase the unemployment rate.

   In the long run, however, the two policy goals *may* be compatible. If the prolonged durations of job search lead to better matches of workers and jobs, the chances that workers will become unemployed in the future will diminish. That is, the better matches will reduce both the probability that workers will quit their jobs and the probability that they will be fired. This reduced probability of entering unemployment will reduce the unemployment rate in the long run. Whether the reduction in the unemployment rate due to the smaller incidence of unemployment outweighs the increase due to the longer spells of unemployment is an open question.

3. An unemployment rate at any given level, say 6 percent, can occur for a number of reasons. At one extreme, everyone in the labor force might be unemployed for slightly over 3 weeks a year. At the other extreme, 6 percent of the labor force might be unemployed for the entire year and 94 percent of the labor force might never be unemployed. More generally, different groups of individuals in the population will have different incidences and durations of unemployment.

One senses that society's concern about the level of the unemployment rate will depend upon how unemployment is distributed; society probably considers the second case (long duration for a small group) more serious than the first (short duration for everyone). Appropriate public policies toward unemployment also depend on these flows. As discussed extensively in the text, public policies to reduce unemployment for groups that have difficulty keeping jobs (high flow into unemployment) are likely to be very different from policies for groups whose unemployment rates are due to labor market entry and exit.

5. There are a number of reasons why unemployed workers' reservation wages may decline as their spells of unemployment lengthen. One is that workers may have finite horizons and plan to be in the labor force for only specific time periods. As their durations of unemployment lengthen, the time they expect to work (once they find jobs) declines, and this shorter expected work life reduces the present value of the benefits obtained from searching longer. As a result, they tend to reduce their reservation wages.

A second reason relates to their changing perceptions about the distribution of wage offers they face. When a worker first becomes unemployed, he or she may be optimistic about employment opportunities and set a high reservation wage. However, if over time only very low wage offers are received, the individual may realize that the distribution of wage offers is lower than initially assumed. This revision of expectations would also cause a downward revision of the reservation wage.

In fact, even if workers' initial perceptions about the distribution of wage offers were correct, this distribution might systematically shift down over time. For example, employers might use the length of time an individual had been unemployed as a signal of the individual's relatively low productivity and might moderate wage offers accordingly. A systematically declining wage-offer distribution that arises for this reason would similarly cause reservation wages to decline as durations of unemployment lengthened.

7. This policy should have two effects on the unemployment rate. First, by reducing the value of benefits to unemployed workers, it should reduce the duration of their spells of unemployment. In other words, by taxing unemployment insurance benefits, the government is in effect reducing those benefits, and the reduction in benefits increases the marginal costs of remaining unemployed for an additional period of time. Thus, workers will tend to be less choosy about job offers they accept and should be induced to reduce the amount of time they spend searching for additional job offers.

However, by reducing job search, the taxation of UI benefits may lead to poorer "matches" between worker and employer, thus creating higher turnover (and more unemployment) in the long run.

Finally, because unemployed workers are now receiving less compensation from the government, those in jobs in which layoffs frequently occur will find them less attractive than they previously did. Employers who offer these jobs will have more difficulty attracting employees unless they raise wages (assuming workers have other job options). This compensating wage differential will act as a penalty for high layoff rates, and this penalty should induce firms to reduce layoffs to some extent. A reduced propensity to lay off workers, of course, should reduce the unemployment rate (other things being equal).

CHAPTER 16

1. The negative relationship between the size of wage increases and the unemployment rate was postulated in the text to arise because of (a) an assumed positive relationship between the level of excess demand for labor and the size of wage increases and (b) an assumed negative relationship between the unemployment rate and the excess demand for labor. Anything that shifts either of these "building block" relationships will shift the wage inflation/unemployment trade-off curve.

Increases in the rate of price inflation are assumed to increase the rate of wage inflation associated with each level of excess demand for labor; as prices increase, larger money wage increases are necessary to keep the change in real wage at its previous level. As a result, increases in price inflation tend to increase the rate of wage inflation associated with any given unemployment rate.

Increases in the labor force participation rate of women may increase the proportion of relatively inexperienced workers (with high incidences of unemployment) in the labor force. As a result, the aggregate unemployment rate associated with any given level of excess demand for labor increases. This, too, shifts up the wage inflation/unemployment trade-off curve.

A whole set of policies that the government can use to reduce the rate of wage inflation associated with any level of unemployment is catalogued in the text. Policies that may shift down the wage inflation/excess demand for labor relationship include incomes policies, policies to increase the competitiveness of labor markets, and "share wages." Policies that may shift down the unemployment/excess demand for labor relationship are those that improve the efficiency of labor markets, including improved job market information, relocation assistance, and training programs to reduce skill bottlenecks. As noted in the text, other policies that aim to reduce the dispersion of unemployment rates may also be useful.

Sophisticated students may develop their answer to this question using different analytical frameworks from that described above. Models of job search and the distinction between anticipated and unanticipated inflation may be stressed, as might a "rational expectations" approach (see Appendix 16A).

3. Whether such a scheme would help reduce the rate of price inflation depends on the factors that are causing inflation. To see this, suppose initially that producers keep their markups constant and that the rate of productivity growth is constant and positive. Then the wage inflation/price inflation process is governed by:

$$(1) \quad \dot{W} = \dot{P}_{-1} \qquad \text{incomes policy}$$
$$(2) \quad \dot{P} = \dot{W} - \dot{q} \qquad \text{pricing rule}$$
$$(3) \quad \dot{P} = \dot{P}_{-1} - \dot{q} \qquad \text{price dynamics}$$

Equation (1) represents the incomes policy and equation (2) the pricing rule (where $\dot{q}$ is the rate of productivity growth). Substituting (1) into (2), we see in (3) that the inflation rate this period equals the inflation rate last period minus the rate of productivity growth. As long as the rate of productivity growth is positive, the price inflation rate will decline over time. However, if instead the rate of productivity growth were zero (negative), the price inflation rate would remain constant (increase) over time. Thus, unless the rate of productivity growth is positive, the incomes policy will fail to work.

The policy may also fail to work if external shocks are responsible for the inflation. Events such as energy price increases will cause producers to increase their markups over unit labor costs. In this case, the process governing inflation would be given by:

$$\text{(1a)} \quad \dot{W} = \dot{P}_{-1} \qquad \qquad \text{incomes policy}$$
$$\text{(2a)} \quad \dot{P} = \dot{k} + \dot{W} - \dot{q} \qquad \text{pricing rule}$$
$$\text{(3a)} \quad \dot{P} = \dot{k} + \dot{P}_{-1} - \dot{q} \qquad \text{price dynamics}$$

Here $\dot{k}$ represents the percentage change in the markup. One can see that positive rates of productivity growth are not sufficient to make the policy work; the rate of productivity growth must exceed the rate of growth of the markup ($\dot{k} - \dot{q} < 0$). If external shocks are large (e.g., a doubling of energy prices), this condition is not likely to be met.

5. Incomes policies specifying that workers should receive percentage wage increases equal to their rate of productivity growth may be doomed to failure, but the reason is not that they will cause management's share of output to fall. In fact, if management holds product prices constant—as it is assumed it will under such a scheme because unit labor cost is unchanged—management's share will remain constant. While it is possible to demonstrate this formally, a simple numerical example should serve to make this point:

	Initially	After 10% Productivity Increase
Output	100 units	110 units
Labor Gets	70 units	77 units
Management Gets	30 units	33 units
Management's Share	30%	30%

In this example, a firm employs a given number of workers, who produce 100 units of output. They are paid 70 units (in real terms), management receives 30 units, and hence management's share of output is 30 percent. Now suppose labor productivity rises by 10 percent. If the same number of workers are employed, output will rise to 110 units. If labor's wage increase is set equal to the rate of productivity growth, labor will receive 77 units of output in the second period, leaving 33 units for management. Management's share will remain at 30 percent (33/110).

7. These laws would increase prices in the short run. Presumably foreign parts and labor are now being used because they are cheaper, so insisting on a certain domestic content would increase consumer prices.

In the long run, the reduced price elasticity of product demand implied by these laws could lead unions to seek greater wage increases (because of less elastic labor demand curves) for any given level of unemployment. This in itself would shift the Phillips curve up, leading to more wage inflation for any given level of unemployment.

9. It was argued in Chapter 16 that firms often adopt a markup rule for setting product prices. If this markup model holds, then prices are closely tied to cost, and inflexible wages would lead to inflexible prices. With profit sharing, however, sectors with declining profits would have reduced labor costs, which would facilitate reductions in product prices. Thus, the price level might actually fall in sectors with reduced demand if workers were paid under a profit-sharing arrangement.

In sectors enjoying prosperity, the current practice of paying workers a fixed hourly wage suggests that if firms are able to raise prices by one dollar, they will increase their profits by one dollar. However, if wages are tied to firms' profits, price increases of one dollar must in effect be partially shared with workers. Given the cost of raising prices—either in terms of lost goodwill or in terms of having to revise one's list of prices—a firm that must share its extra revenues with workers may be deterred from raising prices during periods of prosperity. Because at any given time some sectors are expanding and others are contracting, these profit-sharing effects in expanding and contracting sectors could reduce overall inflationary pressures in the economy.

Name Index

The letter *n* following a page number indicates that the name will be found in a footnote or a source line.

Aaron, Benjamin, 497n, 498n
Abegglen, James C., 169n
Abowd, John M., 133n, 294n, 298n, 417n, 418n, 454n, 486n, 495n, 600n
Abraham, Katharine, 153n, 435n, 479n, 588n, 632n
Abrams, Elliott, 382n
Abrams, Franklin S., 382n
Adams, Arvil, 615n
Adams, Charles, 519n
Addison, John T., 476n, 484n, 487n, 489
Aigner, Dennis J., 548n, 574
Akerlof, George, 420n, 423n, 437, 590n
Alchian, Armen, 76n, 404n
Alibers, Robert, 654n
Allen, Steven G., 183n, 404n, 437, 459n, 483, 483n, 484, 484n, 512n
Alpert, William, 480n
Altonji, Joseph G., 177n, 245n, 435n
Amacher, Ryan C., 12
Anderson, C. A., 306n, 325n
Anderson, John, 182
Archibald, G. C., 633n
Arnould, Richard J., 276n
Aronson, Robert, 588n
Arrow, Kenneth J., 531n
Ashenfelter, Orley, 79n, 94n, 95, 112n, 115n, 117n, 122n, 136, 177n, 191n, 221, 249n, 256, 294n, 298n, 307n, 330n, 362n, 447n, 463n, 463–67, 466n, 467n, 476–77, 478n, 488, 489, 495n, 503n, 505n, 507n, 510n, 523, 528n, 531n, 545n, 600n, 608n, 647n
Asher, Martin, 512n, 513n
Askin, Bradley, 653n
Atherton, Wallace, 455n, 489
Auerbach, Alan, 485n
Azariadis, Costas, 594n

Baily, Martin N., 594n, 640n
Banks, William C., 403n
Barnow, Burt S., 330n, 590n
Barrett, Nancy, 558n

Barringer, R., 552n
Barron, John, 144n
Barrow, R. H., 655, 655n
Bartel, Ann P., 118n, 363n
Bassi, Lauri J., 330n, 518n
Baumol, William J., 312n
Bawden, Lee, 410n
Bazerman, Max, 528n
Bazzoli, Gloria J., 258n
Beach, Charles M., 339n, 343n
Becker, Gary, 4n, 61n, 160, 160n, 173, 227n, 236n, 255, 322n, 347, 542n, 545n, 574
Beer, S., 552n
Behrman, Jere R., 306n
Bell, Linda A., 477n
Beller, Andrea H., 536n, 540n, 551n, 571n
Belous, Richard, 92n, 635n
Benedict, Mary Ellen, 462n
Benhabib, Jess, 312n
Benjamin, Daniel, 611n
Bentham, Jeremy, 265n
Berg, Ivar, 328n, 352n, 354n
Berger, Mark, 118n
Bergmann, Barbara R., 551n, 552n
Berkowitz, Monroe, 330n
Betson, David M., 186n
Bhagat, S., 419n
Bhagwati, J. N., 390n
Bickford, Lawrence C., 417n
Bishop, John, 122n, 124n, 144n, 640n
Bjorklund, Anders, 614n
Black, Dan A., 144n
Blackburn, McKinley L., 343n
Blanchard, Olivier J., 595n, 628n
Blau, Francine, 376n, 536n
Blinder, Alan S., 417n, 437, 534n, 595n
Bloch, Farrell E., 6n, 378n, 379n, 479n, 512n
Bloom, David, 48n, 343n, 510n, 528n
Bluestone, Barry, 339n, 347, 602n
Blum, James, 112n, 117n
Blundell, Richard, 177n
Bodie, Zvi, 249n, 428n

Bognanno, Michael L., 433n
Boissiere, M., 326n
Boorstin, Daniel J., 260n
Borba, Philip S., 291n
Borjas, George J., 118n, 119n, 135, 201n, 214n, 347, 368n, 369n, 370, 370n, 371n, 374n, 386n, 387n, 389n, 393, 394n, 535n, 546n, 574
Borus, Michael, 519n
Boulding, Kenneth, 541n
Bound, John, 199n, 320n, 343n
Bowen, H., 565n
Bowles, Samuel, 325n, 640n
Bowman, M. J., 306n, 325n
Braun, Rudolf, 241n, 390n
Brickley, J., 419n
Briggs, Vernon, 459n
Bronars, Stephen G., 387n
Brown, Charles, 53n, 92n, 95, 274n, 293, 412n, 425n, 483n, 485n, 570n
Brown, Claire, 234n
Brown, James, 435n, 495n
Brown, Martin, 414n
Brown, Murray, 233n
Bulow, Jeremy, 553n
Bunting, Robert L., 79n
Burkhauser, Richard, 92n, 204n
Burtless, Gary, 123n, 249n, 253n
Burton, John F., Jr., 497n, 498n
Butler, Richard, 570n
Bythell, Duncan, 116n

Cagan, Phillip, 643n
Cain, Glen G., 221, 548n, 551n, 574, 579n
Card, David, 330n, 388n, 453n, 495n, 650n
Carey, Max L., 264n
Carliner, Geoffrey, 371n, 535n
Carlson, Leonard A., 534n, 535n, 536n, 574
Carmichael, H. Lorne, 410n, 425n, 593n
Carter, Jimmy, 652, 652n, 653n
Cassidy, Henry, 15n
Cassing, James, 71n
Castro, Fidel, 370
Chang, Hui S., 507n
Cheit, Earl F., 202n
Chelius, James, 438n, 441n
Chiswick, Barry R., 326n, 368n, 371n, 393, 394n, 536n, 547n, 554n, 600n
Chiswick, Carmel Ullman, 246n
Clark, Kim, 483, 483n, 583n, 585n, 607n, 617
Colberg, Marshall R., 250n
Commons, John R., 446n
Conley, Richard, 238n
Connerton, Marie, 483n, 484n
Conyers, John, 148n
Corcoran, Mary, 534n, 539n, 616n
Corson, Walter, 590n, 613n
Cotterill, Philip, 117n
Courant, Paul, 506n, 517n
Cox, James, 459n

Crandall, Robert, 132
Crawford, Vincent, 528n

Dale, Charles, 53n
Dalton, James, 76n
Danziger, Leif, 650n
Danziger, Sheldon H., 330n
Darby, Michael, 607n, 643n
Decker, Paul, 613n
DeFina, Robert H., 482n
DeFreitas, Gregory, 604n, 607n
Delaney, John, 511n
Deming, W. E., 415n
Denison, Edward F., 135
Dertouzos, J. N., 455n
Devine, Theresa, 608n
deVyver, Frank T., 41n
Dickens, William T., 176n, 276n, 455n, 553n, 554n
Dillingham, Alan, 276n
Diocletian, 655
Disney, R., 154n
Doeringer, Peter, 22n, 23n, 167n, 168n, 173, 483n
Dorsey, Stuart, 276n
Douglas, Richard W., 71n
Downs, Anthony, 502n
Duncan, Greg J., 274n, 276n, 293, 322n, 480n, 534n, 539n
Duncan, Greg M., 479n
Dunlop, John, 404n, 455n
Dunston, Shari Miller, 613n
Durden, Garey, 459n

Eaton, Jonathan, 401n
Eatwell, J., 601n
Eberts, Randall, 495n, 508n
Eckstein, Otto, 642n, 648n
Edgeworth, F. Y., 552n
Edwards, Linda, 505n
Edwards, Richard, 553n
Ehrenberg, Ronald G., 75n, 77n, 79n, 92n, 93n, 117n, 150n, 151n, 152n, 154n, 165n, 173, 183n, 215n, 221, 237n, 245n, 296n, 306n, 346n, 370n, 372n, 374n, 393, 404n, 407n, 409n, 410n, 412n, 417n, 419n, 433n, 434n, 437, 441n, 505n, 507n, 508n, 509n, 515n, 516n, 523, 537n, 563n, 566n, 570n, 574, 576n, 577n, 578n, 581n, 589n, 590n, 596n, 603n, 604n, 611n, 612n, 650n
Ellwood, David T., 221, 451n, 606n, 616n
Ethier, Wilfred J., 386n

Farber, Henry S., 435n, 449n, 451n, 455n, 463n, 479n, 511n, 524n, 528n
Fawcett, Millicent, 552n
Feldstein, Martin, 147n, 583n, 596n, 607n
Fellner, William, 371n, 648n

Felstiner, William L. F., 418n
Feuille, Peter, 511n
Field, Barry, 117n
Fields, Gary S., 245n, 249n, 255, 329n, 365n
Filer, Randall K., 387n
Fine, Glenn, 451n
Finegan, T. Aldrich, 92n
Finlay, William, 143n
Fischer, Stanley, 423n
Fishelson, Gideon, 423n
Fisher, Lloyd H., 414n
Fisher, Stanley, 628n
Flaim, Paul, 240n, 582n
Flanagan, Robert J., 409n, 437, 455n, 534n, 593n, 648n, 650n, 658
Flanders, Allan, 460n
Flinn, Christopher J., 374n
Folbre, Nancy, 589n
Ford, E. J., 76n
Ford, Henry, 424
Frank, Robert H., 284n, 285n, 293, 537n
Frantz, John, 483n
Freeman, Richard B., 48n, 118n, 133n, 135, 308n, 314n, 347, 386n, 401n, 443n, 449n, 454n, 476n, 479n, 480n, 481n, 482, 482n, 483n, 484n, 489, 499n, 500n, 505n, 506n, 508n, 509n, 523, 570n, 574, 604n, 606n, 616n, 617
Friedman, Milton, 12, 212n, 625n, 642n, 643n, 654n, 658
Fuchs, Victor R., 304n, 536n, 537n, 538n, 574

Gallaway, Lowell E., 360n
Gauger, William H., 246n
Ghez, G. R., 255
Gilroy, Curtis, 53n
Gintis, Herbert, 325n
Gleick, James, 312n
Goldfarb, Robert, 459n
Goldin, Claudia, 429n, 553n
Goldstein, Gerald S., 507n
Goldstein, Morris, 112n, 117n
Gordon, Anne, 613n
Gordon, David M., 553n, 554n, 574, 640n
Gordon, M. S., 239n, 256
Gordon, R. A., 239n, 256
Gordon, Robert J., 614n, 628n, 637n, 639n, 640n, 653, 653n
Gould, William, 535n
Gramlich, Edward, 107n, 475n, 506n
Grant, James, 118n
Gray, Wayne, 640n
Grebenstein, Charles, 117n
Greenberg, David, 186n
Greenwood, Davydd J., 196n
Greenwood, Michael J., 365n, 372n, 386n, 393
Gregory, Paul R., 275n
Grenier, Gilles, 535n
Gretzky, Wayne, 64

Griesinger, Harriet, 258n
Griliches, Zvi, 322n
Groeneveld, Lyle P., 236n
Gronau, Reuben, 227n, 246n, 255
Grossman, Jean B., 386n
Grossman, Sanford, 594n
Grubb, W. Norton, 343n
Grubel, Herbert G., 390n
Gullickson, William, 640n
Gunderson, Morley, 540n, 571n, 574
Gustafsson, Siv, 222n, 604n
Gustman, Alan, 249n
Gwartney, James D., 186n, 535n
Gyourko, Joseph, 516n

Haber, William, 608n
Hagens, John, 653n
Hall, Robert E., 378n, 420n, 593n, 614n, 638n, 643n
Halloran, Richard, 53n
Haltiwanger, John, 601n, 607n
Ham, John C., 177n, 611n
Hamermesh, Daniel S., 75n, 93n, 115n, 117n, 118n, 121n, 135, 136, 276n, 307n, 362n, 502n, 507n, 519n, 588n
Hannan, Michael T., 236n
Hannan, Timothy, 545n
Hansen, Bent, 56n
Hansen, W. Lee, 565n
Hanushek, Eric A., 291n
Harper, Michael, 640n
Harris, Jeffrey, 482n
Harrison, Bennett, 339n, 347, 602n
Hart, Oliver, 594n
Hart, Robert A., 152n, 153n, 154n, 173
Hartmann, Heidi L., 563n, 578n
Hashimoto, Masanori, 166n, 169n
Hause, John C., 322n
Haveman, Robert, 122n
Hayes, Beth, 468n
Healy, James J., 416n
Heckman, James, 201n, 214n, 222n, 570n
Heigoro, Shoda, 375
Hendricks, Wallace, 650n
Heywood, John S., 76n
Hicks, John R., 109n, 109–12, 112n, 461n, 461–63, 462n
Higuchi, Yoshio, 373n, 374n
Hill, M. Anne, 330n, 539n, 563n, 574, 578n
Hill, Martha S., 274n
Hirsch, Barry T., 476n, 484n, 487n, 489
Hirsch, Werner, 512n
Hirschman, Albert, 482n
Hirshleifer, Jack, 300n, 304n
Hodgson, Alan, 415n
Hoffman, Saul, 534n
Hogue, Carma, 582n
Holmlund, Bertil, 274n, 276n, 293
Holt, Charles, 638n
Holzer, Harry J., 118n, 135, 604n, 606n
Horney, Mary Jean, 233n

Horvath, Francis W., 372n, 537n, 604n
Hotchkiss, Julie, 596n
Hsing, Yu, 507n
Hurd, Richard, 78n
Hurley, Jeremiah E., 258n
Hutchens, Robert M., 75n, 298n, 435n, 461n
Hutchins, Michael, 481n
Hutt, W. H., 555n
Hyclak, Thomas, 479n

Ichniowski, Casey, 506n, 523
Ippolito, Richard A., 515n

Jackson, Peter, 604n
Jacoby, Sanford, 453n
Jakubson, George, 589n
Johnson, George, 320n, 343n, 463n, 463–67, 466n, 488, 519n
Johnson, Harry, 476n
Johnson, Lyndon B., 651, 652, 653, 653n
Johnson, William R., 236n
Johnston, William B., 55n
Jones, Ethel, 178n
Jovanovic, Boyan, 376n, 378n, 379n, 435n
Juhn, Chinhui, 343n

Kagel, John H., 71n
Kahan, Arcadius, 325n
Kahn, Lawrence, 376n, 479n, 546n, 650n
Kahn, Shulamit, 176n
Kasper, Hirschel, 565n
Katz, Harry C., 511n, 524n, 528n
Katz, Lawrence, 386n, 423n, 583n, 588n, 610n, 628n, 658
Kau, James, 459n
Kaus, Mickey, 209n
Keeley, Michael C., 215n, 221
Kehrer, Kenneth, 215n, 221
Kennan, John, 461n, 467n, 468n
Kennedy, John F., 498, 651, 652, 653, 653n
Kessel, Reuben, 76n, 404n
Kiefer, Nicholas, 608n, 611n
Killingsworth, Mark R., 122n, 202n, 215n, 221, 222n, 233n, 237n, 240n, 539n, 563n, 574, 578n
Kim, Sung-Joong, 276n
King, Allan, 459n
King, Sandra, 266n, 414n, 419n
Knight, J., 326n
Kochin, Levis, 458n, 545n, 611n
Korenham, Sanders, 48n
Kornhauser, Arthur, 308n
Kosters, Marvin, 648n
Kostin, Leonid, 331
Kotlikoff, Laurence J., 249n
Koziara, Edward C., 469n
Kraft, John, 653n
Krashevski, Richard, 603n
Kritzer, Herbert M., 418n

Kropp, David, 326n
Krueger, Alan, 512n, 514n
Kruse, Douglas, 417n, 441n
Kunze, Kent, 640n
Kuskin, Mark, 479n

LaLonde, Robert, 330n
Lampman, Robert J., 59
Landes, Elisabeth M., 236n
Landes, William M., 558n
Landon, J. H., 78n
Lang, Kevin, 176n, 326n, 553n, 554n, 617
Lansing, John B., 365n, 367n, 372n
Lawrence, Colin, 478n
Lawrence, Robert Z., 478n
Layard, Richard, 79n, 115n, 136, 191n, 221, 249n, 256, 467n, 505n, 523, 608n
Lazear, Edward P., 249n, 256, 412n, 425n, 428n, 432n, 437, 449n, 593n
Lease, R., 419n
Lee, Lung-Fei, 476n
Leigh, Duane E., 479n
Leigh, J. Paul, 276n, 480n
Leighton, Julia, 589n
Leighton, Linda, 166n, 604n
Lemieux, Thomas, 133n, 454n
Leonard, Jonathan S., 417n, 418n, 571n, 574, 617
Leontief, Wassily, 490n
Levin, Dan, 71n
Levine, Louis, 416n
Levitan, Sar, 92n
Levy, Frank, 339n, 343n, 347
Lewis, H. Gregg, 76n, 404n, 470n, 476n, 477n, 489, 507n
Lewis, John L., 79, 79n
Lewis, Michael, 9n
Li, Jeanne, 154n
Lichtenberg, Frank, 118n, 485n
Lilien, David, 588n, 637n
Lilla, Mark, 342n
Lindbeck, Assar, 12, 418n
Lindsay, C. M., 320n
Lindsay, John, 508n
Link, Albert, 76n, 77n, 484n
Link, Charles R., 78n, 534n
Linneman, Peter, 477n
Lipsey, Richard, 625n, 633n
Lipsky, David, 461n
Livernash, E. Robert, 416n
Lockman, Robert, 261n
Lockwood, Brian, 196n
Loewenberg, J. Joseph, 513n
Long, Clarence D., 175n, 176n
Long, James E., 76n, 77n, 515n, 535n
Lowenstein, Mark A., 144n
Lucas, Robert, 642n, 643n, 647n, 664n
Luce, R. Duncan, 296n
Lundberg, Shelly J., 176n, 191n, 237n, 239n, 548n
Lyons, John S., 116n

McCarthy, Kevin F., 387n
McCloskey, Donald, 12
McDonald, Ian, 490n
McDowell, John M., 386n, 393
McElroy, Marjorie B., 233n, 237n
McGovern, George, 212, 213n
McKersie, Robert, 462n, 588n
McManus, Walter, 369n, 535n
MaCurdy, Thomas, 495n
Madden, Janice F., 291n, 552n
Main, B. G. M., 420n
Malveaux, Julianne M., 540n
Mangum, Garth, 347, 615n
Manser, Marilyn, 233n
Manski, Charles F., 306n, 326n, 348
Marcus, Alan, 92n
Marin, Alan, 276n
Marshall, Alfred, 32, 109n, 109–12
Marshall, F. Ray, 459n, 545n
Marston, Stephen T., 618n
Maskin, Eric, 594n
Mason, William M., 322n
Mattila, J. Peter, 377n, 583n
Maurizi, Alex, 460n
Mauro, Martin, 462n
Medoff, James L., 425n, 443n, 476n, 482,
    482n, 483n, 484n, 485n, 489, 593n,
    632n, 637n, 658
Mehra, Y. P., 650n
Meitzen, Mark, 378n
Mellor, Earl F., 539n
Mellow, Wesley, 425n
Melvin, Michael, 643n
Meyer, Bruce, 583n, 610n, 613n
Meyer, Robert, 616n
Michael, Robert T., 236n, 563n, 578n
Mieszkowski, Peter, 407n, 437, 476n
Milgate, M., 601n
Miller, James, 281n
Mincer, Jacob, 85n, 88n, 96, 169, 169n,
    202n, 239n, 256, 331n, 333n, 334n,
    348, 366n, 373n, 374n, 376n, 378n,
    379n, 472n, 475n, 537n, 539n
Mishan, E. J., 280n
Miskimin, Harry A., 41n
Mitchell, Daniel, 453n, 648n, 649n, 650n,
    658
Mitchell, H., 655n
Mitchell, Olivia S., 93n, 245n, 249n, 255
Modlin, George M., 41n
Moffitt, Robert, 215n, 221, 249n, 253n
Montgomery, Edward, 462n, 604n
Moore, Michael, 276n
Moore, William, 451n, 477n
Morrall, John, III, 459n
Mortensen, Dale T., 608n
Moss, Milton, 227n, 255
Moy, Joyanna, 594n
Mroz, Thomas A., 202n
Mueller, Eva, 365n, 367n, 372n
Mugabe, Robert, 89
Munts, Raymond, 216n
Murphy, Kevin, 343n, 417n, 423n

Murray, Merrill, 608n
Muth, John, 643n

Nardinelli, Clark, 282n
Nathan, Richard, 519n
Nealey, Stanley M., 401n
Neumann, George R., 449n, 468n, 469n,
    590n, 611n
Newman, P., 601n
Newman, Robert, 451n
Nichols, Len M., 276n
Nicholson, Walter, 590n
Nixon, Richard, 652, 653, 653n, 654
Nordhaus, William, 657n
Norsworthy, J. R., 640n
North, Douglass C., 41n
Norwood, Janet, 398n
Nussbaum, Joyce, 151n

Oates, Wallace, 307n, 362n, 503n, 507n
Oaxaca, Ronald L., 459n, 540n, 611n, 612n
O'Connor, Charles J., 264n
O'Farrell, Brigid, 563n, 578n
Oi, Walter, 173, 374n, 375n, 376n, 420n,
    426n
Okun, Arthur M., 216n, 614, 614n, 622n,
    623n, 656n, 658
Olson, Craig, 469n
O'Neill, David, 124n
O'Neill, June, 536n, 537n
Osterman, Paul, 167n, 173, 571n, 605n,
    606n
Oswald, Rudolph, 148n
Owens, Arthur, 321n

Packer, Arnold E., 55n
Palmer, John, 121n, 135
Parsons, Donald O., 165n, 199n, 374n,
    377n, 378n, 379n, 393
Partington, M., 390n
Paxton, Christina H., 177n
Pechman, J. A., 221
Pencavel, John, 6n, 191n, 201n, 215n, 221,
    245n, 393, 418n, 419n, 437, 447n,
    455n, 489, 495n
Pergamit, Michael, 77n
Perloff, Jeffrey, 122n, 136, 512n, 513n
Perry, George, 630n, 633n, 643n, 648n,
    649n, 653, 653n, 658
Peterson, George E., 407n, 437
Peterson, William, 477n
Phelps, Edmund, 642n, 644n
Philips, Peter, 347, 414n
Phillips, A. W., 622n
Pierce, Brooks, 343n
Piore, Michael J., 22n, 23n, 167n, 168n,
    173, 329n, 372n, 393, 483n, 552n
Plant, Mark, 607n
Polachek, Solomon W., 334n, 348, 372n,
    481n, 537n, 539n

Pollak, Robert A., 306n
Popkin, Joel, 512n, 513n
Psacharopoulos, George, 276n, 320n, 327n

Quinn, Joseph F., 512n

Radwan, Samir, 56n
Raff, Daniel, 424n
Raiffa, Howard, 296n
Raisian, John, 169n, 477n
Rapping, Leonard, 647n
Rea, Samuel, Jr., 611n
Reagan, Ronald, 132, 184–85, 501
Reder, Melvin, 449n, 468n, 469n, 502n
Rees, Albert, 481–82, 482n, 531n, 606n,
    617
Reich, Michael, 553n, 554n, 574
Reimers, Cordelia W., 535n
Rissman, Ellen, 449n
Robins, Philip K., 215n
Robinson, Joan, 552n
Roderick, Melissa, 589n
Rosen, Harvey, 401n
Rosen, Sherwin, 147n, 265n, 293, 294n,
    323n, 324, 373, 374n, 376n, 378n,
    409n, 432n, 437, 471n, 600n
Rosenberg, Pamela, 154n
Rosett, Joshua, 485n
Ross, Arthur M., 374n, 455n, 463, 463n
Rottenberg, Simon, 59, 96, 166n, 459n
Royo, Miguel Rodriguez-Pinero, 163n
Ruback, Richard S., 486n
Rubin, Paul, 459n
Rubinfeld, Daniel, 506n
Rufolo, Anthony, 512n
Ruser, John, 276n
Russell, R. Robert, 653n

Sabot, R., 326n
Sahling, Leonard G., 364n
Sahlins, Marshall, 196n
Salisbury, R. F., 196n
Samuelson, Paul A., 622n, 623n
San, Gee, 650n
Sandell, Steven, 372n
Sarat, Austin, 418n
Sargent, Thomas, 643n, 664n
Sayles, Leonard R., 308n
Schmitt, Donald G., 430n
Schroeder, Larry, 363n
Schultz, Theodore W., 222n, 324n, 348
Schumann, Paul L., 150n, 151n, 152n, 173,
    296n
Schuster, J., 565n
Schwartz, Aba, 367n
Schwarz, Joshua L., 79n, 505n, 507n,
    508n, 509n, 523
Scott, Anthony, 390n
Scoville, James G., 329n
Sehgal, Ellen, 171n, 265n, 376n

Seiler, Eric, 415n, 419n
Sellekaerts, Brigitte, 152n
Settle, Russell, 281n
Shabad, Theodore, 331n
Shakotko, Robert, 435n
Sheflin, Neil, 452n
Sherer, Peter, 546n
Sherman, Daniel R., 306n, 508n
Shoven, John B., 249n, 428n
Shultz, George, 654n
Siegel, Donald, 485n
Sieling, Mark, 541n
Silberman, Jonathan, 459n
Simon, Herbert A., 411n
Siow, Aloysius, 314n
Skidmore, Felicity, 410n
Skinner, Jonathan, 236n
Slichter, Sumner H., 416n
Smith, Adam, 274, 274n, 293, 315, 315n
Smith, James P., 532n, 533n, 536n, 570n,
    574
Smith, Ralph E., 558n, 581n
Smith, Robert S., 75n, 94n, 95, 112n, 117n,
    276n, 293, 330n, 407n, 409n, 437,
    438n, 441n, 563n, 566n, 574, 576n,
    577n, 578n
Smith, Sharon P., 52n, 364n, 498n, 511n,
    512, 512n, 514n, 523, 539n
Smith, Shirley, 334n
Solnick, Loren, 151n
Solomon, Lewis, 326n
Solon, Gary, 611n
Solow, Robert M., 490n, 593n, 622n, 623n
Sorenson, Elaine, 539n, 540n, 577n
Spence, Michael, 166n, 173, 348, 349n,
    548n
Spiegelman, Robert, 613n
Stafford, Frank, 222n, 480n
Startz, Richard, 548n
Staudohar, Paul D., 64n
Steinmeier, Thomas, 249n
Stern, Robert, 461n
Stiglitz, Joseph E., 411n, 423n
Stone, Joe, 495n, 508n
Stone, Richard, 477n
Strauss, George, 308n
Stroup, Richard, 186n
Strumilin, S. G., 324–25
Stuart, Robert C., 275n
Studenmund, A. H., 15n
Sullivan, Daniel, 330n
Summers, Lawrence H., 93, 93n, 152n,
    424n, 553n, 583n, 585n, 595n, 607n,
    617, 628n
Svejnar, Jan, 494n, 495n
Swartz, Caroline, 534n, 535n, 536n, 574
Swimmer, Gene, 151n
Szyszczak, E. M., 154n

Taira, Koji, 169n, 235, 235n, 375n
Taubman, Paul, 306n, 322n, 326n
Tauchen, Helen, 258n

Taylor, David P., 545n
Taylor, John, 643n, 649n
Thaler, Richard, 71n, 425n
Thiel, Stuart, 71n
Thomas, Robert Paul, 41n
Thomason, Terry, 497n, 498n
Thompson, Lawrence H., 249n, 256
Thornton, Robert J., 507n
Thurow, Lester, 554n, 608n
Tienda, Mary, 574
Tilly, Charles, 241n, 339n, 390n
Timpane, P. M., 221
Tinto, V., 306n
Tippit, Frank, 614n
Tobin, James, 601n, 603n, 624n, 636n
Tollison, Robert D., 12
Tomola, James, 519n
Topel, Robert, 298n, 365n, 378n, 423n,
    435n, 583n, 596n, 599n, 600n
Tracy, Joseph, 468n, 516n
Tregarthen, Timothy, 546n
Treiman, Donald J., 563n
Triplett, Jack E., 375n, 407n
Troy, Leo, 452n
Trubek, David M., 418n
Tullock, Gordon, 502n
Tuma, Nancy Brandon, 236n
Turnbull, John G., 202n
Turner, Robert, 401n
Twain, Mark, 458, 458n

Unterberger, S. Herbert, 469n

Valdez, R. Burciaga, 387n
Vanderkamp, John, 372n
Vanek, Jaroslav, 416n
Venti, Steven F., 512n
Viscusi, W. Kip, 264n, 276n, 293, 376n
Vroman, Susan, 466n, 648n

Wachter, Michael, 22n, 122n, 136, 477n,
    482n, 512n, 513n
Walker, Ian, 177n
Walker, Kathryn E., 246n
Wallace, Phyllis A., 540n, 541n
Walton, Richard, 462n
Walzer, Norman, 276n

Ward, Michael, 378n, 536n
Warren, Ronald, 282n
Watts, Harold W., 221
Weinberg, Daniel H., 330n
Weinstein, Paul, 460n
Weisbrod, Burton, 496n
Weiss, Andrew, 326n, 376n, 590n
Weiss, Yoram, 423n
Weisskopf, Thomas, 640n
Weitzman, Martin L., 417n, 438n, 592n,
    625n, 657n
Welch, Finis R., 47n, 48n, 92n, 96, 343n,
    532n, 533n, 535n, 570n, 574
Welch, Stephen, 152n
Wellington, H., 499n
Wessels, Walter J., 94n
White, Michelle, 537n
Wigge, Larry, 64n
Willet, Thomas D., 12
Williams, C. Arthur, Jr., 202n
Williams, Harry B., 266n
Williamson, Jeffrey G., 282n
Williamson, Oliver, 167n, 173, 482n
Willis, Robert J., 323n, 324
Wilson, Robert H., 343n
Wilson, Thomas, 648n
Winkler, Donald R., 183n, 404n, 509n
Winter, R., 499n
Wise, David A., 249n, 306n, 326n, 348,
    512n, 523, 563n, 576n, 616n, 617
Wise, Donald, 151n
Witte, Ann Dryden, 258n
Wolfe, John R., 276n
Woodbury, Stephen, 401n, 613n
Worrall, John D., 276n
Wright, John W., 380n
Wright, Randall, 22n, 596n
Wunnava, Phanindra, 481n

Yellen, Janet, 423n, 437, 590n, 593n
Yett, Donald, 57n
Yoshio-Higuchi, 169n

Zarkin, Gary A., 258n, 314n
Zax, Jeffrey, 506n
Ziegler, Philip, 41n
Zimmerman, Martin B., 486n

Subject Index

The letter *n* following a page number indicates that the information will be found in a footnote or a source line.

Above-equilibrium wages, 49, 51–52
Absenteeism
  and employee benefits, 183, 404
  and incentive-pay systems, 419–20
Absolute effect of unions on real wages,
  470–76
Acrylonitrile, benefit/cost analysis of
  standards limiting worker exposure
  to, 281–82
Actual vs. paid hours of work, 177n
Adaptive expectations of inflation, 643,
  659
Added-worker effect, 238–40
Affirmative action plans, 287–92, 558,
  566–71
Age
  and college education, 305
  and gender composition of labor force,
  630–31
  and job tenure, 378–79
  and migration, 365–66
  and voluntary turnover, 378–79
Age discrimination
  in hiring, 168–71
  and mandatory retirement, 434
Age Discrimination in Employment Act,
  428, 434
Age/earnings profiles
  and education/wage relationship, 318
  fanning out by education, 332–33
  hypothetical, for native-born Americans
  and immigrants, 395–96
  post-schooling investments and, 330–33
Agriculture
  employment trends in, 27–28
  and technological change, 126
Airline Deregulation Act of 1978, 453
Airline industry
  deregulation of, 120, 452–54
  strike activity in, 469n
Airline mechanics, earnings of, 453
Airline pilots, earnings of, 120, 453
Airport noise, 259n
Allocation of labor, 2, 260–61
Alternative income streams, 302

American Federation of Labor–Congress
  of Industrial Organizations
  (AFL-CIO), 443, 459
American Medical Association, 460
Amnesty, illegal aliens and, 381–82
Annuity formula, 302n
Antidiscrimination programs, 558–71
Apprenticeship rules, 460
Arbitration and incentive to bargain,
  524–28
Arbitration statutes, effects on wages of
  state and local government
  employees, 509–11
Arbitrators, 500n
Area Redevelopment Act of 1959, 590
Asbestos dust
  benefit/cost analysis of standards
  limiting worker exposure to, 281
  dangers of, 264
Ashenfelter-Johnson model of strike
  activity, 463–67
Asians, earnings disparities of, 535–36
Associations, employee, 445–46, 447, 450
Assumptions of economic models, 4–6,
  61–62
Asymmetric information, and contract
  enforcement, 409–11, 426
Asymmetric information model of strike
  activity, 468
Asymmetry of information, 593–94
Automation, substitution effect of, 125
Automobile industry, import quotas and
  employment in, 132

Baby-boom bulge, 47–48
Backward-bending labor supply curve, 184
Bargaining protocols, 468
Baseball players
  free agents, overpayment of, 70–71
  marginal productivity and allocation of,
  69–70
Basketball players, customer
  discrimination and, 546
Below-equilibrium wages, 53

Benefit/cost studies, 281–82
Benefit streams, 157
Binding arbitration, 509–11
Black Death, 41
Black lung benefits, financing of, 112–13
Blacks
  and affirmative action, 287–88, 557,
    566–68, 570
  as complements and substitutes in
    production, 118–19
  and earnings disparities, 532–35
  educational attainment and salary, 530,
    570
  and eradication of discrimination, 569
  immigration effects on, 386
  migration of, 363–64, 372
  in professional basketball, 546
  unemployment rates for, 601–2
  and union wage effects, 477
Blue-collar workers, 166–67
  and union wage effects, 479
  and working conditions in union vs.
    nonunion firms, 480
Bonus plans, 412, 419
Boom-and-bust cycles, 310–11
Brain drain, 390
Budget constraints, 190–92, 196, 205–8,
  250, 252
Bureau of Labor Statistics (BLS), 603
Business downturns
  effects of share systems on real wages
    in, 438–41
  labor demand in, 438

Cafeteria plans for choosing employee
  benefits, 403
California, piece rates and supervisory
  effort in, 414
Capital, defined, 62
Capital-intensive mode of production, 33
Capital-intensive technologies, 36
Capital market, 10, 32
Capital prices, effect of decline in, 35–36
Capital stock, 61, 62–63, 69
Capital supply, 35
Cardinal utility functions, 296n
Career interruptions of married women,
  171, 242–43, 333, 335
Chain migration, 367
Chaos phenomenon, 312n
Child care, costs of, 222–26
Child-care benefits, 398
Child rearing, 234
  in Switzerland, 241
Chrysler Corporation, 408, 648
Civilian labor force
  availability computation, methods of,
    566–68
  occupational distribution of, 28
  unemployment rates for, 25, 580
Civil Rights Act of 1964, 558–63, 567
Claimant bonus, 613
Clerical jobs, employment trends in, 28

Cliff vesting, 409n
Coal Mine Health and Safety Act, 112
Coal-mining industry, 80, 112–13, 275, 484
  union and association membership in,
    450
Cobb-Douglas production functions, 138n
Cobweb model of a labor market, 312–14
Coefficient of variation, 355
Collective bargaining agreements, 49
Collective bargaining incentive, and
  arbitration, 524–28
Collective bargaining in private sector,
  442–87
  and employee associations, 445–46
  federal legislation governing, 444–45
  issues covered by, 443–44
  and wage/benefit trade-off, 408
Collective bargaining in public sector, 496,
  498–501
Collective voice, unions as institutions of,
  482–87
College education. *See* Education
College professors, earnings of, 45, 564–65
Collusive action model of labor market
  discrimination, 554–56
Colour Bar Act of 1911 (South Africa), 555
Commissions, 412, 413–16
Commuting
  costs of, 222–26
  hedonic model of, 289–92
Comparability legislation, 498
Comparability survey, 511
Comparable jobs, 40
Comparable worth
  earnings gaps, estimating, 575–78
  and labor market discrimination,
    562–63
  and labor market for university
    professors, 45, 564–65
Compensating wage differentials
  and affirmative action planning, 287–92
  and allocation of labor, 260–61
  assumptions and predictions regarding,
    262–65
  as compensation for workers, 261–62
  empirical tests of theory of, 274–77
  for evening and night shifts, 266
  in Great Britain, 282
  hedonic theory of wages, 266–74
  and labor markets, 257–92
  and layoffs, 294–98
  and occupational choice, 257–65
  and occupational safety and health,
    277–87
  and risk of death, 275–78
  and risk of injury, 207n, 266–70, 275–77
  in Soviet Union, 275
Compensation, 2
  deferred, 31, 400–401, 426–27, 430–31
  employee benefits, economics of,
    398–409
  employer expenditures for, 398–99
  and employment contracts, 409–11
  internal labor markets and, 420–35

methods of, in 1890s, 429
nonwage forms of, 93, 94, 144–45
pay, basis of, 411–20
relationship to wages, earnings, and
  income, 29–32
structure of, 397–435
total, 30, 479–81, 511–15
Complements in production, 80–81,
  114–16, 118, 125, 386
Comprehensive Employment and Training
  Act (CETA), 501, 517, 518, 519n, 590
Concession bargaining, in airline industry,
  453
Conspicuous goods, 285
Constant percentage markup, 638–39
Construction industry, unions and, 450,
  484
Consumer Price Index (CPI), 29, 636n
Consumption, household production and,
  231–32
Consumption goods, 301, 328n
Consumption patterns, government
  attempts to influence by changing
  preferences, 180n
Contract curve, 494, 524–28
Contracts. See Employment contracts;
  Labor contracts
Contract zone, 524–28
Conventional arbitration, 510
Corner solution, 192–93, 208n
Corporate takeovers, union wages and,
  485
Cost minimization, 80, 100–103
Cost-of-living adjustment (COLA) clauses,
  649–50
Cost-of-living escalator clauses, 625, 636n,
  649–50, 652
Costs of quitting, 379
Costs of working, 222–26
Cost streams, 157
Council of Economic Advisors, 651
Council on Wage and Price Stability, 652
Craft jobs, employment trends in, 28
Craft unions, 443, 460, 461
Crane operators, recruiting and training
  of, 143
Credentials, in hiring process, 166–67
Cross-sectional data, 13
Cross-sectional studies of labor supply
  behavior, 199, 201–2
Cross-wage elasticity of labor demand,
  113–15, 118, 125
Crowding model of labor market
  discrimination, 551–52
Current labor market discrimination, 531,
  532, 538
Current Population Survey (CPS), 23n,
  581, 603
Customer discrimination, 545–47

Davis-Bacon Act, 459, 637
Death, on-the-job risk of, 275–78
Decentralized marketplace, 21–22

Decertification votes, 447
Decision not to work, 192–93
Decision to work, 174–219
Declining sectors, paradox of large wage
  increases in, 478
Deep-sea divers, earnings of, 260–61
Deferred compensation payments, 31,
  400–401, 426–27, 430–31
Defined benefit pension plans, 407–8
Defined contribution pension plans, 407–8
Demand-deficient unemployment, 591–600
Demand for a good, factors affecting,
  179–80
Demand for labor, 32, 60–94. See also
  Labor demand curve
  in business downturns, 438
  changes in forces affecting, 34–36
  curve, nature of, 33–37, 60, 61, 68
  and degrees of responsiveness, 60
  effect of, on equilibrium wage, 40–46
  effects of quasi-fixed labor costs on,
    141–72
  elasticities of, 106–34, 137–40
  by firms, 36–37, 60, 62–73, 97–105,
    155–60
  by industry, 36–37
  international trade and, 120, 126–34
  and labor shortages, 55–58
  in long run, 37, 61, 79–81, 100–105
  market, 36–37, 60–61, 72–73, 75–79
  and minimum wage legislation, 82–94
  models of, modified, 75–82
  models of, simple, 61–75
  and money wages, 67–69
  and monopoly, 75–77
  and monopsony, 77–79, 90–91
  multiperiod, 158–60
  and payroll taxes, 73–75
  under profit sharing, 439–41
  and real wages, 65–67
  in short run, 37, 61, 62–73, 99–100
  and union behavior, 455–63
  and wage changes, 33–34, 60
Demand for leisure function, 179, 181, 183
Dependent variable, 14
Deregulation, 120, 452–54
Derived demand laws, 109–13, 119–20,
  443
Developing countries
  minimum wages in, 89
  and rate of return on education
    investments, 327
Dichotomous variable, 17
Diminishing marginal productivity, 316
Diminishing marginal returns, 63, 68, 269
Diminishing marginal utility, 524–28
Disability benefits, 202–8
Discounted value of firm earnings, 157
Discouraged-worker effect, 238–40
Discrimination
  age, 434
  collusive action model of, 554–56
  crowding model of, 551–52
  customer, 545–47

defined, 529–31
dual labor market model of, 552–54
and earnings disparities, 531–41
economics of, 529–71
employee, 547–48
employer, 542–45
eradication of, 569
government programs to end, 558–71
in hiring, 168–71
and migration of blacks, 364
monopoly power models of, 551–56
personal prejudice models of, 542–48
power theories of, 551–56
reverse, 567
and state fair employment practice laws,
    556–58
statistical, 123, 167, 171, 548–51, 560n
theories of, 541–56
Disparate impact standard of
    discrimination, 559–61
Disparate treatment standard of
    discrimination, 559–61
Displacement effect, 519
Divorce laws, and human capital
    investments, 321
Divorce rates, 235–36
Domestic content legislation, 457
Domestic jobs, employment trends in, 28
Double time, increasing overtime-pay
    premium to, 148–52
Downturns, business, 438–41
Downward bias on educational
    rate-of-return estimates, 322–23
Dual labor market model of
    discrimination, 552–54
Dumping of farm products, 120

Earnings
  defined, 30
  and experience, 434–35
  incentive pay, 418
  of manufacturing production workers,
      30, 31
  piece vs. time rates, 419
  public vs. private sector, 498, 499,
      511–15
  in regulated industries, 345–46
  relationship to wages, compensation,
      and income, 29–32
Earnings differentials
  and college education, 307–14
  compression by employee benefits, 404
Earnings disparities, 531–41
  for Asians, 535–36
  for blacks, 532–35
  for Hispanics, 535
  for women, 536–41
Earnings distribution
  dispersion of, 337, 339–44
  and family mobility, 342
  human capital and, 336–45
  and inequality measurement, 355–59

and migration, 367–68
  skewness of, 338, 340, 344–45
  statistical concepts, 337–38
Earnings of labor, 29–32
Earplugs, use of on the job, 261–62
Economic immigrants, 370
Economic rents, 53–55, 485
Economists, views of, on incomes policies,
    654
Education
  and age, 305
  and age/earnings profiles, 318, 332–33
  benefits and costs, 301–2, 305–6
  and earnings differentials, 307–14
  estimates of rate of return on, 320,
      322–23, 326
  formal model of choice of investment in,
      303–9
  as investment for individuals, 318–24
  and migration, 366
  of new entrants in labor force, 48
  and present-orientedness, 304–5
  signaling aspects of, 349–54
  as social investment, 324–28
  and wages, hedonic model of, 314–17
  women and, 309, 334
  worker demand for, 301–14
Educational levels. *See* Education
Education/wage relationship
  hedonic model of, 314–17
  market determination of, 317–18
Efficiency wages, 397, 422–24, 590
Efficient contracts, 490–95
Egypt, emigration of construction workers
    from, 56
Elasticities of demand for labor, 106–34.
    See also Wage elasticities of labor
    demand
  technological change and, 124–26
Elasticity of product demand, 110, 114,
    115–17, 124
Elasticity of substitution, 112–13, 114,
    137–40
Elastic labor demand curve, 107–9
Emergency Employment Act of 1971, 501,
    517
Emigration
  consequences of, 390–91
  of construction workers from Egypt, 56
Employee associations, 445–46, 447, 450
Employee benefits, 30–31, 397, 566
  and absenteeism, 183, 404
  availability of various, 398
  cafeteria plans for choosing, 403
  economics of, 398–409
  employee preferences for, 399–401
  employer expenditures for, 398–99
  employer preferences for, 401–5
  and job tenure, 405n
  legally required, 93, 144–45, 146,
      152–54
  pension reform legislation affecting,
      407–9

as percentage of total compensation, 145
and preferential treatment of worker groups, 403
quasi-fixed labor costs and, 144–45, 146, 152–54
tax advantages of, 400–401
union effects on, 401
in union vs. nonunion firms, 480
wages and, joint determination of, 405–7
Employee compensation aggregate, 1
Employee discrimination, 547–48
Employee-initiated mobility, 373–74. *See also* Migration; Quitting; Worker mobility
Employee Retirement Income Security Act (ERISA), 408, 430
Employer bonus experiment, 613
Employer concession schedule, 461
Employer discrimination, 542–45
Employer/employee matching, 270–74, 378–79
Employer-initiated mobility, 361, 373–74. *See also* Layoffs
Employment-at-will doctrine, 410n
Employment contracts
explicit, 409–11, 429–30
implicit, 409–11, 429–30
multiyear, 649
self-enforcing, 411, 426
and sequencing of pay, 425–30
yellow dog, 444
Employment distribution
by industrial sector, 27–28
by occupation, 28
Employment/hours trade-off, 146–54
Employment Protection Act of 1975 (Great Britain), 154
Employment rate, 580
Employment relationship, 1
Employment Service, U.S., 638
Employment subsidies, 121–24
Employment tax credits, 121–24
England. *See* Great Britain
Entry-level jobs, 47, 420
Equal employment opportunity, and affirmative action, 566–71
Equal Employment Opportunity Commission (EEOC), 559, 570, 571
Equal Pay Act of 1963, 558
Equilibrium wage, 40–46, 47, 49, 51–52, 53–54
Error term, 15
Europe, unemployment rates in, 594–95, 628n
Evening and night shifts, compensating wage differentials for, 266
Ex ante vs. *ex post* compensation, 267n
Expected inflation, 643n, 644–47
Expenditure-limitation legislation, effect on public sector labor market, 515–17
Experience, and increased earnings, 434–35

Experience rating, 598
Explanatory variable, 14
Explicit contracts, 409–11, 429–30
Explicit costs of employee training, 143
Explicit employment guarantees, 494

Factfinders, 500n
Factor substitution, 79–80
Fair employment practice legislation, 556–58
Fair Labor Standards Act (FLSA), 8, 82, 92, 148, 151–52
Family labor supply decisions, 233–54
Farm jobs, employment trends in, 28
Farm products, dumping of, 120
Farm workers, wage elasticity of demand for, 120
Featherbedding, 460n
Federal antidiscrimination programs, 558–71
Federal Contract Compliance Program, 566–68, 570–71
Federal government, union and association membership in, 450
Federal labor legislation, 444–45
Feudalism, in Japan, 169
Final-offer arbitration, 510, 528n
Finance industry, union and association membership in, 450
Fire Fighters Local 1784 v. *Stotts*, 562n
Firm demand for labor, 36–37, 60, 62–73, 97–105, 155–60
Firm labor demand curve, 36–37, 60
and cost minimization, 100–103
and demand for labor in long run, 100–105
and demand for labor in short run, 99–100
graphic derivation of, 97–105
and production function, 97–99
and scale effect, 104–5
and substitution effect, 103–4
Firm labor investments, 155–60
Firm labor supply curve, 38–40
Firm-specific training, 160–63, 482
Firm supply of labor, 38–40
Fiscal substitution, 519
Fixed costs of working, 222–26
Flat rate. *See* Piece-rate pay
Flexible time, 414
Flight attendants, earnings of, 453
Flogging, economic implications of, in Korea, 260
Florida, unemployment rates in, 388
Ford Motor Company, 424, 648
Forgone earnings, 301, 305–6, 324
Forgone opportunities, 3
Four-factor method of computing labor force availability, 567–68
Franks v. *Bowman Transportation*, 562n
Frictional unemployment, 585–86, 607–14
Fringe benefits. *See* Employee benefits

Full-employment rate of unemployment, 585, 586, 601–3, 628, 637

Gainsharing plans, 412
Garment workers, wage elasticity of demand for, 119–20
Gender. *See also* Men; Women
 differences in compensation methods in the 1890s, 429
 earnings disparities by, 536–41
 job tenure by, 374, 378–79
 labor force participation rates by, 24, 25
General employment subsidies, 122
General Motors Corporation, 648
General training, 160–63, 165, 331
Geographic imbalances, and structural unemployment, 588
Geographic markets, 634
Geographic mobility, 363–73
Germany, and human capital, 300
Gini coefficient of income distribution, 357–59
Going wage, 41
Golf tournaments, incentive effects of, 433
Goods-producing industries
 employment trends in, 27
 and technological change, 126
Government employment trends, 27, 499–500
Government intervention to overcome transactions barriers, 8–10
Government policy
 and frictional unemployment, 607–14
 and inflation, 651–54
 and labor shortages, 55–58
 and mandatory retirement, 432–34
 and normative economics, 8–10
 and unemployment, 501, 607–14, 637
Government programs to end discrimination, 558–71
Government training programs, 172, 328–30
Great Britain
 and Black Death, 41
 compensating wage differentials in, 282
 and education benefits, 305
 handloom weavers in, 116
 incentive-pay schemes in, 418
 part-time workers in, 154
 unemployment insurance in, 611
 unemployment rates in, 594–95
 and War of 1812, 9
Great Depression, 25–26, 363, 444, 449
Griggs, Willie S., v. *Duke Power Company,* 560n
Gross complements, 80–81, 114–16, 118, 125, 386
Gross-flow data, 603
Gross national product (GNP) implicit price deflator, 634–36, 641, 644
Gross substitutes, 80–81, 114–16, 118, 125

Group incentive pay, 416–19
Guest workers programs, 389

Hamburg, Germany, and human capital, 300
Handloom weavers in England, rise and fall of, 116
Hay Associates, 575
Hay Points, 575–78
Health, and labor supply, 237–38
Health, occupational safety and, 261–62, 277–87
Health and Human Services, Department of, 57–58
Hedonic model of commuting, 289–92
Hedonic model of education and wages, 314–17
Hedonic theory of wages, 266–74
 applications of, 277–92
 empirical tests of, 274–77
 employee considerations in, 266–68
 employer considerations in, 268–70
 employer/employee matching in, 270–74
Hicks' bargaining model, 461
Hicks-Marshall Laws of Derived Demand, 109–13, 119–20, 443
Hidden unemployed, 239–40
High-wage countries, and international trade, 126–34
High-wage recruiting strategy, 143
Hiring costs, 142, 155
Hiring discrimination, 168–71
Hiring investments, 166–68
Hiroshima, Japan, and human capital, 300
Hispanics
 as complements in production, 119
 and earnings disparities, 535
 and migration, 368n, 371–72
 unemployment rates for, 388, 601–2, 604n
Hockey, marginal revenue product and, 64
Holiday pay, 146, 398, 399
Homemakers, evaluation of services performed by, 246
Horizontal supply curve, 38–39, 49
Hourly wages, 29n
 trends in, 30, 31
Hours of work, 174–78, 294–98
Household production
 and consumption, 231–32
 and decision to work, 179
 and husband–wife labor supply decisions, 233–37, 537–41
 in Japan, 235
 life-cycle aspects of labor supply, 242–54
 model of, 228–31
 and sex discrimination, 537–41
 and Social Security retirement test, 249–53
 and supply of labor, 227–42
 theory of, 227–32, 237–42

Human capital
  defined, 299–300
  and distribution of earnings, 336–45
  and earnings in regulated industries,
    345–46
  and Germany, 300
  and Japan, 300
  women and acquisition of, 333–35
Human capital investments
  divorce and, 321
  in education and training, 299–346
  expenditures for, 301
  returns on, 300–301, 307
Human capital theory
  applications of, 330–46
  predictions of, 304–9
Hysteresis, 628n

Ignorance, blocking of mutually beneficial
    transactions by, 7–8
Illegal immigration, 120, 360, 380–85
  analysis of gainers and losers, 384–90
  effect of, on native population, 387–90
  and labor demand curve, 382–86
  and labor supply curve, 382–86
  naive views of, 382–84
Immigrants
  assimilation of, 394–96
  cohort quality changes of, 394–96
  earnings of, 367–68, 394–96
  economic vs. political, 370
  illegal, 120, 360, 380–90
Immigration and Nationality Act, 380
Immigration policy, 379–91
  in 18th-century Switzerland, 390
  history of U.S., 379–82
  union position on, 459
Impasse, in collective bargaining, 500n
Imperfect experience rating, 598–99
Implicit contracts, 409–11, 429–30
Implicit costs of employee training, 143
Implicit employment guarantees, 494
Implicit price deflator, 634–36, 641, 644
Import quotas, and employment in
    automobile industry, 132
Incentive pay
  and absenteeism, 419–20
  and earnings, 418
  and equipment misuse, 415
  group, 416–19
  individual, 413–16
  and output, 416, 418
  and productivity, 421
  and quality standards, 415
  and rate setting, 416
  in Soviet Union, 418
  vs. time rates, 412–13, 419
Income
  defined, 30
  relationship of, to wages, earnings, and
    compensation, 29–32
  unearned, 30
  and wage constraints, 190–92
Income dispersion, 337, 339–44
Income distribution. See Earnings
    distribution
Income effect, 181–84, 194–98, 201–2,
    208–9, 230–31, 252
Income inequality, measurement of,
    355–59
Income maintenance programs, 603n
  immigration and, 387
  and income/earnings distribution, 337,
    339
  and supply of labor, 208–18, 240–42
  and work incentives, 208–18, 240–42
Income replacement programs, 202–8
Incomes policies, 637, 651–54
Independent variable, 14
Index numbers, expression of real wages
    by, 29
Indifference curves, 187–89, 267–68, 270,
    314
Individual Retirement Account (IRA), 400
Industrial distribution of employment,
    27–28, 450–51
Industrial unions, 443
Industry demand for labor, 36–37
Inelastic labor demand curve, 107
Inequality
  of achievement and opportunity, 529–30
  measurement of, 337–38, 355–59
Inexperienced workers, and wages, 47–48
Inferior good, defined, 179n
Inflation
  adaptive expectations of, 643, 659
  expected vs. unexpected, 643n, 644–47
  price, 629–30, 638–43, 659–64
  rational expectations of, 643, 663–64
  structural policies to reduce, 651–57
  and unemployment, 620–57
  unions and, 647–51
Inflation/unemployment trade-off, 621–38
Injury risks
  compensation for, 267n
  employee considerations in, 266–68
  employer considerations in, 268–70
  employer/employee matching in, 270–74
  fatal vs. nonfatal, 275–78
  on the job, 266
  measurement of, 276
  reduction of, 270–74, 277–87
Insider-outsider models of
    inflation/unemployment trade-off,
    628n
Insurance benefits, 31, 93, 146, 152–54,
    398–99, 404
Insurance industry, union and association
    membership in, 450
Interindustry subsidies, 598n
Internal labor markets
  defined, 22
  and delayed rewards, 420
  and efficiency wages, 422–24
  and hiring investments, 167–68

and mandatory retirement, 432–34
and pay in large firms, 424–25
and pensions, 430–31
and promotion tournaments, 431–32
and sequencing of pay, 425–30
and time-based pay systems, 420–35
unemployment and, 593–95
unions and, 482–87
wages in, 420–22
Internal-rate-of-return method of
evaluating returns on education,
303–4
International Brotherhood of Teamsters v.
United States, 562n
International Ladies Garment Workers'
Union (ILGWU), 457
International trade, and demand for labor,
120, 126–34
International trade model, applied to the
family, 233n
International unemployment rate
differentials, 594–95
Intertemporal substitution model of labor
supply, 245, 647n
Inventory costs, 153
Investment behavior, 301
Investment tax credits, 121
Isoexpenditure lines, 101
Isoprofit curves, 269–70, 271, 316–17,
401–2, 405, 492
Isoquants, 97

Japan
automobile industry, and U.S. import
quotas, 132
feudalism in, 169
household productivity and labor supply
in, 235
and human capital, 300
paternalism in, 169
quitting theory in, 375
unemployment rates in, 594
Job satisfaction, 362
Job search, effects of unemployment
benefits on, 607–14
Job tenure
by age and gender, 168–71, 374, 376,
378–79, 450
and employee benefits, 405n
expected, and hiring practices, 168–71
in manufacturing industry, 264–65
and quit rates, 378–79
Job training, 328–30, 332, 334
Job Training Partnership Act (JTPA), 590
Journeymen workers, and apprenticeship
rules, 460

Korea, recruiting strategies in, 260

Labor, U.S. Department of, 123, 261, 277

Labor allocation, 2
and compensating wage differentials,
260–61
Labor categories, 81–82
Labor contracts, 2, 49. *See also*
Employment contracts
Labor costs
quasi-fixed, 141–72
variable, 141
Labor demand. *See* Demand for labor
Labor demand curve, 33–37. *See also*
Demand for labor
for categories of labor, 81–82
and demand by entire labor market,
36–37, 60, 72–73, 75–79
and demand by firms, 36–37, 60,
97–105, 155–60
and demand by industry, 36–37
downward-sloping nature of, 37, 60, 61,
66, 72
and education, 308–14
effect of expenditure- and tax-limitation
legislation on, 515–17
elasticity of, 107–9
and equilibrium wage, 40–46
illegal immigration and, 382–86
long run vs. short run, 37, 61
and monopoly, 75–77
and payroll taxes, 73–75
shift in, vs. movement along, 36
and unemployment, 585–88, 591–92
union effects on, 474
Labor demand schedule, 33
Labor economics
basic concepts, 2–10
defined, 2–3
Labor force
age/gender composition of, effect on
wage inflation/unemployment
trade-off, 630–31
defined, 23
growth of unemployment and, effect on
wage inflation/unemployment
trade-off, 631–32
new entrants in, economic position of
vs. level of schooling, 48
occupational distribution of, 28
and unemployment, 23–26
white female, teenage, and nonwhite
shares of, 630–31, 636
Labor force participation rates, 24, 25,
174, 175, 580
Labor force participation trends, 174–78
decline in actual workweek hours, 176,
177
decrease in length of careers for males,
175
increase in number of women, 24, 175
part-time employment, 152–54, 175–77
Labor hoarding, 165
Labor hours, 62n
Labor investments, 155–60

Labor legislation, 444–45
Labor/leisure choice
  empirical findings on, 199–202
  graphic analysis of, 186–98
  verbal analysis of, 179–86
Labor-Management Relations Act, 444,
    445, 449, 451
Labor-Management Reporting and
    Disclosure Act, 445, 464, 466, 467
Labor market. See also Public sector labor
    market
  and changing industries and
      occupations, 26–28
  and compensating wage differentials,
      257–92
  defined, 22–23
  and demand for labor, 33–37, 60, 72–73,
      75–79
  effect of baby-boom workers on, 47–48
  effects of government training programs
      on, 328–30
  flow between categories of, 23–24
  implications of international trade for,
      131–34
  internal, 22, 167–68, 420–35, 482–87,
      593–95
  local, 22
  loose, 25, 377
  monopsony in, 77–79, 90–91, 504n
  national, 22
  nonpecuniary factors in, 2
  overview of, 21–58
  and price of labor, 29–32
  primary sector of, 27, 552–54
  secondary sector of, 23, 27, 552–54
  signaling in, 166–67, 325–26, 349–54
  stability of, 26
  stock-flow model of, 581–85
  tertiary sector of, 27
  tight, 24, 376–77, 603
  and unemployment, 23–26
  union effects on, 22, 48–50, 455–63,
      504–9
Labor market discrimination. See
    Discrimination
Labor market equilibrium, 40–46, 47,
    49–50, 51–53, 618–19
Labor market flows, and unemployment
    rate, 618–19
Labor market functioning, 2
  accommodation of baby-boom workers,
      47–48
  analysis of, 32–33
  demand for labor, 33–37
  labor shortages, 43–44, 53, 55–58
  overpayment and underpayment of
      workers, 50–55
  supply of labor, 37–40
  union effects, 48–50
  wage determination, 40–46
Labor market hypotheses, statistical
    testing of, 13–20

Labor market stocks, 581
Labor productivity
  slowdown in growth of, 640–41
  and training investments, 165
  union effects on, 481–87, 508–9
Labor share, elasticity of demand for labor
    and, 137–40
Labor share in total cost, 112
Labor share law, 137–40
Labor shortages, 43–44, 53, 55–58
Labor supply. See Supply of labor
Labor supply curve, 47, 54. See also Supply
    of labor
  aggregate, 186
  backward-bending, 184
  and education, 308–14
  effect of expenditure- and tax-limitation
      legislation on, 515–17
  and equilibrium wage, 40–46
  for firms, 38–40
  horizontal, 38–39, 49
  illegal immigration and, 382–86
  for a market, 37–38
  and payroll taxes, 73–75
  and tax cuts, 184–86
  union effects on, 48–50, 470, 471, 474
  upward-sloping nature of, 72–73, 77,
      308–14
  vertical, 74
Labor surplus, 48, 49, 51–52, 391
Labor unions. See Unions
Labour Party (Great Britain), 442
Landrum-Griffin Act, 445, 464, 466, 467
Lawyers, incentive pay and, 418
Layoffs
  advance notice for, 589
  and compensating wage differentials,
      294–98
  and profit sharing, 438–41
  temporary, 583, 592–93
  and training investments, 163–65
  uncertain, effects of, 296–98
  and unemployment compensation, 598,
      599n
  vs. quits, 373, 377
Least squares regression analysis, 15, 576
Legally required employee benefits, 93,
    144–45, 146, 152–54
Leisure function, demand for, 179, 181,
    183
Leisure/labor choice, and supply of labor,
    174–218
Life-cycle aspects of labor supply
  choice of retirement age, 245–49
  interrupted careers of married women,
      242–43
  Social Security retirement test, 249–53
  substitution effect and when to work,
      243–45
Life on the Mississippi (Twain), 458
Localized economic distress, labor
    demand with, 438

Local labor market, 22
Longitudinal data, 480
Long-run labor demand, 37, 61, 79–81, 100–105
Long-run labor demand curve, 33–37, 60, 61, 68
Long-run price inflation/unemployment trade-off, 638–43, 659–64
Long-run profit sharing, 439–40
Loose labor market, 25, 377
Lorenz curve for income distribution, 356–59
Los Angeles Kings, 64
Low-income families, 92
Low-skilled labor
  and mental health, 308
  and minimum wage legislation, 84–86, 88–91
Low-wage workers, 93
Lung cancer, and workers' compensation, 283n

Managerial jobs, employment trends in, 28
Mandatory retirement
  federal policy on, 432–34
  and promotion tournaments, 431–32
Mandatory risk reduction, 277–84
Manpower Development and Training Act (MDTA), 330, 590
Manual jobs, employment trends in, 28
Manufacturing industry
  average wages and earnings of production workers in, 30, 31
  employee benefits in, 399
  employment trends in, 26
  job tenure in, 264–65
  overtime premium in, 149n
  quit rate in, 264, 360
  strikes in, 469
  turnover rate, 264–65, 360
  unions and, 450, 454n, 483–84
  wages in, 266, 424–25
  work hours in, 177
Marginal cost of labor, 63–65, 77, 80
Marginal employment tax credits, 122
Marginal productivity of labor, 62–63, 65, 99, 155
  and baseball, 69–70
Marginal productivity theory of demand, objections to, 70–72
Marginal product of capital, 80–81
Marginal product of labor, 62–63, 65–66, 67, 69, 81
Marginal rate of substitution, 188n
Marginal rate of technical substitution (MRTS), 98, 102
Marginal revenue of labor, 63–65, 75, 76, 79, 80
Marginal revenue product (MRP), 64–69, 75, 77, 78
  hockey and, 64
  in minor league sports, 162–63
Mariel boatlift, 387, 388

Marital dissolution rates, 235–36
Market-clearing wage. *See* Equilibrium wage
Market constraints, union attempts to ease, 455–57, 460–63
Market demand for labor, 36–37, 60–61, 72–73, 75–79
Market labor demand curve, 40, 43, 44, 60–61, 72–73
Market labor supply curve, 38, 40, 43, 44
Market price method of evaluating homemakers' services, 246
Market substitutes, and normative economics, 10
Market supply of labor, 37–38
Markup pricing, 638–39, 656
Marxism, and dual labor markets, 553
Matching, employer/employee, 270–74, 378–79
Maternity leave, 398
Mediators, 500n
Medicare and Medicaid, 57, 58, 283
Men
  decrease in length of careers for, 175, 334
  distribution of earnings for, 330, 339–41, 343–44
  educational level and income of, 306–7, 318
  and household production, 232
  job tenure of, 378
  labor force participation rates for, 24, 175
  labor supply behavior of, 199–201
  migration rates for, 366
  part-time employment of, 177
  public vs. private sector earnings of, 512
  quit rates of, 376n
  starting salaries of, 306–7
  and union wage effects, 477, 478
Men's Professional Golfers' Association, 433
Mental health, and low-skilled labor, 308
Miami, Florida, unemployment rates in, 388
Migration
  and age, 365–66
  of blacks, 363–64, 372
  costs of, 360–61
  and earnings distribution, 367–68
  and economic opportunities, 363–65
  and educational level, 366
  geographic, 363–73
  of Hispanics, 368n, 371–72
  individual returns to international and domestic, 368–72
  international, 367–72
  personal characteristics of movers, 365–66
  rates, for men and women, 366
  regional, 364–65
  return, 372–73
  role of distance in, 367

rural-to-urban, 363
Snowbelt-to-Sunbelt, 451–52
Military pay, 53, 261
Minimum acceptance wage, 54, 224, 609,
    644
Minimum wage effects
    and cross-wage elasticity of demand,
        114–15
    in developing countries, 89
    empirical estimation of, 92–94
    with incomplete coverage, 87–89
    in monopsonized markets, 90–91
    training and, 165–66
    with uniform coverage, 84–87, 90–91,
        107
    unions and, 459
    and youth subminimum, 114–15
Minimum wage legislation, 82–94
    history of, 82–84
    with incomplete coverage, 87–89
    and low-skilled labor, 84–86, 88–91
    social losses resulting from, 89–90
    and teenagers in labor force, 92–93
    with uniform coverage, 84–87, 90–91
Mining industry, union and association
    membership in, 450
Minnesota, comparable worth pay
    adjustments in, 575
Minorities. See also Asians; Blacks;
    Discrimination; Hispanics
    and affirmative action, 287–89, 558,
        566–68, 570–71
    and seniority, 561–62
    and state fair employment practice
        legislation, 556–58
    and statistical discrimination, 548–51
Minor league sports, general training in,
    162–63
Mississippi, unionized steamboat pilots in,
    458
Mobility of workers. See Worker mobility
Monetary costs of working, 223–24, 226
Money wages, 44, 47, 65, 67–69, 72n
Monopoly in the product market, 75–77
Monopoly power models of labor market
    discrimination, 551–56
Monopoly unions, 490–95
Monopsony in the labor market, 77–79,
    90–91, 504n
    and labor market discrimination, 554–56
Moonlighting, 151, 175–76
Multiemployer collective bargaining, 443
Multilayer union contracts, 649
Multiperiod demand for labor, 158–60
Multiple regression analysis, 16–20
Municipal employees, and union wage
    effects, 507n
Mutual benefit, 7
Mutually beneficial transactions, 7–10, 51

National Basketball Association (NBA),
    546

National Education Association (NEA),
    445, 497
National Hockey League, 64
National labor market, 22
National Labor Relations Act (NLRA),
    444, 445, 449, 454, 498
National Labor Relations Board (NLRB),
    444, 447, 454, 486
Natural unemployment rate, 585, 586,
    601–3, 628, 637
Negative income tax, 211–13, 215, 236n
Netherlands, disability programs in, 204
New classical macroeconomics, 630n
New Guinea, and labor supply theory, 196
New Jersey, police officers and arbitration
    in, 510
New Jobs Tax Credit, 122, 124
Noise pollution, 259
Nominal wages, 29
Nonaccelerating inflation rate of
    unemployment (NAIRU), 662
Noncomparable jobs, 40
Nondiscrimination requirement, 558
Nonexperimental studies, 201
Nongovernment services, employment
    trends in, 27
Noninferior inputs, 82n
Nonlabor income, 193–94
Nonpecuniary gains, 3, 4
Nonwage labor costs
    employee benefits, 144–45
    hiring and training costs, 142–44
    quasi-fixed nature of, 141, 142–46
Normal good, defined, 179n
Normative economics, 6–10
    defined, 7
    and government policy, 8–10
    ignorance and, 7–8
    and nonexistence of market, 8
    and overpayment and underpayment of
        workers, 51, 52
    and transaction barriers, 8
    and War of 1812, 9
Normative issues in unemployment,
    614–16
Norris-LaGuardia Act, 444, 449
Nuclear weapons, 462n
Nursing labor market, 56–58, 78–79

Occupational change rates, 265
Occupational choice, 176, 257–65, 346
Occupational distribution of employment,
    28
Occupational illness, 283–84
Occupational licensing laws, 460
Occupational safety and health, 261–62,
    277–87
Occupational Safety and Health Act, 277
Occupational Safety and Health
    Administration (OSHA), 277–84
Occupational segregation, 429, 539–41,
    552

Occupational separation rates, 373
Offer curve, 272–73
Office of Federal Contract Compliance
    Programs (OFCCP), 566–68, 570–71
Ohio, and targeted wage subsidies, 123
Oklahoma State University, and
    professors' salaries, 565
Operative jobs, employment trends in, 28
Opportunity costs method of evaluating
    homemakers' services, 246
Opportunity costs of employee training,
    143
Ordinal utility functions, 296n
Output effect. See Scale effect
Overcompensation for lost income, 203
Overpayment of workers, 50–55
Overtime pay, 141, 147–52
Own-wage elasticity of labor demand,
    106–13, 115–19

Paid vs. actual hours of work, 177n
Panel data, 13n
Parental leave, 93, 398
Partial-coverage minimum wage, 87–89
Partial vesting plans, 409n
Part-time employment trends, 152–54,
    175–77, 224
Paternalism, in Japan, 169
Pay. See Wages
Payments in kind, 30–31, 399, 400
Payoff matrices, 286–87
Payroll taxes, 73–75, 93, 250, 252–53, 403,
    597–98
Payroll-tax liability, 146
Pecuniary gains, 3, 4
Pension benefits, 31, 146, 245–49,
    398–405, 407–9, 430–31
Pension reform legislation, 407–9
Perfect experience rating, 599
Perfect substitution, 232n
Performance attainment plans, 416–19
Permanent income, 180n
Personal prejudice models of labor market
    discrimination, 542–48
Personal protective devices, 261–62
Personal-service jobs, employment trends
    in, 28
Person-hours, 62n
Personnel planning, and government
    training programs, 329
Phillips curve, 622, 635
Physicians, earnings of, 321
Piece-rate pay, 412, 413–16, 419, 429
Pilots' Benevolent Association, 458
Policy analyses
    mandatory retirement, 432–34
    overtime-pay premium, 148–52
Policy analysis, and fundamentals of labor
    economics, 1
Policy applications
    affirmative action planning, 287–92
    employment tax credits, 121–24

hiring discrimination, 168–71
human capital and earnings in regulated
    industries, 345–46
immigration restrictions, 379–91
income maintenance programs, 208–18
income replacement programs, 202–8
investment tax credit to reduce
    unemployment, 121
labor shortages, 55–58
minimum wage legislation, 82–94
occupational safety and health, 277–87
payroll taxes, burden of, 73–75
pension reform legislation, 407–9
Social Security retirement test, 249–53
wage subsidies, 121–24
Political immigrants, 370
Political model of strike activity, 463–67
Population movements, 27, 451–52
Positive economics
    defined, 3
    models and predictions of, 4–6
    rationality, 3–4
    scarcity, 3
    and War of 1812, 9
Postal Reorganization Act, 513
Postal workers, earnings of, 512, 513
Post-industrial state, 27
Post-schooling investments, 330–33
Post-unemployment wages, 608, 610–11
Poverty-level incomes, 215n
Power theories of discrimination, 551–56
Prejudice vs. discrimination, 529
Premarket differences, 531, 532, 538
Present-orientedness of workers, 304–5,
    426
Present value
    concept of, 155–58
    defined, 157
    of employer profits vs. strike length, 461
    of firm earnings, 157–58
    and multiperiod demand for labor,
        158–60
    of net benefits of mobility, 361–62
    and sequencing of pay, 425–30
Present-value method of evaluating
    returns on education, 303–4
Price elasticities of product demand, 110,
    113, 114, 115–17, 124
Price inflation, 629–30, 638–43, 659–64
Price makers, 76
Price takers, 76, 77
Primary sector of labor market, 27, 552–53
Prime-age men, 168, 175
Primitive cultures, and supply of labor,
    196
Prisoner's Dilemma, 286n
Product demand
    changes in, 34
    elasticity of, 110, 113, 114, 115–17, 124
    fluctuations in, 153
Product inventories, 153
Production functions, 61, 97–105, 114,
    137–40

Production possibilities curve, 127–28, 131–33
Productivity. *See* Labor productivity
Productivity bargaining, 460
Product market, 32
  monopoly in, 75–77
Product price, 72n, 75, 110
Professional Golfers' Association, 433
Professional jobs, employment trends in, 28
Profit maximization, 4, 61, 63–65, 90, 159–60, 501–4
  and baseball, 69–70
Profit-maximizing employers, and discrimination, 543–45
Profits, union effects on, 482–87
Profit sharing, 412, 417, 438–41
Promotion tournaments, 431–32
  and golf tournaments, 433
Protective devices, 284
Protective labor laws, 558
Psychic benefits of education, 303, 307, 322–23
Psychic costs of education, 301, 302, 306
Public goods, 8–10
Public sector labor market, 496–522
  arbitration statutes, wage effects of, 509–11
  collective bargaining in, 496, 498–501
  effect of expenditure- and tax-limitation legislation on, 515–17
  employment programs in, 517–22
  employment trends in, 496–501
  model of, 501–4
  pay comparisons with private sector, 498, 499, 511–15
  union effects in, 504–9
  union membership and unionization in, 496–97, 504–5
  wage elasticities of demand in, 505–6
Public service employment (PSE) programs, 501
Public utilities, 51, 52, 344–45
  union and association membership in, 450
Pure income effect, 182
Pure profit sharing, 438–41
Pure public good, 502n
Pure substitution effect, 182

Quality revolution, 415n
Quasi-fixed labor costs, 141–72
  and employee benefits, 144–45, 146, 152–54
  employment/hours trade-off, 146–54
  firm labor investments and demand for labor, 155–60
  and hiring discrimination, 168–71
  and hiring investments, 166–68
  nonwage labor costs, 141, 142–46
  training investments, 160–66
Quit rates
  and age and job tenure, 378–79

and firm size, 374–76
in manufacturing industry, 264, 360
in public vs. private sector, 514–15
and state of labor market, 376–77
and unions, 482
and wages, 373–76
Quitting
  costs of, 379
  theory of, in 19th-century Japan, 375
  vs. layoffs, 373, 377
Quota Law, 379

Racial and ethnic earnings disparities, 532–36
Random demand patterns, 61n
Rational expectations of inflation, 643, 663–64
Rationality, as an assumption of positive economics, 3–4
Real estate industry, union and association membership in, 450
Real wage rate, 65–67
Real wages
  and baby-boom workers, 47
  defined, 29
  effects of share systems in business downturns on, 438–41
  and firm demand for labor, 65–67
  and labor market equilibrium, 44
  and market demand for labor, 72–73
  and payroll taxes, 73–75
  union effects on, 469–79
Recession, 185n
  and demand for labor, 438–41
Recruiting strategies, 143
  in Korea, 260
Refugee Act of 1980, 380n
Regional migration, 364–65
Regression analysis, 575–78
Regulated industries
  earnings in, 345–46
  unions in, 453
Relative wage, 58
  advantages achieved by unions, 469–79
Relief programs. *See* Income maintenance programs
Replacement rate, and unemployment compensation, 597
Reservation wage, 54, 224, 609, 644
Resistance point, union, 466
Resource scarcity, 3, 55–56
Retail trade industry
  employment trends in, 27
  union and association membership in, 450
Retirement
  age, choice of, 245–49
  mandatory, federal policy on, 432–34
  and promotion tournaments, 431–32
  and Social Security benefits, 249–53
Return migration, 372–73
Reverse discrimination, 567
Right-to-work laws, 444–45, 449, 451

Right-to-work states, unionization in, 451–52
Risk-averse party in arbitration, 524–28
Risk aversion, 297–98
Risk-neutral party in arbitration, 524–28
Risk-neutral wait unemployment, 591n
Risk reduction, mandatory, 277–84
Roman Empire, incomes policies during, 655
Rural-to-urban migration, 363

Sales jobs, employment trends in, 28
Scale effect
  and black lung benefits, 112
  and demand for labor, 33–37, 79–80, 104–5, 114, 125
  and immigration, 386
  and overtime pay, 150
Scarcity
  as an assumption of positive economic theory, 3
  and labor shortages, 55–56
Scheduled disability benefits, 203–8
Schooling. *See* Education
Screening devices, 166–67, 325–28, 548–51, 560
Search unemployment, 610
Seasonal unemployment, 600–601
Secondary sector of labor market, 23, 27, 552–53
Select Commission on Immigration and Refugee Policy, report of, 381
Selection bias in educational rate-of-return estimates, 323–24
Selective employment subsidies, 122
Self-employment method of evaluating homemakers' services, 246
Self-enforcing contracts, 411, 426
Seniority, and perpetuation of past discrimination, 561–62
Seniority rights, 427–28, 482–83
Sequencing of pay, employment contracts and, 425–30
Service industries
  employment trends in, 27
  union and association membership in, 450
Sex discrimination in hiring, 168–71
Share wages
  and demand for labor, 438–41
  and inflation, 654–57
Shirking, and efficiency wages, 422–23
Shoplifting, optimal rate of, 67–69
Short-run labor demand, 37, 61, 62–73, 99–100
Short-run labor demand curve, 37
Short-run profit sharing, 438–41
Sick-leave pay, 146, 183, 398, 404
Signaling in the labor market, 166–67, 325–26, 349–54
Skewness of earnings distribution, 338, 340, 344–45

Skills shortage, 55
Skinnerian psychology, 3
Small businesses, growth of employment in, 635
Snowbelt-to-Sunbelt migration, 451–52
Social insurance programs, financing of, 73–75
Social losses resulting from minimum wage laws, 89–90
Social policy, and demand for labor, 60
Social Security (OASDHI) payroll-tax liability, 73, 146n
Social Security retirement test, 249–53
Social Security taxes, 182n, 403n
South Africa, labor market discrimination in, 555
Soviet Union
  incentive pay in, 418
  wage differentials in, 275, 331
Spain, general training in, 162–63
Specific training, 160–66, 168, 331
Spillover effects of unions, 470, 479
Staffing requirements, unions and, 460
Stagflation, 640–41, 656n
Staggered contracts, 649n
Standard deviation, 16, 355
Standard error, 16
Standards of living, 30
Standard-time pay plan, 412n
State and local government (SLG) sector. *See* Public sector labor market
State fair employment practice legislation, 556–58
Statistical discrimination, 123, 167, 171, 548–51, 560n
Status-seeking, 284–87
Steamboat pilots, unionization of, 458
Stock-flow model of labor market, 581–85
Stock prices, unions and, 486
Strike activity, 460–69, 484
Structural policies to reduce inflation, 651–57
Structural unemployment, 586–91
Subcontracting, unions and, 460
Subminimum wage, 92–93, 114–15, 118
Subsequent-period wage, 162
Substitutability of capital and labor, 79–80, 110–13, 125, 137–40
Substitution effect
  and demand for labor, 33–37, 103–4, 114
  and household production, 231–32, 239
  and immigration, 386
  and labor/leisure choice, 181–84, 194–98, 201–2
  and retirement, 248–49, 252
  and welfare system, 209
  and when to work over a lifetime, 243–45
Sunbelt, migration to, 451–52
Supervision of workers, 414–15, 420, 421, 422–23, 426, 432
Supply of capital, effects of changes in on demand for labor, 35

Supply of labor, 32, 174–219
  effects of changes in, on equilibrium
      wage, 40–46
  to entire market, 37–38
  and family considerations, 233–54
  to firms, 38–40
  and health, 237–38
  and household production, 227–42
  and income maintenance programs,
      208–18, 240–42
  and income replacement programs,
      202–8
  intertemporal substitution model, 245,
      647n
  in Japan, 235
  and labor/leisure choice, 174–218
  and labor-market functioning, 37–40
  life-cycle aspects of, 242–53
  primitive cultures and, 196
  shortages in, 55–58
  and tax cuts, 184–86
  union effects on, 50
Supply-side economics, 184–86
Supreme Court, U.S., 560
Survey of Income and Education (1976), 615
Sweden, disability programs in, 204
Switzerland
  child rearing in, 241
  and immigration in 18th century, 390
Symmetry of income distribution, 338

Taft-Hartley Act, 444, 445, 449, 451
Targeted employment subsidies, 121–24
Targeted Jobs Tax Credit Program, 123,
      124
Targeted wage subsidies, 121–24
Target workers, 373
Taxable wage base, 598
Tax credit programs, 121–24
Tax-limitation legislation, effect of on
      public sector labor market, 515–17
Tax rate cuts, and supply-side economics,
      184–86
Tax rate increases, and employee benefit
      growth, 401n
Tax Reform Act of 1986, 408
Teachers, strike activity of, 469
Technical jobs, employment trends in, 28
Technological change, and labor demand
      elasticity, 124–26
Teenagers in labor force, 630–31, 636
  and added worker effect, 239
  as complements and substitutes in
      production, 114–15, 117–18
  and cross-wage elasticity of demand,
      114–15
  labor market equilibrium for, after
      population increase, 47
  and minimum wage legislation, 92–93
  part-time employment of, 177
  and subminimum wage, 92–93, 114–15,
      118

  unemployment rates for, 601–7, 612n,
      614–16
Telephone industry, deregulation of,
      452–54
Temporary layoffs, 583, 592–93
Temporary workers, 153
Tennessee Valley Authority (TVA), 498n
Tenure. See Job tenure
Tertiary sector of labor market, 27
Threat effects of unions, 471, 473, 476,
      479
Tight labor market, 24, 376–77, 603
Time-based pay systems
  vs. incentive-pay plans, 412–13, 419
  and worker motivation in internal labor
      markets, 420–35
Time costs of working, 225–26
Time-series studies, 13n
  of antidiscrimination programs, 570
  of labor supply behavior, 199–201
Timken Company v. Vaughn, 289, 291
Title VII of Civil Rights Act, 558–65, 567
Total compensation, 30
  effect of unions on, 479–81
  in public sector, 511–15
Total cost model of strike activity, 468–69
Trade Act of 1974, 590
Trade Adjustment Assistance Program,
      389n, 590
Trade Expansion Act of 1962, 590
Trade-off curves, 621–38
Training
  firm-specific, 160–63, 482
  general, 160–63, 165, 331
  specific, 160–66, 168, 331
Training costs, 142–43, 155, 172
Training investments, 160–66, 328–30
  in Japan, 169
Training programs, 172, 328–30
Training strategy of recruiting, 143
Transaction barriers
  blocking of mutually beneficial
      transactions by, 8
  government intervention to overcome,
      8–10
Transfer payments, 107n
Transition probabilities, 603–4
Transportation industry, union and
      association membership in, 450
Trucking industry, deregulation of, 452–54
Turnover. See Voluntary turnover
Two-tier wage structures, 55, 453

Uncertain layoffs, 296–98
Underemployment, 610
Underpayment of workers, 50–55
Unearned income, 30
Unemployment, 579–616
  categories of, 583
  defined, 23, 579
  demand-deficient, 591–600
  frictional, 585–86, 607–14

full-employment rate of, 585, 586,
601–3, 628, 637
government policy and, 501, 607–14, 637
inflation and, 620–57
and internal labor market, 593–95
and labor demand curve, 585–88,
591–92
labor force and, 23–26
normative issues in, 614–16
persistence of, 607
reduction by investment tax credits, 121
reduction by overtime-pay premium
increase, 148–52
search, 610
seasonal, 600–601
structural, 586–91
types and causes of, 585–601
Unemployment insurance, 398
and demand-deficient unemployment,
596–600
and demand for labor, 73–75
effects of, on job search, 607–14
and income replacement programs,
202–8
and quasi-fixed nature of nonwage
costs, 146
unions and, 461n
and wage/layoff relationship, 298
and worker incentives, 216–18
Unemployment rates, 579–81
and changes in earnings and prices,
621–22
civilian, 25, 580
defined, 24
demographic structure of, 601–7
dispersion of, effect on wage
inflation/unemployment trade-off,
632–33
full-employment, 585, 586, 601–3, 628,
637
immigration effects on, 388
and inclusion of discouraged workers in
statistics, 238–40
international differentials in, 594–95
and labor market flows, 618–19
and price inflation, 638–43, 659–64
for teenagers, 601–7, 612n, 614–16
and tight labor market, 377
trends in, 25–26
variations across groups, 603–6
Unexpected inflation, 644–47
Unionization
demand for and supply of, 447–49
model of, 445–49
and small firms, 451n
Union resistance curve, 461, 464
Unions
and collective bargaining in private
sector, 442–87
and collective bargaining in public
sector, 496, 498–501
and discrimination, 554–56, 557
and employee benefits, 401, 480
employer resistance to, 454–55

goals of, 119, 455–69
immigration policy of, 459
industrial vs. craft, 443
and inflation, 647–51
and internal labor markets, 482–87
labor by, altering demand for, 457–60
and labor market, 22, 48–50, 455–63,
504–9
and labor supply curve, 48–50, 470, 471,
474
and manufacturing industry, 450, 454n,
483–84
and market constraints, 455–57, 460–63
membership and trends in, 442, 449–55,
496–97
price of membership in, 447–48
and productivity, 481–87, 508–9
and profits, 482–87
in public sector, 496–501, 504–9
in regulated industries, 453
and right-to-work laws, 444–45
spillover effects of, 470, 479
staffing requirements of, 460
and stock prices, 486
strike activity of, 460–69
and subcontracting, 460
threat effects of, 471, 473, 476, 479
and total compensation, 479–81
and voluntary turnover, 482
and wage elasticities of labor demand,
119–20, 455–63
and wages, 48–50, 469–79, 485, 506–8
Unitary elastic labor demand curve, 107n
United Automobile Workers (UAW), 408,
648
United Mine Workers (UMW), 80, 484
Univariate analysis, 13–16
Unjust dismissals, worker protection
against, 410n
Upward bias in educational rate-of-return
estimates, 320–22
U.S. v. County of Fairfax, 291n
Utility maximization, 11, 254, 292, 522,
616
employer discrimination and, 545
household production and, 228–31
human capital investments and, 320n
occupational choice and, 263
positive economics and, 4

Vacation benefits, 31, 146, 398, 399
Variable labor costs, 141
Variance, 355
Vertical labor supply curve, 74
Vesting provisions, of pension plans,
408–9, 430–31
Voluntary turnover, 373–79
and age and job tenure, 378–79
costs of quitting, 379
cyclical effects on, 376–77
in manufacturing industry, 264–65, 360
unexpected outcomes of, 377–78
and unions, 482
wage effects on, 6, 373–76

Wage changes, 33–34, 60, 79–80, 182–84, 194–98, 403
Wage constraints, income and, 190–92
Wage determination
  in nonunionized labor markets, 40–46
  under profit sharing, 438–41
Wage differentials
  compensating, 257–98
  in Soviet Union, 275, 331
Wage/education relationship, 314–17
Wage elasticities of labor demand
  cross-, 113–15, 118, 125
  empirical evidence on, 115–20
  and employment tax credits, 121–24
  and investment tax credits, 121
  laws of derived demand, 109–13, 119–20
  long-run estimates of, 117
  long-run vs. short-run, 110, 111
  own-, 106–13, 115–19
  prediction of, 119–20
  in public sector, 505–6
  union attempts to reduce, 119–20, 455–57
  and wage subsidies, 121–24
Wage/employee benefits combinations
  in collective bargaining process, 408
  determination of, 405–7
Wage guarantee, profit sharing with, 438–41
Wage imitation, 650–51
Wage increases in declining sectors, 478
Wage inflation, 638–43
  inflation/unemployment trade-off, 621–38
  measurement of, 620–21
Wage-layoff relationship, 298
Wage norms, 647–49
Wage rates
  across industries, 425n
  defined, 29
  and firm size, 424–25
  and labor demand curve, 61
  and monopolies, 76
  nonunion, effect of unions on, 469–70
  and payroll taxes, 73–75
Wages. See also Real wages
  basis of, 411–20
  Black Death and, 41
  defined, 30
  and education, 314–17
  efficiency, 397, 422–24, 590
  and employee benefits, joint determination of, 405–7
  and geographic mobility, 363–65
  hedonic model of education and, 314–17
  hedonic theory of, 266–74
  inexperienced workers and, 47–48
  in internal labor markets, 420–22
  and labor shortages, 43–44, 53, 55–58
  in large firms, 424–25
  in manufacturing industry, 30, 31, 266, 424–25
  nominal, 29
  public vs. private sector, 498–99, 511–15

and quit rates, 373–76
and relationship to earnings, compensation, and income, 29–32
  reservation, 54, 224, 609, 644
  rigidity of, 592–95
  sequencing of pay, employment contracts and, 425–30
  with share systems, 438–41, 654–57
  of state and local government employees, 509–11
  union, and corporate takeovers, 485
  unions' effects on, 48–50, 469–79, 485, 506–8
Wage subsidies, 121–24
Wage takers, 40
Wagner Act, 444, 445, 449, 454
Wait unemployment, 472, 474, 476, 479, 588n, 591
Wards Cove v. Atonio, 560n
War of 1812, 9
Wealth of Nations (Adam Smith), 274
Welfare system, 208–13. See also Income maintenance programs
  and work incentives, 213–16
White-collar jobs, 166–67
  employment trends in, 28
  and union wage effects, 479
Wholesale industry
  employment trends in, 27
  union and association membership in, 450
Wildcat strikes, 484
Winner's curse, 70–71
Women
  and added-worker effect, 239
  and affirmative action, 287–88, 291–92, 558, 566–68, 570–71
  career interruptions of married, 171, 242–43, 333, 335
  and comparable worth, 562–63
  as complements and substitutes in production, 118–19
  discrimination in hiring, 168–71
  earnings of, 330, 344, 512, 536–41
  and educational levels, 309, 334
  and Equal Pay Act of 1963, 558
  in high- and low-paying occupations, 58, 539
  and household production, 232, 242–43
  and human capital acquisition, 333–35
  and immigration, 386
  job tenure of, 168–71, 376, 450
  and job training, 334
  labor force participation rates of, 24, 175
  labor force shares of, 630–31, 636
  labor supply behavior of, 199–201, 215
  migration rates of, 366
  part-time employment of, 177
  piece-rate compensation schemes for, 429
  and quit rates, 376
  and seniority, 561–62
  and statistical discrimination, 549–51

unemployment rates for, 602
and union membership, 449–50
and union wage effects, 478
Work, decision not to, 192–93
Work, decision to, 174–219
Worker Adjustment and Retraining
    Notification Act (WARN), 589
Worker demand for education, 301–14
Worker information, 263–64, 411
Worker mobility, 360–92
  and compensating wage differentials,
    264–65
  determinants of, 361–62
  employee-initiated, 373–74
  employer-initiated, 361, 373–74
  geographic mobility, 363–73
  job satisfaction and, 362
  voluntary turnover, 373–79
Worker motivation, under time-based pay
    systems, 2, 420–35
Worker preferences, effect of on labor
    allocation, 54–55
Workers' compensation, 73, 146, 202–8,
    267n, 283, 398, 402
Work hours
  constrained, 295–98
  in manufacturing industry, 177
  trends in, 174–78
  unconstrained, 294–95

Work incentives, 178, 185–86
  and absenteeism, 183, 419–20
  and disability, 203, 204
  and income maintenance programs,
    208–18, 240–42
  and income replacement programs,
    202–8
  and partial benefit unemployment
    compensation, 216–18
  and sequencing of pay, 425–30
  and Social Security retirement test,
    249–53
  welfare and, empirical studies of,
    213–16
  worker adjustment to, 216–18
Working, costs of, 222–26
World War I, 363
World War II, 25–26, 449
Wygant v. *Jackson Board of Education,* 562n

Yellow dog contracts, 444
Youth subminimum wage, 92–93, 114–15,
    118

Zero-profit curves, 269–72, 316, 405
Zimbabwe, minimum wages in, 89

TABLE 6.1 Labor Force Participation Rates of Females over 16 Years of Age, by Marital Status, 1900–1988 (percent)

Year	All Females	Single	Widowed, Divorced	Married
1900	20.6	45.9	32.5	5.6
1910	25.5	54.0	34.1	10.7
1920	24.0			9.0
1930	25.3	55.2	34.4	11.7
1940	26.7	53.1	33.7	13.8
1950	29.7	53.6	35.5	21.6
1960	37.7	58.6	41.6	31.9
1970	43.3	56.8	40.3	40.5
1980	51.5	64.4	43.6	49.8
1988	56.6	67.7	46.2	56.7

TABLE 6.2 Labor Force Participation Rates for Males, by Age, 1900–1989 (percent)

Year	Age Groups					
	14–19	16–19	20–24	25–44	45–64	Over 65
1900	61.1	—	91.7	96.3	93.3	68.3
1910	56.2	—	91.1	96.6	93.6	58.1
1920	52.6	—	90.9	97.1	93.8	60.1
1930	41.1	—	89.9	97.5	94.1	58.3
1940	34.4	—	88.0	95.0	88.7	41.5
1950	39.9	63.2	82.8	92.8	87.9	41.6
1960	38.1	56.1	86.1	95.2	89.0	30.6
1970	35.8	56.1	80.9	94.4	87.3	25.0
1980	—	60.5	85.9	95.4	82.2	19.1
1989	—	57.9	85.3	94.4	80.2	16.6